# THE ENCYCLOPEDIA
## OF
## JUDAISM

# THE ENCYCLOPEDIA
# OF
# JUDAISM

## VOLUME III
## P – Z

Edited by

### JACOB NEUSNER
### ALAN J. AVERY-PECK
### WILLIAM SCOTT GREEN

PUBLISHED IN COLLABORATION WITH THE
MUSEUM OF JEWISH HERITAGE
NEW YORK

CONTINUUM • NEW YORK

1999

The Continuum Publishing Company
370 Lexington Avenue
New York, NY 10017

Copyright © 1999 by Koninklijke Brill NV, Leiden, The Netherlands

Distribution in the United States and Canada by The Continuum Publishing
Company, 370 Lexington Avenue, New York, NY 10017-6503, USA

Distribution in the rest of the world by Brill, Plantijnstraat 2, P.O.Box 9000,
2300 PA, Leiden, The Netherlands

This book is printed on acid-free paper.

Printed in The Netherlands

Library of Congress Cataloging-in-Publication Data

The encyclopedia of Judaism / editors, Jacob Neusner, Alan J. Avery
    -Peck, William Scott Green.
        p.    cm.
    Includes bibliographical references and index.
    Contents: v. 1. A–I.
    ISBN 0–8264–1178–9 (set : alk. paper)
    1. Judaism—Encyclopedias.    I. Neusner, Jacob, 1932–
II. Avery Peck, Alan J. (Alan Jeffery), 1953–    III. Green, William
Scott.
BM50.E63    1999
296'.03—dc21                                          99–34729
                                                        CIP


Volume 3    ISBN 0-8264-1177-0

# TABLE OF CONTENTS

## VOLUMES I-III

# P

**PAGAN HISTORIANS ON JUDAISM IN AN-
CIENT TIMES:** The expansion of Greek civilization to the east, especially from the time
of Alexander the Great onward, involved
contact with many ethnic groups, following
many religions. Judaism, with its monotheism and prohibition of graven images, was
unique among these religions and presented
difficulties for followers of Greek, and later
Roman, polytheism. The Jews worshipped a
God whom they would neither identify with
a Greco-Roman god (syncretism) nor allow
to be worshipped together with such a god.
Historians, writing in Greek and Latin, coped
with these difficulties by attempting to view
the rites and beliefs of Judaism through the
framework of their own sets of beliefs, often
misunderstanding aspects of Judaism, mistakenly identifying Jewish rites and beliefs
with those of their own polytheistic culture,
and, in some cases, fearfully regarding Judaism's monotheistic exclusiveness as a men-
ace to their culture.

The historians described here were followers of polytheistic Greek, Hellenistic, or
Roman belief systems; Christians fall outside
our scope, their attitudes toward Judaism
being substantially different from those of
pagans. All the historians discussed here
lived before Christianity became the official
religion of the Roman Empire in the fourth
century C.E. We look in particular at authors
of material, arranged chronologically, dealing
with political and social developments. Varro
(first century B.C.E.), although generally regarded as an antiquarian, is here treated as
an historian because some of his writings are
historical in nature. Plutarch and Suetonius
(first-second centuries C.E.) are here considered historians because their biographical
works are major historical sources. Strabo,

roughly contemporary, was an historian as
well as a geographer.

Only historians whose extant writings concern Judaism, *the religion*, as opposed to the
politics, ethnicity, and secular culture of the
Jews, are dealt with here; thus Hieronymus of
Cardia, active about 300 B.C.E., is excluded.
Less important historians, including histo-
rians who make only brief and occasional
references to Judaism, as well as historians
who are known only by name, cited in the
writings of other authors, are also excluded.
These excluded historians, from whom ma-
terial survives, listed chronologically, are
Herodotus, Pseudo-Hellenicus, Agatharcides,
Polybius, Laetius, Asinius Pollio, Castor of
Rhodes, Hypsicrates, Timagenes, Nicolaus of
Damascus, Ptolemy, Livy, Valerius Maximus,
Ptolemy of Mendes, Chaeremon, Damo-
critus, Suetonius, Florus, Herennius Philo,
Appian, Cassius Dio, Ammianus Marcelli-
nus, and the author or authors of the *Historia
Augusta*.

**General considerations:** Despite the large
Jewish population in the Hellenistic-Roman
Mediterranean world, extant pagan Greek
and Roman writers say relatively little about
the Jews. Much, of course, has not survived,
and much of what survives is extant only in
citations in the works of other writers; these
may not always be accurate.[1] Thirty-four
pagan historians, of whom twelve are discussed here, ranging chronologically from
the fifth century B.C.E. to the second century C.E., discuss some aspect of Judaism.
A few make only passing references, e.g., to
the Temple of Jerusalem or to circumcision;
others go into considerable detail. Topics
discussed include Moses and the Exodus
(e.g., Hecataeus, Manetho, Diodorus Siculus,
Strabo, Apion, Tacitus), monotheism (nota-

bly Varro and Plutarch), the Sabbath (Strabo, Apion, Tacitus, Plutarch), dietary laws (notably Plutarch and Tacitus; little is said of anything other than the prohibition of pork), and circumcision (notably Hecataeus, Strabo, and Apion). Although many pagan historians discuss the Jerusalem Temple, they do not discuss synagogue services or sectarian divisions within Judaism. It is doubtful whether any of them, except perhaps Nicolaus of Damascus, the confidant of Herod the Great, not discussed in this article since his great knowledge of Jewish matters makes him atypical, had any knowledge of Hebrew or the Septuagint.

**Varying assessments of Judaism:** Much modern scholarship has focused on pagan writers' praise or criticism of Judaism and on the question of antisemitism in antiquity. The most recent study is Peter Schäfer, *Judeophobia: Attitudes toward the Jews in the Ancient World* (Cambridge, 1997). This scholar, like many of his predecessors, considers the preponderance of references to Judaism among ancient pagan writers to be negative. But Louis H. Feldman[2] argues otherwise, ascribing negative attitudes to Judaism to "the refusal of Jews to engage in meaningful dialogue with other religious groups on a plane of equality," which antagonized pagan intellectuals. Schäfer, by contrast, sees these intellectuals as feeling threatened by Jewish "separateness." Indeed, many pagan authors, from Hecataeus (third century B.C.E.) to authors living under the Roman Empire, accused Jews of hatred of foreigners or even of the whole human race and specifically of ass-worship (e.g., Apion, Tacitus) and human sacrifice (Apion). Still, such writers as Plutarch and Varro praised Judaism for its monotheism and prohibition of graven images, so that the overall situation may be more varied than either scholar admits.

**Hecataeus of Abdera:** This Greek philosopher and historian, the first to mention the Jews by name, lived in the time of Alexander the Great and Ptolemy I, the first Hellenistic king of Egypt (ca. 300 B.C.E.). His writings survive only in quotations in the works of later writers, according to whom he wrote a work on the history of Egypt, prob-

ably entitled *Aegyptiaca*. According to Flavius Josephus, he also wrote a book *On the Jews* (*Against Apion* I, 183) and another on Abraham (*Jewish Antiquities* I, 159). The existence of the former book is also mentioned by the third-century Christian writer Origen (*Against Celsus* I, 15), who, however, states that its authenticity was questioned by the pagan Greek historian Herennius Philo of Byblus (in Phoenicia), who was active at the beginning of the second century C.E.

Most modern scholars consider the book on Abraham to have been a Jewish forgery, and many doubt that the work *On the Jews* was written by Hecataeus (Stern, vol. I, pp. 20-25; Feldman, *Jew and Gentile*, p. 8). The passage from *Aegyptiaca*, cited in the later Greek writer Diodorus Siculus' *Historical Library* XL, 3,[3] includes the first Greek account of the Exodus, which states that certain strangers living in Egypt and practicing different religious rites were expelled during a pestilence ascribed to divine punishment for neglect of the traditional, polytheistic, Egyptian religion. Some of the exiles landed in Greece, becoming ancestors of many Greek groups; most went to Judea. The latter group was led by a man called Moses, outstanding both for wisdom and courage. He founded Jerusalem, built the Temple, made rules for Jewish ritual and worship, and established the twelve tribes, the number twelve being "perfect" and equal to the number of months. Moses had no images of the gods made, thinking that God is not in human form but that the heaven that surrounds the earth is itself divine and rules the universe. Moses established sacrifices differing from those of other nations; the Jewish way of living also differs, since Moses, as a result of the expulsion from Egypt, introduced an "anti-social" or "inhuman" (*apanthropon*, literally, "far from human beings") and "xenophobic" or "intolerant" (*misoxenon*, literally, "hostile to strangers" or "foreigners") way of life.

The passage goes on to say that Moses picked out the most refined and able men, appointing them priests and judges and making them guardians of the laws and customs. For this reason, the Jews never have a king, authority being vested in the high priest.

They submit with alacrity to the high priest's decrees, made in the name of Moses. Various praiseworthy ethical requirements, introduced by Moses, are then mentioned, ending with the requirement that Jews rear their children (rather than commit infanticide), as a result of which they are a populous nation.

Hecataeus, as cited by Diodorus, ends by stating that Jews' marriage and burial customs differ from those of other nations, but that later, when under foreign (Persian and Macedonian) rule, many of these customs were overturned due to mingling with other nations. This passage is predominantly sympathetic to the Jews and may have been derived from a Jewish source. Jews are praised by being coupled with two early Greek heroes. The statement about monotheism and graven images praises these concepts in accordance with Greek philosophical ideas. Moses is depicted in terms appropriate to the founder of a Greek city. A number of inaccurate statements, ascribing later developments such as the foundation of Jerusalem and the Temple and high priesthood to Moses as well as inaccuracies about the development of the twelve tribes and the nonexistence of kingship among the Jews, show ignorance of Jewish history before the Persian period. Despite the generally positive tone of the passage, certain themes unfavorable to the Jews appear. These will be repeated, often with variations, by many later writers.

Hecataeus' version of the Exodus story connects the Jews, at least indirectly, with irreligion and pestilence, while for the first time the theme of Jewish *misoxenia*, common in later hostile accounts of the Jews, appears. Scholars have debated the significance of the tension between positive and negative attitudes toward Judaism. Schäfer, p. 17, ascribes the *misoxenia* theme to Hecataeus, adding to existing Egyptian anti-Jewish traditions, perhaps increased by the tension between the Egyptian and Jewish communities in Alexandria, which broke out into violence many times from the period of the early Ptolemies through the first century C.E. Stern, vol. 1, pp. 21-22 and 29-34, emphasizes the philo-semitic aspects of the passage. In antiquity, the reputation of Moses as a magician and wise man extended far beyond Jewish circles, and the lesser but similar reputation of Abraham must be mentioned in connection with Hecataeus and later Greek and Roman historians.

The citation from Hecataeus' doubtful work *On the Jews* in Josephus' *Against Apion* I, 183-204, is of questionable authenticity.[4] Hecataeus (or Pseudo-Hecataeus) discusses the Jewish high priesthood in early Hellenistic times, notes Jewish devotion to the laws of Judaism, describes Jerusalem and the Temple, which he inaccurately locates in the center of the city, and notes that it houses an eternal light but no statue or votive offering or sacred grove (as might be found in Greek temple enclosures). Here priests constantly perform acts of purification, abstaining from wine. The author goes on to say, according to Josephus, that he had seen a Jew deriding the pagan practice of taking omens from the flight of birds.

**Manetho:** The Egyptian priest Manetho wrote a Greek history of his country in the third century B.C.E. This work was a major source of information on Egypt for Greeks and Romans, so remaining until the deciphering of hieroglyphics in modern times. It survives only in citations in Josephus' *Against Apion*, in which all the extant references to Judaism appear, and in the writings of certain Christian authors. In *Against Apion* I, 73-91, Manetho discusses the invasion of Egypt by the Hyksos from Asia, dated by modern scholars to the seventeenth century B.C.E. He notes their cruelty and destruction of Egyptian temples and says they were defeated by the Egyptians, fleeing to Judea and founding Jerusalem. Although Jews are not mentioned by name, this is an Egyptian version of the Exodus story.

A second version of the Exodus story appears in another citation of Manetho in Josephus' *Against Apion* I, 228-252: a seer told the Egyptian king that the king would be able to see the gods if he expelled lepers and other polluted persons. Certain diseased persons, including some Egyptian priests, were cast into stone-quarries; later they were allowed to live in a deserted city formerly inhabited by Hyksos. One Egyptian priest,

Osarseph, became their leader, forbidding them from worshipping the gods and commanding them to eat animals Egyptians considered sacred; they were also forbidden to associate with outsiders. Thus the priest made laws completely contrary to those of Egypt. Eventually, despite opposition from the Egyptian king, these polluted persons joined the Hyksos, who had been expelled from Egypt and were living in Jerusalem. Together they invaded Egypt, pillaging temples and unrestrainedly mutilating images of the gods while roasting the sacred animals worshipped by the Egyptians in the sanctuaries, compelling the priests to sacrifice the sacred animals and then throwing the men out naked.

The passage concludes that the priest who framed the constitution and laws was a native of the Egyptian city of Heliopolis, named Osarseph after the god Osiris, worshipped in that city, but when he joined his people, he changed his name to Moses. Not all scholars ascribe this version to Manetho, although many do (see Stern, vol. I, pp. 63-4). Schäfer, pp. 18-20 and 163-166, believes that an earlier Egyptian story about the expulsion of invaders was later combined with an Egyptian version of the Exodus story; Egyptian antisemitism goes back beyond the Hellenistic period to at least that of Persian domination, and the motifs of *misoxenia* and extreme opposition to Egyptian polytheism, with its divine images and sacred animals, are present.

**Posidonius:** Posidonius of Apamea, a philosopher and historian who lived from about 135 to 51 B.C.E., is said by Josephus (*Against Apion* II, 79, 80, 89, 91-96) to have been a major source for a passage in the works of Apion in which the Jews are accused of human sacrifice in the Temple of Jerusalem. Since scholarly opinion generally rejects Posidonius, who apparently was not directly consulted by Josephus, as the source of this passage (see Stern, vol. I, p. 142 and Schäfer, p. 83), the passage will here be discussed in connection with Apion.

**Alexander Polyhistor:** This Greek historian from Miletus wrote a work *On the Jews* after the Roman general Pompey captured Jerusalem in the first century B.C.E. This

work survives only in citations in Eusebius' *Preparation for the Gospel* (IX, 17-39, Stern, no. 51a) and in Clement of Alexandria's *Miscellanies* (I, 21.130.3, Stern, no. 51b). Alexander seems to have derived his information from a number of Jewish writers in Greek. The first of the two passages refers to the sacrifice of Abraham, the exposure of the infant Moses, and the prophecy of Jeremiah, all in summary form. There is a reference to the "holy book (s)," i.e., the Hebrew Scriptures, which Alexander seems to have heard of but not read. The second passage refers briefly to the building of the Jerusalem Temple. Another citation from Alexander Polyhistor, from his work *Concerning Rome*, appears in the entry for Alexander in the *Suda* ("Fortress of Knowledge"), a tenth-century C.E. Byzantine Greek encyclopedia (Stern, no. 52). This unique and bizarre passages states that Alexander wrote that "there lived a Hebrew woman Moso who composed the Law of the Hebrews." No other extant pagan writer says Moses was a woman. This passage has been variously interpreted as a derisory joke, accusing the Jews of effeminacy, a reference to the Roman prophetesses called Sibyls, and an identification of the name Moses with "Muse."[5]

**Diodorus Siculus:** Diodorus Siculus wrote a *Library of History* in Greek in the first century C.E. This highly unoriginal historian derived much of his material on Judaism from Hecataeus, whom he cites by name at 40, 3 (Stern, no. 65), which goes on to give the passage on the Exodus story discussed above. Two other passages in the *Library of History* (I, 28. 1-3, Stern, no. 55, and I, 55. 5, Stern, no. 57) mention that the Jewish practice of circumcision is of Egyptian origin. At I, 94. 1-2 (Stern, no. 58), Diodorus discusses the divinely-inspired lawgivers of various nations, stating that "among the Jews, Moses referred his laws to the god who is invoked as Iao." This is the first reference to the name Iao in a pagan source, although it appears in Jewish papyri but not in the Septuagint, since the four-letter name for God was regarded as unpronounceable and unwritable. Another passage, 35. 1. 1-5, preserved in the *Library* of Photius (Stern, no. 63), states that when the Seleucid king Antiochus VII Sidetes (reigned 138-129 B.C.E.) besieged Jerusalem, many of the king's friends urged him to capture the city by storm and completely wipe out the nation of Jews, "since they alone of all nations avoided dealings with any other people and looked on all men as their enemies," another example of the recurring theme of Jewish *misoxenia*.

Another theme found in pagan literature appears in the subsequent sentence, where the king's advisors add that the ancestors of the Jews had been expelled from Egypt because they were impious and detested by the gods. People with white or leprous marks on their bodies were driven out, occupied the territory around Jerusalem, made their hatred of humankind into a tradition, and introducing outlandish laws, prohibiting eating with other peoples (a reference to the dietary laws) or showing foreigners any good will at all. The king's friends recalled that when Antiochus IV Epiphanes had captured the Temple (in 168 B.C.E.), he found in its innermost sanctuary, where it was lawful for the priest alone to enter, "a marble statue of a heavily bearded man seated on an ass," which Antiochus thought was a statue of Moses, "founder of Jerusalem and organizer of the nation," who was responsible for the Jews' "misanthropic and lawless customs." The king, shocked by such misanthropy, decided to break down the traditional customs of the Jews and thus sacrificed before the image of Moses and the open-air altar of the god a great sow, pouring its blood over them. He then ordered that the holy books containing the xenophobic laws be sprinkled with the broth of the meat, that the eternal lamp in the Temple be put out, and that the high priest and the rest of the Jews be compelled to eat some of the meat. The passage goes on to say that the friends of Antiochus VII Sidetes, after telling this story, urged the king to exterminate the Jews or at least abolish their laws and make them change their ways.

The king, however, was satisfied with taking a tribute and dismantling the walls of Jerusalem. The source of the passage, apparently unaware of or ignoring the Jewish pro-

hibition against graven images and depicting the Temple of Jerusalem as somewhat resembling a Greek temple, has been identified with Posidonius, perhaps through Nicolaus of Damascus as an intermediate source. Elements of Seleucid propaganda against the second Jewish commonwealth have been thought to appear, but at the end of the passage the arguments of the antisemites are rejected by the king. The ass appears as icon in the Temple but is not depicted as an object of worship, unlike in the later account in Apion. Themes of Jewish xenophobia, expulsion from Egypt due to leprosy, and impiety appear, as they did earlier in the writings of Hecataeus and Manetho. Another passage, from Diodorus 40.2 (Stern, no. 64), excerpted in the writings of the tenth-century Byzantine emperor and writer Constantine Porphyrogenitus, states that the Jewish ruler in Maccabean times should strictly speaking be called high priest, not king (in fact the high priests took the title of king in the second century B.C.E.).

**Varro:** Marcus Terentius Varro (116-27 B.C.E.), "the most learned of the Romans" and a prolific author on many topics, was, strictly speaking, an antiquarian rather than a historian. Since, however, some of his extant writings are substantially historical in nature, he is included here. Since Varro is the first Latin author to be treated in this article, it is appropriate to mention Schäfer's comparison between Greek (or Greco-Egyptian) and Roman attitudes toward Judaism (pp. 193-195). Many Romans, including Tacitus, express favorable attitudes even in highly unfavorable contexts; the Romans place somewhat greater emphasis on abstinence from pork and the Sabbath; they are, unlike the Greeks, concerned with Jewish proselytism; there is somewhat less intolerance of Jewish monotheism, and the Romans never, in extant sources, accuse the Jews of human sacrifice. But there are many exceptions to these rules, including, to a substantial extent, Varro, who is, with the possible exception of Strabo, the most pro-Jewish of the Latin writers here considered as historians.

The extant passages on Judaism in Varro survive only in citations from later Christian writers. Two passages from Varro's *Human and Divine Antiquities* are cited in the writings of Augustine, the famous writer of the *City of God*, who lived at the beginning of the fifth century C.E. The first, cited in *City of God* IV, 31 (Stern, no. 72a), states that the early, uncorrupted Romans worshipped the gods without an image. In support of this opinion, Varro gives "the testimony of the Jewish nation" and, in a number of places in his writings (see Stern, vol. II, p. 209), expresses opposition to divine statues. In three other passages cited in Augustine's *Concerning the Agreement of the Gospels* (I, 22. 30, Stern, no. 72b; I. 23. 31, Stern, no. 72c; I. 27. 42, Stern, no. 72d), Varro identifies the Jewish God with Jupiter, being, according to Augustine (in the first passage), "terrified by his sublimity." The Jews worship the highest God, and the Romans consider Jupiter to be the king of the gods. Here Varro shows Greek philosophical influence. By his time, the Jews were so widespread in the Roman world that it is probable that Varro had personal contact with them. The sixth-century C.E. Greek author John Lydus states that Varro identified the Jewish God with Iao, as did Diodorus Siculus (Lydus, *Concerning the Months* IV. 53, Stern, no. 75).

**Strabo:** Strabo of Amasea (64 B.C.E.-ca. 25 C.E.) was both a historian and a geographer, writing in Greek. The material on Judaism in his *History* survives only in quotations in Josephus' writings, but his *Geography* is extant almost in its entirety. Two citations (Stern, nos. 98 and 100), in Josephus' *Against Apion* II, 83-84, and *Jewish Antiquities* XIII, 319 merely ascribe to Strabo statements about the Temple and circumcision that are also, Josephus notes, attested in other authors, such as Polybius, already discussed. A third citation, in *Jewish Antiquities* XIII, 345-347 (Stern, no. 101), ascribes to Strabo the statement of Nicolaus of Damascus about one of the Ptolemaic king's accusing the Jews of cannibalism. Another passage, cited in the same work, XIV, 111-113 (Stern, no. 102) refers in passing to the Jerusalem Temple. At XIV, 66-68 (Stern, no. 104), Josephus ascribes also to Strabo Nicolaus' statement about the Jews' continuing to practice their rites while Pompey's troops were storming into the Temple, mentioning that the city was captured "on the fast day." Whether this refers to Yom Kippur, which cannot possibly be the day the city was captured, since other evidence indicates that the date was much too early in the year, or the Sabbath, which many pagans thought was a fast day, perhaps because of the prohibition against cooking, is a matter of dispute (Stern, vol. I, p. 277). At XIV, 138-139 (Stern, no. 107), Josephus cites a passing allusion by Strabo to the high priesthood.

Three other passages in Strabo's *Geography* contain more substantial material on Judaism. *Geography* 16. 2. 34-46 (Stern, no. 115) presents a version of the Exodus story completely different from those given by his predecessors among pagan Greek authors and generally more favorable towards Judaism. Strabo notes that the most prevalent of the trustworthy reports in connection with the Temple of Jerusalem says that the ancestors of the present Judeans were Egyptians. Moses, Strabo continues, was an Egyptian priest, holding a part of Lower Egypt, but went to Egypt together with many people who worshipped the divinity (*theion*), because he was dissatisfied with the Egyptian religion and its graven images of gods in animal and human form. He believed that God encompasses us all as well as land and sea, the thing that we call heaven, universe, or the nature of all that exists. Image-worship is therefore wrong, and a sacred precinct and a worthy sanctuary should worship God without an image. People who have good dreams should sleep in the sanctuary for the sake of the community as well as themselves, and only the self-restrained and righteous should expect some blessing from God.

According to Strabo's account, by saying such things, Moses persuaded some thoughtful men, whom he led to the site of Jerusalem. Instead of using weapons, he put forward as a defense his beliefs and worship, promising to give the people a mode of worship and ritual unburdened with unnecessary expenses, divine obsessions, or other "absurd troubles." Because of his dealings with the people and the prospects he held out,

Moses was persuasive and popular, as were his early successors. Later, however, superstitious men were appointed to the priesthood, and then tyrannical ones. From superstition arose abstinence from meat, still their custom, and circumcision and excision (of females) and other such observances. From tyrannies arose bands of robbers, but the people still respected their acropolis, i.e., Jerusalem, honoring it as a holy place, which is natural for people who respect their common traditions. Strabo then goes on to discuss the ancient traditions and law-givers of many nations, noting that many of them were divinely inspired and that prophets frequently became kings. He lists Moses as such a person. Strabo adds that Alexander Jannaeus (103-76 B.C.E.) was the first high priest to declare himself king of Judea, although most scholars agree with Josephus' statement that the previous ruler, Aristobulus, was the first. Further down Strabo mentions members of the dynasty of Herod as priests and kings.

Strabo's statement about Moses' opposition to graven images shows the influence of Hecataeus, cited by Diororus Siculus, XL, 3. 4 (Stern, no. 11). Strabo says nothing about disease or the Hyksos; Moses left because of dissatisfaction with Egyptian religion. The statement about people with good dreams' sleeping in the sanctuary recalls the Greek religious practice of incubation rather than any Jewish custom. The idea of decadence after Moses' time is new, arguably influenced by Greek philosophical ideas about the decadence of religion, reminiscent of Varro's statement about Roman religion in the passage, cited above, about religious images, which also shows resemblances to Strabo's praise of Moses' opposition to them. Opposition to the Jewish dietary laws is also unusual in a Greek author.

But truly unique to Strabo is the reference to female circumcision, unknown in Jewish tradition but found among many ethnic groups in Africa and elsewhere. At two other points, *Geography* XIV, 4. 21 (Stern, no. 118) and XVII, 2. 5 (Stern, no. 124), Strabo specifically states that the Jews practice female excision. The origin of this extraordinary statement is unknown (Stern, vol. I, p. 306).

In general, Strabo has been said to have engaged in "idealizing ethnography" of the Jews, and his mostly favorable evaluation does not exclude elements of hostility, addressed toward the Jews of his own time. Like several of his predecessors, he reveals no knowledge of Jewish history between Moses and the Maccabees.[6]

**Justin-Trogus:** The Latin *Philippic Histories* of Pompeius Trogus, who lived at about the beginning of the common era, deal primarily with the history of the kingdoms founded by Alexander the Great's successors. They are extant only in an *Epitome*, composed in the third or fourth century C.E., and a separate *Prologue*, also composed by Justin. One passage, Book XXXVI, Epitome, 1.9-3.9 (Stern, no. 137), deals with Judaism. According to this passage, the Jews originated in Damascus, early Jewish kings there included Azelus (the biblical Hadad, king of Aram, according to evidence derived from Josephus), Adores (Hazael), Abraham, and Israhel (Israel, Jacob); the latter had ten sons, as a result of which he became more famous than any of his ancestors. He thus divided his people into ten kingdoms, each ruled by one of the sons, and called them Jews in memory of Judas, who died soon after this division and whose portion was divided up among the surviving sons. The youngest brother, Joseph, was feared by his brothers due to his extraordinary abilities and was therefore secretly made prisoner and sold to foreign merchants. He was then, following the biblical account, honored by the king for his mastery of magic and skill in interpreting dreams, foretelling a famine and advising the king to put aside food. The story then diverges from that of Genesis; Joseph is honored so much that his advice seems to proceed from a god rather than a mortal.

Nothing is said about his brothers' entering Egypt. Instead, Trogus says that his son was Moses, who inherited his father's knowledge and was also known for his handsomeness. However, the Egyptians, troubled by scabies and leprosy and warned by an oracle, expelled Moses and those with the disease to avoid contagion. Moses became the leader of the exiles. He carried off the sacred utensils

of the Egyptians, who tried forcibly to recover them but were compelled to return
home by a storm. Having reached his ancestral home, Damascus, Moses took possession
of Mt. Sinai. Upon arrival, having suffered in
the Arabian deserts for seven days without
food, he consecrated the seventh day, which
used to be called Sabbath by the nation's
custom, as a fast day, because that day had
ended their hunger and wanderings. Remembering that they had been driven from Egypt
from fear of spreading infection, they took
care not to become odious to their neighbors
for the same reason, deciding to avoid communication with strangers, a rule that gradually became a religious institution. After
Moses, his son Arruas (Aaron) was made
priest to supervise the Egyptian rites, and,
from then on, same person customarily was
both king and priest. As a result of their justice combined with their religion, it is almost
incredible how powerful they became. After
a digression about the geography of Palestine, Trogus goes on briefly to mention the
Persian conquest followed by later political
developments.

This version of the Exodus tradition is
generally favorable to the Jews, even though
it includes accusations of thievery, xenophobia, and disease, attached to a somewhat
abbreviated and distorted account of the
biblical story of Abraham and Joseph. There
are here ten tribes; Joseph is the youngest
brother, with no mention of Benjamin; Moses
is the son of Joseph; much biblical material is
omitted. The Sabbath is again misconceived
as a fast day but here connected with the
Exodus story. Certain biblical names appear
that are absent from earlier pagan accounts,
but, on the other hand, there is again no
awareness of much of Jewish history, in this
account from Aaron, incorrectly called the
son of Moses, to the Persian conquest. The
Maccabean assumption of the kingship by
the priests is distorted into a tradition dating
back to Moses. Feldman explains this mix of
positive and negative attitudes by arguing
that Trogus used a Jewish source as well as
one on the Exodus that was hostile the Jews.

**Lysimachus:** This author may be identical with an Alexandrian Greek grammarian
and mythographer who lived between the
second century B.C.E. and the first century
C.E. At any rate, the Lysimachus whose
work on Egyptian history is extant in quotations in Josephus' *Against Apion* is cited
by Apion and therefore preceded him. This
author exhibits strongly the antisemitic attitudes of the Alexandrian Greek community.

In a citation from Lysimachus' *Aegyptiaca*
in Josephus' *Against Apion* I, 304-311 (Stern,
no. 158), we hear again about the oracle telling the Egyptian king that lepers, cripples,
and the like were causing crop failures, so
that they were expelled and the temples purified. The lepers and scurvy victims were
drowned and the others driven to the desert
to die; however, they assembled, built bon-
fires at night, fasted and implored the gods
to save them, and, led by a certain Moses,
made a straight track to the nearest inhabited country. Moses advised them to show
goodwill to no one, to offer the worst advice,
and to overthrow any temples and altars of
the gods they found. Following this advice,
they traversed the desert with great hardships, reached inhabited country, maltreated
the inhabitants, plundered and set fire to the
temples, and finally reached Judea, where
they built a city called Hierosyla (*hieros*,
"holy," and *sylao*, "seize, plunder," thus
"temple-robbery," "sacrilege," a word found
in Plato and other pre-Hellenistic authors)
after their sacrilegious habits. Later, having
risen to power, they changed the name to the
less disgraceful, altered form of the name,
Hierosolyma. This version of the Exodus is
even more negative towards the Jews than its
predecessors, perhaps changing the material
from Hecataeus and Manetho in this way.
Descriptions of incidents during the Exodus
from Egypt vaguely recall biblical material,
perhaps distorted for polemical reasons by
the Alexandrian Greeks Lysimachus used as
sources. Three other passages in Josephus'
*Against Apion* briefly castigate Lysimachus,
one (II, 20, Stern, no. 160) for giving the "imaginary" figure of 110,000 exiles, the others
(II, 145, Stern, no. 161; and II, 236, Stern,
no. 162) for vilifying Moses and the Jews.

**Apion:** An Egyptian-Greek writer and
scholar, Apion lived in the first half of the

first century C.E. Unlike other writers who attacked the Jews with words, Apion is known to have been personally involved in antisemitic activities, having represented the Greeks of Alexandria in an embassy to the Roman Emperor Caligula in 39/40 C.E., after the riots of 38. Apion's *History of Egypt* survives only in citations, mostly in Josephus' *Against Apion*. This work (Stern, no. 164) notes that, according to Apion, Moses, a native of Heliopolis in Egypt, following Egyptian custom, set up open-air prayer-houses (*proseuxe*, the normal word for Jewish prayer-houses in the lands of the Hellenistic diaspora; Stern, vol. I, p. 395) in that city, with pillars beneath which was the model of a boat, the shadow cast by the pillars describing a circle corresponding to the sun's course in the heavens.

In a passage cited in *Against Apion* II, 15-17, 20-21, 25, 28 (Stern, no. 165), Apion gives an account of the Exodus somewhat similar to that in Lysimachus, adding that the word "Sabbath" comes from "sabbatosis," an Egyptian term for disease of the groin. The Jews had developed tumors in the groin after a six day's march; therefore, after reaching the country now called Judea, they rested on the seventh day. Josephus goes onto say that, according to another passage in Apion, appearing after the reference to the Exodus' lasting six days, Moses went up into Mt. Sinai, remained concealed there for forty days, and then descended and gave the Jews their laws.

Since, in the opinion of Schäfer, p. 29, Josephus seems to omit many details from Apion's account, it may be speculated, on account of reference to groin disease, that Apion alluded to circumcision. The account of the Sabbath is extremely hostile, while the material on prayer-houses is not, and, as Schäfer notes, there is nothing about either impiety or xenophobia on the part of the Jews, since Apion seems to think that the religion Moses introduced in Jerusalem was Egyptian. Stern (vol. I, p. 397) speculates that Apion added details from the biblical narrative to the common Greco-Egyptian tradition to try to depict Moses' isolation on the mountain as a ruse to fool the people into thinking the laws he invented had a divine origin.

Other passages from Apion's *Aegyptiaca*, cited in the same work of Josephus, attack the Jews for not worshipping the gods of Alexandria or erecting statues of the emperors (II, 65, 68, 73, 78, Stern, no. 169), for not eating pork, for practicing circumcision (II, 137, Stern, no. 176), and for having unjust laws and erroneous religious ceremonies resulting in conquest by foreign nations (II, 125, Stern, no. 174). Elsewhere Apion makes more extravagant assertions. At II, 79-80 (Stern, no. 170), Josephus states that, according to Apion, the Jews kept an ass's head made of gold, which they worshipped and considered worthy of the deepest reverence. This was discovered when the troops of Antiochus Epiphanes looted the Temple.

This account differs from that in Diodorus Siculus XXXIV-XXXV, 1.1-5 (Stern, no. 63), which merely states that a statue of Moses seated on an ass was found in the Temple of Jerusalem. The ass-worship story is traced by modern scholars to the mythographer Mnaseas of Patara in Lycia, who, in about 200 B.C.E., was educator to the royal princes in Alexandria. Mnaseas' collection of myths and amazing tales, cited by Apion according to Josephus, *Against Apion*, II. 112-114 (Stern, nos. 28 and 172), says that in a war between the Jews and the neighboring Idumaeans, one of the latter stole the golden head of the pack-ass from the sanctuary; nothing is said about its being an object of worship. Scholars have attached the charge of ass-worship to various periods of Jewish history, from the Babylonian exile through the early second century B.C.E. and later. The identification by enemies of the Jews of the Jewish God with the Greek god Typhon, who was in turn identified with the Egyptian god Seth, the symbol of the desert and drought, enemy of fertility, associated with the wild ass, which carried Typhon away from battle with the gods, has been put forward by scholars, who note that Plutarch, discussed below, connects this flight of Typhon with Jewish origins.[7]

Apion attacks Judaism even more virulently in the passage quoted in *Against Apion*

II, 89, 91-96 (Stern, no. 171), saying that Antiochus found in the Temple a couch on which a man was reclining before an elaborate banquet. The man asked the king to free him, stating that he, a Greek on a business trip, had been kidnapped, shut up secretly in the Temple, and fattened on elaborate feasts; eventually he heard that, according to Jewish law, at a certain time annually, the Jews kidnapped a Greek, fattened him up for a year, and then sacrificed him in a forest and ate him, swearing an oath of hostility to the Greeks. According to Schäfer, pp. 62-65, this story originates from Alexandrian Greek fear of the Jews rather than Seleucid propaganda, but Stern, vol. I, p. 412, holds the opposite view.[8] Apion again mentions the oath, as cited by Josephus, *Against Apion* II, 121 (Stern, no. 173).

**Plutarch:** This famous philosopher and biographer lived ca. 45 to ca. 125 C.E. A priest of the oracle at Delphi, he is the only resident of Greece proper among the Greek and Latin authors of the Roman imperial period who expressed views on Jews and Judaism. Although he visited Alexandria, his views on Judaism differed from those of many members of that city's Greek communities. Two passages in *On Superstition* 3, p. 166A and 8, p. 169C (Stern, nos. 255 and 256), refer to the Sabbath as superstition, the second noting that refusal to fight on that day led to military defeat. Another passage, in *Convivial Questions* 4, 4.4-6.2, pp. 669C-672B, is part of a work describing a banquet at which the guests, including Plutarch's brother, Lamprias, amuse themselves by discussing obscure questions, one of which is "whether the Jews abstain from pork because of reverence or aversion for the pig." Callistratus says the pig is honored because its snout cuts the soil like a plow or for similar reasons. The Jews, he continues, do not hate pigs: their law forbids killing as well as eating them. Lamprias argues that the Jews abstain from the hare because of its resemblance to the ass, which they honor. He adds that they abominate pork because of fear of leprosy-like diseases, and the underside of the pig is covered with scaly eruptions indicative of such a malady. Additionally, he adduces the filthiness of the pig's habits and the (alleged) fact that their eyes are so twisted downward that they are unable to see the sky or anything above them unless carried upside down, on which occasion the pig, which usually squeals, stands astonished by the sight of the sky. Adonis, believed to be identical with Dionysus, was slain by the boar according to mythology.

The next question concerns the god of the Jews. Moeragenes tries to prove that the Jewish God is actually Dionysus, because the Jews celebrate a so-called fast at the height of the vintage, setting out tables with fruit under tents and huts mostly made of vines and ivy. They call the first of the days of the feast Tabernacles. A few days later they celebrate a feast that, Moeragenes argues, is openly identified with Bacchus (Dionysus), a sort of "procession of branches" or "thyrsus procession," in which they enter the Temple each carrying a thyrsus (branch). What they do after entering "we do not know," but the rite is probably a Bacchic revelry, since they use little trumpets to invoke their god, as do Greek Dionysus-worshippers. Others of them advance playing harps; these players are called in their language "Levites," either from *Lysios*, Releaser, or *Evius*, god of the cry.

The Sabbath is also related to Dionysus, since many Greeks call the Bacchants *Sabi*, who utter that cry when celebrating their god. In addition, the use of wine during the Sabbath proves this connection. The High Priest leads their procession, wearing a miter and dressed in a gold-embroidered fawnskin, a long robe, and high boots, with bells attached to his clothes, all of which correspond to Greek customs related to Dionysus-worship. Also, they have noise as an element in their nocturnal festivals, and a thyrsus is carved in relief on the Temple's pediment; drums are used. All this proves that the Jews have no divinity but Dionysus, as does the non-use of honey at their religious festivals. Finally, people are sometimes punished by being forbidden to drink wine.

This is one of the longest continuous passages on Judaism in extant pagan Greek literature and includes information on Jewish holiday services that, although muddled, is not found elsewhere. The discussion of the prohibition of pork vaguely recalls the Greco-Egyptian charge that the Exodus was actually an expulsion of lepers. Many Greeks, associating any ritual involving vines or wine with Dionysus, thought that god was thus being worshipped; as noted below, Tacitus, unsympathetic to the Jews, argued against the identification of Judaism and Dionysus-worship. Scholars have postulated that another source of this association was the Greeks' identification of Dionysus with Sabazius, who Valerius Maximus in turn had identified with the Jewish God. The idea of syncretism between Dionysiac worship in Judea and Judaism has been generally rejected. The fast is clearly Yom Kippur, which precedes Tabernacles by four days, a fact that may have led Plutarch to confuse these holidays. The thyrsus is the *lulav*, palm-branch, carried on all seven days of the holiday. The trumpets are *shofars*, used in the Temple. The mention of the Levites is unique in pagan literature; that to the use of wine on the Sabbath is found elsewhere only in the Latin poetry of Persius (*Satires* 5, 179-184, Stern, no. 190). The reference to abstention from wine as a punishment is believed to refer to the ascetic institution of the Naziriteship.

Plutarch clearly used a source dating from before the destruction of the Second Temple in 70 C.E. The attitude towards Judaism is generally favorable except for the hints about leprosy and the honoring of the ass.[9] Plutarch also refers to the Exodus by stating in *Concerning Isis and Osiris* 31, p. 363 C-D (Stern, no. 259), that those who say the god Typhon's flight from battle (see above, under Apion) was made on the back of an ass, lasted seven days, and that he had two sons, Hierosolymus and Judaeus, are trying to drag Jewish traditions into legend. The only passage referring to Judaism in Plutarch's *Lives*, *Life of Cicero* 7.6, p. 864 C (Stern, no. 263), relates to Cicero's prosecution of Verres for extortion. Someone involved in the case was suspected of Jewish practices; Cicero said, according to Plutarch, "What has a Jew to do with a Verres," since *verres* is Latin for a castrated pig.

**Tacitus:** Cornelius Tacitus, 56-120 C.E., was one of Rome's greatest historians. A senator nostalgic for the days of the Roman republic and traditional customs, he distrusted foreigners and their alien religious ideas, therefore holding extremely negative views of the Jews and Judaism and apparently fearing proselytization. Most of his references to Judaism appear in his account in the *Histories* of the revolt of 70 C.E. and its suppression. IV, 1-13 (Stern, no. 281) contains a digression on Jewish origins and customs preliminary to the description of the war. Tacitus gives varying accounts of the origin of the Jews, including the theories that they represented the superfluous population of Egypt, emigrating to neighboring lands under the leadership of Hierosolymus and Iuda and that they were the Solymi, an ancient and illustrious people. He concludes that most authors agree that they were expelled from Egypt by a plague causing bodily disfigurement. Considered hateful to the gods, they were abandoned in the desert, weeping. Moses then told them that they would have to fend for themselves, regarding as a guide from heaven whoever gave them escape. They agreed, setting forth in utter ignorance and trusting to chance. Suffering from scarcity of water, they saw a herd of wild asses, which they followed to abundant streams of water. They then marched for six days, reaching and seizing a country on the seventh, expelling its people and founding a city and a temple.

To establish his influence over this people for all times, Moses introduced new religious practices, quite opposed to those of all other religions. The Jews consider profane all that Romans consider sacred, and *vice versa*, dedicating a shrine to the ass, sacrificing animals the Egyptians worship, abstaining from pork because the plague that once afflicted them now afflicts this animal, and frequently fasting to commemorate the hunger they experienced during the flight from Egypt. The unleavened Jewish bread is still used in memory of the haste with which they seized the grain. The Jews say they first chose to rest on the seventh day because that day ended their labors; now they also rest every seventh year due to laziness. Others say they do this in honor of Saturn, because the Ideaeans, according to tradition the ancestors of the Jews, were expelled with (the Roman god) Saturn or because the planet of that name moves in the highest orbit and has the greatest potency.

Tacitus goes on to say that while these rites are supported by their antiquity, the other customs of the Jews are base and abominable, owing their persistence to their depravity. The worst rascals among other religions convert to Judaism, sending tribute to Jerusalem. The Jews are loyal towards one another, always ready to show compassion, but feel only hate and enmity for other peoples. They eat and sleep apart and, although prone to lust, abstain from intercourse with foreign women, while among themselves nothing is unlawful. Adopting circumcision to distinguish themselves from other people, they convert people who follow the same practice. "The earliest lesson they receive is to despise the gods, disown their country, and to regard as of little account their parents, children, and brothers."

Wanting to increase their numbers, Jews consider it a crime to kill any late-born child; they believe the souls of those killed in battle or executed are immortal: hence comes their passion for begetting children and their scorn of death. They bestow care on the dead and bury rather than cremate them, following the Egyptian custom. They also follow Egyptian belief regarding the world below, though they have opposite ideas about heavenly things. Instead of worshipping animals, the Jews conceive of one god, and that with the mind only. Thus they regard as impious those who make graven images. "That supreme and eternal being is to them incapable of representation and without end." Accordingly, they set up no statues in their cities, still less in their temples, honoring neither kings nor Caesars.

Tacitus mentions similarities, as does Plutarch, between Jewish and Dionysiac practices but denies that the Jews worship that god, for Jewish rites, unlike the joyous ones of Dionysus, are preposterous and mean. Tacitus then describes the geography of Judea, mentioning the wealth of Jerusalem and the Temple within the city's innermost wall. Only Jews could approach its doors, and only the priests could cross its threshold. The (Maccabean) kings assumed the priesthood to support their civil authority. The first Roman to subdue the Jews and enter their Temple was Pompey, who found there no representations of the gods. The place was empty, and the secret shrine contained nothing. The walls of Jerusalem, but not the Temple, were torn down. The Jews revolted rather than put up Caligula's statue in the Temple, but his death ended the revolt. The Temple was built like a fortress, because the city's founders expected many wars, since the ways of the people differed so much from those of their neighbors. During a factional struggle between two Jewish generals, one, sending a party under pretext of offering sacrifice, got possession of the Temple. Before the Romans took the Temple in 70 C.E., prodigies occurred. The Jews, according to Tacitus, forbid averting them by victims or vows; although superstitious, they oppose all propitiatory rites. Contending hosts were seen in the skies, the Temple was illuminated with fire from the clouds, and the doors suddenly opened, a superhuman voice crying, "The gods are departing." However, this was interpreted as confirming the prophecy that the east would grow strong and that men starting from Judea should possess the world (Vespasian and Titus, according to Tacitus, but the Jews thought otherwise).

This mostly hostile account of Judaism includes some information not found elsewhere in pagan authors and is, in fact, not entirely unfavorable. This includes material derived from a pro-Jewish source, such as the theory that the Jews are of noble origin, being the Solymi, the observation of the seventh day in honor of Saturn (compare the English word "Saturday"), belief in immortality, and the idea that God cannot be represented and is without end.[10]

The Exodus story follows the negative characterizations of Manetho, Pompeius Trogus, and other writers, with variations. The "herd of wild asses" reference recalls the accusation of ass-worship. Tacitus is the only pagan writer to refer to unleavened bread.

Proselytes are attacked as traitors to their families and country. In connection with the Exodus story, Tacitus says that the Jews dedicated a statue of an ass, while elsewhere he remarks the prohibition of graven images and the absence of them in the Temple, an inconsistency noted by the second- and third-century Christian writer Tertullian (*Apologetic* 16, 1-4). However, Tacitus merely says that "many authors" mention the statue, as Stern notes (vol. II, p. 37). Tacitus is also the only pagan writer to refer unambiguously to the sabbatical year, although he claims that it involves rest from all, not merely agricultural, work. Although Tacitus expresses hostility towards all non-Romans, he uses extreme language against the Jews.

Another passage from Tacitus, cited by the fourth-fifth century Christian writer Sulpicius Severus (*Chronicle* II, 30. 3, 6, 7, Stern, no. 282) has the Emperor Titus favoring the destruction of the Temple in order to destroy both Judaism and Christianity, which, although opposed, stem from the same origin. The expulsion of the Jews from Rome by the Emperor Tiberius in 19 C.E., for proselytizing, it is implied, is mentioned in *Annals* II, 85. 4 (Stern, no. 284).

**Conclusion:** To the pagan Greeks, and, later, the Romans, nations like the Greek city-states and other societies that were equated with them in such works as Aristotle's *Politics* and collection of *Constitutions* had their particular histories, foundation-myths, customs, rituals, and gods, and these were equated with those of the Greeks or Romans. While differing substantially in particulars, they had much generally in common, as did the Greek city-states themselves. Encounters with new peoples in Alexander the Great's time and afterward did not essentially change this way of thinking, since the Greeks had long been aware of the somewhat different society of Egypt, described through Greek eyes by, among others, Herodotus and Plato.

The Jews, however, differed in several essential respects. They worshipped a single God whom they would not equate or worship along with any pagan god and of whom they would not make images. Monotheism in this strict sense, as opposed to the vague, philosophical monotheism of a Plato or Aristotle, was incomprehensible to almost all the pagan Greeks and Romans whose writings survive. Almost equally incomprehensible was Jewish exclusiveness; Jews would neither intermarry nor, owing to their dietary laws, eat with non-Jews. Driven out of Egypt in ancient times (so many if not most pagans believed), the Jews hated the rest of the human race and yet, the Romans believed, tried to convert them to their beliefs. Too often succeeding, the Jews menaced civilization.

Many aspects of the Greek attitude towards the Jews probably stemmed from Egyptian antisemitism, although general anti-foreign prejudices were also present. The Romans often felt threatened by foreign immigration in general and Jewish immigration in particular, as well as proselytization by foreign cults including Judaism. Greek and Roman philo-semitism, as exemplified by Plutarch and Varro, praised Judaism essentially in Greek and Roman terms, comparing, for example, the Jewish prohibition of graven images with the lack of images of the gods among the earliest Romans. But overall, to Greek and Roman pagans, the Jews, to a far greater extent than other foreigners they encountered, were almost wholly "other" and therefore greatly misunderstood. Sadly, some of these misunderstandings, or variants of them, persisted into much later times, often with tragic results.

### Bibliography

Feldman, Louis H., *Studies in Hellenistic Judaism* (Leiden, 1996).

Schäfer, Peter, *Judeophobia: Attitudes Toward the Jews in the Ancient World* (Cambridge, 1997).

Stern, Menahem, ed., *Greek and Latin Authors on Jews and Judaism* (Jerusalem, 1976-84).

### Notes

[1] Menahem Stern's three-volume collection of passages referring to the Jews in ancient Greek and Roman literary sources is substantially complete, presenting each passage under its own number and offering Stern's own comments. Below, citations to the passages are referred to as "Stern, [number of passage]." Citations of Stern's commentaries appear as "Stern, [volume number], [page number]."

[2] *Studies in Hellenistic Judaism* (Leiden, 1996), p. 20; *Jew and Gentile in the Ancient World: Attitudes and Interactions from Alexander to Justinian* (Princeton, 1993), p. 124, 175.

[3] Stern, no. 11. This particular passage itself survives only through an excerpt in a book of readings, the *Library*, written and compiled by the Byzantine scholar Photius.

[4] Stern, vol. I, pp. 23-4, concludes that Josephus may have used a Jewish revision of a work of Hecataeus.

[5] See Feldman, *Jew and Gentile*, pp. 237-238, and Stern, vol. I, pp. 163-164.

[6] On Strabo, see Schäfer, pp. 24-26, 38, 89-94, and 108; Stern, vol. I, pp. 261-267 and 304-311.

[7] Detailed discussion of this material, appears in Schäfer, pp. 55-61, and Stern, vol. I, pp. 97-98 and 410.

[8] See also Louis H. Feldman, "Pro-Jewish Intimations in Anti-Jewish Remarks cited in Josephus' *Against Apion*," in *Studies in Hellenistic Judaism*, pp. 177-236, especially at pp. 205-206.

[9] See Stern, vol. II, pp. 545-548 and 558-62; Schäfer, pp. 53-57 and 72-74; and Feldman, "The Jews as Viewed by Plutarch," *Studies in Hellenistic Judaism*, pp. 529-552.

[10] See Louis H. Feldman, "Pro-Jewish Intimations in Tacitus' Account of Jewish Origins," *Studies in Hellenistic Judaism*, pp. 377-407. Schäfer, p. 41, notes this fact but does not go as far as Feldman regarding Tacitus' pro-Jewish intimations, regarding these passages instead as "the grand synthesis of Roman attitudes toward Jews" (p. 185).

STEPHEN A. STERTZ

**PAGAN PHILOSOPHERS ON JUDAISM IN ANCIENT TIMES:** Within the ancient world, lyric and epic poets were the first to comment on Judea, the Jews, and Judaism,[1] and their comments greatly influenced later Greek, Hellenistic, and Roman views of the Jewish people and their religion. The earliest reference to Palestine in Greek literature is from the writings of the poet Alcaeus (end of the seventh century B.C.E.), who mentions the destruction of the Philistine city Askelon by the Babylonians. Later, Choerilus of Samos (second half of the fifth century B.C.E.) wrote an epic poem on the Persian Wars in which he catalogued all the nations that took part in the expedition of Xerxes against Greece. Among these, he tells us, was a wonderful race that spoke a Phoenician language and lived near a broad lake.

Although it is unlikely that the people to whom Choerilus referred were Jews,[2] the passage turned out to define Greek and Roman views of Jews and Judaism. Since the Solymian mountains are mentioned in the *Odyssey* (V, 283), and a people called Solymi appear in the *Iliad* (VI, 184), these Homeric reminiscences gave rise to the association of the name Solyma with Hierosolyma, that is, Jerusalem. Henceforth, Josephus would quote Choerilus as evidence of the glory of the Jewish people, Manetho would refer to his catalogue as evidence of Jewish enmity towards all things Greek, and Tacitus would use it to connect the Jews with the Solymi, a people celebrated in the Homeric poems, suggesting an illustrious ancestry for the Jewish people (*Historiae* V, 2:3).

**Philosophical and religious background:** The first pagan philosophical studies of the Jews and Judaism were driven by what Aristotle called "the desire to know" (*Metaphysics* I, 980a). Although the existing works of Aristotle do not mention the Jews, his curiosity for geography was complemented by his students' curiosity for ethnography. As a result, the figure of the learned Hellenized Jew dominates the earliest philosophical accounts of Jews and Judaism. For the first Hellenistic philosophers regarded Jews as philosophers and Judaism as an enlightened philosophical religion. While it is unlikely that these reports are historically correct, they offer an accurate "cultural" portrait of how pagan philosophers viewed Jews in the fourth and third centuries B.C.E., especially important since this perspective persisted throughout antiquity.

The Greeks had been a long tradition of tracing their intellectual roots to the East. Even Plato had reported a dialogue between Solon and Egyptian priests (*Timaeus* 22-25), and in the wake of such testimony, later Platonists would identify Pythagoras and implicitly Plato as followers of Moses. Aristotelians, too, viewed Jewish cultic practices as indicative of a higher, philosophical religion. And Philo of Alexandria, drawing from both traditions, claimed that Pythagoras, Plato, Heraclitus, Parmenides, Empedocles, Zeno, and Cleanthes learned their philosophy from Moses, and that Judaism was a higher religion (*Legatio ad Gaium* 356). He thus brought full circle the Greek tradition of apologetic invention regarding the peoples of the orient.[3]

Theophrastus (372-288/7 B.C.E.) declared

Jews to be philosophers devoted to philosophical observation. Speaking of the sacrifices they offered to God, he said, "throughout this time they discourse together about the divine, because they are philosophers by nature, and at night they observe the stars, watching them and addressing them in their prayers" (cited in Porphyry, *De Abs.* II, 26). The Jews' observing of the stars was important because, in the eyes of Aristotelians (and Platonists), the orderly motion of the heavenly bodies constituted one of the chief demonstrations of God's existence. Although he did not explicitly mention the belief in one God, Theophrastus' use of the term "the divine" (*to theion*) to describe Jewish discussions on God suggests admiration. Finally, approving of their cultic practices, he stated that although the Jews introduced animal sacrifice, they practiced it reluctantly. Moreover, the way they did it differs radically from the Greeks. They do not eat meat, but only sacrifice holocausts, and these they do in haste in the darkness of night, when they pour out honey and wine. Theophrastus, at least according to Porphyry, disapproved of animal sacrifice, thinking it unworthy of philosophers.

Aristotle's student Clearchus of Soli (347-345 B.C.E.) reported that Aristotle met a Jew in Asia Minor who was Greek "not only in language but also in spirit." He came from the mountains to the seashore "to meet with the Stagarite and his pupils because he was interested in their philosophy." The Greeks, however, "learned philosophy from him."[4] Clearchus goes on to comment: "The Jews are the descendants of the philosophers of India. They say that the philosophers are *Kalanoi* among the Indians, Jews among the Syrians; the name is derived from their place of habitation, Judah. The name of their town which is very strange is Hierousaleme" (see Josephus, *C. Ap.* 179, 16ff.). A similar estimate of Jews as philosophers is offered by Megasthenes (c. 300 B.C.E.), a contemporary of Seleucus Nicator, who visited India and wrote a book on his encounter with a Jewish philosopher.[5]

Hecataeus of Abdera (c. 300 B.C.E.), perhaps a pupil of Pyrron the Sceptic, closely identified the Jews and Jewish institutions with the Egyptians, and he coupled the Jews with emigrants to Greece led by Cadmus and Danaus. He held Moses (and perhaps Abraham) in high regard, praised Jewish monotheism and its cultic practices, and thought highly of Judaism as a priestly religion.[6]

Shortly afterwards, however, such positive perspectives on Jews and Judaism turned negative. Under Ptolemy II, the Helleno-Egyptian priest Manetho published an Egyptian history that discredited Jewish origins (see Josephus, *C. Ap.* I, 73-91; 93-105; 228-252). In one account, he related the history of the Jews to the Egyptian Hyksos, to whom he connected the building of Jerusalem. In a second account, he identified the Jews of Jerusalem with the hated Hyksos. He characterized them as a mob of degraded lepers, as polluters of traditional Egyptian religion, and identified their leader, Osarsiph, with Moses. The Jews, he proposed, subdued Egypt even more brutally than the Hyksos. They burned down towns and villages, plundered temples, defiled the images of the gods, converted shrines into sties, and roasted the flesh of sacred animals. Ultimately King Amenophis defeated the Jews, and, after a period of slavery, allowed them under the leadership of Osarsiph or Moses to migrate to the frontiers of Syria. Here they built Jerusalem.

Manetho's accounts are significant because they initiate an anti-Jewish attitude in Hellenistic views of the Jews and Judaism. Debate rages over the cause of his hostility towards the Jews and concerning whether it explains the origins of antisemitism in antiquity,[7] especially since Manetho did not invent these "legends" himself. Rather he most likely used them in disputations with Jews over the biblical story of Egyptian bondage. In any case Manetho's views were taken over by later Greeks and Romans, who, for generations, offered even less flattering descriptions, in particular, leveling against the Jews charges of *misanthropia, misoxenia,* and *amixia.*

Josephus reports that Posidonius (135-51 B.C.E.) and Apollonius of Molon (c. first century B.C.E.) also were not sympathetic towards the Jews, and that their stories were used later by Apion in a growing tradition of anti-Jewish propaganda (*C. Ap.* II, 79ff.). The idea of Jewish misanthropy was based on the charge that Jews abstained from worshipping the gods revered by others, worshipping instead an ass-head in the Jerusalem Temple. Most chilling, Damocritos (first century C.E.?) accused the Jews of blood-libel, by annual cultic murder of a Greek. Nicarchus even noted that Moses was called "Alpha" because he was a leper (*De Iudaeis*, cited in Photius, *Lexicon*, s.v. *alpha*.).

Although the social setting of such profiles is difficult to reconstruct, it appears they first arose in literary circles close to Antiochus Epiphanes, who had desecrated the Temple. It is also likely that these tales derived from a literary genre that dealt with "conspiracies" against Antiochus' attempts to Hellenize his empire, including Judea. But this battle against the Jews was largely a "paper war," as early anti-Jewish sources were used assiduously by later pagan writers to verify Jewish antipathy towards all things Greek. The supposed Jewish loathing of and unwillingness to merge with others became standard fare in descriptions of Jews by Diodorus Siculus, Lysimachus, and Philostratus.[8]

Despite such attacks, positive assessments of Jews and Judaism also continued and even accelerated. A positive view is reflected in the Pythagorean work *De Universi Natura* attributed to Ocellus Lucanus (c. second century B.C.E.), who, in a comment on human sexuality, remarked on the customs of the Jews. Referring to the Septuagint translation of Gen. 1:28, Ocellus argued that the organs and impulses of sexual intercourse were supplied by God not for pleasure but to perpetuate the human race.[9] Therefore a man should not leave his home, city, family, or God. Rather, as an intelligent man, he should fulfill his prescribed procreative duty, to insure that the earth is populated by an abundance of good men (*De Universi Natura* 45-46). Thus the Jews are commended for setting an ethical precedent for humanity.

In his *Peri Ioudaion*, Alexander Polyhistor (first century B.C.E.) wrote extensively on the Jews. Josephus refers to him when he quotes from a history of the Jews written by Cleodemus-Malchus (or Malchas), in which a genealogical list from Gen. 25:3-4 is introduced to relate the progeny of Abraham and Keturah. Some of their children are said to have accompanied Heracles in his campaigns against Libya and Antaeus. Moreover, we are told that Heracles married a granddaughter of Abraham and Keturah, and their grandson Sophon gave their name to the African people of Sophakes. The relations between Abraham and Heracles have their counterpart in the legendary traditions of kinship between the Jews and Sparta. In general, the claim by Greeks of genealogical and religious ties to Jews became a commonplace feature among historians and philosophers in this period.

Strabo of Amaseia (c. 64 B.C.E.-20 C.E.) referred to Moses as a legislator of supreme status, placing him alongside such Greek lawgivers such as Minos, Lycurgus, and Tiresias (*Geographica* XVI, 760-765). The Jewish God similarly is viewed most positively, as "that which surrounds us all, also the earth and the sea; we call him the heavens, or the world, or the nature of the whole universe" (XVI, 760-761). Here the elements of Judaism were framed within a pantheistic outlook—imageless worship, the apotheosis of the divine in a modest shrine, all befitting a people and religion of wisdom and righteousness.

The God of the Jews was also viewed as a protector of humankind and the patron of kings. Writing on kingship, the Pythagorean pseudo-Ecphantus (first to second centuries C.E.) alluded to Genesis. First, he noted the fall of man from his pure nature and argued that he was raised from earth by "divine inspiration," which "attached him to the eternal living being, displaying to his better part the holy aspect of the creator."[10] Second, he claimed that while man is the best among earthly creatures, the king is still more divine, for he has been "made by the best craftsman, who wrought him using himself as a model. Thus the king is the one and only creature to represent the king of heaven, being always known to his Creator." Such sources propose that Greek and Jew share common cultural origins, histories, and religions. This is a quite different perspective from the other central one of this period, in which, as we shall see, the Jews and their cult were subjected to significant hostility.

**Greco-Roman philosophy (106 B.C.E.-555 C.E.):** To characterize Hellenic and Roman attitudes towards Jews and Judaism is difficult, for these stretch from amusement to contempt, dislike, and active hostility. For some gentiles, Judaism was so appealing as to invite conversion. For others, Jewish religious rites such as circumcision seemed barbaric, the dietary laws appeared ridiculous, and the refusal to acknowledge other gods was impious atheism. Nonetheless, Roman imperial policy decreed that, as a foreign cult, Judaism comprised an official religion of the empire, an important status since, in the capital, magistrates were charged with prohibiting foreign rites, sacrificers, soothsayers, and books of prophecy other than the Roman (Pliny, *Ep.* 39.16.8, 4.30, 25.1). While this policy focused positively upon Jews as citizens of the empire, it nonetheless looked negatively on Judaism as a tolerated cult.[11] This began to change only in the early fourth century, when Roman imperial policy began to view the Jewish religion favorably. To comprehend this shift we must look at Roman policies towards Judaism.

State religion in the empire was governed by a *princeps* who, as *pontifex maximus*, was responsible for public morals and the well-being of the state. Precisely what both responsibilities entailed shifted from emperor to emperor. What remained constant after Augustus was the Caesars' inclusion of foreign gods and cults in the state religion. Since Judaism was among the earliest of the religions to be recognized, it remained under imperial protection (but not sanction) until the close of antiquity. Even so, traditional Helleno-Egyptian antipathy towards the Jews, alongside Jewish revolts against Roman hegemony in the eastern empire, colored pagan philosophical views of Jews and Judaism in the first two centuries of the *imperium Romanum*. Only the climate of the rise of Christianity in the last three centuries of Roman antiquity led pagan philosophers to

begin to assess Jews and Judaism positively.

**Early Roman philosophy (116 B.C.E.-220 C.E.):** In two main passages on the Jews in his major work, *Res Divinae*, Varro (116-27 B.C.E.) offers the first systematic attempt to explain Judaism from the perspective of an advocate of traditional Roman religion. He identifies the Jewish God with Jupiter and says that he is called Iao in the Chaldean mysteries. We cannot say where Varro got the latter name. It may have been from the neo-Pythagorean Nigidius Figulus. In any case, he attempts to link the God of the Jews with Greek philosophical thought.[12]

The Jewish censure of cult images most impressed Varro. He argued that the iconoclastic Jewish cult exemplifies pure and useful worship and resembles the original cult of old Rome (cited in Augustine, *Civ. Dei* VI, 31). Here he saw a close connection between Greek and Jewish philosophical thought. The cult of images had long been criticized by Aristotelian philosophers, and Stoics from Zeno to Seneca also poured ridicule on images. Add to this the argument that image worship detracts from the fear of the gods, and we have Varro's profile of Judaism's nobility.

Cicero (106-43 B.C.E.) had an ambiguous attitude towards the Jews and Judaism. Unlike Varro, no mention of them appeared in his philosophical works, and he exhibited no appreciation for the incorporeal nature of the Jewish deity. Only in his rhetorical writings—*Pro Flacco* and *De Provinciis Consularibus*—do we encounter Cicero's views, and his comments are most disparaging. But we should remember that these were rhetorical speeches crafted to defend Flaccus and to impugn Gabinius, who was closely connected with the Jews. In brief, Jews were instrumental in the prosecution of Flaccus, siding with Gabinius. Therefore, they were perceived as an enemy of the Roman Publicani and hence as enemies of republican Rome. On this account, Cicero mercilessly attacked the Jews and Judaism.[13]

The judicial and polemical contexts of these speeches define how we should read them. It was a commonplace in forensic rhetoric to denigrate opponents, and Cicero himself stresses the differences between his personal views and those expressed in his speeches (*Pro Flacco* 139). Thus in *Pro Flacco* other "Asians," labeled by the speaker as Phrygians, Mysians, Carians, and Lydians, fare no better than the Jews. Further, since his attack does not even resemble the charges of misanthropy and incompetence brought against the Jews by his acquaintance Apollonius Molon, we need not label Cicero's views as anti-Jewish.[14]

Nonetheless, what Cicero said about the Jews and Judaism was hardly flattering. Laelius had sued Flaccus on behalf of the cities of Roman Syria. Among the charges brought against him was that, while in Asia, he confiscated Jewish money. In defense of his client, Cicero called Judaism a "barbara superstitio." He noted Jews' "raging" in the *cantiones* and claimed that Pompey did not pillage the Jerusalem Temple because he respected the Jews. Rather he did so because of his own sense of honor and political expediency (*Pro Flacco* XXVIII, 67). Finally, he reminds his audience of the barbaric religion of the Jews, of the noble ancestral traditions of the Romans, and of the recent war the Jews waged against Rome (XXVIII, 68).

In the *De Provinciis Consularibus* Cicero impugns the character of Gabinius, the enemy of the *publicani*. He does so by noting Gabinius' association with disreputable peoples such as Syrians and Jews, people born to be slaves (*De Prov. Consul* V:10).[15] He thus cast the Jews as adversaries of the republic and friends of its enemies: Gabinius, Piso, and indirectly Caesar (V:12). Clearly, late republican politics lie behind this attack. The opponents of the *publicani* were supported by the Jews of Rome. Moreover, consuls such as Gabinius in Syria allied himself with Syrians and Jews against the *publicani* and the taxes levied by them.

Their goal was to transfer tax collection from the Roman societies of *publicani* to local authorities. It is likely that the five synhedria were made responsible for the collection of taxes (Josephus, *Ant.* XIV, 91; *BJ* I, 170). Cicero's main argument against the Jews was cast within the context of Gabinius' governorship of Syria and his improper attitude towards the *publicani*. His policies led to the financial and political ruin of Cicero's clients and constituency.

Seneca (c. end of the first century B.C.E.-65 C.E.) was the first Latin philosopher deliberately to attack Jews and Judaism for their negative impact on Roman society. Although he showed antipathy towards oriental religions in general,[16] his critique of Judaism is rather different, standing outside the context of a philosophical critic of the rationality of Judaism as a religion, or a critique of Judaism from a defender of the *mos maiorum*.

Seneca's references to the Jews date from the 60s C.E.[17] This was the height of Jewish proselytizing and the spread of Jewish customs in the Mediterranean world. As a defender of traditional Roman religion, he was disturbed by the spread of the religion of the "gens sceleratissima" throughout the empire, noting that "the vanquished have given laws to their victors" (*De Superstitione*, cited in Augustine, *Civ. Dei* VI, 11). These laws included, for instance, the custom of lighting lamps on the Sabbath. But in the Roman view, the gods do not need light. Nor do they need morning salutations before the doors of temples. For Seneca, rather, "God is worshipped by those who really know him. Let us forbid bringing towels and flesh-scrapers to Jupiter and offering mirrors to Juno; for God seeks no servants. Of course not; he himself does service to mankind everywhere, and to all he is at hand to help" (Plutarch, *Epistula Morales* XCV, 47). These attacks likely were formulated to counter the claims of some Jews that their religion was of a higher type than others and to respond to Romans who were impressed by the abstract monotheism and cultic purity of Judaism.

Seneca stayed for a time with his aunt in Egypt, and there he may have encountered his ideas about Judaism. While there is little evidence that Philo of Alexandria was read outside of Jewish circles in Alexandria, his views, for instance, that Judaism is a philosophy, may comprise the sort of conceptions that Seneca felt it necessary to critique. Seneca clearly held an idea already encountered in Hecataeus and Manetho, that the Jewish religion encourages *amixia*, an unwillingness to merge with others. In Seneca, this notion is located within a specific Roman context. Judaism is in no way a philosophical religion.

In his *Life of Apollonius of Tyana* Philostratus (d. 240 C.E.) presents a less than enthusiastic attitude towards oriental cults, depicting the Jews in particular as in perpetual revolt against Rome and humanity. They are "separated from ourselves by a greater gulf than divides us from Susa or Bactra or the more distant Indies" (*Vita Apollonii* V, 33-34). Their cult is so bloodily abhorrent that the "divine" Apollonius refused to visit Judea (V, 27), so polluted that a Pythagorean's abhorrence of shedding blood prevents him from visiting Judea (VI, 34).

In *Apollonius*, Pythagorean antipathy towards the Jews appears excessive. But again we must be cautious in ascribing to Philostratus the charge of anti-Jewish propaganda. His attitude towards the Jews is conditioned, rather, by his implicit polemic against Christians. Moreover, Pythagorean fervor against blood-letting and taboos against sacrifice were commonly known in antiquity. Indeed, these ideas stretch back to the master himself. The strictest of the Pythagoreans, like Apollonius, called the Pure, rejected all fleshy food and respected only altars unstained by blood. They shunned all contact with hunters, butchers, cooks, and, in this case, priests of the Jerusalem cult.

While Seneca was hostile to the Jews, the other great Stoic, Epictetus (50-130 C.E.), was neutral. In a discussion on the need for a criterion for good and evil he pointed out the differences in the opinions on food of the Jews, Syrians, Egyptians, and Romans (Arrian, *Dissertationes* I, 11:12-13). He went on to note that these nations do not disagree over whether holiness should be pursued but on whether eating pig is holy or not (I, 22:4). A final reference implies that Epictetus knew of the rite of baptism in conversion to Judaism (II, 9:19-21). Striking here is Epictetus' almost casual acquaintance with Jewish customs. By the first century some knowledge of Jews and Judaism was commonplace, particularly at Rome and in the eastern provinces of the empire, as Plutarch and Sextus Empiricus attest.

Plutarch (45-125 C.E.) came from a prominent family of Chaeronea in Boeotia. As a student in around 66-67 C.E. he went to Athens and became a follower of Ammonius, the head of the Academy, who gave him a thorough training in philosophy (*De E.* 387f.). Sent on a political mission to Rome, he eventually returned there to teach and to learn. Later he settled in Chaeronea, where a circle grew up around him.[18]

Plutarch was extremely great loyalty to the temple of Apollo at Delphi. He assumed that all nations worshipped gods who performed similar functions. For Plutarch, most Mediterranean myths and rites thus were good, created by wise men whose insights included all the best that posterity later came to learn in philosophy. At least in *Quaestiones Convivales*, this same view framed his picture of the Jewish God and religion.

Plutarch thus speaks of believers as searching out through reason the truths inherent in the mysteries. Accordingly, in his work *On Isis and Osiris*, dedicated to a friend, Clea, who had been initiated into the mysteries of Dionysus, Isis, and Osiris, Plutarch studies the names, myths, and rituals of the Egyptian gods. He finds in them the same meanings and functions as those in the Greek cults. And Plutarch takes a similar approach to the study of Judaism, which he examines from the perspective of a second century Platonist. To understand his approach, let us briefly outline the salient points of his philosophy.[19]

In his discussion of Apollo, Plutarch argued that the traditional gods were aspects of the one god (*De E* 392eff., *De Is.* 351d, 382b, *De Fac.* 944e), with the Logos comprising the principal intermediary between the intelligible and sensible worlds. He showed this through an allegorization of the two aspects of Osiris (*De Is.* 373ab). Below the primal God and Intelligence, Plutarch posited a World Soul (*De Is.* 373e) and daemons (*Def. Or.* 416cff.). This metaphysical hierarchy is significant because later Platonic philosophers with a little knowledge of Judaism and the Septuagint read Plutarch and identified the God of Genesis with the artificer of the Plato's Timaeus (*Co. Apol.* 109ad).

Following a hint in the *Symposium*, Plutarch also argued that God acts through *daimones*. Good daemons of compact intelligence and passionate soul care for men, give oracles, and appear in visions (*Co. Apol.* 109ad). These daemons are the gods of native religions (*De Is.* 361ae). However, there are also bad or imperfect daemons, which are malevolent (*Def. Or.* 944cd, cf. 415c). As clients of an evil world soul, these powers bring evil into the world (*De Fac.* 945b, *De Is.* 360dff., 361b, *Def. Or.* 417b). Significantly within the context of this study, Plutarch argues that evil daemons cause superstition or *deisidaemonia*, which is fear of the gods brought on by obsession and ignorance. In brief, he holds that superstition separates people from society because the superstitious person does not use reason in affairs of religion (*De Superstitione* 166c). Instead fearful images are created that generate horrible fantasies, and this leads to bizarre and extreme behavior. Superstition manifests itself in rites and taboos, consultations with sorcerers, charms and spells, and unintelligible language in prayers addressed to the gods.

The only antidote to such thought and activity is rational inquiry and teaching. Religion is legitimate for Plutarch only if it is rational and assists one in leading a good life. That is to say, the supreme object of human life is likeness to god, not irrational conformity with nature (*De Sera* 550dff.). This doctrine allows Plutarch to define the virtues and propose an ethical theory of religion, and it is within this specific didactic context that we encounter Plutarch's views of the Jews and their religion.

Plutarch[20] focuses on the dietary habits of the Jews, which give him an opening to comment on Jewish religious beliefs and practices in general. His most extensive treatment of food practices is found in *Quaestiones Convivales*, where the topic arises, not surprisingly, at a symposium held at Aidepsos in Euboea. Interest here is largely limited to the dietary norms of various sects. These include Pythagorean abstention from fish (*QC* VIII, 8), Egyptian priestly avoidance of salt (V, 10:1), and the Jewish prohibition against eating pork (V, 1-2), mentioned in

the course of a conversation between Symmachus, an advocate of seafood, and Lamprias, Plutarch's brother. This leads to a discussion on whether this is done because the Jews honor the pig for its role in the history of agriculture or whether they irrationally abhor it. Callistratus suggests that the Jews honor swine, as they do the ass, which helped them find water during their sojourn in the desert. Lamprias objects and claims that the Jews' abstention from pork arises from a fear of leprosy, a disease associated with this food. Furthermore, the pig is filthy, its living quarters are disgusting, and, in myth, Adonis or Dionysus was killed by a boar. This is why the Jews refuse to eat it.

At this point Plutarch, attempting to understand this aspect of the Jewish cult philosophically, suggests that there is a solid logic behind Jewish dietary practices and a connection between the religions of Jews and Greeks. This tendency continues throughout the rest of the dialogue. Lamprias' suggestion is followed up by Moiragenes, the Athenian, who established links between the Dionysian and Jewish cults. These are centered around the Feast of Tabernacles and the Sabbath. After all, he suggests, many people call the Bacci "Sabboi," the dress worn by the High Priest resembles Dionysian cultic grab, and the sounding of trumpets during nocturnal celebrations sounds like Dionysiac revelry.

The Jews are also mentioned in one of Plutarch's earlier essays, *De Superstitione*. Here the picture is less complementary. The keeping of the Sabbath is listed among the many barbarian customs adopted by the Greeks (*De Superst.* 166a), and it is noted that Jewish inaction on the Sabbath brought disaster upon Jerusalem (169c). Plutarch accordingly deems Judaism a superstitious religion (166a, 169c). In the first and second centuries B.C.E./C.E. this view of Jewish military behavior had become commonplace (Josephus, *Contra Apionem* 1.205-211).

In conclusion, we must be careful to define what Plutarch meant by this. Not all Jewish beliefs were viewed as superstitious, and he thought in general that, if understood rationally, many Greek, Roman, and Oriental rites were comprehensible and beneficial.

In this context, even Jewish dietary and cultic norms are represented as admirable. Only a few Jewish customs, such as Sabbath observance, appear irrational.

For Lucian (120-180 C.E.), by contrast, all religious rituals were worthless vestiges, maintained in an age that had forsaken reason. Except for a few ironical passages in which he depicts the gods as complaining of the new barbarian invaders of Olympus, Lucian held belief in any of the gods to be depravity and consigned philosophy and religion to the realm of the foolish. The *Hermotinus* argues that philosophy is unnecessary to sensible living; in the *Banquet* and the *Lover of Lies* the propositions of Platonists, Stoics, Aristotelians, and Pythagoreans are lampooned for their vacuity, while the philosophers are portrayed as greedy, sexually depraved, quarrelsome, and egocentric; and in *Philosophers for Sale*, with its jumble of contradictory theories, he makes fun of philosophy in the abstract. We thus see a change of mood taking place, with Lucian anticipating the negative attitudes of Celsus, Porphyry, and Julian towards new religions such as Judaism and Christianity.

Lucian criticized philosophy at the level at which it was most vulnerable in later antiquity, its inability to offer a straight-forward explanation of the universe, explain the place of the species in the order of things, and propose a clear-cut program of ethical behavior. Philosophy thus was in danger of becoming a sub-form of rhetoric, in which the validity of its propositions could not be proven either by coherence or correspondence to any manifest truth. Later philosophers such as Porphyry were sensitive to this problem and, like Lucian, had little patience for sects that could not demonstrate the coherence of their propositions.

The reaction against irrationalism was pervasive among the intelligentsia of the second and third centuries, with broad social consequences. The Olympian cult illustrates this, for while, in the imperial era, it continued to have an official and symbolic significance, it was no more metaphysically persuasive than the Roman imperial cult or other Hellenistic cults. Lucian saw this and attempted to undermine the traditional religions by parodying them through reason.

Apuleius (second century C.E.) complements Lucian in two ways. He was born in the provinces, Madauros in Numidia, and was a satirist of contemporary religious movements including Judaism. In his *Apologia* he lists Moses and the magician Iohannes. Both were active in the wake of Zoroaster and Ostanes (*Apologia* 90). In his *Florida* he characterizes the Egyptians as "eruditi" because of their association with the Egyptian Gymnosophists; Nabataeans, Parthians, Ituraeans, and Arabs merely by their dress; while Jews are stigmatized as "superstitiosi" (*Florida* 6). In *Metamorphoses* IX, 14, he tells a story of a miller's wife despised by the gods because she made a sacrilegious claim that there was only one God. Furthermore, in her devotion to this God she feigned empty rites, denounced everyone, deceived her husband, drank wine from dawn to dusk, and lived a life of lewdness.

These descriptions assist us in tracing anti-Jewish typologies in the early empire. Many are familiar from earlier sources, but a few are clearly Roman. These include a connection between the leaders of Judaism and those of other oriental religions. There is also a clear association of Judaism with monotheism. Such perspectives will be interpreted in a more subtle and positive way by the second century philosophers Galen and Numenius.

Galen (130-200 C.E.) authored some five hundred works on philosophy, religion, and comedy, but his main legacy is as a physician who wrote extensive works in anatomy and physiology. Additionally, by his day Judaism and Christianity had made an impact on Roman intellectuals, so that, like Pliny and Lucian, he became one of the earliest Roman witnesses to these religions.[21] He was, indeed, the first Hellenic author who defined these religions as schools and who approached their teachings as a philosophy. His curiosity helped prepare the way for both to be taken seriously in intellectual circles. Numenius, Celsus, Porphyry, and Julian could do no less than recognize what Galen wrought.

While none of them wrote separate treatises on Jews and Christians, they were mentioned in discussions of political and religious concerns. Here Galen offered something new. His criticisms of Jewish and Christian teachings appeared in his works *On the Usefulness of Parts of the Body* and *On the Pulse*.[22] He referred to Judaism and Christianity with the term "school" and characterized both as philosophies that demonstrate their propositions through appeals to faith and the authority of their teachers (3.3). Although Galen finds Jewish and Christian teachings incompatible with reason, nowhere does he make carping remarks about either.

Arguing that Archigenes' theory, to which his own *On the Pulse* responded, was devoid of careful investigation and sound reasoning, Galen claimed that these traits linked him with Jews and Christians (3.3), for each group lacks the capacity to provide a cogent demonstration for what it proposes. Hearing Archigenes thus is like listening to those in "the school (*diatribe*) of Moses and Christ and hearing talk of undemonstrated laws" (2.4). There are physicians "who practice medicine without scientific knowledge . . . who framed laws for the tribe of Israel, since it is his method in his books to write without offering proofs, saying 'God commanded, God spoke'" (*Anat. Hipp.* 3.4).

A familiar rationalist critique emerges. Galen notices these two religions not because they are intellectually novel or socially revolutionary but because they explain reality on the basis of undemonstrated arguments. The followers of Moses and Christ are rationally moribund; their sages do not meet the minimal criteria appropriate to philosophers, let alone physicians. We have, of course, seen this critique before in Lucian's parody of philosophers and the maxims of philosophical schools (*Vitarum Auctio* 2.449-511), which are criticized for their tendency to appeal to oracular tradition and personalities and not to reasoned investigation (*Hermotimus* 16, 27). Galen, by contrast, saw the value of philosophy, like the study of anatomy, physiology, and physics, in its providing rational demonstrations to support all claims (*De usu partium* 11.2.3, 11.5).

In his medical and philosophical investigations, Galen, later echoed by Celsus (*C. Cels.* 5.14) and Porphyry (see Macarius Magnes, *Apoc.* 4.2, 4.24), criticized the assumptions in Genesis that creation was an act of divine will and that God created a universe out of what did not already exist. Both teachings contradict Greek cosmological doctrine, which holds that the world-order and its designer follow perfectly rational principles according to nature and that the demiurge is non-anthropomorphic (see *Tim.* 28a-32c). Viewed from the perspective of Galen's demiurgic theology and cosmology, the Mosaic theology and cosmogony are very primitive indeed, holding, as they do, that the universe and its creator are beyond the laws of nature and that God created the world at will. For Galen, the opinion of Moses is in error because it does not follow the right method in assessing nature or its creator; its views are beyond demonstration. The unreasoned character of the biblical religions particularly struck Galen and the thinkers that followed him. Christians in particular were viewed as dogmatic and uncritical in their thinking, unwilling to submit their teacher and teachings to critical examination.

Around 170 C.E., during the reign of Marcus Aurelius, a work against Christianity called *True Doctrine* appeared. Its author was Celsus, an unknown middle Platonic philosopher of the period. The writing did not survive the war of pamphlets between Hellenes and Christians in late antiquity and exists only in fragments as preserved by the Christian Origen in his *Contra Celsum* (Praef. 4).[23]

Celsus knew the writings of the Jews, the evangelists, and the early Church fathers. His assessment of the first was largely determined by his hostility towards the second. He argues against Judaism's historical messianism, religious anthropocentrism, philosophical creationism, and the low social status of its adherents. These Jewish characteristics, he argued, were passed on to the Christians with disastrous results. Anticipating Porphyry, he noted the Christians' arguments that they were the heirs to Judaism and the embarrassing fact that Jews had rejected these claims (*C. Cels.* 2.1, 2.4, 2.11, 2.28, 7.18).

The *True Doctrine* pullulates with a critique of Judaism, but especially of Christianity, on three broad fronts: political, social, and philosophical. Taking up a familiar criticism, its author viewed Christianity as a marginal political and social movement devoid of any rational principles for articulating a coherent ideological agenda (*C. Cels.* 3.17, 4.10). Christians thus are a gullible and credulous people who espouse a naive fideism and absolutely refuse to subject their teachings to reasoned analysis and lucid argumentation (1.9, 3.55, 5.61-6). This irrational character of Judaism and Christianity makes it impossible for any sensible person to place scriptural teachings within the boundaries of rational religion. To this criticism, Celsus adds that Christianity lacks a system of ancient custom and tradition (*C. Cels.* 1.28, 1.32, 1.41, 2.55), a malady from which Judaism was exempt. Christian tradition thus reflected a particularly irrational faith. Its beliefs were based on the transgression of the laws of Judaism and Hellenism.[24]

These accusations suggested a great and present danger. Celsus argued that the teachings of the Christians would lead to the abandonment of the emperor and the loss of an empire to "lawless and savage barbarians" (*C. Cels.* 8.68), to peoples against whom the emperor and Celsus himself were tenaciously fighting. Even as the Roman emperor and his legions fought wars from Gaul and Dacia to Syria and Parthia to preserve the *imperium Romanum*, Celsus attacked the enemy within to preserve *Romanitas*.

In this setting, the harmony of the world was conceived in political and intellectual terms, for it rested on a culture that was international. Rome was a universal empire under an absolute emperor. Even religion was brought into this universalistic perspective. To the claim that all men could be citizens of a unified empire was added the idea that their gods could be Roman deities as well. Even the gods of the remote regions of the Roman world were made equal to Jupiter Optimus Maximus.

While Jewish attitudes towards these developments remain unknown, past precedents suggest that many second century Jews would have concurred with them. Judaism met the criteria of an ancient religion with commendable *mores*. Jews were loyal to Rome and its emperor, and the Jewish God was seen as part of an almost cosmopolitan *theokrasia*. Among those who concurred with such an assessment were philosophers, who continued to regard Jews and Judaism highly. It is to these writers that we now turn.

Numenius of Apamea (second half of the second century C.E.) was a disciple of Pythagoras and Plato and a precursor of the Neoplatonists. He included Judaism among the oriental religions he most admired and found parallels between the teachings of his masters and the doctrines and rituals of the Brahmans, Magi, Egyptians, and Jews. His praise of the Jews and Judaism echoes the early writers of the Hellenistic era. Indeed, his admiration for Moses is unequaled in the philosophical literature of Mediterranean antiquity. He says: "For what is Plato, but Moses speaking Attic?"[25] Although such sentiments were common in the Alexandrian Jewish philosophers Aristobulus and Philo and the Alexandrian Christian philosophers Clement and Origen, this claim is unprecedented in pagan philosophical literature.

Numenius' knowledge of Judaism included frequent use of both the Pentateuch and the Prophets, which he interpreted allegorically. He also knew of the apocryphal traditions about Moses, including the story of the contest between Moses and the Egyptian magicians (*De Bono*, cited in Origen, *C. Cels.* IV, 51, and Porphyry, *De Antro Nympharum* 10). Most important, Numenius described the Jewish God as the "father of all the gods," and said he was intolerant of all other gods (cited in Lydus, *De Mensibus* IV, 53, 199 [Wuensch]). Unlike Galen, and, later, Iamblichus, Julian, Syrianus, Proclus, and Simplicius, Numenius thus does not explicitly connect the Jewish God to the demiurge, the creator god of the physical universe.

In another vein Vettius Valens (second century C.E.) mentions Abraham as an astrological authority (*Anthologiae* I, 10; II, 28, 29 [Kroll]). Abraham's reputation as an astrologer may go back to Artapanus, who claimed that Abraham taught astrology to the Egyptian king Pharethotes and the

Phoenicians (Eusebius, *PE* IX, 18:1, 2). The prominence of Abraham as an astrologer is also reflected in the later work of Firmicus Maternus (first half of the fourth century C.E.). Firmicus also mentions Abram four times as an astrological authority. Indeed, he is placed among the best-known astrological writers Petosiris, Nechepso, and Critodemus. Moreover, in a surprising turn, Abram is connected with Orpheus.

Finally, the apologetic work *Cohoatio ad Gentiles* (second half of the third century C.E.?) claims that some very ancient Athenian writers—Hellanicus (fifth century B.C.E.) and Philochorus (fourth to third centuries B.C.E.)—referred to Moses' antiquity. He replaces the Egyptian king and legislator Mneus. In addition, we are told that Greek thought and literature are dependent upon Jewish sources, and quotes from Orpheus and Sophocles are adduced as written by Jews (Ps-Iustinus, *Cohoratio ad Gen.* 9). All this is apologetic invention, but it testifies to continued attempts to link Moses and the Jews to Greek origins in the third century C.E.

These testimonies link positive assessments of the Jews and Judaism in the philosophical, scientific, and historical traditions between Numenius and Valens. Clearly, by the end of the second century onwards, pagan thinkers held Moses, Abraham, and the teachings of the Jews in the highest esteem.

**Later Platonism (220-550 C.E.):** Our next thinker, Porphyry, drew deeply from Plotinus, an important Platonist who himself wrote nothing on Jews or Judaism.[26] Plotinus' standard for judging the efficacy of a religion was knowledge, tradition, and custom: the *logos* and *nomos* that had been handed down from antiquity and from the gods. In his day, certain thinkers, like the Gnostics, held profane what the Platonists thought sacred and thus were held to turn people away from "true" devotion to the one high god. Plotinus was convinced that if such associations attracted too many adherents, they could disrupt the cohesion and stability of the *politeia*. These were the values that stood behind Porphyry's defense of Judaism and attack on Christianity.

In the last moments of his life (c. 232-310 C.E.), Porphyry finished a project that had occupied him for much of his over seventy years, a study of the religions of the Roman Empire, including Judaism and Christianity, contained in his *Philosophy from Oracles, Sentences*, and the lost work *Against the Christians*. Early in his life he was sympathetically disposed to the new movements and their teachers, Moses and Jesus. At the end, he maintained his respect only for Judaism (see *Epistula ad Marcell*).

The fragments remaining from *Against the Christians* suggest that Porphyry devoted a major part of the work to the Jewish scriptures, including the historical problem of the date of Moses (see Theodoret of Cyrus, *Affect.* VII, 36) and the vulgarities explicit in the book of Hosea, whom God commanded to marry a whore (see Jerome, *Comm. in Osee* 12). Most important, however, he attacked the historical credibility of the book of Daniel, the sixth century dating of which was central in Christian presentations of history from the beginning of time. Porphyry's goal was to destroy the claim that Daniel prophecized the birth of Christ, the final destruction of the Jewish Temple, and the coming of the anti-Christ. Based on detailed historical proofs culled from Greco-Roman chronology, he claimed that Daniel was pseudepigraphal, not a prophecy about the coming of the Christian messiah at all but about the Maccabean revolt.

Whatever Porphyry may have thought about the Christians, we know in no uncertain terms what later Christians thought of him. Until the end of Mediterranean antiquity *Against the Christians* was not merely feared by Christian bishops, it was burned by Christian emperors. As a result Christian Rome gave Porphyry a prominence he could never have imagined possible. Alongside emperors remembered for their cruelty towards the faith, Porphyry was disliked by Christians as much as the "spine-chilling" Julian.

Part of this judgment likely rested on the fact that Porphyry was a proponent of Judaism. For this Neoplatonist, the Jews' history marked them as pious to an ancestral god, loyal to a cultural tradition, and as bearers of a religion that is philosophical in thought and ethical in behavior. In describing the Essene, his ideal example of the Jew who practices Judaism, he pictures the most sublime example of the virtues of *Romanitas* (*De Abstinentia* 4.11-14). By the dawn of the fourth century, Jews and Judaism thus had become a model people practicing an exemplary religion. The Essene had become for the Neoplatonist a quintessential Roman: loyal, courageous, intelligent, and pious.

Pagan philosophers after Porphyry were strangely silent about Jews and Judaism. Iamblichus (third century C.E.) says only that the God honored by the Hebrews is the demiurge.[27] Sallustius (fourth century C.E.) notes that circumcision was the most characteristic Jewish national custom.[28] From Lactantius and Eusebius we know of the anti-Christian polemicist Hierocles (beginning of the fourth century C.E.), whose work reflects the views of Jews and Christians held by Celsus, Porphyry, and, later, Julian. Hierocles wrote the *Philalethes*, a blistering attack against the Christian Bible and claims made about Jesus by his followers. Eusebius' reply to Hierocles confined itself to the negative comparison he drew between Apollonius of Tyana and Jesus (*PG* XXII, cols. 795ff.). Lactantius also refers to Hierocles' portrait of Christus: "after he had been put to flight by the Jews, he collected a gang of nine hundred men and committed robberies" (Hierocles, *Philalethes*, cited in Lactantius, *Divinae Institutiones* V, 3:4).

Julian (331-363 C.E.), who lived in a divided world, had much to say about both Jews and Christians. While the emperors had been Christian since Constantine's conversion in 313 C.E, the Roman Empire was not yet a Christian state or society. It thus came as a shock to Christians when the young son of Julius Constantius, who was raised a Christian and was a lector in the Church, upon assuming the purple, disowned Christianity, embraced the gods of pagan Rome, and commenced a systematic attack upon the Christian movement.[29]

As was the case with Celsus and Porphyry, Julian's attitude towards the Jews was conditioned by his hostility towards Christianity and admiration for Hellenism. Julian saw in the Jewish scriptures an *atheotes* that advocated exclusivity and was hostile to other religions and their gods (*Con. Gal.* 42e-43b). But he also saw positive elements, such as the truth of their myths (93d), their ancestral customs (238c), and their devotion to ritual practices (354ab).

In brief, Julian held that Jewish teachings and cult activities fell below those of Homer, Hesiod, and Plato (100c). He thought the Jews superior to "the Galilean sect" but inferior to the Hellenes. Jewish theology, eschatological teachings, and prophecy were flawed. Jews think that "all is possible with God," not realizing that God cannot do what is contrary to nature (*Con. Gal.* 96c). God cares not only for the Jews, as Moses claimed, since Egyptians, Chaldeans, and Assyrians also have wise priestly teachers (176ab). Moreover, the Hebrews developed no science, philosophy, or civilization as the did the Greeks. Thus they are an inferior people (178a-184b).

Julian also explains a number of fundamental misconceptions held by Jews and Christians. Jews identify their God with the supreme God worshipped by all when he is only a national or tribal deity (*Con. Gal.* 100c). All peoples had regional gods, Julian argued in typical neoplatonic fashion, but this deity is not the God of all known to all humankind (52b). This is because God does not reveal himself to a particular nation or group, such as in Judea through the prophets or Jesus (141c; 106d). Jews and Christians also anthropomorphize the high God, which Julian finds preposterous (155c; 160d). Finally, Jews' and Christians' creation account is deficient, speaking about the creation of the physical world while neglecting the angels and other spiritual beings (*Con. Gal.* 99e).

Among the positive aspects of Judaism, Julian declared that the Jews carefully observed their ancestral laws, taken by Neoplatonists such as Julian as the greatest sign of their piety (*Con. Gal.* 238ac). In this sense they were viewed as superior even to the Greeks, who had become indifferent to their laws. Julian was aware of the Jewish Temple and priests, whom he viewed as holy men skilled in theurgy, as were Abraham, Isaac, Jacob, and Solomon (354ab-356c). Such facts were of great importance to Julian, who saw theurgy as a practical means to maintain contact with the gods. This suggested that Hellenes and Jews could work together to shift the divine balance in favor of their common religious and political goals.

If Julian's attitude towards Jews and Judaism was ambivalent, this was only because he believed that Judaism had declined as a religion and society. Judaism's acme had been in the period from creation through the time of the first Temple. But beginning with Moses, who obfuscated the original revelation, and through the period of the prophets, whose confusion eventually led to the emergence of the Galileans, or Christians, Judaism has been largely in decline (*Con. Gal.* 176ab-210a; 218a-224e; 238d-351d).

Since Constantine, Judaism and Hellenism had suffered dearly, and Julian, now emperor, offered both Jews and Hellenes a way out of their misfortune (*Fragmentum Epistulae* 89b, 289c-301b). He viewed the Jews as co-religionists whose ancient law was perfectly legitimate. He planned to rebuild the Jewish Temple to return integrity to an *ethnos* within the empire and to challenge Christian claims to Israel and Jerusalem (see Ammianus Marcellinus, *Res Gestae* XXIII, 1:2-3). This initiative was fully consistent with his efforts to restore the offering of sacrifices and to rebuild temples throughout the empire. Julian thought that by re-building the Jerusalem Temple, he literally was bringing the divine to earth, inviting the God of the Jews to dwell among the people once again. Additionally, he had a political motive, to bring the Jews of the Roman east, Mesopotamia, and Babylonia over to his side in his war against the Persians. According to Christian sources, the Jews eagerly responded to Julian's call (see, e.g., Gregory Nazianzenus, V, 4 [*PG* XXXV, col. 668]). But disaster followed. The rebuilding of the Temple ended with an earthquake, Julian was killed in Persia, and this final "pagan" revival came to an end.

The conflict between pagan philosophy and Christianity began in the second century with Celsus and ended in the fourth century with Julian. Apart from its harshness towards Christianity, this polemic carried with it pagan philosophers' increasing admiration for Judaism. With the death of Julian and the consolidation of a Holy Roman Empire, pagan references to Jews and Judaism became less frequent but no less admiring. This is evident in a number of later ancient sources.

Libanius of Antioch, rhetor and teacher of Julian, had many opportunities to meet Jews and had relationships with the Jewish patriarch in Rome and the Jewish community at Antioch. Yoked together under Christian emperors and bishops, Libanius exhibited deep respect for their character and well-being (*Epistulae* 914; 917; 974; 1084; 1097; 1105; 1251).

Damascius of Damascus (first half of the sixth century C.E.), student of Proclus, belonged to the last of the Hellenes who left for Persia after Justinian's closing of the academy at Athens. His *Life of Isidorus*, preserved through Photius and the Suida, includes some allusions to the power of the Jewish God and to the part played by individual Jews in contemporary neoplatonic circles. The God of the Hebrews remains efficacious for magical incantations; and we hear of two Jews who practiced medicine, Domninus of Syria and Gesius of Petra, of another Jew, Zeno of Alexandria, who belonged to the same circles, and of the Samaritan Marinus, who was a philosopher (see Damascius, *Vita Isidori*, cited in Photius, *Bibliotheca* cod. 242, 339a; Suida, s.v., *Gesios*; and Photius, *Bibliotheca* 345b). Zeno, Marinus, and Domninus all left their ancestral religions. Zeno openly attacked Judaism, Domninus no longer followed its precepts, and Marinus left Samaritanism because it had changed from the original religion of "Abramos." Damascius showed respect for their apostasy from Judaism and Samaritanism.

As pagan philosophy came to closure in the Latin West and Greek East, a scholiast and philosopher found occasions to discuss the highest God. Their comments on Jewish conceptions of God are reminiscent of earlier Hellenistic praise of the sublimity of Judaism. Lactantius Placidus (sixth century C.E.) identified the "summus deus" with the demiurge, a claim made about the Jewish God by pagan philosophers from Galen to

Proclus. He suggests that the Persian Magi were correct when they claimed that apart from gods worshipped in temples there is a superior god who rules over all others, like the sun and moon. The name of this god is not known to mankind, Lactantius argued. Only his virtues and powers are known, and they are diffused throughout the world. These powers are worshipped and called by many names. To substantiate his claim of the existence of an unknown ineffable deity who has control over the world, nature, and the many gods worshipped by humankind, Lactantius invokes the authority of the Magi, Orpheus, Moses, and Esaias (*Commentarri in Statii Thebaida* IV, 516).

Simplicius (first half of the sixth century C.E.), the last neoplatonic commentator *par excellence*, wrote a polemic against the Christian neoaristotelian philosopher Philoponus. Philoponus denied the divinity of the heavenly bodies and declared the imminent destruction of the world. Simplicius used the Psalms of David to show that even David contradicts the Christian philosopher's views. The celestial bodies are implicitly connected with God (*Commentaria in Aristotelem Graeca* VII, 90), and the Christian view of the end of the world runs counter to David's assertion that the "heaven and sun are eternal" (VII, 141f.).

**Conclusion:** According to Hegel, "the owl of Minerva spreads its wings only with the falling of the dusk.[30] But Minerva's owl—philosophy—played a morning role also in antiquity, preceding as well as following social and political theory. The ancient philosophers mark out an important epoch in understandings of Jews and Judaism. For their age, these thinkers were crucially important articulators of utopian and dystopian views of the "other." Their assumptions not only became deeply rooted in the intellectual life of their time but also voiced in compelling form notions that framed Christian views of the Jews and Judaism—perspectives that still haunt us.

**Notes**

[1] For a collection of pagan sources on the Jews and Judaism, see M. Stern, *Greek and Latin Authors on Jews and Judaism*, 3 vols. (Jerusalem, 1976). The major studies on this topic are I. Heinemann, "The Attitude of the Ancient World Toward Judaism," in *Review of Religion* 4 [1940], pp. 385-400; A. Momigliano, *Alien Wisdom* (Cambridge, 1975); V. Tcherikover, *Hellenistic Civilization and the Jews* (New York, 1977), and M. Hengel, *Hellenistic Civilization and the Jews* (New York, 1979).

[2] On the authenticity of this passage, see Momigliano, op. cit., p. 77.

[3] On these matters, see Numenius, cited in Clement of Alexandria, *Stromata* I, 22:150:4; Theophrastus, cited in Porphyry, *De Abs.* 11, 26; Clearchus, cited in Josephus, *C. Ap.* I.176, 179; and Philo, *Leg. Alleg.* 1.108.

[4] See Josephus, *C. Ap.* I.179. Scholars are divided on the authenticity of this report. Schürer and Bickermann acknowledge its trustworthiness, while Willrich, Schubart, and Tcherikover deny it.

[5] Megasthenes visited India and spent some time there between 302 and 288 B.C.E. See A. Dahlquist, *Megasthenes and Indian Religion* (Stockholm, Goeteborg, Uppsala, 1962).

[6] The reports of Hecataeus on our topic are in the *Aegyptiaca*, cited in Diodorus Siculus, *Bibliotheca Historica* XL, 3; *De Iudaeis*, cited in Josephus, *C. Ap.* I, 183-204; II, 43.

[7] For an overview, see Tcherikover, *Hellenistic Civilization and the Jews*, pp. 361ff.

[8] See Diodorus Siculus, *Bibliotheca Historica*, Dindorf XXXIV, 1:1; Lysimachus, cited in Josephus, *C. Ap*, I, 309, and Philostratus, *Vita Apollonii* V, 33-34.

[9] See R. Walzer, *Galen on Jews and Christians* (Oxford, 1949), p. 22.

[10] *De Regno*, cited in Stobaeus, IV, 6:22, in Thesleff, *The Pythagorean Texts of the Hellenistic Period* (Abo, 1965), p. 79. On the following, see ibid., IV, 7:64 and Thesleff, pp. 79ff.

[11] See A.H.M. Jones, *The Later Roman Empire* (London, 1986), vol. 2, pp. 948-949, critiqued by Bernard Bachrach, "The Jewish Community of the Later Roman Empire," in Jacob Neusner, ed., *To See Ourselves as Others See Us* (Atlanta, 1985), pp. 402-408.

[12] For Varro's theology, see P. Boyance, *REA* LVII [1955], pp. 57ff. On his connection with neo-Pythagorean philosophers, see W. Aly, *Strabon von Amaseia* (Bonn, 1957), pp. 200f.

[13] For the most detailed study, see J. Lewy, *Studies in Jewish Hellenism* (Jerusalem, 1960), pp. 79ff. Lewy notes that, in 59 B.C.E., the Jewish multitudes in the *contiones* were on the side of Cicero's enemies, the Populares. This only added fuel to the rhetors fire.

[14] Against Tcherikover, *Hellenistic Civilization and the Jews*, p. 364.

[15] *De Prov. Consul* V:10. This charge probably derived from the large number of Jewish slaves brought to Rome by Pompey. See Philo, *Legatio ad Gaium* 155. For the relations between Gabinius and the publicani, see Cicero, *Ad Quintum Fratrem* III, 2:2.

[16] He attacked the followers of Isis and Cybele in the *De Vita Beata* 26:8; and the *galli* of Cybele in the *De Superstitione* (see Augustine, *Civ. Dei* VI, 10).

[17] For *De Superstitione*, see Turcan, op. cit., pp. 12ff.; for *Naturales Quaestiones* and *Epistulae Morales*, see K. Abel, *Bauformen in Senecas Dialogen* (Heidelberg, 1967), pp. 165ff.

[18] See F.E. Brenk, *In Mist Apparelled: Religious Themes in Plutarch's "Moralia" and "Lives"* (Leiden, 1977). For a study Plutarch's career, see D.A. Russell, *Plutarch* (London, 1972); on Plutarch as philosopher, J. Dillon, *The Middle Platonists* (Ithaca, 1974).

[19] See Dillon, *The Middle Platonists*, pp. 199-225.

[20] The most elaborate treatment of Judaism is in the *Quaestiones Conviviales*, 4.4.4-6. For a complete collection of Plutarch's references to Jews and Judaism, see Stern, op. cit., pp. 545-562.

[21] On Galen, see L. Edelstein, *Ancient Medicine* (Baltimore, 1987) and M. Frede, *Essays in Ancient Philosophy* (Minneapolis, 1987), pp. 279-300. For Galen's on Jews and Christians, see Stern, op. cit., pp. 306-328, R. Walzer, *Galen on Jews and Christians* (London, 1949), and R. Wilken, *The Christians as the Romans Saw Them*, pp. 68-93.

[22] There are also two Arabic passages, from Galen's lost work on Hippocrates's *Anatomy* and his work against the theology of Aristotle. Both mention that Jews do not offer proofs for their teachings. See Walzer, op. cit., pp. 24-37. The texts can be found on pp. 10-16.

[23] See Stern, op. cit., pp. 224-231, 293-305.

[24] See Wilken, op. cit., pp. 117-125.

[25] Cited, e.g., in Clement of Alexandria, *Stromata* I, 22:150:4.

[26] See R.M. Berchman, "Rationality and Ritual in Plotinus and Porphyry," in *Incognita* 2.2 (1991).

[27] Cf., Iamblichus, cited in Lydus, *De Mensibus*, IV, 53 [Wuensch]. Following Stern, op. cit., II, pp. 484-485, it seems unlikely that Iamblichus' two passages in *De Mysteriis* II, 3; VII, 4 [des Places] on angels, archangels, and the Assyrians refer to the Jews.

[28] See Sallustius Neoplatonicus, *De Deis et Mundo* IX, 5 [Rochefort]. On Sallustius, see A.D. Nock, *Sallustius— Concerning the Gods and the Universe* (Cambridge, 1926), pp. xlff.

[29] On Julian's reign and attitude towards Jews and Christians, see Wilken, op. cit., pp. 164-196.

[30] Hegel, *Philosophy of Right* (Clarendon Press, 1952), p. 13.

ROBERT BERCHMAN

**PASSOVER HAGGADAH:** The Passover Haggadah contains the text recited at the ritual meal—the seder—held on Passover eve in Jewish homes and communal gatherings ranging from synagogues to the Israeli kibbutzim.

It is probably the most widely used text of the Jewish people, and it has exerted a noticeable influence on Jewish life and thought through the ages. Since the emergence of book printing, the Haggadah has appeared in several thousand editions, and it is represented in manuscripts from the ninth century and on. For more than a century, the Haggadah has been published in bilingual editions, with the original Hebrew and Aramaic languages standing next to translations into the languages of the communities using it.

As is common with liturgical texts, there is no single, uniform Haggadah. Rather, containing quotations from the Hebrew Bible, Mishnah, Talmud, midrash, and other early medieval texts, it is a composition of many different genres, including benedictions, prayers, stories, interpretations of Biblical texts, songs, short dialogues, and so on. Yet whatever passages appear in a particular edition, the main topic remains the story of Israel's departure from Egypt, or, in the Haggadah's metaphor, the passage from slavery to freedom. This central theme, as we shall see, is reflected in many different ways throughout the Haggadah.

**The elements of the Haggadah:** The Haggadah normally is divided into fifteen discrete elements, each marking an act to be performed or a literary passage to be read during the seder (see figs. 102-106). The seder normally begins with a recitation of the names of these sections, and, since they are clearly marked in most printed editions, they also function as dividers within the ritual, marking the passage from one aspect of the ceremony to another. The following elements normally are singled out:

1. Sanctification of the day (*qaddesh* or *qiddush*)
2. Washing of hands (*rahatz*), without benediction
3. Dipping a vegetable in salt water (*karpas*)
4. Breaking the middle matzah (*yahatz*)
5. Recitation of the Haggadah proper (*maggid*)
6. Washing of hands, with benediction (*rahatz*)
7. Reciting the blessing on the matzah (*motzi*)
8. Eating the matzah (*matzah*)
9. Dipping bitter herbs in *haroset* (*maror*)

10. Eating of bitter herbs/horse radish with matzah (*korek*)
11. Passover meal (*shulhan orek*)
12. Eating the *afikoman* (*tzafun*)
13. Grace after meal (*barek*)
14. Recitation of the Hallel-psalms (*hallel*)
15. Ending (*nirtzah*)

The Hebrew names of the elements, indicated in parentheses, are called "signs of the seder" (*simane ha-seder*). As a rule, these acts are accompanied by verbal expressions (mostly benedictions). Others of the acts are themselves verbal expressions, as, for instance, the sanctification of the day, the recitation of the Exodus-story, grace after the meal, etc.

This chain of "signs of the Seder" was delineated by Samuel ben Salomon of Falaise (late thirteenth century), a specialist on the Haggadah. It is the best known and most widely used of several such systems, in which the terminology, as well as the number of elements, varies. These chains were developed so that even those who did not have a text of the Haggadah could remember its order and contents. Thus, a characteristic of all the chains is that they are mnemotechnic aids, with rhyme and assonance easing recollection of the Haggadah's elements and order. This is true of the chain in common use today, which often is sung at the beginning of the seder.

**The text:** The earliest complete text of the Haggadah appears in the tenth century prayer book of Saadiah Gaon. An almost complete text also is embedded in the so-called *Seder* of Amram Gaon, from the ninth century. Through lengthy quotes, this version gives a good picture of the text used in Babylonia, which Amram wanted to be adopted everywhere. Haggadah texts contemporary with or older than the one in Amram's *Seder* are preserved only in fragments, mostly from the Cairo genizah.

Among the early witnesses for the Haggadah also are those embedded in *Mahzor Vitry*, a prayerbook from the eleventh century, and in Maimonides' Mishneh Torah, from the twelfth. The author of the former was close to Rashi, and it is a witness to the shape of the text in the eleventh century and before, showing a clear dependence on Amram's version. It reproduces the text only sketchily, however. In the Mishneh Torah, the Haggadah appears as a separate appendix, after the description of the ritual of the seder evening. Here Maimonides restricts himself to the *maggid* section only, since it constitutes the telling of the story of the Exodus proper. It is not fully clear when separate editions of the Haggadah began to be used. The oldest separate texts originate in the thirteenth century, which is also when illuminated Haggadah manuscripts began to appear.

Despite the relatively late date of these sources, the Haggadah as we know it was in the main put together already in Talmudic times, with some essential parts deriving even from the Mishnaic period. In fact, the final chapter of Mishnah Pesahim contains a basic outline of the Haggadah as well as quotations from some of its passages. Even so, the Haggadah remained in a fluid state through Talmudic times, and, for complete forms and a stable text, we are restricted to sources from the geonic period and later.

It actually turns out that the text of the Haggadah, with the exception of some popular folk songs and some local elaborations of the established text, inserted at the end, remained almost intact from geonic times until the nineteenth century. Then, the vast changes the Jewish populations underwent throughout Europe had repercussions in all fields of activity, especially the liturgy. Nevertheless, among the Orthodox and other traditionalists, the Haggadah has remained almost unchanged, while Liberal and Reform Jews have allowed fairly radical changes. In Israel, especially the kibbutzim have experimented freely with the performance of the Passover ritual. While all this has resulted in the availability of a wide range of divergent texts, here we are confined to an analysis of the text of the traditional Haggadah.

***Qaddesh*—Sanctification:** Passover is one of the great feasts of the year, and the fact that it is different from a weekday is clearly marked—as on all holy days—through a proclamation of its holiness (*qiddush* or *qaddesh*). After festival candles are lit, the first cup of wine is filled, and two central blessings are recited: the blessing over the wine (*birkat ha-yayin*) and the blessing over the day (*birkat ha-qiddush*). According to the Mishnah, Rabbinic opinions were divided on the order of these blessings. Current practice follows the school of Hillel: the blessing over the wine is recited first. The blessing for time (*birkat ha-zeman*; also called *she-hechiyanu*: "... who has preserved us, sustained us, and ...") was added to the other two in the post-Mishnaic period. Drinking the first cup of wine completes the sanctification.

Since Passover may commence on any evening in the week, the Sabbath may need to be taken into account in the *qiddush*. On a Friday evening, the sanctification for Passover is made to encompass the sanctification for the Sabbath primarily through the addition of Gen. 1:31-2:3. If Passover begins at Saturday evening, when Sabbath ends, two blessings of the normal *havdalah*, which concludes all Sabbaths, are inserted, one for the lights (*birkat ha-ner*), another on the separation of Israel from other peoples, the Sabbath from working days and from the festivals, etc. In this way, the symbolism of light is emphasized as well as the simple fact that there is a transition from one hallowed time to another.

**The Aramaic introduction to the Haggadah:** The *maggid*-section, which elaborates the story of the Exodus, is introduced by an Aramaic prose passage that states:

> This is the bread of affliction that our ancestors ate in the land of Egypt. Let all who are hungry come and eat; let all who are in need come and celebrate Passover. Now we are here; next year in the land of Israel. Now we are slaves, next year, free.

Formulations differ in several early manuscripts, and, in some of the earliest, the passage is lacking. From a topical point of view, the three sentences do not hang together well, suggesting that the passage is not unitary. Goldschmidt assumed correctly that, at the earliest, it dates from Talmudic, and probably from geonic, times, even if the sentences, taken separately, are older. The discussion in B. Pes. 36a-b and many other places shows that the expression "the bread of affliction" was in use in the Talmudic period. But it is worth noticing that, in these sources, the expression is given in Hebrew, not Aramaic, and is discussed independently, not in connection with the Aramaic phrases in the Haggadah. The early texts contain detailed discussions of "the bread of affliction," and they all connect it with Passover, as does the Bible. They restrict themselves, however, to the question of what kind of bread is implied. Mostly it is understood as denoting "the bread of poverty" (or "the poor man's bread"), and this results in the ruling that the obligatory matzah, which everyone must eat on Passover night, must not be a "rich matzah," however that is defined.

The leader recites the first sentence of the Aramaic introduction while simultaneously raising the plate of matzah. In many places the custom is to open the door at this moment, appropriate to the invitation for the needy to come and eat. After the recitation, the three matzot are covered, and the second cup of wine is filled. As a situational marker, the introductory sentence refers to the raised matzah, that is, to the ongoing celebration. But it refers also to Deut. 16:3, which dictates the commandment to eat matzah. Thus a bridge is established to the first Passover, when the Israelites "departed from the land of Egypt hurriedly"—a bridge that facilitates identification with the Exodus generation. Indeed, in several Sephardic texts, the Aramaic introduction is preceded by the clause "*we* departed from Egypt with haste."

The Aramaic introduction is intended as an invitation to a meal, in which the hungry and needy are invited to come and take part. Yet it is difficult to find a situation in which this invitation could have been genuine.[1] While the Temple stood, uninvited guests could not take part in the meal at all, since the Passover lamb was eaten only by members of a predetermined group (M. Zeb. 5:8). There was no place for surprise guests, poor or rich. What about after the destruction? Now the invitation appears in the wrong place. In order properly to celebrate the Passover, the individual should participate in the sanctification of the day and the first cup of the wine, that is, the *qiddush*. One could, of course, imagine that some participants might come late and still be allowed to take part. But it is improbable that the order of the ritual itself would *dictate* that those who respond to this invitation break the accepted order. No solution to this oddity is apparent.

The third sentence, with its reference to Israel, clearly was formulated in the diaspora, presumably after the fall of the Second Temple. In the time of the Temple, the recitation concentrated on the Exodus and the people of Israel's celebration of Passover in freedom (even if Jerusalem was governed by foreign powers) and in a functioning temple. After the destruction, the theme of liberation became pertinent in a new way, which has applied to Jews throughout their subsequent history. The third sentence, interestingly, has nothing to do with the first two, but stands alone. Since the seder ends with a similar wish, a unity is created between the commencement and end of the Passover night ritual.

**The child's question:** In Hebrew, the passage is called *mah nishtanah*, in English, commonly, the "four questions." As a matter of fact, there is only *one* question: "Why is this night different from all [other] nights?," followed by four clauses in which the differences are listed. Thus the passage might more accurately be called, "the child's question."

The text belongs to those parts of the Haggadah proper attested from an early time. It is preserved in complete form already at M. Pes. 10:4, though Mishnaic versions—which are numerous in different editions and manuscripts—differ significantly from the current Haggadah. Ancient sources generally list three elements following the question: dipping, matzah, and flesh. Saadiah's Siddur and Amram's Seder have dipping, matzah, maror, and reclining, in that order. This represents an eastern form localized to Babylonia that was a revision of the earlier Mishnaic form, or perhaps it was different from the beginning. The continued history of the text shows that the eastern form eventually superseded its western counterpart. Why the number of elements increased from three to four is not clear. Perhaps it results from the influence of other parts of the Haggadah, in which the number four plays a conspicuous part: the four cups, and, especially, the four sons, referred to below.

In place of the missing element "flesh," the eastern text has "maror" and "reclining." "Maror" appears also in good Mishnah manuscripts, indicating that, from an early time, it was a viable alternative. Maror refers also to the Passover meal eaten from time immemorial, since Exod. 12:8 states that the Paschal lamb should be eaten with matzah and maror, bitter herb. The second "new" element—"reclining"—entered the Haggadah relatively late; it is missing in Mishnaic and Talmudic texts and originates probably not before geonic times. But the custom to which it refers may be much earlier, since it is well known that, in antiquity, one ate at a banquet while reclining on a long sofa at the side of a low table.

M. Pes. 10:4 explains that, at the point at which the *Mah Nishtanah* appears, the son is to take the initiative of asking questions, thus giving the father the opportunity to explain God's great deeds on behalf of the people. The son could ask pretty much anything, but it was supposed that he would ask about something special in the celebration of Passover, for instance, why they mixed a second cup or why they took away the table (B. Pes. 115b). What if he did not ask anything at all? In anticipation of such a situation, the *mah nishtanah* was inserted. The father now could ask on the son's behalf and thus instruct him how to ask (M. Pes. 10:4).

**The first introduction to the midrash:** The son's question is followed by an almost verbatim quotation of Deut. 6:21 ("We were Pharaoh's slaves in Egypt; and the Lord brought us out of Egypt with a mighty hand"), continued by a statement on the importance to later generations of God's earlier saving acts. This explains why all must speak about the Exodus from Egypt, those who already are learned as well as children and those who so far have no knowledge. Here we approach a central theme of the Haggadah, that the Exodus is not only an event that took place long ago. Rather, all who partake in the meal have benefited from and now actually participate in the Exodus. Thus Raba, B. Pes. 116b, emphasizes that the father must say the words, "and *us* did he bring out from there."

**Exemplary stories:** The notion that even the most educated people must linger over the Exodus story is illustrated in the short anecdote about five famous rabbis, who, celebrating the Passover at B'nei Brak, became so absorbed in the telling of the Exodus that they failed to notice that time had come to recite the morning prayers. Illustrating the appropriate way to spend the seder evening, the anecdote appears only in the Haggadah and, in a different version, at T. Pes. 10:12, which reports simply that Gamaliel (not mentioned in the Mishnah's story) and other sages were "occupied with the laws of the Passover that entire night, until the cock crowed." There is no way of knowing whether these anecdotes report a single event, two different events, or whether they have a historical foundation at all.

Next comes an independent statement of Eleazar b. Azariah. Reporting a dispute between Ben Zoma and other sages, this passage has no special connection to Passover night. Its original context is M. Ber. 1:5, where it is preceded by the rule that one must mention the Exodus from Egypt daily in the evening Shema, just as one does in the morning. This is the case even though, since ritual fringes are not worn at night, one might assume that it is unnecessary to recite Num. 15:37-41, which concerns the commandment to wear fringes and the last verse of which mentions the Exodus. The point is that one in all events includes this recitation in the evening Shema.

In the Haggadah, Eleazar b. Azariah's utterance has been detached from the law regarding the Shema. It apparently is here because of his mention of the Exodus and the fact that his name occurs also in the preceding anecdote. The result, in all events, is to strengthen the initial anecdote, making clear the nature of Rabbinic study. It is possible that Eleazar's statement even influenced the wording of the anecdote, which states that the rabbis' discussion concerned the Exodus rather than "the rules about the Passover," as the Tosefta has it.

As for the content of Eleazar b. Azariah's utterance, Ben Zoma's statement that he cites is an example of *halakhic midrash*, which establishes or supports a ruling on the basis of an interpretation of a biblical passage. Here Ben Zoma proves that one must mention the Exodus in the evening Shema based upon the fact that Scripture commands people to remember the Exodus "*all* days of your life." Since it would have been sufficient to say "the days of your life," the apparently extra word "all" must have a special meaning, the Bible being perfect and containing nothing redundant or superfluous. Thus Ben Zoma argues that, in this context, "all" modifies the word "days" so as to include evenings as well.

**Baraita of the four sons:** A short benediction extolling God for giving Torah to the people is followed by a Tannaitic passage in which four types of sons are said to be reflected in the four biblical passages that command the father to teach his son(s) about the Exodus (Exod. 12:26; 13:8; 13:14; Deut. 6:20). Three of the passages contain a question, one does not. Hence the baraita describes three sons who pose questions and one who does not even know how to ask. Each son, except the final one, who does not know how to ask, is presented in a similar way:

    (a) A son, what does he say?
    (b) The question (+ possible comments)
    (c) An answer (+ possible comments).

The questions and answers depend upon biblical quotations. Passages of this sort belong to a genre of numerical sayings common in wisdom writing both in the Bible and in Jewish traditional literature. Some of these lack scriptural proof-texts and reflect human experience or history in general. Others, such as this one, unique to the Rabbinic literature, depend upon proof-texts, which they use in an aggadic context.[2]

Most striking in the passage is the Haggadah's judgment of the wicked son's question[3]—"What do *you* mean by this service?" (Exod. 12:26)—understood to suggest that this son denied God. For modern readers, the sharp reaction to the use of the word "you" seems strange. Yet the rabbis were very sensitive on this point. Heinemann[4] notes that, with the exception of the call to prayer—"Bless the Lord who is blessed"—on no other occasion in the public synagogue service does one group within the congregation address another party in the second person. Such a use of "you," rather than "we" thus was immediately interpreted as the speaker's method of keeping a distance from the community, of rejecting the yoke of heaven and thus of denying God.

Yet, citing Deut. 6:20—"What is the meaning of the testimonies and the statutes . . . which the Lord our God has commanded you?—the wise son also uses the second person, a fact not missed in Rabbinic commentaries on this passage. But many manuscripts and early editions of the Haggadah have "us," which may have only later been changed to "you" in order correctly to cite the biblical verse. Alternatively, the "you" is original and it was often supplanted by "us" specifically to solve the problem of the difference between the wise and wicked sons.

**The second introduction to the midrash:** The passage that starts "In the beginning our ancestors served idols" is composed of at least two, probably three, parts. It explains what is meant by "shame" in M. Pes. 10:4's injunction, "According to the understanding of the son his father teaches him. He begins with the shame and ends with the glory." Then follows a clear new start to the telling of the Exodus story, marked formally with a benediction in the third person—similar to the one that preceded the baraita about the four sons—and topically by the shift of the theme to God's promise to Israel. The imperative "Come and learn . . ." then continues the previous text in that it exemplifies someone who "has risen against us to destroy us." But it also marks a new start in that it shifts to the second person and leaves the theme of promise.

**The midrash:** Like haggadic midrash in general, the passages that follow, interpreting Deut. 26:5-8, aim at edification and theological/philosophical speculation, not at establishing or justifying Halakhic rules. The largest part of this material consists of quotations from biblical texts, mostly from Exodus, that in two different ways throw light on the primary text. Some simply say the same thing as that text; these are not paraphrases but, rather, parallels. Others serve as examples, proving the correctness of *Rabbinic* comments on the meaning of Deut. 26:5-8.

From a formal point of view, the clear shift from one type to the other occurs in the middle of the midrash. One might say that the composition commences at a leisurely tempo, retelling the primary text through references to the narrative in Genesis and Exodus. But in the middle it turns from narrative to explanation, pointing at different passages in Scripture that suggest meanings the rabbis themselves adduce for words and phrases in the primary text. The shift takes place specifically when God appears for the first time as the grammatical subject in the middle of Deut. 26:7. Here God's role becomes active, unlike in the beginning of the passage, where all God does is *hear* and *see* the plight of Israel. For this reason, the beginning of the midrash refers to Israel's plight, the later section, to God's activity.

M. Pes. 10:4 instructs the father to teach the son "according to his understanding." He "begins with shame and ends with glory; he *expounds* from "An Aramean sought to destroy my father" (Deut. 26:5) until he finishes the whole section." According to this rule, all Jewish men were obliged to expound Deut. 26:5-8, a task that only the sages were qualified to do, really. Thus the task was mostly reduced to reciting these fixed and well-known midrashic passages. That the choice fell precisely on Deut. 26:5-8 is understandable, since these verses fit Passover and, from of old, those who offered the first-fruits in the Temple recited this same passage (Deut. 26:1-10). Thus the scriptural passage, at least, was well-known to ordinary people. The obligation to explain the text probably dates from Temple times, and it is commonly held, though with some debate, that the midrash in the present text ultimately derives from the Mishnaic period times, even if it got its present shape after the redaction of the Babylonian Talmud, probably some time in the seventh century.

**The expansion:** The end of the midrash consists of (1) an expansion of the interpretation of Deut. 26:8 in the form of an alternative interpretation and (2) the attribution to Judah of an acronym consisting of the first letter of each of the ten plagues. The alternative interpretation links the five acts of God in Deut. 26:8 to the ten plagues listed in Exod. 7-12, suggesting that each act of God reflects a set number of plagues, which are, in the end, listed. Then comes the passage regarding the acronym, found also in Sifre Deut. 301, suggesting that, from an early time, the first letters of the names of the plagues were grouped in three pseudo-"words." The various interpretations of these groupings shows that the words were conferred a mystical and powerful significance. Indeed, the acronym is quoted widely in Rabbinic literature, where it commonly is connected with the rod of Moses, on which it is said to have been engraved. The acronym also is said to recall the correct order of the plagues, which David, in the Psalms, presented incorrectly.

**Tannaitic expositions on the splitting of the Sea of Reeds:** Two additional passages are not mentioned in the Mishnah and are not mandatory parts of the Haggadah at all. They are missing in the text of Maimonides and also in several of the fragments from the Cairo genizah. The first consists of a series of pronouncements by three well known sages on the punishments God executed upon the Egyptians. Here the center of interest has moved to the crossing of the Sea of Reeds, which is explained as even more miraculous than the Exodus itself. The several passages are almost identical, and they all presuppose the first, which is logically antecedent to the rest. They have a common structure:

(a) Quotation phrase ("So-and-So said. . . .")
(b) Response: "Whence (in Scripture) do you deduce that . . .?"
(c) Citation of the relevant biblical source
(d) Short interpretation
(e) Deduction of the consequences of the reasoning

The question indicated at (b) is quite common in the Rabbinic literature, in which the Bible is said to form the foundation for all knowledge of God, God's acts, and God's demands. Indeed, the pericope dates from Mishnaic times, though it hardly appears before the second part of the second century. Although Maimonides did not accept it in his text of the Haggadah, his son testified that it was recited in his home. Amram accepts it without comment. Saadiah takes a mediating position. He underlines the fact that the pericope is not part of the Haggadah in its true sense, but he allows it explicitly and even quotes the text. Hence we see that although the custom of reciting the pericope probably was well established in the ninth century, at least in Babylonia and the areas under its influence, its position was not secure, and there were presumably many places in the areas under Palestinian influence that only gradually accepted it.

**Dayyenu:** The second addition to the midrash is the song *Dayyenu*. It has two main parts, each introduced by an exclamation of wonder for the many good things God bestows the people. First, after the introductory exclamation, come fourteen strophes with an identical structure, linked to each other in the following way: "Had God done *a* but not *b*— it would have been enough for us; had he *b* but not *c*—it would have been enough for us; . . . ." Each strophe ends with the refrain *Dayyenu* ("it would have been enough for us"), which gives the song an antiphonal character. Then, after a second exclamation, similar but not identical to the first, follows a repetition of the earlier central clauses with statements like "God did *a*, and *b*, and *c*. . . ." The song ends with an appropriate concluding phrase "to atone for all our sins."

The method of repetition and linking both within the first part and between the second and the first part is common in the folklore form called the *chain song*. In such songs, the strophes can be linked to each other in different ways. In *Dayyenu*'s method, the new verse repeats the second half-strophe of the preceding verse and then adds all the central statements of the earlier strophes in a string. It emphasizes that Israel did not *simply* experience a number of great deeds— each of which was sufficient by itself—but all of them together.

In spite of the fact that *Dayyenu* is permeated with allusions to the Bible, no text is close to it in both form and topic, neither in the Bible nor the Rabbinic literature. Indeed, *Dayyenu* is perhaps the most isolated text in the Haggadah, and its date is therefore very difficult to establish. Even so, the Psalms, several of which extol God's acts in history, at least offer several models of such a list of God's deeds in behalf of the people, so that we can have some sense of how this song might have developed. Ps. 136, with its short statements on God's acts in creation and history and its recurrent antiphonal response, "for his steadfast love endures for ever," resembles the structure of *Dayyenu*. After a threefold call to praise God, come several designations of God as the lord of creation (4-9); then there is a jump to the God of Exodus and the sojourn in the wilderness, without any reference to the patriarchs (10-24). Here we find the best resemblances to *Dayyenu*. The topics are fairly limited: creation, Exodus, and wilderness. Interestingly, the gift of land, v. 21, does not refer to the land of Israel but to Bashan and the land of the Amorites, that is, the land west of the Jordan. This psalm speaks before the people has entered the land of Israel.

Chain songs often function primarily as entertainment, which probably is the case with *Had Gadya*—the beloved and well known, "An Only Kid." But just as often, they have a pedagogic function, as do *Ehad mi yodea* ("Who knows one?") and *Dayyenu*. Through repetition, the songs strengthen instruction of important religious lessons. Thus *Dayyenu* contains a series of statements on God's acts on behalf of Israel. Towards the end, the entry into the land is mentioned as well as the building of the Temple. Even though *Dayyenu* does not completely cover the theme of the Haggadah's midrash, it adheres fairly well to it. Thus, while it certainly was not part of the celebration of Passover in biblical times, it probably was composed to be a part of the celebration represented by the Haggadah, and it appropriately concludes the central section of the Haggadah that presents the midrash on the Exodus.

**The teaching of Rabban Gamaliel:** After *Dayyenu*, we turn to the symbolic foods arranged on the seder plate. These are introduced through Gamaliel's statement—taken from M. Pes. 10:5, the basis for the following several sections of the Haggadah—that, during the seder, one is obligated to explain three things: the paschal offering, matzah, and the bitter herb. This introduction is followed by a paragraph regarding each food, the significance of which is explained through biblical references. These three paragraphs may or may not be unitary with Gamaliel's statement, which can stand alone. In any event, understanding these symbols means that each and every person can, and indeed is obligated to, identify with those who went out of Egypt. This is explicit in the following paragraph ("In every generation, a person is obligated to see himself as though he personally left Egypt"), which also is based upon biblical references and which exposes a fundamental feature of the Haggadah, the fusion of the present generation with the one that went out of Egypt. This blurring of distinctions between now and then justifies the duty, expressed next, to praise God for what the deity has done for previous generations as well as the present one ("Therefore, we must revere, exalt, extol . . .").

Codex Kaufmann preserves a more reliable text than is found in standard editions of the Mishnah. The passage that begins "In every generation . . .," absent in Kaufmann, is an interpolation introduced only in late editions of the Mishnah and Talmud. These words appear as a marginal gloss in the Leiden manuscript of the Palestinian Talmud. Similarly, the best manuscripts have the same order of foods as Kaufmann: *pesah, marorim, matzah*. In the final paragraph, the list of verbs praising God varies in the manuscripts. Better, earlier, manuscripts tend to have fewer verbs, though all unvaryingly begin with the same four: revere, exalt, extol, acclaim.

**Hallel:** The Hallel Psalms are recited not only on Passover but on all major festivals, since at least Tannaitic times. The Hallel recited at the Passover seder consists of Pss. 113-118, with Pss. 113-114 recited before the meal and Pss. 115-118 read after grace. In early texts, there is some confusion as to the identification of the Hallel, partly because there are various forms of the Hallel and partly because the texts are sometimes unclear concerning the extent of the Hallel.

The main distinction is between the *full* (or *complete*) Hallel, also called the *Egyptian* Hallel, which comprises Pss. 113-118 in its entirety, and the *half* Hallel, which is the same as the full Hallel except for the omission of Pss. 115:1-11 and 116:1-11. But in addition to the "full" and the "half" Hallel, there is also the "Great Hallel," referring to Ps. 136, which also is recited at the seder, immediately after Pss. 115-118. The concept of the half Hallel appears to be later than that of the full Hallel. Though it is recited on the last six days of Passover, its links to the holiday in early times are tenuous.

Hallel is dealt with at M. Pes. 10:6-7 and the parallel passage at T. Pes. 10:9, which present a Houses-dispute on the extent of the Hallel. The Shammaites say it contains only Ps. 113, while the Hillelites maintain that it contains Pss. 113-114. This text normally is understood to presuppose the division of an already established form of the Hallel—containing Pss. 113-118—into two parts, one before the meal and one after the Grace, as we now have things. The dispute, then, concerns what portion of the Hallel is recited before the meal. But, on the basis of the Mishnaic passage, some scholars maintain that Hallel indeed grew from an original one or two psalms to the six recited today. This view seems at first to have merit: in the Haggadah, Hallel is divided into two parts, recited at some distance from each other, and a natural explanation of this is that the second part is a later addition. But there are good reasons for maintaining the traditional view, that the original form of Hallel indeed comprised Pss. 113-118.

The traditional view is supported, first, by the wording of M. Pes. 10:6, which asks *"up to what point* does one recite the Hallel?" This presupposes that we already know the Hallel's starting point, and that the text reaches beyond the point referred to; otherwise it would be pointless to ask, "up to what point?" Second, the issue in the Mishnah does not appear to be the use of the Hallel in the liturgy in general, but, rather, timing, that is, which psalms are read at what point in the seder. This is supported by the fact that the seder's divided version must be considered a late form of the Hallel, which was first used in the Temple service, from which it migrated to the seder. The texts are oddly silent about the reasons for the division, although it is conspicuous and unique to the seder. The second part of T. Pes. 10:9 states only that, perhaps conscious of the correct sequence of historical events, the Shammaites held that it is not appropriate to mention the Exodus at this point in the service. For the Hillelites, this detail apparently was no problem, and they rebuked the Shammaites for their inconsistency, since they have no qualms about mentioning the Exodus in morning services, even though it took place only later in the day. In all events, this does not explain the division of the Hallel.

**The second cup:** The first part of the Hallel is followed by the "Blessing for Redemption" (*birkat ha-geullah*), when the second cup of wine is raised and then drunk. The blessing thanks God for the redemption from Egypt, an act that explicitly encompasses those present at the seder—". . . who has redeemed *us* and our fathers from Egypt." It continues with a hope that future celebrations of Passover might be observed as before, in a rebuilt Temple through the offering of the Passover sacrifice. The blessing for redemption is mentioned at M. Pes. 10:6, which the Haggadah quotes almost in its entirety.

**Grace after meals:** This is not specific to Passover, but a regular grace after meals, preceded, as on all holidays, by Ps. 126. A long and complicated literary construction, the grace has an equally long and complicated history. In its present form, it begins with an introductory exhortation by the leader to bless God, answered by the others who have dined. This is followed by benedictions that specifically recognize God's provision of nourishment to the whole world. The third part, introduced "We thank you," thanks God for the land of Israel, the Exodus, the covenant, and Torah, and ends with a benediction thanking God for the land and sustenance. The fourth part follows the same pattern, beginning with a prayer for mercy for the Israelite nation and Jerusalem and concluding with a blessing that thanks God for mercifully rebuilding Jerusalem. A paragraph that appears on all holidays is inserted in the middle of the fourth part, requesting that the people's prayers rise up to and be heard by God and begging God to respond to the people in mercy. When the seder coincides with Sabbath evening, a passage appropriate to the Sabbath also is inserted here. The fifth part of the grace commences with a blessing, recognizing God as good.

The final, sixth, section consists of a series of prayers beginning "The Merciful one will . . ." and enumerating Israel's daily and messianic expectations: God will reign throughout all time, will lift the yoke of exile, will bless the table on which the participants have just eaten, will send the prophet Elijah, harbinger of the messiah, will grant the people a share in eternity, etc. Thus, in line with the thematic concerns of the grace as a whole, the people's everyday hopes are tied up with the messianic expectation, the fulfillment of which is vouchsafed by God's trustworthiness in providing food. After the grace, the benediction is recited for the third cup of wine, which then is drunk.

**Conclusion of the Hallel:** The conclusion of the Hallel has grown into a complicated section of the Haggadah, stretching until the blessing of the fourth cup. This long section contains (1) biblical verses that abjure God to pour out wrath on the gentiles; (2) Pss. 115-118, the second section of the Hallel per se; (3) the prayer *yehalleluka* ("May [all your creatures] praise you"); (4) the so-called Great Hallel (Ps. 136); (5) the prayer *nishmat kol hay* ("May all that breathes bless your name"); and (6) the blessing over the fourth cup.

(1) A prayer for revenge, the collection of biblical verses that begins "Pour out your fury" (Ps. 79:6-7; 69:25; Lam. 3:66) belongs among the most debated passages in the Haggadah. Similar collections appear in all local traditions, although great variations occur in the specific selection of verses. But

the collection does not appear in the texts of Amram nor Saadiah, is lacking in the texts of some other early authorities (Rashi and Maimonides), and in most of the genizah texts. But it is present in *Mahzor Vitry* and in almost all subsequent Haggadot. Even if it is lacking in many of the important early texts, it is certainly old and is attested in the Cairo genizah.

(2-4) According to M. Pes. 10:7, Hallel formally extends to the fourth cup, and there is no doubt that by "Hallel" is meant Pss. 113-118 as a whole. Following the second part of Hallel is the "*birkat ha-shir*" ("blessing of the song"). Oddly, Talmudic rabbis disputed which passage is meant by this designation (B. Pes. 118a). Judah held it is the paragraph that begins, "May [all your creatures] praise you, Lord our God," while Yohanan said it is, "May all that breathes [bless your name]." Both these benedictions now are preserved in the traditional Haggadah, with the former, *Yehalleluka*, recited immediately after Ps. 118, and the latter, *nishmat kol hay*, recited after Ps. 136 (the Great Hallel). The benediction over the fourth cup follows, and in practice it is this benediction that today is called the *birkat ha-shir*. But in the earliest texts and commentaries, *birkat ha-shir* as a rule is identified with *yehalleluka*.[5]

Before turning to *nishmat kol hay* it is necessary to deal briefly with the Great Hallel and the question of a fifth cup of wine. Printed editions of B. Pes. 118a read: "Our rabbis taught: Over the fourth [cup] they conclude the Hallel and recite the Great Hallel; the words of R. Tarfon." Manuscripts and statements of geonim and other scholars, however, show that the text should read: "over the *fifth* [cup] they conclude the Hallel. . . ." In later manuscripts and the printed edition, this was corrected to "fourth" following the view of Rashi and his grandson, Rashbam, who were convinced that the text was in error. But if the reading "fifth" indeed is correct, it means that a custom of drinking a fifth cup goes back to Amoraic, perhaps even Tannaitic, times. In any case, in the geonic period, the custom was widespread, even if deemed voluntary. Since then, above all because Rashi and his followers were set against it, a fifth cup has not been drunk. But this cup's heritage remains in two aspects of the seder, the custom of filling a cup for Elijah and the recitation of the Great Hallel, which, as the Talmud states, provided the occasion for the fifth cup.

(5) The content and sequence of the final passages of the Hallel are complex. The Talmud suggests that one could recite either *nishmat kol hay* or *yehalleluka*; or one could use both of them; they could be placed together either before or after the Great Hallel, or separated, one before and the other after; the concluding benediction could be placed in one of them or in both. While the history of this literary unit is unclear, present usage was set in the second half of the twelfth century by Hayyim b. Hananel Ha-Cohen, who established placement of *yehalleluka* after the Egyptian Hallel without a concluding benediction, followed by the Great Hallel and then *nishmat kol hay*, with a long concluding benediction that begins with the words, "Praised be your name forever." This usage was formalized by acceptance in the authoritative code, the *Arbaah Turim*.

**The ending:** The formal grace having already been recited, after the fourth cup of wine, a blessing that is a "summary of the three [first sections of the grace]" is recited, thanking God for the fruit of the vine, the land of Israel, and requesting restoration of the Temple. Now the celebrant turns towards God with the assurance that the seder has been completed according to the rules and with a prayer that God also in future will protect the people. The name of the last passage—*nirtzah*—refers to an offering that has been accepted with pleasure. It is a late passage, actually the ending of a long hymn authored by Yosef Bonfils (Tov Elem), who lived in France in the eleventh century.

**Illuminated Haggadot:** The Haggadah is the most popular of Hebrew illuminated manuscripts. Illuminated Haggadot emerged in the thirteenth century, when the text had become fairly stable, and they were produced until the emergence of printed Haggadot, which also often were illuminated, and for some time after. Since the text is short, it was

relatively cheap to produce, both the text by a scribe and the illuminations by an artist. To be sure, not every family could afford one. But the economic situation for Jews in Spain, France, Germany, and Italy—the home regions for most of the manuscripts, and the best—improved during the high middle ages, so that well-to-do families often could afford to commission an illustrated Haggadah.

The motifs of the illustrations were often culled from the Haggadah itself. Particularly popular motifs are the sages at B'nei Brak, the baraita of the four sons, and different scenes of the family gathered to celebrate the seder evening. Biblical motifs, especially with reference to the Exodus, are clustered around the midrash. Furthermore, the text itself was embellished in the usual manner of manuscript production. The result is that some of the illustrated Haggadot, both manuscripts and printed books, are among the most outstanding examples of book illustration in Jewish, and non-Jewish, literature.

### Notes
[1] Daniel Goldschmidt, *The Passover Haggadah: Its Sources and History* (Jerusalem, 1969), pp. 8-9 [Heb.].
[2] W.S. Towner, *The Rabbinic "Enumeration of Scriptural Examples"* (Leiden, 1973).
[3] This is absent from the version in the Mekhilta, suggesting that the Haggadah's version is later. Similarly, the other additions in the Haggadah's version give an impression of polish. The formulations in the Palestinian Talmud, for their part, depart sufficiently from the other two sources to force one to reckon with the possibility of a parallel, but independent, tradition.
[4] Joseph Heinemann, *Prayer in the Talmud: Forms and Patterns* (Berlin, 1977).
[5] Goldschmidt, op. cit., p. 65.

NILS MARTOLA

**PIETY IN JUDAISM:** Piety fills the life of every Jew and endows it with transcendent meaning. In all forms of Rabbinic Judaism, ancient and modern, piety overshadows faith as the central defining core of the religion. Thus the daily, weekly, and annual routines of the observant Jew as well as the rituals of the life cycle events—each with its own transcendent meanings ascribed within the system of faith—are the concrete signs of the individual's achievement of the standards of piety demanded by Judaism. From Talmudic times until the present, most of the elements of these Rabbinic forms of piety remain commonly prevalent in Orthodox and Hasidic articulations of the religion, less so in today's Conservative Judaism, and only selectively in Reform and Reconstructionist systems of the faith.

**Beginnings and scope:** Early rabbis of the second century C.E. began to emphasize distinctive groups of practices that differentiated their form of Judaism. Some scholars speculate that these rabbis chose to prescribe these practices as a means of maintaining spirituality after the loss of the Temple. These rabbis prescribed, for example, that each Jew recite one hundred blessings each day. The recitation of a blessing prior to the performance of many basic rituals imprints on those rituals a mark of mystical meaning. T. Ber. 6:24-25 spells this out:

> R. Meir used to say, "There is no man in Israel who does not perform one hundred commandments each day [and recite over them one hundred blessings]. . . . And there is no man in Israel who is not surrounded by [reminders of the] commandments: [Every person wears] phylacteries on his head, phylacteries on his arm, has a *mezuzah* on his door post and four fringes on his garment around him. . . ."

**In the home:** The piety Rabbinic Jews practice relates heavily to rituals of the home, village, and fellowship, especially those associated with prayer. Rabbinic Judaism expects all Jews to practice rituals from morning until night. From the first stirring every morning, the Jew begins the day with acts of religious significance.

Hence, washing hands upon arising takes on a special meaning. The individual conducts the washing according to a simple but prescribed practice. Water is poured on the fingers of each hand up to the joint as specified by the masters. The inclusive Rabbinic vision of piety starts here and extends broadly to the individual throughout the activities of the day. Accordingly religious observances are associated with even some bodily functions, such as elimination, not ordinarily considered in the realm of religious ritual. The rabbis said that one has to recite

a blessing after the act as thanks for continued health. This imbues even that normally profane physical process with some aspect of piety.

**Prayers:** In Rabbinic Judaism morning prayers are literally clothed in piety. The man puts on the *tallit* (prayer shawl) and *tefillin* (phylacteries) while reciting the blessings for each (figs. 50 and 107). Every pious male obtains and maintains these prized and essential objects of piety in accord with the prescriptions of the rabbis and scribes. He wears these objects to show compliance with the prescriptions of the verses of the Torah recited in the *shema* (Deut. 6:4-9, 11:13-21 and especially Num. 15:37-41). Each knot on the four fringes of the prayer shawl is tied in accordance with age-old tradition. The phylacteries are crafted of select leather, made into cubical containers to hold the small parchments of biblical paragraphs written by trained scribes. The head-tefillin has to rest on the worshipper's forehead between the eyes, neither too high on the head, nor too low on the face. The leather strap that holds it in place is tied in accordance with known custom. The wearer understands that the knot of leather that sits at the base of his skull is a representation of the letter *yod*, the third letter of *Shaddai*, one of the divine names. On the leather box of the arm-tefillin is inscribed the letter *shin*. The wearer knows that the knot that holds it fast on his left biceps—opposite his heart—is a form of the letter *dalet*. Thus as he recites the prescribed prayers, the Jew is bound head and heart to God, *Shaddai*. He wears these appurtenances each weekday from the time he reaches thirteen, the age of maturity, now commonly called the age of Bar Mitzvah. Obtaining a pair of phylacteries from the scribe is the most significant, overt sign of achieving adult membership in the Rabbinic community. The standard practice is to wear the prayer shawl and phylacteries during the morning prayers and then to remove them. Historically, to show extreme piety, some few virtuoso rabbis wore them all day as they sat immersed in the study of Torah.

An ordinary Jewish man may recite his prayers in a synagogue or study hall or in private, at home or in any orderly place. For optimal piety he goes to the synagogue to pray with the *minyan*, the prayer quorum of ten adult Jewish males. The formalization of the synagogue as a standard communal institution took place over a span from the first century through the middle ages. Rather than on the synagogue *per se*, the emphasis in Jewish custom and law has always been simply on prayer in a public gathering of ten or more men, not on prayer in any specified building (e.g., a synagogue) or in a specifically designated place for gathering (e.g., a sanctuary). Prayer as an aspect of Rabbinic piety thus is considered mainly in terms of a societal association with a community of other Jews. But pious Jews have traditionally placed little emphasis on the need for sacred bricks and mortar to fulfill the spiritual needs of prayer.

Rabbinic piety centers on stability and repetition. On weekdays Jews gather for the morning, afternoon, and evening prayers. Major elements of prayer are repeated with small variations at the three services. A person says the *shema* in the morning and evening services; the *amidah* (standing prayer of eighteen blessings) in the morning afternoon and evening services; the *alenu* (a sublime prayer proclaiming God as king) concludes all three. On Monday and Thursday (and on any festival or fast day) they add to these prayers a morning Torah service, in which they read the first section of the weekly Torah portion that is going to be read in its entirety during the Sabbath morning service at the end of the work week. This focuses attention on the coming Sabbath celebration and gives the men gathered during the week an added opportunity to hear the inspiration of the words of Torah.

A fourth service, the additional prayers, called *musaf*, is added to celebrate special days, including Sabbaths and holy days. On New moons, celebrants add several paragraphs to the regular services and read an appropriate passage from the Torah. They conclude the morning prayers with the recitation of the *amidah*—the standing prayer of eighteen blessings—of the additional service. Likewise on holidays, modifications are made in the regular prayers and the

additional *musaf amidah* is appended.

Evening prayers, optimally recited in the usual quorum, consist of the *shema, amidah,* and *alenu.* A widespread custom is to recite the *shema* once more at bedtime. Many believe this will protect the individual from harm during the night.

**Women's piety:** Women have not been assigned an egalitarian role in traditional Rabbinic piety. In accordance with the profile of Prov. 31:10-31, they are assigned instead a life of valor. Piety for the woman in traditional Judaism thus emphasizes more her personal character as wife, mother, and homemaker, and less her participation in public rituals of prayer and the synagogue. In many Jewish cultures through the course of history, women were not required or expected to attend the synagogue at all. One Rabbinic expression used to justify these choices was that, "The honor of the princess is in the interior (i.e., in the home, not the synagogue)."

For the Jewish woman, developing good character is elevated to a process of piety. Shyness, kindness, and good-heartedness are singled out as desired traits. Modesty is a paramount virtue for the pious woman. The rabbis have translated this expectation into formal custom. The pious woman dresses in accordance with the prevalent rules of modesty. These rules are more rigorous for a married woman. On many occasions and in many places they require that she cover her hair with a hat, kerchief, or wig, cover her arms and legs with suitable clothing, and that she act in a humble and reticent manner. Ideally, to conform to the needs of piety, a woman's speech and conversation at all times are to be modest. The rabbis prohibit a married woman from any form of flirtation or any action that might be misconstrued as an invitation to licentiousness.

Historically, several meaningful prayers were reserved as acts of piety predominantly for women. Saying special chapters from the book of Psalms (*tehillim*), especially on behalf of the sick, was an act of piety more prevalent among women. Characteristically, lighting candles right before the onset of the Sabbath on Friday evening is a woman's act

Figure 102. Women sort unleavened bread prepared under strict rabbinical control *(shmurah matzoh)* into boxes in preparation for the celebration of Passover. Amsterdam, Holland, 1930s.

Figure 103. Burning of remaining unleavened products (*chametz*) in preparation for Passover, Amsterdam, Holland, 1928.

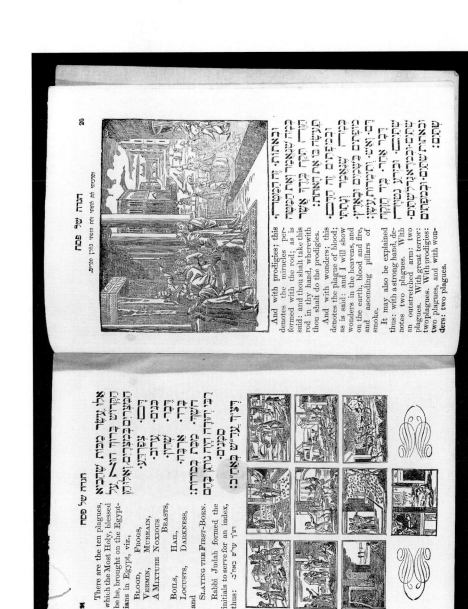

Figure 104. Passover Haggadah, "To honor and welcome refugees," for a seder at Broadway Central Hotel, New York, April 4, 1939.

Figure 105. Sterling silver Passover seder plate made by Albert Dov Sigal, Israel, 1958. Sigal taught in a secret art school in Romania during the Holocaust. After immigrating to Israel in 1947, he became known as an artist in enamel and silver.

Figure 106. Ceremonial wine glass (kiddush cup) used by Isidor and Grete Lefor, Barchfeld, Germany, nineteenth century.

Figure 107. Ritual fringes *(tsitsiot)* for a child, used by Jacob Grunwerg in Kolomea, Austria-Hungary, c. 1900-1910, and brought to the United States when he immigrated before World War I.

Figure 108. Silver spice box belonging to Rabbi Ze'ev Wolf Rosenberg from Debrecen, Hungary. Family members flattened and hid the box when they were deported from Hungary to Florisdorf, a family camp in Austria, and later to the Terezin ghetto in Czechoslovakia.

Figure 109. Wooden clogs with inlaid mother-of-pearl used by Rachel Rabih-Sutton, Aleppo, Syria, 1898. These special clogs *(babouj il-hamman)* were used for a pre-wedding visit to a mikveh, a ritual bath. They were a wedding gift from Moshe Mansoura to his bride.

Figure 110. Moshe Chazanovitch, cantor and shohet (kosher butcher), prepares to slaughter a chicken. Konstantynow, Poland, 1936.

Figure 111. A page from a record book of the Burial Society of Congregation Ahavat Shalom Winitze, 1889, New York.

Figure 112. Yahrzeit calendar for Dr. Moritz Brecher, Vienna, Austria, 1920.

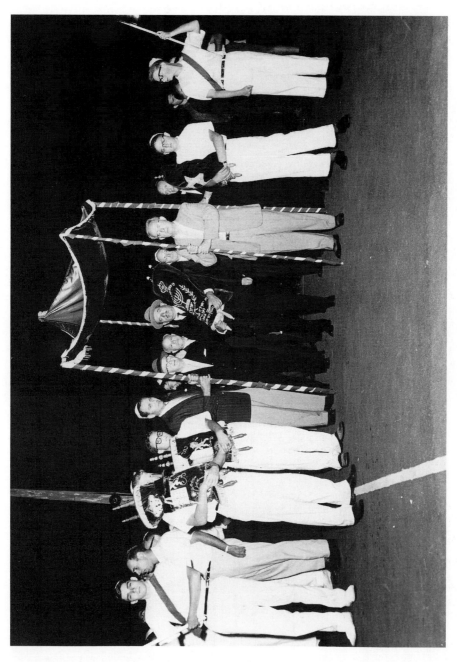

Figure 113. Dedicating a new Torah scroll at Camp Massad, founded in 1941, the first Hebrew language summer camp in the United States; Tannersville, Pennsylvania, undated.

וּבְהֵמָה וּבִשְׂדֵה אֲחֻזָּתוֹ לֹא יִמָּכֵר וְלֹא יִגָּאֵל כָּל חֵרֶם קֹדֶשׁ קָדָשִׁים הוּא לַיהוָה כָּל חֵרֶם אֲשֶׁר
יָחֳרַם מִן הָאָדָם לֹא יִפָּדֶה מוֹת יוּמָת וְכָל מַעְשַׂר הָאָרֶץ מִזֶּרַע הָאָרֶץ מִפְּרִי הָעֵץ לַיהוָה
הוּא קֹדֶשׁ לַיהוָה וְאִם גָּאֹל יִגְאַל אִישׁ מִמַּעַשְׂרוֹ חֲמִישִׁתוֹ יֹסֵף עָלָיו וְכָל מַעְשַׂר בָּקָר
וָצֹאן כֹּל אֲשֶׁר יַעֲבֹר תַּחַת הַשָּׁבֶט הָעֲשִׂירִי יִהְיֶה קֹדֶשׁ לַיהוָה לֹא יְבַקֵּר בֵּין טוֹב לָרַע וְלֹא
יְמִירֶנּוּ וְאִם הָמֵר יְמִירֶנּוּ וְהָיָה הוּא וּתְמוּרָתוֹ יִהְיֶה קֹדֶשׁ לֹא יִגָּאֵל אֵלֶּה הַמִּצְוֹת אֲשֶׁר
צִוָּה יְהוָה אֶת מֹשֶׁה אֶל בְּנֵי יִשְׂרָאֵל בְּהַר סִינָי

**חֲזַק**

סִימָן סְכוּם פְּסוּקֵי דְּסִפְרָא בָּטַח

Figure 114. Folio from the Coburg Pentateuch (Add. 19776, f. 72v) showing a teacher and pupil, copied by Simhah ben Samuel Halevi, dated Kislev 5156 (1395).

Figure 115. The Eisensteins leaving on a honeymoon trip to Palestine in June, 1934: (from left) Naomi Kaplan, Lena Kaplan, Ira Eisenstein, Judith Kaplan Eisenstein, Mordecai Kaplan, Selma Kaplan, Hadassah Kaplan.

Figure 116. Mordecai M. Kaplan affixes the mezuzah at the dedication of the Reconstructionist Rabbinical College, 1968.

Figure 117. Judith Kaplan Eisenstein in 1992, at the seventieth anniversary of her Bat Mitzvah celebration. Dr. Eisenstein was the first female to participate in a Bat Mitzvah service, which was created by her father, Mordecai M. Kaplan.

of piety on behalf of her entire household.

Rabbis gave serious attention to obligations and exemptions for women in all acts of piety and religious commandments (*mitzvot*). The rabbis distilled their concept down to the principle that women are exempt from all pious acts that must be accomplished at a fixed time of day. Women thus are not expected to attend the synagogue and, in part because they were not obligated to recite the prayers in the first place, are not counted in the official quorum. The common expectation is that women will not join with men in the professional study of Torah. With rare exceptions, until the emergence of modern, non-Orthodox forms of Judaism, they could not study alongside men in the yeshiva and could not be ordained as rabbis.

**The pious home:** The woman's main role in traditional Jewish culture is to aid her husband in building a household among the people Israel. It is deemed a significant act of piety to marry, raise children, and to maintain a pious family life. Thus the goal of the union of a man and woman is to create a Jewish home. Simple rites of piety mark the life cycle rituals of passage in Rabbinic tradition. The wedding ceremony creates the pious state of matrimony in a few symbolic stages. At the betrothal, the woman is designated for marriage to her intended husband. In medieval and later times, the betrothal and wedding were combined into one event. Bride and groom often fast and repent from wrongdoing on their wedding day, which some rabbis compare to Yom Kippur.

The writing of the Ketubah—the marriage contract—formalizes the matrimony. This Aramaic legal document is given to the wife to protect her interests within the marriage. The writ is often read aloud by a rabbi during the wedding ceremony. During this brief ceremony, the groom places a ring on the bride's finger and recites, "Behold you are sanctified to me in accord with the laws of Moses and Israel." The presiding rabbi or distinguished members of the family or community then recites seven blessings that allude to the cosmic and mythic biblical accounts of the beginning and end of time, which sanctify the present moment of piety.

The concluding blessing in a series of seven declares:

> Blessed art Thou Lord our God King of the Universe who created joy and happiness, bride and groom, gladness, jubilation, cheer and delight, love, friendship, harmony and fellowship. Lord our God soon may there be heard in the cities of Judah and the streets of Jerusalem the sounds of joy and happiness, bride and groom, exultation of grooms from their wedding canopy and of children from their joyous banquets. Blessed are you Lord our God who gladdens the groom with the bride.

Traditionally the wedding was held out-of-doors under a canopy, the *chuppah*, and even today, in the case of weddings held indoors, the use of the canopy continues. Thus the wedding is imbued with the cosmic symbolism of the heavens, on the one side, and a metaphor for the new home, represented by the *chuppah*, on the other. According to tradition, the divine presence comes down upon the canopy and angels of heaven cry out that it be God's will that the bride and groom rejoice with one another. After the ceremony it is a common custom to break a glass, symbolizing both the fragility of the relationship and the sufferings of the Jewish people. The bride and groom then go briefly into a private room, to embody their intimacy. After the wedding feast, the couple continues to celebrate the marriage for one week with special blessings and customs at every festive dinner.

**Pious relationships:** A peaceful home and harmonious family life are a simple ideal for Rabbinic society, and these goals are elevated to acts of piety. A husband has to make efforts to understand and cater to the needs of his wife, to control his anger and his ego. The wife in turn must strive continually to fulfill her roles within the family. Biblical models of loyalty, like that of Ruth, and bravery, like that of Esther, guide the actions of the pious woman. The rabbis said that sanctity resided in the correct union of partners.

Childbearing and rearing are imbued with elements of piety, making it incumbent upon both partners to provide a nurturing environment for their children. The obligation to educate one's children is also elevated to the level of an act of piety. The Talmud prescribes that a father must teach his son Torah, a trade, and how to swim, that is survival skills, and self-defense.

More so than other religions, Rabbinic Judaism asserts that religious piety governs sexuality and intimacy between partners in a marriage, an area of piety called "family purity." Couples are urged to observe the rules both out of promises of merit and threats of dire consequences both to those who violated them and to their offspring. Based on Lev. 18:19, the rabbis formalized a taboo against sexual relations during a woman's monthly menstrual cycle. A piety thereby governs the most intimate physical relations between husband and wife.

Intricate rituals govern the period of abstinence. During the wife's menstrual period, the husband and wife do not touch each other casually, or at meals, or share the same bed. The separation is compared to a hedge of roses erected between lovers, and mastery of one's desires is considered a sure sign of piety. The rabbis taught that the laws of family purity will continually renew the love between husband and wife. After the prescribed period of abstinence during menstruation and the following seven clean days, the wife immerses in the specially constructed *miqvah*-bath (fig. 109), under the supervision of another woman, before she resumes intimacy with her husband. Traditionally, if there are uncertainties about the menstrual period, a rabbi was consulted to judge whether the emission required abstinence. This was done through the anonymous submission of test cloths to the authority. Maimonides in the Middle Ages urged Jews to observe these laws, not based on fact or logic but out of "the devotion of one's heart."

The rights and expectations of husband and wife are formulated into Rabbinic prescriptions for the pious to observe. Elements of a relationship, like love, devotion, and faithfulness, are not merely character traits to be admired. They are integral to fulfillment of a pious life within the parameters of a marital relationship.

**The pious household:** Piety extends to nearly all aspects of life in the Rabbinic home. The symbolic *mezuzah*—a sort of amulet—hangs on every doorway, sanctifying the space of the house and protecting its inhabitants. It contains passages from Deut. 6:4-9 and 11:13-21, written on parchment in 22 lines as in the phylacteries. The rabbis noted that the *mezuzah, tefillin*, and fringes of the prayer shawl remind a person of the need to be pious and protect one from sin. A person has thirty days from the time of occupancy to affix a *mezuzah* to his home.

Especially noteworthy is the extensive reach of practices of piety into the cuisine of the Rabbinic home, which is governed by the laws of kashrut. Kosher food categories and rules require constant attention to the sources and preparation of food in the household. Meats may only be obtained from a trusted butcher who knows that the item from a kosher species, a healthy animal, and that it was properly slaughtered and prepared. A Jew may not consume *treifa*, unfit meat or foods not prepared under the stringencies of the dietary restrictions (fig. 110).

The taboo against cooking or eating milk and meat together necessitates that homes have two sets of utensils and dishes, one for the preparation of meat meals, the other for dairy. The theory behind this is that a pot, utensil, or other dish absorbs the flavor when milk or meat is cooked in, or even just placed on, it and imparts that flavor to whatever food subsequently is in contact with it. Thus a dish used for milk may not thereafter be used for meat or *vice versa*. The details of maintaining separate utensils for dairy and meat are complex and require extensive Rabbinic guidance.

Kosher preparation of foods requires that, to remove the blood, which may not be consumed, meat is soaked in water, carefully salted with coarse salt, and washed. Further, specific veins must be removed. Liver in particular must be cut, washed, salted, and broiled over a fire. Eggs with a spot of blood in them are deemed forbidden. Vegetables must be carefully inspected for insects and worms that would render them unfit for consumption. Alongside the requirement that milk and meat foods neither be prepared together nor eaten at the same meal, Rabbinic law required the immersion in a *mikvah* of new metal or glass cooking utensils prior to initial use.

In an effort to perpetuate some of the rules of the destroyed Jerusalem Temple and its priestly cult, the rabbis symbolically extended the laws of dough offerings, tithes, and heave-offerings. When baking bread it is necessary to separate *challah*, a small piece of dough that in ancient times would have been designated as the priest's share but which today is burned rather than consumed. This serves as a memorial of the priestly dues that may no longer be brought to the Temple and as a sign of hope for the redemption of Israel and the restoration of the Temple service. Any bread dough made of wheat, barley, spelt, rye, or oat flour is liable to this obligation.

In addition, the rabbis recommend as an act of piety that a Jew donate a tithe of his income to charity as a memorial of the Levitical tithes described in Scripture.[1] Much has been written and preached about the piety of giving generously to charity. Maimonides extolled the virtues of anonymous donation as the most pious form of charity.

Every occasion for eating is transformed by Rabbinic precept into a pious meal. Before partaking of bread, pious Jews wash their hands and recite a blessing, a symbol of the purity once associated with the priests' entering the Temple to perform the sacred rites of the cult. Indeed, in accordance with the system developed in the Mishnah and Talmud, pious Jews recite blessings and prayers before and after eating or drinking any food.

The rabbis determined that what makes the consumption of food a meal is the breaking of bread. This brings with it the blessing, "Blessed art thou, O Lord our God, who brings forth bread from the earth," a blessing that is held to encompass thanks for all foods eaten during that meal. In the case of a meal beginning with bread, accordingly, no blessings beyond the one for bread are recited for the individual foods that are consumed. But after such a meal, at which bread has been consumed, the full grace after meals must be recited.

Snacks or other occasions for eating that do not involve bread are subject to different rules. These acts of consumption are not treated as unitary meals, and for their case, accordingly, Rabbinic authorities developed a system of blessings appropriate to each individual type of food or drink. When consumed outside of the context of a meal including bread, that is, individual blessings are specified for vegetables, fruits, baked goods, wine, and drinks. Piety additionally requires that one recite short blessings of thanksgiving after the eating baked goods or individual foods.

Group meals create a formal fellowship. At the completion of a meal at which a minimum of three men ate bread together, one diner is designated to recite an invitation to the others to recite the grace together. Good table manners thus become a matter of piety as well.

A righteous Jew is to uphold the imperative of hospitality. One who engages in the kindness of welcoming guests is understood to emulate the character of Abraham the patriarch, who welcomed the three messengers of God (Gen. 18:1-8). Opening one's house to the poor is the highest form of the piety of welcoming the stranger. Proper behavior towards animals also is expected as a matter of piety. Causing any suffering to an animal is a transgression. Indeed one is not permitted to eat before first feeding his animals.

Part of the Rabbinic way of life is devotion to children. This starts with the fundamental commandment that a father circumcise his son on the eighth day. This practice goes back to Abraham as the most ancient sign of the covenant between God and his chosen people. If the father cannot fulfill this role, he designates a professional circumcizer, *mohel*, to carry out the rite. Most often the ceremony is occasion for a public celebration and an obligatory feast. Traditionally all members of the community were expected to participate in the celebration. Members of the family and distinguished guests received the honors of carrying and holding the infant before, during, and after the procedure. All the assembled guests would bless the child that he might enter into a life of Torah, marriage, and good deeds. The child's name was then announced in public for the first time.

Historically, there was no formal ritual to mark the birth of a daughter. However it has become a common practice to name one's daughter in the synagogue after being called to the Torah on the Sabbath following the birth.

Alongside circumcision, another symbolic act harking back to biblical times is the practice of redeeming one's first born son from a priest. This is based on Num. 3:11-13 and 44-48, where God declares that all the first born of the people of Israel are his, but that he has taken into his service in their stead the Levitical priests. Rather than turn their first born sons over for service in the priestly cult, Israelites may accordingly pay redemption money. This practice is carried out to our own day, when, thirty-one days after the birth of a first born son, the father symbolically presents to a Jew of priestly lineage (*Cohen*) five shekel coins, or their equivalent value, for his son.

The caring roles of mother and father are demarcated clearly within the pious family structure. Caring for infants traditionally is thought to be the role of the mother. Discipline of children is evenly shared between mother and father. Education of the young up to a certain age is entrusted to the mother. An example of a Jewish lullaby captures the spirit of pious child rearing:

> Run my son, run hard
> Enter the house of your teacher.
> Search and seek only in the Torah
> For her wealth is better than all wares.

When old enough, boys are educated by the father or sent off to formal training with a rabbi or suitable teacher. Historically, girls were afforded a less intensive education.

The bar mitzvah, or coming of age ceremony, was a late development in Judaic ritual and piety. As noted above, it marks the first occasion for boys to put on *tefillin* and to be called in public to read from the Torah. The bat mitzvah ceremony for girls is an even later practice, developing within the past hundred years. Some communities mark a girl's coming of age with a celebration in the synagogue or, in orthodox circles, more commonly by a public feast.

Finally, filial piety, or honor of one's parents, is a hallmark of all Jewish piety. Some rabbis expressed this in mystical terms. Rav Joseph, hearing his mother's footsteps approaching, would say, "I rise before the Shekhinah (Divine Presence) that draws nigh."

**Philosophical meanings of piety:** Within Judaism, the obligations of what modern Western people would call a life of piety are clear. Yet it bears noting that, within this context of Judaism, the definition of the term "piety" itself is fraught with difficulties. For piety is a classical category of Western discourse related to religious action and ethics (cf., Plato, *Euthyphro*). But it is not a category native to classical Judaism at all.

We have proposed that for Rabbinic Judaism piety implies living in accordance with a faith in the validity and relevance of the Torah as taught and expanded by the rabbis. This means that in all aspects of day-to-day life one acts in a manner and maintains vivid moods and motivations that are in keeping with the teachings of the law, written and oral. Piety endows everyday activities, decisions, and attitudes with special significances associated with historical, mystical, and redemptive beliefs. Piety requires that new practices that might emerge from age to age be based on these same ideals.

The motives and goals of piety within the Judaic system lead to several outcomes: Piety leads to a life of sanctification—*qedushah*—in accordance with the Halakhah. It leads to a life of awe, of both love and fear of God. It results in submission to a higher power, engendering a sense of creatureliness. It enables the believer to insure entry into paradise, that is, the "World to Come" (i.e., the afterlife or heaven). The collective piety of the community of the people Israel is understood to aid in bringing about the messianic era. On the most basic level, many believe that acts of piety also result in material gain for their practitioners.

Yet most aspects of Jewish piety are performed not as the free choice of an individual who desires a special reward but because these behaviors are viewed as God's commandments and, hence, as obligations. A majority of the practices that comprise Jewish piety, that is, have official status, are binding on the entire community of the faithful, as *mitzvot*, divine duties. God's command both compels the Jew to live a pious life and endows daily activities with transcendent meanings. Even the Judaic notion of custom, *minhag*, gives quasi-official status to pious practices that emerge over time and are not directly associated with God and the original revelation at Sinai. The obligation to carry out such customs might technically be limited in time and place, and these practices might, by the letter of the law, be less authoritative than other pious acts. But often such distinctions are unrecognized in the life of a pious Jew, who sees all traditional Jewish behaviors as essentially obligatory.

**Categories of Piety:** The ultimate yardstick of piety is the *Zaddiq*, the righteous saint who we would call purely ethical, who flourishes as a proper human, and who achieves true virtue. The extent to which one adheres to all of the norms of piety marks how closely one proximates this standard of perfect righteousness.

Cognitive piety is a subset of the general category. Its highest form is the perpetual study of the Torah, the source and authoritative basis of all Judaic piety. The well-known epigram that expressed this notion asserts that, "The study of Torah is as important as all other acts of piety combined."

Another dimension of piety may be referred to as "mind-piety," i.e., the desirability of maintaining perpetually pure thoughts, of harboring thoughts of Torah at all times. Along these lines, the rabbis emphasized the centrality in the daily life of the Jew of meditation, prayer, and contemplation.

Body-piety is another aspect of the larger concern. Physical actions endowed with piety include bowing and other specific bodily postures in prayer; washing for the purposes of ritual purity rather than simple hygiene; wearing proper clothing and appurtenances of pious living: *tzitzit* (fringes), *tefillin, yarmulke*, hat; other forms of dress; haircut, beard, or side locks. Naturally all aspects of

sexuality can be included in this subset, as discussed above.

Synagogue piety is a third major area of the subject. Many acts associated with prayer in the synagogue define elements of this type of piety. Blowing and hearing the shofar on the New Year and shaking the *lulav* on the festival of Tabernacles constitute two examples of this area. All acts of prayer come under this rubric.

Some modern, secular, attitudes deny the value of the wide range of religious practices that define piety. Some even argue that constant piety and familiarity with the sacred in fact devalue the worshipper's relationship to the deity and render it rote and mechanical. Apologists for piety respond that such attitudes denigrate one important means of fulfilling a basic human need: acts of piety connect individuals to the past and future, to heaven and earth, to family and community. In this view, the modern, secular person, bereft of modes of enacting piety, lives a more lonely, detached life with less passion and devotion. Proponents of piety thus ask if the rise in secularization has in fact been accompanied by an increase in levels of individual or communal happiness or by a decline in economic oppression or psychological dysfunction?

The believer-practitioner of the pious life emphasizes a main advantage afforded by the intimacy of piety. In the Judaic notion, God wants constant contact with the believer, akin to an obsessive love affair, renewed frequently through expected daily affirmations. Constant devotion to the divine provides the perpetual training and conditioning for that relationship. Piety invigorates all the devotions of life, marriage, raising children, advancing one's vocation, and contributes to the well-being and wholeness of one's community.

**Notes**
[1] See also CHARITY.

TZVEE ZAHAVY

**POLITICS, JUDAISM AND, [I] THE NORMATIVE STATEMENT IN SCRIPTURE AND THE TALMUD:** The political theory of Judaism emerges in the Hebrew Scriptures of ancient Israel as these writings are interpreted by the rabbis of the first six centuries C.E. in the Talmud of Babylonia and related documents. The Pentateuch portrays Israel as "a kingdom of priests and a holy people" and further takes for granted that this "kingdom" or "people" forms a political entity, exercising legitimate violence. Scripture therefore understands Israel not merely as a church or a voluntary community but an empowered society, with a government, laws, and institutions. Scripture's own portrait of the type of government varies. The Pentateuch read whole takes for granted that Israel is governed by God through the prophet Moses. Moses further appoints an administration to deal with conflict and to secure the public order, and that administration exercises authority and inflicts the death penalty for civil and religious infractions. Other writings describe an Israelite monarchy; still others, a government by the priesthood based on the Temple in Jerusalem. The picture of Israel as a family, descended from Abraham and Sarah, conflicts with this account of Israel as an empowered and political entity. That picture plays no role in the articulation of the politics of the holy people.

However Scripture portrays matters, the politics of Judaism are shaped in the legal documents of late antiquity, which take over and recast Scripture's account. The Mishnah, ca. 200 C.E., a philosophical law code that portrays a utopian Israel in the manner of Plato's Republic or Aristotle's Ethics, with its commentaries in the Talmud of the Land of Israel, ca. 400 C.E., and the Talmud of Babylonia, ca. 600 C.E., carries forward the premise of Scripture that the holy people forms a political entity in the here and now, not merely a supernatural community of the faithful, such as is the conception of Israel in the Dead Sea library. The Mishnah's Judaism speaks of a social entity treated as a political one as well, of "Israel" classified as a state. This social entity (called, as the social entity of every Judaism is called, "Israel") is not merely a mythic and theological picture but also a political structure.

When people would speak of "the state of (being) Israel," therefore, they would also refer to "the State of Israel," the Jewish State, understanding that they spoke of a political entity like other such political entities. Accordingly this Judaism became in mind and imagination a state not only of (autonomous) being but also of (shared and social) doing, not alone of ontology but of society. That is why this Judaism defines a locus for inquiry into more than theological science, but into, especially, the social sciences as well: economics, politics, and philosophy. The key generative problematic of the Mishnah is the interplay of divine will and the human will, and the relationships that require political scrutiny are between God and Israel, not among citizens or between the state and its citizens. Religion and politics are integrated.

The encompassing framework of rules, institutions, and sanctions is explained and validated by appeal to the myth of God's shared rule. That dominion, exercised by God and his surrogates on earth, is focused partly in the royal palace, partly in the Temple, and partly in the court. The political myth of Judaism explains who exercises legitimate violence and under what conditions and furthermore specifies the source for differentiation. Indeed, the Judaic political myth comes to expression in its details of differentiation, which permit us to identify, and of course to answer, the generative question of politics: who has power, whence does that power derive, and how may they use that power to commit legitimate violence? Analyzing myth by explaining sanctions draws our attention to the modes of legitimate violence that the system identifies.

Here we find four types of sanctions, each deriving from a distinct institution of political power, each bearing its own mythic explanation. The first comprises what God and the heavenly court can do to people. The second comprises what the earthly court can do to people. That type of sanction embodies the legitimate application of the worldly and physical kinds of violence of which political theory ordinarily speaks. The third comprises what the cult can do to people. The cult through its requirements can deprive people of their property as legitimately as can a court. The fourth comprises conformity with consensus—self-imposed sanctions. Here the issue is, whose consensus and defined by whom? Across these four types of sanction, four types of coercion are in play. They depend on violence of various kinds—psychological and social as much as physical. Clearly, then, the sanctions that are exercised by other than judicial-political agencies prove violent and legitimately coercive, even though the violence and coercion are not the same as those carried out by courts.

Predictably, when we search for the mythic premises sanctions, we begin with God's place in the institutionalization and execution of legitimate violence. Of course, the repertoire of sanctions does encompass God's direct intervention, but that is hardly a preferred alternative or a common one. Still, God does commonly intervene when oaths are violated, for oaths are held to involve the person who invokes God's name and God. Further, whereas, when faced with an insufficiency of valid evidence, under strict rules of testimony, the earthly court cannot penalize serious crime, the heavenly court can and does impose a penalty. Clearly, then, God serves to justify the politics and account for its origin. Although God is never asked to join in making specific decisions effecting policy in the everyday politics of the state, deliberate violation of certain rules provokes God's or the heavenly court's direct intervention. Thus obedience to the law clearly represents submission to God in heaven. Further, forms of heavenly coercion suggest a complex mythic situation, with more subtle nuance than the claim that, overall, God rules would indicate. A politics of rules and regulations cannot admit God's *ad hoc* participation, and this system did not do so. God joined in the system in a regular and routine way, and the rules took for granted God's part in the politics of Judaism.

In the Mishnah's picture, some of the same crimes or sins for which the heavenly court imposes the penalty of extirpation—death at the hands of the divine—are those that, under appropriate circumstances (e.g., sufficient evidence admissible in court) the earthly court imposes the death-penalty. That is, the heavenly court and the earthly court impose precisely the same sanctions for the same crimes or sins. The earthly court therefore forms down here the exact replica and counterpart, within a single system of power, of the heavenly court up there.

The earthly and heavenly courts share jurisdiction over sexual crimes and over serious religious crimes against God. The heavenly court penalizes with its form of the death-penalty religious sins against God, in which instances a person deliberately violates the taboos of sanctification. This fact calls our attention to a third partner in the distribution and application of power, the Temple with its system of sanctions that cover precisely the same acts subject to the jurisdiction of the heavenly and earthly courts. Heaven's counterpart on earth is now not the earthly court but the Temple. This is the institution that, in theory, automatically receives the appropriate offering from the person who inadvertently violates these same taboos of sanctification.

But this is an odd choice for the Mishnah, since in its authors time no Temple stood on earth. The juxtaposition of courts and Temple thus suggests that both are equally matters of theory. In the theory at hand, then, the earthly court, for its part, penalizes social crimes against the community that the heavenly court, on the one side, and the Temple rites, on the other, do not take into account at all. These are murder, apostasy, kidnapping, public defiance of the court, and false prophecy. The earthly court further imposes sanctions on matters of particular concern to the heavenly court, with special reference to taboos of sanctification (e.g., negative commandments). These three institutions, therefore, exercise concrete and material power, utilizing legitimate violence to kill someone, exacting penalties against property, and inflicting pain. The sages' modes of power, by contrast, stand quite apart, apply mainly to their own circle, and work through the intangible though no less effective means of inflicting shame or paying honor.

Power flows through three distinct but intersecting dominions, each with its own concern, all sharing some interests in common.

The heavenly court attends to deliberate defiance of heaven, the Temple to inadvertent defiance of heaven. The earthly court attends to matters subject to its jurisdiction by reason of sufficient evidence, proper witnesses, and the like, and these same matters come under heavenly jurisdiction when the earthly court is unable to act. Accordingly, we have a tripartite system of sanctions: heaven cooperating with the Temple in some matters, with the court in others, and, as noted, each bearing its own distinct media of enforcing the law as well. What, then, can we say concerning the systemic myth of politics? The forms of power and the modes of mediating legitimate violence draw our attention to a single political myth. The unity of that myth is underlined by the simple fact that the earthly court enters into the process right along side the heavenly court and the Temple. So a single myth must serve all three correlated institutions.

The myth of God's authority infuses the institutions of heaven and earth alike, an authority diffused among three principle foci or circles of power, heaven's court, the earthly court, and the Temple in-between. Each focus of power has its own jurisdiction and responsibility, heaven above, earth beneath, the Temple in the position of mediation, transmitting as it does from earth to heaven the penalties handed over as required. And all media of power in the matter of sanctions intersect at some points as well: a tripartite politics, a single myth drawing each component into relationship with a single source and origin of power, God's law set forth in the Torah. The point of differentiation within the political structures, supernatural and natural alike, lies in the attitude and intention of a human being. We differentiate among the applications of power by reference to the attitude of the person who comes into relationship with that power. A person who comes into conflict with the system, rejecting the authority claimed by the powers that be, does so deliberately or inadvertently. The myth accounts in the end for the following hierarchization of action and penalty, infraction and sanction: [1] If the deed is deliberate, then one set of institutions exercises jurisdiction and utilizes supernatural power. [2] If the deed is inadvertent, another institution exercises jurisdiction and utilizes the power made available by that same supernatural being.

A sinner or criminal who has deliberately violated the law has by his or her action challenged the politics of Judaism. Consequently, God or God's surrogate imposes sanctions—extirpation (by the court on high), or death or other appropriate penalty (by the court on earth). A sinner or criminal who has inadvertently violated the law is penalized by the imposition of Temple sanctions—lose of valued goods. People obey because God wants them to and has told them what to do, and when they do not obey, a differentiated political structure appeals to that single hierarchizing myth. The components of the myth are two: first, God's will, expressed in the law of the Torah, second, the human being's will, carried out in obedience to the law of the Torah or in defiance of that law. The political myth of Judaism has to explain the differentiation of sins or crimes, with their associated penalties or punishments, and so sanctions of power. And in Scripture there is a very precise answer to the question of how to differentiate among sins or crimes and why to do so. Given the position of the system of the Mishnah, the point of differentiation must rest with one's attitude or intentionality.

We have a well-known story of how the power of God conflicts with the power of humanity so as to invoke penalties and sanctions in precisely the differentiated modes we have before us. That story of power differentiated by the will of the human being in communion or conflict with the word of the commanding God comes to us from the Garden of Eden (Gen. 2:1ff.), where what was at stake was responsibility: not only who has violated God's commandment, but who bears responsibility for deliberately violating the law. Here the ultimate responsibility lies with the snake, because it acted deliberately, not under constraint or on account of deception or misinformation, as did Adam and Eve. The sanction applies most severely to the one who by intention and an act of will violated God's intention and will.

The political myth of Judaism now emerges in the Mishnah in all of its detail as a reprise—in consequential and necessary, stunning detail—of the story of God's commandment, humanity's disobedience, God's sanction for the sin or crime, and humanity's atonement and reconciliation. The Mishnah omits all explicit reference to myths that explain power and sanctions but invokes in its rich corpus of details the absolute given of the story of the distinction between what is deliberate and what is mitigated by an attitude that is not culpable, a distinction set forth in the tragedy of Adam and Eve, in the failure of Moses and Aaron, and in countless other passages in the Pentateuch, Prophetic Books, and Writings. The Mishnah's is a politics of life after Eden and outside of Eden. The upshot of the matter is that the political myth of Judaism sets forth the constraints of freedom, the human will brought to full and unfettered expression, imposed by the constraints of revelation, God's will made known.

Since the freedom of humanity to make decisions and frame intentions forms the point of differentiation among the political media of power, we are required to return to the paradigmatic exercise of that same freedom, that is, to Eden, to the moment when Adam and Eve exercise their own will and defy God. Since the operative criterion in the differentiation of sanction—that is, the exercise of legitimate violence by heaven, earth, or the Temple—is the human attitude and intention in carrying out a culpable action, we must recognize that the politics before us rehearses the myth of Adam and Eve in Eden—it finds its dynamic in the correspondence between God's will and humanity's freedom to act however it chooses, thus freely incurring the risk of penalty or sanction for the wrong exercise of freedom.

At stake is what Adam and Eve and numerous others intend, propose, plan, for that is the point at which the politics intervenes, making its points of differentiation between and among its sanctions and the authorities that impose those penalties. For that power to explain difference, which is to say, the capacity to represent and account for hierarchy, we are required to turn to the story of the fall of Adam and Eve from Eden and to counterpart stories. The reason is that the political myth derives from that myth of origins its points of differentiation, and it explains by reference to the principal components of that myth—God's and humanity's will and power—the dynamics of the political system at hand. God commands, but humanity does what it chooses, and in the interplay of those two protean forces, each power in its own right, the sanctions and penalties of the system apply. Power comes from two conflicting forces, the commanding will of God and the free will of the human being. Power expressed in immediate sanctions is also mediated through these same forces, heaven above, human beings below, with the Temple mediating between the two. Power works its way in the interplay between what God has set forth in the law of the Torah and what human beings do, whether intentionally, whether inadvertently, whether obediently, whether defiantly. That is why the politics of Judaism is a politics of Eden.

To examine the politics of the Mishnah in its historical context, we must recall that, among prior Judaisms, only the scriptural system had set forth a politics at all. The appeal to politics in setting forth a theory of the social order of their particular "Israel" will have provoked some curiosity among, for one example, the framers of the Judaism portrayed by the Essene library uncovered at Qumran, and, for another, the framers of the Christianity of the land of Israel in the first century. Both groups, heirs of the ancient Scriptures as much as were the framers of the Mishnah, found in politics no important component of the systemic structure they set forth. By contrast, the integration, within a systematic account of the social order, of a politics will not have surprised the great figures of Greco-Roman philosophy, Plato and Aristotle for example. That fact takes on consequence when we note that the Pentateuch simply does not prepare us to make sense of the institutions that the politics of Judaism for its part designs. The Pentateuchal politics invokes priest and prophet, Aaron and Moses, but knows nothing of a tripartite government involving king, priest, and sage; nor do the royal narratives concede empowerment to the priest or sage. On the other hand knowledge of Aristotle's Politics and Plato's Republic gives perspective upon the politics of the Mishnah.

The Pentateuch contributes nothing to the Mishnah's scheme of routine government by king, high priest, and sages' court. The Pentateuch's prophetic rule and constant appeal to God's immediate participation in the political process, and, in particular, in the administration of sanctions and acts of legitimate violence, by contrast, falls into the category of a politics of charisma. The difference is not merely that the Pentateuchal institutions appeal to prophet and priest; it also is a difference in how the structure works as a political system. For the Pentateuchal myth that serves to legitimate coercion—rule by God's prophet, in the model of Moses, governance through explicitly revealed laws that God has dictated for the occasion—plays no active and systemic role whatsoever in the formulation and presentation of the politics of Judaism. Philosophical systems use politics, by contrast, to set forth the rules and unchanging order of legitimate exercise of power, its teleology and its structure. Plato and Aristotle make no place for godly intervention on any particular occasion.

And for their part, among the types of political authority contained within the scriptural repertoire, the one that the Mishnah's philosophers reject is the prophetic and charismatic, and the one that they deem critical is the authority governing and governed by rules in an orderly, rational way. The principal political figures—king, high priest, the disciple of the sage—are carefully nurtured through learning of rules, not through cultivation of gifts of the spirit. The authority of sages in the politics of Judaism in particular does not derive from charisma, e.g., revelation by God to the sage who makes a ruling in a given case, or even general access to God for the sage. So the politics of the Pentateuch—structure and system alike—in no way forms the model for the politics of the Mishnah.

**The politics of the Talmud:** The next and definitive politics emerged in the interpretation of the Mishnah by the Talmud. There, in the Talmud of the Land of Israel, we find a politics that exhibits none of the traits of the Mishnah's politics, but sets forth those of its own. Where the Mishnah's politics is orderly and hierarchical, the Yerushalmi's scarcely effects differentiation within the Israelite sphere at all; it has one political entity and class, not three on earth, corresponding to the one in heaven. The Talmud of the Land of Israel and related writings portray not the (imagined) orderly and innerfacing politics of Israel living by themselves under God, king, priest, and sage, but the palpable chaos of Jews living among gentiles, governed by a diversity of authorities, lacking all order and arrangement. The politics of the Mishnah is classified with that of philosophers, in abstract terms thinking about logic and order. The politics of the successor-documents shows us politicians deeply involved in the administration of the concrete social group, describing its "Israel" as a real-life community. The later authorships, in the fourth and fifth centuries, prove analogous not to philosophers but to men of affairs, judges, lawyers, bureaucrats, heads of local governments.

True, both the Mishnah's and the successor-documents' politics in the end put sages in charge of everything. But in the first system sages formed one component of a well-ordered structure, in which monarchy, priesthood, and clerkdom formed a cogent structure and together, each doing its assigned task, administered an orderly world in an orderly way. In the second, sages are represented as the sole legitimate authority, competing to be sure with such illegitimate authorities as the patriarch within and the gentile government of Rome beyond. The practical politics then dealt with Jews who lived under both rabbis near at hand, settling everyday disputes of streets and households, and also distant archons of a nameless state, to be manipulated and placated on earth as in heaven. But the Yerushalmi's portrait of legitimate power, as distinct from illegitimate violence, appeals then to the legitimation of the Torah serving solely for the sages, while the Mishnah's account differs in ways now entirely obvious. While legitimate power is carefully parceled out, illegitimate power is ignored. In the Yerushalmi's politics, by contrast, the issue is the distinction between illegitimate power, worked by patriarch within and Rome beyond, and legitimate power, focused solely upon sages. The issues thus shift even while the category remains the same. That shift indicates a decay in categorical cogency; the Mishnah's category of politics is preserved but then bypassed as issues not formerly considered intervene and drastically revise the character of the whole—even in its initial context and definition.

The Mishnah's politics breathes the pure air of public piazza and stoa, the politics of the Talmud of the Land of Israel and its associated Midrash-compilations, the ripe stench of private alleyway and courtyard. That is why the comparison of the Mishnah's politics with philosophical politics, the Yerushalmi's with an other-than-philosophical politics is amply justified. The image of the Mishnah's politics is evoked by the majestic Parthenon, perfect in all its proportions, conceived in a single moment of pure rationality. The successor-system is a scarcely-choate cathedral in process, the labor of many generations, each of its parts the conception of diverse moments of devotion, all of them the culmination of an on-going and evolving process of revelation in the here and now. The Mishnah's system presents a counterpart to Plato's Republic and Aristotle's Politics, a noble theory of it all. In literary terms, in the transition from the Mishnah to the successor-writings we leave behind the strict and formal classicism of the Mishnah, like Plato's Republic describing for no one in particular an ideal society never, in its day, to be seen. We come, rather, to focus upon the disorderly detail of the workaday world, to be sure taking the utopian Mishnah along with us in our descent into the streets where people really do commit acts of violence against one another, and where authority really does have to sort out legitimate acts and on-going institutions able to perform such acts from illegitimate ones.

While, therefore, the politics of the Yerushalmi and related writings carries forward that of the Mishnah, a quite separate conception of political institutions and relationships also comes to expression. It is a political structure in which sages administer sanctions, a system in which sages make decisions; where others intervene, their sanctions—whether those of the patriarch or of the gentile—are illegitimate. Legitimate violence is executed solely by one political entity, which is the sages' court.

This draws our attention to the question of the sanctions legitimately in the hands of sages alone. These are differentiated not in principle but only in context: what works. And the differentiation is circumstantial, expressed through description of cases, never theoretical and principled. But there should be no doubt that violence, not merely voluntary acquiescence, is at stake. Sages' power is political, not merely moral, routine and not charismatic in any sense. Thus sages are portrayed by the Talmud of the Land of Israel as exercising authority effected through concrete sanctions not only over their own circles, people who agreed with them, but over the Jewish community at large.

This authority was practical and involved very specific powers. The first and most important sort of power a rabbi under some circumstances and in some cases maintained he could exercise was to sort out and adjudicate rights to property and personal status affecting property. The rabbi is described as able to take chattels or real estate from one party and to give them into the rightful ownership of some other. The second power rabbis are supposed to have wielded was to tell people what to do, or not to do, in matters not involving property rights. They could administer floggings, that is, violence in its most personal form. The Talmud alleges that rabbis could tell people outside the circles of their own disciples and estate how to conduct themselves. A rabbi is presented as able to coerce someone to do what that ordinary Jew might otherwise not wish to do or to prevent him from doing what he wanted. That other authorities existed, and even competed with rabbinical authorities, is taken for granted. What is important is that the Yerushalmi portrays legitimate violence in a manner quite asymmetrical with the pattern set forth in the Mishnah.

The Talmud of the Land of Israel takes for granted that rabbis could define the status of persons in such ways as to affect property and marital rights and standing. It is difficult to imagine a more effective form of social authority. The Talmud treats as settled fact a range of precedents out of which the law is defined. In those precedents, rabbis declare a woman married or free to marry; permitted as wife of a priest to eat food in the status of leave-offering or prohibited from doing so; enjoying the support of a husband's estate or left without that support; having the right to collect a previously contracted marriage settlement or lacking that right. In all of these ways, as much as in their control of real estate, commercial, and other material and property transactions among Jews, the rabbis held they governed the Jewish community as effective political authorities. Whatever beliefs or values they proposed to instill in the people or realize in the collective life of the community, they effected not through moral suasion or pretense of magical power. It was not hocus pocus but political power resting on the force of government authority. They could tell people what to do and force them to do it.

The Talmud of the Land of Israel is remarkably reticent about the basis for rabbis' power over the Jews' political institutions: who bestowed this-worldly legitimacy and supplied the force? But the systematic provision of biblical proof texts for Mishnaic laws presents an ample myth for the law and its enforcement: sages acted by right of their mastery of the Torah and therefore in the status of heaven. Given by God to Moses at Sinai, the law of the Torah, including the Mishnah's laws, represents the will of heaven. But with all the faith in the world, on the basis of such an assertion about God's will, the losing party to a litigation over a piece of real estate will surely have surrendered his property to the other side only with the gravest reservations—if at all. He more likely will have complained to some

other authority, if he could. Short of direct divine coercion, upon which a legal system cannot be expected to rely, there had to be more reliable means of making the system work.

What these were, however, the Talmud of the Land of Israel hardly tells us. That silence underlines the political theory of the document: the sage now acts for heaven, in the way in which, in the Mishnah's politics, the king, high priest, and sage represented on earth a counterpart power and activity to the power and activity of God. Then each party, on earth as in heaven, carried out its assigned and proper task. Now, it seems clear, the sage is the sole focus of legitimate authority on earth, and heaven's rule is no more explicit than the role of the king (or high priest) is legitimate. The differentiated foci of the Mishnah's philosophical politics give way to the unitary focus of the Yerushalmi's theory of the same matter. What is clear is that politics, in theory, in the Mishnah represents a diffusion of power within an articulated order and hierarchy; the focus of power is no longer cogent but multiple and incoherent; but legitimacy, by contrast, is now single and singular, and therein lies the shift.

The Talmud of the Land of Israel therefore is clear that rabbis competed with other authorities for rule over the Jewish community. But sages alone exercised power legitimately; all other political institutions by definition were illegitimate. True, the relationship of the rabbis as judges and administrators to other Jewish community judges and administrators who may have carried out the same tasks and exercised the same responsibilities in regard to the Jewish nation of the land of Israel is not clarified either in cases or as to theory. But here too the silence is indicative: it is a tacit judgment, and a devastating, eloquent one. The Talmud's picture of legitimate violence comes to concrete expression in its account of what rabbis could force people to do because of their political power and position. The sovereignty of rabbinical courts in property disputes derived from the power of the courts not only to persuade or elicit general support but also to call upon the power of the state to transfer ownership of real and movable property from one party to another. In medieval and modern times, the emergence, out of Scripture, the Mishnah, and the Talmuds, of a politics administered by rabbis—portrayed as both holy men and sages—would carry forward the model adumbrated here.

JACOB NEUSNER

**POLITICS, JUDAISM AND, [II] IN MEDIEVAL AND MODERN TIMES:** The Jewish people and its religious and political traditions span at least 3300 years, perhaps 500 more. During this period, Jews have comprised a tribal polity, an enslaved caste, a simple agrarian republic, a state that was also a regional power, a community in exile, an imperial province, a vassal state, a revolutionary polity, a congeries of dispersed communities bound together by a common law, a set of co-religionists, an ethnic group, and, today, a modern state. While each of these configurations has had its own uniqueness, certain threads have run through every one of them, dating back to the earliest days of Jewish existence.

From its very roots, Judaism has been a theo-political phenomenon. According to Jewish tradition, God called upon Abraham to establish a new family in a new country. Within that land, this family would expand into a group of tribes and then a people with its own polity, shaped by God's communications given directly to their leaders and them. The Bible is a theo-political book, for it provides the foundations for the relationship between Judaism and politics and describes four different regimes of government: the patriarchal (Genesis), a tribal federal republic (Exodus through Judges, Ruth), a federal monarchy (Samuel, Kings, Chronicles, the prophetic books), and a restored republic (Ezra, Nehemiah), at times referred to as a nomocracy. Each of these regimes emerged as a response to a particular situation that confronted the Jewish people at a particular time. Each had to maintain the set of relationships set forth in the Bible, which we know as the fundaments of Judaism. Indeed, the political thought of Judaism begins in the presentation of a proper set of relationships required by God that the people can then shape into appropriate regimes, depending upon conditions at the time.

In the first centuries C.E., under the rabbis, Judaism's biblical foundations were modified through a system of law that constructed a complete yet evolving legal context for the relationship between the people and God, on the one hand, and the people and each other, the land, and other nations, on the other. As in the case of the biblical foundations, through the legal process, for approximately two millennia, Rabbinic Judaism maintained and even strengthened the close intertwining between Judaism and politics. Rabbinic Judaism served at least four different regimes in the diaspora and in Israel under diaspora conditions: patriarchate and Sanhedrin in Roman Palestine, exilarch and yeshivot and their variations in Babylonia and the Middle East, the Kehillah—holy community—and (con)federations of communities in Europe from Spain to Russia.

Only with the coming of the modern era was an element of separation introduced between Judaism and politics, especially from the latter years of the eighteenth century onward. Judaism was redefined in sacral and ritual terms as a "religion" in the Christian sense, while responsibility for the political needs of the Jews as a people was transferred to civil, essentially secular, institutions. This separation reached its apogee at the end of the nineteenth century, when, in community after community as well as world-wide, a formal institutional separation was made between "religious" and "political."

Yet even in modern times, when efforts at separation have been at their greatest, it remains essentially impossible to separate the Jews as a people from Judaism as a religion. Being Jewish is conventionally and properly recognized both as being a part of the Jewish people—regardless of one's other political loyalties—and being identified with the Jewish religion—regardless of the degree of one's religious belief or practice. Efforts to treat the two as separate continue to be overwhelmingly rejected by the vast majority of Jews, who thus deny the validity of the enterprises of those who have tried to define a totally secular Jewishness, or who, for instance, imagine that it is possible to be Jewish while accepting the religious claims of Christianity ("Messianic Jews," "Jews for Jesus"). While modern Jews have been preoccupied with the discussion of the relationship between peoplehood and religion, they share the idea that the two are intertwined in some way.

**Kinship and consent:** Just as Jews as a people and Judaism as a religion have always gone hand and hand, so was the Jewish people formed and continues to exist as an amalgam of kinship and consent. Jews are Jews by virtue of their common descent (converts to Judaism are traditionally considered to have acquired that kinship through their conversion, which is why they are traditionally given the names of Abraham and Sarah as their immediate forbears). At the same time being Jewish is also a matter of consenting to live according to the Sinai covenant and the system of norms and law that flows from it, the consent that every individual Jew must affirm and reaffirm. In essence, kinship leads to Jewish peoplehood and ethnicity, while consent underlies the Jews' Judaism. Both are considered critically necessary, and Jewish religion is rooted in both.

The contrary view, that Judaism can stand apart from Jewish peoplehood, was first advanced in Western Europe as a strategy to achieve Jewish emancipation from the ghettoization imposed by the majority Christian society. This became especially necessary as modernity brought down the medieval divisions in the general society and as Jewish communities lost their autonomy as well. Most Jews did not want to be left out of the new opportunities that the emergence of the nation-state, which recognized individual citizens only, in theory without regard to other divisions, offered.

Hence, except for those who remained strictly Orthodox and wished to continue to live in self-contained communities, the Jews sought integration into the new nation-states. They could do so only if they emphasized Judaism as a religious identity rather than Jewishness as a national one. This approach worked only partially and was defeated by the rise of modern antisemitism. In the end, the Jews could survive as a group only by recognizing their corporate character to at least some degree.

While Zionism emphasized Jewish nationhood to its fullest, it still made the concession to modernity of separating this nationalism from religion. But this too was a first time venture, and, for the same reasons, yielded mixed results. Just as Judaism rested and rests on Jewish peoplehood, so, too, as even those thoughtful Israelis who thought otherwise are beginning to find, does Jewish peoplehood rest on Judaism. Neither can maintain itself without the other. No matter how one chooses to view it, this is fundamental: neat divisions between ethnicity, culture, and religion have proved impossible to maintain in Jewish life, past or present.

The crises of the past few years have generated renewed interest on the part of Jewish publics in Israel and the diaspora in the character of the state of Israel as a Jewish state and in the Jewish people as a corporate entity. As a consequence, the modern Jewish search for roots and meaning has been intensified. In the twentieth century, the most practical aspects of this search have involved the restoration of Jewish political independence through the state of Israel and the revival of the sense of Jewish peoplehood based on religious affiliation throughout the diaspora. Precisely because large numbers of contemporary Jews have moved increasingly towards self-definition in terms that must be considered political, a significant part of the contemporary Jewish search for roots and meaning must take place within the political as well as the religious realm.

**Biblical foundations of the Jewish political tradition:** The Bible provides the enduring foundations of the Jewish political tradition. In one sense, this is because the foundations of all of Jewish tradition are found there. In many respects, however, the Jewish political tradition has been even more enduringly influenced by the Bible than other aspects of Judaism. Notably, the effort of the sages to diminish the biblical political tradition in the wake of the disastrous Roman wars meant that the tradition was transformed by them into an undifferentiated part of the halakhic tradition, so much so that with the revival of explicit political inquiry in the Middle Ages, Jewish thinkers and leaders who otherwise relied exclusively on the Talmud went back to biblical sources for ideas on proper political behavior and institution building. Centuries later, we find an echo of that process in the way that Zionists sought to base on biblical sources their quest for renewed Jewish statehood in the land of Israel.

Perhaps most compelling about the Jewish political tradition is that Jews continue in no small measure to function on its basis in the political arena, albeit usually without conscious awareness that they are working within a living tradition of their own or any tradition at all. The striking similarities in the structure of Jewish institutions in Israel and the diaspora, present and past, the continuities in the basic characteristics of Jewish political behavior, the persistence of certain fundamental beliefs and practices embedded in Jewish political culture, all attest to the persistence of a Jewish political tradition even if it remains for the most part unrecognized.

**Covenant and the Jewish political tradition:** Like every political tradition, the Jews' is concerned with power and justice. But, as a product of Judaism, it differs from the political traditions growing out of classical Greek thought in that it begins with a concern for relationships rather than regimes. It is less concerned with determining the best form of government (in Aristotelian terms, the best constitution) than with establishing the proper relationship between the governors and the governed, power and justice, God and humanity. This concern for relationships is embodied in the principle of covenant that lies at the root of the Jewish political tradition and that gives the tradition its form. In the Jewish political tradition, as in Jewish tradition as a whole, all relationships are rooted in the covenant between Israel and God.

The concept of covenant is deceptively simple. The Hebrew term *brit* conveys the sense of a morally grounded perpetual (or at least indeterminate) compact between parties having independent but not necessarily equal status. The covenant establishes certain mutual obligations and a commitment to undertake joint action to achieve defined ends, which may be limited or comprehensive, under conditions of mutual respect and in such a way as to protect the fundamental integrity of all parties involved. A covenant is much more than a contract—though our modern system of contracts is related to the covenant idea—because it involves a pledge of loyalty and a morally grounded obligation beyond that demanded for mutual advantage, often involving the development of community among the partners. It is also more than a compact in that it involves God as either a party or as a witness and guarantor. In its fullest sense, a covenant thus creates a holy or divinely sanctioned partnership community, based upon a firm, legally defined relationship delineating the authority, power, and integrity of each of the partners but requiring more than a narrow legalistic approach to make the community a real one.

This covenant idea is of great importance because of how it builds relationships. The Bible develops a whole system of relationships based upon covenants, beginning with the covenants between God and humankind, which create the conditions under which regimes can be constituted. The Sinai covenant, for example, transformed the Jewish people from a family of tribes into a body politic that could develop its constitution and regime. Exod. 18-20, which describes the Sinai experience, provides us with a clear picture of this process. On one hand, it describes the covenant that institutionalizes the fundamental relationship between God and Israel, establishing the new body politic over which God assumes direct rule. On the other hand, the actual institutions of the regime are portrayed as coming from distinctly non-divine, even non-Jewish, sources, partly from the inherited tradition of tribal government and partly from Jethro, Moses' father-in-law, who suggests the way to structure the judicial branch of the national government.

The fact that these stories are intertwined and placed parallel to one another is of the utmost significance. It suggests that the political basis for the constitution is the covenant, which is more than a social compact. But the covenant does not dictate or establish the form of the regime. Rather, the form of the regime is taken from human sources on the basis of necessity and convenience. This is the pattern of interaction between covenant and regime throughout Jewish history. On the one hand, we find the continuity of the fundamental covenant and the constitution that flows from it, the Torah. On the other hand, within the latitude established by the Torah, Jews are free to adopt the form of regime they wish.

The interaction between the two elements is ongoing. The model of this post-Sinai interaction is found in Joshua 24, where a covenanting act takes place to confirm the reorganization of the tribal confederacy after the conquest of the land. Subsequent Jewish historical experience brought with it a variety of adaptations of covenantal principles, with a new one for each new era of Jewish political adjustment.

In its classical form, the Jewish polity is an *edah*—an assembly or congregation, a coming together, perhaps best understood as the Hebrew equivalent of a commonwealth—constituted by God and Israel through the Sinai covenant. The powers of this polity traditionally were shared by God, the people of Israel in their character as an *edah*, and those designated as governors by both (e.g., David, who is anointed by Samuel in God's name but whose rule is confirmed only after he enters into covenants with the tribal elders of Judah and Israel). The powers are further divided among several domains: the magistrates (Moses, Joshua, the judges, the kings), the prophets, and the priests.

The result of all this is a separation of powers, not in the modern sense of executive, legislative, and judicial (although the Bible is cognizant of those three basic divisions, cf., Is. 33:22—"For the Lord is our Judge, the Lord is our Lawgiver, the Lord is our King; He will save us"), but as an intricate set of power relationships among separate yet linked bodies that must work together for the good of both the religious and political dimensions of Jewish life. In several ways, the Jewish liturgy reflects this intricate set of relationships covering both religious and political matters: in the daily morning service where the heavenly hosts grant (or acknowl-

edge) each other's authority to praise God and in the blessing after meals when the leader requests authority to take the lead from the others at the table (and, in the Sephardic ritual, from heaven as well), to name but two examples.

Perhaps the best example of all is found in the mode of delivery of the priestly blessing in prayer services of Sephardic Jews. Under Jewish law, those descended from the priestly families are required by God to administer the blessing; this is a purely ministerial task in which they have no discretion. When they are called upon to perform this task in the synagogue, a non-priest (an "Israelite") calls them to it; they respond by asking for *reshut* (authority) from the congregation, which, in turn, indicates that the authority is really granted by heaven. The one who called upon them then leads them in the blessing word by word. The script is as follows:

| | |
|---|---|
| Israelite: | Cohanim (priests)! |
| Priests: | *B'reshut rabbotai* (By the authority of the congregation)! |
| Congregation: | *B'reshut shamayim* (By the authority of heaven)! |
| Israelite: | *Y'varechacha* (May you be blessed). . . . |
| Priests: | *Y'varechacha.* . . . |

This pattern of interlocking authorities is paradigmatic of the Jewish polity; no single person or body has final authority; instead various bodies share powers.

It is in this original sense that the Jewish political tradition is federal (from the Latin *foedus*, meaning "covenant") in orientation. Fundamentally, federalism involves the coming together of separate elements to compound a common entity in such a way that their respective integrities are preserved. Appropriately, federal arrangements emphasize relationships as the key to proper structures of a lasting character. For that reason, the variety of structures animated by the federal principles is substantial. Jewish history attests to that variety, since the Jewish political tradition has emphasized federal arrangements in the more conventional sense of the term as well. There has hardly been an age in which the Jewish *edah* has not been organized on a federal basis, beginning with the tribal confederacy and including the federated kingdom of the tribes; the *politeuma* of the Hellenistic diaspora, which stood in federal relationship to the city in which it was located as well as to the rest of *Knesset Yisrael* (the Hebrew equivalent of *Kenishtay*, the Arab translation of *Edah*); the *yeshivot* of Babylonia and their respective communities; the medieval federations of communities, the Council of the Four Lands; the post-emancipation European federations of *cultesgemeinden*; the Latin American federations of country-of-origin communities; and the contemporary North American federations of Jewish functional agencies. And this is not an exhaustive list by any means.

The Jewish political tradition is republican in the original sense of the term—the body politic is held to be a *res publica*, a public thing, and not anyone's private preserve. Significantly, the Jewish political tradition in its classical expression has no idea of the state as a reified entity—that would be challenging God, from a religious point of view, idolating; there are only the varieties of political relationships that create polity. Indeed, the Jewish political tradition does not recognize state sovereignty as such: no state—a human creation—can be sovereign. Classically, only God is sovereign, and God entrusts the exercise of sovereign powers mediated through the Torah-as-constitution to the people as a whole, the magistrates, priests, and prophets or sages as provided in God's covenant with Israel.

In the last analysis, the Jewish political tradition is based upon what S.D. Goitein has termed "religious democracy," using the term religious in its original sense of "binding." At the same time, the Jewish political tradition has a strong aristocratic current, again not in the sense of aristocracy as a political structure but as a relationship whereby those who hold powers of government are trustees for both the people and the law, selected on the basis of some qualification—divine sanctification, scholarship, lineage or, de facto, wealth—the particular mix varying according to time and place.

**Exploring the Jewish political tradition:** The record of the Jewish political tradition is to be found in the Jewish people's sacred and subsidiary texts and in their collective behavior. It can even be argued that the survival of a committed Jewry, at least outside of the Orthodox camp, depends in no small measure on the Jewish political tradition. It is one of the ironies of the post-modern age that, just at the time when all Jews outside of Israel, some two-thirds of the world Jewish population, have lost all formal corporate political status, a new political focus of Jewish identification has suddenly reemerged.

The modern epoch—three hundred years from the middle of the seventeenth to the middle of the twentieth centuries—found Jews shedding their corporate status and forms of corporate organization. In the process, they also shed the political links that were part and parcel of Jewish tradition and that held Jews together as one people, even in dispersion. On the intellectual plane, Jews tried to transform those links into theological-cum-ritual ("religious") links of various kinds and, on the practical plane, into social-cum-philanthropic ones.

Now, rather suddenly, these various links created by Jewish moderns as the source of Jewish identity and identification have begun to weaken for many Jews. In their place, ironically enough, both the political and spiritual have increasingly become the focal points of Jewish identity and interest. The first is clearly true in the state of Israel, and, particularly in the past decade, the last has been particularly true in the United States. A new political concern is also evident in the diaspora, where Jews are increasingly bound to one another only by formal associational ties that, while not of the old corporate kind, are political in the sense of reflecting such common interests as combating antisemitism, supporting Israel, and maintaining the Jewish right to be different.

As a result, the political dimension is rapidly emerging as a major unifying force that links virtually all Jews at a time at which secularization, assimilation, and movement away from tradition are rampant. Were Jews to derive their political ideas from philosophy (in the classical or technical sense of the term), perhaps it would be appropriate to talk about a Jewish political philosophy or competing Jewish political philosophies. This is the way of European civilization and, indeed, is characteristic of many peoples who have undergone a revolutionary break with their past that they must ground ideologically. However, Jews derive their framework from midrash and halakhah, not from philosophy, and are not dependent for their existence on ideology. Hence, they cannot rely upon philosophy to provide a grounding for Jewish political life. (Jews can philosophize, i.e., use the tools of philosophy, but only by grounding them in different set of assumptions, methods, and results.)

Significantly, the two great phenomena of twentieth-century Jewry, the reestablishment of a Jewish state in the land of Israel and the establishment of a great Jewish community in North America, represent interesting and important adaptations of the covenant idea. A look at the foundation of the early institutions and settlements of the new *yishuv* in Israel reveals that their basis in almost every case was covenantal. Borrowing from the established patterns of congregational *askamot*, Jews established their associations on the basis of formal compacts and constitutional documents often explicitly referred to as covenants. This continued to be the standard form of organization in the Jewish *yishuv* even after the British became the occupying power in the country. Until the emergence of the state in 1948, the *yishuv* was governed internally through a network of covenants and compacts.

In the United States, the organization of congregations follows the traditional form even though the congregations themselves may be untraditional in their religious practices. Similarly, the organization of social agencies and educational institutions and their coming together in local Jewish federations or countrywide confederations are simply extensions of what has been the standard pattern of Jewish organization for several millennia. One might be hard put to prove that, in either the Israeli or the American case, there was a conscious desire to maintain

a particular political tradition. Rather, the shared political culture of Jews involved in situations that made its application feasible led to the new adaptation of the traditional pattern.

It is more than a little ironic that in the United States, where the government does not care how Jews organize themselves so long as they do not go beyond certain constitutional restrictions applicable to all Americans, the traditional covenantal pattern has expressed itself fully, whereas in Israel, where it was felt necessary to build authoritative state institutions on the model of the modern nation-state, this process has run into something of a dead end, stifled by the strong statist inclination toward centralized control of every aspect of public life brought from the European experiences of the state's molders and shapers. Nevertheless, by the mid-1960s, a reaction against that statism arose and a reassertion of the demands of Jewish political culture emerged.

**Humanity, government, politics:** To understand these developments, we must comprehend the religious conceptual basis upon which Jewish political activity rests and the ends toward which it is directed. From the religious perspective, humans are partners with God, the Sovereign of the Universe (*Ribbon ha-Olam*), in the development and governance of the world, a partnership established by the covenant. Humans have both good and evil inclinations (*yetzer ha-tov* and *yetzer ha-ra*). Because of the inclination to evil, they require laws to guide them; and because they are more good than bad, their behavior can be improved by proper institutions. At the same time, people, when unrestrained, are capable of utilizing government and politics to institutionalize their evil inclinations, thereby greatly increasing their capability to do evil.

Government and politics are necessary parts of human existence, but, necessary and important as they are, they are not ends in themselves but merely tools for the achievement of more sacred goals. Politics is a universal and serious human activity but only as a means to achieve holy purposes (*tiqqun olam*—reform of the world). Since politics is part and parcel of the human way (*derekh ha-adam*), it is a mixture of the petty and the grand. Its importance must be recognized, but always with a certain ambivalence, given its propensities to serve excessive ambitions. In the last analysis, however, full achievement of the goals of political activity is dependent upon God's intervention to redeem (*geulah*) humanity. Hence it is necessary to look to a better future in the messianic age (*yemot ha-mashiah*).

**Law and justice:** Law, in the sense of the divine constitutional teaching (the *Torah*), provides the foundation of the good human polity. Divine law is comprehensive and immutable, but properly constituted human agency has been granted broad powers of interpretation that, when used fully, are essentially legislative *de facto*. This strong commitment to constitutionalism and the rule of law tends to elevate judges to a position of special authority within the body politic. In its most narrow application, this commitment encourages hairsplitting legalism. On the other hand, it can be coupled with an equally strong operational commitment to the idea that all individuals must ultimately decide for themselves to what extent particular laws apply in their case, i.e., a kind of rule of law by repeated acts of consent. In certain ways, law is understood as a norm to be attained as much as a fixed rule or boundary.

Justice is intimately associated with divine law, but the association extends beyond a simple one-to-one relationship to involve practical considerations of covenant obligation (*hesed*) and mercy (*rahamim*). This often leads to a paradoxical condition whereby legal support for doing justice formally exacts the strongest penalties for unjust acts, which penalties are rarely if ever applied on grounds of tempering justice with mercy.

**Political authority and obligation:** The universe and its parts are under divine sovereignty (*malkhut shamayim*), and hence all human institutions possess only delegated authority and powers. That is the essence of Jewish theocracy. In fact, the good political order is a complex of interlocking authorities the legitimacy of which derives from the covenant-established partnership between God and humanity. In some cases the former elects and the latter ratifies; in others the process is reversed. But in every one, the two sides are somehow represented. This can lead to power-sharing at its best or, in extreme manifestations, to near-anarchy. Part of the theocratic character of the Jewish political tradition is reflected in a constant tension between the divine (*shamayim* or *theo*) and rule (*malkhut* or *cratos*), which must be reconciled by federal or covenantal linkage.

The basis for political authority is invariably covenantal, and political obligation flows from that covenantal base. Covenanting makes divine sovereignty concrete and human self-government possible in this world, but removal of the former can lead to the institutionalized expression of Faustian ambition on the part of humans.

**The polity:** A legitimate polity is an extension of the covenantal relationship, constituted consensually through a pact, as a partnership or metapartnership of its constituents. There is no "state" in the Jewish political tradition, in the sense of a reified political entity complete and presumed self-sufficient in and of itself. The contemporary Hebrew term for state, *medinah*, refers in the Bible to a political unit with its own jurisdiction (*din*) within a larger entity, e.g., a province. While the term *medinah* is today used for politically sovereign states, its classical echoes still remind us that "polity" would be a better translation. The latter term offers wider and narrower expressions of meaning consistent with the Hebrew original—wider in that all entities with their own political-legal jurisdiction are polities and narrower in that no polity exists apart from its component elements, nor does it possess absolute sovereignty. Both dimensions are vital elements in the Jewish political tradition. In fact, the Jewish political tradition does not recognize state sovereignty in the modern sense of absolute independence. No state—a human creation—can be sovereign. In Judaism, only God is sovereign and furdeus, entrusting the exercise of sovereign powers to the people as a whole, mediated through the Torah-as-constitution, as provided through the divine covenant with Israel.

The Jewish people is a polity of equals, a commonwealth (*edah*), with all that implies for the organization and conduct of Jewish political affairs. While no single form of political organization is mandated by Jewish law or tradition, any form chosen must embody this basic republican principle. Jewish regimes have not always been democratic republics; because of the emphasis on God's role, they have aristocratic tendencies that often have degenerated into oligarchic patterns of rule. But with rare local exceptions, they have not been autocratic. The republican foundations of the Jewish political tradition have prevented that.

A proper Jewish polity embodies a suitable set of political relationships rather than any particular structure or regime. This emphasis on relationships is particularly relevant to a covenantal polity and helps reinforce Jewish republicanism, but it can also lead to the ignoring of structures that do not create extreme difficulties. The Jewish people as an *edah* takes as its point of departure a strong commitment to bargaining as the basic mode of political decision-making. In its best sense, this leads to negotiated cooperation based upon covenantal obligation; in its worst, to a willingness to haggle over everything, with minimum regard for norms or accepted procedures.

**Political tradition and the language of political discourse:** The Bible is rich in political terminology, as any close reading reveals. Indeed it remains the primary source of Hebrew political terms, many of which have been transmitted over the millennia with no or minimum change in meaning. The terminology as such and in context has substantial implications for understanding the sources of the Jewish political tradition and deserves full treatment on its own. Among those terms and phrases are several that are of special importance because they give meaning to fundamental political relationships and the regimes they shape. In essence, they are the Hebrew equivalents of the classic political terminology of ancient Greek and Latin. Summarizing what we have seen so far, the classic Jewish political world-view can be summarized as follows:

The kith (*moledet*) of tribes (*shevatim*) descended from Abraham, Isaac, and Jacob, which God raised up to be a nation (*goy*), became the Jewish people (*Am Yisrael*) through its covenant (*brit*) with God, which, in turn, laid the basis for the establishment of the Jewish commonwealth (*edah*) under divine sovereignty (*malkhut shamayim*), bound by the divine constitutional teaching (*Torah*). The *am* so created must live as a community of equals (*kahal*), whose locus is the land of Israel (*Eretz Israel*), under the rule of law (*hukah, hok*) that applies to every citizen (*ezrah*), defined as a partner to the covenant (*ben-brit*). All citizens are linked to their neighbors (*rea*) by covenant obligation (*hesed*). Within these parameters there is latitude in choosing the form of government or regime as long as the proper relationships between the various parties are preserved. That, in turn, requires a system of shared authorities (*reshuyot*)—what today would be termed "checks and balances." These *reshuyot* are combined under three authoritative categories (*ketarim*): the authority of Torah (*keter torah*), the authority of civil governance (*keter malkhut*), and the authority of the priesthood (*keter kehunah*), each of which plays a role in the government of the *edah* through a system of shared powers. At any given time, different religious and political camps (*mahanot*) and parties (*miflagot*) within those camps compete for control of the governing institutions of the *edah*. Moreover, since the full achievement of its religio-political goals requires reformation of the existing order (*tiqqun olam*) and redemption (*geulah*), the Jewish political world-view is messianic, looking towards a better future rather than a golden past.

What is important about Jewish political terminology is not only that it exists in such abundance, had its origins in the very earliest epochs of Jewish history, and has remained extraordinarily consistent in meaning for some three millennia, but that it is so thoroughly rooted conceptually in the covenantal world-view that pervades the Jewish political tradition. Not only are there many obvious covenantal terms of political importance (e.g., *brit* and *hesed*). Rather, other terms also abound whose covenantal dimension is not usually recognized until they are examined more deeply (e.g., *edah, haver, va'ad*). In other words, Judaism is permeated with covenantal echoes, and nowhere more than in its Hebrew vocabulary.

**Brit and *Hesed*: The covenant or federal base:** The basic simplicity of the covenant idea masks important complexities. The Hebrew term *brit* (covenant) conveys the sense of both separation and linkage, cutting and binding. The prophet Ezekiel referred to *masoret ha brit*—the covenant tradition (or bond)—as the central thread of Jewish existence (Ezek. 20:35-37). In his highly sensitive commentary to the Bible, Meir Loeb ben Yehiel Michael (1809-1879) offers us a good summary of the covenantal relationship between God and Abraham, described in Gen. 17: This covenant will be "between Me and thee," meaning that the binding obligation rests on both parties to the covenant, because Abraham also obligated himself to be a partner with God in the act of creation by perfecting what was created and by participating in its improvement.

This idea is of great importance because of what it offers in the way of building relationships. The Bible posits and develops a whole system of relationships based upon covenants, some of which, it suggests, were actual covenants between God and humankind and some of which seem to be figurative covenants between God and inanimate objects, such as the heavenly bodies. Inevitably present within the covenant idea is the sense of a contractual partnership in which the partners must, by definition, share in the implementation of certain common tasks and, at the same time, are able to preserve their respective integrities.

In some cases the partners are equals, in some they are not. Obviously, covenants between God and people, even between God and Israel, ultimately are covenants between unequals, who are redefined as relatively equal for the covenantally defined task at hand. The quite radical covenant idea thus inevitably suggests that God limits himself drastically by recognizing the freedom of humans to contract an obligation with God

and to maintain their own integrities, doing so not simply to obey God but to hearken to God's word as covenant partners. The implications of this are developed in the biblical and Rabbinic literature to suggest that, under the terms of the *brit*, in matters of *tiqqun olam*, God and humans are considered equal. Indeed, covenantal people are then required to choose whether or not to live up to the terms of the covenant. The Puritans, interestingly, understood this when they interpreted the covenantal basis of the biblical worldview as the *federal theology*, which emphasizes that the same covenant that tightly binds people to God also radically emancipates humanity and enables it to act on its own accord.

**Edah and *Kahal*: The republican base:** The covenant not only transformed a *goy*—primarily a kinship group with its own land and culture—into an *am*—a kinship group united through some vocation—but the *am* became an *edah*—a body politic based on consent. The term literally implies an assembly of all citizens that meets at regular times or frequently. Moshe Weinfeld has argued that the term *edah* actually described the regime prior to the introduction of the monarchy. In this respect it parallels (and historically precedes) similar phenomena, such as the *landesgemeinde* in Switzerland, the Icelandic *althing*, and the town meeting the United States. Crucial is that it continued to be used to describe the Jewish body politic in every period down to the present. Only in contemporary Israel has the term lost its authentic meaning, becoming a sociological expression intentionally devoid of political content. In all events, the original *edah* can be summarized as follows:

1. Political equality existed for those capable of bearing arms.
2. Decisions were made by an assembly that chose its own leaders.
3. The *edah* was portable and transcended geography.
4. Nevertheless, for it to function completely, the *edah* needed the land of Israel.
5. The Torah was the constitution of the *edah*.

These basic characteristics have been pre-served with a minimum of modification over the centuries. After the end of Jewish politi-cal independence, the arms-bearing measure of political equality gave way to one of Torah study. In the twentieth century state of Israel, it reaquired its original meaning, while, in the rest of the world, its equivalent was activ-ity and monetary support for Jewish causes. The principles of assembly, leadership, and decision-making have remained the same, although modes of assembling, leadership recruitment, and leaders' roles and responsi-bilities obviously have changed from time to time. The portability of the desert-born *edah* is a notable, continuing characteristic, as is attachment to Zion. The Torah of course has persisted as a constitution.

The documentary literature of every age is full of the classical usage of the term *edah*. Moreover, that body was invariably defined as including all adult males as participants in fundamental decision-making. At the very least, the *edah* as a whole was responsible for actions of a constitutional character, whether electing kings in ancient Israel, constituting the Council of the Four Lands in the medi-eval Poland, or forming communities in the modern United States. The *edah* offered a variety of adaptations of covenantal princi-ples, with a new one for each new era of Jewish political adjustment. A high point was reached in the Jewish communities of the Middle Ages. The congregational form it-self—the *kahal* or *kehillah*—is a subsidiary product of the linkage of the covenant and the *edah*. Thus the term *kahal*, in the Bible used almost synonymously with *edah*, be-came the terminological subsidiary of *edah* in its constituted local dimension.

***Edah, Medinah,*** and ***Kehillah***—The are-nas of Jewish political organization: From earliest times, the Jewish polity has been or-ganized in three arenas, generally definable as national, regional or intermediate, and local. The first form in which these three arenas was constituted was nationally, in the form of the *edah*, constituted by the tribes, each with its own government institutions. Each tribe was, in turn, a union of extended households (*batei av*). After the Israelite set-

tlement in Canaan, the most prominent form of local organization was the city or town-ship (*ir*), with its own assembly and council (*sh'ar ha-ir* or *ziknei ha-ir*).

Once formulated in early Israelite history, this division of governance has remained a permanent feature of Jewish political life. This is so despite frequent changes in the forms of organization of the several arenas and in the terminology used to describe them. Thus just as the *bet av* gave way to the *ir*, the latter gave way to the *kehillah* (local community). In turn, the *kehillah* became the molecular unit of organization for all post-biblical Jewry, especially since a *kehillah* could be established by any ten adult Jewish males who so constituted themselves. While the *kehillah* survives in the diaspora, in con-temporary Israel it has once again reemerged as an *ir*.

Similarly, the breakdown of the traditional tribal system (a phenomenon that long pre-ceded the first exile) resulted in the replace-ment of the *shevet* (tribe) by the *medinah* (the autonomous jurisdiction or province), a re-gional framework that embraces a congeries of *kehillot* that it unites within an organiza-tional structure, as in *Medinat Yehud* (Judea in the Persian Empire). In the diaspora, *medinah* became virtually interchangeable with *eretz* (country) to describe the intermediate arena, as in *Eretz Lita* (the organized Jewish com-munity in late medieval Lithuania). In mod-ern times, the term came to mean a politically sovereign state, as it is precisely used in con-nection with *Medinat Yisrael* (the State of Israel).

Actions of constitutional import taken by and for the *edah* as a whole are binding on ev-ery one of its constituent parts. One illustra-tion of this rule is provided by the connected biblical narratives relating to the settlement of the two and a half tribes on the eastern bank of the Jordan (Num. 32 and Josh. 22). It is significant that the initial approach, by the Reubenites and Gadites, was to Moses, Eleazar the priest, and the tribal magistrates (*nesiim*, Num. 32:2). Similarly, it was in the name of *Adat Adonai*, "The Congregation of the Lord," that the two and a half tribes were subsequently upbraided for the construction of an altar on their way home from Joshua's wars. At issue, as Josh 22:16-20 makes explicit, was the contention that the original commitment to worship the one God had been undertaken by the entire *edah* and that the entire *edah* would be held responsible for any violation—even if it be on the part of a minority.

The system is not, however, a hierarchy and certainly not centralized, since all the important lines of political communication and decision-making are not controlled by a unitary government transmitting its directives through a clearly stratified system of regional and local instruments. Rather, the *edah* is a framing institution that, among its various tasks, establishes boundary rules for the pursuit of political objectives but leaves to its constituent parts considerable leeway in the conduct of their political affairs. Individual *medinot* and *kehillot* are not merely aspects of the *edah*. Like the *edah*, they derive their authority directly from the series of covenants periodically entered into by God and the entire Jewish people. That is why, to quote another biblical example, divine sanction could be granted for secession from an overwhelming centralized monarchy and why, during the High Middle Ages, individual communities could enact highly particularistic *taqqanot ha-qahal* (communal ordinances). Moreover, and notwithstanding the very special place allotted to the land of Israel in all Jewish thought, the preeminence of the *medinah* in matters constitutional has never been taken for granted. On the contrary, it proved to be a bone of serious contention in talmudic times, as in our own.

Of the many implications of this organizational framework, the most important is that the traditional system of Jewish government might best be described as a matrix rather than a pyramid. It does not posit "high" and "low" power centers, with gradations of power flowing down from the top (or out from the center). Rather, it forms a matrix of larger and smaller arenas of authority, linked through common adherence to a single recognized constitutional framework and through formal and informal lines of mutual communication. Furthermore, the texture of the lines of communication between and within the various arenas has, over the long haul, provided the system with the flexibility necessary to its stability and resilience. Since the system was not dependent on the maintenance of any single central institution, it did not disintegrate the moment an individual locus of power was destroyed (as happened when the first two Jewish commonwealths were destroyed) or withered away (the fate of the subsequent patriarchate in the land of Israel and exilarchate in Babylonia). These were undoubtedly severe blows to the Jewish polity, but they did not prove fatal because survival of the *edah* had never been dependent on such mechanisms.

To take a positive example, in the eleventh-fourteenth centuries C.E., when the older seats of jurisdiction in Babylonia and the land of Israel lost all authority outside of their immediate geographic perimeter and before the newer centers of the Iberian Peninsula (Sepharad) and West-Central Europe (Ashkenaz) had developed, substitute organizational frameworks emerged. The fact that institutional authority had been vested almost exclusively in the *kehillah* did not vitiate the continuity of the *edah*. The "nerves" of the system continued to exist and, indeed, precisely during this epoch, flourished, with the legal-religious correspondence between individual legal decisors serving as a communications network of extraordinary efficiency and repute.

The Jewish organizational framework thus differs from the models of centralization and decentralization dominant in much of the current literature of political science. Instead, it posits an appropriate noncentralization, found to be characteristic of all federal systems based—as in the Jewish tradition—on the notion of a covenantal relationship between partners. In this scheme, the diffusion of power is not a matter of grace (dependent upon the whim—or weakness—of a central authority) but a matter of right. The rank order of the several arenas of government is deliberately left flexible, allowing the system as a whole to adapt to the changing circumstances of its environment. The history of the

Jewish polity indicates that some concentration of governmental power in the founding institutions of the *edah* may have been permissible; but this was never mandatory. Far more entrenched is the tradition whereby authority is spread widely (even if not in equal proportions) among a range of regional authorities, each with the right to independent self-expression.

**Judaism and politics among the nations:** Biblical Judaism emphasized the separation of the Jewish people from the nations because of its special vocation. Indeed the Hebrew word *am* in the Bible essentially signifies a nation (*goy*) with a vocation. This is true not only for Israel, the *am* of God, who gives the Israelites their vocation, but also for Moab, the *am* of Chemosh, who gives the Moabites their vocation. In one respect, the Bible is a record of the struggle between the demands of Judaism and the political reality that prevented the Jewish polities from ignoring their neighbors. Israel's leaders regularly sought to reach an accommodation with some of those neighbors in order to resist the designs of others against them.

During the Second Commonwealth, sages devised the legal system that later became known as Judaism, designed to separate the Jewish people not only as a collectivity but as individuals. At the same time, their more prudent leaders pursued a general policy of accommodation, punctuated by periodic seizures of power by less prudent figures, which led to disastrous revolts against the power (Persian, Seleucid, or Roman) within whose sphere of influence either Judea or the Jewish people fell. After the last of those revolts, under Bar Kokhba in 132-135 C.E., Rabbinic sages depoliticized the Jewish people insofar as it was possible to do so. This was a political strategy to preserve them from their follies and a political effort to keep them from pursuing disastrous actions that, as a vigorous and believing people, they constantly were willing to try but at which, as a small people, they were not capable of being successful.

Over the next 1700 years, this Judaism of accommodation dominated Jewish political thinking, reinforced at every turn by the situation of exile and the lack of rooted political power. At certain times and places Jewish leaders could supplement their accomodationist politics with a politics of maneuver that gave the Jewish community just enough room to survive. Halakhic Judaism went so far as to declare that except in a few utterly impermissible spheres, Jews were to follow the principle "*Dina Demalkhuta Dina:*" the law of the kingdom is the law. Acceptance of the law of the foreign suzerain thus was made a halakhic requirement.

With emancipation, Jewish efforts moved from simply seeking accommodation to struggling for equal rights and citizenship. Often, this included forging alliances with non-Jews who had similar aspirations. Now the previously conservative Jewish community—whose conservatism stemmed from a fear that change would upset the hard won right to live by their own laws and institutions—adopted a politics of revolution and liberalism, which the experiences of early modernity suggested could only improve the Jews' position through the extension of emancipation and equal rights.

Judaism accordingly was reinterpreted by its more liberal adherents as fundamentally supportive of liberalism and its goals. The Bible, especially the prophetic message of social justice, became the source of this new ideology. While the results of European revolutionary movements were distinctly mixed and often worked to the disadvantage of the Jews as well as the general population, enough good came out of these efforts to reinforce Jewish expectations and wed Jews to the idea that the problems resulted from the revolutions' not going far enough.

The only dissenting voices in the community were of those few Jews who saw in Jewish emancipation and equality an invitation to extensive assimilation and who desired to preserve Jewish separateness so that the Jews could continue to fulfill their religious vocation. Increasingly, this group was limited to the Ultra-Orthodox, whose very existence could be understood as a religiously fostered political response to the new reality of modernity. Prior to emancipation, traditional Judaism had a flexibility that enabled it to adapt to changing times and conditions without any sense of internal disruption. Now, arguing and fighting for a more rigid definition of Judaism, the traditionalists developed the idea that any change toward greater accommodation with the external environment at the price of Jewish separatism was bad.

The traditionalists were opposed by Jewish religious liberals, who also sought a new political accommodation that involved abjuring the political dimension of Judaism and reforming Jewish ideas and institutions, so that its religious dimension would not be incompatible with the surrounding Christian world or with modern trends. These Jews developed Reform Judaism as their religious and political response. A third group held that Judaism as it had developed historically should be maintained but interpreted with a liberal spirit and that Jewish political life should be tempered in consideration of modern realities. While in many respects, this is an ideologically satisfying position, it was difficult to actualize on a practical level.

In essence, because of the political and religious realities of the world in which Jews found themselves, all three approaches had limited success. Ultra-Orthodoxy proved too rigid to attract or hold more than a small minority of all Jews. And for their part, the modern Orthodoxy that emerged from it and the more liberal Conservative Judaism, while willing and able to accommodate secular forces outside the Jewish community, lost credibility in the eyes of the traditionalists while failing to inspire those attuned to Reform. Reform Judaism in the nineteenth century, on the other hand, rapidly turned into a creed the idea that Jews are only adherents of Judaism, a religion, and not members of a nation with political aspirations at all. Only the new political realities of the twentieth century drove the vast majority of Jews back to a sense of Jewish peoplehood and common Jewish political interests, if only for physical survival. Thus, by the latter part of the twentieth century, it is all but agreed within world Jewry that, while Jews have plural religious expressions of Judaism, they are united through their politics, that all Jews who either wish to remain Jewish or feel they have no choice come together around common political interests.

The Jewish revolutionary left has collapsed in the wake of the general failure of the movements of the revolutionary left. At the same time, Jewish liberalism has been reinforced both by those who remain liberal because they see liberalism as best both ideologically and in terms of Jewish self interests and those who come to liberalism from collapsed positions further left. It would not be unfair to say that at the twentieth century's end, despite the rise of political conservatism in much of the western world where almost all Jews live, over three-fourths of all Jews remained firmly entrenched in the liberal camp as strong supporters of both human rights and the welfare state. For many, whatever the role political self interest has to play in their liberalism, they understood it as a reflection of their Judaism. For that matter, Jews who remained or became conservative more often than not have also made that ideological decision based upon their understanding of what Judaism requires of them. Both positions reinforce the close link between Judaism and politics in the sphere of external Jewish relations as much as Judaism and politics have always been linked on Jewish internal matters.

**Bibliography**
Cohen, Stuart, *The Three Crowns: Structures of Communal Politics in Early Rabbinic Jewry* (New York, 1990).
Elazar, Daniel J., and Stuart A. Cohen, *The Jewish Polity: Jewish Political Organization from Biblical Times to the Present* (Bloomington, 1985).
Elazar, Daniel J., *Covenant and Polity in Biblical Israel: Biblical Foundations and Jewish Expressions* (New Brunswick, 1995).
Elazar, Daniel J., ed., *Authority, Power and Leadership in the Jewish Polity: Cases and Issues* (Lanham, 1991).
Elazar, Daniel J., ed., *Kinship and Consent: The Jewish Political Tradition and Its Contemporary Uses* (New Brunswick, 1997).

DANIEL J. ELAZAR

**PSYCHOLOGY AND JUDAISM:** The title of this essay immediately raises the question of the possible relationship between psychology, imagined to be a universal scientific discipline, and Judaism. How, that is, might a profession usually associated with medicine be affected by religion at all? When we recall that our perceptions of psychology as a scientific discipline are still largely shaped by the methodologies of the natural sciences and medicine,[1] we see that this question is no less relevant today than it would have been in the nineteenth century, when psychology was deemed "the offspring of philosophy and experimental physiology."

We must be clear at the outset, therefore, that the term psychology here does not refer to neuro-physiological parameters that may affect human behavior. Rather, we take up psychology as an idea that guides systems of normative conduct, emanating from one's beliefs about the meaning of life and death. In introducing psychology as a system of ideas affecting behavioral patterns of everyday life, we have in mind not only Jerome Burner's notion of "folk psychology" (*Acts of Meaning*, Cambridge, 1990) but also the idea of psychology as a set of culturally shaped Platonic ideas that mold one's world view, nowadays internalized very early in life due to the socializing power of the media. Our underlying assumption is that deeply entrenched beliefs about what makes society and psychological growth possible operate today as Platonic ideas, or meta-codes, for interpreting and assigning meanings to life. These codes usually are inculcated through the religio-cultural environment surrounding people during crucial periods of their life.

That events and personal experiences always take on meanings that are socially determined was best argued by Gregory Bateson (*Steps to an Ecology of Mind*, New York, 1972), who equated the processes of interpretation to a telecommunication mechanism. In such a mechanism, a signal is differentiated from noise because the former constitutes an accepted pattern of redundancy that helps the receiver (who recognizes it as a signal only because it is redundant) understand the meaning of the message. The repetitive regularity of a telecommunicative noise turns it into a perceptible, meaningful message, a fact that implies, in turn, that "the concept of redundancy is at least a partial synonym of meaning" (p. 414). Similarly, to

make sense of their world, people acquire redundant regularities of meaning from the religious-cultural systems to which they are repetitively exposed. This means that if you scratch the surface of any norm regulating psychology or psychotherapy, you will find behind it a theology or a theosophy that has manifested itself in various secularized norms and interpretations of reality. The result is that, through Max Weber's sociology of religion, which argues that social norms usually are secularized patterns of religious ethics, we may comprehend, for instance, how, in Iranian-Shiite culture, death in a suicidal war can be perceived as a direct path to paradise and as a desirable form of self-actualization. Similarly, by tracing the Calvinist-Protestant work ethos, we can understand the American secular WASP's contrary view that salvation and actualization come only through hard work and that one belongs to the "elect" only if he succeeds materially.

What emerges from this approach is the recognition that there is, in fact, a distinctive psychology of Judaism and that, contrary to the misguided notion of the "Judeo-Christian tradition," we must differentiate between the conventional Christianized psychological norms predominating in the west and the Jewish ethical system. Arthur Cohen points out in *The Myth of the Judeo-Christian Tradition* (New York, 1971, p. XVIII) that, "the Jewish factor in Christian civilization . . . was all but obliterated." It was "reclaimed, rather like a prehensile tail" largely through the fiction that whatever was once Jewish is now Christian, such that Christianity itself constitutes the "larger more sophisticated economy" of the "new Jews." But contrary to this pervasive view, an examination of how the Christianized West was affected in the sixteenth century by Protestant individualism, while Judaism remained highly collective, shows how two essentially different psychological systems emerged.

In this regard Matthew Arnold's classic distinction between Hebraism and Hellenism is pertinent. William Barrett (*Irrational Man*, New York, 1962), who studied Arnold's dichotomizing conceptualizations, explains that the core differences between the two cultures revolve around the phenomenon of "detachment." While, allegedly, "detachment was for the Hebrew an impermissible state of mind, a vice rather than a virtue" (p. 76), Greek philosophy was constructed on the ideal of detachment: "the word 'theory' derives from the Greek verb *theatai* which means . . . to see and is the root of the word theater. At a theater we are spectators of an action in which we ourselves are not involved . . . the man of theory . . . looks upon existence with detachment" (p. 77).

Consequently, we might argue that the contemporary individualistic psychology summed up in the motto "do your own thing" is embedded in a Greco-Christian idea of detachment. By contrast, the still dominant collective Jewish I-Thou doctrine of "Arevim" (bondsmanship), discussed in detail below, which deems each Jew responsible for his brother, is unique and serves as a canonical guide within Jewish institutional life, represented, for instance, in operations such as Hadassah and the United Jewish Appeal, which take care of and responsibility for Israel.

Before speaking more specifically about the uniquely Jewish psychology, let us better understand how, through a process of apologetic compartmentalization, many Jewish psychologists have disguised the specific Jewish ethic and the distinctive psychological paradigms it created. This apologetic process begins with Freud himself, who, in *Moses & Monotheism* in describing the psychology of the "Oedipal man," posited that human growth is possible only through symbolically killing—that is, detaching oneself from—one's father. This approach continues in the work of contemporary Jewish psychologists (among them orthodox rabbis), who, in their attempts to reconcile Freud's Christianized Oedipal psychology, must apologetically bracket their own Jewish ethical orientation.

Freud, an emancipated nineteenth century Jew, accepted the Hegelian-Marxian idea of progress, which postulated that the world's history develops deterministically through a continuing series of conflicts in which the young and fit *replace* the old, decaying class or nation. In positing his parallel Oedipal

theory, Freud explicitly understood that the religion of the new "Pauline Oedipal" son *replaced* the religion of the old Mosaic father, now to be considered a fossil (pp. 109, 111, 113, 175). In portraying psychoanalysis as an unavoidable confrontation with one's "Oedipal original sin"—the guilt of killing and replacing the old unfit father—Freud argued:

> Paul, a Roman Jew from Tarsus, seized upon this feeling of guilt. . . . This he called original sin: it was a crime against God. . . . In reality this crime . . . has been the murder of the Father. . . . Paul, by developing the Jewish religion further became its destroyer. . . . Christianity marked a progress in history. . . . From now on, the Jewish religion was, so to speak, a fossil. . . . The way in which the new religion came to terms with the ancient ambivalency in the father-son relationship is noteworthy. . . . The fate of having to displace the father it could not escape.

Deeming this process of Oedipal development to be universal, Freud repeatedly stated that "it is the fate of all of us to direct our . . . first hatred and our first murderous wish against our father" (*Complete Psychological Works*, Vol. 4, London, p. 262).

Two patterns of detachment emerge clearly from Freud's Oedipal psychology and from western individualism at large:

1) the Hegelian-Marxian intergenerational detachment following from Freud's developmental theory of Oedipal growth, and
2) the interpersonal theory of Darwinian egoistic detachment via the process of survival of the fittest, which may be recognized today as the psychology of detachment that says, "Do your own thing."

To illuminate how these doctrines impinge on Jewish psychological formulations, we turn to two cases involving a contemporary Orthodox psychologist. Through these examples we shall see how reconciling Freud with Judaism leads to a distorting of the unique Jewish psychology of *teshuva* (repentance) and, moreover, blurs the differences between the western notion of an ego-centered psychological Darwinism and the Jewish collective psychology of bondsmanship, referred to above, which recognizes the possibility of self actualization in helping the other (alter-centrism).

The Freudian psychologist Moshe Spero, an Orthodox Jew, describes his treatment of a *Baal-Teshuva*—a secular Jew who came to accept Orthodox religious beliefs and practices—who identified with the Talmudic rabbis Aqiba and Resh Laqish.[2] The former, who started his studies at the age of 40 years, gave the newly observant Jew the hope that he might still be able to master the intricacies of Talmud study; the latter was a fitting model because he became a known Talmudic scholar even though he once was a highway gangster. Spero (p. 152), probably one of the most prolific writers in Jewish psychology, reports proudly that instead of fostering this man's identification with these Talmudic heroes, whom Spero denounced as folkloristic figures, he helped him succeed "over the course of several months" to excavate his "deeply suppressed hate for his parents."

In a second case,[3] Spero attempted to reconcile the Jewish notion of bondsmanship, which refers to a condition under which "the *arev*-bond undertakes almost completely the role and obligations of the other" with the psychoanalytic process of "transference." The problem is that, by superimposing apologetically the Jewish communal notion of bondsmanship on the individualistic process of psychoanalytic "transference," the *collective, egalitarian* idea of mutuality inherent in bondsmanship is distorted. Transference refers by definition to a non-egalitarian process in which a powerful psychoanalyst uses his "knowledge" (as Michel Foucault indicated) to control, or, better, to manipulate, the analysand to take responsibility for his or her unconscious "resistance:" projections and sexual attraction toward the analyst. The state of bondsmanship, by contrast, especially in the common Talmudic notion that "All of Israel are bonded to (and so responsible for) each other" (B. San. 27b), refers to the egalitarian notion of unconditional mutual responsibility that each Jew has for his or her fellow. To be sure, in transference the psychoanalyst undertakes an overall measure of responsibility for the total psychotherapeutic process. But transference, in which an analysand is manipulated to accept the analyst's

interpretations of his or her unconscious drives (because, after all, laymen are unable to decipher the language of the unconscious), constitutes an apologetic and cynical reduction of the *communal* psychology of the Jewish doctrine of bondsmanship.

**Paradoxical dialogues in midrashic interpretation:** Contrary to this apologetic trend, in which Jewish psychologists bracket their Jewish commitments and attempt to prove that the Jewish heritage illustrates Freudian ideas, it is possible to trace to the Rabbinic system of midrashic exegesis the roots of the contrary, pluralistic-democratic idea of freedom to choose one's own interpretation of life and worldly events. A definitive account of how this psycho-philosophical principle of dia-logic co-existence derives from the midrashic system of hermeneutic pluralism is in order.

Diverse hermeneutic systems take different stands on the ability of a single datum to support more than one meaning. Some psychological hermeneutics adhere to a *dialectic* either/or principle, which finds it necessary to replace a false interpretation that is eliminated with the one true explanation that has been identified. In *dia-logic* systems, by contrast, two interpretations may co-exist. The first, Aristotelian either/or system is embedded in the idea of conflict; the hyphen in the dia-logic principle of paradox, on the other hand, is rooted in the Platonic or Buberian I-thou idea, according to which truth stands between two co-existing, alternating or even opposing positions.

Interestingly, this principle of paradoxical interpretations stands at the foundation of many ideas central to Judaism. These ideas include the notions, for instance, that God's *midat hadin* (quality of rigorous sternness) and *midat harachamim* (quality of merciful compassion) co-exist. At the very heart of Rabbinic Judaism, indeed, stands the concept of the written and oral Torahs, both revealed by God even though, prima facie, their texts seem sometimes to contradict each other. In interpreting canonical documents, the principle of paradoxical interpretations is further invoked, for instance, to explain the fact that, while the written Torah often specifies the death penalty, the oral Torah condemns as murderous any Jewish court that carries out this penalty even once in seventy years (B. Mak. 7a).

Even as it was used to comprehend contradictions between the oral and written Torahs, so the principle of paradoxical interpretations applied in the resolution of apparent contradictions within the written Torah itself. A classic example is the verse, "And the Lord God said, it is not good that the man should be alone, I will make him a help against him" (Gen. 2:18). Gen. Rab. 17:3 explains the two seemingly contradictory concepts, "help" and "against," by applying a hermeneutic principle that reads them independently of each other. The woman will become man's righthand "help" if he deserves it; but if he does not deserve it, she will turn "against" him. A similar interpretation makes Israel's deservingness of future redemption dependent on the freedom of choice to do good or evil. Here the two contradicting words *beita achishena* (Is. 60:22), which mean literally "I shall hasten it" (*achishena*) and "in its due time" (*beita*), were also read independently (Song Rab. 8:12) to mean: redemption will occur in due time if Israel does not deserve it (*beita*); but if they deserve salvation, I will hasten it (*achishena*).

This principle of paradoxical interpretations stands in opposition to "double bind" theories,[4] which postulate that socialization via "double messages" may lead to psychotic breakdowns. By contrast, we refer to the Midrashic principle of "*Al-tikrei*," which means literally "don't read," and is a catchphrase for the full sentence, "Don't read (the biblical text) as it is written, but, by switching or changing the letters, read it in a different way to reveal an alternate meaning." The relevance of this paradoxical principle in the present context is that it entails the possibility of retaining two contradictory interpretations of a textual passage. This hermeneutic, which has extensive psychological implications, appears about 180 times in the Rabbinic literature,[5] and some of its occurrences, in prayers and/or turned into popular slogans, remarkably affected socialization of Jews throughout the ages.

One of the most famous uses of the *al-tikrei* passages, recited by traditional Jews daily in the morning prayers, refers to Is. 54:13: "All your sons shall be taught by the Lord, and great shall be the peace of your sons." Concerning this verse, B. Ber. 64 says, "Do not read 'your sons' (*banayich*) but 'your builders' (*bonayich*)." Thus, while Isaiah states that peace shall be brought upon the Israelites' children ("sons") in general, the Talmud rereads his words to refer to "your builders" in particular, thus establishing a distinct ethical imperative to participate in the rebuilding of the Jewish nation.

In our current discussion, at issue is whether this mode of interpretation intends completely to replace and erase the original textual reading or only to add to it another level of meaning. Judah Eisenstein, editor of the *Otzar Yisrael* encyclopedia, answers this question by noting that both Maimonides and Nachmanides stressed that such formulations add an alternative interpretation to the biblical text but do not negate the original reading. Indeed, Nachmanides held that the hermeneutic idea inherent in the "*al-tikrei*" form allows even two *contradictory* interpretations both to be true. This is possible insofar as the biblical text is sufficiently powerful to endure both meanings. It is, accordingly, exactly the possibility of such an alternative that creates what I have termed a dia-logic, or alternating, hermeneutic system. The reading "your builders" does not replace dialectically the original words, "your children." The new reading, rather, facilitates the dia-logic possibility of accumulative progress, according to which "your children" become "your progressing developers."

Having posited that this ancient midrashic system of hermeneutic pluralism possibly comprised the bedrock of the democratic notion of dialogic co-existence, we may proceed now to introduce four different psychological dimensions, the first two entailing a time element and the subsequent two relating to space. The four subtitles, formulated in a comparative style, are articulated as four systems of psychological dialogues that people usually maintain on various levels with their surrounding environment:

1. *The intergenerational psychology of Abraham's binding of his son, Isaac ("Aqeda")*: Here the possibility of maintaining a total personal identity by rearranging the intergenerational continuity between the "Abrahams" and "Isaacs" will be compared to the Oedipal psychology of intergenerational conflict.
2. *The intrapersonal psychology of return to Judaism ("Teshuva")*: In this section the possibility of recomposing one's failing past according to the idea of repentance will be compared to the deterministic linear time conception of one's past that follows from the concept of "original sin."
3. *The interpersonal psychology of bondsmanship ("Arevim")*: In this section the communal idea of self-actualization via helping the other (alter-centrism) will be discussed by comparing it to the ego-centered actualization psychology of Darwinian Survival of the Fittest.
4. *The superpersonal psychology of "PaRDeS"*: This section discusses two dialogical levels: a) the hermeneutic notion of *PaRDeS* which provides a dialogical bridge between the rational-physical world and one's irrational-mystical world, and b) the dialogical system of sexuality, which provides a bridge for regulating the flow of energy between the *yetzer* (carnal desire) and the *yetzira* (spiritual creativity).

We discuss each of these psychological paradigms in turn.

**The intergenerational psychology of Abraham's binding of his son, Isaac ("Aqeda"):** While not oblivious to the universal phenomenon of intergenerational tension, based on the story of Abraham's binding of this son Isaac, the Jewish *Aqeda* psychology nonetheless assumes that maintaining a consistent total identity depends at least partially on people's ability to reconnect their life story to their ancestral roots. This is hardly to say that Jewish Oedipal tales, as well as Biblical and Talmudic interpretations, evaded the phenomenological possibility of intergenerational tension, including the presumed incestual drive; they clearly did not. Of interest to us here, rather, is the differential pattern of the proposed religio-cultural *solution* Judaism offered to this intergenerational tension.

Since the Oedipal psychology of inter-generational detachment appears to be congruent with the Hegelian Marxist idea of progress via conflict that can be resolved only by eliminating the old unfitting father, nation or class, the neo-Freudian scenario of psychotherapeutic patricide follows. As a result, the approach taken in the following excerpt from Fritz Perls' Gestaltist therapeutic dream analysis (*Gestalt Therapy Verbatim*, Lafayette, 1969, pp. 221-222) seems not an exception but the rule in most neo-Freudian therapies (F = therapist; J = patient):

> F: So find somebody else to kill . . .
> J: My mother . . . how can I kill her? I want it to hurt. . . . Oh! I killed her. . . . Into the swimming pool, all filled with acid, and she dove in. There's nothing left. . . . You deserved it. I should have done it a long time ago. There aren't even any bones left. She just disappeared. . . . And then I sorta felt *good*. I should have done it a long time ago.
> F: Say this to the group.
> J: It felt good! I should have done it *a long time ago*.

One need not be a professional therapist in order to realize that the therapist's encouragement of this thirty-five year old patient to "say this to the group" is geared to help her to kill her mother symbolically and publicly in order to become "healthy" by separating from her according to the prescribed individualistic Western-American social norm of "detachment."

Since the idea that psychological or psychotherapeutic growth is possible only via patricide permeates most western theories of personality, it is interesting to compare this idea, available in various versions of the classic Oedipal myth, with Isaac myths. For though it appears that most of the thematic elements comprising the Oedipal myth were quite popular in medieval tales and fables, these stories are quite different from those presented from a Jewish point of view. In the Greek Oedipal myth and the Judas Iscariot legend,[6] the sons (Oedipus and Judah) marry their mothers, who according to some versions even bear their children. In various Jewish Oedipal myths, by contrast, the consummation of the incestuous relations is miraculously prevented at the last moment.

Let us follow the sequence of events in a medieval legend about the biblical Joshua, son of Nun (see *Rav Pealim*, 1894):

> The father of Joshua lived in Jerusalem, and his wife was childless, and this righteous man was praying in the presence of his wife, and God listened to him. And it was so that while she was pregnant, this righteous man tormented himself and weeped day and night non-stop; and this was bad in the eyes of his wife, and she said to him: you should have been happy because God listened to your prayers . . . and he told her . . . that he was told from Heaven that this son that will be born to him will decapitate him. . . . And it was so that when she gave birth and it was a son and his mother took for him a basket (ark) . . . and she put the child in it and she threw it into the river (Nile), and God arranged for a big fish (whale) to swallow the basked. . . . And it was the day when the king made a feast for his ministers and slaves and he caught this fish . . . and opened it and there was a boy crying . . . and the boy grew up in the king's palace and he made him the hangman. . . . And after these things this righteous man (Joshua's father) sinned against the king of Egypt and the king ordered the hangman to decapitate him and take his wife, sons and property to himself, as was customary those days. And as he approached his mother to copulate with her, then the whole bed filled up with milk from her breasts. And he became very alarmed, and he took a spear to kill her, because he thought that she was a witch, but his mother remembered the words of his father, the late righteous man, and she answered him saying: it is not witch-craft but the milk with which I nursed you, because I am your mother, and she told him the whole event, and he immediately separated from her . . . as he did not know that it was his father, and he repented . . . and followed Moses our Rabbi blessed be his memory (p. 23).

Notably, in many non-Jewish medieval versions of the Oedipal myth, the father-killing theme is entirely lacking, and the incestuous marrying of the mother ends in a dialogic rearranging continuity. An example is the famous Gregory legend, in which the son, after discovering that he is married to his mother, not only repents but is allowed to become Pope (see *Gesta Romanorum*, 1891). The fact that Freud, nonetheless, chose the patricidal Oedipal myth as a key narrative for the construction of his dialectic paradigm of growth and progress demonstrates that it was not only the incest theme but its concomitant theme of patricide that Freud believed characterized human development.

Again, while in the famous medieval legend about Pope Gregory, an incestuous relationship between mother and son is actually enacted, in the Jewish version of this tale, which appears in various anthologies under the title *Mamzer Talmid Chacham* ("The Talmudic Scholar Bastard"), the actual consummation of the incestuous relationship is prevented at the last moment, as happened in the fable concerning Joshua. In one version for example:[7]

> the husband sat and heard the whole story, and he was utterly startled: it became clearly known to him that this woman was his mother . . . and (he) gave praise and gratitude to God, for bestowing upon him great charity, so that he did not commit such a grave sin as to depend sexually on his mother.

Nonetheless, as alluded to earlier, it is not the denial of the intergenerational tension—including the incestual drive—that characterizes Jewish socializing dicta. Rather, the focus of those dicta is the need to overcome this natural trend. Indeed, B. Shab. 130a states:

> It was taught: R. Simeon b. Gamaliel said: "Every precept that [the Israelites] accepted with joy, e.g. circumcision . . . they still observe with joy. But every precept that they accepted with displeasure, e.g. the forbidden degrees of consanguinity [incest] . . . they still perform with strife [quarrel]."

Even commentators such as the famous *Maharal* of Prague (see *Chidushey Agadot Hamaharal*, part 1) note that it is natural for people to be sexually attracted to their immediate kin. It appears, therefore, that only the Hegelian theme of progress via patricidal replacement is distinctive in the story of Oedipus.

It further is clear that Freud chose the patricidal story of Oedipus as his paradigmatic narrative even though he was familiar with Judah's legend, which was cited by his student Otto Rank. Similarly, he most probably was acquainted with Pope Gregory's legend, about whom Thomas Mann wrote his famous novel, *The Holy Sinner*. It seems, rather, that the focus upon the Oedipus story, which includes the patricidal element, reflects Freud's desire to create an emancipated "Godless" universal psychology of personal development, which concurs with Hegel's dialectic idea of progress via replacement.

Furthermore, it is important to point out evidence showing that the dialogical norm of intergenerational continuity was known already in ancient midrashic texts and fostered in the Jewish tradition. Emphasizing how Israel's anti-incestuous nature differed from the dialectic mode of progress of gentile nations, the ancient (first or second century) Midrash Tanhuma (Vayeshev) stated:

> Why did the Scripture engage in writing their [the gentiles'] genealogy . . . except . . . to publicize that they are all the children of incest. And so it says: "The sons of El'phaz: Teman, Omar, Zephi, Gatam, Kenaz, Timna, and Am'alek" (1 Chron. 1:36) and [in the Torah it says], "Timna was a concubine of El'iphaz" (Gen. 36:12). It teaches us that [Elifas] married his daughter . . . and later it says [about someone else's genealogy], "Ana the son of Zivon. . . ." This teaches that Zivon copulated with his mother, and she gave birth to Ana so that he was his brother and son. . . . But God brought Israel close to him . . . as it is written, "Yet I had planted thee a noble vine, wholly a right seed" (Jer. 2:21).

To understand how an appropriate resolution to intergenerational tensions was consistently inculcated in Jews, we now may examine the "Aqeda" paradox. The Aqeda is presented in most Jewish texts as a Kierkegaardian test of faith, meant to condition Jewish "Isaacs" stubbornly to retain faith in the biblical promise of dialogic continuity with Abraham, "even when a sharp sword is laid upon their neck" (B. Ber. 10a).

With this theory of dialogic continuity of progress in mind, we may understand why, on the one hand, even those rare interpretative texts that depict Isaac as having been killed report that he subsequently was brought back to life,[8] while, on the other hand, massive child sacrifice, modeled by the Aqeda, was relatively permissible only during the Middle Ages, when, for instance, Jewish continuity was concretely threatened by the Crusaders' coercion of Jewish children to convert to Christianity.

What we have then are two models of progress:

1. the dialectic paradigm, in which the idealization of the actual filicidal killing-sacrificing of the son-Jesus may trigger progress via the actual Oedipal elimination of the father-generation, so that the son rules *instead* of the father;
2. the dialogic paradigm that idealizes Isaac's "patricidal" faith in a last-minute avoidance of Abraham's "filicidal" pressure to facilitate continuity of the son's ruling *after* the father.

In conclusion, let us emphasize that the recomposition of total identities by using the Aqeda theme to reestablish intergenerational continuity has been used successfully by many psychotherapists and educators.

**The intrapersonal psychology of return to Judaism ("Teshuva"):** This inner time dimension purports to encounter the cyclistic meta-code of *teshuva* with the deterministic linear intrapersonal time dimension of the "original sin" meta-code. Concurrent with the intergenerational time dimension inherent in the Aqeda psychology, the *teshuva* meta-code begins from the assumption that in order to maintain a coherent total identity, people need a normative system for re-biographing or recomposing their past failures so that they may be linked into a personal life-story with which they can live. Thus, if people have internalized the Christian "original sin" meta-code, which, according to Ricoeur (*The Conflict of Interpretation*, Evanston, 1981, p. 269), represents "a hereditary vice" and "an original guilt," then this "Oedipal guilt" cannot be shaken off. However, if people internalize a belief in the cyclistic *teshuva* (repentance) meta-code, which means literally "turning," then they may reinterpret their past failures so that their life story will be recomposed into a new resonant melody. But how does this cyclistic possibility for recomposing life-stories emerge from a Jewish psycho-philosophy, which the *teshuva* psychology presumably epitomizes? One of the most quoted socializing statements about the possibility of *teshuva* is cited in the name of Resh Laqish, who prior to becoming a major Talmudic sage was allegedly a highway gangster. He asserts that "repentance (*teshuva*) is so great that premeditated sins are accounted as though they are merits" (B. Yoma 86b).

*Prima facie* the translation of this Talmudic assertion into psychotherapeutic terms would mean that from a curative-rehabilitative perspective, a person who experienced failures may declare that he "hopes to have a good past in the future." Having been reared to think in Western, historically based terms, we would probably dismiss such a declaration as senseless, because we were taught to believe that our past is a closed book. Accordingly, we train our ex-criminals or ex-mental patients to redeem themselves either in a present based on a "here and now" existential salvation or in a "not yet here and not yet now" futuristic "clean leaf" rehabilitation scheme, asking them, in essence, to erase or accept their unchangeable failing past. By advocating such rehabilitation formulas, however, we rarely come to full terms with the problem of whether and how people are really capable of trading or integrating their old "Mr. Hyde" selves with reborn, "clean leaf, Dr. Jekyl" ones.

In essence the question is why Western people must hide their past failings. Why should we not be able to correct our past in order either to bridge the cognitive gap that separates the amnestic death of that failing past from an existential "here and now" rebirth, or to minimize the "cognitive dissonance" brought about by the psychoanalytic confrontation between our conscious, guiltful past and our neurotic present? Indeed, by examining the possibility of rehabilitation within the political sphere, we may learn that powerful people are rarely satisfied with a "clean leaf" schema that allows them only to do their best in the future without erasing the possible social stigma that they incurred in their doubtful past. Consequently, we feel sympathetic to such people if they demand a re-reading of their failed past. Similarly, in concluding his study about federal witnesses whose past life and identity had to be buried and erased in order to protect them from potential revengers, Fred Montanino stated:[9]

> the witnesses' protection experience tells us that . . . we construct reality from the world around us, and past life and interaction are essential parts of this construction. . . . The protected witness experience teaches us further that . . . we cannot escape responsibility for our own past performance, nor can we easily assume a rightful place in collective social life without some recognition of it. We cannot totally divorce ourselves from others who have been part of our social life without losing the part from which we seek to divorce them.

Thus, the dialectic divorce from past identity, be it criminal or "schizophrenic," advocated by the "new leaf" rehabilitation formula seems insufficient and even unworkable when examined through such extreme cases as Protected Federal Witnesses or degraded political personalities seeking rehabilitation.

Accordingly, Resh Laqish's statement about *teshuva* must be understood as a Talmudic effort to institutionalize a social-cultural norm by which repenters will not merely be given a new chance from now on but will be granted full "biographic rehabilitation," actually being permitted to correct, reinterpret, or assign new meaning to their past failures. Otherwise, it would be impossible for premeditated sins committed in the *past* retroactively to be "accounted as merits."

This psychology for recomposing one's failing life history would seem inconceivable if it did not derive its normative social legitimation from a canonical system of hermeneutic tradition. Indeed, a careful examination of Talmudic and midrashic interpretative methods reveals that this is precisely how biographies of Biblical sinners are retroactively recomposed. While the Rabbinic literature provides abundant examples of rebiographing, here I introduce by way of example only the classic case of King David.

**David's adulterous sin:** The story is related succinctly at 2 Sam. 11:3-4: "And David sent and inquired about the woman. And one said, "Is not this Bathshe'ba, the daughter of Eli'am, the wife of Uri'ah the Hittite? And David sent messengers and took her; and she came in unto him, and he lay with her." But while the Biblical description is straightforward in describing David's sin of adultery, B. Shab. 56a offers an initial revisioning of the episode:

R. Samuel the son of Nahman said in the name of Jonathan: "Whoever maintains that David sinned is nothing but mistaken; for it is written, 'And David behaved himself wisely in all his ways, and the Lord was with him' (1 Sam. 18:14). Is it possible that sin came to his hand, yet the Divine Presence was with him?"

The Talmud reconciles this seeming contradiction by offering a rereading of another biblical verse: "Then how do I interpret [the verse], 'Why have you [David] despised the word of the Lord, to do what is evil in his sight?' (2 Sam. 12:9)." The Talmud concludes that, "David only wished or intended to do evil [adultery] but actually didn't:"

> Rab observed: Rabbi, who is descended from David, seeks to defend him and [so reads 2 Sam. 12:9 in] reverse in David's favor. [Thus] the "evil" [mentioned] here is unlike every other "evil" [mentioned] elsewhere in the Torah. For of every other evil in the Torah it is written "and he did," whereas here it is written "to do;" [this means] that he desired to do, but did not.

In presenting this creative rereading, the Talmud does not hesitate to admit that Rabbi's familial loyalty ("who is descended from David") contributed to his willingness to interpret the verse in David's favor. Yet the very subtle distinction between the intention or desire to do evil and the evils that were actually committed is an important step in David's rehabilitation.

Interestingly while the notion that there was only intention to do evil appears here as a mitigating reinterpretation of what the Bible presents as an actual sin, matters are not so simple as this at all. Rather, the midrashic re-biographing of David epitomizes the infinite possibilities inherent in a hermeneutic multiple-choice system. This is clear since, according to a much cited Talmudic dictum (B. Yom. 29a), formulating the "intention" to sin is worse than actually sinning. To reconcile this apparent problem, in interpreting the continuation of 2 Sam. 12:9, B. Shab. 56a states the following:

> "You have smitten Uri'ah the Hittite with the sword:" you should have had him tried by the Sanhedrin but did not. "And have taken his wife to be your wife:" you have marriage

rights in her, for . . . everyone who went out in the wars of the house of David wrote a bill of divorce for his wife.

This passage reflects the Talmudic principle that "there is no early and no late in the Torah" (B. Pes. 6b), everything having been conceived in God's mind at the same time and revealed together at Sinai. Otherwise it would be impossible to claim that the Talmudic dictum that soldiers must deposit a tentative writ of divorce before going into battle (to avoid unresolved widowhood) was already known and followed during David's time. The impact of this reading is to claim that there was neither sin nor even intention to sin.

As in most other cases, the Talmud and the Midrash use David's subsequent full repentance as a pivotal point to begin to reverse, via various hermeneutic methods, the meaning of David's earlier sins, so that it becomes possible to present him retrospectively as a perfect role model for other prospective repenters. Indeed, along these lines, one passage states (Shocher Tov, Tehilim 51): "This is what David said to God, '. . . if you accept me, all criminals will make up with you, and everybody will look to me, and I shall testify that you accept repenters.'"

Thus, the *hermetic* approach to the past embedded in the Christianized "original sin" meta-code and the *hermeneutic* approach to the past rooted in the midrashic *teshuva* meta-code produce two diametrically opposed psychological systems. The linear conception of the past constitutes a *hermetic* inner time perspective, while the *hermeneutic* orientation to one's past emanates from a cyclistic orientation concerning one's intrapersonal rehabilitative recomposition of his past.

To be sure, according to the *hermetic* model, reinterpretation of the past is possible. It differs however from the open *hermeneutic* paradigm in that it allows only one fundamentalistic, predetermined interpretation. For example, the psychoanalytic psychologist Roy Schafer (*The Analytic Attitude*, New York, 1983, pp. 219-224) describes openly how he manipulates his analysands to accept only one reinterpretation of the past, grounded in the "sex-aggression" cause inherent in the "Oedipal original sin" meta-code:

> The analyst's retellings progressively influence the what and the how of the stories told by analysands. . . . The analyst slowly and patiently develops an emphasis on infantile or archaic modes of sexual and aggressive action.

Moreover, by stressing that in contrast to the *hermetic* conception of the past only the *hermeneutic* perception of past failures allows "re-biographing," one should not be misled to believe that biographic recomposition of one's past is possible without behavioral changes in the present. Rather, the first step in the sequence of re-biographing is repentance in a specific present. This is a prerequisite for re-composing the past, which can be only a second step.

The story of Jacob's sons' callous selling of their brother Joseph (Gen. 37:18-28) serves as a good case in point. What first appeared to be a sinful act subsequently was reinterpreted by Joseph himself, who assured his brothers retroactively, "As for you, you meant evil against me; but God meant it for good, to bring it about that many people should be kept alive, as they are today" (Gen. 50:20). As step no. 1 in this process of re-biographing, Joseph subjected his brothers to the severest test of repentance, their ability to resist the same temptation to sell or turn in a brother even when circumstances seemed to demand and warrant it. This was the case when presumably only Benjamin had sinned by stealing Joseph's cup, leading Joseph to declare, "Only the man in whose hand the cup was found shall be my slave; but as for you, go up in peace to your father." (Gen. 44:17). Only after his brothers withstood the test of "absolute repentance"[10] did Joseph use retrospective reinterpretation, step no. 2, to rehabilitate his brother's, asserting, "God meant it for good."

Indeed, in a series of studies of Israeli exconvicts who became repenters (*baalei teshuva*), interviewees frequently used the midrashic reinterpretation method to indicate how their behavioral change in the present allowed them to recompose their past. One repenter said: "I want to remember this [criminal] period in my life so that I shall be reminded from where I came and to where I was able to go, from a low pit to a high roof." Another noted: "I don't have to forget my past. . . . Out of bitterness came forth sweetness."

In the first citation, the famous Talmudic slogan "from a high roof to a low pit" (B. Hag. 5b), which refers to a disgraceful fall from a highly respectable position, was reversed and rephrased to depict "ascent through descent." In the second citation, Judg. 14:14—"from the strong came forth sweetness"—was paraphrased by inserting the word *bitterness* in place of the word *strong*. Likewise, using this method of recomposing life stories in psychotherapy was found to help people to reestablish a comprehensive biographical identity with which they could better live. In one case, a patient's frequent visits with his mother previously had been interpreted as inappropriate dependency; the recomposition process rebiographed these visits as favorable efforts to honor the mother. In another case, a mother's voluntary devotion to taking care of a sick, lonely woman was perceived by her daughter as a testimony to her own being neglected by that mother; the process of retroactive recomposition facilitated her perceiving of her mother's conduct as an appropriate "role-modeling" act.

In conclusion, since a similar pattern of successful recompositions of failing life stories was noticed when people suffering from mental disturbances adopted the cyclistic meta-code inherent in the *teshuva* psychology, it appears that the Midrash provides a reversed law of causality. Indeed, the late J.B. Soloveitchick, a leading authority in Jewish philosophy and law, appears to state this unequivocally (*The Halakhic Man*, Philadelphia, 1983, pp. 114-115):

> the law of causality, from this perspective, also assumes a new form. The future imprints its stamp on the past and determines its image. . . . The cause is interpreted by the affect, moment *a* by moment *b*. The past itself is indeterminate. . . . It is only the present and the future that can pry it open and read

its meaning. . . . The main principal of repentance is that the future dominates the past and then reigns over it in unbounded fashion.

At the heart of repentance, as we have seen, thus is not the forgetting of the past but the ability to recompose the past so as to use it in constructing a better future.

**The interpersonal psychology of bonds-manship ("Arevim"):** The communal dimension of the motto "Kol Yisrael arevim ze baze" ("all the people of Israel are sureties one for another," B. B.Q. 92a) shifts individuals' focus from psychological time to their interaction with their psycho-social surrounding. The idea of "Arevim," which puts the *other* (alter) in the center, constitutes a diametric opposition to the ego-centered "do your own thing" psychology that emanates from the Darwinian concept of the survival of the fittest. Accordingly, a clear distinction can be made between the *ego-centered* psychology emanating from the Protestant self-actualizing-salvation ethic and the Jewish psychology that follows from the *alter-centered* "Arevim" ethic of self actualizing-salvation through the other. For generations, accordingly, Talmudic imperatives such as "one who solicits mercy for his fellow while he himself is in need of the same thing will be answered first" (B. Shav. 39a) have expressed the Jewish attitude towards communal welfare.

It is possible to demonstrate how the alter-centered "Arevim" psychology was systematically inculcated from the tribal structure that functioned during ancient times, continued in the interpersonal psychology that facilitated the survival of Hasidic communities, and appears still in such contemporary voluntary associations as Hadassah or the United Jewish Appeal. To be sure, the interpersonal "Arevim" psychology of alter-centered actualization is not to be confused with a collectivizing psychology such as comprised communism. While it has been claimed that in collectivizing systems the individuality of the self may be undermined, in the interpersonal psychology inherent in the "Arevim" system, the self—the "I"—is never obliterated but retains a dialogical position

*vis a vis* the "thou" through a process that may be termed "reciprocal-individualism."

The crux of reciprocal-individualism, the desire to facilitate alter-centered actualization in the "Arevim" community where people are *different* from each other but not *indifferent* to each other, was used by the philosopher Hugo Bergman (*Dialogical Philosophy*, Jerusalem, 1974, pp. 247-248) to explicate the differences between the Hegelian dialectic principle and Buber's I-thou philosophy: "It is worthwhile to compare the dialogical principle and the dialectic principle of Hegel . . . [for] Hegel's synthesis swallows . . . the thesis and the antithesis into a more engulfing synthesis . . . [whereas] this is not so among those dialogic philosophers, according to whom the engulfment really preserves both." In this way, the "I" remains "I" and the "thou" remains a "thou." But what are the ideological-theosophical roots of the alter-centered "Arevim" psychology?

To apprehend the historical components of Jewish alter-centrism, it seems useful to consider the dynamics of give and take. In his introduction to the Zohar, Ashlag explains how the human desire to receive divine influx would be impossible without perceiving God's equal or even greater desire, even his need, to give or bestow holiness on the human world. Similarly, according to Hasidic ethics, the best context for actualizing the pleasure one may derive through interpersonal giving is relationships involving education or love. In such relationships, self-fulfillment is meaningless until the interacting partner provides the proper feedback to indicate that the message was fully received and perceived. To visualize how two unequal partners (child and father, student and teacher) can fully convey what they feel or think only through narrowing and contracting the matter or theme to be conveyed, one may use the "funnel" metaphor provided by the Maggid of Mezeritz (*Maggid Devarav Le-Yaacov*, Lublin, 1927, p. 47), the successor of the Besht, the founder of the eighteenth century Hasidic movement:

> When the Rabbi wants his student to understand his broad mind, and the student cannot apprehend it then the Rabbi-teacher

contracts his mind in talk and letters. For example, when a person wants to pour from one container to another and he is afraid to spill, then he takes an instrument called a funnel, and by this the liquid is contracted . . . and he will not spill. So it is when the Rabbi's mind is contracted in talk and letters which he says to the student, and through this the student can apprehend the teacher's broad mind.

Thus, contraction is a prerequisite to alter-centered revelation—giving—in the human and divine worlds. Divine contraction as a precondition for emanation is best illuminated in Buber's poetic words (*Bepardes Hachasidut*, Tel Aviv, 1963, p. 104):

How could the divine infinite (*eyn-sof*) become a contracted God which roams the worlds to carry out His creation through acts of contraction? . . . Why did the infinite divine, as an absolute personality, vis-a-vis stand nothing, become a personality which stands vis-a-vis a receiver? . . . [It is] because of the desire to find a receiver, so that the divine will be able to bestow His light upon it.

Following the above it appears that western ego-centered "do-your-own-thing" psychology encompasses a basic misunderstanding of the need to give. The kabbalistic analogy of God's need to give or to bestow may be understood on a human level by picturing an artist's incurable need to "give" the pictures he paints. One may imagine that if an artist were locked up for life in his studio to paint as much as he desired but that no human eye was permitted to glance at his work, he would eventually die or attempt suicide. Consider the self-endangering risks anti-establishment writers are willing to take in totalitarian states when they distribute underground copies of their work.

Self-actualization thus would be largely self-defeating if it culminated in a simplistic psychology of "doing my own thing." If I follow literally the "democratic" imperative of "doing my own thing as long as I do not hurt others," those others might still hurt me by obstructing "my own actualizing thing," for instance, if they refuse to receive what I want to give as an expression of my self-actualization. In this sense, then, the line

between giving and receiving becomes considerably blurred, with giving becoming *ipso facto* receiving. Indeed, reception theory,[11] which shifted focus from studying the text and its author to assessing the role of the reader, suggests by its very definition that if there would be no reader to receive the author's writing ("giving"), his text would be quite meaningless. Similarly, the declarations "I am a therapist!" or "I am a teacher!" would be rather meaningless if there were no one to receive the therapy or the teaching. Giving, in this dialogic sense, is not a unilateral altruistic act of good Samaritanism but a reciprocal process of mutual dependency: A might be willing to receive B's actualizing-giving under the condition that B or C is willing to receive A's actualizing-giving.

Now, if reciprocal-individualism, which concurs with Buber's I-thou stance, stands neither for massifying collectivism (in which one runs away from one's self into the mob) nor for isolating ego-centered individualism (in which one runs away from the mob), how are we to envision the interpersonal "Arevim" psychology of egalitarian or balanced give and take? One model can be referred to as the Zebulun and Issachar exchange contract.

**The Zebulun and Issachar exchange contract:** The earliest sources concerning the contract between the tribes Issachar and Zebulun are the legends and commentary that evolved around the biblical descriptions of these two tribal brothers. The first elements of the legend were based on Jacob's blessings of his sons ("Zebulun shall dwell at the haven of the sea; and he shall be a haven of ships. . . . Issachar is a strong ass crouching down between two burdens;" Gen. 49:13-14) and Moses' blessings of the tribes ("of Zebulun he said, 'Rejoice, Zebulun, in thy going out; and Issachar, in thy tents;'" Deut. 33:18).

In the Talmudic period of the second to fifth centuries C.E., Zebulun was described as a merchant, and Issachar's burden and tents were described as the burden and tents of Torah. The fact that Zebulun was mentioned first in both blessings, although he was younger than Issachar, gave birth to the famous interpretation that Zebulun and

Issachar made a partnership. Zebulun dwells at the haven of the sea and goes out sailing with his merchandise and earns and gives into the mouth of Issachar, who sits and studies the Torah. Zebulun came before Issachar, since Issachar's Torah was due to Zebulun (Rashi on Deut. 33:18). From a historical point of view it is of interest to stress that, in spite of some evidence indicating that Zebulun was indeed a sea merchant and Issachar a judge, it was a legend, gradually transformed into an ideology, that was translated into a contractual and contractional tradition instructing the rich (not necessarily of the tribe of Zebulun or sea merchants) to purchase their salvation by supporting poor Talmudic scholars.[12]

To lead the reader directly to our major paradigmatic case study, let us skip now from the Talmudic period to eighteenth century Hasidic culture to demonstrate how the Issachar and Zebulun model was revived in Hasidic spiritual-material terms as an alter-centered contract model.

According to Yaacov Yosef (*Toldot Yaacov Yosef*, Jerusalem, 1963), the student and friend of the Besht, early Hasidim used the doctrine of "form" and "matter" strictly to reestablish the alter-centered contractional relationship that prevailed between Issachar and Zebulun. Indeed, according to him, an exchange system should prevail between Issacharian form and Zebulunian matter on the *inter*personal and the *intra*personal levels. Hence, he stresses (p. 243):

> Since similar to the individuality within one person, the soul and form are not to feel superior over the body and say that it is a holy soul, . . . and even more so the body is not to be arrogant over the soul as it holds the soul . . . as they need each other like a man and a woman, each one being half a body— so it is in the collective, the Talmudic scholars and righteous are not to say that there is no need for the masses, since they support the Torah, . . . and even more so the masses are not to say there is no need for Talmudic scholars, or to feel arrogant against them since their livelihood is due to them, . . . and so, each one is half and with both together, matter and form whether in the collective or within the individual, it becomes one full person.

The interpersonal "Arevim" psychology exposes the *futility* of the equality myth that is predicated only on one materialistic salvation ideal as compared to the apparent *utility* of a social structure with a multiple (Zebulun and Issachar) actualization system. The difference between the Protestant-Darwinian ego-centered salvation psychology and the alter-centered Zebulun and Issachar actualizing exchange system distinguishes accordingly between multiple *roads* to one salvation ideal and multiple *modes* of actualization.

Nonetheless, by tracing the roots of the Zebulun and Issachar interpersonal exchange system, one may realize that the "Arevim" paradigm also comprises an organic socio-psychological theory. Accordingly, the Hasidic notion of organic interdependency between matter and form (body and soul), which portrays for example the "people of matter" as the congregation's feet and the "people of form" as its eyes, seems to concur with Emile Durkheim's conception of modern society in the terms of organic solidarity between various functional sections (organs).

In socio-psychological terms, this organic interdependence may be conceptualized as a two directional process, leading both outside the self and inside the self. Accordingly, the *Zaddik* ("righteous teacher") may reach the other by going outward to meet that other on the other's level or by going inward to correct his own self, because, in light of the organic "Arevim" principle, the process of *"tikun"* (self correction) includes correction of the other.

While reaching out on the other's level constitutes today a popular dictum in various practice theories adhering to the postulates of group dynamics, it is interesting to note that this principle was formulated already in the eighteenth century as a canonical imperative of Hasidic ethics. This is expressed in Nahman of Bratzlav's parable of the "indic" (turkey),[13] used nowadays as a classic metaphor for psychotherapeutic oriented groups geared to enhancing human relations. The parable, which speaks of a prince who believed himself to be a turkey and so sat naked under a table and ate only sunflower seeds, is as follows:

While all the doctors hired by his father, the king, could not cure the prince, there was one wise man who got also undressed, sat with the prince under the table, introduced himself as a turkey, and ate sunflower seeds until the prince found it strange that a wise man should behave in such a fashion. Thus they both decided that turkeys could dress, eat other food, etc., and finally both came out from under the table and behaved like humans again.

The symbolic alter-centered idea of uplifting the other by going down to his level is quite clear in this parable and is conveyed in the very idea that the *Zaddik* must go down to reach the masses by telling them simple allegoric stories. But let us turn now to the more radical "Arevim" principle of "tikkun," which posits the possibility of changing the other's conduct via self correction.

Although the Hasidic imperative of *tikkun* refers primarily to the human capacity and obligation to correct the divine disorder caused during the primordial "breaking of the vessels," it entails also self-correction. Thus the Besht (*Keter Shem Tov*, Jerusalem, 1975, p. 21) states, "If a person had the opportunity to observe a transgression and he should feel [the need] to correct himself . . . then he will bring back the wicked person after he includes him through unification." Upon initial consideration of this imperative, one may wonder why the *a*normative behavior of the other should be casually related to the same *a*normative behavior in myself, and, further, how should *my* correction of this particular behavior simultaneously correct the other's behavior? To understand this process we should distinguish between the one-directional "copying" model of Albert Bandura or between the passive, reflective, looking glass metaphor of Charles Cooley and George Herbert Mead,[14] and the double-mirror model of the Besht. While Bandura construes the possibility of "identification" as one-way role-modeling or "copying" and while, in the Meadian looking-glass model, the self evolves from a social mirroring process, there are no assumptions as to whether and how a role-taker (the one who looks at the social mirror) or the copier affects the significant other's or model's behavior in an interactive situation. However, the double-mirroring paradigm, which may be termed the Beshtian mutual-emulating scheme, proposes a reflective process of double-mirroring, in which both interacting partners are affected simultaneously. The active-dynamic double-mirror concept assumes that if my interacting partner persistently repeats a certain kind of *a*normative behavior, then my performance in regard to this specific behavior must have been similarly *a*normative or insufficiently normative and persistent to serve its reflective modeling purpose. My correction of this behavior should reverse the process, for unlike modeling, emulation is a two-directional mirroring process. Indeed, Yaacov Yosef (p. 259) interprets the verse "who is a wise man? He who learns from everybody" (M. Ab. 4:1) by using the mirror metaphor (about two hundred years before Charles Cooley) by noting: "A wise man is the one who learns from everybody like someone that looks in the mirror and knows his own faults by seeing the faults of his fellow man."

A common example of such mutual self-correction is when a teacher suddenly lowers his voice to bring attention to the fact that both he and his students have been shouting over one another's heads. A similar example involves a parent who notices a child eating in an unmannerly way while important guests are present. Rather than reprimand the child in front of the visitors, the parent corrects his or her own eating habits in the hope that the child will emulate that behavior. Mutual-emulation via double-mirroring, by contrast, occurs in a case, for instance, in which a father or politician preaches observance of rules such as traffic laws or honest reporting of one's income. If the child or follower indeed corrects his driving or tax reporting, the father or politician may in turn be forced to adhere to his own preaching and to correct a second time a behavior that, at first, he may not in fact have been that concerned about at all.

Indeed, in a research project that compared various clinical supervision methods in family psychotherapy it was found that therapists' self-corrections (enacted according to instructions received via earphones) were enhanced (corrected twice) when the person treated improved his conduct via emulation that functioned as a mirror for the therapist.

**The Superpersonal "PaRDeS" Psychology:** If a consensus could be established that at one time or another, and especially during periods of crisis and uncontrollable predicaments, all people have a need to communicate with the transcendental world of metaphysics, then the ecstatic experience should be conceived as the major means for bridging the natural and the super-natural worlds. The term *ex-stasis*, meaning to stand outside oneself, is known among students of mysticism as *unio mystica*, which refers to an effort of the soul to depart from the body in order to unite with a higher divine entity.

Since the process of the soul's departure from the body encompasses on the one hand the human perception of the death experience while on the other hand it comprises a state of exaltation, our discussion of the superpersonal dimension will be divided into two sections:

   a) The first will present the Jewish "PaR-DeS" as a psychological bridge between people's material-rational world of *Peshat* ("surface meaning") and the mystic-irrational language of the Kabbalistic *Sod* (mystical meaning), which may help them to deal with unexpected calamities and their fear of death.
   b) The second section introduces the ecstatic bridge between the energy producing *yet-zer* (sexual drive) and the super-material state of *yetzira* (spiritual creativity), which encompasses the mental experience of attaining the muse or the exuberant feeling of romantic love.

Together, these two sections concern the preventative-immunizing aspect of dealing with the irrational fear of death or inexplicable personal predicaments and the possibility of reaching ineffable elated experiences of mental inspirations.

**Ecstasy for experiencing mystic "Sod":** To present the Jewish concept of "PaRDeS" (which will be explained below) as a psychological bridge between the rational-material world and the irrational supernatural world of the unknown, let us pose the following rhetorical questions: If Max Weber is correct that since the rise of Protestantism in the sixteenth century we are witnessing in the West the gradual predominance of rational, calculated thinking as a sole criteria and evidence for salvation and divine election, then is it not plausible that socialization would aim to inculcate only the language of rationality? Likewise, if Michel Foucault (*Madness and Civilization*, New York, 1967, p. X) is correct that until the Renaissance "madness and non-madness, reason and non-reason are inextricably involved: inseparable," while "the end of the eighteenth century affords the evidence of a broken dialogue . . . in which the exchange between madness and monologue of reason about madness has been established only on the basis of such a silence," then has not Protestantism indeed banned the irrational thought system? Consequently, if Western Protestantism has excluded the mystic-irrational language from its text, what happens to people's eternal irrational fears of the transcendental unknown and the unexpected unrationalizable predicaments that will forever haunt people in our "imperfect world," as Weber posited?

Now, since ecstatic-mysticism was not banned by Jews, Eastern Shamanists, and pre-Protestant Westerners, our next query could be the nature of the Jewish impact, if any, on conceptions of the ecstatic *unio mystica* experience, which was perceived as the attempt of the soul to depart from the body. To begin with, it is of interest to point out that Michael Screech (*Erasmus: Ecstasy and the Praise of Folly*, London, 1988, p. 49), for example, who studied Erasmus' classic pre-Protestant *Praise of Folly*, stresses that "for centuries before Erasmus, ecstasy had come to mean the state of a Christian who had been raptured outside himself, his soul 'leaving his body' in the process." Screech emphasizes nonetheless that Christian notions of ecstasy owe their understanding not only to Platonic thought but also to Jewish scholars, such as the first century philosopher Philo, whose writings were highly influential in shaping the Greco-Western formulations of ecstasy. One example, Philo's interpretation of God's "leading Abraham outside" (Who is the Heir 76-85), will suffice:

He led him outside and said "Look up into heaven" (Gen. 15:5). . . . [He led him] outside of the prison-houses of the body, of the lairs where the senses lurk, of the sophistries of the deceitful word and thought; above all He led him out of himself, out of the belief that he thought and apprehended through intelligence which acknowledged no other authority and owed no allegiance to any other than itself.

Following the brief accounts of the nature of ecstatic *unio mystica*, construction of a theory that construes ecstasy as a psychological bridge between the natural and the supernatural worlds could be accomplished only by using rational terms to expound irrational experiences, such as fear of death, because our present psychological orientation is by definition rational. Accordingly, the analogy of the immunization procedure against physical epidemics may be applied to portray ecstatic exercises as immunizations against the fear of death on the metaphysical level.

Thus, if the prescription against the possible contraction of a disease in the physical world requires the introjection of small doses of bacteria, which are presumed to cause a specific disease so that the human organism will develop natural antibodies against the illness under consideration, the same process may be envisioned on a metaphysical level. If ecstatic *unio mystica* is perceived in experiential terms that simulate the death experience, during which the soul presumably leaves the body, then the experiencing of doses of "temporary death" may be perceived as an immunization against the fear of permanent death. On a clinical level this means a reversal of a principle practiced by behavioral therapists. Instead of asking people to accompany an imagined experience of phobia with relaxation exercises, they are instructed to experience a guided state of ecstasy following their imagined fear of death simulation. Indeed, in *Dialogue with Deviance*, my study of the psychosocial dynamics of kabbalistic Hasidism, I interpret the famous Hasidic notion of descent for the sake of ascent as a desensitizing immunization device. I suggest, accordingly, that one may understand Hasidic normative prescriptions as instructions for overcoming depression or the feeling of failure. Thus the Besht states, for example, that the verse "'There is no righteous man on earth who will do good without sinning' (Eccl. 7:20) [means] that when a person does only good the evil impulse seduces him, whereas when the evil impulse realizes that he has in him a part of the evil inclination, he will leave him alone." The prescription against the disease of temptation described by the Besht is thus portrayed as a straightforward immunization manual that may be read as follows: Consume or inject a small dose of germs (e.g., anti-evil impulse germs) that cause the disease that threatens to contaminate you, and your organism will develop natural antibodies against the illness under consideration.

Moreover, the kabbalistic-Hasidic immunization model may be expanded now to include a variety of irrational experiences. Thus, acquiring the irrational language of mystic *Sod* may be instrumental in preventing permanent psychotic detachments from reality. If individuals encounter stress, disaster, or manic joy, for instance, they need not be overly alarmed if they are allowed to understand their resultant experiences (delusions or hearing voices) either in the rational language of reason or in the mystic language of unreason, which they learned to master in the course of their socialization.

Nonetheless, a Cartesian linguistic model will be of little help to the modern person unless a linking dimension is available to enable the bridging between such rational and irrational thought systems. This linking dimension may be found in the Jewish multifaceted interpretative system known as PaRDeS. The etymological history of the concept PaRDeS is insignificant, but it is important to know that the term refers generally to the concept that the Torah and other sacred texts may be interpreted on four levels or, rather, according to four different thought systems: P(*eshat*) ("simple") stands for the simple, straightforward, literal and rational meaning of a verse, which could be understood as going by the written letter. R(*emez*) ("implication") refers to the philosophical truth inherent in an allegoric or symbolic meaning of a word, derived either by reading the word or several words as an abbreviation of other words, by breaking a word into its constituent elements, or by recombining the letters of the word into a new word in order to derive a new meaning. D*(erash)* ("search," "interpret") refers to the narrative and ethical interpretation of a word or paragraph by using an analogic story and parable or by using any other method that activates the imagination to expand, broaden, or change the meaning of the text according to traditional midrashic methods. S*(od)* ("secret") refers to specific texts that include mystical-irrational interpretations of the scripture according to prestructured paradigms as outlined, for instance, in Kabbalistic books. For our psychotherapeutic purposes, PaRDeS may be conceived as a threefold scheme in which one may incorporate *remez* under the general heading of *derash*, because, on the one hand, it means literally "hint or allusion," which pertains to mystic *sod*, and, on the other hand, in actual usage it comprises specific narrative and hermeneutic techniques.

From the present psychological perspective, let us demonstrate that, by incorporating the mystic language of *Sod* as a normative interpretation outlet, the "PaRDeS" provides a psychotherapeutic bridge between the rational and irrational worlds. In practical terms this means that if a frightened person rushes to a psychotherapist because he or she heard the voice of or was persecuted by Satan, the therapist could say, "Relax! You will not be excommunicated as a schizophrenic, for we have a normative bridging system that legitimizes the alternating use of the rational *Peshat* interpretation and the mystical *Sod* language." Accordingly, this therapist might then proceed to help our frightened "patient" by using Job's dialogue with God, which ended in God's justifying and compensating Job, or by using kabbalistic or midrashic paradigms for normalizing the hearing of voices.

The predominate efforts to use ecstatic and other mystical experiences appear to have been geared towards energizing and nourishing the mind. A classical case involves Joseph Karo, the sixteenth-century author of the monumental Jewish legal code book, the *Shulchan Aruch*, who communicated with an angel, called by him the *Maggid*, apparently in order to energize his intellectual system. However, insofar as Abraham Abulafia, the thirteenth-century father of ecstatic mysticism, advocated the use of *devekut* (the Hebrew term for *unio mystica*) for attaining prophecy by portraying this ecstatic experience in erotic terms, this is the place for moving to our final account of how sexual ecstasy may function as an energizing bridge for reaching superpersonal spirituality.

**Ecstasy for reaching spiritual creativity:** Michael Screech (p. XVII) has already indicated "how powerful a contribution Plato had made to the doctrines of ecstasy with his teachings in the *Phaedrus* about the divine forms of madness which produce prophets, poets and lovers." Plato's all embracing observation that ecstasy produces prophets, poets, and lovers may in fact be understood as the natural other side of perceiving ecstasy in terms of an immunizing procedure against the fear of death. If by consuming "temporary death" in small doses one learns to control the fear of a permanent death, then it is only logical that the sexual act, which produces life, may be attained via a similar ecstatic experience.

The notion that *devekut* (*unio mystica*) represents two opposites—a temporary death and the life producing experience of sexual ecstasy—might now be better understood by considering how the Kabbalah tackled the affinity between life and death. In the kabbalistic literature the idea of death by a kiss (*mitat neshika*) is so taken for granted and deeply established that it does not require further qualification and documentation. Indeed, in the kabbalistic literature, the soul's departure from the body, which occurs in the process of dying, is often termed life (*chayim*), and consequently the ecstatic experiences of sexual orgasm and "dying" appear almost as synonymous terms, because both are described in the anthropomorphic terms of the sexual union. As a matter of fact, the first reference in the Torah to the term *devekut* as a verb explicates the natural drive for matrimonial sexuality: "Therefore shall a man leave his father and his mother, and shall cleave (*vedavak*) unto his wife: and they shall be one flesh" (Gen. 2:24). Hence, the prescribed sexual cleaving (*vedavak*) unto one's wife entails also the idea of separation and union according to the biblical command to "be one flesh," which concurs with the required procedure for attaining *unio mystica* or *devekut*. Thus, the soul's separation from the body or man's separation from his parents in order to cleave to his wife or to God symbolize the meeting point between life and death.

The enigmatic declaration "love is strong as death" (Cant. 8:6) thus may be better understood by interpreting it in light of another statement, "But ye that did cleave unto the Lord . . . are alive" (Deut. 4:4), suggesting that those who know the secret of cleaving (*devekut*) know the secret of life. Sigmund Freud was accordingly on the right track in signifying the sexual drive as a pivotal life producing parameter. It seems doubtful however whether the physician Freud succeeded in breaking open the chains imposed on him by the nineteenth century's over emphasis on the natural sciences in order to incorporate also the spiritual dimension emanating from the sexual energy.

One need only to follow Freud's own definition of neurosis as a mechanical disability to discharge the tension reducing sexual drive to realize that he defined sexuality exclusively in motoric instinctual terms. When Freud (*General Psychological Theory*, New York, 1963, p. 180) states that "the . . . neuroses . . . came about by sexual instinctual impulses being rejected" and when he subsequently adds (p. 186), "All our analyses go to show that the . . . neuroses originate from the ego's refusing to accept a powerful instinctual impulse existing in the *id* and denying it motor discharge" (p. 186), he reflects an unequivocally narrow physiological model of sexuality.

It seems needless to reiterate here what has been claimed so often, that according to Freud's narrow instinctual theory of sexuality, spiritual creativity must be understood as a gloomy sublimated neurotic result of one's incapacity to satisfy his tension reducing need for sexual discharge. Silvano Arieti (*Creativ-* *ity: The Magic Synthesis*, New York, 1976, p. 22), an internationally recognized authority on psychopathology, has for example attacked Freud's formulation of creativity as follows:

> The concept of sublimation or diversion of sexual energy from the original aim plays an important role in Freud's concept of creativity. Thus, when sexual energy is not spent in the proper sexual activity, it is displaced and invested in pursuits, like the creative, which do not seem to be related to sex. The creative person is a frustrated individual who cannot find fulfillment in sexual gratification or other aspects of life and who therefore attempts to find it in creativity. In contrast to Freud's view, however, the biographies of many gifted people who also had a rich sexual life seem to contradict such assumptions.

Concomitant with Arieti's position, Anthony Storr (*The Dynamics of Creation*, Tel Aviv, 1983) cites a psychoanalytic study that describes Van Gogh's creativity as an attempt to sublimate his conflicting inner torments that presumably evolved from his compulsive masturbation and frustrated sexuality. Consequently, Storr asks ironically whether we would have lost Van Gogh's artistic contribution if he would have gone through a successful process of psychoanalysis.

Although Freud's theory of sexuality is intricate, from the present perspective it is significant that he joined with other western scholars who pointed a blaming finger at the Christian religion as the "bedrock" for western neurotic repressed and oppressed sexuality. Since Judaism as such never repressed sexuality or spiritual mysticism, our focus on the *yetzer-yetzira* sequence as a broader sexual paradigm that incorporates the possibility for reaching super natural ecstatic creativity becomes highly significant.

While the Jewish psycho-philosophy of sexuality is complex, a brief presentation will suffice to demonstrate how the physical sexual drive, *yetzer*, may nourish the spiritual creative *yetzira*. Etymologically, the Hebrew words *yetzer*, referring to the physical drive or sexual impulse, and *yetzira*, literally meaning creation and creativity, are derived from the same root. It is, however, the multiple use of this term that demonstrates how the sexual physical union provides a structural model for the broader union between the *yetzer* and the *yetzira*. Thus, the word *zur*, which means rock or hard stone, is linked to the word *zura*, meaning *form*, in a way that comprises the essence of the relationships that, according to the philosophers, are to prevail between form and matter.

In *The Guide of the Perplexed*, the twelfth century Jewish philosopher Maimonides used, for example, a passage from Isaiah to indicate how the sexual union must be understood as a paradigm for the broader creative notions associated with the terms *form* and *matter*. Isaiah stated: "Look unto the rock [*zur*] from which you were hown, and to the quarry from which you were digged. Look to Abraham your father and to Sarah who bore you" (Is. 51:1-2).

Because the term *zur* is also used as a verb, *yatzar* (to form), we find also at Is. 43:7 a reference to God's creation of the human species: "And whom I have created for my glory, if have formed [*yetzartiv*] him, yea, I have made him." Accordingly, David Bakan's conclusion (*Maimonides on Prophecy*, Northvale, 1991) appears plausible that, in order to understand the sexual that is brought to mind as an allegory of a greater principle, "Maimonides thus seeks . . . to raise it to being a matter of the relationship between form and matter, with Abraham contributing the form, and Sarah contributing the matter" (p. 84). If we add the terms *yetzur*, referring to the human being, and the term *zir*, meaning pivot, we have indeed an all-engulfing model of creativity that unifies the physical and spiritual under the roof of one term. A person needs his or her *yetzer*, the drive that he or she may use freely and willingly as a *zir* (pivot) for infinite possibilities of *yetzira* (spiritual creativity or *ziyur* [painting]), for without these components he or she is not a *yetzur*—a human being.

Indeed, a classical aphorism that urges people to keep their sexual drive alive is cited in the name of the late thirteenth century Kabbalist Isaac of Acre, who declared that "a person who does not desire [or who has not longed for] a woman is lower than a *chamor* [donkey]."[15] The word *chamor* sym-

bolizes *chomer*—that is, materiality—and the implication is that such a person lacks the spiritual component of desire. This anti-repressive imperative, claimed Isaac of Acre, is only the first step in reaching the level of spiritual creativity. To inculcate how the sexual desire of *yetzer* may be channeled, he used the popular tale about a street corner idler whose desire for a princess he saw coming out of a bathhouse turned into spiritual passion. More specifically, when the idler attempted a pass at the princess, she responded by stating, "In the cemetery that thing will take place." Accordingly, the idler's experience of desire while waiting in the cemetery for the princess who never showed up turned presumably into spiritual passion.

Thus, the idea that the *yetzer* as "physical desire" (*cheshek gufani*) should be neither repressed nor fully expressed but contracted so that the *yetzira*, "spiritual desire" (*cheshek ruchani*), may expand became practically a folk psychology that for hundreds of years exerted its canonical impact on all Jewish and some non-Jewish ethical systems. The *yetzer-yetzira* sequence was inculcated to keep the *yetzer* alive by popular teachings such as one that emphasizes that, "were it not for the *yetzer hara* (evil), a person would not build a house and would not marry, procreate, and . . . deal in business" (Gen. Rab. 9:7).

Its psychotherapeutic applicability may be recognized in such cases as that of Mr. E.,[16] a lawyer diagnosed as a schizophrenic, who was able to maintain a steady job by interpreting his revived sexual fantasies as spiritual energizers. Thus, the *yetzer* as an energizer for the spiritual *yetzira* concurs with the Kabbalistic idea that emotional-ecstatic activities should nourish and enhance the intellectual-spiritual possibility of creativity but never control it.

**Conclusion:** The semantic association between the physical *yetzer* and the spiritual *yetzira* epitomizes the essence of the Jewish psycho-philosophy that is grounded in a search for a dialogical co-existence between matter and form. While the terms *yetzer, devekut, daat* (copulating and knowing), *mila* (phallus and word), and *arel* (uncircumcised) encompass both the sexual-physical and the spiritual-metaphysical reality, this dialogic relationship refers to all four psychological dimensions presented in this essay.

Accordingly, a coherent total identity may be reestablished by reorganizing the psychological co-existence between one's incorporeal past (ancestors and auto-biography) and one's corporeal present. And likewise the psychological well being may be maintained via the interpersonal co-existence between the material *Zebuluns* and the spiritual *Isaachars* much the same as the *yetzer-yetzira* continuum may preserve the intrapersonal balance between carnality and spirituality.

### Bibliography

Rotenberg, Mordechai, *Damnation and Deviance* (New York, 1978).

Rotenberg, Mordechai, *Dia-Logo Therapy: Psychonarration and PaRDeS* (New York, 1991).

Rotenberg, Mordechai, *Dialogue with Deviance* (Philadelphia, 1983).

Rotenberg, Mordechai, *Re-Biographing and Deviance* (New York, 1987).

Rotenberg, Mordechai, *The "Yetzer": A Kabalistic Psychology of Eroticism and Human Sexuality* (Northvale, 1997).

### Notes

[1] See C.S. Hall and G. Lindzey, *Theories of Personality* (New York, 1970), p. 4.

[2] "The Use of Folklore as a Developmental Phenomenon in Nouveau-Orthodox Religions," in *The American Journal of Psychoanalysis* 42(2), 1982, pp. 149-158.

[3] M. Spero, *Religious Objects as Psychological Structures* (Chicago, 1992), p. 111.

[4] See G. Bateson, *Steps to an Ecology of Mind*, New York, 1972.

[5] M. Zipor, "*Al gilguleyhen shel derashat 'Altikrei,'*" in Y. Refael, ed., *Yovel Sinai* (Jerusalem, 1987).

[6] The latter, according to Otto Rank's much neglected important work on the incest theme (1912), "was declared by most researchers as the Christian interpretation (formulation) of the Oedipus fable" (p. 143). It appears in Jacobus de Voragine's *Golden Legend* (1941).

[7] M. Ben Yechezkel, *Sefer Hamasiot*, vol. 4 (Tel-Aviv, 1951).

[8] S. Shpiegel, "*Meagadot Haaqeda*," in *Sefer Hayovel Le A. Marks* (New York, 1950).

[9] "Protecting the Federal Witness," in *American Behavioral Scientist* 27(4), 1984, pp. 501-528.

[10] Maimonides, *Teshuva* 2:1, applies this designation to circumstances in which, even given the opportunity, one does not again sin as one previously had.

[11] See W. Iser, *The Act of Reading* (Baltimore, 1978).

[12] See M. Beer, "Issachar and Zebulun" in *Bar-Ilan Year Book* (Ramat Gan, 1968).

[13] See M. Rotenberg, *Dialogue with Deviance* (Philadelphia, 1983), p. 124.

[14] See A. Bandura, *Principles of Behavior Modification* (New York, 1969) and C.H. Cooley, *Human Nature and Social Order* (New York, 1902).

[15] Quoted in Pierkarz, *The Beginning of Hasidism* (Tel Aviv and Jerusalem, 1978), p. 209.

[16] See M. Rotenberg, *Dia-Logo Therapy: Psychonarration and PaRDeS* (New York, 1991) and *The "Yetzer": A Kabalistic Psychology of Eroticism and Human Sexuality* (Northvale, 1997).

MORDECHAI ROTENBERG

**PURITY AND IMPURITY IN JUDAISM:** In Classical Judaism, purity (*tohorah*) and uncleanness (*tum'ah*) carry forward Pentateuchal commandments that the holy people, Israel, when eating, procreating, and worshiping God in the Temple, is to avoid certain sources of contamination. The principal one of these is the corpse (Num. 19). Lev. 11, further, catalogues foods that are clean and those that are unclean; Israelites eat the former, not the latter. Lev. 12 goes over the uncleanness that results from childbirth; Lev. 13-14 deal with a skin-ailment that Scripture deems analogous to the condition of the corpse; and Lev. 15 discusses the uncleanness of the woman in her menstrual period and analogous uncleanness brought about by excretions other than in the menstrual period of a woman and counterpart excretions from the flaccid penis.

In the Pentateuch uncleanness affects the conduct of three activities: eating, procreation, and attendance at the Temple. When the priests ate their priestly rations, they were to do so in a condition of cultic cleanness. Furthermore, all Israelites were to abstain from unclean foods and from sexual relations during a woman's menstrual period or when affected by the uncleanness of the sexual organs to which Lev. 15 makes allusion. All Israelites also were to become clean to participate in the Temple cult, which would affect many at the time of the pilgrim festivals, Passover, Pentecost, and Tabernacles. In addition, among the Judaisms that flourished before 70 C.E. when the Temple was destroyed, some groups, such as the Pharisees, the Essenes, and some represented by law codes found in the Dead Sea Scrolls, kept the rules of cultic purity in eating food at home, not in the Temple, a practice that did not characterize the bulk of the communities of Judaism. After 70, when attaining cleanness to participate in the cult no longer pertained, uncleanness-rules governing food and sexual relations continued to apply, as they do in Judaism to the present day. But in matters of public worship it was the Temple, not the synagogue, to which considerations of cleanness pertained, and no one would refrain from attending synagogue worship by reason of having contracted uncleanness, e.g., having attended a funeral and so contracted corpse-uncleanness.

The Mishnah, ca. 200 C.E., the principal legal document of Judaism beyond Scripture, greatly amplifies the definition of what is affected by uncleanness, how uncleanness is transmitted, and the way in which uncleanness is removed. The Mishnah's Division of Purities treats the interplay of persons, food, and liquids. Dry inanimate objects or food are not susceptible to uncleanness (Lev. 11:34, 37). But what is wet is susceptible, so that liquids activate the system. What is unclean, moreover, emerges from uncleanness through the operation of liquids, specifically, through immersion in fit water of requisite volume and in natural condition. Liquids thus also deactivate the system, with water in its natural condition concluding the process by removing uncleanness. The uncleanness of persons, furthermore, is signified by body liquids or flux in the case of the menstruating woman (Niddah) and the *Zab* (Zabim). Corpse uncleanness is conceived to be a kind of effluent, a viscous gas, which flows like a liquid. Utensils for their part receive uncleanness when they form receptacles able to contain liquid. So the invisible flow of fluid-like substances or powers serves to put food, drink, and receptacles into the status of uncleanness and to remove those things from that status. Thus, in material terms, the effect of liquid is upon food, drink, utensils, and humans. The consequence has to do with who may eat and drink what food and liquid and what food and drink may be consumed in which pots and pans. These loci are speci-

fied by tractates on utensils (Kelim) and on food and drink (Tohorot and Uqsin).

In Judaism, overall, what is unclean is abnormal and disruptive of the economy of nature, and what is clean is normal and constitutive of the economy and the wholeness of nature. What is unclean is restored to a condition of cleanness through the activity of nature, unimpeded by human intervention, in removing the uncleanness, through the natural force of water collected in its original state. Accordingly, if to be clean is normal, then it is that state of normality that is restored by natural processes themselves. So to be unclean is abnormal and is the result of what was deemed to be unnatural processes: death, menstrual blood, flux of blood outside of the menstrual cycle, and a flow from the penis outside of the normal reproductive process. Procreation and sustenance of life define what is at stake in the condition of cleanness, en route to the state of sanctification, as in the hierarchical statement of Pinhas b. Yair at M. Sot. 9:15:

> R. Pinhas b. Yair says, "Heedfulness leads to cleanliness, cleanliness leads to cleanness, cleanness leads to abstinence [*perishut*, a.k.a., Pharisaism], abstinence leads to holiness, holiness leads to modesty, modesty leads to the fear of sin, the fear of sin leads to piety, piety leads to the Holy Spirit, the Holy Spirit leads to the resurrection of the dead, and the resurrection of the dead comes through Elijah, blessed be his memory, Amen."

Uncleanness and sanctification form opposites, because the one stands for death, the other, the predisposition, the preparation, for eternal life.

**The impurity of bodily excretions:** In the halakhah of the Oral Torah we deal with semen or vaginal blood that cannot carry out the purpose that by nature the one or the other realizes, which is participation in the process of procreating life. Such nonproductive semen, such vaginal flow outside of the normal cycle of procreation—these violate their own innate teleology. They do so on their own, not by man's or woman's intervention. Of such violations of the natural law and the purposive definition of the media of procreation, the Israelite has to take heed. Man or woman cannot generate by an act of deliberation an unclean body fluid, whether genital semen or genital blood, which is deemed unclean only if it flows naturally, nor can they form by an act of will a source of uncleanness represented by the corpse or the dead creeping thing. Were we to simplify matters and say, as to what contracts uncleanness, humanity disposes, but as to what imparts uncleanness, nature imposes, we should not be far off the mark.

Of the animate sources of uncleanness, the person afflicted with the skin ailment is the only one for whom the sexual organs do not define the source and focus of uncleanness. But such a person proves interstitial, since he or she is like the corpse but not wholly so. The exegetical fulcrum of the halakhah governing animate sources of uncleanness is indicated, then, by the comparison of the animate to the inanimate, persons who produce uncleanness to the corpse that produces uncleanness. The comparison of corpse-matter to flux, then, provides a governing analogy for our interpretation of the matter, and, as usual, the halakhah itself identifies the focus of analogical-contrastive thinking and spells out its result. But we have gotten ahead of our story.

The *Zab* and *Zabah* of Lev. 15 transmit uncleanness to that on which they sit or lie, even though they do not touch the chair or bed. So we shall wonder what is special about the bed and comparable objects that subjects those objects to a particular kind of uncleanness, transmitting in a quite distinctive way: using those objects for the purpose for which they are manufactured. That classification of uncleanness, called *midras*- or pressure-uncleanness, pertains only to objects that ordinary are used to bear weight or pressure, that is, beds and chairs and things analogous to them. The halakhah of Kelim shows that objects not used for sitting or lying, e.g., pots and pans, are not susceptible to the *midras*-uncleanness transmitted by a *Zab* or a *Zabah*. And that is a severe uncleanness, comparable to the corpse-uncleanness that affects receptacles and persons, requiring a period of seven days in which the source of uncleanness does not renew itself, on the

one side, and a rite of purification in the Temple, on the other. Accordingly, in Zabim we deal with the animate form of uncleanness that falls into the classification of the counterpart inanimate form, that is, *zob* (flux) compares with corpse-matter, the *Zab* or the *Zabah* with the corpse. And, as the logic of the halakhah requires, the media of dissemination will prove comparable as well.

The inanimate and the animate sources of uncleanness bear each its own distinctive traits as well. While the former, the corpse, constitutes a Father of Fathers of uncleanness, turning what touches it into a Father of uncleanness, the latter is a mere Father of uncleanness, and what touches it is in the first remove of uncleanness. Then the process is simple. Once the mere pressure of the *Zab* or *Zabah* has sufficed to transmit uncleanness to something used for lying or sitting, and the chair or bed imparts uncleanness to one who touches it, it has rendered such a one unclean in the first remove, and then the clothing of such a person is unclean in the second remove. How further does an animate source of uncleanness affect others in a way in which a corpse or a dead creeping thing does not? The spit of such a person conveys uncleanness, as much as does his touch (contact), as much as does his pressure or weight to the object or person bearing that weight.

The purification process for the person afflicted with flux-uncleanness takes seven days, just as does the purification process of a person who is a Father of uncleanness by reason of contact with a corpse. Immersion now is required, and the uncleanness passes at sunset.

The rules of the matter to this point derive mainly from Scripture. The relevant verses are, first, Lev. 12:1-8, for the woman after childbirth, then Lev. 15:1-33, encompassing in a single statement both the flux (*zob*) of the *Zab* and the *Zabah*, and semen and menstrual blood, that is, excretions of the sexual organs that do not, and that do, pertain to the cycle of procreation, the former breaking, the latter establishing, that cycle. At Lev. 12:1-8 we have vaginal blood that for seven or fourteen days is deemed unclean in the classification of menstrual blood and then for thirty-three or sixty-six days is deemed altogether clean. The important point to note is that vaginal blood is not always deemed a mark of uncleanness. But, we also notice, a rite of purification is required for the vaginal flow that is classified as unclean. So in that regard—the cultic purification-rite—the woman after childbirth is comparable to the *Zabah* and not to the woman who has menstruated, so Lev. 15:1-33. Scripture's point of emphasis throughout is on three matters, [1] the character of the discharge that signifies flux-uncleanness; [2] the effects of the status of uncleanness: objects that are subject to uncleanness; and [3] how the uncleanness is transmitted; and the mode of purification and attendant cultic rite signifying the regaining of the normal status of cleanness. The variable that will guide us concerns whether a woman is excluded from, or included within, the procreative cycle. If her vaginal flow does not remove her from acts of procreation (in fact or at least in theory), then no purification-rite is called for; if she is utterly excluded from the process, then it is. The *Zabah*, it is assumed, simply cannot become pregnant and will not engage in sexual relations; the Torah makes no provision for that possibility. The menstruating woman may find herself in a situation in which, inadvertently, she has sexual relations during her period, with the consequence for her mate that he enters her status as to uncleanness.

The contribution of the Oral Torah in the articulation of these facts proves not only formidable but intellectually fructifying, as sages explore the teleology embedded in Scripture's statement. Whether sages have penetrated into the logic inherent in the Written Torah, or whether they have brought to bear a set of considerations all their own in re-framing the inherited Torah into the dense and subtle formation that they set forth, remains to be seen. It suffices to say at the outset that here, as everywhere, the halakhah shows itself to constitute a tight and extremely cogent system, everywhere cognizant of its own pervasive rationality.

**The Halakhah of Zabim:** What classification of animate beings produces *zob*, that is, contaminating flux from the genitals? What is that *zob*? And how is such *zob* produced? These are the critical questions that the Oral Torah undertakes to answer.

The first question is answered through the intersection of the Mishnah's and the Tosefta's rule. The entire system of differentiated sources and effects of uncleanness that envelops the household and classifies its food, clothing, utensils and furniture as clean and cult-worthy or unclean and not pertains only to Israel and forms a vast system that realizes in the details of the here and now the sanctification of Israel. The Tosefta makes that statement in its own laconic language: All are susceptible to uncleanness through flux, even converts, even slaves, whether freed or not freed, a deaf-mute, imbecile, or minor, a eunuch by castration and a eunuch by nature. Gentiles and the convert and the resident alien are not susceptible to uncleanness through flux. That is because the gentiles form a vast undifferentiated world, unclean with corpse-uncleanness by nature, a realm of death; gentiles' uncleanness is inherent. So when it comes to the uncleanness of the *Zabah* and the *Zab*, we deal only with Israelites. And, given the nature of *zob*—a genital excretion—we deal with Israelites in the household in particular, in their normal, licit marital relationships.

Let us answer the second question, What is that *zob*? It is, in the case of a male, semen emitted by a flaccid penis, and, in the case of a female, blood emitted by the genitals not during the established menstrual period. So, as usual, the system of sanctification and uncleanness forms an exercise in classification: semen and blood, like food and drink and clothing and furniture, may fall into one or another taxon, as circumstances defined by nature dictate.

And what differentiates semen classified as unclean in a minor way from the semen deemed to fall into the category of *zob*? The answer is made explicit—again by the Tosefta—as follows: And what is the difference between flux and semen? Flux comes from a limp penis, and semen from an erection. The uncleanness that results from a healthy ejaculation, meaning, one that at least potentially can accomplish its purpose, procreation, is routine and minor, as Scripture states explicitly, and as M. Zab. 5:11 recapitulates: One who has had a seminal emission is like one who has touched a dead creeping thing. Purification then requires mere immersion and sunset, nothing more. By contrast, one confirmed as a *Zab* or *Zabah* undergoes a purification rite comparable to that required after corpse-uncleanness, a seven-day period, immersion, then an offering on the eighth day—a considerable difference. The key is the imputation of a seven-day process of purification, guaranteeing that the victim has fully recovered from his affliction. When *zob* can realize its teleologically-dictated purpose, it is unclean in a minor way. But when it violates that teleology, it is unclean in the league of a corpse.

Who or what differentiates between the teleologically-valid semen (that capable of impregnating a woman) and semen deemed invalid *zob*? This question is answered with equal clarity: *zob* of either male (semen) or female (blood) comes about solely by nature; it cannot derive from an extrinsic cause of the flow of semen, let alone from his own engagement. If a man ejaculated after eating, drinking, jumping, or fantasizing, this is not unclean semen in the category of *zob*. Physical or psychological causes may produce a flow of semen, but that semen does not qualify as *zob*. So in *Zabim* we deal with Israelites who produce genital flux through no activity of their own. It is nature's own flawed semen, semen that violates its own teleology. Man cannot bring it about by an act of will, any more than by an act of will he turns himself into a source of corpse-uncleanness, releasing his soul to contaminate until contained.

The halakhah of the Oral Torah contributes fundamental considerations to the definition of uncleanness deriving from the sexual parts. Scripture speaks of a man's discharge; the halakhah wants such a discharge to take place on three successive days or in three ample, distinct flows even on one day. When it comes to flux of a woman, the halakhah likewise concerns itself with three such appearances on three successive days; only then is the matter confirmed. The consequent, abundant possibilities of doubt preoccupy sages. Much of the law concerns itself with interstitial cases of one kind or another.

**The woman:** A flow of vaginal blood may bear diverse significations; it may be menstrual blood, it may be *zibah*-blood, and it may be natural blood. Blood that flows during a regularly-established period is classified as menstrual. Blood that flows in the eleven days between periods—called *zibah*-days—is classified as *zob*, hence *zibah*-days' blood. Now, if blood appears on one of the eleven *zibah*-days, what is the consequence? The woman immerses in the evening. Then she has to wait out the next day to make sure that there is no further flow of blood. If there is none, she is clean and permitted to have sexual relations with her husband. If there are appearances of blood on the three successive days during the period of the *zibah*-days, the woman is classified as a *Zabah*. In both cases—differentiated menstrual- or *zibah*-blood—the consequence, uncleanness, is the same.

Much of the law pursues the question of ambiguous data on the matter. That is the way of the halakhah in general. What is at stake is the woman's status as to procreation. If she is established as unclean for her period, then, after the period, for the next eleven days, she is permitted to have sexual relations, until the advent of the next regular period. If the blood flows during the *zibah*-days, however, then an irregular flow, from day to day, prevents her from participating in the procreative process, and that exclusion from normal sexual relations, by reason of the intermittent, irregular flow, may continue for a long time. So the distinction between menstrual- and *zob*-blood makes a great difference. By the latter the woman is marked as not a fit vehicle for procreation.

**The man:** A flow of semen from the flaccid penis forms the counterpart to the vaginal flux of the woman. He who sees semen does not become susceptible to uncleanness by flux for twenty-four hours. One such flow does not establish uncleanness, three on successive days do. The issues must be separate and distinct from one another but need not appear on different days. Questions therefore arise when "clean days," that is, days on which no flux makes an appearance, intervene between days of flux. But the Torah also treats as unclean the flow of semen from the erect penis, though it is uncleanness in a different classification. The former uncleanness persists; it yields contamination through pressure, not only contact; only when the discharge stops for a week is the man clean, and then a rite of purification is required. But contrast, an emission of semen in the normal manner produces uncleanness removed through immersion and sunset. So we need to differentiate the relationship of semen to flux. Then we face the sequence of interstitial cases—not clean, but not confirmed as unclean—that the details of the law address. Here again, a man who produces semen not in the normal framework of the reproductive life is excluded from the procreative process. The *Zab* and the *Zabah* belong to holy Israel, but nature removes them from the natural processes by which the sanctity of Israel is propagated.

**The media for transmitting uncleanness:** The special medium, pressure, that transmits the uncleanness of the sexual organs matches the way by which those organs realize their teleology. As sexual activity takes place through not only making contact or touching but also exerting pressure—the penis upon the vagina bringing about procreative ejaculation—so uncleanness is transmitted through not only contact but also pressure, specifically, to objects bearing the weight of a person afflicted with the uncleanness of flux. Since sexual activity commonly takes place where people lie, objects used for lying (and, concomitantly, for sitting) are susceptible to the pressure-uncleanness of the sexually-based sources of uncleanness. So a fully-realized logic governs.

But how to sort out the diverse media that take effect for the dissemination of diverse, differentiated sources of uncleanness? The halakhah forms the ideal instrument for acute, systematic differentiation, through analogical-contrastive logic, between and among things that are both alike and not alike. And, as usual, the framers of the authorita-

tive statement of the law, the Mishnah, provide a systematic statement of the matter. That brings us to the exquisite exposition of the halakhah that is provided by *Zabim* Chapter Five. There we deal with the means for transferring uncleanness, direct contact, pressure, carrying, shifting, and overshadowing. Of these modes, it is the last item that is of special interest, because it is the point at which the comparison of *zob-* and corpse-uncleanness becomes necessary, and, with that comparison we reach the exegetical key for understanding the law of *Zabim*.

Let us begin with the summary that the Tosefta—true to its character as the source of generalizations of the Mishnah's exemplary cases—provides (at T. Zab. 3:3):

> More strict is the rule applying to the *Zab* than to one unclean by corpse-uncleanness, and more strict is the rule applying to the one unclean by corpse-uncleanness than to the *Zab*: For the *Zab* makes a bed and chair under him render man unclean and render garments unclean and imparts to what is above him *maddaf*-uncleanness [affecting objects not used for sitting or lying that are located above a *Zab*] and makes food and drink unclean—forms of uncleanness which the corpse does not impart. His flux and his spit and his urine impart stringent uncleanness. And he imparts uncleanness by means of contact to a utensil which is subject to purification by rinsing, and by means of shifting to a clay utensil. And he is liable for a sacrifice and is required to enter running water for his purification, which is not the case for the one who is unclean by reason of corpse-uncleanness. More strict is the rule applying to one unclean by corpse-uncleanness: For the one suffering corpse-uncleanness requires sprinkling with purification-water on the third and seventh day, which is not the case for the *Zab*.

The work of hierarchical classification is never more beautifully accomplished than by a passage such as this elegant statement.

How does the Mishnah frame matters? The Mishnah's key rule is at M. Zab. 5:2: Whatever is carried above the *Zab* is unclean. And whatever the *Zab* is carried upon is clean, except for something which is suitable for sitting and lying, and except for man. Here we find a striking paradox. If something is used for lying or sitting and the *Zab* is carried thereon, the object is unclean; but if it is food or drink that bears his weight, the food or drink is unaffected by him. And then a mirror-image is taken: whatever is carried above the *Zab*, not bearing his weight, is unclean, inclusive of food and drink. So the *Zab* possesses no power of transmitting uncleanness by overshadowing, but he transmits uncleanness to what overshadows him (thus: *maddaf*-uncleanness). First comes the teleological definition of what is subject to his pressure, which is, what can be used for lying and the like, then comes the antithesis; first comes the location, what is beneath, then comes the antithesis, what is above. It is an amazingly logical system that is set forth, each point then generating its consequence within the same simple logical structure.

So *zob*-uncleanness is transmitted through direct contact, carrying (pressure), shifting, and overshadowing, while corpse-uncleanness is transmitted through direct contact and overshadowing. In both cases, we meet our old friend as we distinguish removes of uncleanness, that is to say, we make a distinction between the situation that prevails when one is in actual contact with the source of uncleanness from that which prevails after one lets go. We further distinguish modes of transmission of uncleanness to the various sorts of objects that receive the uncleanness—a critical point for corpse-uncleanness, when it comes to receptacles, and for *zob* and other pressure-uncleanness when it comes to the matter at hand. We then identify the bed and the chair, things used for lying and sitting, other objects not used for sitting and lying (*maddaf*-objects) and food and drink. The *Zab* imparts uncleanness to objects that bear his weight and that are not shifted by him, which, absent contact or overshadowing, corpse-matter cannot do.

That is the point of T. Zab. 5:1: the Torah has imposed a more stringent rule upon food and drink and *maddaf* not used for sitting and lying that are above the *Zab*, than upon food and drink and maddaf that are under the *Zab*; upon bed and chair that are under the *Zab*, than upon bed and chair that are above the *Zab* and upon *maddaf* not used for lying and sitting that is above the *Zab*, than upon bed and chair that are above the *Zab*; upon man, whether above the *Zab* or below the *Zab*, than upon bed and chair that are above the *Zab*.

**The effects of Zob-uncleanness, such as is transmitted by pressure (*Midras*):** What are the consequences of *zob*-uncleanness for the Israelite household? An object appropriate to receive uncleanness from the *Zab* or *Zabah*—the bed and analogous objects—becomes unclean when the *Zab* or *Zabah* has stood, sat, lain, leaned upon, or been suspended from said object. Then the object imparts uncleanness to another person who stands, sits, lies upon, or is suspended from the object itself; the bed or analogous object likewise imparts uncleanness to one who carries its weight or to one who touches it ("contact"). It does not convey uncleanness to one who overshadows it, or to one whom it overshadows; it does not function as does corpse-uncleanness. The uncleanness of *Zabim* bears its own message, aligned alongside, but distinct from, the message of the uncleanness conveyed by a corpse within a tent (Ohalot). This is stated at M. Nid. 6:3 as follows: Whatever is susceptible to *midras* uncleanness is susceptible to corpse uncleanness, but there is that which is susceptible to corpse uncleanness and is not susceptible to *midras* uncleanness. The Talmud to the same passage proceeds:

III.1A. Whatever is susceptible to *midras* uncleanness is susceptible to corpse uncleanness, but there is that which is susceptible to corpse uncleanness and is not susceptible to *midras* uncleanness:

B. What is encompassed by that statement? What is encompassed is a seah-measure and a tarqab-measure, for it has been taught on Tannaite authority:

C. "And he who sits on any thing" (Lev. 15:6)—might one suppose that if one turned over a seah-measure and sat down on it, or a tarqab-measure and sat down upon it, it will be unclean?

D. Scripture states, "On which he who has an issue has sat" (Lev. 15:6), meaning, that which is designated as an object for sitting, which then excludes something concerning which people may say, "Get up and let us do our work with that object."

So while the two sources of uncleanness—the corpse, *Zob*—produce a single consequence, uncleanness, each functions in its own way, and that must be each for its own reasons, as we shall see.

But first we must incorporate into our account the other form of vaginal blood that serves as a source of uncleanness, the blood that appears in the seven days of the menstrual cycle. Only when we encompass blood of all three classifications—blood that is not a source of uncleanness at all, blood that signifies the menstrual period, and blood that signifies status as a *Zabah*—shall we find possible the identification and systemic interpretation of the religious statement made through the halakhic discourse on vaginal excretions.

**The halakhah of Niddah:** Life is to be created in conditions of cultic cleanness such as the Written Torah defines. Ordinary sexual activities, as much as ordinary meals, raise issues of cultic cleanness. But in the case of sexuality, the cult does not define the point at which such issues make an impact upon everyday life; ordinary sexual relations do. This is the one area of the law of cultic cleanness and uncleanness laid out at Leviticus Chapters Eleven through Fifteen that Scripture itself declares in so many words to pertain to the household, not only the cult. In concrete terms, Scripture is explicit that sexual relations may not take place during the menstrual period: "And if a man lies with her, her impurity is communicated to him; he shall be unclean seven days, and any bedding on which he lies shall become unclean." Whether or not the governing consideration pertains to entry into the tabernacle is not specified; but the Oral Torah takes for granted that sexual relations may not take place in the woman's menstrual period, and considerations of cleanness, made explicit in Scripture, then pertain to preserving cultic cleanness at home, not only in connection with entry into the Temple. The upshot is, sexual relations, like eating, involve considerations of cleanness and invoke avoidance of some of those very same sources of un-

cleanness that close off the Temple to the person affected by them.

For the Oral Torah, when it comes to menstrual uncleanness, the main problem comes at the start of the period. In the clean or *Zibah*-days (when any blood that is excreted is classified as *Zob*), the woman may have sexual relations without scruple; as soon as the menstrual cycle commences, a single drop of blood marks the change in her status to that of a menstruant. Then how do we deal with cases of unclarity as to the exact point at which the period has begun? It is that interstitial period that defines the topic of Tractate Niddah—a topic that the law of *Zabim* did not treat, since the *Zabah* generates no cases of uncertainty.

Tractate Niddah discusses the uncleanness of certain vaginal flows and considers cases of doubt in connection with that same matter. These fluids are menstrual blood, the abortion, and the like; the women are classified as Israelite, Samaritan, Sadducean, and so on. The animate source of uncleanness—here, the woman—has to take precautions to ascertain her status, and the net effect is to require the woman to pay close attention to the condition of her vagina. The woman who has a fixed period still has to examine herself in the morning, at twilight, and before having sexual relations. That imposes considerations of cultic cleanness on a variety of homely situations. A man concerned with seminal emission, by contrast, is discouraged from doing the same, but if his motive is to look out for flux, he is praised as well. While considerations of eating priestly rations in the state of cultic cleanness register, the premise of the halakhah throughout places us in the home of an ordinary caste-Israelite. Then, if a drop of blood is found on the man's cloth, the man is assumed to have had sexual relations with a menstruating woman; so too, if it is found on hers at the time of intercourse. But if it is found on hers later on, the matter is not certain. The upshot is, sexual relations are subject to considerations of cultic cleanness, even when the prevailing assumption is that both parties are cultically clean for the act.

Here again, considerations of uncleanness

require that we sort out the sources of an uncleanness that is, physically, undifferentiated—what class of woman with an affiliation in Israel has produced the blood? But it goes without saying, it is in the setting of holy Israel that the entire matter is worked out. Gentile women are unclean by definition, and considerations of Niddah- or *Zibah*-blood do not pertain. Scripture speaks of Israel, not gentiles. But the spit and urine of the gentile are unclean, for the gentile is classified as a *Zab*, and the blood of the gentile woman is unclean just as are the urine and spit of the *Zab* (when wet, not when dry). But Samaritan and Sadducean women are Israelites and the pertinent distinctions among types of blood do apply. Because they continue unclean for any sort of blood, Samaritan women miscalculate, not differentiating one type of blood from another, and hence impart uncleanness to everything on which they sit or lie. In their power to differentiate among types of blood, knowing the difference between menstrual and other classifications of vaginal excretions, sages thus distinguish (their) Israel from all others claiming to form part of Israel.

Since the menstruating woman takes her position in-between the two poles—wholly participating in the procreative process, wholly excluded from it—we must find entirely predictable that a principal problematic of the law concerns cases of doubt. That is to say, since in the sequence from the menstrual period to the clean days and back to the menstrual period, a woman participates in the cycle of procreation, what we need to know is how to deal with uncertainty as to her particular status at a given moment. How do we deal with the status of objects the woman has touched in the interval between the moment at which she knew for certain she was clean and the one at which she discovered she was menstruating? The Niddah's procreative interstitiality—she can procreate, as a *Zabah* cannot, and for that reason is deemed at some moments clean, at some, unclean, in a way in which a *Zabah* is never deemed clean—then accounts for what is at stake in the Oral Law. What is involved is retrospective, and thus retroactive contamina-

tion, that is to say, how do we classify persons or objects that have had contact with the woman at the time at which her status is uncertain?

The solution is to mediate between two points of certainty. The woman is assumed to remain perpetually alert as to her status, inspecting her sexual organs for spots of blood. So if we look backward from the moment of discovery of blood, we come to a point at which the woman has last inspected herself and found herself clean. Then all objects she has touched from that last inspection to the point of discovery of the blood may be deemed unclean. Or we may impose an arbitrary standard of twenty-four hours, in the assumption that the woman is unlikely to have missed a vaginal flow for longer than that span of time. The halakhah takes the view that each span of time—the period from the last inspection, the arbitrary period of twenty-four hours—lessens the other, so that the longest interval of uncertainty is twenty-four hours. But if a woman has a fixed period, that establishes the presumptive fact and decides the issue. She then assumes that at no time prior to the advent of her regular period has she produced vaginal blood, inspection or no. Once the period is established, we have ample evidence on how to resolve situations subject to doubt. Thus, if a woman habitually saw blood at the beginning of [symptoms of] periods, all things requiring cleanness that she prepared while the symptoms of periods are in progress are unclean. If she usually saw blood at the end of symptoms of periods, all the things requiring cleanness that she prepared while the symptoms of the periods lasted are deemed clean. Rules of this kind present no surprises, working out commonsense distinctions as they do.

Sages distinguish categories of blood produced by an abortion, determining whether or not the vaginal blood derives from childbirth or from the menstrual period. Thus, if the fetus bears human form, it is deemed to have been a birth and the rules of Lev. 12 apply; if not, the woman is clean, or, if the event takes place during her menstrual period, is regarded as nothing more than a menstruant. But then the sex of the fetus has to be determined, and sages supply rules for doing so. So too if a woman excretes blood during labor not in her menstrual period; then the blood is attributed to labor, and the woman is not deemed a menstruant.

Because they fall into the classification of substances that impart uncleanness, the blood of the menstruating woman, the flux and blood of the *Zab*, the dead creeping thing, carrion, and semen all have to be compared and contrasted as well. The point of differentiation concerns the power to contaminate whether wet or dry. The blood of the menstruating woman and the flesh of a corpse impart uncleanness wet or dry. But the *Zab*'s flux, phlegm, spit, and the dead creeping thing, carrion, and semen impart uncleanness only when they are wet, unless they can be soaked and return to their former condition, in which case they impart uncleanness even when dry. So the difference is not absolute but relative. If the substances that do not impart uncleanness when dry can in fact be restored through soaking, they revert to their original virulence.

The real question then pertains to what menstrual blood and corpse-matter bear in common, and once we ask that question, we find ourselves with a possible, if only tentative answer, already supplied in Tractate Ohalot: the interplay of soul and body must come into consideration. Menstrual blood now is treated as equivalent to corpse-matter, meaning, both contain remnants of the soul, the one having been permeated by the soul, which is now the principal source of uncleanness, the other (so it appears) deriving from the cache of potential souls; but that is only a guess.

What happens when death overtakes one of the animate sources of uncleanness under consideration here? If a *Zab* or *Zabah*, a menstruating woman or a woman unclean after childbirth or a person suffering the skin ailment dies, how does the uncleanness emanating from them disseminate? It is through carriage, even without contact; the same is so for a gentile. That is so until the flesh rots. In this aspect, then, the named animate sources of uncleanness differ from the corpse. The upshot is, the particular kind of unclean-

ness affecting the named classes of persons continues to classify the persons at hand, and they are not now deemed mere corpses along with all other corpses. The uncleanness that has enveloped them defines the working of the uncleanness that exudes from them, even after death; only when the flesh rots do they enter the taxon of ordinary corpses.

Except at the specified times, cultic cleanness defines the natural condition of the Israelite. Thus all the eleven days that follow the seven days of menstruation a woman is in the assumption of being clean, unless evidence to the contrary presents itself. On that basis, if a virgin who has not yet menstruated is married, she is assumed to be cultically clean through the honeymoon; any blood is held to derive from the hymen. So too if a woman has completed her period and examined herself and found that she was clean, but did not immerse at twilight at the end of her seventh day, and later on found she was unclean, she is assumed to have been clean to that point.

**The religious principles of Zabim and Niddah:** At issue is the character of a woman's vaginal secretions or blood: when does it appear, how is it classified? The distinction between menstrual or *Niddah*-blood and *Zibah*-blood, the former part of the procreative cycle, the latter not, yields very little difference in actuality, except at the point of purification. The one is vaginal blood that flows during the woman's established menstrual cycle. The other is vaginal blood that flows during the eleven clean days between one cycle and another; these are called *Zibah*-days, in that blood that flows during the eleven days between menstrual cycles is deemed *Zob*, as we have already established. In some ways—those that have to do with actualities—the two types of vaginal flow are comparable, in others, they contrast.

If we compare Scripture's presentation of the two forms of animate female-sources of uncleanness, we see how they relate, starting with the menstruating woman. The first thing we notice is that while the menstrual period is limited, the uncleanness attaching to the *Zabah* is indeterminate. The woman who menstruates may before and afterward

engage in sexual relations and become pregnant. The *Zabah* may not engage in sexual
relations and so may not become pregnant.
She is removed from the entire procreative
process so long as her excretions continue.
The second thing we see is that while the
Niddah accomplishes purification through
immersion and sunset, the *Zabah* undergoes
an elaborate cultic rite, comparable to the
rite of purification after contracting corpse-
uncleanness. So while the signification of
the uncleanness—vaginal flux—is the same,
the circumstances as to timing and longev-
ity vastly distinguish the one from the other,
and, as I shall suggest presently, the distinction makes a massive difference in our reading of what is at stake. Here is Scripture's
presentation of the pertinent laws:

MENSTRUAL UNCLEANNESS: When a
woman has a discharge, her discharge being
blood from her body, *she shall remain in her
impurity seven days*;
　1. whoever touches her shall be unclean
until evening.
　2. Anything that she lies on during her impurity shall be unclean; and anything that she
sits on shall be unclean.
　3. Anyone who touches her bedding
shall wash his clothes, bathe in water, and
remain unclean until evening; and anyone
who touches any object on which she has
sat shall wash his clothes, bathe in water,
and remain unclean until evening. Be it the
bedding or be it the object on which she
has sat, on touching it he shall be unclean
until evening.
　4. And if a man lies with her, her impurity is communicated to him; he shall be
unclean seven days, and any bedding on
which he lies shall become unclean.

The *Zabah* is presented as follows:

THE *ZABAH*: When a woman has had a discharge of blood for many days, not at the
time of her impurity, or when she has a discharge beyond her period of impurity, *she
shall be unclean as though at the time of her
impurity, as long as her discharge lasts.*
　2. Any bedding on which she lies while
her discharge lasts shall be for her like bedding during her impurity; and any object on
which she sits shall become unclean as it
does during her impurity;
　3. whoever touches them shall be unclean;
he shall wash his clothes, bathe in water, and
remain unclean until evening.

　4. When she becomes clean of her discharge, she shall count off seven days, and
after that she shall be clean. On the eighth
day she shall take two turtledoves or two
pigeons and bring them to the priest at the
entrance of the tent of meeting. The priest
shall offer the one as a sin-offering and the
other as a burnt-offering; and the priest shall
make expiation on her behalf, for her unclean
discharge, before the Lord.
　You shall put the Israelites on guard
against their uncleanness, lest they die
through their uncleanness by defiling my tabernacle which is among them.

The menstruating woman and the *Zabah*
convey uncleanness through touch, and both
serve as Fathers of uncleanness, setting into
the first remove of uncleanness whatever they
touch. One who touches what they have lain
upon or sat upon immerses, awaits sunset,
and is then clean. As to sexual relations, the
menstruating woman imparts her own status
to the one with whom she has sexual relations, and he imparts pressure-uncleanness by
sitting and lying as well. As to the *Zabah*,
touching produces the same result; no provision is made for sexual relations. A cultic
purification-rite is provided for her, but not
for the menstruating woman, who, at the end
of her period, simply immerses and waits for
sunset. She is then in the first remove, her
period having concluded.
　So while the concrete effects of the respective sources of vaginal uncleanness coincide,
the purification-rite contrasts sharply. The
*Zabah* purifies herself in a blood-rite at the
tabernacle. The purification-rite, not required
for the menstruating woman, marks the
woman as suitable to reenter the procreative
cycle; the flux has removed her from that
cycle, the cessation signifies her suitability
once more. We have, therefore, to distinguish
*Niddah*- from *Zibah*-blood (*Zob*). The facts
at hand suffice to show that *Zibah*-blood signifies an aberration in the procreative cycle,
Niddah-blood proves integral to that cycle.
The one is irregular and disrupts normal sexual relations, marking the woman as one
who, at that point, may not reproduce life
(any more than, from sages' view, the semen emitted by a flaccid penis can reproduce
life). The other is regular, integral to the normal sexual cycle, and marks the woman as

one wholly integrated to the cycle of repro-
duction. Then the entire sequence—eleven
*Zibah*-days, seven *Niddah*-days—forms an
account of the woman's relationship to the
procreative cycle, which involves three possibilities: she wholly participates, having
sexual relations, receiving semen and not
emitting blood; she is wholly excluded, not
having sexual relations at all, and she is
temporarily excluded but remains sexually
accessible, which is why the Torah makes
provision for the status of one who, in her
period, does have sexual relations with her.

Viewed together, the halakhah of Zabim
and that of Niddah together make a single
coherent statement, just as Moses arranged
matters at Lev. 15. The contrast between
blood in the *Niddah*-days and blood in the
*Zibah*-days frames the issue at hand. We
cannot understand Tractate Niddah outside of
the framework of Tractate Zabim, and, in the
nature of things, the contrary is also the case.
The points of intersection—the consequences
of uncleanness imparted by vaginal blood—
and the points of differentiation—sexuality and the purification rite, respectively—
leave no choice but to consider Niddah and
Zabim a single statement within the halakhah,
of which Zabim forms the main lines of
thought, Niddah the subordinated and secondary results thereof.

The character of *Zob* and of its flow guides
us to the center of the religious world-view
at hand. It is genital discharge that by its
nature cannot accomplish that for which it
is created. In a word, the physical world
portrayed here finds its definitive traits in
the teleology of things, which yields the
meetings and the matchings that produce the
halakhah of Zabim. The uncleanness generated by sexual fluids that do not realize
their teleology passes via pressure, analogous
to that of the sexual relation, to objects that
serve for sexuality. When the teleological
physics of sexual fluids accomplish their
goal, they bring about life. Then, consequently, a minor uncleanness is brought
about by semen properly ejaculated, and so
too with vaginal blood of an episodic character outside the regular period.

When the teleology—the procreation of

life—of the sexual parts, encompassing further the objects used for sexual intercourse,
and extending even to the activities and ex-
ertions characteristic thereof—when that
teleology is not realized, then severe uncleanness results. That uncleanness then
overspreads each of the components of procreation that has not realized its purpose:

> [1] the fluid itself, now source of unclean-
> ness analogous to corpse-uncleanness;
> [2] the activity, exerting pressure, now me-
> dium for disseminating not life but un-
> cleanness, and
> [3] the bed and analogous objects, now the
> focus of not procreative activity but con-
> tamination.

Now, not realizing their tasks within the
teleological physics at hand:

> [1] the fluid is unclean,
> [2] the bed and analogous objects become
> the unique foci of the uncleanness of said
> fluid, and
> [3] the activity—pressure—serves as the me-
> dium not of life but of anti-life, such as,
> we now realize, cultic uncleanness dis-
> seminated through *midras*-uncleanness
> in particular represents.

How are we to compare and contrast the uncleanness of the soul, the seven-day uncleanness of the corpse and corpse-matter, with the
uncleanness of *Zob*? When we examine, the
uncleanness exuding from the *Zab* or *Zabah*, encompassing not only the flux itself,
whether semen or blood, but the body-fluids,
e.g., the spit, the urine, of a person so afflicted, we find an interesting fact. *Zob* does
not constitute a Father of Fathers of Uncleanness as the corpse does. The *Zabah* or *Zab*
is a Father of uncleanness, contaminating
the garments and utensils of someone who
touches her or him, also those things that bear
her or his weight. These are made unclean in
the first remove. So the virulence of the escaping soul vastly exceeds that of the genital
excretions that do not realize their purpose.

Different in degree, they form a common
genus. The character of *Zob*-fluid and the
uncleanness of the soul that we examined
in the context of corpse-uncleanness share
the common quality that, when touched, both
sorts of fluid impart uncleanness. If there is
an object suitable to serve as a bed or chair

or saddle that lies underneath a stone, and a *Zab* or *Zabah* bears down on the stone, e.g., stands, sits, lies or leans on it or hangs from it, because he is supported by the stone, the bed or chair that bears the weight of the intervening stone is itself contaminated. But corpse-uncleanness—e.g., a receptacle containing a bone—not touched but nonetheless the weight of which is carried produces no effect, e.g., through an intervening layer of disconnected material, while *Zob*-uncleanness that is not contacted but the weight of which is carried does produce its uncleanness. So corpse-uncleanness possesses a tangibility, a tactility, that *Zob*-uncleanness lacks, and *Zob*-uncleanness responds to forces that affect corpse-uncleanness little or not at all. What is the difference?

Using our imagination of the workings of the physics of liquids in this odd context, we may on that basis differentiate the uncleanness of the corpse from the uncleanness of flux. The one, while thick, diffuses into the air of a contained space. It is therefore comparable to a gaseous substance; but, as we noted, it flows like a viscous fluid, along fairly firm lines, within a sizable space, a squared handbreadth. So while comparable to a gaseous substance, it remains, if invisible, thick and tactile. *Zob*, by contrast, does not diffuse in the air. It permeates the objects that are congruent to its effects. Then, if a clean person bears down, the *Zob* under pressure is excreted upward onto the clean person, even through intervening, disconnected layers of material; the transmission takes place by reason of pressure, not contact.

Now how are we to differentiate the gaseous corpse-uncleanness, which does not respond to pressure, from comparable *Zob*-uncleanness, which does? A difference in (imagined) viscosity ought to explain matters. Corpse-uncleanness flows within a guiding framework (under pressure, spurts upward and downward). But it does not permeate and pass through intervening fabric ("tent") or other materials. *Zob*-uncleanness under pressure is not guided along the lines of that which conveys the pressure—the tent for example—but flows right into, and through, the fabric or other material that

contains it. Hence seen in physical terms, the former is dense, glutinous and semi-fluid, the latter attenuated, spare and light.

But those physical traits on their own do not suffice to explain the difference as to the modes of movement between the uncleanness exuding from the corpse and that emitted by the sexual organs, male or female. Specifically, why should the latter classification of uncleanness flow so as to pass through a stone on which the *Zab* exerts pressure through direct contact, as well as weight, to the bed beneath? Why should a receptacle contain corpse-uncleanness but not the uncleanness of *Zob*, that is, why should a receptacle be unaffected by *midras*- or pressure uncleanness of a *Zab* or *Zabah*? Asked in that way, the question bears its own answer. We deal in *Zob* with a kind of uncleanness that matches, that responds to, its own origin, assignment, and character: origin in sexual organs, assignment, procreation, and character defined by a dysfunction in those organs. Sexually-generated fluid that, by (sages') definition cannot accomplish the purpose that, by nature, sexually-generated fluid is supposed to achieve—procreation of life—affects, as we have noted, those sorts of objects that serve sexually, ones used for lying and the like, but not those sorts of objects that under normal circumstances do not serve sexually, receptacles, for example.

As with the corpse and as we shall see again in connection with the uncleanness of the person afflicted with the skin ailment described at Lev. 13—the uncleanness is transmitted through spatial relationships not involving direct, physical contact: overshadowing the corpse or being overshadowed by it, so too the *Zab* or *Zabah* in relationship to a bed or chair, so too the person afflicted with the skin ailment within a contained space. In all three instances, location within a demarcated spatial relationship with the source of uncleanness, not only actual contact, direct or through pressure (as the case requires), serves as cause of dissemination of uncleanness from the source to the focus thereof. Let us address the particular rule of spatial relationship in the transmission of uncleanness of a *Zab* or *Zabah*, because there we shall see the inexorable operation of the principle of realized or unrealized teleology as the key to all else, affecting both the source and the subject of contamination.

That brings us to the paradoxical fact of the rule that overshadowing serves corpse-uncleanness and Zob-uncleanness, but with powerful distinctions, and each in its own way. What overshadows a corpse contracts corpse-uncleanness, and what a corpse overshadows is contaminated by corpse-uncleanness. That is without regard to the character of the objects. We do not, furthermore, differentiate between the two locations of the corpse relative to the object in relationship thereto. So locative relationship and substantive character play no role in the transmission of corpse-uncleanness through overshadowing. The corpse that overshadows or is overshadowed produces its effects without regard to what is affected. But that is not how matters are with Zob-uncleanness. Here we do differentiate, in the situation of overshadowing, between the character of classes of objects. And, concomitantly, we also differentiate locatively, between the two locations that said classes of objects, above or below the Zab. So we have two variables as to the character of objects, and two variables as to their location, and, further, these variables produce opposite results, the locative for the substantive, as the case requires.

Here are some of the exemplary facts. If a Zab overshadows food and drink, unlike the corpse he has no affect upon them. But if food or drink are located above the Zab, they are made unclean. Why the mirror-relationships? What is located where the Zab lies or sits but cannot serve for lying or sitting is unaffected by him; what is located where the Zab cannot lie or sit and cannot serve for lying or sitting—thus what in relationship to the Zab is in its natural location, not in its unnatural location—is affected by him. So he functions as does a corpse in conveying uncleanness, the medium is the same; but he does not impart uncleanness as does a corpse. What does not conform in relationship to the Zab to its natural location is affected by him; what conforms is not.

Here again, a teleological logic comes into play through analogical-contrastive dialectics, with the things that enjoy their natural relationship to the Zab subject to his effect, those not, not; and the opposite also comes into force: what the Zab cannot use for lying that is located where the Zab cannot lie down is affected by the Zab! So considerations of fulfilling the physical purpose for which the thing is shaped take over, even here. To state matters simply: teleological physics dictates the course of contamination by Zob and the results, for things affected by that contamination, as well. And it is a simple teleology, which we identified at the very outset: what serves for procreation is distinguished, in respect to Zob-uncleanness, from what does not. And the rest follows.

What we confront, therefore, is a physics permeated by teleology: the flow of fluids in response to the condition or purpose of that to which, or from which, they flow, and not in response only to their own character, e.g., to the density of the atoms that comprise the fluid and define its viscosity. That which matches the character of an object or its purpose flows to that object or its purpose, and the invisible flow itself conforms to the character of the activity conducted with said object. The bed, used for lying or sitting, then is affected by pressure, carried on in acts of lying or sitting; the particular uncleanness at hand, sexual excretions in a non-procreative framework, affects those objects that by their nature serve, through those actions that by their nature produce, procreation.

When sexual activity bearing the potential of procreation takes place, a transient uncleanness results—that of healthy semen, which passes upon immersion and sunset, as Scripture says. When sexual excretions lacking that potential take place, a virulent uncleanness takes over, life replaced by anti-life, by a form of death nearly as virulent as the death that takes over the life of a man and causes the excretion of the soul. The soul of the fully-realized man or woman is thick, the unrealized, proto-soul of Zob, thin. But the former can be contained in physical limits, as it was in the body, while the latter flows teleologically, its character and therefore its purpose overriding the substantive, physical traits, or physical traits responding to teleological matches (whichever formulation better serves).

In this same context, moreover, the difference in the rite of purification of the Niddah and the *Zabah* emerges as entirely rational within the system. The Niddah's purification-rite is analogous to the purification-rite of the man who has emitted semen in the normal course of procreation, and for the same reason: the Niddah has passed through a natural stage in the procreative cycle. When menstrual uncleanness ends and she reverts to the condition of cleanness required for propagation of life in conditions of sanctification, she immerses and awaits sunset. She need not undergo a cultic rite of purification because she has never been removed from the cycle of life. Niddah-blood then bears no analogy to the blood of a corpse, but *Zabah*-blood does. That is because, within the teleological physiology as much as the teleological physics of the system, Niddah-blood fulfils its teleology, Zob-flux (*Zabah*-blood) does not.

The goal of nature, its telos in procreation, pertains to Israel and the propagation of the holy people. Sages make that point explicitly, because their perfect mastery of the Written Torah so instructed them. Let me explain. With a system so permeated by the conviction that things bear a natural purpose and accomplish a goal that is set for them by their very nature, we must identify the central and generative focus of the teleology realized in uncleanness or sanctification. So we ask ourselves, Who matters, who makes a difference? The answer, repeated in one sector of the halakhah after another, is, only the Israelite. It is his or her life-force that comes under scrutiny. It is that life-force, that blood, that accomplishing its teleology procreates life and yields a minor form of uncleanness, but, not accomplishing its teleology, is deemed analogous to the departing soul. What does it take to constitute an animate source of uncleanness, affecting the Israelite household, when it comes to the sexual organs? The first and most important consideration is, only Israelites produce flux capable of effecting contamination under the laws of *Zabim*.

Gentiles do not. The halakhah of Niddah makes that point explicit. Their body fluids contaminate under other rubrics of uncleanness, but in general they contaminate like corpses and not like animate beings. They, their body-fluids, their land—all represent a realm of undifferentiated death, contrasting with the highly differentiated life attaching to holy Israel. In the articulation of the halakhah of animate sources of uncleanness, therefore, we see the consequence of the basic problem, the generative tension of the Oral Torah, with its conviction about the sanctification and sanctity of the Israelite household in the model of the holy Temple. Once issues of sanctification encompass not only the family and genealogy, but also the bed and the table, procreation and sustenance of life, then those who keep the entire Torah, oral and written, have to work out those governing patterns of behavior that will guide toward the realization of sanctification and the preservation of sanctity. Such patterns then order and regularize relationships between the cultically-clean and the cultically unclean, specifying the causes and consequences of contamination.

Having focused upon what we do find, we ought not miss what we do not find. Intentionality plays no role in the capacity to transmit uncleanness imputed to the animate beings; the corpse transmits uncleanness *ex opere operato*, from the moment of death, about which the deceased was not consulted, and so too the menstruating woman, man afflicted with flux or the *Zab*, and the woman or the *Zabah* afflicted with flux outside of her regular period, effect uncleanness willy-nilly. The woman's period does not depend upon her intentionality. And equally probatively, the law stresses that the flux of the *Zab* and the *Zabah* that bears the power to contaminate—semen from the one, blood from the other—make its appearance on its own. The blood or semen must come about without the connivance of the afflicted party. The teleological principle that permeates the whole underscores the exclusion of man's or woman's will.

And that leads us at the very heart of the halakhah of *Zabim*, the analogy to death.

Why does the halakhah defining sources of uncleanness exclude all consideration of the attitude or intentionality of the animate being, the man or woman, who becomes a source of uncleanness? Because of the governing analogy, death: we die willy-nilly, neither by intention nor by plan, and to death our attitude is null. What by its nature compares with death also contaminates like death, which comes whether or not it is wanted. Then the details of the law flow from the natural teleology that governs: excretions of the sexual organs that by their nature cannot procreate life, affect objects used in that process, and that is accomplished by means of activities analogous to the sexual act or integral thereto: *Zob* or semen from a flaccid penis affect beds and like objects through pressure.

The systemic goal is for life to be created and maintained as if it were lived in the holy Temple, protected from the sources of contamination that pollute the Temple. Perhaps, embodying the perfection of the natural world, the Temple as if here and now stands for Eden then and there. For the paramount aspiration of the halakhah is to restore humanity to Eden, Israel to the land of Israel. That conclusion is hardly far-fetched within the analogical-contrastive mode of thought of the halakhah. For if, as is blatant, uncleanness closes off access to the Temple and its surrogates and counterparts in the households of Israel: their tables and their beds, then cleanness—counterpart and opposite—must open the way to sanctification. Uncleanness attended to, cleanness attained, all media of restoration of cleanness, Israel's natural condition, set the household of Israel *en route* to sanctification, localized in the Temple down below, matched by heaven up above, realized by the household here and now of bed and table, Eden then and there. And these terms invoke no ineffable abstractions, but, we must constantly recall, the concrete activities that routinely take place in bed and at table: the labor of Adam and Eve in making and maintaining life.

JACOB NEUSNER

# R

**RABBI IN CLASSICAL JUDAISM:** All attempts to describe the rabbi—the religious virtuoso of ancient Judaism—must begin with the nature of the sources and, first and foremost, with the recognition that virtually all of our information about these figures comes from documents formulated, written, and redacted within their own circles. Fashioned and molded by rabbis, these texts constitute the material remains of Rabbinic Judaism and are the primary evidence for its existence. A precise understanding of Rabbinic textual constructions therefore provides the foundation and justification for all other inferences from the texts.

Rabbinic literature, made up of documents dated from the third century C.E. to early medieval times, treats two broad subjects: halakhah (Rabbinic praxis, the way of doing things) and the interpretation of Scripture. The documents consist of large numbers of distinct, usually self-contained passages of varying length and character grouped in patterns of thematic, topical, or scriptural arrangement. Within these writings, the stories about rabbis are always presented in the setting of discussions of unrelated events, for, uniquely in western antiquity, Rabbinic literature is devoid of biography or hagiography. Indeed, Rabbinic documents are anonymous, and all include significant numbers of pericopae that are not associated with the names of specific masters. No document claims to be the writing of an individual rabbi in his own words, and all contain the ostensible sayings of, and stories about, many rabbis of diverse generations. Selected to suit the purposes of compilers and redactors, the documents' components are not pristine and natural. They have been revised and reformulated in the processes of transmission and redaction, with the consequence that the actual words of any rabbi are beyond recovery. Rabbinic literature is severely edited, anonymous, and collective.

Use of Rabbinic documents to recover Rabbinic biography is further limited by the fact that the literature as a whole, especially in the area of halakhah, is terse and formulaic, presented in a lean and disciplined vocabulary that constitutes a scholastic shorthand. Even the most elementary halakhic statement presumes a tacit dimension of Rabbinic knowledge, attitudes, behaviors, and motivations. The result of this is that the Rabbinic literature virtually ignores the world beyond its own preoccupations. Its documents obscure their origin by neglecting the events that led to their formation, and they report remarkably little about ordinary Jews or non-Jews. This insularity is reinforced by the nearly total absence of external witness to Rabbinic religion, culture, and society. The documents thus present the restricted discourse of a small number of men who appear primarily engaged in observing discussing, and analyzing ideas, opinions, and behaviors, sometimes those recounted in Scripture, but most often those promoted within the Rabbinic group itself. Rabbinic writing addresses Rabbinic specialists; it is a parochial literature wholly obsessed with itself.

The technical knowledge presupposed by most of Rabbinic literature shows that rabbis produced their texts not for the world at large, nor for strangers and outsiders, but for themselves. In the texts, selected reports of the opinions, arguments, and activities of generations of rabbis are encased in anonymous, synchronic, and rhetorically disciplined frameworks. It follows that the documents' picture of the world and of the rabbis themselves necessarily is overdetermined, manipulated, and incomplete. Rabbinic editors offer no comprehensive and nuanced report, no mirror image, of their colleagues and precursors. They produce instead a vision of their world as they imagined it and described it to themselves. With language as their principal representational tool, the producers of Rabbinic documents create the world they reveal.

Rabbinic literature thus emerges not as an essentially neutral and inerrant record of "what actually happened" in Rabbinic antiquity but rather as an enormous labor of intellect and imagination that codifies a particular Jewish conception of reality in a distinctive mode of discourse that both derives from and generates that conception.

These substantive and literary traits, which inform the presentation of all persons in Rabbinic documents, make the construction of portraits of ancient rabbis extremely problematic. The sources at best provide the barest hint of the relations between rabbis and the non-Rabbinic social and economic world, and they thus block our perception of the rabbis at work in society. A truly critical analysis of Rabbinic religious leadership becomes difficult, for, without evidence of followers, little of certainty can be said about leaders. The absence of biography obscures evidence of family lineage, local origin, economic status, and other marks of social identification. Indeed, Rabbinic masters are never introduced, and, while there is a habit of referring to rabbis as "X son of Y, these patronymic surnames, though known in most cases, are sparingly applied.

In the Rabbinic sources, rabbis simply appear from nowhere, speaking and arguing as if everyone knows who they are. The absence of biography, however, hardly exhausts the problem. The texts offer a fragmented picture of rabbis. The dicta and opinions assigned and the stories told about any given master are nowhere collected under his name but are scattered throughout the documents, often in different versions that serve the varied purposes of compilers and redactors. Particularly in the earlier documents, rabbis appear in disagreement with one another, but the disputes tend to remain unresolved. The conflicting opinions remain in endless juxtaposition and their relative importance is uninflected. This mode of representation suppresses evidence of authority, domination, and power among the disputants and makes rabbis appear as equals. This is despite the fact that, as Richard Kalmin suggests, in the Babylonian Talmud, ". . . very likely, most interactions between rabbis involve colleagues . . . of widely different status. Colleagues of approximately equal status, particularly the most important leaders of their generation, rarely interact."[1] But this trait is obscured by the distinctive literary character of that document, which homogenizes all named authorities and obscures evidence of individuality.

Rabbinic literature, indeed, is largely indifferent to the presentation of distinctive individuality. No document pays homage to a particular rabbi. None celebrates one man's virtue, reflects his thoughts, or recounts his deeds. The sources offer no museum of well-rounded Rabbinic portraits, only a gallery of partial sketches and disjointed images. Rabbinic literature presents its protagonists paratactically, in pieces. It is a literature of contention without victors, in which the sense of separate existences is minimal. This massive labor of homogeneity suggests that devotion to individual masters played little role in the motivations of the men who made the texts. In all of the literature, no rabbi emerges as central, dominant, determinative; none appears to symbolize, guide, or shape Rabbinic destiny. No Rabbinic texts claims to be the product of the life, career, or inner struggle of a single great man. Rather, the men appear as products of the sources.

No doubt, individual rabbis achieved importance, decisively shaped Rabbinic culture, and affected the lives of their contemporaries. No doubt stories about rabbis are not wholly fabrications and falsehoods, literary inventions grounded in no historical reality. But, whatever their origin, the segments of Rabbinic lives thought worthy of narration and transmission appear in their present form for purposes other than hero worship, dedication to a particular master, or a desire to recount and preserve the past. A representative narrative illustrates the extent to which these traits inhibit our ability to discern the exact nature of the early rabbi and to discern his true place within early Jewish culture. The story, which appears at M. R.H. 2:8-9, reads:

A. Rabban Gamaliel had pictures of the shapes of the moon on a tablet and on the wall of his upper chamber, which he would show untrained observers [who came to give evidence that, on the preceding night, they had seen the appearance of the new moon, which would determine the beginning of the next Hebrew month] and say, "Did you see it like this or like that?"

B. It happened that two came and said, "We saw it in the east in the morning and in the west in the evening."

C. Said R. Yohanan b. Nuri, "They are false witnesses."

D. When they came to Yavneh, Rabban Gamaliel accepted them.

E. And again two came and said, "We saw it at its [expected] time, but on the next night it did not appear."

F. And Rabban Gamaliel accepted them.

G. Said R. Dosa b. Harkinas, "They are false witnesses."

H. "How can they testify that a woman has given birth when the next day her belly is [still] between her teeth?"

I. R. Joshua said to him, "I approve your words."

J. Rabban Gamaliel sent a message to him: "I decree that you shall come before me with your staff and your money on the day that falls as the Day of Atonement according to your reckoning [on which day such travel, carrying these objects, would be forbidden]."

K. R. Aqiba went and found him upset.

L. He said to him, "I am able to learn that whatever Rabban Gamaliel has done is done,

M. "as it is written, 'These are the appointed seasons of the Lord, the holy assemblies which you shall proclaim' (Lev. 23:4), [meaning]: Whether in their time or not in their time, I have no other appointed seasons but these."

N. He came to R. Dosa b. Harkinas.

O. He said to him, "If we come to judge the court of Rabban Gamaliel, we will have to judge each and every court that has stood from the days of Moses until now,

P. "as it is written, 'Moses went up with Aaron, Nadav, and seventy of the elders of Israel' (Exod. 24:9). And why were the names of the elders not made explicit? Rather, it is to teach that each and every [group of] three who stood as a court over Israel, lo, they are like the court of Moses."

Q. And he took his staff and his money in his hand and went to Yavneh on the day that fell as the Day of Atonement according to his reckoning.

R. Rabban Gamaliel stood up and kissed him on the head.

S. He said to him, "Come in peace, my
master and my disciple—my master in
wisdom, and my disciple, since you have
accepted my words."

This account is particularly useful since it
reports an alleged historical event with political consequences for the Rabbinic movement. It also treats an issue crucial in the
history of Judaism, the determination of the
sacred calendar after the destruction of
the Jerusalem Temple.

In Judaism, the yearly calendar is calculated according to the sun, but the months,
and therefore the dates of the annual holy
days, are determined by the appearance of
the moon. Before the fall of the Jerusalem
Temple in 70 C.E, the priests proclaimed the
sacred times of the year. In the aftermath of
the Temple's destruction, the new Rabbinic
movement appropriated that priestly task to
itself. This story reports a conflict on this
issue between Gamaliel II, the patriarch and
ostensible leader of the rabbis at Yavneh, and
two other Yavnean masters, Dosa b. Harkinas and Joshua b. Hananiah.

The story can be divided into three sub-
stantively related but formally unintegrated
segments, A, B-D, and E-S. A sets the stage
and supplies the halakhic topic of the pericope, the examination of witnesses about
the appearance of the new moon. B-D is a
brief prelude to the longer account at E-S.
In B-D, Gamaliel examines two witnesses
and accepts their testimony, presumably for
the beginning of a new month, despite the
objection of Yohanan b. Nuri. In the bar-
renness of B-D, so typical of Rabbinic narratives, we are told the rationale neither for
Yohanan b. Nuri's judgment nor for Gamaliel's rejection of it. The opinions simply are
juxtaposed without being brought into explicit interaction.

At issue in both B-D and E-I is the correct evaluation of testimony about the new
moon. Gamaliel accepts even irregular testimony. Yohanan b. Nuri and Dosa b. Harkinas oppose such practice and are supplied
with identical language. At no point in either
B-D or E-I does anyone deny or even question the patriarch's authority to proclaim the
dates of festivals. The addition of Joshua's

comment at I does not change matters; the
issue still is not who decides but how one
decides. At J this matter is dropped, never
to be resolved, and the focus of concern
abruptly shifts to the question of patriarchal
authority. The issue is not who is right but
who is in charge. Gamaliel commands Joshua to violate what the latter regards as the
correct Day of Atonement.

Aqiba's appearance at K-M is a surprise. He plays no role in the disagreement,
and his apparent support of the patriarch on
this matter conflicts with the testimony of
M. R.H. 1:6, in which he attempts to prevent
witnesses from testifying before him. K-M
obviously is an intrusion into the narrative.

According to N, Joshua goes to Dosa. The
identity of the speaker at O-P is unclear, but
H. Albeck supposes it to be Dosa. This reading is questionable, since the ruling against
Gamaliel is attributed to Dosa, not Joshua.
Q-S complete the narrative. The actor at Q
must be Joshua, for the language at Q is identical to that of J. At R-S, Gamaliel appears
the magnanimous victor.

The uncertain identity of the speaker at O
calls attention to Joshua's place in the story.
His name and words appear only once, at I,
where he affirms Dosa's judgment. After that,
he becomes an invisible figure whose presence is never made explicit. Talmudic literature contains many accounts of Joshua's
opposition to Gamaliel, the most famous of
which tells of Gamaliel's deposition from
the patriarchate. In such cases, Joshua typically propounds his own opinion, which is
reported in his own name. His role here, then,
is highly unusual, and this suggests that his
name has been inserted into an earlier account of a Gamaliel-Dosa dispute. Dosa b.
Harkinas is an obscure figure who appears
only eleven times in the Mishnah. At M.
Ket. 13:1-2, however, he sides with priestly
authority in civil matters, and after 70 C.E.,
he may have represented priestly claims in
religious matters as well. If so, then the earlier account on which this version is based,
something like E-G, J, and Q, would have
been a straightforward story about Gamaliel's dominance of the priestly party after
70. If this be the case, then the addition of

Joshua and Aqiba to the account has preserved the plot of the original, something difficult to alter if the earlier version were well known, but the addition has dramatically redirected the implications of the plot. This analysis, which is necessarily speculative because of the nature of the sources, shows the difficulty of constructing the historical background of Rabbinic texts. Even if accurate, it does not explain what the narrative is about. Let us return to the story in its present form and read it as a whole.

In a conventional narrative about Gamaliel, G would precede F, on the model of B-D. The reversal of those elements here establishes that the point at issue is Gamaliel's ruling. At G, Dosa demurs, and the graphic imagery supplied at -H, a common Rabbinic expression, adds bite to his judgment. Gamaliel cannot be right. At I, Joshua endorses Dosa's view, to be made the object of Gamaliel's displeasure at J. The point of J is clear; Gamaliel's decree is a blatant exercise of authority. At K, Aqiba enters to find Joshua "upset." Early Rabbinic stories normally eschew such nonessential detail, so the description of Joshua's mood is uncharacteristic. Its presence here highlights the dispute and fixes the context for Joshua's action at the end of the story. Aqiba supports Gamaliel at I-M with the exegesis of Lev. 23:4, but he endorses Gamaliel's position as patriarch, not his opinion. Indeed, the exegesis at M makes clear that Gamaliel is wrong. If the appointed seasons were observed "in their time," that is, properly, there would be no reason to apply the verse. Aqiba takes the verse to mean that Israel's appointed seasons are only those proclaimed by human agency, and, since Gamaliel is the recognized leader of the rabbis, what he "has done is done," whether or not it conforms to the times revealed by nature. Aqiba's conclusion is presented as the result of intellection; it is something he has been "able to learn."

N-P contains the exchange between Joshua and Dosa, but the identity of the speaker is unclear. In the flow of the narrative the words at P make better sense if said by Joshua than to him. Since, at K-L, Aqiba "went" and "said," N-O ought to read likewise. Joshua,

therefore, goes to Dosa to withdraw his support and offer his reasons. His rationale and the exegesis of Exod. 24:9 assume the existence of a line of Rabbinic courts that extends back to Moses. If the decision of one court can be held to question, so can the decisions of all courts, an approach that would undermine the coherence and credibility of Rabbinic (self-)government. The issue in O-P, then, is the welfare of the Rabbinic movement, not the objective correctness of Gamaliel's opinion.

At Q-S, Joshua goes to Gamaliel in apparent submission and is received with generosity. Gamaliel rises to greet him, a gesture of respect, and welcomes him warmly. But the words of greeting assigned to him blunt the effect of his victory. Joshua is both "master" and "disciple," at best an ambiguous status. By calling Joshua his "master in wisdom," in the story's context a clear reference only to the halakhic conflict between them, Gamaliel implicitly acknowledges the error of his own decision. Joshua is Gamaliel's "disciple" by virtue of his acceptance of the latter's words, but the exegesis at O-P leaves no doubt that Joshua's "discipleship" is voluntary, motivated neither by fear of nor personal devotion to Gamaliel, nor by regard for his halakhic acumen, but by a concern for the solidarity of Rabbinic collectivity.

In the end it is not clear who has won. Joshua and Gamaliel are both "master" and "disciple" to one another, a relation that blurs any hierarchy. Gamaliel's position remains intact, but his authority results from Joshua's refusal to judge his court, not from Gamaliel's qualities of intellect, charisma, or power. Indeed, it could be argued that the real hero of the narrative is Joshua, and secondarily Aqiba. It is Joshua who is able to suppress his correct opinion for the sake of the collective welfare, and Aqiba who calls the matter to his attention.

Although doubtless grounded in some event of conflict between the new Yavnean patriarch and other rabbis, the story actually says little about it. We do not know where or when the conflict took place and are told nothing of its broader social, religious, or political ramifications. Indeed, its very presence in the Mishnah, in the midst of legal rulings and disputations, suggests that Rabbinic authorities did not want such consequences as part of their record. The protagonists appear in a skeletal paratactic narrative framework that allows characters to be added to the story without altering the plot. They speak in clipped, truncated phrases that may indicate what they think but expose nothing of why they think it. The motives, passions, reasons, and principles that make the confrontation possible are wholly obscured. Finally, from J onwards, the protagonists are identified by pronouns the antecedents of which are not clear. As readers, we cannot be certain who speaks and who listens, but this ambiguity obstructs neither the story's progress nor its intelligibility. At one level, then, although the narrative includes the names of Gamaliel, Dosa, Aqiba and Joshua, it really is about no one in particular. Its images consequently tell us less about life as lived than about life as imagined.

But if this story tells us little about history as we would like to know it, it does reveal much about the contours and values of Rabbinic culture and religion. It portrays rabbis as imagining themselves to be the heirs and, for their own time, equivalents of Moses. To judge one of their courts is, of necessity, to judge the court of Moses. Rabbis, not God, fix the boundaries of sacred time, and God has "no other appointed seasons but these." The story exposes a powerful recognition that the rabbis are creating something new in their culture, something they, not God, are responsible to maintain. The persistence of that creation depends on the voluntary cooperation and mutuality of numbers of rabbis and can be destroyed by contrary attitudes and behaviors. In such a context no rabbi can appear to dominate others, and disputes among rabbis must be resolved without humiliation to any party. In this narrative, the medium for such resolution is the exercise of intellect. Joshua changes his mind neither because he fears Gamaliel's power nor because he respects the person of Aqiba. He does so because of the exegesis Aqiba has "learned." In idealized Rabbinic life, it is through the discipline of "learning" that the sharp and projecting edges of individuality and ego are blunted, controlled, and directed in pursuit of some larger goal.

The attempt to describe the rabbis of antiquity yields a result disappointing for conventional history but fruitful for the study of culture. The virtual anonymity of persons in Rabbinic literature reveals a powerful cultural disinclination, perhaps an incapacity, to construe Rabbinic culture and religion as the work of powerful individuals. It is as if, when they came to put their story down on paper, rabbis could not bring themselves to tell it and therefore were unable to imagine it in terms of themselves. In Rabbinic documents there is no place for the expression of private ego, no room for the imposing, charismatic personality, and no occasion for the emergence of any single, great man who represents the fate and destiny of the many in his own life and person.

The content of Rabbinic documents virtually certifies that they were produced for an internal audience. They are of rabbis, by rabbis, and for rabbis; they constitute a Rabbinic conception of Rabbinic culture, composed for itself and addressed to itself. Rabbinic texts present their contents, whether halakhic teaching or images of persons, in pieces, in fluid literary frameworks that exhibit little temporal dimension. Rabbinic discourse shields itself from intellectual penetration by others; it is the work of a group bounded and set apart. It would be derelict to claim that these texts existed in precisely their present form throughout Rabbinic antiquity. The diachronic range of most documents indicates that their production is not contemporary with the events described and the persons depicted in their pages. But it also is gratuitous to argue that the present form of the texts is unrelated to or at variance with the ways their contents initially were composed, received, transmitted and redacted. Rather, the generations of rabbis who produced, preserved accepted, and believed the materials contained in Rabbinic documents apparently found this mode of depicting reality credible. Unless we suppose all of Rabbinic writing to be one massive literary artifice, we must assume that to some degree the texts reflect and conform to rabbis' experience of and in the world.

This proposition can be tested by a consideration of some aspects of Rabbinic social life. Unfortunately, Rabbinic social life in Palestine after 200 remains substantially unexplored. But in Sasanian Babylonia,[2] as well as in the land of Israel in Roman times,[3] Rabbinic instruction was effected through disciple-circles rather than schools. Rabbinic disciples, that is, apparently did not attend institutions with corporate identities but clustered, rather, around individual masters whom they served, at least in part, as apprentice lawyers. Rabbinic disciples could change teachers either for intellectual or personal reasons. While masters could be abusive and demanding, some attracted students through special expertise in particular subjects.

The picture of a network of relatively autonomous disciple-circles suggests that in order to attract students rabbis had to be figures of forceful personality and distinctive individuality. But the very possibility that students could change teachers at will, the apparent movement of disciples among masters, implies a system of social relations in which rabbis theoretically were equivalent to one another. In a world of face-to-face relationships in which rabbis had to compete with one another for students, no master could fail to be aware of his colleagues' skills, none could escape public scrutiny within the movement. In such a system, individual claims to special power and authority are easily refuted and rendered fragile.

Hints that the realities of Rabbinic social life restrained Rabbinic claims to special power and encouraged the literary suppression of individuality also appear in the rabbis' treatment of themselves as miracleworkers. During the first two centuries, charismatic types who claimed miraculous powers were antithetical to and played little role in Rabbinism. God could perform miracles, but rabbis could not. By the middle of the third century, that picture had changed, and miracle-power became a conventional component in the rabbinical dossier. This shift corresponds to a general development among religious virtuosi in the late Roman world. The third century is witness to the emergence of a class of charismatic individuals, holy men, "friends of God," who claim a special power, an intimate relation with the divine, that definitively sets them off from other men.

In late antique Christianity and paganism, this claim accompanies a vigorous expression of individuality and is recounted, in individual lives, in the literary portraiture of hagiography. In Rabbinism, however, miracle-working does not generate hagiography and appears not to have had the socially disruptive effects it did in pagan and Christian manifestations. This failure of Rabbinism to adopt the pagan and Christian model and portray itself in terms of great and powerful individuals is partly a function of the social system sketched above. But it also is a consequence of the distinctly intellectual character of the Rabbinic enterprise. Whatever personal traits, magnetism, or charisma a rabbi possessed, his standing and credibility within the Rabbinic movement initially depended on his learning. Rabbinical status derived not from the exercise of mysterious and arbitrary divine favor but from the result of intellectual labor. Whatever else being a rabbi meant, it meant the publicly demonstrable mastery of a considerable body of Scripture and halakhic material. Rabbis did not hide from one another in the desert, nor did they seclude themselves behind cloister walls. The evidence of the sources suggests that they lived in a world of persistent mutual scrutiny, a world of continual evaluation and judgment. In such a world, rabbis could not help but be aware of their mortality and could not possibly maintain the illusion of special power, at least, and especially, among themselves.

What, then, can we know overall of the Rabbinic class of antiquity? The rabbis constituted a recognized group of intellectual specialists in ancient Jewish society. By their own description, they developed a set of behavioral patterns that set them off from ordinary people and apparently were designed to identify them as a distinct group. The following Talmudic narrative, at B. Qid. 70a-b, illustrates both the rabbis' claims to use special vocabulary and the potential consequences of their words:

A. There was a man from Nehardea who went into a butcher shop in Pumbedita. He said to them, "Give me meat."

B. They said to him, "Wait until the servant of R. Judah bar Ezekiel gets his, and then we'll give to you."

C. He said, "So who is this Judah bar Sheviskel who comes before me to get served before me?"

D. They went and told R. Judah.

E. He excommunicated him.

F. They said, "He is in the habit of calling people slaves."

G. He proclaimed concerning him, "He is a slave."

H. The other party went and sued him in court before R. Nahman.

I. When the summons came, R. Judah went to R. Huna, he said to him, "Should I go, or shouldn't I go?"

J. He said to him, "In point of fact, you really don't have to go, because you are an eminent authority. But on account of the honor owing to the household of the patriarch [of the Babylonian Jews], get up and go."

K. He came. He found him making a parapet.

L. He said to him, "Doesn't the master concur with what R. Huna bar Idi said Samuel said, 'Once a man is appointed administrator of the community, it is forbidden for him to do servile labor before three persons'?"

M. He said to him, "I'm just making a little piece of the balustrade."

N. He said to him, "So what's so bad about the word, 'parapet,' that the Torah uses, or the word 'partition,' that rabbis use?"

O. He said to him, "Will the master sit down on a seat?"

P. He said to him, "So what's so bad about 'chair,' which rabbis use, or the word 'stool,' which people generally use?"

Q. He said to him, "Will the master eat a piece of citron-fruit?"

R. He said to him, "This is what Samuel said, 'Whoever uses the word "citron-fruit" is a third puffed up with pride.' It should be called either etrog, as the rabbis do, or 'lemony-thing,' as people do."

S. He said to him, "Would the master like to drink a goblet of wine?"

T. He said to him, "So what's so bad about the word 'wineglass,' as rabbis say, or 'a drink,' as people say?"

U. He said to him, "Let my daughter Dunag bring something to drink?"

V. He said to him, "This is what Samuel said, 'People are not to make use of a woman.'"

W. "But she's only a minor!"

X. "In so many words said Samuel, 'People are not to make use of a woman in any manner, whether adult or minor.'"

Y. "Would the master care to send a greeting to my wife, Yalta?"

Z. He said to him, "This is what Samuel said, 'Even the sound of a woman's voice is [forbidden as] lustful.'"

AA. "Maybe through a messenger?"

BB. He said to him, "This is what Samuel said, 'People are not to inquire after a woman's health.'"

CC. "Through her husband?!"

DD. He said to him, "This is what Samuel said, 'People are not to inquire after a woman's health in any way, shape, or form.'"

EE. His wife sent word to him, "Settle the man's case for him, so that he not make you like any other fool."

FF. He said to him, "So what brings you here?"

GG. He said to him, "You sent me a subpoena." He said to him, "Now if even the language of the master I don't know, how in the world could I have sent you a subpoena?!"

HH. He produced the summons from his bosom and showed it to him: "Here is the man, here is the subpoena!"

II. He said to him, "Well, anyhow, since the master has come here, let's discuss the matter, so people should not say that rabbis are showing favoritism to one another."

JJ. He said to him, "How come the master has excommunicated that man?" "He harassed a messenger of the rabbis."

KK. "So why didn't the master flog him, for Rab would flog someone who harassed a messenger of the rabbis?"

LL. "I did worse to him."

MM. "How come the master declared the man that he was a slave?"

NN. "Because he went around calling other people slaves, and there is a Tannaite statement: Whoever alleges that others are genealogically invalid is himself invalid and never says a good thing about other people. And said Samuel, 'By reference to a flaw in himself he invalidates others.'"

OO. "Well, I can concede that Samuel said to suspect such a man of such a genealogy, but did he really say to make a public declaration to that effect?"

PP. In the meanwhile, the litigant from Nehardea came along. Said that litigant to R. Judah, "You called me a slave, I, who descend from the royal house of the Hasmoneans!"

QQ. He said to him, "This is what Samuel said, 'Whoever says that he comes from the house of the Hasmoneans is in fact a slave.'"

RR. [Nahman] said to him, "Doesn't the master concur with what R. Abba said R. Huna said Rab said, 'Any disciple of a sage who teaches a law, if it is prior to the case that he said it, [his teaching] is listened to, but if not, it is not listened to'?"

SS. He said to him, "Well, there's R. Mattenah, who concurs with me." Now R. Mattenah had not seen the town of Nehardea for thirteen years, but on that very day, he paid a visit. Said [Judah] to him, "Does the master remember what Samuel said when he was standing with one foot on the bank and one foot on the bridge?"

TT. He said to him, "This is what Samuel said, 'Whoever says that he comes from the house of the Hasmoneans is in fact a slave, for of that family survived only one woman, who climbed up to the roof and shouted in a loud voice, "Whoever says that he comes from the house of the Hasmoneans is in fact a slave." She then fell from the roof and died.'" So they issued a proclamation concerning the litigant that he was a slave.

UU. Now, on that day, many marriage contracts were ripped up in Nehardea. So when R. Judah came out, they came out after him to stone him. He said to them, "So if you'll shut up, just shut up, but if not, I'm going to tell concerning you what Samuel said, namely, 'There are two families in Nehardea, the household of the dove and the household of the raven, and the mnemonic is: The unclean is unclean, the clean, clean.'"

VV. So they tossed away their stones, and that made a dam in the royal canal.

WW. [Then] R. Judah declared in Pumbedita, "Adda and Jonathan are slaves, Judah bar Pappa is a *mamzer*, Bati bar Butiah arrogantly refused to accept a writ of manumission."

XX. Raba proclaimed in Mahoza, "The households of Bela, Dena, Tela, Mela, and Zega all are unfit."

YY. R. Judah said, "The household of Guba are Gibeonites; Durunita is a village made of Netins."

ZZ. Said R. Joseph, "The household of Kubi in Pumbedita is made up entirely of slaves."

Despite the rabbis' claims to control Israel's destiny, they lacked the political power to direct their society or to enforce the myriad laws and scriptural interpretations they believed held the key to redemption. Their literature's manifest lack of interest in that society suggests its reciprocal lack of interest in them. In the absence of real power, rabbis exerted what influence they could but devoted themselves primarily to forging their own collective identity. The bulk of their literature is recondite and insular, bespeaking the shared privacy of the initiated. Its obsession with detailed scriptural exegesis and halakhic disputation means that rabbis needed each other as an audience. Their sense of social credibility and group membership, therefore, in large measure depended on how they treated one another. To alienate a colleague by arrogance, humiliation, or claims to special power was to risk losing an audience and consigning the work of collective identity to failure.

The search for the rabbis of antiquity suggests a degree of conformity among the ways rabbis lived with one another, imagined one another, and represented one another in their literature. It leads not into the lives and careers of great men but into a self-absorbed community of intellectuals who competed with each other but needed each other and strove to maintain at least the illusion of each other's dignity.

### Notes

[1] Richard Kalmin, *Sages, Stories, Authors, and Editors in Rabbinic Babylonia* (Atlanta, 1994), p. 198.

[2] David M. Goodblatt, *Rabbinic Instruction in Sasanian Babylonia* (Leiden, 1975).

[3] Martin Goodman, *State and Society in Roman Palestine: 120-200* (Totowa, 1985).

WILLIAM SCOTT GREEN

**RABBINIC JUDAISM, FORMATIVE CANON OF: [1] DEFINING THE CANON:** The Judaism of the dual Torah, which took shape in the first seven centuries C.E., rests upon its adherents conception of Torah, meaning revelation. The literature produced by the rabbis is understood to form a part of that Torah, and this literature therefore is highly valued. Because it is part of the Torah, that is, in its Judaism, Rabbinic literature is important. In the Torah God reveals ("gives") God's self-manifestation in one aspect: God's will, expressed in particular in an account of the covenant between God and Israel. That refers to the identification of the contracting parties, on the one side, and what the covenant entails for the life of Israel with God, on the other. That is the religious context defined by the Judaism of the dual Torah in which the literature of Rabbinic Judaism is written, valued and studied.

While it is only one among several Judaic systems of antiquity, the Judaism of the dual Torah set forth the most important canon of a Judaism to emerge from ancient times. For it is the Judaism that proved normative from its formative centuries to our own day, and it produced most of the Judaic systems that now flourish. That Judaism, drawing upon older materials of course, beginning with the Old Testament itself, finds its definitive symbol in the Torah, written and oral. Its distinctive myth appeals to the story that at Sinai God revealed revelation, or "Torah," to Moses in two media. One medium for revelation was in writing, hence "the written Torah," *Torah shebikhtab*, corresponding to the Old Testament of Christianity. The other medium for revelation was through oral formulation and oral transmission, hence through memorization, yielding "the oral Torah," *Torah shebe'al peh*, the memorized Torah. The Judaism of the dual Torah bestows upon its authorities, or sages, the title of "rabbi," hence is called Rabbinic Judaism; it appeals for its ultimate authority to the Talmud of Babylonia, or Bavli, hence is called talmudic Judaism; it enjoys the status of orthodoxy, hence is called "normative" or "classical" Judaism. Today, the Rabbinic literature valued as canonical by the Judaism of the dual Torah forms the court of final appeal to all Judaisms, from Orthodoxy both integrationist and segregationist, to Reform, Conservative, Reconstructionist, and all other

known Judaic systems of a religious character. Each invokes in its own way and for its own purposes the received writings of the Judaism of the dual Torah.

**The concept of a holy book in the Judaism of the Dual Torah:** The literature of Rabbinic Judaism therefore takes its place as a component of that Torah: part of God's revelation to Israel. But it is only one of the three parts that comprise the Torah. In the Judaism of the dual Torah, the Torah is set forth and preserved in three media, [1] a book, the Hebrew Scriptures or Old Testament, [2] a memorized oral tradition, first written down in the Mishnah, ca. 200 C.E., and other ancient documents, and [3] the model of a sage who embodies in the here and now the paradigm of Moses, called a rabbi. Other Judaic systems identified other holy books, in addition to Scripture, for their canon. The canon of Rabbinic Judaism is only one, distinct and autonomous corpus of writings; other Judaisms defined their own canons in accord with their systems' requirements. Each canon then recapitulated its system and no other.

That is to say, since in antiquity, as in modern times, diverse sets of books have been defined as the canon of one Judaism or another, we recognize at the outset a simple fact. No single, unitary, linear "Judaism" ever existed, from the beginnings to the present, defining an "orthodoxy." Quite to the contrary, a variety of Judaisms—Judaic systems, comprising a way of life, world view, and definition of a social entity, an "Israel"—have flourished. Comparison of one Judaic system with another shows that each is autonomous and freestanding. Each Judaic system appeals to its distinctive symbolic structure, explains itself by invoking its particular myth, sets forth its indicative way of life, accounts for its way of life by appealing to its own world view. The Judaic system revealed by Philo side by side with the one preserved in the Essene library found at the Dead Sea, or the Judaic system presented by the ancient rabbis with the Judaic system defined by the Pentateuchal editors in the fifth century B.C.E., makes the point quite clear. Harmonizing all of the diverse Judaisms into a single Judaism imposes a theological construct upon diverse and discrete historical facts. Since (except in the theological context) there never has been a single, "orthodox", unitary and harmonious "Judaism," against which all "heterodox" or "heretical" Judaisms have to be judged, we recognize that each Judaism is to be described in its own terms, meaning, in the context of its literature or other enduring evidences.

The concept of a sacred text in the Judaism of the dual Torah therefore finds definition in the myth of the dual Torah. In fact, all components of that Torah are secondary. What comes first is the myth of the memorized Torah, what follows is the identification of the documents that enjoy the status of components of that memorized Torah. The Judaism of the dual Torah by definition does not find its definition in a book—e.g., the Old Testament. Its generative principle is quite the opposite: God did not resort solely to a book to convey and preserve the divine message. It was through teachings, which could be transmitted in more than a single form. Consequently, a way lay open to encompass more than the Old Testament as Torah, and, indeed, in late antiquity, Torah found ample room not only for truth formulated in words—whether written down or memorized—but also for gestures, indeed, also for persons. Consequently the sage could be received as a Torah and treated as such.

An important and simple statement of that fact will prove the point. A sage himself was equivalent to a scroll of the Torah—a material, legal comparison, not merely a symbolic metaphor.

> A. He who sees a disciple of a sage who has died is as if he sees a scroll of the Torah that has been burned.

> Y. M.Q. 3:7.X.

> I. R. Jacob bar Abayye in the name of R. Aha: "An elder who forgot his learning because of some accident which happened to him—they treat him with the sanctity owed to an ark [of the Torah]."

> Y. M.Q. 3:1.XI.

The sage therefore is represented as equivalent to the scroll of the Torah, and, turning the statement around, the scroll of the Torah is realized in the person of the sage. The conception is not merely figurative or metaphorical, for, in both instances, actual behavior was affected. Still more to the point, what the sage *did* had the status of law; the sage was the model of the law, thus once again enjoyed the standing of the human embodiment of the Torah. Since the sage exercised supernatural power as a kind of living Torah, his very deeds served to reveal law, as much as his word expressed revelation. That is a formidable component of the argument that the sage embodied the Torah, another way of saying that the Torah was incarnated in the person of the sage.

The capacity of the sage himself to participate in the process of revelation is illustrated in two types of materials. First of all, tales told about rabbis' behavior on specific occasions immediately are translated into rules for the entire community to keep. Accordingly, he was a source not merely of good example but of prescriptive law.

> X. R. Aha went to Emmaus, and he ate dumpling [prepared by Samaritans].
> Y. R. Jeremiah ate leavened bread prepared by them.
> Z. R. Hezekiah ate their locusts prepared by them.
> AA. R. Abbahu prohibited Israelite use of wine prepared by them.

> Y. A.Z. 5:4.III

Along with hundreds of parallels in the Rabbinic literature, these reports of what rabbis had said and done enjoyed the same authority as citations of traditions in the names of the great authorities of old or of the day. What someone did served as a norm, if the person was a sage of sufficient standing. The precedent entered the Torah, and what a sage said became part of the oral component of the one whole Torah that God gave to Moses at Sinai. That is the mythic premise on which these and similar stories are told and preserved.

It follows that the Judaism of the dual Torah is not a religion of a book, though that Judaism does venerate books as well as orally formulated and orally transmitted teachings. The reason is that that Judaism does not take form solely through sacred texts. It is not a religion that appeals to a book for its authority and definition of truth. It appeals to truth that is preserved in diverse media, books, words preserved not in books but in memorized formulas, and, finally, the lives, gestures, and deeds of holy persons. It follows that the Judaism of the dual Torah appeals not solely to texts, oral or written, and it is assuredly not a religion that derives from a book in particular. It is a religion that receives its revelation in a variety of media, and, by definition, it is therefore not a religion of a book. But it does refer to a canon, which serves to recapitulate the system just now adumbrated. Let us rapidly survey the canonical writings that comprise Rabbinic literature.

**Defining the canon of Rabbinic literature:** A simple definition follows from what has been said. Rabbinic literature is the corpus of writing produced in the first seven centuries C.E. by sages who claimed to stand in the chain of tradition from Sinai and uniquely to possess the oral part of the Torah, revealed by God to Moses at Sinai for oral formulation and oral transmission. This they possessed in addition to the written part of the Torah possessed by all Israel. Among the many, diverse documents produced by Jews in the first seven centuries C.E., only a small group cohere and form a distinctive corpus, called "Rabbinic literature." Three traits together suffice to distinguish Rabbinic literature from all other Jewish (ethnic) and Judaic (religious) writing of that age:

[1] These writings of law and exegesis, revered as holy books, copiously cite the Hebrew Scriptures of ancient Israel ("written Torah").

[2] They acknowledge the authority, and even the existence, of no other Judaic (or gentile) books but the ancient Israelite Scriptures.

[3] These writings promiscuously and ubiquitously cite sayings attributed to named authorities, unique to those books themselves, most of them bearing the title "rabbi."

Other Judaic writings ordinarily qualify under the first plank of the definition, and the same is to be said for Christian counterparts.

The second element in the definition excludes all Christian documents. The third dismisses all writings of all Judaisms other than the one of the dual Torah. Other Judaisms' writings cite Scriptural heroes or refer to a particular authority; none except those of this Judaism sets forth, as does every Rabbinic document, extensive accounts of what a large number of diverse authorities say, let alone disputes among them. "Rabbinic" is therefore an appropriate qualifier for this Judaism, since what distinguishes it from all other is the character of its authorities (the matter of title being a mere detail) and the myth that accounts for its distinctive character.

Any book out of Judaic antiquity that exhibits these three traits—focus upon law and exegesis of the Hebrew Scriptures, exclusion of all prior tradition except for Scripture, and appealing to named sages called rabbis, falls into the category of Rabbinic literature. All other Jewish writings in varying proportions exhibit the first trait, and some the second as well, but none all three. It goes without saying that no named authority in any Rabbinic writing, except for scriptural ones, occurs in any other Judaic document in antiquity (excluding Gamaliel in Acts), or in another Jewish one either (excluding Simeon b. Gamaliel in Josephus's histories).

Having defined the traits that distinguish all Rabbinic documents from non-Rabbinic ones, let us examine the characteristics that distinguish the documents within the Rabbinic corpus. Rabbinic literature is divided into two large parts, each part formed as a commentary to a received part of the Torah, one oral, the other written. The written part requires no attention here: it is simply Scripture (Hebrew: "the written Torah," TaNaKH, Torah, Nebiim, Ketubim, a.k.a. "the Old Testament" part of the Bible). The oral part begins with the Mishnah, a philosophical law code that reached closure at the end of the second century C.E. Promulgated under the sponsorship of the Roman-appointed Jewish authority of the Land of Israel ("Palestine"), Judah the Patriarch, the Mishnah formed the first document of Rabbinic literature and therefore of the Judaic system, "Rabbinic Judaism," or "the Judaism of the dual Torah," that took shape in this period. The attributed statements of its authorities, named sages or rabbis called Tannaites ("repeaters," "memorizers," for the form in which the sayings were formulated and transmitted), enjoyed the standing of traditions beginning at Sinai. Numerous anonymous sayings, alongside the attributed ones and bearing upon the same controverted questions, appear as well.

**The Mishnah and the exegetical tradition of the Oral Torah:** Comprising six divisions, dealing with agriculture, holy seasons, women and family affairs, civil law and politics, everyday offerings, and cultic purity, the Mishnah served as the written code of the Patriarch's administration in the Land of Israel, and of that of his counterpart, the Exilarch, in Iranian-ruled Babylonia as well. Alongside the Mishnah's compilation of sages' sayings into well-crafted divisions, tractates, and chapters, other sayings of the same authorities circulated, some of them finding their way, marked as deriving from Tannaite authority, into three exegetical documents that formed around parts of the Mishnah. These were, specifically:

[1] the Tosefta, a compilation of supplementary sayings organized around nearly the whole of the Mishnah as citation and gloss, secondary paraphrase, and freestanding complement thereto, of no determinate date but probably concluded about a century after the closure of the Mishnah, hence ca. 300.

[2] the Talmud of the Land of Israel (Yerushalmi), which reached closure in ca. 400, a commentary to most of the tractates of the Mishnah's first four divisions,

[3] the Talmud of Babylonia (Bavli), concluded in ca. 600, providing a sustained exegesis to most of the tractates of the Mishnah's second through fifth divisions.

The Tosefta's materials occasionally form the basis for exegetical compositions in the two Talmuds, but the second Talmud's framers know nothing about the compositions, let alone compositions, of the prior Talmud, even though they frequently do cite sayings attributed to authorities of the Land of Israel as much as of Babylonia. So the line of the exegesis and extension of the Mishnah extends through the Tosefta and then to the two, autonomous Talmuds.

**Scripture and the exegetical tradition of the Written Torah:** Parts of the written Torah attracted sustained commentary as well, and, altogether, these commentaries, called Midrash-compilations, form the counterpart to the writings of Mishnah-exegesis. It should be noted that both Talmuds, in addition, contain large composites of Midrash-exegesis, but they are not organized around books or large selections of Scripture. The part of Rabbinic literature that takes Scripture, rather than the Mishnah, as its organizing structure covers the Pentateuchal books of Exodus, Leviticus, Numbers, and Deuteronomy, and some of the writings important in synagogue liturgy, particularly Ruth, Esther, Lamentations, and Song of Songs, all read on special occasions in the sacred calendar. Numbering for late antiquity twelve compilations in all, the earliest compilations of exegesis, called midrash, were produced in the third century, the latest in the sixth or seventh.

**Sages and the exemplary Torah:** There is a third type of writing in Rabbinic literature, which concerns teachings of sages on theological and moral questions. This comprises a very small, freestanding corpus, tractate Abot ("the fathers," or founders) and Abot deRabbi Nathan ("the fathers according to Rabbi Nathan"). The former collects sayings of sages, and the later contributes in addition stories about them. But the bulk of Rabbinic literature consists of works of exegesis of the Mishnah and Scripture, which is to say, the principal documents of the Torah, oral and written respectively. But throughout the documents of the oral Torah also are collected compositions and large compilations that are devoted to the sayings and exemplary deeds of named sages. No documents took shape to be made up out of that kind of writing, which, nonetheless, was abundant.

**Mishnah and Midrash, *Halakhah* and *Aggadah*:** Viewed as a whole, therefore, we see that the stream of exegesis of the Mishnah and exploration of its themes of law and philosophy flowed side by side with exegesis of Scripture. Since the Mishnah concerns itself with normative rules of behavior, it and the documents of exegesis flowing from it ordinarily are comprised of discussion of matters of law, or, in Hebrew, *halakhah*. Much of the exegesis of Scripture in the Midrash-compilations concerns itself with norms of belief, right attitude, virtue and proper motivation. Encased in narrative form, these teachings of an ethical and moral character are called *aggadah*, or lore.

Midrash-exegesis of Israelite Scripture in no way was particular to the Rabbinic literature. To the contrary, the exegesis of the Hebrew Scriptures had defined a convention of all systems of Judaism from before the conclusion of Scripture itself; no one, including the sages who stand behind Rabbinic literature, began anywhere but in the encounter with the Written Torah. But collecting and organizing documents of exegeses of Scripture in a systematic way developed in a quite distinct circumstance.

For Rabbinic literature, the circumstance was defined by the requirement of Mishnah-exegesis. The Mishnah's character itself defined a principal task of Scripture-exegesis. Standing by itself, providing few proof texts to Scripture to back up its rules, the Mishnah bore no explanation of why Israel should obey its rules. Brought into relationship to Scriptures, by contrast, the Mishnah gained access to the source of authority by definition operative in Israel, the Jewish people. Accordingly, the work of relating the Mishnah's rules to those of Scripture got under way alongside the formation of the Mishnah's rules themselves. It follows that explanations of the sense of the document, including its authority and sources, would draw attention to the written part of the Torah.

We may classify the Midrash-compilations in three successive groups: exegetical, propositional, and exegetical-propositional (theological).

**[1] Exegetical discourse and the Pentateuch:** One important dimension of the earliest documents of Scripture-exegesis, the Midrash-compilations that deal with Leviticus, Numbers, and Deuteronomy, measures the distance between the Mishnah and Scripture and aims to close it. The question is persistently addressed in analyzing Scripture: precisely how does a rule of the Mishnah relate to, or rest upon, a rule of Scripture? That question demanded an answer, so that the status of the Mishnah's rules and, right alongside, of the Mishnah itself could find a clear definition. The collecting and arranging of exegeses of Scripture as these related to passages of the Mishnah first reached literary form in Sifra, to Leviticus, and in two books, both called Sifré, one to Numbers, the other Deuteronomy. All three compositions accomplished much else. For, even at that early stage, exegeses of passages of Scripture in their own context and not only for the sake of Mishnah-exegesis attracted attention. But a principal motif in all three books concerned the issue of Mishnah-Scripture relationships.

A second, still more fruitful path in formulating Midrash-clarifications of Scripture also emerged from the labor of Mishnah-exegesis. As the work of Mishnah-exegesis got under way, in the third century, exegetes of the Mishnah and others alongside undertook a parallel labor. They took an interest in reading Scripture in the way in which they were reading the Mishnah itself. That is to say, they began to work through verses of Scripture in exactly the same way—word for word, phrase for phrase, line for line—in which, to begin with, the exegetes of the Mishnah pursued the interpretation and explanation of the Mishnah. Precisely the types of exegesis that dictated the way in which sages read the Mishnah now guided their reading of Scripture as well. And, as people began to collect and organize comments in accord with the order of sentences and paragraphs of the Mishnah, they found the stimulation to collect and organize comments on clauses and verses of Scripture. This kind of verse-by-verse exegetical work got under way in the Sifra and the two Sifrés, but reached fulfillment in Genesis Rabbah, which presents a line-for-line reading of the book of Genesis. Characteristic of the narrowly-exegetical phase of Midrash-compilation is the absence of a single, governing proposition, running through the details. It is not possible, for example, to state the main point, expressed through countless cases, in Sifra or Sifré to Deuteronomy.

**[2] From exegesis to proposition:** A further group of Midrash-compilations altogether transcends the limits of formal exegesis. Beyond these two modes of exegesis—search for the sources of the Mishnah in Scripture, line-by-line reading of Scripture as of the Mishnah—lies yet a third, an approach we may call "writing with Scripture," meaning, using verses of Scripture in a context established by a propositional program independent of Scripture itself. To understand it, we have to know how the first of the two Talmuds read the Mishnah. The Yerushalmi's authors not only explained phrases or sentences of the Mishnah in the manner of Mishnah- and Scripture-exegetes. They also investigated the principles and large-scale conceptual problems of the document and of the law given only in cases in the Mishnah itself. That is to say, they dealt not alone with a given topic, a subject and its rule, the cases that yield the rule, but with an encompassing problem, a principle and its implications for a number of topics and rules.

This far more discursive and philosophical mode of thought produced for Mishnah-exegesis sustained essays on principles cutting across specific rules. Predictably, this same intellectual work extended from the Mishnah to Scripture. Exegesis of Scripture that focused on words, phrases, and sentences produced discursive essays on great principles or problems of theology and morality. Discursive exegesis is represented, to begin with, in Leviticus Rabbah, a document that reached closure, people generally suppose, sometime after Genesis Rabbah, thus ca. 450 and that marked the shift from verse-by-verse to syllogistic reading of verses of Scripture. It was continued in Pesiqta deRab Kahana, organized around themes pertinent to various holy days through the liturgical year, and Pesiqta Rabbati, a derivative and imitative work.

Typical of discursive exegesis of Scripture, Leviticus Rabbah presents not phrase-by-phrase systematic exegeses of verses in the book of Leviticus, but a set of thirty-seven topical essays. These essays, syllogistic in purpose, take the form of citations and comments on verses of Scripture to be sure. But the compositions range widely over the far reaches of the Hebrew Scriptures while focusing narrowly upon a given theme. They moreover make quite distinctive points about that theme. Their essays constitute compositions, not merely composites. Whether devoted to God's favor to the poor and humble or to the dangers of drunkenness, the essays, exegetical in form, discursive in character, correspond to the equivalent, legal essays, amply represented in the Yerushalmi. The framers of Pesiqta deRab Kahana carried forward a still more abstract and discursive mode of discourse, one in which verses of Scripture play a subordinated role to the framing of an implicit syllogism, which predominates throughout, both formally and in argument.

**[3] Saying one thing through many things:** Writing with Scripture reached its climax in the theological Midrash-compilations formed at the end of the development of Rabbinic literature. A fusion of the two approaches to Midrash-exegesis, the verse-by-verse amplification of successive chapters of Scripture and the syllogistic presentation of propositions, arguments, and proofs deriving from the facts of Scripture, was accomplished in the third body of Midrash-compilations: Ruth Rabbah, Esther Rabbah Part I, Lamentations Rabbah, and Song of Songs Rabbah. Here we find the verse-by-verse reading of scriptural books. But at the same time, a highly propositional program governs the exegesis, each of the compilations meaning to prove a single, fundamental theological point through the accumulation of detailed comments.

**Halakhah and Aggadah, Mishnah and Midrash in a single definitive document:** The Talmud of Babylonia, or Bavli, which was the final document of Rabbinic literature also formed the climax and conclusion of the entire canon and defined this Judaism from its time to the present. The Talmud of Babylonia forms the conclusion and the summary of Rabbinic literature, the most important document of the entire collection. One of its principal traits is the fusion of Mishnah- and Scripture-exegesis in a single compilation. The authors of units of discourse collected in the Talmud of Babylonia or Bavli drew together the two, up-to-then distinct, modes of organizing thought, either around the Mishnah or around Scripture. They treated both Torahs, oral and written, as equally available in the work of organizing large-scale exercises of sustained inquiry. So we find in the Bavli a systematic treatment of some tractates of the Mishnah. And within the same aggregates of discourse, we also find (in somewhat smaller proportion to be sure, roughly 60% to roughly 40% in a sample made of three tractates) a second principle of organizing and redaction. That principle dictates that ideas be laid out in line with verses of Scripture, themselves dealt with in cogent sequence, one by one, just as the Mishnah's sentences and paragraphs come under analysis, in cogent order and one by one.

**Dating Rabbinic documents:** While we have no exact dates for the closure of any of the documents of Rabbinic literature—all the dates we have are mere guesses—we have solid grounds on setting them forth in the sequence [1] Mishnah, Tosefta, [2] Yerushalmi, [3] Bavli for the exegetical writings on the Mishnah, and the three corresponding, and successive groups—[1] Sifra and the two Sifrés, [2] Leviticus Rabbah, Pesiqta deRab Kahana, Pesiqta Rabbati, then [3] Ruth Rabbah, Esther Rabbah Part One, Lamentations Rabbah, and Song of Songs Rabbah—for the exegetical writings on Scripture. The basis in the case of the sequence from Mishnah is citation by one compilation of another, in which case, the cited document is to be dated prior to the document that does the citing. The basis in the case of the sequence from Scripture is less certain; we assign a post-Mishnah date to Sifra and the two Sifrés because of the large-scale citation of the former in the latter. The rest of the sequence given here rests upon presently-accepted and conventional dates and therefore cannot be regarded as final.

Study of the history of Rabbinic Judaism through the literature just now set forth must proceed document by document, in the sequence presently established for their respective dates of closure. In such a study of documentary sequences, e.g., how a given

topic or theme is set forth in one writing after another, we learn the order in which ideas came to expression in the canon. We therefore commence at the Mishnah, the starting point of the originally-oral part of the canon. We proceed systematically to work our way through tractate Abot, the Mishnah's first apologetic, then the Tosefta, the Yerushalmi, and the Bavli at the end. Along the same lines, the sequence of Midrash-compilations is to be examined and the results, if possible, correlated with those of the Mishnah and its companions. In tracing the order in which ideas make their appearance, we ask about the components in sequence so far as we can trace the sequence. The traits of documents govern, and the boundaries that separate one from another also distinguish sayings from one another. The upshot is the study of the documents one by one, with emphasis on their distinguishing traits.

JACOB NEUSNER

**RABBINIC JUDAISM, FORMATIVE CANON OF: [2] THE HALAKHIC DOCUMENTS:** "Halakhah" refers to laws, norms of conduct, and halakhic documents are those that present rules of correct behavior and belief for holy Israel. These form continuations of the laws that the written Torah sets forth. Many derive from the exegesis and amplification of the laws of the written Torah, some from tradition of Sinai set forth by "our sages of blessed memory." The halakhic documents of the Rabbinic canon are the Mishnah, Tosefta, Talmud of the Land of Israel, and Talmud of Babylonia.

**The Mishnah:** The Mishnah is a philosophical law code, covering topics of both a theoretical and practical character. It was produced at about 200 C.E. under the sponsorship of Judah, Patriarch (*nasi*) or ethnic ruler of the Jews of the Land of Israel. It comprises sixty-two tractates, divided by topics among six divisions, as follows:

1. AGRICULTURE (Zeraim): Berakhot (Blessings); Peah (the corner of the field); Demai (doubtfully tithed produce); Kilayim (mixed seeds); Shebiit (the seventh year); Terumot (heave offering or priestly rations); Maaserot (tithes); Maaser Sheni (second

tithe); Hallah (dough offering); Orlah (produce of trees in the first three years after planting, which is prohibited); and Bikkurim (first fruits).

2. APPOINTED TIMES (Moed): Shabbat (the Sabbath); Erubin (the fictive fusion meal or boundary); Pesahim (Passover); Sheqalim (the Temple tax); Yoma (the Day of Atonement); Sukkah (the festival of Tabernacles); Besah (the preparation of food on the festivals and Sabbath); Rosh Hashshanah (the New Year); Taanit (fast days); Megillah (Purim); Moed Qatan (the intermediate days of the festivals of Passover and Tabernacles); Hagigah (the festal offering).

3. WOMEN (Nashim): Yebamot (the levirate widow); Ketubot (the marriage contract); Nedarim (vows); Nazir (the special vow of the Nazirite); Sotah (the wife accused of adultery); Gittin (writs of divorce); Qiddushin (betrothal).

4. DAMAGES or civil law (Neziqin): Baba Qamma, Baba Mesia, Baba Batra (civil law, covering damages and torts, then correct conduct of business, labor, and real estate transactions); Sanhedrin (institutions of government; criminal penalties); Makkot (flogging); Shabuot (oaths); Eduyyot (a collection arranged on other than topical lines); Horayot (rules governing improper conduct of civil authorities);

5. HOLY THINGS (Qodoshim): Zebahim (every day animal offerings); Menahot (meal offerings); Hullin (animals slaughtered for secular purposes); Bekhorot (firstlings); Arakhin (vows of valuation); Temurah (vows of exchange of a beast for an already consecrated beast); Keritot (penalty of extirpation or premature death); Meilah (sacrilege); Tamid (the daily whole offering); Middot (the layout of the Temple building); Qinnim (how to deal with bird offerings designated for a given purpose and then mixed up);

6. PURITY (Tohorot): Kelim (susceptibility of utensils to uncleanness); Ohalot (transmission of corpse-uncleanness in the tent of a corpse); Negaim (the uncleanness described at Lev. 13-14); Parah (the preparation of purification-water); Tohorot (problems of doubt in connection with matters of cleanness); Miqvaot (immersion-pools); Niddah (menstrual uncleanness); Makhsirin (rendering susceptible to uncleanness produce that is dry and so not susceptible); Zabim (the uncleanness covered at Lev. 15); Tebul-Yom (the uncleanness of one who has immersed on that self-same day and awaits sunset for completion of the purification rites); Yadayim (the uncleanness of hands); Uqsin (the uncleanness transmitted through what is connected to unclean produce).

In volume, the sixth division covers approximately a quarter of the entire document. Topics of interest to the priesthood and the Temple, such as priestly fees, conduct of the cult on holy days, conduct of the cult on ordinary days and management and upkeep of the Temple, and the rules of cultic cleanness, predominate in the first, second, fifth, and sixth divisions. Rules governing the social order form the bulk of the third and fourth. Of these tractates, only Eduyyot is organized along other than topical lines, rather collecting sayings on diverse subjects attributed to particular authorities. The Mishnah as printed today always includes Abot (sayings of the sages), but that document reached closure about a generation later than the Mishnah. While it serves as its initial apologetic, it does not conform to the formal, rhetorical, or logical traits characteristic of the Mishnah overall.

**Main points of stress in the Mishnah:** The stress of the Mishnah throughout on the priestly caste and the Temple cult point to the document's principal concern, which centered upon sanctification, understood as the correct arrangement of all things, each in its proper category, each called by its rightful name, just as at the creation as portrayed in the Priestly document, and just as with the cult itself as set forth in Leviticus. Further, the thousands of rules and cases (with sages' disputes thereon) that comprise the document upon close reading turn out to express in concrete language abstract principles of hierarchical classification. These define the document's method and mark it as a work of a philosophical character. Not only so, but a variety of specific, recurrent concerns, for example, the relationship of being to becoming, actual to potential, the principles of economics, the politics, correspond point by point to comparable ones in Graeco-Roman philosophy, particularly Aristotle's tradition. This stress on proper order and right rule and the formulation of a philosophy, politics, and economics, within the principles of natural history set forth by Aristotle, explain why the Mishnah makes a statement to be classified as philosophy, concerning the order of the natural world in its correspondence with the supernatural world.

**The Mishnah's philosophy—Method and propositions:** The system of philosophy expressed through concrete and detailed law presented by the Mishnah, consists of a coherent logic and topic, a cogent world-view and comprehensive way of living. Its world-view speaks of transcendent things, a way of life in response to the supernatural meaning of what is done, a heightened and deepened perception of the sanctification of Israel in deed and in deliberation. Sanctification thus means two things, first, distinguishing Israel in all its dimensions from the world in all its ways; second, establishing the stability, order, regularity, predictability, and reliability of Israel in the world of nature and supernature in particular at moments and in contexts of danger. Danger means instability, disorder, irregularity, uncertainty, and betrayal. Each topic of the system as a whole takes up a critical and indispensable moment or context of social being. Through what is said in regard to each of the Mishnah's principal topics, what the system as a whole wishes to declare is fully expressed. Yet if the parts severally and jointly give the message of the whole, the whole cannot exist without all of the parts, so well joined and carefully crafted are they all. The details become clear in our survey of the document's topical program, in which we review the six divisions as they were finally spelled out.

THE DIVISION OF AGRICULTURE treats two topics, first, producing crops in accord with the scriptural rules on the subject, second, paying the required offerings and tithes to the priests, Levites, and poor. The principal point of the Division is that the Land is holy, because God has a claim both on it and upon what it produces. God's claim must be hon-

ored by setting aside a portion of the produce for those for whom God has designated it. God's ownership must be acknowledged by observing the rules God has laid down for use of the Land. In the temporal context in which the Mishnah was produced, some generations after the disastrous defeat by the Romans of Bar Kokhba and the permanent closure of Jerusalem to Jews' access, the stress of the division brought assurance that those aspects of the sanctification of Israel—land of Israel, Israel itself and its social order, the holy cycle of time—that survived still remained holy and subject to the rules of Heaven.

THE DIVISION OF APPOINTED TIMES carries forward the same emphasis upon sanctification, now of the high points of the lunar-solar calendar of Israel. The second division forms a system in which the advent of a holy day, like the Sabbath of creation, sanctifies the life of the Israelite village through imposing on the village rules on the model of those of the Temple. The purpose of the system, therefore, is to bring into alignment the moment of sanctification of the village and the life of the home with the moment of sanctification of the Temple on those same occasions of appointed times. The underlying and generative logic of the system comes to expression in a concrete way here in the rule of like and opposite, comparison and contrast. What is not like something follows the rule opposite to that pertaining to that something. Here, therefore, since the village is the mirror image of the Temple, the upshot is dictated by the analogical-contrastive logic of the system as a whole. If things are done in one way in the Temple, they will be done in the opposite way in the village. Together the village and the Temple on the occasion of the holy day therefore form a single continuum, a completed creation, thus awaiting sanctification. The village is made like the Temple in that on appointed times one may not freely cross the lines distinguishing the village from the rest of the world, just as one may not freely cross the lines distinguishing the Temple from the world. But the village is a mirror image of the Temple. The boundary lines prevent free entry into the

Temple, so they restrict free egress from the village. On the holy day what one may do in the Temple is precisely what one may not do in the village.

So the advent of the holy day affects the village by bringing it into sacred symmetry in such wise as to effect a system of opposites; each is holy, in a way precisely the opposite of the other. Because of the underlying conception of perfection attained through the union of opposites, the village is not represented as conforming to the model of the cult, but of constituting its antithesis. The world thus regains perfection when on the holy day heaven and earth are united, the whole completed and done: the heaven, the earth, and all their hosts. This moment of perfection renders the events of ordinary time, of "history," essentially irrelevant. For what really matters in time is that moment in which sacred time intervenes and effects the perfection formed of the union of heaven and earth, of Temple, in the model of the former, and Israel, its complement. It is not a return to a perfect time but a recovery of perfect being, a fulfillment of creation, which explains the essentially ahistorical character of the Mishnah's Division on Appointed Times. Sanctification constitutes an ontological category and is effected by the creator.

This explains why the division in its rich detail is composed of two quite distinct sets of materials. First, it addresses what one does in the sacred space of the Temple on the occasion of sacred time, as distinct from what one does in that same sacred space on ordinary, undifferentiated days, which is a subject worked out in Holy Things. Second, the Division defines how for the occasion of the holy day one creates a corresponding space in one's own circumstance, and what one does, within that space, during sacred time. The division as a whole holds together through a shared, generative metaphor. It is the comparison, in the context of sacred time, of the spatial life of the Temple to the spatial life of the village, with activities and restrictions to be specified for each, upon the common occasion of the Sabbath or festival. The Mishnah's purpose therefore is to correlate the sanctity of the Temple, as defined by

the holy day, with the restrictions of space and of action which make the life of the village different and holy, as defined by the holy day.

THE DIVISION OF WOMEN defines the women in the social economy of Israel's supernatural and natural reality. Women acquire definition wholly in relationship to men, who impart form to the Israelite social economy. The status of women is effected through both supernatural and natural, this-worldly action. Women formed a critical systemic component, because the proper regulation of women—subject to the father, then the husband—was deemed a central concern of Heaven, so that a betrothal would be subject to Heaven's supervision (Qiddushin, sanctification, being the pertinent tractate); documents, such as the marriage-contract or the writ of divorce, drawn up on earth, stand also for Heaven's concern with the sanctity of women in their marital relationship; so too, Heaven may through levirate marriage dictate whom a woman marries. What man and woman do on earth accordingly provokes a response in heaven, and the correspondences are perfect. So women are defined and secured both in heaven and here on earth, and that position is always and invariably relative to men.

The principal interest for the Mishnah is interstitial, just as, in general, sanctification comes into play at interstitial relationships, those that require decisive classification. Here it is the point at which a woman becomes, and ceases to be, holy to a particular man, that is, enters and leaves the marital union. These transfers of women are the dangerous and disorderly points in the relationship of woman to man, therefore, the Mishnah states, to society as well. The division's systemic statement stresses the preservation of order in transactions involving women and (other) property. Within this orderly world of documentary and procedural concerns a place is made for the disorderly conception of the marriage not formed by human volition but decreed in heaven, the levirate connection. Mishnah-tractate Yebamot states that super-nature sanctifies a woman to a man (under the conditions of the levirate connection).

What it says by indirection is that man sanctifies too: man, like God, can sanctify that relationship between a man and a woman, and can also effect the cessation of the sanctity of that same relationship.

Five of the seven tractates of the Division of Women are devoted to the formation and dissolution of the marital bond. Of them, three treat what is done by man here on earth, that is, formation of a marital bond through betrothal and marriage contract and dissolution through divorce and its consequences. The Division and its system therefore delineate the natural and supernatural character of the woman's role in the social economy framed by man: the beginning, end, and middle of the relationship. The whole constitutes a significant part of the Mishnah's encompassing system of sanctification, for the reason that heaven confirms what men do on earth. A correctly prepared writ of divorce on earth changes the status of the woman to whom it is given, so that in heaven she is available for sanctification to some other man, while, without that same writ, in heaven's view, should she go to some other man, she would be liable to be put to death. The earthly deed and the heavenly perspective correlate. That is indeed very much part of larger system, which says the same thing over and over again.

THE DIVISION OF DAMAGES comprises two subsystems, which fit together in a logical way. One part presents rules for the normal conduct of civil society. These cover commerce, trade, real estate, and other matters of everyday intercourse, as well as mishaps, such as damages by chattels and persons, fraud, overcharge, interest, and the like, in that same context of everyday social life. The other part describes the institutions governing the normal conduct of civil society, that is, courts of administration, and the penalties at the disposal of the government for the enforcement of the law. The two subjects form a single tight and systematic dissertation on the nature of Israelite society and its economic, social, and political relationships, as the Mishnah envisages them. The main point of the first of the two parts of the Division is that the task of society is to maintain perfect stasis, to preserve the prevailing situation, and to secure the stability of all relationships. To this end, in the interchanges of buying and selling, giving and taking, borrowing and lending, it is important that there be an essential equality of interchange. No party in the end should have more than what he had at the outset, and none should be the victim of a sizable shift in fortune and circumstance. All parties' rights to, and in, this stable and unchanging economy of society are to be preserved. When the condition of a person is violated, so far as possible the law will secure the restoration of the antecedent status.

The goal of the system of civil law is the recovery of the prevailing order and balance, the preservation of the established wholeness of the social economy. This idea is powerfully expressed in the organization of the three tractates that comprise the civil law, which treat first abnormal and then normal transactions. The framers deal with damages done by chattels and by human beings, thefts and other sorts of malfeasance against the property of others. The civil law in both aspects pays closest attention to how the property and person of the injured party so far as possible are restored to their prior condition, that is, a state of normality. So attention to torts focuses upon penalties paid by the malefactor to the victim, rather than upon penalties inflicted by the court on the malefactor for what he has done. When speaking of damages, the Mishnah thus takes as its principal concern the restoration of the fortune of victims of assault or robbery. Then the framers take up the complementary and corresponding set of topics, the regulation of normal transactions. When we rapidly survey the kinds of transactions of special interest, we see from the topics selected for discussion what we have already uncovered in the deepest structure of organization and articulation of the basic theme.

The other half of this same unit of three tractates presents laws governing normal and routine transactions, many of them of the same sort as those dealt with in the first half. At issue are deposits of goods or possessions that one person leaves in safe-keeping with another. Called bailments, for example, cases of such transactions occur in both wings of the triple tractate, first, bailments subjected to misappropriation, or accusation thereof, by the bailiff, then, bailments transacted under normal circumstances. Under the rubric of routine transactions are those of workers and householders, that is, the purchase and sale of labor; rentals and bailments; real estate transactions; and inheritances and estates. Of the lot, the one involving real estate transactions is the most fully articulated and covers the widest range of problems and topics. The three tractates of the civil law all together thus provide a complete account of the orderly governance of balanced transactions and unchanging civil relationships within Israelite society under ordinary conditions.

The character and interests of the Division of Damages present probative evidence of the larger program of the philosophers of the Mishnah. Their intention is to create nothing less than a full-scale Israelite government, subject to the administration of sages. This government is fully supplied with a constitution and bylaws. It makes provision for a court system and procedures, as well as a full set of laws governing civil society and criminal justice. This government, moreover, mediates between its own community and the outside ("pagan") world. Through its system of laws it expresses its judgment of the others and at the same time defines, protects, and defends its own society and social frontiers. It even makes provision for procedures of remission, to expiate its own errors. The (then non-existent) Israelite government imagined by the second-century philosophers centers upon the (then non-existent) Temple, and the (then forbidden) city, Jerusalem. For the Temple is one principal focus. There the highest court is in session; there the high priest reigns.

The penalties for law infringement are of three kinds, one of which involves sacrifice in the Temple. (The others are compensation, physical punishment, and death.) The basic conception of punishment, moreover, is that unintentional infringement of the rules of society, whether "religious" or otherwise, is not penalized but rather expiated through an offering in the Temple. If a member of the people of Israel intentionally infringes against the law, to be sure, that one must be removed from society and is put to death. And if there is a claim of one member of the people against another, that must be righted, so that the prior, prevailing status may be restored. So offerings in the Temple are given up to appease heaven and restore a whole bond between heaven and Israel, specifically on those occasions on which without malice or ill will an Israelite has disturbed the relationship. Israelite civil society without a Temple is not stable or normal, and not to be imagined. And the Mishnah is above all an act of imagination in defiance of reality.

The plan for the government involves a clear-cut philosophy of society, a philosophy that defines the purpose of the government and ensures that its task is not merely to perpetuate its own power. The Israelite government, within the Mishnaic fantasy, is supposed to preserve a perfect, steady-state society. That state of perfection which, within the same fantasy, the society to begin with everywhere attains and expresses forms the goal of the system throughout: no change anywhere from a perfect balance, proportion, and arrangement of the social order, its goods and services, responsibilities and benefits. This is in at least five aspects:

First of all, one of the ongoing principles of the law, expressed in one tractate after another, is that people are to follow and maintain the prevailing practice of their locale.

Second, the purpose of civil penalties is to restore the injured party to his prior condition, so far as this is possible, rather than merely to penalize the aggressor.

Third, there is the conception of true value, meaning that a given object has an intrinsic worth, which, in the course of a transaction, must be paid. In this way the seller does not leave the transaction any richer than when he entered it, or the buyer any poorer (parallel to penalties for damages).

Fourth, there can be no usury, a biblical prohibition adopted and vastly enriched in the Mishnaic thought, for money ("coins") is what it is. Any pretense that it has become more than what it was violates, in its way, the conception of true value.

Fifth, when real estate is divided, it must be done with full attention to the rights of all concerned, so that, once more, one party does not gain at the expense of the other.

In these and many other aspects the law expresses its obsession with the perfect stasis of Israelite society. Its paramount purpose is in preserving and ensuring that that perfection of the division of this world is kept inviolate or restored to its true status when violated.

THE DIVISION OF HOLY THINGS presents a system of sacrifice and sanctuary. The division centers upon the everyday rules always applicable to the cult: the daily whole offering, the sin offering and guilt-offering which one may bring any time under ordinary circumstances; the right sequence of diverse offerings; the way in which the rites of the whole-, sin-, and guilt-offerings are carried out; what sorts of animals are acceptable; the accompanying cereal offerings; the support and provision of animals for the cult and of meat for the priesthood; the support and material maintenance of the cult and its building. We have a system before us: the system of the cult of the Jerusalem Temple seen as an ordinary and everyday affair, a continuing and routine operation. That is why special rules for the cult, both in respect to the altar and in regard to the maintenance of the buildings, personnel, and even the whole city, will be elsewhere—in Appointed Times and Agriculture. But from the perspective of Holy Things, those divisions intersect by supplying special rules and raising extraordinary (Agriculture: land-bound; Appointed Times: time-bound) considerations for that theme which Holy Things claims to set forth in its most general and unexceptional way: the cult as something permanent and everyday.

THE DIVISION OF PURITIES presents a very simple system of three principal parts: sources of uncleanness, objects and substances susceptible to uncleanness, and modes of purification from uncleanness. So it tells the story of what makes a given sort of object unclean and what makes it clean.

Viewed as a whole, the Division of Purities treats the interplay of persons, food, and liquids. Dry inanimate objects or food are not susceptible to uncleanness. What is wet is susceptible. So liquids activate the system. What is unclean, moreover, emerges from uncleanness through the operation of liquids, specifically, through immersion in fit water of requisite volume and in natural condition. Liquids thus deactivate the system. Thus, water in its natural condition is what concludes the process by removing uncleanness. Water in its unnatural condition, that is, deliberately affected by human agency, is what imparts susceptibility to uncleanness to begin with. The uncleanness of persons, furthermore, is signified by body liquids or flux in the case of the menstruating woman and the *zab* (the person suffering from the form of uncleanness described at Lev. 15:1ff.). Corpse uncleanness is conceived to be a kind of effluent, a viscous gas, which flows like liquid. Utensils for their part receive uncleanness when they form receptacles able to contain liquid.

In sum, we have a system in which the invisible flow of fluid-like substances or powers serve to put food, drink, and receptacles into the status of uncleanness and to remove those things from that status. Whether or not we call the system "metaphysical," it certainly has no material base but is conditioned upon highly abstract notions. Thus in material terms, the effect of liquid is upon food, drink, utensils, and man. The consequence has to do with who may eat and drink what food and liquid, and what food and drink may be consumed in which pots and pans. These loci are specified by tractates on utensils and on food and drink.

The human being is ambivalent. Persons fall in the middle, between sources and loci of uncleanness, because they are both. They serve as sources of uncleanness. They also become unclean. The *zab*, suffering the uncleanness described in Leviticus Chapter 15, the menstruating woman, the woman after childbirth, and the person afflicted with the skin ailment described in Leviticus Chapters 13 and 14—all are sources of uncleanness. But being unclean, they fall within the system's loci, its program of consequences. So they make other things unclean and are subject to penalties because they are unclean. Unambiguous sources of uncleanness never also constitute loci affected by uncleanness. They always are unclean and never can become clean: the corpse, the dead creeping thing, and things like them. Inanimate sources of uncleanness and inanimate objects convey uncleanness *ex opere operato*; their status of being unclean never changes; they present no ambiguity. Systemically unique, man and liquids have the capacity to inaugurate the processes of uncleanness (as sources) and also are subject to those same processes (as objects of uncleanness).

Having reviewed the system of the Mishnah and its points of stress, we hear a single message. It is a message of a system that answered a single encompassing question, and the question formed a stunning counterpart to that of the sixth century B.C.E. The Pentateuchal system addressed one reading of the events of the sixth century, highlighted by the destruction of the Jerusalem Temple in 586 B.C.E. At stake was how Israel as defined by that system related to its land, represented by its Temple, and the message may be simply stated: what appears to be the given is in fact a gift, subject to stipulations. The precipitating event for the Mishnaic system was the destruction of the Jerusalem Temple in 70 C.E., the question turned obsession with the defeat of Bar Kokhba and the closure of Jerusalem to Jews. The urgent issue taken up by the Mishnah was, specifically, what, in the aftermath of the destruction of the holy place and holy cult, remained of the sanctity of the holy caste, the priesthood, the holy land, and, above all, the holy people and its holy way of life? The answer was that sanctity persists, indelibly, in Israel, the people, in its way of life, in its land, in its priesthood, in its food, in its mode of sustaining life, in its manner of procreating and so sustaining the nation.

The Mishnah's system therefore focused upon the holiness of the life of Israel, the people, a holiness that had formerly centered on the Temple. The logically consequent question was, what is the meaning of sanc-

tity, and how shall Israel attain, or give evidence of, sanctification. The answer to the question derived from the original creation, the end of the Temple directing attention to the beginning of the natural world that the Temple had embodied. For the meaning of sanctity the framers therefore turned to that first act of sanctification, the one in creation. It came about when, all things in array, in place, each with its proper names, God blessed and sanctified the seventh day on the eve of the first Sabbath. Creation was made ready for the blessing and the sanctification when all things were very good, that is to say, in their rightful order, called by their rightful name. An orderly nature was a sanctified and blessed nature, so dictated Scripture in the name of the Supernatural. So to receive the blessing and to be made holy, all things in nature and society were to be set in right array. Given the condition of Israel, the people, in its land, in the aftermath of the catastrophic war against Rome led by Bar Kokhba in 132-135 C.E., putting things in order was no easy task. But that is why, after all, the question pressed, the answer proving inexorable and obvious. The condition of society corresponded to the critical question that obsessed the system-builders.

**The critical place of the Mishnah in Rabbinic literature:** When, in ca. 200, the Mishnah reached closure and was received and adopted as law by the state-sanctioned Jewish governments in both the Roman empire, in the land of Israel, and Iran, in Babylonia, respectively, the function and character of the document precipitated a considerable crisis. Politically and theologically presented as the foundation for the everyday administration of the affairs of Jewry, the Mishnah ignored the politics of the sponsoring regimes. Essentially ahistorical, the code hardly identified as authoritative any known political institution, let alone the patriarchate in the land of Israel, the exilarchate in Babylonia.

True, that political-institutional flaw (from the viewpoint of the sponsoring authorities) scarcely can have proved critical. But silence of the authorship of the Mishnah on the theological call for their document presented not a chronic but an acute problem. Since Jews generally accepted the authority of Moses at Sinai, failure to claim for the document a clear and explicit relationship to the Torah of Moses defined that acute issue. Why should people accept as authoritative the rulings of this piece of writing? Omitting reference to a theological, as much as to a political myth, the authorship of the Mishnah also failed to signal the relationship between their document and Scripture. Since, for all Judaisms, Hebrew Scriptures in general, and the Pentateuch, in particular, represented God's will for Israel, silence on that matter provoked considerable response. Let me now spell out in some detail the political, theological, and literary difficulties presented by the Mishnah to any theory that the Mishnah formed part of God's revelation to Moses at Sinai.

Laws issued to define what people were supposed to do could not stand by themselves; they had to receive the imprimatur of Heaven, that is, they had to be given the status of revelation. Accordingly, to make its way in Israelite life, the Mishnah as a constitution and code demanded for itself a theory of beginnings at (or in relation to) Sinai, with Moses, from God. The character of the Mishnah itself hardly won confidence that, on the face of it, the document formed part of, or derived from Sinai. It was originally published through oral formulation and oral transmission, that is, in the medium of memorization. But it had been in the medium of writing that, in the view of all of Israel until about 200 C.E., God had been understood to reveal the divine word and will. The Torah was a written book. People who claimed to receive further messages from God usually wrote them down. They had three choices in securing acceptance of their account. All three involved linking the new to the old.

In claiming to hand on revelation, they could, first, sign their books with the names of biblical heroes. Second, they could imitate the style of biblical Hebrew. Third, they could present an exegesis of existing written verses, validating their ideas by supplying proof texts for them. From the closure of the Torah literature in the time of Ezra, circa 450

B.C.E. to the time of the Mishnah, nearly seven hundred years later, we do not have a single book alleged to be holy and at the same time standing wholly out of relationship to the Holy Scriptures of ancient Israel. The Pseudepigraphic writings fall into the first category, the Essene writings at Qumran into the second and third. We may point also to the Gospels, which take as a principal problem demonstrating how Jesus had fulfilled the prophetic promises of the Old Testament and in other ways carried forward and even embodied Israel's Scripture.

Insofar as a piece of Jewish writing did not find a place in relationship to Scripture, its author laid no claim to present a holy book. The contrast between Jubilees and the Testaments of the Patriarchs, with their constant and close harping on biblical matters, and the several books of Maccabees, shows the differences. The former claim to present God's revealed truth, the latter, history. So a book was holy because in style, in authorship, or in (alleged) origin it continued Scripture, finding a place therefore (at least in the author's mind) within the canon, or because it provided an exposition on Scripture's meaning. But the Mishnah made no such claim. It entirely ignored the style of biblical Hebrew, speaking in a quite different kind of Hebrew altogether. It is silent on its authorship through sixty-two of the sixty-three tractates (the claims of Abot are post facto).

In any event, nowhere does the Mishnah contain the claim that God had inspired the authors of the document. These are not given biblical names and certainly are not alleged to have been biblical saints. Most of the book's named authorities flourished within the same century as its anonymous arrangers and redactors, not in remote antiquity. Above all, the Mishnah contains scarcely a handful of exegeses of Scripture. These, where they occur, play a trivial and tangential role. So here is the problem of the Mishnah: different from Scripture in language and style, indifferent to the claim of authorship by a biblical hero or divine inspiration, stunningly aloof from allusion to verses of Scripture for nearly the whole of its discourse—yet authoritative for Israel.

The Mishnah was not a statement of theory alone, telling only how matters will be in the eschaton. Nor was it a wholly sectarian document, reporting the view of a group without standing or influence in the larger life of Israel. True, in some measure it bears both of these traits of eschatology and sectarian provenance. But the Mishnah was (and is) law for Israel. It entered the government and courts of the Jewish people, both in the motherland and also overseas, as the authoritative constitution of the courts of Judaism. The advent of the Mishnah therefore marked a turning in the life of the nation-religion. The document demanded explanation and apology. And the one choice one did not face, as a Jew in third-century Tiberias, Sepphoris, Caesarea, or Beth Shearim, in Galilee, was ignore the Mishnah and the issues inherent in its character as a piece of writing given political standing by the ethnarch.

True, one might refer solely to ancient Scripture and tradition and live life out within the inherited patterns of the familiar Israelite religion-culture. But as soon as one dealt with the Jewish government in charge of everyday life—went to court over the damages done to a crop by a neighbor's ox, for instance—one came up against a law in addition to the law of Scripture, a document the principles of which governed and settled all matters. So the Mishnah rapidly came to confront the life of Israel. The people who knew the Mishnah, the rabbis or sages, came to dominate that life. And their claim, in accord with the Mishnah, to exercise authority and the right to impose heavenly sanction came to perplex. There were two solutions to the problem set forth by the character of the Mishnah.

[1] THE MISHNAH AS AN AUTONOMOUS, FREESTANDING COMPONENT OF THE TORAH OF SINAI: One response was represented by the claim that the authorities of the Mishnah stood in a chain of tradition that extended back to Sinai; stated explicitly in the Mishnah's first apologetic, tractate Abot, that circulated from approximately a generation beyond the promulgation of the Mishnah itself, that view required amplification and con-

crete demonstration. This approach treated the word *torah* as a common noun, as the word that spoke of a status or classification of sayings. A saying was *torah*, that is, enjoyed the status of torah or fell into the classification of *torah*, if it stood in the line of tradition from Sinai.

[2] THE MISHNAH IS SUBORDINATE TO THE WRITTEN PART OF THE TORAH BUT CAN BE SHOWN TO STAND ON THE WRITTEN TORAH'S AUTHORITY: A second took the same view of *torah* as a common noun. This response was to treat the Mishnah as subordinate to, and dependent upon, Scripture. Then *torah* was what fell into the classification of the revelation of *Torah* by God to Moses at Sinai. The way of providing what was needed within that theory was to link statements of the Mishnah to statements ("proof texts") of Scripture. The Tosefta, ca. 300, a compilation of citations of, and comments upon the Mishnah, together with some autonomous materials that may have reached closure in the period in which the work of redaction of the Mishnah was going on, as well as the Talmud of the Land of Israel, ca. 400, fairly systematically did just that.

The former solution treated Torah with a small t, that is to say, as a generic classification, and identified the Mishnah with the Torah revealed to Moses at Sinai by claiming a place for the Mishnah's authorities in the process of tradition and transmission that brought torah—no longer, the Torah, the specific writing comprising the Five Books of Moses—to contemporary Israel, the Jewish people. It was a theological solution, expressed through ideas, attitudes, implicit claims, but not through sustained rewriting of either Scripture or the Mishnah.

The latter solution, by contrast, concerned the specific and concrete statements of the Mishnah and required a literary, not merely a theological, statement, one precise and specific to passages of the Mishnah, one after the other. What was demanded by the claim that the Mishnah depended upon, but therefore enjoyed the standing of, Scripture, was a line-by-line commentary upon the Mishnah in light of Scripture. But this too treated *torah* as a common noun.

[3] THE REDEFINITION OF THE TORAH: The third way emerged in Sifra, a sustained and profound philosophical reading of the book of Leviticus. Sifra's solution would set aside the two solutions, the theological and the literary, and explore the much more profound issues of the fundamental and generative structure of right thought, yielding, as a matter of fact, both Scripture and the Mishnah. This approach insisted that *torah* always was a proper noun. There was, and is, only The Torah. But this—The Torah—demanded expansion and vast amplification. When we know the principles of logical structure and especially those of hierarchical classification that animate The Torah, we can undertake part of the task of expansion and amplification, that is, join in the processes of thought that, in the mind of God, yielded The Torah. For when we know how God thought in giving The Torah to Moses at Sinai and so accounting for the classifications and their ordering in the very creation of the world, we can ourselves enter into The Torah and participate in its processes.

Presenting the two Torahs in a single statement constituted an experiment in logic, that logic, in particular, that made cogent thought possible, and that transformed facts into propositions, and propositions into judgments of the more, or the less, consequential. While the Mishnah's other apologists wrote the written Torah into the Mishnah, Sifra's authorship wrote the oral Torah into Scripture. That is to say, the other of the two approaches to the problem of the Mishnah, the one of Sifra, to begin with claimed to demonstrate that the Mishnah found its correct place within the written Torah itself. Instead of citing verses of Scripture in the context of the Mishnah, the authorship of Sifra cited passages of the Mishnah in the context of Scripture, Leviticus in particular.

What the three accounts of the Mishnah's relationship to the Torah achieved, each in its own way, cohered to yield a single consequence. All three insisted on a privileged position for the Mishnah within, or at least in intimate relationship to, the Torah of Sinai. That explains two facts that together demonstrate the absolute uniqueness of the Mishnah in Rabbinic literature. First, the Mishnah as a document acknowledged no prior writing, except—and then only episodically—for Scripture itself. Second, the Mishnah alone among Rabbinic documents itself received sustained and systematic commentaries in the model of those accorded to Scripture. Every document that followed the Mishnah, that is to say, the entirety of Rabbinic literature except for the Mishnah, took shape as a commentary to a prior document, either Scripture or the Mishnah itself. So the entirety of Rabbinic literature testifies to the unique standing of the Mishnah, acknowledging its special status, without parallel or peer, as the oral part of the Torah.

**The Tosefta:** A huge supplement to the Mishnah, four times larger than the document it amplifies, the Tosefta, ca. 300, exhibits none of the documentary traits that mark as autonomous the other Rabbinic writings. Wholly depending upon the Mishnah for its rhetoric, topical program, and logic of coherent discourse, the Tosefta is like a vine on a trellis. It has no structure of its own but most commonly cites and glosses a passage of the Mishnah, not differentiating its forms and wording of sentences from those of the cited passage. Only seldom—for somewhat under a sixth of the whole of its volume—does the Tosefta present a statement that may be interpreted entirely independent of the Mishnah's counterpart (if any). The Tosefta covers nearly the whole of the Mishnah's program but has none of its own.

What marks the document as dependent, further, is that its sentences by themselves do not hold together at all. Their order consistently refers to that of the Mishnah's statements. The logic of coherent discourse, affecting more than two or three sentences at a time, is wholly fixed-associative. The dependent status of the Tosefta derives from the simple fact that, for most of the document we simply cannot understand a line without first consulting the Mishnah's counterpart statement. Once a text derives from some other document not only its coherence, but even the first level of meaning of its sentences one by one, we no longer can maintain that we have a freestanding statement, let alone a systemic one. The document contains three kinds of writings:

[1] The first consists of verbatim citations and glosses of sentences of the Mishnah.

[2] The second is made up of freestanding statements that complement the sense of the Mishnah but do not cite a Mishnah-paragraph verbatim. These statements can be fully understood only in dialogue with the Mishnah's counterpart.

[3] The third comprises freestanding, autonomous statements, formulated in the manner of the Mishnah but fully comprehensible on their own.

The editors or compilers of the Tosefta arranged their materials in accord with two principles, and these govern the order of the Tosefta's statements in correspondence to the Mishnah's. First will come statements that cite what the Mishnah's sentences say, and this ordinarily will occur in the order of the Mishnah's statements. Second, in general Mishnah-citation and gloss will be succeeded by Mishnah-amplification, which is to say, sentences that do not cite the Mishnah's corresponding ones, but that cannot be understood without reference to the Mishnah's rule or sense. The first two kinds of statements are the ones that cannot be fully understood without knowledge of the Mishnah, which defines their context. Third in sequence, commonly, will be the small number of freestanding statements, which can be wholly understood on their own and without appeal to the sense or principle of the corresponding Mishnah-passage; and in some few cases, these compositions and even composites will have no parallel in the Mishnah at all.

Autonomous statements require attention in their own right. These comprise paragraphs that make their own point and can be fully understood in their own terms. These freestanding materials are of two kinds. First, some autonomous materials work on topics important to a passage in the Mishnah and are placed by Tosefta's framers in a position corresponding to the thematic parallel in the Mishnah. What marks these materials as autonomous is that, while they intersect with the Mishnah's topic, their interest in that topic bears no point in common with the Mishnah's treatment of the same topic. A second

criterion, which is complementary, is that we can understand what follows without referring to the Mishnah for any purpose. The second type of autonomous materials addresses topics omitted in the Mishnah, and that type is included only because, in the Mishnah, there may be a tangential reference to the topic treated by Tosefta's composition. The criterion of classification, then, is even simpler than that governing the first type. The Tosefta's authorship has collected this kind of material we know not where. It can have been composed in the same period as the writing of the Mishnah.

While these freestanding statements that can as well have stood in the Mishnah as in the Tosefta itself may have reached final formulation prior to the closure of the Mishnah, most of the document either cites the Mishnah verbatim and comments upon it, or can be understood only in light of the Mishnah even though the Mishnah is not cited verbatim, and that is sound reason for assigning the formulation of most of the document and the compilation of the whole to the time after the Mishnah was concluded. The first two types of materials certainly were written after the closure of the Mishnah. The Tosefta as a whole, covering all three types, was compiled sometime after the conclusion of the Mishnah in ca. 200 but before the formation of the Talmud of the Land of Israel, ca. 400, which frequently cites materials found in the Tosefta and interprets the Mishnah in light of the Tosefta's complements. The compilation therefore is a work of the third century, 200-300.

But in substance the document's claim proves still stronger. The Tosefta's materials, coherent and cogent not among themselves but only in relationship to the Mishnah, serve as the Mishnah's first commentary, first amplification, and first extension. If by "a talmud," we mean, a sustained, systematic commentary to the Mishnah, following a program of exegesis and analysis, then the Tosefta must be called the first talmud, prior to the ones done in the Land of Israel by ca. 400 or completed in Babylonia by ca. 600. Since both Talmuds read Mishnah-passages through Tosefta-complements to the Mishnah, the Tosefta forms the bridge between the Talmuds and much of the Mishnah.

But that does not mean the Tosefta is a very accessible document. The opposite is the case. And the reason derives from the Tosefta's very character as a document of mediation, expansion, and extension of another piece of writing. The Tosefta as is now clear makes sense only in relationship to the Mishnah. That is so not only for its program and order, which are defined by the Mishnah, but also for its individual compositions. Each completed unit of thought of the Tosefta is to be understood, to begin with, in relationship with the Mishnah: is it a citation of and commentary to the Mishnah-passage that forms its counterpart? Is the passage fully to be comprehended on its own or only in relationship to a counterpart passage of the Mishnah? Or is the passage freestanding? The answers to these three questions define the first step in making any sense at all of a passage of the Tosefta.

The Tosefta, as is already clear, stands nearly entirely within the circle of the Mishnah's interests, only rarely asking questions about topics omitted altogether by the Mishnah's authors, always following the topical decisions on what to discuss as laid down by the founders of the whole. One cannot write about the Tosefta's theology or law, as though these constituted a system susceptible of description and interpretation independent of the Mishnah's system. At the same time, the exegetes of the Mishnah, in the Tosefta, and in the two Talmuds, stand apart from, and later than, the authors of the Mishnah itself. Accordingly, the exegetes systematically say whatever they wish to say by attaching their ideas to a document earlier than their own, and by making the principal document say what they wish to contribute.

The system of expressing ideas through reframing those of predecessors preserves the continuity of tradition and establishes a deep stability and order upon the culture framed by that tradition. The Tosefta not only depends for structure, order, and sense, upon the Mishnah, but, in general, the materials assembled in the Tosefta set forth no viewpoint other than that of the Mishnah's counterpart

materials, clarified, refined, and improved. No study has as yet shown a sustained tendency in the Tosefta to execute a distinct exegesis of the Mishnah in such wise as to recast the sense or character of the Mishnah's program, though in numerous passages, the work of commentary shades over into a fresh reading of a specific problem.

**The Talmuds:** We come now to the two Talmuds, the Talmud of the Land of Israel, ca. 400 C.E., and the Talmud of Babylonia, ca. 600 C.E. Since the second of the two forms the definitive statement of the Judaism of the dual Torah and defines the curriculum of Torah-study in the very centers in which the Torah is studied as God's word and will for Israel, we do well to begin by considering the purpose that these documents were meant to serve. In a word, the Talmuds propose to state in writing the basic rules of the social order, and to show us how to discover the right rule, based on the principles God has made known in the Torah, for the affairs of everyday life. The Talmuds are documents full of debates on erudite and esoteric questions. But in the debates about fine points of law, ritual, and theology, "our sages of blessed memory" formulated through concrete examples the rules of right thinking and accurate formulation in words of God's will for the here and now. For they held that the Torah is given to purify the hearts of humanity, and that what God really wants is the heart. But there, in the center of life, in the streets and homes of the holy community, Israel, what does that mean? It is through close and careful thinking about little things that "our sages" brought the Torah's great principles into the everyday world of ordinary people. The media of language, logic, and law express the message of the Torah of Sinai. The Talmuds show us how, for the purposes of portraying the entirety of the social order, its culture and its politics alike, people write in signals an account of their modes of thought and how these are to be replicated any time and anywhere.

First, to define matters: a talmud—generically defined—is a sustained, systematic amplification and analysis of passages of the Mishnah and other teachings alongside the

Mishnah, inclusive of the Tosefta, that are accorded the status of Tannaite authority. Of the genus, talmud, there are two species, the Tosefta, on the one side, the two Talmuds, on the other. These further subspeciate into the Talmud of the Land of Israel (Yerushalmi), ca. 400, and the Talmud of Babylonia (Bavli), ca. 600. The former treats the first four divisions of the Mishnah; the latter, the second through the fifth; each is independent of the other, the two meeting only at parts of the Mishnah and sharing, further, some sayings attributed to authorities after the Mishnah; but these the documents' respective authorships read each in its own way.

The genus, talmud, as a source of information in clarification of the Mishnah was established by the Tosefta; but there information was left inert, the Tosefta's framers' knowing nothing of dialectics (other than what they found on rare occasion in the Mishnah itself). What characterizes the other species of talmud, the one that encompasses the two Talmuds, is the transformation of information into principle, the systematic formation of argument, the transformation of facts, the raw materials of analytical inquiry, through the modes of thought of applied reason and practical logic, into systemic truth.

The subspecies of the species formed of the two Talmuds must be differentiated. What the first Talmud contributed was the definition of a talmud in which received facts ("traditions") were treated as active and consequential, requiring analysis and deep thought. The second Talmud transformed thought into argument, subordinating fact to the fully-realized processes of dialectical argument and reasoning. So the three talmuds, the Tosefta, the Talmud of the Land of Israel, and the Talmud of Babylonia, in sequence expanded the definition of the genus, talmud, each adding an important component of that definition.

Both Talmuds-strictly-speaking—the Yerushalmi, the Bavli—are formed into commentaries to some of the same passages of the Mishnah (tractates in the divisions of Appointed Times, Women, and Damages, but not in Agriculture or Holy Things; neither Talmud takes up Purities, except for trac-

tate Niddah). Both are laid out in the same way, that is, as ad hoc treatments of phrases or even whole paragraphs of the Mishnah; the two Talmuds are identical in form, species of a genus. The two Talmuds defined Mishnah-commentary in a distinctive way, through their active program of supplying not merely information but guidance on its meaning: a program of inquiry, a set of consequential issues, in place of mere information. That program would be fully realized only in the second, and last, of the two Talmuds.

But both Talmuds in common exhibit definitive traits as well. Specifically they share the program of harmonizing one rule or principle with another. Both, furthermore, propose to uncover the scriptural foundation of the Mishnah's rules. In common therefore they undertake the sustained demonstration of the theology of the Torah: its perfection, on the one side, its unity (oral and written), on the other. Because of that fact, we may properly speak of "the Talmuds," since both do one thing, though the second does another in addition.

To begin with, the two Talmuds look alike. That is because both comment on the same prior text, the Mishnah. Both take up a few sentences of that prior text and paraphrase and analyze them. Both ask the same questions, e.g., clarifying the language of the Mishnah, identifying the scriptural foundations of the Mishnah's rules, comparing the Mishnah's rules with those of the Tosefta or other texts of Tannaite status, that is, presented with attributions of sayings solely to names that occur also in the Mishnah or Tosefta. They furthermore are comparable because they organize their materials in the same way. They moreover take up pretty much the same topical agenda, in common selecting some divisions of the Mishnah and ignoring others, agreeing in particular to treat the matters of everyday practice, as distinct from theory, covered by Mishnah's divisions of Appointed Times, Women, and Damages. Both documents moreover are made up of already-available compositions and composites, which we may identify, in each document, by reference to the same literary traits or indications of completion prior to inclusion in the Talmuds. So they exhibit traits of shared literary policy.

In both, moreover, we find not only the same received document, the Mishnah, but occasionally also citations of, and allusions to, the same supplementary collection to the Mishnah, the Tosefta, and also a further kind of saying, one bearing the marks of formalization and memorization that serve to classify it as authoritative ("Tannaite") but external to the composition of the Mishnah and the compilation of the Tosefta. The points of coincidence are more than formal, therefore, since both Talmuds cite the same Mishnah-tractates, at some points the same Tosefta-passages, and also, from time to time, the same external Tannaite formulations.

Not only are the two Talmuds alike, but in their canonical context, the two Talmuds also are different from all other documents of the Judaism of the dual Torah in the formative age. First of all, among Mishnah-centered writings in the canon—the Tosefta, Sifra, the two Sifres, the Bavli and the Yerushalmi—only the two Talmuds conduct sustained analytical inquiries over a broad range of problems. The Tosefta is not an analytical document; we have to supply the missing analytical program (as the authors of the two Talmuds, but particularly the Bavli, themselves discovered early on). Sifra treats the Mishnah in only a single aspect, while the two Talmuds cover that aspect generously, along with a far more elaborate program. They pursue no encompassing exegetical program. So the two Talmuds are unique in context.

While set forth in a manner that implicitly bears the attributes of a commentary, that is a mere amplification of received truth, as a commentary to the Mishnah, the two Talmuds express, in a cogent and coherent way, the topical, rhetorical, and logical choices, forming the well-crafted statement and viewpoint, of their respective authorships. The two Talmuds therefore comprise a genus, talmud, made up of two species, the Talmud of the Land of Israel and the Talmud of Babylonia. But what speciates vastly overrides what unites the species into a genus; the form is common, and, we shall see, so is much of the thought. Where the Talmuds

differ is in the deepest layers of discourse but not on the surface of the medium or in the messages they set forth.

Both Talmuds invariably do to the Mishnah one of these four things, and each of these procedures will ordinarily be expressed in patterned language. It suffices here to classify the types of patterns:

[1] text criticism;
[2] exegesis of the meaning of the Mishnah, including glosses and amplifications;
[3] addition of Scriptural prooftexts of the Mishnah's central propositions; and
[4] harmonization of one Mishnah passage with another such passage or with a statement of Tosefta.

Each of these types of compositions follows a well-defined form, so that, if we were given only an account in abstract terms of the arrangement of subject and predicate or a simple account of the selection of citation language (e.g., "as it is said," "our rabbis have taught") we could readily predict the purpose of the composition or composite. So formal traits accompany the purpose of the commentary-compositions and other compositions and composites and permit differentiation of one type from another.

The first two of these four procedures remain wholly within the narrow frame of the Mishnah passage subject to discussion. Therefore, in the natural order of things, what the two Talmuds will find interesting in a given Mishnah-passage will respond to the same facts and commonly will do so in much the same way. The second pair take an essentially independent stance vis-a-vis the Mishnah pericope at hand. Part of the rhetorical convention of the Talmuds governs the order in which types of compositions— Mishnah-text-criticism, exegesis, Scriptural prooftexts, and the like—are set forth. Ordinarily, the order for both Talmuds is the same as given above. While both Talmuds conform to complex and distinctive rhetorical programs, what makes them different from all other documents of Rabbinic literature is not only rhetoric but logic, to which we turn forthwith.

**The composition of the two Talmuds:** The two Talmuds are made up of compositions, complete in themselves, which have been formed into composites. The framers of the Talmuds then resort to two distinct logics of coherent discourse to form of their materials whole and cogent documents. Philosophical logic ordinarily holds together into cogent paragraphs the discrete sentences of a given composition. The logic of fixed association then connects into protracted statements of a cogent character otherwise unrelated sequential sentences. It also joins into sizable compositions entire paragraphs that, on their own, through their own propositions, in no way coalesce. The authorship of the Talmuds in the making of medium- and large-scale logical connections thus resorted to two distinct principles of cogent discourse: the one of propositional connection within completed units of thought, a connection discovered through the pursuit of reasoned speculative inquiry, and the second of the fixed associative connection between and among those same completed units of thought, producing large-scale compositions.

Sizable numbers of the completed units of thought of the Talmuds find inner cogency through the development of a proposition concerning a given theme. Overall, these units of completed thought are linked to one another through the connections supplied for the Talmuds extrinsically by both the Mishnah and Scripture. The framers of the Talmuds had in hand a tripartite corpus of inherited materials awaiting composition into a final, closed document. First, they took up materials, in various states and stages of completion, pertinent to the Mishnah or to the principles of laws that the Mishnah had originally brought to articulation. Second, they had in hand received materials, again in various conditions, pertinent to Scripture, both as Scripture related to the Mishnah and also as Scripture laid forth its own narratives. And that fact points to the way in which the logic of fixed association governed their work.

Little of what the Talmuds' authorships present in a propositional form derives cogency and force from a received statement. True, many of the propositions of the two Talmuds, in the nature of things, address the meaning of paragraphs of the Mishnah, and most of the documents are laid out as a commentary to either the Mishnah or Scripture. But the authorship of each of the compositions and the framer of the respective composites has selected out of Scripture and the Mishnah the passages or topics it wishes to amplify. At stake is the reformation of the (oral part of the) Torah in a way not envisaged by its writers. The Talmuds do not merely clarify the Mishnah; both of them in point of fact re-present the Torah—a very different thing.

The writers of the Mishnah created a coherent document, with a topical program formed in accord with the logical order dictated by the characteristics of a given topic, and with a set of highly distinctive formulary and formal traits as well. But these are obscured when the document is taken apart into bits and pieces and reconstituted in the way in which the Talmuds do. The redefinition of the Torah accomplished by the Talmuds therefore represented a vast revision of the initial writing down of the oral component of the Torah—a point at which the hermeneutics shaded over into a profoundly theological activity.

**What happens to the Mishnah in the Talmuds:** For the Mishnah is read by the Talmuds as a composite of discrete and essentially autonomous rules, a set of atoms, not an integrated molecule, so to speak. In this reading, the most striking formal traits of the Mishnah are obliterated. More important, the Mishnah as a whole and complete statement of a viewpoint no longer exists. Its propositions are reduced to details. But what is offered instead? The answer is, a statement that, on occasion, recasts details in generalizations encompassing a wide variety of other details across the gaps between one tractate and another. This immensely creative and imaginative approach to the Mishnah vastly expands the range of discourse. But the consequence is to deny to the Mishnah both its own mode of speech and its distinctive and coherent message. So the two Talmuds formulate their own hermeneutics, to convey their theological system:

[1] defining the Torah and
[2] demonstrating its perfection and compre-

hensive character: unity, harmony, lineal origin from Sinai.

What the second Talmud would later on add to that first stage in theological re-presentation of the Torah is instantiation of modes of analysis of the unity, lineal formation, and harmony of the Torah. But the framers of the first Talmud assuredly affirmed the same points.

Both authorships take an independent stance when facing the Mishnah, making choices, reaching decisions of their own. Both Talmuds' framers deal with Mishnah-tractates of their own choice, and neither provides a Talmud to the entirety of the Mishnah. What the Mishnah therefore contributed to the Talmuds was not received in a spirit of humble acceptance by the sages who produced either of the two Talmuds. Important choices were made about what to treat, hence what to ignore. The exegetical mode of reception did not have to obscure the main lines of the Mishnah's system. But it surely did so. The discrete reading of sentences, or, at most, paragraphs, denying all context, avoiding all larger generalizations except for those transcending the specific lines of tractates—this approach need not have involved the utter reversal of the paramount and definitive elements of the Mishnah's whole and integrated world view (its "Judaism"). But doing these things did facilitate the revision of the whole into a quite different pattern. That represents a re-presentation of the Torah, one of considerable originality indeed.

A second trait, already familiar to us, joins with the foregoing. The Mishnah rarely finds it necessary to adduce prooftexts from the written Torah in support of its statements. The Talmuds, by contrast, find it appropriate whenever possible to cite Scriptural proof-texts for the propositions of the Mishnah. While the various tractates of the Mishnah relate in different ways to Scripture, the view of the framers of the Talmud on the same matter is not differentiated. So far as they are concerned, prooftexts for Mishnaic rules are required. These will be supplied in substantial numbers. And that is the main point. The Mishnah now is systematically represented as not standing free and separate from Scripture, but dependent upon it. The authority of the Mishnah's laws then is reinforced. But the autonomy of the Mishnah as a whole is severely compromised. Just as the Mishnah is represented in the Talmud as a set of rules, rather than as a philosophical essay, so it is presented, rule by rule, as a secondary and derivative development of Scripture. It would be difficult to imagine a more decisive effort to re-formulate the Torah than is accomplished by this work.

The undifferentiated effort to associate diverse Mishnah laws with Scripture is to be viewed together with the systematic breakup of the Mishnah into its diverse laws. The two quite separate activities produce a single effect in both Talmuds. They permit the Talmuds to represent the state of affairs pretty much as the framers of the Talmuds wish to do. Theology as a creative venture here determines to (re)define the Torah. And how is this done? Everything is shown to be continuous: Scripture, Mishnah, the Tosefta where cited, the authoritative sayings labeled Tannaite where used, ending in the Talmud itself (whichever Talmud we examine, the effect being the same)! Then all things, as now shaped by the rabbis of the Talmud(s), have the standing of Scripture and represent the authority of Moses (now called "our Rabbi"). Accordingly, once the Mishnah enters either of the two Talmuds it nowhere emerges intact. It is wholly preserved, but in bits and pieces, shaped and twisted in whatever ways the Talmuds wish. The Torah now forms a single, continuous statement. And that is the work of the first Talmud, not only of the second.

**The Talmuds distinct from the Mishnah:** The question has now to be asked, when do the Talmuds speak for themselves not for the Mishnah? Second, what sorts of units of discourse contain such passages that bear what is "Talmudic" in the two Talmuds? These two questions produce the same answers for both Talmuds, allowing us to characterize the topical or propositional program of the two Talmuds.

[1] THEORETICAL QUESTIONS OF LAW NOT ASSOCIATED WITH A PARTICULAR

PASSAGE OF THE MISHNAH. In the first of the two Talmuds there is some tendency, and in the second, a very marked tendency, to move beyond the legal boundaries set by the Mishnah's rules themselves. More general inquiries are taken up. These of course remain within the framework of the topic of one tractate or another, although there are some larger modes of thought characteristic of more than a single tractate.

[2] EXEGESIS OF SCRIPTURE SEPARATE FROM THE MISHNAH. It is under this rubric that we find the most important instances in which the Talmuds present materials essentially independent of the Mishnah.

[3] HISTORICAL STATEMENTS. The Talmud contains a fair number of statements that something happened, or narratives about how something happened. While many of these are replete with biblical quotations, in general they do not provide exegesis of Scripture, which serves merely as illustration or reference point.

[4] STORIES ABOUT, AND RULES FOR, SAGES AND DISCIPLES, SEPARATE FROM DISCUSSION OF A PASSAGE OF THE MISHNAH. The Mishnah contains a tiny number of tales about rabbis. These serve principally as precedents for, or illustrations of, rules. The Talmuds by contrast contain a sizable number of stories about sages and their relationships to other people.

When the Talmuds present us with ideas or expressions of a world related to, but fundamentally separate from, that of the Mishnah, that is, when the Talmuds wish to say something other than what the Mishnah says and means, they will take up one of two modes of discourse. Either we find exegesis of biblical passages, with the value system of the rabbis read into the Scriptural tales; or we are told stories about holy men and paradigmatic events, once again through tales told in such a way that a didactic and paranetic purpose is served. It follows that the Talmuds are composites of three kinds of materials, [1] exegeses of the Mishnah (and other materials classified as authoritative, that is, Tannaite), [2] exegeses of Scripture, and [3] accounts of the men who provide both.

Both Talmuds constitute elaborate reworkings of the two antecedent documents: the Mishnah, lacking much reference to Scripture, and the Scripture itself. The Talmuds bring the two together into a synthesis of their compilers' own making, both in reading Scripture into Mishnah, and in reading Scripture alongside of, and separate from, Mishnah.

If, therefore, we want to point to what is Talmudic in either of the two Talmuds it is the exegesis of Scripture, on the one side, and the narration of historical or biographical tales about holy men, on the other. Since much of the biblical exegesis turns upon holy men of biblical times, we may say that the Talmuds speak for themselves alone, as distinct from addressing the problems of the Mishnah, when they tell about holy men now and then. But what is genuinely new in the Talmuds, in comparison and contrast to the Mishnah, is the inclusion of extensive discourse on the meaning imputed to Scripture.

It follows that the two Talmuds stand essentially secondary to two prior documents: Mishnah (encompassing for this purpose the whole corpus labeled Tannaite, whenever and wherever produced, much being later than the Mishnah and some being Babylonian), on the one side, and Scripture, on the other. The Mishnah is read in the Talmuds pretty much within the framework of meaning established by the Mishnah itself. Scripture is read as an account of a world remarkably like that of the rabbis of the Talmuds. When the rabbis speak for themselves, as distinct from the Mishnah, it is through exegesis of Scripture. (But any other mode of reading Scripture, to them, would have been unthinkable. They took for granted that they and Scripture's heroes and sages lived in a single timeless plane.)

**Talmudic exegesis of the Mishnah:** Let us now turn to three more questions, the answers to which equally characterize both Talmuds' programs of exegesis, the counterpart to the topical program of the Mishnah:

[1] What do rabbis in the two Talmuds do in common when they read the Mishnah?

[2] What are their modes of thought, their characteristic ways of analysis?

[3] What do we learn about their world view from the ways in which they receive and interpret the world view they have inherited in the Mishnah?

These are the very questions, we now realize, that the Talmuds answer on their own account, not only the Mishnah's. The Talmudic exegetes of the Mishnah brought to the document no distinctive program of their own. The exegetes did not know in advance of their approach to a law of the Mishnah facts about the passage not contained within the boundaries of the language of the Mishnah passage itself (except only for facts contained within other units of the same document). Rejecting propositions that were essentially *a priori*, they proposed to explain and expand precisely the wording and the conceptions supplied by the document under study.

In not a single instance did the Mishnah-exegetes in either Talmud appear to twist and turn the language and message of a passage, attempting to make the words mean something other than what they appear to say anyhow. The framers of both Talmuds' reading of the Mishnah take as the measure of truth the clear and present sense of the Mishnah's own language and formulations, rarely asking the Mishnah's rule to confirm a judgment extrinsic to the Mishnah's message. While the Talmuds follow a coherent hermeneutics that is very much their own, there is no exegetical program revealed in the Talmuds' reading of the Mishnah other than that defined, to begin with, by the language and conceptions of one Mishnah-passage or another. Seen whole, the Talmuds appear to be nothing more than secondary developments of the Mishnah. If there is nothing *in particular* that is Talmudic, nonetheless, there is much *in general* that in both Talmuds is Talmudic. This is in entirely familiar respects.

First, the Mishnah was set forth by Judah the Patriarch, who sponsored the document, whole and complete, a profoundly unified, harmonious document. The Talmud insists upon obliterating the marks of coherence. It treats in bits and pieces what was originally meant to speak whole. That simple fact constitutes what is original, stunningly new and, by definition, Talmudic. Second, the Mishnah, also by definition, delivered its message in the way chosen by Judah the Patriarch. That is to say, by producing the document

as he did, the Patriarch left no space for the very enterprises of episodic exegesis undertaken so brilliantly by his immediate continuators and heirs.

True, a rather limited process of explanation and gloss of words and phrases, accompanied by a systematic inquiry into the wording of one passage or another, got underway, probably at the very moment, and within the very process, of the Mishnah's closure. But insofar as the larger messages and meanings of the document are conveyed in the ways Judah the Patriarch chose through formalization of language, through contrasts, through successive instances of the same, normally unspecified, general proposition, the need for exegesis was surely not generated by his own program for the Mishnah. Quite to the contrary, Judah chose for his Mishnah a mode of expression and defined for the document a large-scale structure and organization, which, by definition, were meant to stand firm and autonomous. The Mishnah speaks clearly and for itself.

The true power of the two Talmuds emerges when we realize that the Mishnah did not merely come to closure. At the very moment at which it was completed, the Mishnah also formed a closed system, that is, a whole, complete statement that did not require facts outside of its language and formulation, so made no provision for commentary and amplification of brief allusions, as the Talmuds' style assuredly does. The Mishnah refers to nothing beyond itself except, episodically, Scripture. It promises no information other than what is provided within its limits. It raises no questions for ongoing discussion beyond its decisive, final, descriptive statements of enduring realities and fixed relationships.

The Talmuds' single irrevocable judgment is precisely opposite: this text needs a commentary. The Talmuds' first initiative is to reopen the Mishnah's closed system, almost at the moment of its completion and perfection. That is what is Talmudic about the Talmuds: their daring assertion that the concluded and completed demanded clarification and continuation. Once that assertion was made to stick, nothing else mattered very much. The two Talmuds' message was conveyed in the very medium of the Talmud: a new language, focused upon a new grid of discourse to re-view a received writing.

In the two Talmuds in common we address a program of criticism of the Mishnah framed by independent and original minds. How is this made manifest? Let us quickly bypass the obvious points of independent judgment, the matter of insistence that the very word choices of the Mishnah require clarification, therefore prove faulty. The meanings and amplification of phrases represent the judgment that Judah's formulation, while stimulating and provocative, left much to be desired. These indications of independence of judgment among people disposed not merely to memorize but to improve upon the text provided by Judah the Patriarch hardly represent judgments of substance. Rather, let us turn to the two most striking: [1] the provision of Scriptural prooftexts for the propositions of various passages of the Mishnah; [2] the rewriting, in the Mishnah's own idiom, if not in its redactional and disciplinary patterns, of much of the law.

As to the former, of course, the message is familiar and clear. The propositions of the Mishnah cannot stand by themselves but must be located within the larger realm of Scriptural authority. As to the latter, the Tosefta's compositions and other Tannaite passages, serving as an exegetical complement to the Mishnah's corresponding passages, imitate the Mishnah. For they are phrased in the way in which the Mishnah's sentences are written (as distinct from the utterly different way in which the Talmuds' own sentences are framed, e.g., in Hebrew rather than in the Talmuds' Aramaic). And yet they show equivalent independence of mind. They indicate that, where sages of the time of the Talmuds took up Mishnaic passages, they were not at all limited to the work of gloss and secondary expansion. They recognized and exercised a quite remarkable freedom of initiative. They undertook to restate in their own words, but imitating the Mishnah's style, the propositions of the Mishnah passage at hand.

That is, they both cite what the Mishnah had said and also continue, in imitation of the Mishnah's language, the discourse of the Mishnah passage itself. These Toseftan or other Tannaite complements to the Mishnah—a vast number of them demonstrably written after the closure of the Mishnah—are Talmudic in two senses. First, they come to expression in the period after the Mishnah had reached closure, as is clear from the fact that the exact language of the Mishnah is cited prior to the labor of extension expansion and revision. So they are the work of the Talmuds' age and authority. Second, they derive from precisely the same authorities responsible for the formation of the Talmud as a whole.

Accordingly, both the insistence upon adducing prooftexts for passages the Patriarch judged not to need them and the persistent revision and expansion of the Mishnah, even in clumsy imitation of the Mishnah's syntax, rhetoric, and word choices, tell us once more this simple truth: the Talmuds are distinctively Talmudic precisely when the Mishnah itself defines the Talmuds' labor, dictates its ideas, displays its rhetoric, determines its results.

The very shift in usable language, from "the Mishnah" (as a whole) to "the Mishnah passage" or "the Mishnaic law at hand" indicates the true state of affairs. On the surface, in all manner of details, the two Talmuds are little more than secondary and derivative documents, explaining the Mishnah itself in trivial ways, or expanding it in a casuistic and logic-chopping manner. But viewing that same surface from a different, more distant perspective and angle, we see things quite differently. In detail the Talmuds changed nothing. Overall, the Talmuds left nothing the same. And, it follows, in general, the two Talmuds stand close together, not only in form, but in program and much else.

In the two Talmuds we find little to deem Talmudic in particular. But in them both, equally, there is much that is talmudic in general. The particular bits and pieces are Mishnaic. But the Talmuds leave nothing of the Mishnah whole and intact. Their work upon the whole presents an essentially new construction. Through the Mishnah, Judah contributed to the Talmuds most of the bricks, but little of the mortar, and none of the joists and beams. The design of the whole bore no relationship to the Patriarch's plan for the Mishnah. The sages of the Talmud did the rest. They alone imagined, then built, the building. They are the architects, theirs is the vision. The building is a monument to the authority of the sage above all.

What is most definitively indicative of the Talmudic sages' freedom of imagination is the exercise—by each set of authors—of free choice even among the Mishnah's tractates awaiting exegesis. We do not know why some tractates were chosen for Talmudic expansion and others left fallow. We may speculate that the Yerushalmi's omission of all reference to the entire division of Holy Things, on the everyday conduct of the Temple, and to most of the division of Purities, on the sources of uncleanness, objects subject to uncleanness, and modes of removing contamination, constitutes a radical revision of the law of Judaism. What for Judah the Patriarch was close to 50% of the whole story in volume, forming two of his six divisions in structure, for that Talmud's designers was of no importance. That is an amazing fact, attesting on its own to the Talmuds' formulation of their own program and statement, independent of that of the Mishnah even while expressed wholly in the form of a commentary to the Mishnah. Here too, we find the Torah once more subject to (re)definition; nothing of course would be omitted; but choices clearly were made about what is to be brought to the fore.

**The Mishnah's program and the Talmuds' program:** Both Talmuds in common address the tractates of Appointed Times, Women, and Damages, the second, third, and fourth divisions of the Mishnah. That is then where the comparisons and contrasts have to take place. Interest in the division of Appointed Times involved extensive discussion of the conduct of the cult on extraordinary days. Perhaps at issue here was not what had to be omitted (the cult on appointed times) but what people wanted to discuss, the home and village on those same holy occasions. So the former came in the wake of the latter. Inclusion of the divisions of Women, on the

family and the transfer of women from father to husband and back, and Damages, on civil law and institutions, is not hard to explain. The sages fully expected to govern the life of Israel, the Jewish people, in its material and concrete aspects. These divisions, as well as some of the tractates of the division on Appointed Times, demanded and received attention. Ample treatment of the laws in the first division, governing the priests' rations and other sacred segments of the agricultural produce of the Holy Land, is to be expected among authorities living not only in, but also off, the Holy Land.

If we stand back and reflect on the Mishnah's program, we recognize how different is that of the respective Talmuds. The Mishnah covers a broad variety of topics. The Talmuds contribute none of their own, but trawl across the entire surface of the Mishnah. The Mishnah is organized topically. The Talmuds may be broken down into discrete compositions and neatly-joined composites, none of them framed as freestanding, topical formations, all of them in one way or another depending upon the Mishnah for order and coherence. The Mishnah lays out rules and facts about a world beyond itself. The Talmuds negotiate rules and recast facts into propositions that concern the Mishnah— a different focus of discourse and perspective altogether. Continuous with the Mishnah, the two Talmuds in point of fact redirect the Mishnah not only by destroying its integrity and picking and choosing with its topical (and propositional) program, but also by forming of the detritus of the received writing a statement of their own. But it was not a statement that, in the end, concerned the Mishnah at all, rather, a statement about the Torah, and a statement of the Torah.

In accepting authority, in centering discourse upon the ideas of other men, in patiently listing even the names behind authoritative laws from olden times to their own day, the sages and framers of the Talmud accomplished exactly the opposite of what we might have supposed they wanted to do. They made a commentary. On the surface, that suggests they wanted merely to continue and strengthen the received tradition.

But they obliterated the text. They loyally explained the Mishnah. But they turned the Mishnah into something else than what it had been. They patiently hammered out chains of tradition, binding themselves to the authority of the remote and holy past. But it was, in the end, a tradition of their own design and choosing. That is, it was not tradition but a new creation. And so these Talmuds of ours, so loyal and subservient to the Mishnah of Judah the Patriarch, turn out to be less reworkings of received materials than works—each one of them—of remarkably independent judgment. The Talmuds speak humbly and subserviently about received truth, always in the name only of Moses and of sages of times past. But in the end it is truth not discovered and demonstrated, but determined and invented and declared.

The redactional program of the men responsible for laying out the materials of Talmuds may now be described. There is a pronounced tendency in both Talmuds to move from close reading of the Mishnah and then Tosefta outward to more general inquiry into the principles of a Mishnah passage and their interplay with those of some other, superficially unrelated passage, and, finally, to more general reflections on law not self-evidently related to the Mishnah passage at hand or to anthologies intersecting only at a general topic. Unlike the Mishnah, the Talmuds reveal no effort to systematize sayings in larger constructions, or to impose a pattern upon all individual sayings. If the Mishnah is framed to facilitate memorization, then we must say that the Talmuds' materials are not framed with mnemonics in mind. If the Mishnah focuses upon subsurface relationships in syntax, the Talmud in the main looks like notes of a discussion. These notes may serve to recreate the larger patterns of argument and reasoning, a summary of what was thought and perhaps also said. The Talmud preserves and expresses concrete ideas, reducing them to brief but usually accessible and obvious statements. The Mishnah speaks of concrete things in order to hint at abstract relationships, which rarely are brought to the surface and fully exposed.

The Mishnah hides. The Talmuds spell out. The Mishnah hints. The Talmuds repeat *ad nauseam*. The Mishnah is subtle, the Talmuds are obvious; the one restrained and tentative, the others aimed at full and exhaustive expression of what is already clear. The sages of the Mishnah rarely represent themselves as deciding cases. Only on unusual occasions do they declare the decided law, at best reticently spelling out what underlies their positions. The rabbis of the Talmuds harp on who holds which opinion and how a case is actually decided, presenting a rich corpus of precedents. They seek to make explicit what is implicit in the law. The Mishnah is immaterial and spiritual, the Talmud earthy and social. The Mishnah deals in the gossamer threads of philosophical principle, the Talmud in the coarse rope that binds this one and that one into a social construction.

The Mishnah speaks of a world in stasis, an unchanging, eternal present tense where all the tensions of chaos are resolved. The Talmuds address the real Israel in the here and now of ever-changing times, the gross matter of disorder and history. Clearly, the central traits of the Mishnah, revealed in the document at its time of closure in ca. 200 C.E., were revised and transformed into those definitive of the Talmud at its time of closure in ca. 400 C.E. for the earlier Talmud, 600 for the later. We know only that when we compare the Mishnah to the Talmuds we find in each case two intertwined documents, quite different from one another both in style and in values. Yet they are so tightly joined that the Talmud appears in the main to provide mere commentary and amplification for the Mishnah. So in important, superficial traits the two Talmuds are indistinguishable.

JACOB NEUSNER

**RABBINIC JUDAISM, FORMATIVE CANON OF [3]: THE AGGADIC DOCUMENTS. MIDRASH: THE EARLIER COMPILATIONS:** We consider the documents that are generally considered to belong to the first period in the collection and preservation of exegeses of Scripture. These cover Exodus, Leviticus, Numbers, and Deuteronomy. (Important scholarly opinion assigns the compilation on Exodus to a much later period.)

**Mekhilta Attributed to R. Ishmael (Exodus):** Mekhilta Attributed to R. Ishmael seen in the aggregate presents a composite of three kinds of materials concerning the book of Exodus. The first is a set of *ad hoc* and episodic exegeses of some passages of Scripture. The second is a group of propositional and argumentative essays in exegetical form, in which theological principles are set forth and demonstrated. The third consists of topical articles, some of them sustained, many of them well crafted, about important subjects of the Judaism of the dual Torah. The document forms a sustained address to the book of Exodus, covering Exod. 12:1-23:19, Exod. 31:12-13, and Exod. 35:1-3. It comprises nine tractates, Pisha (Exod. 12:1-13:16), Beshallah (Exod. 13-17, 14-31), Shirata (Exod. 15:1-21), Vayassa (Exod. 22-17:7), Amalek (Exod. 17:8-18:27), Baho-desh (Exod. 19:1-20:26), Neziqin (Exod. 21:1-22:23), Kaspa (Exod. 22:24-23:19), and Shabbata (Exod. 31:12-17 and 35:1-3). There are eighty-two sections, subdivided into paragraphs. The division of the book of Exodus has no bearing on the lections read in the synagogue as we now know them. The document is variously dated, but ca. 250 is presently favored by many scholars, but rejected with reason by others.

In Mekhilta Attributed to R. Ishmael, we find a compilation of Midrash-exegeses the authorship of which did not write with Scripture at all. Providing this encyclopedia of information concerning theology and normative behavior for the authorship of Mekhilta Attributed to R. Ishmael did not require a sustained demonstration of a position, whether whole or even in part, distinctive to that authorship and distinct from positions set forth by other authorships. These compilers encountered and utilized Scripture in a very different way. For the authorship of Mekhilta Attributed to R. Ishmael, Scripture is inert. That is to say, it is a source of information, texts that prove propositions. It also is the foundation of the organization of discourse. But when people wish to say things, they say them *about* Scripture, not through Scripture or with Scripture.

Accordingly, what we have in Mekhilta Attributed to R. Ishmael falls into a different category altogether: the document comprises the first scriptural encyclopedia of Judaism. A scriptural encyclopedia joins together expositions of topics, disquisitions on propositions, in general precipitated by the themes of scriptural narrative or the dictates of biblical law, and collects and arranges in accord with Scripture's order and program the exegeses—paraphrases or brief explanations—of clauses of biblical verses. The nine authorships of Mekhilta Attributed to R. Ishmael treat as a given, that is to say, a corpus of facts or, more aptly, a body of tradition, what the other authorships or compilers of Midrash-compositions set forth as components of a system that requires defense and demands apologetic exposition. For our authorship, the facts comprise a corpus of information, to which people require ready access. By setting forth an important component of information, that is, the data of revealed truths of the Judaism of the dual Torah, that authorship provides such access. What is needed, then, is an encyclopedia of things one should know on themes Scripture dictates, and the sequence of topics and propositions, in the order demanded by Scripture, results.

A model for long centuries to come Mekhilta Attributed to R. Ishmael attracted many imitators and continuators. The conception of collecting information and holding it together upon the frame of Scripture attracted many, so that a vast literature of Midrash-compilation much like this compilation came into being in succeeding periods. Not one but dozens, ultimately hundreds, of Midrash-compilations, interesting, traditional, and, of course, pointless and merely informative, would fill the shelves of the library that emerged from the canon of the Judaism of the dual Torah. Accordingly, Mekhilta Attributed to R. Ishmael stood at the beginning of centuries of work carried on in the pattern set by that authorship. There would be only one Bavli, but many, many Midrash-compilations: Mekhiltas, Yalquts, Midrash-this and Midrash-that, and, in due course, a secondary development would call into being commentaries to Scripture (as to the Bavli) as well. So Mekhilta Attributed to R. Ishmael formed not only a scriptural encyclopedia of Judaism, but, as it turned out, the first of many, many such compilations of revealed, received truth, set forth in the framework of the written Torah.

Lacking all interest in cogent and sustained argumentation and demonstration of propositions set forth for argument, the authorship of Mekhilta Attributed to R. Ishmael scarcely aspires to make a full and important, well-composed and proportioned statement of its own. The nine tractates of Mekhilta Attributed to R. Ishmael, moreover, prove discrete. We have to take account of a document behind which, even at the end product, stand nine authorships, not one single authorship whose hand is evident through. For in formal and logical traits, all the more so in topical program, the nine tractates are scarcely cogent when seen whole and complete. They make no one point over and over again. They undertake no sustained, methodical analysis that joins bits and pieces of exegesis into a large-scale composition, bearing meaning. They do not pursue a single range of problems in such a way as through discrete results to demonstrate in many ways a single cogent position.

It follows that, while the authorship of Mekhilta Attributed to R. Ishmael sets forth propositions, these overall do not serve to organize or impose cogency upon the document as a whole. That is why it is an encyclopedia, cogent in the pieces, but not overall. Only one tractate, Neziqin, clearly exhibits fundamental cogency, since, in the main, it follows a single program of exegesis, aimed at establishing a set of uniform conceptual results. These, briefly stated, point to the conclusions that [1] cases may be generalized into rules; [2] Scripture does not repeat itself even when it covers the same legal subjects more than once; [3] the categories that make sense of reality derive from Scripture's classification of things, not from the traits of things viewed independently of Scripture. The other eight tractates into which the document is divided present a variety of conclusions.

That miscellaneous character of the whole should not obscure the fact that the parts really do form coherent statements, each on its own. Indeed, what makes the document interesting is the laconic and uncontroversial character of its discourse. Its framers clearly take for granted that what they are telling us are the established, accepted truths of the faith. That is why they can find it appropriate just to collect and present information, certain of the knowledge that everyone knows what they say is so. The main points that this Midrash-compilation makes in its several parts may be conveniently divided into three classifications: [1] generalizations about the character of Scripture, [2] rules for correct conduct, and [3] theological teachings, with special reference to the relationship between Israel and God and the implications of that relationship for the fate of Israel among the nations. The first two are in volume and intellectual dimensions not imposing, the third is enormous and important, bearing the weight of the burden of our document.

*Traits of Scripture*: The order in which Scripture sets forth two or more propositions does not necessarily indicate the priority assigned to those items. Scripture itself will dictate priority. Scripture uses euphemistic language. Scripture is not bound by temporal considerations, e.g., of sequence.

*The moral life in Israel*: When one party pays respect to another, they speak in harmony. With the measure with which one metes out to others is one's own reward meted out. Whoever welcomes a fellow is as if one welcomed the face of the Presence of God. Do not favor either rich or poor in judging a case.

*Theological Convictions*: These add up to a great collection of the basic theses of the theology of the Judaism of the dual Torah.

Through doing religious duties Israel was redeemed, and preparation of the rite well in advance was the religious duty to which redemption for Israel would serve as reward. What God says he will do, he does. Wherever Scripture indicates that God has said something, we can find in some other passage precisely where and what he had said. The upshot, of course, is that by carefully reading Scripture, we are able to identify the rules that govern history and salvation. The vindication of Moses's demands turns the demands into prophecies of precisely what would come about. This further is underlined by the careful delineation of the degradation and humiliation of Pharaoh, portrayed as running about. And then comes the striking contrast between the reverence in which Israelites hold the rule of God and the humiliation of the Egyptian ruler. People get what is coming to them. Divine punishment is inexorable, so too divine reward. When God exacts punishment on the nations, his name is made great in the world. Merit saved Israel at the sea. The issue to be pursued is, what sort of merit, e.g., deriving from what actions or persons? The acts of healing of the Holy One, blessed be he, are not like the acts of healing of mortals. The redemption at the sea prefigures the redemption at the end of time. Faith in God is what saves Israel.

God punishes the arrogant person by exacting a penalty precisely from that about which such a person takes pride. With that in which the nations of the world take pride before him he exacts punishment from them. Numerous cases on a long line of instances, based upon historical facts provided by Scripture, serve to demonstrate that proposition. Israel is unique among the nations. Mortals have the power to praise and glorify God. God takes many forms. The Lord is master of all media of war. The Lord needs none of those media. The Lord is a man of war, but the Lord is in no way comparable to a man of war, making war in a supernatural way, specifically by retaining, even while making war, the attributes of mercy and humanity. God is just, and God's justice insures that the worthy are rewarded and the unworthy are penalized. God responds to human actions and attitudes. Those who oppose Israel are as though they opposed God. God is unique and God's salvation at the sea will be repeated at the end of time.

Israel gained great merit because it alone was willing to accept the ten commandments. The Israelites deserve praise for accepting the Torah. The "other gods" are not really gods at all. They are called "other" for various theological reasons. Suffering is precious and will not be rejected. One must not act in regard to God the way the outsiders treat their gods. They honor their gods in good times, not in bad, but Israel, exemplified by Job, honors God in bad time as much as in good. These fundamental principles of faith hardly exhaust the allusions to, or representations of, theological and normative statements in Mekhilta Attributed to R. Ishmael. They represent only those convictions that are spelled out in massive detail and argued with great force, the points of emphasis within a vast fabric of faith.

While familiar, these propositions form a miscellany. The characterization of the propositional message of our authorship(s) strongly suggests that we are dealing with a repertoire of standard and established, normative dogmas of the Judaism of the dual Torah. Nothing in the representation just now set forth points toward controversy or can be shown to contradict convictions contained within other documents. In Mekhilta Attributed to R. Ishmael we deal with a compilation of teachings, not a sustained argument: a systematic presentation of conventions, not a focused argument in behalf of distinct and urgent propositions.

Compared to other Midrash-compilations Mekhilta Attributed to R. Ishmael therefore is abnormal in two aspects. First, it is animated by no paramount questions and does not lay out compelling and sharply-etched responses to them. Second, it is not predominantly a propositional writing at all. So in its topical and propositional character, this document differs from others of its classification. If the others bear singular messages, Mekhilta Attributed to R. Ishmael speaks in eternal verities, which, in the context of controversy, enjoy the authority of accepted commonplaces, or, less cordially classified, mere banalities—theological truths, but routine and broadly-acknowledged ones. If the others employ as their paramount mode of discourse propositional compositions, this compilation is first of all exegetical and miscellaneous, and only in moderate measure, propositional at all. Other compilations prove points and bear a weighty message; this one does not.

**Sifra (to Leviticus)** Sifra, a compilation of Midrash-exegeses on the book of Leviticus, forms a massive and systematic statement concerning the definition of the Mishnah in relationship to Scripture. Unlike the other Midrash-compilations that concern the Pentateuch, the two Sifrés and Mekhilta Attributed to R. Ishmael, the document is programmatically cogent, beginning to end, in its sustained treatment of the issues defined by the Mishnah. For the heirs of the Mishnah, the relationship of the Mishnah with Scripture—in mythic language, of the oral to the written part of the Torah—required definition. The authorship of Sifra composed the one document to accomplish the union of the two Torahs, Scripture, or the written Torah, and the Mishnah, or the oral Torah.

This was achieved not merely formally by provision of proof texts from Scripture for statements of the Mishnah—as in the two Talmuds—but through a profound analysis of the interior structure of thought. It was by means of the critique of practical logic and the rehabilitation of the probative logic of hierarchical classification (accomplished through the form of *Listenwissenschaft*) in particular that the authorship of Sifra accomplished this remarkable feat of intellect. That authorship achieved the (re-)union of the two Torahs into a single cogent statement within the framework of the written Torah by penetrating into the deep composition of logic that underlay the creation of the world in its correct components, rightly classified, and in its right order, as portrayed by the Torah.

This was done in two ways. It involved, first of all, systematically demolishing the logic that sustains an autonomous Mishnah, which appeals to the intrinsic traits of things to accomplish classification and hierarchization. Secondly, it was done by demonstrating the dependency, for the identification of the correct classification of things, not upon the traits of things viewed in the abstract, but upon the classification of things by Scripture in particular. The framers of Sifra recast the two parts of the Torah into a single coherent statement through unitary and cogent discourse. So in choosing, as to structure, a book of the Pentateuch, and, as to form, the

exegetical form involving paraphrase and amplification of a phrase of a base-text of Scripture, the authorship of Sifra made its entire statement *in nuce*. Then by composing a document that for very long stretches simply cannot have been put together without the Mishnah and at the same time subjecting the generative logical principles of the Mishnah to devastating critique, that same authorship took up its position. The destruction of the Mishnah as an autonomous and freestanding statement, based upon its own logic, is followed by the reconstruction of (large tracts of the Mishnah) as a statement wholly within, and in accord with, the logic and program of the written Torah in Leviticus. That is what defines Sifra, the one genuinely cogent and sustained statement among the four Midrash-compilations that present exegetical discourse on the Pentateuch.

The dominant approach to uniting the two Torahs, oral and written, into a single cogent statement, involved reading the written Torah into the oral. In form this was done through inserting into the Mishnah (that is, the oral Torah) a long sequence of proof texts. The other solution required reading the oral Torah into the written one, by inserting into the written Torah citations and allusions to the oral one, and, as a matter of fact, also by demonstrating, on both philosophical and theological grounds, the utter subordination and dependency of the oral Torah, the Mishnah, to the written Torah—while at the same time defending and vindicating that same oral Torah. Sifra, followed unsystematically to be sure by the two Sifrés, did just that. Sifra's authorship attempted to set forth the dual Torah as a single, cogent statement, doing so by reading the Mishnah into Scripture not merely for proposition but for expression of proposition. On the surface that decision represented a literary, not merely a theological, judgment. But within the deep structure of thought, it was far more than a mere matter of how to select and organize propositions.

That judgment upon the Mishnah forms part of the polemic of Sifra's authorship—but only part of it. Sifra's authorship conducts a sustained polemic against the failure of the Mishnah to cite Scripture very much or systematically to link its ideas to Scripture through the medium of formal demonstration by exegesis. Sifra's rhetorical exegesis follows a standard redactional form. Scripture will be cited. Then a statement will be made about its meaning, or a statement of law correlative to that Scripture will be given. That statement sometimes cites the Mishnah, often verbatim. Finally, the author of Sifra invariably states, "Now is that not (merely) logical?" And the point of that statement will be, Can this position not be gained through the working of mere logic, based upon facts supplied (to be sure) by Scripture?

The polemical power of Sifra lies in its repetitive demonstration that the stated position, citation of a Mishnah-pericope, is not only not the product of logic, but is, and only can be, the product of exegesis of Scripture. That is only part of the matter, but that component of the larger judgment of Sifra's authorship does make the point that the Mishnah is subordinated to Scripture and validated only through Scripture. In that regard, the authorship of Sifra stands at one with the position of the authorships of the other successor-writings, even though Sifra's writers carried to a much more profound level of thought the critique of the Mishnah. They did so by rethinking the logical foundations of the entire Torah.

The framers of the Mishnah effect their classification-structures (sets of things that are alike, therefore follow the same rule, by contrast to sets of things that are unlike and follow the opposite rule) through the traits of things. The authorship of Sifra insists that the source of classification is Scripture. Sifra's authorship time and again demonstrates that classification cannot be carried out without Scripture's data, and, it must follow, hierarchical arguments based on extra-scriptural taxa always fail. In the Mishnah we seek connection between fact and fact, sentence and sentence, by comparing and contrasting two things that are like and not alike. At the logical level the Mishnah falls into the category of familiar philosophical thought. Once we seek regularities, we propose rules. What is like another thing falls under its rule, and

what is not like the other falls under the opposite rule. Accordingly, as to the species of the genus, so far as they are alike, they share the same rule. So far as they are not alike, each follows a rule contrary to that governing the other.

So the work of analysis is what produces connection, and therefore the drawing of conclusions derives from comparison and contrast: the *and*, the *equal*. The proposition then that forms the conclusion concerns the essential likeness of the two offices, except where they are different, but the subterranean premise is that we can explain both likeness and difference by appeal to a principle of fundamental order and unity. To make these observations concrete, we turn to the case at hand. The important contrast comes at the outset. The high priest and king fall into a single genus, but speciation, based on traits particular to the king, then distinguishes the one from the other. All of this exercise is conducted essentially independently of Scripture; the classifications derive from the system, are viewed as autonomous constructs; traits of things define classifications and dictate what is like and what is unlike.

In Sifra no one denies the principle of hierarchical classification. That is an established fact, a self-evident trait of mind. The argument of Sifra's authorship is that, by themselves, things do not possess traits that permit us finally to classify species into a common genus. There always are traits distinctive to a classification. Accordingly, it is the argument of Sifra's authorship that without the revelation of the Torah, we are not able to effect any classification at all, are left, that is to say, only with species, no genus, only with cases, no rules. The thrust of Sifra's authorship's attack on the Mishnah's taxonomic logic is readily discerned. Time and again, we can easily demonstrate, things have so many and such diverse and contradictory indicative traits that, comparing one thing to something else, we can always distinguish one species from another. Even though we find something in common, we also can discern some other trait characteristic of one thing but not the other. Consequently, we also can show that the hierarchical logic on which we rely, the argument *a fortiori* or *qol vehomer*, will not serve. For if on the basis of one set of traits that yield a given classification, we place into hierarchical order two or more items, on the basis of a different set of traits, we have either a different classification altogether, or, much more commonly, simply a different hierarchy. So the attack on the way in which the Mishnah's authorship has done its work appeals not merely to the limitations of classification solely on the basis of traits of things. The more telling argument addresses what is, to *Listenwissenschaft*, the source of power and compelling proof: hierarchization. That is why, throughout, we must designate the Mishnah's mode of *Listenwissenschaft* a logic of hierarchical classification. Things are not merely like or unlike, therefore following one rule or its opposite. Things also are weightier or less weighty, and that particular point of likeness of difference generates the logical force of *Listenwissenschaft*.

Sifra's authorship repeatedly demonstrates the formation of classifications based on monothetic taxonomy. What that means is this: traits that are not only common to both items but that are shared throughout both of the items subject to comparison and contrast, simply will not serve. These shared traits are supposed to prove that the items that are compared are alike, and therefore should be subjected to the same rule. But the allegation of comparability proves flawed. The proposition maintains that the two items are alike, because they share one trait in common (thus: "monothetic taxonomy"). But they also exhibit traits that are different for the respective items. Then we have both likeness and difference.

Then, the argument proceeds, at every point at which someone alleges uniform, that is to say, monothetic likeness, Sifra's authorship will demonstrate difference. Then how to proceed? Appeal to some shared traits as a basis for classification: this is not like that, and that is not like this, but the indicative trait that both exhibit is such and so, that is to say, polythetic taxonomy. The self-evident problem in accepting differences among things and insisting, nonetheless, on their mono-

morphic character for purposes of comparison and contrast, cannot be set aside: who says? That is, if we can adduce in evidence for a shared classification of things only a few traits among many characteristic of each thing, then what stops me from treating all things alike? Polythetic taxonomy opens the way to an unlimited exercise in finding what diverse things have in common and imposing, for that reason, one rule on everything. Then the very working of *Listenwissenschaft* as a tool of analysis, differentiation, comparison, contrast, and the descriptive determination of rules yields the opposite of what is desired. Chaos, not order, a mass of exceptions, no rules, a world of examples, each subject to its own regulation, instead of a world of order and proportion, composition and stability, will result.

**Sifra and the Mishnah:** While setting forth its critique of the Mishnah's utilization of the logic of comparison and contrast in hierarchical classification, the authorship of Sifra is careful not to criticize the Mishnah. Its position favors restating the Mishnah within the context of Scripture, not rejecting the conclusions of the Mishnah, let alone its authority. Consequently, when we find a critique of applied reason divorced from Scripture, we rarely uncover an explicit critique of the Mishnah, and when we find a citation of the Mishnah, we rarely uncover linkage to the ubiquitous principle that Scripture forms the source of all classification and hierarchy. When the Mishnah is cited by our authorship, it will be presented as part of the factual substrate of the Torah. When the logic operative throughout the Mishnah is subjected to criticism, the language of the Mishnah will rarely, if ever, be cited in context. The operative language in dealing with the critique of the applied logic of *Listenwissenschaft* as represented by the framers of the Mishnah ordinarily is, "is it not a matter of logic?" Then the sorts of arguments against taxonomy pursued outside of the framework of Scripture's classifications will follow. When, by contrast, the authorship of Sifra wishes to introduce into the context it has already established a verbatim passage of the Mishnah, it will ordinarily, though not always, use, *mikan amru*, which, in context, means, "in this connection [sages] have said." It is a simple fact that when the intent is to demolish improper reasoning, the Mishnah's rules in the Mishnah's language rarely, if ever, occur. When the authorship of Sifra wishes to incorporate paragraphs of the Mishnah into their re-presentation of The Torah, they will do so either without fanfare or by the neutral joining-language "in this connection [sages] have said."

The authorship of Sifra never called into question the self-evident validity of taxonomic logic. Its critique is addressed only to how the Mishnah's framers identify the origins of, and delineate, classification-units. But that critique proves fundamental to the case that that authorship proposed to make. For, intending to demonstrate that *The Torah* was a proper noun, and that everything that was valid came to expression in the single, cogent statement of The Torah, the authorship at hand identified the fundamental issue. It is the debate over the way we know things. In insisting, in agreement with the framers of the Mishnah, that there are not only cases but also rules, not only species but also genera, the authorship of Sifra also made its case in behalf of the case for The Torah as a proper noun. This carries us to the theological foundation for Sifra's authorship's sustained critique of applied reason.

At stake is the character of The Torah. We may phrase the question in this way: exactly what do we want to learn from, or discern within The Torah? And the answer to that question requires theological, not merely literary and philosophical, reflection on our part. For in their delineation of correct hierarchical logic, our authorship uncovered within The Torah (hence by definition, written and oral components of The Torah alike) an adumbration of the working of the mind of God. That is because the premise of all discourse is that The Torah was written by God and dictated by God to Moses at Sinai. And that will in the end explain why our authorship for its part has entered into The Torah long passages of not merely clarification but active intrusion, making itself a component of the interlocutorial process. To what

end we know: it was to unite the dual Torah. The authorship of Sifra proposed to regain access to the modes of thought that guided the formation of the Torah, oral and written alike: comparison and contrast in this way, not in that, identification of categories in one manner, not in another. Since those were the modes of thought that, in our authorship's conception, dictated the structure of intellect upon which the Torah, the united Torah, rested, a simple conclusion is the sole possible one.

In their analysis of the deepest structures of intellect of the Torah, the authorship of Sifra presumed to enter into the mind of God, showing how God's mind worked when God formed the Torah, written and oral alike. And there, in the intellect of God, in their judgment humanity gained access to the only means of uniting the Torah, because that is where the Torah originated. But in discerning how God's mind worked, the intellectuals who created Sifra claimed for themselves a place in that very process of thought that had given birth to The Torah. Our authorship could rewrite the Torah because, knowing how The Torah originally was written, they too could write (though not reveal) The Torah.

For its topical program the authorship of Sifra takes the book of Leviticus. For propositions Sifra's authorship presents episodic and ad hoc sentences. If we ask how these sentences form propositions other than amplifications of points made in the book of Leviticus itself, and how we may restate those propositions in a coherent way, nothing sustained and coherent emerges. Sifra does not constitute a propositional document transcending its precipitating text. But that in no way bears the implication that the document's authorship merely collected and arranged this and that about the book of Leviticus. For three reasons, we must conclude that Sifra does not set forth propositions in the way in which the Rabbah-compilations and Sifré to Deuteronomy do.

First, in general there is no topical program distinct from that of Scripture. Sifra remains wholly within Scripture's orbit and range of discourse, proposing only to expand and clarify what it found within Scripture. Where the authorship moves beyond Scripture, it is not toward fresh theological or philosophical thought, but rather to a quite different set of issues altogether, concerning the Mishnah and Tosefta. When we describe the topical program of the document, the blatant and definitive trait of Sifra is simple: the topical program and order derive from Scripture. Just as the Mishnah defines the topical program and order for the Tosefta, the Yerushalmi, and the Bavli, so Scripture does so for Sifra. It follows that Sifra takes as its structure the plan and program of the written Torah, by contrast to the decision of the framers or compilers of Tosefta and the two Talmuds.

Second, for sizable passages, the sole point of coherence for the discrete sentences or paragraphs of Sifra's authorship derives from the base-verse of Scripture that is subject to commentary. That fact corresponds to the results of form-analysis and the description of the logics of cogent discourse. While the Mishnah holds thought together through propositions of various kinds, with special interest in demonstrating propositions through a well-crafted program of logic of a certain kind, Sifra's authorship appeals to a different logic altogether.

The third fundamental observation draws attention to the paramount position, within this restatement of the written Torah, of the oral Torah. We may say very simply that, in a purely formal and superficial sense, a sizable proportion of Sifra consists simply in the association of completed statements of the oral Torah with the exposition of the written Torah, the whole re-presenting as one whole Torah the dual Torah received by Moses at Sinai (speaking within the Torah-myth). Even at the very surface we observe a simple fact. Without the Mishnah or the Tosefta, our authorship will have had virtually nothing to say about one passage after another of the written Torah. Far more often than citing the Mishnah or the Tosefta verbatim, our authorship cites principles of law or theology fundamental to the Mishnah's treatment of a given topic, even when the particular passage of the Mishnah or the Tosefta that sets forth those principles is not cited verbatim.

That brings us to the positive side of the picture. While Sifra in detail presents no paramount propositions, as a whole it demonstrates a highly-distinctive and vigorously-demonstrated proposition. We should drastically misunderstand the document if the miscellaneous character of the parts obscured the powerful statement made by the whole. For while in detail we cannot reconstruct a topical program other than that of Scripture, viewed in its indicative and definitive traits of rhetoric, logic, and implicit proposition, Sifra does take up a well-composed position on a fundamental issue, namely, the relationship between the written Torah, represented by the book of Leviticus, and the oral Torah, represented by the passages of the Mishnah deemed by the authorship of Sifra to be pertinent to the book of Leviticus. Sifra joins the two Torahs into a single statement, accomplishing a re-presentation of the written Torah in topic and in program and in the logic of cogent discourse, and within that rewriting of the written Torah, a re-presentation of the oral Torah in its paramount problematic and in many of its substantive propositions. Stated simply, the written Torah provides the form, the oral Torah, the content. What emerges is not merely a united, dual Torah, but *The* Torah, stated whole and complete, in the context defined by the book of Leviticus.

The three basic and definitive topical traits of Sifra, are, first, its total adherence to the topical program of the written Torah for order and plan; second, its very common reliance upon the phrases or verses of the written Torah for the joining into coherent discourse of discrete thoughts, e.g., comments on, or amplifications of, words or phrases; and third, its equally profound dependence upon the oral Torah for its program of thought: the problematic that defines the issues the authorship wishes to explore and resolve.

**Sifre to Numbers:** Sifré to Numbers provides a miscellaneous reading of most of the book of Numbers, but examining the implicit propositions of the recurrent forms of the document yields a clear-cut purpose. The document follows no topical program; but it also is unlike Mekhilta Attributed to R. Ishmael because of its recurrent effort to prove a few fundamental points. True, these are general and not limited to a given set of cases or issues, so that the successive compositions that comprise Sifré to Numbers yield no propositional program. But the recurrent proofs of discrete propositions that time and again bear one and the same implication do accumulate and when we see what is implicit in the various explicit exercises, we find a clear-cut and rather rich message indeed.

The document as a whole through its fixed and recurrent formal preferences or literary structures makes two complementary points. Reason unaided by Scripture produces uncertain propositions, and reason operating within the limits of Scripture produces truth. These two principles are never articulated but left implicit in the systematic reading of most of the book of Numbers, verse by verse. The exegetical forms stand for a single proposition: the human mind joins God's mind when humanity receives and sets forth the Torah. The Torah opens the road into the mind of God, and our minds can lead us on that road, because our mind and God's mind are comparable. We share a common rationality. Only when we examine the rhetorical plan and then in search of the topical program reconsider the forms of the document does this propositional program emerge.

As with Sifra, therefore, Sifré to Numbers follows no topical program distinct from that of Scripture, which is systematically clarified. An interest in the relations to Scripture of the Mishnah and Tosefta, a concern with the dialectics characteristic of Sifra—these occur episodically, but scarcely define the character of the document. Its topical program and order derive from Scripture. As with Sifra, here too the sole point of coherence for the discrete sentences or paragraphs derives from the base-verse of Scripture that is subject to commentary. At the same time, if we examine the incremental message, the cumulative effect of the formal traits of speech and thought revealed in the uniform rhetoric and syntax of the document, we may discern a propositional program that is implicit in the rhetoric and logic of the compilation.

The rhetorical form underlines the priority of not proposition, hence reason, but process, hence the exegesis of Scripture. The

way chosen to accomplish this goal is to begin at all points with a verse of Scripture and demonstrate that only by starting with the word-choices and propositions of that verse of Scripture, all further progress of interpretation commences. But the second proposition, that man has a place in the process of revealing the Torah of Sinai, comes to expression in the careful separation of the cited verse of the written Torah from the contribution of the contemporary exegete. In that formal preference too, the authorship made a major point and established—if implicitly—a central syllogism: God's will follows the rules of reason. Man can investigate the consequences of reason as expressed in God's will. Therefore man can join in the labor of exploring God's will in the Torah. The appeal to Scripture, however, comes once the proposition is established, and that appeal then dictates the rhetoric and topic alike. Only when we know what question we bring to Scripture may we devise appropriate formal and programmatic policies for our Midrash-exegesis and Midrash-compilation alike. A second formal preference in all three documents, in addition to the exegetical form, makes the same point. The other form involves citation of a passage of the Mishnah followed by an extensive discourse on how the verse of Scripture that pertains to the topic of that Mishnah-passage must contribute its facts, revealed at Sinai, if we wish to know the truth. Reason alone, which is systematically tested through a sequence of propositions shown to fail, will not serve.

**Sifre to Deuteronomy:** Out of cases and examples, sages seek generalizations and governing principles. Since in the book of Deuteronomy, Moses explicitly sets forth a vision of Israel's future history, sages in Sifré to Deuteronomy examined that vision to uncover the rules that explain what happens to Israel. That issue drew attention from cases to rules, with the result that, in the book of Deuteronomy, they set forth a systematic account of Israel's future history, the key to Israel's recovery of command of its destiny. Like Sifra, Sifré to Deuteronomy pursues a diverse topical program in order to demonstrate a few fundamental propositions. The survey of the topical and propositional program of Sifré to Deuteronomy dictates what is truly particular to that authorship. It is its systematic mode of methodical analysis, in which it does two things. First, the document's compilers take the details of cases and carefully re-frame them into rules pertaining to all cases. The authorship therefore asks those questions of susceptibility to generalization ("generalizability") that first-class philosophical minds raise. And it answers those questions by showing what details restrict the prevailing law to the conditions of the case, and what details exemplify the encompassing traits of the law overall. These are, after all, the two possibilities. The law is either limited to the case and to all cases that replicate this one. Or the law derives from the principles exemplified, in detail, in the case at hand. Essentially, as a matter of both logic and topical program, our authorship has reread the legal portions of the book of Deuteronomy and turned Scripture into what we now know is the orderly and encompassing code supplied by the Mishnah. To state matters simply, this authorship "mishnaizes" Scripture. We find in Sifré to Numbers no parallel to this dominant and systematic program of Sifré to Deuteronomy.

But in other aspects, the document presents no surprises. In the two Sifrés and Sifra we find a recurrent motif, intense here, episodic there, of how the written component of the Torah, that is, revelation in written form, serves as the sole source of final truth. Logic or reason untested against Scripture produces flawed or unreliable results. The Torah, read as rabbis read it, and that alone proves paramount. Reason on its own is subordinate. For their search for the social rules of Israel's society, the priority of the covenant as a reliable account of the workings of reality, and the prevailing laws of Israel's history decreed by the terms of the covenant, their fundamental claim is the same. There are rules and regularities, but reason alone will not show us what they are. A systematic and reasoned reading of the Torah—the written Torah—joined to a sifting of the cases of the Torah in search of the regularities and points of law and order—these are what will tell the pre-

vailing rule. A rule of the Mishnah and its account of the here and now of everyday life rests upon the Torah, not upon (mere) logic. A rule of Israel's history, past, present, and future, likewise derives from a search for regularities and points of order identified not by logic alone, but by logic addressed to the Torah. So there are these modes of gaining truth that apply equally to Mishnah and Scripture. There is logic, applied reason and practical wisdom, such as sages exhibit; there is the corpus of facts supplied by Scripture, read as sages read it. These two together form God's statement upon the world today.

The topical program of the document intersects at its fundamental propositions with programs of other authorships—beginning, after all, with those of Scripture itself. The writers and compilers and compositors of Deuteronomy itself will have found entirely familiar such notions as the conditional character of Israel's possession of the land of Israel, the centrality of the covenant in Israel's relationship with God and with the other nations of the world, and the decisive role of the covenant in determining its own destiny, and the covenantal responsibilities and standing of Israel's leadership—surely a considerable motif in the very structure of the book of Deuteronomy itself, beginning and end in particular. The reader may well wonder how we may treat as a distinctive authorship a group of writers who simply go over ground familiar in the received literature. In some important ways the authorship of Sifré to Deuteronomy makes a statement that is very much its own. That fact becomes clear when we consider the document's rhetorical, logical, and topical characteristics.

Four principal topics encompass the document's propositions, of which the first three correspond to the three relationships into which Israel entered: with heaven, on earth, and within. These yield systematic statements that concern the relationships between Israel and God, with special reference to the covenant, the Torah, and the land; Israel and the nations, with interest in Israel's history, past, present, and future, and how that cyclic is to be known; Israel on its own terms, with focus upon Israel's distinctive leadership. The fourth rubric encompasses not specific *ad hoc* propositions, that form aggregates of proofs of large truths, but rather, prevailing modes of thought, demonstrating the inner structure of intellect, in our document yielding the formation, out of the cases of Scripture, of encompassing rules.

ISRAEL AND GOD: THE IMPLICATIONS OF THE COVENANT: The basic proposition, spelled out in detail, is that Israel stands in a special relationship with God, and that relationship is defined by the contract, or covenant, that God made with Israel. The covenant comes to particular expression, in our document, in two matters, first, the land, second, the Torah. Each marks Israel as different from all other nations, on the one side, and as selected by God, on the other. In these propositions, sages situate Israel in the realm of heaven, finding on earth the stigmata of covenanted election and concomitant requirement of loyalty and obedience to the covenant.

First comes the definition of those traits of God that our authorship finds pertinent. God sits in judgment upon the world, and his judgment is true and righteous. God punishes faithlessness. But God's fundamental and definitive trait is mercy. The way of God is to be merciful and gracious. The basic relationship of Israel to God is one of God's grace for Israel. God's loyalty to Israel endures, even when Israel sins. When Israel forgets God, God is pained. Israel's leaders, whatever their excellence, plead with God only for grace, not for their own merit. Correct attitudes in prayer derive from the need for grace, Israel having slight merit on its own account. Israel should follow only God, carrying out religious deeds as the covenant requires, in accord with the instructions of prophets. Israel should show mercy to others, in the model of God's merciful character.

Second, the contract, or covenant, produces the result that God has acquired Israel, which God created. The reason is that only Israel accepted the Torah, among all the nations, and that is why God made the covenant with Israel in particular. Why is the covenant made only with Israel? The gentiles did not accept the Torah, Israel did, and that

has made all the difference. Israel recognized God forthwith; the very peace of the world and of nature depends upon God's giving the Torah to Israel. That is why Israel is the sole nation worthy of dwelling in the palace of God and that is the basis for the covenant too. The covenant secures for Israel an enduring relationship of grace with God. The covenant cannot be revoked and endures forever. The covenant, terms of which are specified in the Torah, has duplicate terms: if you do well, you will bear a blessing, and if not, you will bear a curse.

That is the singular mark of the covenant between God and Israel. A mark of the covenant is the liberation from Egypt, and that sufficed to impose upon Israel God's claim for their obedience. An important sign of the covenant is the possession of the land. Part of the covenant is the recognition of merit of the ancestors. In judging the descendants of the patriarchs and matriarchs, God promised, in making the covenant, recognition of the meritorious deeds of the ancestors. The conquest of the land and inheriting it are marks of the covenant, which Israel will find easy because of God's favor. The inheritance of the land is a mark of merit, inherited from the ancestors. The land is higher than all others and more choice. All religious duties are important, those that seem trivial as much as those held to be weightier.

God always loves Israel. That is why Israel should carry out the religious duties of the Torah with full assent. All religious duties are equally precious. Israel must be whole-hearted in its relationship with God. If it is, then its share is with God, and if not, then not. But Israel may hate God. The right attitude toward God is love, and Israel should love God with a whole heart. The reason that Israel rebels against God is prosperity. Then people become arrogant and believe that their prosperity derives from their own efforts. But that is not so, and God punishes people who rebel to show them that they depend upon God. When Israel practices idolatry, God punishes them, e.g., through exile, through famine, through drought, and the like. Whether or not Israel knows or likes the fact, it is the fact that Israel therefore has no choice but to accept God's will and fulfill the covenant.

The heaven and the earth respond to the condition of Israel and therefore carry out the stipulations of the covenant. If Israel does not carry out religious duties concerning heaven, then heaven bears witness against them. That centers on the land of Israel in particular. Possession of the land is conditional, not absolute. It begins with grace, not merit. It is defined by the stipulation that Israel observe the covenant, in which case Israel will retain the land. If Israel violates the covenant, Israel will lose the land. When Israel inherits the land, in obedience to the covenant and as an act of grace bestowed by God, it will build the Temple, where Israel's sins will find atonement. The conquest of the land itself is subject to stipulations, just as possession of the land, as an act of God's grace, is marked by religious obligations. If Israel rebels or rejects the Torah, it will lose the land, just as the Canaanites did for their idolatry.

The land is not the only, or the most important, mark of the covenant. The fact that Israel has the Torah shows that Israel stands in a special relationship to God. The Torah is the source of life for Israel. It belongs to everyone, not only the aristocracy. Children should start studying the Torah at the earliest age possible. The study of the Torah is part of the fulfillment of the covenant. Even the most arid details of the Torah contain lessons, and if one studies the Torah, the reward comes both in this world and in the world to come.

The possession of the Torah imposes a particular requirement, involving an action. The most important task of every male Israelite is to study the Torah, which involves memorizing, and not forgetting, each lesson. This must go on every day and all the time. Study of the Torah should be one's main obligation, prior to all others. The correct motive is not for the sake of gain, but for the love of God and the desire for knowledge of God's will. People must direct heart, eyes, ears, to teachings of the Torah. Study of the Torah transforms human relationships, so that strangers become the children of the master of the Torah whom they serve as disciples. However unimportant the teaching or the teacher, all is as if on the authority of Moses at Sinai. When a person departs from the Torah, that person becomes an idolater. Study of the Torah prevents idolatry.

ISRAEL AND THE NATIONS: THE MEANING OF HISTORY: The covenant, through the Torah of Sinai, governs not only the ongoing life of Israel but also the state of human affairs universally. The history of Israel forms a single, continuous, cycle, in that what happened in the beginning prefigures what will happen at the end of time. Events of Genesis are reenacted both in middle-history, between the beginning and the end, and also at the end of times. So the traits of the tribal founders dictated the history of their families to both the here and now and also the eschatological age. Moses was shown the whole of Israel's history, past, present, future. The times of the patriarchs are reenacted in the messianic day. That shows how Israel's history runs in cycles, so that events of ancient times prefigure events now. The prophets, beginning with Moses, describe those cycles. What happens bears close ties to what is going to happen. The prophetic promises too were realized in Temple times, and will be realized at the end of time.

The periods in the history of Israel, marked by the exodus and wandering, the inheritance of the land and the building of the Temple, the destruction, are all part of a divine plan. In this age Rome rules, but in the age to come, marked by the study of the Torah and the offering of sacrifices in the Temple cult, Israel will be in charge. That is the fundamental pattern and meaning of history. The Holy Spirit makes possible actions that bear consequences only much later in time. The prefiguring of history forms the dominant motif in Israel's contemporary life, and the reenacting of what has already been forms a constant. Israel therefore should believe, if not in what is coming, then in what has already been. The very names of places in the land attest to the continuity of Israel's history, which follows rules that do not change. The main point is that while Israel will be punished in the worst possible way, Israel will not be wiped out.

But the cyclical character of Israel's history should not mislead. Events follow a pattern, but knowledge of that pattern, which is provided by the Torah, permits Israel both to understand and also to affect its own destiny. Specifically, Israel controls its own destiny through its conduct with God. Israel's history is the working out of the effects of Israel's conduct, moderated by the merit of the ancestors. Abraham effected a change in God's relationship to the world. But merit, which makes history, is attained by one's own deeds as well. The effect of merit, in the nation's standing among the other nations, is simple. When Israel enjoys merit, it gives testimony against itself, but when not, then the most despised nation testifies against it.

But God is with Israel in time of trouble. When Israel sins, it suffers. When it repents and is forgiven, it is redeemed. For example, Israel's wandering in the wilderness took place because of the failure of Israel to attain merit. Sin is what causes the wandering in the wilderness. People rebel because they are prosperous. The merit of the ancestors works in history to Israel's benefit. What Israel does not merit on its own, at a given time, the merit of the ancestors may secure in any event. The best way to deal with Israel's powerlessness is through Torah-study; the vigor of engagement with Torah-study compensates for weakness.

It goes without saying that Israel's history follows a set time, e.g., at the fulfillment of a set period of time, an awaited event will take place. The prophets prophesy concerning the coming of the day of the Lord. Accordingly, nothing is haphazard, and all things happen in accord with a plan. That plan encompasses this world, the time of the Messiah, and the world to come, in that order. God will personally exact vengeance at the end of time. God also will raise the dead. Israel has overcome difficult times and can continue to do so. The task ahead is easier than the tasks already accomplished. Israel's punishment is only once, while the punishment coming upon the nations is unremitting. Peace is worthwhile and everyone needs it. Israel's history ends in the world to come or in the days of the Messiah. The righteous inherit the Garden of Eden. The righteous in the age to come will be joyful.

God acts in history and does so publicly, in full light of day. That is to show the nations who is in charge. The Torah is what distinguishes Israel from the nations. All the nations had every opportunity to understand and accept the Torah, and all declined it; that is why Israel was selected. And that demonstrates the importance of both covenant and the Torah, the medium of the covenant. The nations even had a prophet, comparable to Moses, who was Balaam. The nations have no important role in history, except as God assigns them a role in relationship to Israel's conduct. The nations are estranged from God by idolatry. That is what prevents goodness from coming into the world. The name of God rests upon Israel in greatest measure. Idolaters do not control heaven. The greatest sin an Israelite can commit is idolatry, and those who entice Israel to idolatry are deprived of the ordinary protections of the law. God is violently angry at the nations because of idolatry. As to the nations' relationships with Israel, they are guided by Israel's condition. When Israel is weak, the nations take advantage, when strong, they are sycophantic. God did not apportion love to the nations of the world as he did to Israel.

ISRAEL AT HOME: THE COMMUNITY AND ITS GOVERNANCE: A mark of God's favor is that Israel has (or, has had and will have) a government of its own. Part of the covenantal relationship requires Israel to follow leaders whom God has chosen and instructed, such as Moses and the prophets. Accordingly, Israel is to establish a government and follow sound public policy. Its leaders are chosen by God. Israel's leaders, e.g., prophets, are God's servants, and that is a mark of the praise that is owing to them. They are to be in the model of Moses, humble, choice, select, well-known. Moses was the right one to bestow a blessing, Israel were the right ones to receive the blessing.

Yet all leaders are mortal, even Moses died. The saints are leaders ready to give their lives for Israel. The greatest of them enjoy exceptionally long life. But the sins of the people are blamed on their leaders. The leaders depend on the people to keep the Torah, and Moses thanked them in advance for keeping the Torah after he died. The leaders were to be patient, honest, give a full hearing to all sides, make just decisions, in a broad range of matters. To stand before the judge is to stand before God. God makes sure that Israel does not lack for leadership. The basic task of the leader is both to rebuke and also to console the people.

The rulers of Israel are servants of God. The prophets exemplify these leaders, in the model of Moses, and Israel's rulers act only on the instruction of prophets. Their authority rests solely on God's favor and grace. At the instance of God, the leaders of Israel speak, in particular, words of admonition. These are delivered before death, when the whole picture is clear, so that people can draw the necessary conclusions. These words, when Moses spoke them, covered the entire history of the community of Israel. The leaders of Israel address admonition to the entire community at once. No one is excepted. But the Israelites can deal with the admonition. They draw the correct conclusions. Repentance overcomes sin, as at the sin of the golden calf. The Israelites were contentious, nitpickers, litigious, and, in general, gave Moses a difficult time. Their descendants should learn not to do so. Israel should remain united and obedient to its leaders. The task of the community is to remain united. When the Israelites are of one opinion below, God's name is glorified above.

**General considerations: Midrash defined:** The word *midrash*, translated "exegesis," presents confusion, since it is routinely used to convey three distinct, if related, meanings. If people say "the *midrash* says," they may refer to

[1] a distinctive *process* of interpretation of a particular text, thus, the hermeneutic,
[2] a particular compilation of the results of that process, thus, a book that is the composite of a set of exegeses, or
[3] a concrete unit of the working of that process of scriptural exegesis, thus the write-up of the process of interpretation as it applies to a single verse, the exegetical composition on a particular verse (or group of verses).

It follows that for clear speech the word *midrash*, standing by itself, bears no meaning. Let us consider the three distinct usages.

[1] The word *midrash* refers to the processes of scriptural exegesis carried on by diverse groups of Jews from the time of ancient Israel to nearly the present day. Thus people say, "He produced a *midrash* on the verse," meaning, "an exegesis." A more extreme usage produces, "Life is a *midrash* on Scripture," meaning that what happens in the everyday world imparts meaning or significance to biblical stories and admonitions. It is difficult to specify what the word *midrash* in Hebrew expresses that the word *exegesis* in English does not. It follows that just how "exegesis" in English differs from *midrash* in Hebrew is not self-evident. Nor is there any reason that the Hebrew will serve better than the more familiar English.

[2] The word *midrash* further stands for a compilation of scriptural exegeses, as in "that *midrash* deals with the book of Joshua." In that sentence, *midrash* refers to a compilation of exegeses, hence the statement means, "That compilation of exegeses deals with the book of Joshua." *Compilation* or composite in the present context clearly serves more accurately to convey meaning than *midrash*. That is why in this Introduction we speak of Midrash-compilation, as in "the Midrash-compilation on Exodus. . . . ."

[3] The word *midrash*, finally, stands for the written-out result of a process of scriptural exegesis, that is to say, a composition (e.g., a paragraph with a beginning, middle, and end, in which a completed thought is laid forth), resulting from the process of *midrash*. In this setting *a midrash* refers to a paragraph or a unit of exegetical exposition, in which a verse of the Hebrew Scriptures is subjected to some form of exegesis or other. In this usage one may say, "Let me now cite the *midrash*," meaning, a particular passage of exegesis, a paragraph or other completed whole unit of exegetical thought, a composition that provides an exegesis of a particular verse. We use the word composition in this sense, that is, Midrash-composition, the particular presentation of a given passage.

**Types of Midrash-compilations:** The relationship to Scripture and modes of use of verses of Scripture yield a classification of Midrash-compilations. In the Midrash-compilations of Rabbinic literature, verses of Scripture serve not merely to prove but to instruct. Israelite Scripture constituted not merely a source of validation but a powerful instrument of profound inquiry. The framers of the various Midrash-compilations set forth propositions of their own, yet in dialogue with Scripture. Scripture raised questions, set forth premises of discourse and argument, supplied facts, constituted that faithful record of the facts, rules, and meaning of humanity's, and Israel's, history that, for natural philosophy, derived from the facts of physics or astronomy.

Whether or not their statement accorded with the position of Scripture on a given point, merely said the simple and obvious sense of Scripture, found ample support in proof texts—none of these considerations bears material consequence. These authorships made use of Scripture, but they did so by making selections, shaping a distinctive idiom of discourse in so doing. True, verses of Scripture provided facts; they supplied proofs of propositions much as data of natural science proved propositions of natural philosophy. Writing with Scripture meant appealing to the facts that Scripture provided to prove propositions that the authorships at hand wished to prove, forming with Scripture the systems these writers proposed to construct.

Classifications of relationships to Scripture are three.

[1] The first approach shows that a verse of the Israelite Scriptures illustrates a theme, that is to say, provides *information* on a given subject. In the context of the statement of a document, that information is systemically inert. That is markedly characteristic of Mekhilta According to R. Ishmael. The first mode of relationship therefore is to develop an anthology on a theme. One way of forming a comprehensible statement is to draw together information on a single theme. The theme then imposes cogency on facts, which are deemed to illuminate aspects of that theme. Such a statement constitutes a topical anthology. The materials in the anthology do not, all together, add up to a statement that transcends detail. For example, they do not point toward a conclusion beyond themselves. They rather comprise a series of facts, e.g., fact 1, fact 2, fact 3. But put together, these three facts do not yield yet another one, nor do they point toward a proposition beyond themselves. They generate no generalization, prove no point, propose no proposition.

[2] A second mode of relationship will tell us that a verse of the Israelite Scriptures defines a *problem* on its own, in its own determinate limits and terms. In the setting of a document, the problem will be identified and addressed because it is systemically active. That is not at all common in Mekhilta Attributed to R. Ishmael, while Sifra for its part takes a keen interest in verses and their meanings. Yet in doing so, its authorship weaves a filigree of holy words over a polished surface of very hard wood: a wood of its own hewing and shaping and polishing.

[3] Yet a third mode points toward that utilization of Israelite Scriptures in the formation and expression of *an independent proposition*, one autonomous of the theme or even the facts contained within—proved by—those Scriptures. This characterizes the relationship between Scripture and Sifra, which is not extra-scriptural but meta-scriptural. Scripture in this function is systemically essential yet monumentally irrelevant. Sifra in that way addresses and disposes of Scripture by rewriting it in ways of Sifra's authorship's design. That is the wonder of this marvelous writing: its courage, its brilliance, its originality, above all, its stubbornness.

The routine relationship to Scripture is indicated when the focus of interest is on the exegesis of Scripture. In Mekhilta Attributed to R. Ishmael, as well as in Sifra and Sifré to Deuteronomy, we have composites of materials that find cogency solely in the words of a given verse of Scripture but in no other way. These materials string together, upon the necklace of words or phrases of a verse, diverse comments; the comments do not fit together or point to any broader conclusion;

they do not address a single theme or form an anthology. Cogency derives from the (external) verse that is cited; intelligibility begins—and ends—in that verse and is accomplished by the amplification of the verse's contents. Without the verse, the words that follow form gibberish. But reading the words as amplifications of a sense contained within in the cited verse, we can make good sense of them.

JACOB NEUSNER

**RABBINIC JUDAISM, FORMATIVE CANON OF [4]: THE AGGADIC DOCUMENTS. MIDRASH: THE LATER COMPILATIONS:** While Mekhilta Attributed to R. Ishmael, Sifra, and Sifre to Numbers, like the Mishnah, cover many topics and yield no prominent propositional program but only implicit principles of thought, the second and later set of Midrash-compilations, produced in the fifth and sixth centuries (ca. 450-600 C.E.), which accompany the Talmud of the Land of Israel, form highly propositional statements. The first of the group, Genesis Rabbah, makes the same point many times and sets forth a coherent and original account of the book of Genesis. The next set, Leviticus Rabbah, Pesiqta deRab Kahana, and Pesiqta Rabbati, provide well-argued syllogistic arguments, entirely leaving behind the structure of verse-by-verse exposition. Let us examine each document in turn.

**Genesis Rabbah:** Generally thought to have been closed ("redacted") at ca. 400-450 C.E., sometime after the Talmud of the Land of Israel had been redacted, Genesis Rabbah transforms the book of Genesis from a genealogy and family history of Abraham, Isaac, Jacob, then Joseph, into a book of the laws of history and rules of the salvation of Israel: the deeds of the founders become omens and signs for the final generations. In Genesis Rabbah, thus, the entire narrative of Genesis is so formed as to point toward the sacred history of Israel, the Jewish people: its slavery and redemption; its coming Temple in Jerusalem; its exile and salvation at the end of time—the whole a paradigm of exile and return. In the rereading by the authorship of Genesis Rabbah, Genesis proclaims

the prophetic message that the world's creation commenced a single, straight line of significant events, that is to say, history, leading in the end to the salvation of Israel and, through Israel, of all humanity. The single most important proposition of Genesis Rabbah is that, in the story of the beginnings of creation, humanity, and Israel, we find the message of the meaning and end of the life of the Jewish people in the here and now of the fifth century. The deeds of the founders supply signals for the children about what is going to come in the future. So the biography of Abraham, Isaac, and Jacob also constitutes a protracted account of the history of Israel later on.

Genesis Rabbah is a composite document. As with the Talmud that it accompanies, so in Genesis Rabbah, some of the material in the compilation can be shown to have been put together before that material was used for the purposes of the compilers. Many times a comment entirely apposite to a verse of Genesis has been joined to a set of comments in no way pertinent to the verse at hand. Proof for a given syllogism, furthermore, will derive from a verse of Genesis as well as from numerous verses of other books of the Bible. Such a syllogistic argument therefore has not been written for exegetical purposes particular to the verse at hand. On the contrary, the particular verse subject to attention serves that other, propositional plan; it is not the focus of discourse; it has not generated the comment but merely provided a proof for a syllogism. That is what it means to say that a proposition yields an exegesis. That fundamental proposition, displayed throughout Genesis Rabbah, which yields the specific exegeses of many of the verses of the book of Genesis and even whole stories, is that the beginnings point toward the endings, and the meaning of Israel's past points toward the message that lies in Israel's future. The things that happened to the fathers and mothers of the family, Israel, provide a sign for the things that will happen to the children later on.

What is at stake is the discovery, among the facts provided by the written Torah, of the social rules that govern Israel's history.

At stake is the search for the order yielded by the chaos of uninterpreted data. It follows that, as with the Mishnah, the governing mode of thought is that of natural philosophy. It involves the classification of data by shared traits, yielding descriptive rules, the testing of propositions against the facts of data, the whole aimed at the discovery of underlying rules out of a multiplicity of details, in all, the proposing and testing, against the facts provided by Scripture, of the theses of Israel's salvation that demanded attention just then. But the issues were not so much philosophical as religious, in the sense that while philosophy addressed questions of nature and rules of enduring existence, religion asked about issues of history and God's intervention in time. Within that rough and ready distinction between nature, supernature, and sanctification, typified by the Mishnah and the Tosefta and the legal enterprise in general, on the one side, and society, history, and salvation, typified by Genesis Rabbah, Leviticus Rabbah, Pesiqta deRab Kahana, and the theological inquiry into teleology, on the other, we may distinguish our documents.

Specifically, we may classify the document before us and its successors and companions as works of profound theological inquiry into God's rules for history and society in the here and now and for salvation at the end of historical time. That fundamental proposition concerning the search, in the account of the beginnings, of the ending and meaning of Israel's society and history—hence the rules that govern and permit knowledge of what is to come—constitutes the generative proposition that yielded the specific exegesis of the book of Genesis in Genesis Rabbah.

Genesis Rabbah in its final form emerges from that momentous century in which the Roman Empire passed from pagan to Christian rule, and, in which, in the aftermath of Julian's abortive reversion to paganism, in ca. 360, which endangered the Christian character of the Roman empire, Christianity adopted that politics of repression of paganism that rapidly engulfed Judaism as well. The issue confronting Israel in the Land of Israel therefore proved immediate: the meaning of the new and ominous turn of history, the implications of Christ's worldly triumph for the other-worldly and supernatural people, Israel, whom God chooses and loves. The message of the exegete-compositors addressed the circumstance of historical crisis and generated remarkable renewal, a rebirth of intellect in the encounter with Scripture, now in quest of the rules not of sanctification—these had already been found—but of salvation. So the book of Genesis, which portrays how all things had begun, would testify to the message and the method of the end: the coming salvation of patient, hopeful, enduring Israel.

That is why in the categories of philosophy, including science and society, and religion, including a prophetic interpretation of history and teleology, Genesis Rabbah presents a deeply *religious* view of Israel's historical and salvific life, in much the same way that the Mishnah provides a profoundly *philosophical* view of Israel's everyday and sanctified existence. Just as the main themes of the Mishnah evoke the consideration of issues of being and becoming, the potential and the actual, mixtures and blends and other problems of physics, all in the interest of philosophical analysis, so Genesis Rabbah presents its cogent and coherent agendum as well. That program of inquiry concerns the way in which, in the book of Genesis, God set forth to Moses the entire scope and meaning of Israel's history among the nations and salvation at the end of days. The mode of thought by which the framers of Genesis Rabbah work out their propositions dictates the character of their exegesis, as to rhetoric, logical principle of cogent and intelligible discourse, and, as is clear, even as to topic.

Sages read Genesis as the history of the world with emphasis on Israel. So the lives portrayed, the domestic quarrels and petty conflicts with the neighbors, all serve to yield insight into what was to be. Why so? Because the deeds of the patriarchs taught lessons on how the children were to act, and, it further followed, the lives of the patriarchs signaled the history of Israel. Israel constituted one extended family, and the metaphor of the family, serving the nation as it did, imparted to the stories of Genesis the character of a family record. History become genealogy conveyed the message of salvation. These propositions really laid down the same judgment, one for the individual and the family, the other for the community and the nation, since there was no differentiating one from the other. Every detail of the narrative therefore served to prefigure what was to be, and Israel found itself, time and again, in the revealed facts of the history of the creation of the world, the decline of humanity down to the time of Noah, and, finally, its ascent to Abraham, Isaac, and Israel.

In Genesis Rabbah the entire narrative of Genesis is so formed as to point toward the sacred history of Israel, the Jewish people: its slavery and redemption; its coming Temple in Jerusalem; its exile and salvation at the end of time. The powerful message of Genesis in Genesis Rabbah proclaims that the world's creation commenced a single, straight line of events, leading in the end to the salvation of Israel and through Israel all humanity. Israel's history constitutes the counterpart of creation, and the laws of Israel's salvation form the foundation of creation. Therefore a given story out of Genesis, about creation, events from Adam to Noah and Noah to Abraham, the domestic affairs of the patriarchs, or Joseph, will bear a deeper message about what it means to be Israel, on the one side, and what in the end of days will happen to Israel, on the other. So the persistent theological program requires sages' to search in Scripture for meaning for their own circumstance and for the condition of their people. The single most important proposition of Genesis Rabbah is that, in the story of the beginnings of creation, humanity, and Israel, we find the message of the meaning and end of the life of the Jewish people. The deeds of the founders supply signals for the children about what is going to come in the future. So the biography of Abraham, Isaac, and Jacob also constitutes a protracted account of the history of Israel later on. If the sages could announce a single syllogism and argue it systematically, that is the proposition upon which they would insist.

As a corollary to the view that the biography of the fathers prefigures the history of the descendants, sages maintained that the deeds of the children—the holy way of life of Israel—follow the model established by the founders long ago. So they looked in Genesis for the basis for the things they held to be God's will for Israel. And they found ample proof. Sages invariably searched the stories of Genesis for evidence of the origins not only of creation and of Israel, but also of Israel's cosmic way of life, its understanding of how, in the passage of nature and the seasons, humanity worked out its relationship with God. The holy way of life that Israel lived through the seasons of nature therefore would make its mark upon the stories of the creation of the world and the beginning of Israel.

Part of the reason sages pursued the interest at hand derived from polemic. From the first Christian century theologians of Christianity maintained that salvation did not depend upon keeping the laws of the Torah. Abraham, after all, had been justified and he did not keep the Torah, which, in his day, had not yet been given. So sages time and again would maintain that Abraham indeed kept the entire Torah even before it had been revealed. They further attributed to Abraham, Isaac, and Jacob rules of the Torah enunciated only later on, for example, the institution of prayer three times a day.

The world was created for Israel, and not for the nations of the world. At the end of days everyone will see what only Israel now knows. Since sages read Genesis as the history of the world with emphasis on Israel, the lives portrayed, the domestic quarrels and petty conflicts with the neighbors, as much as the story of creation itself, all serve to yield insight into what was to be. The lives of the patriarchs signaled the history of Israel. Every detail of the narrative therefore served to prefigure what was to be, and Israel found itself, time and again, in the revealed facts of the history of the creation of the world, the decline of humanity down to the time of Noah, and, finally, its ascent to Abraham, Isaac, and Israel. In order to illustrate the single approach to diverse stories, whether concerning Creation, Adam, and Noah, or concerning Abraham, Isaac, and Jacob, we focus on two matters: Abraham, on the one side, and Rome, on the other. In the former we see that Abraham serves as well as Adam to prove the point of it all. In the latter we observe how, in reading Genesis, the sages who compiled Genesis Rabbah discovered the meaning of the events of their own day.

Genesis is read as if it portrayed the history of Israel and Rome. For that is the single obsession binding sages of the document at hand to common discourse with the text before them. Why Rome in the form it takes in Genesis Rabbah? And how come the obsessive character of the sages' disposition of the theme of Rome? Were their picture merely of Rome as tyrant and destroyer of the Temple, we should have no reason to link the text to the problems of the age of redaction and closure. But now it is Rome as Israel's brother, counterpart, and nemesis, Rome as the one thing standing in the way of Israel's, and the world's, ultimate salvation. So the stakes are different, and much higher. It is not a political Rome but a Christian and messianic Rome that is at issue: Rome as surrogate for Israel, Rome as obstacle to Israel. Why? It is because Rome now confronts Israel with a crisis, and the program of Genesis Rabbah constitutes a response to that crisis. Rome in the fourth century became Christian. Sages respond by facing that fact quite squarely, saying, "Indeed, it is as you say, a kind of Israel, an heir of Abraham as your texts explicitly claim. But we remain the sole legitimate Israel, the bearer of the birthright—we and not you. So you are our brother: Esau, Ishmael, Edom."

By rereading the story of the beginnings, sages discovered the answer and the secret of the end. Rome claimed to be Israel, and, indeed, sages conceded, Rome shared the patrimony of Israel. That claim took the form of the Christians' appropriate of the Torah as "the Old Testament," so sages acknowledged a simple fact in acceding to the notion that, in some way, Rome too formed part of Israel. But it was the rejected part, the Ishmael, the Esau, not the Isaac, not the Jacob. The advent of Christian Rome precipi-

tated the sustained, polemical, and rigorous and well-argued rereading of beginnings in light of the end. Rome then marked the conclusion of human history as Israel had known it. Beyond? The coming of the true Messiah, the redemption of Israel, the salvation of the world, the end of time. So the issues were not inconsiderable, and when the sages spoke of Esau/Rome, as they did so often, they confronted the life-or-death decision of the day.

**Leviticus Rabbah:** When we come to Leviticus Rabbah, we find the interest in verse succeeding verse has waned, while the proposition comes to the fore as the dominant organizing motif throughout. With Genesis Rabbah, the Sifra's and Sifré's mode of exegesis of verses and their components, one by one in sequence, comes to its conclusion and a new approach commences. The mixed character of Genesis Rabbah, joining propositional to exegetical rhetoric in order to make points of both general intelligibility and also very specific and concrete amplification of detail, marks a transitional moment in the workings of Midrash. Exactly what did the framers of Leviticus Rabbah learn when they opened the book of Leviticus? To state the answer in advance, when they read the rules of sanctification of the priesthood, they heard the message of the salvation of all Israel. Leviticus became the story of how Israel, purified from social sin and sanctified, would be saved.

The framers of Leviticus Rabbah, closed in the mid-fifth century, set forth, in the thirty-seven *parashiyyot* or chapters into which their document is divided, thirty-seven well-crafted propositions. They made no pretense at a systematic exegesis of sequences of verses of Scripture, abandoning the verse by verse mode of organizing discourse. They struck out on their own to compose a means of expressing their propositions in a more systematic and cogent way. Each of the thirty-seven chapters proves cogent, and all of them spell out their respective statements in an intellectually economical, if rich, manner. Each *parashah* makes its own point, but all of them furthermore form a single statement.

The message of Leviticus Rabbah—

congruent with that of Genesis Rabbah—is that the laws of history may be known, and that these laws, so far as Israel is concerned, focus upon the holy life of the community. If Israel obeys the laws of society aimed at Israel's sanctification, then the foreordained history, resting on the merit of the ancestors, will unfold as Israel hopes. So there is no secret to the meaning of the events of the day, and Israel, for its part, can affect its destiny and effect salvation. The authorship of Leviticus Rabbah has thus joined the two great motifs, sanctification and salvation, by reading a biblical book, Leviticus, that is devoted to the former in the light of the requirements of the latter. In this way they made their fundamental point, which is that salvation at the end of history depends upon sanctification in the here and now.

To prove these points, the authors of the compositions make lists of facts that bear the same traits and show the working of rules of history. It follows that the mode of thought brought to bear upon the theme of history remains exactly the same as in the Mishnah: list-making, with data exhibiting similar taxonomic traits drawn together into lists based on common monothetic traits or definitions. These lists through the power of repetition make a single enormous point or prove a social law of history. The catalogues of exemplary heroes and historical events serve a further purpose. They provide a model of how contemporary events are to be absorbed into the biblical paradigm. Since biblical events exemplify recurrent happenings, sin and redemption, forgiveness and atonement, they lose their one-time character. At the same time and in the same way, current events find a place within the ancient, but eternally present, paradigmatic scheme. So no new historical events, other than exemplary episodes in lives of heroes, demand narration because, through what is said about the past, what was happening in the times of the framers of Leviticus Rabbah would also come under consideration.

This mode of dealing with biblical history and contemporary events produces two reciprocal effects. The first is the mythicization of biblical stories, their removal from the framework of ongoing, unique patterns of history and sequences of events and their transformation into accounts of things that happen all the time. The second is that contemporary events too lose all of their specificity and enter the paradigmatic framework of established mythic existence. So (1) the Scripture's myth happens every day, and (2) every day produces re-enactment of the Scripture's myth.

The focus of Leviticus Rabbah's laws of history is upon the society of Israel, its national fate and moral condition. Indeed, nearly all of the *parashiyyot* of Leviticus Rabbah turn out to deal with the national, social condition of Israel, and this in three contexts: (1) Israel's setting in the history of the nations, (2) the sanctified character of the inner life of Israel itself, (3) the future, salvific history of Israel. So the biblical book that deals with the tabernacle in the wilderness, which sages understood to form the model for the holy Temple later on built in Jerusalem, now is shown to address the holy people. That is no paradox, rather a logical next step in the exploration of sanctification. Leviticus really discusses not the consecration of the cult but the sanctification of the nation—its conformity to God's will laid forth in the Torah, and God's rules. Leviticus Rabbah executes the paradox of shifting categories, applying to the nation—not a locative category—and its history the category that in the book subject to commentary pertained to the holy place—a locative category—and its eternal condition. The nation now is like the cult then, the ordinary Israelite now like the priest then. The holy way of life lived now, through acts to which merit accrues, corresponds to the holy rites then. The process of metamorphosis is full, rich, complete. When everything stands for something else, the something else repeatedly turns out to be the nation. This is what our document spells out in exquisite detail, yet never missing the main point.

The message of Leviticus Rabbah paradoxically attaches itself to the book of Leviticus, as if that book had come from prophecy and addressed the issue of salvation. But it came from the priesthood and spoke of sanctification. The paradoxical syllogism—the as-if reading, the opposite of how things seem—of the composers of Leviticus Rabbah therefore reaches simple formulation. In the very setting of sanctification the authors find the promise of salvation. In the topics of the cult and the priesthood they uncover the national and social issues of the moral life and redemptive hope of Israel. The repeated comparison and contrast of priesthood and prophecy, sanctification and salvation, turn out to produce a complement, which comes to most perfect union in the text at hand.

What we have in Leviticus Rabbah is the result of the mode of thought not of prophets or historians, but of philosophers and scientists. The framers propose not to lay down, but to discover, rules governing Israel's life. As we find the rules of nature by identifying and classifying facts of natural life, so we find rules of society by identifying and classifying the facts of Israel's social life. In both modes of inquiry we make sense of things by bringing together like specimens and finding out whether they form a species, then bringing together like species and finding out whether they form a genus—in all, classifying data and identifying the rules that make possible the classification. That sort of thinking lies at the deepest level of list-making, which is work of offering a proposition and facts (for social rules) as much as a genus and its species (for rules of nature). Once discovered, the social rules of Israel's national life yield explicit statements, such as that God hates the arrogant and loves the humble. The logical status of these statements, in context, is as secure and unassailable as the logical status of statements about physics, ethics, or politics, as these emerge in philosophical thought. What differentiates the statements is not their logical status—as sound, scientific philosophy—but only their subject matter, on the one side, and distinctive rhetoric, on the other.

FROM COMMENTARY TO PROPOSITIONAL STATEMENTS: The framers of Leviticus Rabbah treat topics, not particular verses. They make generalizations that are freestanding. They express cogent propositions through extended compositions, not episodic ideas. In Genesis Rabbah things people wished to

say were attached to predefined statements based on an existing text, constructed in accord with an organizing logic independent of the systematic expression of a single, well-framed idea. That is to say, the sequence of verses of Genesis and their contents played a massive role in the larger-scale organization of Genesis Rabbah and expression of its propositions. Now the authors of Leviticus Rabbah so collected and arranged their materials that an abstract proposition emerges. That proposition is not expressed only or mainly through episodic restatements, assigned to an order established by a base text (whether Genesis or Leviticus, or a Mishnah-tractate, for that matter). Rather it emerges through a logic of its own.

What is new is the move from an essentially exegetical mode of logical discourse to a fundamentally philosophical one. It is the shift from discourse framed around an established (hence old) text to syllogistic argument organized around a proposed (hence new) theorem or proposition. What changes, therefore, is the way in which cogent thought takes place, as people moved from discourse contingent on some prior principle of organization to discourse autonomous of a ready-made program inherited from an earlier paradigm. When they read the rules of sanctification of the priesthood, the sages responsible for Leviticus Rabbah heard the message of the salvation of all Israel. Leviticus became the story of how Israel, purified from social sin and sanctified, would be saved.

The authors of Leviticus Rabbah express their ideas, first, by selecting materials already written for other purposes and using them for their own, second, by composing materials, and third, by arranging both in parashiyyot into an order through which propositions may reach expression. This involves both the modes of thought, and the topical program, and also the unifying proposition of the document as a whole. To summarize:

[1] The principal mode of thought required one thing to be read in terms of another, one verse in light of a different verse (or topic, theme, symbol, idea), one situation in light of another.

[2] The principal subject of thought is the moral condition of Israel, on the one side, and the salvation of Israel, on the other.

[3] The single unifying proposition—the syllogism at the document's deepest structure—is that Israel's salvation depends upon its moral condition.

It follows that Leviticus Rabbah constitutes not merely diverse thoughts but a single, sustained composition. The authors do so through a rich tapestry of unstated propositions that are only illustrated, delineated at the outset, by the statement of some propositions. And these also are illustrated. It is, in a word, a syllogism by example—that is, by repeated appeal to facts—rather than by argument alone. For in context, an example constitutes a fact. The source of many examples or facts is Scripture, the foundation of all reality. Accordingly, in the context of Israelite life and culture, in which Scripture recorded facts, we have a severely logical, because entirely factual, statement of how rightly organized and classified facts sustain a proposition. In context that proposition is presented as rigorously and critically as the social rules of discourse allowed.

The authors of the document's compositions and composites transformed Scriptural history from a sequence of one-time events, leading from one place to some other, into an ever-present mythic world. No longer does Scripture speak of only one Moses, one David, one set of happenings of a distinctive and never-to-be-repeated character. Now whatever happens of which the thinkers propose to take account must enter and be absorbed into that established and ubiquitous pattern and structure founded in Scripture. It is not that biblical history repeats itself. Rather, biblical history no longer constitutes history at all, that is, history as a linear, purposeful, continuous story of things that happened once, long ago, and pointed to some one moment in the future. Rather it becomes an account of things that happen every day— hence, an ever-present mythic world. In this way the basic trait of history in the salvific framework, its one-timeness and linearity, is reworked into the generative quality of sanctification, its routine and everyday, ongoing

reality. When history enters a paradigm, it forms an exercise within philosophy, the search for the rules and regularities of the world. That is the profound achievement of the document before us.

And that is why, in Leviticus Rabbah, Scripture—the book of Leviticus—as a whole does not dictate the order of discourse, let alone its character. In this document the authorship at hand chose in Leviticus itself an isolated verse here, an odd phrase there. These then presented the pretext for propositional discourse commonly quite out of phase with the cited passage. The verses that are quoted ordinarily shift from the meanings they convey to the implications they contain, speaking about something, anything, other than what they seem to be saying. So the as-if frame of mind brought to Scripture precipitates renewal of Scripture, requiring the seeing of everything with fresh eyes. And the result of the new vision was a re-imagining of the social world envisioned by the document at hand, the everyday world of Israel in its Land in that same difficult time at which Genesis Rabbah was taking shape, sometime in the fifth century and the first century after the conversion of Constantine and the beginning of the Christian chapter of Western civilization. For what the sages now proposed was a reconstruction of existence along the lines of the ancient design of Scripture as they read it. What that meant was that, from a sequence of one-time and linear events, everything that happened was turned into a repetition of known and already experienced paradigms, hence, once more, a mythic being. The source and core of the myth derive from Scripture—Scripture reread, renewed, reconstructed along with the society that revered Scripture.

The recurrent message of the document may be stated in brief way. God loves Israel, so gave them the Torah, which defines their life and governs their welfare. Israel is alone in its category (sui generis), so what is a virtue to Israel is a vice to the nations, life-giving to Israel, poison to the gentiles. True, Israel sins, but God forgives that sin, having punished the nation on account of it. Such a process has yet to come to an end, but it will culminate in Israel's complete regeneration. Meanwhile, Israel's assurance of God's love lies in the many expressions of special concern, for even the humblest and most ordinary aspects of the national life: the food the nation eats, the sexual practices by which it procreates. These life-sustaining, life-transmitting activities draw God's special interest, as a mark of his general love for Israel. Israel then is supposed to achieve its life in conformity with the marks of God's love.

These indications moreover signify also the character of Israel's difficulty, namely, subordination to the nations in general, but to the fourth kingdom, Rome, in particular. Both food laws and skin diseases stand for the nations. There is yet another category of sin, also collective and generative of collective punishment, and that is social. The moral character of Israel's life, the treatment of people by one another, the practice of gossip and small-scale thuggery—these too draw down divine penalty. The nation's fate therefore corresponds to its moral condition. The moral condition, however, emerges not only from the current generation. Israel's richest hope lies in the merit of the ancestors, thus in the Scriptural record of the merits attained by the founders of the nation, those who originally brought it into being and gave it life.

The world to come will right all presently unbalanced relationships. What is good will go forward, what is bad will come to an end. The simple message is that the things people revere, the cult and its majestic course through the year, will go on; Jerusalem will come back, so too the Temple, in all their glory. Israel will be saved through the merit of the ancestors, atonement, study of Torah, practice of religious duties. The prevalence of the eschatological dimension in the formal structures, with its messianic and other expressions, here finds its counterpart in the repetition of the same few symbols in the expression of doctrine.

The theme of the moral life of Israel produces propositions concerning not only the individual but, more important, the social virtues that the community as a whole must exhibit. First of all, the message to the individual constitutes a revision, for this context,

of the address to the nation: humility as against arrogance, obedience as against sin, constant concern not to follow one's natural inclination to do evil or to overcome the natural limitations of the human condition. Israel must accept its fate, obey and rely on the merits accrued through the ages and God's special love. The individual must conform, in ordinary affairs, to this same paradigm of patience and submission. Great men and women, that is, individual heroes within the established paradigm, conform to that same pattern, exemplifying the national virtues. Among these, Moses stands out; he has no equal. The special position of the humble Moses is complemented by the patriarchs and by David, all of whom knew how to please God and left as an inheritance to Israel the merit they had thereby attained.

If we now ask about further recurring themes or topics, there is one so commonplace that we should have to list the majority of paragraphs of discourse in order to provide a complete list. It is the list of events in Israel's history, meaning, in this context, Israel's history solely in scriptural times, down through the return to Zion. The one-time events of the generation of the flood, Sodom and Gomorrah, the patriarchs and the sojourn in Egypt, the exodus, the revelation of the Torah at Sinai, the golden calf, the Davidic monarchy and the building of the Temple, Sennacherib, Hezekiah, and the destruction of northern Israel, Nebuchadnezzar and the destruction of the Temple in 586, the life of Israel in Babylonian captivity, Daniel and his associates, Mordecai and Haman—these events occur over and over again. They turn out to serve as paradigms of sin and atonement, steadfastness and divine intervention, and equivalent lessons.

We find, in fact, a fairly standard repertoire of scriptural heroes or villains, on the one side, and conventional lists of Israel's enemies and their actions and downfall, on the other. The boastful, for instance, include the generation of the flood, Sodom and Gomorrah, Pharaoh, Sisera, Sennacherib, Nebuchadnezzar, the wicked empire (Rome)—contrasted to Israel, "despised and humble in this world." The four kingdoms recur again and again, always ending, with Rome, with the repeated message that after Rome will come Israel. But Israel has to make this happen through its faith and submission to God's will. Lists of enemies ring the changes on Cain, the Sodomites, Pharaoh, Sennacherib, Nebuchadnezzar, Haman.

At the center of the pretense, that is, the as-if mentality of Leviticus Rabbah and its framers, we find a simple proposition. Israel is God's special love. That love is shown in a simple way. Israel's present condition of subordination derives from its own deeds. It follows that God cares, so Israel may look forward to redemption on God's part in response to Israel's own regeneration through repentance. When the exegetes proceeded to open the scroll of Leviticus, they found numerous occasions to state that proposition in concrete terms and specific contexts. The sinner brings on his own sickness. But God heals through that very ailment. The nations of the world govern in heavy succession, but Israel's lack of faith guaranteed their rule and Israel's moment of renewal will end gentile rule. Israel's leaders—priests, prophets, kings—fall into an entirely different category from those of the nations, as much as does Israel. In these and other concrete allegations, the same classical message comes forth. Israel's sorry condition in no way testifies to Israel's true worth—the grandest pretense of all. All of the little evasions of the primary sense in favor of some other testify to this, the great denial that what is, is what counts. Leviticus Rabbah makes that statement with art and imagination. But it is never subtle about saying so.

Salvation and sanctification join together in Leviticus Rabbah. The laws of the book of Leviticus, focused as they are on the sanctification of the nation through its cult, in Leviticus Rabbah indicate the rules of salvation as well. The message of Leviticus Rabbah attaches itself to the book of Leviticus, as if that book had come from prophecy and addressed the issue of the meaning of history and Israel's salvation. But the book of Leviticus came from the priesthood and spoke of sanctification. The paradoxical syllogism—the as-if reading, the opposite of how

things seem—of the composers of Leviticus Rabbah therefore reaches simple formulation. In the very setting of sanctification we find the promise of salvation. In the topics of the cult and the priesthood we uncover the national and social issues of the moral life and redemptive hope of Israel. The repeated comparison and contrast of priesthood and prophecy, sanctification and salvation, turn out to produce a complement, which comes to most perfect union in the text at hand.

**Pesiqta deRab Kahana:** A compilation of twenty-eight propositional discourses, Pesiqta deRab Kahana (pisqa yields "chapter," so the plural can be rendered, "chapters attributed to R. Kahana), innovates because it appeals for its themes and lections to the liturgical calendar, rather than to a Pentateuchal book. Pesiqta deRab Kahana marks a stunning innovation in Midrash-compilation because it abandons the pretense that fixed associative connections derive solely from Scripture. Rather, the document follows the synagogal lections. The text that governs the organization of Pesiqta deRab Kahana comprises a liturgical occasion of the synagogue, which is identical to a holy day. This occasion has told our authorship what topic it wishes to take up—and therefore also what verses of Scripture (if any) prove suitable to that topic and its exposition.

| | |
|---|---|
| *Adar-Nisan-Sivan*: | Passover-Pentecost: *Pisqaot* 2-12 [possible exception: *Pisqa* 6] |
| *Tammuz-Ab-Elul*: | The Ninth of Ab: *Pisqaot* 13-22 |
| *Tishré*: | Tishré 1-22: *Pisqaot* 23-28 |

Only *Pisqa* 1 (possibly also *Pisqa* 6) falls out of synchronic relationship with a long sequence of special occasions in the synagogal lections. The twenty-eight parashiyyot of Pesiqta deRab Kahana in order follow the synagogal lections from early spring through fall, in the Western calendar, from late February or early March through late September or early October, approximately half of the solar year, 27 weeks, and somewhat more than half of the lunar year. On the very surface, the basic building block is the theme of a given lectionary Sabbath—that is, a

Sabbath distinguished by a particular lection—and not the theme dictated by a given passage of Scripture, let alone the exposition of the language or proposition of such a scriptural verse. The topical program of the document may be defined very simply: expositions of themes dictated by special Sabbaths or festivals and their lections.

| PISQA | BASE-VERSE | TOPIC OR OCCASION |
|---|---|---|
| 1. | *On the day Moses completed* (Num. 7:1) | Torah-lection for the Sabbath of Hanukkah |
| 2. | *When you take the census* (Exod. 30:12) | Torah-lection for the Sabbath of Sheqalim first of the four Sabbaths prior to the advent of Nisan, in which Passover falls |
| 3. | *Remember Amalek* (Deut. 25:17-19) | Torah-lection for the Sabbath of Zakhor second of the four Sabbaths prior to the advent of Nisan, in which Passover falls |
| 4. | *Red heifer* (Num. 19:1f.) | Torah-lection for the Sabbath of Parah third of the four Sabbaths prior to the advent of Nisan, in which Passover falls |
| 5. | *This month* (Exod. 12:1-2) | Torah-lection for the Sabbath of Hahodesh fourth of the four Sabbaths prior to the advent of Nisan, in which Passover falls |
| 6. | *My offerings* (Num. 28:1-4) | Torah-lection for the New Moon which falls on a weekday |
| 7. | *It came to pass at midnight* (Exod. 12:29-32) | Torah-lection for the first day of Passover |
| 8. | *The first sheaf* (Lev. 23:11) | Torah-lection for the second day of Passover on which the first sheaves of barley were harvested and waved as an offering |
| 9. | *When a bull or sheep or goat is born* (Lev. 22:26) | Lection for Passover |
| 10. | *You shall set aside a tithe* (Deut. 14:22) | Torah-lection for Sabbath during Passover in the Land of Israel or for the eighth day of Passover outside of the Land of Israel |
| 11. | *When Pharaoh let the people go* (Exod. 13:17-18) | Torah-lection for the Seventh Day of Passover |
| 12. | *In the third month* (Exod. 19:1ff.) | Torah-lection for Pentecost |
| 13. | *The words of Jeremiah* (Jer. 1:1-3) | Prophetic lection for the first of three Sabbaths prior to the Ninth of Ab |
| 14. | *Hear* (Jer. 2:4-6) | Prophetic lection for the second of three Sabbaths prior to the Ninth of Ab |
| 15. | *How lonely sits the city* (Lam. 1:1-2) | Prophetic lection for the third of three Sabbaths prior to the Ninth of Ab |
| 16. | *Comfort* (Is. 40:1-2) | Prophetic lection for the first of three Sabbaths following the Ninth of Ab |
| 17. | *But Zion said* (Is. 49:14-16) | Prophetic lection for the second of three Sabbaths following the Ninth of Ab |
| 18. | *O afflicted one, storm tossed* (Is. 54:11-14) | Prophetic lection for the third of three Sabbaths following the Ninth of Ab |
| 19. | *I even I am he who comforts you* (Is. 51:12-15) | Prophetic lection for the fourth of three Sabbaths following the Ninth of Ab |
| 20. | *Sing aloud, O barren woman* (Is. 54:1ff.) | Prophetic lection for the fifth of three Sabbaths following the Ninth of Ab |
| 21. | *Arise, Shine* (Is. 60:1-3) | Prophetic lection for the sixth of three Sabbaths following the Ninth of Ab |
| 22. | *I will greatly rejoice in the Lord* (Is. 61:10-11) | Prophetic lection for the seventh of three Sabbaths following the Ninth of Ab |
| 23. | *The New Year* | No base verse indicated. The theme is God's justice and judgment. |
| 24. | *Return O Israel to the Lord your God* (Hos. 14:1-3) | Prophetic lection for the Sabbath of Repentance between New Year and Day of Atonement |
| 25. | *Selihot* | No base verse indicated. The theme is God's forgiveness. |

| 26. | *After the death of the two sons of Aaron* (Lev. 16:1ff.) | Torah-lection for the Day of Atonement |
| 27. | *And you shall take on the first day* (Lev. 23:39-43) | Torah-lection for the first day of the Festival of Tabernacles |
| 28. | *On the eighth day* (Num. 29:35-39) | Torah-lection for the Eighth Day of Solemn Assembly |

This catalogue draws our attention to three eccentric *pisqaot*, distinguished by their failure to build discourse upon the base verse. These are No. 4, which may fairly claim that its topic, the red cow, occurs in exact verbal formulation in the verses at hand; No. 23, the New Year, and No. 25, *Selihot*. The last-named may or may not take an integral place in the structure of the whole. But the middle item, the New Year, on the very surface is essential to a structure that clearly wishes to follow the line of holy days onward through the Sabbath of Repentance, the Day of Atonement, the Festival of Tabernacles, and the Eighth Day of Solemn Assembly.

It follows that, unlike Genesis Rabbah and Leviticus Rabbah, the document focuses upon the life of the synagogue. Its framers set forth propositions in the manner of the authorship of Leviticus Rabbah. But these are framed by appeal not only to the rules governing the holy society, as in Leviticus Rabbah, but also to the principal events of Israel's history, celebrated in the worship of the synagogue. What we do not find in this Midrash-compilation is exposition of Pentateuchal or prophetic passages, verse by verse; the basis chosen by our authorship for organizing and setting forth its propositions is the character and theme of holy days and their special synagogue Torah-lections. That is, all of the selected base verses upon which the *parashiyyot* or chapters are built, Pentateuchal or prophetic, are identified with synagogal lections for specified holy days, special Sabbaths or festivals.

The contrast to the earlier compilations—this one is generally assigned to ca. 500—is striking. The framers of Sifra and Sifré to Numbers and Sifré to Deuteronomy follow the verses of Scripture and attach to them whatever messages they wish to deliver. The authorship of Genesis Rabbah follows suit, though less narrowly guided by verses and more clearly interested in their broader

themes. The framers of Leviticus Rabbah attached rather broad, discursive and syllogistic statements to verses of the book of Leviticus, but these verses do not follow in close sequence, one, then the next, as in Sifra and documents like it. That program of exposition of verses of Scripture read in or out of sequence, of organization of discourse in line with biblical books, parallel to the Tosefta's and Talmuds' authorships' exposition of passages of the Mishnah, read in close sequence or otherwise, we see, defines what our authorship has not done. Pesiqta deRab Kahana has been assembled so as to exhibit a viewpoint, a purpose of its particular authorship, one quite distinctive, in its own context (if not in a single one of its propositions!) to its framers or collectors and arrangers.

These synagogal discourses, read in their entirety, form a coherent statement of three propositions:

[1] God loves Israel, that love is unconditional, and Israel's response to God must be obedience to the religious duties that God has assigned, which will produce merit. Israel's obedience to God is what will save Israel. That means doing the religious duties as required by the Torah, which is the mark of God's love for—and regeneration of—Israel. The tabernacle symbolizes the union of Israel and God. When Israel does what God asks above, Israel will prosper down below. If Israel remembers Amalek down below, God will remember Amalek up above and will wipe him out. A mark of Israel's loyalty to God is remembering Amalek. God does not require the animals that are sacrificed, since man could never match God's appetite, if that were the issue, but the savor pleases God, as a mark of Israel's loyalty and obedience. The first sheaf returns to God God's fair share of the gifts that God bestows on Israel, and those who give it benefit, while those who hold it back suffer. Observing religious duties, typified by the rites of Sukkot,

Tabernacles, brings a great reward of that merit that ultimately leads to redemption. God's ways are just, righteous and merciful, as shown by God's concern that the offspring remain with the mother for seven days. God's love for Israel is so intense that he wants to hold them back for an extra day after Sukkot in order to spend more time with them, because, unlike the nations of the world, Israel knows how to please God. This is a mark of God's love for Israel.

[2] God is reasonable, and when Israel has been punished, it is in accord with God's rules. God forgives penitent Israel and is abundant in mercy. Laughter is vain because it is mixed with grief. A wise person will not expect too much joy. But when people suffer, there ordinarily is a good reason for it. That is only one sign that God is reasonable and that God never did anything lawless and wrong to Israel or made unreasonable demands, and there was, therefore, no reason for Israel to lose confidence in God or to abandon him. God punished Israel to be sure. But this was done with reason. Nothing happened to Israel of which God did not give fair warning in advance, and Israel's failure to heed the prophets brought about her fall. And God will forgive a faithful Israel. Even though the Israelites sinned by making the golden calf, God forgave them and raised them up. On the New Year, God executes justice, but the justice is tempered with mercy. The rites of the New Year bring about divine judgment and also forgiveness because of the merit of the fathers. Israel must repent and return to the Lord, who is merciful and will forgive them for their sins. The penitential season of the New Year and Day of Atonement is the right time for confession and penitence, and God is sure to accept penitence. By exercising his power of mercy, the already-merciful God grows still stronger in mercy.

[3] God will save Israel personally at a time and circumstance of his own choosing. Israel may know what the future redemption will be like, because of the redemption from Egypt. The paradox of the red cow, that what imparts uncleanness, namely touching the ashes of the red cow, produces cleanness, is part of God's ineffable wisdom, which man cannot fathom. Only God can know the precise moment of Israel's redemption. That is something man cannot find out on his own. But God will certainly fulfill the predictions of the prophets about Israel's coming redemption. The Exodus from Egypt is the paradigm of the coming redemption. Israel has lost Eden—but can come home, and, with God's help, will. God's unique power is shown through Israel's unique suffering. In God's own time, he will redeem Israel.

To develop this point, the authorship proceeds to further facts, worked out in its propositional discourses. The lunar calendar, particular to Israel, marks Israel as favored by God, for the new moon signals the coming of Israel's redemption, and the particular new moon that will mark the actual event is that of Nisan. When God chooses to redeem Israel, Israel's enemies will have no power to stop him, because God will force Israel's enemies to serve Israel, because of Israel's purity and loyalty to God. Israel's enemies are punished, and what they propose to do to Israel, God does to them. Both directly and through the prophets, God is the source of true comfort, which he will bring to Israel.

Israel thinks that God has forsaken them. But it is Israel who forsook God; God's love has never failed and will never fail. Even though he has been angry, his mercy still is near and God has the power and will to save Israel. God has designated the godly for himself and has already promised to redeem them. He will assuredly do so. God personally is the one who will comfort Israel. While Israel says there is no comfort, in fact, God will comfort Israel. Zion/Israel is like a barren woman, but Zion will bring forth children, and Israel will be comforted. Both God and Israel will bring light to Zion, which will give light to the world. The rebuilding of Zion will be a source of joy for the entire world, not for Israel alone. God will rejoice in Israel, Israel in God, like bride and groom.

**Song of Songs Rabbah:** The Song of Songs, called in the Christian Bible, "the Song of Solomon"—with both titles referring to the opening line, "The Song of Songs, which is Solomon's"—finds a place in the Torah because the collection of love-songs is understood to speak about the relationship between God and Israel. The intent of the compilers of Song of Songs Rabbah is to justify that reading. What this means is that Midrash-exegesis turns to everyday experience—the love of husband and wife—for a metaphor of God's love for Israel and Israel's love for God. Then, when Solomon's song says, "O that you would kiss me with the kisses of your mouth! For your love is better than wine" (Song 1:2), sages of blessed memory think of how God kissed Israel. Reading the Song of Songs as a metaphor, the Judaic sages state in a systematic and orderly way their entire structure and system.

The sages who compiled Song of Songs Rabbah read the Song of Songs as a sequence of statements of urgent love between God and Israel, the holy people. How they convey the intensity of Israel's love of God forms the point of special interest in this document. For it is not in propositions that they choose to speak, but in the medium of symbols. Sages here use language as a repertoire of opaque symbols in the form of words. They set forth sequences of words that connote meanings, elicit emotions, stand for events, form the verbal equivalent of pictures or music or dance or poetry. Through the repertoire of these verbal-symbols and their arrangement and rearrangement, the message the authors wish to convey emerges: not in so many words, but through words nonetheless. Sages chose for their compilation a very brief list of items among many possible candidates. They therefore determined to appeal to a highly restricted list of implicit meanings, calling upon some very few events or persons, repeatedly identifying these as the expressions of God's profound affection for Israel, and Israel's deep love for God. The message of the document comes not so much from stories of what happened or did not happen, assertions of truth or denials of error, but rather from the repetitious rehearsal of sets of symbols.

In reading the love-songs of the Song of Songs as the story of the love affair of God and Israel, sages identify implicit meanings

that are always few and invariably self-evident; no serious effort goes into demonstrating the fact that God speaks, or Israel speaks; the point of departure is the message and meaning the One or the other means to convey. To take one instance, time and again we shall be told that a certain expression of love in the poetry of the Song of Songs is God's speaking to Israel about the Sea, Sinai, and the world to come; or the first redemption, the one from Egypt; the second redemption, the one from Babylonia; and the third redemption, the one at the end of days. The repertoire of symbols covers Temple and schoolhouse, personal piety and public worship, and other matched pairs and sequences of coherent matters, all of them seen as embedded within the poetry. So Israel's holy life is metaphorized through the poetry of love and beloved, Lover and Israel. Long lists of alternative meanings or interpretations end up saying just one thing, but in different ways. The implicit meanings prove very few indeed. When in Song of Songs Rabbah we have a sequence of items alleged to form a taxon, that is, a set of things that share a common taxic indicator, what we have is a list. The list presents diverse matters that all together share, and therefore also set forth, a single fact or rule or phenomenon. That is why we can list them, in all their distinctive character and specificity, in a common catalogue of "other things" that pertain all together to one thing.

What do the compilers say through their readings of the metaphor of—to take one interesting example—the nut-tree for Israel? First, Israel prospers when it gives scarce resources for the study of the Torah or for carrying out religious duties; second, Israel sins but atones, and Torah is the medium of atonement; third, Israel is identified through carrying out its religious duties, e.g., circumcision; fourth, Israel's leaders had best watch their step; fifth, Israel will be in glory in the coming age; sixth, Israel has plenty of room for outsiders but cannot afford to lose a single member. What we have is a repertoire of fundamentals, dealing with Torah and Torah-study, the moral life and atonement, Israel and its holy way of life, Israel and its coming salvation. A sustained survey of these composites shows the contradictory facts that the several composites are heterogeneous, but the components of the composites derive from a rather limited list, essentially scriptural events and personalities, on the one side, and virtues of the Torah's holy way of life, on the other. Here is a survey:

Joseph, righteous men, Moses, and Solomon.

Patriarchs as against princes, offerings as against merit, and Israel as against the nations; those who love the king, proselytes, martyrs, penitents.

First, Israel at Sinai; then Israel's loss of God's presence on account of the golden calf; then God's favoring Israel by treating Israel not in accord with the requirements of justice but with mercy.

Dathan and Abiram, the spies, Jeroboam, Solomon's marriage to Pharaoh's daughter, Ahab, Jezebel, Zedekiah.

Israel is feminine, the enemy (Egypt) masculine, but God the father saves Israel the daughter.

Moses and Aaron, the Sanhedrin, the teachers of Scripture and Mishnah, the rabbis.

The disciples; the relationship among disciples, public recitation of teachings of the Torah in the right order; lections of the Torah.

The spoil at the Sea = the Exodus, the Torah, the Tabernacle, the ark.

The patriarchs, Abraham, Isaac, Jacob, then Israel in Egypt, Israel's atonement and God's forgiveness.

The Temple where God and Israel are joined, the Temple is God's resting place, the Temple is the source of Israel's fecundity.

Israel in Egypt, at the Sea, at Sinai, and subjugated by the gentile kingdoms, and how the redemption will come.

Rebecca, those who came forth from Egypt, Israel at Sinai, acts of loving kindness, the kingdoms who well-balanced rule Israel, the coming redemption.

Fire above, fire below, meaning heavenly and altar fires; Torah in writing, Torah in memory; fire of Abraham, Moriah, bush, Elijah, Hananiah, Mishael, and Azariah.

The Ten Commandments, show-fringes and phylacteries, recitation of the Shema and the Prayer, the tabernacle and the cloud of the Presence of God, and the mezuzah.

The timing of redemption, the moral condition of those to be redeemed, and the past religious misdeeds of those to be redeemed.

Israel at the sea, Sinai, the Ten Commandments; then the synagogues and school houses; then the redeemer.

The Exodus, the conquest of the Land, the redemption and restoration of Israel to Zion after the destruction of the first Temple, and the final and ultimate salvation.

The Egyptians, Esau and his generals, and, finally, the four kingdoms.

Moses' redemption, the first, to the second redemption in the time of the Babylonians and Daniel.

The palanquin of Solomon: the priestly blessing, the priestly watches, the Sanhedrin, and the Israelites coming out of Egypt.

Israel at the sea and forgiveness for sins effected through their passing through the sea; Israel at Sinai; the war with Midian; the crossing of the Jordan and entry into the Land; the house of the sanctuary; the priestly watches; the offerings in the Temple; the Sanhedrin; the Day of Atonement.

God redeemed Israel without preparation; the nations of the world will be punished, after Israel is punished; the nations of the world will present Israel as gifts to the royal messiah, and here the base-verse refers to Abraham, Isaac, Jacob, Sihon, Og, Canaanites.

The return to Zion in the time of Ezra, the Exodus from Egypt in the time of Moses.

The patriarchs and with Israel in Egypt, at the Sea, and then before Sinai.

Abraham, Jacob, Moses.

Isaac, Jacob, Esau, Jacob, Joseph, the brothers, Jonathan, David, Saul, man, wife, paramour.

Abraham in the fiery furnace and Shadrach Meshach and Abednego, the Exile in Babylonia, well-balanced with reference to the return to Zion.

These components form not a theological system, made up of well-joined propositions and harmonious positions, nor propositions that are demonstrated syllogistically through comparison and contrast. The point is just the opposite; it is to show that many different things really do belong on the same list. That yields not a proposition that the list syllogistically demonstrates. The list yields only itself, but then the list invites our exegesis, with the connections among these items require. What this adds up to is not argument for proposition, hence comparison and contrast and rule-making of a philosophical order, but rather a theological structure—comprising well-defined attitudes.

**Ruth Rabbah:** Like the other Midrash-compilations of its class, Ruth Rabbah makes one paramount point through numerous exegetical details. Ruth Rabbah has only one message, expressed in a variety of components but single and cogent. It concerns the outsider who becomes the principal, the Messiah out of Moab, and this miracle is accomplished through mastery of the Torah. The main points of the document are these:

[1] Israel's fate depends upon its proper conduct toward its leaders.
[2] The leaders must not be arrogant.
[3] The admission of the outsider depends upon the rules of the Torah. These differentiate among outsiders. Those who know the rules are able to apply them accurately and mercifully.
[4] The proselyte is accepted because the Torah makes it possible to do so, and the condition of acceptance is complete and total submission to the Torah. Boaz taught Ruth the rules of the Torah, and she obeyed them carefully.
[5] Those proselytes who are accepted are respected by God and are completely equal to all other Israelites. Those who marry them are masters of the Torah, and their descendants are masters of the Torah, typified by David. Boaz in his day and David in his day were the same in this regard.
[6] What the proselyte therefore accomplishes is to take shelter under the wings of God's presence, and the proselyte who does so stands in the royal line of David, Solomon, and the Messiah. Over and over again, we see, the point is made that Ruth the Moabitess, perceived by the ignorant as an outsider, enjoyed complete equality with all other Israelites, because she had accepted the yoke of the Torah, married a great sage, and through her descendants produced the Messiah-sage, David.

Scripture has provided everything but the main point: the Moabite Messiah. But sages impose upon the whole their distinctive message, which is the priority of the Torah, the extraordinary power of the Torah to join the opposites—Messiah, utter outsider—into a single figure, and to accomplish this union of opposites through a woman. The femininity of Ruth seems to me to be as critical to the whole as the Moabite origin: the two modes of the (from the Israelite perspective) abnormal, outsider as against Israelite, woman as against man, therefore are invoked, and both

for the same purpose, to show how, through the Torah, all things become one. That is the message of the document, and, seen whole, the principal message, to which all other messages prove peripheral.

Ruth Rabbah is a commentary in the narrowest sense—verse by verse amplification, paraphrase, exposition—as it is a compilation in the working definition of this inquiry of mine. What holds the document together and gives it, if not coherence, then at least flow and movement, after all, are the successive passages of (mere) exposition. All the more stunning, therefore, is the simple fact that, when all has been set forth and completed, there really is that simple message that the Torah (as exemplified by the sage) makes the outsider into an insider, the Moabite into an Israelite, the offspring of the outsider into the Messiah: all on the condition, the only condition, that the Torah governs. This is a document about one thing, and it makes a single statement, and that statement is coherent.

The authorship decided to compose a document concerning the book of Ruth in order to make a single point. Everything else was subordinated to that definitive intention. Once the work got underway, the task was not one of exposition so much as repetition, not unpacking and exploring a complex conception, but restating the point, on the one side, and eliciting or evoking the proper attitude that was congruent with that point, on the other. The decision, viewed after the fact, was to make one statement in an enormous number of ways. It is that the Torah dictates Israel's fate, if you want to know what that fate will be, study the Torah, and if you want to control that fate, follow the model of the sage-Messiah. As usual, therefore, what we find is a recasting of the Deuteronomic-prophetic theology.

Three categories contain the topical and propositional messages of the document, as follows:

ISRAEL AND GOD: Israel's relationship with God encompasses the matter of the covenant, the Torah, and the Land of Israel, all of which bring to concrete and material expression the nature and standing of that relationship. This is a topic treated only casually by our compilers. They make a perfectly standard point, that Israel suffers because of sin (I:i). The famine in the time of the judges was because of Israel's rebellion: "My children are rebellious. But as to exterminating them, that is not possible, and to bring them back to Egypt is not possible, and to trade them for some other nation is something I cannot do. But this shall I do for them: lo, I shall torment them with suffering and afflict them with famine in the days when the judges judge" (III:i). This was because they got overconfident (III:ii).

Sometimes God saves Israel on account of its merit, sometimes for his own name's sake (X:i). God's punishment of Israel is always proportionate and appropriate, so LXXIV:i: "Just as in the beginning, Israel gave praise for the redemption: 'This is my God and I will glorify him' (Exod. 15:2), now it is for the substitution [of false gods for God]: 'Thus they exchanged their glory for the likeness of an ox that eats grass' (Ps. 106:20). You have nothing so repulsive and disgusting and strange as an ox when it is eating grass. In the beginning they would effect acquisition through the removal of the sandal, as it is said, 'Now this was the custom in former times in Israel concerning redeeming and exchanging: to confirm a transaction, the one drew off his sandal and gave it to the other, and this was the manner of attesting in Israel.' But now it is by means of the rite of cutting off." None of this forms a centerpiece of interest, and all of it complements the principal points of the writing.

ISRAEL AND THE NATIONS: Israel's relationship with the nations is treated with interest in Israel's history, past, present, and future, and how that cyclical pattern is to be known. Only one nation figures in a consequential way, and that is Moab. Under these circumstances we can hardly generalize and say that Moab stands for everybody outside of Israel. That is precisely the opposite of the fact. Moab stands for a problem within Israel, the Messiah from the periphery; and the solution to the problem lies within Israel and not in its relationships to the other, the nations.

ISRAEL ON ITS OWN: Israel on its own concerns the holy nation's understanding of itself: who is Israel, who is not? Within the same rubric we find consideration of Israel's capacity to naturalize the outsider, so to define itself as to extend its own limits, and other questions of self-definition. And, finally, when Israel considers itself, a principal concern is the nature of leadership, for the leader stands for and embodies the people. Therein lies the paradox of the base-document and the Midrash-compilation alike: how can the leader most wanted, the Messiah, come, as a matter of fact, from the excluded people and not from the holy people?

And, more to the point (for ours is not an accusatory document), how is the excluded included? And in what way do peripheral figures find their way to the center? Phrased in this way, the question yields the obvious answer: through the Torah as embodied by the sage, anybody can become Israel, and any Israelite can find his way to the center. Even more—since it is through Ruth that the Moabite becomes the Israelite, and since (for sages) the mother's status dictates the child's, we may go so far as to say that it is through the Torah that the woman may become a man (at least, in theory).

The sin of Israel, which caused the famine, was that it was judging its own judges. The Israelites were slothful in burying Joshua, and that showed disrespect to their leader (II:i). They were slothful about repentance in the time of the judges, and that is what caused the famine; excess of commitment to one's own affairs leads to sin. The Israelites did not honor the prophets (III:iii). The old have to bear with the young, and the young with the old, or Israel will go into exile (IV:i). The generation that judges its leadership ("judges") will be penalized (V:i). Arrogance to the authority of the Torah is penalized (V:i). Elimelech was punished because he broke the peoples' heart; everyone depended upon him, and he proved undependable (V:iii); so bad leadership will destroy Israel. Why was Elimelech punished? It is because he broke the Israelites' heart. When the years of drought came, his maid went out into the market place, with her basket in her hand.

So the people of the town said, "Is this the one on whom we depended, that he can provide for the whole town with ten years of food? Lo, his maid is standing in the marketplace with her basket in her hand!" So Elimelech was one of the great men of the town and one of those who sustained the generation. But when the years of famine came, he said, "Now all the Israelites are going to come knocking on my door, each with his basket." The leadership of a community is its glory: "The great man of a town—he is its splendor, he is its glory, he is its praise. When he has turned from there, so too have turned its splendor, glory, and praise" :(XI:i.1C).

A distinct but fundamental component of the theory of Israel concerns who is Israel and how one becomes a part of Israel. That theme proves fundamental to our document, so much of which is preoccupied with how Ruth can be the progenitor of the Messiah, deriving as she does not only from gentile but from Moabite stock. Israel's history follows rules that are to be learned in Scripture; nothing is random and all things are connected (IV:ii). The fact that the king of Moab honored God explains why God raised up from Moab "a son who will sit on the throne of the Lord" (VIII:i.3). The proselyte is discouraged but then accepted. Orpah, who left Naomi, was rewarded for the little that she did for her, but she was raped when she left her (XVIII:i.1-3). When Orpah went back to her people, she went back to her gods (XIX:i).

Ruth's intention to convert was absolutely firm, and Naomi laid out all the problems for her, but she acceded to every condition (XX:i). Naomi said to her, "My daughter, it is not the way of Israelite women to go to theaters and circuses put on by idolators." She said to her, "Where you go I will go." She said to her, "My daughter, it is not the way of Israelite women to live in a house that lacks a mezuzah." She said to her, "Where you lodge I will lodge." "Your people shall be my people:" This refers to the penalties and admonitions against sinning. "And your God my God:" This refers to the other religious duties. And so onward: "for where you

go I will go:" to the tent of meeting, Gilgal, Shiloh, Nob, Gibeon, and the eternal house. "And where you lodge I will lodge:" "I shall spend the night concerned about the offerings." "Your people shall be my people:" "so nullifying my idol." "And your God my God:" "to pay a full recompense for my action." I find here the centerpiece of the compilation and its principal purpose. The same message is at XXI:i.1-3.

Proselytes are respected by God, so XXII:i: "And when Naomi saw that she was determined to go with her, [she said no more]:" Said R. Judah b. R. Simon, "Notice how precious are proselytes before the Omnipresent. Once she had decided to convert, the Scripture treats her as equivalent to Naomi." Boaz, for his part, was equally virtuous and free of sins (XXVI:i). The law provided for the conversion of Ammonite and Moabite women, but not Ammonite and Moabite men, so the acceptance of Ruth the Moabite was fully in accord with the law, and anyone who did not know that fact was an ignoramus (XXVI:i.4, among many passages). An Israelite hero who came from Ruth and Boaz was David, who was a great master of the Torah. Ruth truly accepted Judaism upon the instruction, also, of Boaz (XXXIV:i). Ruth had prophetic power (XXXVI:ii). Ruth was rewarded for her sincere conversion by Solomon (XXXVIII:i.1).

Taking shelter under the wings of the Presence of God, which is what the convert does, is the greatest merit accorded to all who do deeds of grace. The language that Boaz used to Ruth, "Come here," bore with it deeper reference to six: David, Solomon, the throne as held by the Davidic monarchy, and ultimately, the Messiah. Boaz instructed Ruth on how to be a proper Israelite woman (LIII:i). So did Naomi encompass Ruth within Israel. Moab, whence Ruth came, was conceived not for the sake of fornication but for the sake of Heaven (LV:i.1B). Boaz, for his part, was a master of the Torah and when he ate and drank, that formed a typology for his study of the torah (LVI:i). His was a life of grace, Torah study, and marriage for holy purposes. Whoever trusts in God is exalted, and that refers to Ruth and Boaz; God put it in his heart to bless her (LVII:i). David sang Psalms to thank God for his great-grandmother, Ruth (LIX:i.5). Because of the merit of the six measures that Boaz gave Ruth, six righteous persons came forth from him, each with six virtues: David, Hezekiah, Josiah, Hananiah-Mishael-Azariah (counted as one), Daniel and the royal Messiah.

God facilitated the union of Ruth and Boaz (LXVIII:i). Boaz's relative was ignorant for not knowing that while a male Moabite was excluded, a female one was acceptable for marriage. The blessing of Boaz was, "May all the children you have come from this righteous woman" (LXXIX:i), and that is precisely the blessing accorded to Isaac and to Elkanah. God made Ruth an ovary, which she had lacked (LXXX:i). Naomi was blessed with messianic blessings (LXXXI:i). On account of the blessings of the women, the line of David was not wholly exterminated in the time of Athaliah. David was ridiculed because he was descended from Ruth, the Moabitess (LXXXV:i). David referred to and defended his Moabite origins (LXXXIX:i). Just as David's descent from Ruth was questioned, so his descent from Judah via Tamar could be questioned too, and that would compromise the whole tribe of Judah.

**Lamentations Rabbah:** The theme of Lamentations Rabbati is Israel's relationship with God, and the message concerning that theme is that the stipulative covenant still and always governs that relationship. Therefore everything that happens to Israel makes sense and bears meaning; and Israel is not helpless before its fate but controls its own destiny. This is the one and whole message of this compilation, and it is the only message that is repeated throughout; everything else proves secondary and derivative of the fundamental proposition that the destruction of the Temple in Jerusalem in 70 C.E.—as much as in 586 B.C.E.—proves the enduring validity of the covenant, its rules and its promise of redemption.

Lamentations Rabbah's is a covenantal theology, in which Israel and God have mutually and reciprocally agreed to bind themselves to a common Torah; the rules of the relationship are such that an infraction triggers its penalty willy-nilly; but obedience to the Torah likewise brings its reward, in the context envisaged by our compilers, the reward of redemption. The compilation sets forth a single message, which is reworked in only a few ways: Israel suffers because of sin, God will respond to Israel's atonement, on the one side, and loyalty to the covenant in the Torah, on the other. And when Israel has attained the merit that accrues through the Torah, God will redeem Israel. That is the simple, rock-hard and repeated message of this rather protracted reading of the book of Lamentations. Still, Lamentations Rabbah proves nearly as much a commentary in the narrowest sense—verse by verse amplification, paraphrase, exposition—as it is a cogent, thematic compilation.

What holds the document together and gives it, if not coherence, then at least flow and movement are the successive passages of (mere) exposition. All the more stunning, therefore, is the simple fact that, when all has been set forth and completed, there really is that simple message that God's unique relationship with Israel, which is unique among the nations, works itself out even now, in a time of despair and disappointment. The resentment of the present condition, recapitulating the calamity of the destruction of the Temple, finds its resolution and remission in the redemption that will follow Israel's regeneration through the Torah—that is the program, that is the proposition, and in this compilation, there is no other.

Israel's relationship with God is treated with special reference to the covenant, the Torah, and the land. By reason of the sins of the Israelites, they have gone into exile with the destruction of the Temple. The founders of the family, Abraham, Isaac, and Jacob, also went into exile. Now they cannot be accused of lacking in religious duties, attention to teachings of the Torah and of prophecy, carrying out the requirements of righteousness (philanthropy) and good deeds, and the like. The people are at fault for their own condition (I:i.1-7). Torah-study defines the condition of Israel, e.g., "If you have seen [the inhabitants of] towns uprooted from their places in the land of Israel, know that it is because they did not pay the salary of scribes and teachers" (II.i).

So long as Judah and Benjamin—meaning, in this context, the surviving people, after the northern tribes were taken away by the Assyrians—were at home, God could take comfort at the loss of the ten tribes; once they went into exile, God began to mourn II:ii) Israel (now meaning not the northern tribes, but the remaining Jews) survived Pharaoh and Sennacherib, but not God's punishment (III:i). After the disaster in Jeremiah's time, Israel emerged from Eden—but could come back. (IV:i). God did not play favorites among the tribes; when any of them sinned, he punished them through exile (VI:i). Israel was punished because of the ravaging of words of Torah and prophecy, righteous men, religious duties and good deeds (VII:i). The land of Israel, the Torah, and the Temple are ravaged, to the shame of Israel (Jer. 9:19-21) (VIII:i). The Israelites practiced idolatry, still more did the pagans; God was neglected by the people and was left solitary, so God responded to the people's actions (X:i). If you had achieved the merit (using the theological language at hand), then you would have enjoyed everything, but since you did not have the merit, you enjoyed nothing (XI:i).

The Israelites (throughout referring to the surviving Jews, after the northern tribes were taken into exile) did not trust God, so they suffered disaster ((XIII.i). The Israelites scorned God and brought dishonor upon God among the nations (XV:i). While God was generous with the Israelites in the wilderness, under severe conditions, he was harsh with them in civilization, under pleasant conditions, because they sinned and angered him (XVI:i). With merit one drinks good water in Jerusalem, without, bad water in the exile of Babylonia; with merit one sings songs and Psalms in Jerusalem, without, dirges and lamentations in Babylonia. At stake is peoples' merit, not God's grace (XIX:i). The contrast is drawn between redemption and disaster, the giving of the Torah and the destruction of the Temple (XX:i). When the Israelites went into exile among the nations of the world, not one of them could produce a word of Torah from his mouth; God punished Israel for its sins (XXI:i). Idolatry was the cause (XXII:i). The destruction of the Temple was possible only because God had already abandoned it (XXIV:ii). When the Temple was destroyed, God was answerable to the patriarchs for what he had done (XXIV:ii). The Presence of God departed from the Temple by stages (XXV:i).

The Holy One punishes Israel only after bringing testimony against them (XXVII:i). The road that led from the salvation of Hezekiah is the one that brought Israel to the disaster brought about by Nebuchadnezzar. Then the Israelite kings believed, but the pagan king did not believe; and God gave the Israelite kings a reward for their faith, through Hezekiah, and to the pagan king, without his believing and without obeying, were handed over Jerusalem and its Temple. (XXX:i). Before the Israelites went into exile, the Holy One, blessed be he, called them 'bad. But when they had gone into exile, he began to sing their praises (XXXI:i). The Israelites were sent into exile only after they had defied the Unique One of the world, the Ten Commandments, circumcision, which had been given to the twentieth generation [Abraham], and the Pentateuch (XXXV:ii, iii). When the Temple was destroyed and Israel went into exile, God mourned in the manner that mortals do (XXXV:iv). The prophetic critique of Israel is mitigated by mercy. Israel stands in an ambiguous relationship with God, both divorced and not divorced (XXXV:vi, vii).

Before God penalizes, he has already prepared the healing for the penalty. As to all the harsh prophecies that Jeremiah issued against the Israelites, Isaiah first of all anticipated each and pronounced healing for it (XXXVI:ii). The Israelites err for weeping frivolously, "but in the end there will be a real weeping for good cause" (XXXVI:iv, v). The ten tribes went into exile, but the Presence of God did not go into exile. Judah and Benjamin went into exile, but the Presence of God did not go into exile. But when the children went into exile, then the Presence of God went into exile (XXXIX:iii). The great men of Israel turned their faces away when they saw people sinning, and God did the same to them (XL:ii). When the Israelites carry out the will of the Holy One, they add strength to the strength of heaven, and when they do not, they weaken the power of the One above (XL:ii). The exile and the redemption will match (XL:ii). In her affliction, Jerusalem remembered her rebellion against God (XLI;i).

When the gentile nations sin, there is no sequel in punishment, but when the Israelites sin, they also are punished (XLII:i). God considered carefully how to bring the evil upon Israel (XLVIII:i). God suffers with Israel and for Israel (L:i), a minor theme in a massive compilation of stories. By observing their religious duties the Israelites became distinguished before God (LIII:i). With every thing with which the Israelites sinned, they were smitten, and with that same thing they will be comforted. When they sinned with the head, they were smitten at the head, but they were comforted through the head (LVI:i). There is an exact match between Israel's triumph and Israel's downfall. Thus: "Just as these—the people of Jericho—were punished through the destruction effected by priest and prophet [the priests and Joshua at Jericho], so these—the people of Jerusalem in the time of the Babylonian conquest—were subject to priest and prophet [Jeremiah]. Just as these who were punished were penalized through the ram's horn and shouting, so Israel will be saved through ram's horn and shouting" (LVII:ii).

God's relationship to Israel was complicated by the relationship to Jacob, thus: "Isn't it the fact that the Israelites are angering me only because of the icon of Jacob that is engraved on my throne? Here, take it, it's thrown in your face!" (LVII:ii). God is engaged with Israel's disaster (LIX:ii). The Israelites did not fully explore the limits of the measure of justice, so the measure of justice did not go to extremes against them (LX:i, LXI:i). God's decree against Jerusalem comes from of old (LXIV:i). God forewarned Israel and showed Israel favor, but it did no good (LXIX:i). God did to Israel precisely what he had threatened long ago (LXXIII:i). But God does not rejoice in pun-

ishing Israel. The argument between God and Israel is framed in this way. The Community of Israel says that they are the only ones who accepted God; God says, I rejected everybody else for you (LXXIX:ii). Israel accepted its suffering as atonement and asked that the suffering expiate the sin (LXXV:i).

God suffers along with Israel, Israel's loyalty will be recognized and appreciated by God, and, in the meantime, the Israelites will find in the Torah the comfort that they require. The nations will be repaid for their actions toward Israel in the interval. Even though the Holy One, blessed be he, is angry with his servants, the righteous, in this world, in the world to come he goes and has mercy on them (LXXXVI:i). God is good to those that deserve it (LXXXVII:i). God mourns for Israel the way human mourners mourn (LXXXVIII:i). God will never abandon Israel (LXXXIX:i). The Holy Spirit brings about redemption (XCV:i). It is better to be punished by God than favored by a gentile king (CXXII:i).

The upshot here is that persecution in the end is good for Israel, because it produces repentance more rapidly than prophecy ever did, with the result that the redemption is that much nearer. The enemy will also be punished for its sins, and, further, God's punishment is appropriate and well-placed. People get what they deserve, both Israel and the others. God should protect Israel and not leave them among the nations, but that is not what he has done (CXXIII:i). God blames that generation for its own fate, and the ancestors claim that the only reason the Israelites endure is because of the merit of the ancestors. (CXXIX:i). The redemption of the past tells us about the redemption in the future (CXXX:i). "The earlier generations, because they smelled the stench of only part of the tribulations inflicted by the idolatrous kingdoms, became impatient. But we, who dwell in the midst of the four kingdoms, how much the more [are we impatient]!" (CXXXI:i).

God's redemption is certain, so people who are suffering should be glad, since that is a guarantee of coming redemption. So if the words of the prophet Uriah are carried out, the words of the prophet Zechariah will be carried out, while if the words of the prophet Uriah prove false, then the words of the prophet Zechariah will not be true either (CXL:i). The Temple will be restored, and Israel will regain its place, as God's throne and consort (CXLI:i). Punishment and rejection will be followed by forgiveness and reconciliation (CXLII:i). The Jews can accomplish part of the task on their own, even though they throw themselves wholly on God's mercy. The desired age is either like that of Adam, or like that of Moses and Solomon, or like that of Noah and Abel; all three possibilities link the coming redemption to a time of perfection, Eden, or the age prior to idolatry, or the time of Moses and Solomon, the builders of the Tabernacle and the Temple, respectively (CXLIII:i). If there is rejection, then there is no hope, but if there is anger, there is hope, because someone who is angry may in the end be appeased. Whenever there is an allusion to divine anger, that too is a mark of hope (CXLIV:i).

Israel's relationship with the nations is treated with interest in Israel's history, past, present, and future, and how that cycle is to be known. But there is no theory of "the other," or the outsider here; the nations are the enemy; the compilers find nothing of merit to report about them. Israel's difference from the other, for which God is responsible, accounts for the dislike that the nations express toward Israel; Israel's present condition as minority, different and despised on account of the difference, is God's fault and choice. Israel was besieged not only by the Babylonians but also the neighbors, the Ammonites and Moabites (IX:i), and God will punish them too. The public ridicule of Jews' religious rites contrasts with the Jews' own perception of their condition. Even though the nations of the world go into exile, their exile is not really an exile at all. But as for Israel, their exile really is an exile. The nations of the world, who eat the bread and drink the wine of others, do not really experience exile. But the Israelites, who do not eat the bread and drink the wine of others, really do experience exile (XXXVII:i).

The Ammonites and Moabites joined with the enemy and behaved very spitefully (XLIV:i). When the Israelites fled from the destruction of Jerusalem, the nations of the world sent word everywhere to which they fled and shut them out (LV:i). But this was to be blamed on God: "If we had intermarried with them, they would have accepted us." LXIX:i There are ten references to "might" of Israel; when the Israelites sinned, these forms of might were taken away from them and given to the nations of the world. The nations of the world ridicule the Jews for their religious observances (LXXXIII:i). These propositions simply expose, in their own framework, the same proposition as the ones concerning God's relationship to Israel and Israel's relationship to God. The relationship between Israel and the nations forms a subset of the relationship of Israel and God; nothing in the former relationship happens on its own, but all things express in this mundane context the rules and effects of the rules that govern in the transcendent one. All we learn about Israel and the nations is that the covenant endures, bearing its own inevitable sanctions and consequences.

Our authorship has little interest in Israel out of relationship with either God or the nations. Israel on its own forms a subordinated and trivial theme; whatever messages we do find take on meaning only in the initial framework, that defined by Israel's relationship with God. Israel is never on its own. The bitterness of the ninth of Ab is contrasted with the bitter herbs with which the first redemption is celebrated (XVIII:i). The same contrast is drawn between the giving of the Torah and the destruction of the Temple (XX:i). If Israel had found rest among the nations, she would not have returned to the holy land (XXXVII:ii). The glory of Israel lay in its relationship to God, in the Sanhedrin, in the disciples of sages, in the priestly watches, in the children (XL:i). Israel first suffers, then rejoices; her unfortunate condition marks the fact that Israel stands at the center of things (LIX:iii). Israel has declined through the generations (CXXXVII:i).

**Esther Rabbah Part One:** In Esther Rabbah Part One (that is, covering the book of Esther's first two chapters), we find only one message, and it is reworked in only a few ways. It is that the nations are swine, their rulers fools, and Israel is subjugated to them, though it should not be, only because of its own sins. No other explanation serves to account for the paradox and anomaly that prevail. But just as God saved Israel in the past, so the salvation that Israel can attain will recapitulate the former ones. On the stated theme, Israel among the nations, sages set forth a proposition entirely familiar from the books of Deuteronomy through Kings, on the one side, and much of prophetic literature, on the other.

The proposition is familiar, and so is the theme; but since the book of Esther can hardly be characterized as "Deuteronomic," lacking all interest in the covenant, the land, and issues of atonement (beyond the conventional sackcloth, ashes, and fasting, hardly the fodder for prophetic regeneration and renewal!), the sages' distinctive viewpoint in the document must be deemed an original and interesting contribution of their own. But the message is somewhat more complicated than merely a negative judgment against the nations. If I have to identify one recurrent motif that captures that theology, it is the critical role of Esther and Mordecai, particularly Mordecai, who, as sage, emerges in the position of messiah. And that is a message that is particular to the exposition of the book of Esther's opening chapters.

Like Lamentations Rabbah, Esther Rabbah Part One is as much a commentary in the narrowest sense—verse by verse amplification, paraphrase, exposition—as a cogent compilation. It too is held together and given coherence by successive passages of (mere) exposition. Here the single message that emerges is that the Torah (as exemplified by the sage) makes the outsider into an insider, the woman into a heroic leader (just as, in the book of Ruth, we see how the Moabite is turned into an Israelite, the offspring of the outsider into the Messiah). These paradoxes come about on the condition, the only condition, that the Torah govern. This is a document about one thing, and it makes a single statement, and that statement is coherent, just as is the case with Ruth Rabbah, the

counterpart and complement. Where we find a woman in the systemic center of a document's statement, there we uncover the document's critical message, that which can account for everything and its opposite, and for the transformation of otherwise fixed values, e.g., in this case, the exclusion of women from the center of consideration.

Gender thus defines the focus for both Esther Rabbah I and Ruth Rabbah, yielding the opposite of what is anticipated. Ruth Rabbah has the Messiah born of an outsider, Esther Rabbah has salvation come through a woman. For Esther and Mordecai, woman and the sage-Messiah, function in this document in much the same way that Ruth and David, woman and sage-Messiah, work in Ruth Rabbah. While the sages of Ruth Rabbah face their own, distinctive problem, the way the outsider becomes the insider, the Moabite-Messiah, still, Ruth Rabbah and Esther Rabbah Part One deal with the same fundamental fact: the Messiah-sage dictates the future of Israel, because he (never she) realizes the rule of the Torah. In Esther Rabbah Part One many things say one thing: the Torah dictates Israel's fate, if you want to know what that fate will be, study the Torah, and if you want to control that fate, follow the model of the sage-Messiah.

These episodic propositions comprise the document's single message. Bad government comes about because of the sins of the people (VII:i). But that proposition is realized in discourse mainly about bad government by the nations, and, given the base-document, that is hardly surprising. God was neglected by the people, so he is left solitary through his own actions, which responded to the people's actions (XVIII:iii). This serves Lamentations Rabbah as its Petihta 10; but the proposition surely is not alien to our base-document. The contrast between the relative neglect of this inviting topic and the intense interest in another, the one that follows, which characterize Esther Rabbah Part One, and the opposite emphases and interests revealed in Lamentations Rabbah, is readily discerned.

Our compilation concentrates upon this one subject, and all of its important messages present the same proposition, in several parts. Israel's life among the nations is a sequence of sorrows, each worse than the preceding. But through Torah, Israel can break the cycle. When Israel is subjugated by the nations, God will not spurn, abhor, destroy them or break his covenant with them—in the age of Babylonia, Media, the Greeks, and the wicked kingdom; of Vespasian, Trajan, Haman, the Romans (II;i.1). The same is repeated at III:i.1-5.

In comparing the ages through which the Jews had lived, Babylonian, Median, Greek, Roman, the same position recurs. When the righteous achieve great power, there is joy in the world, and when the wicked achieve great power, there is groaning in the world; this is so of Israelite and gentile kings (IV:i). Gentile kings may do good things or bad things (VI:i). But even the good kings are not without flaws. When a bad king rules, it is because of the sins of the people, those who will not do the will of the creator (VII:i). God worked through whomever he chose. From the beginning of the creation of the world, the Holy One blessed be he designated for every one what was suitable. Ahasuerus the first of those who sell [people at a price], Haman the first of those who buy [people at a price] (VIII:i). There are decisions made by God that determine the life of nations and individuals; Israel's history follows rules that can be learned in Scripture; nothing is random, all things are connected, and fundamental laws of history dictate the meaning of what happens among the nations (VIII:ii).

Ultimately, God will destroy Israel's enemies (IX:i). God will save Israel when not a shred of merit will be found among the nations of the world (X:i.15). The prosperity of the nations is only for a time; then the nations will be punished and Israel redeemed (XI:i). There will be full recompense, and the contrast between Israel's subjugation and the nations' prosperity will be resolved. The principle of measure for measure governs. Pagan kings propose to do what God himself does not claim to be able to do. They cannot accomplish their goal; if God wanted to, God could do it. But in the age to come, God will accomplish the union of opposites, which in this time pagan kings claim to be able to do but cannot accomplish (XVII:i). Pagan kings rebel against not only God but also their own gods (XVIII:i). But for the slightest gesture of respect for God they are rewarded (XVIII:i).

God is in full control of everyone at all times. The salvation in the time of Ahasuerus was directly linked, detail by detail, to the punishment in the time of Nebuchadnezzar (XVIII:ii). Israel's relationship with one empire is no different from its relationship to the other. The same base-verse, Ps. 10:14, accounts for both Rome and Sasanian Iran, the world-empires of the day. The relationship of each to Israel is the same. Both of them call into question Israel's faith in the power of God by showing off their own power. Esau/Romulus and Remus pay back God's blessing by building Temples of idolatry in Rome. Belshazzar/Vashti/Iran do the same by oppressing Israel. Both intend by their power to prove that they are stronger than God. But, the premise maintains, God will show in the end who is the stronger. The upshot is to underline the irony that derives from the contrast between the empires' power and God's coming display of his power; that and one other thing: the challenge facing God in showing his power over theirs (XVIII:iv).

Israel possesses wise men, the nations' sages are fools thus. There is a correspondence between how Israel suffers and how the nations prosper (XXVIII:I). Saul lost the throne because he did not destroy Amalek, Esther got it back because she did. Obedience to divine instructions made the difference. Persian women suffered and were humiliated because they had ridiculed Israelite women (XXXIV:i). Those who do righteousness at all times are going to be the ones who will carry out God's salvation. They that they that do righteousness at all times are to be remembered when God's salvation is required and it is performed through them. Accordingly, Mordecai in his generation was equivalent to Moses in his generation.

God always responds to Israel's need. The reason this point is pertinent here is the repeated contrast, also, of Mordecai and Haman; the upshot is that ultimately Israel gets what it has coming just as do the nations; and when Israel gets its redemption, it is through people of a single sort, Moses, Abraham, Mordecai. The redemptions of Israel in times past then provide the model and paradigm for what is going to happen in the future. None of this has any bearing on the land and nothing invokes the covenant, which is why I see the entire matter in the present context. When God saves Israel, it is always in response to how they have been punished (XXXVIII:i.9).

As to Israel's distinctive leadership and its life within its own boundaries, the nature of the book of Esther, with its concern for its heroes, Mordecai and Esther, secures for this subject a more than negligible place in the propositional program of the midrash-compilation. Israel's leadership consistently follows the same norms, and what the ancestors taught, the descendants learn. Thus Esther behaved as had Rachel (LI:i), who kept silent when she saw her wedding band on the hand of her sister. Benjamin, her son, kept silent, even though he knew of the sale of Joseph. Saul, from whom Esther descended also kept silent (1 Sam. 10:16). What happens now therefore has already happened, and we know how to respond and what will come in consequence of our deeds.

**Tractate Abot, The Fathers:** Tractate Abot is made up of five chapters of wisdom-sayings, neither legal nor exegetical in character, but mainly a handbook of wise sayings for disciples of sages, especially those involved in administration of the law. These sayings, miscellaneous in character, are assigned to named authorities. The rhetoric of The Fathers is dictated by aphoristic style, producing wise sayings presented as a list. The topic, over all, derives from the realm of wisdom: right conduct with God, society, self. The logic of cogent discourse derives from the notion that a list of sages constitutes a principle of coherent composition, and the diverse sayings fit together within the sustaining logic of a list of authorities of a given classification. The list holds together because everything on it is part of a chain of formulation and transmission—tradition—beginning with Moses on Sinai. So one sentence joins the next because all the sentences enjoy the same status, that imparted by the Torah. That logic deriving from authority makes it possible for the audience of the document to see relationships of order, proportion, and sustained discourse, where we see merely a sequence of essentially discrete sayings. The rhetorical device rests upon the same principle of cogent discourse: the listing of authorities suffices as a principle of rhetorical composition—and persuasion. The topical program—with its recurrent emphasis on Torah-study and the social, intellectual, and personal virtues required for Torah-study—is equally cogent with the logical and rhetorical decisions made by the authorship of the whole.

Always published along with the Mishnah but autonomous of that document in all differentiating formal and programmatic attributes, the compilation cites authorities of the generation generally assumed to have flourished after the closure of the Mishnah and hence may be situated at ca. 250 C.E.—a mere guess. The Mishnah's rhetorical program exercised no influence whatsoever on the formulation of tractate Abot. The mnemonic patterns characteristic of the Mishnah are not to be found. The topical division and organization of the Mishnah-tractates one by one and as a set play no role. Tractate Abot therefore bears no formal, or substantive, relationship to the Mishnah. Its rhetoric, logic of coherent discourse, and topic mark the document as utterly anomalous in Rabbinic literature; it has no parallel.

But its proposition and message form the keystone and centerpiece of that literature. The document serves as the Mishnah's first and most important documentary apologetic, stating in abstract and general terms the ideals for the virtuous life that are set forth by the Mishnah's sages and animate its laws. Its presentation of sayings of sages extending from Sinai to figures named in the Mishnah itself links the Mishnah to Sinai. The link consists of the chain of tradition handed on through the chain of sages itself. It follows that, because of the authorities cited in its pages, the Mishnah constitutes part of the Torah of Sinai, for by the evidence of the chain of tradition, the Mishnah too forms a statement of revelation, that is, "Torah revealed to Moses at Sinai." This is expressed in the opening sentence (M. Ab. 1:1):

> Moses received the Torah at Sinai and handed it on to Joshua, Joshua to elders, and elders to prophets. And prophets handed it on to the men of the great assembly. They said three things: Be prudent in judgment. Raise up many disciples. Make a fence for the Torah.

The verbs, receive . . . hand on . . ., in Hebrew yield the words *qabbalah*, tradition, and *masoret*, also tradition.

The theological proposition that validates the Mishnah is that the Torah is a matter of tradition. The tradition goes from master to disciple, Moses to Joshua. And, further, those listed later on the same list include authorities of the Mishnah itself. That fact forms an implicit claim that part of the Torah was, and is, orally formulated and orally transmitted, and the Mishnah's authorities stand in the tradition of Sinai, so that the Mishnah too forms part of the Torah of Sinai.

This position is different from that taken by pseudepigraphic writers, who imitate the style of Scripture, or who claim to speak within that same gift of revelation as Moses. It is one thing to say one's holy book is Scripture because it is like Scripture, or to claim that the author of the holy book has a revelation independent of that of Moses. These two positions concede to the Torah of Moses priority over their own holy books. The Mishnah's first apologists make no such concession, when they allege that the Mishnah is part of the Torah of Moses. They appeal to the highest possible authority in the Israelite framework, claiming the most one can claim in behalf of the book which, in fact, bears the names of men who lived fifty years before the apologists themselves. The sages' apologia for the Mishnah, therefore, rests upon the persons of the sages themselves: incarnations of the Torah of Sinai in the here-and-now.

Unlike Mishnah-tractates, tractate Abot deals with no single topic, and, it follows, the document also contains no proposition that is argued in detail. But the first two chapters

do set forth a proposition, which is to be discerned not from what is said but from the chain of names that is set out in those chapters. Specifically, the list of names and the way in which they are arranged contains the claim that the two great pillars of the Mishnah—the patriarch of the Jewish community in the Land of Israel, that is, Judah the Patriarch (Hebrew: nasi), sponsor of the document and recognized by the Roman government as ruler of the Jewish ethnic group in the country, and the sages, who studied and, where relevant, applied the laws of the Mishnah, stand equally in the chain of tradition backward to Sinai. This union of the patriarch and the sages forms the document's proposition concerning the sponsorship of the Mishnah and the divine authority that is accorded to its sages.

In Chapter One's list of names there is a clear logic of fixed association in play. The names of the listed sages form a coherent pattern. What is attributed to the sages exhibits a certain topical coherence but in substance is random and episodic. Major authorities of the Mishnah stand in a chain of tradition to Sinai; hence, the Mishnah contains the Torah of Sinai. The order of the names is therefore deliberate and unites what is attributed, though the sentences themselves bear slight connections among themselves:

> 1:2 Simeon the Righteous was one of the last survivors of the great assembly. He would say: On three things does the world stand: On the Torah, and on the Temple service, and on deeds of loving-kindness.
>
> 1:3 Antigonus of Sokho received [the Torah] from Simeon the Righteous. He would say: Do not be like servants who serve the master on condition of receiving a reward, but [be] like servants who serve the master not on condition of receiving a reward. And let the fear of Heaven be upon you.
>
> 1:4 Yose ben Yoezer of Zeredah and Yose ben Yohanan of Jerusalem received [the Torah] from them. Yose ben Yoezer says: Let your house be a gathering place for sages. And wallow in the dust of their feet, and drink in their words with gusto.
>
> 1:5 Yose ben Yohanan of Jerusalem says: Let your house be open wide. And seat

the poor at your table ["make the poor members of your household"]. And don't talk too much with women. (He referred to a man's wife, all the more so is the rule to be applied to the wife of one's fellow. In this regard did sages say: So long as a man talks too much with a woman, he brings trouble on himself, wastes time better spent on studying the Torah, and ends up an heir of Gehenna.)

1:6    Joshua ben Perahyah and Nittai the Arbelite received [the Torah] from them. Joshua ben Perahyah says: Set up a master for yourself. And get yourself a companion-disciple. And give everybody the benefit of the doubt.

1:7    Nittai the Arbelite says: Keep away from a bad neighbor. And don't get involved with a bad person. And don't give up hope of retribution.

1:8A   Judah ben Tabbai and Simeon ben Shetah received [the Torah] from them.

1:8B   Judah ben Tabbai says: Don't make yourself like one of those who advocate before judges [while you yourself are judging a case]. And when the litigants stand before you, regard them as guilty. But when they leave you, regard them as acquitted (when they have accepted your judgment).

1:9    Simeon ben Shetah says: Examine the witnesses with great care. And watch what you say, lest they learn from what you say how to lie.

1:10   Shemaiah and Avtalyon received [the Torah] from them. Shemaiah says: Love work. Hate authority. Don't get friendly with the government.

1:11   Avtalyon says: Sages, watch what you say, lest you become liable to the punishment of exile, and go into exile to a place of bad water, and disciples who follow you drink bad water and die, and the name of Heaven be thereby profaned.

1:12   Hillel and Shammai received [the Torah] from them. Hillel says: Be disciples of Aaron, loving peace and pursuing grace, loving people and drawing them near to the Torah.

1:13A  He would say [in Aramaic]: A name made great is a name destroyed, and one who does not add, subtracts.

1:13B  And who does not learn is liable to

death. And the one who uses the crown, passes away.

1:14   He would say: If I am not for myself, who is for me? And when I am for myself, what am I? And if not now, when?

1:15   Shammai says: Make your learning of the Torah a fixed obligation. Say little and do much. Greet everybody cheerfully.

1:16   Rabban Gamaliel says: Set up a master for yourself. Avoid doubt. Don't tithe by too much guesswork.

1:17   Simeon his son says: All my life I grew up among the sages, and I found nothing better for a person [the body] than silence. And the learning is not the thing, but the doing. And whoever talks too much causes sin.

1:18   Rabban Simeon ben Gamaliel says: On three things does the world stand: on justice, on truth, and on peace. As it is said, Execute the judgment of truth and peace in your gates (Zech 8:16).

The intent of the list is not only to establish the link to Sinai; the fixed associative list bears a second polemic, which emerges in the pairs of names and how they are arranged:

    Moses
    Joshua
    Elders
    Prophets
    Men of the Great Assembly
    Simeon the Righteous
    Antigonus of Sokho
      1. Yosé ben Yoezer     Yosé b. Yohanan
      2. Joshua b. Perahyah  Nittai the Arbelite
      3. Judah b. Tabbai     Simeon b. Shetah
      4. Shemaiah            Avtalyon
      5. Hillel              Shammai
    Gamaliel
    Simeon his son [that is, Simeon b. Gamaliel]
    Rabban Simeon b. Gamaliel

Once the pairs end, we find Gamaliel, who is (later on) represented as the son of Hillel, and then Gamaliel and Simeon, his son, Hillel's grandson.

The cogency of the list emerges when we realize that the names Gamaliel, then Simeon, continued through this same family, of primary authorities, through Gamaliel II, ruler of the Jewish community after the destruction of the second Temple in 70 and into the second century, then his son, Simeon b. Gamaliel, ruler of the Jewish community after the defeat of Bar Kokhba in 135—and also, as it happens, the father of Judah the Patriarch, this same Judah the Patriarch who sponsored the Mishnah. Judah the Patriarch stands in the chain of tradition to Sinai. So not only the teachings of the sages of the Mishnah, but also the political sponsor of the document, who also was numbered among the sages, formed part of this same tradition. The list itself bears the message that the patriarch and sages employed by him carry forward the tradition of Sinai.

**Abot deRabbi Natan. The Fathers According to Rabbi Nathan:** In 250, Mishnah-tractate Abot, The Fathers, delivered its message through aphorisms assigned to named sages. A few centuries later—the date is indeterminate but it is possibly ca. 500—the Fathers According to Rabbi Nathan, a vast secondary expansion of that same tractate, endowed those anonymous names with flesh-and-blood-form, recasting the tractate by adding a sizable number of narratives. The authorship of the Mishnah-tractate, the Fathers, presented its teachings in the form of aphorisms, rarely finding it necessary to supply those aphorisms with a narrative setting, and never resorting to narrative for the presentation of its propositions. The testamentary authorship, The Fathers According to Rabbi Nathan, provided an amplification and supplement to The Fathers and introduced into its treatment of the received tractate a vast corpus of narratives of various sorts. In this way, the later authorship indicated that it found in narrative in general, and stories about sages in particular, modes of discourse for presenting its message that the earlier authorship did not utilize. And the choice of the medium bore implicit meanings, also, for the message that would emerge in the later restatement of the received tractate.

The work of The Fathers according to Rabbi Nathan was defined by the fact that the authorship of The Fathers presented the message of sages solely in aphoristic form. Apophthegms bore the entire weight of that authorship's propositions, and—quite consistently—what made one saying cogent with others fore and aft was solely the position of the authority behind that saying: here,

not there. The framers of the successor writing vastly augmented The Fathers by recasting aphorisms in narrative form, and, more important, according to the names of sages listed in the prior writing the rudiments of biography.

Among the types of narrative (in a moment defined in detail in our treatment of the teleological logic of coherent discourse that prevails) we find in The Fathers According to Rabbi Nathan, precedent, precipitant, parable, and story (whether an expansion of one that was scriptural or one that concerned sages), three have no counterpart in The Fathers, and therein lies the definition, as a talmud, of The Fathers According to Rabbi Nathan. The authorship of the Fathers completely neglected three. The authorship of The Fathers fully acknowledged the importance of the past, referring to historical events of Scripture. But they did not retell and include in their composition the scriptural stories of what had happened long ago. They understood that their predecessors lived exemplary lives. But they did not narrate stories about sages. They had every reason to appreciate the power of parable. But they did not think it necessary to harness that power for delivering their particular message, or even for stating in colorful ways the propositions they wished to impart. The framers of The Fathers resorted to narrative, but only to serve as a precipitant, with great economy to describe the setting in which a stunning saying was set forth. They did not cite narratives in the form of precedents.

Given a saying of an apophthegmatic character, whether or not that saying is drawn from The Fathers, the authorship of the Fathers According to Rabbi Nathan will do one of the following:

[1] give a secondary expansion, including an exemplification, of the wise saying at hand;

[2] cite a proof-text of Scripture in that same connection;

[3] provide a parable to illustrate the wise saying (as often as not instead of the proof-text).

These three exercises in the structuring of their document—selecting materials and organizing them in a systematic way—the authors of The Fathers According to Rabbi Nathan learned from the framers of The Fathers. In addition they contributed two further principles of structuring their document:

[4] add a sizable composition of materials that intersect with the foregoing, either by amplifying on the proof-text without regard to the wise saying served by the proof-text, or by enriching discourse on a topic introduced in connection with the base-saying;

[5] tack on a protracted story of a sage and what he said and did, which story may or may not exemplify the teaching of the apophthegm at hand.

The Fathers According to Rabbi Nathan presents two types of materials and sets them forth in a fixed order. The document contains amplifications of sayings in The Fathers as well as materials not related to anything in the original document. The order in which The Fathers According to Rabbi Nathan arranges its types of material becomes immediately clear. First that authorship presents amplifications of the prior document, and, only second does it tack on its own message. The Fathers According to Rabbi Nathan first of all presents itself as continuous with the prior document, and then shows itself to be connected to it. That is the strategy of both Talmuds in connecting with the Mishnah. And where the authorship gives us compositions that are essentially new in rhetoric, logic and topic, it is in that second set of materials that we find what is fresh. Let me spell out matters as they will soon become clear. Where the authorship of the later document has chosen [1] to cite and amplify sayings in the earlier one, that exercise comes first. There may be additional amplification, and what appears to augment often turns out to be quite new and to enter the second of our two categories, in the form of proof-texts drawn from Scripture, or parables, other sorts of stories, sometimes involving named sages, that illustrate the same point, and sequences of unadorned sayings, not in The Fathers, that make the same point. These come later in a sequence of discourses in The Fathers According to Rabbi Nathan. Where an appendix of secondary materials on a theme introduced in the primary discourse occurs, it will be

inserted directly after the point at which said theme is located in the counterpart, in the later document, to that passage in the earlier one, and only afterward will the exposition of the saying in The Fathers proceed to a further point. This general order predominates throughout.

The authorship of The Fathers According to Rabbi Nathan clearly found inadequate the mode of intelligible discourse and the medium of expression selected by the framers of the document they chose to extend. The later writers possessed a message they deemed integral to the unfolding Torah of Moses at Sinai. They resorted to a mode of intelligible discourse, narrative, that conveyed propositions with great clarity, deeming the medium—again, narrative—a vehicle for conveying propositions from heart to heart. Not only so, but among the narratives utilized in their composition, they selected one for closest attention and narrative development. The sage-story took pride of place in its paramount position in The Fathers According to Rabbi Nathan, and that same sub-classification of narrative bore messages conveyed, in the document before us, in no other medium. The framers made ample use of formerly neglected matters of intellect, aesthetics, and theology, specifically, to compose their ideas through a mode of thought and cogent thought, so as to construct intelligible discourse through a medium, meant to speak with immediacy and power to convey a message of critical urgency.

Accordingly, they found place for all four types of narrative, and, of greatest interest, they made use of the sage-story to convey powerful propositions lacking all precedent in The Fathers and, in context, therefore of an utterly fresh order. That they made the shift from a document that articulated propositions principally through aphorisms to one that made points through narrative and particularly through sage-stories is entirely clear. Three traits define the sage-story in this document.

[1] the story about a sage has a beginning, middle, and end, and the story about a sage also rests not only on verbal exchanges ("he said to him . . ., he said to

him . . ."), but on (described) action.

[2] the story about a sage unfolds from a point of tension and conflict to a clear resolution and remission of the conflict.

[3] the story about a sage rarely invokes a verse of Scripture and never serves to prove a proposition concerning the meaning of a verse of Scripture.

What about Scripture-stories? The traits of stories about scriptural figures and themes prove opposite:

[1] in the story about a scriptural hero there is no beginning, middle, and end, and little action. The burden of the narrative is carried by "he said to him . . ., he said to him. . . ." Described action is rare and plays slight role in the unfolding of the narrative. Often the narrative consists of little more than a setting for a saying, and the point of the narrative is conveyed not through what is told but through the cited saying.

[2] the story about a scriptural hero is worked out as a tableau, with description of the components of the stationary tableau placed at the center. There is little movement, no point of tension that is resolved.

[3] the story about a scriptural hero always invokes verses from Scripture and makes the imputation of meaning to those verses the center of interest.

So the Fathers According to Rabbi Nathan systematically enriches The Fathers with a variety of narratives, each with its own conventions. When the narrators wish to talk about sages, they invoked one set of narrative conventions, deemed appropriate to that topic, and when they turned to make up stories about scriptural heroes and topics, they appealed to quite different narrative conventions.

The topical program of The Fathers According to Rabbi Nathan in particular emerges only in identifying topics treated in the successor-compilations but not in the principal one. Points of emphasis in The Fathers lacking all counterpart in restatement and development in the Fathers According to Rabbi Nathan are three. First, the study of the Torah alone does not suffice. One has also to make an honest living through work. In what is peculiar to The Fathers According to Rabbi Nathan we find not that point but

its opposite: one should study the Torah and other things will take care of themselves—a claim of a more supernatural character than the one in The Fathers. A second point of clear interest in the earlier document to which, in the later one, we find no response tells sages to accommodate their wishes to those of the community at large, to accept the importance of the government, to work in community, to practice self-abnegation and restraint in favor of the wishes of others. The sage here is less a supernatural figure than a political leader, eager to conciliate and reconcile the other. The third and most important, indicative shift in the later document imparts to the teleological question an eschatological answer altogether lacking in the earlier one.

If we were to ask the authorship of Abot to spell out their teleology, they would draw our attention to the numerous sayings about this life's being a time of preparation for the life of the world to come, on the one side, and to judgment and eternal life, on the other. The focus is on the individual and how he or she lives in this world and prepares for the next. The category is the individual, and, commonly in the two documents before us when we speak of the individual, we also tend to find the language of "this world" and "the world to come," *olam hazzeh, olam habba*. The sequence of sayings about this world and the next form a stunning contrast to the ones about this *age* and the next age, *olam hazzeh, le'atid labo*. In general, though not invariably, the shift in language draws in its wake a shift in social category, from individual to social entity or group, nation, or people. The word *"olam"* bears two meanings, "world," and "age." In context, when we find the word bearing the sense of "world," the category under discussion is the private person, and where the required sense, in English, is "age," then—as a rough rule of thumb—what is promised is for the nation.

We can tell that the definitive category is social, therefore national, when at stake is the fate not of the private person but of holy Israel. The concern then is what will happen to the nation in time to come, meaning the coming age, not the coming life of the resurrection. The systemic teleology shifts its focus to the holy people, and, alongside, to the national history of the holy people—now and in the age to come. So in the movement from *this world* and *the world to come*, to *this age* and *the age to come*, often expressed as *the coming future, le'atid labo*, we note an accompanying categorical shift in the definitive context: from individual and private life of home and family, to society and historical, public life. That shift then characterizes the teleological movement as much as the categorical change. It is contained both in general and in detail in the differences we have noticed between The Fathers and The Fathers According to Rabbi Nathan.

The national-eschatological interest of the later document, with its focus on living only in the Land of Israel, on the one side, and its contrast between this age, possessed by the gentiles, and the age to come, in which redeemed Israel will enjoy a paramount position, which has no counterpart in the earlier composition, emerges not only in sayings but also in stories about the critical issue, the destruction of Jerusalem and the loss of the Temple, along with the concomitant matter, associated with the former stories, about repentance and how it is achieved at this time.

Yet a further point of development lies in the notion that study of the Torah combined with various virtues, e.g., good deeds, fear of sin, suffices, with a concomitant assurance that making a living no longer matters. Here too the new medium of the later document—the stories about sages—bears the new message. For that conviction emerges not only explicitly, e.g., in the sayings of Hananiah about the power of Torah-study to take away many sources of suffering, Judah b. Ilai's that one should treat words of the Torah as the principal, earning a living as trivial, and so on, but also in the detail that both Aqiba and Eliezer began poor but through their mastery of Torah ended rich.

The Fathers According to Rabbi Nathan differs from The Fathers in one aspect so fundamental as to change the face of the base-document completely. While the earlier authorship took slight interest in lives and deeds of sages, the later one contributed in a systematic and orderly manner the color and life of biography to the named but faceless sages of The Fathers. The stories about sages make points that correspond to positions taken in statements of viewpoints peculiar to The Fathers According to Rabbi Nathan. The Fathers presents an ideal of the sage as model for the everyday life of the individual, who must study the Torah and also work, and through the good life prepare now for life after death, while The Fathers According to Rabbi Nathan has a different conception of the sage, of the value and meaning of the study of the Torah, and of the center of interest—and also has selected a new medium for the expression of its distinctive conception. To spell this out:

[1] the sage is now—in the Fathers According to Rabbi Nathan—not a judge and teacher alone but also a supernatural figure.

[2] Study of the Torah in preference to making a living promises freedom from the conditions of natural life.

[3] Israel as the holy people seen as a supernatural social entity takes center-stage.

And these innovative points are conveyed not only in sayings but in stories about sages.

What follows is that the medium not only carries a new message but also forms a component of that new message. The sage as a supernatural figure now presents Torah-teachings through what he does, not only through what he says. Therefore telling stories about what sages did and the circumstances in which they made their sayings forms part of the Torah, in a way in which, in the earlier document, it clearly did not. The interest in stories about sages proves therefore not merely literary or formal; it is more than a new way of conveying an old message. Stories about the sages are told because sages stand for a message that can emerge only in stories and not in sayings alone. So we turn to a close reading of the stories themselves to review that message and find out why through stories in particular the message now emerges. For what we see is nothing short of a new mode of revelation, that is, of conveying and imparting God's will in the Torah.

People told stories because they wanted to think about history, and, in their setting, history emerged in an account of what happened, with an implicit message of the meaning of events conveyed in the story as well. They further conceived of the social entity, Israel, as an extended family, children of a single progenitor, Abraham, with his son and grandson, Isaac and Jacob. Consequently, when they told stories, they centered on family history. That accounts in general for the details of what the authorship of The Fathers According to Rabbi Nathan have chosen to add to the topical program of The Fathers. The sage in the system of The Fathers According to Rabbi Nathan constituted the supernatural father, who replaced the natural one; events in the life of the sage constituted happenings in the history of the family-nation, Israel. So history blended with family, and family with Torah-study. The national, salvific history of the nation-family, Israel, took place in such events as the origins of the sage, i.e., his beginnings in Torah-study; the sagacity of the sage, the counterpart to what we should call social history; the doings of the sage in great turnings in the family's history, including, especially, the destruction of the Temple, now perceived as final and decisive; and the death of the sage, while engaged in Torah-study. And these form the four classifications of story in this document.

JACOB NEUSNER

**RABBINIC LITERATURE IN MEDIEVAL AND MODERN TIMES:** The writing of commentary upon the literature of the oral Torah begins within the earliest layers of that literature itself. The Talmud itself preserves statements in which such second century Tannaim as Meir and Judah comment on the earlier first century teachings of the Houses of Hillel and Shammai, teachings that appear in the Mishnah without commentary. The result of this continuing process of exegesis is that in later Rabbinic writings we often find several tiers of interpretation on earlier material. The Talmuds of Babylonia (the "Babli") and of the Land of Israel ("the Palestinian Talmud" or the "Yerushalmi"), that

is, contain elucidations of earlier legal and non-legal matters found in the Mishnah, the Tosefta, in other Tannaitic traditions, and of passages of both legal and homiletical midrash. Through these interpretations, the Talmudic authorities ("Amoraim") explained in detail the teachings of their own masters as well as the teachings of the earlier rabbis ("Tannaim"), sometimes clarifying the apparent original intent of the materials they explained but also, at times, reinterpreting those traditions to fashion the diversity of disparate materials into a unified whole. Thus Rabbinic masters emended traditions, forced readings, reversed names of tradents, and utilized other methods to resolve contradictions and so systematize the materials they inherited. The result is a complicated maze of winds and turns that is often unintelligible to all but the dedicated specialist, and even to such an expert, large portions remain difficult.

To help resolve these difficulties, the geonim and later commentators to the Talmud developed formulations by which they could interpret complex passages and distill a legal system from the maze of debated Talmudic statements. Often these commentators and decisors did not agree with each other, so that, in questions of interpretation, students are left to consult the works that best satisfy their own approaches and, often, to develop their own solutions. In questions of practical law, of course, there is no such latitude, as the *halakhah* resides in the hands of current authorities.

The following lists in chronological order the most outstanding Talmudic commentators. Due to space constraints, commentators on the midrashic literature are not included. Considered of secondary importance in Rabbinic scholarship, Midrash was known for the most part through the works of the great biblical commentators.[1] Nevertheless, many popular commentaries were written on the midrashim, though these have not been covered here.

**Geonim:** With the Islamic conquests, the old academies of Sura and Pumbedita became rejuvenated with a spirit of centralized authority. The heads of the academies, now called geonim ("Excellent authorities"), disseminated teachings far and wide concerning normative *halakhic* practice. Where the Talmud lacked clarity or did not offer a specific guideline on a topic, people addressed questions to the geonim, and they, in turn, wrote detailed answers. The institution of responsa literature that resulted has its roots in the Talmud, where we hear that, to clarify proper practices, certain rabbis asked questions of other authorities. These responsa form the first commentaries to the Talmud, and it appears that at times scribes allowed geonic comments to creep into the Talmudic texts themselves. At the same time, geonim helped fix the Talmudic text, determine meaning, and organize communal custom by fixing the order of the liturgy. *Seder Tikkun Shetarot, Halakhot Pesukot,* and *Halakhot Gedolot* are all geonic legal works that shaped the direction of legal practice in the post-Talmudic era.

**Saadiah ben Joseph Gaon (882-942):** The head of the Sura academy, a scholar of Torah and secular sciences, Saadiah was considered the greatest author of the geonic period. His major philosophic work, *The Book of Beliefs and Opinions*, was among the first philosophic classics of Judaism and the earliest to survive intact. His translation of the Bible into Arabic, which incorporates his commentary into a paraphrase of the literal text, is still used today by many Arabic-speaking Jews. He wrote commentaries to other biblical works as well and compiled the liturgy for the year into a comprehensive volume, still consulted today for its variant readings. His *Sefer Ha-Zikaron* and *Sefer Ha-Moadim* depict the dispute between the Babylonian and Jerusalem academies over the fixing of the Jewish calendar, which was ultimately resolved in accordance with the traditions of Babylonian Jewry. Saadiah's halakhic decisions took the form of monographs, and he established a standard format for his books of halakhic decisions. As a result of his belligerent character, he had many political enemies who succeeded in upsetting his career. His greatest victories were in discrediting the Karaite stances of biblical interpretation and anti-Rabbinic polemic.

**Sherira ben Hanina Gaon (tenth century):** The prolific head of the Pumbedita academy in 968-1006, he wrote many responsa. He and his son, Hai ben Sherira, are believed to be the authors of one third to one half of the geonic responsa literature. Sherira is known to have composed a commentary on the Bible and on several tractates of the Talmud. He also assembled a glossary on the first and last orders of the Mishnah. His *Iggeret Rav Sherira Gaon* attempts to reconstruct the processes of redaction of the Mishnah and Talmud, as well as of the Tosefta and *beraitot*. The work is extant in French and Spanish recensions, which differ on key issues. Sherira established the pre-eminence of the Babylonian Talmud as the universal source of authority in Jewish legal tradition.

**Hai ben Sherira Gaon (939-1038):** The head of the academy 998-1038, he composed commentaries on several tractates of the Babylonia Talmud and authored numerous responsa. Ranking as the most influential of the geonim, among his major works are treatises on commercial transactions, marriage, divorce, and other contracts and documents in prescribed format. He also composed approximately two dozen poems, including five *selihot* for the Ninth of Av, and several liturgical poems. He argued for the metaphorical interpretation of anthropomorphic passages in the Talmud and Midrash, on the one hand, and against the search for reasons for the commandments, on the other. His responsa disavowing the literal truth of miraculous tales in the Talmud and describing the practices of Merkava mystics are vital in the study of the history of philosophy and mysticism.

**Rishonim:** The period of the Rishonim—earliest Talmudic commentators—began in the tenth century in Spain and Germany, when some centers of Jewish habitation moved far from the orbit of Palestine and the Fertile Crescent and developed their own academies, independent of the existing central authorities. Marked at first by relative tranquillity but then marred by Muslim and Christian persecutions, this period was one of social and political unhappiness, on the one hand, but of scholarly stability, on the other. The one avenue Jews had to express themselves as Jews was in the autonomy of their religious and civil administrations. The task of the Rishonim was to render the traditional intelligible to the novice, who could gain enlightenment through the written works of Responsa and commentary. The Rishonim edited texts, commented on them, decided law according to their own methods of analysis, and provided leadership for the masses while maintaining their own specialized institutions of learning. The responsa, codes, and commentaries of this period stabilized Jewish teaching, doctrine, and practice.

**Gershom ben Judah (c. 965-1028):** He became renowned as the foremost Jewish scholar in the West and is referred to as Meor Ha-Golah ("Light of the Diaspora"). His decrees, cited to this day, include one mentioned by Rashi that forbids people from reminding returned apostates of their past. While Gershom's liturgical hymns survive, commentaries attributed to him apparently were written by his students. One of them, Jacob bar Yakar, was the primary teacher of Rashi, who reports what was written in the Talmud of Rabbenu Gershom, which he had seen. Gershom is widely cited by early scholars, but none of his legal writings have reached us directly. His responsa were collected from citations in other works and published in 1955 by S. Eidelberg. There is some literary evidence that his son and wife converted to Christianity, and he endured many tragedies.

**Hananel ben Hushi'el of Kairouan (died c. 1055):** This prolific master wrote a commentary on the Babylonian Talmud that paraphrased, summarized, and analyzed the discussions and noted the current legal practices. He was the first commentator regularly to include the discussions found in the Palestinian Talmud. The extant portions of his commentaries, on Berakhot and Seders Nashim, Moed, and Nezikin, focus on issues with practical applications. They includes material from the Tosefta as well as legal midrash. Hananel's Talmud commentary was highly regarded by the scholars of North Africa, particularly Isaac Alfasi in Spain. His commentary to the Pentateuch was also quoted extensively, although only fragments are extant, and some have been published. He also is known to have composed *Sefer Dinim*, which is no longer extant.

**Isaac ben Jacob Alfasi (1013-1103):** Known as Rif, he compiled a guide to all of the laws of the Talmud in practice in his time. His *Sefer Ha-Halakhot* codified the applicable legal material, quoting and commenting on the discussion in the Talmud as well as the interpretations of the geonim and his own opinions. Alfasi was also the author of numerous responsa, several hundred of which have survived. He is the major source for subsequent codes, and his decisions more than those of any other single individual shaped the future of Jewish legal practice.

**Joseph Tov Elem Bonfils (eleventh c.):** One of the great liturgical poets and scholars of France in the period of Rashi's youth, he appears to have been the copyist of geonic works such as *Halakhot Pesukot, Halakhot Gedolot, Teshuvot Ha-Geonim,* and *Seder Tannaim ve-Amoraim.* Only a few sections from his works have survived. He was a master talmudist who composed a commentary to the Talmud that occasionally is cited by Rashi and the Baalei Ha-Tosafot. His responsa sometimes are cited by Maharam Rothenberg. He is sometimes confused in the legal literature with another scholar of the same name who lived in the twelfth century.

**Isaac ibn Geat (died c. 1089):** A Spanish poet and halakhist, his major works have not survived, although we do have a collection of his legal expositions, known as *Meah Shearim* or *Shearei Simha,* which covers the topics of Jewish law in the order their tractates appear in the Talmud. His exposition is chronological, beginning with the Talmudic discussions, then citing the geonic understandings of the Talmud, and then those of the subsequent commentators. Modern scholars have found much useful information in his variants to the Talmud and geonic literature. Many of the most important decisors cite his works: Rabad, Ramban, Rashba, Rosh, and others. We know he composed commentaries to biblical books and literally hundreds of liturgical poems incorporating mystical themes, of which most have been lost.

**Solomon ben Isaac (c. 1040-1105):** Rashi, as he is called, was a native of Troyes in France in the area of Champagne. He often praises his teachers, such as Isaac ben Eleazar, but has no reservation about differing from their interpretations. Rashi's grandsons (he had no sons of his own) were great scholars who founded the methods and schools of the Baalei Ha-Tosafot. Besides his biblical commentaries, Rashi composed a masterful commentary to the Talmud. This has supplanted all others and remains to this day the definitive work on the Talmud, alongside which it is printed. The commentaries bearing his name to some tractates, however, are not his, his own work having been lost or perhaps, in some cases, never composed. Rashi's command of the Talmud and ability to explain Talmudic discussions succinctly allows us to see the weakness of the commentaries, erroneously ascribed to him, to Horayot, Nazir, Taanit, Nedarim, and Moed Qatan (his actual commentary to which has now been located and printed).

Rashi's renditions of difficult pericopae, which he deciphers by reference to other Talmudic passages, show his genius and perceptive mind. He explains difficult words and usages and argues against weak explanations. In the course of his exegetical work, he suggested emendations to the Talmudic texts used in France and Germany and soon afterwards. To the horror of his grandsons, his admirers copied these emendations, offered as mere comments and not corrections, into the actual text of the Talmud. His legal rulings are preserved in collected responsa, such as that of Elfein (who also edited other rulings in *Sefer Ha-Sedarim* [Horeb, 1951]). Most often cited in connection with Rashi's legal decisions are *Sefer Ha-Pardes, Machzor Vitry, Sefer Issur ve-Heter,* and *Siddur Rashi*. It became the practice of legal commentators to cite Rashi's understandings of details of laws in Caro's authoritative *Shulhan Arukh*, although Caro often adopted *verbatim* the rulings of Maimonides. The commentary of Obadiah Bertinora to the Mishnah is largely borrowed from Rashi's commentary to the Talmud. As a result, Rashi's influence on modern halakhah is enormous.

**Samuel ben Meir (c. 1080-1165):** Rashbam was born in Northern France (Ramerupt), the grandson and student of Rashi and the brother of the illustrious Jacob, commonly referred to as Rabbenu Tam. Yet he, in his own right, was both a Talmudic commentator, not in the manner of Rashi's crisp glosses, but as a propounder of new ideas used to reconcile Talmudic passages that seemed in conflict. His interpretations were used to supplement Rashi's sparse commentary to tractate Baba Batra and the tenth chapter of Pesahim. Rashbam's Talmudic commentaries were much different in method from his biblical ones. The latter focused on the most apparent meanings of texts and eschewed such forced comments as ran through Rabbinic tradition to reconcile biblical and Rabbinic teachings. In his explanations of the Talmud, by contrast, he does not spare his imaginative impulses, reconciling disparate sources and producing an interpretation that justified both Rabbinic tradition and contemporary practice. A proficient halakhist, he ranks as a leader, perhaps the founder, of the school of the Baalei Ha-Tosafot.

**Jacob ben Meir (1100-1171):** Rabbenu Tam was the younger brother of Rashbam and the grandchild of Rashi. His work on the Babylonian Talmud laid the foundations for the work of the Baalei Ha-Tosafot. Suffering much during the crusades, he wrote liturgical hymns as well as some Bible commentaries. His Talmudic pronouncements became the basis for Jewish law in Ashkenazic lands, and his extra-Talmudic decrees were accepted widely. His major work, *Sefer Ha-Yashar*, reconciled apparent discrepancies among various Talmudic pericopae by identifying a single principle that would account for all the passages. Much of his effort was aimed at emending corrupted passages in the Talmudic text and, in this way, making the Talmud more lucid. He was careful to insist that his emendations be kept in commentaries and not introduced into the main body of texts passed down from generation to generation, since no one had the right to interfere in the natural transmission of texts.

His comments took into account contemporary social relevance and communal needs, and he did not value the interpretations of past or present masters on the simple basis of their perceived authority or reputation. Rather, he viewed the cogency and usefulness of the argument alone as paramount. His arguments with his grandfather Rashi are well known, and his ideas about the proper order of the texts contained in the phylacteries are still followed today, alongside the view of Rashi (so that some Jews don two sets of phylacteries daily).

Jacob ben Meir produced works beyond his Talmudic comments, including a liturgical manual containing all the laws of prayer and their texts. He also wrote comments to Alfasi's work. The *Machzor Vitry* contains his *Hilkhot Sefer Torah*. References are found in the writings of other scholars to his *Sefer Ha-Pesakim*, but no copies of the work exist. A scholar of Hebrew grammar, his *Sefer Ha-Hakhraot* defended Menahem ibn Saruk in his grammatical dispute with Dunash ibn Labrat.

**Isaac ben Samuel of Dampierre (died c. 1185):** He was the major figure in promoting the study methods of the Tosafists. His students produced the major volumes of the writings of the Baalei Ha-tosafot. He is called Ri Ha-Zaken (that is, Rabbi Isaac the elder) and was the nephew of Rashbam and Rabbenu Tam. His work remains the basis of the Tosafists' commentaries to the Talmud, edited by his student, Samson of Sens, the famed author of a commentary to the Mishnaic Division of Zeraim. He was also the teacher of Barukh, the author of *Sefer Ha-Truma*. His responsa often are cited by halakhic authorities of the period and repeatedly in the halakhic compendium *Or Zarua* by Isaac of Vienna. His bible commentaries and commentary to Alfasi's compendium have not survived.

**Jacob ben Samson (died c. 1130):** A student of Rashi and teacher of Rabbenu Tam, he wrote many commentaries, and citations of his work on Abot are interpolated into a commentary on Abot in *Machzor Vitry*. He composed a commentary to *Sefer Yetzira* and a work, *Seder Olam*, listing the chronologies of the Talmudic rabbis. He was a noted collector of ancient liturgical poetry and composed liturgical hymns himself. Most

of his work has not as yet been published.

**Isaac ben Asher Ha-Levi (eleventh-twelfth centuries):** Known as the Riva, this master Tosafist and student of Rashi composed novellae to most of the Talmud. Although no longer extant, his commentary to the Pentateuch and his responsa are cited by early authorities. He was the teacher Eliezer ben Joel Ha-Levi, the author of the *Ravya*, a notable halakhic work still cited by modern decisors.

**Abraham ben David of Posquieres (1125-1198):** The Rabad was the leader of his generation in France, Germany, and Spain and forged new methods and understandings in the method of Talmudic analysis and law. His colleagues were very prominent scholars, such as Abraham ben Isaac the author of the *Sefer Ha-Eshkol*, but he nevertheless operated under his own inspiration, without consulting others. He even wrote a book, *Issur Mashehu*, to show the mistakes of his teacher.

He wrote legal expositions such as *Baalei Nefesh* on the laws of menstruation and ritual immersion. He composed lengthy criticisms on Zerahiah Ha-Levi's *Sefer Ha-Meor*, in which Rabad defends Alfasi against well-taken and perceptive attacks. Nevertheless Rabad finds fault with Alfasi too at times. Ramban defended Alfasi against the comments of Rabad in his *Sefer Zekhut*. Some responsa of Rabad are found in *Sefer Ha-Tashbatz*. He is best known for his critiques of Maimonides' *Mishneh Torah*, which are printed in standard editions of Maimonides' work. His commentaries to Mishnah tractates Eduyyot and Kinim, to Sifra, and to the Talmud (of which we have only a few works extant) are of the highest order.

**Zerahiah ben Isaac Ha-Levi (died 1186):** He wrote the *Sefer Ha-Meor* at a young age and thereby established himself as a genius of the first rank. His colleague Rabad saw his arguments against the great work of Alfasi as impudence. Rabbi Zerahiah, or Raza as he is called, wrote the *Sefer Ha-Meor Ha-Gadol* on the orders of Nashim and Nezikin and the *Sefer Ha-Meor Ha-Qatan* on the order of Moed. His comments are published in standard editions of the Talmud beneath the work of Alfasi, and alongside it is published Ramban's defense, called *Milhamot Ha-Shem*. Although Raza's *Hilkhot Shehita, Hilkhot Bedika*, and some other works are no longer extant, we have his notes to Mishnah tractate Kinim, printed alongside Rabad's commentary in standard editions of the Talmud. Raza was an accomplished poet, both liturgical and secular. His *Sefer Ha-Tsava* criticizes Alfasi and Rabad for at times ignoring thirteen basic rules of Talmudic study.

**Isaac ben Abba Mari of Marseilles (c. 1122-1193):** He is the author of the *Ittur*, or *Ittur Sofrim*, a magnificent work of which our printed texts are poorly edited and presented. A new edition from good manuscripts is necessary. He was the first French or Provencal scholar to use the Palestinian Talmud extensively, and his work contains a wealth of information taken from the responsa of geonim. It is a legal compendium covering almost all the topics of daily living: civil law, religious law including the festivals, circumcision, phylacteries, and ritual fringes. His glosses to Alfasi's massive compendium is called *Meah Shearim* and can be found is standard editions of the Babylonian Talmud.

**Eliezer ben Nathan of Mainz (1090-1170):** Ravan was one of the most outstanding of the Baalei Ha-Tosafot and has left us a number of important works. *Sefer Ha-Ravan* (or *Even Ha-Ezer*) is a compendium of laws in the form of a code in which he cites texts and readings from the Talmud and midrash that are of immense importance for understanding the period of the Baalei Ha-Tosafot. He wrote an important commentary to the entire liturgy, which has been partially published.

**Eliezer ben Samuel of Metz (1115-1198):** A student of Rabbenu Tam, he analyzed the 613 commandments. His *Sefer Yeraim* preserves early variant readings of the classics of Rabbinic Judaism. He has left other works as well, which contain historical information of his period. His interpretations are cited in the *magnum opus* of Mordecai ben Hillel.

**Moses ben Maimon (1135-1204):** In his early years, Rambam, or Maimonides, wrote his commentary to the Mishnah in Arabic to explain the principles of legal decision making. His introduction to the Division of Agriculture, for example, summarizes the entire history of the oral law from the time of Moses to his own, while his introduction to Abot, called *Shemoneh Perakim*, reconciles Aristotelian ethics and Jewish law. Maimonides' "Thirteen Articles of Faith" are presented in his introduction to Sanhedrin Chapter 10 and became the model for subsequent formulations of Jewish belief. In his *Sefer Ha-Mitzvot*, also written in Arabic, Maimonides identifies and classifies the 613 commandments according to his own system. His *Mishneh Torah*, or *Yad Ha-Hazakah*, was his definitive halakhic compendium, written in clear and precise Hebrew but lacking any designation of sources. For this he was criticized by his scholarly contemporaries, who were concerned that students would depend upon Maimonides and abandon the study of the Talmud and its commentaries. Maimonides also wrote responsa, many of which have been published, a commentary to the Babylonian Talmud, which is no longer extant, a halakhic analysis of the Palestinian Talmud, which has not survived, treatises on logic and medicine, and important letters to communities. His *Guide for the Perplexed* in Arabic seeks to reconcile the principles of Jewish faith with those of philosophy.

**Judah ben Samuel he-Hasid (1150-1217):** He was the teacher of Eleazar ben Judah of Worms and the principal author of the *Sefer Hassidim*, which has set many practices for the naming of children and mourning rituals. He was a mystic, pietist, legal decisor, liturgist, and ascetic. Many mystical works of his remain in manuscript as well as works of piety and moral instruction. His will has been published many times but, at the hands of many editors, has suffered additions and omissions.

**Isaac ben Moses of Vienna (1180-1250):** This great scholar studied in the finest academies of Germany and France, but his foremost teacher was Isaac Sir-Lyons of Paris. He studied mysticism under Judah he-Hassid and is the author of *Or Zarua*, a massive halakhic work that suffered badly at the hands of copyists. He was able to consult the *Ravya* of Eliezer ben Joel Ha-Levi, under whom he had studied.

**Samson ben Abraham of Sens (died c. 1220):** His great contribution was the compiling of the works of the Tosafists of France and Germany, which are now printed on the pages of standard editions of the Babylonian Talmud. His teachers were Rabbenu Tam and Isaac ben Samuel Ha-Zaken. His commentary to the Mishnah is simply called Commentary of Rash Mi-Shantz and covers every book of the Mishnah to which there is no Babylonian Talmud. It is a thorough and massive work that utilizes both the Palestinian Talmud and the Tosefta to elucidate the Mishnah, as well as citing places in the Babylonian Talmud where these passages of the Mishnah are tangentially mentioned.

**Isaiah ben Mali of Trani (died c. 1260):** Known as the Rid, this Italian scholar exchanged many letters with Isaac ben Moses. His explanations of Talmudic passages, called *Tosafot Ha-Rid*, have been printed covering the majority of tractates in the Babylonian Talmud, though some are not yet in print. He authored several halakhic works, such as *Sefer Ha-Machria*, but many of his works, such as his commentary to Sifra, have not yet been printed. His grandson was called Elijah (Riaz) and wrote a copious halakhic work, *Piskei Halakhot*, encompassing all the practical laws.

**Menahem ben Solomon Ha-Meiri (1249-1316):** This Provencal scholar was one of the most prolific writers of all times. His *Beit Ha-Behira* commentary to the Talmud encompasses 37 tractates. After elucidating a particular passage of the Mishnah, he collects all the materials pertinent to any Talmudic discussions concerning that passage and lays them out before reporting what every major commentator has had to say about them. His work is replete with citations from the geonim and the Yerushalmi. Instead of calling commentators by their names he describes them with adjectives that capture the essence of their endeavors. He indicates preferred legal practice and reinterprets some fantastic Talmudic tales as metaphors for rational experiences.

He incorporated chronologies of the great rabbis into a section of his work in one place and in another collects the laws of washing hands. He wrote other commentaries to the Talmud as well and to some books of Scripture, such as Proverbs and Psalms. One of his most masterful works, *Hibbur Ha-Teshuvah*, is on the methods and value of repentance. He also wrote works dealing with legal and customary matters as well as liturgical and philosophical issues. When the Maimonidean controversy began to rage in Provence, he defended the philosophic approach to life, including the study of the natural sciences and rational philosophy.

**Moses ben Nahman (c. 1194-1274):** Ramban achieved lasting fame as a halakhist, Talmudic expositor, biblical commentator, and early Kabbalist. He also composed treatises on halakhic subjects not covered by Alfasi. His *Milhamot Ha-Shem* was a major undertaking that defended Alfasi against the perceptive critiques of Zerahiah Ha-Levi Gerondi's lengthy and penetrating *Meor*, while his *Sefer Zekhut* defended Alfasi against the onslaught of David of Posquieres (Rabad). He also defend the methods in the Halakhot Gedolot against the criticisms found in Maimonides *Sefer Ha-Mitzvot*, on which Ramban wrote an extensive commentary, differing with Maimonides on many issues. His encounter with Pablo Christaini in the Barcelona disputation is well known, and Ramban's summary of the debate is widely printed.

Ramban utilized the methods of German and French Tosafists and introduced into Spain their approach of brilliant harmonization of conflicting Talmudic passages. Solomon ben Abraham Adret (the Rashba) continued these methods and at the same time was a staunch adherent to the quite different methods of Alfasi. Ramban created a synthesis between the French/German and Spanish schools, so that eventually the great German Talmudist, the Rosh, could gain a strong following in Spain. Ramban's magisterial command of the totality of Jewish learning, his exacting scholarship which pierced to the very heart of Talmudic methods and discerned the various chronological layers in the Talmudic texts, makes him a valuable source for the modern study of Talmud.

Kabbalistic works attributed to Ramban are those of contemporaries and not his. His great love for the Land of Israel (where he eventually settled) is reflected in many of his commentaries. He considered the commandments as more functional in the Land of Israel but still binding outside of the Land, if only to keep the method of practice vibrant among the people until they resettled there.

**Meir ben Barukh of Rothenberg (1215-1295):** Maharam of Rothenberg was a student of Jehiel of Paris and other Tosafists. His students wrote commentaries to the works of the great masters utilizing methods of analysis. Even when imprisoned and held for ransom for seven years he continued to lead the Jewish community and forbade them to pay his ransom, lest other scholars be captured and held hostage afterwards. His students, Moses Parnas and Samson ben Zadok, put together major works that Meir supervised during the prison years. The first is *Sefer Ha-Parnas*, the second *Sefer Tashbatz*. The responsa from the years of imprisonment were compiled from his amazing memory of the entire sea of Jewish learning. Thousands of his responsa are known, and his students cite his decisions constantly in their works. Four major volumes of his responsa are in print, but many works quote his other responsa. His comments to the Talmud are lost except for that on Yoma, which has been printed, as are some interpretations of various tractates from his major commentary to the Mishnah. While much has been lost or remains in manuscript, some of his smaller works were published, such as *Mahneh Leviah*, on the laws of mourning. His student, Moses Shneur, collected some responsa concerning various laws, which were published in *Ha-Goren* (1908). His liturgical hymns are still recited on the Ninth of Av. His students produced the major halakhic works of Ashkenazic Jewry: *Rosh, Mordecai, Or Zarua, Tashbatz.*

**Joel ben Isaac Ha-Levi (twelfth-thirteenth c.):** His son composed the book *Ravyah*, which preserves his father's responsa and some of his Talmudic commentaries. He was an eminent Tosafist, the student of Meir of Rothenberg. His liturgical poetry dating from the Second Crusade and commemorating the slaughters of Jews in the Rhineland are recited to this day. His major book, *Or Zaruah*, is a halakhic guide based on the order of the tractates of the Talmud. He was familiar with all the responsa of his own and preceding generations. His son produced an abridged version of his work. This work remains an important source for halakhah of the Middle-Ages.

**Eliezer ben Joel Ha-Levi of Bonn (1140-1225):** He was the teacher of the author of the *Or Zarua* (Isaac ben Moses) and the author of *Ravya* (or *Avi Ha-Ezri*), which analyzes legal decisions in the order they appear in the Talmud. He wrote many responsa and commentaries to the Talmud and Pentateuch, which were used by scholars throughout the Middle Ages. His responsa have been collected and published. He utilized the Palestinian Talmud in his researches.

**Isaac ben Joseph of Corbeil (d. 1280):** While the great code of Moses of Coucy, the *Sefer Mitzvot Gadol*, was a work of importance for the masters of scholars, the short work by Isaac ben Joseph, called *Amudei Golah* or *Sefer Mitzvot Qatan*, was aimed at lay people. Divided into seven sections, laymen could study a part each day. It contained short notices on the many laws of Judaism and did not enter into analytical discussion and abstract principles but rather presented the laws succinctly.

**Solomon ben Abraham Adret (1235-1310):** The head of Spanish Jewry, known as Rashba, he opposed philosophical works that he thought undermined the authority of Rabbinic teaching. He put to death, through due process, an informer to the Christian authorities. His Talmudic commentaries and responsa (about 3000 are extant) are widely read to this day. His commentaries were not only brilliant expositions of halakhah but also of the lore found in the Talmud. Jacob ben Habib cites the latter in his *Eyn Yaacov* commentary to the lore of the Talmud.

Rashba's major halakhic work, constantly cited by decisors, is *Torat Ha-Bayit*. Critical comments were written by his colleague Aaron Ha-Levi (Rahah), called *Bedek Ha-Bayit*, which Rashba in turn anonymously criticized in his *Mishmeret Ha-Bayit*. Rashba wrote a work on the laws of Sabbath and festivals, called *Avodat Ha-Bayit*, and some other works.

**Mordecai ben Hillel Ha-Kohen (1240-1298):** The prominent student of Maharam of Rothenberg and Rabbenu Peretz of Corbeil, his major work is a compendium based on the discussions of halakhic material distilled in the great work of Alfasi. To depict the laws as practiced in France and Germany, he assembled the writings of the most prominent Ashkenazic legal decisors. His full work is very detailed and lengthy and only connected to Alfasi's work as a way of organizing his topics. His work has been edited into longer and shorter versions. The original has not been preserved well, although some manuscripts exist that are much less corrupt than what has been printed.

**Moses ben Jacob of Coucy (c. 1240-1300):** His great code, known as *Smag*, that is, the *Sefer Mitzvot Gadol*, categorized all commandments under the rubric of 365 negative prohibitions and 248 positive injunctions. After the great conflagration of the Talmud following the forced disputation of Jehiel of Paris with Donin, Moses composed the *Smag* to serve as a replacement for the Talmud, study of which was now banned in France. He thought Maimonides' great code was insufficient, for it failed to prove its assertions by citing the necessary sources, and it utilized a different approach to Talmudic study from that of the Tosafists. Moses also included aggadic materials to make the reading more enjoyable. His work became a classic throughout the generations of Jewish scholarship and still is cited by modern decisors. He also wrote a full body of comments to the Talmud, of which those to tractate Yoma have been preserved under the title *Tosafot Yeshanim*. He set out what he saw as the great threats to Jewish survival in his day: intermarriage and neglect of the basic rituals of phylacteries, fringes, and mezuzah.

**Asher ben Jehiel (1250-1327):** Rosh, also known as Asheri, was a renowned German talmudist who spread the Tosafists' approach to Talmud study when he came to Spain.

He synthesized Ashkenazic and Spanish halakhic practices. His extant responsa number well over a thousand and reveal much about the process of halakhic development in western Europe. His major halakhic work, *Piskei Ha-Rosh*, summarized the conclusions of previous codifiers and commentators. As Alfasi had done, he arranged the halakhot in the order of the Talmudic tractates in which they appeared.

He composed commentaries to orders Tohorot and Zeraim of the Mishnah and compiled interpretations to the Babylonian Talmud that are more extensive than the ones printed on the Talmudic page. At times he incorporated the views of Spanish scholars and also of Meir of Rothenberg. He was the author of an ethical work, known as *Hanhagot Ha-Rosh* or *Orhot Hayyim*, which set down the rules for proper behavior in the home and community.

Among the best of the commentaries to *Piskei Ha-Rosh* is *Korban Netanel* by Nethanel ben Naphtali Zevi Weil (b. 1687) on Seder Moed and Nashim. His comments often have been incorporated into current legal practice. He wrote many responsa as well.

**Isaac ben Meir Dueren (died c. 1390):** His major work, *Shaarei Dura*, deals with the laws of kashrut and menstruation. Later decisors regarded it as one of the highest authorities, and many wrote commentaries to it. Isaac also wrote a book of customs for the whole year, published as *Minhagim Mi-Kol Ha-Shannah*, and commentaries to some Talmudic tractates.

**Yom Tov ben Abraham Ishbili (1250-1330):** The Ritva was the student of the spiritual leader of Spain, Solomon ben Abraham Adret. He composed a brilliant analytical commentary to almost the entire Babylonian Talmud, although as of yet not all of it has been printed. He also wrote commentaries to the halakhic compendium of Alfasi and the major halakhic treatises of Nahmanides, most of which have not yet been printed. Many of his halakhic works and his commentary to *Sefer Yetzirah* have not been preserved. He had a penchant for Kabbalistic thought but, in his *Sefer Ha-Zikharon*, did not hesitate to defend the philosophical, non-

Kabbalistic positions of Maimonides against his detractors.

**Jeroham ben Meshullam (c. 1290-1350):** This great halakhic master was a student of the Rosh. His written works include *Sefer Mesharim* and *Toldot Adam ve-Hava*, a discussion of all laws from birth to death. It was used as an authority by the major decisors and codifiers.

**Nissim ben Reuben Gerondi (1310-1375):** The Ran was the greatest scholar of his period and answered questions from Jewish communities everywhere. Seventy-five of his responsa have been preserved along with fourteen tractates of his great commentary on Alfasi's compendium, published beside it in almost every edition of the Talmud. (The comments on Moed Katan and Makkot are mistakenly attributed to him.) His commentary to Nedarim also is printed on the page, although, with few exceptions, his commentaries to other tractates remain in manuscript. His book of philosophic expositions, called *Derashot Ha-Ran*, shows him to be an able philosopher in the Jewish-Aristotelian mode. Many of Ran's ideas are contained in the responsa of Isaac ben Sheshet, his outstanding student.

**Isaac ben Sheshet Perfet (1326-1408):** The Rivash was the major decisor in Spain in the fourteenth century. He was a student of Nissim Gerondi and Hasdai Crescas. During the horrendous persecutions in Spain he fled to Algiers. His collected responsa have remained masterpieces, and his decisions and commentaries are mentioned by every major decisor. His Talmudic commentaries and his work on the Pentateuch have not survived.

**David ben Joseph Abudarham (fourteen century):** This magisterial scholar wrote an extensive commentary on the content and customs connected with prayer, *Sefer Abudarham* (1340). Working from an original copy of the prayer book of Saadiah Gaon, Abudarham commented on the various prayers and the rituals connected with their recitation according to the Talmud, the geonim, and other authoritative decisors. He preserved French, Spanish, German, and Provencal variants of prayers and practices. He also wrote liturgical poems and a commentary, *Tashlum Abudarham*, on the Yom Kippur liturgy.

**Simeon bar Zemah Duran (1361-1444):** The Rashbatz was a towering figure in Talmudic and legal study, with close to a thousand of his responsa preserved in the *Sefer Tashbatz*. His method was to elucidate every aspect of a case, looking at the question historically, socially, and legally, so that his responsa contain a wealth of historical information. He wrote treatises about ritual slaughter (*Yavin Shemuah*), a commentary to the Haggadah of Passover, and Talmudic commentaries (*Hidushei Ha-Rashbatz*). Besides his halakhic writings he has left us some major philosophic works, such as *Or Ha-Hayyim* and *Leviat Hen*, voicing opposition to some of the ideas of Crescas and Levi ben Gershom. His *Zohar Ha-Rakia* defends Maimonides' ideas in *Sefer Ha-Mitzvot* against Nahmanides' assaults. His commentary to Job is called *Ohev Mishpat*, and he wrote a polemic against Christianity and Islam, called *Keshet Magen*. He also wrote liturgical poetry and a major work of theology discussing such topics as revelation and the nature of God.

**Jacob ben Moses Moellin (1360-1427):** Known as the Maharil, he was accepted as the foremost Jewish religious authority in Western Europe. His major work, *Sefer Maharil*, a collection of customs that he gathered and explained, was transcribed and edited by one of his students. This work was unprecedented and was used by subsequent legal authorities such as the Rama to establish prevailing custom in western and eastern European communities. Much of his writing has been lost.

**Israel ben Pethahiah Isserlein (1390-1460):** Known as the Maharai, this great grandson of Israel of Kreimz wrote the *Hagahot Asheri* (notes on the halakhic compendium of the Rosh utilizing *Or Zarua* and other works) and was the head of a famous academy in Neustadt. He led a life of abstinence and piety. One of his students recorded his customs and manner of living in a work called *Leqet Yoshar*. Isserlein's magnum opus, *Trumat Ha-Deshen* is cited by the major authorities. It contains 354 responsa that deal with many matters that no one else had ever discussed prior to him. The appendix to the work contains another 267 of his responsa that were edited by one of his students. Some of his works are now lost, but his comments concerning Rashi's commentary on the Torah was printed under the title *Beurim*.

**Aharonim:** The period of the Aharonim—later commentators—is characterized by the work of organizing and systemizing the ideas of the Rishonim. An important aspect of this activity was the use of the methods of the Baalei Ha-Tosafot to explain Talmudic problems and to make sense of the diverse legal decisions of the Rishonim. This was done by pointing out fine legal distinctions and proposing limiting circumstances in order to resolve apparent contradiction in the cases presented in the Talmud and earlier commentators. The result was an impetus to create novel interpretations and the emergence of a new method, *pilpul*, which attracted many fine minds and produced a spate of works. Many commentaries to Rishonim now appeared. Additionally, Caro's *Shulhan Arukh* engendered a host of commentaries, which either supplemented the work or argued with Caro's approach. A spiral of additional analysis of the sources and interpretations of the Code ensued. Elijah, the Gaon of Wilna, by contrast, developed fine tools for analyzing the Talmuds and Rishonim and, in the end, opposed excessive *pilpul*-analysis. The Hassidic master Shneur Zalman of Lyady, although thoroughly hassidic in his approach to custom and theology, exhibits an affinity for the legal analysis of the Gaon in his *Shulhan Arukh Ha-Rav* and places his code in the forefront of halakhic digests for the layman.

With the Enlightenment, the stresses on traditional life were met by Aharonim who rallied around the *Shulhan Arukh* as the basis of Jewish life. But the Code and its commentaries became too unwieldy for the average layman, so that other abbreviated codes soon appeared, such as *Hayye Adam* and the later *Kitzur Shulhan Arukh*. The responsa literature continued to grow, as the leaders of the generation were left to settle

many issues introduced by modernity and modern technology: how, for instance, were electric lights, automobiles, elevators, and new food-processing techniques to be treated under Jewish law? Modern decisors of halakhah are quite conservative, and they have not dared to follow the path of those Aharonim who introduced new laws based on common practice. They focus instead upon the Babylonian Talmud, the writings of the major Rishonim who are cited by the Aharonim, and the works of the outstanding Aharonim. The halakhic midrashim, the Palestinian Talmud, newly published manuscripts of Rishonim, and critical historical methods—all tools utilized in modern Talmudic research—are generally ignored as irrelevant to the thrust of traditional halakhic momentum, which is rooted in the printed texts of the commentaries of the Rishonim.

For the most part, because of space constraints, we do not here mention the extensive legal and Talmudic traditions of Sephardic and Yemenite Jews in the period of the Aharonim. It is to be noted that while Rabbinic authority was removed in Ashkenazic communities in Eastern and Western Europe in the 1800s, so that modern responsa were limited in the area of civil law, Sephardic and Yemenite rabbis continued to deal with all areas of law. Their responsa thus are very important. Ovadya Yosef, a current Sephardic rabbi, enjoys high status among his Ashkenazic colleagues for his mastery of precedents in Sephardic law as well as for his knowledge of Ashkenazic authorities.

**David ben Solomon ibn Abi Zimra (1480-1573):** Radbaz was the Chief Rabbi of Egypt. He introduced the practice of counting years on documents from the *Anno Mundi* as was the custom in the West, and he reintroduced the silent recitation of prayer that Maimonides had abolished in Egypt. He left there and resettled in the Holy Land, where he had first gone after he was expelled from Spain in the great expulsion of 1492. His printed responsa number close to 2500, but there are more in manuscript. He deals with questions of every type, and his personal authority is stamped in every answer. He defended the study of philosophy and science and was an avid student of Kabbalah himself, so that his commentaries are in a Kabbalistic manner. His comments on issues in Talmudic study are cited in *Shita Mekubetzet* by Bezalel Ashkenazi, his student. *Keter Malkhut*, his work on the liturgy for Yom Kippur, remains very popular.

**Obadiah ben Abraham Yare of Bertinoro (1447-1505):** His work on the Mishnah is the standard commentary in the major printed editions. He based it on the discussions of the Mishnah found in the Babylonian Talmud, and he often cited Rashi's comments verbatim. His commentary to the Torah is also well known. He composed a commentary to Abot and a book, *Or Amim*, which was translated into Latin, that argued that Aristotelian philosophy is opposed to the basic tenets of Judaism.

**Jacob ibn Habib (died c. 1516):** This Castillian scholar fled the Spanish persecution of 1492 and settled in Salonica. He excerpted all the midrashic and aggadic materials from the Babylonian Talmud, from beginning to end, and wrote an extensive commentary to them, called *Eyn Yaacov*. He composed his own interpretation by citing the major Talmudic commentaries and then adding his own ideas. After his death, the work was carried on by his son. He wrote much, and his halakhic commentaries to the *Tur* are preserved in citations by Joseph Caro other major scholars.

**Moses Cordovero (1522-1570):** Focusing upon Talmudic and legal commentators, we have not discussed important figures such as Moses de Leon, whose role in the production of the Zohar cannot be minimized, or Israel Baal Shem Tov, the founder of the Hassidic Movement. Still, we cannot ignore the special contributions of Moses Cordovero, known as Ramac, whose role is pivotal in the history of Jewish understanding of sacred texts. Ramac was the student of Joseph Caro, the composer of the *Shulhan Arukh*, and of the great Kabbalist Solomon Alkabez. His students were the powers behind the school of Lurianic Kabbalah in Sefad, which wholly integrated Kabbalah into a halakhic framework. What is generally viewed as the great,

new impulse of Isaac Luria—the Ari—was already expounded, without detail, by Ramac: the mystical doctrines of *tzimtzum*, the four levels or worlds of emanation, and the configurations of the *sefirot*. The Ari developed and refined these ideas and became the master teacher of the new movement in Kabbalah. Ramac's *Or Yakar* is a complete commentary to the *Zohar*, and he wrote many other books as well, such as *Or Ha-Shamayim, Sefer Shiur Ha-Koma, Tfilah le-Moshe, Or Neerav*, and *Tamar Devora*. Sermons of his and a commentary to the Pentateuch remain in manuscript, as yet unpublished.

**Isaac ben Solomon Luria Ashkenazi (1534-1572):** The Holy Ari was the foremost master of Kabbalistic doctrines. His teachers were the illustrious David ben Zimra, known as Radbaz, and Bezalel Ashkenazi, compiler of the *Shita Mekubetzet*. He was given to spending long periods of time in silence and meditation and had a penchant for telling future events. When Luria came to Sefad in the Holy Land to hear the lectures of Moses Cordovero, the foremost expositor of the Zohar, he fulfilled his life's wish. Cordovero, however, passed away shortly after the two met. Luria's students spread their master's customs and ideas far and wide, and his halakhic ideas were incorporated into his own teacher's *Shita Mekubetzet*. His student, Hayyim ben Joseph Vital, wrote *Etz Hayyim* further to circulate the teachings of Rabbi Luria.

Luria laid stress upon the doctrines of reincarnation of the soul and the coming of the messiah through the perfection of the soul and the cosmic orders tied to the soul. Over 25 Kabbalistic works have been attributed to him, whether directly or through the records of his students. He stands behind unique forms of liturgy, distinctive shapes of letters in Torah scrolls, and special Kabbalistic meditations.

**Joseph ben Ephraim Caro (1488-1575):** The author of the great code of Jewish law, the *Shulhan Arukh*, first gained prominence with his *Beit Yosef*, a commentary on the *Arbaah Turim* of Jacob ben Asher. Caro's purpose was to standardize Jewish practice by researching every law from its Talmudic origin through its divergent interpretations and variant practices in later Jewish communities, concluding with a decisive ruling on how the law ought to be observed. To decide among divergent customs, Caro turned to the opinions of Alfasi, Rambam, and the Rosh, defining normative practice as the majority opinion of the three. Because Alfasi and Maimonides were both of the Spanish tradition, the *Beit Yosef* minimized the opinions of Ashkenazic scholars. Caro also composed *Kesef Mishneh*, a commentary to eight books of Maimonides' *Mishneh Torah*. In it he often reads the understanding of Tosafot and Rashi into the words of Maimonides. In addition to two volumes of responsa and *Avkat Rokhel*, Caro wrote two books published posthumously: *Kelalei Ha-Talmud*, on Talmudic methodology, and *Bedek Bayit*, which contains corrections and supplements to the *Beit Yosef*.

**Moses ben Israel Isserles (c. 1527-1572):** The esteemed giant of Polish legal minds, Rama reacted in a fine, critical manner to the masterful works of Joseph Caro. In his *Darkei Moshe*, Rama adroitly wrote improvements to Caro's complex and detailed masterpiece, the *Beit Yosef*. His *Mapa* not only explains the *Shulhan Arukh* but also adds views other than Caro's, especially appending the fixed customs of Ashkenazic Jewry. In this way, Isserles radically altered the thrust of Caro's code. He wrote another great work, *Torat Ha-Olah*, to explore the philosophical, mystical aspect of Jewish ceremonial laws, especially those connected to the Jerusalem Temple. His Kabbalistic writings, like his commentaries to the Zohar and to Talmudic tractates, remain in manuscript, unpublished. His work on Jewish ritual law, *Torat Hatat*, his collected responsa, and his commentary to the book of Esther have proven very popular.

**Moses of Trani (1500-1580):** He was in dialogue with Joseph Caro, whom he replaced as chief judge, and also communicated with Radbaz, Bezalel Ashkenazi, Moses Alshekh, and others. His well over 800 responsa are important historical documents as well as learned decisions in Jewish law. His *Kiryat Sefer* deals with the arrange-

ment of Maimonides' *Mishneh Torah*, and his *Beit Elohim* is an important theological work on faith and prayer.

**Azariah ben Moses del Rossi (1511-1578):** His work on the history of the Jews utilizes the critical methodologies of the renaissance rather than the methods of folklore and legend common among his Rabbinic colleagues. His major study, *Meor Eynaim*, establishes a chronology of second temple times and the Jewish sects of that period. He sought archaeological evidence and rejected Talmudic calculation as a credible way of determining truth when there was counter evidence. He was sharply rebuked by many of his colleagues, and there was a ban against his works. But they were read and eventually helped pave the way for the Jewish Enlightenment.

**Bezalel ben Abraham Ashkenazi (1520-1592):** A student of Radbaz, he was the major legal decisor in Egypt and the teacher of the Ari. His *Asafat Zekenim* became known as *Shita Mekubetzet* and preserves the interpretations of major Talmudic commentators from the ninth to the thirteenth century. His work was completed by great scholars, so that most of the Talmudic tractates could be studied with the aid of one major commentary. Nevertheless, his work on some tractates still is unpublished. His emendations of *Seder Qodashim* are printed in standard Talmud editions. Some of his responsa have been published; other works of his are lost.

**Solomon Luria (1510-1573):** The Maharshal is the famed author of *Yam Shel Shelomo*, a Talmudic commentary studied widely in Europe and today in Lithuanian style Yeshivot in Israel and the U.S.A. He lays out the threads of legal decisors and their decisions for sixteen tractates, explaining how they interpreted passages in the Talmud to arrive at their understandings of the law. Providing a wealth of sources unknown to us from other places, he tested current laws against their original sources to proclaim them valid or invalid. In his important *Hokhmat Shelomo* he emends and corrects the texts of the Talmud, Rashi, and Tosafot by eliminating copyist and printing errors. He also emended the works of Alfasi, Rosh, Rambam, *Smag*, *Tur*, and the common prayer-book. His *Yeriat Shelomo* is a super-commentary on Rashi's commentary to the Torah; his *Amudei Shelomo* is a commentary to the *Smag*; and *Ateret Shelomo* is a commentary to *Shaarei Dura*.

**Judah Loew ben Bezalel (c. 1520-1609):** Known as Maharal of Prague, he was a master talmudist and theologian of Polish or German extraction. At his final Rabbinic post, in Prague, he established a renowned Talmudic academy, which brought him to the notice of all. His originality shines through his treatises on God, Israel, exile, and redemption—the major themes of Jewish thought. His works include a concise super-commentary on Rashi's commentary to the Pentateuch, known as *Gur Aryeh*; a highly intricate work on Jewish theosophy of the Exodus (and the Passover Haggadah), called *Gevurot Ha-Shem*; and his commentary to Abot in *Derekh Hayyim*, which is philosophically intricate. His responsa remain of interest, and his mastery of halakhah is evident in his *Tiferet Yisrael* as well as in his work on moral instruction, *Netivot Olam*. One gets a sense of his homiletic genius in his works on Esther (*Or Hadash*) and Hannuka (*Ner Mitzvah*). His study of redemption, *Netzah Yisrael*, is major work of theology. Some of his sermons have been published as have some of his legal works, notably on the *Tur*, *Yoreh Deah*, and Talmudic tractates of Moed (also called *Gur Aryeh*).

His influence is apparent on his student Yom Tov Lipmann Heller, who commented on the Mishnah and Talmud, as well as in the legal works of major decisors such *Magen Avraham*, *Bah* (*Bayit Hadash*), and *Taz* (*Turei Zahav*); his mystical directions are evident in the works of the masters of Hassidei Gur and Isaac Abraham Kook. A pedagogue, he established a curriculum that proceeded from the study of all of Scripture and its grammar to the Mishnah and then, in the mid-teenage years, to the Talmud. That program had already been recorded in Mishnah Abot as the proper sequence. The legend of the Golem of Prague shows the Maharal to have been in the popular imagination a towering figure of piety and learning.

**Mordecai ben Abraham Jaffe (1530-1612):** Taught by Solomon Luria and Moses Isserles, the two central legal minds in Poland, he was well schooled in the natural sciences and in Kabbalistic works. He wrote commentaries to Maimonides' *Guide for the Perplexed* and the laws of new moons as well as other books that required scientific knowledge. He also wrote a commentary to the Kabbalistic writings of Recanati, to the Torah commentary of Rashi, and other works as well. He wrote magnificent halakhic works based on the *Tur*. These presented the various laws according to definitive principles he had rigorously determined from his study of the Talmud and subsequent halakhic authorities. Collectively called *Levushim*, these works were the subject of commentaries by fine halakhic authorities. They remain standard references for modern decisors. However, *Levushim* was not printed in many editions, since Caro's briefer *Shulhan Arukh* was fixed as the accepted authority by Sephardic communities, and, as glossed by Moshe Isserles, by Ashkenazic communities as well.

**Joshua Falk (c. 1550-1614):** The author of *Sefer Meirat Eynaim* on *Shulhan Arukh Hoshen Mishpat*, and *Prisha* and *Drisha* on *Tur Shulhan Arukh*, his critical notes and corrections were esteemed and accepted as authoritative. A few of his responsa are preserved in *Geonei Batraye* and *Bayit Hadash*. Lost are his Talmudic novellae, commentaries to the Rif and the Ran, his Kabbalistic writings, his biblical commentaries, and his responsa. He had studied under the greatest scholars of his age, Solomon Luria and Moses Isserles. His daughter, Beila, also was known as a halakhist, and her legal opinions were entertained by the leading authorities of the times.

**Meir ben Gedaliah of Lublin (1558-1616):** A prominent scholar, he is referred to as the Maharam Lublin. His son collected some of his responsa and published them under the name *Manhir Eynei Hakhamim*. His major work, comments to the entire Babylonian Talmud, is printed in standard editions, under the title *Meir Eynei Hakhamim*. His other works were never published: a commentary to the entire *Tur*, another to the *Sefer Mitzvot Gadol*, and other homiletic and legal works. Maharam opposed using codes to decide the law, maintaining that only one who knows the entire Talmudic literature can understand how to apply legal principles to individual cases.

**Joel Sirkes (1561-1640):** He is known as the *Bah* after his classic work on the *Tur*, called *Bayit Hadash*. He analyzes the sources of each law in the *Tur* and decides its proper application according to the logic of the Talmudic system. He intended to justify community practices that seemed at odds with the written, legal traditions, e.g., the prohibition against eating winter wheat before the second day of Passover. A master talmudist and legal decisor, his work is noted in every intricate legal decision to this day. His students were David Ha-Levi (author of the *Turei Zahav*), Menahem Mendel Krochmal, and Menahem Mendel Auerbach (author of *Ateret Zekenim*). He insisted that Talmudic scholars had to be proficient in Hebrew language and grammar, and he set up a curriculum similar to that of the Maharal of Prague. His contributions to Talmudic studies are staggering. He wrote critical notes (called *Hagahot Ha-Bah*) to correct copyists errors he identified in the texts of the Talmud, the Rosh, the *Tur*, the *Beit Yosef*, the *Shulhan Arukh*, and the Rama. We have two volumes of his collected responsa, which for the most part reveal a liberal and lenient approach to some areas of Jewish law. Besides his notes to Falk's *Meor Eyneim*, called *Quntres Aharon*, he composed notes to the Mishnah's commentators: Maimonides, Samson of Sens, and Rabad. He also wrote biblical commentaries, *Meshiv Nefesh* to Ruth and *Beer Mayim* to Rashi's commentary to the Pentateuch, and *Shealot u-Teshovot Bayit Hadash*. His Kabbalistic works, novellae to the Talmud, treatise on the *Shulhan Arukh*, and liturgical commentaries still await publication.

**David ben Samuel Ha-Levi (1586-1667):** Forced to flee persecutions, wars, and upheavals, he journeyed from city to city. He often cites his father-in-law, the Bah. He wrote a super-commentary to Rashi's interpretation of the Torah, called *Divre David*, and composed a work called *Daf Aharon* to defend himself against the attacks of Shabbetai Ha-Kohen (the Shach). His major work, a commentary to the entire *Shulhan Arukh*, is all in print. The best known sections are on *Orah Hayyim*, called *Magen David* (published together with the *Magen Avraham* commentary as *Meginei Aretz*), and to *Yoreh Deah*, called *Turei Zahav*, on which basis David was simply called the Taz. The *Turei Zahav* was printed with the commentary of the Shach in a volume known as *Ashlei Ravravi*. Later in his life he wrote further clarifications to his commentaries on *Orah Hayyim* and *Yoreh Deah*.

**Isaiah Horowitz (1560-1630):** A Talmud student under Joshua Falk, he learned Kabbalah from the son of Hayyim Vital. Thus combining the best talents of talmudist and Kabbalist, he achieved lasting fame through his magisterial *Shnei Luhot Ha-Brit*. This work analyzes the entire range of commandments using philosophical, ethical, and Kabbalistic methods. In the process Horowitz gives detailed information concerning the proper method of performing every commandment and custom. He also wrote a commentary to the *Sefer Mordecai* on Seder Moed (called *Bigdei Yesha*), composed notes to the *Zohar*, produced legal works such as the laws of phylacteries, and authored a prayer book with commentary, *Shaar Ha-Shamayim*. His life was filled with turmoil and persecution, and he was even held hostage for a time.

**Samuel Eliezer Edels (1555-1631):** This master commentator, known as Maharsha, wrote his *Hidushe Halakhot* to expound the sense of Rashi's or Tosafists' comments to the Talmud. Maharsha clarifies, explains, and even emends texts, so that students gain a lucid grasp of the Talmudic passage. In his *Hidushe Aggadot* he goes to great lengths to clarify Talmudic stories and to fit them into the matters at hand. His ethical and moral teachings are framed in these works. The greatness of these works was so evident that they are published in all standard editions of the Talmud. He had a fine critical mind and was able to see that the Targum of Pseudo-Jonathan was not composed by the translator of the prophets. He also discerned later glosses in the works of Rashi and Tosafot, and he emended the texts accordingly. He wrote other works, but his Talmudic commentaries are crucial for the understanding of the Talmud. For the student, these rank in usefulness next to those of Rashi and the Baalei Ha-Tosafot.

**Menahem Mendel ben Abraham Krochmal (1600-1661):** The Zemah Zedek studied together with David Ha-Levi under the tutelage of Joel Sirkes. A champion of social justice, he introduced many economic and social reforms for the Jews of Moravia. Many of his writings were lost in a fire. His responsa, *Sheelot u-Teshuvot Zemah Zedek*, cover the entire range of the *Shulhan Arukh* of Joseph Caro and remain an important source for modern decisors.

**Yom Tov Lipmann ben Nathan Ha-Levi Heller (1579-1654):** The famed student of the Maharal of Prague, his work shows a masterful Hebrew style of intricate grammatical constructions. His commentaries also reveal a wide knowledge of mathematics and the natural sciences as well as of philosophical and legal works. An ardent Kabbalist, he offered many original interpretations in his commentary to the Mishnah, *Tosafot Yom Tov*.

He composed a guide, in Yiddish, for salting meat (*Brit Meleh*), which was abridged and printed in many standard editions of the Mishnah. His major halakhic contributions are massive commentaries to the Rosh, known as *Maadnei Yom Tov*, *Divrei Hamudot*, and *Pilpulei Harifta*. He composed works on the architecture of the temple and other works including an autobiography, *Megillat Eyvah*. He also wrote critical notes to the *Levush Orah Hayyim*. Unprinted as of yet are many works on Kabbalah, commentaries to medieval works, legal works, parts of his commentaries to the Rosh, and even a super-commentary to Abraham ibn Ezra's commentary to the Pentateuch.

**Shabbetai ben Meir Ha-Kohen (1621-1662):** The Shach wrote extensive commentaries to *Yoreh Deah* and *Hoshen Mishpat* of the *Shulhan Arukh*. This work, called *Siftei Kohen*, encompassed the entire literature of Jewish law, and his decisions were based on clear reasoning, not simply the chain of accepted and authoritative decisors. In a perceptive work called *Nekudot Ha-Kesef*, he criticized the commentary of *Turei Zahav* on *Yoreh Deah*. The author of *Turei Zahav*, David ben Samuel Ha-levi, defended himself in *Daf Aharon*, and Shabbetai refuted this response in his *Kuntres Aharon*. In future years the greatest minds debated his positions, so that he is the subject of much controversy in the legal literature. Living during the persecutions of 1648, when whole communities were butchered, he wrote dirges to commemorate their slaughter. An account of the great tragedy is in his *Megillat Afah*. His commentary to the *Tur Yoreh Deah* is in print. His long work *Takfo Kohen* was abridged by Jonathan Eybeschuetz, who added his own commentary to it. Shabbtai also authored a commentary to the Passover Haggadah and wrote other works, such as *Poel Tzedek*, concerning the *Sefer Ha-Mitzvot* of Maimonides.

**Abraham Abele Gombiner (1637-1683):** In his lifetime, Abraham was not a world renowned scholar but a simple teacher of children. But when he died, his son sought to publish his commentary to the *Shulhan Arukh*, which he called *Magen Avraham*. The publisher was so amazed by the work that he printed it together with the commentary of David Ha-Levi on the very pages of the *Shulhan Arukh* itself. Subsequently, all standard editions of the *Shulhan Arukh* have come to be printed that way. The commentary does four major things: 1) It explains the rulings of Caro and Isserles, in instances of discrepancies usually deciding in favor of Isserles and arguing frequently against the rulings of Mordecai Jaffe's *Levush*. 2) It enhances all legal codes by citing Kabbalistic customs, which were becoming widespread, and introducing them into the accepted practice. 3) It reviewed the entire tradition of law and fills in omissions in the works of Caro and Isserles. 4) It introduces an ethical and moral dimension relevant to the performance of the laws. Alongside the approaches of Caro and Isserles, this work became the standard for all practice in subsequent generations.

Abraham also penned the *Zayit Raanan* commentary to Yalkut Shimoni. This work examined older commentaries and showed which were more accurate. An abridged form is printed in standard editions of Yalkut Shimoni.

**Jacob ben Samuel Hagiz (1620-1674):** This Sephardic sage was the head of the most famous academy in the Land of Israel and produced many exceptional Talmudic scholars. His major work was *Etz Hayyim*, a commentary to the entire Mishnah. His *Halakhot Ketanot* contains his many responsa. In his *Tehilat Hokhmah* he organized the principles necessary for a clear understanding of the Talmud. He composed around twenty works, of which only ten have been printed. He is the author of a major commentary to the Shulhan Arukh known as *Lehem Ha-Panim*.

**Moses ibn Jacob Hagiz (1672-1751):** His great works covered law and lore, biblical commentary, and ethics. He was an expert linguist and proficient in the natural sciences. He is best known for his *Leket Ha-Kemah*, a commentary to half of Caro's *Shulhan Arukh*, his *Shetei Ha-Lechem*, responsa to all areas of law, as well as for his comments to the Mishnah, called *Zikharon li-Vnei Yisrael*. His *Eleh Ha-Mitzvot* is an exposition of the 613 commandments of the Torah as compiled by Maimonides. He wrote many other books, but the most interesting is his *Sfat Emet*, in which he talks about the great spiritual value of living in the Land of Israel.

**Isaac Hezekiah Lampronti (1679-1756):** A renowned physician and Italian halakhist, he composed an encyclopedia of halakhah, called *Pahad Yitzhak*, arranged alphabetically, in which he cites and analyzes the responsa of scholars on many topics. The work remains a classic until this day. Many other works of his still remain in unpublished.

**Jacob Joshua ben Zevi Hirsch Falk (1680-1756):** Known as the Pnei Yehoshua, after the name of his magnum opus commenting on the Talmud, he was the great great grandson on his mother's side of Joshua Heschel and is also the author of responsa and the *Meginei Shelomo*, a work defending Rashi's commentary against the questions raised by the Baalei Ha-Tosafot. Because of his uncompromising nature, Falk was forced to leave Poland and take up posts in Germany. His wife was also an accomplished Talmudic scholar. His Talmudic commentaries are major sources of discourses in the world of Jewish learning to this very day. Unfortunately his commentaries to several tractates remain unpublished, as do his collected responsa and his commentary to the Pentateuch.

**Jonathan Eybeschuetz (1690-1764):** The master of Prague's most illustrious Talmudic academy, Eyebschuetz was one of the most prodigious minds to influence the Jews of Poland, Austria, and Germany in the eighteenth century. He was a master of Talmud and all legal works, but also of Zohar, Kabbalah, and the natural sciences. His amulets were thought to contain allusions to the infamous messianic pretender, Shabbetai Zevi. Jacob Emden sought to prove he was a follower of the banned sect of Shabbateans, and there may be some truth to those allegations. Although he was cleared of wrong-doings by formal inquiries, his son, Wolf, publicly admitted he was a follower of the banned sect, and a Shabbatean work was ascribed to him.

Eyebschuetz's legal works, mainly edited by his students, include the well known *Kreti u-Fleti* on *Tur Yoreh Deah*, *Urim ve-Tumim* on *Hoshen Mishpat*, *Bnei Ahuvim* on Maimonides' laws of marriage and divorce, *Bina La-itim* on laws pertaining to festivals, and a couple of dozen more. His homiletic works include *Yearat Dvash*, *Tifferet Yehonaton*, *Ahavat Yehonaton*, and *Keshet Yehonaton*. *Shem Olam*, on Kabbalistic themes, has been attributed to him, and this work shows an affinity to the Shabbatean work mentioned above.

**Jacob ben Zevi Emden (1698-18c):** Rabbi Emden, known as Yavetz, was a brilliant, critical scholar with a fiery personality. His *Mitpahat Sefarim* examines the classics of Judaism and comes to the conclusion that parts of the Zohar could not possibly come from Simeon bar Yochai, the reputed author of the Zohar. Besides such works, he wrote responsa (*Sheelat Yavetz*), a commentary on the Mishnah called *Lehem Shamayim*, a comprehensive prayer book for the entire year with legal notations, notes to selected Talmudic tractates, and many other works. He has even left us an autobiography, called *Megillat Sefer*.

**Jair Hayyim Bacharach (1638-1702):** His *Etz Hayyim* contains nine separate works, the first of which is *Havat Yair*. His 238 responsa show his mastery of mathematics, science, and music. He wrote glosses to Alfasi's compendium, which are published in standard editions of the Talmud. He composed a commentary on tractate Hagigah, notes to Maimonides' *Guide*, a commentary to *Orah Hayyim* of the *Shulhan Arukh*, and some forty other works, most of which are not printed.

**Moses ben Simeon Margoliot (1715-1781):** He is best known as the author of *Pnei Moshe, a* commentary to the Talmud Yerushalmi. He exerted untiring efforts to ascertain the exact meaning of the Yerushalmi, deeply studying sources from the Land of Israel, such as the Tosefta, and delving into botanical sciences. (We know he took university courses at Frankfort to clarify passages in the Yerushalmi). He also composed *Mareh Panim*, which harmonizes apparent contradictions in the Yerushalmi. Modern scholars find his commentary at times too superficial, since it utilizes the Babylonian Talmud and its commentators as a frame through which to understand the Yerushalmi. Unfortunately we do not have his commentary *Beer Mayim Hayyim* to Babli tractates Shabbat and Erubin.

**Aryeh Leib ben Asher Gunzberg (1695-1785):** His *Shaagat Aryeh* presents 120 responsa to *Orah Hayyim*, utilizing acute analysis and finding fine distinctions. His Talmudic novellae, *Turei Even* and *Gevurat Ari*, and his collected responsa are widely cited in Rabbinic literature.

**Elijah ben Solomon Zalman (1720-1797):** The Gra, or Wilna Gaon, authored over seventy books and commentaries, including an interpretation of almost the entire bible. He wrote a commentary to several books of the Mishnah, called *Shnot Eliyahu*, and to the Mekhilta, Sifra, Sifre, both the Jerusalem and Babylonian Talmuds, as well as on parts of the Tosefta, the aggadot of the Talmud, Pirke de Rabbi Eliezer, Abot de Rabbi Natan, Pesikta, Seder Zuta Rabbah, and Seder Olam Rabbah. His major work is a commentary to the entire *Shulhan Arukh*. A virulent opponent of Hassidism, he wrote extensively on Kabbalah, including commentaries to *Sefer Yetzira, Sefer Ha-Bahir, Sifra de Tzeniuta, Raaya Mehemna,* Zohar, and *Tikkunei Ha-Zohar*. He greatly influenced his student Hayyim ben Isaac of Volozhin (1749-1821), author of *Nefesh Ha-Hayyim* and *Ruah Hayyim* on Abot, who in 1802 founded a Yeshiva based on the methods of the Wilna Gaon. This determined the scholarly methods of analysis of Lithuanian scholarship until the brutal murders of Lithuanian Jewry in the 1940s.

**Joseph ben Meir Teomim (1727-1792):** Renowned in Poland and Germany as a halakhist, he wrote a commentary, *Pri Megaddim*, on works of the Taz, the Shach, and the Magen Avraham. He also wrote commentaries on Talmud tractates Yebamot, Ketubot, and Baba Qamma, known as *Porat Yosef*, as well as commentaries to Hulin (*Rosh Yosef*), to Berakhot, and to all of seder Moed. Of great importance is his *Ginat Veradim*, which sets forth seventy rules that are basic for understanding the methodology of the composition of the Babylonian Talmud. It is printed in most standard editions of the *Shulhan Arukh*. His *Rav Pnenim* collects his explanations of Scriptures. Many other works of his have not been printed, including commentaries to several Talmudic tractates. He wrote a dictionary of Hebrew and Aramaic and offered insights into the Pentateuch and Haftorot.

**Ezekiel ben Judah Landau (1713-1793):** Renowned for his piety and his learning, this Polish sage became the leading teacher and authority in his generation in Prague. He was the teacher of Abraham Danzig, the author of the very lucid code of Jewish law known as *Hayye Adam*. He subsisted on small morsels of food and fasted for long stretches of time. His method of learning was based on the methods of Rashi in the study of Talmud and Isserles in his methods of deciding halakhic norms. He established the *Shulhan Arukh* and the Rama as the foremost authorities to be followed and thereby began the process of unifying Jewish custom in Poland and Germany. He opposed the nascent hassidic movement and entered into disputations with its leaders. His printed works include *Sheelot u-Teshivut Nodeh be-Yehudah* (responsa), *Tsiun le-Nefesh Hayya*, extensive commentaries to tractate Berakhot, much of seder Moed, and all of seder Qodashim. Commentaries to tractates in seder Nezikin and seder Nashim remain unpublished. We have his *Degel mi-Revava* to the *Shulhan Arukh*, printed right on the page in many editions of that work. Extant also are various collections of his sermons and addresses and a work in German discussing the civil marriage laws of Kaiser Josef II of Austria.

**Hayyim Joseph David Azulai (1724-1806):** Known as Hida, he was an extraordinarily gifted bibliophile, talmudist, decisor, and Kabbalist. His autobiography-diary, *Maagal Tov*, reports on five years of his travels. His major halakhic writings are found in *Birkei Yosef, Makhzik Berakha*, and *Shiyyurei Berakha*. But he is best known for his bibliographies, *Vaad la-Hakhamim* and *Shem Gedolim*. He prepared extensive folklore collections, biblical commentaries, sermons, and he mentions many works that he saw in manuscripts on his travels but which are no longer extant.

**Aqiba Eiger ben Moshe Guens (1761-1837):** A staunch opponent of the reform movement in Germany, this great Talmudic scholar used his great erudition and understanding to keep his community distant from the movement he saw as heretical. His own works show he had a keen and critical mind, and students such as Jacob Levy made important linguistic contributions to the study of Talmudic philology. Aqiba Eiger is best known for his brilliant notes to the Babylonian Talmud, called *Gilyon Ha-Shas*, which are printed in the margins of standard editions. His glosses to the Palestinian Talmud, by contrast, have been lost. His responsa are widely used as are his glosses to the *Shulhan Arukh*. His published works include *Hilluka de-Rabbanan*, notes to the Mishnah, *Hiddushei Rabbi Akiva Eiger*, and novellae.

**Moses Sofer (1762-1839):** Known as Hatam Sofer, the creator, in Pressburg, of the greatest Yeshiva in the world, he raised a generation of outstanding scholars who followed his opposition to the modernizing spirit of the reform movement and the liberalism of Moses Mendelssohn. He promoted the authority of the *Shulhan Arukh* as a means of standardizing religious practice, so that people could accurately be judged as "observant" or "non-observant." Today, his volumes of Talmudic and biblical commentary, his many volumes of collected responsa, and his ethical will are studied carefully by Yeshiva students the world over.

**Israel ben Gedaliah Lipschutz (1782-1860):** He wrote an extensive commentary to the entire Mishnah, called *Tiferet Yisrael*, and introduced each of the orders of Moed, Qodashim, and Tohorot by summarizing its principles. His main commentary, titled *Yakhin*, gives the plain meanings of the text; a more penetrating analysis appears in a second commentary, titled *Boaz*. He appended the pertinent halakhic rulings of the *Shulhan Arukh* at the end of each chapter, in a section titled *Hilkheta Gevirta*. His brief commentary on the Mishnah is called *Zera Yisrael*.

**Joseph ben Moses Babad (1800-1875):** He is the author of *Minhat Hinnukh* (1869), a commentary on the thirteenth century *Sefer Ha-Hinnukh*. Babad quotes halakhic authorities and commentators on each biblical commandment but does not attempt to arrive at any conclusions or determine the halakhah. His aim is simply to raise questions that challenge the reader, so as to stimulate further study of the principles, laws, and customs of the commandments.

**Joseph Baer Soloveichik (1820-1892):** Known as the Beit Ha-Levi, he developed extremely acute methods of Talmudic analysis, which would be systematized and organized by his son, Rav Hayyim. He personally lacked those methodological skills. Many of his works have been published under the name *Beit Ha-Levi*, including comments on the Talmud, responsa, homiletic materials, and halakhah.

**Naphtali Zevi Judah Berlin (1817-1893):** The Netziv was head of the Volozhin Yeshiva for over 40 years and was a leading halakhic authority of the nineteenth century. His method stressed study of the works of the geonim and Rishonim. His reputation was founded on his learned *Emek* commentaries to the Mechilta and Sifre as well as his *Haamek Sheelah* on the *Sheiltot* of the Gaon Rabbi Aha of Shabha. More popular among the masses is his *Haamek Davar*, a commentary to the Torah. He wrote a commentary on the Song of Songs, called *Rinnah shel Torah*, and wrote many responsa, a small number of which are published in *Meshiv Davar*. Unlike his colleague Hayyim of Brisk, he did not analyze Jewish laws by breaking them into precise qualitative components but rather by understanding them as functional and practical expressions of spiritual life.

**Hayyim Soloveichik of Brisk (1853-1918):** Known simply as Rav Hayyim, he created from his father's methods an extremely powerful tool for analyzing all problems in the Jewish legal literature, thus bringing a new trend to wide acceptance in Talmud study. He divided passages of the Talmud into component categories that he showed were operative everywhere. His methods, which offered new solutions to old problem, thus explained every Talmudic passage and even every commentator of note. Many of his commentaries to the Talmud have been printed as well as his analysis of topics in Maimonides' *Mishneh Torah*.

**Israel Meir Ha-Kohen (Kagan) (1838-1933):** Hafetz Hayyim was popularly named after the title of his first book, on the importance of the laws prohibiting slander, talebearing, and gossip. His *Mishnah Berurah*, a commentary on *Orah Hayyim* of the *Shulhan Arukh*, is a comprehensive handbook devoted to practical halakhah for daily living. It remains his most highly regarded and most studied book. He was the author of 21 books, including *Mahaneh Yisrael*, a spiritual guide for the Jewish soldier in the Russian army; *Ahavat Hesed*, on charity; *Niddehei Yisrael*, an appeal for Jews who had left Eastern Europe to maintain their Jewish traditions and practices; and a number of other books devoted to daily observances, including Torah study and the dietary laws. He

wrote a commentary to Sifra and encouraged the study of the order Qodashim, on the laws of the Temple. This subject had been neglected in the Lithuanian Yeshivot, and forecasting the approach of the Messianic Era he revitalized their study. He also was influential in the maintenance of Beth Jacob Schools for young women, so they would be able to withstand the lure of secularism and apostasy that was rife in Western Europe.

**Abraham Isaac Kook (1865-1935):** A deeply philosophical and mystical thinker, he was attached to the Zionist cause, which he infused with the resources of Jewish tradition. His philosophic writings are masterpieces, about a dozen of which have been published. His halakhic responsa, legal writings, and treatises on a variety of subjects are very popular. Though his Talmudic works have not survived, his responsa concerning the observance of laws in the modern land of Israel are very important. He was a student of the Netziv.

**Avraham Yeshayahu Karelitz (1878-1953):** He is known as the Hazon Ish, after the title of his first work, a commentary on the *Shulhan Arukh* focused primarily on *Orah Hayyim*, published anonymously in 1911. The depth and breadth of Karelitz's knowledge had a major impact on the Rabbinic world. Although he published few responsa, he was highly esteemed throughout the Jewish world as a halakhic authority and wrote over forty books on Jewish law.

**Hayyim Ozer Grodzinski (1863-1940):** He wrote a three volume collection of responsa, entitled *Ahiezer*, which exercises much influence on current trends in Jewish law. His mastery of the whole tradition, his personal piety, and his untiring leadership of European Jewry established him as the leader of traditional Jewry after the death of Hafetz Hayyim.

**Jehiel Michael ben Aaron Isaac Ha-Levi Epstein (1829-1908):** Although he wrote novellae on the Talmud and responsa, his great fame derives from his *Arukh Ha-Shulhan*, which supplements the *Shulhan Arukh* by summarizing major rulings from the time of the Talmuds to the nineteenth century. His volume of laws dealing with the future, rebuilt Temple is called *Arukh Ha-Shulhan le-Atid*. Epstein was also the author of a commentary on Rabbenu Tam's *Sefer Ha-Yashar*, called *Or Yerushalayim*, and a commentary to the Passover Haggadah.

**Baruch Ha-Levi Epstein (1860-1942):** He was the son of Jehiel Michael Epstein and the nephew of the Netziv. His *Torah Temimah* cites and analyzes relevant midrashic and Talmudic materials pertinent to each verse of the Pentateuch. He also wrote other books, such as a commentary on the liturgy, called *Barukh Sheamar*, and an autobiography, *Mekor Barukh*.

**Isaac Ze'ev Ha-Levi Soloveichik (1866-1960):** He was the son of Rav Hayyim of Brisk. His students have passed on his teachings on the order of Qodashim and his other Talmudic lectures, which were based on the methods of his father.

**Jehiel Jacob Weinberg (1855-1966):** One of the greatest decisors of the twentieth century, his four volume *Sridei Esh* discusses many modern problems. His *Mehkarim ba-Talmud* show a blend of approaches of traditional piety and modern methods of Talmudic research. He esteemed the works of David Zevi Hoffmann and emulated him in many ways, combining both a traditional and a critical-historical outlook.

**Hanokh Albeck (1890-1972):** In the nineteenth and twentieth centuries the study of Rabbinic texts found its way into secular universities, where professors of Talmud produced important, critical editions of Jewish classics and investigated such works from historical viewpoints. Hanokh Albeck studied almost all areas of Tannaitic literature and the Talmud. Author of many scholarly books and essays in German and in Hebrew, he believed that the objective of the redactors of the Talmud had been to compile scattered materials, not to edit or abridge them. He also suggested that differences in halakhic midrashim were the result of different redactions and that the Tosefta and halakhic midrashim were unknown to the compilers of the Babylonian and Jerusalem Talmuds. His annotated editions based on manuscripts include Meiri's *Beit Ha-Behira* on Yebamot, Gen. Rabbah, Gen. Rabbati, and the Mishnah,

with introduction, commentary, and notes. His studies on the Mishnah, Tosefta, Baraita, Midreshie Halakhah, and the Talmuds are: *Mavo la-Mishnah, Mavo la-Talmudim, Untersuchungen über die Redaktion der Mischna, Untersuchungen über die halkischen Midrashm*, and *Mehkarim bi-Veraita ve-Tosefta*. He also annotated works by earlier scholars. His views have many critics, but his editions of texts are universally accepted.

**Moses Feinstein (1895-1986):** His responsa, *Igerot Moshe*, were collected and published in four volumes. His studies in Talmud were published under the title *Dibrot Moshe*, and some of his sermons on the Pentateuch were collected and published as *Darash Moshe*. His Talmudic novellae to Baba Qamma, Baba Mezia, and briefer notes to some other tractates have also been published.

**Joseph Baer Soloveichik (1903-1992):** Named after his great grandfather, he was the spiritual mentor of the Orthodox Synagogue Rabbis in the 1950s and 1960s. His writings include theological essays such as "*Ish Ha-Halakhah*," "The Lonely Man of Faith," "*Kol Dodi Dofek*," "*Torah u-Melucha*," "*U-Vikashtem mi-Sham*," and several volumes of published addresses. His students have also edited many volumes of essays based on his lectures, such as a treatise on the topic of repentance and some of his Talmudic lectures.

His methods of analysis resembled, at the outset of a lecture, those of his grandfather, Rav Hayyim. Typically he began his lectures with a Talmudic passage and posed a mass of problems involved in the reading of the passage. He would then analyze the passage utilizing the categories established by Rav Hayyim and showing them to be operative by recourse to the comments of Rishonim on the passage. He would then develop halakhic principles, based on his analysis, which he showed lay behind the passage at issue. When these principles were now read back into the passage, the mass of problems would dissolve into a structure very different from the initial reading he gave. He would, in turn, fit these operative principles into his own constructs of socio-religious categories. These constructs usually expressed a personal theology of the place of the individual and the community within the abstract universe of the halakhah. For the Rav, the halakhic universe expressed the Jew's relationship to the divine and the divine's relationship to the Jew.

The passing of towering talmudists such as Rabbis Kotler, Kamenetzky, and Auerbach marks the inception of an age of talmudic commentators and decisors not educated in the European mold. The next millennium thus begins with a sizable population of Jews growing more and more passionate about talmudic civilization even as the breaches left by the passing of the last generation have not been wholly filled.

### Bibliography

Margalioth, M., ed., *Encyclopedia of Great Men in Israel* (Hebrew: Tel Aviv, 1977).
Halperin, S., *Seder Ha-Dorot* (Reprinted, Jerusalem, 1956).

### Notes

[1] See EXEGESIS OF SCRIPTURE, MEDIEVAL RABBINIC.

HERBERT W. BASSER

**RECONSTRUCTIONIST JUDAISM:** Reconstructionism is a religious ideology and fourth American Jewish movement that was initiated in the early decades of the twentieth century and has experienced dramatic growth since the 1970s. Following the teachings and writings of Rabbi Mordecai M. Kaplan, Reconstructionists define Judaism as the evolving religious civilization of the Jewish people. Based on that definition, they seek to understand the historical contexts in which Jewish beliefs and practices emerged and changed and to adapt and reinvigorate those ideas and practices in the lives of contemporary Jews. Under Kaplan's leadership, Reconstructionism was a school of thought that sought to transform and bring together the existing Jewish movements. Beginning in the 1950s, however, with the establishment of the Jewish Reconstructionist Federation, the Reconstructionist Rabbinical College, and the Reconstructionist Rabbinical Association, it has emerged as a distinct organizational movement.

**Historical development:** Reconstructionist Judaism dates back to 1922, when Kaplan founded the Society for the Advancement of Judaism (SAJ), a synagogue in New York City, with the goal of addressing the disparity between inherited Jewish traditions and the outlook of most American Jews of the time. The members of the SAJ shared Kaplan's dissatisfaction with the Jewish community of the day and were committed to reconstructing Judaism in ways that would enable it to sanctify and transform Jewish lives in the new American environment. The congregation experimented with changes in the traditional liturgy, with the inclusion of women, including the introduction of the bat mitzvah ceremony in 1922, with the "revaluation" of Jewish ritual, and with the application of Jewish values to current political and social issues.

Jewish intellectuals, both those affiliated with other movements and those who were otherwise unaffiliated, were drawn by Kaplan's sermons and lectures. He applied current social scientific theory to an analysis of the challenges faced by Jews in an open, democratic culture, and he proposed a program of reconstruction that entailed a radical reconceptualization of Judaism. Many of these early ideas were published in the *SAJ Review*, which was distributed far beyond the SAJ membership.

In 1934, Kaplan published his first book, *Judaism as a Civilization*, which projected his ideas more widely. A comprehensive and critical analysis of modern Judaism and a passionate proposal for its reconstruction based on current theories of culture and community, the book had a powerful impact on the American Jewish world. It continues to stand as an influential classic of Jewish thought. On the heels of the book's initial reception, in 1935, the *Reconstructionist* magazine was founded as a vehicle to encourage the development of Reconstructionist ideas. Edited first by Kaplan and then by Rabbi Ira Eisenstein (fig. 115), the magazine influenced the thinking of many Jewish leaders who were not associated with Kaplan.

The Jewish Reconstructionist Foundation was founded in 1940 to publish materials that would promote the Reconstructionist program. Kaplan and his preeminent disciples,

Eisenstein and Eugene Kohn, then published a series of prayer books. The first of these—*The New Haggadah* (1941) and *The Sabbath Prayer Book* (1945)—created heated controversy because they revised the wording of traditional Hebrew prayers. The latter, which deleted or revised liturgical references to Israel as the Chosen People, to the messiah, and to the resurrection of the dead and the restoration of the Jerusalem Temple, was burned in 1945 by several Orthodox rabbis in a public ceremony of *herem* (excommunication). Kaplan, the son of a prominent Orthodox rabbi, had received rabbinical ordination under Orthodox auspices after being ordained by the Conservative Jewish Theological Seminary. He served on the JTS faculty for five decades and so represented a threat to traditional practice that could not be ignored. Subsequently, prayer books for daily services, the pilgrimage festivals, and the High Holy Days were published.

In 1954, four synagogues, including the SAJ, joined to form a synagogue organization, the Reconstructionist Federation of Congregations (now re-named the Jewish Reconstructionist Federation [JRF]). In 1960, the idea of *havurot*—small, participatory groups of Jews who would meet without Rabbinic leadership for study, worship, and celebration—was introduced with the establishment of the Whittier (California) Havurah. The Federation subsequently has grown following a pattern in which affiliated *havurot* grow into congregations and then seek Rabbinic leadership. JRF growth was gradual through the 1970s under the leadership of Eisenstein and Rabbi Ludwig Nadelmann. Then, in 1982, under the direction of Rabbis David Teutsch and Mordechai Liebling, it developed as an independent organization that has expanded rapidly, doubling in size in five years and growing at a rate of 20% each year in the mid-1990s.

Beginning in 1989, the JRF began to publish *Kol Haneshamah*, a series of prayer books for Sabbath and festivals, home ceremonies, daily services, and the High Holy Days. Teutsch served as editor of the series, whose decision-making Prayer Book Commission included, notably, a balance of rabbis and Reconstructionist lay leaders. Designed to be used by Jews who do not have strong traditional backgrounds and are in the process of re-embracing ritual practice, the series includes transliterations of all Hebrew that is customarily sung, extensive commentaries about the meaning of the prayers, and a new gender-neutral, contemporary translation by poet Joel Rosenberg. It also includes a variety of suggestions about how to modify the Hebrew text to avoid exclusively masculine God-language. Whereas the first series of Kaplan-edited prayer books explained revisions of the text only in the introduction, *Kol Haneshamah* places those explanations below the line on the same page and sometimes includes the traditional wording as an option. This reflects an increasingly diverse attitude towards ritual practice. The result of the series' approach to prayer is that these prayer books have been warmly received not only by Reconstructionist congregations but by many unaffiliated synagogues, campus foundations, and communal organizations.

The Reconstructionist Rabbinical College (RRC) was founded in Philadelphia in 1968 by Eisenstein, who served through 1981 as its first president (fig. 116). The decision to establish a rabbinical program was made by those who despaired about the possibility of influencing the other movements and who felt the need to cultivate an indigenous Reconstructionist leadership. It marked a decisive turning point that has led to the subsequent growth of Re-constructionist Judaism as a movement. The College's charter articulates its dual mission: to ordain rabbis to lead in the synagogues of the Reconstructionist movement and to serve the greater Jewish community in other settings: as campus rabbis, chaplains, academics, educators, and professionals in Jewish communal organizations.

Its core curriculum reflects the Reconstructionist view of Judaism as the evolving religious civilization of the Jewish people, with each of the five years devoted to a study of the texts, thought, history, and culture of a particular period: biblical, Rabbinic, medieval, modern, and contemporary. Thus, students study texts, beliefs, and practices in their historical contexts and through their ongoing evolution, on the premise that this will better prepare them to lead Jews in the continuing evolution and reconstruction of Jewish life. Students also thus acquire an intense empathy with their forebears, whose responses to perennial questions, understood in historical context, speak directly to contemporary challenges.

Committed to providing rabbis who will serve wherever Jews congregate, not exclusively in synagogues, the RRC's Practical Rabbinics curriculum offers specialized training for those who intend to serve in the campus rabbinate, chaplaincy, Jewish communal organizations, and education. The RRC has been a pioneer among rabbinical training programs in the excellence and sophistication of its professional training in such areas as counseling, administration, group work, and outreach.

The education of Reconstructionist rabbis extends beyond the curriculum to the community of RRC students and faculty, which is meant to model the communities the rabbis will serve after ordination. Decision-making power is shared with students, experimentation with re-interpreted practices and beliefs is encouraged, and community observances and celebrations are promoted. RRC graduates are thus trained to be open, welcoming leaders with a deep respect for Jewish diversity and with the expectation that vital communities are created when individuals are encouraged to find their own way while engaged in communal study and decision making.

By the mid-1990s, the movement's rate of growth exceeded the College's ability to provide Rabbinic leaders. A 1996 demographic study of members of JRF affiliates revealed that they join Reconstructionist congregations because the quality of JRF adult education programs allows them to deepen their levels of Jewish study and practice and because of the communities' warmth, gender equality, and embrace of new members. Most respondents indicated that their level of ritual practice was greater than that of their parents; over one-third observed kashrut, an extraordinary percentage, significantly higher than in other non-Orthodox movements.

The Reconstructionist Rabbinical Association (RRA) was founded in 1974 by RRC alumni. In 1997, its membership approaches 250 and includes like-minded graduates of other rabbinical seminaries. The RRA has pioneered in its conversion, divorce, intermarriage, and professional ethics guidelines, has taken a leadership role in the movement, and is now a voice heard clearly on the North American and international Jewish scene.

**Reconstructionist approaches to Jewish belief—Evolving civilization:** The starting point of Kaplan's approach to Judaism was the insight that Judaism is an evolving civilization, and this has remained central to Reconstructionist Judaism. This perspective acknowledges that Jewish civilization in all of its facets has developed and changed throughout the generations, as the Jewish people has adapted to ever new challenges: external cultural developments that influenced the thinking and customs of Jews; political developments that necessitated changes in the governance of Jewish communities and their notions of authority; social developments that altered Jews' views of women, family, slaves, and non-Jews; and religious developments that led to new forms of religious and spiritual practice. This recognition of evolution runs contrary to the traditional Jewish assertion that the Torah was divinely revealed at Sinai and that all subsequent interpretations were contained in that original revelation.

The Reconstructionist approach, by contrast, fundamentally embraces the perspective of the modern historian and social scientist and transforms the relationship of the contemporary Jew to the Jewish heritage. Inherited laws and practices are no longer seen as being literally the commandments of God and therefore authoritative, but, rather, as the accumulated wisdom of generations of Jewish communities that pursued lives of sanctity and justice, permeated by ultimate meaning. Jewish texts and traditions are therefore invaluable treasures, but they reflect, by necessity, the human and historical limitations of prior generations. The evolution must continue, and every generation has the obligation to reconstruct.

**Civilization:** Reconstructionists affirm that, much more than a religion, Judaism is the civilization of the Jewish people. It has always included far more than religious faith and ritual practice: languages, art, music, foods, community structures, social services, sacred study, folk practices. Jewish civilization has flourished through the centuries because it has been an all-embracing way of life, fostered in autonomously governed Jewish communities. Every aspect of Jewish communal culture immersed Jews in a structure of symbolic meaning that implicitly and subliminally reinforced the community's values.

When Kaplan began to write, all of the North American Jewish movements had imitated the Protestant Christian separation of religious Christianity from secular culture, redefining Judaism as a religion, with its primary sphere confined to the synagogue. In this way, the movements legitimated Jews' equal participation in western society. But Reconstructionists fear that, because Jewish identity has always been an outgrowth of Jews' participation in the fullness of Jewish civilization, the conceptualization of Judaism as exclusively a religion will prove an insurmountable obstacle to Jewish survival. A Judaism that is reduced to a belief in God, ritual practice, and moral behavior is not capable of being transmitted organically across generations. Reconstructionist Judaism therefore defines Judaism as a religious civilization and expands the scope of Jewish communities beyond ritual, to include, for example, the full range of cultural programs, support systems that involve members in each other's lives in times of need, ethical decision making that dares to challenge members, and social action based on Jewish study.

**Peoplehood:** If every facet of Jewish civilization is viewed as evolving, the constant that provides for continuity across the centuries and within a generation is, in the Reconstructionist view, the Jewish people itself. We cannot claim that Isaiah's belief about God was identical to that of Maimonides or the Baal Shem Tov, or that the text of our prayers dates back unchanged to the period of the Second Temple. All that is constant in Jewish civilization is the Jewish people,

which has weathered the centuries and remains the source of everything Jewish. Even in the people's encounters with God's presence, the message heard and commandments received are best understood as human refractions of divine imperatives, reflecting the social, cultural, and historical context of the people involved in the encounters.

The primacy of peoplehood is reflected in the Reconstructionist belief that belonging is prior to belief or behavior. Beliefs and behaviors emerge from the context of a community in whose culture one is immersed and from which one internalizes the narratives in which values are imbedded. Before the modern era, this acculturation occurred naturally, as Jews lived in Jewish communities. Reconstructionists seek to create new forms of Jewish community that can function similarly today. Unless Jews belong to functioning communities, they are not likely to internalize Jewish beliefs or values or to find Jewish ritual and culture meaningful.

**Need for reconstruction:** In the view of Reconstructionism, Jewish civilization has always evolved as successive generations of Jews have adapted to unprecedented circumstances, and that evolution must continue today if the Jewish people is to survive. The current challenge, however, is more formidable than ever, because of the radical dislocations in Jewish life caused by the enlightenment, political emancipation, and the technological revolution. Prior to 1800, Jews lived in autonomous Jewish communities, granted sovereignty by Muslim and Christian rulers to govern their members in accordance with Jewish law. People were born into Jewish communities that established enforceable norms and provided a full range of social, economic, educational, and cultural services, for which there were no alternatives. Jews had no choice, short of apostasy, but to live as members of the Jewish community. Moreover, for thirteen centuries, the competing surrounding cultures were of a piece with traditional Judaism in their assertions of a divinely revealed Scripture, a divinely commanded way of life, the primacy of religion, the authority of the clergy, the existence of a God who intervenes supernaturally to reward and punish, and the promise of an other-worldly recompense for one's deeds in this life.

Kaplan was the first to observe that the Jewish crisis of modernity is a direct result of the loss of these social and cultural circumstances. Socially, since the beginning of the nineteenth century, Jews in various places have undergone political emancipation that has granted them citizenship as individuals in their nations of residence. They participate fully in the surrounding society and thus now have a choice their ancestors lacked about whether and how to identify and participate as Jews. Jewish law is no longer the law by which they are governed, and it is therefore no longer functional as a legal system. A new mode for establishing community norms accordingly is needed, one that does not depend on the authority of Rabbinic decisions.

Additionally, the predominant world view in the societies in which Jews now live is no longer supportive of traditional Jewish teachings. In its belief in natural causes, modern science undercuts traditional supernaturalism. The primacy of individual autonomy conflicts with the traditional virtue of obedience to commandments and communal norms. The teachings of democracy make Jews reluctant to have decisions made by those with the authority of Halakhic learning. Ecumenicism invalidates traditional notions of separatism and chosenness. Secularism renders counter-intuitive the traditional view that God's presence is everywhere. In this setting, with Jews fully integrated into their surrounding cultures, Reconstructionists seek to reconstruct traditional teachings so that they can continue to influence Jews' hearts and minds.

**Theology:** Beginning with Kaplan, Reconstructionists have constructed a naturalist or transnaturalist theology, reinterpreting the traditional personal and supernatural images of God as a person who governs history, aware of the details of our lives, intervening supernaturally in human affairs to reward and punish us. ("Transnaturalism" is a naturalism that assumes that God is greater than the sum of natural principles in which God is manifest.) Supernaturalism has been regarded as a vestige of the pre-modern era, when Jews,

Muslims, and Christians alike shared a belief in the reality of miracles and differed only with regard to which miracles had in fact occurred. Living after the scientific revolution, when everyday life has been secularized and people believe in the causation of nature, Reconstructionists have sought to rescue religious faith from being discarded as entirely irrelevant.

Kaplan defined God as a Power or a Process inherent in the universe that makes for salvation or human fulfillment. In this, he was influenced by such process theologians as Alfred North Whitehead, who identified God as the impersonal Sum of the totality of forces in the world. He was also influenced by the Pragmatism of John Dewey, and, thus, more than on the nature of God, he focused on how a person's belief affects the way he or she lives.

Reconstructionists' belief in God has been questioned by those who affirm more conventional conceptions of God and think that in denying God's supernatural power, Reconstructionists are denying the existence of God altogether. Reconstructionists have been emphatic, however, in their insistence that they experience the reality of God's presence in the world and in their lives. Both in his writings and in his life, Kaplan possessed a passionate faith in the existence of an impersonal God-Force, not identical with nature, that is the source of the human impulse to virtue. His god, however—like that of such medieval Jewish philosophers as Maimonides—does not intervene supernaturally to reward and punish. God rather underlies all of existence, serving as a source of energy and inspiration to those who seek divine ends. The human impulse, he argued, to act with justice or love, for example, or to build community or fight for freedom, stems from God, and not meaninglessly from laws of nature. When people transcend self-interest and act nobly, when they act to realize their potential, they are partners with God in revealing the otherwise hidden divine presence in the world.

Rabbi Harold Schulweis, a disciple of Kaplan, articulated what he calls Predicate Theology, which has been very influential among Reconstructionists. Schulweis argues that we cannot know what God is as Subject. Such knowledge is beyond the human ability to know. What we can know is *when* God is present. We can't know that God is just, for example, but we can know that justice is divine. Thus, when we act justly or we witness justice, we experience the presence of God. In this way, our quest for faith focuses not on the unanswerable questions relating to the definition of God as Subject but rather on the ways in which we can live to make God's presence manifest in our lives.

In many important ways, this theological approach resembles the teachings of Maimonides and other classical medieval Jewish philosophers. Maimonides believed that we can know nothing about God's essence and that the only legitimate, non-idolatrous things we can say positively about God derive from our observation of the effects of God's causation in the world of creation—what he called God's "attributes of action." Thus, when we affirm that God is a healer, for example, that means that the effects of God's causation are such that, if God were a human being, we would call that person a healer—and not that God in God's essence resembles, in any way, a human healer. In other words, we can know only that the world is created such that God's presence is made manifest in healing. But God is so absolutely other from the world of creation that any literal association of God's attributes with the characteristics of creatures, in Maimonides' view, is tantamount to idolatry.

The Reconstructionist approach to God is therefore not as radical or unprecedented as it may first appear. As the fields of the anthropology of religion and, more recently, post-modern hermeneutics have developed, Reconstructionists have grown more comfortable affirming the transformative power of the myths and symbols of traditional Jewish prayer and Rabbinic theology—even as they remain naturalists. Kaplan is now seen as having been limited by the tools of social science available to him in his day, so that his descriptions of the function of symbols and rituals, for example, following such sociologists as Emile Durkheim, were confined to analyses of the way they built community. While his ritual practice was extremely traditional and he worshipped with great fervor, he did not have the vocabulary of mythic power and spirituality that are available to non-supernaturalists today.

**Ritual practice:** The Reconstructionist view of God rejects the traditional belief that the Torah and its subsequent reinterpretations are literally revealed by God. Therefore, the mitzvot are not literally divine commandments reflecting the will of God, and Jews are not rewarded or punished for their level of observance. Nevertheless, Reconstructionists affirm ritual observance as an essential component of Jewish identity and life.

The rationale for ritual practice derives directly from the definition of Judaism as a civilization. Jewish civilization is the cumulative result of the collective quest of successive generations of Jews to pursue lives of sanctity and ultimate meaning. The only way to gain access to that wisdom is to study Jewish texts and enter into the symbolic world of Jewish practice and celebration. In this way, we can live in Jewish time and see the world through Jewish lenses. The insights and values of previous generations cannot be acquired by reading descriptions of what they believed, but, rather, by having one's sense of God's presence transformed by reciting traditional blessings throughout the day, for example, or altering one's sense of time and priorities by viewing each day in relation to the Sabbath. Indeed, if Judaism is a civilization, the dichotomy commonly made between ritual practice and ethical behavior is false. Religious insights have ethical correlatives, and ethical norms emerge out of communal narratives transmitted subliminally through ritual observance and celebration. The greater one's immersion in ritual practice, the greater one's access to cultural, psychological, and spiritual treasures that are largely absent from secular western culture.

Hence the apparent disparity between the progressive thinking of Reconstructionists and their apparently traditional practice. The format of the worship services of many Reconstructionist congregations is traditional. Hebrew prayers predominate, and they are sung and chanted with great fervor. All of this reflects the conviction that inherited texts, as well as sacred objects and observances, are the most powerful points of access to the Jewish universe, perhaps the only way for contemporary Jews to avoid being cut off from the pre-modern Jewish world that presents itself as an extraordinarily foreign culture.

The fact that one does not believe that God is literally aware of one's every action need not prevent one from experiencing life through a symbol system expressed by a ritual discipline that emphasizes God's presence. In fact, Reconstructionists would argue that an authentic reconstruction of the traditional meaning of ritual practices depends exactly on such an immersion. The goal is to understand the meaning of inherited practices in a contemporary idiom that is equivalent, in our universe, to the meaning that traditional supernatural intentions (kavvanot) carried in the universe of discourse of previous generations. The story of the Exodus from Egypt re-enacted at the Passover Seder, for example, carries with it the value of freedom, which, in another time, meant the hope for a miraculous divine redemption from oppressive exile. That same re-enactment today continues to serve as a powerful experience of the value of freedom, but interpreted differently: a resolve to work for the rescue of oppressed Jewish communities; a commitment to the struggle against the oppression of all peoples; an opportunity to reflect upon the way you, yourself, are enslaved in your personal life.

Much is worthy of recovery among inherited Jewish traditions, and Reconstructionists believe that traditional practices should not be changed as long as they can be redeemed through reinterpretation of their meaning. There also are, however, many practices that require reconstruction because the values they convey are beyond redemption, from the point of view of the highest values of the contemporary Jewish community. Within the Reconstructionist movement, there is and will always be a great deal of disagreement about when this line is crossed. The drawback of discarding or revising a ritual practice that appears morally objectionable is that one may be blinded by one's own cultural and historical biases from noticing nuances of meaning that might open up realms of insight and experience. That is why the movement is perpetually rediscovering rituals that were once ignored.

Nevertheless, on key points, there is agreement about the need for change. The moral imperative of gender equality is illustrative. Since Kaplan introduced the first bat mitzvah ceremony for his eldest daughter, Judith, in 1922, Reconstructionists have been committed to full gender equality, including women in all the roles and practices from which they have been excluded traditionally by Jewish law (fig. 117). The RRC has admitted women into its Rabbinical program since its founding in 1968. The wedding ceremony has been equalized, and divorces have been transformed so that each partner has an equal role.

With few exceptions, one of which is gender equality, most ritual decisions are left to individual communities. Members of communities engage in a process of collective study of traditional sources and ta'amei ha-mitzvot (rationales for practice), eventually reaching agreement about norms for public practice. The role of the rabbi in this process is to share his or her knowledge, leading participants first in Torah study that provides an intimate level of acquaintance with the voices of the past, and then through an exploration of their own values and the extent to which they may be deepened by inherited Jewish perspectives. In the end, however, the rabbi does not serve as an authoritative halakhic decisor. The community of lay participants reaches its own informed conclusions. Philosophically, this participatory decision-making process reflects the Reconstructionist commitment to the very un-traditional value of democracy. Strategically, it leads Jews to a commitment to Jewish study and practice that is not be achieved when the rabbi makes the decision for the community.

The ritual practice of individuals in Reconstructionist communities varies widely, reflecting members' diverse backgrounds. While one of the ultimate objectives of a Reconstructionist community is to encourage and support its members through a journey of ongoing experimentation with increasing ritual practice that will intensify their immersion in Jewish civilization, it is central to the Reconstructionist approach that members are not judged for what they do and don't observe ritually. There is, after all, no claim that God has literally commanded us to observe these practices. Rather, members are more likely to be supported by one another in their diversity, and to learn from one another in non-coercive ways. When communities function effectively, their members gradually internalize their overt and implicit values.

**Prayer:** Given the Reconstructionist understanding of God, there is no question of prayer's serving as a direct petition with the hope for a response from a God who is listening. Worship services are nevertheless central to the life of most Reconstructionist communities. A list of some of the reasons Reconstructionists pray also exemplifies Reconstructionism's revaluation of traditional ritual forms:

*Spiritual discipline.* Most Jews might go through the day without experiencing God's presence. A spiritual sense is a faculty that must be developed and maintained. Focusing regularly on our sacred encounters helps us to notice them as they occur.

*Meditation.* Living at a very rapid pace, people welcome the opportunity to slow down to remember what has deeper meaning beyond our daily distractions.

*Group connection.* Our daily lives rarely afford opportunities to let our guard down and express what is really important. People want to be connected to a group, all of whom are seeking together.

*Celebration.* Given the individualism and privatism of the general culture, group worship and song provides an all-too-rare opportunity to express, uninhibited, the joys of living.

*Group support.* Similarly, our lives are filled with disappointment, illness, and tragedy. People need the support of a caring group to cope with and recover from family discord, depression, and physical illness. Many Reconstructionists believe praying for a sick person is efficacious even though they don't believe God intercedes supernaturally.

*Rededication to principles.* It is easy to lose perspective, to lose sight of who you are and what you stand for. Praying draws one out and restores the larger picture.

*Acknowledgment of need.* At the end of the twentieth century, most people are raised to think they have control of their lives and, therefore, are responsible for what happens to themselves—good or bad. Prayer allows us to ask for help, admitting we need help, that we are frightened, overwhelmed, or desperate. Removing our defenses before God can move us to the honest self-awareness we require to get past our personal obstacles.

In the best of circumstances, individual worshippers grow in their familiarity with the structure and meaning of the traditional worship service—by regular participation, through study in classes, or by means of the commentaries provided in the *Kol Haneshamah* prayer books. The yearnings and emotions expressed in the traditional fixed prayers and contemporary readings that accompany them serve as particularly effective mnemonics, infused with the sacred power of their history, to lead the worshipper in all of the above directions.

In addition, Reconstructionist services are often enriched by spirited singing and dancing, contemporary poetry, guided meditation, and chanting. The overwhelming majority of North American Jews initially approach the traditional prayerbook as a mystifying and intimidating text that reminds them of many of the reasons they feel alienated from their Jewish identity. To re-open the closed book, Reconstructionist communities are committed to a variety of innovative media.

**The Chosen People:** Among the most controversial hallmarks of Reconstructionist Judaism is its rejection of the traditional claim that the Jews are the Chosen People. Theologically, the Reconstructionist view follows directly from an understanding of God in naturalistic terms. If God does not govern and intervene in human affairs, God could neither have chosen the Jewish people from among all others nor revealed the Torah.

In light of this perspective, Reconstructionists have altered the blessing Jews recite when called up to the Torah, from "Blessed are you, Lord our God . . . who has chosen us from among all peoples" to "Blessed are you, Lord our God . . . who has brought us near to God's service." Other related changes include the elimination from the *Alenu*, which concludes all worship services, of the words thanking God, "Who has not made us like the nations of the land," and the excision of the reference to "God's people, Israel" from the blessing recited prior to the chanting of the Haftarah.

These liturgical changes and the Reconstructionist insistence on the rejection of the doctrine of chosenness provide a revealing example of how and when the ritual is changed. In many other instances, by contrast, ritual is left in its traditional form and given a new meaning. For instance, the God who could not have chosen Israel also could not "love His [sic] people Israel" or be "the Redeemer of Israel." Yet these phrases have not been rewritten, and the Reconstructionist prayer book indeed is replete with such traditional liturgical language, which the worshipper is expected to reconceptualize to correspond to Reconstructionist theology.

Thus, it is primarily references to Israel's exclusive relationship to God that have been revised or removed, and this is because of the objectionable ethical value they convey, particularly when transposed into a naturalistic key. In traditional Jewish teaching, the doctrine of the Chosen People emphasized the superiority of Torah rather than the distinctiveness of Jews. Jews were not seen as intrinsically better that non-Jews; they had a special relationship with God only because they followed the commandments and lived a life of Torah. In the Jewish world today, however, in which the overwhelming majority of Jews do not believe literally in the revelation of the Torah at Sinai or in the binding nature of the commandments, the doctrine of chosenness becomes, in the Reconstructionist view, a chauvinistic, often racist, affirmation that Jews—no matter how they act—are closer to God than other people.

Reconstructionists believe instead that all peoples and civilizations have equal access to the divine and that each, like Judaism, should be encouraged to evolve in ways that approximate the divine will more closely. Jews are not privileged by birth or genetic heritage, and the teachings of Jewish civilization are not infallible. While much in the Jewish heritage leads us to live according to the noblest values, much needs reconstruction. Similarly, other civilizations and religions have both admirable and unfortunate teachings and practices. Following Kaplan's description of Judaism as "the religion of ethical nationhood," Reconstructionists seek to influence other peoples not by claiming superiority but by modeling ethical and spiritual values. They affirm their commitment to Judaism because it is their heritage, even though they view aspects of that heritage critically.

**Living in two civilizations:** Reconstructionists part ways with those who lament the corrosive effects of political emancipation on Jewish life. While noting the problems, they embrace the political culture of western democracy as a welcome advance over a past in which Jews lived in forced segregation. They believe the modern west has much to offer Jews in the enterprise of reconstructing Jewish civilization in accord with democratic values and that working for a vital Jewish community is entirely in harmony with the goals of pluralism.

Kaplan was entirely at peace with the fact that Jews in western democracies live primarily in the civilization of their surrounding cultures and only secondarily in Jewish civilization. For him, the best of American and Jewish values coincide, and he developed liturgies for celebrations of American civil religion.[1] He was outspoken in his criticism of capitalism, for example, but he believed that Jews, working with other peoples, could effect a transformation of the culture of the United States so that its noblest ideals could be realized. More recently, the Reconstructionist embrace of American culture has been less optimistic. The values of democracy are affirmed even as Reconstructionists work to correct the insidious effects of American secularism, materialism, and individualism upon Jewish values and practices.

**A new Zionism:** Kaplan's definition of Judaism as a civilization led him and his early disciples to an emphatic advocacy of Zionism long before most other American Jewish leaders. If Jews in the U.S. lived in two civilizations, where the primary civilization was inevitably American and the Jewish one only secondary, he embraced the resettlement of Palestine as a welcome opportunity for Jews to live in a society in which Jewish civilization was primary. Only there could a full reconstruction of the totality of Jewish civilization be achieved according to modern, democratic values and a renaissance of Jewish culture come to pass. Kaplan was a fervent Hebraist, and he seriously contemplated making *aliyah*.

Kaplan was heavily influenced by Ahad Ha'am, the champion of Cultural Zionism who was less concerned about political independence than about the opportunities presented by the *Yishuv* (the pre-state Jewish community in Palestine) for a Jewish cultural renaissance unimpeded by the disabilities of the diaspora mentality. Following Ahad Ha'am, Kaplan conceived of the Jewish world as a wheel in which Jews in Palestine (and after 1948, Israel) are at the center, connected by Jewish "spokes" to Jews around the world. The latter, living in two civilizations, gain cultural and spiritual sustenance from the one community in which Jewish civilization is primary.

Despite the early leadership of Reconstructionists in the pre-state Zionist movement, Reconstructionist Judaism did not establish an institutional presence in Israel during the first decades of statehood, at least until the movement joined the World Union for Progressive Judaism in the 1980s. This was due, in part, to a lack of resources when the movement was in the early stages of growth in the U.S. and, in part, to the conviction that Reconstructionist Judaism is a North American phenomenon that cannot be transplanted to Israeli society without significant modification. Much of the Reconstructionist program in North America—the emphasis on culture and community, for example—exists naturally in Israeli society.

The other component of Reconstructionist Judaism—the revitalization of Jewish religious and spiritual life in accordance with contemporary naturalist and democratic values—did not speak for many decades to an Israeli society in which the religious

lines were divided clearly between Orthodox and secular Jews. Beginning in the 1990s, however, responding to the new interest of non-Orthodox Israeli Jews in tradition and spirituality, the Reconstructionist movement has initiated outreach efforts in Israel.

**Community:** The ultimate success of the Reconstructionist approach to Judaism depends upon its emphasis on the centrality of community. If, as Reconstructionists believe, Judaism is a religious civilization that has evolved organically in the daily lives of generations of Jewish communities, then, for the evolution to continue, the breakdown of those communities after the political emancipation of the Jews in the nineteenth century must be effectively addressed. Jews no longer live in Jewish communities governed by Jewish law. They are no longer educated in Jewish languages and texts. They no longer depend on social services provided by the Jewish community. In fact, their decision to affiliate Jewishly at all is voluntary, just as they are free whenever it suits them to leave communities they have joined. Complicating the challenge yet further is contemporary western culture's dominant emphasis on autonomy and individualism.

Reconstructionism responds by fostering development of small communal units in which members become deeply involved. Since about 1960, most affiliated groups have begun as participatory, lay-led *havurot* for study, worship, and celebration. To promote close community, during worship services chairs often are arranged in a circle or semicircle. Services often are led by lay members, who also take turns reading Torah, teaching classes, and delivering homilies. Reconstructionist rabbis work to foster an environment in which the maximum number of members are able actively to participate in the service and lead the congregation. This is encouraged, of course, by the process of participatory decision making described above.

As groups grow into larger congregations, participation and intimacy remain preeminent values. This has led to careful thinking about lay-Rabbinic relations and democratic governance and to the development of support systems within congregations, in which members help one another in times of need—in coping with illness, in parenting teenagers or caring for elderly parents, in finding employment, etc.[2] Under David Teutsch's leadership in the early 1980s, the JRF developed a process for democratic, movement-wide decision making. Each affiliated group discusses an issue and sends delegates to the annual convention, where decisions are made by majority vote. There has thus been much success in increasing the commitments of members and heightening their involvement in the study and thinking required by decision-making processes at the local and movement-wide levels. To the extent that Jews become intensely involved in the lives of Jewish communities, the practices and values of those communities are effectively transmitted.

In recent years, Reconstructionists have also begun to adopt the approach of communitarian theorists and to speak the language of obligation. That is, when individuals become seriously involved in communities they have voluntarily joined, they become responsible to follow the decisions of the community, both those related to communal policy and those related to ethical and ritual norms. The obligations derives neither from a belief in divine commandment nor from the community's ability to act coercively. Rather, they derive from the community's ethos, which creates a culture of expectations.

To be sure, all of this takes place in the context of an affirmation of diversity with regard to religious belief and ritual practice—and in the context of the autonomy of each community to reach decisions independent of movement-wide policies. The movement's statements of policy on key issues, which are written by lay-Rabbinic commissions, are issued in the form of Guidelines that are based on the study of traditional and contemporary texts and that elaborate the values and issues with which each community should struggle on its own. Nevertheless, in such areas as the expectation that community members participate in programs, services, and on committees, and in the affirmation of ethical principles, the communitarian ideal is often realized.

**Feminism:** In recent decades, the Reconstructionist movement has moved beyond its earlier affirmation of the equality of men and women in all areas of Jewish life. Based on advances in the fields of feminist theory, social history, and women's history, the original Kaplanian analysis of the evolution of Jewish civilization has been expanded. The traditional Jewish heritage, transmitted by successive generations of rabbis, is now seen as a very selective and incomplete representation of the totality of the experience of the Jewish people through the ages. The direct voices of the majority of Jewish men and all Jewish women are silent.

In response, Reconstructionists have advanced on a number of fronts. In the area of Jewish history, they utilize contemporary academic methods to rediscover previously ignored traces of the experiences of Jewish women, thereby to reconstruct Jewish women's history. Where no such traces are recoverable, they remain acutely aware that when "Jews" are described, it is really Jewish men, not women, who are under discussion. This problem has been addressed in part, since the 1970s, by the creation of many new rituals to mark previously ignored passages in women's lives. KOLOT, the Center for Jewish Women's and Gender Studies at the RRC, maintains an ever growing file of such rituals, which it makes available to the Jewish community.

In the liturgy, within the *Amidah*, the matriarchs are named as well as the patriarchs, and, in general, the English translation in the *Kol Haneshamah* prayer book series is gender-neutral. The Hebrew includes much experimentation with the use of feminine grammatical forms to refer to God alongside the traditional masculine ones. Similarly, the traditional masculine images and names of God are supplemented by feminine ones—*ru'ah ha'olam* ("spirit of the universe") for *melekh ha'olam* ("king of the universe"), for example, or *Shekhinah* ("Presence") for *Adonai* ("Lord"). Reconstructionists do not believe God is more accurately described as feminine than masculine. Rather, since all images are understood metaphorically, there is a sensitivity to the negative, idolatrous impact of becoming attached to one set of metaphors rather than another.

Theologically, the movement is now engaged in a full-fledged exploration of the ways in which the very structure of the Jewish heritage reflects an exclusively male, and thus partial, perspective on the experience of God and system of Jewish values. How would the story of the Binding of Isaac (Gen. 22) read if it had been told from Sarah's point of view? How would the Jewish experience of God be different if God had been portrayed as a nursing mother rather than a jealous husband, or as the builder of relationships rather than the creator of hierarchies? How would the customs of the Jewish holidays have been different if they hadn't been intended for men who depended on the support of women excluded from those customs?

Such questions are now addressed in Reconstructionist circles in weekly discussions of the Torah portion, monthly *Rosh Hodesh* groups (women's gatherings at the beginning of each lunar month), and through the composition of new midrashim. The application of feminist insights to Jewish civilization has unleashed an extraordinary amount of enthusiasm and commitment from women and men previously alienated by Judaism's patriarchal form.

**Ethics:** Kaplan coined the phrase "The Religion of Ethical Nationhood" to describe his conviction that Jewish civilization's greatest contribution to the betterment of humankind is in the realm of ethics. Accordingly, his revaluations of Jewish rituals generally located the core ethical value each of them expressed and judged every theological formulation in terms of the ethical behavior of its proponents. Schulweis's Predicate Theology similarly locates God's presence in the manifestation of ethical values. In Kaplan's grand but unrealized vision of a reconstituted Jewish community, he yearned for the creation of communities of Jewish business persons who would develop and adhere to a Jewish system of business ethics, of Jewish physicians who would formulate a Jewish system of medical ethics, and so on.

In place of Kaplan's vision of an organic Jewish community, Reconstructionists are now seriously engaged in articulating a new Jewish ethics that extracts from traditional sources core values that can be applied to contemporary ethical dilemmas. The Center for Jewish Ethics at the RRC is now publishing a comprehensive series of adult education curricula on the Ethics of Speech, Business Ethics, Biomedical Ethics, Sexual Ethics, and other areas, designed to be used by study groups of lay Jews. Each module collects the traditional sources and raises issues for contemporary discussion, with the goal of immersing Jews in a process of making ethical choices in the context of struggling with the wisdom of inherited texts.

**Social justice:** From its earliest days, the editorials and articles of the *Reconstructionist* assumed a progressive political stance, in which Kaplan and his early followers spoke out forcefully against the excesses of capitalism and in favor of labor and unionization. That heritage continues today. In the last two decades, the Reconstructionist movement has led on such issues as the Middle East peace process, the nuclear freeze, Judaism and the environment, creating sanctuaries for Central American refugees, and protesting the genocide in Bosnia. JRF communities remain committed to the principle that the social activism of their members ought to take place in a Jewish context, informed by Jewish study and Jewish values. As the politics of the American Jewish community as a whole has become less liberal, Reconstructionist progressive commitments have remained firm.

**Outreach and inclusion:** The recent growth of the movement reflects its commitment to establishing communities that welcome Jews searching seriously for a Jewish home who have previously felt excluded or alienated. Initial Jewish ignorance is no barrier, so long as there is an ongoing commitment to Jewish learning. Hebrew is taught, and prayers and rituals are offered as means to gain access to the spiritual treasures of Jewish civilization, without the expectation of familiarity or prior commitment to observance. Questions and doubts are welcome, and communities measure their effectiveness by the degree to which they are able to address their members in their diversity.

What members share in common is a commitment to learning and participation.

The pioneering work of the movement in the inclusion of women serves as a model for its approach to other previously excluded groups. In 1982, the RRA passed a set of Guidelines on Intermarriage that recognized that Jews who marry non-Jews do not thereby signal their desire to abandon their Jewish heritage. Often enough, rather, their choice of spouse moves them back into the Jewish orbit. It also recognized that the likelihood of the non-Jewish partner's subsequent choice of Judaism increases dramatically when the couple becomes involved in a Jewish community. Intermarried households have since been welcomed without prejudice, with non-Jewish partners honored for supporting their Jewish families. While achieving a balance between welcome and maintaining boundaries is always challenging, the effect of the effort has been to provide a Jewish communal home for countless Jews and their children who might otherwise have been lost to the Jewish people. In 1997, a JRF Commission on the Role of the Non-Jew published a set of Guidelines designed to assist local communities in addressing these challenges.

As early as 1968, the JRF voted to recognize as Jewish the children of a Jewish father and a non-Jewish mother who are raised as Jews. Patrilineal descent was affirmed by the RRA in 1978. In part, the decision was made on the basis of a commitment to gender equality—in this instance, the tradition privileged the mother over the father. More broadly, the policy was justified as an attempt to address a yawning disparity between the law and reality. In other periods of Jewish history, children could reasonably be assumed to adopt the religion of their mother. But this assumption no longer corresponds to the facts, and a law that requires the conversion of a child who is living a Jewish life is counterproductive. The policy has been assailed as threatening the unity of the Jewish people, and many within the movement therefore have hesitated to embrace it. The fact that conversions under Reconstructionist (or any non-Orthodox) auspices are not recognized in the Orthodox world, however, bolsters the argument that it is not Reconstructionist Judaism that is responsible for splintering the Jewish people.

In 1984, the RRC instituted a non-discrimination policy for admitting rabbinical students who are openly gay or lesbian. In 1992, a movement-wide Commission on Homosexuality concluded its deliberations by publishing guidelines that committed JRF communities to the ideal of becoming "welcoming communities," in which lesbian and gay Jews can find a comfortable home. The Commission made its case on the basis of traditional Jewish core values that overrode, in its argument, the historically limited and ethically objectionable assumptions on which Jewish law has traditionally been based. These policies have led lesbian and gay Jews to find their way back to the Jewish community and also have empowered people who were already members to acknowledge their own sexual orientation or that of their children and relatives. Communities' courses of study on the issue of sexual orientation have dispelled preconceptions and gone a long way to overcoming homophobia. Most transformative, however, has been the effect on communities of the participation of serious, committed Jews who are openly gay.

**Future outlook:** There is every reason to expect that the current rapid growth of the Reconstructionist movement will continue for the foreseeable future. At a time when the majority of Jews in the U.S. is unaffiliated, Reconstructionist Judaism is clearly appealing to a segment of the population that has not been satisfied elsewhere. The movement's institutional base has become much more stable in recent years with the growth of its financial support and the tripling of the RRC endowment. Moreover, if the trend revealed in the 1996 demographic survey, which shows that movement members are more Jewishly educated and observant than their parents, continues to hold true, Reconstructionist communities clearly will remain pockets of Jewish energy that defy the current weakening of Jewish life in North America.

If the movement's prospects are evaluated on the basis of its own theory, however, then its chief challenge will continue to be to overcome the predominance of personal autonomy as a supreme value. Only then can it succeed in the formation of cohesive, though voluntaristic, communities to which members feel responsible and in which they engage in meaningful Jewish study, worship, ritual practice, and ethical decision making.

### Bibliography

Alpert, Rebecca T., and Jacob J. Staub, *Exploring Judaism: A Reconstructionist Approach* (New York, 1985).

Goldsmith, Emanuel S., Mel Scult, and Robert M. Seltzer, eds., *The American Judaism of Mordecai M. Kaplan* (New York, 1990).

Goldsmith, Emanuel S., and Mel Scult, eds., *Dynamic Judaism: The Essential Writings of Mordecai M. Kaplan* (New York, 1985).

Scult, Mel, *Judaism Faces the Twentieth Century: A Biography of Mordecai M. Kaplan* (Detroit, 1993).

Teutsch, David, ed., *Kol Haneshamah* (Wyncote, 1998).

### Notes

[1] See Mordecai M. Kaplan, ed., *The Faith of America* (New York, 1951).

[2] On these matters, see Sidney H. Schwarz, "Operating Principles for Reconstructionist Synagogues," in *Reconstructionist* 53/4 (1988), pp. 28-31, 34, and Harriet Feiner, "The Synagogue As Support System," in *Reconstructionist* 50/4 (1985), pp. 25-30.

JACOB J. STAUB

**REFORM JUDAISM:** Reform Judaism, also known as Liberal or Progressive Judaism, sets forth a Judaic religious system that takes as its critical task the accommodation of Judaism to political changes in the status of the Jews from the late eighteenth century onward. These changes, particularly in Western Europe and the USA, accorded to Jews the status of citizens like other citizens of the nations in which they lived. But they denied the Jews the status of a separate, holy people, living under its own laws and awaiting the Messiah to lead it back to the Holy Land at the end of history. Reform Judaism insisted that change in the religion, Judaism, in response to new challenges represented a valid continuation of that religion's long-term capacity to evolve. Reform Judaism denied that any version of the Torah enjoyed eternal validity. It affirmed that Jews should adopt the politics and culture of the countries where they lived, preserving differences of only a religious character, narrowly construed.

**Emancipation:** In the nineteenth century sweeping changes in the political circumstances in which Jews made their lives as well as in the economic conditions in which they made their living made urgent issues that formerly had drawn slight attention, and rendered inconsequential claims that had for so long demanded response. The Jews had formerly constituted a distinct group. Now in the West they formed part of an undifferentiated mass of citizens, all of them equal before the law, all of them subject to the same law. The Judaism of the dual Torah rested on the political premise that the Jews were governed by God's law and formed God's people. The two political premises—the one of the nation-state, the other of the Torah—scarcely permitted reconciliation. The consequent Judaic systems, Reform Judaism, Orthodox Judaism, Positive Historical Judaism (in the USA: Conservative Judaism), each of them addressing issues regarded as acute and not merely chronic, in the nineteenth century alleged that they formed the natural next step in the unfolding of "the tradition," meaning the Judaic system of the dual Torah.

From the time of Constantine to the nineteenth century, Jewry in Christendom sustained itself as a recognized and ordinarily-tolerated minority. The contradictory doctrines of Christianity—the Jews as Christ-killers to be punished, the Jews as witnesses to be kept alive and ultimately converted at the second coming of Christ—held in an uneasy balance. The pluralistic character of some societies, for instance, that in Spain, the welcome accorded entrepreneurs in opening territories, for instance, Norman England, Poland and Russia, White Russia and the Ukraine, in the early centuries of development—these account still more than doctrine for the long-term survival of Jews in Christian Europe. The Jews, like many others, formed, not only a tolerated religious minority but something akin to a guild, specializing in certain occupations, e.g., crafts and commerce in the East. True, the centuries of essentially ordinary existence in the West ended with the Crusades, which forced Jewry

Figure 118. Gary M. Bretton-Granatoor is installed as rabbi of the Stephen Wise Free Synagogue, New York City, September 15, 1995. Photograph by Peter Goldberg.

Figure 119. Members of He-Halutz, a Zionist youth group, Zhitomir, Ukraine, 1921.

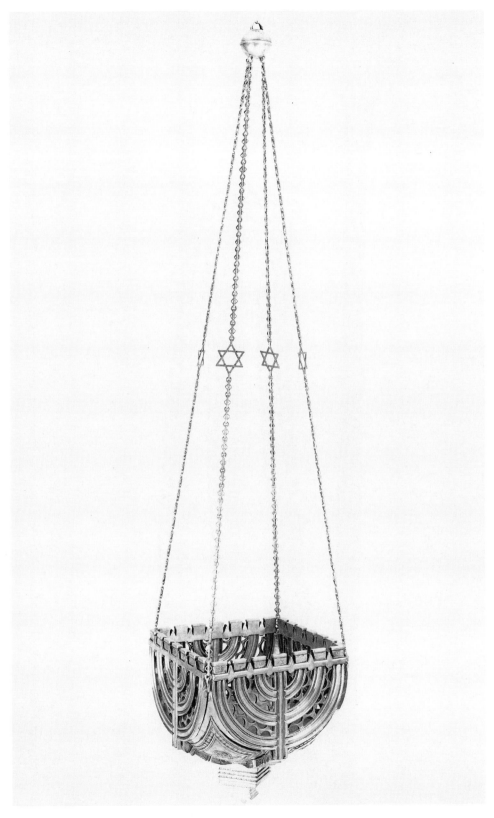

Figure 120. Silver engraved eternal light *(ner tamid)* with chain made by the workshop of Barta and Nash, Cluj, Romania, 1930. A ner tamid burns perpetually in a synagogue in front of the ark that holds the Torah scrolls.

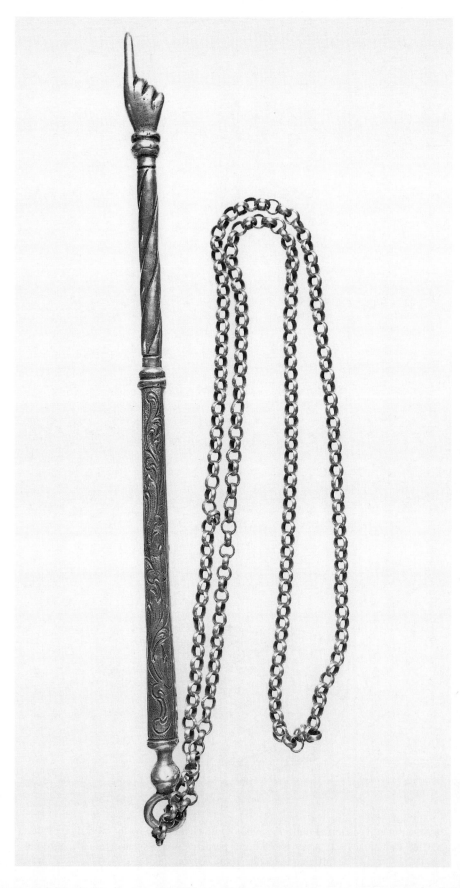

Figure 121. Torah pointer brought to the United States from Germany by the Bamberger family, Hamburg, Germany. The Hebrew name for a Torah pointer, *yad*, means hand, and pointers often are fashioned in the shape of a pointing hand.

Figure 122. A student reads from the Torah at the Brandeis-Bardin Institute in Simi Valley, California, 1991. Photograph by Bill Aron.

to migrate to the eastern frontier of Europe. But, until the twentieth century, the Jews formed one of the peoples permanently settled in Europe, first in the West, later in the East. Still it was only in modern times that the Jews as a whole found, or even aspired to, a position equivalent to that of the majority population in European societies.

Prior to that time the Jews found themselves subjected to legal restrictions controlling where they might live and how they might earn a living. They enjoyed political and social rights of a most limited character. In the East, where most Jews lived, they governed matters of personal status and other aspects of the life of their own communities through their own administration and law. They spoke their own language, Yiddish; wore distinctive clothing; ate only their own food; controlled their own sector of the larger economy and ventured outside of it only seldom; and, in all, formed a distinct and distinctive group. Commonly, the villages in which they lived found Jews and Christians living side by side, but in many of those villages Jews formed the majority of the population. These facts made for long-term stability and autonomy. In the West, the Jews formed only a tiny proportion of the population, but, until modern times, lived equally segregated from the rest of the country, behind the barriers of language, custom, and economic calling. So the Jews for a long time formed a caste, a distinct and clearly defined group— but within the hierarchy ordered by the castes of the society at hand.

A process called "emancipation," part of a larger movement of emancipation of serfs, women, slaves, Catholics (in Protestant countries, for instance, England and Ireland), encompassed the Jews as well. Benzion Dinur defines this process of emancipation as follows:[1]

> Jewish emancipation denotes the abolition of disabilities and inequities applied specially to Jews, the recognition of Jews as equal to other citizens, and the formal granting of the rights and duties of citizenship. Essentially the legal act of emancipation should have been simply the expression of the diminution of social hostility and psychological aversion toward Jews in the host nation . . . but the antipathy was not obliterated and constantly hampered the realization of equality even after it had been proclaimed by the state and included in the law.

The political changes that fall into the process of the Jews' emancipation began in the eighteenth century and, in a half-century, affected the long-term stability that had characterized the Jews' social and political life from Constantine onward. These political changes raised questions not previously found urgent, and, it follows, also precipitated reflection on problems formerly neglected. The answers to the questions flowed logically and necessarily from the character of the questions themselves.

Dinur traces three periods in the history of the Jews' emancipation, from 1740-1789, ending with the French revolution, then from 1789-1878, from the French revolution to the Congress of Berlin, and from 1878 to 1933, from the Congress of Berlin to the rise of the Nazis' to power in Germany. The adoption of the American Constitution in 1787 confirmed the U.S. position on the matter. Jewish males enjoyed the rights of citizens, along with all other whites. The first period marks the point at which the emancipation of the Jews first came under discussion, the second marked the period in which Western and Central European states accorded to the Jews the rights of citizens, and the third brought to the fore a period of new racism that in the end annihilated the Jews of Europe.

In the first period advocates of the Jews' emancipation maintained that religious intolerance accounted for the low caste-status assigned to the Jews. Liberating the Jews would mark another stage in overcoming religious intolerance. During this first period the original ideas of Reform Judaism came to expression, although the important changes in religious doctrine and practice were realized only in the earlier part of the nineteenth century. In the second period, the French revolution brought Jews political rights in France, Belgium, Netherlands, Italy, Germany, and Austria-Hungary. As Germany and Italy attained unification and Hungary independence, the Jews were accorded the rights and duties of citizenship. Dinur explains:

It was stressed that keeping the Jews in a politically limited and socially inferior status was incompatible with the principle of civic equality . . ."it is the objective of every political organization to protect the natural rights of man," hence, "all citizens have the right to all the liberties and advantages of citizens, without exception."

Jews at that time entered the political and cultural life of the Western nations, including their overseas empires (hence Algerian Jews received French citizenship).

During this second period Reform Judaism reached its first stage of development, beginning in Germany. It made possible for Jews to hold together the two things they deemed inseparable: their desire to remain Jewish, and their wish also to be one with their "fellow citizens." By the middle of the nineteenth century, Reform had reached full expression and had won the support of a sizable part of German Jewry. In reaction against Reform ("the excesses of . . ."), Orthodoxy came into existence. Orthodoxy no less than Reform asked how "Judaism" could co-exist with "German-ness," meaning citizenship in an undifferentiated republic of citizens. A centrist position, mediating between Reform and Orthodoxy, was worked out by theologians in what was then called the Historical School, and what, in twentieth-century America, took the name of Conservative Judaism. The period from the French Revolution to the Congress of Berlin therefore saw the full efflorescence of all of the Judaisms of political modernization. All of these Judaisms characterized the Jews of Western Europe, and, later on, America. But in America Reform, Orthodoxy, and the Historical School or Conservative Judaism radically changed in character, responding to the urgent issues of a different circumstance, producing self-evidently valid answers of a character not compatible with the nineteenth century statements of those same systems.

In the third period, anti-Semitism as a political and social movement attained power. Jews began to realize that, in Dinur's words, "the state's legal recognition of Jewish civic and political equality does not automatically bring social recognition of this equality." The Jews continued to form a separate group; they were racially "inferior." The impact of the new racism would be felt in the twentieth century. The Judaisms of the twentieth century raised the questions of political repression and economic dislocation, as these faced the Jews of Eastern Europe and America.

Clearly, in the nineteenth century, particularly in Western countries, a new order revised the political settlement covering the Jews, in place for nearly the entire history of the West. From the time of Constantine forward, the Jews' essentially autonomous life as a protected minority had raised political questions that found answers of an essentially supernatural and theological character. But now the emancipation redefined those questions, asking about Jews not as a distinct group but Jews as part of some other polity altogether than the Jewish one. Those Jews who simply passed over retain no interest for us; Karl Marx, converted to Christianity at an early age, produced no ideas important in the study of Judaism(s). But vast numbers of Jews in the West determined to remain Jewish and also to become something else. Their urgent question addressed the issue of how to be both Jewish and something else: a citizen of Germany or France or Britain. That issue would not confront the Jews of the Russian Empire until World War I, and, together with the Jews the Austro-Hungarian Empire, Rumania, and other Eastern European areas, these formed the vast majority of the whole.

The Jews of the West, preoccupied with changes in their political position, formed only a small minority of the Jews of the world—the Western frontier (extending, to be sure, to California in the farthest west of all) of the Jewish people. But their confrontation with political change proved paradigmatic. They were the ones to invent the Judaisms of the nineteenth century. Each of these Judaic systems exhibited three characteristic traits. First, it asked how one could be both Jewish and something else, that is, also a citizen, a member of a nation. Second, it defined "Judaism" as a religion, so leaving ample space for that something else, namely, nationality, whether German ("*Deutschtum und Judentum*," German-ness and Jewish-ness), or British, or French, or American. Third, it appealed to history to prove the continuity between its system and the received Judaism of the dual Torah. The resort to historical fact, the claim that the system at hand formed the linear development of the past, the natural increment of the entire "history" of Israel, the Jewish people, from the beginning to the new day—that essentially factual claim masked a profound conviction concerning self-evidence. The urgent question at hand—the political one—produced a self-evidently correct answer out of the history of politics constituted by historical narrative.

**Appeal to history:** That appeal to history, particularly historical fact, characterizes all three Judaisms. The Reformers stated explicitly that theirs would be a Judaism built on fact. The facts of history, in particular, would guide Jews to the definition of what was essential and what could be dropped. History then formed the court of appeal—but also the necessary link, the critical point of continuity. The Historical School took the same position, but reached different conclusions. History would show how change could be effected, and the principles of historical change would then govern. Orthodoxy met the issue in a different way, maintaining that "Judaism" was above history, not a historical fact at all. But the Orthodox position would also appeal most forcefully to the past in its claim that Orthodoxy constituted the natural and complete continuation of "Judaism" in its true form. The importance of history in the theological thought of the nineteenth century Judaisms derives from the intellectual heritage of the age, with its stress on the nation-state as the definitive unit of society, and on history as the mode of defining the culture and character of the nation-state. History as an instrument of reform, further, had served the Protestant Reformation, with its appeal to Scripture as against (mere) tradition, its claim that it would restore Christianity to its (historical) purity. Finally and most important, the supernaturalism of the inherited Judaism of the dual Torah, its emphasis upon God's active intervention in history, on miracles, on a perpetual concern for the natural implications of the supernatural will and covenant—that supernaturalism contradicted

the rationalism of the age. The one thing the Jewish thinkers wished to accomplish was to show the rationalism, the reason—the normality—of the Judaisms they constructed. Appealing to (mere) facts of history, as against the unbelievable claims of a Scripture placed upon a positive and this-worldly foundation that religious view of the world that, in the received system of the dual Torah, rested upon a completely supernatural view of reality.

For the three Judaisms of the age took as their task the demonstration of how they formed out of the received and unwanted old Judaism something new, different, and acceptable. The Judaisms of the nineteenth century were born in the matrix of the received system of the dual Torah, among people who themselves grew up in a world in which *that* Judaism defined what people meant by Judaism. That is why the questions of analysis address the fact that the framers of the Judaisms of continuation could not evade the issue of continuity. They wished both to continue and also to innovate—and to justify innovation. And that desire affected Orthodoxy as much as Reform. In making changes, they appealed to the past for justification. But they pointed to those changes also as proof that they had overcome an unwanted past. The delicate balance between tradition and change attained by each of the Judaisms of continuation marks the genius of its inventors. All worked out the same equation: change but not too much, whatever the proportion a group found excessive.

**Reform Judaism as traditional:** The view that the Judaisms of the nineteenth century from a later perspective look remarkably alike will have surprised their founders and framers. For they fought bitterly among themselves. But the three Judaisms of continuity exhibit striking traits in common. All looked backward at the received system of the dual Torah. All sought justification in precedent out of a holy and paradigmatic past. All viewed the documents of that system as canonical, differing, of course, on the relative merit of the several components. They concurred that texts to prove propositions deemed true should derive from those canonical writings (or from some of them). All took for granted the enduring, God-given authority of those writings. None doubted that God had revealed the (written) Torah at Sinai. All looked for validating precedent in the received canon. Differing on issues important to both world view and way of life, all three Judaisms concurred on the importance of literacy in the received writings, on the lasting relevance of the symbolic system at hand, on the pertinence of the way of life (in some, if not in every detail), on the power of the received Judaism of the dual Torah to stand in judgment on whatever, later, would serve to continue that Judaism.

True, the differences among the three Judaisms impressed their framers and with good reason. The Reformers rejected important components of the Judaism of the dual Torah and said so. Written Torah, yes, Oral Torah, no. The Orthodox explicitly denied the validity of changing anything, insisting on the facticity, the givenness, of the whole. The Conservatives, in appealing to historical precedent, shifted the premise of justification entirely. Written Torah, yes, Oral Torah, maybe. They sought what the Orthodox thought pointless and the Reform inconsequential, namely, justification for making some few changes in the present in continuation of the processes that had effected development in the past. None of these points of important difference proved trivial. But all of them, all together, should not obscure the powerful points of similarity that mark all three Judaisms as continuators of the Judaism of the dual Torah.

Continuators, but not lineal developments, not the natural next step, not the ineluctable increment of history, such as all claimed to be—each with good reason, and, of course, all wrong. The points at which each Judaism took its leave from the received system do not match. In the case of Reform, the break proved explicit: change carried out by articulate, conscious decision, thus change as a matter of policy, enjoys full legitimacy. And as for the positive Historical School and of its continuators in Conservative Judaism, the gulf between faith and fact took the measure of the difference between the received sys-

tem of the dual Torah and the statement of mere historical facts that, for the Historical School, served to document the faith.

While the differences in the grounds of separation from the received system prove formidable, still more striking and fresh are the several arguments adduced once more to establish a firm connection to the Judaism of the dual Torah, or, more accurately, to "the tradition" or to "Judaism." For the Judaisms of continuation characteristically differ in the several ways in which each, on its own, proposed to establish its continuity with a past perceived as discontinuous. All three Judaisms enjoyed ample justification for the insistence, each in its way, that it carried forward the entire history of Judaism and took the necessary and ineluctable step beyond where matters had rested prior to its own formation. Reform in this regard found itself subjected to vigorous criticism, but in saying that "things have changed in the past, and we can change them too," Reform established its primary position. It too pointed to precedent, and implicitly conceded the power of the received system to stand in judgment. All the more so did the Orthodox and Conservative theologians affirm that same power and place themselves under the judgment of the Judaism of the dual Torah. All three established a firm position within the continuation of that Judaism. While the allegation made by each of priority as the next step in the linear and incremental history of Judaism scarcely demands serious analysis, the theory, for each one respectively, enjoys ample, if diverse, justification.

**The Pittsburgh Platform:** For Reform Judaism in the nineteenth century the full and authoritative statement of the system— its world view, with profound implications on its way of life, and its theory of who is Israel—came to expression not in Europe but in America, in an assembly of Reform rabbis in Pittsburgh in 1885. At that meeting of the Central Conference of American Rabbis, the Reform Judaism of the age, by now about a century in aborning, took up the issues that divided the Judaism and made an authoritative statement on them, one that most people could accept.

The very fact that the Judaism before us could conceive of such a process of debate and formulation of a kind of creed tells us that this Judaism found urgent the specification of its systemic structure, testimony to a mature and self-aware frame of mind. We look in vain for equivalent convocations to set public policy, for example, in the antecedent thousand years of the Judaism of the dual Torah. Statements of the world-view, as these would emerge in diverse expressions of the received system, did not take the form of a rabbis' platform, on the one side, and did not come about through democratic debate on public issues, on the other. That world-view percolated upward and represented a rarely-articulated and essentially inchoate consensus about how things really are and should be. The received system came to expression in how things were done, what people found needless to make articulate at all: the piety of a milieu, not the proposition of a theological gathering. That contrast tells us not merely that Reform Judaism represented a new Judaism, but, of greater interest, that the methods and approaches of Reform Judaism enjoyed their own self-evident appropriateness. And from that fact we learn how the qualities people found self-evidently right had changed over time.

So we begin our trip in Pittsburgh, U.S.A., among rabbis who could point to three or even four generations of antecedents. These were not the founders of the new faith—the Judaism before us came to birth about a generation before anyone said a new thing had been born—but the authorities of an established and enduring one. For the end of the nineteenth century found Reform Judaism a major component of the Judaic religious life of America as well as of Germany, and making inroads elsewhere as well. The American Reform rabbis, meeting in Pittsburgh in 1885, issued a clear and accessible statement of their Judaism. We want to know about this Judaism one thing in particular: its formulation of the issue of Israel as political circumstances defined it. For critical to the Judaism of the dual Torah was its view of Israel as God's people, a supernatural polity, living out its social existence under God's Torah.

The way of life, one of sanctification, and the world view, one of persistent reference to the Torah for rules of conduct, on the one side, and of the explanation of conduct, on the other, began in the basic conception of who is Israel. Here too we find emphasis on who is Israel, with that doctrine exposing for all to see the foundations of the way of life and world view that these rabbis had formed for the Israel they conceived:

> We recognize in the Mosaic legislation a system of training the Jewish people for its mission during its national life in Palestine, and today we accept as binding only its moral laws and maintain only such ceremonies as elevate and sanctify our lives, but reject all such as are not adapted to the views and habits of modern civilization. . . . We hold that all such Mosaic and rabbinical laws as regulate diet, priestly purity, and dress originated in ages and under the influence of ideas entirely foreign to our present mental and spiritual state. . . . Their observance in our days is apt rather to obstruct than to further modern spiritual elevation. . . . We recognize in the modern era of universal culture of heart and intellect the approaching of the realization of Israel's great messianic hope for the establishment of the kingdom of truth, justice, and peace among all men. We consider ourselves no longer a nation but a religious community and therefore expect neither a return to Palestine nor a sacrificial worship under the sons of Aaron nor the restoration of any of the laws concerning the Jewish state. . . .

The Pittsburgh Platform takes up each component of the system in turn. Who is Israel? What is its way of life? How does it account for its existence as a distinct, and distinctive, group? Israel once was a nation ("during its national life") but today is not a nation. It once had a set of laws that regulate diet, clothing, and the like. These no longer apply, because Israel now is not what it was then. Israel forms an integral part of western civilization. The reason to persist as a distinctive group was that the group has its work to do, namely, to realize the messianic hope for the establishment of a kingdom of truth, justice, and peace. For that purpose Israel no longer constitutes a nation. It now forms a religious community.

What that means is that individual Jews do

live as citizens in other nations. Difference is acceptable at the level of religion, not nationality, a position that accords fully with the definition of citizenship of the Western democracies. The world-view then lays heavy emphasis on an as-yet unrealized but coming perfect age. The way of life admits to no important traits that distinguish Jews from others, since morality, in the nature of things, forms a universal category, applicable in the same way to everyone. The theory of Israel then forms the heart of matters, and what we learn is that Israel constitutes a "we," that is, that the Jews continue to form a group that, by its own indicators, holds together and constitutes a cogent social entity. All this in a simple statement of a handful of rabbis forms a full and encompassing Judaism, one that, to its communicants, presented truth of a self-evident order. But it was, also, a truth declared, not discovered, and the self-evidence of the truth of the statements competed with the self-awareness characteristic of those who made them. For they could recognize the problem that demanded attention: the reframing of a theory of Israel for that Israel that they themselves constituted: that "we" that required explanation. No more urgent question faced the rabbis, because, after all, they lived in a century of opening horizons, in which people could envision perfection. World War One would change all that, also for Israel. By 1937 the Reform rabbis, meeting in Columbus, Ohio, would reframe the system, expressing a world view quite different from that of the half-century before.

Let us briefly summarize this picture of the program of urgent issues and self-evident responses that constituted the first of the new Judaisms of the nineteenth century. Questions we find answered fall into two categories, first, why "we" do not keep certain customs and ceremonies but do keep others, second, how "we relate to the nations in which we live." So the system of Reform Judaism explained both why and why not, that is, why this, not that: the mark of a fully framed and cogent Judaism. The affirmative side covered why the Jews would persist as a separate group, the negative would account for the limits of difference. These two questions deal with the same urgent problem, namely, working out a mode of Judaic existence compatible with citizenship in (for these rabbis) America. Jews do not propose to eat or dress in distinctive ways. They do seek a place within "modern spiritual elevation . . . universal culture of heart and intellect." They impute to that culture the realization of "the messianic hope"—a considerable stake. And, explicit to the whole, the Jews no longer constitute a nation. They therefore belong to some other nation(s). The single self-evident proposition taken fully into account by the Judaism at hand is that political change has changed the entirety of "Judaism," but the Judaism at hand has the power to accommodate to that change. So change in general forms the method for dealing with the problem at hand, which is change in the political and social standing the Jews now enjoy. On the very surface, Reform Judaism formed a Judaic system that confronted immense political change and presented a world-view and way of life to an Israel defined in those categories opened up by the change at hand. Two questions demand attention. We want to know how this Judaism came into being and how its intellectuals explained their system.

**The urgent questions answered by Reform Judaism:** From the perspective of the political changes taking place from the American and French Revolutions onward, the received system of the Judaism of the dual Torah answered the wrong questions. For the issue no longer found definition in the claims of regnant Christianity. A new question, emerging from forces not contained within Christianity, demanded attention from Jews affected by those forces. For those Jews, the fact of change derived its self-evidence from shifts in political circumstances. When the historians began to look for evidence of precedents for changing things, it was because their own circumstance had already persuaded them that change matters—change itself effects change. What they sought, then, was a picture of a world in which they might find a place, and, it went without saying, that picture would include a portrait of a Judaic system—a way of life, a world view, a definition of the Israel to live the one and believe the other. The issue confronting the new Judaism derived not from Christianity, therefore, but from political change brought about by forces of secular nationalism, which conceived of society not as the expression of God's will for the social order under the rule of Christ and his Church or is anointed king (emperor, Tsar), but of popular will for the social order under the government of the people and their elected representatives, a considerable shift. When society does not form the aggregate of distinct groups, each with its place and definition, language and religion, but rather undifferentiated citizens (male, white, wealthy, to be sure), then the Judaism that Jews in such a society will have to work out also will account for difference of a different order altogether. That Judaism will have to frame a theory of who is Israel consonant with the social situation of Jews who will to be different, but not so different that they cannot also be citizens.

The original and enduring Judaic system of Reform correctly appeals to Moses Mendelssohn for its intellectual foundations, and Mendelssohn presented, in the words of Michael A. Meyer, an appeal "for a pluralistic society that offered full freedom of conscience to all those who accepted the postulates of natural religion: God, Providence, and a future life."[2] The protasis presents the important component: a pluralistic society, which, in the nature of things, constitutes a political category. Issues dominant from Mendelssohn's time forward concerned as we have said "emancipation," the provision, for Jews, of the rights of citizens. Reform theologians took the lead in the struggle for such rights. To them it was self-evident that Jews not only should have civil rights and civic equality. It also was obvious that they should want them. A Judaism that did not explain why the Jews should want and have full equality as part of a common humanity ignored the issues that preoccupied those who found, in Reform Judaism, a corpus of self-evident truths. To those truths, the method—the appeal to historical facts—formed a contingent and secondary consideration.

To the Reform rabbis in Pittsburgh, Chris-

tianity presented no urgent problems. The open society of America did. The self-evident definition of the social entity, Israel, therefore had to shift. The fourth century rabbis balanced Israel against Rome, Jacob against Esau, the triumphant political messiah, seen as arrogant, against the Messiah of God, humble and sagacious. So Israel formed a supernatural entity and in due course would enter into that final era in God's division of time, in which Israel would reach its blessing. The supernatural entity, Israel, now formed no social presence. The Christian world, in which Christ ruled through popes and emperors, kings claimed divine right, and the will of the Church bore multiform consequences for society, and in which, by the way, Israel too was perceived in a supernatural framework—if a negative one—no longer existed. So the world at large no longer verified that category, Israel, as supernatural entity at all. Then the problem of the definition of what sort of entity Israel did constitute, and, by the way, what sort of way of life should characterize that Israel, what sort of world view explain it—that problem produced a new set of urgent and ineluctable questions, and, in the nature of things, also self-evidently true answers, such as we find in Pittsburgh.

**Changes in synagogue worship:** This brings us back to the birth of this Judaism. Reform Judaism dates its beginnings to the nineteenth century with changes, called reforms and regarded as the antecedents of Reform, in trivial aspects of public worship in the synagogue.[3] The motive for these changes derived from the simple fact that many Jews rejected the received system. People were defecting from the synagogue. Since, it was taken for granted, giving up the faith meant surrendering all ties to the group, the beginning of change made reform and ultimately Reform address two issues at one time: [1] making the synagogue more attractive so that [2] defectors would return, and others would not leave. The reform of Judaism in its manifestation in synagogue worship— the cutting edge of the faith—therefore took cognizance of something that had already taken place. And that was the loss for the received system—way of life, world-view, addressed to a defined Israel—of its standing as self-evident truth. That loss manifested itself in two ways. First, people were simply leaving. Second and more important for the group, the many who were staying looked in a new way on what, for so long, had scarcely demanded examination at all. But, of course, the real issues involved not the synagogue but society at large. It would take two generations before Reform Judaism would find the strength to address that much larger issue, and a generation beyond for the power of the ideas ultimately formulated in the Pittsburgh Platform to be felt.

To begin with the issue involved not politics but merely justification for changing anything at all. But that issue asked the wrong question in the wrong way. The Reformers maintained that change was all right because historical precedent proved that change was all right. But change long had defined the constant in the on-going life of the Judaism of the dual Torah. Generative causes and modes of effecting change marked the vitality of the system. The Judaism of the dual Torah endured, never in tact but always unimpaired, because of its power to absorb and make its own the diverse happenings of culture and society. So long as the structure of politics remained the same, with Israel an autonomous entity, subordinated but recognized as a cogent and legitimate social group in charge of some of its own affairs, the system answered the paramount question. The trivial ones could work their way through and become part of the consensus, to be perceived in the end as "tradition" too. A catalogue of changes that had taken place over fifteen hundred years, from the birth of Judaism to its death, therefore will list many more dramatic and decisive sorts of change than those matters of minor revision of liturgy, e.g., sermons in the vernacular, that attracted attention at the dawn of the age of change become Reform.

**From change to reform:** We must wonder, therefore, what made the difference then, so that change could be perceived as reform and transformed into the Reform of Judaism, hence, Reform Judaism. The answer is that, when people took a stance external to the received mode and effected change as a matter of decision and policy, rather than as a matter of what is restorative and purported to be timelessly appropriate, for those people, Judaism in its received form had already died. For the received system no longer defined matters but now become subject to definition. And that marks the move from self-evidence to self-consciousness.

What had brought about the demise of the received system as definitive and normative beyond all argument is something we do not know. Nothing in the earliest record of reform of liturgy tells us. The constructive efforts of the first generation, only later on recognized not as people who made changes or even as reformers but as founders of Reform Judaism, focused upon synagogue worship. The services were too long; the speeches were in a language foreign to participants; the singing was not aesthetic; the prayers were in a language no one understood. But that means some people recited the prayers as a matter of duty, not supplication; did not speak the language of the faith; formed other than received opinions on how to sing in synagogue; saw as alien what earlier had marked the home and hearth. Those people no longer lived in that same social world that had for so long found right and proper precisely the customs now seen as alien.

When the heritage forms an unclaimed, unwanted legacy, out of duty people nonetheless accept it. So the reform that produced Reform Judaism introduced a shortened service, a sermon in the language people spoke, a choir and an organ, prayers in the vernacular. Clearly, a great deal of change had taken place prior to the recognition that something had changed. People no longer knew Hebrew; they no longer found pleasing received modes of saying the prayers. We look in vain to the consequent reforms for answers to the question of why people made these changes, and the reasons adduced by historians settle no interesting questions for us. The more interesting question concerns why the persistence of engagement and concern. For people always had the option, which many exercised, of abandoning the received Judaism of the two Torahs and all other Judaisms too. Among those for whom these cosmetic changes made a difference, much in the liturgy, and far more beyond, retained powerful appeal. The premise of change dictated that Jews would say the old prayers in essentially the old formulation. And that premise carried much else: the entire burden of the faith, the total commitment to the group, in some form, defined by some indicators, if not the familiar ones then some others. So we know that Reform Judaism, in its earliest manifestation in Germany in the early nineteenth century, constituted an essentially conservative, profoundly constructive effort to save for Jews the received Judaism by reforming it in some (to begin with) rather trivial ways.

**Justifying Reform. Historical study as an instrument of Reform:** The justification for these changes was the theory of the incremental history of a single, linear Judaism, a theory that played a powerful role in the creative age of Reform Judaism. The ones who made changes (it is too soon to call them Reformers, or the changes Reforms) to begin with rested their case on an appeal to the authoritative texts. Change is legitimate, and these changes in particular wholly consonant with the law, or the tradition, or the inner dynamics of the faith, or the dictates of history, or whatever out of the past worked that day. The laymen who made the changes tried to demonstrate that the changes fit in with the law of Judaism. They took the trouble because Reform even at the outset claimed to restore, to continue, to persist in, the received pattern. The justification of change always invoked precedent. People who made changes had to show that the principle that guided what they did was not new, even though the specific things they did were. So to lay down a bridge between themselves and their past they laid out beams resting on deep-set piles. The foundation of change was formed of the bedrock of precedent. And more still: change restores, reverts to an unchanging ideal. So the Reformer claims not to change at all, but only to regain the correct state of affairs, one that others, in the inter-

val, themselves have changed. That forms the fundamental attitude of mind of the people who make changes and call the changes Reform. The appeal to history, a common mode of justification in the politics and theology of the nineteenth century, therefore defined the principal justification for the new Judaism: it was new because it renewed the old and enduring, the golden Judaism of a mythic age of perfection. Arguments on precedent drew the Reformers to the work of critical scholarship as they settled all questions by appeal to the facts of history.

We cannot find surprising, therefore, the theory that Reform Judaism stood in a direct line with the prior history of Judaism. Judaism is one. Judaism has a history. That history is single and unitary, and it was always leading to its present outcome: Reform Judaism. Others later on would challenge these convictions. Orthodox Judaism would deny that Judaism has a history at all. Conservative, or positive Historical Judaism, would discover a different goal for history from that embodied by Reform Judaism. But the mode of argument, appealing to issues of an historical and factual character, and the premises of argument, insisting that history proved, or disproved, matters of theological conviction, characterized all the Judaisms of the nineteenth century. And that presents no surprises, since the Judaisms of the age took shape in the intellectual world of Germany, with its profoundly philosophical and historical mode of thought and argument. So the challenge of political change carried with it its own modes of intellectual response: in the academic, scholarly framework. The challenges of the twentieth century exhibited a different character altogether. They were not intellectual but wholly political, and they concerned not matters of political status, but issues of life or death. The Judaic systems of the age then would respond in their own way: through forming instrumentalities of collective action, political power, not theory. But we have moved ahead of our story.

**Abraham Geiger:** The original changes, in the first decades of the nineteenth century, produced a new generation of rabbis. Some forty years into the century, these rabbis gave to the process of change the name of Reform and created those institutions of Reform Judaism that would endow the inchoate movement with a politics of its own. In the mid-1840s a number of rabbinical conference brought together the new generation of rabbis. Trained in universities, rabbis who came to these gatherings turned backward, justifying the changes in prayer rites long in place, effecting some further, mostly cosmetic changes in the observance of the Sabbath and in the laws covering personal status through marriage and divorce. In 1845 a decision to adopt for some purposes German in place of Hebrew led to the departure of conservative Reformers, typified by Zacharias Frankel. But the Reformers appealed for their apologia to the received writings, persisting in their insistence that they formed a natural continuation of the processes of the "tradition." Indeed, that point of insistence—that Judaism formed, in Petuchowski's words in regard to Geiger, "a constantly evolving organism"[4]— formed the centerpiece of the nascent Judaism at hand.

Abraham Geiger enjoyed the advantage of the finest argumentative mind in Jewry in the nineteenth century. If we want to understand the new Judaisms of the age, therefore, we turn to the leading intellect to show us how people reached their conclusions, not merely what they said or why they found self-evident the positions that they took. Geiger's life presents facts of less interest than his work, and, in his work, his way of asking and answering questions tells us what matters in Reform Judaism. For that is the point at which we gain access to what people found self-evident, on the one side, and urgent on the other. The urgency accounts for the questions, the self-evidence, the mode of discovering the answer. To those two matters, everything else takes second place. The question Geiger found ineluctable takes simple form: how can we explain what has happened to us. The answer: what has taken place—change become Reform—forms the natural and necessary outcome of history. In his emphasis upon the probative status and value of the facts of history we find those self-evident principles that lead us deep into

the consciousness of the man and the Judaism he embodied. What Geiger took for granted, in our terms, held as self-evident, is that history proved propositions of theology. Whatever the particular matter of conviction or custom takes a secondary place. The primary source of verification, therefore, of appropriate and inappropriate traits in Judaism, that is to say, the origin of the reliable definition of Judaism, lies in not revealed records of God's will but human accounts of humanity's works. To that principle, everywhere taken for granted, occasionally enunciated, but never systematically demonstrated, Geiger's mode of argument and inquiry took second place.

Since the earliest changes changed into reforms, and reforms of Judaism into Reform Judaism, to Geiger we address our principal questions: old or new? And how did people explain themselves? Abraham Geiger presented in clearest form the argument that Reform carried forward the historical processes of Judaism, hence position both a single, linear Judaism and a Judaism affected by history, that is, by change. He appealed to the facts of history, beginning with the critical study of the Bible. Petuchowski summarizes his view as follows:

> Judaism is a constantly evolving organism. Biblical Judaism was not identical with classical rabbinic Judaism. Similarly, the modern age calls for further evolution in consonance with the changed circumstances. . . . The modern rabbis are entitled to adapt medieval Judaism, as the early rabbis had the right to adapt biblical Judaism. . . . He found traces of evolution within the Bible itself. Yet for Geiger changes in Judaism had always been organic. . . . The modern changes must develop out of the past, and not represent a revolutionary break with it.[5]

Geiger therefore recognized change as "traditional," meaning, that changing represents the way things always were and so legitimately now goes forward. The Jews change, having moved from constituting a nation to a different classification of social entity. The messiah-idea now addresses the whole of humanity, not only speaking of national restoration. Revelation then turns out to form a progressive, not a static fact. In these diverse ways Geiger—and with him, Reform Judaism through its history—appealed to history to verify its allegations and validate its positions. So facts turn into the evidence for faith.

Geiger was born in 1810 and died in 1874.[6] Growing up in Frankfurt, he undertook university studies at Heidelberg, then Bonn, with special interest in philosophy and Semitics. University study formed the exception, not the rule, for Jews. By definition, therefore, the change Geiger had to explain in fact came about through the decision of the former generation. Geiger explained change. His parents made it. But among the intellectual leaders in Geiger's day, not only he, but his arch-opponent, Samson Raphael Hirsch, founder of Orthodox Judaism, also acquired a university education. So Orthodox Judaism too emerged as the result of the decision of the generation prior to the age of the founders. To both sets of parents therefore the value of an education in the sciences of the West proved self-evident; the ways of harmonizing that education and its values with the education in the Judaic sciences considerably less clear. Earlier generations had not sent their sons to universities (and their daughters would have to wait until nearly our own day for a similar right). So before Geiger and Hirsch could reach the academy, their parents had to find self-evident the value of such an education. But prior to that generation, most parents found self-evident the value of education in the established institutions of the Judaism of the dual Torah—there alone. Knowledge of another sort, under other auspices, bore no value. So prior to the advent of the reformer, whether the great intellect of Reform Judaism or the courageous leader of Orthodoxy, change had already characterized modes of self-evident truth.

Geiger served a parlous life in synagogue pulpits, not always appreciated for the virtues he brought to them: flawless German and his questioning of routine.[7] What he did with most of his time, however, concerned not the local synagogue-community but the constituency of Judaic learning. He produced a periodical, the *Scientific Journal for Jewish Theology*, from 1835 onward. The purpose of scientific knowledge Wiener epitomizes

in the following statement: "They were convinced that, given the historical facts, it would be possible to draw the correct practical conclusions with regard to the means by which their religion could best be served and elevated to the level of contemporary culture."[8] That is to say, through systematic learning Judaism would undergo reform. Reform Judaism rested on deep foundations of scholarship of a certain sort, specifically, of a historical character.

What Geiger had in mind was to analyze the sources of Judaism and the evolution of Judaism. If science (used in its German sense, systematic learning) could uncover the sources of the Jewish "spirit," then, in Wiener's words, "the genius of his people and . . . its vocation" would serve "as a guide to the construction of a living present and future." Geiger's principle of Reform remained fixed. Reform had to emerge from *Wissenschaft*, "a term which he equated with the concept of the understanding of historical evolution."[9] To him "Judaism in its ideal form was religion per se, nothing but an expression of religious consciousness. Its outer shell was subject to change from one generation to another."[10] All things emerge out of time and of change. But when it comes to trace the history of time and change, contemporary categories assuredly defined the inquiry. Thus Geiger produced, out of ancient times, portraits suspiciously congruent to the issues of his own day.

**A new Judaism or renewed Judaism?** Do the framers of the Judaisms of the nineteenth century claim to renew the received Judaism of the dual Torah or to invent a Judaism? And if they allege that they stand as the natural next step in "the tradition," does that claim stand? Geiger represents the answer of Reform Judaism in his day, a powerful and one-sided answer. Reform Judaism renews, it does not invent. There was, and is, only a single Judaism. In the current age, Reform undertakes the discovery of that definition. The answer to the question, On what basis does the claim stand? is clear. Reform lays its foundations on the basis of history, which is to say, tradition. Propositions of a theological character, for example, concerning the dual Torah revealed at Sinai, the sanctified and therefore supernatural character of Israel, the holy people, the coming Messiah-sage at the end of times—these take their place in the line of truths to be investigated through historical method, in historical sources. Some may see an incongruity between the propositions at hand and the allegations about the decisive, probative character of historical inquiry in evaluating them. For the facts of history hardly testify, one way or another, concerning the character of revelation at Sinai (though we may know what people recorded in that connection), the status and sanctity of Israel (though the social facts and political issues surely pertained to this-worldly Israel), let alone that event at the end, on the other side, of history altogether, the coming of the Messiah.

We cannot ask whether the claim of Reform Judaism finds justification in "the facts." The question proves beside the point. Of course it does: the facts are what people make of them, whether discovered in history or imputed in revealed and holy writings, in a canon of truth. We can scarcely say that the position of Reform Judaism, as outlined by a brief sketch of Geiger's thought, even intersects or connects with what had gone before.

Old or new? Not only new, but out of all relationship to the old. The appeal to the old—to history—turns out to come after the fact, the system, had already come to ample formation. Once the Judaism at hand had come into being, people knew what they wanted to find out from history, and that was whether or not things change. Geiger followed a far more sophisticated program, of course, since, knowing that things do change (to whom would the proposition have brought surprise?), he asked exactly how, in Judaism, change takes place, and in what direction. What then do we find to be the point of self-evidence? It is that the categories defined in Geiger's day pertained a long time ago. That is the mark of the new Judaism called Reform Judaism: its powerful capacity without a trace of self-consciousness to impose anachronistic issues and categories. So to claim a movement, in modern times, from self-evidence to self-consciousness distorts the

matter. What changes is the repertoire of self-evident truths.

*"Reform Movements in Judaism:"* **The appeal to historical precedent:** Clearly, Reform Judaism, once well under way, would have to situate itself in relationship to the past. Geiger's powerful appeal to precedent left no choice. For not all precedents sustained contemporary choices—the system as it had already emerged—and some of the more recent ones surely called it into question. So as learning rolled forward, the question emerged, Precisely what, in history, serves as a precedent for change become Reform? The answer came down to the appeal to continuing traits of change, the search for constants about change. To advance our understanding of Reform Judaism we move once more to America, the country in which Reform Judaism enjoyed massive success in the last half of the twentieth century. There we see in full and articulate formulation the world-view of Reform Judaism as it unfolded in a straight line from Geiger's day to our own.

Specifically, in his preface to Abraham Cronbach's *Reform Movements in Judaism*,[11] Jacob Rader Marcus, a principal voice in Reform Judaism in the twentieth century, provides a powerful statement of the Reform view of its own place in history. Marcus recognizes that diverse Judaisms have flourished in the history of the Jews. What characterizes them all is that each began as a reform movement but then underwent a process we might characterize as "traditionalization." That is to say, change becomes not merely reform but tradition, and the only constant in the histories of Judaisms is that process of transformation of the new to the conventional, or, in theological language, the traditional. This process Marcus describes as follows:

> All [Judaisms] began as rebellions, as great reformations, but after receiving widespread acceptance, developed vested "priestly" interests, failed their people, and were forced to retreat before the onslaught of new rebellions, new philosophies, new challenges.

Nothing in Marcus's picture can have presented a surprise to Geiger. So the fundamental theological method of Reform Judaism in its initial phase, the appeal to facts of history for the validation of theological propositions, endures. But the claim that everything always changes yields a challenge, which Marcus forthrightly raises:

> Is there then nothing but change? Is change the end of all our history and all our striving? No, there is something else, the desire to be free . . . In the end [the Jew] has always understood that changelessness is spiritual death. The Jew who would *live* must never completely surrender himself to one truth, but . . . must reach out for the farther and faint horizons of an ever Greater God. . . . This is the meaning of Reform.

Marcus thus treats as self-evident—obvious because it is a fact of history—the persistence of change. And, denying that that is all there is to Reform, at the end he affirms the simple point that change sets the norm. It comes down to the same thing. The something else of Marcus's argument presents its own problems. Appeal to the facts of history fails at that point at which a constructive position demands articulation. "The desire to be free" bears a predicate: free of what? Free to do, to be what? If Marcus fails to accomplish the whole of the theological task, however, he surely conveys the profoundly constructive vision that Reform Judaism afforded to its Israel.

For his part, Cronbach sets forth as the five precedents for the present movement the Deuteronomic Reformation, the Pentateuchal Reformation, the Pharisaic Reformation, the Karaite Reformation, and the Hasidic Reformation. His coming reformation appeals to social psychology and aims at tolerance: "Felicitous human relationships can be the goal of social welfare and of economic improvement. . . . Our Judaism of maturity would be dedicated to the ideal of freedom. Corollary of that ideal is what we have just observed about courtesy toward the people whose beliefs and practices we do not share. . . ."[12] We now have moved far from the position outlined by Geiger, in which a constant conversation with the received canon of the dual Torah yielded important propositions. But our interest in Reform Judaism hardly requires us to criticize the constructive efforts of its theologians. What we want to know

is two things: first, is it old or is it new? It is new. Second, if a Judaism turns out to be new, as shown by its essentially distinctive principle of selection, then we ask how that Judaism establishes its claim to form the natural, the necessary next step in "Judaism." We find the answers to both questions near at hand. First, does this Judaism ask the questions that for the Judaism of the dual Torah demanded answer, or does it ask other questions? That is a matter of fact. Second, does this Judaism find self-evidently valid the answers of the Judaism of the dual Torah, or do other propositions prove self-evidently true? That too is a matter of fact.

**Urgent questions, self-evident answers:** In the new Judaism at hand, what place do we find for the Judaism of the dual Torah? What questions prove so urgent as to make self-evident the answers of the Judaism in process of emerging? The answers to both questions lie right on the surface. Given its intellectual strength, Reform Judaism had no difficulty saying precisely what it wished on classic issues. As to the Judaism of the dual Torah, its questions proved no more compelling than its answers. The whole turned from the self-evident statement of God's will to a source of precedents, available for selection and rearrangement. How to pick and choose formed the principal issue of method. The distinction between written and oral Torah provided the answer. Pick the written, drop the oral. So the Reform theologians rejected the claim that the oral part of the Torah came from God. It was the work of men, time-bound, contingent, possessed of a mere advisory authority. Whatever precedents and antecedents Reform historians and theologians sought, they would not look in the rabbinic writings that, all together, fall under the name, "the Talmud," because there their enemies found their principal ammunition. The Judaism from which Reform took its leave, the one that required the changes become reforms yielding Reform—that Judaism found its definition in the dual Torah of Sinai, as written down from the Mishnah onward. So, quite naturally, when the Reformers addressed the issue of continuity, they leapt over the immediate past, represented by the

Judaism of the dual Torah, and sought their antecedents in the processes of change instead.

### Notes

[1] Benzion Dinur, "Emancipation," *Encyclopaedia Judaica*, vol. 6, cols. 696-718.
[2] Michael A. Meyer, *The Origins of the Modern Jew. Jewish Identity and European Culture in Germany, 1749-1824* (Detroit, 1967), p. 48.
[3] Jakob J. Petuchowski, "Reform Judaism," *Encyclopaedia Judaica*, vol. 14, cols. 23-28.
[4] Ibid., col. 25.
[5] Ibid., col. 25.
[6] Max Wiener, *Abraham Geiger and Liberal Judaism. The Challenge of the Nineteenth Century* (New York, 1962).
[7] Ibid., p. 11.
[8] Ibid., p. 13.
[9] Ibid., p. 40.
[10] Ibid., p. 42.
[11] (New York, 1963.) Quotations on pp. 7-9.
[12] Ibid., p. 132.

JACOB NEUSNER

**REPENTANCE IN JUDAISM:** The word "repentance" renders into English the Hebrew theological word, *teshuvah*, meaning, "turning," in the sense of a turning away from sin, a turning toward God. Repentance in Judaism when properly carried out erases the consequences of sin and reconciles God and the sinner. That means the one who has sinned regrets the sin and resolves not to repeat it, and, further, when the occasion to repeat the sinful deed comes once more, the penitent does not then revert to the prior sinful action or condition. The power of repentance or teshuvah is unlimited, for a remarkable statement from the Talmud shows that sin is not indelible either upon one's family or upon oneself (B. Git. 57B).

> Grandsons of Haman studied Torah in Bene Beraq. Grandsons of Sisera taught children in Jerusalem. Grandsons of Sennacherib taught Torah in public. And who were they? Shemaiah and Abtalion [teachers of Hillel and Shammai].

To understand the power of this statement, we have only to say, "Hitler's grandson teaches Torah in a yeshiva of Bene Beraq." Or: "Eichmann's grandson sits in a Jerusalem Yeshiva, reciting prayers and psalms and learning Talmud."

If the sinner repents the sin, atones, and attains reconciliation with God, the sin is wiped off the record, the sinner forgiven, the sinners' successors blameless. The mark of repentance comes to the surface when the one-time sinner gains the chance to repeat the sinful deed but does not do so; then the repentance is complete. True, Scripture refers to God as ". . . visiting the guilt of the parents upon the children, upon the third and upon the fourth generations of those who reject me" (Ex. 20:5). But the Torah—the oral Torah reading the written Torah—qualifies that judgment: if the third and fourth generations continue the tradition of the fathers in rejecting the Lord, they too suffer punishment—for their own sins.

The sins of the fathers reach closure with the repentance of the children, their determination to make their own future. That is what the sinner who repents also does. Such statements represent the outcome of repentance, which is, moral regeneration for oneself, based upon genuine regret, fully realized in deed. These statements instruct the current generation of Judaism upon its moral duties towards those of its enemies, in the aftermath of the Holocaust, who repent and seek reconciliation. The message declares that sinners who repent are to be forgiven.

The Hebrew word is *teshuvah*, from the root for return, and the concept is generally understood to mean returning to God from a situation of estrangement. The turning thus is not only from sin. Sin rather serves as an indicator of a deeper pathology, utter estrangement from God. Teshuvah then involves not humiliation but reaffirmation of the self in God's image, after God's likeness. It follows that repentance in Judaism forms a theological category encompassing moral issues of action and attitude, wrong action, arrogant attitude, in particular. Repentance forms a step in the path to God that starts with the estrangement represented by sin: doing what I want, instead of what God wants, thus rebellion and arrogance. Sin precipitates punishment, whether personal for individuals or historical for nations; punishment brings about repentance for sin, which, in turn, leads to atonement for sin and, it follows, reconciliation with God. That sequence of stages in the moral regeneration of sinful humanity, individual or collective, defines the context in which repentance finds its natural home.

True, repentance is a far cry from loving and forgiving one's unrepentant enemy. God forgives sinners who atone and repent and asks of humanity that same act of grace— but no greater. For forgiveness without a prior act of repentance not only violates the rule of justice but also humiliates the law of mercy, cheapening and trivializing the superhuman act of forgiveness by treating as compulsive what is an act of human, and divine, grace. Sin is to be punished, but repentance is to be responded to with forgiveness, as the written Torah states explicitly: "You shall not bear a grudge nor pursue a dispute beyond reason, nor hate your brother in your heart, but you shall love your neighbor as yourself" (Lev. 19:18). The role of the sinful other is to repent, the task of the sinned-against is to respond to and accept repentance, at which point loving one's neighbor as oneself becomes the just person's duty. Repentance therefore forms the critical center of the moral transaction in a contentious and willful world. The data we shall examine indicate that, for Judaism, repentance without atonement bears no meaning whatsoever, indeed lies beyond all rational comprehension. And atonement, it goes without saying, requires the presence of God, with whom reconciliation is sought.

In Judaism, the conception of repentance—regretting sin, determining not to repeat it, seeking forgiveness for it—defines the key to the moral life with God. No single component of the human condition takes higher priority in establishing a right relationship with God, and none bears more profound implications for this-worldly attitudes and actions; the entire course of a human life, filled as it is with the natural propensity to sin, that is, to rebel against God, but comprised also by the compelled requirement of confronting God's response, punishment for sin, takes its direction, finds its critical turning, at the act of repentance, the first step in the regeneration of the human condition as it was meant to be. The concept takes on

specificity when atonement comes to the fore: in the Temple, atonement involved correct offerings for sin; for the prophets, repentance would characterize the entire nation, Israel, come to its senses in the aftermath of God's punishment, and, as we shall see, in the oral part of that one Torah—revelation— that defines Judaism, repentance takes on a profoundly this-worldly, social sense. But in all statements of the matter, the single trait proves ubiquitous: repentance defines a stage in the relationship of Man and God, inclusive of repentance to one's fellow for sin against him or her.

Let us turn first to the classic statement of repentance and examine the context in the law and theology of Judaism in which the concept takes on concrete and this-worldly form. To understand the context, we recall that God's revelation, the Torah makes its normative statements to holy Israel in two media, one written, the other orally formulated and orally transmitted until being written down long after Sinai. The Hebrew Scriptures ("Old Testament," "Tanakh") set forth the written part of the Torah. The documents that record in writing the originally oral Torah begin with the Mishnah, a late second century C.E. philosophy in the form of a law code, to which, over the next four centuries, was appended a large and systematic commentary, the Talmud; alongside, compilations of Scriptural exegeses called Midrashim recorded other components of this same Torah. All together, the two Torahs, oral and written, set forth the full and exhaustive account of God's self-manifestation to humanity through holy Israel, the supernatural community bearing God's blessing from Abraham to the end of time. That this formulation of the religious myth carries us deep into the world of not history and ethnicity, but eternity and transcendent, holy community of the faithful, alerts us to the theological framework in which repentance will make its appearance.

Moving beyond Scripture, we find in the Mishnah (Yom. 8:8-9) the appropriate starting point in the presentation of the moral dimensions of the Day of Atonement (Yom Kippur):

A. A sin offering and an unconditional guilt offering atone.
B. Death and the Day of Atonement atone when joined with repentance.
C. Repentance atones for minor transgressions of positive and negative commandments.
D. And as to serious transgressions, [repentance] suspends the punishment until the Day of Atonement comes along and atones.

A. He who says, "I shall sin and repent, sin and repent"—
B. they give him no chance to do repentance.
C. [If he said,] "I will sin and the Day of Atonement will atone"—the Day of Atonement does not atone.
D. For transgressions done between man and the Omnipresent, the Day of Atonement atones.
E. For transgressions between man and man, the Day of Atonement atones, only if the man will regain the good will of his friend.

The process of reconciliation with God—at-one-ment so to speak—encompasses a number of steps and components, not only repentance; and repentance, for its part, does not reach concrete definition in the formulation of the process. A sin offering in the Temple in Jerusalem, presented for unintentional sins, atones, and therein we find the beginning of the definition of repentance. It lies in the contrast between the sin-offering at A, that is, atonement for unintentional sin, and those things that atone for intentional sin, which are two events, on the one side, and the expression of right attitude, *teshuvah*, returning to God, on the other. The role of repentance emerges in the contrast with the sin-offering; what atones for what is inadvertent has no bearing upon what is deliberate. The willful sin can be atoned for only if repentance has taken place, that is to say, genuine regret, a turning away from the sin, after the fact therefore transforming the sin from one that is deliberate to one that is, if not unintentional beforehand, then at least, unintentional afterward. Then death, on the one side, or the Day of Atonement, on the other, work their enchantment.

But that provision for reconciliation even after the fact raises the question of deliberate and willful violation of the law, encom-

passing repentance—before the fact. And that is the point at which repentance loses its power. If to begin with one has insinuated repentance into the sinful act itself, declaring up front that afterward one will repent, the power of repentance is lost, the act of will denying the post facto possibility altogether. That is the point of 8:9A-C. For, we now observe, the issue of attitude takes over, and is in the end the fundamental attitude that governs: if to begin with the willful act is joined to an act of will affecting the post facto circumstance, then that attitude nullifies all further possibilities—except an ultimate act of repentance, to which, for Judaism (as for Christianity) God is always prepared to respond.

Thus far the Mishnah has treated the act of repentance or turning as if it had come to a full and complete definition. But that premise presupposes a rich set of a priori definitions. These come to full articulation in a document that reached closure at the same time as the Talmud of Babylonia, a commentary on Mishnah-tractate Abot (The Fathers), called Abot deRabbi Nathan, The Fathers According to Rabbi Nathan (XXIX:VIII.1):

3.A. In Rome R. Matia b. Harash asked R. Eleazar b. Azariah, "Have you heard about the four types of atonement that R. Ishmael expounded?"
B. He said to him, "I heard indeed, but they are three, but with each of them repentance is required.
C. "One verse of Scripture says, 'Return, you backsliding children, says the Lord, I will heal your backsliding' (Jer. 3:22). A second says, 'For on this day shall atonement be made for you to cleanse you' (Lev. 16:30). And a third says, 'Then I will visit their transgression with the rod and their iniquity with strokes' (Ps. 89:33), and a fourth: 'Surely this iniquity shall not be expiated by you until you die' (Is. 22:14).
D. "How so? If someone has violated a religious duty involving an act of commission but has repented, he does not move from that spot before he is forgiven forthwith. In this regard it is said, 'Return, you backsliding children, says the Lord, I will heal your backsliding' (Jer. 3:22).
E. "If someone has transgressed a negative commandment but has repented,

G. "repentance suspends the punishment and the Day of Atonement atones. In this regard it is said, 'For on this day shall atonement be made for you to cleanse you' (Lev. 16:30)."

F. "If someone has transgressed a rule, the penalty of which is extirpation or judicially inflicted capital punishment, but has repented, the repentance and the Day of Atonement suspend the matter, and suffering on the other days of the year effect atonement, and in this regard it is said, 'Then I will visit their transgression with the rod and their iniquity with strokes' (Ps. 89:33).

G. "But one who has profaned the name of heaven—repentance has not got the power to effect suspension of the punishment, nor suffering to wipe it out, nor the Day of Atonement to atone, but repentance and suffering suspend the punishment, and death will wipe out the sin with them, and in this regard it is said, 'Surely this iniquity shall not be expiated by you until you die' (Is. 22:14)."

The issue of repentance now takes concrete form. The secondary articulation takes on a legal aspect, as the Mishnah's formulation (Repentance atones for minor transgressions of positive and negative commandments . . . as to serious transgressions, repentance suspends the punishment until the Day of Atonement comes along and atones) leads us to anticipate. Once the cited distinctions are made, then the exegete will specify how the distinctions work themselves out, thus D, E, F. Here we see how repentance takes its place in the hierarchical process.

The talmudic discussions, for their part, move from law to theology, deeming each to transmit the same message as the other, the one in the form of norms of behavior, the other, of belief. The problem is how the victim is to respond to a genuine act of repentance, formed in conformity to the religious norms that we have examined: a statement of regret for the past and a resolve not to repeat the sins of the past. This is how the Talmud deals with precisely the problem of intransigence on the part of the victim (B. Yom. 87a):

VI.2.A. Said R. Isaac, "Whoever offends his fellow, even if through what he

says, has to reconcile with him, as it is said, 'My son, if you have become surety for your neighbor, if you have struck your hands for a stranger, you are snared by the words of your mouth . . . do this now, my son, and deliver yourself, seeing you have come into the power of your neighbor, go, humble yourself, and urge your neighbor' (Prov. 6:1-3). If it is a money-claim against you, open the palm of your hand to him [and pay him off], and if not, send a lot of intermediaries to him."

B. Said R. Hisda, "He has to reconcile with him through three sets of three people each: 'He comes before men and says, I have sinned and perverted that which was right and it did not profit me' (Job 33:27)."

C. Said R. Yosé bar Hanina, "Whoever seeks reconciliation with his neighbor has to do so only three times: 'Forgive I pray you now . . . and now we pray you' (Gen. 50:17).

D. "And if he has died, he brings ten people and sets them up at his grave and says, 'I have sinned against the Lord the God of Israel and against this one, whom I have hurt.'"

The sinner must do his or her best to reconcile with the victim, who is expected to accept the genuine act of repentance. But the matter has its own limits. Beyond the specified point, the penitent has carried out his obligation as best he or she can, and nothing more is to be done.

How the canonical literature of Judaism defines the concept of repentance emerges, finally, in a systematic composite of statements on the matter. A sizable abstract allows the Talmud of Babylonia, the final and authoritative statement of the Torah of Sinai, to portray the conception in its usual, systematic way. For, organizing topical presentations on such theological themes, the Talmud makes its statement on the subject in the following terms, a sequence of sayings expressing the main components of the concept (B. Yom. 86b):

8.A. Said R. Yohanan, "Great is repentance, for it overrides a negative commandment that is in the Torah: 'If a man put away his wife and she go from him and become another man's wife, may he return to her again? Will not the land be greatly polluted? But you have played the harlot with many lovers, and would you then return to me, says the Lord' (Jer. 3:1)."

9.A. Said R. Jonathan, "Great is repentance, for it brings redemption near: 'And a redeemer shall come to Zion and to those who return from transgression in Jacob' (Is. 59:20)—how come 'a redeemer shall come to Zion'? Because of 'those who return from transgression in Jacob.'"

10.A. Said R. Simeon b. Laqish, "Great is repentance, for by it sins that were done deliberately are transformed into those that were done inadvertently: 'And when the wicked turns from his wickedness and does that which is lawful and right, he shall live thereby' (Ezek. 33:19)—now 'wickedness' is done deliberately, and yet the prophet calls it stumbling!"

12.A. Said R. Isaac, [or] they say in the West in the name of Rabbah bar Mari, "Come and take note of how the characteristic of the Holy One, blessed be he, is not like the characteristic of mortals. If a mortal insults his fellow by something that he has said, the other may or may not be reconciled with him. And if you say that he is reconciled with him, he may or may not be reconciled by mere words. But with the Holy One, blessed be he, if someone commits a transgression in private, he will be reconciled with him in mere words, as it is said, 'Take with you words and return to the Lord' (Hos. 14:2). And not only so, but [God] credits it to him as goodness: 'and accept that which is good' (Hos. 14:2); and not only so, but Scripture credits it to him as if he had offered up bullocks: 'So will we render for bullocks the offerings of our lips' (Hos. 14:2). Now you might say that reference is made to obligatory bullocks, but Scripture says, 'I will heal their backsliding, I love them freely' (Hos. 14:4)."

14.A. How is a person who has repented to be recognized?

B. Said R. Judah, "For example, if a transgression of the same sort comes to hand once, and second time, and the one does not repeat what he had done."

C. R. Judah defined matters more closely: "With the same woman, at the same season, in the same place."

The act of repentance commences with the sinner, but then compels divine response; the attitude of the penitent governs, the motive—love, fear—making the difference. The power of repentance to win God over, even after recurring sin, forms the leading theme—the leitmotif—of the composite. Israel's own redemption depends upon Israel's repentance. The concluding statement proves most concrete. Repentance takes place when the one who has sinned and declares his regret ("in words") faces the opportunity of repeating the sinful action but this time refrains, so No. 14.

That we deal with the critical nexus in the relationship between God and humanity emerges in one composition after another, e.g., repentance overrides negative commandments of the Torah (the more important kind); brings redemption; changes the character of the already-committed sins; lengthens the life of the penitent. Not only so, but the power of repentance before the loving God of grace is such that mere words suffice. The upshot is, we deal with a matter of attitude that comes to the surface in concrete statements; but as to deeds, the penitent cannot repeat the sin, so no deed can be required; the penitent has a more difficult task: not to do again what he has done before. The whole complex then draws us deep into an enchanted and transcendent universe. To be human is to sin, to acknowledge and respond to repentance is to exhibit that which, in humanity, is to act like God. So, to summarize the position of Judaism on repentance: it is human to sin, it also is human to repent—an act of humility to wipe out an act of arrogance—and that is why it is divine to respond to repentance with an act of forgiveness, whether the response comes from God or from us.

JACOB NEUSNER

**REWARD AND PUNISHMENT IN CLASSICAL JUDAISM:** God's will is rational, within humankind's understanding of reason, because it is just. And by "just," the sages of classical Judaism understood the commonsense meaning: fair, equitable, proportionate. In place of fate or impersonal destiny, chance or irrational, inexplicable chaos, God's purpose is seen everywhere to come to realization. The Oral Torah thus identifies God's will as the active and causative force in the lives of individuals and nations.

But how do sages know that God's will is realized in the moral order of justice, involving reward and punishment? Of the various types of scriptural evidence—explicit commandments, stories, prophetic admonitions—available to show how the moral order prevailed in all being, the one bearing the greatest probative weight derived from the exact match between sin and punishment. That body of evidence recorded human action and divine reaction, on the one side, and meritorious deed and divine response and reward, on the other. It was comprised by consequential cases, drawn from both private and public life, to underscore sages' insistence upon the match between the personal and the public, all things subject to the same simple rule.

That demonstration of not only the principle but the precision of measure for measure, deriving from Scripture's own record of God's actions, takes priority of place in the examination of the rationality of the sages' universe, for it permeates their system and frames its prevailing modes of explanation and argument. The principle that all being conforms to rules and that these rules embody principles of justice—exact punishment of each sin and precise reward of each act of virtue—defined the starting point of all rational thought and the entire character of sages' theological structure and system.

Sages deemed it a fact that good is rewarded and evil punished. Since the world in which they lived knew better, and since sages themselves created a system that explained why, though justice is supposed to prevail, present matters are chaotic, we may take for granted that they too knew better. Only their theology—the logic of God, systematically expounded—taught them to see matters as they did. That is why we seek to identify the sources for their conviction of the order of society, natural and supernatural alike. Since no one in the history of humanity has offered as a simple fact of everyday reality

such a principle of natural justice, but many have found the opposite, we are forced to ask why these sages conceived matters as they did.

What endowed them with certainty that they lived in a trustworthy world of reason and order defined by justice is readily apparent. This conviction emerged from their systematization of the facts of the written Torah. In Scripture, sages found the pervasive purpose of the rule of justice, resting on reason and on equity. From that generative principle, all else followed, the structure stood firm, the system worked.

To understand how the judge of all the world is bound by the rules of justice and does justice, the sages framed a null-hypothesis, that is, a hypothesis they would test to prove the opposite of what they sought to show. They asked: if justice did not govern, how should we know it? The answer is, we should find not a correlation but a disproportion between sin and consequent result, or penalty, between crime and punishment. But, by contrast, they understood that, in line with God's justice, the penalty must fit the crime, measure must match measure, and the more exact the result to the cause, the more compelling the proof of immediate and concrete justice as the building block of world order. In this approach, justice is transformed from a vague generality—a mere sentiment—to a precise and measurable dimension of the actual social order of morality: how things hold together when subject to tension, at the pressure-points of structure, not merely how they are arrayed in general.

Let us turn to a systematic statement of the main point: when God judges and sentences, not only is the judgment fair but the penalty fits the crime with frightening precision. So too, when God judges and awards a decision of merit, the reward proves exact. These two together, the match of sin and penalty, meritorious deed and reward, then are shown to explain the point and purpose of one detail after another, and, all together, they add up to a portrait of a world order that is fundamentally and essentially just—the starting point and foundation of all else, as M. Sot. 1:7 illustrates:

A. By that same measure by which a man metes out [to others], do they mete out to him:

B. She primped herself for sin, the Omnipresent made her repulsive.

C. She exposed herself for sin, the Omnipresent exposed her.

D. With the thigh she began to sin, and afterward with the belly, therefore the thigh suffers the curse first, and afterward the belly.

E. But the rest of the body does not escape [punishment].

These are the sages' general observations based on the facts set forth in Scripture. The response of the woman accused of adultery to her drinking of the bitter water—which produces one result for the guilty, another for the innocent (Num. 5:20-22)—in the Mishnah is amplified and expanded, extended to the entire rite, where the woman is disheveled; then the order, thigh, belly, shows the perfect precision of the penalty. What Scripture treats as a case, sages transform into a generalization, so making Scripture yield governing rules.

At T. Sot. 4:1-6 we again see that reward is governed by exact justice, the precision of the deed matched by the precision of the response:

4:1G. And so you find in the case of Abraham that by that same measure by which a man metes out, they mete out to him.

H. He ran before the ministering angels three times, as it is said, "When he saw them, he ran to meet them" (Gen. 18:2), "And Abraham hastened to the tent" (Gen. 18:6), "And Abraham ran to the herd" (Gen. 18:7).

I. So did the Omnipresent, blessed be he, run before his children three times, as it is said, "The Lord came from Sinai, and dawned from Seir upon us; he shone forth from Mount Paran" (Deut. 33:2).

4:2A. Of Abraham it is said, "He bowed himself to the earth" (Gen. 18:2).

B. So will the Omnipresent, blessed be he, respond graciously to his children in time to come, "Kings will be your foster-fathers, and their queens your nursing mothers. With their faces to the ground they shall bow down to you and lick the dust of your feet" (Is. 49:23).

C. Of Abraham it is said, "Let a little water be brought" (Gen. 18:4).

D. So did the Omnipresent, blessed be he, respond graciously and give to his children a well in the wilderness, which gushed through the whole camp of Israel, as it is said, "The well which the princes dug, which the nobles of the people delved" (Num. 21:18), teaching that it went over the whole south and watered the entire desert, which looks down upon the desert" (Num. 21:20).

E. Of Abraham it is said, "And rest yourselves under the tree" (Gen. 18:4).

F. So the Omnipresent gave his children seven glorious clouds in the wilderness, one on their right, one on their left, one before them, one behind them, one above their heads, and one as the presence among them.

4:3A. Of Abraham it is said, "While I fetch a morsel of bread that you may refresh yourselves" (Gen. 18:5).

B. So did the Omnipresent, blessed be he, give them manna in the wilderness, as it is said, "The people went about and gathered it . . . and made cakes of it, and the taste of it was like the taste of cakes baked with oil" (Num. 11:8).

4:4A. Of Abraham it is said, "And Abraham ran to the herd and took a calf, tender and good" (Gen. 18:7).

B. So the Omnipresent, blessed be he, rained down quail from the sea for his children, as it is said, "And there went forth a wind from the Lord, and it brought quails from the sea, and let them fall beside the camp" (Num. 11:31).

4:5A. Of Abraham what does it say? "And Abraham stood over them" (Gen. 1 8:8).

B. So the Omnipresent, blessed be he, watched over his children in Egypt, as it is said, "And the Lord passed over the door" (Exod. 12:23).

4:6A. Of Abraham what does it say? "And Abraham went with them to set them on their way" (Gen. 18:16).

B. So the Omnipresent, blessed be he, accompanied his children for forty years, as it is said, "These forty years the Lord your God has been with you" (Deut. 2:7).

The evidence is of the same character as that adduced in the Mishnah: cases of Scripture. But the power of the Tosefta's treatment of Abraham must be felt: finding an exact counterpart in Israel's later history to each gesture of the progenitor, Abraham, shows the match between the deeds of the patriarchs and the destiny of their family later on. Once more, we note, a systematic effort focuses upon details. Justice is not a generalized expectation but a very particular fact, bread/manna, calf/quail, and so on.

The principle of commensurate response to each action extends also to the atonement of the holy people of God, Israel. Israel is punished for its sin. But when Israel repents and God forgives and restores the holy people's fortunes, then that same principle that all things match takes over. Hence we should not find surprising the logical extension to the character of God's forgiveness and comfort of Israel of the principle of measure for measure. When, specifically, Israel sins, it is punished through that with which it sins, but it also is comforted through that with which it has been punished. What is important is not only the logical necessity of sages' reaching such a position. It also is the character of their demonstration of that fact. Here is a remarkably successful exposition in which sages assemble out of Scripture facts that, all together, demonstrate the moral order of reward and punishment along with the merciful character of God and his justice (Pesiqta deRab Kahana XVI:XI.1):

A. "[Comfort, comfort my people, says your God.] Speak tenderly to the heart of Jerusalem and declare to her [that her warfare is ended, that her iniquity is pardoned, that she has received from the Lord's hand double for all her sins]" (Is. 40:1-2).
B. When they sinned with the head, they were smitten at the head, but they were comforted through the head.
C. When they sinned with the head: "Let us make a head and let us return to Egypt" (Num. 14:4).
D. ... they were smitten at the head: "The whole head is sick" (Is. 1:5).
E. ... but they were comforted through the head: "Their king has passed before them and the Lord is at the head of them" (Mic. 2:13).

The construction is pellucid, the triplet of sin, punishment, and comfort, applied first to the head, and, predictably, in the following, to the body's other principal parts. Why predictably? Because sages wish to match nature with supernature, the components of the natural world with the parts of the body, the components of the body with the paradigmatic actions of Israel through time. All things match in exact balance: the natural world and the body of humankind, the body of humankind and the actions of Israel. From the head we proceed to the eye, ear, nose, mouth, tongue, heart, hand, foot—the agencies of the expression of human will (Pesiqta deRab Kahana XVI:XI.2-13.):

2.A. When they sinned with the eye, they were smitten at the eye, but they were comforted through the eye.
B. When they sinned with the eye: "[The daughters of Zion ... walk] ... with wanton eyes" (Is. 3:16).
C. ... they were smitten at the eye: "My eye, my eye runs down with water" (Lam. 1:16).
D. ... but they were comforted through the eye: "For every eye shall see the Lord returning to Zion" (Is. 52:8).
3.A. When they sinned with the ear, they were smitten at the ear, but they were comforted through the ear.
B. When they sinned with the ear: "They stopped up their ears so as not to hear" (Zech. 7:11).
C. ... they were smitten at the ear: "Their ears shall be deaf" (Mic. 7:16).
D. ... but they were comforted through the ear: "Your ears shall hear a word saying, [This is the way]" (Is. 30:21).
4.A. When they sinned with the nose [spelled *af*, which can also mean "yet" or "also"], they were smitten at the nose, but they were comforted through the nose.
B. When they sinned with the nose: "And, lo, they put the branch to their noses" (Ezek. 8:17).
C. ... they were smitten at the word *af* [also]: "I also will do this to you" (Lev. 26:16).
D. ... but they were comforted through the word *af* [now meaning yet]: "And yet for all that, when they are in the land of their enemies, I will not reject them" (Lev. 26:44).
5.A. When they sinned with the mouth, they were smitten at the mouth, but they were comforted through the mouth.
B. When they sinned with the mouth: "Every mouth speaks wantonness" (Is. 9:16).
C. ... they were smitten at the mouth: "[The Aramaeans and the Philistines]

devour Israel with open mouth" (Is. 9:11).

D. ... but they were comforted through the mouth: "Then was our mouth filled with laughter" (Ps. 126:2).

6.A. When they sinned with the tongue, they were smitten at the tongue, but they were comforted through the tongue.

B. When they sinned with the tongue: "They bend their tongue, [their bow of falsehood]" (Jer. 9:2).

C. ... they were smitten at the tongue: "The tongue of the sucking [child cleaves to the roof of his mouth for thirst]" (Lam. 4:4).

D. ... but they were comforted through the tongue: "And our tongue with singing" (Ps. 126:2).

7.A. When they sinned with the heart, they were smitten at the heart, but they were comforted through the heart.

B. When they sinned with the heart: "Yes, they made their hearts as a stubborn stone" (Zech. 7:12).

C. ... they were smitten at the heart: "And the whole heart faints" (Is. 1:5).

D. ... but they were comforted through the heart: "Speak to the heart of Jerusalem" (Is. 40:2).

8.A. When they sinned with the hand, they were smitten at the hand, but they were comforted through the hand.

B. When they sinned with the hand: "Your hands are full of blood" (Is. 1:15).

C. ... they were smitten at the hand: "The hands of women full of compassion have boiled their own children" (Lam. 4:10).

D. ... but they were comforted through the hand: "The Lord will set his hand again the second time [to recover the remnant of his people]" (Is. 11:11).

9.A. When they sinned with the foot, they were smitten at the foot, but they were comforted through the foot.

B. When they sinned with the foot: "The daughters of Zion ... walk ... making a tinkling with their feet" (Is. 3:16).

C. ... they were smitten at the foot: "Your feet will stumble upon the dark mountains' (Jer. 13:16).

D. ... but they were comforted through the foot: "How beautiful upon the mountains are the feet of the messenger of good tidings" (Is. 52:7).

10.A. When they sinned with "this," they were smitten at "this," but they were comforted through "this."

B. When they sinned with "this:" "[The people said ... Go, make us a god], for as for *this* man Moses ..., [we do not know what has become of him]" (Exod. 32:1).

C. ... they were smitten at "this:" "For *this* our heart is faint" (Lam. 5:17).

D. ... but they were comforted through "this:" "It shall be said in that day, lo, *this* is our God" (Is. 25:9).

11.A. When they sinned with "he," they were smitten at "he," but they were comforted through "he."

B. When they sinned with "he: "They have denied the Lord and said, It is not he" (Jer. 5:12).

C. ... they were smitten at "he:" "Therefore he has turned to be their enemy, and he himself fought against them" (Is. 63:10).

D. ... but they were comforted through "he:" "I even I am he who comforts you" (Is. 51:12).

12.A. When they sinned with fire, they were smitten at fire, but they were comforted through fire.

B. When they sinned with fire: "The children gather wood and the fathers kindle fire" (Jer. 7:18).

C. ... they were smitten at fire: "For from on high he has sent fire into my bones" (Lam. 1:13).

D. ... but they were comforted through fire: "For I, says the Lord, will be for her a wall of fire round about" (Zech. 2:9).

13.A. When they sinned in double measure, they were smitten in double measure, but they were comforted in double measure.

B. When they sinned in double measure: "Jerusalem has sinned a sin" (Lam. 1:8).

C. ... they were smitten in double measure: "that she has received from the Lord's hand double for all her sins" (Is. 40:2).

D. ... but they were comforted in double measure: "Comfort, comfort my people, says your God. [Speak tenderly to the heart of Jerusalem and cry to her that her warfare is ended, that her iniquity is pardoned, that she has received from the Lord's hand double for all her sins]" (Is. 40:1-2).

The basic proposition—when they sinned with this, they were smitten at this, but they were comforted through this—maintains that an exact match unites sin and punishment;

through that with which one sins, one is punished. But then, that same match links the modes of consolation as well, that is, through that trait through which one is punished, one also will be comforted. So the conviction of an orderly and appropriate set of correspondences setting forth a world in balance and proportion generates the details. The proofs for the proposition involve an extensive survey of both the media of sin and the character of punishment therefor.

Two motifs overspread the theology of the Oral Torah, the destruction of Jerusalem and its Temple and the cessation of Israel's sacrificial service to God, and the fate of the individual; public and private affairs are governed by those same principles of order flowing from justice. When it comes to the manifest punishment represented by the loss of Jerusalem and its medium for divine service, the precision noted in the cases above gives way to a generalized conviction that an entire list of sins found a single punishment. But all of these sins fall into a single category: they are public and for them the community of Israel at large bears responsibility. That accounts for the various specific sins linked to the general ruin of Jerusalem, e.g., by B. Shab. 16:2II.42/119b:

A. Said Abbayye, "Jerusalem was ruined only because they violated the Sabbath therein: 'And they have hidden their eyes from my Sabbaths, therefore I am profaned among them' (Ezek. 22:26)."

B. Said R. Abbahu, "Jerusalem was ruined only because they stopped reciting the Shema morning and evening: 'Woe to them that rise up early in the morning, that they may follow strong drink . . . and the harp and the lute, the timbrel and the pipe and wine are in their feasts, but they do not regard the works of the Lord; therefore my people have gone into captivity for lack of knowledge' (Is. 5:11-13)."

C. Said R. Hamnuna, "Jerusalem was ruined only because they neglected the children in the schoolmaster's household: 'pour out . . . because of the children in the street' (Jer. 6:211). Why pour out? Because the children are in the streets."

D. Said Ulla, "Jerusalem was ruined only because they were not ashamed on account of one another: 'Were they ashamed when they committed abomination? No, they were not at all ashamed, therefore they shall fall' (Jer. 6:15)."

E. Said R. Isaac, "Jerusalem was ruined only because they treated equally the small and the great: 'And it shall be, like people like priest' and then, 'the earth shall be utterly emptied' (Is. 24:2-3)."

F. Said R. Amram b. R. Simeon bar Abba said R. Simeon bar Abba said R. Hanina, "Jerusalem was ruined only because they did not correct one another: 'Her princes are become like harts that find no pasture' (Lam. 1:6)—just as the hart's head is at the side of the other's tail, so Israel of that generation hid their faces in the earth and did not correct one another."

G. Said R. Judah, "Jerusalem was ruined only because they humiliated disciples of sages therein: 'But they mocked the messengers of God and despised his words and scoffed at his prophets, until the wrath of the Lord arose against his people till there was no remedy' (2 Chr. 36:16)."

None of these identified sins proves private or particular to one person only. But when it comes to the private person, by contrast, sages aim at a more precise match of sin to punishment. So far as is possible, they match the character of the one with the definition of the other (M. Shab. 2:6): "On account of three transgressions do women die in childbirth: because they are not meticulous in the laws of menstrual separation, in those covering the dough offering, and in those covering the kindling of a lamp for the Sabbath." The first clearly matches in a particular way, the second and the third are more general. Various specific penalties are incurred for specific sins, and these are specified in the Talmud of Babylonia's amplification of that same Mishnaic passage (B. Shab. 2:6I.12ff./32B):

I.12A. It has been taught on Tannaite authority:

B. R. Nathan says, "On account of the sin of a man's unfulfilled vows, a man's wife dies: 'If you have nothing with which to pay your vows, why should he take away your bed from under you?' (Prov. 22:27)."

C. Rabbi says, "On account of the sin of a man's unfulfilled vows, a man's children die when they are young: 'Suffer not your mouth to cause your flesh to sin, neither say before the angel that it was an error. Wherefore should God be angry at your voice and destroy the work of your hands?' (Eccl. 5:5). What is 'the work of a man's hands'? Say: It is his sons and daughters."

I.13A. Our rabbis have taught on Tannaite authority:

B. "On account of the sin of unfulfilled vows children die," the words of R. Eleazar b. R. Simeon.

C. R. Judah the Patriarch says, "It is on account of the sin of neglect of the Torah."

I.16A. Said R. Simeon b. Laqish, "Whoever is careful about the requirement of show fringes will in response enjoy the merit that two thousand eight hundred slaves will serve him: 'Thus says the Lord of hosts, in those days it shall come to pass that ten men shall take hold, out of all the languages of the nations, shall even take hold of the skirt of him who is a Jew, saying, we will go with you' (Zech. 8:23)." [The skirt is the fringe, there are four corners of the garment, and there are seventy languages, hence seventy languages times ten men times four corners, or two thousand eight hundred.]

The next item holds that, if one preserves a grudge, his own household will be disrupted by discord as well. What the man does will in the end affect his own home:

I.17A. It has been taught on Tannaite authority:

B. R. Nehemiah says, "For the sin of nursing a grudge, discord grows in someone's house, his wife will miscarry, and his sons and daughters will die young."

The dough-offering, a bit of dough removed before baking the bread, gives back to the priesthood, one of God's surrogates, part of the grain that is used. Since it is a mark of abundance of food, failure to give that offering leads to a scarcity of food:

II.1A. R. Eleazar b. R. Judah says, "For the sin of neglect of the dough-offering, no blessing comes upon what is in storage, prices are cursed, seed is sown but others eat it up: 'I also will do this to you: I will visit you with terror, even consumption and fever, that shall consume the eyes and make the soul to pine away, and you shall sow your seed in vain, for your enemies shall eat it' (Lev. 26:16). Read the word translated as terror as though it were written, dough-offering.

B. "But if they give it, they are blessed: 'You shall also give to the priest the first of your dough, to cause a blessing to rest on your house' (Ezek. 44:30)."

The gathered crops are liable to the separation of grain for heave-offering and tithes, which represent God's share of the crop; these are given to God's surrogates, the priests, Levites, or poor, and some of the tithes also are to be consumed by the farmer in Jerusalem; here too, God has a claim, and if that is not met, then rain is withheld. So violation of the laws governing agriculture brings a concomitant end to successful farming of the land:

II.2A. For the sin of neglect of heave-offering and tithes, the heavens are shut up from bringing down dew and rain; prices are high; wages low; people pursue a living but don't succeed: "Drought and heat consume the snow waters, so does the grave those who have sinned" (Job 24:19).

Locusts represent thieves of the farmers' crops; for robbery, locusts come up and steal the crops:

II.4A. For the sin of robbery, locusts come up and famine follows, and people eat the flesh of their sons and daughters: "Hear this word, you cows of Bashan, who are in the mountain of Samaria, who oppress the poor, who crush the needy" (Amos 4:1).

B. And it is written, "I have smitten you with blasting and mildew; the multitude of your gardens and your vineyards and your figs trees and your olive trees has the palmer-worm devoured" (Amos 4:9); and further, "That which the palmer-worm has left has the locust eaten; that which the locust has left, the cankerworm has eaten; that which the cankerworm has left, the caterpillar has eaten" (Joel

1:4); "And one shall snatch on the right hand and be hungry and he shall eat on the left hand and they shall not be satisfied; they shall eat every man the flesh of his own arm" (Is. 9:19).

C. Don't read the consonants that yield "the flesh of his own arm" in that way but as though they bore vowels to yield "the flesh of his own seed."

The failure of the political system—of the just use of the sword for acts of legitimate violence in recompense for violation of the just law—produces political crisis, war and disruption:

II.5A. For the transgressions of the delay of judgment, perversion of judgment, spoiling judgment, and neglect of the Torah, sword and spoil increase, pestilence and famine come, people eat and are not satisfied, and they measure out the bread that they eat by weight: "And I will bring a sword upon you, that will execute the vengeance of the covenant" (Lev. 26:25). Covenant refers only to the Torah: "But for my covenant of day and night, I had not appointed the ordinances of heaven and earth" (Jer. 33:25), and "When I break your staff of bread, ten women shall bake your bread in one oven and they shall deliver your bread again by weight" (Lev. 26:26), "Because, even because they rejected my judgments" (Lev. 26:43).

II.6A. For the sin of vain oaths, false oaths, profanation of the divine name, and desecration of the Sabbath, wild beasts multiply, domestic ones become few, the population declines, the roads become desolate: "And if by these things you will not be rebuked by me" (Lev. 26:23); read the letters translated by "these things" as though they bore vowels to yield "by reason of oaths" [that are false].

B. Further, "and I will send the beast of the field among you" (Lev. 26:22). In regard to false oaths it is written, "And you shall not swear by my name falsely, so that you profane the name of God" (Lev. 19:12), and of the profanation of the divine name it is written, "that you do not profane my holy name" (Lev. 22:2), and the profanation of the Sabbath is set forth, "every one who profanes it shall surely be put to death" (Exod. 31:15), and the penalty for profana-

tion derives from the penalty for a false oath, [with both punished by the sending of wild beasts].

If the Temple is not kept pure and holy, God's presence will depart from there:

II.7A. For the sin of bloodshed the Temple was destroyed and the presence of God left Israel: "So you shall not pollute the land in which you are, for blood pollutes the land. And you shall not defile the land which you inhabit, in the midst of which I dwell" (Num. 35:33-4). Lo, if you do make it unclean, you won't live there, and I won't live there.

Public sins against the social order, such as incest, idolatry, and neglect of the Sabbatical Year, are penalized by exile; others, more worthy to live in the Holy Land than Israel, will take over:

II.8A. For the sin of incest, idolatry, and neglect of the years of release and Jubilee, exile comes into the world, they go into exile, and others come and take their place: "For all these abominations have the men of the land done" (Lev. 18:27), "and the land is defiled, therefore I visit the iniquity thereof upon it" (Lev. 18:25), "that the land vomit you not out also when you defile it" (Lev. 18:28). With regard to idolatry: "And I will cast your carcasses upon the carcasses of your idols" (Lev. 26:30), "and I will make your cities a waste and will bring your sanctuaries into desolation" (Lev. 26:31), "and you will I scatter among the nations" (Lev. 26:33). In regard to the years of release and Jubilee Years: "Then shall the land enjoy her Sabbaths, as long as it lies desolate, and you shall be in your enemies land" (Lev. 26:34), "as long as it lies desolate it shall have rest" (Lev. 26:35).

II.9A. For the sin of a foul mouth, troubles multiply, evil decrees are renewed, Israel's youth die, and the fatherless and widows cry out and are not answered: "Therefore shall the Lord not rejoice over their young men, neither shall he have compassion over their fatherless and their widows; for every one is profane and an evil doer, and every mouth speaks folly. For all this his anger is not turned away, but his hand is stretched out still" (Is. 9:16).

So too B. Shab. 5:3 XII.12/55a-b adds the more general statement of the governing rule of justice: sin brings on death, transgression, suffering; as is the manner of the Talmud of Babylonia, the proposition is not only stated but systematically analyzed and subjected to provocative challenge:

A. Said R. Ammi, "Death comes about only through sin, and suffering only through transgression.
B. "Death comes about only through sin: 'The soul that sins, it shall die; the son shall not bear the iniquity of the father, neither shall the father bear the iniquity of the son; the righteousness of the righteous shall be upon him and the wickedness of the wicked shall be upon him' (Ezek. 18:20).
C. "And suffering only through transgression: 'Then will I visit their transgression with the rod and their iniquity with stripes' (Ps. 89:33)."

The rationality of the system requires not only that sin be punished appropriately, but that the punishment fit the crime in detail. Some trait must join the sin to the penalty, even though the precise trait may not be self-evident. This is clearest in the moral failures that follow a sin of morality, e.g., nursing a grudge produces miscarriage, neglecting dough-offering produces famine, and the like. Some of the facts of the matter derive from Scripture, but the principle as a principle is developed systemically only in the Oral Torah.

If sages had to state the logic that imposes order and proportion upon all relationships—the social counterpart to the laws of gravity—they would point to justice: what accords with justice is logical, and what does not is irrational. The principal documents of the Oral Torah provide ample evidence that, in sages' view, the moral order, based on justice, governs the affairs of people and nations. A more extensive survey than can be presented here will readily uncover ample testimony to the prevalence of this view at the foundation of every document of the Oral Torah. For the principle of justice does more than pervade the account of the world that sages set forth. Rather, it defines the first principle, the governing logic, of sages' system.

By that claim I allege that all else takes its leave from the conviction that by the term "good" (Gen. 1:31), God characterizes creation as *just*, that an entire system of the social order coheres as an amplification and exegesis of that principle, and that justice dictates the primary point of self-evidence: the system's unmoved mover, the point before which there is no appeal, and beyond which, no point unaffected, no refuge for the irrational. How to show that that conviction is not only normative but generative? It is by asking about what sages deem to require attention and explanation, and what they take for granted as a given. The answer to this question is clear: in sages' discourse, justice never requires explanation, but violations of justice always do. When what happens seems to violate the expectations of justice, then sages pay close attention and ask why. When what happens does conform, they do not have to: their unarticulated conviction of self-evidence is embodied, therefore, in the character of their discourse: not only the speech but the silence. Justice defines the rational, and injustice, the irrational.

JACOB NEUSNER

**RUSSIA, UKRAINE, BELARUS AND THE CAUCASUS, JEWISH EDUCATION IN FROM CZARIST TIMES UNTIL THE PRESENT:** Traditional orthodox Jewish education endured in Russia and the Soviet Union until the communist regime took control in 1917. This schooling primarily included the *cheder* and yeshiva and was directed exclusively to the Jewish male population. Most girls studied at home, learning basic reading skills and how to run a Jewish household. Secular education, which was scorned and considered heretical in the orthodox community, had begun to spread only after the 1860s, when Czar Alexander II liberalized the laws that controlled Jewish activity and participation within the empire. This education took place primarily in the Russian educational system, not in government sponsored Jewish schools. The same developments that led to this education also destroyed the traditional fabric of Jewish life, as secularly educated Jews, with Russification as their motto, did not recognize any tie or connection with their people. In this environment, several Jewish responses to the new social realities emerged, including Haskalah (enlightenment), Zionism (fig. 119), and socialism. Each directly influenced the educational system.

Socialism in particular attracted many Jews. The growth of industrialization in the Pale, Jewish artisans' previous experience in their guilds, and the desire for education were factors in socialism's growth and led to the formation of a Jewish socialist organization, the Bund, in 1897. In 1901, this group adopted an official position, emphatically condemning Zionism and demanding instead its own Jewish language and national-cultural autonomy with Russian society. Under the Czar, few Yiddish schools, which were illegal, existed. After the revolution, the situation changed. As part of a party of the masses, the Bund had to concern itself with the development of a language of the masses, Yiddish, and so began to develop secular Yiddish schools, providing teacher training and publishing its own text books.

Despite its relatively small size, the Russian Haskalah movement attempted to reform Judaism from within. Enlighteners believed that by using Hebrew language as a cultural tool, Jewish identity could be preserved. The revival of Hebrew in turn inspired Jewish nationalism and was considered the forerunner of Zionism in Russia.

Nationalistic in character, the *cheder metukan* (reformed elementary school) did not eliminate religious studies entirely. But modern Hebrew was emphasized, and, while Hebrew texts in the traditional *cheder* were studied for their content, in the new school, nationalism was primary. In addition to Jewish studies, as in the Russian schools, the *cheder metukan's* curriculum included secular studies, even taught in Russian. But the creation of these schools introduced new issues. While the *cheder*, a religious school, did not require governmental supervision, the *cheder metukan*, which included secular studies, required exactly such supervision.

An organization called Mefitzei Haskalah offered financial strength, assisting with and shaping the curriculum of the modern Jew-ish schools. Further interest in the Hebrew schools grew with the establishment, in 1897, of the World Zionist Congress and the subsequent Zionist Congress meetings. These meetings emphasized development of Hebrew and secular and cultural educational institutions. By 1902, the *cheder metukan* had spread throughout the Jewish communities, so that relatively few municipalities in the Pale, the area in which most Russian Jews resided, lacked one. Still, this expansion did not unify the school system or create an appropriate central educational organization; the schools developed their own curricula and independent emphases. Some focused on Russian while others even included Yiddish. Only in 1907 did such a central committee begin to function. The *cheder metukan* succeeded to a greater extent in the areas in which Jews were more affluent and students from middle and upper class homes comprised most of the school population. Tuition covered the majority of the expenses of these modern schools, with contributions from individuals and public events making up the rest. The salary of faculty teaching in the *cheder metukan* was far higher than that of the *melamed* (teacher) in the traditional *cheder*.

During this period, a war raged between supporters of Hebrew and those who favored Yiddish as the Jewish national language. Hebrew's supporters were further divided between those who accepted a synthesis between Yiddish and Hebrew and Hebraists, who demanded use of Hebrew alone. In 1907, the government legalized the "Lovers of the Hebrew Tongue Society" (*Choveve Safat Ivri*), which strengthened the Hebrew school movement. During this same year, the Mefitzei Haskalah Hebrew teacher training courses were developed, which continued until 1915. At the conference of Russian Zionists in 1913, a proposal of Jabotinsky was adopted that established all Hebrew schools. But if such schools were impossible to operate in Russian, Yiddish would be given preference over other languages.

**The Bolshevik Revolution and Communism:** Russian Jews saw the fall of the Czarist government as portending an improved Jewish life, and, indeed, on March 17, 1917, the Provisional Government annulled all religious and national restrictions. All streams of Jewish organizations immediately began expanding their activities. On November 2, 1917, the Zionist and Hebrew culture movements received an additional boost with the signing of the Balfour Declaration. Even as the strength of the Hebraists increased, the Yiddishists were weakened. *Choveve Sfat Ivri* changed its name to *Tarbut* ("Culture") and played a wider role in the teaching of Hebrew as well as other cultural activities. This organization flourished through schools, teacher seminaries, courses, and culture. *Tarbut* sponsored more than two hundred institutions and educational activities.

But Lenin and other leaders of the Bolshevik movement did not view Jewish nationalism positively. Instead, the ideologists of the new Soviet state refused to recognize the Jews as a nation and perceived Jewish culture as reactionary and anti-socialist. They therefore assailed all efforts to preserve Jewish culture. On December 1, 1918, a law allowing instruction in one's native language made government controlled minority schools possible. While greatly reducing *Tarbut's* influence over the schools, at least this allowed them to exist, as many of the schools became part of the government educational system. But even this did not last. In the middle of 1919, the schools were deemed illegal, and all education now had to be in the mother tongue, which ruled out Hebrew.

The Bolsheviks sought internal Jewish support as a foundation for Jewish indoctrination. Since most Jews spoke only Yiddish, they supported a Yiddish school system through which they hoped to bring Jewish youth and the masses to accept Bolshevism. The schools, portrayed as "true people's schools," were organized by a Jewish Commissariat through a body called the "Culture and Education Section" and aspired to develop the physical and moral attitudes of poor children. The School Division thus undertook the overall task of organizing the Yiddish elementary and secondary schools, including curriculum, personnel, training faculty, budget, and books. Higher education in Yiddish also developed, including pedagogic institu-

tions and the opening of faculties in state universities and some of the Academies of Science. Between 1921 and 1927, these schools grew and flourished.

But the October Revolution and the coming to power of the Bolsheviks were disastrous for Jewish life and education. The *Jewish* system of universal education, including the *cheder* and yeshiva system, was virtually destroyed by the Bolsheviks' anti-religious campaign. In 1919, a new law prohibited religious education for youngsters under age eighteen. Although deemed illegal and subject to continual harassment, the traditional *cheder* survived until 1921, when a major attack was directed against it, with teachers and rabbis tried, convicted, and sentenced to prison. Even so, a network of illegal Jewish establishments persisted until 1936, primarily organized by the Habad movement. In the same period, the 1920s and early 1930s, the expansion of Yiddish schools can be attributed to the policy of compulsory attendance for Yiddish-speaking children, the result of Stalin's desire for the allegiance of the nationalistic intellectuals. In addition, it was hoped that such an education would suppress the influence of Jewish nationalism, Zionism, Hebraism, clericalism, and Yiddishism.

In the 1930s, the Yiddish schools began their decline and final closing, the result of Stalin's official policy of oppression that marked the change in the Soviet government's attitude towards national cultures. The emphasis now was towards a "socialistic content" rather than "national form." Stalin took absolute power, destroyed opposing factions, and began his first fivesyear plan for the reconstruction of Russia. He no longer had to placate the minorities, so that a policy of cultural assimilation could be introduced, concentrating primarily upon national languages, literature, art, and culture in the fight against manifestations of "bourgeois nationalism." 1934 marks the end of the Yiddish schools as well as of most other Jewish cultural institutions. In 1938, through an administrative order, Stalin officially closed the Yiddish schools.[1]

During the Second World War, the Nazis destroyed whatever Stalin did not, for instance, closing whatever schools in distant areas of the Soviet Union had managed to remain open. Until the Perestroika of the 1980s, Jewish education in the Soviet Union was, with few exceptions, finally ended. One exception was the Soviet Authorities' permitting of the opening in Moscow in 1957 of the Kol Yaacov rabbinical seminary, intended to train rabbis and ritual slaughterers. In the first year, the thirty five students who enrolled were carefully screened by the KGB. This does not mean that they became agents of the intelligence unit, but, rather, that they would be no threat and were potentially willing to be intelligence agents. In the early 1960s, in the face of problems of religious persecution, enrollment ceased. In 1969, the school had only six students; though officially open, in reality, it did not function.

Similarly, Hebrew was taught under governmental supervision in institutions of higher learning. For example, the Institute for Asian and African Studies, part of Moscow University, and the Institute for International Relations ran Hebrew classes. But no Jewish students were permitted to enter these institutions. In addition, government supervised Russian Orthodox schools taught Hebrew. In the theological school in Leningrad (now St. Petersburg) and Yagorsk, where Russian Orthodox priests were trained, Hebrew also was taught, as it was, officially, in the Yeshiva Kol Yaacov.

In 1963, the Soviet authorities permitted publication of a Hebrew-Russian dictionary prepared by the Russian scholar P. Shapiro. Hebrew teachers, however, were not officially recognized and could not receive permits—required for any language teacher—to function in this capacity. While Soviet law provided no foundation for the refusal to issue these licenses, various excuses were offered, including the applicant's lack of formal higher education in the field or the fact that Hebrew was not part of the educational curriculum of the Ministry of Education. Throughout this period, formal classes thus were prohibited by the Soviet authorities, and Hebrew teachers and students were harassed and persecuted, often on trumped up charges. Persecution and arrests fell un-

der the criminal code paragraph 190, which prohibited the circulation of anti-Soviet materials, or paragraph 70, prohibiting incitement and anti-Soviet propaganda.

Despite official actions and the danger of imprisonment, Hebrew classes increasingly were organized and, in some instances, included fundamentals of Judaism. The 1967 Six Day War in Israel was a turning point in the struggle for the knowledge of Hebrew, which went hand in hand with Russian Jews' struggle for the right to emigrate to Israel.

**Perestroika and later:** Only in the late 1980s, during the period of Perestroika, did the situation for Hebrew teachers and Jewish education began to change. In 1988-1989, Jewish culture societies were set up in many cities to organized Hebrew and Yiddish classes. In 1989, the first Jewish school was opened, in Riga, with classes held in Russian. At first only Yiddish was taught, but after a petition to the authorities, non-obligatory Hebrew lessons were introduced. In Vilnius that same year, a Jewish kindergarten was opened, and Sunday schools and afternoon classes were opened in Jewish centers throughout the Soviet Union, including such places as the Moscow and Leningrad central synagogues. By the beginning of 1991, over twenty Jewish schools functioned in the Soviet Union.

The revival was bolstered by the participation of Israeli and world Jewish organizations as well as private Jewish philanthropists. These included the Liaison Office of the Foreign Ministry of the government of Israel (although never officially registered in Russia), the Jewish Agency, the Jewish Joint Distribution Committee, the Reichman Charitable Trust, and, later, the Canadian Foundation for the Education and Welfare of Jews in the Soviet Union, Rabbi Adin Steinzaltz, who organized a yeshiva, called Mikor Chaim (which burned down in 1997), Mr. Zev Wolfson, who sponsored high schools in different cities of Russia, Agudath Israel and its affiliate, Open Curtain, which sponsored a day school for boys and girls, a teachers seminary, and a yeshiva called Ohaley Yaakov, Rabbi Moshe Solovetchik from Switzerland, who organized both a yeshiva called Torat Chaim and girls seminary, Bet Yehudit, in

Moscow, and Dr. Bernard Lander, president of Touro College, which sponsored the first Jewish university in Moscow. Two Hasidic groups also were very active in the revival of Jewish life, Habad (with its different factions) and Karlin Stolin. A private Russian businessman, Leonid Roitman, sponsored a Jewish day and high school in Moscow. The major centers for Jewish education were developed in Moscow, St. Petersburg, and Kiev.

The Ulpan system developed to include classes taught in the evenings and/or on weekends in Hebrew studies, Jewish religion, tradition, history, calendar, and festivals. They provided adults, teenagers, and children with a place to experience an Israeli-Jewish atmosphere. Many of the students were in the process of emigrating to Israel. Both the Israel Liaison Office and the Jewish Agency trained and sent sorely needed teachers. At first, the Jewish Agency sought teachers in Israel who were fluent in Russian or the local languages and who had the necessary teaching certification. Their purpose was both to instruct their pupils and to encourage emigration to Israel. But by 1992, the demand for Hebrew teachers was so great that enough teachers could not be recruited in Israel. Now Hebrew training courses were organized and, in 1992, the Joint Authority for Zionist Education, a branch of the Jewish Agency, trained approximately two thousand teachers in the Soviet Union itself. Permanent teacher training centers were set up in Moscow, St. Petersburg, and Kiev in conjunction with the Jewish universities in these cities. The major center for teachers training was developed by Touro College, School of Jewish Studies in Moscow.

The Jewish Joint Distribution Committee provided educational materials, which reportedly reached more than 21,000 students in 296 schools in the Former Soviet Union (FSU). These schools included forty five day schools, thirty five pre-schools, and over two hundred Sunday schools. Since 1993, these materials have included 220,000 textbooks for student use and teacher training. The JDC also supported teacher training seminars both in Russia and Israel as well as university student organizations such as Hillel and Sefer.

A 1993/94 census of kindergartens, day schools, and supplementary schools (run after normal school hours) showed that the FSU had 218 schools with a total of 17, 809 pupils and 2,041 teachers. 42% of the schools were in Russia. 58% over all were day schools; in Russia, 27% were day schools, encompassing 47% of the 8,342 pupils. Eighty-five percent of the schools were affiliated with a non-orthodox group; the remaining 15%, with an orthodox organization, mostly (73%) identified as ultra-orthodox (*haredi*). Viewed from the perspective of the students, 8,999 (51%) were in secular schools, 4,813 (21%) in communal schools, 2,723 (15%) in *haredi* schools, 731 (4%) in mainstream orthodox schools, and 543 (3%) in schools oriented towards reform. A similar pattern was found in Russia and other republics of the FSU. The distribution of teachers was quite similar to that of the pupils. The census also showed a growth of 45% in enrollment since the previous year. This is in spite of the earlier mass emigration to Israel and the beginning of a considerable decrease in this emigration.[2]

A 1995 survey of the Jewish schools in the FSU reported the following:[3]

| Republic | School type | Number of schools | Number of students |
| --- | --- | --- | --- |
| Azerbaijan | Day School | 0 | 0 |
| | Pre-School | 1 | 40 |
| | Supplementary | 3 | 210 |
| Belarus | Day School | 2 | 227 |
| | Pre-school | 2 | 54 |
| | Supplementary | 15 | 1116 |
| | Yeshiva | 1 | ? |
| Estonia | Day School | 1 | 351 |
| | Pre-school | 1 | 16 |
| | Supplementary | 5 | 98 |

*cont.*

| | | | |
|---|---|---|---|
| Georgia | Day school | 1 | 90 |
| | Pre-school | 0 | 0 |
| | Supplementary | 5 | 276 |
| | Yeshiva | 1 | 10 |
| Kazakhstan | Day School | 0 | 0 |
| | Pre-school | 0 | 0 |
| | Supplementary | 11 | 539 |
| Kirgizstan | Day School | 1 | 130 |
| | Pre-school | 0 | 0 |
| | Supplementary | 1 | 92 |
| Latvia | Day School | 1 | 460 |
| | Pre-school | 3 | 59 |
| | Supplementary | 7 | 255 |
| Lithuania | Day School | 1 | 168 |
| | Pre-school | 1 | 36 |
| | Supplementary | 4 | 160 |
| | Yeshiva | 2 | 53 |
| Moldova | Day School | 3 | 501 |
| | Pre-school | 3 | 132 |
| | Supplementary | 6 | 349 |
| Russia | Day School | 16 | 2629 |
| | Pre-school | 6 | 246 |
| | Supplementary | 85 | 3853 |
| | Yeshiva | 7 | 135 |
| | Teacher College and Girl Seminar | 4 | 131 |
| Ukraine | Day School | 13 | 3232 |
| | Pre-school | 11 | 419 |
| | Supplementary | 51 | 2883 |
| | Yeshiva | 7 | 146 |
| | Teachers College | 1 | 42 |
| Uzbekistan | Day Schools | 2 | 402 |
| | Pre-school | 0 | 0 |
| | Supplementary | 3 | 283 |
| | Yeshiva | 2 | 47 |

In 1995, almost 20,000 students were enrolled in Jewish institutions.

The first institution of Jewish higher education in the FSU, the St. Petersburg Jewish University, was founded in 1989 by A. Dworkin. Dworkin sought the right to the license of the original Jewish university in that city, which years earlier had been closed by the authorities. A few years later, the first Jewish university in Moscow offering an American accredited baccalaureate degree and recognized by the Russian Ministry of Higher education was Touro College. This author, Simcha Fishbane, served as dean and organized the program, financed solely by Touro College. At first the program was intended to be the Jewish affiliate of a business school, but the large student enrollment encouraged the formation a separate school, and the opening day of classes in October,

1991, attracted more than a hundred students. Within two years, enrollment reached five hundred. Instructors of Judaism were recruited primarily from foreigners then living in Moscow, while language teachers were local. Hebrew and English were taught, with the emphasis on Hebrew. In the second year of the school, a department was organized to train Yiddish teachers. Students for this program came primarily from Moscow and Biribijan.

The mission of the school, in line with the mission of Touro College's main branch, was to serve the Jewish community, and the emphasis thus became the training of Hebrew teachers. Eighty-five percent of teachers of Hebrew and Judaism in Moscow were students in Touro College. The program ran in conjunction with the Department for Religious Education of the World Zionist

Organization (WZO), the Pincus Fund, the Joint Fund, and the WZO's Department for Eastern Europe. In addition to general Jewish studies, teacher training for other programs, such as social work for the Jewish community, was introduced. After Dr. Fishbane returned to the U.S.A., the chief rabbi of Moscow, Pinchas Goldschmidt, took on responsibility for the program, and Shlomo Gendelman was appointed dean. The first graduation was held in 1996 in the Moscow Choral Synagogue.

The Aleph organization, headed by Rabbi Steinsaltz, opened almost immediately after the Touro College branch, under the direction of Dr. Greenberg. This university saw itself as serving Jews rather than teaching only Jewish studies or areas that would serve the Jewish community. In 1992, Maimonides Academy was founded, offering a few Judaism courses and receiving state recognition and support. Yivo and the Jewish Theological Seminary similarly sponsored a small Jewish studies program in conjunction with the Moscow Humanitarian University. Approximately six hundred students study full and part time at these institutions. Outside of Moscow and St. Petersburg, Solomon University was opened in Kiev.

Even as emigration to Israel has dropped significantly, Jewish communities throughout the FSU continue to develop. In each one, Jewish education on all levels is a priority. While financial aid, teachers, and materials continue to come from world Jewry, these local communities now have begun to produce their own teachers and to locate funding from the Jews of their country. It appears, accordingly, that after nearly a century, the study of Hebrew and Judaism in Russia and the rest of the former Soviet Union is once again becoming a normal and central aspect of Jewish life.

### Bibliography

Halevy, Zvi, *Jewish Schools Under Czarism and Communism* (New York, 1976).
Korey, William, "Hebrew in the U.S.S.R.," in *Jewish Intelligentsia in the Soviet Union* (vol. 5; Israel, 1981).

### Notes

[1] The above has been adapted primarily from Zvi Halevy, *Jewish Schools Under Czarism and Communism* (New York, 1976).

[2] The census data was adapted from S. Dellapergola, E. Bassan, et al., "A Census of Jewish Schools in the Former Soviet Union for the 1993/94 School Year," in *Journal for Jewish Education*, vol. 63, Nos. 1-2, 1997.

[3] This data was adopted from *Jewish Schools in the Former Soviet Union* (St. Petersburg, 1995).

SIMCHA FISHBANE

**RUSSIA, UKRAINE, BELARUS AND THE CAUCASUS, THE PRACTICE OF JUDAISM IN:** Before 1990, it would not have been possible to write an article on the practice of Judaism in the USSR. World Jewry (including Soviet Jewry) was not allowed access to information about Soviet Jews, and those who did manage to collect some information were never sure of its accuracy or reliability. Jews in the world's third largest Jewish community were cut off from any normal flow of contact with Jews around them and in other parts of the world. The price often paid for contacts that were discovered (or even suspected) was severe—loss of job, exile to Siberia, even death.

The situation changed during Mikael Gorbachev's policy of Perestroika and Glasnost. Beginning in 1989, Jewish community organizations began to form within the USSR and to register officially as Jewish cultural associations. In addition, several world Jewish organizations, such as the American Jewish Joint Distribution Committee (JDC), the Jewish Agency for Israel, Habad, and B'nai B'rith, were allowed, or even invited, to visit and engage officially in religious and humanitarian programs. Now, comprehensive information began to be gathered about the Jews of the USSR. Since 1991, after the break-up of the Soviet Union, even more has become known about the Jews of Russia, Ukraine, Belarus, Moldova, and the Caucasus. The process is still unfolding, as tiny Jewish communities are discovered in remote towns throughout the vast geographical expanses of Russia's Siberia, Urals, and Volga region and in the villages of Ukraine and Belarus.

Still, no one knows definitively the number of Jews now living in what, for lack of a better term, generally is called the former Soviet Union (FSU). Estimates range from one and a half to four million, depending on whether one includes all those who have even one Jewish grandparent on either side (an echo of Hitler's criteria, now used in the state of Israel to determine a person's right to citizenship under the Law of Return) as well as those who live among Jews (generally by intermarriage) and feel themselves part of the Jewish people. Indeed, the dramatic and poignant re-entry of Soviet Jewry into the Jewish mainstream after an absence of seventy years has forced the Jewish world to confront anew the question of who is a Jew.

**Background:** At the beginning of the twentieth century, approximately five million Jews lived in an area called the Pale of Settlement, extending from the Baltics (Estonia, Latvia, and Lithuania) to the Black sea, and including Belarus, Ukraine, and Moldova. Regions of what is now the territory of Russia—the Uolga, Urals, Siberia, Moscow, and the St. Petersburg regions—were not within the Pale of Settlement and only certain categories of Jews (i.e., lawyers, doctors, and guilded craftsmen) were officially allowed to live there until the fall of the Romanov Empire in 1917. Therefore, with the exception of the Caucasus Jews who had for centuries been living in the region now known as Georgia, Uzbekistan, Azerbaijan, and Southern Russia (Dagistan) and were allowed to remain despite occasional threats of evacuation, the practice of Judaism had no immediate historical roots within Russian territory.

Jews living within the Pale of Settlement were widely dispersed in cities, towns, and tiny villages (shtetls), where, despite their separate status, they lived in close proximity to the local peasants. The Jewish communities maintained ongoing contact with one another, but within their shtetls they led an autonomous, self-contained existence. Jews were often victims of antisemitic violence but were generally allowed to live by the regulations of traditional Judaism, which shaped all aspects of their daily lives. However, the winds of western emancipation were reaching eastward, and, since the nineteenth century, not all Jews in the Pale of Settlement continued to follow the precepts of the Halakhah.

While many welcomed the opportunity to leave the ghetto and enter the life of the society about them, relatively few wished to do so at the expense of their Jewish identity. Many wanted to remain Jewish but not to be encumbered with all the regulations of Jew law. This was possible insofar as, in addition to religious practices, Judaism encompasses a wealth of cultural and ideological traditions. Therefore, prior to WWI, in many large and small Jewish communities in the Pale of Settlement, organizations were formed representing a range of Jewish religious, ideological, and cultural outlooks. Nonetheless, the Jewish day school (*cheder*) in every Jewish community continued to provide many generations of Jewish boys a religious education that prepared them for study of Jewish sacred texts and for Orthodox Jewish lives. The more serious students continued to study in centers for advanced learning (yeshivot), many of which were famous for producing great Rabbinic leaders and scholars. Still, as the secular world became more accessible to Jews in the Pale of Settlement, a demand grew for vocational education that would more adequately prepare youth for the modern world.

Despite increasing opportunities for assimilation in pre-revolution years, even the most secular Jews had some knowledge of Jewish religion. Those who chose not to practice it usually remained in contact with the traditional Jewish community through family ties and a common knowledge of Yiddish. Even a secular Jew asked to participate in a prayer quorum could do so with some familiarity. Many centuries of religious adherence and intensive Jewish community living had left their mark all individuals. The knowledge thus absorbed was not always valued by those who lived secular lives. But it became the sole surviving source of Jewish knowledge for the generations that followed, who no longer had any access to Jewish tradition and practice.

Before the Bolshevik revolution and the implementation of its plan to abolish all non-Communist religious practice and belief, came World War I and its aftermath of chaos and famine. Everyone in its path of destruction suffered. The majority of Jews from

Belarus and Ukraine became refugees, forced to flee their homes because of the advancing battle front, with its gangsterism and plundering. Hundreds of thousands moved into Russia, where they were restricted from free movement. Over 500 towns in the Pale of Settlement were abandoned as the Czarist, Polish, German, White Russian, Ukrainian, and Bolshevik armies advanced and retreated. Refugees fled without adequate transportation, order collapsed, and pogroms against Jews were common, as scapegoats were sought. Within a short time there were 500,000 Jewish refugees in the Russian interior, 200,000 Jews were killed, 75,000 wounded, half a million economically ruined, and 200,000 Jewish orphans in Ukraine alone. This was part of the tragic backdrop that preceded the Menshevik and then Bolshevik revolutions.

**1917-1939—The early Communist era:** As is well known, the Communist Party exercised strict control over its minorities, who were required to register. The practice of Judaism, or any other religion, was absolutely forbidden under the Communist regime or, at best, controlled by the State. Although the Bolsheviks officially repudiated anti-semitism, they believed that integration and assimilation were the only solution to the Jewish problem. The goal was to blend all minorities into the mass of devoted Communist subjects, and no spontaneous expression of religious belief or practice was tolerated. This could be achieved only by creating and preserving an ideological monopoly for the Communist Party. Contact with the outside world was forbidden, so that the two and a half million Jews then living within the newly defined, tightly sealed borders of the Soviet Union found themselves cut off from world Jewry.

In August, 1919, all Jewish communities were officially dissolved, and over the years their properties were confiscated. Religious institutions were prohibited, and most of the synagogues were gradually seized and converted into clubs or warehouses. In the mid-1920s over a thousand synagogues still existed within the borders of the Soviet Union; only 62 remained open in 1965.

These were needed to maintain control over the Jewish population and as symbolic proof of the government's official, constitutional guarantee of full religious freedom to all creeds.

Religious life was regulated mainly by the law of April 8, 1929, which defined the status of voluntary societies, called Dvadsatkas. These were composed of twenty members who were allowed to rent a building for the conduct of religious and burial services, but only with the permission of the authorities. The religious activities of these Dvadsatkas were, of course, closely monitored, and they could be summarily disbanded according to stricter or more lenient enforcement of whatever policy was currently determined by the ruling Soviets. Throughout the years, Jews, for instance, were required to work on the Sabbath. This was one of the unyielding requirements that effectively destroyed a basic underlying spiritual, philosophical, and practical expression of Jewish religious life. Not all Jews, of course, opposed these developments. During the early years, after so much suffering under autocratic czars, many young Jewish idealists believed in the Communist utopian dream. They accepted the dictates of religious suppression as a necessary step towards greater equality for all and often cooperated willingly with government decrees.

Still, the Jews did not fair well under this "utopian dream." Bolshevik ideology gave the highest status to those engaged in manual and agricultural labor. Since Jews had not been allowed to own land, and since Judaism places a high value on scholarship, Jewish intellectuals and tradesmen suddenly found themselves defined as class enemies, *lishentsy*, deprived of all civil rights because they were not "productively occupied." This, of course, included all Jewish religious functionaries. The number of Jewish declasses was estimated at 830,000, and they were heavily stigmatized. Since standard policy during the 1920s was a pressure towards agricultural colonization, Jews were also included in the campaign. By 1928, about 100,000 Jews were in Jewish colonies around southern Ukraine and in Eastern Siberia (the Birobidjan Jewish Autonomous Region). The practice of religion was not allowed here, although the proximity of Jews to one another in communal settings helped preserve a sense of Jewish consciousness.

With the edict of August, 1919, which officially decreed the dissolution of all religious institutions, the formal Jewish education of Soviet Jews also had come to an end. Without permission of the authorities, which was rarely granted, even the Dvadsatkas were not permitted to maintain educational facilities for children, print prayer books, or produce any other articles needed for ritual. Since Hebrew was connected with prayers, Jewish holidays, Jewish study, and with the competing ideology of Zionism, the Bolsheviks decreed it a counter-revolutionary language. For seven decades, the study of Hebrew was strictly forbidden, and any violation of that prohibition was severely punished. As late as 1987, Jewish students discovered carrying Hebrew textbooks were expelled from universities. The zeal to enforce the ban on Hebrew led to some paradoxical situations, such as the attempt on the part of a Belarus Bolshevik Commissary for Jewish affairs, in the 1930s, to have the Mishnah translated into Russian.

Yiddish, on the other hand, a cultural expression of Jewish life, underwent periods of greater and lesser acceptance. In the early 1920s for example, the municipal authorities in various Belarus towns made its study compulsory in local schools. Jewish children were forced to attend these schools, and any attempt to boycott them because of their inferior quality brought communal punishments for counter-revolutionary behavior. Throughout the Soviet regime, Yiddish teaching and the publication of Yiddish literature were tightly controlled by the authorities, and it was never known when the Yiddish language would be more or less in favor. This same variable policy applied to other aspects of Jewish educational and cultural life, for instance, the Yiddish theater. This at least kept alive hopes for a Jewish educational revival despite the actuality of the situation.

Crushing religious autonomy was an ongoing pursuit, and religious functionaries were generally singled out as prime targets.

When the devastating famine of the early 1920s in Ukraine, Belarus, and the Volga region reached proportions that even the Soviet government could no longer ignore, food aid was allowed to be brought in by the American government and by the American Jewish Joint Distribution Committee. In an unanticipated twist, the Yiddish Landsmannschaft bureau in New York, through the JDC, was able to aid rabbis in hundreds of Russian towns. This avenue of outside aid was soon closed by local patriots, who decided that aid should not be distributed according to the priorities of the donors but according to Communist ideological standards. Jewish Communist ideologues saw to it that rabbis, cantors, and ritual slaughterers did not get preferential treatment, even though, as the least likely to have work permits or hope for a livelihood, they were, in fact, in even more desperate straits than others.

In 1917, as a sign of their long-term egalitarian intentions, the Soviet regime gave Jews the right to enter any Russian town. In order to escape the desperate situation in the former Pale of Settlement, over 100,000 Jews found their way to towns in Siberia, and many more went to the big cities like Moscow and Petrograd (later Leningrad and now St. Petersburg). Over 100,000, mostly young, came to Moscow, including 200 refugee rabbis from shtetls and at least four ritual slaughterers. Most had no work and managed to rent apartments on the outskirts of the city, where rents were more moderate. The "Dvadsatka" prayer groups that formed all around Moscow thus were headed by refugee rabbis from Ukraine, Belarus, or Moldova.

Prior to this mass influx, a small community of 8,000 Jews lived in Moscow— officially only lawyers, doctors, and guild merchants—with four synagogues. The first, the Choral Synagogue, was built in 1891, closed 1892, and reopened in 1906. The others were Zaryadye (mostly Sephardic), Bolshaya Bronaya, and a fourth synagogue on Pyatnitskaya street. After the refugees arrived, almost every street in the Jewish neighborhoods had its prayer group, but no synagogues were allowed to be built. Living in great poverty, the Jews began to form work cooperatives that employed fellow "disenfranchised" Jews, and they helped one another scrape out a living. Some of these urban work cooperatives functioned over a period of many years.

As the Stalin persecutions intensified during the 1930s, many Jews in Belarus and Ukraine, including rabbis and ritual slaughterers who were threatened with arrest or expulsion, continued to flee to Moscow, and, by 1939, the Jewish population their reached 400,000. Under continually deteriorating conditions, most of the neighborhood prayer groups were unable to continue their activities. Some of the Jewish work cooperatives became substitute Jewish communities and attempted to preserve Jewish traditions, holding prayer services and not working on the Sabbath. But this was not easy. For instance, in 1936, the supervisor of one such cooperative arrived on a Saturday and found the management in a private home after prayer. There was a public scandal, the cooperative was closed, and most of the workers fled Moscow for Eastern communities.

Before World War II, most Jews who fled to Moscow and St. Petersburg remembered the religious practices of their home communities. Although public observance of Jewish holidays was prohibited, for many years, they were allowed to bake matzot for Passover. Indeed, as part of the continuing policy of religious suppression that was coupled with appearance of religious freedom, in March, 1937, the government announced that an unlimited supply of matzot would be baked, but only in state bakeries, without Rabbinic supervision. Since these matzot would not be kosher, Orthodox Jews were forced to bake their own at home. Over time, this policy continued, and the vast majority of Jews grew unaware of the fact that they were eating unkosher matzah. Nonetheless, buying and eating matzah on Passover continued, and, for many Jews, this practice became the only way to express continuing identification with the Jewish tradition.

Similarly, despite official edicts, through the establishment of traditional Jewish councils, Jewish communities early on attempted

to preserve the continuity of communal life. Thus, on July 19, 1920, 133 delegates from 39 communities around Russia gathered at a conference in Moscow to create a Jewish National Council and to introduce a uniform system of communal administration and taxation. Petrograd established a Jewish Communal Council, and, on September 6, 1920, a Union of Jewish Communal Councils was established in Moscow to coordinate the activities of the existing councils, form new ones, and introduce uniformity of organization in social, economic, and cultural activities. Had these councils been allowed to function, Jewish religious practice might have been maintained. But since this was precisely what the Soviets wished to suppress, all such efforts were short circuited, and, for close to seventy years, the only *officially* recognized local or national Jewish organ-izations were those organized by the Communist regime: the Jewish Anti-Fascist Committee and, later, the highly controversial Jewish Anti-Zionist Committee, which communicated only what was government approved.

Stamping out all remnants of religious revival required the authorities' continual vigilance. On August 18, 1937, Emes, the Yiddish Communist newspaper, claimed that there was renewed evidence of religious revival in the Ukraine, where one and a half million Jews lived. Rabbis there were carrying out an energetic religious campaign, and, as a result, children in Moghilev-Podolsk had stayed away from school during Passover and had participated in the seder. Many children in the country were receiving instruction from Jewish religious teachers, and the paper called for more anti-religious instruction from the regular school teachers. A campaign of massive arrests of rabbis followed both in Ukraine and in other areas of the Soviet Union.

While the policy of religious control and suppression was universal in all regions of the Soviet empire, during the 1930s one region, where the Jews simply refused to comply, was granted somewhat more autonomy. The Sephardic Jews of the Caucasus (Bukharan, Georgian, and Tat "Mountain Jews") had lived traditional Jewish lives there for centuries (Jewish tombstone inscriptions on the shores of the Black Sea date to the fifth century C.E.). Even during the worst period of Stalin's suppression, Jewish functionaries in Bukhara, Samarkand, and Tashkent slaughtered meat ritually, circumcised newborn sons, and led the daily and Sabbath services. Like religious functionaries in other parts of the country, they often paid for their services with their lives. Still, throughout the past century, Caucasian Jews participated in the Zionist movement and in the ingathering to Israel. (In 1892 there was already a Bukharan quarter in Jerusalem.) They were among the first to spearhead the dissident movement that began in the late 1960s and early 1970s.

Unexpectedly, in November, 1938, the Minister of Education approved a series of lectures on Talmudic, medieval, and modern Hebrew literature, delivered to the Jewish section of the Moscow Pedagogic and Literary Institute. This sanctioning was seen as foreshadowing a lifting of the government's ban on Hebrew and Zionism, but not on religion. In fact, it was the beginning of far greater repressions.

**1939-1989—Synagogue life, religious observance, and Jewish education:** After a quarter century of unrelieved agony, World War II presented Soviet Jews another period of unimaginable suffering. Although no concentration camps were on Soviet soil, Hitler's extermination campaign was systematically carried out in all areas of German occupation. The German troops marched into Belarus and Ukraine, and, within a matter of days, with ample local cooperation, they rounded up the Jewish population of each town, marched them to a nearby ravine, and shot them. Only those who fled to the East were saved, and, by the end of the war, over a million Soviet Jews had been killed. In Odessa, Ukraine, for example, where a third of the inhabitants were Jewish, there had been 165,000 Jews in 1914, over 50 synagogues, and 92 Jewish schools. By 1939, there were no Jewish schools and only a few synagogues, but refugees had swollen the number of Jews to 180,000. None of these

remained after the Nazi invasion in 1941. Virtually all who did not escape beforehand to Western Siberia were slaughtered. No memorials of any kind were set up, and no Jewish mourning was allowed.

During the war years, tens of thousands of Ukrainian and Belarussian Ashkenazic Jews fled eastward from Hitler's advancing troops and settled in the traditionally Sephardic region of the Caucasus. Most of these refugees remained after the war, but the dissolution of their home communities, the struggle to survive in a new environment without communal support, and the ongoing campaign of terror waged by Stalin appeared to have succeeded in stamping out any sparks of interest in preserving a Jewish identity or integrating into the Sephardic Jewish communities. Since the Gorbachev years, these Jews have been among the most difficult to locate or identify.

Stalin, who had a paranoid suspicion of people with Western contacts, was convinced that all Jews were Zionist agents bent on the destruction of the Soviet regime. His pre-war campaign against "cosmopolitanism," which was basically antisemitism, accelerated. Over the next eight years, until he died in 1953, all remnants of Jewish culture and religion were eradicated, and Soviet Jews lived in constant terror. Prominent Jews were exiled to slave labor camps or killed, together with an estimated 600,000 others, thirty percent of the Soviet Jewish population. Midnight raids were carried out throughout the Ukraine, Belarus, Georgia, and Dagistan, and in some districts, such as Rovno and Zdolbunov in the Ukraine, all Jews were rounded up and transported to Siberia.

By 1951, no autonomous Jewish cultural organizations or activities of any kind existed, the last Jewish school in Birobidjan was closed, and any association of Jews or Jewish communal activity was considered treasonable. In deference to the now faint whispers of world pressure, Jews ostensibly were allowed to associate in a few remaining synagogues, maintained to demonstrate to foreign visitors that there was "freedom of religion." All foreigners were shown these same synagogues and entertained by the same rabbis. The few elderly Jews found in these places were generally afraid to speak to the visitors, and Rabbi Shlomo Shleifer, from the Choral synagogue in Moscow, was called to represent the "Jewish faith" whenever the purposes of Soviet propaganda made this necessary.

A short period of quiet ensued after Stalin's death in 1953, during Khrushchev's reign. Some faint stirrings of hope even arose that the Jewish community might be allowed to revive after the devastating blows forty years. A few Yiddish books were published, and the authorities allowed a yeshiva to open in the Moscow Choral synagogue. Had Jewish hopes been realized at that time, while difficult, the process of healing and rehabilitation would have been based on solid knowledge and some memory of actual Jewish life and practice. But these hopes were not realized for another thirty five years, and by then almost no Jews remained with any knowledge of Jewish religion and practice.

After a short respite, the small number of synagogues that survived both the Stalinist terror and Nazi onslaught again were endangered. Khrushchev distrusted the Jews, considering them a foreign element with strong international ties, and so closed synagogues in Ukraine, the Caucasus, Lithuania, Belarus, Moldova, and Russia proper. Then, in 1960, a wave of arrests occurred of Jews who attended prayer groups. In 1961, in Kiev, Minsk, Vilna, Tashkent, and Riga, individuals holding synagogue positions were removed from their posts. Only Western protest brought this campaign to a halt. However, during the 1960s, the Kiev matzah factory, which had been an essential source of continuing identification with Jewish practice, was closed down.

Even so, as just noted, during this time, permission was granted by the Moscow authorities for Rabbi Shleifer to open a yeshiva in the Moscow Choral Synagogue. As the sole source of potential Jewish learning, Yeshiva Kol Yaakov began optimistically in 1957 with thirty five students from Odessa, Kiev, Riga, Georgia, Bukhara, and Moscow, and a small staff. A few of the students were studying for the rabbinate, the others stud-

ied to be cantors and ritual slaughterers. But there were insufficient prayer books, religious articles, and books with which to study, and, within three or four years, after some harassment and provocations, such as the refusal to renew residence permits of those from the Caucasus, the numbers dwindled, to twenty in 1960 and five in 1965. The yeshiva closed for a time, reopening in the summer of 1974 with eighteen adult and ten younger students.

There is no precise information on the number of synagogues in the Soviet Union during this period. According to official Soviet sources, 97 existed in 1965, but apparently at least a third of them functioned as Dvadsatkas, without a physical structure. Of the 62 remaining, almost half were Sephardic synagogues in the Caucasus, where a remnant of Jewish religious practice remained even during the worst years of terror. However, even here, as religious functionaries grew older and died, they had no replacements. Jews gathered each Sabbath in the synagogue, but fewer and fewer knew the prayers or how to lead the worship. There also was virtually no institution for the training of circumcisors—mohalim—and when those who were trained died, no further circumcisions were performed throughout the country.

In 1965, forty rabbis lived in the Soviet Union, including some trained in Poland and Lithuania. By 1977, only five remained, two in Ashkenazic synagogues (including a Karliner-Stoliner Hasidic rabbi in Kiev), and three Sephardis. The Lubavitcher Hasidim played an important, though strictly monitored, role, until Rav Tversky, the last remaining Lubavitcher Rebbe in the Soviet Union, left for Israel in 1964. Thus, there were almost no competent rabbis to educate young scholars, no formal preparation for Bar or Bat Mitzvah took place, and religious marriage, let alone divorce, was virtually impossible. In 1973, the Soviet authorities gave permission for two men, Khaim Levitas and Adolf Shayevich, to leave for rabbinical training and ordination in Budapest at the only remaining rabbinical seminary in Eastern Europe, and they were later joined by a candidate from Riga. But the situation remained bleak.

No accurate information is available for the Jewish population during these years, but the estimate is two and a half million. This means that, at best, there was one synagogue, without a rabbi, for every 25,000-30,000 Jews. The Dvadsatka remained an option for those who wanted to create a religious community, and the Soviets acknowledged the existence of three hundred such synagogue groups. But the authorities always had an eye on their composition, participants were regularly brought to trial for violating laws regulating religious organizations, and membership was controlled by the government, which brought in non-religious individuals with only a remote interest in Judaism.

The Brezhnev-Kosygin years, beginning in October, 1964, are called the years of stagnation, and, at first, nothing happened to reverse the gradual process of assimilation within the Jewish community. Indeed, lest hopes of revival be reignited, acts of suppression here and there reminded Jews that all was still far from well. For example, although Jewish burial had been one of the very few rites permitted by the Soviet authorities over the years, in 1966, under various pretexts, they closed Jewish cemeteries in all the central cities. In Minsk, Kiev, Leningrad, and Moscow, Jewish families were refused parcels of land for burials, and they were forced to cremate the bodies of their relatives. This became the accepted practice throughout the Soviet Union.

Nonetheless, several small but significant signs of life deserve note. In a rare show of lingering erudition and devotion to Jewish religious tradition, Rabbis Z. Garkavi and A. Shauli published in Israel a small volume, "Shoere ha-Gahelet," that contained responsa and theological essays from the Soviet Union, where religious Jews continued to ask rabbis questions about the application of religious law in a Communist dominated society. On a more popular level, a tradition began during this period that, over the next few decades, swelled to a mass scale. In Moscow, Leningrad, Kiev, Tbilisi, and other cities, crowds of Jews, including many young people, appeared in front of the synagogues on Saturday mornings, on the High Holi-

days, and on Simhat Torah. Although these crowds were not harassed, all knew that KGB agents were among them, photographing all who were there. Apparently those who appeared only on holidays were not punished, but a person who entered the synagogue during the year for services ran the risk of losing his or her job.

In the mid- to late 1960s, all over the world, young people began to question the established order of things, and these winds of dissent even blew eastward toward the Ukrainians, Tatars, and Jews in the Soviet Union. In 1965, two respected Soviet writers, Andrei Sinyavsky and Yuli Daniel, were tried for anti-Soviet writings. Both were sentenced to hard labor, which set off waves of anxiety among the Jews in Russia and was strongly protested in the west. As the protests from the west became more organized, they were heard by those Eli Weisel had named "The Jews of Silence." Despite the very palpable iron curtain, communication began to be established between some Soviet Jews and the western world.

In this setting, the momentous victory of Israel in the 1967 Six Day War had an almost electrifying impact. Soviet Jews who barely knew of Israel's existence, who had never been allowed to learn anything about their rich Jewish heritage, and who had always been made to feel ashamed of being Jewish felt a surge of pride. This was the beginning of the Jewish dissident movement and the underground network of Hebrew classes and Samizdat (illegal, hand-copied publications of Jewish books and Hebrew texts).

For a number of years following the Six Day War, intermarriage, which was estimated to have reached up to seventy percent, decreased significantly, and there was more Jewish awareness. However, it was almost impossible to satisfy the need for meaningful Jewish education. Virtually no Jewish schools stood in the Soviet Union, including Birobidjan. In these circumstances assimilation also rose visibly, and more children of intermarried parents, when given the choice, chose to remove the label "Hebrew" from their internal passport. In addition, despite the growing Jewish awareness, attraction arose among the Jewish intelligentsia to Russian or Greek Orthodoxy. The lack of ordained rabbis and modern Jewish schools that could interpret religious doctrine to younger Jews prompted many who knew nothing of Judaism but were interested in religion to turn to Christian thought. Boris Pasternak, the poet Osip Mandelstam, and the writer Mikhail Merson-Aksnov all converted to Christianity, as had a popular Moscow priest, Father Aleksandr Men.

Harassment for religious practices continued unabated. In Tashkent, after the synagogue had been damaged by an earthquake and could not be used, the authorities thwarted an attempt by local Jews to rebuild within walking distance of the community's Orthodox elderly. In Riga, the entrance to the Jewish mass graves at Rumboli was closed, and, in Kiev, the Ukrainian administration forbade Hebrew inscriptions on tombstones in the Jewish cemetery. Despite these interferences, however, during the early 1970s, an upsurge of religious interest and feeling occurred among younger Soviet Jews. In 1971, the first seders were celebrated in Moscow, and the synagogue streets were crowded during the High Holy days with many younger Jewish men and women. Tens of thousands danced and sang Hebrew songs outside the Moscow Central Synagogue on Simhat Torah, among them Jews from Kiev, Riga, Rostov, and other places. Clearly this outpouring of religious and national feeling had become an open expression of Jewish religious and national identification, despite the presence of police agents all around. This tradition continued during all the years that followed.

In 1979, Adolph Shayevich returned from Budapest and became deputy chief rabbi of Moscow under Yaakov Fishman. In 1983, another Budapest graduate became the rabbi of Riga. The Soviet Council of Religious Affairs gave permission for two more students to receive rabbinical training in Budapest, and, by 1985, there were ten to twelve ordained rabbis in the Soviet Union. This was an improvement, but certainly far from adequate for an estimated two and a half million Jews. Still, interest in religion increased among Jews and non-Jews alike, and, for the first time in at least six decades, it was estimated that in Moscow about three hundred young people were involved in the systematic study of the Bible, Talmud, and other religious works, many in underground dissident yeshivot.

During the final years of the Soviet Union, authorities claimed that fifty synagogues functioned. The thirty five that were known were in Baku (Azerbaijan); Bukhara, Samarkand, and Tashkent (Uzbekistan); Chernovtsi, Dnepropetrovsk, Kiev, Odessa, Slavuta, Sverdlovsk, Ujgorod, Vinnitsa, and Zhitomer (Ukraine); Dushanbe (Tajikistan); Gori, Kutaisi, Sukhumi and Tbilisi (two) (Georgia); Irkutsk and Kuibishev (Siberia-Russia); Kaunas and Vilnius (Lithuania); Kazan and Rostov (Volga-Russia); Kishinev, Moldova, Leningrad (two), Moscow (two) (Russia); Makhakala, Dagistan, Minsk, Belarus, Riga (Latvia); and Tallin (Estonia). The official list did not, of course, include a growing number of underground dissident groups that met regularly, under conditions of danger, to study their religious heritage as they awaited exit visas to Israel.

**1989-1997—Recent developments in Jewish religious practice:** In 1989, the gates of the Soviet Union opened for large-scale Jewish emigration to Israel, and, for the first time in seventy years, spontaneous expressions of religious revival were given official sanction. A major turning point for Jewish religious practice came on May 26, 1988, when the Jerusalem scholar Adin Steinsaltz negotiated an agreement with Yevgeny P. Velikov, vice president of the Soviet Academy of Sciences, to create an independent Jewish religious training institute in Moscow. Unlike the yeshiva at the Moscow Choral Synagogue, which had been under the control of the Soviet authorities, the new institute would be under the aegis of the Academy of World Civilizations, which planned departments of Islam, Christianity, and Judaism. Until a new generation of Soviet Jewish scholars and religious leaders could be educated, it would be staffed largely by teachers from Israel and the west.

The Steinsaltz Yeshiva, as it came to be called, opened in February, 1989, with thirty five full-time students, selected from over a hundred and fifty applicants, and up to a hundred part-time participants. It was the first of many religious educational institutions opened during the next decade in response to the overwhelming demand of Soviet Jewry for a reconnection with their Jewish heritage. For almost seven decades, they had no way to learn about or to experience Jewish religious practices, and without such knowledge and experience they could develop no positive appreciation for their traditions and culture. For most, being born Jewish meant discrimination and had been a source of shame. Through the new exposure to Jewish history, culture, and tradition, a sense of pride and pleasure could be reawakened.

This budding process of revival, however, required not only the withdrawal of suppressive measures. After so many years of intensive indoctrination against religious beliefs and practices, most Soviet Jews felt, and still feel, extremely uncomfortable with the idea of God and religious worship. Secular Jewish culture, however, was a different matter, and the newly offered opportunities for religious revival were often expressed during these early revival years through the formation of local cultural associations, duly registered with the Ministry of Religion and given official recognition. By the end of 1989, fifty such associations existed and many more were in process of formation.

During the euphoria of the early months, it did not seem to be significant whether a Jewish association formed around a local synagogue or a local cultural society. Within a year, however, the ideological differences between these groups became sharply delineated, and, all over the Soviet Union, the newly formed Jewish communities found themselves embroiled in highly emotional turf battles between religious and cultural associations. In spring, 1988, the Public Council of Jewish Religious Affairs, chaired by Dr. Gregory Rozenshtein, was officially founded as an umbrella organization to help local groups negotiate issues of everyday Jewish religious life around the country.

However, in response to the growing factionalism between the culturalists and religionists, this early council was soon succeeded by two separate organizations.

In December, 1989, the first Congress of USSR Jewish Cultural Organizations (the Va'ad) was held in Moscow with representatives from the fifty local cultural associations throughout the Soviet Union. Mikhail Chlenov was elected chair. A month later, on January 22, 1990, at the initiative of the Moscow Choral Synagogue, the National Council of Synagogues held its first conference, also in Moscow, with representatives of fifty nine synagogues from Russia, Moldova, Georgia, Belarus, Uzbekistan, and Azerbaijan. Vladimir Federovsky, lay leader of the Moscow Choral Synagogue, became the national chair.

From the beginning, each of the two national associations claimed to represent Soviet Jewry and challenged the legitimacy of the other. Federovsky, though himself not an observant Jew, claimed that Jewish organizations unwilling to cooperate with synagogues and insensitive to religious needs cannot represent Soviet Jewry. He pointed out that at the Va'ad's first Congress, elections for officers were scheduled late on a Friday afternoon, precluding observant Jews' participation. Religious groups attending the congress had walked out in protest. On the other side, only the Council of Synagogues, not the Va'ad, was officially recognized by the Soviet government, and the Va'ad's leadership challenged this cooperation with the authorities, claiming their own independence from Communist doctrines and arguing the importance of their ideological heritage, based on the struggles of thousands of Jewish dissidents. In spite of such immediate and emotionally charged challenges to mutual cooperation and acceptance, a process of healing and religious revival soon began.

Neither of these umbrella organizations was free from its own internal problems, and both were regarded with suspicion by outlying Jewish communities, wary of Moscow leadership. This leadership was further challenged after the summer of 1991, with the break-up of the Soviet empire. In addition, although the Moscow Choral Synagogue's leadership was deemed well suited for its mediating role with the authorities, it was not seen as an appropriate leader in the spiritual revival of Soviet Jewry. Over time, as the dynamics of religious life and practice developed, the centrality of the three major pioneer institutions—the Steinsaltz Yeshiva, the Va'ad, and the Council of Synagogues—thus was not sustained. Still, they must be credited for helping set in motion the activities and institutions that marked the end of officially sanctioned religious suppression and for initiating the first steps towards the revival of communal religious life.

In these early years of reconnection, it was known that Soviet Jews were more widely dispersed than the Jews of other Eastern European countries. But only two or three years after international Jewish organizations began to work with Jewish communities in what had by then become the former Soviet Union (from September, 1991), did the extent of Jewish dispersion became clear. Throughout the FSU, Jews were discovered living in hundreds of small villages, medium sized towns, and large Siberian, Ural, and Volgan cities far from the center of the country. In Russia, seventy urban centers had a combined Jewish population minimally of more than half a million Jews, including eleven cities with from ten thousand to two hundred thousand. In Ukraine, there were close to half a million Jews in sixty seven urban centers and over three hundred villages. One community led to another, and, by 1995, most outlying Jews were connected to one another through organized regional networks that collected information for welfare assistance and supplied information about centrally organized Jewish religious and cultural events. The problem of identifying Jews in the large, central urban areas remains more complex, and over eighty percent may still remain unidentified and totally unconnected to any Jewish association.

Community organization has intensified issues of physical space and facilities. Synagogue buildings throughout the Soviet Union needed to be located and claimed by the local Jewish community through a recognized legal procedure. Although the Ministry of Religious Affairs, with its constant surveillance and control, was officially abolished in 1991, and all dealings were with the Ministry of Internal Affairs, it often took years for the legal process to unfold, especially as many former synagogues now housed firms or families that were difficult to evict. All these synagogues, including those that had remained open and functioning, were in need of significant repair. Standards for public as well as private buildings were not high, and many of the structures were in dangerously unstable condition and could not be used for communal purposes. Therefore, over the course of time, two parallel processes were set in motion, the registration of Jewish religious congregations without buildings and the registration of synagogue congregations. By 1997, 133 congregations possessed and 144 religious communities lacked a synagogue structure. Although this comprised only a quarter the number of such functioning religious communities that had existed before the Soviet regime, it was far more than anyone had dreamed of less than a decade before.

The explosion of interest in Israel, Hebrew, and Jewish culture also made the need for communal study and meeting space urgent, and it often was necessary to rent space for rapidly expanding Jewish schools, community events, and religious services. Even where synagogue structures had been reclaimed, funds were needed for renovations and repairs. But, despite extremely low prices in those early years, particularly before the 1991 coup, funds were not available for this purpose. The new Russian middle and upper class had not yet developed, Soviet Jews, like most Soviet citizens, had no available capital, and world Jewry still concentrated almost exclusively on helping Soviet Jews emigrate, particularly to Israel. "Operation Exodus" was in full gear, and aside from several foundations interested in the preservation of Eastern European Jewish historical sites, no world Jewish organization had on its agenda an investment in physical structures within the Soviet Union.

Indeed, the idea of a future for Soviet

Jewry within the Soviet Union was generally dismissed as either an unthinkable absurdity, an unrealistic reading of the political and economic situation, or anti-Zionist treachery. Even the American Jewish Joint Distribution Committee, which strongly supported emigration to Israel but was assigned the primary goal of reconnecting Soviet Jewry with its Jewish heritage and the Jewish people, had relatively limited funds. The JDC urgently needed this money to help Soviet Jewish organizations function and to supply religious, educational, and cultural materials. Little money remained for synagogue renovation.

A second need—synagogue leadership's openness to a broad community role—also was often a problem. On the one hand, synagogue association leaders at first tended to be conservative and suspicious of change, not aware of their potential role in the revival of Jewish life. On the other, religious functionaries who had been associated with the synagogues during the years of suppression were often in compromised positions, generally not trusted by Jews who had been either unconnected with Jewish religious life or who were involved in the dissident movement. Also, these synagogue leaders' attempts to follow traditional Orthodox Jewish practices made most Jews feel uncomfortable and unwelcome. Indeed, during the 1990 Passover holiday, all necessary religious and culinary aspects of the seder were set up at the Riga synagogue. But instead of welcoming all who wished to participate, the local religious committee carefully guarded the entrance and only admitted those who could prove they had a Jewish mother.

The role of those few synagogues with Rabbinic leadership depended on the rabbi's openness to community involvement. Those who were open had a major impact. When Jacob Bleich, a young Karliner-Stoliner Orthodox rabbi, was sent to Kiev in 1990, his dynamic, warm, and inclusive approach affected not only the Jews of Kiev but Jewish communities throughout Ukraine. He cooperated with local cultural associations, and his synagogue building became a center of educational and welfare activities.

Jewish communities in each of the independent former Soviet Republics gradually created their own umbrella organizations, even as forums for inter-republic cooperation and contact were maintained. Each of the religious movements, such as Habad and the Reform congregations, remained in on-going contact with members all over the FSU, and new organizations were created specifically to allow networking among former Soviet Jews with similar interests. For example, in 1995, Sefer, the International Center for University Teaching of Jewish Civilization, an independent academic organization hosted by the highly prestigious Russian Academy of Sciences, became the central address for Jewish scholarship and took on the task of coordinating information on Jewish and non-Jewish scholars working in Judaic studies and on all courses offered in this field throughout the FSU. In addition, in order to deal with overall Jewish religious matters and to coordinate contact with Israel's chief rabbinate, thirty FSU rabbis (almost all from abroad) met in 1992 with rabbis from Israel and France and formed the organization Rabbis of the CIS. After years of imposed isolation, maintaining contact with Jewish communities both within the FSU and abroad remained a high priority.

**Modes of Judaic expression and religious observance:** Towards the end of the 1980s, when the open expression of Jewish religious practice was no longer suppressed and punished, four religious movements operated in the Soviet Union. First was the Orthodox Habad (Lubavitch) movement, which had originated in the Pale of Settlement and had remained in Ukraine until 1964. In 1987, Habad began to send young rabbis to live in Jewish communities around the FSU, generally in very difficult circumstances, and, by 1997, forty Habad representatives resided from the Baltics to Siberia. The second was the traditional Orthodox synagogues that had managed to keep a small flame alive throughout the Soviet years and to maintain some tie with the Jewish world through official visits, governmental recognition, and whatever form of religious practice was officially approved.

The third religious movement was a series

of underground study groups formed by Jewish dissidents who met regularly through the 1970s and 1980s. One of these groups, called Machanayim, operated a religiously oriented kindergarten in Moscow and worked towards Jewish revival through educational and religious activities. After most of these dissidents emigrated to Israel, some continued their contact with the Steinsaltz Yeshiva through their organization in Jerusalem that sent Russian-speaking Judaica teachers to Moscow. Finally, a small community of Reform Judaism had been developed by another group of Jewish dissidents who met at one another's homes for Jewish holidays. On October 2, 1989, they officially registered as Congregation Hineini, with Zinovy Kogan as congregational leader. Over the years, the Reform movement grew slowly, and, by 1997, thirty five synagogues in the FSU claimed to be Reform; seventeen in Russia, nine in Ukraine, six in Belarus, two in Estonia, and one in Kazakhstan. In Russia, Ukraine, and Belarus, regional associations of Reform congregations were organized, headed by a lay leader from that region, and their umbrella organization, the Union of Reform Congregations, was registered in 1995 with the Ministry of Religion.

During the 1990s, other Jewish religious movements sent representatives from abroad. By 1997, the Orthodox Agudat Yisrael was operating twelve schools with kindergartens and day centers, summer Torah retreat seminars for adults, and summer camps for 10,000 children, as well as programs for college-aged youth. The modern Orthodox B'nai Akiba movement established seven branches in major cities around the FSU. Conservative Judaism was represented by a Camp Ramah in Moscow, by Midreshet Yerushalayim, which ran four supplementary schools in Ukraine and one in Moscow as well as a Tali day school in Chernovtsy, Ukraine, and by the Conservative movement's Jewish Theological Seminary graduate program in advanced Jewish studies, called Project Judaica, operated in conjunction with YIVO in Moscow's prestigious University for the Humanities. In addition, branches of the International Federation of Secular Humanist

Jews held a conference in Moscow in 1994 with eighty participants from twenty six affiliated FSU groups.

Although not a religious movement, Hillel associations for students existed in Moscow, St. Petersburg, Kiev, and Minsk, and at least five more such associations were in process of formation. Unlike in North America, the model developed in the FSU was regionally, not university, based, and, despite some early resistance to involvement in religious practice, these Hillel groups have experimented with Sabbath and holiday services and have been involved in community projects such as organizing Purim celebrations. In order to help reach the more remote Jewish communities, young Jewish students were trained through the national Hillel and, since 1994, have been sent to lead Passover seders in some sixty small communities in which there had been no Jewish religious practice for decades. The response to these seders was overwhelming, both for the participants and for the young leaders, who were themselves new to such practices.

To meet the enthusiastic demand for knowledge of Jewish religion and traditions, each aspect of Jewish culture had to be introduced from an outside source. A major public seder program was organized by the JDC, which, in 1991, reached 15,000 people through 52 seders in 28 cities. Passover matzah, though not necessarily kosher, had been available for purchase in the Soviet Union since the late 1930s, and, for many Jews, this had been the only tangible way to show identification with the Jewish people. With the revival of religious life, the demand grew, and Moscow, St. Petersburg, and Kiev had to significantly increase production. Chanukah became another source of organized community celebration. In 1991, the lighting of a large menorah in Moscow near the "White House" was seen by millions on national TV. This was the first in a series of large public menorah lighting ceremonies over the following years. In addition, kits for each holiday were developed by the educational branch of the JDC, and thousands were sent to community associations and schools with instructions and explanations about the religious traditions and their historical context. To reach as many Jewish homes as possible, a Shabbat-at-home program was launched by the JDC in 1993 and continued until the funds were more urgently needed for welfare emergencies. The interest in these programs remained great; only budgetary constraints prevented wider coverage.

Jewish life cycle traditions had completely vanished and required reintroduction. Ritual circumcision, virtually unknown, was gradually reintroduced so that, within a few years, most sons born in the Sephardic community were circumcised, although this was far less widespread among Ashkenazic Jews. Three clinics for ritual circumcision have been set up, two in Moscow, one in St. Petersburg, and surgical teams come regularly from England to train circumcisors in outlying areas and to circumcise adult males and teenagers. There have been instances of three generations—grandfather, father, and son—coming together for the ceremony.

Bar and Bat Mitzvah celebrations for boys of thirteen and girls of twelve were introduced as community events since 1990 and have been widely adopted. The ceremonies culminate a period of intensive Jewish studies, in which parents are strongly encouraged to participate. During the early years of Jewish revival, it was generally the grandparent, rather than the parent, who brought the child to the synagogue for the ceremony. This has changed as outreach programs from day schools, camps, and supplementary schools involve parents in Jewish learning. Already in 1991, community celebrations took place in Moscow, Rostov, Ekaterinburg, Perm, Derbent, Samara, Kiev, Kharkov, Gomel, Tblisi, Dnepropetrovsk, Simpferpol, Minsk, Bobruisk, Kishinev, Alma Ata, Samarkand, Tashkent, Baku, and St. Petersburg. Each participant received a Hebrew-Russian Bible and a prayer book for personal use. In response to the unique situation of Soviet Jews, world rabbinical councils have made the humane and courageous decision to allow uncircumcised boys to celebrate Bar Mitzvah.

Other areas of Jewish practice have remained minimal. Jewish weddings are extremely rare. Intermarriage was the norm and endures as a major problem, and even religious couples seem to resist a traditional wedding; almost a decade after the beginning of Jewish revival, the vast majority of FSU Jews had never witnessed one. As for rituals of death and mourning, burial in a cemetery plot reserved for Jews has now been made possible in most major cities. The majority of Jews, however, still practice cremation, to which they became accustomed over the past decades. Few know Jewish mourning traditions, and sitting Shiva—the seven days of home mourning—is almost unknown, although there is a growing awareness of the practice of recitation of the mourner's Kaddish.

Summer and winter camp programs were early on seen as a unique way to introduce and allow people to experience Jewish traditions. Since 1990, such camps provided several weeks of intense Jewish living and learning for tens of thousands of children of all ages. Working together with young leaders-in-training, counselors were brought from Israel, North America, and even Australia, and every moment was considered a precious opportunity to instill pride, enthusiasm, and knowledge. Within an exhilarating two week period, children who knew absolutely nothing about the Jewish heritage learned about the holidays, Jewish life cycle rituals, and the state of Israel. These camps were generally run by the local communities with the help of the Jewish Agency, the Lubavitch movement, B'nai Akiba, the JDC, and the Israeli government. The impact has been significant. In 1990, for instance, the Jewish community of Tallin prepared to open a day school with about twenty five students. After summer camp, the number increased to 120. In Vitebsk, Ukraine, after their first camp experience in 1993, fifty young people began attending synagogue regularly.

Although each community's reconnection with the Jewish people and religious practice was unique, a growing network of contacts between families and community leaders in remote areas increased the extent of Jewish awareness even among those who were last to be reached by world Jewry. The small, agrarian community of Oguv in the Caucasus is an example of the process of Jewish community revival. In the summer of 1994, a JDC representative in the Caucasus region arrived for a first visit to the four hundred Jews of Oguv. Through local initiative, the large central synagogue had been restored to the community the previous year and was in process of repair by Jewish volunteers. There were no religious texts, no Torah scroll, and no religious functionaries, but many Jews gathered near the synagogue in enthusiastic anticipation of the JDC representative's visit. He installed mezuzot on all the doors and entrances of the synagogue, promised to supply the community with prayer books and Hebrew texts, and discussed the possibility of securing a Torah scroll and sending a rabbi-teacher for a period of time. A young man who seemed to be the recognized community leader took him to the home of his parents, who brought him to an old wooden chest and proudly took out two red velvet bags embroidered with silver thread, containing a prayer shawl and phylacteries. No one in the town knew what to do with these treasures, which had somehow been smuggled in several decades previously and guarded carefully. They were hopeful that a rabbi would be sent to teach them how these objects could be used.

Clearly, against all odds, Jews in the FSU have managed to keep live a spark of Jewish identity, and, during the first decade of their religious revival, they have, by and large, eagerly participated in those religious observances to which they have been exposed. As with most Jewish communities around the world, they are in the process of choosing to express their Jewish identity within a variety of religious forms and movements.

**Religious education and religious functionaries:** In 1989, when Jewish studies became possible, Soviet Jews had no Jewish schools for children or adults, no texts or books on Jewish tradition, and only a few rabbis, religious functionaries, and enthusiastic self-educated dissidents with some knowledge to communicate. Therefore, the developments and achievements in this field during the first decade of religious revival have been perhaps the most dramatic of all.

World Jewry was called upon to help meet the pressing and almost insatiable educational demands of Soviet Jews and responded, on the whole, with courage, ingenuity, and skill. Since Soviet Jews were well educated in most other areas, the JDC responded to their great thirst for knowledge of Jewish history and tradition by bringing Jewish libraries to towns and cities with Jewish associations prepared to house and distribute the books. These libraries contained hundreds of books in Russian on subjects ranging from modern Israeli literature to the history of Russian Jewry. By 1992, the JDC had distributed 187,000 Jewish books in 141 full libraries and 23 mini-libraries to more than 120 communities and schools throughout the FSU. In addition, in response to the urgent need for prayerbooks and basic texts, the JDC commissioned a reprinting of the most popular Hebrew-Russian Bible and a new translation of a Hebrew-Russian prayer book. While most Judaica publications were still imported from Israel or the US, the Steinsaltz Yeshiva, which was destroyed by fire in 1996, still maintained a publication center in Moscow, and the Russian Synagogue Council was in the process of publishing several traditional texts, including a Sabbath prayerbook with Hebrew transliteration.

For most Soviet Jews, however, the first stage in the search for Jewish education came when the gates of emigration to Israel were opened, and an urgent need to learn Hebrew as a beginning connection to world Jewry and Jewish practice was felt. With the cooperation of the Israeli government and its Liaison Bureau, the newly formed cultural associations first responded to this need, starting Hebrew classes for adults and children. An enthusiastic Soviet Hebrew Teacher's Union was created by former dissidents with over twenty branches active in towns like Kharkov and Kiev in Ukraine. As soon as it was legally possible, Israel, through the Liaison Bureau, began to send hundreds of Hebrew teachers to communities all over the Soviet Union. Jewish supplementary schools were created in tens and then hundreds of communities, and the first of almost fifty day schools opened in Riga in 1989. Although these schools were substantially helped through contributions from the Jewish Agency, the Israeli government, Habad, Agudat Israel, the Israeli Masorti movement, and the JDC, the majority, including the day schools, were largely locally initiated, sponsored, and funded.

But most of these schools remained dependent on outside teachers, mainly from Israel, who were sent for periods of one to three months, did not speak Russian, and were unfamiliar with Russian culture. Though dedicated and able to teach under difficult conditions, they were mainly secular Israelis, not attuned to the spiritual questions of the young and old or knowledgeable in the religious traditions Soviet Jewry sought to know. They wished to teach Hebrew and promote Aliyah, and the language books they used did not emphasize Jewish tradition and values. Still, during those early years, the exultant enthusiasm of the students—children and adults—made up for the absence of knowledgeable educators and appropriate educational materials and classroom space. Only over time did it became more important to integrate Judaic values into secular studies. This challenge still faces Soviet Jewish, Israeli, and diaspora educators.

From 1989 through 1997, a clear indication of the growth in commitment to Jewish practice and tradition were the forty nine day schools that functioned with 8,200 pupils, with new schools opening each year. Twenty two of these schools were Orthodox, one was Conservative, eleven were sponsored solely by their local communities, and the rest were either sponsored by Israel or by private foundations. Jewish supplementary schools were even more widespread. Few towns in the FSU with more than a thousand Jews did not have some form of supplementary Jewish education for children or for children and adults. In 1997, 205 such schools existed in 174 communities. The large majority were either sponsored by Israel, by the local Jewish community, or by both, with a minority sponsored by organizations like the World Union for Progressive Judaism, Midreshet Yerushalayim, the Jewish Agency for Israel, and various independent organizations.

Introducing Judaic studies into the academies of higher learning also expressed Jewish religious practice. The challenge was first taken up in St. Petersburg by Ilya Dworkin, a dedicated Jewish scholar and activist, who started the Jewish University of St. Petersburg, so that young Jewish intellectuals could answer their spiritual and intellectual questions. In 1992, the Jewish University of Moscow, affiliated with the prestigious Moscow State University, was created with the help of Professor Nehemia Levzion of the Israeli National Academy of Sciences. During the next few years, Jewish universities were opened in Kiev, Kishinev, and Minsk as well. In 1996, seventeen students graduated Project Judaica with degrees in advanced Jewish studies, and the western scholars who had been the faculty during the programs' first years were gradually replaced by a strong core of Russian instructors. Over a hundred courses in fields of Jewish Studies were located by Sefer, the organization that coordinates information on academic Jewish study programs, and, in 1995, their first Conference of Judaic Studies drew over a hundred scholars from all over the FSU.

Thirty institutes of advanced Orthodox learning (including two for women) existed in the FSU, some recognized as yeshivot, with well over five hundred students. Twelve of these were in Ukraine, eleven in Russia, and the rest in Belarus, Moldova, and the Asian Republics. Twelve were sponsored by the Lubavitch movement, two by Agudat Israel, and the rest were either affiliated with a synagogue or supported by a foundation. These institutes offered two kinds of rabbinical programs. The first was the pulpit ordination program called Rav U-Manhig Semicha, which educates rabbis to be congregational leaders. The second was the more traditional ordination program, called Yoreh Yoreh, which educates authoritative Jewish religious functionaries. The first of these programs, under the leadership of Rabbi Pinchas Goldschmidt, produced the initial generation of local religious functionaries who graduated from the Moscow Choral Synagogue's yeshiva, renamed Ohalei Yaakov. Over the years, many gifted young Soviet Jews have left to study in Israeli, European, and American yeshivas, and, within the next decade, some are expected to return to the FSU as religious educators.

As the normalization of Jewish religious life unfolded, the need for religious functionaries—rabbis, ritual slaughterers, and Jewish communal leaders—became most urgent. Communities like Tashkent, Bukhara, and Samarkand (in the Caucasus) and Kharkov (in Ukraine) had maintained religious communities in which Sabbath services existed even in the absence of anyone who could read Hebrew or lead the worship. Some local candidates were willing to learn, but in insufficient numbers to meet even the immediate need. In 1992, the Russian Council of Synagogues turned to world Jewry for help in finding rabbis willing to serve such isolated communities. The response was not overwhelming, and primarily Habad rabbis agreed to commit to a sufficient period of residence to learn the language and culture. To meet the challenge, in coordination with the Soviet Jewish Religious Community association, the JDC began to send itinerant rabbis to outlying communities in Siberia and the Urals. Traveling from community to community for a week at a time, they developed synagogue activities, ran summer and winter camps for children and adults, and taught and conducted services. The first of these itinerant rabbis, Yehuda Zeidenfeld, served during 1992-1993 in Krasnayarsk, Irkutsk, Novosibirsk, Ufa, Penza, Saratov, Samara, and Kubishev. These are large, isolated cities (some with over a million inhabitants), and each has populations of over 5,000 Jews.

Rabbinic education takes a minimum of six or seven years, and the immediate need for religious functionaries made long-term planning a lower priority. Instead, ritual slaughterers, circumcisors, and prayer leaders were sent to Jerusalem for group and individualized training. Similarly, a training seminar for Soviet cantors was held in May, 1989, which initiated an ongoing Cantorial Academy in Moscow. In 1992, the Jewish communities of the Caucasus, where knowledge of ritual slaughtering had passed from father to son over many generations, sent 54 candidates from 35 cities to Jerusalem for the religious functionary course. To supplement their education and increase their support, in 1993, fifteen religious functionaries were brought together in Baku, where, with rabbis and teachers from Moscow, they spent six days in workshops on weddings, funerals, and High Holiday services.

The next step was to help organize local and regional training programs. Some of those who returned early from the Jerusalem course to places like Minsk displayed real leadership potential and over time had a significant impact on Jewish religious practice in their home communities and the surrounding region. The tremendous leadership vacuum led to the development of a training course called the Buncher program, which prepared potential leaders in all spheres of Jewish communal life, including tradition and practice. One of the course requirements was a community project planned, researched, and implemented with on-going follow-up supervision in the home community. Gradually, a generation of local Jewish communal leaders and religious functionaries was educated and supervised.

In 1997, ten communities in the Russian Republic had traditional rabbis, another twelve, from the Habad Lubavitch. Only three were Russian born, the rest from abroad. In Ukraine and Belarus were another twelve communities with rabbis. Since FSU students interested in intensive Orthodox studies require a more basic curriculum than those who have attended Jewish schools all their lives, only three or four of the schools of Orthodox learning functioning in the FSU grant Orthodox ordination. Nonetheless, in 1997, eleven Orthodox places of learning exist in Russia, with almost 250 students. Ukraine, with its rich tradition of yeshiva study, has twelve Orthodox places of learning with 175 students, Belarus has one with twenty students, Moldova has two with fifty students, and there are four in the Caucasus with about sixty students. Twelve of these thirty Orthodox seminaries are sponsored by the Lubavitch movement, two by Agudat Israel, and the rest are affiliated with a synagogue or supported by a foundation.

Recognizing that educated lay leaders are essential to vigorous, well functioning congregations, the Congress of Russian Jewish Religious and Community Organizations in Moscow, founded in 1994 under the leadership of Chief Rabbis Adolph Shayevich and Pinchas Goldschmidt, began to hold monthly seminars for groups of fifteen to twenty synagogue leaders around Russia. During a week in Moscow, they learn intensively about Jewish traditions and practices. The Russian Jewish Congress, a new group of wealthy Russian Jewish community leaders, supports this seminar together with the JDC. Most local Jewish communal leaders view with interest and hope these wealthy Russian businessmen's assuming of responsibility for communal religious life.

**Conclusion:** Jews in the former Soviet Union experienced some of the cruelest, most tragic periods of Jewish history. Completely isolated from the world Jewish community, they were singled out for brutal collective punishment and were systematically denied access to their rich religious heritage. When it became possible to leave the Soviet Union in the late 1980s, hundreds of thousands chose to emigrate, mainly to Israel, where they were welcomed as citizens. World Jewry, which for seven decades had been cut off from all contact with relatives in the third largest Jewish community, rallied in support of the exodus of Soviet Jewry. Most Jews who have heard stories of the horror of life behind the former iron curtain find it difficult to imagine that several million Jews willingly would remain behind. As a result, the dramatic revitalization of the Jewish communities in the former Soviet Union is not well known. The facts, however, are undeniable and deserve to be communicated. Although it may well be too early to summarize the modes of Jewish religious expression taking shape in the FSU, some apparent trends are worth mentioning:

a) Although levels of emigration to Israel have declined steadily in recent years, both familial and geographical closeness have given the Jews of the FSU more immediate ties to the state of Israel than those of any other diaspora community. Most FSU Jews have family members and friends in Israel, and almost ten percent of the tourists who visited Israel during the past few years have been from the FSU. Hebrew language is generally highly valued, and it is spoken by many young FSU Jews who are involved in Jewish community life.

b) The many outreach programs created to reconnect Soviet Jews with their Jewish heritage have succeeded in reaching only ten to twenty percent of Soviet Jewry. The vast majority of Jews, particularly those living in Russia's central cities, Moscow and St. Petersburg, are either so assimilated that they are unaware of the outreach or deliberately remain unconnected.

c) Prayer and synagogue worship remain a problem for most FSU Jews, who feel more comfortable with Jewish culture and history.

d) Many Jews living in the FSU remain deeply suspicious of governmental acceptance of religious expression, which they are convinced cannot last. Indeed, a bill presently under debate would make it illegal to start a new religious organization. Only those in existence fifteen years ago would be recognized by the authorities. Intended to protect the Russian Orthodox church from competition with modern cults, the bill has been vetoed by President Yeltzin and may or may not pass. But even its proposal has reinforced fears that religious expression will once again be in jeopardy.

e) Jews born and brought up in the former Soviet Union were not exposed to Jewish religious dogma of any kind. Therefore, all religious educators, from Lubavitch to Reform, who come from Israel, Europe, or North America, engage in basic Jewish education. This contributes to a cooperative atmosphere uncharacteristic of the distinct Jewish movements elsewhere in the world. An example of such applied cooperation is in Chelyabinsk in the Russian Urals. The Jewish community of about 8,000 Jews has only one synagogue building but two congregations, one Orthodox and one Reform. On Friday evenings and holidays, the synagogue accommodates both congregations through two shifts of prayer services.

f) By 1997, it seems clear that, in the

future, most of the FSU's rabbis will be locally born and educated. An example of this trend is the newest Sephardic congregation in Moscow, which proudly engaged a local Sephardic rabbi, educated in the Moscow Choral Synagogue's yeshiva. The main problem for these rabbis and all other Jewish religious and community functionaries will be the ability of the community to provide them with adequate, middle-class salaries. Such community support requires an assumption of financial responsibility and a growing community awareness and sophistication, both of which are in a slow process of development.

In other words, preparing local religious functionaries is not sufficient. Work still is needed to prepare the Jewish communities of the FSU to maintain their religious and community leaders. With the passing of the initial period of euphoria and enthusiasm for all things Jewish, the emphasis needs to be on quality in education and religious practice. This can be achieved only if gifted young people have confidence that there is a future for them in Jewish community work and that the Jewish community will support them financially, emotionally, and intellectually. This is the main challenge now facing the revitalizing Jewish communities of the FSU.

### Bibliography

Gitelman, Zvi, *A Century of Ambivalence: The Jews of Russia and the Soviet Union—1881 to the Present* (New York, 1994).

Shapiro, Leon, "Soviet Jewry Since the Death of Stalin: A Twenty-Five Year Perspective," in Find, Morris, and Milton Himmelfarb, eds., *American Jewish Year Book* (New York and Philadelphia, 1979).

ANITA WEINER, EUGENE WEINER

# S

**SACRIFICE AND TEMPLE IN RABBINIC JUDAISM:** Scripture (in the context of Rabbinic Judaism, "the Written Torah") sets forth God's explicit statement that he will meet Israel "at the door of the tent of meeting," where he dwells, e.g., Exod. 29:38ff.: "Now this is what you shall offer upon the altar . . . at the door of the tent of meeting before the Lord, where I will meet with you to speak there to you. There I will meet with the people of Israel . . . And I will dwell among the people of Israel and will be their God." Rabbinic Judaism regarded the Temple as the place at which God and Israel meet. From 70 C.E., when the Temple was destroyed, that Judaism therefore focused upon the restoration of the Temple, the hopes of the holy people. A principal task of the messiah who would come at the end of days would be to rebuild the Temple and restore the priesthood to the altar, the Levites to their platform, where they sang psalms, and Israel to the courtyards of the rebuilt edifice. The reason that the sacrifices in the Temple mattered was that, through them, Israel atoned for sin, and the Torah explicitly said so in many ways.

Why did sin and atonement play so critical a role in Rabbinic Judaism that the principal act of piety should involve sacrifice? The answer lies in what, in the Scriptural narrative, led to the sacrificial cult. In the beginning, God created nature for the encounter with humanity, Eden standing for nature, Adam and Eve for humanity. But, through disobedience, Adam and Eve lost Eden, and with the sin of Man began the long quest for regeneration. But even as it was only Israel that presented itself for the meeting with God, Israel showed itself to be like the rest of Man. For on the other side of Sinai came the idolatrous celebration of the Golden Calf. As a result of this sin, Israel was commanded to sacrifice that which it had chosen to worship in place of God: the calf and comparable beasts. That is, in response to Israel's sin, God provided for Israel, surrogate of humanity, sacrifices as a means of atonement for sin. Then, freed of sin through offerings that signified obedience to God's will, God and humanity might meet in mutual and reciprocal commitment. Where Israel atoned for sin and presented itself as ready for the meeting, there God and Israel would found their Eden.

No wonder, then, that the offerings at the Temple altar commemorate and celebrate creation—the new beginning of God's and humankind's transaction. And that explains why the sacrificial cult is celebrated as a memorial to creation, and the Psalms the Levites sing identify the particular aspect of creation that took place on a given day of the week. The entire rhythm of the relationship of Israel with God—and of humanity through Israel—then was to be recapitulated in the weekly celebration of creation (B. R.H. 4:4A-E I.2/31A):

A. It is taught on Tannaite authority [see M. Tam. 7:4]: R. Judah says in the name of R. Aqiba:

B. "On the first day what did they sing? [Ps. 24, which begins]: 'The earth is the Lord's and the fullness thereof, [the world and they who live therein].' [This psalm was used] because [on Sunday, God] took possession and gave possession and was ruler over his world [without the heavenly hosts, who were created on the second day].

C. "On the second day what did they sing? [Ps. 48, beginning]: 'Great is the Lord and highly to be praised [in the city of our God, even upon his holy hill].' [This psalm was used] because [on Monday, God] divided that which he created [into the upper and lower worlds] and was sovereign over them.

D. "On the third day they did sing [Ps. 82, which begins]: 'God stands in the congregation of God, [he is a judge among the gods].' [This psalm was used] because [on Tuesday, God] revealed the dry land in his wisdom and prepared the earth for his congregation.

E. "On the fourth day they did sing [Ps. 94, which begins]: 'Lord God to whom vengeance belongs, [you God to whom vengeance belongs, show yourself].' [This psalm was used] because [on Wednesday, God] created the sun and moon and was destined to exact punishment from those who serve them.

F. "On the fifth day they did sing [Ps. 81, which begins], 'Sing aloud to God our strength, [make a joyful noise to the God of Jacob].' [This psalm was used] because [on Thursday, God] created birds and fish, which bring glory to his name.

G. "On the sixth day they did sing [Ps. 92, which begins], 'The Lord reigns; he is robed in majesty.' [This psalm was used] because [on Friday, God] finished his work and ruled over all [he created].

H. "On the seventh day they did sing [Ps. 92, which begins], 'A Psalm, a song for the Sabbath day'—[a psalm] for the day that is wholly Sabbath rest [for eternity]."

I. Said R. Nehemiah, "What was sages' understanding [that led them] to distinguish between these passages? [Why, that is, do they say that the first passages refer to God's acts in the past, at the time of creation, while the passage for the Sabbath, they say, refers to the future?] Rather [the passages should be explained as follows, in which only the interpretation of Ps. 92, for the Sabbath differs from what has preceded]: On the first day [Ps. 24 was used] because [on Sunday, God] took possession and gave possession and was ruler over his world. On the second day [Ps. 48 was used] because [on Monday, God] divided that which he created [into the upper and lower worlds] and was sovereign over them. On the third day [Ps. 82 was used] because [on Tuesday, God] revealed the dry land in his wisdom and prepared the earth for his congregation. On the fourth [Ps. 94 was used] because [on Wednesday, God] created the sun and moon and was destined to exact punishment from those who serve them. On the fifth [Ps. 81 was used] because [on Thursday, God] created birds and fish, which bring glory to his name. On the sixth [Ps. 92 was used] because [on Friday, God] finished his work and ruled over all [he created]. On the seventh [Ps. 92 was used] because [on the Sabbath, God] rested."

Nature, then, is embodied in the sequence of the days of the week of creation, and the Temple sacrifices celebrate creation, leading to Eden. But the Temple cult embodies both the natural and the social order: Eden in which Israel, in particular, forms the human counterpart to God's presence. Here the invocation of Psalms to be sung in the Temple that correspond to events in the creation of the world underscores that same sense of the integrity of all reality, natural and social.

Then how does Israel figure? The key-motif, as we have seen, concerns sin and atonement. In the conflict of God's word and human will, the drama of the cult takes its cue in the particular role of Israel, sinful but, because Israel possesses the Torah, also repentant and seeking to atone. If Israel represents humanity at large, the regenerate part thereof, then the priesthood stands for Israel. Priests serve as bearers of the sin and embodiment of the atonement of Israel. The priesthood in the cult takes on the garments of Israel's atonement, to offer the atoning sacrifices. That proposition is made entirely particular and concrete in this account of how the garments that the priest wears atone for particular sins that Israel commits:

4.A. For we have learned in the Mishnah:
   B. The high priest serves in eight garments and an ordinary priest in four:
   C. tunic, underpants, head-covering, and girdle.
   D. The high priest in addition wears the breastplate, apron, upper garment, and frontlet [M. Yom. 7:5A-C].
   E. The tunic would atone for bloodshed: "And they dipped the coat in the blood" (Gen. 37:31).
   F. Some say, "It atoned for those who wear mixed varieties: 'And he made him a coat of many colors' (Gen. 37:3)."
   G. The underpants atone for fornication: "And you shall make them linen underpants to cover the flesh of their nakedness" (Exod. 27:42).
   H. The head-covering atones for arrogance: "And he set the head-covering on his head" (Lev. 8:9).
   I. For what did the girdle atone?
   J. For double-dealers.
   K. Others say, "For thieves."
   N. The breastplate would atone for those who pervert justice: "And you shall put in the breastplate of judgment the Urim and the Thummim" (Exod. 28:30).
   O. The apron [ephod] would atone for idolatry: "And without ephod or teraphim" (Hos. 3:4).
   P. The upper garment [robe] would atone for slander.
5.A. R. Simon in the name of R. Jonathan of Bet Gubrin: "For two matters there was no atonement, but the Torah has provided atonement for them, and these are they:
   B. "Gossip and involuntary manslaughter.
   C. "For gossip there was no atonement, but the Torah has provided atonement for it, specifically through the bell of the robe: 'And it shall be upon Aaron to minister, and the sound thereof shall be heard' (Exod. 28:35).

   D. "Let the sound that this makes come and atone for the sound of slander.
   E. "For involuntary manslaughter there was no atonement, but the Torah has provided atonement for it, specifically through the death of the high priest: 'And he shall dwell therein until the death of the high priest' (Num. 35:25)."
6.A. The frontlet would atone for impudence.
   B. Some say, "It was for blasphemy."
   C. The one who says it was for impudence cites the following verse of Scripture: "And it shall be upon Aaron's forehead" (Exod. 28:38), and also, "Yet you had a harlot's forehead" (Jer. 3:3).
   D. The one who says it was for blasphemy cites the following verse of Scripture: "And it shall always be upon his forehead" (Exod. 28:38) along side, "And the stone sank into his forehead" (1 Sam. 17:49).

Accordingly, God abides in Israel. Where heaven and earth intersect, at the altar, whence the flames rising from burning meat, grain, oil, wine, and, above all, blood, from fires burning day and night ascend toward heaven, there in the fragrance of the incense and in clouds of smoke, Israel encounters God. The parties to the transcendent transaction are God, the priest as mediator, and any Israelite or even (for some offerings) a gentile. The priests act in behalf of Israelites individually and severally.

The Temple and its activities of sacrifice encompass a profusion of contradictions or paradoxes. God is one but ubiquitous, universal but localized. The land of Israel defines the arena of encounter, but the tent of meeting is situated, to begin with, in no-man's land, the wilderness possessed by none and all. And the Temple reaches toward heaven from earth, and Jerusalem is distinct from the rest of the Land. Not only so, but while God dwells among the whole people of Israel, the priesthood is singled out. How then to mediate between the special position of the genealogical caste and the paramount standing of the people of Israel, among all of whom God dwells? The priests do not act on their own. For the most part, they work in behalf of all Israel in carrying out the liturgy for the public offerings or of individuals subject to obligation for the personal ones. In this negotiation between the presence of the entire holy people and the priority of the priesthood, we find the model for other negotiations that are required: the God of all creation, ubiquitous and omnipotent, declaring that he will dwell among the people of Israel, the God of all humanity identifying himself as "their God."

Then and there, at the altar when the Israelite presents his offering, the priest receives and prepares it, and God responds with favor, three parties intersect. These are God, the priesthood, and Israel, one by one and also *en masse*. They come together spatially, but the encounter takes place—can only take place—when all three concur about the purpose of the exchange. So space does not suffice, nor even the time of a particular occasion, though both matter much. In the wrong space, at the wrong time, nothing happens to affect Israel's relationship with God. An offering at the Temple of Onias, which Egyptian Jews built in competition with the Jerusalem Temple, or a celebration of the Day of Atonement on any day but the tenth of the lunar month of Tishre would prove null. Then what precipitates the transaction of meeting? What brings about the intersection is concurrence. God, the Israelite, the officiating priest must agree, each in the free exercise of his will. The transaction takes place through animal offerings. The Israelite designates the beast for the correct, sacred purpose, so sanctifies it. He then delivers the beast to the priest. The priest takes the beast, cuts the neck organs and veins, catches the blood, and sprinkles some of it at the appropriate part of the altar, then places the animal or entrails of the animal on the altar. And God receives the scent of the sacrificial parts as they are burned on the altar. The transaction then encompasses agreement on all parties, beginning with the Israelite's act of will: the sanctification of a beast to atone for sin (and for certain other purposes). So much for the sequence of actions.

What—apart from the shared project, the activity itself and its outcome—links the one party to the other two and about what do the three parties concur? What the Israelite desires, what the priest intends, and what God requires—these three acts of will must coincide. Sages here translate into rites their deepest convictions about what joins God to people, which is, God's will and humankind's corresponding will, each capable of free, uncoerced choice. Here, at the points at which the Written Torah falls silent, the halakhah of the Oral Torah in the particular idiom chosen for its statement turns eloquent. Setting forth in the context of the transcendent transaction of the altar and its rites and offerings, the halakhah patiently lays out, through sharply-etched cases, the thickest layers of thought of the entire halakhic structure and system. Most of the facts that are invoked and systematized, e.g., definitions of the classification of offerings and their hierarchy, derive from the Written Torah. What the halakhah of the Oral Torah contributes are layers of construction upon deep foundations of reflection. What rises up is a towering account of the role of Israel's and the priests' and God's will in the blood-rite conducted to propitiate God and win his good will. The Land transcended, Israel transformed, in silence but for the Levites' singing, in smoke and blood and fire God is approached, propitiated, pleased, as in the Torah he said he could and would be.

Since the basic account of sacrifice and the Temple simply recapitulates the Written Torah's story and laws, we must wonder what the Oral Torah contributes. The answer is, the systematization of the Written Torah's facts into a cogent, profound set of norms, for it is in law, halakhah, that Rabbinic Judaism sets forth its theology of belief and behavior alike. That is to say, Scripture sets forth a variety of facts. The halakhah of the Oral Torah identifies what is implicit in those facts, picking out the indicative traits that open the way to generalization, to identification of the principle embodied by the case. Then the halakhah of the Oral Torah regularizes, orders, systematizes, classifies, and above all, hierarchizes, the discrete facts. These the halakhah shapes into a single, utterly cogent structure. And then the halakhah shows how the structure sustains a working system. Just as any thoughtful person will find much to admire in the acumen and perspicacity of the halakhah of the Oral Torah throughout, its power to construct data into coherent and logical order, here (and at the corresponding halakhah of cultic cleanness) we encounter the acme of halakhic thinking: what it can accomplish, through applied reason and practical law, in the translation of theology into concrete conduct. This we see when we consider fundamental questions concerning sacrifice and the Temple, starting with the basic issue: how does all Israel participate in the rites of the holy place?

The halakhah speaks through well-ordered details. It answers the question, how does Israel participate in the sacrifices at the altar, by specifying who pays the Sheqel-Tax, which the Written Torah commands be collected in support of the atonement-offerings. Exod. 30:11-16 describes the half-sheqel in this language:

> The Lord said to Moses, "When you take the census of the people of Israel, then each shall give a ransom for himself to the Lord when you number them, that there be no plague among them when you number them. Each who is numbered in the census shall give this: half a sheqel, according to the sheqel of the sanctuary . . . half a sheqel as an offering to the Lord. Every one who is numbered in the census, from twenty years old and upward, shall give the Lord's offering. The rich shall not give more, and the poor shall not give less, than the half-sheqel, when you give the Lord's offering to make atonement for yourselves. And you shall take the atonement money from the people of Israel and shall appoint it for the service of the tent of meeting; that it may bring the people of Israel to remembrance before the Lord, so as to make atonement for yourselves."

The collection of the half-sheqel as a ransom "that there be no plague . . . when you number them" plays no role in the halakhah of the Oral Torah. The conception that, through the half-sheqel, everyone acquires a share in the atonement offering predominates. And the stress on the public offerings as atonement offerings, which the halakhah of the Oral Torah picks up, clearly begins in the Written Torah. Like Scripture, the Oral Torah clearly understands the half-sheqel as a tax in support of the Temple and its atonement-offerings in behalf of Israel. Here, then, is one

medium of Israel's relationship with God that transcends place, genealogy, and condition; the half-sheqel, unlike first fruits, comes from any location, even beyond the Land, and comes from all Israelites.

All adult Israelite males—those from puberty onward—pay the tax, and that is without regard to where they are located. Money-changers' facilities are set up, first in the provinces, then in the Temple. People who do not pay have to supply a pledge, and these are Levites, Israelites, proselytes, and freed slaves. Women, slaves, and minors may pay the sheqel if they choose to do so; gentiles and Samaritans may not. Pledges may not be taken from women, slaves, and minors. Gentiles may contribute money for burnt-offerings or peace-offerings but not money for the upkeep of the Temple house. That is, they do not participate within Israel in the atonement offering. But if they sanctified something for that purpose, it is a valid action. People may pay the half-sheqel in behalf of third parties, e.g., for the poor or for friends. The half-sheqel supports the daily whole- or burnt-offerings, and these atone, as the halakhah states in so many words: "Whatever is brought because of sin or guilt—with it burnt offerings are purchased." So at stake throughout is the atonement of the sin of all Israel.

Then Israel relates to God not only one by one but all together. That principle, implicit throughout, is made explicit in the following rule: If people volunteered the funds on their own, they are valid, on condition that they [to begin with, explicitly] donate the funds to the community for public use. And, it follows, not only do Israelites sin and atone one by one, but Israel as a whole sins and requires atonement, and that is the purpose of the daily whole-offerings, as Scripture makes explicit. So the sacrifices of the Temple atone for corporate Israel, not only for individual Israelites. The public offerings—the daily whole offerings—atone for Israel's sin: public offerings appease and effect atonement between Israel and their father in heaven, just as is stated in the Written Torah. It is the collectivity of Israel that is embodied in the half-sheqel offering. And that statement of the corporate character of Israel comes to expression in the half-sheqel in particular. No wonder the half-sheqel forms the counterpart to the agricultural tithes and offerings, representing as they do enlandised Israel. But then the difference cannot be missed: the half-sheqel embodies the offering of all Israel equally, wherever located, however situated within the genealogical and social order.

Gentiles may sanctify as an act of volition, but only Israel as an act of responsibility and obligation. More to the point, gentiles act one by one, only Israel forms a moral entity all together, and, in the act of taking up the heave-offering of the half-sheqels, all at once. So the corporate action, transcending individual householders, priests, and the poor, represents the entire social entity. That, in detail, the sheqel-tax derives from, and stands for, all Israel, both within and without the Land, is stated explicitly in the halakhah of Sheqalim: He took up the heave-offering of sheqels the first time and said, "Lo, this is from the land of Israel in behalf of the whole people of Israel." Then he took up the heave-offering the second time and said, "Lo, this is from the lands of Ammon and Moab and from the cities surrounded by a wall in the Land of Israel." He took up the heave-offering the third time and said, "Lo, this is from Babylonia and Medea and from places distant from the Land of Israel, in behalf of all Israelites." But he did not cover it up. This was the richest fund of all of them.

That is not to say individual Israelites from near and far, formed into a corporate entity before God, play no personal role in Israel's relationship with God. Not only do all Israelites share in the public offerings and in common prayer, but everyone has the right to present on the altar a votive or peace- or thanksgiving offering, on the one side, and an obligatory sacrifice, e.g., a sin- or guilt-offering, on the other. But, realized and utilized in particular in connection with the pilgrim festivals, the half-sheqel obliterates the distinctions of place, class, and genealogy, that, in the setting of sanctification of this world's goods and services, individuate persons and demarcate family-units. Then Israel, abstracted from Land, takes shape at the transcendent location.

Israel convenes, specifically, with God three times a year, ascending upward above the Land to do so. On pilgrim festivals, holy Israel gathers in the Temple, coming from overseas and from gentile territories, entering a condition of purity to carry out duties of sanctification in the Temple. True, the offerings that they bring to the Temple and its priesthood ordinarily come from the Land, first fruits of its crops and the tithe of its flocks and herds. But the value that those offerings represent, transported to Jerusalem in the form of money and converted into the produce of the Land, originates without the Land as much as within. So Israel beyond all enlandisement relates to God through the building that towers above the Land and the offerings of every Israelite, wherever situated as well. It follows that the most intensely locative venue of the encounter with God, Jerusalem, Zion, the Temple, the inner sanctum, also forms the center for all Israel defined as sanctified without reference to place of origin or of residence.

Then what is at issue? As usual, the Tosefta makes explicit what is at stake in the matter: They exact pledges from Israelites for their sheqels, so that the public offerings might be made of their funds. This is like a man who got a sore on his foot, and the doctor had to force it and cut off his flesh so as to heal him. Thus did the Holy One, blessed be he, exact a pledge from Israelites for the payment of their sheqels, so that the public offerings might be made of their funds. For public offerings appease and effect atonement between Israel and their father in heaven. Likewise we find of the heave-offering of sheqels that the Israelites paid in the wilderness, as it is said, "And you shall take the atonement money from the people of Israel land shall appoint it for the service of the tent of meeting; that it may bring the people of Israel to remembrance before the Lord, so as to make atonement for yourselves" (Exod. 30:16). So what the sheqel accomplishes is to form of all Israel a single entity before God: all have sinned, all atone, *all together*.

Collective sin, collective atonement—

these categories of the relationship with God, defined by Scripture from the story of the Golden Calf forward—transcend class, genealogy, and location. But that comes about not for the merely adventitious consideration that Israel encompasses vast populations beyond the limits of the Land, on the one side, and vast social diversity within, as much as beyond, the limits of the Land, on the other. To be Israel, wherever one is situated geographically and socially, is to participate in the collective character of Israel, its capacity to sin, its vocation of atonement. God views Israel as a mutually-responsible social entity, not as a collection of individuals of shared convictions and origins, but as a collectivity that encompasses individuals and forms of them something else, something other than what, as individuals, they are. Among the innumerable statements of that view, Amos 3:2 suffices in its use of the plural: "Only you have I known of all the families of Man, therefore I will visit on you all your iniquities." The half-sheqel provides for that collective guilt and collective atonement that makes Israel Israel.

If the generative myth of the halakhah retells the story of Man and Woman in Eden and their counterpart, Israel in the Land, then the logic of the tale requires the *incorporation* of Israel in a very precise sense: the formulation of Israel as a single responsible body, a collectivity culpable as a whole and not solely by reason of the activities of the individual parts. Israel then emerges not as the sum of the parts but on its own a whole moral entity, viewed, by God, in its own terms and framework: culpable but capable of atonement. By analogy, the Torah, written and oral, will view other principal players in world history as collectively capable of guilt. But Israel alone, possessed of the Torah, is obligated to, and can, carry out atonement all together. It is the Temple and its cult that set the stage for the embodiment of entire Israel and that mediate between Israel and God, and now we know precisely why that is so and how corporate Israel, confronting the God of all creation, comes about. To Israel alone has God given not solely the possibility but, as a matter of obligation, the very power to carry

out an act of sanctification of the goods of this world, things of value, translated whether into produce designated for God's purposes, whether coins for the purchase of what God requires.

That brings us to the second question that the halakhah answers, this time in the category of Zebahim, animal offerings. This question concerns precisely where and how Israel encounters God. The answer is, the link between Israel and God is effected by the attitude or intentionality of the Israelite and of the priest, each in his position in the transaction. God responds to the Israelite's and the priest's feelings and plans, and the offering is acceptable to him only so far as these are correct in a particular, specific way. At what points, in connection with what specific actions, does the intentionality of the donor and the priest register? The halakhah makes its statement solely through its cases, and here, by what it says, it also eliminates many possibilities. The offering is offered for six purposes, and the priest acting in behalf of the donor must have in mind the proper attitude concerning all six. The attitude of the officiating priest governs, and if the priest expresses no improper attitude, that suffices to validate the offering on these points. For the sake of six things is the animal offering sacrificed: (1) for the sake of the animal offering, (2) for the sake of the one who sacrifices it, (3) for the sake of the Lord, (4) for the sake of the altar fires, (5) for the sake of the odor, (6) for the sake of the pleasing smell. And as to the sin offering and the guilt offering, for the sake of the sin expiated thereby. That is to say, the officiating priest has to have in mind the particular offering at hand, offering a burnt-offering as a burnt-offering and not as peace-offerings. The one who sacrifices it is the donor of the animal, who benefits, e.g., from the expiation. The intent must be for God, not for an idol (!). The intent must be to roast the meat on the fire of the altar, not at any other location. One must intend an odor to ascend from the roast. And in the case of the sin- or guilt-offering, the particular sin that is expiated must be in mind. As to the particular actions at which these six aspects of intentionality must conform, they involve these deeds: cutting the pertinent organs, collecting the blood in a bowl, conveying the blood to the altar, and tossing the blood on the altar.

The priest is required for preparation of an offering; a non-priest cannot carry out the critical procedures of the blood-rite. An invalid priest likewise spoils the rite by his participation, e.g., one who was unclean, improperly dressed, and the like. But if the status of the priest weighs heavily on the rite, the attitude of the priest carries still greater consequence. Specifically, as just now noted, four processes integral to the rite, killing the beast, collecting the blood, conveying the blood to the altar, and tossing the blood on the altar, must be carried out by the officiating priest in accord with the intentionality of the *sacrifier*—the person who benefits from the offering, as distinct from the sacrificer, the priest who carries out the offering. There must be an accord between the will of the sacrifier in designating the beast and the will of the sacrificer in carrying out the rite. Should the priest declare that he carries out the action for some purpose other than the designated one, e.g., conveying the blood of a lamb for the purpose of peace-offerings when it is the fourteenth of Nisan and the beast has been designated for a Passover, the rite is spoiled.

Why does the attitude of the officiating priest bear so heavily on the matter? To find the answer, we take the classic case of how intentionality invalidates a deed. What we see is that what one intends before the fact governs the status of the act itself, and even though one performs the act correctly and ultimately acts in accord with the law, the initial intentionality still dictates the outcome. There can be no more powerful way of stating that what one intends in advance, and not what one does in fact, dictates the outcome of a transaction. Before us then is an extreme position, one that imposes its own perspective upon all else: the intentionality that motivates an action, not what is really done, governs. The way this is said is not complicated. It involves a rule about the priest's consuming the meat of the offering that he presents and how, at the moment

of slaughter (encompassing the other phases of the blood rite) he intends to eat that meat: when and where.

Specifically, the meat of the offerings that the priests receive must be eaten by them within a specific span of time, two nights and the intervening day. If the priest when slaughtering the beast (or wringing the neck of a bird) says that he will eat the meat later on, that very act of intentionality suffices to render the act of slaughter one of abomination, and the status of the offering is determined—without any action whatsoever on the priest's part. Now we see what it means to evaluate what happens solely by reference to what one intends to make happen: not what one actually does after the fact, but what one is thinking in advance of it. The rule is framed in terms of not what the priest does but what he is thinking of doing later on: He who slaughters the animal offering intending to toss its blood outside of the Temple court, to burn its sacrificial portions outside, to eat its meat outside, or to eat an olive's bulk of the skin of the fat tail outside—it is invalid. He who slaughters the animal offering, intending to toss its blood on the next day, to burn its sacrificial portions on the next day, to eat its meat on the next day, or an olive's bulk of the skin of the fat tail on the next day—it is refuse. And that is without regard to the actual deed of the priest. If, after the fact of the declared intention, he did the deed at the correct time or place, it changes nothing. With such remarkable power over the status of the beast that the mere intention to eat the meat outside of its proper time or to dispose of it outside of the proper place suffices to ruin the offering, the priest's intentionality in connection with immediate, concrete actions in other aspects of the offering will make a massive difference as well.

What about the transaction of the priest in behalf of the sacrifier? Here too, the action is evaluated by the intention, so that even if all the rites are correctly carried out, if the priest does not do them with the right attitude, the sacrifier loses out. This is expressed in the formulation that follows. If a beast, designated as sanctified by its own for a particular classification of offering, is actually slaughtered for a purpose other than that for which it was originally designated, what is the result? If the officiating priest does not carry out the intention of the Israelite who purchased and sanctified the beast, the offering remains valid; the blood is collected, conveyed to the altar, and tossed there. So far as the beast is concerned, the act of sanctification is irrevocable. So far as the householder is concerned, his obligation has not yet been carried out; he must present another animal to accomplish his purpose, e.g., to present a sin-offering or carry out a vow. There are two exceptions to this rule. If on the afternoon of the fourteenth of Nisan an Israelite's animal, designated to serve as a Passover offering, is offered for some other purpose, e.g., as peace-offerings, it is null. So too an animal designated as a sin-offering must be presented for that purpose and for no other. In both cases, the specificity of the occasion—the Passover, the sin—takes over; the animal that has been mis-classified by the priest is lost.

It follows that the blood-rite forms the center of the transaction between Israel and God at the altar. That is shown in the answer to the question, At what point is the offering validated, so that the disposition of the animal bears consequences? It is when the blood has been properly sprinkled or tossed. Then the offering is "permissible," meaning, the blood is burned on the altar and so the meat is eaten by the priest and (where appropriate) the Israelite sacrifier. The proper sprinkling or tossing of the blood therefore marks the turning point. Then the sacrifice comes within the category of being subject to the rule of refuse and extirpation. But if what permits the meat to be eaten is not properly offered, the blood not having been properly tossed so that the sacrificial portions of the animal may be burned up and the edible portions eaten, the sacrifice is not subject to the rule of refuse. If the blood-rite is improperly performed, therefore, issues of attitude and intention prove null. The decisive deed dictates the disposition of the initial intention.

The basic conception is that when the rite is performed properly with the correct intentionality, it accomplishes its goals (it is

"valid"). When the rite is performed properly but classified incorrectly, it is invalid. Resting as it does on the facticity of Scripture, the halakhah of the Oral Torah bears no messages concerning the meaning of the blood-rite, only the conditions that are required for its effective accomplishment. These Scripture has already set forth. The halakhah takes as its problem an issue on which the Written Torah makes no statement within the framework of normative prescriptions, but it makes an elaborate statement indeed within the setting of narrative of exemplary events and transactions from the beginning to the end. So in the present setting, the halakhah takes as its task the embodiment in ritual of the Written Torah's myth.

Why the stress on intentionality, and what outcome for Israel's relationship with God do we discern? The simple fact is, the Israelite has the power to change the status of a beast from secular to sacred, and this he does by an act of will. He designates a beast as sacred, specifying the purpose of the act of sanctification. So the entire process of presenting personal offerings (as distinct from the public ones) depends upon the act of will effected by the individual Israelite. And since the rites are carried out at the critical turnings by the priest, the attitude that governs his activities likewise must register. Neither the Israelite nor the priest is portrayed as an automaton, nor do the actions of the two parties emerge as coerced or automatic. What the Israelite does realizes his will, which is why the deed makes a difference, and, the halakhah takes for granted, the priest too engages through an act of will. Both are deemed to have, and to make, choices, and these choices respond to the intentionality that motivates the entire transaction, start to finish. So the halakhah portrays the cult as the stage on which Israel—priest and Israelite alike—work out in concrete actions the results of their interior reflections.

Since, as with the daily whole-offerings of all Israel all together, the entire rite is time and again represented as an exercise in expiation of sin, even though a variety of offerings serves another purpose altogether (e.g., celebration, service, and the like), we do well to recall the principal (but not sole) occasion for individual participation (M. Ker. 1:2):

> For those [thirty-six classes of transgressions] are people liable, for deliberately doing them, to the punishment of extirpation, and for accidentally doing them, to the bringing of a sin offering, and for not being certain of whether or not one has done them, to a suspensive guilt offering (Lev. 5:17).

The cult expiates sin only when the sin is inadvertent; deliberate sin is expiated through the sacrifice of years of life ("extirpation"). Then the entire transaction at the altar, so far as the expiation of sin forms the center, concerns those actions that one did not intend to carry out but nonetheless has done. The intentionality governing the deed therefore proves decisive, and we may not find surprising the focus upon attitude accompanying the action of sacrifice.

Just as the offering expiates an inadvertent sin, so the attitude that motivates the sacrifier (and, correspondingly, the priest too) will define matters: it is for this particular sin that I did not mean to do that I have deliberately designated as holy that particular beast. An unintentional, sinful act provokes an intentional act of expiation. Then, what God follows with close anticipation is how this act of will is realized—confirmed in actuality; that occasion of acute advertence is what concludes the transaction begun inadvertently. And that means in the concrete arrangements of the cult, how the actions of the priest conform in the priest's intentionality to the original act of sanctification brought about by the Israelite's intentionality. The entire relationship between Israel and God works itself out as a match of the intentions of the several parties, each of them qualified to form an independent act of will, all of them conforming to bring about the successful result, the expiation of sin or the fulfillment of commitment.

Accordingly, in the offerings of the altar, the Israelite relates to God by an act of will in designating as sacred for a specific purpose defined as acceptable by God for purposes of propitiation an animal and related materials. The priest then mediates this act of will by realizing, in actions resulting in the tossing of the animal's blood on the altar, the intentionality of the Israelite. And God relates to the Israelite, in that same transaction, by paying closest possible attention to the interplay of the Israelite's initial intentionality in the act of sanctification and the concrete outcome, in the priest's realization of that same intentionality, in the act of offering.

We should not miss the negative, for it yields a positive result. It is not enough that the Israelite designate the animal; God must know that the priest has prepared it in accord with the definition of the sanctification that has taken hold of that animal by reason of the Israelite's act of sanctification: the priest must carry out the action within the same framework of purpose established by the Israelite for the beast. So it does not suffice for the priest to impose his judgment upon the disposition of the beast; the initial act of sanctification has imposed limits upon his purpose. The Israelite requires priestly conformity to his, the Israelite's, act of will in designating the beast. The priest effects the correct offering only when he subordinates his will to that of the Israelite. The Israelite attains atonement and reconciliation with God only when, after an unintended violation of the Torah, he demonstrates that, in giving something back (whether a costly beast, whether a bird of no account), he subordinates his will to that of God. We find matched acts of willful and deliberate subordination—the priest's to the Israelite's, the Israelite's to God's.

The sequence of acts in conformity with the will of another having been worked out, God then accepts the actions that come about by reason of right thought and responds by accepting the blood-offering as an act of propitiation and atonement, on the one side, or of fulfillment of obligation, on the other. What is required in a valid act of fulfillment of the Israelite's act of consecration is uniform conformity of deed to will. When it comes to characterizing Israel's relationship with God, what counts, then, is that God follows this sequence of steps, this process leading the beast from the secular herd to the sacred altar, its blood turned into the reagent to wash away the inadvertent sin of the sacrifier. Everyone must concur in sequence, the sacrifier, the sacrificer, and God in confirmation to the correct intention of both. It is as though God wished to set up a system carefully to monitor the will of successive participants in the process, each exposing for God's inspection the contents of his hearts.

The premise of the halakhah is fully exposed here: God closely attends to the match of deliberation and deed, and only when the Israelite's and priest's intent coincide does God confirm his gracious acceptance of the result, propitiation resulting. So while the presentation of offerings superficially places the human side of the transaction at the center—it is the Israelite's, then the priest's parts that effect the relationship—in fact, it is God's engagement with the same transaction, his close and careful surveillance of the match of intent and action, word and deed, that makes all the difference. In the cult Israel relates to God intimately and concretely. Once the Israelite undertakes by an act of will to engage in a deed of sanctification, God's participation in the process, step by step, his close attention to the interior of the activities consequence upon the undertaking—these responses embody God's intense interest in the Israelite's attitude, to which God responds.

That is why "intentionality" takes on very concrete and specific meanings in the setting of the offering to God of the gifts of the Land, meat, wine, oil, grain and the like. When an Israelite expresses his intentionality to sanctify a particular animal for a specified offering, that consecrates the beast for God's service at the altar. But the intentionality of the Israelite then requires a corresponding attitude on the part of, with a confirming action by, the officiating priest. If he does the deeds of the sacrifice for some purpose other than the announced one of the Israelite, he denies the Israelite the benefit of confirmation of his intentionality by a cultic action. What is the result of the priest's mis-conceiving of matters? Where the beast can serve for some appropriate cultic purpose, it does so. That is to say, the original action of the Israelite in sanctifying the beast is not nullified by the contradictory intentionality of the

priest. But where the beast is designated for a very particular purpose and can then serve no other, the sacrificial act is lost.

Then when is a beast sanctified with such specificity as to be lost by the priest's contradictory intentionality? It is when either the time or the circumstance intervenes and so defines the status as to sanctification of the beast as to render the beast useless for all other purposes. For the Passover-offering in particular, the time is the eve of the Passover, when the lamb designated for the Passover offering must be offered up under that designation and no other. Any other time, the same lamb may serve as peace-offerings. So the time makes all the difference in avoiding confusion as to the intent of the sacrifier.

The other consideration—the circumstance—appeals to much weightier concerns, confirming what has already been said about why intentionality registers in so weighty a way. The circumstance is the inadvertent commission of a particular sin. The beast designated as the sin-offering for a given sin can serve to expiate no other. It is the demonstration of correct intention—the good will, not the rebellious will—that the offering embodies. The correlation of the sin-offering with the inadvertent sin is expressed in the following way (T. Ker. 2:4):

> [If] it is a matter of doubt whether or not one has sinned, he brings a suspensive guilt-offering [M. Ker. 4:1, 2A-B]. [If] he has sinned, but is not certain what particular sin he has committed, he brings a sin-offering. [If] he has sinned and is informed of the character of his sin but he has forgotten what sin he has committed, lo, this one brings a sin-offering [M. Ker. 4:2C-D], and it is slaughtered for the sake of whichever [sin he has committed] and it is eaten. Then he goes and brings a sin-offering for that sin of which he is informed, and it is slaughtered for the sake of whatever [particular sin he has done] and it [too] is eaten.

A very particular occasion then has precipitated the act of will involved in designating the beast as a sin-offering, and that same purpose must govern throughout.

In both cases, then, the act of sanctification takes on a particularity that drastically limits options in case of priestly error. The reason for the latter—the sin-offering—is self-evident. God permits the man who has inadvertently sinned to atone for the sin he did not mean to commit or even know that he committed. Once he finds out what he has done, he wishes to show the true state of his will, and that is through the sin-offering. The offering then is linked to that action and no other. Sin is particular, concrete, and delimited—an action, not a condition. And so is the intention to be made manifest: that act I did not intend to commit, shown by this act, which I fully will.

That negative rule—the sin-offering and Passover are invalidated if the priest's intentionality does not conform to the occasion (the will of the sacrifier) or the time (the afternoon of the fourteenth of Nisan) yields a striking, positive result: God pays exceedingly close attention to the act of will exercised by both the sacrifier and the sacrificer, responding to what is in the heart of each in assessing the effect of the act viewed whole. Then the activity that yields the event—the sacrifier's selection of the beast, designation of its purpose in an act of consecration, his presentation to the priest with the sacrifier's laying on of hands, then the priest's cutting of the beast's throat and collection of its blood, conveyance of its blood to the altar and the splattering of its blood thereon—all of these activities must be uniformly animated by the initial intention of the Israelite, and the continuation of the program by the priest is at issue. It would be difficult to formulate a more concrete and far-reaching statement that God pays the closest possible attention to the Israelite's will than the rule at hand. The offerings at the altar accomplish their goal because God attentively engages with, responds to, the Israelite's and the priest's intentionality. God will respond, the halakhah takes for granted, and accord atonement, register the fulfillment of an obligation for example, only when these coincide: the will of the sacrifier, the will of the sacrificer.

Sacrifices thus do not accomplish atonement merely because they are offered, but only when offered with the correct attitude. That bears a deep implication: sanctification is not a condition that inheres but a status that

is invoked. That conception is expressed in the rule that the altar sanctifies what is appropriate to it but has no affect upon what is not appropriate to it. Sanctification does not inhere in the altar, such that mere contact with the altar transforms what touches the altar into something permanently sacred. The full meaning of that rule of the halakhah emerges only when we consider the Written Torah's judgment of the same matter, which is stated at Exod. 29:37: "the altar shall be most holy; whatever touches the altar shall become holy." That halakhah of the Oral Torah significantly qualifies that statement, adding the language "that is appropriate" to the phrase, "whatever touches. . . ." The issue is whether sanctification is indelible or stipulative. Sanctification affects status, not substance.

Then we must ask, does not the Land sanctify? Does not the city sanctify? Does not the altar sanctify? We know that all three do have that power; to take one case, produce designated as second tithe is sanctified upon entry within the walls of Jerusalem. So introducing the principle of appropriateness qualifies what we should have anticipated would represent an absolute condition. Since Scripture explicitly declares the altar itself to be not only holy but capable of imparting holiness to whatever touches it, we cannot miss the drastic way in which the halakhah mediates the meaning of sanctification. It is now not a condition but a transaction, subject to variables and stipulations; it is no longer locative and place-bound, nor, indeed, is it utopian (the altar is unique and singular, where it is and no where else, as Deuteronomy has made the fact).

What is at stake is the insistence of the normative halakhah that, while the altar alone serves as the nexus of Heaven and earth, not even the altar embodies let alone transmits what is intrinsically holy. What can become holy realizes its potential upon the altar: the right place, the right time, confirmed by the right intentionality. Then some things are relative to others, and location, time, and attitude all together coincide: then the potential sanctity becomes actual, then alone. We cannot speak in the halakhic framework of "the

Holy," only the status of holiness, which depends upon meeting specified conditions and turns out to be relative and stipulative.

The religious meaning of the halakhah focuses upon atonement for sin, just as Scripture says time and again. The blood-rite and all the elaborate arrangements of a spatial character round about it are represented, time and again, as essentially a medium for atoning for sin; that is explicitly why the daily whole-offerings are required, and whatever other motivations animate God's commandments concerning the sacrificial cult, the main one, the governing one, repeatedly is, atonement for sin. It is not only the halakhah, but also the aggadah, that takes the view of the blood-rite: it is principally an act of atonement for sin, and when the rite was brought to an end, another medium of atonement had to be identified (Fathers according to Rabbi Nathan IV.V.2):

    A. One time after the destruction of the Temple, Rabban Yohanan ben Zakkai was going forth from Jerusalem with R. Joshua following after him. He saw the house of the sanctuary lying in ruins.

    B. R. Joshua said, "Woe is us for this place that lies in ruins, the place in which the sins of Israel used to come to atonement."

    C. He said to him, "My son, do not be distressed. We have another mode of atonement, which is like atonement through sacrifice, and what is that? It is deeds of loving kindness."

    D. "For so it is said, 'For I desire mercy and not sacrifice, and the knowledge of God rather than burnt offerings' (Hos. 6:6)."

With its recapitulation of the Written Torah's presentation of matters, the Oral Torah makes explicit the critical factor that will bring about the restoration, which turns out to be the same power that in the offerings on the altar brings about expiation and reconciliation: the realization in actuality of the required intention, which only Israel has the power to bring into being. It is once more the act of will—this time, the act of mercy, which God cannot coerce but only crave.

JACOB NEUSNER

**SCRIPTURE IN CLASSICAL JUDAISM:** The Hebrew Bible had a fundamental place in classical Judaism (for modern examples, see

figs. 120-122) and constituted an important component of its conceptual background: indeed, no Rabbinic document could have been written without knowledge of Scripture. And yet, the rabbis' exegetical interest in Scripture was not comprehensive. Although they absorbed nearly the whole of Scripture, they commented only on selected parts. Thus, large portions of Scripture, including segments of prophecy and the Deuteronomic history, escaped formal Rabbinic exegesis. This suggests that, in Rabbinic Judaism, the truth of Scripture does not depend on, or emerge from, *ad hoc* comments on discrete passages. Rather, it comes from the rabbis' grasp of what they judged to be Scripture's comprehensive message. That message, in turn, determined which passages rabbis would subject to close reading.

Scripture alone neither determined the sole agenda nor provided the ubiquitous focus of Rabbinic literary activity and imagination. It was the major—but certainly not the only—source rabbis used to produce their literature. They also drew extensively on their own materials. Indeed, M. Hag. 1:8 baldly asserts that substantial portions of Rabbinic teaching—for example, on matters as basic and important as Sabbath observance—have scant scriptural support. A saying attributed to the Tannaitic master Simeon b. Yohai goes so far as to value study of Rabbinic teachings over study of Scripture (Y. Shab. 16:1 [15c]; B. B.M. 33a):

    A. "He who occupies himself with Scripture [gains] merit (*mdh*) that is no merit.

    B. He who occupies himself with Mishnah [gains] merit for which they receive a reward (*skr*).

    C. He who occupies himself with Talmud— you have no merit greater than this."

To account for the varied roles of Scripture in Rabbinic literature, it helps to remember that Rabbinism's initial catalyst was neither the canonization of the Hebrew Bible nor readerly research into Scripture. It was, rather, the demise of the Second Temple and its divinely ordained cult, the rites of which guaranteed God's presence in Israel's midst. The loss of the Holy of Holies—the principal locus of Israel's invisible and silent God—

meant the absence of a stable cultural center and generated an acute religious crisis, primarily in the realm of behavior.

The kind of religion manifested by the Temple and advocated by its priestly personnel—"levitical religion"—conceived of Israel's life as a comprehensive and integrated system of disciplined engagement with God. That engagement largely took the form of prescribed and repeated behaviors, directed by a caste of priests, that revolved around and focused attention on a sacred center, a stable reference point, where access to God was certain to occur. Levitical religion mapped out a system of categories, usually binary opposites such as clean/unclean, fit/unfit, holy/profane, in which everything that mattered had its place. Its preferred literary form was the list rather than narrative. In its ritual and its writing, levitical religion promulgated a synchronic vision of a centered, structured, hierarchical, and orderly reality. Its practitioners celebrated precision, lineage, precedent, and concreteness and had an exceedingly low tolerance for uncertainty, confusion, and ambiguity.

The pre-70 Jewish religious groups in the land of Israel about whom we know the most—Sadducees, Pharisees, the Dead Sea Sect—all operated within the sphere of levitical religion. In early Christian writing, levitical religion was a primary negative, and therefore defining, focus; it remained so well after the Temple's destruction. For example, Paul's early discarding of "the Law" sought to render levitical categories nugatory, and the evangelists could not tell of Jesus' death without recording that the curtain of the Holy of Holies "was torn in two, from top to bottom" (Mark 15:38; Mat. 27:51; cf., Luke 23:45). Other Christian writers, from the author of the Epistle of Barnabas to Justin Martyr and Irenaeus, made the rejection of routine levitical rituals a central theme of their compositions.

In contrast to their patristic counterparts, the post-70 founders of Rabbinism aimed to perpetuate a levitical system. Rabbinic piety comprised a host of attitudes, ethics, and rituals—food, purity, and kinship taboos; ethical practices; observance of Sabbaths, holy days, and festivals; prayer, etc.—that depended on and promulgated levitical categories. The Rabbinic use of Scripture was thus embedded in a complex of rabbinically ordained practices, many of which—including most of the rules for the treatment of Scripture itself—are not in, and do not derive from, Scripture at all. Rabbinism's initial concern was the elaboration and refinement of its own system. Exegetically attaching the system to Scripture was secondary.

Rabbinic Judaism did not emerge from a circle of scriptural exegetes. Rather, it began as the work of a small, ambitious, and homogeneous group of pseudo-priests who professed to know how to maintain Israel's ongoing engagement with God—its life of sanctification—in the absence of a cult, and who, on that basis, aspired to lead the Jews. By the third century, rabbis expressed their self-conception in the ideology of the "oral Torah," which held that a comprehensive body of teachings and practices (*halakhot*) not included in Scripture had been given by God to Moses and, through Moses, only to the Rabbinic establishment. Thus, ancient rabbis advanced the proposition that even without a temple, Israel could still achieve holiness if the people's conduct conformed to Rabbinic expertise and authority. Though rabbis articulated this claim in the language of the "oral Torah," they made it stick through their manipulation of the written one.

To achieve their goals, rabbis had to conquer a difficulty the pre-70 groups avoided: the absence of a sacred center. The community at Qumran at least had a real building in Jerusalem about whose recovery and control it could fantasize. But particularly after the Bar Kokhba debacle in 132-135 C.E., rabbis must have known that the Temple was gone for good. To compensate for that loss and to preserve the sacred center required by their piety, Rabbinic Judaism developed a distinctive theory of the sanctity of Scripture.

This is not to claim that only Rabbinic Judaism conceived the scroll of Scripture as sacred, but rather that the complex of restrictions discussed below is not present in other ancient Jewish writings. The Community Rule and Damascus Document, for instance, are silent on the question of the production and handling of Scripture, and the common storage of what we regard as Scripture together with writings produced by the sectaries themselves suggests that they may have given equal treatment to all writings they deemed valuable. Though the "Law of Moses" has authority in the Damascus Document, for instance, the sectarians' own writings may have for them what we would identify as a scriptural authority.

In classical Judaism, Scripture had a sacred status, and human dealings with it were hedged about with behavioral restrictions. M. Yad. 3:5 declares that "all the holy writings render the hands unclean" (also see M. Kel. 15-6; M. Yad. 3:2, 4:6). A scroll's sanctity was not limited to its text but extended to its blank margins (M. Yad. 3:4; T. Yad. 2:11) and its wrappings and containers (T. Yad. 2:12). The sanctity of Scripture outweighed even the Sabbath, and people were expected and permitted to violate Sabbath restrictions to save the scroll and its wrappings from fire (M. Shab. 16:1)—an exemption otherwise applied only to save a human life. Also, it was acceptable to make heave-offering unclean to rescue Scripture from harm (T. Shab. 13:2, 6). A damaged, worn, or unfit scroll retained its sanctity and therefore was to be buried, by itself or in the coffin of a sage, but not burned or otherwise destroyed (B. Meg. 26b).

Although the category "holy writings" apparently could include works in Hebrew and in translation (M. Shab. 16:1), rabbis gave the scroll of the Hebrew Pentateuch, the *Sefer Torah*, pride of place. It was the scriptural paradigm and prototype. Every Jew was obliged to write or possess a *Sefer Torah* (B. San. 21b). According to M. Meg. 3: 1, a Jewish community could do without a synagogue, an ark, Scripture wrappings, or other books of Scripture, but not a Torah scroll. The Talmud's elaborate rules for the scroll's production and treatment decisively distinguish its content from ordinary writing. The *Sefer Torah* was used in synagogue worship and was to be written without vocalization. It had to be transcribed on specially prepared parchment marked with lines (B. Meg. 19a), in a par-

ticular script (B. Shab. 104a; B. San. 21b-22a; Y. Meg. 1:11 [71b]), and with orthographic uniformity (B. Erub. 13a; B. Meg. 18b; B. Yeb. 79a; B. Ket. 19b). In the scroll, seven Hebrew letters, each time they appeared, were to be drawn with *tagin*, three-stroke decorative crowns or titles at the top of the letter (B. Men. 29b). A sheet that contained four errors was to be buried, not corrected (B. Meg. 29b), but scrolls produced by Jews deemed heretics or sectarians were to be burned (B. Git. 45b). Worshipers were expected to rise in the presence of the Torah scroll (Y. Meg. 4:1 [12a]; B. Mak. 22b; B. Qid. 33b), and no other type of scroll could be placed on top of it (T. Meg. 3:20). To touch the parchment of a Torah scroll with bare hands was judged an outrage (B. Shab. 14a; B. Meg. 32a).

Rabbis used the Torah-writing for purposes other than reading. They wore it in phylacteries and affixed it to dwellings in *mezuzot*. On account of the segments of Torah-writing they contained, these items too had sacred status. Along with the bags and straps of phylacteries, sacks for holding Scripture, and the mantle of the Torah scroll, they were labeled "instruments of holiness" and had to be buried, but neither burned nor discarded, when worn out (B. Meg. 26b). M. Ta. 2:12 requires that prayers for rain be recited in front of the ark containing the Torah scrolls, which was to be brought to the public square, and M. San. 2:4 imagines that the scroll itself would accompany the Israelite king in battle, when he judged, and when he ate.

Other passages illustrate the special position of the Torah scroll in Rabbinic culture. Sifra (Behuqotai, Pereq 8:10) asserts that the possession of the "*Sefer Torah* distinguished Israel from the peoples of the world" and is the reason for God's persisting loyalty. Finally, rabbis were expected to perform the mourning rite of *qeri'ah*, the ritual tearing of one's garment, at the sight of a burned Torah scroll (B. Meg. 25b), and, on seeing a torn scroll, they were to perform *qeri'ah* twice, "once on account of the parchment and once on account of the writing" (B. M.Q. 26a; also Y. M.Q. 3:7 [83b]).

Figure 123. Poster advertising a performance of "Orphan of the Streets" at the Theater Ludowy, Vilna, Poland, 1920s-1930s. The poster heralds an appearance by American artist Anna Jakubowicz (Jackubowitz) in the first Vilna production of a popular play from Warsaw.

Figure 124. Theater poster announcing performances at the Palas Theater, Vilna, Poland, probably 1930. Featured were the plays "Two Millionaires" and "Three Kopecks a Pound of Bread."

Figure 125. Culture League Drama School graduation performance of an I.L. Peretz one-act play, Warsaw, Poland, c. 1929. Graduates formed the socially conscious Yiddish Experimental Studio-Yung Theater in 1932.

Figure 126. Rabbi Cyril Harris, Chief Rabbi of South Africa. Photograph by Ryan Noik.

Figure 127. Waverly Shul, Johannesburg, South Africa. Photograph by Ryan Noik.

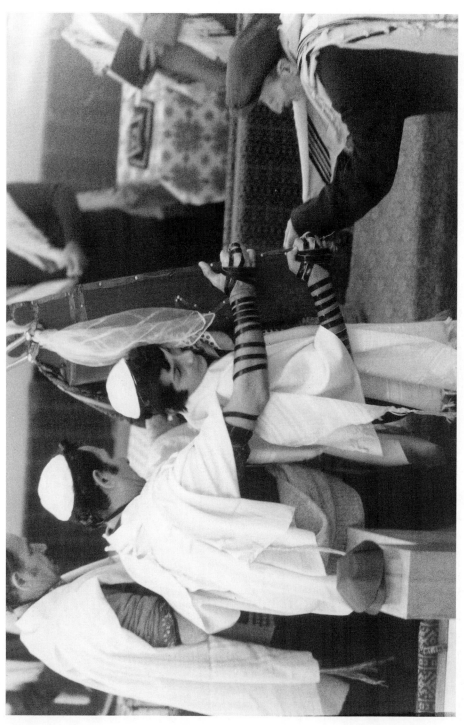

Figure 128. Four generations of Iranians participate at a bar mitzvah celebration, Jerusalem, Israel, 1970s. Photograph by Barbara Pfeffer

Figure 129. Yemenites celebrating the festival of Sukkot, Ein Kerem, Israel, 1970s. Photograph by Barbara Pfeffer.

Figure 130. Hasidic Jews celebrate the reunification of Jerusalem after the Six Day War, Mt. Zion, Israel, June, 1967. Photograph by Leonard Freed.

These regulations suggest that rabbis regarded the Torah-writing itself as a sacred object. The idea that a missing or added letter in the Torah's transcription could "destroy the world" (B. Erub. 13a) and the notion that one grieves for damaged writing as one does for a deceased human being imply that rabbis construed the very letters of the Torah writing not as mere signs of an immaterial discourse but as sacred in themselves.

Although a scroll required writing in order to be sacred, the writing apparently did not have to constitute a discourse. Consider, for example, M. Yad. 3:5:

A. A scroll (*spr*) that was erased and in which there remain eighty-five letters, like the section "And it came to pass when the ark set forward" (Num. 10:35-36), renders the hands unclean.
B. A sheet (*mglh*) [of a scroll] on which was written eighty-five letters, like the section "And it came to pass when the ark set forward" (Num. 10:35-36), renders the hands unclean.

T. Yad. 2:10 (ed. Zuckermandel, p. 683, lines 2-5) adds:

A scroll that wore out—if one can glean (*llqt*) from it eighty-five letters, like the section "And it came to pass when the ark set forward" (Num. 10:35-36), it renders the hands unclean.

On this issue, the late-third-century Babylonian masters Huna and Hisda are said to have agreed that if the eighty-five letters appeared as words, the scroll would make hands unclean if the words were randomly scattered, and Hisda declared the scroll sacred even if it contained eighty-five scattered letters (B. Shab. 115b). Moreover, rabbis supposed it possible to deduce "mounds and mounds" of behavioral practices (*halakhot*) from the *tagin* attached to the top of certain letters (B. Men. 29b). Since these titles were strictly ornamental markings, their interpretation did not require discerning a discourse. They were deemed meaningful nevertheless, and the Babylonian Talmud certifies their significant by imagining that they were affixed to the Torah writing by God.

Finally and most important, the "official" Torah writing, that used in worship, contained, and could contain, no vowels. It thus did not and could not "fix" a discourse in writing and was not a text in Ricoeur's sense. Constituted solely of unvocalized consonants—only half a language—the writing in the *Sefer Torah* was mute. Like the scroll and the *tagin*, it was envisioned as a material object. In Rabbinic Judaism, therefore, the sanctity of Scripture appears to have depended neither on what the writing said nor even on its being read, but rather on how and by whom it was produced. A scroll of heretics or sectarians, after all, was not inspected for accuracy but was simply condemned to burning on the *a priori* grounds that its producers were untrustworthy.

Whatever else it may have been, the writing we would call "Scripture" was conceived by Rabbinic culture as a holy object, a thing to be venerated. The Torah scroll was Rabbinism's most revered and sacred artifact, and its sanctity was socially demonstrated, objectified, and certified by a network of Rabbinic behavioral injunctions. Thus, the *Sefer Torah*—both as scroll and as writing—constituted the ubiquitous material reference point of Rabbinic religion. As an artifact, the Torah scroll, with its holy and allegedly unchanged and changeless writing, formed the requisite stable center for Rabbinism's system of piety. In the absence of the Temple and its Holy of Holies, the scroll and its writing became for ancient rabbis primary repositories and conveyers of social legitimacy, cultural authenticity, and religious meaning.

Since properly inscribed Torah-writing was sometimes—perhaps often—not a text (as with phylacteries and *mezuzot*) but was always a sacred object, its artifactual status dominated and defined its use as a text. Because it was a holy artifact, the Torah-writing by definition was heavy with significance; it was meaning-full. But because it had no vowels, and hence contained no discourse, in another way the Torah-writing was also meaning-less—evocative but profoundly inarticulate.

The Torah scroll could not be read by itself because its writing was indeterminate script. To transform that script into a text, to make it readable, necessarily meant imposing a determinate discourse on it. For rabbis, in addition to supplying the absent vowels to make the letters into words, this transformation entailed the tradition of qere' ("what is read") and ketiv ("what is written"), in which some words were read differently from their written form, euphemisms were substituted for offensive written words (T. Meg. 3(4):39-40; B. Meg. 25b), and some written words and passages were not read at all. It also involved knowing how to divide lines of script into verses, when to introduce accents, stresses, and pauses (M. Meg. 4:4; B. Meg. 3a; B. Ned. 37b; Y. Meg. 4:1 [7d]; Genesis Rabbah 36), and the customary melody in which the scroll was chanted (B. Ber. 62a; B. Meg. 32a). Since none of these, including the essential vowels, could ever be the property of the script, in Rabbinic Judaism reading the Sefer Torah was less a matter of deciphering an inscription than of reciting a previously known discourse and applying it to the writing.

For rabbis, reading the Sefer Torah thus could not be the consequence of ordinary literacy, although that surely was a prerequisite. Because the Torah-writing was both sacred and illegible, making it intelligible was a highly disciplined activity that demanded specialized knowledge. Since rabbis could neither recite what they wrote nor write what they recited, the determination of Scripture's discourse had to reside almost entirely with them. Some sources suggest Rabbinic awareness of this implication. For instance, B. San. 3b-4b reports a lengthy dispute about whether authority is given to the vowels or to the consonants in delineating Scripture's discourse. Although the discussion favors the authority of vowels—and thereby confirms that Scripture's discourse was not fixed by writing—the disagreement itself shows that rabbis appealed to both principles and outlawed neither. It thus depicts the sages, not the rules, as the final arbiters of discourse. More explicitly, an important saying, attributed to Isaac, a third century Palestinian master, holds that (B. Ned. 37b-38a):

A. The vocalization (mqr') of the scribes, the [orthographic] omissions ('ytwr) of the scribes, and the [Scripture words that are] read but not written and the [Scripture passages that are] written but not read

B. [are] practice[s] (hlkh) [revealed] to Moses from Sinai.

The phrase that concludes the saying at B is a standard Rabbinic expression that refers to the "oral Torah." The passage thus claims that not only qere and ketiv but also the orthography and vocalization of Scripture—its writing and its discourse—are not in Scripture; rather they are the possession solely of Rabbinic tradition. For rabbis, the credibility of Scripture's discourse was guaranteed only by proper acculturation and training, in short, by Rabbinic discipleship.

The Rabbinic theory of Scripture thus contained three complementary components that aimed to justify both the sages' vision of themselves and their claim to leadership over Israel. First, by declaring Scripture sacred, rabbis endowed it with a unique and unassailable status. As a holy object, Scripture possessed a givenness, a fixity, and a substantiality that made it seem independent of rabbis or their traditions. Second, rabbis reinforced the impression of Scripture's autonomy and centrality by making ownership of a Sefer Torah a religious obligation for every Jew. From a Rabbinic perspective, Scripture was not only the distinctive possession of all Israel; more important, it was the personal property of each individual Israelite. Finally, while they affirmed Scripture as the heritage of all Jews, rabbis simultaneously claimed that its writing and its discourse were part of "oral Torah." They thereby asserted their singular mastery over, indeed, their exclusive right to manipulate the sacred artifact they deemed the emblem of Israel's identity. In effect, rabbis proclaimed themselves coextensive with Scripture and sought to acquire for themselves and their own discourse the same objectivity they attributed to it. Y. M.Q. 3:7 [87b] makes the identification explicit: "He who sees a disciple of a sage who has died is like one who sees a Torah scroll that has been burned."

In their theory and use of Scripture, rabbis had it both ways. As much as Scripture was the general legacy of all Israel, it also was intimately and inextricably bound to

Rabbinism's particular tradition. In the Rabbinic view, in order to be "Israel," Jews had to invest themselves in Scripture; but to do so they had equally to invest themselves in the sages' authority. Since all these components were realized in concrete and prescribed behaviors, the effect of the theory becomes clear. With their use of Scripture, rabbis sought to develop and sustain a sociology of knowledge that made them indispensable.

Within classical Judaism, the sanctity of Scripture accordingly gave its writing an intrinsic efficacy, an almost totemic quality. The discourse attached to it had an unimpeachable authenticity and the power of authentication; it could make other discourses legitimate. Thus, in Rabbinic Judaism, the writing and discourse of Scripture had to be inherently separable from, and could be neither merged nor confused with, the commentary upon them. To mix the two would have deprived rabbis of an artifact to control and violated the basic levitical distinction between the sacred and the profane. In Rabbinic writing, therefore, passages and words of Scripture tend to be identified as such by an introductory formula, such as "thus Scripture says," "as it is written," "as it is said," or "a [scriptural] teaching says." The routine and nearly ubiquitous marking of scriptural passages is distinctive in antiquity. For example, in contrast to early Christian materials such as Luke's infancy narrative or the Book of Revelation, which subtly appropriate various Old Testament images, the rabbi's' use of Scripture is explicitly referential.

The rabbis not only distinguished Scripture from other kinds of writings, they also developed literary forms that seem to give Scripture an autonomous voice. The following passage illustrates this point. Mekhilta of Rabbi Ishmael, Tractate Shirta, Chapter 8 (ed. Horowitz-Rabin, p. 144, lines 14-22) comments on the last two words of Exod. 15:11, "Who among the gods is like you, Lord? Who is like you, majestic in holiness, awesome in praises, *doing wonders*."

A. "Doing wonders"
B. "Did ('sh) wonders" is not written here, but "doing ('wsh) wonders—in the Age to Come."
C. As it is said, "Therefore, says the Lord, the time is coming when men shall no longer swear, 'By the life of the Lord who brought the Israelites up from Egypt,' but, 'By the life of the Lord who brought the Israelites back from a northern land and from all the lands to which he had dispersed them;' and I will bring them back to the soil which I gave to their forefathers" (Jer. 16:14-15).
D. Another interpretation: "Doing wonders"
E. He did wonders for us and he does wonders for us in each and every generation.
F. As it is said, "I will praise you, for I am filled with awe; you are wonderful and your works are wonderful; and you know my soul very well" (Ps. 139:14).
G. And it says, "You have done many things, Lord my God, your wonders and your thoughts towards us" (Ps. 40:6).
H. Another interpretation: "Doing wonders"—
I. He does wonders for the fathers, and in the future [he will] do [them] for the sons.
J. As it is said, "As in the days of his going forth from the land of Egypt, I will show him wonders" (Micah 7:15).
K. "I will show him"—what I did not show to the fathers.
L. For, look, the miracles and mighty acts that in the future I [will] do for the sons, they [will be] more than what I did for the fathers.
M. For thus Scripture says, "To him who alone does great wonders, for his mercy endures forever" (Ps. 136:4).
N. And it says, "Blessed is the Lord God, God of Israel, who alone does wonders, and blessed be his glorious name forever, and may the whole earth be filled with his glory. Amen and Amen" (Ps. 72:18-19).

The passage begins at B by noting a difference between the orthography and the vocalization of Scripture—its writing and its discourse. The word 'sh can be vocalized—and these are not the only alternatives—as a third-person masculine singular perfect ("did," "has done") or as a masculine singular present participle ("doing," "does"). Its defective spelling favors the former, but the discourse tradition, for good reason, affirms the latter. The passage exploits the discrepancy and, by the mere gloss with the Rabbinic term "Age to Come, imputes an eschatological intention to the participle. The verses from Jeremiah, appended without comment at C, make "the Age to Come" refer to the return from exile.

The second interpretation (D-G), which focuses on the noun "wonders," consists of an assertion (E) that God's wonders for Israel are constant, which is then bolstered by two verses from Psalms. Considered apart from the statement at E, however, the verses discuss only God's wonderful qualities and actions, but neither Israel nor her generations. The third interpretation (H-N), also on the theme of God's wonders, asserts at I, with support from the verse from Micah at J, that Israel's past will be replicated in her future ("As in the days of his going forth . . ."). K-L makes this mean that God's acts for Israel's "sons" will be greater than those for the "fathers." The identifying formula at M ("For *thus* Scripture says") suggests that the Psalm citations at M-N support this idea, but, as above, the verses simply praise God as the sole worker of wonders and make no reference to the future.

Although the interpretations in this passage are formally distinguished from one another at D and H by the disjunctive device *davar aher* ("another interpretation"), they operate within a limited conceptual sphere and a narrow thematic range. As is typical of most lists of *davar aher* comments in Rabbinic literature, the three segments not only do not conflict but are mutually reinforcing. Taken together, B-C, D-G, and H-N claim that God's past wondrous acts in Israel's behalf will continue, and be even greater, in the future. Thus, they ascribe to the words "doing wonders" multiple variations of a single meaning.

The literary technique for presenting that meaning is worth noting. Instead of providing an actual exegesis of the words from Exod. 15:11, the passage strategically juxtaposes verses from prophecy and Psalms and pre-interprets them with brief comments and glosses that are in no way integral to the verses themselves. The verses at C, F, G, M, and N stand alone, without elaboration. By gathering discrete verses from Scripture's three divisions—the Pentateuch, the Prophets, and the Writings—the list form makes Scripture itself seem naturally and ubiqui-

tously to articulate a single message about God's persistent devotion to Israel. By providing multiple warrant for that message, the form effectively restricts the interpretive options. In this case, it excludes the possibility that God's miraculous acts for Israel have ceased.

The following passage illustrates another form that accomplishes the same interpretive end (Sifre to Numbers, Pisqa' 117 [ed. Horowitz, p. 134, lines 11-13]):

A. "And the Lord spoke to Aaron" (Num. 18:8)
B. I understand [from this] that the speech was to Aaron.
C. A [scriptural] teaching says (*tlmwd lwmr*),
D. "It is a reminder to the children of Israel, so that an unqualified man, not from Aaron's seed, should not approach to burn incense before the Lord, and should not be like Qorah and his company; [this was done] as the Lord instructed (*dbr*) him through (*byd*) Moses" (Num. 17:5 [16:40]).
E. This teaches us that the speech was to Moses, who told [it] to Aaron.

C-E use Num. 17:5 to counter the obvious meaning of the discourse of Num. 18:8. The words recited there as "The Lord spoke to Aaron" are to be understood to mean that God did so "through Moses." Thus, the clear sense of the verse is effaced, and a single contrary meaning, suggested by Num. 17:5, is assigned to replace it. The form of the passage presents that judgment not as an interpretation but as a fact of Scripture.

The rhetorical pattern of this brief passage is typical of much Rabbinic scriptural interpretation, especially of Sifra, Sifre to Numbers, and Sifre to Deuteronomy, and its effect should not be overlooked. The structure provided by B, C, and E ("I might think. . . . But Scripture teaches. . . . Therefore. . . .") limits rather than multiplies the possibilities of Scripture's meaning and clearly is designed to reject what rabbis regarded as erroneous understandings. In this case, since Rabbinic ideology held that God spoke directly only to Moses, Num. 18:8 had to mean something other than what its discourse plainly said. A different but very representative and forceful demonstration of the Rabbinic limitation of Scripture's meaning occurs in a famous passage at B. B.Q. 83b-84a. There, rigorous talmudic argument that skillfully manipulates verses from Leviticus and Numbers shows that the famous *lex talionis* of Exod. 21:24 ("An eye for an eye, and a tooth for a tooth") does not mean what it says but refers instead to pecuniary compensation.

By juxtaposing discrete biblical verses in the form of a list and by strategically placing them in established rhetorical patterns and propositional frameworks, Rabbinic interpretation made Scripture appear to speak by itself and for itself and also to restrict its own connotation. Much Rabbinic use of Scripture was kaleidoscopic. Unlike Irenaeus's Rule of Faith, in which the theological value of the "Old Testament" requires the reader's acceptance of a fixed narrative line, Rabbinic rules of interpretation (*middot*) provide instruction on how fragments of the holy writing can be mixed and matched to reveal patterns of signification. But the patterns can be meaningful only if they are constructed within a sealed sphere of reference. If the sphere is broken or corrupted, the pieces scatter randomly or fall into a heap. For Rabbinism, Scripture's sphere of reference was constituted of Rabbinic practice, ideology, and discourse, but, most important, of the community of sages themselves.

As heirs and practitioners of a levitical piety, rabbis could afford little tolerance of ambiguity, uncertainty, or unclarity. The holy writing on the sacred scroll that was the stable center of their system could not appear to speak, as it were, with a forked or twisted tongue. By controlling Scripture both as sacred artifact and as intelligible text, sages guaranteed that it would always refer to their concerns and interests, that it would always validate and justify—but never contradict— their halakhah and the religious ideology that undergirded it. In their various literary compositions, rabbis did not so much write about or within Scripture as they wrote with it, making it speak with their voice, in their idiom, and in their behalf.

WILLIAM SCOTT GREEN

**SCRIPTURE, PRIVILEGED TRANSLATIONS OF:** In antiquity, Jews translated their sacred scriptures into two languages: the Greek translations, called the Septuagint, and the Aramaic translations, called the targums. Jews were the first in the Mediterranean world to translate their sacred texts, and they used these translations to study and teach about their relationship with God, to define their world view, and to carry out their liturgical practices. The earliest translated document was the Pentateuch, rendered in Greek in the third century B.C.E. and followed later by the rest of the Hebrew Bible. The translation apparently was done in Egypt and came to be known as the Septuagint (often abbreviated as LXX). Over the following centuries the Septuagint became the Bible for Greek-speaking Jews throughout the Mediterranean world.

The targums (sg., targum) had a more widespread and longer lasting impact on Judaism. These Aramaic translations became important in Rabbinic Judaism, first in the land of Israel and then in Babylonia, Syria, and beyond. The earliest extant Rabbinic targums date to the second century C.E. at the earliest (although fragments of a Job targum found among the Dead Sea Scrolls come from the first century C.E.). Some such translations were not created until the seventh century C.E. or later. Because of the importance of the Rabbinic movement to all Jewish life after the Temple's destruction in 70 C.E., the targums adopted by the rabbis had a long period of relevance. Although their heyday was well over by the thirteenth century, some targums, such as Onkelos, remain part of Jewish education even today.

Early translations of the Hebrew Bible are important not only from a religious point of view but also from a historical perspective, as they provide insight into the world in which the translators lived. It is commonly understood that all translations are interpretations, and the Septuagint and the targums are no exception. In passages we can clearly identify as interpretations, we discover what Jews believed, how they wrestled with the pressing issues of their time and place, and, in some cases, how they practiced their religion.

**The Septuagint:** The world "Septuagint" is singular, implying that there is only one Bible in Greek. But this is not the case. Although most Septuagint scholars agree that there was one initial translation of the Hebrew Bible into Greek, in the first few centuries of its existence, this translation underwent many revisions, some of them, beginning in the second century C.E., identified with specific people. This complex situation has led to two different definitions of the term "Septuagint," one that identifies all Greek versions of the Bible from antiquity as "Septuagint," and one that limits the term to the earliest period of translation, before extensive revisions took place. This text is sometimes called the "Old Greek" or the "Old Greek Bible."

A third definition comes from Christianity, which identifies the Septuagint with the "Greek Bible" or, more specifically, the "Greek Old Testament." Since the Greek Old Testament includes books from outside the Hebrew Bible, this designation goes beyond translation. Indeed the Septuagint as the "Bible in Greek" contains (1) books translated from the Hebrew Bible, (2) Greek additions to those books (most notably in Esther and Daniel), and (3) books written in, or known only in, Greek (such as 1 and 2 Maccabees, Judith, and Ben Sira). Parts 2 and 3 together are often termed the Apocrypha or the deutero-canonical books.

**Approach to translation:** The Septuagint was the first sustained translation into Greek of a lengthy oriental religious text. Since there was no direct precedent for this kind of translation, the translators drew upon the general practice of translation within the Hellenistic world. The principles that guided their method depended (1) on the genre of the source text and (2) on the assumed knowledge of the source language among the translation's readers.[1] The two main genres of translated works during the Hellenistic period were literary texts and legal documents. The translation of literary texts assumed no knowledge of the source language on the part of the readers and so aimed to produce a text intelligible to them. The translation therefore was fairly free, with emphasis placed on rendering the original's sense rather than its actual wording. But legal texts—such as government and administrative documents—required a different approach. Since their legal character necessitated maintenance of the exact form of the document, a careful word-for-word translation was used to preserve the document's language and the formal character. Since the resulting translation often contained passages unintelligible in Greek, the translator presumed that the recipients could understand the original language. Later Roman practice ensured that this was the case by making certain that an *expositor* was always on hand to interpret and expound the translation, usually from the Latin original to which the translation was attached.

So the choice facing the Septuagint's first translators was essentially to decide whether the Bible's genre was literary or legal and to translate accordingly. They came down in the middle, at times translating literally and at other times paraphrastically. Later translators were more decisive, aligning Scripture with either legal or literary writings and revising the Greek translation accordingly.

The Greek translations of the Hebrew Bible were important in Hellenistic Judaism. Not only was the Bible translated by Jews for Jews, but the early revisers—Theodotion, Aquila, and Symmachus—were probably also Jewish. They all worked in the second century C.E., in the context of growing awareness of the Christian use of the Septuagint. After the second century C.E., revisions were done primarily by Christians, with Origen, Hesychius, and Lucian prominent in this activity. Origen also created a six-column parallel text—the *Hexapla*—that contained the Hebrew text, the Hebrew text transliterated into Greek, and the four versions then widely known: the Old Greek and the revisions of Theodotion, Aquila, and Symmachus.

**The Old Greek:** The Hebrew Pentateuch was first translated into Greek sometime in the early- to mid-third century B.C.E. in Alexandria. Most scholars believe that the Jews of this Egyptian city were losing their knowledge of Hebrew and so had a translation of the text done for them to use in study and worship. Over the next century, the books of the Prophets were also translated, as were most of the books of the Writings. By 116 B.C.E., the grandson of Ben Sira (who translated Ben Sira/Ecclesiasticus into Greek) refers to Greek versions of all but a few books of the Writings. The Old Greek translations contained much free translation, since the Alexandrian Jews spoke primarily Greek and knew little Hebrew. The Greek Septuagint thus became the Bible they knew and used.

As use of the Septuagint spread, Jews who knew both Hebrew and Greek became aware of the many passages in which the Greek differed from the original Hebrew. Although many of the divergences could be attributed to scribal errors or to differences between Hebrew manuscripts used for translation and comparison, most of the problems resulted from the translators' technique. This caused a certain amount of debate between Jews who knew only Greek and bilingual Jews who knew Greek and Hebrew, and it resulted in two contradictory developments: the defense of the existing translation and attempts to correct it.

The defense of the Septuagint took the form of stories of how the translation originated. The earliest version of the story appeared in the *Letter of Aristeas* in the second century or early in the first century B.C.E. It was later retold by Philo (*Vita Mosis* 2:25-44) and Josephus (*Jewish Antiquities* 12:12-118) in the first century C.E. and, afterwards, by a number of early Christian writers. The main story line is that, wishing to put a Greek copy of the Hebrew Bible into the great library at Alexandria, King Ptolemy commissioned the most knowledgeable Jewish scholars from the land of Israel, seventy-two in number, and brought them to Egypt. After a great feast, they went out to an island where they worked for seventy-two days to produce the translation. The resulting work was received with high praise by the king, the Jewish community, and the priests, that is, the leaders of the Jewish community. In Philo's version, the translators worked in isolation from each other. Even so, through divine inspiration, they all composed exactly the same translation; Philo thus calls them "prophets."

These versions of the story proved that the Septuagint had the approval of human authority—that of the royal government and of Jewish scholarship—as well as of God, seen as the translation's actual author. Thus the Septuagint was viewed as revealed in its own right; it could stand on its own without reference to the Hebrew Bible.

By contrast to this supportive attitude, the critics' approach was to correct the Greek text to make it more closely match the original Hebrew. Many early attempts to accomplish this were carried out, but the main attempts are traditionally identified as "The Three:" Aquila, Theodotion, and Symmachus.

**Aquila's revision:** A convert to Judaism who, according to tradition, studied under Aqiba, some scholars identify Aquila with the Rabbinic figure Onkelos, who is credited with composition of the Aramaic Targum Onkelos (B. Meg 3a). Aquila composed his revision using the translation practices usually applied to legal edicts. This produced a highly literal translation, with the Greek echoing the Hebrew syntax and with the same Greek word's being consistently used to replace each Hebrew word, no matter what the context or meaning. But the result is a translation that is often so literal as to be unintelligible and, for comprehension, to demand familiarity with the underlying Hebrew text. Written around 130 C.E., Aquila's translation remained in use among some Jews until at least the sixth century. Even so, apart from quotations in secondary sources, it now exists in only a few extended passages, primarily in the Psalms and Kings.

**Theodotion's revision:** Theodotion is usually identified as an Ephesian convert to Judaism (although one witness portrays him as an Ebionite Christian) who worked in the late second century C.E. He reformulated much of the Septuagint, bringing it closer to the Hebrew text. His goal seems to have been to provide a more systematic translation of the Hebrew while keeping a readable text for his Greek audience. The translation is known for its frequent transliterations, apparently used as an alternative to guessing when Theodotion was unsure of the meaning of a Hebrew word.

**Symmachus' revision:** Scholars usually date Symmachus' work to around 170 C.E. While Epiphanius describes him as a convert to Judaism, both Jerome and Eusebius identify him as an Ebionite Christian. One scholar has identified him with Sumchos, a disciple of Meir. In his translation, Symmachus reacted against the trends of his time, viewing the Septuagint as akin to a literary text. Thus, rather than bringing his translation more into line with the Hebrew Bible, he worked to improve its Greek style and make it more intelligible. He clearly had a broad knowledge of Jewish midrashic exegesis as well as familiarity with Greek writings. He therefore created a translation that was felicitous in Greek style, knowledgeable of Jewish interpretation, and faithful to the Hebrew text. The work today is known only from a few fragments of Origen's *Hexapla*.

***Kaige* Theodotion:** "The Three," scholars now know, based their revisions on a previously unidentified work, known as the *Kaige*. Identification with Theodotion comes from some quotations of this version that appear to derive from Theodotion, even though they now are included in texts written before Theodotion's birth. Portions of the Minor Prophets of this version were found in the Judean Desert at Nahal Hever. These suggest how Theodotion, Aquila, and Symmachus used the *Kaige* in their own work.

**Relationship of the Septuagint to the Hebrew Text:** Scholars have long used the Septuagint as a key tool in the search for the original Hebrew text of Scripture. Such a search is necessary because the Masoretic text, which forms the basis for all modern Hebrew Bibles, was not regularized until the early Middle Ages, and the earliest complete manuscript of the Masoretic text dates to 1008 C.E. By comparison, the Septuagint was translated from a Hebrew text sometime in the third to second century B.C.E., and it is nearly totally preserved in a fourth century C.E. text, with several partial texts dating to the fourth and the fifth century C.E. Given its age, the reasoning goes, the Septuagint's text is much closer in time to the period during which the books of the Hebrew Bible were composed, and it is thus more likely to give an accurate picture of the original biblical text.

But the fact that the Septuagint's age makes it possible for it to be accurate does not mean that it necessary is. It could equally be based on an early but corrupt manuscript or simply be a poor translation. Accordingly, it is only in comparison with other versions and manuscripts that the Septuagint can really be used. Much of the time, it agrees with the Masoretic text, and so supports its accuracy. Other times, it disagrees with it while agreeing with other ancient texts, such as the biblical manuscripts found at Qumran. This is the case, for instance, where the Septuagint agrees with the Qumran fragments of Samuel against the Masoretic text, suggesting that they preserve an earlier reading. Qumran fragments of other biblical books, however, show closer affinity with the Masoretic text than with the Septuagint. The Septuagint thus cannot be simply assumed to reveal an earlier, and therefore more accurate, version of the Bible.

Another problem is that, to-date, no critical edition is available for much of the Septuagint. With the different revisions and copying mistakes, it is quite difficult to determine the Septuagint's own original text, let alone the relationship of that text to the Hebrew Bible. In particular, nine short fragmentary manuscripts of the Septuagint and related texts found at Qumran reveal the difficulties faced by scholars trying to reconstruct the original Septuagint. These fragments, nearly all from the Pentateuch, constitute by several centuries the oldest Septuagint texts known. Even though their fragmentary state limits their usefulness, they reveal fifteen variants in only 28 lines; seven of these variants are unique.[2] This suggests that even the best critical editions of the Septuagint may not be as close to the original as we thought.

**Relationship to other biblical translations:** The early Christian Church adopted the Greek Bible (in its many versions) as Holy Scripture from the beginning, considering it inspired and authorized by God. For this reason, over the earliest centuries, many translations were made from it, including the Syro-Hexaplar (Syriac), the Coptic, Armenian,

Georgian, Arabic, Ethiopic, and Old Latin Version. Although Jerome created the Vulgate by translating from the Hebrew, he regularly consulted the Septuagint and the three revisions. Similarly, the Syriac Peshitta was translated directly from the Hebrew but with consultation of the Septuagint. By contrast to the situation in Christianity, after the second century C.E., the Septuagint fell from importance in the Rabbinic Jewish world and was largely ignored. No Jewish translations were made from it.

**Relationship to non-canonical writings:** The Septuagint appears prominently in some Greek works, such as those of Philo and Josephus, while little awareness of it appears in texts first written in Hebrew or Aramaic, such as the Apocrypha or Pseudepigrapha or those found at Qumran. It constitutes Josephus' biblical source in his *Jewish Antiquities*, many scholars have argued, once he begins to discuss the events related in the historical books (i.e., the Former Prophets). Some scholars have even argued that Josephus' Septuagint source was an early (therefore Jewish) version of the Lucian revision. Philo relies even more heavily on the Septuagint; it is the only Bible he knows. Even in his books of Biblical exegesis, he interprets the Greek text rather than the Hebrew.

The Pseudepigrapha and texts from Qumran, by contrast, make little use of the Septuagint. Occasionally similar beliefs and ideas appear in these texts and the Septuagint, but there is no indication of any textual links. Even where such use might be obvious— as in the texts of the so-called "Rewritten Bible" (e.g., Jubilees, Enoch, the Genesis Apocryphon, and Pseudo-Philo)—no indication appears that the writers knew the Greek Bible. Ironically, this also holds true for the books of the Apocrypha. Only the Testament of Job shows any awareness of the Septuagint, from which it draws extensively.

In the later world of Rabbinic Judaism, beginning in 70 C.E. and culminating in the creation of the Babylonian Talmud in the sixth century, matters are slightly more complex. On the one hand, the rabbis developed their biblical exegesis straight from the Hebrew text. Indeed, one of the ideals of Rabbinic Judaism is the ability to read the Hebrew Bible, preferably before one reaches puberty. On the other hand, a few exegeses are shared between the Septuagint and Rabbinic midrashic interpretation.

**Status and use of the Septuagint in Judaism:** Among the Greek-speaking Jews of the Mediterranean diaspora, the Septuagint and its revisions continued in use into the early Middle Ages. As previously mentioned, Jews used Aquila's version as late as the sixth century. But in the land of Israel, Syria, and Babylonia—the world of Rabbinic Judaism— the use of the Septuagint ceased. Instead, the rabbis relied primarily upon the Hebrew text itself, with secondary interest in the Aramaic targums discussed below. However, even the Babylonian Talmud recognizes the importance of the translation of the Torah into Greek and knows Jews use it in worship. Through a version of the Aristeas story (B. Meg. 9a), the rabbis therefore give it a status above that of other translations. The Palestinian Talmud even records a brief passage of praise for Aquila and his translation in (Y. Meg. 1:9, 71c).

Little explicit evidence indicates the role of Scripture in the Hellenistic Judaism of the Mediterranean world outside the land of Israel, let alone the place of any translations. The Babylonian Talmud suggests that Greek versions of Esther were sometimes read in synagogue worship during Purim, and Josephus links synagogues with the study of Scripture. But apart from these hints, little is known. By analogy with developing post-Temple, Rabbinic Judaism in the land of Israel, most scholars believe that Scripture, probably in the form of the Septuagint, was read in synagogue worship, studied by children in educational settings, and perused by educated individuals in private meditation.

**The Targums:** While Egypt and the rest of the Eastern Mediterranean adopted Greek as their *lingua franca*, the Jewish communities of the land of Israel, Syria, and Babylonia retained and even increased their use of Aramaic, which had been introduced into those regions by the Persians. Among Jews, Aramaic supplanted Hebrew in everyday usage. Its use remained high until the arrival of Arabic under Islam in the seventh century and then only gradually declined—a process taking many centuries. Manuscript finds at Qumran and literary references indicate that Bible translation into Aramaic may have begun as early as the first century B.C.E. But only in the Rabbinic period, starting in the late first century C.E., did translation into Aramaic became widely practiced. These ancient Aramaic translations of the Hebrew Bible were called targums (sg., *targum*, pl., *targumim*).

In modern Hebrew, the noun *targum* means "translation." But the meaning it bears from antiquity includes both "translation" and "explanation." This double meaning fits the targums, for they regularly combine translation of the biblical text with explanations of it. This combination signals the different choices that targum translators (pl., *meturgemanim*, sg., *meturgeman*) made from the models of translation in antiquity. Rather than locate their work on a continuum between literal and paraphrastic, like different versions of the Septuagint, targums belong on a line between literal and expository. Just as a Roman administrative *expositor* often had to explain the meaning of laws or edicts translated overly literally, so the literal translation of many targums contained insertions—sometimes just a word or two, other times as much as a paragraph or two—to explain or signal the passage's correct meaning.

The development of targums can be divided into three main stages, Galilee in the second and third centuries, Babylonia in the second through fourth centuries, and Greater Syria in the fourth century and later. In particular, during the Rabbinic period, the importance of the Torah made it the most popular text for translation, such that its books received new targums in each stage. These are divided into two groups: the Babylonian Targum Onkelos and the Palestinian targums—which include Targum Neofiti, Targum Pseudo-Jonathan, the Fragmentary Targums, the targum fragments from the Cairo Geniza, and the targumic *toseftot*. Targum Neofiti and the Cairo Geniza targum fragments were composed in the land of Israel during the first stage. Targum Onkelos was com-

pleted in Babylonia in stage two, while the remaining Palestinian Targums were created in stage three.

**Stage 1: Galilee in the second and third centuries:** Targum Neofiti is written in the dialect of Jewish Palestinian Aramaic and provides a continuous translation the Torah, except for some verses that are missing due to copyist errors or the activities of censors. The targum combines a highly literal translation with additional interpretive material, a primary feature of all Palestinian Targums. Often these two aspects are woven together so skillfully that the additions can only be identified through comparison with the Hebrew text. In this way, Targum Neofiti combines with exposition a legal approach to translating Scripture. That is, the additions are not paraphrase—giving the sense of the passage—but instead expound its true meaning as understood by the translator.

The first Cairo Geniza targum fragments were found by Solomon Schechter in the geniza of the Ibn Ezra Synagogue in Cairo. Fragments from seven different Palestinian Targums have been found, all written in Jewish Palestinian Aramaic. The manuscripts date from the ninth to the fourteenth centuries, but they copy Palestinian targums written before the fourth century. Unfortunately, the fragments are few; none of the manuscripts comprise even half of Genesis, the book best represented. But enough remains to show that these targums were composed in the same manner as Neofiti, combining word-for-word translation with additional material. Indeed, where extant, they contain the same expansions as Targum Neofiti. With few exceptions, we can say that where Neofiti has an expansion, so do the extant Geniza fragments, and where Neofiti just translates, so do the existing Geniza fragments.

Targum Neofiti and the Cairo Geniza fragments contain the same additions because, scholars claim, they acquired them from the same source. Scholars call this presumed source Proto-PT, and they understand it to comprise all the shared additional material among the Palestinian Targums to the Pentateuch. This material thus is seen as representing the earliest known stratum of the pentateuchal targums. Some scholars think Proto-PT was an actual written document, while others imagine it only as an oral stage in the development of the targums.

**Stage Two: Babylonia in the second through fourth centuries:** Targum Onkelos to the Pentateuch and Targum Jonathan to the Prophets were completed in this stage. Targum Onkelos, as we know it, derives from Babylonia, where it served as the approved targum of the Rabbinic movement. The Babylonian Talmud attributes its composition to Onkelos, a student of Eliezer b. Hyrcanus and Joshua b. Hananiah (B. Meg. 3a). This attribution is probably a misunderstanding of the Palestinian Talmud's comment about Aquila (Y. Meg. 1:9, 71c). That Targum Onkelos was composed in Babylonia is clear from its Aramaic dialect, however, which contains eastern grammatical forms and vocabulary.

In addition to this eastern identification, Targum Onkelos contains features that link it to the west and, specifically, to the Palestinian Targums. First, Onkelos contains many elements suggesting a Palestinian dialect of Aramaic, specifically, that found at Qumran, which scholars call Standard Literary Aramaic. Second, while Onkelos has a consistently literal approach to translation—clearly viewing Scripture translation as comparable to that of legal documents—it occasionally inserts extra words or phrases or renders a verse in an interpretive manner. These non-literal elements often occur in passages in which the Palestinian Targums contain additional material. Indeed, Onkelos' additional material often echoes or alludes to Palestinian expansions found in other targums to the same verses.

To explain the evidence for both western and eastern features, scholars suggest that Targum Onkelos originated in the land of Israel and was later revised in Babylonia. The first stage of what became Targum Onkelos was probably written in the land of Israel prior to 135 C.E., which accounts for the association of its Aramaic with that found at Qumran. The exact nature of this text, sometimes designated Proto-Onkelos, is unclear. Its links with the expansive material of the Palestinian Targums suggest that it

may derive from the Proto-PT source of the Palestinian Targums to the Pentateuch. The second stage of Targum Onkelos came about when Proto-Onkelos was brought to Babylonia. There, sometime prior to the end of the fourth century, it was revised, with the targumist removing most of the non-translation material and reworking the Aramaic with eastern dialectical forms. This revised version became authoritative among Babylonian Jewry and comprises the text we know today as Targum Onkelos.

**Targums to the Prophets:** The compositional history of Targum Jonathan to the Prophets—apocryphally attributed to Jonathan b. Uziel (B. Meg. 3a)—parallels that of Targum Onkelos. Written in Babylonia, Targum Jonathan's translation tends to be literal, but it contains more expansive renderings than Onkelos. This is because the literary character of prophetic books—many of which contain large sections of poetry—forced the *meturgemanim* to pay more attention to meaning and less to exact wording. Targum Jonathan also parallels Targum Onkelos in its two-stage composition. Jonathan's first version was composed in the land of Israel about the same time as Proto-Onkelos, probably between 70 and 200 C.E. In the second stage, this targum was taken to Babylonia, where, in the fourth century, it underwent extensive revision. These revisions enabled it to become the authoritative translation of the Prophets among Babylonian Jewry.

Two types of evidence support the conclusion of a two-stage development of Targum Jonathan. First, the targum combines two dialects of Aramaic: a Palestinian form close to Standard Literary Aramaic and a Babylonian form. This dialectical mix directly parallels that of Targum Onkelos. Second, study of key theological terms in the Targum to Isaiah also suggests that it was composed in two stages.[3] The first stage was created in the land of Israel between 70 and 200, and the second in Babylonia between the third and fifth centuries (the Amoraic period). The convergence of these two types of evidence supports the conclusion that Targum Jonathan took shape in two stages and in different geographical locations.

**Stage Three: Greater Syria in the fourth century and later**. In this stage, several types of Palestinian Targums to the Pentateuch were created in reaction to Targum Onkelos, and the Targums to the Writings were composed. After their acceptance among Babylonian Jewry, Targum Onkelos and Targum Jonathan moved westward into the eastern Mediterranean region (Syria, the land of Israel, and Egypt). Here, both targums rose to predominance and ultimately supplanted the Palestinian Targums. This movement began sometime between the fourth century and seventh centuries and was probably complete by the ninth century.

Jews in the eastern Mediterranean experienced several different reactions to the rising ascendancy of Targum Onkelos. These reactions can be seen in the different Palestinian Targums to the Pentateuch that developed. First, a version was created that could be used alongside Onkelos without competing with it, the so-called Fragmentary Targums. These targums are not continuous but appear to contain "extracts" from a continuous targum, arranged in the order of the Pentateuch and sometimes including words or phrases from a few verses in a chapter while at other times skipping several chapters at once. The largest number of extracts derive from the Proto-PT source, while the remainder explain technical terms, define words that occur only once in the Bible, or correct supposed errors. Although most of the literal translation has been left out, a few extracts contain simply translation. Like Neofiti, the two main recensions of the Fragmentary Targums—represented by manuscripts in the Paris and Vatican libraries—are written in Jewish Palestinian Aramaic. Thus, with Onkelos supplying the literal translation and a Fragmentary Targum supplying the interpretive material, the two targums could be used together without competition.

While the Fragmentary Targums were arranged in pentateuchal order, other collections of Proto-PT expansions—called Festival Collections—were organized by liturgical criteria. This second targumic form brings together expansions of the Proto-PT type to be read on specific holidays. For ex-

ample, one collection found in the Cairo Geniza contains readings for Pentecost, Purim, and the seventh day of Passover, while another has readings for Pentecost, Passover, and New Year. These collections apparently comprise the forerunners of the medieval Mahzorim—prayer books for the holidays, some of which contain targums to the biblical readings. The medieval Mahzor Vitry, in fact, presents the readings for the Passover liturgy (Exod. 13:17-15:26 and Exod. 19:1-20:26) by interweaving the literal translation of Onkelos with the Proto-PT expansions found in the Fragmentary Targum of the Paris manuscript. The Festival Collections were probably organized sometime after the seventh century.

Targum Pseudo-Jonathan comprises the third reaction to the new importance of Targum Onkelos in the west. It combines an Onkelos-like translation with Proto-PT additions and with other interpretive material. This results in a complete targum to the Pentateuch with significantly more expansive material than Targum Neofiti. Some new additions derive from known Rabbinic writings, such as Sifra and the Babylonian Talmud, while other additions are unparalleled. Usually, the new material is simply placed into the targum, but Pseudo-Jonathan's targumist occasionally uses it to recast the older Proto-PT material. The combination of these sources results in a targum containing three different types of Aramaic: the dialect of Onkelos, the Jewish Palestinian Aramaic of Proto-PT, with most of the newer additions written in Late Jewish Literary Aramaic. The exact date of this targum is unclear, with scholars arguing for dates ranging from the mid-fourth up to the late eighth century.

The fourth reaction to Onkelos' ascendancy appears in the Tosefta targums, also known as targumic *toseftot*. These are individual Proto-PT expansions that have been recast into an Onkelos-like dialect. Some appear in manuscripts of Targum Onkelos—either written into the text, inserted into the margins, or placed at the end. Others have been compiled into independent collections. They probably date to the medieval period.

**Targums to the Prophets:** Targum Jonathan to the Prophets accompanied Onkelos in its westward movement. Following Onkelos' example, it supplanted the Palestinian Targum of the Prophets among eastern Mediterranean Jewry. More successful than Onkelos, Jonathan obliterated almost all traces of the Palestinian Targum. Only one body of evidence remains to indicate that the earlier targum even existed, namely, the targumic *toseftot* of the prophets found in Targum Jonathan manuscripts. Just as the Palestinian Targum of the Pentateuch provided non-translation material that was transformed into targumic *toseftot*, so the Palestinian Targum of the Prophets provided material that was likewise transformed. Some eighty of these *toseftot*—labeled "Targum Yerushalmi" or "Another Targum"—appear in Codex Reuchlinianus and other manuscripts. Like the Pentateuchal *toseftot*, these are Palestinian expansions recast into a dialect matching that of Targums Onkelos and Jonathan.

**Targums to the Writings:** Unlike the Pentateuch and Prophetic books, the books of the Writings apparently were not translated until stage three. Indeed, containing material borrowed from the Babylonian Talmud and other Rabbinic texts, most of the targums to the Writings are quite late, probably composed between the sixth and the ninth centuries. Another indication of their late date is that, whereas the Talmud speaks of targums to the Pentateuch and the Prophets, it explicitly states that God refused to permit composition of targums to the Writings (B. Meg. 3a). Furthermore, many of these targums have been influenced by both types of Pentateuchal Targums and occasionally even by Targum Jonathan to the Prophets. Finally, most Writings targums blend characteristics from eastern and western dialects of Aramaic, as well as Late Jewish Literary Aramaic and the Aramaic of the Babylonian Talmud. All these factors support the conclusion that the several Writings Targums were composed in the eastern Mediterranean region after the Babylonian Talmud and the Babylonian Targums of Onkelos and Jonathan came west.

Nearly every book of the Writings has it own targum—no single targum covers all the Writings—and only Ezra, Nehemiah, and Daniel (two of which have Aramaic portions of their own) have no targum at all. The targums to the Writings fall into three general categories: (1) the Five Megillot ("Scrolls"), (2) Job and Psalms, and (3) Proverbs and Chronicles.

The targums to the Five Megillot—Ecclesiastes, Song of Songs, Lamentations, Ruth, and Esther (which has two targums)[4]—are quite expansive and contain material derived from the Babylonian Talmud and other Rabbinic texts. Except for the Lamentations Targum, they primarily contain exposition, eschewing translation almost entirely and instead providing extensive eisegetical interpretations. These often are drawn from Rabbinic midrash, in particular, from the Midrash Rabbah of their particular book (Targum to Ecclesiastes draws from Ecclesiastes Rabbah; Targum to Ruth from Ruth Rabbah, and so on). They thus give what the *meturgeman* sees as the text's true meaning, often without even providing the text. While their language has Palestinian features, they also contain elements of the eastern dialects found in Targum Onkelos or the Babylonian Talmud.

By contrast, the Targums to Job and Psalms mix expansive material with literal translation, somewhat like the Palestinian Pentateuchal targums. They also show a midrashic influence in their style, for instance, in several verses presenting two or more different translations and/or interpretations. Each is marked by the words, "another targum," or "another wording," echoing the common midrashic phrase "another matter." These constitute the only targums in which the text's narrative flow is interrupted, signaling that the targum does not present a single, seamless translation. Thus, instead of hiding additions by interweaving them with the translation, these targums identify the different translations and interpretations. These targums are written in the dialect of Late Jewish Literary Aramaic, which is also found in Targum Pseudo-Jonathan.

The targums to Proverbs and Chronicles belong to neither of the previous categories. First, the highly literal targum to Proverbs has a pronounced link to the Christian Syriac translation of this book (the Peshitta), with nearly a third of its verses word-for-word identical to what is found in the Peshitta. It contains no Rabbinic exegesis at all, not even any material identifying wisdom as Torah—a theme prevalent in the Rabbinic literature and emphasized in most other targums. Second, the Targum to Chronicles consists of a literal translation that occasionally incorporates expansive material, often borrowed from the Babylonian Talmud. It frequently happens that where the Hebrew text of Chronicles shares material with the books of Samuel and Kings, the base translation of the Chronicles Targum is copied from Targum Jonathan to these books. The Chronicles Targum also has borrowed some material from a Palestinian Targum to the Pentateuch, probably Pseudo-Jonathan.

**Targums at Qumran:** While most of the documents and fragments found at Qumran were written in Hebrew, a few were written in Aramaic. Several contain biblical passages in Aramaic, though only one targum has been identified for certain, a targum of Job. A large section of one manuscript covers Job 37:10-42:11 (plus fragments starting in 17:14), while pieces of a second cover Job 3:4-5 and 4:16-5:4. The translation in this targum provides a word-for-word rendering of the Hebrew and shows no links to the Rabbinic targum of Job. Archaeologists also found a few Aramaic fragments of Lev. 16:12-15 and 18-21. Unfortunately, the brevity of these pieces makes it difficult to ascertain whether they constitute a targum or are simply biblical quotations within another type of work, such as a prayer or a theological text. In addition to these items, excavations unearthed a few Aramaic fragments of Tobit. Joseph Fitzmyer thinks these constitute remains of Tobit in its original language and should not be classed as a targum.

The *Genesis Apocryphon*, one of the earliest texts to be published from Qumran, is an Aramaic rewriting of Genesis, for which we now possess portions covering Gen. 12-15. Its free treatment of the subject matter places it in the category of Rewritten Bible, like Josephus' *Jewish Antiquities* and the book of Jubilees. In places, however, it produces a translation that adheres closely to the Hebrew, suggesting some connections to the targum genre.

**Targums and the text of the Hebrew Bible:** In their attempts to establish the original text of the Hebrew Bible, scholars have made little use of the targums. Even though nearly all targums were composed before the Middle Ages and so can bear witness to the Hebrew text in its pre-Masoretic form, their non-literal tendencies make scholars less than willing to trust them. This is especially true for the Palestinian Targums to the Pentateuch and the targums to the Writings, less so for the more literal targums, Onkelos and Jonathan to the Prophets. The problem is the difficulty in determining which differences between a targum and the Masoretic text result from the targum's knowledge of a different Hebrew original and which stem from the *meturgeman's* intentional providing of an interpretative or expository translation.

**Relationship of the Targums to other biblical translations:** The targums reveal little contact with the other biblical translations of late antiquity. There are no textual links whatsoever with the Septuagint, although there are a few parallel interpretations that probably emerged independently. The same observation applies to the targums' relationship to the Peshitta, with one exception. By-and-large there are no textual links between any book of the Peshitta and any targum, although most books have a few passages in which the targum and the Peshitta contain the same interpretative understanding of the Hebrew text. The only exception is the Targum to Proverbs, mentioned above, which is clearly copied from the Peshitta. Nearly a third of that targum's verses are word-for-word identical with the Peshitta's.

**Relationship to non-canonical writings:** Three sets of Jewish writings have links with the targums: the Rabbinic literature, the New Testament and other first and second century Christian works, and the literature of the Apocrypha, Pseudepigrapha, and Qumran.

We already have noted the Rabbinic literature's extensive contacts with the targums. Not only does the Babylonian Talmud occasionally quote from Targum Onkelos and

Targum Jonathan to the Prophets, but nearly every Rabbinic text finds some echoes in at least one targum. Sometimes a Rabbinic text repeats elements of a story found in the targums or vice versa. The targumic exchange between Tamar and Judah in Gen. 38:25-26, for example, contributes several story elements to the midrashic discussion found in B. Sot. 10b. At other times, the parallels are less explicit, being limited to shared theological ideas, exegetical techniques, or characterization of important biblical figures.

The New Testament and other early Christian literature similarly reveal many contacts with ideas and interpretations found in the targums. This is only rarely explicit, but the targums shed light on the origins of a number of early Christian exegeses of Scripture. For example, targumic concepts of the Shekhina—God's indwelling presence—shed light on the idea of the *logos* at the beginning of John's Gospel. There additionally are revealing parallels concerning the messiah in the two types of documents.

Jewish works of the Second Temple period—the Apocrypha, the Pseudepigrapha, and the Dead Sea Scrolls—exhibit many links with the targums. These range from parallel understandings of important biblical figures—such as Abraham in the Pentateuchal targums, the Genesis Apocryphon, and the book of Jubilees—to non-canonical characters—such as Jannes and Jambres. They include theological concepts, such as the messiah and afterlife, and interpretations of specific words in specific passages. Nearly all the points of contact between the targums and Second Temple literature are exegetical, not textual.

**Place of the Targums in Judaism:** Targum Onkelos constituted the official pentateuchal targum of the Babylonian rabbis. In the Babylonian Talmud, the rabbis refer to it as "our targum" (B. Qid. 49a), and whenever an Aramaic translation of a pentateuchal passage appears here, the quote matches Targum Onkelos. The rabbis even considered Onkelos a valid foundation for deciding issues of law. Targum Onkelos' importance inspired the Babylonian rabbis formally to fix its text, so as to ensure its accurate copying, much as the Hebrew Bible's text was fixed. Thus,

Targum Onkelos has a more stable textual tradition than the Palestinian Targums. Similarly, Targum Jonathan became the authoritative Babylonian targum to the Prophets, so that, at several places, the Talmud gives the correct rendering of a biblical passage by citing a verse from Targum Jonathan. For example, in B. M.Q. 28b, Targum Jonathan's rendering provides the correct interpretation of Zech. 12:11, which Joseph claims would be unknown without the targum.

The Palestinian Targums never achieved this level of acceptance. In fact, no direct mention of them appears in any Palestinian Rabbinic text, whether legal or exegetical. When Targums Onkelos and Jonathan moved west from Babylonia into the Mediterranean world, they supplanted the Palestinian targums already there.

**Use of Targums in Judaism:** Rabbinic texts refer to the use of translation in three situations. Although these texts do not explicitly refer to the use of written targums, they clearly establish contexts in which such documents will have religious importance: in synagogue worship, education in the schools, and private study. M. Meg. 4:4-6, first, states that, in synagogue worship, the Torah and Prophetic lections should be read in Hebrew and then translated into Aramaic; other Rabbinic texts supply numerous guidelines for this public translation of Scripture, including Y. Meg. 4:1, 74d, which forbids use of written texts in the service (although this does not prevent their use by the translator in preparation). Second, Sifre Deut. 161 reveals that, although education begins with Torah, it is followed by translation (lit., *targum*). It is not clear whether translation in this passage means the practice of translating or the study of a written translation. Third, B. Ber. 8a-b states that individuals are expected to review the weekly Torah portion twice in Hebrew and once in translation (again: *targum*). Here too, it is not clear whether "translation" refers to the use of a written text or to the individual's own act of translating.

Although we cannot definitively determine whether any of the above situations involved written targums, evidence suggests that written targums were used in the Rabbinic period.

The Tosefta provides the earliest Rabbinic evidence of the existence of written targums in Aramaic, showing that they were sometimes used for studying (T. Shab. 13:2-3). Furthermore, the Tosefta approves of the use of Scripture translations in any language, permitting people who know no Hebrew to read Esther in their own language on Purim (T. Meg. 2:6) and to read most of the weekly Torah portion in their own language (T. Meg. 3:13). The similarity between the synagogue worship here and that discussed in the previous paragraph suggests that, until the time of the Palestinian Talmud, written Aramaic targums may have been used in synagogue worship. Even more significantly, the Babylonian Talmud mentions the use of written targums in legal discussions, acknowledging their authority and adhering to their interpretations (e.g., B. Naz. 39a and B. San. 94b). In the Palestinian Rabbinic texts, we thus see evidence of translations' being used in synagogue worship, while in the Babylonian documents, we find that targums are valid even for establishing religious law.

### Bibliography

Jellicoe, Sidney, *The Septuagint and Modern Study* (Oxford, 1968).

Beattie, D.R.G., and M.J. McNamara, eds., *The Aramaic Bible: Targums in their Historical Context* (Sheffield, 1994).

Flesher, Paul V.M., ed., *Targum Studies: Textual and Contextual Studies in the Pentateuchal Targums* (Atlanta, 1992).

### Notes

[1] Sebastian Brock, "Aspects of Translation Technique in Antiquity," in *Greek, Roman, and Byzantine Studies* 20:1 (1979), pp. 69-87.

[2] E.C. Ulrich, "The Septuagint Manuscripts from Qumran: A Reappraisal of their Value," in G.J. Brooke and B. Lindars, eds., *Septuagint, Scrolls and Cognate Writings* (Atlanta, 1992), pp. 49-80.

[3] Bruce D. Chilton, *The Glory of Israel* (Sheffield, 1983).

[4] R. Le Déaut and B. Grossfeld, "The Origin and Nature of the Esther Targum in the Antwerp Polyglot: Exit Targum Esther III?" in *Textus* 16 (1991), pp. 95-115.

PAUL V.M. FLESHER

**SIN IN JUDAISM:** In Judaism a sin is any act that violates the stipulations of the covenant with God. This means that, within Judaism, sin encompasses not only religious or ritual offenses, which people today commonly think of as sins, but also includes all other crimes as well, whether they are against individuals or are violations of any of the community laws described in the Torah as a whole.

Judaic thinking about sin grows out of the Hebrew Scriptures' comprehension that human beings are by nature morally flawed.[1] People, this is to say, have an innate disposition to transgress God's commandments, so as to sin. This perception of human nature emerges explicitly in Scripture's depiction of the earliest history of humankind. The primeval history at Gen. 1-11 depicts God's gradual realization that people are morally undeveloped, that they cannot achieve the level of perfect obedience that God apparently expected when he placed Adam, and then Eve, in the Garden of Eden. God's initial reaction to the realization that "every imagination of the thoughts of his heart was only evil continually" (Gen. 6:5) is entirely to wipe out the human race and to start again, presumably attempting to create a being that is human but that does not sin. Only after the flood does God seem to grasp the hopelessness of this task. What makes people "human" in the first place is their capacity to violate the divine will. It accordingly is impossible even to imagine a kind of person who is not prone to sin; such a being would not be "human" at all. Thus, through God's affirmation that "I will never again curse the ground because of man, for the imagination of man's heart is evil from his youth; neither will I ever again destroy every living creature as I have done" (Gen. 8:21), Scripture expresses early Israel's keen awareness that sinfulness is an inherent trait of humankind. It is a necessary result of the intellectual and physical freedoms that make people human, and hence a trait that even God cannot change.

The concept of the inherent sinfulness of humans appears throughout the Hebrew Scriptures. Indeed, in petitionary passages, this most human of traits frequently is adduced as a mitigating circumstance that, it is hoped, God will take into account in determining punishment for sin. Since people are constrained by their nature to break the law, their punishment should be lessened from what would be deserved if they acted totally freely. In line with this thinking, during the dedication ceremony for the Temple he built to God in Jerusalem, Solomon reminds God that "there is no man who does not sin" (1 Kgs. 8:46). Solomon therefore prays that, when the people of Israel sin, their sincere acts of repentance will be accepted by God. Similarly, Ps. 143:2 begs: "Enter not into judgment with thy servant; for no man living is righteous before thee," and Ps. 78:38-39 assures the reader that God indeed takes human nature into account:

> Yet he, being compassionate, forgave their iniquity, and did not destroy them; he restrained his anger often, and did not stir up all his wrath. He remembered that they were but flesh, a wind that passes and comes not again.

As Ec. 7:20 states, "Surely there is not a righteous man on earth who does good and never sins." While striving to act righteously, the Israelite thus was assured that God was conscious of the inevitability of sin and so acted mercifully towards those who, though they sinned, repented sincerely.

While taking for granted humankind's sinful nature, the Hebrew Bible shows little interest in sin's origin. Of course the story of the Garden of Eden depicts the sin of Adam and Eve as central in explaining the nature of all later human existence: why people die, why they must labor, etc. But at its heart, the story only *assumes*, and does not *explain*, the human propensity to violate rules. Thus Scripture's depiction of Adam and Eve's quick surrender to the serpent's subtle logic and to the desirability of the fruit reveals the willingness to sin, perhaps the ease with which people can be drawn into sin, but not sin's intellectual or moral source. Only in Christian thinking, with its notion that the snake represents Satan, who constantly incites humans to sin, does Gen. 3 become significant as an explanation of the ultimate cause of sinfulness. But, by contrast to this approach, in which the story of the "fall" becomes foundational to all thinking about human nature, the episode is not even referred to elsewhere in the Hebrew Bible. This is a clear indica-

tion that the story of the Garden of Eden was hardly at the heart of Israel's overall thinking about sin.

Indeed, rather than explaining sin through reference to the actions of Adam and Eve, other passages in the Hebrew Scriptures usually associate the predilection to sin simply with human nature. This approach is especially explicit in a number of passages in the book of Job that reflect upon human weakness and mortality. At Job 4:17-21, for instance, Job's companion Eliphaz the Temanite states:

> Can mortal man be righteous before God? Can a man be pure before his Maker? Even in his servants he puts no trust, and his angels he charges with error; how much more those who dwell in houses of clay, whose foundation is in the dust, who are crushed before the moth. Between morning and evening they are destroyed; they perish for ever without any regarding it. If their tent-cord is plucked up within them, do they not die, and that without wisdom?

In this same vein, at Job 15:14-16 Eliphaz continues:

> What is man, that he can be clean? Or he that is born of a woman, that he can be righteous? Behold, God puts no trust in his holy ones, and the heavens are not clean in his sight; how much less one who is abominable and corrupt, a man who drinks iniquity like water!

These passages reflect and make explicit the overall view we have seen expressed elsewhere in Scripture, that people's mortality and their human nature entails by definition a propensity to sin. If, compared to God, even heavenly beings are not perfect, then how much the moreso must we accept sin as a paramount trait of the human condition. Robin Cover explains this comprehension of the nature of humanity as follows:[2]

> [H]uman sinfulness was related merely to creaturliness. Humans were made of dusty chthonic substance (hence, frail and ephemeral), born of impure women in a tainted birth process (hence, morally tainted) and made to inhabit a polluted, lower-than-celestial realm called earth (hence, having even more natural proclivity to sin than celestial creatures, who themselves all to frequently fall into error).

At the heart of this perspective is the view that, because they are not divine, people by definition cannot be perfect. This imperfection is expressed in their tendency to sin, that is, to violate the perfect order in which the perfect God established the world.

Job, for his part, disagrees only with the relevance of this depiction of human nature to his own circumstance and punishment, for he is certain that he himself has behaved with absolute righteousness. But except for this caveat regarding his own character, Job fully accepts the description of humanity offered by his friends in the above-cited passages (Job 14:1-6):

> Man that is born of a woman is of few days, and full of trouble. He comes forth like a flower, and withers; he flees like a shadow, and continues not. And dost thou open thy eyes upon such a one and bring him into judgment with thee? Who can bring a clean thing out of an unclean? There is not one. Since his days are determined, and the number of his months is with thee, and thou hast appointed his bounds that he cannot pass, look away from him, and desist, that he may enjoy, like a hireling, his day.

The human condition—born in uncleanness, limited by mortality—prevents humans from achieving God's standard of moral perfection. Recognizing this circumstance of humanity, God should accept humankind as it is and expect from people no more than they can achieve.

**Scripture's terminology for sin:** In referring to sin, Scripture uses about twenty different words, of which three are central.[3] Chief among these is *het*, which occurs 595 times in the Hebrew Bible. *Het*'s root meaning connotes "missing the mark or specified goal." The term accordingly can refer to the performance of an archer (Judg. 20:16) or to an individual's following the wrong road (Prov. 19:2). But its most frequent use is in signifying a person's being mistaken or at fault, in the sense of having missed a specified goal or failed to carry out a duty.[4] The term accordingly refers frequently to a failure in mutual relations, that is, to one individual's failing to treat another appropriately either by showing proper courtesy or by meeting a social or economic obligation. In this usage, the Isra-

elites' inability to make sufficient bricks for the Egyptians is described as the latters' "*het*." The Egyptians did not provide sufficient straw and so are "at fault." Similarly, the failure of a vassal to pay tribute is referred to as "*het*" (2 Kgs. 18:14).

The term *het*'s theological significance—its use to mean "sin" rather than simply "fault" or "misdeed"—emerges when the offense is committed against God in particular. Use of this term to describe a failed relationship with God suggests the extent to which, in the Israelite conception, obligations to God were of the same standing and nature as those to people. Accordingly, a failure to follow God's law is not viewed abstractly but, rather, as a concrete offense with a real victim. It is similar to all failures in interpersonal or international relations. Thus 1 Sam. 2:25 uses the same root to refer to offenses against people and God: "If a man sins against a man, God will mediate for him; but if a man sins against the Lord, who can intercede for him?"

The fact that a crime against God was conceived in the same terms as a violation of the rules that control relationships with other people suggests (1) that, like all other offenses, sin is an act with consequences and (2) that just as in the case of offenses against people, so in the event of sins against God, God could be recompensed and the relationship set right. This conception of the nature of offenses against God is highlighted by the additional use of the term *het* to signify not just the abstract concept "sin" but also the cognate concepts of "guilt," "punishment," and, most important, "sin-offering" (*hata'at*), that is, the central mode of expiation before God, the sacrifice through which the sinner purifies him or herself and atones for the infraction. Jer. 17:1 thus uses the term to refer to the condition of being sinful: "The guilt[5] of Judah is written with a pen of iron;" Zech. 14:19 uses the term to refer to punishment: "This shall be the punishment to Egypt and the punishment to all the nations that do not go up to keep the feast of booths;" and 2 Kgs. 12:16 uses the term to speak of a monetary gift made to compensate for sin: "The money from the guilt offerings and the money from the sin offerings was not brought into the house of the Lord; it belonged to the priests."

The term *het* refers to both intentional and unintentional mistakes. By contrast, *pesha*, a second term meaning sin, which appears 134 times in the Hebrew Bible, always refers to an intentional breach of responsibility. Thus, rather than indicating simply that one has "missed the mark," as is suggested by *het*, this term signifies willful rebellion. The word accordingly is a political term that is used, for instance, to describe breach of a treaty (see, e.g., 2 Kgs. 1:1). *Pesha* takes on its theological significance when that treaty is the covenant with God, to whom the people of Israel are understood to constitute a vassal nation. Although commonly translated "transgression," in such settings the term more accurately conveys the sense of purposeful rebellion against God.

*Pesha* appears at Gen. 31:36 in reference to the breaking down of previously peaceful relationships between two people: "Then Jacob became angry, and upbraided Laban; Jacob said to Laban, "What is my offense (*pesha*)? What is my sin, that you have hotly pursued me?" A cognate usage is at Prov. 28:24: "He who robs his father or his mother and says, 'That is no transgression' (*pesha*), is the companion of a man who destroys." The use of the term to signify a misdeed of Israel against God is similar. 1 Kgs. 8:50 uses the term in the context of the dedication of the Jerusalem Temple and the recitation of the covenant agreement between God and the people of Israel. In this setting, Solomon prays that, in the future, when the people sin, God will "forgive thy people who have sinned (*het*) against thee, and all their transgressions (*pesha*) which they have committed against thee; and grant them compassion in the sight of those who carried them captive, that they may have compassion on them." While the meanings of the English terms "sin" and "transgression" are undifferentiated, the Hebrew text suggests a range of misdeeds for which the people may become culpable: willful or unintentional failure to behave appropriately towards God and intentional rebellion against the terms of the covenant.

Unlike *het* and *pesha*, which can signify transgressions against people or God, the term *avon* almost always refers to an error or iniquity committed when one acts contrary to the will of God.[6] Appearing 229 times in the Hebrew Bible, the word's root meaning is unclear, although it may be associated with crookedness. In Scripture, *avon* refers to both the transgression—"sin"—and to its consequences—"guilt" and "punishment." Indeed in certain contexts it is difficult to discern which connotation is intended, and it may be that all three are at play. This is the case, for instance, at Gen. 4:13, where Cain, having killed his brother, says to God, "My *avon* is greater than I can bear." Cain thus refers to his sin in killing Abel, to the feeling of guilt that results from that sin, and to the punishment God has just meted out in response to that sin.

While the distinctions pointed out here in the meanings of the biblical terms used for sin are important, it must also be clear that in later biblical and post-biblical texts these terms frequently are used to refer to sin in general. The distinctive connotations attributable to their root meanings and to their original uses often times appear to have been lost, so that in later contexts, the words simply function as synonyms.

**Sin in the Rabbinic literature:** Unlike the Hebrew Bible, the Rabbinic literature most commonly refers to sin with the term *averah*, from a root meaning "to pass over" or "transgress." This usage appears to emerge from the Rabbinic notion that the law of God—embodied in the Torah—has been given into human hands and made clear. This means that sin always is an act of disregard for—"going over"—this law.

Alongside this meaning, Rabbinic interpretation adds a separate dimension to the word by noting its relationship to the concepts of "passing forth" or "making public." B. Sot. 3a states that, though a person might sin in private, God will make the matter known in public:

> A. It has been taught on Tannaite authority:
> B. R. Meir would say, "If a person oversteps the bounds in secret, the Holy One, blessed be he, makes the matter public.
> C. "For it is said, 'And the spirit of jealousy overstepped him' (Num. 5:14).

D. "And the word 'overstep' bears only the meaning of public display,

E. "as it is said, 'And Moses commanded and they brought the report about the camp' (Exod. 36:6)."

F. R. Simeon b. Laqish said, "A person commits a transgression only if a spirit of foolishness enters him.

G. "For it is said, 'If a man's wife goes aside' (Num. 5:12).

H. "The word for 'go aside' is written so that it can be read 'act foolishly.'"

We see here the underlying ideology of sin detailed in the Rabbinic literature. The rejection of God's will results from the individual's loss of focus upon the demands of Torah. Referred to here as "the spirit of foolishness," this loss of focus normally is attributed to the *yetser ha-ra*, "the inclination to do evil," which is discussed in full below. The larger point of the passage, made at B, is that, whether the sin regards a cultic ("religious") obligation or a violation of the broader economic, social, political, and familial rules encompassed by Torah, the matter ultimately will be revealed in public. As a violation of the covenant that binds all of Israel to God, sin, this is to say, always has communal implications, besmirching not only the relationship between the individual sinner and God but tainting the covenant relationship as a whole. Thus, in the Rabbinic system that understands all law to emerge from divine revelation, all "crimes" are sins against God and affect the relationship of the people of Israel to God. All sins for this reason are matters of public concern.

**The inclination to do evil:** The rabbis concur with the inherited scriptural view that people have an inclination to engage in wrong actions. This inclination, which they term the *yetser ha-ra*, is recognized as an aspect of the human condition, a temptation to which all people are subject. The idea of the existence of such an inclination is suggested by the specific wording of Gen. 8:21, where God speaks following the conclusion of the flood, after Noah emerges from the ark and offers sacrifices:

And when the Lord smelled the pleasing odor, the Lord said in his heart, "I will never again curse the ground because of man, for the inclination[7] (*yetser*) of man's heart is evil

(*ra*) from his youth; neither will I ever again destroy every living creature as I have done.

Indeed, the rabbis go beyond the understanding of Scripture, which sees the propensity to sin as a human trait that God came to recognize only as a result of his concrete experiences with humankind. The rabbis suggest, rather, that the inclination to do evil was actually a creation of God himself (B. Suk. 52b):

A. Said R. Hana bar Aha, "In the school house they say, There are four things that the Holy One, blessed be he, regrets he created, and these are they:

B. "Exile, the Chaldeans, the Ishmaelites, and the inclination to do evil.

C. "'Exile,' as it is written, 'Now, therefore, what am I doing here says the Lord, since my people is taken away for nothing' (Is. 52:5).

D. "'The Chaldeans,' as it is written, 'Behold the land of the Chaldeans, this is the people that was not' (Is. 23:13).

E. "'The Ishmaelites,' as it is written, 'The tents of the robbers prosper, and they who provoke God are secure since God has brought them with his hand' (Job 12:6).

F. "'The inclination to do evil,' as it is written, '[And I will gather her that is driven away] and her that I have afflicted' (Mic. 4:6)."

God presumably regrets having created these things, because they have caused the world to take on a character contrary to that which God intended. While the present text is silent on the point, the broader Rabbinic theology of God explains why the rabbis did not expect the deity to change things, that is, to destroy those aspects of creation that he regrets. Insofar as the rabbis understand the continued existence of the world to depend upon the partnership of God and humans, God was not understood any longer to exercise the power to interfere in worldly matters so as entirely to change the nature of creation. Conquering the inclination to do evil thus was viewed not as God's obligation but as the responsibility of humans. The people of Israel in particular, by following and studying Torah, would need to work to dissolve the grip the inclination to do evil had on them.[8]

While the Rabbinic idea of the evil inclination suggests that people have the innate tendency to sin, this notion should not be confused with the Christian concept of original sin, to which it is not equivalent. Contrary to the concept of original sin, according to Rabbinic Judaism people do not have an inherited, corrupt nature. This is made clear at B. Shab. 145b-146a, which appears to comprise a direct polemic against the idea of original sin:

A. [Said R. Hiyya bar Abba to R. Assi], "How come gentiles lust?"
B. [R. Assi replied], "Because they didn't stand at Mount Sinai. For when [146A] the snake had sexual relations with Eve, he dropped into her a filthy drop [of lust]. When the Israelites stood at Mount Sinai, their lust came to an end.
C. "But since the gentiles did not stand at Mount Sinai, their lust did not come to an end."
D. Said R. Aha b. Raba to R. Ashi, "So how about converts?"
E. He said to him, "Even though they weren't there, their stars were there, [as Scripture states]: 'Neither with you only do I make this covenant and this oath, but with him who stands here with us this day before the Lord our God and also with him who doesn't stand here with us this day' (Deut. 29:14-15)."
F. This [B] differs from R. Abba bar Kahana, for said R. Abba bar Kahana, "For three generations lust didn't come to an end for our fathers. After all, Abraham begat Ishmael, Isaac begat Esau, but Jacob begat the twelve tribal progenitors, in whom there was no flaw at all."

The result of Adam's sin was not to bind people to sin forevermore. The giving of the Torah, B, or the evolving merit of the patriarchs, F, removed from the people of Israel (and from converts to the Jewish faith, D-E) any taint that resulted from the actions of the first human beings. Of course, following the explicit theory of Scripture, the rabbis do recognize the reason for the existence of death to be the sin of Adam and Eve. Because Adam and Eve disregarded God's commandment not to eat of the fruit of knowledge of good and evil, they were removed from the Garden of Eden and made mortal (Gen. 3:1-22). But while the rabbis recognize that all people suffer the consequences of Adam and Eve's misdeed, so as now to live as mortals in a

non-utopian world, the sages recognize as the proximate cause of each person's death his or her own actions alone. Death, that is, was instituted as a result of Adam and Eve's violation of God's will. But each person dies as a consequence of his or her own sins (Tanhuma Bereshit 29, Tanhuma Hukkat 39). People are not besmirched by sin from birth. But they are continually subject to temptation, a heinous force that they must constantly fight.

The rabbis describe sinfulness as a condition that people who begin to disregard the law increasingly accept for themselves. One consequence of sin thus is its growing power over the sinner, leading one who at first commits a minor infraction to greater and greater offenses, culminating with idolatry (T. B.Q. 9:31):

A. R. Simeon b. Eleazar says in the name of R. Hilpai b. Agra which he said in the name of R. Yohanan b. Nuri, "If a person pulled out his own hair, tore his clothing, broke his utensils, scattered his coins, in a fit of anger, he should be regarded by you as though he performed an act of service for an idol.
B. "For if his temper should say to him, 'Go do an act of service for an idol,' he would go and do it.
C. "And that is the sort of thing that the evil impulse can do: Today it says to him, 'Do this,' tomorrow, 'Do that,' until it tells him, 'Go serve idols,' and he goes and does just that."

Committing one transgression inevitably leads to committing another, just as performance of one religious duty leads to the performance of another (see M. Ab. 4:2). Thus, while at first sin may be called a passerby, it later is viewed as a guest and, finally, as a member of the household (B. Suk. 52a):

A. Said R. Assi, "The inclination to do evil to begin with is like a spider's thread and in the end like cart ropes.
B. "For it is said, 'Woe to them who draw iniquity with cords of vanity and sin as with cart ropes' (Is. 5:18)."

A similar point is made in a subsequent section of this text, at B. Suk. 52b, which describes how an outside force, the tendency to do wrong, quickly becomes internal and natural:

A. R. Huna contrasted the following verses of Scripture: "It is written, 'For the spirit of harlotry has caused them to err' (Hos. 4:12) [thus the cause is external to the person].

B. "But it also is written, '[For the spirit of harlotry] is within them' (Hos. 5:4).

C. "In the beginning, it caused them to err, but in the end, it is within them."

D. Said Raba, "In the beginning one calls it a passerby, then a guest, and, finally, a man [of the household].

E. "For it is said, 'And there came a passerby to the rich man, and he spared to take of his own flock and of his own herd, to dress for the guest [no longer passerby],' and [at the end] the verse states, 'But he took, the poor man's lamb and dressed it for the man [now a household member] who had come to him' (2 Sam. 12:4)."

Rabbinic authorities thus see the temptation towards sin as a force that must consistently be fought. This is illustrated in the following (B. Suk. 52a-52b):

A. Said R. Isaac, "A man's inclination [to do evil] overcomes him every day.

B. "For it is said, 'Only [52B] evil all day long' (Gen. 6:5)."

C. Said R. Simeon b. Laqish, "A man's inclination [to do evil] prevails over him every day and seeks to kill him.

D. "For it is said, 'The wicked watches the righteous and seeks to slay him' (Ps. 37:32).

E. "And if the Holy One, blessed be he, were not there to help him, he could not withstand it.

F. "For it is said, 'The Lord will not leave him in his hand nor suffer him to be condemned when he is judged' (Ps. 37:32)."

The inclination to do evil appears as a physical, external force that all people must constantly combat. Victory over this force is possible only through the support of God, who helps the individual withstand the danger presented by sin. Within the Rabbinic context, this support offered by God is understood to be available in the form of the laws of Torah, adherence to and study of which, as we shall see below, the rabbis believed to be the only certain ways of protecting oneself from sin.

Before evaluating the ways in which the rabbis understand Torah to be a prophylactic against sin, we should be clear that they did not all see the inclination to sin in an entirely negative light. That is, while deeply concerned for the potential devastation the inclination to do evil could do to a person over whom it gained a hold, some Rabbinic authorities also recognized in this temptation one of life's motivating powers. In their view, the inclination to sin stands behind people's desire to improve their own circumstance, to fulfill sexual needs and so to raise families, and to acquire in appropriate ways that which is currently beyond their means. Were it not for such desires, these authorities argued, most productive human activity would cease. The rabbis accordingly saw the inclination to sin—however dangerous and evil—as an important component of the human psyche. In this vein, B. Yom. 69b relates that, when the men of the great synagogue succeeded in capturing the yetser ha-ra for three days, they discovered that, during that time, no productive activity took place. Even chickens ceased laying eggs. Similarly, Gen. Rab. 9:7 states that, were it not for the yetser ha-ra, people would not be motivated to engage in business, marry, raise a family, or construct a house.

A. R. Nahman bar Samuel bar Nahman in the name of R. Samuel bar Nahman said, "[As for the statement at Gen. 1:31, 'And God saw everything that he had made], and behold, it was very good'—this [refers to] the inclination to do evil."

B. [Samuel bar Nahman said], "'And behold, it was very good'—this [refers to] the inclination to do evil"?!

C. Now, is the inclination to do evil in fact "very good"?

D. What a surprising statement!

E. Rather [here is what it means]: If it were not for the inclination to do evil, a person would neither build a house, nor get married, nor have children, nor engage in commerce.

F. And [reflecting on this fact] Solomon said [Ec. 4:4], "Then I saw that all toil and all skill in work come from a man's envy of his neighbor."

Human productivity thus is a positive result of people's envy, on the one hand, and sexual desires, on the other. This being the case, the rabbis see the need not simply to obliterate these desires but rather constantly to rise above them. This is accomplished when the individual fights the inclination to do evil by recognizing the ever present eyes and ears of God (see M. Ab. 2:1) and by following the law. But, above all, the rabbis hold that one protects oneself from falling into evil by engaging in study of Torah, as this passage at B. Sot. 21a reflects:

A. There is the possibility that merit suspends the curse [that comes upon an adulteress woman] for three years, etc. [M. Sot. 3:4E]:

B. Merit on what count?

C. If one should propose that it is merit on account of study of Torah, lo, [a woman] is not subject to the commandment of the religious duty of doing so [and hence merit will not accrue, since merit accrues from doing what one is commanded to do].

D. Hence it must be the merit of such religious duties [as she has carried out].

E. But does the merit accruing for performing a religious duty afford all that much protection?

F. And has it not been taught on Tannaite authority:

G. This is what R. Menahem b. R. Yose expounded, "'For the commandment is a lamp, and Torah is light' (Prov. 6:23).

H. "Scripture has treated the matter of the religious duty as comparable to a lamp, and the Torah, to light.

I. "A religious duty is made comparable to a lamp to tell you that just as a lamp affords protection only for a moment, so a religious duty affords protection only for a moment.

J. "And [it treats] Torah [as comparable] to light, to tell you, just as light serves as protection for all time, so the Torah serves as protection for all time."

K. And it says, "When you walk, it will lead you, when you sleep, it will watch over you, and when you awake, it will talk with you" (Prov. 6:22).

L. "When you walk, it will lead you" in this world; "when you sleep, it will watch over you" in death; and "when you awake it will talk with you" in the age to come.

M. There is the following parable. The matter may be compared to a man who was walking along in the depths of the night and gloom and feared on account of thorns, pits, thistles, wild beasts, and thugs, and he does not know which road to take.

N. A lighted torch [that is, religious practice] comes to hand, so he is saved from thorns, pits, thistles, but still fears on account of wild beasts and thugs, and does not know which road to take.

O. But once the morning star [that is, Torah] comes up, he is saved also from wild beasts and thugs. He still does not know which road to take.

P. When he reaches the crossroads [that is, death], he is saved from all [fear and doubt].

Q. Another matter: A transgression extinguishes [the merit accruing on account of carrying out] a religious duty, but a transgression does not extinguish [the merit accruing on account of] studying Torah, for it is said, "Many waters cannot quench love" (Song 8:7).

R. Said R. Joseph, "Doing a religious duty, when one is doing it, serves as a shield and affords protection, but when one is no longer doing it, while it continues to serve as a shield [from suffering], it does not afford protection [from the evil inclination].

S. "But as to Torah, whether one is actually engaged in studying it or not, it both serves as a shield and affords protection."

T. Raba objected to that statement, "But then how about the following case: Did not Doeg (see 1 Sam. 22) and Ahitophel (see 2 Sam. 15-16) engage in study of Torah? Then did it not serve as a shield for them?"

U. Rather, said Raba, "As to the study of Torah, when one is engaged in studying it, it serves as a shield and affords protection. But when one is not engaged in studying it, while it serves as a shield, it does not afford protection.

V. "But as to the doing of a religious duty, whether one is engaged in carrying it out or not, while it serves as a shield, it does not afford protection."

W. Rabina said, "Indeed [as for the water's not having effect, A], it is, as you have stated [B-C], that the merit of the study of Torah [suspends the effects of the water].

X. "And as to your objection that a woman is not commanded to carry out [the study of Torah and so does not attain merit from her act], granted that she is not subject to a commandment on that account; still, as a reward for having their sons taught to recite Scripture and to repeat Mishnah, and for their waiting for their husbands until they come back from the study house, do women not have a share [of the merit] with them?"

Study of Torah is the single greatest antidote against the temptation to sin and against the punishments that come from sin. Study of Torah is viewed as much more powerful in this regard than any righteous deed: the latter will keep the individual from sin only during the moment that he or she is actually engaged in that act, while the study of Torah acts as a constant prophylactic. Further, righteous deeds offer no continuing merit that balances the punishment owed for sins. This is unlike study of Torah, which accrues to the scholar's benefit whenever he might become deserving of some punishment.

This idea that the study of Torah is the only truly effective means of combating the inclination to sin is made concrete in the belief that such study fights sin as surely as a medication prevents a wound from festering (B. Qid. 30b):

26.A. Our rabbis have taught on Tannaite authority:
B. "Therefore impress these my words upon your very heart; [bind them as a sign on your hand and let them serve as a symbol on your forehead; and teach them to your children, reciting them when you stay at home and when you are away, when you lie down and when you get up, and inscribe them on the doorposts of your house and on your gates, to the end that you and your children may endure in the land that the Lord swore to your fathers to assign to them, as long as there is a heaven over the earth]" (Deut. 11:18-21):
B. This use of the word [impress, which can be read to sound like "medicine" or "ointment"] indicates that words of Torah are compared to a life-giving medicine.
C. The matter may be compared to the case of a king who grew angry with his son and gave him a severe blow, but then put a salve on the wound and said to him, "My son, so long as this bandage is on the wound, eat whatever you like, drink whatever you like, and wash in either warm or cold water, and nothing will do you injury. But if you remove the bandage, the sore will immediately begin to produce ulcers."
D. So the Holy One, blessed be he, said to Israel, "My children, I have created in you an impulse to do evil, than which nothing is more evil.
E. "'Sin couches at the door and to you is its desire' (Gen. 4:7).

F. "Keep yourselves occupied with teachings of the Torah, and [sin] will not control you.
G. "But if you leave off studying words of the Torah, lo, it will control you, as it is said, 'and to you is its desire' (Gen. 4:7).
H. "And not only so, but all of its undertakings concern you. But if you want, you will control it, as it is said, 'But you may rule over it' (Gen. 4:7)."
I. And Scripture says, "And if your enemy is hungry, give him bread to eat, and if he is thirsty, give him water to drink, for you will heap coals of fire upon his head" (Prov. 25:21-22).

The power of the inclination to do evil, which the study of Torah alone can negate, is further defined in the continuation of the discussion at B. Sot. 21a:

27.A. Our rabbis have taught on Tannaite authority:
B. So formidable is the lust to do evil that even its creator has called it evil, as it is written, "For that the desire of man's heart is evil from his youth" (Gen. 8:21).
C. Said R. Isaac, "The desire to do evil renews itself daily against a person: 'every imagination of the thoughts of his heart was only evil every day' (Gen. 6:5)."
D. And said R. Simeon b. Levi, "A man's inclination [to do evil] prevails over him every day and seeks to kill him. For it is said, 'The wicked watches the righteous and seeks to slay him' (Ps. 37:32). And if the Holy One, blessed be he, were not there to help him, he could not withstand it. For it is said, 'The Lord will not leave him in his hand nor suffer him to be condemned when he is judged' (Ps. 37:32)."

The inclination to do evil is so powerful that it continually attempts to kill a person. The only sure place in which a person can overcome that inclination is the study house (B. Sot. 21a):

28.A. A Tannaite of the household of R. Ishmael: "If that vile one meets you, drag it to the house of study. If it is a stone, it will dissolve. If it is iron, it will be pulverized. If it is a stone, it will dissolve, as it is written, 'Lo, everyone who is thirsty, come to water' (Is. 55:1). And it is written, 'The water wears down stones' (Job.

14:19). If it is iron, it will be pulverized, as it is written, 'Is not my word like fire, says the Lord, and like a hammer that breaks the rock into pieces' (Jer. 23:29)."

Together these passages from B. Sot. 21a encapsulate the theory of sin found in Rabbinic Judaism. Sin is a concrete, physical force that derives from the human inclination to violate the precepts of God. An individual's observing of religious commandments alongside his or her acts of righteousness offers some protection from this inclination. These behaviors, of course, are expected of all members of the people of Israel. But the only true antidote to the inclination to do evil is intense engagement in the study of God's precepts, that is, in Torah. Within the study house, in the setting of Rabbinic learning, the inclination to sin is powerless.

**Atonement from sin:** While rabbis held that people, and in particular those like rabbis who studied Torah, could escape the inclination to sin, they also understood that the tendency to stray from divine law is an inevitable part of life.[9] As a result, in Rabbinic Judaism the concept of sin was intimately tied to the notion of atonement, and just as the rabbis recognized that all people, by nature, have a propensity to sin, so they held that atonement for sin was always possible. The Rabbinic term for atonement, "*teshubah*," meaning, literally, "return," refers to an individual's breaking away from sinful conduct and turning to proper behavior before God. *Teshubah* thus describes the process through which the sinner atones for past actions and returns to proper modes of behavior. Judaism views this process as a central and natural aspect of religious and social life. Indeed, the rabbis list repentance as one of the seven things God made before Creation (B. Pes. 54a; B. Ned. 39b), and they hold that sincere repentance is equivalent to the rebuilding of the Jerusalem-Temple and to the restoration of the sacrificial cult (B. San. 43b):

A. Said R. Joshua b. Levi, "Whoever sacrifices his impulse to do evil and confesses regarding [his sins] is regarded by Scripture as though he had honored the Holy One, blessed be he, in the two worlds, this world and the world to come, for it is written, 'Who offers the sacrifice of confession honors me' (Ps. 50:23)."

B. R. Joshua b. Levi said, "When the Temple stood, a person would offer a burnt offering, and the reward of a burnt offering would go to his credit, or he would do the same with a meal offering, and the reward of a meal-offering would go to his credit."

C. "But he who is humble is regarded by Scripture as though he had offered up all sacrifices.

D. "For it is said, 'The sacrifices of God are a broken spirit' (Ps. 51:19).

E. "And his prayers are not rejected, for it is written, 'A broken and contrite heart, O God, you will not despise' (Ps. 51:19)."

Repentance thus represents the most direct and efficacious manner of placating God and assuring God's continued protection.

Repentance is a precondition of atonement (*kaparah*), which signifies the actual forgiving of sin by God. The Day of Atonement, which annually provides an opportunity for forgiveness by God, is particularly important only insofar as it marks an annual conclusion of the continuing process through which people repent and correct their ways. But the Day of Atonement is efficacious only if the individual already has repented. Thus M. Yom. 8:8 states:

A. Death and the Day of Atonement atone when joined with repentance.

B. Repentance [by itself] atones for minor transgressions of positive and negative commandments.

C. And, as to serious transgressions, [repentance] suspends the punishment until the Day of Atonement comes along and atones.

We see that the advent of the Day of Atonement by itself has no expiatory power. Sins are forgiven by God, rather, only if the sinner has completed the process of repentance. Once this has occurred, the advent of the Day of Atonement cleans the individual's slate before God.

Repentance itself entails confession of the sin before God and formulation of a resolve not to commit the same sin again. In the case of a sin against another person, forgiveness by God is possible only after full restitution or correction of the wrong deed has been made and a pardon from the other person has been obtained. In Scripture's sacrificial system, the process of repentance had been completed by an expiatory offering sacrificed in the Jerusalem Temple. After the destruction of the Temple and the cessation of the sacrificial cult in 70 C.E., the rabbis found a replacement for the expiatory offering in charitable deeds. Rabbinic authorities consequently viewed repentance and charity together as a person's greatest advocates before God (B. Shab. 32a).

Forgiveness is available to all who repent, and the hand of God is continually stretched out to those who seek atonement (B. Pes. 119a):

> A. Said R. Kahana in the name of R. Ishmael b. R. Yose, and our rabbis in the name of R. Judah the Patriarch, "What is the meaning of the verse of Scripture, 'And they had the hands of a man under their wings' (Ezek. 1:8)?
>
> B. "What is written is 'his hand,' referring to the hand of the Holy One, blessed be he, which is spread out under the wings of the living creatures [who bore the divine chariot], so as to accept penitents [and protect them] from the attribute of justice."

Recognizing the dramatic change of behavior and intense commitment to God's will that stand behind true repentance, Rabbinic authorities praise those who have sinned and repented even beyond those who have never sinned, stating, B. Ber. 34b, "In a place in which those who repent stand, those who are completely righteous cannot stand." Repentance is accomplished neither through a linguistic formula nor through simple participation in a rite of expiation. It depends, rather, upon a true change in the life of the one who seeks atonement. That person must make the commitment to continue to fight what the rabbis understand to be the most powerful negative trait of the human being, the innate tendency to sin.

**The High Holidays—sin and repentance in Jewish worship:** Through the rituals and holiday celebrations of Judaism, Rabbinic notions of sin and repentance continue today to shape Jews' understanding of sin and repentance. This is especially the case insofar as the Jewish liturgy firmly expresses the idea

that Israel's exile and the delayed coming of the messianic redemption are the result of sin, that is, of the nation's failure fully to follow the stipulations of God's covenant. Sin thus has a clear and direct impact upon the life of individual Jews as well as upon the nation as a corporate entity, as this passage from the festival liturgy makes clear:

> Because of our sins were we exiled from our land, far from our soil. May it be your will, Lord our God and God of our ancestors, compassionate king who restores his children to their land, to have compassion for us and for your sanctuary; rebuild it quickly and enhance its glory! Accept with compassion the prayer of your people Israel, wherever they dwell.[10]

Exile, the result of sin, will end when, in response to Israel's prayers and acts of repentance, God compassionately restores the people to their land.

This idea of the very real presence of sin as a devastating force in the people's life and of the power of repentance to undo its consequences emerges directly and powerfully in the rituals and liturgy of Rosh Hashanah and Yom Kippur, the holidays that together form the Days of Awe or Ten Days of Repentance.[11] These days proclaim that God annually judges each person's sins, determining whether or not the individual's conduct has earned him or her another year of life.[12] By making concrete the dramatic impact of sin, the Days of Awe create an opportunity for deep introspection and honest self-evaluation. Recognizing their shortcomings, people determine to correct their paths and give up their sinful habits.

On Rosh Hashanah and Yom Kippur, the Rabbinic conception of the pervasiveness of sin and the seriousness of its consequences is expressed through the metaphor of a trial. Beginning on Rosh Hashanah, God is understood to evaluate the behavior of each person. Especially on the Day of Atonement, because of sin, the individual's life stands in the balance. This perception is made concrete through a metaphorical confrontation with death that occurs on that day. Wearing a burial shroud, leaving aside the pleasures of life (eating, drinking, washing, sex), facing the reality of God's judgment—through these rituals and perceptions the person recognizes life as a gift, given to those who use it properly, to be given up if sin is allowed to overpower one's capacity for doing good. But there is no escaping this propensity to sin, as this passage recited after the silent prayer at each service on Yom Kippur makes clear:

> My God, before I was born, I was unworthy; and now that I have been born it is as though I have not been born. During my life I am as dust; all the moreso after my death. I stand before you like a vessel full of shame and disgrace. May it be your will Lord, my God, and God of my ancestors that I not sin again. And the sins I already have committed against you—nullify them in your great mercy, but not through harsh afflictions and diseases.

And later, a passage that reflects the biblical and Rabbinic understanding of the inevitability of sin as a result of the human condition itself:

> You know our sins, whether deliberate or not, whether committed willingly or under compulsion, whether in public or in private. What are we? What is our piety? What is our righteousness, our attainment, our power, our might? What can we say Lord our God and God of our Fathers? Compared to you, all the mighty are nothing, the famous are nonexistent, the wise lack wisdom, the clever lack reason. For most of their actions are meaninglessness, the days of their lives emptiness. Man's superiority over the beast is an illusion. All life is a fleeting breath.[13]

In the sight of the perfect God, all people are sinners. Their hope is in their knowledge of God's merciful willingness to offer another chance to even the worst offender. This perception of God's nature turns a somber and potentially morbid ritual into an occasion for hope, a hope that emerges from the knowledge that God desires not the death of the sinner but that he or she repent:

> On Rosh Hashanah it is written
> And on Yom Kippur it is sealed
> How many shall leave this world and how many shall be born into it, who shall live and who shall die, who shall live out the limit of his days and who shall not. . . .

> But penitence, prayer and good deeds can annul the severity of the decree.

> Your glory is Your nature: slow to anger, ready to forgive. You desire not the sinner's death, but that he turn from his path and live. Until the day of his death you wait for him. Whenever he returns, You welcome him at once. Truly You are Creator, and know the weakness of your Creations, who are but flesh and blood.[14]

Repentance thus is not granted by God so much as it is earned by sinners who, recognizing and admitting their shortcomings, determine to return to God, who, mercifully, is always waiting, always ready to accept sincere repentance.

Confronting one's mortality and dependence upon God encourages the reevaluation of priorities and values, the recognition of life as a fragile gift, the turning away from sin that allows one to use that gift wisely. As the Talmudic passages on sin lead us to anticipate, the ultimate focus of the Days of Awe thus is not simply human failings and sinfulness but, rather, the knowledge that people can overcome their nature so as to act righteously. The willingness to confront their tendency to sin empowers people to stop sinning, so as to better themselves and improve the world around them. And God, conscious of people's tendency to sin, is seen as choosing not to pursue punishment and death but, instead, to encourage and accept repentance. God, the prosecutor and judge, does not delight in proving the case and imposing the harshest sanctions. Rather, like a merciful parent, God most desires to remove sin and demands only that people take the first step, engaging in penitence, prayer, and good deeds as the prerequisite to God's reducing the severity of the decree. They will die. But it need not be now.

While recognizing the human propensity to sin, at its heart, Judaism thus presents a positive view of humankind and a hopeful perspective on the human future. The Days of Awe take advantage of the metaphor of death and the certainty of each individual's death to offer the assurance expressed in the idea of rebirth. By appeasing those they have wronged and by engaging in acts of repentance before God, people correct their relationship with God. They thereby make possible individual, as well as national, redemption. The Days of

Awe, like Judaism's view of humankind in general, thus are ultimately positive. Their attention to sin and death provides the opportunity for *Heshbon ha-Nefesh*, taking account of one's deeds and honestly assessing the sort of life one is leading and should lead. Just as Judaism rejects the notion that people are condemned to live out a destiny shaped by their innate inclination to sin, so it denies that past sin necessarily shapes their future actions or controls their relationship with God. Honest assessment leads to future righteousness, under the watchful eye of a God who desires not the deaths of sinners but that they repent.

### Notes

[1] On the following, see Robin Cover, "Sin, Sinners (OT)," *ABD*, vol. 6, pp. 32-34.

[2] Ibid., p. 33.

[3] See ibid., pp. 31-32.

[4] The root interestingly forms a perfect antonym to the root meaning of the term Torah (*yrh*). Besides referring to instruction, *yrh* designates "hitting the mark." Like the root *ht'*, it can refer to the performance of an archer.

[5] RSV translates "sin." See Francis Brown, et al., *A Hebrew and English Lexicon of the Old Testament* (Oxford, reprint, 1974), p. 309.

[6] Cf., 1 Sam. 20:1, 20:8, and 25:24, which refer to the guilt of one person against another.

[7] RSV: imagination.

[8] See also the discussion below of Gen. Rab. 9:7, where some Rabbinic authorities argue that the inclination to do evil has an important role in assuring human productivity. In this view, destruction of that inclination would bring an end to all human endeavor.

[9] For a complete discussion of this topic, see REPENTANCE.

[10] Adapted from Jules Harlow, ed., *Siddur Sim Shalom* (New York, 1985), p. 463.

[11] On the following, see Irving Greenberg, *The Jewish Way. Living the Holidays* (New York, 1993), pp. 182-215.

[12] Thus, unlike other Jewish festivals, these days have no link to historical events of redemption, liberation, or catastrophe. They focus, rather, on the meaning of life in general, viewed outside of the context of history and politics. Later tradition, however, links the forty days from the beginning of the month of Elul to Yom Kippur to the period of Moses's visit on Sinai to get the second tablets and to ask for forgiveness for the people's creating and worshipping of the golden calf. Yom Kippur thus is recognized as the anniversary of God's forgiveness.

[13] Jules Harlow, ed., *Mahzor for Rosh Hashanah and Yom Kippur* (New York, 1972), p. 463.

[14] Ibid., pp. 537-538.

ALAN J. AVERY-PECK

**SOCIALISM-YIDDISHISM, JUDAISM AND:** Jewish Socialism was a nineteenth and twentieth century movement that joined the social and economic ideals of Socialism to a deep commitment to the formation of a way of life and a world view for an Israel, specifically, the impoverished and working class Jews of Eastern Europe. It is comparable to a Judaism because it presented a complete picture of how one should live life, namely, as an active worker for political change and social improvement, how one should see the world, namely, as something to be perfected within the ideals of the biblical prophets and the program of Socialist theorists, and how to so form a new people Israel, this one a component in the united working people of the world. This new Israel would take its place within the international working classes, but as a distinct component, just as the Russian or the Polish Socialists recognized their ethnic origins as well. Forming a Jewish wing of Socialism, focused on the Yiddish language, yielded a secular Jewish system comparable to the religious Judaic systems of modern times such as Reform, Orthodox, and Conservative Judaism. Like Zionism, another secular Jewish system, Jewish Socialism-Yiddishism put forth a way of life, a world view, and a theory of who and what is "Israel," a system that coalesced into a coherent account of the social order formed by its constituents. Jewish Socialism was born within the framework of international Socialism at the end of the nineteenth century. In 1897, Jews of Poland formed the Jewish Union, the Bund, which embodied Jewish Socialism and gave the movement its institutional expression. Jews derived from Jewish Socialism not merely economic benefits or political identity but a life's ideal, a view of the future, a reason for action in the present, in short, all of the components that define a system of Judaism.

**Jewish secularists and secular Jews:** But can we in fact call it a Judaism? It was not a Judaism for Communists and Socialists who happened to be Jews, that is, who happened to have come from Jewish families. For these entirely secular Jews had no special relationships to other Jews, and Socialism had no bearing on their Jewish origins. But for Jews who opted for a Socialist ideal, who organized labor unions and other institutions in particular for the betterment of the life of the Jewish masses, Socialism bonded with certain components of the received holy literature to form a distinctively Jewish version of Socialism indeed, one that in the lives of the participants formed their way of "being Jewish." They were Jewish secularists, and Socialism, formulated in Yiddish, formed their Judaic system.

One considerable component of that way of life involved the Yiddish language, which formed the vehicle for bringing Socialism to the Jewish masses. Hence, Jewish Socialism joined to Yiddishism—an ideology of turning a language into the foundation for a way of life—constituted a powerful and important Judaism. Before taking up the ideology of Yiddishism presently, we first consider the world-view, the life-ideal, of the Jewish Socialists. For a statement of the world view of the radicals—this one in Hebrew, but an example of Socialist poetry, we turn to a poem, "We Believe," published in 1872. Here we find that set of truths that express the way of explaining the world and the purpose of life that made Jewish Socialism a statement of meaning comparable to a religion:

> We believe
> — that misdeeds, injustice, falsehood, and murder will not reign forever, and a bright day will come when the sun will appear.
> — there is hope for mankind; the peoples of the world will not destroy each other for a piece of land, and blood will not be shed for silly prestige.
> — Men will not die of hunger, and wealth not created by its own labor will disappear like smoke.
> — People will be enlightened and will not differentiate between man and man; will no longer say, "Christian, Moslem, Jew," but will call each other "Brother, friend, comrade."
> — The secrets of nature will be revealed and people will dominate nature instead of nature dominating them.
> — Man will no longer work with the sweat of his brow; the forces of nature will serve him as hands.[1]

The world-view of the Jewish Socialists laid emphasis on the building of a better world

through science and technology. It elicited commitment and generated hope because of this powerful promise of a better tomorrow. Jewish Socialism promised a bright future, so described a better tomorrow; spoke of an eschatology; addressed the issues of economic justice; took up the Jews' concern for anti-Semitism as part of a larger ideal of universal tolerance; expressed a commitment to science and technology. All of this frames a world-view: an amalgam of the Jews' social aspirations and contemporary complaints, a solution to the Jewish problem as part of a solution to the problem of class conflict.

**Yiddishism:** This brings us to the other component of the Judaism at hand, the Yiddish component of Socialism and Yiddishism. Yiddishism was the Judaic movement that identified in the Yiddish language a set of cultural values and ideals of personal conduct that, all together, comprise a way of life and a world view, based in an "Israel" constituted, of course, by Yiddish-speaking persons (figs. 123-125). The union of Jewish Socialism and Yiddishism formed the single most popular Judaism of the first half of the twentieth century, enjoying mass appeal to Jews in both Poland and Russia and in America.

In a classic essay, Ruth R. Wisse defines Yiddishism as a system: "*Yiddishkeyt* [that is, the ideology of Yiddish] has come to signify both the culture that is embodied in the Yiddish language and a standard of ethical conduct that preserves the essence of Judaism without the requirements of ritual and law."[2] Since the language is treated as the bearer of ideals and values, the speaking of that language constitutes the principal component of a way of life, and those values, the world-view. The connection to Socialism, moreover, proves critical. Jewish Socialists pointed to the Yiddish language and its supposedly distinctive values of compassion and socialist idealism as the cultural vehicle for their movement. They espoused Yiddish as the language of Jewish Socialism. So Yiddishism and Jewish Socialism joined together, even though each Judaism preserved its particular points of stress and concern. As to the special ideology of Yiddishism, again in Wisse's words, we find, ". . . an ideal of behavior in which the whole religious discipline of Jewish life is transmuted into the practice of kindness and decency." In Yiddishism, then, one deals not with yearning for a language but for a social and political ideal.[3] That ideal, moreover, for its holders serves in Wisse's words as "a model for the present and the future."

The appeal to language as an ideology, Wisse points out, has its roots in the end of the nineteenth and beginning of the twentieth century in Eastern Europe. Compensating for the loss of religious credence and the absence of a territorial unity and an autonomous politics, advocates of Yiddish would resort to language to "express . . . cultural autonomy, so that same language would now cement a culturally autonomous community." Wisse observes, in this connection, that the recognition of language as a separate category for Jews runs parallel to the recognition of religion as something subject to discrete definition.[4] This again indicates that the language-nationalism represented by Yiddish forms an encompassing system, not merely a matter of adventitious choice.

The linking of Yiddishism to Socialism requires explanation. For whom did that choice turn into a system? Wisse explains the appeal of Yiddishism to the Socialist:

> A Jew who lived in accordance with the religious tradition could presumably maintain his Jewishness in Spanish as well as English, in German as well as Yiddish, or even in modern Hebrew. A secular Zionist could abandon religious practice and many of the "trappings" of Jewish culture, secure in the belief that statehood would generate a new national identity. The Jewish Left, however, had only its culture to set it apart from the Polish Left and the Russian Left, and that culture, stripped of its religious content, added up to Yiddish—the language, the folklore, the literature.[5]

That accounts for the formation of Yiddishism, now no longer an ideology of language but an ideology of the people. The Jewish Socialist-Yiddishist Zhitlowsky held, Wisse points out, that "Yiddish had absorbed the Jewish ethics to such a degree that anyone who spoke it was permeated by the Jewish spirit."[6] The difficulty with the ideology

at hand, both on its own and when joined to Socialism, hardly escapes notice. Wisse states it very simply:

> Yiddish had developed out of the religious way of life of the Jews, both to express and to protect Jewish separateness. Yiddishists now hoped that a secular way of life, with no other ideological justification for separateness, could be sustained by language alone.[7]

Joined to Socialism and class struggle, treated as the language of oppressed classes, Yiddish found itself bearing a still heavier burden. Again Wisse: "The transfer of a system of values from religion, where it was appropriately lodged, to language, where it was assuredly not, placed upon Yiddish a new burden of exceptionalism, and one for which there was no national consensus."

**The system of Jewish Socialism:** Clearly, Jewish Socialism formed a Jewish component of international Socialism. That was the claim of the Jewish Workers Union, the Bund. But then what place for a Jewish sector or version of a general movement, systems bearing no particular message to Jews and addressing no problem unique to concerns of Jewish social entities? Jewish Socialism and Yiddishism formed a distinctive ideology out of aspects of the received system of the dual Torah as defined in Eastern Europe, the Yiddish language and the social ideals of the prophets and rabbis of old. Jewish Socialism demands attention in the study of the birth of Judaisms beyond the death, for many, of Talmudic Judaism because the movement at hand when reshaped to the special interests of Jews—hence, Jewish Socialism—offered to Jews in particular an ideology, a mode of social organization, a way of life and a world view, explaining who is Israel and what the Jews must do: a Judaism. That is not to suggest that all Jews who joined socialist parties or movements formed a single movement, Jewish Socialism, for the opposite is the case.

Many Socialists who happened to derive from Jewish families explicitly rejected that heritage of Jewish origin. In Germany, Poland, and Russia, important Socialist and Communist figures derived from Jewish parents but in no way sought in Socialism or Communism a mode of "being Jewish."

Quite to the contrary, Rosa Luxemberg, a leading German Socialist, and Leon Trotsky, a major Bolshevik leader in the early stages of the Russian Revolution, and the Jews in the leadership of the Polish Communist Party, though afflicted by anti-Semitism, treated particularly Jewish concerns as trivial or distasteful and said so. Nor does anyone imagine that because, in some circumstances, Socialism constituted a movement particularly attractive to Jews, Socialism demands attention in the study of the Judaisms of modern and contemporary provenance. Not everything Jews adopt as a way of life and a world view constitutes a Judaism, and most such things, in the nature of modern life, do not.

True, Jews were attracted to socialism in Western Europe partly by the appeal of "building a 'just society' based on the teachings of the prophets, partly by the hope that socialism would overcome and provenience anti-Semitism."[8] Still others turned to socialism as an instrument for their own exodus from the Jewish group, so Schneier Zalman Levenberg: "There were also Jews who saw in it a way of getting rid of their Jewish heritage and serving the cause of the 'Brotherhood of Man.' Socialism was particularly attractive for Jews anxious to leave the ghetto behind them and who, disappointed with the slow progress of 19th century liberalism, were keen to embrace a new universal faith."[9] None of this has any bearing on our subject, though these themes take a considerable place in the study of the ideas and politics of Jews in modern Europe and the U.S.A., as well, of course, as the State of Israel.

Ezra Mendelsohn describes the matter as follows: "[Jewish Socialism] refers to specifically Jewish movements and parties which envisaged the creation of a socialist society as an essential aspect of the solution to the Jewish question. This definition, while far from perfect, has the virtue of excluding Jews who happened to be socialist as well as socialist movements in which many Jews were active but which had no specifically Jewish content or aims."[10] Mendelsohn's definition amply justifies asking whether and how a Jewish Socialism took shape as a Judaic system. By every criterion, Jewish Socialism

serves. Informing its adherents how to conduct their lives, supplying them with a purpose and a meaning to existence, providing them with an explanation for history and a world-view encompassing the entirety of existence, defining for them the meaning of Israel and the place of Israel, the people, in the world, Jewish Socialism qualifies as a Judaism. In ways in which psychoanalysis did not form a Judaism, despite its appeal to Jewish practitioners, the Jewish Socialist system did. As Mendelsohn stresses, in addressing "the Jewish question," Jewish Socialism developed a system that would not only function like a Judaism but would exhibit those indicative traits that, all together, denote a Judaism.

When through the nineteenth and into the twentieth century, Jews in Eastern Europe ceased to find self-evident the system of the dual Torah, they did not become Reform, Conservative, or Orthodox. Reform answered questions of political definition that those Jews did not face, since no one ever offered them the promise of political "emancipation." Conservative Judaism relied upon Reform for its motive energy. Reacting against what it deemed excess, Conservative Judaism drew its power from the tensions of the center-position. But in Eastern Europe (as in the State of Israel today) it is difficult to locate that center among contending groups of a religious order. Orthodoxy had no message not delivered more eloquently by the life of the villages and the streets imbued with the received system. To explain to Jews within that system that the facts of nature and of supernature were equally facts answered a question of faith in a context of doubt that few within the received system perceived. And those who did come to doubt in the main sought some system other than the one retained and intellectually enriched by Orthodoxy in its philosophical mode. Those who found the Judaism of the dual Torah self-evidently irrelevant did not then seek a revisioning of that Torah. The reason is that the problems that occupied their lives scarcely intersected with the issues of that Torah, in any of its versions. What defined those problems was a long-term depression, severely aggravated by political stress in the very regions of Jewish settlement, the decline of agriculture and the economy that served it, the growth of population and consequent unemployment, for Jews in particular the growing and violent anti-Semitism of the state, of one ethnic identification, the Russian, and the population, of several others, Polish, Ukrainian, Lithuanian, Hungarian, and Rumanian, for instance. These constituted a crisis of a different order from the one addressed by the dual Torah.

One of the several interesting systemic alternatives derived from Socialism, and it was the Jewish kind that mattered. It mattered because it constituted a kind of "anti-Judaism," a systemic response, of a negative order, to the received system among those choosing to reject that system. Again Mendelsohn:

> Jewish socialism, so understood, could originate only in Eastern Europe, [where there were] . . . thousands of workers, the Yiddish-speaking "masses" so evident in the cities of western and southern Russia. Moreover, by the late nineteenth century a secular Jewish intelligentsia had developed in the Pale, consisting of students and professionals, many of whom were influenced by radical Russian ideologies. That they should be so was quite predictable, given the all-pervasive anti-Semitism which awakened their demands for social justice and made public activity, outside of radical circles, impossible. These Jewish intellectuals . . . were in revolt against the values and traditions of the ghetto. In many cases socialism, the acceptance of which in itself was a sign of assimilation, led them to discover the Jewish proletariat; this discovery, in turn, led them back to the Jewish people, to whom they preached the new doctrine.[11]

So much for the audience. What can one say of the doctrine and the way of life and address to (an) Israel?

The first stages in the formation of a doctrine of Jewish Socialism, of course, had to take up the issue: how can an internationalist movement recognize a particular ethnic group? The special needs of the Jewish working class, Jewish Socialists maintained, made Jewish Socialism not a kind of nationalism but a legitimate outgrowth of international socialism. What was needed, however, constituted no more—in the earliest phase of the movement—than Jewish unions. The original aim of the movement was to establish a school for socialism among Jews.[12] By the early 1890s, however, a distinct Jewish Socialist movement began to take shape. In 1897, the year of the formation of the Zionist Organization, the Jewish Socialist movement founded the General Jewish Workers Union in Russia and Poland, known as the Bund. Russian Marxists in the Russian Social Democratic Workers' Party declined to recognize the Jewish Union, a position consistently taken by Lenin and the Bolsheviks.

The ideology of the Bund took the shape of a Jewish national program, so Mendelsohn explains: "the Jewish proletariat, bearer of the Marxist mission, was also seen as the bearer of the Jewish national tradition as against the assimilated, Russified, or Polonized Jewish middle class."[13] The mode of expression? Celebration of the Yiddish language and literature. The Jewish Socialists adopted the Yiddish language as the language of the working class, maintained that reading Yiddish literature formed an expression of the movement, and argued that the Jews formed a group deserving national self-determination, like the other ethnic nations of Eastern Europe in both the Russian and the Austro-Hungarian empires. The Bund moved into system-building as it began to speak of the Jews' national rights, so forming a doctrine of Israel, aiming at the right to foster Yiddish cultural activities, so beginning to define a distinctive, public way of life for the Jewish entity ("People"? "nation"?) of the Russian and Austrian empires.

So, in all, the marriage of socialism and nationalism yielded that Jewish Socialism that formed an absorbing and encompassing system: way of life, world view, addressed to the people Israel. The way of life involved a panoply of institutions, unions, youth groups, and the like, that the Jewish Socialist movement formed for the organization of the working class. These organizations, with their meetings, rehearsals of the faith, enactment of recurrent rites, defined a kind of Jewish "civil religion," and that civil religion appealed to the ideals and emotions of the faithful in much the same spirit as the received system of the dual Torah. That is, as is clear, Jewish Socialism absorbed the devotee, explained what the adherent should do with his or her life (with women enjoying a more substantial role than in the Judaism of the dual Torah), and how that person should understand and interpret national and personal existence, so, again, a way of life and a world view. These claims of the Judaic-systemic classification of Jewish Socialism await the evidence of how, in a given system of life and thought, they worked themselves out: the concrete system as an interesting intellect gave it substance.

**The Judaic system of Yiddishism:** Just as Jewish Socialism developed a distinctively Judaic world-view and a way of life out of recalcitrant materials, so nothing can have proved less likely to yield an ideology than a language. But in the age in which (merely) speaking Yiddish became a statement of meaning, rather than a vehicle for the expression of meaning, one can identify a long list of languages that, in their respective settings, served the same purpose. Indeed, one of the recurrent traits of group life in the twentieth century would come to exemplary expression in Yiddishism, namely, the position that the language bears the meaning—the world-view, the way of life—of the group. Whether the celebration of Afrikaans, marking the inauguration of a renaissance of Afrikaans national politics in the Republic of South Africa, or the strong affirmation of Flemish in Belgium, or French in Canada, among numerous candidates world-wide, the picture proves uniform. What marks Yiddishism as especially interesting is the joining of linguistic assertion to the values of the class struggle espoused in Jewish Socialism. In the study of Judaic systems, that is the aspect of Yiddishism that attracts our interest.

The use of the Yiddish language as a vehicle of reaching the Jewish working class and of organizing the labor movement became a matter of ideology. Yiddish found itself transformed from an instrument of communication into a "cultural asset of national and intrinsic value."[14] Clearly, for speaking Yiddish to constitute a statement, then speaking some other language had also to matter, and,

among the Jews of Eastern Europe, the choice was Yiddish or Hebrew or the vernacular (Polish, Russian, for example). Yiddish, the language of the working class, took on the status of a symbol of a broader position, that outlined in our look at Jewish Socialism, and speaking Yiddish rather than some other language became an instrument of self-identification. Because speaking Hebrew stood for the Zionist position, speaking Yiddish constituted a mode of identification with the Jewish Socialist movement. The writers of Yiddish then enunciated an ideology of struggle against the exploitation of the worker, summoning the Jew "to struggle against his exploiters within and without and to sacrifice himself for social, political, and national liberation."[15] If then people ask who participated in that system identified as Yiddishism, we point first of all to writers and poets, but, then, to those to whom they spoke: who spoke the language and throughout asserted the values of system at hand, class struggle within Jewry, aiming at a liberation of all workers everywhere, so an international movement's Jewish section. Any Judaism has to identify its distinctive type of hero. For Jewish Socialism it was the labor union leader. For Yiddishism it was the poet, the writer. That the writers and poets served as counterparts to the rabbis and saints of the received Rabbinic Judaism found proof in their treatment among the enemies of Yiddishism and Jewish Socialism. On August 12, 1952, the most important Yiddish authors living in the Soviet Union were put to death by the Communist government of that country, which, for its reasons to be sure, thereby liquidated proponents of a world-view and a way of life to which it took exception.

Accordingly, speaking and writing a language form definitive components of a world view and a way of life. And that conception, so difficult of access for the speakers of American English, a homogenizing force in the life of diverse groups, finds its best proof in the Soviet government's recognition of Yiddish as a competing force. When Lenin declared his implacable opposition to Jewish Socialism, he gave evidence of discerning precisely the same trait: namely, that that set of organizations and views constituted a competing system, with its distinctive world-view and way of life. Nonetheless, these external testimonies to the character of Jewish Socialism with Yiddishism as a mode of organizing life and making sense of it leave open the question of how the system at hand actually worked. To answer that question, we turn to the testimony of individuals who expressed in their own words that larger world view and way of life by which they formed their identity.

**The union of Socialism and Yiddishism—Medem and Zhitlovsky:** The definition of the joined system of Jewish Socialism and Yiddishism gains concreteness when we consider the lives of important heroes of the system(s). These tell us in a vivid way how the Judaic system at hand functioned. What we see in the two figures before us is a trait characteristic of the Judaisms of the twentieth century: the creative power of once-alienated Jews in the forming of Judaic systems. Both of the exemplary heroes of the Judaic system before us began their lives and careers as outsiders and came back to a Judaism, but not to the Judaism of the dual Torah or of its continuators. What they came back to and what they brought with them would define the Judaic systems at hand: they came back to the group, and they brought with them things they had learned elsewhere, much as Moses came back to Israel but was identified, by the Israelites, as an Egyptian.

Vladimir Medem (1879-1923), after an upbringing in the Orthodox Church and as a Russian, identified himself as a Jew only through Jewish Socialism. He rejoined the Jews in his early twenties and identified, as a Jew and a Marxist, with the Bund. He spent his life in the service of the Jewish union, as writer and organizer and public speaker. That way of life encompassed his existence, much as, a generation before, spending his days in the study of the Talmud might have absorbed his life's energies. He represented the Bund at the second convention, in 1903, of the Russian Social Democratic Party in London,[16] served on the Committee Abroad of the Bund, contributed to Bund newspapers, served on the Bund Central Committee, and

on and on. So the way of life of Jewish Socialism, for the elite at least, involved a life of public activity in organizations. Medem took the view that the Bund should take an interest in Jewish community organization and should encourage the teaching of Yiddish. He strongly opposed Zionism while favoring Jewish national-cultural autonomy in the countries of Eastern Europe. He also opposed Communism in the Bund.

Medem, raised as a gentile by converted parents, regained his identification with Jews through Jewish Socialism, and the movement of his life—from one system to the other—strongly points to the comparability, in terms of his existence, between the one and the other. That is not to argue that Jewish Socialism for Medem formed a religion comparable to the (Russian, Christian) Orthodoxy of his youth. The two cannot have differed more radically. One was a religion in the narrow and accepted sense: a system of sacred duties in the service of God, the other was a secular identity. But Medem moved from the one to the other and to the second gave precisely those energies and commitments he had devoted to the first. So for him one world view and way of life gave way to another, each addressing the enduring issues of human life and society that he found required sorting out. And in his movement from outside to inside via the media of Jewish Socialism and Yiddishism, he typified the passage of Jews of the twentieth century, indeed, prefigured what would be the norm: traveling the road back. For characteristic of the movement in the nineteenth century was the way out, and in the twentieth (for those who sought the path), the way back. For many already outside, Yiddishism and Jewish Socialism showed the way.

How did Medem express this "Jewishness" that he discovered in Jewish Socialism? For one thing, he learned Yiddish. Speaking that language formed his entry into the Israel he would serve. For another, he identified with the Jews, describing the worship of a synagogue in these terms:

> . . . it was as though I had fallen among torrential waves. Hundreds upon hundreds of worshippers—each one taking his own case

to God, each in a loud voice with passionate eagerness. Hundreds of voices ascended to the heavens, each for himself, without concord, without harmony, yet all joining together in one tremendous clamorous sound. No matter how strange to the Western ear, it makes a deep impression and has a great beauty derived from the passion of mass feeling.[17]

The power that brought him to the Jews derived from "constant association with Jews and Jewish life:"

I cannot exactly determine how this "nationalizing" influence of the Jewish labor circles expressed itself. It was the quiet effect of day to day living. This life became dear and important to me. It was Jewish and it drew me into its environs.[18]

To be sure, we see no clear ideology comparable to the theology that identifies with God's will the way of life so cherished by Medem; no well-defined way of life emerges from (merely) associating with other Jews. Yet for Medem, exemplary of a great many, that is what Jewish Socialism provided: association, together with an articulated appreciation of that association; an ideal of life in the service of the laboring masses; a teleology of class struggle to which were imputed strong affinities with prophetic texts; a definition of Israel as apart from the international working classes; an ideal of how to use one's life on earth, and with whom: a Judaism, as self-evidently valid to Medem as was Orthodoxy to Samson Raphael Hirsch.

The joining of Yiddishism to Socialism finds its best representative in Chaim Zhitlowsky (1865-1943). Lucy Dawidowicz describes him as "the example par excellence of the modern radical Jew drawn to non-Jewish intellectual and revolutionary society, yet reluctant, despite his ambivalence toward the Jewish group, to divorce himself from it."[19] Hostile to Judaism as a supernatural religion, Zhitlowsky provided for Yiddish the ideological position as the foundation for the renewal of Jewish culture, parallel to a renewal of the Jewish people along economic lines: "Jews were to become 'productive' and 'nonparasitic' elements in a socialist economy."[20] So Yiddish would serve as the vehicle of national cultural identity, along with Socialism as the definition of the entity's organization of its productive life. Yiddish was meant to serve as a weapon in the class-war, Dawidowicz points out. Since, in later times, ideologists identified the Jews' participation in socialism, or, in the U.S.A., in liberal politics, as part of their prophetic heritage, it is important to note that that identification, for the thinker at hand, came much after the fact:

Did I assimilate this concept of internationalism from our Jewish prophets? True, the best of them first promulgated the pure internationalist ideal of a fraternizing society. . . . But I knew almost nothing of the prophets. We had learned about them in heder, but only incidentally and according to the interpretation of a later Jewry uninterested in such "trivialities." . . . . Did my internationalism originate in a Jewish religious world view which reigned in our world of Jewish ideas? . . . . First, Jewish religion was of no interest to me . . . the idea of chosenness was conspicuous for its glaring chauvinism. Second, national diversity in the Jewish world view was distorted to mean that Jews differed from Gentiles, but all Gentiles were alike. Third, even nationalism, a basic element of internationalism, was not quite a pure element because it was pervaded with religion. . . .[21]

Any claim, therefore, that the received system took its natural next steps toward Socialism finds little proof in Zhitlovsky's memoirs; he is quite explicit to the contrary. Zhitlovsky found in Socialism a road out of the Jewish condition of being victim of anti-Semitism: "For me personally, the idea of cosmopolitanism was for a time like healing balm for the pain I had felt ever since it had been explained to me that we Jews lived a parasitic existence."[22] What struck Zhitlovsky was the need for a language and a literature that would explain to Jews the life, ideas, hopes, and aspirations, of the Jews. What Zhitlovsky sought was a socialist theory "that harmoniously united socialist ideals with the problems of Jewish life." Describing a sequence of conversion-experiences, Zhitlovsky explains that, to carry out his moral responsibility to remain faithful to the Jewish people, he would devote his life to a work of "enlightenment and struggle for those universal foundations of human progress which could be advocated even under Russian censorship:"[23]

The decision to issue the journal in Yiddish did not originate from any conscious Yiddishism. The theoretical works on nationality . . . gave no particular importance to language. . . . My reasoning then went something like this: One must talk to a people in its own language. But our people use two languages, Hebrew and Yiddish. In the world in which I grew up, both languages had the same prestige. . . . The question facing me was to decide in which language to appeal to Jews, not just the ignorant masses, but the whole people, to train an avant-garde to fight for the ideals of universal progress and for their realization in Jewish life. I decided on Yiddish. This was my calculation: We, the carriers of ideas of universal human progress, had to appeal to the people with our message about quite a new world, the world of modern, progressive, West European culture. Vis a vis this world, the whole Jewish people were like the ignorant masses. . . . One had to use the language that everyone understood. That was Yiddish, the vernacular of every Jew. . . .[24]

Zhitlovsky's contribution, therefore, was the advocacy of Yiddish as the instrument of Socialism and reform. Others held that the use of Yiddish would form an obstacle to the assimilation of the Jews. Zhitlowsky for his part demanded equal national rights for the Jews, as a distinct national group in the Russian empire.[25] These rights would be effected through their sustaining their own national language. Socialism would transform the Jews into part of the working class. The Yiddish language would express their ideals of productive labor and solidarity with humanity. Socialism did not require cosmopolitanism but allowed nations to develop in a multi-national community. So Melech Epstein states: Yiddish literature . . . did not originate in a drawing room. . . . Yiddish literature was a people's art, a conscious medium for uplifting. It carried an impelling social and moral message to the ordinary man and woman. . . .[26]

The Yiddishists found themselves drawn by humanitarian impulses, the Socialists by a more rigorous theoretical vision, but together they formed a powerful phalanx within Jewry. But did they add up to a Judaism? The Jewish Socialists, in the definition of Mendelsohn, assuredly thought so. They clearly formed a consciousness of "uniquely Jewish needs and dilemmas."[27] They did make the effort to draw on inherited writings, "a past culture which could not be totally denied or repressed," and they recognized the need of Jewish workers "to find a Jewish, as well as socialist, identity."[28] Language of this kind points to the formation of a Judaism: a way of life, joined to a world view, addressed to an Israel. The way of life involved union activity and political agitation in causes in no way distinctively Jewish; the world view was taken over from socialism in its Eastern European redaction; the people Israel was the working class of Jewish origin. Yet Medem and Zhitlovsky found in these components common to all Socialist lives, all socialist systems of thought, the wherewithal for what they regarded as a distinctive doctrine, which accounted for a life particular to Jews: encompassing, ample, adequate to the purpose.

**Socialism-Yiddishism as a Judaism:** The claim that in Jews' particular expression of Socialism a Judaism emerged and that in Jews' framing of the linguistic nationalism of the age another is to be found must puzzle people who take for granted that a Judaism must be a religion. In such a definition of a Judaism, one may invoke the classification of religion, then treat as a subdivision of that classification, Judaism, and, within Judaism, diverse Judaisms. But that conception of matters imposes on Jews categories alien to their diverse historical cultural expressions. Singling out as a distinct and distinctive aspect of culture something one defines as religion violates the classification-system of the Judaism of the inherited sort, the system of the dual Torah, and indicates—by itself—the hegemony of a peculiarly nineteenth century and Protestant view of matters. That same stress on a Judaism as a type of a religion moreover lays enormous emphasis on systems of ideas, theology or ideology, since, when people define a religion, they ordinarily focus upon things people believe rather than things they do, and they treat belief as an aspect of the definition of the individual's world-view rather than as the principal component of a whole society's conceptual basis.

But if one comes at matters from the angle of the society—the particular "Israel" at hand—there is no difficulty in treating as a Judaism something that in no way constitutes a religion. A Judaism addresses a particular people that defines itself as Israel, and an Israel finds its self-understanding in the world-view of a Judaism, its way of living as a society in the way of life posited by a Judaism. Among the three components of a social and cultural system, way of life, world view, and social definition, the third takes priority, and that explains why a massive movement made up only of Jews who claim to speak a Jewish language and form a Jewish social entity should constitute a Judaism. Yiddishism therefore forms a critical component in under-standing why Jewish Socialism and Yiddishism constitute a Judaism, just as the Zionist ideal of resurrecting the Hebrew language and the Jewish State makes Zionism— a Jewish movement of national emancipation—into a Judaism.

Claiming a continuity in values with the received Rabbinic Judaism, Yiddishism, both with and without Socialism, to its founders and framers solved important problems. These problems, for those who confronted them, proved urgent and pressing. The way of life—the use of language, the devotion to organizations or to writing or to reading— and the world view, bound up with a particular evaluation of the Jews and their values do coalesce and present a cogent and coherent answer to a large and encompassing question. Self-evident? To those who found the question urgent, the answer scarcely demanded argument and apology. It was beyond all doubt a Judaism. But the urgent questions in no way corresponded to those answered by the received system, and the answers originated in places other than the Torah. So in Yiddishism and Socialism is discerned a Judaism out of all relationship with the Judaism of the past, articulately and explicitly alienated from the Judaism of the dual Torah.

In no way do Yiddishism and Socialism, severally or jointly, develop in an incremental relationship to the Rabbinic Judaism regnant for fifteen hundred years, and in no way do they mark the natural next step out of that earlier and established system. The difference between this Judaism and the nineteenth

century Orthodoxy and Reform Judaisms is blatant. No one carried out the pretense of claiming continuities that people in any case did not want. And no one found in the received literature more than a set of evocative and useful texts for the persuasion of people who, unlike those who made the selections, responded to the authority and to the values of those words. Socialism and Yiddishism did not trouble to explain how they related to the received Judaism, because to begin with their framers proposed to break the ties utterly and completely. That is why they undertook their labor of shaping and defining a system of their own. And that is precisely what they accomplished. And yet none can deny that they set forth a Judaic system, precisely as they claimed to do. They specified their Israel, the Yiddish-speaking working classes, they worked out their world view, the amalgam of socialist theory and sherds and remnants of appropriate sayings, and above all, they knew just who Israel was. Some would question characterizing Socialism and Yiddishism as a Judaism. But the framers of the system maintained that one can and should. In its founders' view, the union yielded a new entity, but, unlike the Judaisms of the nineteenth century, a born, not a reborn Judaism. It did posit a way of life. It told them the meaning of history and linked the individual to the large movement of time.

To be sure, Jewish Socialism and Yiddishism did not enjoy staying power. Their way of life served only the first generation of Jewish Socialists and Yiddishists, which proved to be a transitional generation. The Judaic system of social action and linguistic preference did not produce a second generation for itself, again Wisse: "It is not simply that the children of the Yiddishists no longer speak to their children in Yiddish. . . . Yiddishism, which was meant to serve Jewish cohesion, had no . . . self-regenerating powers, and Yiddishkeyt was but a transitional phase in which a secular generation enjoyed the fruits of a religious civilization."[29] But for that first generation the system did answer the same questions as did other systems. And that is what marks as a Judaism the set of ideas, the doctrine of how life is to be lived, the definition of the Israel at hand. How long a system lasts, where it comes from, where it heads—these form the epiphenomena of description, not the center and heart of analysis. Had the vast populations to whom these mated Judaisms proved self-evidently true survived World War II and endured in societies prepared to accommodate them on their own terms, who knows the terms those populations might have defined for themselves? Jewish Socialism and Yiddishism, in their nature, would have formed the single most powerful force within whatever Judaisms the reconstituted Jews of Poland, Rumania, Hungary, not to mention the lands of the former Soviet empire, might have made for themselves. But they are all dead.

### Notes

[1] Quoted by Melech Epstein, *Profiles of Eleven. Profiles of Eleven Men Who Guided the Destiny of an Immigrant Society and Stimulated Social Consciousness among the American People* (Detroit, 1965), p. 17.

[2] Ruth R. Wisse, "The Politics of Yiddish," in *Commentary* 1985, 80, 1, pp. 29-35. Quotation on p. 29.

[3] Ibid., p. 30.

[4] Ibid., p. 31.

[5] Ibid., p. 32.

[6] Ibid., p. 33.

[7] Ibid., p. 33.

[8] Schneier Zalman Levenberg, "Socialism," in *Jewish Encyclopaedia*, vol. 15, cols. 24-29.

[9] Op. cit., col. 25.

[10] Ezra Mendelsohn, "Socialism, Jewish," in *Encyclopaedia Judaica*, vol. 15, cols. 38-52. Quotation: col. 38.

[11] Ibid., col. 38.

[12] Ibid., col. 39.

[13] Ibid., col. 42.

[14] Chone Shmeruk, "Yiddish Literature," in *Encyclopaedia Judaica*, vol. 16, cols. 798-833. Quotation: col. 811.

[15] Ibid.

[16] Moshe Mishkinsky, "Vladimir Medem," in *Encyclopaedia Judaica*, vol. 11, cols. 1175-1176.

[17] Lucy S. Dawidowicz, ed., *The Golden Tradition. Jewish Life and Thought in Eastern Europe* (New York, 1967), p. 432.

[18] Ibid., p. 434.

[19] Ibid., p. 411.

[20] Ibid., p. 411.

[21] Ibid., p. 412.

[22] Ibid., p. 415.

[23] Ibid., p. 421.

[24] Ibid., pp. 421-422.

[25] Yerucham Tolkes, "Chaim Zhitlowsky," in *Encyclopaedia Judaica*, vol. 16, cols. 1009-1011.

[26] Melech Epstein, *Jewish Labor in the U.S.A. An Industrial, Political and Cultural History of the Jewish Labor Movement* (New York, 1969), p. 275.

[27] Nora Levin, *While the Messiah Tarried. Jewish Socialist Movements, 1871-1917* (New York, 1977), p. ix.

[28] Ibid., p. x.

[29] Ibid., p. 35.

JACOB NEUSNER

**SOUL IN JUDAISM:** The inner, animating element of human beings, the soul stands in contrast to the physical body, generally comprehended as the vehicle that contains the soul. Within this general definition, cultures throughout the world express a wide range of understandings of the meaning and function of the soul. In ancient near-eastern cultures, for instance, the soul was broadly associated with physical appearance, destiny, and power. Within the culture of ancient Israel, by contrast, rather than being seen as an aspect of personality or identity, the soul was associated primarily with respiration, narrowly signifying the life force. This is reflected in the root meanings of Hebrew words generally translated as soul: *nefesh* ("breath"), *neshamah* ("breathing"), and *ruah* (literally, "wind"). Having to do primarily with respiration, these terms encompass the Latin terms for soul, *anima*, which is close to the Hebrew concept of *ruah*, and *spiritus*, which parallels the Hebrew terms *nefesh* and *neshamah*.

The Hebrew Bible conceives every living thing to have a soul, that is, a "life-force." This life-force is associated with the creature's blood and is understood to derive ultimately from God's own *ruah*, that is, the "spirit" or "wind" from God that Gen. 1:2 describes as moving over the face of the waters at the time of God's creation of the world. It is this *ruah* that God breathed into the first man's nostrils so as to give him life: "Then the Lord God formed man of dust from the ground, and breathed into his nostrils the breath of life; and man became a living being" (Gen. 2:7). Death, comparably, is understood in the Bible to occur when the soul (*nefesh*) leaves the body, as Gen. 35:18 makes explicit: "And as her soul was departing (for she died), she called his name Ben-o'ni. . . .''

Scripture's associating of the soul or life-force—that aspect of all living creatures that derives from God—with blood accounts for the prohibition against eating meat from which all blood has not been drained. Gen. 9:4 and Lev. 17:14, among other similar verses, are specific in making this connection between the soul and blood: "Only you shall not eat flesh with its life (*nefesh*), that is, its blood" (Gen. 9:4). This same association undoubtedly accounts for the taboos against menstrual blood (Lev. 15:19) as well as for the important function of the blood of sacrifices in cultic rituals. In these rituals, the animal's life force, represented by its blood, has expiatory power, as Lev. 17:11 makes explicit: "For the life of the flesh is in the blood; and I have given it for you upon the altar to make atonement for your souls; for it is the blood that makes atonement, by reason of the life."

In the case of humans in particular, Scripture assigns to the soul an additional function that exists alongside its association with breath (the "life-force") and blood. Additionally, Scripture uses the term "soul"—*nefesh*—to stand for the person him or herself. In this usage, the term soul stands for the essential substance of the human being, the seat of emotions, passions, appetite and, on occasion, even knowledge. The soul feels love and longs for another person, as at Gen. 34:3: "And [Shechem's] soul was drawn to Dinah the daughter of Jacob; he loved the maiden and spoke tenderly to her;" the soul experiences distress, as at Gen. 42:21: ". . . we saw the distress of his [that is, our brother's] soul, when he besought us and we would not listen;" the soul belongs to or, as a result of sin, is cut off from the people of Israel, as at Exod. 31:14: "whoever does any work on it [that is, the Sabbath], that soul shall be cut off from among his people;" and the soul is the seat of true knowledge, e.g., of God, as at Deut. 11:18: "You shall therefore lay up these words of mine in your heart and in your soul."

Even as we are conscious of the broad and very common biblical usage of the term "soul," we must be clear that Scripture does not present even a rudimentarily developed *theology* of the soul. The creation narrative is clear that all life originates with God. Yet the Hebrew Scripture offers no specific understanding of the origin of individual souls, of when and how they become attached to specific bodies, or of their potential existence, apart from the body, after death. The reason for this is that, as we noted at the beginning, the Hebrew Bible does not present a theory of the soul developed much beyond the simple concept of a force associated with respiration, hence, a life-force. As the life-force, the soul represents the sum and substance of the person, such that Ps. 11:5 can even depict God as having a soul: "The Lord tests the righteous and the wicked, and his soul hates him that loves violence." But beyond this general association, in which "soul" refers to the essence of the individual, the Hebrew Bible offers no conception of the soul as an independent creation. The notion of the soul as an independent force that animates human life but that can exist apart from the human body—either prior to conception and birth or subsequent to life and death—is the product only of later Judaism.

**The concept of the soul in Rabbinic Judaism:** Like Scripture, the Talmudic literature envisions a close connection between body and soul. Rabbinic authorities do not conceive of the soul's immortality separate from that of the body. Nor do they imagine the transmigration of the soul from one body to another. Body and soul, rather, are seen as separate only in origin, with the body deriving from human parents and the soul originating with God. In practice, the soul, created and bestowed upon the body by God, is taken back to God at death. At the time of the resurrection, it will be restored to that same body (see Y. Kil. 8:4, 31c, and B. Ber. 60a).

The rabbis continue in the overall perspective of the soul presented in the Hebrew Scriptures, including the use of the same terminology, explained as follows (Gen. Rabbah 14:9):

1.A. "[. . . and breathed into his nostrils] the breath of life" (Gen. 2:7):
   B. It is called by five names: spirit (*nefesh*), wind (*ruah*), soul (*neshamah*), unique, and life.

C. "Spirit" refers to the blood: "For the blood is called the spirit" (Deut. 12:23).

D. "Wind," because it goes up and down [like the wind]: "Who knows the soul [*ruah*] of man, whether it goes up, [and the wind of the beast whether it goes downward to the earth]" (Ec. 3:21).

E. "Soul" refers to [the person's] disposition, as people say, "He has a good disposition."

F. "Life," because even though all the limbs perish, it continues to live on in the body.

G. "Unique," for all the limbs in the body are two, but it is unique in the body [two arms, two legs, but one soul].

As in Scripture, the rabbis associate the soul with the animating elements of the body, represented by the blood (C) and breath (D). The soul further represents the person him or herself, standing for the individual's disposition or, more broadly, character (E). What this Rabbinic passage adds to the biblical conception appears at F, a rudimentary expression of the notion that the death of the body does not signify (or result from) the death of the soul. This is an idea that receives full expression within the Rabbinic literature, as we shall see below.

The Rabbis understand all human souls to have been brought into existence during creation, as aspects of the wind or spirit (*ruah*) of God referred to at Gen. 1:2. Accordingly, the messiah will come either when these prepared souls have been used up or, alternatively, when God has finished creating all of the souls that he intended to create from the beginning. B. A.Z. 5a makes the point as follows:

A. And said R. Yose, "The son of David will come only when all of the souls that are stored up in the *Guf*[1] will be used up: 'For I will not contend for ever, neither will I be always angry, for the spirit should fall before me and the spirits which I have made' (Is. 57:16)."

B. Hag. 12b makes the same point:

A. [Explaining one of the items on Simeon b. Laqish's list of the seven firmaments:] "heavy cloud": that is where there are right, judgment, and righteousness, the treasures of life and the treasures of peace and the treasures of blessing, the souls of the righteous and the spirits and souls that are yet to be born, and dew with which

the Holy One, blessed be he, in the age to come will revive the dead.

The soul, in Talmudic thought, thus exists prior to the conception of the corporeal body. As the product of human sperm, the body, unlike the soul, is subject to decay. Still, in the Rabbinic ideology, despite the soul and body's separate origins and the fact that they will again be separated at death, the soul's destiny is tied directly to that of the body. A highly developed depiction of the relationship between soul and body appears in the late Rabbinic midrashic compilation Tanhuma, which describes the procedure through which God determines the characteristics of a person who is about to be conceived. Tanhuma Exod., Piqudei 3, holds that God chooses whether the person will be male or female, strong or weak, and selects as well a range of other characteristics. But the question of whether the individual is to be wicked or righteous is left open to the person's own free will. This aspect of the person's life, that is to say, will be determined by the course selected by the soul:

A. The Holy One, blessed be he, motions to the angel in charge of the souls (*ruahot*) and tells him, "Bring me this certain soul, which is in the Garden of Eden, whose name is Such-and-So, and whose appearance is such-and-such."

B. For all of the souls that were ever to be created, all of them were created on the day that [God] created the world.

C. Before the world will come to an end, they will be assigned to [specific] people, as it is written [Ec. 6:10]: "Whatever will come to be has already been named."

D. Immediately, the angel goes and brings the soul before the Holy One, blessed be he.

E. And when it comes, immediately it bends down and bows its knees before the king of kings of kings, the Holy One, blessed be he.

F. Then the Holy One, blessed be he, says to that soul, "Enter into this drop [of semen] of so-and-so!"

G. The soul opens its mouth and says to him: "Master of the universe! The world in which I have lived from the day on which you created me is good enough for me! Why do you wish to place me in that decaying drop, for I am holy and pure, and I have been hewn from your glory."

H. Immediately, the Holy One, blessed be he, says to this soul (*neshamah*), "The world into which I am going to place you is better for you than the one in which you have lived until now."

I. "And, at the time at which I created you, I created you only for this [particular] drop!"

J. Immediately, the Holy One, blessed be he, places it there against its will, and then the angel goes and places the soul in the womb of its mother.

K. And they call upon two [other] angels, which watch over [the soul], so that it does not leave there and so that it does not miscarry.

L. And they place there a lit candle on its head, as Scripture states [Job 29:3], "Oh, that I were as in the months of old, as in the days when God watched over me; when his lamp shone upon my head [and by his light I walked through darkness]."

M. And [by that candle's light] it can look and see from one end of the world to the other.

N. The angel takes it from there and brings it to the Garden of Eden, and shows it the righteous sitting in glory with their crowns on their heads, and the angel says to that soul, "Do you know who these are?"

O. Says to him the soul, "No, my lord."

P. So the angel continues and says, "They that you see were created in the beginning just like you, within the wombs of their mothers, and they went out into the world and observed the Torah and the commandments. Therefore, they were deemed worthy and this good that you see came to them.

Q. "Know, that you are destined to leave the world, and if you are worthy and observe the Torah and the commandments of the Holy One, blessed be he, you will be worthy of this and of the same place they have [earned]."

R. "But if not, know and realize that you will be worthy of a different place."

The continuation of the passage describes how the soul, now residing within the growing embryo, is shown all of the world and the potential for doing good and evil. The important point is that while the rabbis understand the soul to preexist the body and to be eternal, they also view it as having no meaningful existence outside of the body. Prior to placement in the womb, and following death, it is neither intrinsically good nor evil. It is

judged, rather, by the actions of the body that was its home. Hence while the rabbis hold that the soul is of divine origin and gives life, as in the conception of the Hebrew Scripture they understood it very much to be the embodiment of the person, good or evil depending upon the life and choices of that person.

The rabbis' notion that the soul participates in the choice of how the person lives his or her life is made clear at B. San. 91a-91b, which holds that, at the time of the resurrection, the soul and the body will be brought back together for judgment:

A. Antoninus said to Rabbi, "The body and the soul both can exempt themselves from judgment.

B. "How so? The body will say, 'The soul is the one that has sinned, for from the day that it left me, lo, I am left like a silent stone in the grave.'

C. "And the soul will say, 'The body is the one that sinned. For from the day that I left it, lo, I have been flying about in the air like a bird.'"

D. He said to him, "I shall draw a parable for you. To what may the matter be likened? To the case of a mortal king who had a lovely orchard, and in it were [91b] luscious figs. He set in it two watchmen, one crippled and one blind.

E. "Said the cripple to the blind man, 'There are luscious figs that I see in the orchard. Come and carry me, and let us get some to eat. The cripple rode on the blind man and they got the figs and ate them. After a while the king said to them, 'Where are the luscious figs?'

F. "Said the cripple, 'Do I have feet to go to them?'

G. "Said the blind man, 'Do I have eyes to see?'

H. "What did the king do? He had the cripple climb onto the blind man, and he inflicted judgment on them as one.

I. "So the Holy One, blessed be he, brings the soul and places it back in the body and judges them as one, as it is said, 'He shall call to the heavens from above and to the earth, that he may judge his people' (Ps. 50:4).

J. "'He shall to call to the heavens from above'—this is the soul.

K. "'And to the earth, that he may judge his people'—this is the body."

This close connection between body and soul explains the rabbis' notion that, upon death, the soul would have a place either in the

Garden of Eden or Gehennah, depending on whether, during life, it had been wicked or righteous (B. Shab. 152b):

    A. It has been taught on Tannaite authority:

    B. R. Eliezer says, "The souls of the righteous are hidden away under the throne of glory: 'Yet the soul of my lord shall be bound up in the bundle of life with the Lord your God' (1 Sam. 25:29). And those of the wicked are kept in prison. One angel stands at one end of the world, and another angel stands at the other end of the world, and they sling their souls from one to the other: 'And the souls of your enemies, them shall he sling out, as from the hollow of a sling'" (1 Sam. 25:29)."

    C. Said Rabbah to R. Nahman, "So what about the middling ones?"

    D. He said to him, "If I'd not died, I couldn't have told you this fact: this is what Samuel said, 'These and those [the souls of the middling and of the wicked] are handed over to Dumah. These get rest, those get no rest.'"

While immortal, a direct creation of God, even the soul's destiny is not predetermined. It reflects, rather, the manner in which the particular soul made use of the free will that the rabbis understood people to have.

During life, the soul's divine origin remains significant. While the body sleeps, for instance, the soul nourishes it to keep it from dying. The rabbis debated how this was accomplished (Gen. Rabbah 14:9):

    2.A. ["The breath of life . . ." (Gen. 2:7)]: That is in line with the following verse of Scripture: "If he set his heart upon man, if he gather unto himself his spirit and his soul, all flesh shall perish together, and man shall return to the dust" (Job 34:14).

    B. R. Joshua b. R. Nehemiah and Rabbis.

    C. R. Joshua b. R. Nehemiah said, "'If he,' meaning God, 'set his heart upon man,' refers to this man, Adam. 'His spirit' then indicates that [in the evening, God] already had [man's] spirit. 'And gather to himself his soul' means into [one part of] his body [instead of having it pervade all his limbs] 'then all flesh shall perish together.' Thus when a man is asleep, his soul heats up his body, so that he should not waste away and die."

    D. Rabbis say, "'If he,' meaning God, 'set his heart upon man,' refers to this man, Adam. 'His spirit' then indicates that [God] already had his spirit. 'And if he gather to himself his soul' above, then all men should perish equally. Thus when a man goes to sleep, the soul warms his blood so that he should not grow cold and die."

    E. R. Bisni, R. Aha, R. Yohanan in the name of R. Meir: "The soul fills the body, and when man is asleep, it goes up and draws life for him from above."

    F. R. Levi in the name of R. Haninah, "It goes up and down [at each breath]. For each breath that a man takes, it therefore is proper to praise the Holy One, blessed be he. What is the verse of Scripture that so indicates? 'Let every breath praise the Lord' (Ps. 150:6). That is, on account of each and every breath [one should praise the Lord]."

While disagreeing on the specifics of how this works, all Rabbinic authorities concur that the soul is that part of the human that belongs to God and gives the body life. Without the soul, the body would become cold and perish. At the same time, as the other cited passages make clear, the rabbis do not view the soul as uniquely pure or unaffected by the same inclination to sin that affects the body. While separate in origin, rather, during life, the soul and body comprise a single entity, the person as a whole. At the time of death, the soul, which is immortal, returns to God. But it there must wait for the time of the resurrection, when it will be replaced in that same body, within which it will undergo God's final judgment.

**The concept of the soul in medieval Judaism:**[2] Medieval Jewish philosophers argued that all living things have souls, including plants and animals as well, of course, as humans and even heavenly bodies.[3] Indeed, the human soul was understood to have affinities with those of plants and animals, and was differentiated from these forms of living things only through its distinctive connection to a larger, encompassing emanation. In the Neoplatonists' system, this is the World Soul, which emanates from the Universal Intellect. In the Aristotelian theory, by contrast, the human soul is associated with the souls of the celestial spheres, which, in the Aristotelian view, comprise the rational principle that stands behind all movement. In both of these theories, the human soul frequently was pictured as the body's ruler, the source of perception and the principle of life. And yet, following the Talmudic picture and comprehending the soul as immortal and perfect, derived from God and destined to survive the death of the body, the medieval Jewish thinkers also understood the soul to be a stranger on earth, longing to return to its place of divine origin.

Following a mixture of Platonic and Aristotelian thought, Saadiah Gaon (882-942) understood the soul to be created by God from nothing at the moment of the completion of the body. Body and soul formed an inseparable unit during life and, again, in the coming world. The soul provided the body with the faculties of reason and sensation, even as the body, through its moral acts, allowed the immaterial substance of the soul to fulfill its purpose. Solomon ibn Gabirol (1021-1058) and others who followed Plato generally viewed the soul as a distinct entity that was joined to the body. Others, for instance, Abraham ibn Daud (1110-1180), who followed Aristotle, argued that the soul was an aspect of the body and not separable from it. This view stands in contrast to the earlier Talmudic perspective.

In keeping with the earlier Rabbinic view, medieval Jewish philosophers in general rejected belief in the transmigration of souls, a view that they deemed incompatible with the doctrine of resurrection. For if a soul could, over time, animate more than one body, then bodily resurrection would not appear to be possible, there being fewer souls than bodies. Kabbalistic mystics, however, disagreed on this point, making the transmigration of souls a central doctrine of their system of Judaism.

The Zohar, for its part, understood the three Hebrew terms that refer to soul each to designate a different human faculty.[4] Access to the world of intellect is provided through the *neshamah*, which the Zohar identified as the rational faculty and understood to emanate from the sphere called the "Crown" (*keter*). *Ruah* is the moral faculty, emanating from the sphere called "Beauty" (*tiferet*) and

giving people knowledge of the world of creativity. Emanating from the sphere called "Foundation" (*yesod*), the vital faculty, *nefesh*, is related to the world of practical action.

### Notes
[1] Literally, "body," the name of the storehouse of souls in heaven (Rashi). See Marcus Jastrow, *A Dictionary of the Targumim, the Talmud Babli and Yerushalmi . . .* (New York, reprint, 1971), p. 225, s.v., *gwp*.
[2] See also JUDAISM, PHILOSOPHY AND THEOLOGY OF, IN MEDIEVAL TIMES.
[3] On the following see Alfred Ivry, "Soul" in *EJ*, vol. 15, cols. 172-174.
[4] On the following see Gershom Scholem, "Soul, Immortality of . . ., In Kabbalah" in *EJ*, vol. 15, cols. 180-181.

ALAN J. AVERY-PECK

**SOUTH AFRICA, PRACTICE OF JUDAISM IN:** "South African Judaism" refers to the religious beliefs and practices of the approximately 70,000-80,000 Jews living in South Africa today. For a number of reasons, this local Jewish community is unique. First, it exists in the only country in the world in which a substantial Jewish community lives within a black majority, a fact made more significant by the unique transition from apartheid to democracy that has occurred in the past decade. Second, South African Jewry is English-speaking, so that—especially in light of the periodic return of many emigrants—the community has knowledge of and, theoretically, should be open to at least some of the trends and innovations currently taking place in other English-speaking Jewish communities, such as the United States and England.

Yet South African Jews are deeply insular. Some scholars attribute this conservatism to the Anglo-Lithuanian origins of the community, a spirit that is still very much evident and provides the conceptual basis for the power of an Orthodox rabbinate. Others have focused on the legacy of apartheid in conditioning the community, and yet others note as a contributing factor the historical existence in South Africa of only two denominations, Orthodoxy and, more recently, Reform. Conservative Judaism and other contemporary movements—including Reconstructionism, Jewish Renewal, Havurot, and Jewish

Humanism—that have developed in the United States and elsewhere are for the most part completely absent from and virtually unknown in South Africa.

**The Litvak "invasion:"** The earliest Jews to build communities in South Africa were British, arriving when the British first settled the Cape around 1820. But since their numbers remained small, the character of South African Jewry was significantly changed beginning in 1880, when the first of the some 70,000 Eastern European, primarily Lithuanian, Jews who would arrive prior to 1948 came to the country.

Although many of the Lithuanian immigrants settled in urban areas, many other "pioneers" sought their fortunes in less developed areas, such as Natal, the Transvaal, and the Orange Free State. Many became peddlers on the veld (the great southern African plains), eventually opening prosperous country stores. Particularly successful and well known were the Lithuanian Jews in the town of Oudshorn in the Karoo province area, who were pioneers in the ostrich feather trade and developed an important import-export business. Although these early Jewish settlers could not legally hold public office or be in the civil service, many of them became respected leaders in their communities.

The Jewish immigrants quickly began building their own communities. Previously the synagogues had performed most of the educational, financial, and social functions in addition to religious ones. Now separate institutions were formed to facilitate life in the community. Jewish day schools were first established in the 1880s. A number of social welfare institutions were founded in the 1890s, in particular in Cape Town and Johannesburg. These included traditional *chevras* for Torah and Talmud study and a Jewish hospital with a kosher kitchen and Yiddish-speaking staff. The pressure to provide even more services was intensified during the Anglo-Boer War (1899-1902), when some ten thousand Jews fled the Transvaal and took refuge in Cape Town. After the war, federations of existing organizations were modeled on the Anglo-Jewish pattern. Jewish Boards of Deputies were established for

Transvaal and Natal in 1903 and the Cape Colony in 1904.

**Immigration in the twentieth century:** Jews were allowed to immigrate to South Africa fairly freely until immigration was severely curtailed by the Quota Act of 1930 and effectively stopped by the Aliens Act of 1937. As a result, from the 1930s until the early 1970s there was no significant immigration to the Jewish community of South Africa, a circumstance that led to the creation of a native-born Jewish population even more homogenous than the existing immigrant community, comprised primarily of Jews from Lithuania who had adopted certain British institutional models. Now that homogeneous background was reinforced and exaggerated, creating a highly cohesive and unified Jewish community that sees its origins in very definitive terms. The majority of South African Jews feel that they share similar roots and values. No influx of newcomers has created a need for pluralistic models that would integrate different types of Jews into the Jewish community.

**The synthesis of Anglo-Jewish religions and institutional forms:** The so-called "British" Jews[1] were the founders and leaders of all of the institutions of South African Jewry in the early years. As Lithuanian Jews arrived in greater numbers, they joined these institutions and, as in other British colonies, such as Australia, New Zealand, and even the United States, they initially looked to Britain as a religious model.

This English influence was evident—and to some extent still is—in a number of important areas. First is the institution of Chief Rabbi. For a long time, the Chief Rabbi of Britain was looked to as the ultimate spiritual and religious head of the local community; even since that time, all Chief Rabbis have come from Great Britain. Aspects of South African Jewish liturgical ritual also parallel the British model. Services contain a prayer, in the vernacular, for the government and generally used the Singer, and later, the Adler prayer books. Only very recently were these books replaced by the Birnbaum edition and, finally, after 1980, by the Art Scroll prayer book. Until 1945, when they were banned by Chief Rabbi Louis Rabinowitz, there was a tradition of mixed choirs in many Orthodox synagogues, and, until recently, rabbis and cantors wore robes and caps.[2] Further, most synagogues use the Hertz Pentateuch, a product of English-style modern Orthodoxy that has been overwhelmingly used in English-speaking countries for over half a century, though today it is regarded as outmoded and somewhat apologetic. Finally, there is a preference for large, ornate synagogues and a more elaborate worship service than is found in the Litvak tradition, for example, with much pomp and ceremony surrounding the Torah procession prior to the Sabbath Torah reading.

These Briticisms, however, have always been matched by a strong Lithuanian influence on the beliefs and practices of South African Jews. South African Jews, for example, have a cerebral attitude toward religion and are not given to passionate outpourings of spirit in prayer and worship. Many specifically Lithuanian-influenced synagogues therefore are modest places of worship, and South African Jewry may be characterized overall by what Shimoni describes as its "non-Hassidic religious Orthodoxy." Although South African Jews typically congregate around religious activity, they are not, as a whole, devoutly religious. They tend, rather, towards what has been called "conservative traditionalism" or "non-observant Orthodoxy." The more expressive Hasidic movement did not come on the scene until the 1970s, with the arrival of Lubavitch, which is very much of an American import.

**The role of the day schools:** Following World War II, South Africa's day school system increased dramatically in importance, even as the system of afternoon schools declined. This new commitment to day school education was made possible by the development of a traditional-national orientation that became the hallmark of the day schools.

The traditional-national orientation to Jewish education stresses that Jews are a distinct national group, bound together by a connection to classical Judaism. Nevertheless, there is the recognition that different students will take the tradition more or less seriously as

something they actually practice and totally believe in. Despite these differences, the consensus among South African Jews is that traditional Judaism is the cornerstone of their national identity. In practice, the schools have taught this tradition not so much to emphasize the religion but as a means of instilling a distinct Jewish identity.

The day school system began with the establishment of the King David School in Johannesburg in 1948 and, by the late 1960s, had grown to seventeen day schools, some linked together in school systems such as King David and Herzelia. It has become increasingly common for Jewish parents to send their children to a day school, so that, by the late 1970s and certainly the 1980s, it became more the rule than the exception. Especially as more and more Jews began to emigrate, many of the government schools, which once boasted considerable numbers of Jewish children, contained fewer and fewer of them. This, in turn, increased Jewish parents' feeling that their children would feel more comfortable in a Jewish day school. Currently, between seventy-five and eighty-five percent of Jewish students attend a day school, primarily in Johannesburg and Cape Town.

Notably, this shift has had a catastrophic impact on the Progressive movement, since most parents who send their children to a day school—where a traditional Jewish perspective is presented—do not see the need also to bring the child to an afternoon Hebrew School—where the child might learn about Progressive Judaism. The move to day school education accordingly has severely weakened parents' ability to commit to Reform temples and Progressive Judaism.

**South African Orthodoxy:** The Orthodox community constitutes the vast majority of the Jewish population of South Africa. In the most recent comprehensive socio-demographic survey, conducted in 1991, Professor Allie Dubb found that almost four-fifths of Jews in South Africa describe their religious orientation as Orthodox. Dubb lists 78.5 percent of all Jews as Orthodox, 12.7 percent as Reform, and the rest as not identified with a specific movement. In Johannesburg, 90.1 percent of all those affiliated with a synagogue were affiliated with an Orthodox one. The Orthodox affiliation rate for Pretoria was 89.1, for Cape Town, 84, Port Elizabeth, 75.4, and Durban, 73.4. Overall, 86.8 percent of all affiliated Jews were Orthodox by affiliation, an extremely high percentage. The figure today is almost certainly even higher.

The high percentage of Orthodox affiliation does not, however, indicate just how active the Orthodox community is and how much more active it is today than it was twenty years ago. In a 1974 study by Dubb, half of all respondents stated that they had attended 7.6 or more synagogue services in the previous year. While, in 1991, the median frequency was only a slightly higher, other numbers had risen significantly, so that, for instance, the percentage of those who attended services during the week had increased from 2.5 percent to 8.4 percent, and those who attended at least one Sabbath service per week had increased from 14 percent to 21.7 percent.

This trend toward greater involvement is very pronounced among the young. Dubb's two younger age groups, 18 to 29 and 30 to 44, attended synagogue about twice as frequently as their 1974 counterparts. In contrast, the median attendance of the oldest age group, 65 years old plus, had dropped in 1991 to half its 1974 levels.

In Dubb's 1991 socio-demographic study, 14.3 percent of respondents rated themselves highly observant, 74.4 as moderately observant, and 11.3 as being low in observance. Ninety-two point four percent always have a Passover Seder, and another 5.6 sometimes do; 90.8 percent fast on Yom Kippur; 74.3 percent always light Sabbath candles, and another 12.8 sometimes do. These percentages are high and reflect the very traditional nature of South African Jews.

Nevertheless, other observances have lower percentages of participation. The study indicates that only 45.1 percent always light Hanukkah candles, and another 15.4 percent sometimes do; 40.6 percent keep separate meat and dairy utensils strictly, 4.0 do "to some extent;" 37.7 percent purchase kosher meat only, and another 17.9 percent sometimes do. One marker of observance is whether people handle money on Sabbath. Seventeen point seven percent do not, which is a few percentage points *above* the 14.3 percent who had rated themselves as highly observant. A greater measure of concern with a halakhic lifestyle is fasting on the minor fast days: 8.3 percent report that they do.

South African Jews have been described as adhering to both "non-observant Orthodoxy" and the "national-traditional orientation," both of which are particular to South African Jewry. These terms are different ways of saying that many of the roughly eighty percent of South African Jews who consider themselves Orthodox want to hold to Jewish tradition rather than follow halakhah strictly. Such people find it important that one's primary identity be as a member of the Jewish community, and part of that identity is the emotional connection with traditional Judaism.

For example, most South African Orthodox Jews like to go to synagogue on Friday nights; in fact, many of the big synagogues draw hundreds of people on Friday nights, with lesser numbers attending on Saturday mornings. Once in synagogue, however, people do a lot of talking, which is shocking to anyone raised in the Reform or Christian traditions, where being in a house of worship requires reverential respect. For South African Jews, by contrast, simply being in an Orthodox synagogue seems to fulfill a need for identity with their tradition. Whatever their actual behavior in the synagogue, by attending they reinforce their visceral ethnic identity.

To cite another example of South African Jewry's non-observant Orthodoxy, until the last few decades, South African Jews often celebrated a child's becoming bar mitzvah in an Orthodox synagogue but then hosted a reception that was not kosher. This practice was halted only when the Beit Din—religious court—prohibited it, demanding that such receptions be strictly kosher and under Rabbinic supervision. Interestingly, despite people's personal lack of concern for kashrut, no opposition was expressed to this new policy. They apparently saw this observance as the right thing to do, despite the added cost and possible inconvenience and even if they continued otherwise not to follow the dietary restrictions.

Similarly, for many decades, most South African Jews have driven to synagogue on Sabbath and made little effort to hide that fact. But, as South African Orthodoxy has become more strict, Orthodox synagogues have been locking their parking lots. Again, there is little complaint, but also no change in people's personal observance; they still drive and simply park as near to the synagogue as they can. This willingness to accept the Orthodox approach is especially surprising in light of the high crime rate in Johannesburg, which makes walking even a block potentially dangerous. Still, there has been virtually no opposition to the policy; people accept the tradition because they recognize it as authentic and legitimate, even if they do not personally follow it.

Even Orthodox leaders, who might be highly critical of the apparent hypocrisy of South African Jewish practice, understand the social pressures that created this non-observant Orthodoxy. Indeed, in some regards, they view this synthesis positively, as evidence that South African Jews consider the Orthodox tradition alone to represent true Judaism. While it would be better if more South African Jews were truly observant, these leaders understand the social realities that created this unusual synthesis and consider it the best possible outcome, far preferable to the trends that have emerged in the United States, where Jews are moving toward Conservative and Reform Judaism, total assimilation, and a high degree of intermarriage.

Notably, just as most South African Jews continue to see Orthodox Judaism as the only legitimate expression of historical Judaism, they maintain the traditional rabbinate as the only rightful source of religious authority. Accordingly, the Orthodox rabbinate, in particular the Orthodox Chief Rabbi and the Beit Din, continues to exercise power over a wide range of issues, such as conversion, kashrut, and synagogue standards. Until about two decades ago, this rabbinate was divided into separate hierarchical structures for Johannesburg and Cape Town. Shortly before Chief Rabbi Cyril Harris (fig. 126) and the current Beit Din, these two structures were unified, so that a single Orthodox policy can be applied throughout the country.

**The Progressive movement:** In England, as in the United States, the Reform and Conservative movements developed during the course of the nineteenth century. In England, the Reform movement was separate from the Liberal movement. In Australia, Liberal, Reform, and Progressive were all synonymous terms. In South Africa, the term Reform was the preferred term in the early years. Liberal Judaism was used occasionally and then disappeared from usage entirely as liberalism became a negative concept. Over the past fifteen years, Progressive has become the preferred term, with Reform continuing to be used some of the time.

Reform movements developed around the same time in Australia and South Africa and in countries nearby, that is, New Zealand and Rhodesia (now Zimbabwe), respectively. These early Reform movements were encouraged by the World Union for Progressive Judaism, which was established in 1926 and headquartered in London. The support of the World Union allowed Reform movements to establish themselves on turf that until that time had been completely Orthodox.

The World Union had much reason to believe that Reform Judaism could attract a substantial number of South African Jews. Although before the advent of Reform all affiliated Jews were nominally Orthodox, many were completely non-observant. Thus, in 1932, the World Union agreed to provide a small stipend for a limited period to Moses Cyrus Weiler, a Latvia-born Palestinian national who was about to receive ordination at Hebrew Union College in Cincinnati. In South Africa, however, Weiler confronted a campaign of hostility from the Orthodox rabbinate, which charged that Reform was an illegitimate form of Judaism that would undermine both authentic Judaism and Zionism. Indeed, since no Jewish organization allowed his congregation to hire a room for prayers, Weiler initially had to use a Freemasons' hall.

Weiler's approach to building his community reflected a certain sense of decorum and equality among his growing community. He requested that services be more than a fashion parade, that members of the congregation respect the synagogue as a place of worship, and that seats be neither sold nor assigned. He also introduced children's services and helped organize a choir. Under Weiler, despite Orthodox opposition, the Progressive movement developed rapidly, establishing temples in Johannesburg, and later Cape Town, Durban, Pretoria, Springs, Bloemfontein, Port Elizabeth, East London, and elsewhere. At its zenith in the 1950s, this large and vibrant movement had as much as eighteen percent of South African Jews. Only Kimberley and Pietermaritzburg remained as medium- or large-sized cities without reform congregations.

But in the late 1950s, after Weiler emigrated to Israel, the movement began to decline. This decline, which paralleled that of the South African Jewish community in general, was the direct result of the political turmoil in the country. Thus, by 1993, it had become very apparent that a number of Reform congregations in some of the smaller cities would close. As of 1998, there were officially only ten Reform congregations: one in Cape Town, three in Johannesburg, and one each in Port Elizabeth, East London, Durban, Bloemfontein, Pretoria, and East London. However, Bloemfontein is defunct in all but name, and East London is nearly so. Port Elizabeth's congregation is quite small and unable even to consider supporting a rabbi. Some of these smaller congregations will undoubtedly close in the coming years.

**The Conservative Movement:** A form of Conservative Judaism began in Johannesburg in 1985, when Temple Shalom on Louis Botha Avenue, one of four congregations forming the United Progressive Congregation of Johannesburg, invited Rabbi Aby Assabi to officiate at High Holy Day services. Assabi previously had led an Orthodox-style congregation in Germany and a Reform congregation in Netanya, Israel, where he simultaneously served for eight years as Executive Director of the Israeli Progressive Movement.

Assabi became Temple Shalom's full-time rabbi and soon presided over the congregation's merger with Temple Emanuel, of Houghton, Johannesburg. The newly formed alliance, Imanu-Shalom, began in 1986 as a Progressive congregation with two temples under the rubric of one congregation. According to the congregation's newsletter, it numbered 1350 families, including a number of wealthy and influential business people and Jewish lay leaders. Rabbi Assabi served as Senior Rabbi, rotating on alternating Sabbaths between Shalom and Emanuel. By 1991, his leadership had resulted in a dramatic transition from a reform-style service to a traditional, Conservative one. A new prayer book was being used in place of the Reform Gates of Prayer, and other Conservative ritual innovations were in place.

In 1995, Imanu-Shalom broke completely with the South African Union for Progressive Judaism, citing its refusal to adapt a more traditional approach to Judaism. But a disagreement with some members of the former Temple Emanuel regarding religious ideology soon led the two congregations again to be separated. Temple Shalom remained until 1998 under the religious leadership of Rabbi Assabi, and, since 1994, it has been loosely affiliated with the Conservative/Masorati Movement. But, in recent years, the congregation's membership has dropped precipitously, from fourteen hundred families to around three hundred fifty, the apparent result of a vacuum in leadership.

It appears, then, that building a Conservative congregation in isolation from a broadly based Conservative movement is very difficult. In addition, Conservative Judaism in South Africa faces all of the same problems that Reform Judaism faced and faces in terms of being seen as illegitimate and inauthentic. As long as Orthodox affiliation imparts a higher social status, non-Orthodox Judaism will remain a fringe phenomenon. This is the case especially as conservatism's strict standards on conversion close off a main potential source of new members, intermarrieds and potential Jews-by-choice who find no place within the Orthodox community.

**The German Orthodox in Johannesburg:** The perception in South Africa, as in other English-speaking communities that received German Jewish immigrants prior to World War II, was that the German Jews tended to be Reform or at the very least to be highly assimilated. There is in fact no evidence that German Jews joined Reform in any disproportionate numbers. To the contrary, some of the German Jews who arrived in South Africa had been followers of Rabbi Samson Raphael Hirsch, who had built a modern Orthodox movement in Germany. In September, 1936, this group established the Adath Jeshurun Shul on Fortesque Road in Yeoville, Johannesburg. Beginning with no more than about a score of committed members, at its height Adath Jeshurun probably numbered around one hundred twenty or thirty families.

When Rabbi Yaakov Salzer came in 1953, he attempted to establish independent religious standards. For example, in 1954 he set up procedures to produce milk products under rabbinical supervision and, rejecting the broader Orthodox community's standards, also established an independent facility for slaughtering animals for meat. In response, the *Federation Chronicle*, which represented the more mainstream Orthodox in South Africa, launched a biting attack on Adath Jeshurun's alleged exclusivity. The newspaper accused its members of causing a rift in the unity of the Jewish people. Although both the Chief Rabbi and Beit Din immediately disassociated themselves from the articles, many people developed an image of Adath Jeshurun as a bastion of intolerant fanaticism.

Still, over the years, the Adath Jeshurun community was responsible for innovations that brought the standards of Orthodox observance to higher levels. Along with more stringent kashrut standards, it established an ultra-Orthodox Talmud Torah and a women's *tahara* service at the burial society, initiated informal training of *gabboim* (ritual directors) who began serving at various Orthodox synagogues throughout Johannesburg, and set up a laboratory for checking for *shatnes* (the prohibited mixture of wool and linen in a single cloth).

Adath Jeshurun was not the only synagogue that catered to German Jews. In the 1930s, Etz Chayim was the most popular congregation for German Jews arriving in Johannesburg. Whereas Adath Jeshurun catered almost exclusively to those who were disciples of Samson Raphael Hirsch and who were ultra-Orthodox in their religious perspective, Etz Chayim catered to the vast majority of German Jews. Some of the immigrants who had been Reform in Germany may have joined one of the Progressive synagogues, which were English-speaking. However, even though Etz Chayim was Orthodox, being in fellowship with other German Jews and hearing the sermon in German was probably much more important than theological principles or specific ritual practices. The congregation remained strong until the end of the 1950s, by which time it was half German and half Lithuanian. In the 1960s and 1970s, though, it declined as Jews moved out of the neighborhood, and, around 1993, it closed, although a *minyan* was maintained until 1997, when the remaining congregants joined with the remaining congregants of the Wolmarans Street Shul.

**Sephardic Jews:** When, after years of colonial status, the countries in which they were living became independent, many Sephardic Jews moved to South Africa. The majority came from Zaire and settled in Cape Town, although a number from Zimbabwe settled in Johannesburg. In Cape Town today there is a two hundred-family Sephardic Orthodox congregation. Increasing numbers of Israelis are now joining this congregation, creating conflicts regarding ritual policy and other issues between the relatively newly arrived Sephardic Israelis and the founders, who are Sephardic central Africans originally from Rhodes.

The Sephardim from Rhodes have also had to face the recent increased stringency of Orthodox standards in South Africa. While the Rhodes Jews, like the Jews of Italy, were Orthodox, their traditionalism was very liberal and accepting of all levels of observance and manners of theological belief. Now, with the increasing control of the Beit Din over all religious questions, their congregations are being pushed into adopting more stringent halakhic requirements, ranging from the demand for a higher barrier to separate men and women at prayer to the application of additional kashrut standards that apply to food brought into the synagogue.

**The growth of ultra-Orthodoxy: The Baal Teshuva movement:** One very noticeable trend in recent times, primarily in Johannesburg, has been the growth of institutions promoting a return of young, assimilated Jews to an observant Jewish lifestyle. One such institution, Ohr Somayach, began in Johannesburg in February, 1986, with the work of Rabbi Shmuel Mofson, who was the official campus rabbi at the University of the Witwatersrand, where he played a direct and active role in the programs run by the South Africa Union of Jewish Students (SAUJS). In February, 1987, the beginning of the academic year in South Africa, Ohr Somayach, together with Yeshiva College, established an own institution in the suburb of Glenhazel. Together these would form the nucleus of what became known as a "new Yeoville," or the new Orthodox center, Yeoville having been the center of Orthodox Jewish life in Johannesburg prior to the dismantling of apartheid and the movement of Jews to the suburbs.

Ohr Somayach initially catered to young adults by creating a learning center that met three times a week, at first in the home of one of the rabbis. The group quickly outgrew the space, its popularity stemming from its ability to establish a trend by which it became not only acceptable but socially advantageous to attend Ohr Somayach lectures. These lectures were delivered by guest speakers from abroad and usually focused on the immediate emotional concerns of the audiences, in particular, on psychological issues such as interpersonal skills, relationships, and how to deal with the stresses of modern life.

Such programs began to attract an average of at least two hundred fifty people. In addition, Ohr Somayach sponsored daily worship services and classes that drew between fifty and sixty mostly young people who had not previously been observant. In 1989, a separate study program was instituted for women and, shortly thereafter, a Jewish marriage education program. This was considered an important innovation in South African Jewish educational programming, especially in light of the very high divorce rate in the country in general and among the Jewish population in particular. After this program was established, the Beit Din, which had no specific link to the Ohr Somayach organization, began insisting that all prospective marriage couples attend this four-week course.

Ohr Somayach also tried to avoid conflicts with various subgroups within the Orthodox community. So, for example, when the Lubavitcher Rebbe passed away in 1995, the Lubavitchers were deeply in mourning. The Adath Jeshurun group, totally opposed to the Lubavitchers, ignored this milestone. In contrast, the Ohr Somayach organization held lectures to mark the passing of the Rebbe. In general, Ohr Somayach tried to do things to appeal to as broad a spectrum of Orthodox people as possible.

In 1992, the organization established a yeshiva program with a full morning study session. The program quickly grew to include twenty-five full-day students and a large number who studied half day. The yeshiva had four separate morning prayer services, two afternoon prayer services, and two evening prayer services. Also in 1992, a separate branch was established in Gallo Manor (in Sandton, a suburb of Johannesburg) and, in 1993, another branch opened in Savoy. In 1995, the group established a kollel—a yeshiva for married men—with eight South African families, augmented with five more brought from Ohr Somayach in Israel. The group's first rabbinical ordination took place in 1997.

Ohr Somayach has thus created a tight religious community that, by the late 1990s, had become a highly influential element of Johannesburg Jewish life, duplicating what Aish Hatorah—another center encouraging return to Judaism—was doing overseas and, indeed, leading Aish Hatorah in 1996 to open its own branch in Johannesburg. There, as elsewhere, Aish Hatorah specializes in reaching out to the uninitiated and combating assimilation by "injecting understanding in Jewish practice and by increasing Jewish pride." By mid-1997, after only a year in existence, over thirty-five hundred people had attended at least one Aish Hatorah seminar.

The development of the Baal Teshuva movement is connected with a related phenomenon, the growth of the *shtibl*. While South African Orthodoxy has always been characterized by large formal synagogues typical of the British Commonwealth (fig. 127), the new trend is toward small, traditionalist houses of prayer. Such *shtibl*-style communities in Johannesburg include Kollel Yad Shaul, Keter Torah, Yeshivah Gedolah, Yeshivah MaHarShA, and the various Lubavitch *shtibls*. In this model, worship services lack the elaborate ritual and ceremony of the large Orthodox shuls. Without choirs and professional cantors, the services involve the lay membership in ways that do not occur in the traditional synagogues, in which there is a barrier between the officiants and the congregants, who play a passive role.

The Baal Teshuva organizations have tremendous potential in South Africa. On the one hand, the community is already strongly sympathetic to Orthodoxy; on the other, most of the children have been raised in homes in which there was more sympathy for Orthodoxy than knowledge of it. Many of these young adults are candidates for a more intense version of Orthodox Jewish belief and practice. Further, South African parents typically encourage and are proud of their children's greater involvement in and allegiance to Orthodoxy. Even those South African parents who practice virtually none of Jewish law nonetheless generally accept the legitimacy and authenticity of Orthodox belief and practice. This makes them much more willing to accept their children's decision to embrace Orthodoxy.

**Prospects for the future:** For South African Jews, South Africa's social transformation of the past years has been quite traumatic. As in white homes in general, the recent dramatic increases in crime, including hijacking and break-in murders in affluent white suburbs, have produced renewed paranoia and sometimes hysteria. One of the consequences of this climate of instability and fear has been the increasing Jewish emigration. In the years before the 1994 elections, tens of thousands of Jews left South Africa. Though just how many Jews left is subject to speculation, one of the most widely quoted—though often debated—sources, the 1991 Dubb Report, holds that, between 1970 and 1991, 39,000 Jews emigrated from South Africa.

In this period, the largest number of those who left moved to Israel. However, by 1991, this trend shifted, and the largest proportion of émigrés from South Africa were to be found in the United States. The country with the next largest proportion remained Israel, followed by Australia, where the number of South African emigrants was growing. The other two countries with significant populations of South African émigrés were the U.K. and Canada.

Just as there are no reliable statistics on the exact number of Jewish emigrants, there are no statistics on who is emigrating. Still, the South African Jewish community feels it has lost "the cream of the community," that is, a high percentage of younger couples with children as well as a high percentage of those who are professionals and well educated. Indeed, according to the 1991 Dubb report, the émigrés are predominantly young couples and singles aged 18 to 44, and they are more likely to be engaged in professional occupations than the average South African Jew.

In the past twenty years there has also been migration within the country, from small towns and medium-sized cities—Port Elizabeth, Bloemfontein, East London, Pretoria, and even Durban. Because very few Jews remain in these towns, dozens of small synagogues have closed or function only on high holidays. Thus, not only is South African Jewry smaller than it was twenty years ago, it is also much more concentrated, with the vast majority of Jews in just two cities, Johannesburg and Cape Town. Durban, for example, had a Jewish community of some six to seven thousand in 1980; today there are only about three thousand to thirty-five hundred.

Largely as a result of the increasing crime rate in Johannesburg, Jewish religious and social life there has shifted out of the city center and to the northern suburbs. This migration from traditional Jewish neighborhoods, such as Hillbrow, has left those once-vibrant centers of Jewish life and culture deteriorating and crime-ridden. A striking symbol of the Jewish desertion of the city is the Wolmarans Street Shul in Hillbrow, until recently Johannesburg's central synagogue, which now is deserted and up for sale.

Parallel with the decline of the Wolmarans Street Shul and another result of the northward flight of Jews into the suburbs is that Yeoville, once the nerve center of Orthodox Jewish life, is now in the final stages of disintegrating. In the recent past, three Jewish bookstores, two bakeries, two kosher delis, and a Jewish restaurant have all either closed or moved out. In addition, nonprofit Jewish organizations are leaving; the Beit Din itself has sold its building and moved. These changes are significant since Yeoville was South Africa's first truly ultra-Orthodox community. Today most of its founders and their children are living outside of South Africa.

Hillbrow, site of the Wolmarans Street shul, had become one of the most densely populated square miles in the world and was particularly attractive to young, single Jewish professionals enjoying urban lifestyles. But today the only Jews who remain—and there are still Jews in many of the apartment buildings in the neighborhood—are elderly and poverty stricken. Many are religiously devout, but they fear walking on the streets of Hillbrow, even on Sabbath morning when it is light outside.

Besides the enormous negative impact of this circumstance on the Jewish elderly who remain in these neighborhoods, it appears that the rising violence again is causing many Jews, in particular younger ones, to contemplate emigration. This, in conjunction with the fact that many who previously had received visas valid for a limited number of years must now use or lose them, has meant a renewal of what has derogatorily been referred to as "the chicken run." While the same forces pressure all whites to leave the country, Jews, who are more likely to own their own businesses or have professional training, find it easier to relocate. It bears noting that this exodus of Jews and other whites is of great concern to the government,

such that, for example, in 1995, speaking to an audience of two thousand people, including prominent members of the Jewish community, at Temple Emanuel, a large Reform Congregation in Parktown, Johannesburg, President Nelson Mandela said, "Don't leave, don't let us down." He assured whites, including Jews, that they were "marked for leadership in the new multiparty, multiracial South Africa." Their skills were desperately needed, and they should not abandon the country in its time of rebuilding.

Although the Jewish community is certainly having difficulties and is contracting numerically, some believe that the situation is by no means catastrophic. Before, during, and after the 1994 elections, the South African Jewish Board of Deputies consistently argued that there is a positive future for South African Jewry, and the leadership of the community has been strongly supportive of the movement for democracy. In 1994, the National Director of the Board, Seymour Kopelowitz, said, "A mood of optimism has swept across the Jewish community in South Africa since the last elections. . . . The results have exceeded expectations and are a benefit not only to South African Jewry but to all South Africans. In spite of the gloom and doom which emanated from local sources and from various agencies in Israel, one thing is nevertheless clear: there is a future for Jews in South Africa and there will be a viable Jewish community here."

In a recent report, Russell Gaddin, who holds office in a number of Jewish organizations, argued that although the demographics of the Jewish community in South Africa may be changing, the numbers that have been lost to emigration are, in fact, considerably less than those lost to the simple process of assimilation that naturally occurs throughout the diaspora. Gaddin believes that the community in South Africa is quite stable and has managed to build up a sound infrastructure sufficient for it to flourish. He concedes that this infrastructure demands continued support from the community but that there is no question that facilities for Jews are in any danger of collapsing.

One thing is clear, and this is that many

South African Jews are active in helping to build the new South Africa. As Chief Rabbi Cyril Harris, in his testimony before the Truth and Reconciliation Commission in November, 1997, noted, they are operating many programs under the broad umbrella of Tikkun, a Hebrew word meaning "repairing" or "trying to put things right." These include the distribution of food to the hungry, support of homes for the mentally and physically disabled in Alexandra Township and in Johannesburg, and an agricultural project at Rietfontein, based on the principle of empowerment.

Other projects include helping develop solar heating, preserve water, and plant crops. There are educational programs in schools in black neighborhoods, preschool enrichment programs, adult literacy programs, and teacher training programs. Jewish business people are sharing their entrepreneurial and banking skills with young people. Harris concludes saying, "It is our job as religious people to try to apply the antidotes . . . to display the best that human beings can do to fellow human beings. . . . If Apartheid was divisive, the antidote is building bridges and coming together—a togetherness which will spell the great future of our country." For those Jews who remain, the religious obligation of *tikkun olam*-of repairing the world—is felt alongside the fear of being engulfed by problems so massive that the only solution is individual emigration. The Jews of South Africa are living under unparalleled conditions, and their Judaism is developing in a number of patterns that directly respond to the unique challenges facing the new South Africa.

### Bibliography

Elazar, D.J., and P. Medding, *Jewish Communities in Frontier Societies: Argentina, Australia, and South Africa* (New York and London, 1983).

Saron, G., and L. Hotz, eds., *The Jews in South Africa* (Cape Town, 1956).

Shain, M., *The Roots of Antisemitism in South Africa* (Johannesburg, 1994).

Shimoni, G., *Jews and Zionism: The South African Experience, 1910-1967* (Cape Town, 1980).

### Notes

[1] Notably, these were not in fact all of British origin. Some were Eastern European Jews who passed through Britain on their way to the Cape Colony.

[2] This is extremely rare today, the result of the increasing numbers of Orthodox rabbis who hail from the United States or are locally trained.

DANA EVAN KAPLAN

**STATE OF ISRAEL, THE PRACTICE OF JUDAISM IN:** Formally a secular democratic state, Israel has no established religion nor any provisions in its laws requiring a particular religious affiliation, belief, or commitment—Jewish or other—as a prerequisite for holding office. In this way Israel differs from many other Middle Eastern countries, whose constitutions provide that only Christians or Muslims may hold any, or at least certain, public offices. But despite the absence of such requirements, Israel still manifests a close interconnection between religious communities and the state. This interconnection includes a special status by consensus for the majority Jewish religious community as well as state support for all recognized religions that do not explicitly reject such support. In Israel, any religious community can apply for and receive official recognition and state support. Israel's *Ministry of Religions*, in the plural, is just that, serving the communities of Jews, Muslims, Druze, and Christian denominations.

The Israeli parliament, the Knesset, grants individual religions authority in matters of personal status (marriage, divorce, etc.) and in other matters pertaining to the governance of their respective communities. Yet as a matter of constitutional principle, no Israeli Knesset could interfere in any systematic way with those prerogatives, since all the religious communities would present a unified front to prevent this. Indeed, members of individual religious communities do not recognize the Knesset as a source of authority in religious matters at all, but only as the regularizer of that authority within the context of the state. For them, the real source of authority is their religion's divine source, represented, e.g., by the Jewish rabbinate, which obtains its authority through Jewish religious law—halakhah—or by the Muslim imams, who obtain theirs through Muslim religious law, the Sharia. In this sense religion in Israel is rooted in the constitutional fabric of the state, which no regime can seriously disrupt.

In addition, no less than Islam does for

other Middle Eastern countries, Judaism legitimates the existence of Israel as a homeland of Jews. People accordingly speak of Israel as a Jewish state, which the majority of Israelis want it to be. Virtually all Israelis recognize the connection between Israel and religious Judaism as well as secular Jewishness. Certainly, many of the founders of Israel were secularists, who saw Israel as Jewish only in the national sense of the term. But this approach to Jewishness has not become dominant, however much it has helped loosen the bonds of religion on the behavior of most of Israel's Jews.

**Religious and national commitments:** The Israeli understanding of religion defies conventional definition. On the one hand, Israeli Jews reflect the usual modern ambivalences regarding the relationship between religion and society, though perhaps less with regard to religion and politics. At the same time, since Jewish religious tradition is associated with patterns that are quite at home in modern society, there has not been the kind of undiluted confrontation between traditional religion and modernization that has occurred in other countries. One sees this in the way that even ultra-Orthodox Jews in Israel fit into modern economic and political life. There have been some conflicts, but, for the most part, the problems of confrontation and contradiction found in the Islamic world, for example, have not occurred in Israel.

Indeed, while outside observers may have an impression of two tight camps—the religious and the non-religious—the situation actually is much more complex. Among Israelis who call themselves religious, there is great diversity in attitudes towards religious observance, the state, and the modern world. Similarly, among Israelis who call themselves non-religious are large groups that are extremely close to the tradition as well as others those who have only minimal contact with Judaism.

This variety of religious expressions in Israel is hidden to some extent by the use of the term *dati*, "religious," to signify one who punctiliously observes religious law. To be "religious" in Israel, that is, means to accept the traditional Jewish world view and to follow the ritual practices recorded in the Bible and developed by Rabbinic authorities. In Israel, the word "religious" thus does not carry its broader Western sense of being spiritual, without regard for whether or not one observes religious ritual. Similarly, the term "non-religious" does not imply the same thing in Hebrew as it does in English. In Israel, to be "non-religious" signifies that one is not *entirely* observant, even if one believes in God and observes some—or even many—religious traditions. Unlike in the majority of the western world, in Israel anyone who is not *strictly* traditional is deemed "non-religious." This is the case even though many in this category accept certain traditional views and preserve substantial elements of Jewish tradition.

More accurately to depict what Israeli Jews actually do and believe, another usage has emerged that demarcates groups within the otherwise undifferentiated"non-religious" category. The term *masorti* ("traditional") identifies somewhat observant people who do not declare themselves atheists or agnostics. Only such people, termed *hiloni* ("secularist"), are accurately to be considered non-religious—even though many of them selectively maintain Jewish religious practices, particularly in their homes. But despite the availability of these distinctions, the Israeli public continues generally to identify "religious" commitment by the traditional criterion of ritual behavior, without regard for the beliefs that underlie such behavior or that might be present among those who do not observe ritual practices. To tell the complete story of Israeli Jews' beliefs and practices, we must therefore move behind these standard categories, which is accomplished when we review the latest survey on the subject, published in 1993 by the prestigious Guttman Institute of Applied Social Research.

**The practice of Judaism in Israel:** Israel's Jews fall into four groups: ultra-Orthodox (*haredim*), religious Zionists (*datiim*), traditional (*masortiim*), and secular (*hilonim*). The ultra-Orthodox—the traditionally garbed, black hatted Jews often featured in pictures meant to convey "Judaism"—represent only eight percent of Israel's Jewish population.

Another seventeen percent, the religious Zionists, generally are lumped with everyone else and so, in most studies and statistics, are lost to view. These Jews are similar to the modern or centrist Orthodox Jews of the diaspora, enjoying most aspects of modern civilization even as they maintain Orthodox observance of Jewish religious law and tradition.

The third group, those who define themselves as "traditional," comprises the vast majority of Israeli Jews, some 55 percent. While coming from many backgrounds, most of these Jews are Sephardim, from the Mediterranean or Islamic worlds (figs. 128-129). They value traditional Jewish life but are prepared to modify the required Jewish practices in cases in which they find it personally necessary or attractive to do so. They cover the whole range of belief and observance, from people of fundamentalist belief but quite minimal religious practice to people who interpret Judaism in the most modern manner but retain many of its traditional customs and ceremonies. Many of these "traditional" Jews drive their cars, use electricity, watch television, or go to a soccer game or to the beach on the Sabbath, frequently after attending religious services in the morning and the evening before. Many of the men follow traditional patterns of daily prayer and use of ritual garments. What is critical is that, like the ultra-orthodox, they are committed to a major religious component in the definition of their Jewishness and the Jewishness of the Jewish state.

Many of these traditional Sephardic Jews have been drawn to the ultra-orthodox Shas (Sephardic Torah Guardians) movement, which has grown from a small handful of Jerusalemites dissatisfied with the then Ashkenazic-dominated National Religious Party to become the third largest political party in the country, with seventeen seats in the present Knesset. Shas has an extraordinarily active educational system that reaches into neighborhoods neglected by the "establishment," including the religious establishment. A good half of the country's population lives in these neighborhoods, largely invisible to diaspora communities. Shas has revived religious traditions, presented in a more Orthodox way than older Sephardic customs demanded. This growth in religious practice has been encouraged by the warm-hearted activities of Shas-appointed rabbis, educators, and preachers, many of whom have far larger followings than all of the non-Orthodox religious movements in Israel combined.

The fourth group within Israel consists of the self-defined secular Jews, some twenty percent of the Jewish population. But while these people's beliefs are secular, their practices are often quite similar to those of traditionalists, even if they are maintained for familial and national reasons rather than for religious ones. Since Jewish religious observance has a strong national component, it remains central to the identity even of Jews who no longer see themselves as believing in the tenets of the Jewish religion.

The Guttman study shows that an astounding three-quarters of these "secular" Jews follow the most common traditional religious practices. Only a quarter of them—five percent of the total Jewish population—say they observe no religious practices whatsoever. But even this figure is belied by data showing that 98 percent of Israeli Jews have *mezuzot* on the doorposts of their houses, that 92 percent circumcise their male children, and that almost all Israeli Jews have some form of Passover Seder, to mention only three of a number of observances that are so deeply entrenched in the culture that hardly anyone thinks of them as religious at all.

Notably almost all the elites in Israeli society—cultural, intellectual, political, and economic—are found within the secular twenty percent, and this shapes the picture outsiders get of Israel. Moreover, this twenty percent is overwhelmingly Ashkenazic—Jews from Eastern and Central Europe or descended from them—who are most likely to know English, to have relatives in the diaspora, or to be contacted by journalists coming to the country. Accordingly, a skewed picture emerges, depicting Israeli Jews as much more secular than they actually are.

**Patterns of Israeli belief:** Let us look at the statistics more closely. Nearly two-thirds of Israelis believe there is a God, and another quarter believe there may be ("not sure"). Fifty-five percent believe in the literal revelation of the Torah by God to the Jewish people at Mt. Sinai, while those who see this as possible ("not sure") raise the total to 86 percent. Other measures of religious belief yield similar results, and there undoubtedly are many fewer atheists in Israel today than when it was founded. Still, believers should not take too much comfort from these figures, for they essentially parallel those found in other modern Western countries. Indeed, while 55 percent believe the commandments have a divine origin, only 27 percent believe God will punish them for not observing the law.

Yet, all told, most Israelis observe far more of Jewish tradition than the average Reform or even Conservative Jew of the diaspora. And since a majority in Israel is Sephardic, from a world that never experienced religious reformation and the division of Judaism into three or more "denominations," even those who do are not themselves Orthodox believe that Jewish tradition should stand relatively unchanged and not be fragmented. While they reserve for themselves the right to pick and choose, they define Judaism exactly as do the Orthodox. Thus, in the entire history of the rebuilding of Israel, no indigenous movement to reform Jewish religion has emerged, despite the Zionists willingness to reform almost everything else. This is telling, as is the fact that the 1993 survey largely replicates the results of earlier surveys going back some thirty years. The amount of observance has dropped over time, but not appreciably.

**Religious pluralism in Israel:** Diaspora Jews who say there is no religious pluralism in Israel, refer to pluralism of the American kind. In fact, Israel is hardly monolithic in any respect and enjoys a deeply rooted religious pluralism that must be recognized for what it is. Israel recognizes at least half a dozen different religio-ethnic communities, to be viewed, in the Middle Eastern way, as the primary manifestations of pluralism. These include Jews; Arabs who are Muslim, Bedouin, or Christian; non-Arab Christians of various denominations from Armenians to Mormons; Druze; and Circassians (Muslims of Russian rather than Arab background).

Perhaps most overlooked by outsiders is the pluralism within the Jewish ultra-Orthodox/Orthodox camp. Despite the outside view of all Orthodox Jews as dressed in black, whether they are or not, there are something like a dozen different Hasidic "courts," ranging from the unbendingly anti-Zionist Satmar, to Habad, which is strongly Zionist and dedicated to bringing all Jews closer to Judaism as Habad understands it (fig. 130). There are Hasidic courts like Bratslav, who are highly spiritual and quietist, and others like Gur and Belz, noted for their political activity both within the ultra-Orthodox world and often outside of it. And there are small courts such as Sadigorer, the preserve of certain families, including family members who may not be in any way ultra-Orthodox in their behavior.

Other communities gather around "Lithuanian" yeshivot, ranging in orientation from ultra-religious and nationalist, like Mercaz HaRav Kook, to the militantly anti-Zionist yeshivot of groups like Toldos Aharon. There are also *misnagdim*, who, since the eighteenth century, have opposed Hasidism, and who have become more active in Israeli affairs over the last decade and a half. For their part, the *haredim leumiim—hardal*, Orthodox nationalists—pride themselves on their Orthodox devotion and their willingness to take on such obligations of national existence as combat service in the Israeli army and settlement in the territories. Then there are the very moderately religious of the religious kibbutzim, most of whom come out of the socialist religious Zionist background of Poalei Mizrahi, long-time allies of the Labor camp. And there is the Meimad group of peace-oriented modern Orthodox intellectuals. Overall, in certain respects, the differences between the extremes among these groups are far greater than those between Conservative and Reform Jews in the diaspora. At the same time, they are all united in their acceptance of the traditional understanding of *halakhah* and Torah and in their rejection of non-Orthodox claims to religious legitimacy. All told, these groups represent about 25 percent of Israel's population.

Conservative, Reform, and humanistic Jews, a very small number but with their own functioning and successful congregations and associations, are normally undisturbed in their worship, even by the most fanatical of the Orthodox establishment (unless that worship takes on a public dimension, for instance, in prayer services involving women's participation at the Western Wall in Jerusalem). Yet Reform and Conservative Judaism, so successful in the United States and elsewhere, have not had an impact in Israel and are not likely to improve their position in the near future. This is despite the fact that both movements can freely establish congregations and receive funds from the Jewish Agency and, because of pressure from American Jewry, from the Israeli government as well. The conventional explanation for these movements' modest growth in Israel blames the Israeli government's refusal—the result of political necessity—to recognize Reform and Conservative rabbis. But the answer more likely lies in the overall Israeli outlook on Jewish religious practice.

The sticking point is recognition under Israeli law of marriages and conversions performed in Israel by Conservative and Reform rabbis. The Orthodox monopoly has denied this, even as it has recognized Conservative and Reform marriages and conversions performed abroad. In this area, the status quo seems to promote the Orthodox monopoly in Israel even as it recognizes the reality and legitimacy of Jewish life in the diaspora. Israelis of all stripes normally signify one group or another within Orthodoxy, the only religious parties in the country are Orthodox, and control of publicly supplied religious services is exclusively in the hands of the Orthodox. Thus, while there is great religious pluralism in Israel, there also is an Orthodox monopoly in the formal arenas of religious power.

Secular Israeli Jews and at least some traditionalists would not object to official recognition of Conservative and Reform Judaism. But, except for a handful, these same Israelis do not seek to affiliate with these movements and do not respond to them positively. One example of this attitude was seen recently in *Kal Ha'ir*, a Jerusalem weekly news-

paper that hardly ever misses an opportunity to criticize ultra-Orthodox Jews and the Orthodox establishment. Weekly, a column in the paper "reviews" the prayer services at different synagogues, just as a critic would review and rate a movie or play. The kinds of synagogues the columnist has identified is overwhelming, ranging from a classical Sephardic congregation in Talbieh, where the president and prime minister of Israel reside, to a Moroccan Bratslaver Hasidic synagogue in the Katamonim, a working class neighborhood. Yet the reviewer, who himself is not Orthodox and writes for a paper that is often anti-Orthodox, wrote his most critical review about one of Jerusalem's Reform synagogues, saying in essence that he thought he was in a church and did not understand what was Jewish about the service. This, for better or worse, is a typical Israeli attitude.

After more than sixty years of struggle, Conservative and Reform Judaism remain confined to a few public institutions supported by and principally serving their diaspora adherents. There are only a few dozen small congregations, some with devoted members, but many active only for the High Holidays, and primarily serving immigrants from English-speaking countries. They may involve a few distinguished intellectuals, attracted to the particular combination of ideas and observances that these movements promote, and their presence often gives the movements some visibility despite their size. But try as they might, they have been unable to broaden their appeal among religiously moderate, traditional or secular Jews.

The issues that dominate the Conservative movement today, especially those of egalitarianism and liturgical reform, simply do not speak to many Israeli Jews. Even Israel's Sephardim, many of whom are moderate and more accepting of the contemporary world than the militant Ashkenazic Orthodox, are not concerned with either of those issues. They do not seem to want to end separate seating for men and women within the synagogue and do not accept the practice of the Bat Mitzvah ceremony, let alone of active women's participation in the service. Indeed, even though they do themselves make personal choices, Reform's notion of voluntary, individual religious choice is incomprehensible to these people. Most Israelis accept that an individual may choose what he or she will observe. But they hold that the religious *tradition* is fixed by unchanging divine law. Thus even those who reject the tradition in their own lives have a set definition of "authentic" Judaism. While there have been exceptions to this approach, they have been too few to make a difference.

**Israel and Mediterranean religion:** The ideas that lie behind Reform and Conservative Judaism can be traced back to the Protestant Reformation, to a need that arose in Central and Western Europe not only to purify the church but to reconcile belief and practice in a way that never found expression in Eastern Europe, the Mediterranean world, or the Islamic world. In Eastern Europe and the Christian Mediterranean, for the average person, the emphasis was on impressive church rituals and not on personal piety or doctrine; the Islamic world, like the Jewish, emphasized the communal, legal, and traditional character of religious behavior over matters of individual attitudes.

Thus, while Northern European Protestantism influenced the Jews in that part of the world to seek greater consistency in their religious lives, something that became absolutely critical in the United States, where anything less is considered hypocrisy, in Israel's part of the world, what counts are critical behavioral acts, such as birth, marriage, and burial rites, performed not necessarily for reasons of belief. In Judaism this is compounded by the intimate connection between nationality and religion that has been substantially severed in the Protestant world and most especially in the United States. Thus Israeli Jews perform for national reasons acts that would be deemed "religious" in the United States. This eliminates the need for them to confront disparities between belief and action and also makes it more difficult to change tradition without damaging national as well as religious ties.

Within this setting, some ritual observance emerges naturally, as an aspect of civil religion. Because the atmosphere of the Sabbath descends upon the entire country, for most people, some observance seems appropriate. Since the entire country prepares for holidays and celebrates them in some traditional ways, some observance naturally takes place in the home. Because many communities, indeed entire cities, have a traditional orientation, those inclining towards tradition anyway are pushed towards increased religious practice as a mode of better conforming to the environment in which they live. This same pressure towards religious observance comes from the need even of secularists to justify the existence of Israel as a Jewish state.

In Israel, the power of Jewish symbols deepens this process of sanctification, linking the nation to a force and history beyond itself. For some Israelis, especially the religious and traditional groups, Israel is a nation under God. For others, the reference to God has been dropped. But the idea that the state must be directed towards a goal beyond itself remains. In either case, religious elements are interwoven with national ones: continuity with Jewish national culture implies continuity with the religious tradition. The sources to be confronted are religious sources. The consciousness and sensibility are religious. Consequently, Judaism remains a live force that drives, and divides, people, even as it in many ways legitimates the state.

**Providing religious services:** In order to provide services to the Jewish and non-Jewish populations, the State of Israel has established a Ministry of Religions, whose head is a cabinet minister, responsible for the government's role in providing religious services to all recognized religious groups. All recognized non-Jewish communities conduct their own law courts for religious matters, maintain their own religious schools, and conduct their own marriages, divorces, and burials. The Israeli Government guarantees their freedom in all these areas and attempts to facilitate relations between all religious communities.

An extensive statewide and local structure provides services for the Jewish sector of the population. Its officials are appointed by the Ministry of Religions or elected by bodies outside the Ministry but funded by it in all or part. The highest governing Jewish religious body is the Supreme Rabbinical Council, consisting of four Sephardic and four Ashkenazic rabbis, including the Chief Rabbis of both groups. These men deal with religious questions that reach the state plane, although their power is not absolute. Questions involving state legislation are reviewed by the Knesset, which does not always accept their decision, and, on occasion, the decisions of the Chief Rabbis or the Rabbinical Council have not even been accepted by the religious parties. Agudat Yisrael, for instance, has never recognized the Rabbinical Council and the chief Rabbinate altogether, but has established its own independent Council of Torah Greats, which rules on problems that arise in the ultra-Orthodox community. Shas, for its part, has established a Council of Torah Sages, which, increasingly, is authoritative for the Sephardic religious community.

On the local plane, every major city has two chief rabbis as well as a local rabbinical court. The country additionally is divided into special districts, generally following municipal boundaries, in which religious services are provided. Here too the ultra-Orthodox do not accept the authority of the religious councils, but turn to their own courts. Conservative and Reform Jews, because they do not want to be viewed as separate religious bodies standing outside of the Jewish fold, do not have their own courts. They utilize the state's Orthodox mechanisms.

These arrangements hide certain real tensions between the religious and non-religious sectors of the population. Of course, intellectual arguments occur over the place of Judaism in the State of Israel generally. But even as these battles are fought mostly in journals and newspapers, on occasion the conflict emerges in heated public debate or even in street violence. This has occurred especially when a change in the strategic balance of power appears to be occurring, so that the status quo may be upset. Thus the determination of the Orthodox community to expand the number of streets closed in Jerusalem on the Sabbath will incense the non-Orthodox community and lead to verbal and even physical arguments. People on both sides generally accept the status quo, grudgingly or willingly. But when it appears that the status quo is being altered, both sides fear being pushed around, and violence may result.

**Israel's religious camp:** Prior to the founding of the state, religious Jews in the diaspora awaited the end of the exile and return to Zion as part of the process of God's redemption. For these Jews, the central question concerned whether or not one may participate in a non-Orthodox led effort to end the exile. Additionally, these Jews asked whether such efforts might actually be contrary to the will of God. The tradition had warned Jews against rebelling against foreign powers, so as to impel the coming of the end-time.

But a significant number of moderate Orthodox rabbis found a theological grounding to support the Zionist movement and even formed their own party within that movement. Accepting the Zionist principle of acting to achieve return to the land of Israel, they worked within the Zionist movement as religious Jews. In 1902, under the leadership of Rabbi Isaac Joseph Reines, they formed the Mizrahi party, its name, an abbreviation of *Merkaz Ruhani*, meaning "spiritual center," also a play on words meaning "of the east." From the beginning, the religious Zionists wished to influence Zionism in a religious direction, as they defined it, and to influence Orthodox Jews to support Zionism. This they would do by legitimating the movement in the eyes of the Orthodox public, which still included a majority of world Jewry.

So long as the aim of the Zionist movement was almost exclusively political, the disagreements between religious and non-religious Zionists over religious and cultural matters could be ignored. But when the Zionists began to focus upon a cultural program of national renaissance, the religious issue could no longer be avoided. But despite the conflicts, the religious Zionists always responded from within Zionism. The unifying ideal of "Love of Israel" predominated over the centrifugal tendencies that emerged from sharp ideological conflicts.

Still, many Orthodox Jews could not accept what they regarded as the compromising posture of Mizrahi. Following the Tenth

Zionist Congress, in which a cultural program for the Zionist movement was approved, these oppositionists organized Agudat Yisrael (1912), which opposed the Zionists as secular but promoted activities meant to build Israel from a fully Orthodox position. Immigration was deemed important, but only within the framework of a Torah-true community. There could be no possibility of cooperating with non-observant Jews.

The Sephardic Yishuv that dominated the land of Israel throughout the period of Ottoman rule until the British conquest during World War I constituted a traditional community, headed by a chief rabbi and a council of householders. The Sephardim also sought to rebuild the land and extended their hands to the Zionist pioneers, especially those who came during the First Aliyah (1880-1904), who for the most part combined observance of Jewish religious tradition with Zionist aspirations and so were compatible with the Sephardic Yishuv.

The Ashkenazim who came to the country primarily from the 1830s onward tended to be ultra-Orthodox but also committed to resettling the land, albeit in a way very different from that of the Zionists. They tried to separate themselves both from the Sephardic Yishuv and from the new Yishuv of the Zionist movement. However, the separation could not be clear-cut, since the institutions of the Old Yishuv needed money to survive, and the control of such funds was delegated by the British to the Zionist-sponsored *Vaad Leumi* (National Council), composed of non-religious and religious Zionists. Throughout the 1920s, great efforts were made by Chaim Weizmann and others to bring the Orthodox anti-Zionists into the *Vaad Leumi* in order to gain unity of the Jews in Palestine and in order to increase the religious legitimation of the Zionist organization. But these efforts came to naught. In the end, the Zionists agreed to fund religious academies in return for tacit cooperation, securing a truce between the two sides.

These differences regarding the meaning of the Zionism continue to be manifest today in the battle between the National Religious Party (*Mafdal*; NRP), built around the Miz-

rahi party, and the Agudat Yisrael. Throughout the Mandate period, the religious Zionists participated in Zionist activities and were integrated into the new Yishuv. The Mizrahi organization brought to Israel many Orthodox settlers and developed the concept of the integration of Torah and labor, which encouraged religious immigrants to engage in agricultural work and thereby to become part of the major developing thrust of the new Jewish society. Whereas Orthodox Jews had lived almost exclusively in cities and engaged in petty crafts, artisanry, and business, this movement projected a new ideal, in tune with the general Zionist focus upon physical labor and agricultural settlement. Thus, out of Mizrahi developed a new party, *HaPoel Ha-Mizrahi* ("Mizrahi Labor"), for those engaged in agricultural pioneering, and the religious Zionists succeeded in establishing a number of important *kibbutzim* (collective agricultural settlements) and *moshavim* (cooperative agricultural settlements), based upon the concept of a life of both labor and study.

Throughout the 1930s, Agudat Yisrael maintained its posture of aloofness and separation. Later this stance underwent great changes, although not without an internal struggle. The immediate cause of the change was the influx of Orthodox immigrants from Central Europe, who, in their approach to modernization and Zionism, were more moderate than the old settlers. Second, the burning threat of Nazism forced Agudah leaders to consider ways of cooperating with the Zionists in bringing Jews out of Europe. Some of the old-time Agudah leaders remained firm in their opposition to Zionism and continued to block all changes. Others, however, altered their position as the situation seemed to demand.

Following World War II, Agudat Yisrael entered into an agreement with David Ben-Gurion, backing the establishment of the state. This agreement is very important, since it set the basic lines followed ever since to enable the religious parties to remain within the government. The agreement largely continued practices embodied in legislation or customary during the Mandatory period: the Sabbath would be the official day of rest in the Jewish State, *kashrut* laws would be maintained in all public institutions, religious school systems would be operated and funded by the state, national public transportation would not run on Sabbaths and holy days, and matters of personal status—primarily marriage and divorce—would be controlled exclusively by religious law. At the same time, the religious camp conceded that the state radio would operate on Sabbaths and holidays, and local practices with regard to public transportation would be maintained.

In agreeing to these conditions, Ben-Gurion certainly sought to avoid conflicts within the Jewish population, even as he gained the support of the religious community. He felt he had provided a national minimum in the area of religion, guaranteeing that observant Jews and secular Jews could live as they desired without coercing each other or violating each others' principles in any intolerable way. This minimum also guaranteed the Jewish character of the state. Both religious parties accepted the arrangement and represented their constituencies in the provisional government formed by Ben-Gurion in 1948.

This status quo lasted with very little change until the late 1960s, but since then it has been eroded in ways small and large. While the religious parties have succeeded in reversing this erosion from time to time, the overall thrust has been to reduce the restrictiveness of the status quo, for example, with regard to the opening of places of entertainment on the Sabbath and the requirement of kashrut in restaurants. This is the case even though the number of exemptions to the rules restricting work on Sabbaths and holidays has been reduced each time a new government has come to power and needed to make a new coalition agreement with the religious parties. Yet these agreements always specify that the status quo to be protected is the current one, not what existed in earlier years, a sure sign that the changes are meaningful enough to be matters of political negotiation.

Given its reservations about a Jewish state not entirely founded on religious law, Agudat Yisrael not surprising has sought and received exemption from military service for its young people: male *yeshivah* students and all women who choose exemption need not serve. It is not clear according to halakhah that the students should be exempt. Agudat Yisrael persuaded Ben-Gurion by claiming that the students were needed desperately to rebuild in Israel the academies destroyed in Europe. Sympathetic to this goal and knowing that the total number of boys involved was no more than a thousand, Ben-Gurion granted the exemption. This exemption, which now extends to thirty thousand *yeshivah* students, still is respected by the Israeli government. Seeking of a military exemption reflects more than a fear of any halakhic violation that might be incurred during military service. Rather, exemption from the armed forces reflects a suspicion of and withdrawal from the state and its political efforts as well as withdrawal from secular elements of the society, represented by the army.

In contrast, the Mizrahi party and its successor, the NRP, have regarded service in the armed forces as an act of devotion to the state and the land, since for them the state is a positive religious value and an irreversible step in the messianic process. Moreover, while Mizrahi and the NRP joined government coalitions from the first, until the 1980s, Agudat Yisrael refused to take any responsibility for governing. Even today it carefully restricts its political responsibility though not its political activities.

**The secular camps:** In understanding the status quo agreement and the position of Judaism in Israel, one must consider why the non-Orthodox majority has sanctioned the presence and influence of the religious in Israeli society. Why has there not been a real *Kulturkampf*, as is so often suggested will occur, against the powers of "religious coercion"?

Jews who defined themselves as socialist Zionists brought with them from Europe a combination of rationalist and socialist ideals, the former determining a rejection of the traditional understanding of revelation, history, and messianism, the latter providing a humanistic surrogate for them. However, within the workers' movement several approaches to religion and tradition occurred, and these must be distinguished from each other. First was the negative approach of the group that rejected religion and tradition totally. These radical Zionists deemed Judaism a survival from primitive times and a brake upon the progress of the Jewish people. They considered it necessary to break loose from the entire religious framework before the work of national and individual reconstruction could begin. While this approach flourished for a generation or so in certain prominent circles, it soon began to decline. Spokesmen for it can still be found, but it is no longer a significant force in the country.

Another approach was ambivalent, its ideas far more complicated than the call for the abrogation of religious practices or the denial of religious concepts would seem to indicate. This approach remains characteristic of the leadership of Israel and prevalent among the non-Orthodox population. The roots of this ambivalence lie first in the socialist Zionists' deep attachment to their immediate past, their sense of warmth and nostalgia for what had been received at home. From the first, these sentiments moderated a staunchly negative ideological stance against Judaism. Yet far more significant than this passive, reflexive, appreciation was these Jews' active sense that, as pioneers in *Eretz Yisrael*, they were actualizing selected but core elements of the Jewish tradition. They saw themselves as builders of a Jewish society and culture that would be freer, healthier, and more universal than had been possible within the fettered conditions of exile. Finally, they considered themselves as a group to be a vital link in the historical continuity of the Jewish people, identifying themselves romantically with the ongoing historical spirit of Israel and invoking history and destiny when speaking of the meaning of the Zionist activity.

The sense of participation in a redemptive process, the longing to establish a utopian society, and the feeling of being actors in a drama that had world-historic significance linked even the secular pioneers with traditional religious ideals, ideas, and attitudes. Still, these religious associations must not disguise the secular grounding of the workers'

movement and the secular approach of its leaders. Alongside a deeply felt need to maintain historical continuity and even to receive legitimation from Jewish history existed a conscious attempt to dismiss the religious base of the Jewish tradition as meaningless or irrelevant.

National settlement facilitated and made real the transition from a religious to a national self-definition. Here the sense that the sacred was a social force whose manifestations are confined to society itself could be experienced easily and naturally. Zionism as an experience and as a project could be considered a mode of Jewish being that needed no external legitimation because it was the natural fulfillment of the Jewish struggle for survival. Some socialist Zionists appreciated the tradition while feeling free to abandon its religious framework or use it selectively, finding in their own national self-definition a sufficient substitute for the national-religious self-definition of their fathers. The apparent self-evidence of this transition from religious to national categories within the Zionist framework may account for the pioneers' almost total lack of interest in religious questions.

The Jewish people thus became the carrier of sanctity, the representative of the sacred. Particular cultural values, previously religious values also, were now sanctified simply because of their association with the nation. During the period of the Second Aliyah a process of selection took place in which certain values from the religious tradition were sorted out to be retained in the new Hebrew culture. Those selected were chosen because they could be interpreted as meaningful to the national or socialist vision of the pioneers. Thus, the Bible retained its sacred quality but was interpreted in terms of its national value, as a Jewish cultural monument, a link to Jewish history, the legitimator of Jewish claims to the land of Israel, and as a source of universalist humanistic ideals. It was emptied of its explicit meaning as the record of Israel's breakthrough to transcendence, becoming instead a treasure of Israel's national past.

The inescapable ambivalence towards Judaism derived from these developments was characteristic of Israeli society until recently and remains important today. While not accepting the entire world view and structure of Judaism, large groups want to maintain ties to the tradition that was once identified with Jewish national religious culture; they want to preserve elements and aspects of that tradition as part of Israeli culture and as values in Israeli society. No clear consistency is manifest in how either the Zionist pioneers or contemporary "non-religious" Israelis accomplish this. Various customs, ideals, attitudes, and values are maintained, often for reasons that are not conscious and in ways that are not explicit. This is the hold of a living and dynamic tradition upon its descendants. The result in Israel today is continuity despite rebellion. Both the pioneers of earlier immigrations and the citizens of today feel the pull of ancient and submerged loyalties towards the Jewish tradition.

Traditionalist citizens of contemporary Israel may not be concerned with the definitions or justifications the Zionist revolution brought to the Jewish tradition. They are concerned, however, with the character of the Jewish state and its legitimation. More and more in recent years they have come to recognize that both depend upon some link to the Jewish tradition. Judaism is somehow constitutive of Jewish identity, and the State of Israel is identified as a Jewish State. The non-believer—even the rabid anti-believer—has grasped this, and it has become the source of much inner anguish. This essential core character of Judaism inclines the non-religious within the Israeli population towards the tradition of those who are not nonreligious but who are also not Orthodox, that is, the traditionalist parts of the population.

**The peace process and Judaism in the State of Israel:** Recent years thus have brought changes in Israeli society, perhaps more at the expense of Zionism than Judaism. These changes have been highlighted in particular by the shift in the peace process after the first Oslo agreement between Israel and the Palestine Liberation Organization (PLO). The trends brought into sharp relief by the peace process all antedate that process and probably would have come into play in any case. But the peace process has hastened their development, and they will be exacerbated by the peace process and its consequences even if the peace is only partially successful. Some Israelis are pleased with the unfolding of these trends. Others have doubts, some of them grave, and are worried about their potential and even likely consequences.

The peace process is a landmark that may signify the end of Zionism, at least of Zionism as an effective means of pursuing the goals the Zionist founders of the State set out a hundred years ago and more. Importantly, Zionism's end will come because of its success. Of all the ideologies to come out of the nineteenth century and to have an impact on the world in the last century, Zionism was the most successful, even though it began from the least promising position. Its ideological competitors have long since died out; Zionism, by contrast, now reaches its end because of what it achieved, far more than because of its failures.

Zionism's success was as great as it was generally unanticipated: a more than hundredfold increase in the Jewish population of the land of Israel; the transformation of a barren, poverty-stricken land into a green and pleasant one, among the most prosperous in the world; the establishment of an independent Jewish state and the revival of the Hebrew language and a culture to go with it; construction of more Jewish religious institutions and at a higher level in every field than had ever existed before, or at least for thousands of years. Even the non- and anti-Zionists have benefited from Zionism. There are more students studying in yeshivot today than there were in Eastern Europe in its heyday. Synagogues in Israel and throughout the world, regardless of their form of Judaism and degree of identification with the State, draw upon it for inspiration and expressions of Jewish culture at every level. The list goes on.

**The new privatism:** Yet given the trends in the world against the old ideologies, the end of Zionism was bound to come, replaced by a new privatism that does not encourage great public purposes or individual sacrifice. Zionism's demise is the result of the decline of religious or national exclusivism in a world increasingly interdependent in every way, where mass communications and pop culture enter into every corner and drive out local cultures, even those rooted from centuries. All of these trends have been exacerbated by the non- or anti-Zionists within the Israeli peace camp, who see the goals and values of Zionism, like those of Judaism much more generally, as their greatest enemy. They have been trying to undermine Zionism for years, painting the Zionist enterprise in the blackest of hues. The peace process has allowed them to speak much more sharply on behalf of a goal that seems equally popular with much of the Israeli public. So harsh has been their message that it has provoked a response from some of the most seemingly unlikely sources, not only religious but secular Jewish intellectuals and artists for whom Zionism is, if not a sufficient answer, at the very least the faith of their fathers.

Secular Zionism has had to bear the brunt of this failure. In earlier times, it offered its adherents great tasks and grand challenges, equivalent to the tasks and challenges of religious Judaism and so equally, if not more, compelling, at least momentarily. But as those tasks have been completed and the predominate challenges overcome, Zionism has gone the way of every other Jewish movement that has made secularism its goal. It has ceased to be either necessary or sufficient to motivate the next generation or to deflect Jews—who are after all only human—from the natural paths towards normalcy: to seek peace, ease, security and prosperity, and to pursue happiness however they define it, as individuals.

Indeed, Zionism always had within it two great camps, those who saw the Zionist enterprise of restoring the Jewish people to their land as the first step toward normalcy, and those who saw it as a means of restoring the Jewish spirit in its most productive sense. Those two camps go back to the very beginnings of Zionism and, regardless of what other divisions existed in the Zionist movement, represented the main and greatest division. Until the peace process began, while Israel was under siege, those two camps had enough in common to hold themselves together as one. Today, the prospect of peace

has divided them in the most profound and contradictory ways, placing them in strong opposition to one another.

What we can say is that this is a historic struggle, not only within the Zionist movement but throughout Jewish history, between Jews who seek normalcy and those who feel in some way obligated or bound by their Jewishness. Indeed, much of the falling away of Jews in the past as well as the present probably has had to do with that struggle and the sides different people are on.

Normalcy may be good for Jews but, left alone to unfold, will bring an end to the Jewish state as such. Still, many Israeli Jews and half of the Israeli leadership thirst for that normalcy, either for private reasons as people or because they are simply tired—legitimately in many respects. Both the people and leaders are acting on that thirst for normalcy, whether we are speaking of the everyday citizens who flood the beaches and highways on Sabbaths and holidays or of the most powerful judges on Israel's Supreme Court, who set the pace in Israeli constitutional law according to interpretations that follow the most liberal trends in the west.

Increasingly, therefore, those who want the Jewish state to remain Jewish are forced into a corner. None of this was dependent upon acquiring and holding the administered territories in 1967; but it is all exacerbated by the necessity to withdraw from them in 1994 and beyond.

**The maintenance of the State's Jewishness:** Outside of a few small religious peace groups, those most active in promoting the Jewishness of the State (or, at least, their view of it) are the ultra-Orthodox *haredim*, their Shas offshoot, and the National Religious Party (NRP), joined also by the non-religious "Complete Land of Israel" group. Since 1967, the major interest of the NRP has been the administered territories, both in terms of settlements and as a means of intensifying the significance of the Land in the eyes of Israelis. The NRP thus became the heir of the Labor-initiated settlement movement that was the backbone of Zionism for nearly a century. But now, in the face of the peace process, it is on the defensive.

In the last analysis, all of this is part of the struggle to transform the Jewish state from a commonwealth to a civil society. This is not a clash between democracy and something else, for both a commonwealth and a civil society are species of democracy and both can be equally faithful to or abusive of democratic principles. The difference is the manner in which each combines communal solidarity and individualism. The commonwealth seeks a more homogeneous society, in which individuals express themselves as parts of a community, showing great solidarity and a willingness to accept manifold obligations in order to maintain their rights. A civil society is far more heterogeneous. It seeks communal solidarity in only a minimal sense, desiring, rather, to foster the individual's private pursuit of happiness almost without regard to the communal whole.

Since the emergence of modern democratic republicanism in the Protestant Reformation, both types of society have been democratic and republican in character but based on very different fundamental principles of societal structure and norms of communal relationships. For Jews, the matter goes even deeper. From their very beginning over three thousand years ago, Jews organized themselves as a commonwealth, marked by democratic and republican ideals but demanding communal solidarity built around Jewish monotheism and divine law. The modern Zionist movement attempted to secularize that commonwealth, not replace it. Even as its leaders retained the model of the commonwealth, they thought that modern ideology, particularly socialist ideology, could replace the older religious convictions as a source of communal solidarity.

But as the Zionist ideologies lost their potency, both because of success and of changing times, the heirs of those secular notions tended to adopt highly individualistic western, particularly American, ideas of social organization and relationships. They sought to reduce the demand for communal solidarity in favor of the individual's pursuit of happiness, particularly in the material sense but also in the sense of personal freedom to pursue more hedonistic ends. This squares well with the modern idea of a civil society, in which the polity frames an essentially private social order and in which the government's power to intervene in matters deemed to be the private preserve of individuals is drastically limited. From the first, civil society placed religion in the realm of the private. By the late twentieth century, most moral standards have been relegated to the private realm as well. This is quite different from the commonwealth ideal, which holds that matters of morality, at least, if not matters of religion as well, have a significant public dimension.

In a general way, at least, much earlier in the modern epoch the western world, led by the United States, embraced the idea of civil society as opposed to that of commonwealth. Israel has only now reached the point of open struggle between the two conceptions. The peace process makes that struggle possible, since it apparently removes one of the major justifications of absolute Jewish solidarity, the presence of an external threat. The elimination of that threat may be an illusion; we hope it is not. Nevertheless, a consequences of its elimination is the loss to those for whom traditional reasons are not compelling of a significant motivation for communal solidarity.

The struggle will be decided over the next generation. In part it will depend upon the degree of success of the peace process, but in most respects it will depend upon Israeli Jews' own expectations. It will be a struggle regardless, and it is important for Israeli Jews and, indeed, the entire Jewish people to understand accurately the struggle that awaits us.

**The interplay of religion and politics:** The religious population in Israel hopes that the entire population eventually will become Orthodox and that the state will conform in its laws and behavior to the demands of the religious tradition. In the meantime, the Orthodox groups have had to compromise and to operate with the reality of a non-halakhic state governed by a non-Orthodox leadership. Both religious parties, the NRP and Agudat Yisrael, have attempted to influence government policy in two areas. First, they have worked to establish by law their own institutions and separate services. Second, they have defined certain areas in the public realm to be governed by religious law and have established this fact through government legislation.

On the institutional plane, this means that the Orthodox have constructed their own school systems and have gained government support for their separate existence. The NRP-backed religious school system is part of the state system and receives its funding from state taxes. The extreme Orthodox do not want their schools to be part of the state system and so have gained recognition and funding for their own independent schools. The rabbinate and law courts are under the control of the Orthodox and are free of government interference except insofar as the courts are subject to the review of the Supreme Court. As noted above, religious law dictates that all public institutions be kosher, that certain restrictions of the Sabbath be imposed upon the entire population, and that marriage and divorce of Jews be regulated by Jewish law. The imposition of religious tradition in these areas has been accepted by Israelis, religious and non-religious. The acquiescence of large parts of the non-religious population together with the efforts of the religious parties have resulted in an obvious continuity between the modern state and Jewish tradition. While Israel has no established church and all religions are equal before the law, the state is not exactly neutral or secular and is not divorced from the symbols and institutions of Judaism.

This is not to say that the state is a religious entity or that it fulfills the ideals of Judaism. In fact, some Israelis argue from a religious perspective that the Jewish symbols and public celebrations of Jewish ritual are mere window-dressing for a basically secular state and society, that to call Israel a Jewish state in any religious sense its a distortion. On the other side, ideological secularists argue that the religious presence is hypocritical and offensive. In either case, it is clear that the relation between Judaism and society in Israel is complex and not easily analyzed.

Still, the religious parties exist because of the intense politicization of public life in Israel and the heavy involvement of government in almost all spheres of public activity. A major segment of the religious leadership is convinced that it must remain in politics simply in order to guard the Jewish character of the sate and the religious institutions that exist, that the alternative is to withdraw and permit these areas to be secularized. The power of the religious parties lies in Israel's system of coalition-governance. From the rise of the state in 1948 until the election of 1977, the majority party in that coalition was Labor, which, however, never received enough votes to form a government alone and so was forced time and again to reach an agreement with other smaller parties. Every coalition sought to include the religious parties, which, in each election, secured between ten and fifteen percent of the vote. In fact, every coalition included the NRP. Accordingly, it always received support for its special interest, religious affairs, even as its dominant coalition partner received the support of the religious in economic affairs and foreign policy.

While the NRP received around eight to ten percent of the vote, Agudat Yisrael along with the small Poalei Agudat Yisrael together received between three and five percent. Both electorates remained fairly stable. But NRP and Agudat Yisrael were often at odds, reflecting NRP's choice to be a coalition partner, with responsibility to maintain coalition loyalty, while Agudah remained independent and so can maintain its religious principles at all costs. NRP almost continuously ran the Ministry of Religious Affairs and the Ministry of the Interior and sometimes controlled the Education portfolio as well.

Both major religious parties dedicated themselves to preserving the status quo referred to above. However, while the NRP adopted a "go-slow" policy in certain areas, Agudat Yisrael pushed for immediate and total action, often seeking to embarrass the NRP in its conciliatory approach. Sensitive to charges of seeking to coerce the non-religious population in religious maters, the NRP has been willing to compromise. Thus, instead of a comprehensive national Sabbath observance law that would ban all business activities, a compromise permits local buses to run and certain businesses to open in specific localities and under specific conditions. In the area of kashrut, for many years the NRP attempted to pass a law banning the breeding of pigs. In 1962, when a coalitional balance permitted, this law was passed.

Without any cabinet seats to lose, the Agudah had a greater opportunity to make demands upon the government and sometimes even proposed bills just to demonstrate the NRP's willingness to compromise. Thus, Agudah proposed that, on the Sabbath, all flights of El-Al, the national airline, be stopped and that no airplanes from foreign fleets be allowed to land or take off in Israel. Given the conditions of international commercial aviation, both proposals were obviously impossible. An embarrassed NRP was forced to abstain, not being able to vote for the unworkable bill or against the government of which it was a part.

In the past, the NRP concentrated its efforts within the rather confined areas of its specific religious interests. Its thrust was mainly defensive: to protect gains rather than to seek new ones. Recognizing the non-religious character of the majority of the population, the party's larger goal was seen as the distant end of a long process of change. In the interim, the immediate goal of guaranteeing the maximal influence of religious precepts upon public life and the optimal support for separate religious institutions was pursued. This has required a posture of adaptation, compromise, and adjustment rather than aloofness, intransigence, and inflexibility.

The integration of Shas into this equation since the 1980s has meant that a religious party that seeks to be in government and control ministries but whose demands are close to those of the ultra-orthodox has now become the largest party at a time at which the religious parties hold one quarter of the Knesset seats. This has made them seemingly more powerful even as their status has eroded.

The religious parties are convinced that

withdrawal from the political sphere would not create a neutral state. Rather, it would produce a secular society whose state-funded institutions would have an inherent advantage over religious institutions and whose secular way of life and world view would compete with religion and inevitably dominate the marketplace. The American experience, in which, in principle, religion and state are separated completely, witnesses the necessary diminution of religion. This may be workable in a largely Christianity society, in which religion makes relatively few practical demands on a daily basis. But in the case of Judaism, where the scope of religion is total, the withdrawal of the state from the public sphere would mean a serious threat to the Jewish character of the society.

A number of legal cases in the Israeli court system or debated in the Knesset have tested the long range issues involved in the current religions-state arrangement. The first concerned a written constitution for the state, taken up in the Knesset in 1949. Proponents of a written constitution argued that the new state needed to guarantee individual rights and democratic governmental arrangements and that certain values of the Zionist revolution should be recorded so as to perpetuate the original vision of the state's founders. The Orthodox were among the strongest opponents of this idea, for they did not want the values of secular Zionism to be immortalized in a constitution. For the Orthodox, the Torah of Israel remained the eternal basis of the Jewish people, which must eventually be recognized by all. While the Jewish state might enact secular legislation, technically only interim measures, a full-blown constitution was another matter.

In this debate, not only the religious parties countered the pro-constitution forces. For their own reasons, other ideological groups also opposed a written constitution. Hashomer Hatzair, for instance, opposed any document that would not declare a radical socialist foundation of the state. Finally, Ben-Gurion himself opposed the proposed constitution, feeling a fight in its favor was premature. A compromise solution empowered the Knesset to enact "basic laws" that would ultimately form a complete constitution. Six such laws have been enacted to date, none touching on questions of religious principle. This leaves the issue of religious or secular authority unresolved in a sense but permits various factions to live together on a day-to-day basis.

Another conflict that gave expression to the debate over national self-definition concerns the question of "who is a Jew." As in many European countries, Israelis are registered at birth and possess an identity card that records religion and nationality. Jews normally have "Jewish" in both categories. The question is what defines a person as a Jew and whether the category "Jew" should refer to both nationality and religion at all. These issues have been tested in several cases in the Israeli courts and have aroused intense interest and concern, not only in Israel but throughout the world. The matter is weighty because it epitomizes the most basic question of who has the right to define Judaism in the modern Jewish State. Although it has not always pressed the issue, the religious leadership consistently has demanded that the only criteria be halakhic and that this criteria be applied without exception.

The most famous test case resulted in a non-*halakhic* decision, but one that the Orthodox accepted. The case of Brother Daniel challenged the meaning of the Law of Return, which recognizes anyone who is Jewish as an *oleh*, an immigrant. This is a privileged status, and for those possessing it citizenship and certain material benefits are automatic, which is not the case for non-Jews, who must undergo normal procedures for citizenship. Thus, the Law of Return guarantees all Jews (except those sought as criminals by foreign countries) the right to enter and be citizens of Israel and to receive national services from the moment of entry into the country.

In 1962, a Polish monk, Brother Daniel, applied for entry into Israel as an *oleh*, on the grounds that he was Jewish. He was born Oswald Rufeisen in Poland to Jewish parents and had been hidden in a monastery during the Holocaust, where he converted to Catholicism. Daniel claimed that because his mother was a Jew and he considered himself

a Jew nationally, even though he had become a Christian, he was entitled to be registered as a Jew and was eligible for the privileges of an *oleh*. The court recognized the halakhic position claimed by Daniel, for under Rabbinic law, one born of a Jewish mother remains Jewish, no matter what. Yet the court departed from this strict interpretation of the halakhah, which it distinguished from the law of the state, in this case, the Law of Return. The Court stated that the law "has a secular meaning, that is as it is usually understood by the plain and simple Jew. . . . A Jew who has become a Christian is not a Jew."

That majority opinion of the court rested upon the notion that a Jew is what is understood by the simple Jew on the street. The national history of the Jewish people demonstrates that one cannot be a Jew in nationality and a Christian in religion. Religious conversion to Christianity implied, according to the judges, that Daniel had indeed rejected his Jewish national past. The decision was that he could become a citizen of the Jewish State only by going through procedures of naturalization and citizenship, which he subsequently did.

Secular versus religious authority in matters of Jewish self-definition has been tested on other occasions, always causing complicated and emotional debate within the country. The cabinet crisis of 1958 is another example of such a test case, this time raised over the issue of how one registers children of mixed marriages. Is the simple declaration of both parents that they consider the child Jewish and want him or her registered as such sufficient for the government to recognize the child as Jewish? The Interior Minister declared that he would accept this self-definition and not insist on halakhic standards. This meant that a person essentially could intend or will his child to be Jewish, so long as one parent were Jewish. But in this case, the government ruled in favor of halakhic criteria and against the Minister of the Interior, who subsequently revoked his directive. The immediate crisis was settled, while the basic problem was only postponed.

While the religious definition of who is a Jew has been accepted by the government, new cases have arisen and undoubtedly will continue to test the halakhic definition. The Eitani case was similar to that of Brother Daniel. Ruth Eitani was born of a Jewish father and non-Jewish mother. During the Holocaust, the mother identified herself with her husband and suffered along with the family. After the war, Ruth immigrated to Israel, fought in the Haganah, raised a family, and became active in politics. Only then it became known that her mother was not Jewish and that, according to Rabbinic law, she and her own children would need to convert, despite their honest self-identification as Jews. After long debates, Ruth Eitani and her children underwent formal conversion.

The Shalit case challenged the registration of Jews in Israel. Benjamin Shalit, a naval officer, had married a non-Jewish woman and sought to have his children registered as Jews in nationality alone, thus asserting a new conception, of a Jew by nationality who rejects any religious profession. The government maintained its earlier view. Despite any profession on the part of the individual, objective criteria determine one's status. Born a Jew, in the eyes of the state, one remains a Jew in both religion and nationality. But one born a non-Jew may become a Jew, even nationally, only through a religious conversion.

None of the legal cases or Knesset debates has altered the government's commitment to the status quo, which supports a halakhic interpretation in matters of status, divorce, and marriage. And the majority of the population appears either to agree with or at least to acquiesce to this policy. The reason is as suggested above, a sense that the religious definition protects the Jewish character of the state and the desire to maintain the unity of the Jewish people, religious or non-religious, in the diaspora or Israel.

**Conclusion:** The Israeli government does not control or seek to control the state's religious establishment, even though the two are clearly and continually engaged with each other. Rather, the various religious communities and groups utilize state instrumentalities to further their own ends and to relate to other groups as parts of the compound or federation of communities that form Israel as a state.

What is the future of this compound? A more serious split appears likely between those who reject Judaism in their pursuit of normalcy and those who seek to be Jews through Judaism in some form. In particular, the shift of a part of the pace-setting elements of Israeli society towards greater concern for Jewish tradition reflects at least two factors, the perennial search for meaning that is characteristic of Jews, including Israeli Jews, and the concern for the Jewish future of Israel. These factors are mutually reinforcing, and both are appropriate in a world in which religious concerns seem to be on the rise.

But just as it is difficult to define or delimit Judaism in Israel, it is almost impossible to predict its future. The words *dati*—religious—and *hiloni*—secular—are useful only as labels and often hide as much as they reveal. While those who call themselves *dati* generally believe in and practice Judaism, those who are called or who call themselves *hiloni* do not necessarily fail to believe or practice. Similarly, while the State of Israel is officially secular, the meaning of this designation, applied to a self-proclaimed Jewish state, is not clear. From the earliest period of the Zionist movement until today, the "non-religious" Zionists have not been able to govern without the votes of religious groups. So God and the covenant have always been a part of the government, just as they are somehow a part of the state. This makes the religious condition of Israel extremely complicated, even to the point of challenging comprehension.

Two elements underlie the complex religious situation in Israel. Alongside the enlightenment ideals of pioneer Zionism, which have left so visible a mark upon present day Israel, ran a deep sense of and concern for Jewish identity. This sense, however obscured, was substantial and experienced by all Zionists. The second element was the sense of at least some Zionists that a Jewish state could not dispense with Judaism, recognized as constitutive of Jewish identity even for the unbeliever. This recognition, conscious or unconscious, inclined the secular Zionists towards cooperation with the Orthodox, no matter how annoying they found their specific demands. Most important, the centrality of Judaism, the religion, for Jewishness, a secular identity, has continued to be recognized, and with this recognition has come the awareness of the importance of Judaism in Jewish survival overall. The role of Judaism in the personal lives of Israelis and in Israeli politics and governance reflects all of this.

### Bibliography

Elazar, Daniel, *Israel: Building a New Society* (Bloomington, 1986).

Liebman, Charles, and Don-Yehiyah, Eliezer, *Civil Religion in Israel: Traditional Judaism and Political Culture in the Jewish State* (Berkeley, 1983).

Liebman, Charles and Don-Yehiyah, Eliezer, *Religion and Politics in Israel* (Bloomington, 1984).

DANIEL J. ELAZAR

**SYNAGOGUES, ANCIENT TIMES:** Researchers on the origins of the synagogue have not come to unanimity, although the traditions connecting its founding with Ezra (Neh. 8:1-10) are clear. One standard assertion is that the synagogue originated in the Babylonian exile. While this is plausible, it remains unproved. More recently some have argued for a third century B.C.E. date, and others for a second century B.C.E. origin of the synagogue. Of some help in dating the origins of the synagogue are Greek inscriptions, several of which, mentioning synagogues, are known from the Fayyum in Egypt and date as early as the second century B.C.E. The term they normally use for a synagogue is *proseuchê*, or place of prayer.

For example, a second or first century B.C.E. Greek inscription from ancient Athribis, about 150 km southeast of Alexandria in Egypt, reads:

> ON BEHALF OF KING PTOLEMY AND QUEEN CLEOPATRA, PTOLEMY SON OF EPHIKYDES, CHIEF OF POLICE, AND THE JEWS IN ATHRIBIS [DEDICATED] THE PLACE OF PRAYER (*proseuchê*) TO THE MOST HIGH GOD.

In this case, we have a dedicatory inscription that memorializes the dedication of the "Place of Prayer." A second inscription from Athribis of approximately the same date recounts the addition of an exedra to the Place of Prayer.

> ON BEHALF OF KING PTOLEMY AND QUEEN CLEOPATRA AND THEIR CHILDREN, HERMIAS AND HIS WIFE PHILOTERA AND THEIR CHILDREN [GAVE] THIS EXEDRA TO THE PLACE OF PRAYER.

The "exedra" is understood to be a room open on one side, annexed to the main hall and provided with seating. It may resemble the apsidal end of the Sardis synagogue (see below).

An early Greek inscription from Jerusalem (the Ophel) uses the Greek word *synagogê* for "synagogue." The pre-70 C.E. date of this inscription has recently been challenged, but further research tends to vindicate the early date. The text, carefully chiseled into a limestone block, was discovered in 1913 and is on display in the Rockefeller Museum in Jerusalem:

> THEODOTOS THE SON OF VETTENOS, PRIEST AND HEAD OF A SYNAGOGUE (*archisynagogos*), SON OF A HEAD OF A SYNAGOGUE, GRANDSON OF THE HEAD OF A SYNAGOGUE, BUILT THE SYNAGOGUE (*synagogê*) FOR THE READING OF THE LAW AND FOR INSTRUCTION IN THE COMMANDMENTS, AND THE GUEST HOUSE, AND THE ROOMS, AND THE WATER REQUIREMENTS AS A LODGING FOR THOSE NEEDING IT FROM ABROAD, WHICH (SYNAGOGUE) HIS FATHERS AND THE ELDERS AND SIMONIDES FOUNDED.

Likewise, a Greek inscription from North Africa dating to 56 C.E. uses the term *synagogê* once to mean the "congregation" and once to mean the "building." Therefore the word *synagogê* can indeed refer to architecture in the diaspora in the first century C.E. The inscription in question, from Berenice of Cyrenaica, reads:

> IN THE SECOND YEAR OF THE EMPEROR NERO CLAUDIUS CAESAR DRUSUS GERMANICUS, ON THE SIXTEENTH OF CHORACH, IT WAS RESOLVED BY THE CONGREGATION (*synagogê*) OF THE JEWS IN BERENICE THAT [THE NAMES] OF THOSE WHO

DONATED TO THE REPAIRS OF THE SYNAGOGUE (*synagogê*) BE INSCRIBED ON A STELE OF PARIAN MARBLE.

These inscriptions make clear that the word *synagogê* was known in the first century in North Africa and in ancient Palestine and used to refer to a building. But they do not make clear precisely for what purpose the building was used. Indeed, whatever the synagogue's origins, the earliest concrete archaeological evidence for actual synagogue buildings is in the diaspora. Let us consider four such buildings: on the island of Delos, in ancient Ostia, in Sardis, and the well known synagogue of Dura-Europos.

**The synagogue of Delos:** The earliest known synagogue building, from the Greek island of Delos, dates from the first century B.C.E. to the end of the second century C.E. (Drawing 1). The building is surely a private, peristyle courtyard house built as early as the second century B.C.E. but renovated for Jewish community use about the beginning of the first century B.C.E. The house had been situated near the shore in a domestic neighborhood during the course of the second century B.C.E. The building continued in use as a synagogue at least until some time during the second century C.E.

After the renovations, three entrances led into the assembly worship area, sometimes understood to be the synagogue proper (Room A) from Room B to the south. Another entry opened from the east from the courtyard and its porch. This main hall (room A) is a simple rectangle about 14.4 × 16.9 m., quite large by ancient standards but half as large as the original room formed of Rooms A and B. The excavators found marble benches both on the northern wall and on the western wall of the Main Hall. This is a provision for a seated congregation.

In the published plans, there is also a evidence that marble benches were found on the south wall of Room B. These benches are about 45 cm. wide. In the middle of the extant bench on the west is a fine marble "throne," designated a "Seat of Moses" in some publications, though probably erroneously. This throne resembles most strongly the throne of the priest of Dionysos in the theater at Athens. It doubtless was for the president or presiding officer of the synagogue at some of the meetings held there. He may have been flanked by other dignitaries on the western marble bench. In any case it is clear that the architecture followed the social structure of the gathering.

The rooms to the south of the main room contained no identifiable furniture. A cistern beneath the floor of the middle room contained lamps with many pagan motifs on the depressed discus of each. These attest to the Roman context in which the synagogue operated.

The identification of this building as a synagogue rests upon inscriptional evidence. Many inscriptions "in accordance with a vow" (*ex voto*) were found on marble columns and bases in the building. These contain references to "the highest God" (*theos hypsistos*), taken to refer to the God of Judaism. One of the inscriptions on an inscribed base also contained the Greek word *proseuchê*, again a common word for synagogues in the diaspora. The inscription reads: AGATHOCLES AND LYSIMACHUS (GAVE THIS) TO THE HOUSE OF PRAYER.

**The synagogue of Ostia:** Another early building identified as a synagogue is from ancient Ostia, the port city of Rome (Drawing 2). It was founded in the first century C.E., and whether it was intended from the beginning to be a gathering place for the Jewish community is still open to debate. Still, it seems clear that the first renovation of the building for use by the Jewish community resulted in the general lay-out of the Main Hall (D) with the center of interest being the bema, or raised platform, against the west wall. Benches lined the north and south walls, but not for their entire lengths. The Main Hall was about 16.3 × 12.5 m. in maximum extent, which compares favorably to the synagogue at Delos. If the inscription of Mindius (or Mindus) Faustus at Ostia refers to this renovation (see below), then an ark was installed on the bema. This renovation dates to the late second or early third century C.E.

Late in the third century or early in the fourth century C.E., a second renovation took place. This time the building was "monumentalized:" the ceiling in the Main Hall was raised, columns were installed, and the shell of the Main Hall thickened. New walls were added so as to incorporate the Vestibule (A), Kitchen (G), Utility Room (F), and Dining Hall (E) into the total structure. The entry area was redesigned so that three portals opened off the Vestibule (A) into areas B and C, which conducted worshipers into the main hall down a kind of nave and two side aisles.

A second major change occurred in the orientation of the Main Hall (D) when an aedicula was built against the south wall as a Torah Shrine. In this change the new Torah Shrine moved the center of interest from the west to the south-east. The new shrine blocked the south aisle, necessitating other changes, namely, the addition of low balustrades between area B and the south aisle to block traffic. These additions may have occurred early to mid-fourth century C.E.

Other embellishments and decorations occurred after this last addition, but the outlines of the building were firm until it went out of use. Some of these later decorations included menorah reliefs on architectural elements of the Torah Shrine. The building was abandoned at some point in the fifth century C.E.

The synagogue inscription from Ostia was found in re-use as a repair tile in the last stages of the building. It was originally cut into the tile near the end of the second century C.E. or the beginning of the third century C.E., that is, about 200 C.E. The first line is in Latin, the remaining six are in Greek, but cut by the same hand, though there is a suggestion that the last two lines containing the name of Mindius Faustus are in a second hand.

FOR THE WELL-BEING OF THE EMPEROR. MIND<I>US FAUSTUS ME[. . .] [. . .]DIO[. . .] CONSTRUCTED [THE SYNAGOGUE] AND MADE [IT] FROM HIS OWN FUNDS, AND HE DEDICATED THE ARK FOR THE SACRED LAW.

The additional "I" in the name Mindius was suggested from the find of the name "Mindius" in other inscriptions in the environs of Ostia. This is a large plaque, about 29 × 54.5 cm., presumably originally installed in a wall.

It is noteworthy that the Greek word translated "ark" was evidently already used as a technical term in this inscription.

**The synagogue at ancient Sardis:** This is the largest and most impressive of any so far excavated (fig. 131). In the late third century, an already existing basilica space on the south side of a block in the recreation area of Sardis (baths and palaestra) was acquired by the Jewish community. It is not clear whether this space was a civil court or other public space at this time, though it had been public space from 17 C.E. In any case, in the third century C.E., the Jewish community completely transformed the space for its own requirements. The Jews added a large podium to the apse at the western end, built of finely fitted marble and limestone ashlars, or stone blocks cut on all six faces. Doorways into the neighboring baths were sealed up, as were two niches, one on either side of the apse. Three tiers of benches were added to the apse, presumably for the seating of dignitaries and possibly others during meetings.

Also at this time, though precisely in what sequence is open to interpretation, piers replaced the columns that held up the roof. The floor was paved with fine mosaics within the apse and extending into the nave of the building. Two inscriptions from this renovation present names from the past. The first was originally quite long, but only three lines in Greek have been pieced together. The letters, 6 cm. high, were cut into a marble plaque that originally adorned the south wall. The three lines read:

. . . WITH MY WIFE REGINA AND MY CHILDREN . . . GAVE FROM THE GIFTS OF ALMIGHTY GOD THE ENTIRE MARBLE REVETMENT . . . OF THE HALL AND THE PAINTING (OF THE WALLS).

"The marble revetment" refers to a marble facing several centimeters thick that covered the lower half of the walls of the main hall. Another revetment covered the walls of the apse. Since some of the revetment was made of small colored stones cut as circles, triangles, etc., and set in geometric patterns (*opus sectile*), it is possible that the revetment refers also to the *opus sectile*.

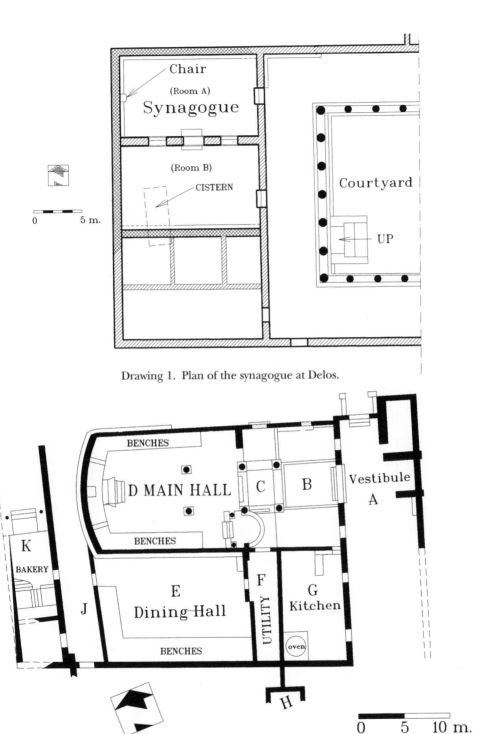

Drawing 1. Plan of the synagogue at Delos.

Drawing 2. The synagogue from Ancient Ostia.

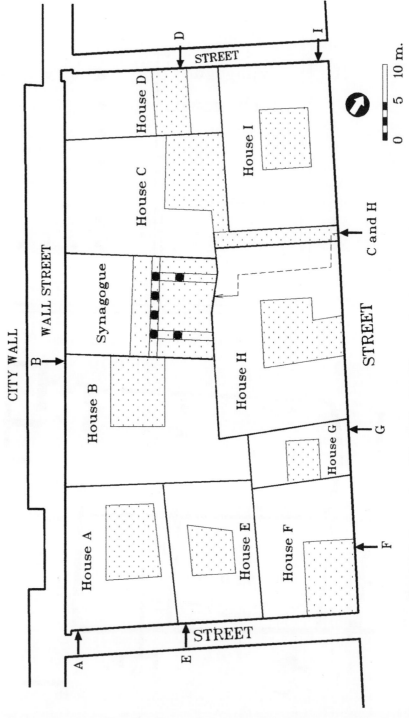

Drawing 3.  Restoration of Block L7 at Dura-Europos showing courtyards and street entrances.

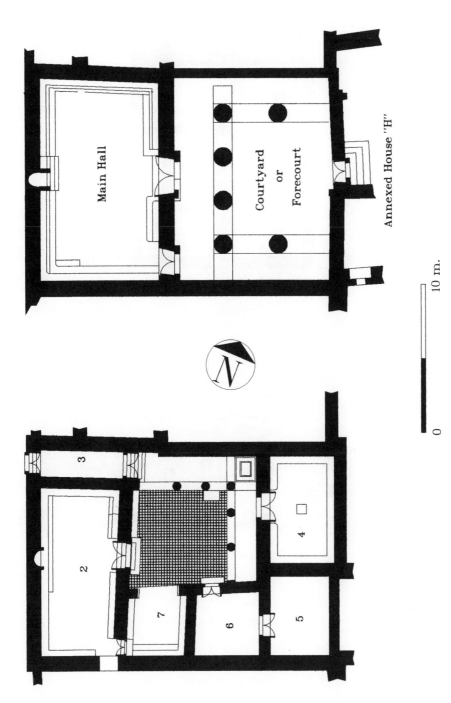

Main Hall

Courtyard
or
Forecourt

Annexed House "H"

*N*

0          10 m.

Drawing 4. Dura, early synagogue (left) and late synagogue (right).

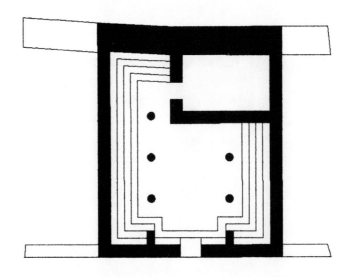

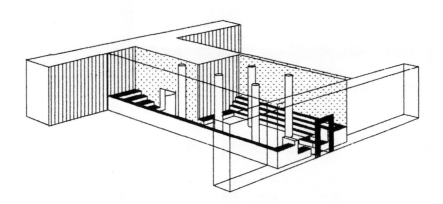

Drawing 5. Plan and perspective of the Masada synagogue.

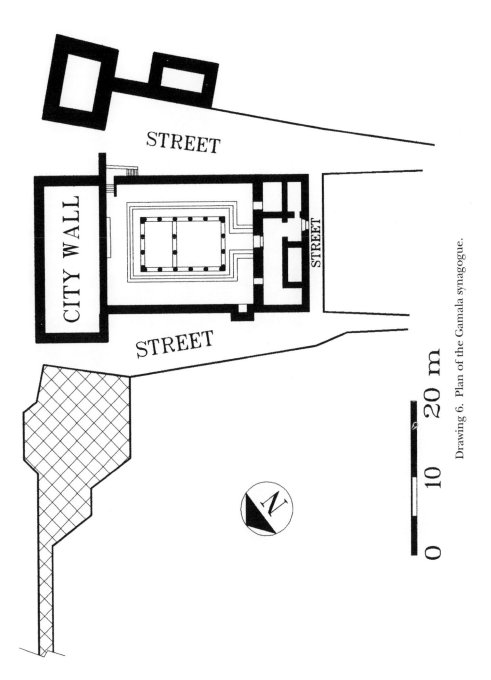

Drawing 6. Plan of the Gamala synagogue.

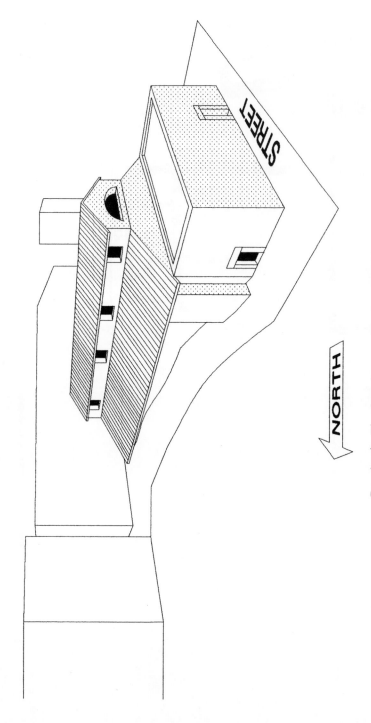

Drawing 7. The Gamala synagogue in perspective.

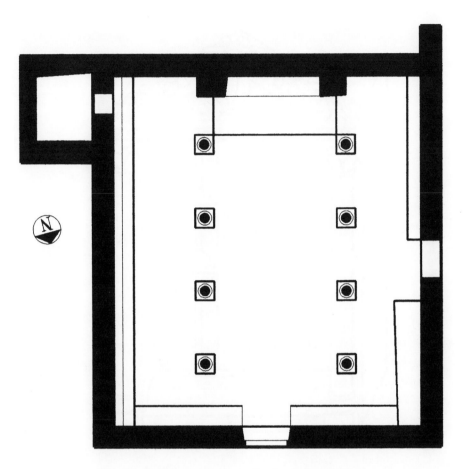

Drawing 8. The synagogue at Qasrin, Golan Heights.

Drawing 9. A Torah shrine adapted from the mosaic floor of the synagogue at Hammath-Tiberias showing a double-leaf door.

Figure 131. Overview of excavated synagogue at Sardis, Turkey, c. fourth-sixth century C.E. A vast urban complex was discovered including a bath, gymnasium, palaestra, and the largest ancient synagogue yet discovered. The building consisted of a colonnaded forecourt and a main hall. Situated on the eastern end were two aediculae, which possibly served as the Torah shrines.

Figure 132. Infant Moses discovered in the bulrushes, detail from the mural on the western wall of the synagogue at Dura Europos, Syria, c. 244-245 C.E. According to the biblical text, the infant Moses was discovered by Pharaoh's daughter and her servants. This panel depicts the child's rescue and presentation before Pharaoh.

Figure 133. Moses reading the Law, detail from the murals on the western wall of the synagogue at Dura Europos. Dressed in typical Greco-Roman tunic and toga, Moses holds an open Torah scroll. By late antiquity, reading of the Torah was an essential part of synagogue worship.

Figure 134. The Ark at Dagon, detail from the murals on the western walls of the synagogue at Dura Europos. The pagan statues and ritual implements of the temple of Dagon lay broken before the triumphant Ark of the Covenant, showing the greatness and power of the God of Israel.

Figure 135. Detail of the Torah Shrine panel from a synagogue mosaic at Beth Shean, Israel, c. fourth-fifth century C.E. The central feature of this mosaic pavement is a Torah Shrine in the form of an aedicula. Torah scrolls were probably stored within a wooden cabinet, positioned behind the curtain. The Shrine is flanked by two free-standing menorahs, which are in turn flanked by an incense shovel and shofar. This assemblage appeared in many synagogue pavements in ancient Palestine.

Figure 136. Interior of restored Ben Ezra Synagogue, Fostat, nineteenth century.

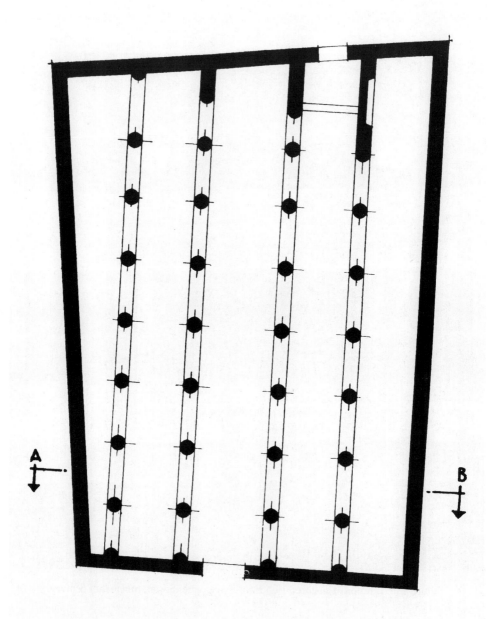

Figure 137. Ground plan of Santa Maria de la Blanca, Toledo, ca. 1200.

Figure 138. Interior of Santa Maria de la Blanca, Toledo, ca. 1200.

Figure 139. Destroyed Synagogue, Segovia, thirteenth century.

Figure 140. Columns of former Synagogue, Seville, thirteenth century.

Figure 141. Interior of Synagogue, Cordoba, 1315.

Figure 142. Interior of El Transito, Toledo, 1360.

Figure 143. Interior of Synagogue, Tomar, ca. 1460.

Figure 144. Interior of Synagogue, Worms, 1175 .

Figure 145. Artist's rendering of the interior of Altneuschul, Prague, ca. 1260.

The second inscription lay in the mosaic floor of bay three on the south wall, counting from the apse at the west end of the hall. The letters are black on a white background, each letter from 5.5 to 7.5 cm. High. The inscription reads:

> AURELIOS ALEXANDROS, ALSO CALLED ANATOLIOS, A CITIZEN OF SARDIS AND A CITY COUNCILLOR, PAVED THE THIRD BAY WITH MOSAIC.

It is interesting to see that this man occupied a seat on the city Council. Other dedicatory inscriptions in the Sardis synagogue list donors who held equally important civic positions. Some of the titles held include Count (*comes*), Procurator (*epitropes*), members of the Decurionate or municipal senate (*sardionoi, bouleutai*), and civic administrators (*boethoi taboulariou*).

During the fourth century, a second major renovation was carried out. This time a certain Hippasios gave funds for the construction of a colonnaded atrium or forecourt at the east end of the building. A large sculpted crater stood in the center of the atrium and functioned as a water fountain. Now when one entered from the street, one was not standing in the main hall, but in a beautifully decorated forecourt partitioned off from the main hall by a cross wall with three portals leading into the main hall. The floors of the forecourt were paved in mosaics, and low balustrades closed the spaces between the columns.

In terms of understanding worship in the synagogue, perhaps the most important addition was two aediculae or shrines with two columns in front, rather like the aedicula at Ostia in Italy. These stood with their back to the west wall of the forecourt but inside the main hall. Each aedicula flanked the main portal leading into the main hall. Two recessed steps led up to each platform within each aedicula to a height of 55 cm. above the floor of the main hall.

Another addition was a marble table, which stood in bay 1 near the west end of the main hall. The legs of this table were sculpted in the form of standing eagles. Two stone lions found in the excavation probably stood on either side of this table. Perhaps contemporary with the Eagle Table was a bema or raised platform of marble constructed in bay 4. Another marble table stood before the shrine on the south side of the central door. Finally, Corinthian columns and an architrave stood on a circular base in bay 1. This may have held a menorah, though a menorah could have also stood in one of the aediculae. Mosaic floors stood everywhere in the main hall, organized in panels corresponding to the bays between the piers. In each panel appeared a dedicatory inscription for the person who had donated so many feet of mosaic.

**The synagogue at Dura-Europos:** The ancient city of Dura-Europos was laid out in blocks of houses commonly called *insulae*. The particular block in which the synagogue stood was labeled L7 by the excavators (Drawing 3). It stood beside Wall Street, which ran along the west city wall and between two gates. The synagogue therefore stood on the west side of the approximately 40 × 77 m. block. Between 150 and 200 C.E., the synagogue was built by renovating a house. Entrance to the synagogue from Wall Street was through a small doorway that let into a long, narrow hall (marked 3 in Drawing 4). The hall led about six meters to a set of steps that led down to the north porch of a peristyle court with a second porch on the east.

There were five rooms around the peristyle court, three of which were equipped with benches for assemblies of various sizes and for various purposes. These were Room 4, a dining room about 6.8 × 4.1 m. with benches on four sides, Room 7, a meeting room open on the north measuring about 3.9 × 3.7 m., equipped with benches on three sides and a small doorway into Room 2, and Room 2 itself, understood to function as the main hall (about 10.7 × 5 m).

Room 7, because of the benches all around, because of wall decoration reminiscent of the main hall, and because it opened into the main hall, has been understood to be a repository for biblical scrolls. This room was decorated with a floral motif painted on its plastered walls, beginning about one meter above the floor. The ceiling was painted to resemble tiles with floral designs. Three Aramaic graffiti found in Room 7 contain names of men, perhaps donors, who took part in formalities associated with assembly and worship.

The floor of Room 2 was nearly half a meter higher than the floor of the courtyard. This main hall was therefore entered by steps and a doorway from the courtyard. Benches allowed for seating on all four walls, and the floor itself was plastered. In the center of the west wall there stood a small Torah shrine or aedicula with two columns in front and a niche cut into the back. An Aramaic dipinto (painted inscription) from the niche of the later synagogue uses the term "House of the Ark" (*byt arona*), which was likely the local name for such a niche.

The second renovation of the synagogue, which corresponds to the third renovation of the space where it stood, took place during the year 244/245 C.E. This was a major change, requiring the complete clearing of the internal walls of the structure and transformation of the space into a forecourt (courtyard) and main meeting hall. Entry was from the other side of the block into House H, which was now annexed by the Jewish community. Worshippers and others climbed up steps from House H into the open and colonnaded forecourt. There was a roof between the columns and the side walls.

South of the forecourt, one entered the main hall through either of two doors. The middle portal featured double leaf doors and let directly into the center of the hall on its long side. The room was equipped with plastered benches on all four walls for assembly. Directly opposite the entrance, and therefore opposite the entering worshiper, was a niche with a shell motif above, the successor to the niche in the early Dura synagogue. This is the niche mentioned in the Aramaic dipinto. The inscription has been constructed in two different ways:

> I, UZZI, MADE THE REPOSITORY OF THE TORAH SHRINE. JOSEPH SON OF 'ABBA MADE THE. . . .

> MARTIN MADE THE PAINTINGS (work) OF THE "HOUSE OF THE ARK;" SISA' MADE THE HOLY ARK.

If we follow closely Du Mesnil's reading of the Aramaic, we translate:

> MARTIN WHO MA[DE] THE WORK OF THE HOUSE OF THE ARK, AND SISA' MADE THE HOLY ARK.

A second entrance let into the main hall at its southeast end, or at the left end of the wall at the back of the forecourt. There is no formal clue in the plaster or floor to indicate who might use this entrance instead of the one in the center of the wall.

The ceiling was plastered in imitation of floral tiles. However, three ceiling tiles from the renovation of 244/245 C.E. were inscribed in Aramaic and preserve the names of the major benefactors of this third century C.E. renovation of the building. The first few lines of the Aramaic inscription read:

> THIS HOUSE WAS BUILT IN THE YEAR 556 (= 244/245 C.E.), THIS CORRESPONDING TO THE SECOND YEAR OF PHILIP JULIUS CAESAR, IN THE ELDERSHIP OF THE PRIEST SAMUEL BAR YEDA'YA THE ARCHON. AND THOSE WHO SUPERVISED THE WORK WERE ABRAM THE TREASURER, AND SAMUEL BAR SAPHARAH, AND [SILAS?] THE PROSELYTE.

The Caesar Philip Julius in question today is usually called "Philip Senior" to distinguish him from his son and successor. Three other ceiling tiles are inscribed in Greek and contain in brief the same information. For example, one reads: "SAMOUEL SON OF EIDDEOS, ELDER OF THE JEWS, MADE [IT]."

The most spectacular features of the room were the professionally executed wall paintings of biblical scenes. These appeared in four registers of twenty panels, though the top register was badly destroyed. These paintings have been well studied, and the present consensus is that they are major representations of the piety of the Jews at Dura (figs. 132-134). A central motif appears to be the ark of the covenant, perhaps as a symbol of revelation.

The entire city of Dura-Europos was destroyed in a siege in 256 C.E. The synagogue and all other buildings for worship were destroyed at this time.

**The ancient vocabulary for synagogue:**
The rich Greek vocabulary for synagogues in the diaspora in the Second Temple period surely reflects how synagogues were conceived by their communities and, on occasion, how they were viewed by outsiders. The vocabulary also gives clues as to what went on inside them. The most commonly found Greek term is one of the common words for prayer, used in the sense of "[place of] prayer" (*proseuchê*). We find this term used in this sense about thirty times in inscriptions and in papyri. It also appears twice in Acts 16 for a place of prayer at Philippi. Other synonyms for "place of prayer" occur. For example, at least once in the papyri it is called a "*eucheion*," and at least once in Philo it is called a "*proseukterion*." Both these terms imply a space set aside for public, congregational prayer.

In inscriptions in North Africa, the word "amphitheater" is used for a synagogue four times. This may suggest that the seating was arranged in a circle or ellipse, though it is more likely that use of this term was simply a local custom. Philo twice calls the synagogue a "school" (*didaskaleion*), indicating that instruction was a second major function of the institution.

Three times in the *Jewish Wars* (7.3.3, §45; 4.7.2, §408, 7.5.5., §144), Josephus uses the word "holy [place]" or "sanctuary" (*hieron*). The word "place" (*topos*), which appears three times in Josephus, once in Philo, and perhaps once in 3 Maccabees, may be shorthand for "holy place" (*hieros topos*), which eventually became a synonym for synagogue in Greek as well as in the Byzantine period in Hebrew and Aramaic synagogue inscriptions. Once in Philo and once in an Egyptian papyrus (and probably once in a Ptolemaic inscription), the term "holy space" or "holy enclosure" appears (*hieros peribolos*). These two terms and "holy place" (*hieros topos*), which appears twice in inscriptions, suggest that the space is set aside as sacred. In archaeological terms, this need mean no more than that it was enclosed with a stone wall so that outsiders could not enter at inopportune moments. The special term translated "Sabbath meeting place" (*sabba-*

*teion*) occurs once in Josephus, once in a papyrus, and once in an inscription. The word confirms that gathering took place on the Sabbath. Once in Josephus the word "dwelling place" occurs (*oikema*). The Latin word "*templum*" also occurs once (Tacitus, *History* 5.5.4), reflecting nothing more than a Roman cultural perception of a Jewish place of worship.

In the New Testament, the most common word is "*synagogê*," usually translated "synagogue." The word appears more than fifty times in the four gospels and in Acts. In these contexts it seems to signify a building, though some have argued that the use of the word in the gospels for architecture is anachronistic. In any case it seems an irresistible conclusion that the preferred name for the institution in ancient Palestine was "synagogue," whereas in the diaspora it was "place of prayer" (*proseuchê*).

From ancient literature, we can deduce some of the ritual activities that took place in synagogues. Philo has informed us that on the Sabbath in Jewish schools in every city, the congregation sat in a fitting fashion while a knowledgeable or wise person stood to instruct (*Spec. Leg.* 2.62). Josephus also informed his Roman audience that reading and study of the ancient holy books was an important part of Jewish life (*Contra Apion* 1.42). In the New Testament, Luke 4:16-20 placed Jesus in a synagogue, understood both as a gathering and as a building. There he stood up to read (v. 16), he had access to a scroll of Isaiah (v. 17), and an attendant was present to give the scroll to the reader and then to receive it back (v. 20). Apparently Jesus and the congregation had been seated. Thus we infer that synagogues provided congregational seating while at least one leader (and perhaps the attendant) stood. We also expect to find a special space for the congregation to stand for congregational prayer, since public prayer in the ancient world was normally executed standing.

In later discussions of synagogues much is taken for granted that is absent in these texts. The texts make no assumption about any specific decoration, either inside or outside. So long as the Jerusalem Temple was standing with its art and ritual equipment, there seems to have been no impetus to draw or carve representations of this equipment in the synagogue. Not even the menorah is mentioned. There is also no gallery for women and no separate entrance for women. There is no raised center of interest or bema and no specific orientation of the building to the east or towards Jerusalem. Furthermore the texts do not assume that worshipers in synagogues first went to a ritual bath. Any or all of these items may be presupposed; but they are not supported by concrete textual evidence.

**Archaeological evidence for early synagogues in the land of Israel:** It seems that the debate about the plausibility of calling the structures at Gamala, Masada, Magdala, and Herodium "synagogues" in some narrow sense is not resolving one way or the other. All these halls were identified as synagogues by circumstantial evidence. They resemble in general Roman or Byzantine synagogues in the land of Israel, known as such from their decoration and/or inscriptions. Many of the Late Roman or Byzantine synagogues were oriented toward Jerusalem. Finally, some of these presumed synagogues were found at Jewish sites and were clearly designed for public gatherings, so that they seem correctly to be called "synagogues."

We leave Magdala out of the discussion, since there is some debate about its function. On the other hand, the three possible synagogue buildings at Masada, Herodium, and Gamala all seem to meet the requirements for space referred to above. Further, they have more in common than not:

(A) These buildings organize innermost space in a similar manner, namely, it is rectangular and surrounded on three or four sides by rows of columns, then by ranges of benches on three or four sides.

(B) One must use the benches as steps to move from the top bench or landing to the floor. In other words, there is no separate staircase to lead the worshiper up from the lowest floor. This calls to mind a saying attributed to Simeon ben Azzai (about second century C.E., but preserved in a much later context), "Descend from your place two

or three steps and sit down. It is better that you should be told 'ascend' than 'descend'" (Abot dR. Nathan 25.4). It also recalls texts in the synoptic gospels that speak of preferred seating in synagogues (Mark 12:39, et al.).

(C) Perhaps the most revealing feature of inner space is that worshipers sitting or standing on the benches must look through a balustrade of columns to see what is going on centrally. This is echoed in the construction of the diaspora synagogues at Priene in Greece and at Ostia in Italy.

(D) The "Jewishness" of these structures is not expressed by building elements or decorations but by their sitting in a Jewish town or village or even in a Jewish fortress. (It is possible that the palm tree decoration on the lintel at Gamala is intended as a Jewish symbol.)

(E) Although parts of these buildings resemble structures in the Roman empire, their total organization is novel. For example, a Council Chamber (*bouleuterion*) could be thought of as a progenitor of this synagogue space, for such a chamber was built with concentric, square ranges of benches for seating and a central, rectangular space, presumably for the leader or speaker. One may also think of a Roman basilica as the natural parent of the synagogue, as witness the adoption of the Sardis basilica by the Jewish congregation. The similarity between synagogue buildings, particularly Late Roman and Byzantine synagogues, and the basilica is precisely in the organization of inner space. Both divided inner space into a nave and aisles by columns and often by the placement of the principal entrances on the narrow end of the building. Yet neither in a Council Chamber nor in a basilica is one required to look between the columns to watch a ritual or spectacle. Rather, in either of these two types of buildings, one stands in the nave within the space of the ritual or spectacle.

Since these four buildings resemble one another more than other buildings, they may represent a type. This resemblance extends to structures in the diaspora, notably at Sardis (which is itself a basilica, see above), Ostia, and Priene. The commonality among them also suggests strongly that their builders were seeing some structure or structures that gave them the extraordinary idea of arranging seating between the columns and the walls.

An examination of Drawings 5, 6, and 7 brings home the point of how odd such organization of space really is. One is presented virtually with a forest of columns, and it is between these rows of columns that the important business of the synagogue is transacted.

(F) The most prominent source of this idea is the porticos of the Temple Mount, including the "Royal Portico." But, according to Josephus (*BJ* 5.5.2, §199), the Court of Women, the Court of Israel, and the Court of the Priests were also surrounded by porches with columns. Furthermore, one would pass through the Nicanor Gate, a gate with three portals, into space surrounded with porticoes and columns, rather like the majority of synagogues from the first to the sixth centuries C.E. Although we know nothing of benches for seating inside the colonnades on the Temple Mount, the similarities of the buildings at Gamala, Masada, Magdala, and Herodium to the porches on the Temple Mount strongly suggest that the synagogue building, as erected in Israel, is a Jewish invention based upon the porches or colonnaded spaces of the Temple, especially the Nicanor Gate and the Court of Israel. This observation pertains even if these first century halls were sometimes used for ritual purposes and sometimes for non-ritual purposes, such as community meetings.

**Other synagogue excavations in the land of Israel:** More than fifty synagogues from the second to the seventh centuries C.E. have been excavated or surveyed in Israel, Jordan, and Syria as well as in the diaspora. The greatest density of synagogues is found in the Galilee and the Golan Heights. Most of these appear to have been founded about the middle of the third century C.E. Some of them go out of use by the fourth century C.E.; others are in use through the seventh or eighth century C.E. They seem to follow no rigid plan, except that the majority of them place the rows of columns between the benches and the central space, usually

understood to be the area in which worshipers stood to pray. The columns are most commonly Ionic, though the Corinthian and Doric orders are represented.

Most synagogues are rectangular. About one-fourth of them (often sixth century C.E.) have an apse at the focus of interest, and about half are built so that their facades are oriented on Jerusalem. Most commonly it is theorized that those with an apse are in imitation of basilicas or of Christian churches, themselves basilicas.

Often synagogues of the third and fourth centuries have a facade furnished with three portals, reminiscent of the Temple Mount's Triple Gate, one of the two Hulda Gates, or suggesting the Nicanor Gate. Of course many buildings in the Greco-Roman world also featured three portals, so this element in and of itself only has significance in a Jewish context. In this arrangement, the central and tallest portal leads directly into the nave between the columns. The two side portals lead into the side aisles. This arrangement is sometimes called a "Triple Portal" and describes about three-fourths of published synagogue plans. On occasion the "Triple Portal" is found on one of the long sides. Ordinarily, the builders decorated the door posts and lintels of these portals with elaborate multiple moldings.

Most of the synagogues of the Golan Heights were entered through a single door in the center of the facade (Drawing 8). This door lets directly into the nave between the two rows of columns. A few other synagogue buildings in ancient Palestine were entered on the long side, giving rise to the term "broadhouse" synagogue. This is true at Khirbet Shema in Upper Galilee, for example, but also at Ma'oz Hayim east of Beth She'an, and at Eshtemoa in Judea.

**Synagogue art:** The facades of some synagogues were lavishly decorated with geometric or floral carvings in relief, carvings in the round, sometimes of lions and eagles, incised designs, sometimes repeating what was carved in relief, or carved and incised inscriptions on lintels. The finest examples of such decoration are from Capernaum and Chorazin, both near the north and west shores of the Sea of Galilee. Lintels might be decorated with garlands, palms, palm fronds, flowers, nikes or genii, birds, and other artistic motifs. Usually the stones of the facade, though not necessarily all of the building, were very carefully chiseled to present a finished face to approaching worshippers. For example the facade of the synagogue at Gush Halav in Upper Galilee is very finely cut across the entire front and for an additional 2.6 m. around the southeast corner, that is, on the east side. The remainder of the building presents well-fitted and trimmed field stones to the worshipper but does not present ashlars.

Floors of these prayer halls are about equally divided between those paved with stone slabs and those paved with mosaics. Suffice to say here that mosaics sometimes depict biblical scenes, but often also animals, the zodiac and four seasons, menorahs with a Holy Ark, and other such motifs (Fig. 135).

Probably one of the most famous of these mosaic floors is from Hammath-Tiberias from the ancient city of that name south of Tiberias. The floor is laid out in three panels in the worship area. As one moves south towards the center of the entrance, one traverses first a panel 3.3 m. wide with two lions standing guard on either side of nine quadrilaterals containing inscriptions honoring eight benefactors, all in Greek. The central two panels, which are upside down relative to the vision of those entering, read:

> SEVE[ROS] DISCIPLE OF THE MOST IL-
> LUSTRIOUS PATRIARCHS FULFILLED
> (IT, presumably a vow). BLESSINGS UPON
> HIM. AMEN.

The excavator believes that Severos was the main benefactor of this synagogue, about 325 C.E.

The next panel contains a round zodiac surrounded by a square, with the four seasons in the corners. The twelve signs of the zodiac appear as figured art, and their names are given in Hebrew. The center of the zodiac presents the Greek god Helios driving his four-horse chariot (quadriga) directly towards the viewer. He holds the orb and a whip in his left hand and has his right hand raised with palm outward in salute. His head is surrounded by a nimbus (halo), from which rays of sun-light stream. The moon and a single star are still visible to the left and to the right. The later construction of a wall destroyed many details in the zodiac and the Helios panel.

The final panel as one walks towards the center of interest on the south wall of the main hall depicts a Torah Shrine (Drawing 9) flanked by two menorahs. With the menorah one sees two incense shovels, ram's horns (shofar), and bound branch of myrtle (lulav). A curtain tied in a knot hangs from a horizontal rod at the top of the Torah Shrine. (This rod is omitted in Drawing 9.) An elegant, double-leaf door with fine paneling conceals the Torah scrolls and scrolls of the prophets. In the center of the pediment of the Torah Shrine is a scallop shell, usually called a "conch" in scholarship. Two columns on either side complete the architectural form of the Torah Shrine, uniting its form with that of the aedicula, as we have seen at Ostia in Italy.

The interiors of synagogue buildings were not all treated the same. Some featured a plain interior, though pleasant and well-designed. Others were elaborately decorated with painted plaster in fresco or seccho or decorated with intricate carvings in low relief, Corinthian or Ionic capitals, repeated moldings, and other art. Three synagogues in the land of Israel excavated so far (Hammath-Tiberias, Chorazin, and En-Gedi) featured a special stone chair to the side of the ark, with its back against the wall that the congregation faced. These chairs have been found in the diaspora at Delos and Dura-Europos. The example from Chorazin has hand-rests decorated with a lion and eagle. Rachmani argues that the stone chairs found so far (except at Delos) were for a fourth century C.E. ritual of enthronement of the Torah during worship.

By far the most important artifact in the synagogue, however, and the architectural focal point of worship, was the Torah Shrine (Drawing 9). The general form of such a shrine has been known for some time, as they have been found in Jewish art in gold glass, molded on ceramic lamps, molded on glass vessels, incised on a bowl, carved in low relief on ossuaries and sarcophagi, set into mosaic floors, carved on stone plaques, and carved in relief or incised on lintels. In general the Torah Shrine stood on a raised platform or bema. Those that survive are of stone, but some argue that wood platforms were used before their construction in stone. On top of the bema stood an aedicula of two columns (sometimes four) in front, sometimes with a lintel above the columns, the whole fitted with a roof, and with a shell carved into the pediment. Inside the aedicula stood a chest with double-leafed doors, which, when the doors were opened, showed the ends of scrolls on shelves. Often two heraldic lions stood rampant on the ground on either side of the shrine, though on the Nabratein pediment they crouch on either side of the top.

Only the pediment from the aedicula of the Nabratein synagogue was identified as such by its excavators. In earlier surveys and excavations, virtually identical architectural fragments were found but identified as lintels for windows. Fragments of columns about 30 cm. in diameter, also found in synagogue excavations, may have been from a Torah Shrine, though they may also have decorated windows. Fragments of lions sculpted in the round at Capernaum and other sites may also have been from those guarding the aedicula and its ark. Apparently one portable aedicula was represented on a lintel at Capernaum. It is decorated with a simple shell motif in front and Ionic columns on the long side.

A few synagogues have been reconstructed from the evidence of their own fragmented remains with two aediculae, one on either side of the main entrance, as at Sardis in Turkey or at Capernaum in Lower Galilee. It is tempting to surmise that one contained the ark or chest for scrolls and the other held a menorah, though other uses are possible.

Mosaic floors often depict a menorah on either side of an aedicula with its ark, the whole often covered by a curtain (*parokhet*). In later synagogues of the Byzantine and Arab periods the ark seems to have stood by itself in an apse. The portals of the facade and other architectural features are not depicted in these mosaic floors. Nevertheless,

the constancy of this lay-out wherein a Torah Shrine is flanked by menorahs raises at least the possibility that this scene reflected reality, and that the center of interest of a synagogue, perhaps in the fourth century C.E. and later, included a Torah Shrine and two menorahs, perhaps even with two lions rampant.

**Bibliography**
Goodenough, Erwin. R., *Jewish Symbols in the Greco-Roman Period*, 13 vols. (New York, 1952-65).
Gutman, Joseph, *Ancient Synagogues: The State of Research* (Chico, 1981).
Meyers, Eric M., Meyers, Carol L., and Strange, James F., *Excavations at the Ancient Synagogue at Gush Halav* (Winona Lake, 1990).

JAMES F. STRANGE

SYNAGOGUES, MEDIEVAL AND MODERN: The history of synagogue architecture in the medieval and modern periods is characterized by variety and discontinuity. Variety of style, even within a single chronological period, is due to the dispersion of the Jewish people among both Muslim and Christian cultures, each with its own architectural traditions and local variants. Additionally, the lack of continuity in the development of synagogues as building types, even in a single locale during the medieval and early modern periods, is due to historical circumstances, such as expulsions from European cities and readmissions at a later date when the prevailing architectural style had changed. In the modern period, the adoption of new styles reflects the proud sense of Jewish identity resulting from Emancipation and changes in the liturgy of reformed congregations.

Until the nineteenth century, all synagogues housed traditional congregations. Whatever their geographic location and stylistic milieu, architects and builders faced a common set of design issues. Chief among these was how to accommodate two major foci: the Torah ark and the reader's desk (*bimah*). Other considerations were the desirability of placing the ark, the focus of prayer, in the direction of Jerusalem; the need to provide seats for the lengthy services; the relationship of the separate women's seating to that of the men; and the necessity of adequate windows to provide light for reading, given the entire congregation's participation in services. Solutions to these issues were often shaped by government ordinances concerning the height or placement of a Jewish house of worship or by the constraints of a building site.

The architecture of each synagogue depends then on its location in a particular country at a specific time and, further, on its surroundings, whether in a large city with sophisticated buildings or in a smaller population center with a tradition of rural architecture. At times when Jews were free to build as they wished, the wealth of the congregation affected the size of synagogues and their furnishings. In the nineteenth and twentieth centuries, the religious orientation of the congregation also became a factor.

**The Middle Ages and later—North Africa and the Iberian Peninsula:** While written records attest to the existence of medieval synagogues centuries earlier, the first extant buildings belong to the High Middle Ages. Medieval synagogue structures still exist in the two major areas of Jewish settlement on the European continent, the Iberian Peninsula and central Europe, while the appearance of a slightly earlier synagogue in Fostat, Cairo, can be reconstructed from archaeological remains and extensive documentary evidence.

When, after the destruction of an earlier house of worship on the same site, the Palestinian Synagogue of Cairo—now known as the Ben Ezra—was rebuilt in 1039-1041, it was the most important Jewish institution in the capital of Muslim power in the eastern Mediterranean. The interior was basilical, as were many ancient synagogues in the Land of Israel, and was divided by impressive columns into a nave and side aisles oriented toward the southeast wall, which housed the ark (fig. 136).[1] The cabinet for the Torah scrolls was inset into this wall, its front masked by wooden doors carved with inscriptions, portions of which survive. Near the ark hung a silver candelabrum, while thirty bronze lamps and 51 chandeliers hung throughout the synagogue.[2] The other major furnishing mentioned in documents from the famous geniza of this synagogue was the *bimah* or almemor reached by twelve steps.

Presumably, it resembled the wooden pulpit made in Cordoba between 1125-1130 for a mosque in Marrakech Jewish usage of almemors similar to those placed in mosques is demonstrated by miniatures in early fourteenth-century Spanish haggadot.[3] In the Ben Ezra synagogue, women sat in galleries above the aisles that were reached through a separate entrance to the synagogue. The spaces were lit by small, round windows.

In comparison with the wealth of documentary material related to the Ben Ezra synagogue, for our meager knowledge of the Grand Synagogue in Baghdad we are dependent on the travelogue of Benjamin of Tudela (twelfth century). According to Benjamin, the building was a columned hall with a courtyard in front, a description that recalls medieval mosques. Hebrew inscriptions dominated the interior decoration, a practice typical both of mosques and of Spanish synagogues of the thirteenth century.

The earliest extant Spanish synagogue, in Toledo, dates ca. 1200, and was converted into a church, Santa Maria de la Blanca, two centuries later, after the campaigns of Vincente Ferrer. The outer walls of this synagogue form a trapezoid 26/28 × 19/23 meters that is subdivided into five parallel aisles by arcades of horseshoe piers (fig. 137). The pier capitals, the spandrels of the arcade, and its upper wall are covered with stucco decoration (fig. 138). The plan of Santa Maria de la Blanca and its relatively austere stucco ornamentation compared to other Mudejar buildings of the period seem to derive from those of North African mosques, perhaps brought to the Peninsula along with the Almohad invasion of 1125.[4] A similar multi-aisled synagogue with octagonal piers, pine cone capitals, and horseshoe arches stood in Segovia until the nineteenth century (fig. 139).

In 1252, Alfonso el Sabio of Castile awarded three former mosques to the Jewish community of Seville for use as synagogues. Following the expulsion of the Jews from Spain, one later became the Church of Santa Cruz. This building, like the earlier Ben Ezra in Cairo, was basilical and had two rectangular apses, one at either end: that on the side toward Jerusalem housed the Torah ark, the other, the *bimah* or almemor.[5] Closed or screened areas were set aside for the women. Today, only the columns of the former mosque/synagogue remain, incorporated into later public structures in Seville (fig. 140).

An entirely different building type was erected in Cordoba in 1314-1315 by an individual patron, Isaac Mehab ben Ephraim (fig. 141). This private synagogue is small, measuring only 6.5 × 7.1 meters. It is preceded by a forecourt and a later vestibule above which is a women's gallery that fronts on the main hall through a series of large, arched openings. The ark, in the western wall, is accented by a delicate, polylobed stucco arch. The remaining wall surfaces were entirely covered with stucco in relief, mostly expanding stars and interlace punctuated by Hebrew inscriptions. This scheme of decoration emulates the interior ornament of contemporaneous Mudejar buildings erected for the Muslim rulers of Granada.[6]

Between 1357 and 1360, another private patron, Samuel Abulafia, treasurer to King Pedro the Cruel of Castile (1350-1369), built a larger single-hall synagogue with a woman's gallery along one side (23 × 9.5 m) that functioned as a palatine chapel (fig. 142). Three niches for Torah scrolls punctuate one of the narrow ends of the building, an arrangement known from North African and Middle Eastern synagogues. The walls of El Transito still bear most of their elaborate stucco decoration that incorporates the elements found in the Cordoba synagogue, together with heraldic shields bearing the arms of Pedro I and flowering vines. The dedicatory inscription indicates the one-time existence of other furnishings and auxiliary spaces:

> See the sanctuary which was dedicated in
>     Israel
> and the house which Samuel built,
> and the wooden tower for reading the law in
>     its midst,
> and its Torah scrolls and their crowns to God,
> and its lavers, and its lamps for illumination
> and its windows like the windows of Ariel.[7]
> And its courts for those diligent in the per-
>     fect law,

and a residence for those who would sit in
    the shade of God . . .

The wooden tower is a reference to the raised platform used as a reader's desk that was similar to the pulpits in medieval mosques. Contemporaneous Rabbinic texts state that seating was on mats, and that the congregants of one Toledan synagogue occasionally decorated the walls adjacent to the Torah ark with Muslim carpets, although repeatedly forbidden to do so by the rabbis.[8] Samuel Halevi's dedication indicates that scholars studied or taught in the courtyard, which also accommodated a hospice, functions known from ancient synagogues in the land of Israel and from the Ben Ezra synagogue in Cairo. Recent archaeological investigations adjacent to El Transito have revealed the existence of a *mikveh* (ritual bath).

A small synagogue of nearly square proportions, 9.5 × 8.2 meters, dated ca. 1460, is in Tomar, Portugal (fig. 143). Its plan is similar to that of small, privately built mosques throughout the Islamic world: a central square bay surrounded by other vaulted bays. The support of the vaults with stone columns and capitals and the austere decoration of the walls, however, point to Christian builders working with a Moslem ground plan. Even this late expression of synagogue architecture on the Peninsula suggests the mix of cultures that characterized medieval Iberia and, in particular, the era of Christian hegemony during which most of the existing synagogues were erected.

The synagogues of North Africa are later than those of Spain, but have some similarities of plan that suggest a common source and/or mutual influences. One feature is the tripartite Torah shrine that may have come westward with Jews who followed the Islamic conquest of North Africa and the Iberian Peninsula.[9] In Morocco, one can be seen in the ibn Danan Synagogue of Fez, which was built in the sixteenth century. Other common features are the high *bimah*, which was used in synagogues like the Ben Toah in Algiers, and the use of multiple decorative patterns.[10] Both of these features can also be seen in the Synagogue of Rabbi Joshua

Berdugo in Meknes, which is some four hundred years old. The patterning still extant in Morocco is generally of tile, rather than of stucco as in medieval Spain.

**The Middle Ages—Central Europe:** Jews first came to Central Europe with the Roman armies and administration and were numerous enough in some cities, like Cologne, to establish organized communities. Not until the ninth century, however, was there continuous Jewish settlement, principally along the Rhine River. As was true in Iberia, documents attesting to the existence of synagogue buildings precede the few extant buildings.

Until Kristallnacht, the oldest extant medieval synagogue was that of Worms, a city renowned as the home of Rashi (1040-1105), the great scholar and commentator on the Torah and the Talmud. The synagogue building of 1174-1175 was erected on the site of an earlier structure dated 1034 (fig. 144). The main space of the twelfth-century building was a double-nave hall, a form used in Worms for the first time, that was probably chosen because it was not used by Christians for churches but for council chambers, audience halls, refectories, and chapter houses.[11] The *bimah* was placed between the two columns that supported the vaulted ceiling and bisected the space. Although this arrangement aligned the reader's desk with the main focus of the ark and placed it in the midst of the congregation, the surrounding columns obscured its form. To enhance the appearance of the *bimah* and to modernize it in accord with Baroque taste, ca. 1634 a stone grillwork was built around the desk, whose height gave the platform a greater sense of monumentality.

A women's section (*Frauenschul*) was added in 1212/1213. Narrow slits provided the only openings on the main synagogue. Some of the *Frauenschul* windows were framed by Gothic moldings, a stylistic change from the originally round-headed Romanesque windows of the men's prayer hall.

The twin-nave plan of Worms and the placement of its reader's desk between columns were repeated in the Regensburg synagogue erected before 1227, and destroyed by order of the City Council in 1519. Prior to its demolition, the artist Albrecht Altdorfer (1480-1538), a council member, recorded the interior and the vestibule. His drawings show a six-bay structure of groin vaults supported by a range of three columns and clustered wall colonnettes, all raised on high plinths. A small high window punctuates the wall of each bay, while a longer, lancet window surmounted by an oculus appears above the Torah ark.

The only twin-nave Gothic synagogue to survive is the Altneuschul of Prague, dated ca. 1265.[12] Despite its small size, 14.3 × 8.7 meters, the architect achieved a sense of verticality in the main synagogue by lowering the level of the floor beneath that of the surrounding buildings, and through the lines of the ribbed vaults that continue the verticality of the supporting piers (fig. 145). Floral sculptural decoration in the Altneuschul is confined to the pier capitals, the consoles of the ribs, and the keystones, and to the original gable above the Torah ark and the tympanum of the main entrance, both of which are carved with Tree of Life motifs. The figurative sculpture of Christian Gothic buildings is absent. In the fourteenth century a *Frauenschul* was added, and major renovations were carried out a century later. The building's distinctive crenellated gable was constructed, and the original stone reader's desk was replaced by a wooden platform surrounded by a wrought-iron superstructure in Gothic style.

An even earlier example of a *Frauenschul* is at Sopron in western Hungary, whose main synagogue and women's section both date to the early 1300s. The main space is rib vaulted, and the ark is surrounded by a framing band of Gothic foliate ornament. In the tympanum of the ark is an oculus filled with trilobed forms, a translation into stone of a design seen in roundels of stained glass and metalwork of the period.

Another twin-naved Gothic synagogue was discovered in Buda; it is dated by inscription to the year 1461. The three large flamboyant Gothic pillars that subdivided the 26.5 × 10.7 meters space are in the style of buildings erected by King Matthias I, Corvinus (r. 1458-1490). After the Ottoman occupation of

Buda in 1541, the Jews of the city were allowed to return from the exile Sultan Suleyman had imposed in 1526, and they regained their synagogue. A terrible siege ended Ottoman rule over Buda in 1686. Archaeological investigations of the building remains confirm the eyewitness account of Izsak Schulhof who wrote that the Jews of Buda sought refuge in the synagogue.[13] The bodies of those who had been killed were placed in the geniza; the corpses could not be buried because they had been consumed by fire.

Perhaps as the result of the influence of Bohemian Jews who migrated eastward after the Prague pogrom of 1389, or due to the adoption of local Polish church models, the twin-nave plan was later used for the Old Synagogue in Kasimierz, Cracow, erected ca. 1400 (fig. 146). As in the Altneuschul, a wrought iron superstructure emphasizes the reader's desk situated between two columns.

**The influence of Renaissance architecture on Transalpine Synagogues:** Italian influence on the cultural life of Prague in the sixteenth century and on the Jewish community in particular resulted in the replacement of the old Pinkas Synagogue of the thirteenth century with a new building of mixed Gothic and Renaissance elements in the years 1520-1535 (fig. 147). Renaissance pilasters support the late Gothic rib vaults of the Pinkas, and the outer windows have classical moldings. The main portal is a round arch flanked by fluted pilasters. In the early seventeenth century, a woman's balcony and other modifications were added by the Jewish architect Judah Goldsmith de Hertz, who, according to the inscription on his tombstone dated 1626, also worked on the rebuilding of the Maisel Synagogue.

Two interesting Prague documents reveal aspects of congregants' involvement in synagogue life. One is an inventory of the Maisel Synagogue written in 1684 that records the textile holdings of this well-endowed synagogue: twenty-two Torah curtains, twenty-nine mantles and twenty-three Torah covers, all made of expensive silk weaves and silk, gold, and silver threads.[14] The numbers reflect the significance of textiles as an art form in Bohemia, and the willingness of individuals and corporate bodies in the community, such as the Burial Society, to commission expensive furnishings for their house of worship. The second document, dated 1709, is known as *The Book of Seats* and consists of 471 pages documenting controversies regarding ownership of seats in the Pinkas Synagogue.[15] Each place in the synagogue was owned by the individual who sat there, its worth determined by its location. There were 187 places for men, but 237 seats for women, a very unusual ratio. Seats were bought and sold and left for inheritance. The listings reveal the somewhat haphazard arrangement of the seats, which means that they were not oriented according to religious strictures. A rabbinical court and a lay commission with both male and female members were established to resolve the divisive issues. The seat controversy in the Pinkas synagogue was not unique; instances of serious disagreements over synagogue seats appear in the responsa literature as well.[16]

The Pinkas Synagogue is not the only instance of Italian influence on transalpine synagogues during the sixteenth century. The residence of the royal court of Sigismond I in Cracow and his marriage to Bona Sforza in 1518 drew Italian scholars, artists, and architects to the Polish capital. In 1553, Matteo Gucci rebuilt the Remo Synagogue, whose name derives from the initials of the halakhist Moses Isserles (1525-1572), but which was financed by his father Israel, banker to Sigismund II Augustus. Israel donated the rather large single-naved synagogue, 17.7 × 12.4 meters, to the Jewish community of Cracow. Gucci replaced the wooden exterior of the original synagogue with more permanent materials, stone and brick, and added a parapet with blind arcades, an architectural feature that had been used for guild and town halls and castles and which became characteristic of Polish masonry synagogues (fig. 148). A Renaissance aedicula frames the Torah ark. In 1638-1644, another Italian builder, Francesco Olivieri, designed the Izak Synagogue in Cracow, named for its founder, Isaac Jacobowics (d. 1673), banker to King Wladislaw IV. The synagogue is a barrel-vaulted structure with a lateral arcade and a women's gallery separated from the men's space by an arcade of Tuscan columns.

**Baroque synagogues in Italy:** Jews have lived continuously on the Italian peninsula since Roman times. During the Empire, they constituted ten percent of the population of Rome, equaling a community of 100,000. Those whose family histories trace to this early period were known as Romaniot. In the fourteenth century, they were joined by a significant number of Ashkenazic Jews drawn southward by economic opportunities, particularly in banking. The largest waves of immigration took place following the Spanish pogroms of 1391; the expulsions from Spain and Portugal and their dominions, which included nearly all of southern Italy (the Kingdom of Naples), Sicily, and Sardinia, between 1492 and 1497; and the westward move of Sephardic Jews who had first settled in the Levant under the welcoming rulers of the Ottoman Empire. By the second half of the sixteenth century, it was common for Italian Jewish communities to build several synagogues to accommodate the various rites of their members: the Roman, the Ashkenazic or Tedesco, the Sephardic, and the Levantini. Depending on the size of the community and local regulations, these several synagogues could be accommodated in one multiple structure as at Rome and Ferrara, or each congregation occupied an independent building as in Venice. The community's tenacity in maintaining its membership's original religious identity and practice was expressed not only in the services and customs of separate congregations but in their segregation within discrete synagogue spaces. The resulting need for many buildings stimulated a burst of building activity in the second half of the sixteenth that continued through the seventeenth century.

The most impressive grouping of synagogues is in the area of the former Venetian ghetto. It includes five separate buildings: an Italian synagogue, the Sephardic, the Levantine, and two Ashkenazic synagogues, the Scuola Grande Tedesca and the Scuola Canton, as well as a number of auxiliary buildings, such as the study hall (*Beit Midrash*) of Rabbi Leone Modena. To escape the crowded conditions at street level and damage from periodic flooding of the canals, Venetian synagogues were placed on the second story of buildings, with auxiliary spaces below.[17] Most of these synagogues are bipolar spaces with the reader's desk and the Torah ark given equal emphasis by being placed at opposite ends of the main prayer hall, both spanning the full width of the building. All of the Venetian synagogues are lavishly decorated with carved wooden furnishings, often gilt, and with numerous silver and brass lamps, and silk textiles, many embroidered with silver and gold metallic threads.

In contrast to the medieval Ashkenazic confinement of female worshippers in a separate *Frauenschul*, the Jewish women of sixteenth- and seventeenth-century Venice were accommodated in the main space, albeit in a high balcony behind a balustrade or perforated screens. The vertical distance between the seating of the men and women is mediated by the raised reader's desk and ark, so that while the men gaze upward towards the *bimah* during the reading from the Torah scroll, the women gaze downward at the text. Women's sense of inclusion is further enhanced by the Venetian custom of passing the Torah binder to the women for rerolling and by the blessing that refers to "every daughter of Israel who makes a mantle or cover in honor of the Torah," incorporated into the weekly Sabbath prayers of the Italian rite.

The earliest Venetian synagogue is the Scuola Grande Tedesca, built in 1528-1529, just twelve years after the establishment of the ghetto. To mask its trapezoidal shape, the architect created an elliptical women's balcony that obscures the walls behind and gives an illusion of spatial regularity (fig. 149). As with many of the Venetian synagogues, the Scuola Grande Tedesca was refurbished in the seventeenth century when a new ark was donated. At the same time, its reader's desk appears to have been moved from a traditional Ashkenazic placement in the center of the prayer hall to a position opposite the Torah ark, the Italian practice.

These refurbishings common in Venetian synagogues during the seventeenth century and the building of two new synagogues may have been due to the doubling of the ghetto population between 1630 and 1655.[18] Some of the renovations were designed by major Venetian architects or their workshops. The ark, ceiling panels, and gallery of the Spanish synagogue dated ca. 1655 appear to have been the work of an assistant of Baldassare Longhena (1598-1682) (fig. 150). In the nearby Levantine Synagogue, a monumental *bimah* rises above the men's congregation (fig. 151). It is reached by two curved staircases that meet below a canopy supported by four massive, baroque, twisted columns, a composition that may have been inspired by Bernini's monumental Baldacchino in St. Peter's, Rome of 1624-1633, which was designed to emphasize the altar within the vast space of the premier church of Christendom. Just as is true of the Baldacchino, the open curving columns of the *bimah* both penetrate and shape the space of the synagogue. This reader's desk, as well as the ceiling panels, were by Andrea Brustolon (1662-1732), who worked as a woodcarver for churches and private patrons.

Synagogues like those of Venice—relatively small but richly decorated with elaborate woodcarvings, rich textiles, sculpted arks, and readers' desks—were used into the modern period by the many scattered Jewish communities in the northern half of Italy. The populations of many smaller communities decreased in the nineteenth century as the Jews of rural Italy emigrated to large cities. The Baroque synagogues of these depleted congregations were abandoned, while in the large cities, massive temples were built to serve expanded urban communities and to express pride in the fact of Jewish emancipation.

**The classic Baroque of the Netherlands, England, and the Colonies:** The relatively small Jewish population of sixteenth-century Amsterdam swelled in the seventeenth century with the arrival of numerous Converso families from Spain and Portugal, who took advantage of Dutch tolerance to return to Judaism. The growth in population was expressed in the building of several large synagogues. In contrast to the dynamic spaces and elaborate ornament of Italian Baroque synagogues, Jewish houses of worship in Amsterdam are characterized by regular ground plans, plain walls, and classical forms. In time, the synagogues of Amsterdam served as models for Jewish houses of worship in countries with governmental and cultural links to the Netherlands in both the Old and New Worlds.

The earliest Amsterdam synagogue, the Sephardic congregation of 1639, introduced an interior scheme that became a model for later synagogues: large galleries that were integrated with the space of the main prayer hall, an arrangement that may have been inspired by Dutch galleried churches built in the first decades of the century.[19] Unlike modern orthodox practice, men and women occupied different sections of the gallery, with the women shielded by perforated screens. In 1670-1671, an Ashkenazic synagogue, the Grote Sjoel, which may have been designed by the municipal architect Daniel Stalpaert, was erected nearby according to the same scheme. The plan was given its most monumental expression in the building that replaced the Sephardic synagogue of 1639, that built in 1671-1675 according to the plans of Elias Bouman. A sense of monumentality is imparted by the large size of the synagogue, 38 × 26 meters accommodating nearly two thousand seats, and is emphasized by means of large-scale furnishings (fig. 152). Massive Ionic columns thirteen meters tall subdivide the main space into a large central nave and aisles. The Torah ark of dark red Brazilian wood is an elongated cabinet, nearly the width of the nave (fig. 153); at the opposite end of the central space is a large reader's desk. During the day, light passes through seventy-two tall, arched windows; at night, candles placed in brass holders along the benches illuminated the prayer books.

The plan and austere appearance of seventeenth-century Dutch synagogues spread along trade routes emanating from Amsterdam. Similar synagogues were built in London and in Newport, Rhode Island, for Sephardic congregations. In England, the rule of William of Orange that began in 1688 encouraged the arrival of increased numbers of Jewish immigrants from the Netherlands, so that by 1700 the Sephardi community was large enough to commission a synagogue, the first house of worship built for Jewish use since the expulsion of 1290. It came to be called Bevis Marks from its location on an obscure street. William's simultaneous rule of Holland and England facilitated the influence of Dutch architectural models on English building, and the rectangular plan of Bevis Marks is one instance of this development (fig. 154). It is similar to that of the Amsterdam Sephardic synagogue of 1671-1675, and like it has a monumental, tripartite ark with a tall, gabled center carved of dark wood, set against a series of large windows. The men's seating on both of the long sides faces inward toward the center. Well into the second half of the eighteenth century, the Bevis Marks was the most often used model for other Jewish houses of worship built in Britain and its colonies.

Among its most noteworthy copies, is Temple Yeshuath Israel, in Newport, Rhode Island, designed by an English architect, Peter Harrison (1716-1775), and called the Touro Synagogue after its first rabbi, Isaac Touro. The main space is rectangular with two rows of superimposed columns, Corinthian above Ionic, that support the women's galleries on three sides. As in Bevis Marks, the gabled ark is set against a large arched window, with similar windows on either side, and is aligned with the bimah. Harrison appears to have derived details of his design from English architectural handbooks available in the American colonies, as was true of other Newport buildings he designed.[20] Some of the monies for the building of the Touro synagogue came from the Sephardic congregation of Curacao, whose house of worship still stands, one of two early Caribbean synagogues still in existence.[21]

The Ashkenazic population of London grew in numbers and prominence in the first decades of the eighteenth century, leading to the establishment in 1722 of a congregation independent of Bevis Marks. In 1765-1766, the Ashkenazic synagogue doubled in size through the combination of its original space with a new addition.[22] Architect James Spiller created a circular staircase in one corner, pro-

viding access to the women's gallery. On the ground floor, the reader's desk was placed on axis with the ark, with the space between them devoid of seats to allow for processions. Two columns carrying an entablature framed the ark, and two more framed the bimah and bisected the synagogue horizontally. A further, major reconstruction took place in 1790. The resulting interior was based on the Grote Sjoel, the Sephardic synagogue of Amsterdam of 1665. Like its Dutch model, the London synagogue was supported by tall Ionic columns, with the women's galleries set between the columns and the outside walls. The London ark, however, was set within a half-dome supported by Corinthian columns and was flanked by a seat for the rabbi, a borrowing from English church architecture. The synagogue seated a thousand congregants.

The Great Synagogue of London was the model for colonial congregations like the Great Synagogue of Sydney, Australia, whose architecture, ritual, and even its many governing principles were based on those of the London congregation.[23] The Sydney ark, like that in London, sits beneath a half-dome, but one that is two stories high, which establishes one end of the axis that terminates in the centrally placed reader's desk. As in London, an empty processional space is left between. Like the Great Synagogue, the Sydney building has women's galleries the full length of the long sides, with the difference that the Australian galleries are supported by two rows of superimposed columns, each one story high, rather than by a single row of monumental columns as in London.

**East European synagogues:** A great number of synagogues of both timber and masonry were built in Poland from the first half of the seventeenth century into the nineteenth century. The first, built in Lublin in 1636/1638, was known as the Maharshal synagogue after Solomon Luria, head of the city's yeshiva. It was destroyed in a Russian attack of 1656 and then rebuilt, but its original plan may have been the earliest focused around a small central bay supported by four large columns that enclosed the reader's desk. This bay was surrounded by eight larger groin-vaulted bays that together formed a square interior. The groins of the center vault rested on columns supporting a tabernacle above the reader's desk. As a result, the *bimah* was integrated into the center of the architectural system in a rare synthesis of form and meaning, and gave an unobstructed view of the ark.[24] The synagogue accommodated 3,000 worshippers. The widespread adoption of this plan throughout Poland may be attributed to the prestige of the Lublin community which was based on the scholarship of the Maharshal and his great yeshiva and on the presence there of the seat of the Council of the Four Lands, the self-governing institution of East European Jewry.

The earliest surviving example of the same design is at Lańcut in southern Poland.[25] Its women's gallery is above the vestibule that flanks one side of the synagogue. In the main interior, the eight bays are alternately capped by barrel and groin vaults. The synagogue walls and supports are decorated with both paintings and relief plasterwork.

An alternate central bay plan developed at Lvov and Vilna during the 1630s. In these synagogues, the bay housing the *bimah* is equal in size to the other bays of the main space. This plan was made possible by the separation of the *bimah* tabernacle from the vaulting system and its design as an independent structure.[26]

Ashkenazic immigrants introduced to Palestine the plan of a central bay masonry building supported by four columns. Examples are the Ari Synagogue in Safed, the Avraham Avinu Synagogue of Hebron, and two Jerusalem synagogues, that dedicated to the prophet Elijah the prophet, and the Istanbul, founded by immigrants from the capital after the Ottoman conquest of Jerusalem in 1517.

During the seventeenth century, the first wooden synagogues were built in Poland along the same plan, a central tabernacle surrounded by full- or half-barrel vaults. Which building type was primary is unknown, although the greater flexibility of wood as a medium allowed for the creation of variant forms impossible in masonry synagogues.

Since, in wooden synagogues, the columns were not needed to support the roof, their inclusion around the reader's desk expresses the spiritual value ascribed to this monumental grouping of architectural forms.[27] The structure and ornamentation of East European wooden synagogues drew on the vernacular architecture of the region, but their spatial arrangements and decoration are specific to synagogues. Relevant documents indicate that Jewish craftsmen designed and created these houses of worship.

The Synagogue at Wolpa was one of the most outstanding examples of this genre. Built in the early eighteenth century, its ceiling rose in three stages; the last tier was in the form of an octagonal cupola (fig. 155). By reducing the sizes of the successive tiers and their decoration, the builders created an illusion of great height. The three stages of the ceiling appeared as three curved tiers in the roof when seen from the outside (fig. 156). On the facade, raised pavilions flank the roofs above the paired doorways. Although the enclosure of the *bimah* at Wolpa was formed of relatively simple balustrades and a cornice, the Torah ark, ten meters tall, was a Baroque composition of architectural elements overlaid with a teeming world of carved foliage and animals in painted wood.

Many wooden synagogues had ceilings painted with murals. One hundred such buildings existed in Poland alone in 1939; but not one in Poland, Lithuania, Belorussia, or the Ukraine survived World War II. After the Chmielnicki pogroms of 1648, Jewish craftsmen migrated westward creating in Germany a version of East European synagogues. Eliezer Zussman, active in the 1730s, painted the interior murals and the readers' desks of the wooden synagogues in Bechhofen and Kirchheim, both in Franconia (fig. 157). The four-columned central tabernacle plan in masonry was the other dominant East European architectural scheme that came to be used in the west, for example, at Nikolsburg, Bohemia, whose synagogue was built in 1550 and remodeled in 1723.

**Eighteenth-century synagogues in German lands:** The services provided by Court

Jews (*Hofjuden*) to their rulers often necessitated their residence in capital cities from which Jews had previously been expelled. The Court Jew, his family, business associates, and employees became the nucleus of new Jewish communities, many of which were numerous enough by the early eighteenth century to require a separate house of worship to replace the small synagogue spaces in use in private homes.

During the early years of the century, the Berlin Jewish community was dominated by the Court Jew Esther Liebmann, who had inherited her husband's office upon his death in 1701.[28] Her treatment of the synagogue in their home as a personal fiefdom led members of the community to agitate for the right to build a public house of worship. The synagogue on the Heidereutergasse designed by Michael Kemeter was completed in 1714, shortly after Esther Liebmann's death. It was set in a courtyard, hidden from view, a setting typical of many European synagogues (fig. 158). The single hall interior was lit by very tall windows along the sides and behind the Torah ark, which was two-storied and resembled contemporaneous church altarpieces. The coved ceiling centered on an octagonal panel situated directly above the central *bimah*. Women sat in a gallery on the short wall opposite the ark. The decoration of the Heidereutergasse Synagogue was sober, reminiscent of Protestant church interiors, and very different from the colorful, dense decoration of East European houses of worship.[29]

One of the donors to the Berlin synagogue was Berend Lehmann, Court Jew of Halberstadt and patron of the arts. His support of a synagogue in another city was typical of the Court Jews. In the late seventeenth century, Samuel Oppenheimer of Vienna donated an ark to the Klausen Synagogue in Prague and contributed to the Ashkenazic synagogue of Mantua. Lehmann took a very active role in the building of a synagogue in his home city. It was completed in 1712 after three years of construction. He assured the finances of the project and even ordered special materials, like the marble columns from Russia that supported the Torah ark. His patronage of communal and domestic buildings was a hallmark of Lehmann's Court Jew status and emulated the architectural patronage of the German nobility that was an expression of wealth and power.[30]

**Nineteenth-century eclecticism:** As Edward Jamill has noted, "While the 19th century was distinguished by advances in political thought and in sciences and industry, these were accompanied by a marked decline in architectural standards . . . the art of building sank into a morass of revivals."[31] What was true in general was also true of synagogues, with the caveat that the choices of architectural styles, of building sites, and of modes of interior spatial organization for a Jewish house of worship were usually determined by ideological considerations. The Gothic style which typified church architecture was avoided. On the other hand, there was a desire to indicate the Near Eastern origins of the Jewish people and thus to emphasize their possession of a lengthy history and civilization. And by choosing to erect grand buildings on main thoroughfares, Jewish patrons expressed their equality with the rest of the population, the result of Emancipation. Finally, the spatial arrangement of reformed synagogues signified their break with tradition.

In the late eighteenth century and the early decades of the nineteenth, which were marked by an enthusiasm for ancient Greece and Rome that permeated various scholarly disciplines, a number of synagogues were built in a neo-classical style that sought to emulate ancient forms. Emperor Leopold III Friedrich Franz (r. 1758-1817) commissioned neo-classical buildings on his estate in Wörlitz, near Dessau, from Friedrich Wilhelm von Erdmannsdorff (1736-1800). Among them was a round synagogue, built in 1789-1790, that was modeled on the Temple of Vesta in Rome, whose architecture had been studied by von Erdmannsdorff.

Perhaps the best known classical synagogue is that on the Seitenstettengasse in Vienna, built in 1825-1826 by Josef Körnhausel (1782-1860), architect to Archduke Karl (fig. 159). Its oval, domed main hall with galleries is supported by massive Ionic columns on tall plinths. Their regular place-

Figure 146. Interior of Old Synagogue, Kasimierz, ca. 1400.

Figure 147. Interior of Pinkas Synagogue, Prague, 1520-1535.

Figure 148. Exterior of Remo Synagogue, Cracow, after 1553.

Figure 149. Interior of Scuola Grande Tedesca, Venice, 1528-1529

Figure 150. Interior of Spanish Synagogue, Venice, after 1655.

Figure 151. Interior of Levantine Synagogue, Venice, ca. 1700.

Figure 152. Interior of Sephardi Synagogue, Amsterdam, 1671-1675.

Figure 153. Interior of Sephardi Synagogue, Amsterdam, 1671-1675.

Figure 154. Interior of Bevis Marks Synagogue, London, 1700.

Figure 155. Interior of Synagogue, Wolpa, early eighteenth century.

Figure 156. Exterior of Synagogue, Wolpa, early eighteenth century.

Figure 157. Interior of Synagogue, Bechhofen, 1730s.

Figure 158. Interior of Synagogue on the Heidereutergasse, Berlin, 1714.

DER ISRAELITISCHE TEMPEL. №74. LE TEMPLE DES ISRAELITES.

Figure 159. Interior of Seitenstettengasse Synagogue, Vienna, 1825-1826

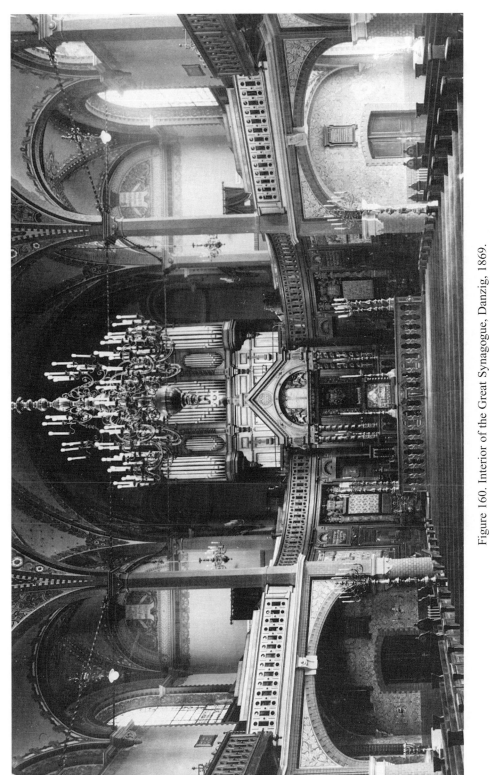

Figure 160. Interior of the Great Synagogue, Danzig, 1869.

Figure 161. Interior of Tempio Israelitica, Florence, 1874-1882

Figure 162. Interior of Congregation Emanu-el of New York, 1929.

Figure 163. Edmund Körner, exterior of Reform Synagogue, Essen, 1913.

Figure 164. Edmund Körner, interior of Reform Synagogue, Essen, 1913.

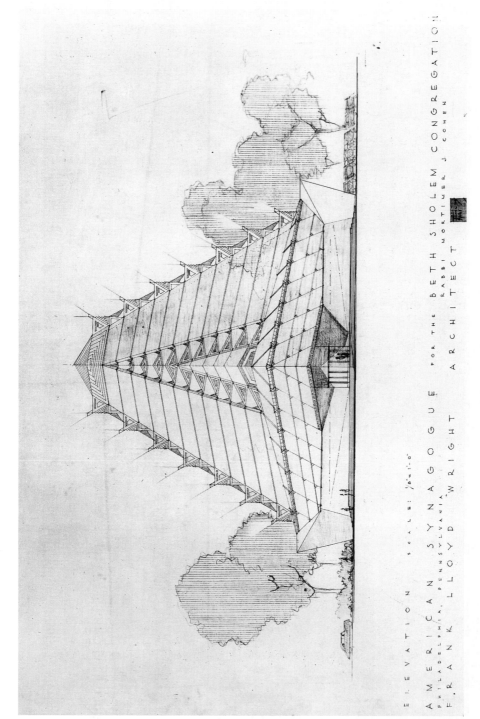

ELEVATION SCALE: 1/8"=1'-0"

AMERICAN SYNAGOGUE FOR THE BETH SHOLEM CONGREGATION
PHILADELPHIA, PENNSYLVANIA. RABBI MORTIMER J. COHEN
FRANK LLOYD WRIGHT ARCHITECT

Figure 165. Frank Lloyd Wright, plan for Temple Beth Shalom, Elkins Park, Pennsylvania, 1959.

Figure 166. Frank Lloyd Wright, interior of Temple Beth Shalom, Elkins Park, Pennsylvania, 1959.

Figure 167. Interior of North Shore Congregation, Glencoe, Illinois, 1964.

Figure 168. Exterior of Israel Goldstein Synagogue, the Hebrew University, Givat Ram, Jerusalem, 1957.

ment lends a sense of rhythm to the interior and leads the eye of the worshipper toward the ark, which is seen through two of the columns and framed by Doric pilasters. The synagogue was built in a courtyard in order not to offend the Catholic majority of the city.

In 1869, eighteen years after the synagogues of Danzig (now Gdansk) united in accord with Prussian law, the community built a large neo-Romanesque structure holding two thousand seats on the main street of the city, signifying by its size and location the place of the Jewish community in the life of the city (fig. 160).[32] The rejection of Gothic in favor of Romanesque-style synagogues was a decision followed in many communities. To express the unity of the community, the Great Synagogue of Danzig was built with a large platform surrounding the Torah ark on which were hung four additional ark curtains symbolic of the amalgamation of the congregations the new building represented. In accord with Reform principles, the reader's desk was incorporated into the ark platform, and all of the seats on the main floor and in the galleries faced frontward. One of the five prior congregations remained open for orthodox members of the community. Following Hitler's invasion of Poland, the Jews of Danzig, a Free City, in cooperation with municipal authorities, organized to assist all members to emigrate. As part of these efforts, communal properties were liquidated. The Great Synagogue was dismantled, brick by brick, its furnishings sold to churches and synagogues in the East.

Other communities chose as the basis of new synagogues a Byzantine church plan in the form of a Greek cross, thus avoiding the Latin cross plan, more familiar in the West and, therefore, more objectionable. This was the case in Florence. Following the granting of civil rights in Italy and the establishment of the city as Italy's capital (1864-1870), the Jewish community inaugurated an architectural competition to determine who would build a new synagogue expressive of their emancipated status and their feelings of loyalty to the nation. A team of three architects was chosen, of whom only Marco Treves (1814-1898), an architect and professor, was

Jewish. Their design for the interior featured a domed Byzantine shell overlaid with Mooresque ornament expressive of the ancient Near Eastern origins of the Jewish people (fig. 161). Numerous cusped arches serve as doorways and articulate the walls, whose surfaces are densely covered with repeat designs drawn from Islamic art. Two towers flank the facade, while the striped stonework of the exterior recalls the city's Duomo.

The Moorish revival had begun in Dresden when, in 1838-1840, Gottfried Semper designed a synagogue of relatively simple form, "Romanesque on the outside," but with an interior cloaked in Islamicizing motifs. The appropriateness of the style was articulated by Otto Simonson, a pupil of Semper and architect of a Moorish synagogue in Leipzig. The synagogue, he said, "was built in the Moorish style which I believe is the most characteristic. Judaism is faithful to its history; its law, its customs and practices, the organization of its ritual; its whole substance is embedded in the east, its motherland."[33] Similarly decorated synagogues were built later in Berlin, Cologne, Vienna, Budapest, New York, Philadelphia, and other cities. Most were based on a Byzantine ground plan.

Egyptian revival synagogues were built in Karlsruhe, 1798, in Canterbury, and in Philadelphia, where the second Mikveh Israel congregation of 1822-1825 was designed by William Strickland, who also created a church in the same style, while the imposing Congregation Emanu-el of New York was built as late as 1929 as a Romanesque-Gothic revival structure (fig. 162). It is the grandest and largest (2,350 seats) manifestation of the eclectic nineteenth-century revivalism. Emanu-el exemplifies the changes in synagogue architecture wrought by the German Reform movement in the nineteenth century. The reader's desk was amalgamated with the platform supporting the Torah ark, resulting in a synagogue with a single focus. As the rabbi assumed greater importance in the conduct of the liturgy, his seat was placed close to the ark. As a result, the entire congregation now faced forward along a single axis toward one altar-like center.

**The twentieth century:** In the modern period innovative technologies revolutionized the field of architecture. New materials freed architects from the constraints of wood and stone and made possible a variety of new designs, such as soaring interior spaces without internal supports. Yet as Richard Meier has written, "[The] unlimited opportunities open to the architect . . . [also] impeded the formulation of fixed types of buildings for particular uses."[34]

One of the first large-scale synagogue projects to experiment with new technology was built in Turin, Italy. In 1863, the architect Alessandro Antonelli (1798-1888) designed the building that came to be known as the "Mole Antonelliana." As in Florence, the Turinese community wished to express gratitude for Emancipation and to create a building worthy of their city, the capital of Italy in the years 1860-1864. The lower two stories of Antonelli's creation were supported on columns; above them rose a square base and a soaring cupola 250 feet high. He devised new systems of masonry construction to achieve the building's extraordinary height and size; it was to accommodate 1,500 seats and facilities for a school, the ritual bath, for life cycle events, and administrative offices. In the middle of construction, the Jewish community's funds ran out, and the city of Turin took over the unfinished synagogue and completed it for civic purposes.

In twentieth-century synagogues, new spatial arrangements reflect the expanded role of the rabbi in Reform services and the more passive role of the congregation. The move of the reader's desk to the front near the Torah ark rendered the frontal emphasis of Christian churches palatable, with the result that some congregations purchased church buildings for use as synagogues.[35] A theater arrangement of spaces also became appropriate.[36] Many Reform synagogues are in the form of auditoriums with raking floors; all lines focused on the Torah ark-reader's desk platform and the officiating rabbi.

During the first two decades of the century, the most innovative synagogues were built in Germany. The Reform synagogue erected in Essen, Germany, in 1913 was situated on a prominent but difficult triangular building site whose broad side faced a main thoroughfare (fig. 163). As in Florence, an architectural competition was held, which was won by the Essen architect Edmund Körner (1875-1925). He created a broad exterior of massive stonework that led to a series of interior spaces that gradually diminished in width, filling nearly all the available area in the converging portion of the plot. At the same time that they decrease in breadth, the interior spaces rise in height and increase in light, until they culminate in a polygonal-domed prayer hall whose theater-like arrangement of seats ascends in a gradual slope toward the ark and *bimah* in the front (fig. 164). Körner also created new, modern ornaments for the building. His contemporaries regarded the Essen synagogue as a cohesive, modern design whose emphasis was on space-forming masses rather than on small details.[37]

A 1931 synagogue competition in Zilina, Slovakia, engaged two prominent architects, Peter Behrens of Berlin and Josef Hoffman of Vienna. Behrens was eventually chosen, but some of the ideas present in Hoffmann's designs were adopted by later architects. His hemispherical dome on a low base was used by Eric Mendelsohn in Cleveland, and his glass pyramidal Tent of the Tabernacle was taken up by Frank Lloyd Wright outside Philadelphia.

In the United States, virtually no synagogues were built from the beginning of the Depression until the end of World War II. In the post-war period, changes in lifestyles and religious practice severed the traditional ties between members and a neighborhood synagogue. The move to the suburbs characteristic of post-war America created greater distances between homes and community facilities than had been true in cities. Since Reform and Conservative Judaism allowed for travel on the Sabbath, synagogues, too, could be at a distance from the residences of their membership, often in near-rural locations.[38] Another consequence of the placement of synagogues outside the constraints of densely populated cities was that the house of prayer could be surrounded by a complex of spaces that served ancillary functions: schools, catering halls, libraries, offices, and, sometimes, small museums. An early example is Congregation B'nai Amoona, St. Louis, designed in 1945 by Eric Mendelsohn, who had developed an expressionistic modernism in his native Germany before emigrating to Palestine and then to the United States, where he authored seven synagogue projects. The St. Louis synagogue, completed in 1950, is the first to have a flexible seating plan based on movable walls, which allowed the prayer hall of six hundred seats to expand into auxiliary spaces accommodating 1,500 on days when the congregation was largest.

A unique collaboration between artists and architect marked the building of Congregation Bnai Israel in Millburn, New Jersey, in 1950-1951. The building was designed by Percival Goodman of New York, who was to become one of the most prolific synagogue architects of the post-war period, creating over fifty Jewish houses of worship. He invited three rising artists to decorate Bnai Israel: Adolph Gottlieb designed the Torah curtain, which was sewn by women of the congregation; Robert Motherwell created paintings for the entry area; and Herbert Ferber sculpted "A Burning Bush" for the exterior wall. Throughout his career, Goodman continued to collaborate with other artists who fashioned Judaica and decorations for the synagogues he designed.

As was true of many of his colleagues, Goodman eventually turned away from the depersonalized International Style toward one that was more expressive.[39] In 1964, in the North Suburban synagogue Beth El of Highland Park, Illinois, he used modern materials like pre-cast concrete to create a circular sanctuary with elliptical clerestory windows based on the form of the olive leaf, which was meant to symbolize both the land of Israel and universal peace. Unlike inner-city synagogues that incorporated stained glass windows to block out adjacent buildings,[40] suburban synagogues like Beth El were lit by expanses of clear glass that admitted views of its vernal surroundings. The Torah ark and menorah of the sanctuary were created by Ludwig Wolpert (1900-1980),

who had emigrated from Israel in the 1950s to head the Tobe Pascher Workshop in the Jewish Museum, New York. Goodman and Wolpert had a long, creative partnership in the design and decoration of synagogues.

The theme of the Tent of the Tabernacle in the wilderness shaped numerous American synagogues of the post-war period. A monumental example is Frank Lloyd Wright's last executed commission, Temple Beth Shalom in Elkins Park, Pennsylvania, built in 1959, which he saw also as an embodiment of Mt. Sinai: ". . . At last a great symbol! Rabbi Mortimer J. Cohen gave me the idea of a synagogue as a 'traveling Mt. Sinai'—a 'mountain of light.'"[41] The tent-mountain is a corrugated glass roof supported by aluminum-faced supports, the whole rests on concrete buttresses (fig. 165). A triangle motif underlies the whole design, even the interior furnishings (fig. 166). Elkins Park's symbolic meaning is expressed in its structural form, not by means of additive decoration, as was true of the synagogues built in a pure International Style.

Poured concrete was used to create the soaring vaults of one of the more expressive "tent" synagogues of the period, North Shore Congregation Israel in Glencoe, Illinois, created in 1964 by Minoru Yamasaki (b. 1912) (fig. 167). A series of segmented arches meet in the vaults, their interstices filled with patterned glass. These vaguely Islamicized forms create a rhythmic movement toward the front, their shapes echoed in the Torah ark that dominates the broad pulpit. Yamasaki thus manipulated structural forms to create a spiritual ambiance for the worshippers.[42]

In 1957, a variant tent shape was employed to form the Israel Goldstein Synagogue at the Hebrew University, Givat Ram, Jerusalem, designed by Heinz Rau (fig. 168). A domical canopy anchored by posts set at regular intervals creates an enclosed synagogue. In contrast to Yamasaki's ethereal use of light-filled openings admitting views of the heavens, the windows of Rau's synagogue are near the floor, yielding only views of the ground and contributing to a sense of oppressive weightiness.

The referential nature of the modern tent

synagogues is echoed in the only synagogue project by Louis Kahn that was actually built, Beth El of Chappaqua, New York, dedicated in 1972. The building is a two-story octagon beneath a thirty-foot clerestory that was adapted from the plans of Polish wooden synagogues. Polish models were used for synagogues all over America, their plans generally evocative of the originals, but in no way slavish copies. M. Louis Goodman designed the latest in this series, Temple Israel in Greenfield, Massachusetts. Working in a region where wooden architecture is dominant, Goodman turned to Polish synagogues for models. The resulting building is entirely of wood, and, according to the architect, it "recalls and extends the characteristic forms of Eastern Europe and synthesizes them with modern concepts."[43]

**Conclusion:** As is true of Jewish art in general, no single style characterizes the architecture of the medieval and modern synagogue. Each building is a melange of influences from surrounding architecture and from the necessity of accommodating furnishings in traditional spatial relationships. The Torah ark generally is fixed in the direction of Jerusalem, but there have been many exceptions. Crucial to the arrangement of the interior is the axis between the ark and the reader's desk and the relationship of the seats to both. After the fourteenth century, seating for women was another variable that had to be factored in to the total plan. But only beginning in the nineteenth century was synagogue architecture largely freed from traditional concerns. This was a result of the growth of the reformed movement, in which new definitions of the relative roles of the rabbi, cantor, and congregation led to a reformulation of synagogue spaces.

**Bibliography**

Bernstein, Gerald, and Gary Tinterow, *Two Hundred Years of American Synagogue Architecture* (Waltham, 1976).
de Breffny, Brian, *The Synagogue* (New York, 1978).
Kadish, Sharman, ed., *Building Jerusalem. Jewish Architecture in Britain* (London, 1996).
Krinsky, Carole, *Synagogues of Europe. Architec-*

*ture, History, Meaning* (Cambridge and London, 1985).
Wischnitzer, Rachel, *The Architecture of the European Synagogue* (Philadelphia, 1964).

**Notes**
[1] Menahem Ben Sasson, "The Medieval Period: The Tenth to Fourteenth Centuries," in Phyllis Lambert, ed., *Fortifications and the Synagogue. The Fortress of Babylonia and the Ben Ezra Synagogue, Cairo* (London, 1994), pp. 212-214 and 219-223.
[2] Shlomo Dov Goitein, "The Synagogue Building and Its Furnishings according to the Records of the Cairo Genizah," in *Eretz Israel* (1964), pp. 81-97, 171.
[3] For the Cordoba almemor, see Jerrilyn Dodds, *Andalus* (New York, 1992), no. 115. For the synagogue almemor, see Bezalel Narkiss, *Hebrew Illuminated Manuscripts in the British Isles*, vol. 1, pt. 2, pls. 187 and 241.
[4] Jerrilyn S, Dodds, "Mudejar Tradition and the Synagogues of Medieval Spain: Cultural Identity and Cultural Hegemony," in *Convivencia: Jews, Muslims, and Christians in Medieval Spain* (New York, 1992), pp. 116-117.
[5] Rafael Comez, "La Antigua Synagoga del Barrio de Santa Cruz en Sevilla," in *Madrider Mitteilungen* 33 (1991), pp. 189-190.
[6] Dodds, op. cit., p. 122.
[7] Ariel is a name for Jerusalem; Is. 29:1-2, 7.
[8] Vivian B. Mann, "Jewish-Muslim Acculturation in the Ottoman Empire: The Evidence of Ceremonial Art," in Avigdor Levi, ed., *The Jews of the Ottoman Empire* (Princeton and Washington, 1994), pp. 562-564.
[9] For an example from sixteenth-century Isfahan, see Norman L. Kleeblatt and Vivian B. Mann, *Treasures of The Jewish Museum* (New York, 1985), pp. 38-39.
[10] Jacob Pinkerfeld, *Synagogues in North Africa. Tunisia, Algeria, Morocco* (Hebrew: Jerusalem, 1974), p. 54.
[11] Richard Krautheimer, *Mittelälterliche Synagogen* (Berlin, 1927), pp. 102-107.
[12] Zdenka Munzer, *Die Altneuschul in Prag* (Prague, 1932), p. 36.
[13] Laszló Zolnay, *Buda középkori zsidósága* (Budapest, 1968), pp. 66 and 70.
[14] Ludmila Kybalová, "Die ältesten Thoramäntel aus der Textiliensammlung des Staatlichen jüdischen Museums in Prag (1592-1750)," in *Judaica Bohemiae* 9,1 (1973), pp. 24-25.
[15] Hana Volavková, *The Pinkas Synagogue* (Prague, 1955), pp. 70-80.
[16] For example, *She'elot u-Teshuvot lehaRav Rabeinu Asher* (New York, 1954), nos. 3-7; *She'elot u-Teshuvot haRitba*, ed. Joseph Kapach (Jerusalem, 1958), nos. 18, 101, 182-183; *She'elot u-Teshuvot lehaRashba* (Lvov, 1811), no. 52; *She'elot u-Teshuvot haRashba*, Part 1 (Vienna, 1812), no. 581 (582); Jair Hayyim Bacharach, *Havvat Yair* (Jerusalem, 1967), no. 90; *Teshuvot*

*veHiddushei Akiva Eger* (New York, 1952), nos. 10, 32, 36, 42.

[17] Brian de Breffny, *The Synagogue* (New York, 1978), p. 95.

[18] Carole Krinsky, *Synagogues of Europe. Architecture, History, Meaning* (Cambridge and London, 1985), p. 383.

[19] Ibid., p. 387.

[20] de Breffny, op. cit., p. 140.

[21] For a survey of early Caribbean and South American synagogues, see Gunther Böhm, "The First Sephardic Synagogues in South America and in the Caribbean Area," in *Studia Rosenthaliana* 22 (1988), pp. 1-14.

[22] Clarence Epstein, "Compromising Traditions in Eighteenth-Century London: The Architecture of the Great Synagogue, Duke's Place," in Sharman Kadish, ed., *Building Jerusalem. Jewish Architecture in Britain* (London, 1996), pp. 65-69.

[23] R. Apple, "The Great Synagogue of Sydney, History and Heritage," in *Los Muestros*, 4 (1996), p. 25.

[24] On this synagogue, see Krinsky, op. cit., p. 206; Aharon Kashtan, "Synagogue Architecture of the Medieval and Pre-Emancipation Periods," in Cecil Roth, ed., *Jewish Art* (Greenwich, 1972), p. 110; Rachel Wischnitzer, *The Architecture of the European Synagogue* (Philadelphia, 1964), p. 115.

[25] For other examples, see Krinsky, op. cit., p. 206.

[26] Wischnitzer, op. cit., p. 119.

[27] Kashtan, op. cit., p. 111.

[28] On Esther Liebmann, see Deborah Hertz, "The Despised Queen of Berlin Jewry, or the Life and Times of Esther Liebmann," in Vivian B. Mann and Richard I. Cohen, eds., *From Court Jews to the Rothschilds* (New York, 1996), pp. 67-77.

[29] Krinsky, op. cit., p. 262.

[30] Richard I. Cohen and Vivian B. Mann, "Melding Worlds: Court Jews and the Arts of the Baroque," in Mann and Cohen, op. cit., pp. 119-120.

[31] Edward Jamill, "The Architecture of the Contemporary Synagogue," in Roth, op. cit., p. 273.

[32] Gershon C. Bacon, "Danzig Jewry: A Short History," in Vivian B. Mann and Joseph Gutmann, eds., *Danzig 1939: Treasures of a Destroyed Community* (Detroit and New York, 1980), p. 27.

[33] Wischnitzer, op. cit., p. 201. On the historical events that contributed to the Islamic revival in synagogue architecture, see de Breffny, op. cit., pp. 156-165.

[34] Richard Meier, *Recent American Synagogue Architecture* (New York, 1963), p. 7.

[35] de Breffney, op. cit., p. 149.

[36] Jamill, op. cit., pp. 280-281.

[37] Krinsky, op. cit., p. 285.

[38] Jamill, op. cit., p. 284.

[39] Lauren Weingarden Rader, "Synagogue Architecture in Illinois," in *Faith and Form* (Chicago, 1976), p. 70.

[40] Alfred Werner, "Synagogues for Today's Jews," in *Readings on Jewish Art* (New York, n.d.), p. 15.

[41] Meier, op. cit., p. 25.

[42] Rader, op. cit., p. 72.

[43] Evelyn Greenberg, "Sanctity in the Woodwork," in *Hadassah Magazine*, October, 1996, pp. 30-31.

VIVIAN B. MANN

# T

**TALMUD, NINETEENTH AND TWENTIETH CENTURY APPROACHES:** The interpretation of Halakhah occupies a central place in Rabbinic Judaism, and over the centuries several methods of interpretation have evolved and been formalized, ranging within the tradition of Judaism from Midrash Halakhah to pilpul—a term used to describe various kinds of casuistry or dialectic. But, towards the end of the nineteenth century in the yeshivot of Lithuania and Belorus, particularly Volozhin, the way people studied the legal sections of the Talmud underwent a radical transformation. In the century since its origin, this new approach, associated with the name of Hayyim Soloveitchik and the circle of talmudists around him, has become the dominant approach to advanced Talmudic study in the yeshiva world. The distinguishing feature of this approach is its emphasis on conceptual analysis, so that it is appropriately designated the "Analytic Movement" and its practitioners called "the Analysts."[1]

**How the Vilna Gaon studied Torah:** The towering figure in Torah learning in the eighteenth century was Elijah ben Solomon Zalman, the Vilna Gaon (1720-1797).[2] Totally committed to belief in the divine origin of

Torah, including the traditions of the sages, he reacted against the conventional methods of learning in the lower and higher Talmudic academies, feeling that they distracted from the search for truth. He criticized the lack of systematic instruction, the neglect of Bible, the neglect of Rabbinic source texts other than the Babylonian Talmud, the lack of a comprehensive approach to the Babylonian Talmud itself, and the failure to connect study with practice. He is also said to have rejected the pilpul method, or "arid Rabbinic dialectics," though what exactly is meant by these descriptions is not entirely clear.

To counter this catalogue of errors, he developed within his own select circle of disciples a systematic approach to textual study, commencing with Bible, working through the Tannaitic texts (Mishnah, Tosefta, Halakhic Midrashim), then the Jerusalem Talmud, the Babylonian Talmud, and the Rishonim ("early" authorities, before the sixteenth century). He placed great stress on Hebrew grammar as an aid to textual comprehension and on the acquisition of knowledge of astronomy, geometry, algebra, and geography in order to understand Talmudic laws and discussions. He encouraged the translation into Hebrew of works on the natural sciences, but he opposed philosophy and the Jewish enlightenment, seeing them as threats to faith and tradition. Above all, he championed the accurate reading of texts to ascertain the law. Study of Torah was a sort of science devoted to revealing, through texts, the divine will.

The Gaon's legacy contained within it the seeds of its own destruction. His program rested on the assumption that careful, systematic study of the texts of Torah would yield truth in perfect conformity with tradition. This did not happen. On the one hand, he himself undermined tradition by virtually ignoring the Aharonim (later authorities), especially the "pilpulists," and by taking sides among, or even flatly contradicting rulings of, the Rishonim. On the other hand, his program of careful textual study, with attention to previously ignored texts and to historical development of the Halakhah, fed directly into the agenda of the despised Enlightenment, the

Haskala, and the new "critical" study of Judaism, the *Wissenschaft des Judentums*. Paradoxically, the model defender of the faith thus was himself perceived, with some justification, as a precursor of the historical criticism that undermined that faith.[3]

Indeed, the story of the new, nineteenth century approach to Talmud study is the story of how the revolution of the Gaon was received and modified within one section of his own faith community. That another revolution had to be accomplished in order to save the first is not surprising when we bear in mind the inherent ambivalence of the Gaon's reform of learning.

**The growth and character of the Volozhin yeshiva:** The little town of Volozhin, Belorus, about 100 km. south-east of the Lithuanian capital, Vilnius, has few claims to fame. Indeed, it may well be its relative obscurity, and its distance from the influence of the Vilna community administration, then rent by severe internal discord, that led the Gaon's disciple, Rabbi Hayyim "Volozhiner," to establish there in 1803 the yeshiva that was to become the model and inspiration for Torah study throughout the nineteenth century. This yeshiva was to number among its alumni not only great rabbis but literary figures of the caliber of Bialik and Berdyczewski and to close its doors finally only when its 64 remaining students perished in the Holocaust.[4]

The establishment of the Volozhin yeshiva was conceived as a defense of true Torah in the face of Hasidism. Some say it was founded on the instructions of the Gaon; certainly its founder emphasized systematic study, careful investigation of the texts, and the acquisition of "outside" knowledge, for instance of mathematics and astronomy, as was necessary for their comprehension.

After Hayyim's death in 1821, his son Isaac served as principal of the yeshiva. Isaac eventually became occupied with public matters and the administrative and financial affairs of the yeshiva, so that he delegated the task of teaching to his sons-in-law, Eliezer Isaac Fried and Naftali Zvi Yehuda Berlin (the Netziv; 1817-1893). By then a controversy had arisen in the yeshiva because, contrary to the tradition laid down by its founder, Fried favored an approach dismissed by his detractors as casuistic.[5] Even so, he had attracted a following among the students.

In 1849, Fried succeeded his father-in-law as principal of the yeshiva, and Berlin became vice-principal. After Fried's death in 1854, Berlin and Hayyim's grandson, Joseph Baer Soloveitchik,[6] were appointed joint principals. The pilpul controversy then came to a head, as the two principals were of incompatible temperament and opposing views.[7] Towards the end of 1857, a delegation of prominent Lithuanian rabbis, including Isaac Elhanan Spektor of Kovno, ruled that Berlin should be sole principal of the yeshiva and Soloveitchik his deputy. This uncomfortable situation contributed to Soloveitchik's departure to serve as rabbi of Slutsk in 1865.

Not only the pilpul controversy shook the yeshiva in its years of glory. Zionism and Musar both from time to time raised hackles. The threat perceived as most serious was no longer Hasidism, which was successfully kept at arm's length, but the maturing and increasingly confident Russian Jewish Enlightenment—Haskala. Students read Haskala literature in Hebrew and other languages despite the energetic opposition of the principal, Berlin. The Enlighteners—Maskilim—began to demand changes in the yeshiva's regime, which finally brought intervention by the Russian educational authorities. On December 22, 1891, the Russian minister of education published the *Regulations Concerning Volozhin Yeshiva*, in which the yeshiva was defined as a private open educational institution, and its pupils were required to study general subjects to elementary school standard. Berlin did not agree to the regulations, and, on January 22, 1892, the authorities announced the closure of the yeshiva. Berlin and his students were expelled.

The re-opening and subsequent history of the yeshiva do not concern us. By 1892, many yeshivot—notably Mir, Telz, and Slobodka (Kovno)[8]—had been established along similar lines, and the study of Torah continued regardless of the Czar and his minions, if not entirely unaffected by the ongoing love-hate relationship with Haskala.

**Origins of the Analytic Movement— Jacob Isaac Reines and conceptual analysis:** It seems likely that the first individual consciously to develop the techniques of conceptual analysis that characterize the Analytic Movement was Jacob Isaac Reines (1839-1915).[9] Born in Karelin, Lithuania, in addition to a traditional Talmudic education, Reines took an early and lasting interest in secular studies, including languages, law, and science, and was imbued with a love of Zion by his father, who had emigrated to Safed from Lithuania but returned on account of difficult economic circumstances.

Reines' memory continues to be honored in Zionist circles, but he has been forgotten in the yeshiva world. In his major Halakhic work, *Hotam Tokhnit*, published in 1880/1, and again in his *Urim Gedolim* (Vilna, 1886), he set out a novel conceptual basis for Jewish law, aiming to demonstrate both its logical integrity and its coherence with universal principles of jurisprudence. For his vocabulary, he drew heavily and consciously on medieval Jewish philosophical literature, particularly the writings of Maimonides. His methodology, though broader, incorporates virtually all the features that came to be attributed to the Analytic School.

Reines must have profoundly influenced Joseph Rozin (1858-1936), the Rogatshover Gaon.[10] A common feature of the systems of Reines and Rozin is their utilization in a Halakhic setting of logical and scientific terminology derived in the main from Judah ibn Tibbon's Hebrew translation of Maimonides' *Guide for the Perplexed*. Another aspect of Reines' work, his awareness of other law systems and the possibility of universal concepts of law, may well have influenced I.H. Herzog, who, in his *Main Institutions of Jewish Law* (2 vols., 1935), presents Halakhah within the framework of western jurisprudence.

Yet Reines is ignored by Hayyim Soloveitchik and other members of the Analytic School. He studied, and probably taught for a time, at Volozhin, though he had left by the time Soloveitchik returned there in 1873. Undoubtedly part of the reason for his being shunned was his commitment to secular studies as necessary for the better understanding of Torah. An unremitting opponent of secular Haskala, he would have felt that his attitude to secular studies was that of the Vilna Gaon, on the basis of which Volozhin yeshiva had been set up; but, meanwhile, Orthodox attitudes had hardened in reaction to the growth of enlightenment thinking.

In 1905, Reines founded a yeshiva in Lida, Poland, to implement his ideas.[11] One can gauge the hostility this aroused from the words with which Zvi Hirsch Levinsohn, head of the Hafetz Hayyim's yeshiva in nearby Radin, opposed the opening of this rival institution: "Our yeshiva and the yeshiva of Lida are two different ways, at Radin the way of life, at Lida another way, and even though at the beginning of the journey they are close to one another . . . as with any parting of the ways the further they go the greater the distance and the gulf between them."[12]

Like Naftali Zvi Yehuda Berlin, Reines joined the *Hibbat Zion* movement. But the mainstream Orthodox leaders were scandalized by his close friendship with Theodore Herzl and by his founding, in 1904, of the movement of acculturated religious Zionists eventually known as Mizrahi. The Hafetz Hayyim is said to have visited Reines personally to dissuade him from supporting the Zionists, and further pressure was exerted by excluding him from the counsels of the *Gedolei Hatorah*, the "Torah Greats."

A glance at Reines' work will demonstrate his method, in particular the use of the method called *haqira*. Though this term and its cognates were in common use—particularly among the Maskilim—to signify "investigation" or "research," with Reines and, as we shall see, the Analysts who followed, it became the technical term that denoted a characteristic type of distinction between two possible formulations of a juristic concept.

Chapter 13 of *Urim Gedolim* is headed *Sha'ar ha-Haqirot* ("the section on *Haqirot*"); in a footnote to his introduction, Reines draws special attention to the chapter, part of which has been detached from the rest and printed at the end of the volume. The chapter focuses on the law for the defendant who admits the partial truth of a claim. B. B.M. 5a, based on M. Shav. 6:1, prescribes an oath. For instance, if A claims that B owes him $100, and B admits that he owes $50, and no evidence can be produced, B is obliged to swear that he owes A not less than $50, and to pay the $50.

The first *haqira* is this: Does the obligation to take the oath arise as a *positive* effect of the admission, as a *negative* effect, or from the combination of positive and negative effects?

In an earlier part of the work (chapters 1:2 and 5:4), Reines divided obligations into two classes, the duty to compensate and the duty to clarify or establish facts. The oath belongs to the latter category. He also established the principle that no duty can arise without a cause (chapter 5:5). Evidently, in the case under discussion, the cause, or ground, of the obligation to take an oath is the partial admission by the defendant. Such a partial admission has both a positive component (the admission of half the debt) and a negative component (the denial of the other half). Which of these leads to the duty to take an oath? Or does only the combination of both factors have that effect?

Reines does not resolve the issue but draws attention to its relevance for the laws of evidence and restitution. Only when he has clarified several related issues—understood within the concept of *haqirot*—is he ready to tackle systematically the debates of the earliest Talmudic commentators on these laws and to demonstrate that many of the disputes depend on implicit assumptions as to the resolution of the *haqirot*. As we shall see, this is precisely the use to which the subsequent Analysts put their own *haqirot*.

**Hayyim Soloveitchik:** Born in Volozhin at the time his father, Joseph Baer, was vice-principal, Soloveitchik (1853-1917) was twelve when the family departed for Slutsk, within a few years establishing himself as a prodigy. The aforementioned rift between his father and Berlin was to some extent healed by Hayyim's marriage in 1873 to Berlin's granddaughter. After his marriage, he returned to Volozhin, and, in 1881, succeeded Raphael Shapira as vice-principal. For a time, the first lecture of the day was given by Hayyim in the first part of the week and by Berlin in the second. Volozhin Yeshiva was temporarily closed by the Russian government in 1892; on 4 Iyar that year Hayyim's father died, and he succeeded him as rabbi of Brisk (Brest, Belorus).

His standing as a political figure among the orthodox was very high, and there is scarcely a Rabbinical conference of any importance in which he did not take a leading part. His general attitude was one of devotion to Torah, manifesting itself in unbending determination to follow traditional principles, refusal to compromise, yet realistic understanding of the difficulties involved. He despised secular Haskala but was less than outspoken in his opposition to the introduction of Musar into the yeshiva curriculum. Though not himself a Hasid, he is reputed to have sent many of his disciples to pray at the synagogue of the Karliner Hasidim, for whose devotion in prayer he had a special regard.

Yet he was uncompromising in his belief in the necessity to regard all problems in the strictest light of the Halakhah. This "pan-halakhism," as A.J. Heschel[13] called it, is a corner-stone of the Analytic movement. Indeed, Joseph D. Soloveitchik's portrayal of Halakhic Man is modeled on the life of his grandfather.[14] Though much material attributed to him has appeared in print, he prepared only one script for publication, his *Novellae* on Maimonides' Mishneh Torah, and even that was not published until 1936, nineteen years after his death.

Alongside Hayyim Soloveitchik, the following were all active in the formative phase of the movement:

> Jacob Isaac Rabbinowitz ("Reb Itzeler Poniewezer") (1854-1918)
> Shimon Yehuda Ha-Cohen Shkop (1860-1939)
> Joseph Leib Bloch (1860-1929)
> Moshe Mordecai Epstein (1860-1933)
> Baruch Dov Leibowitz (1867-1939)
> Isser Zalman Meltzer (1870-1953)
> Naftali Trop (1871-1928)
> Elhanan Bunem Wasserman (1874/5-1941)
> Hayyim Rabbinowitz ("Hayyim Telzer") (1877-1931)
> Moshe Avigdor Amiel (1883-1946)
> Abraham Isaac Bloch (1891-1941)

Of these, Soloveitchik himself, Hayyim Rabbinowitz, Shkop, Epstein, J.L. Bloch, Leib-owitz, Meltzer, and, for a short time, Wasserman, studied at Volozhin. All of them came under the direct influence either of Soloveitchik or of Shkop, who together with J.L. Bloch re-established the yeshiva of Telz, Lithuania, in the mid-1880s.

**Characterization of the Analytic approach:** Six broad features distinguish the approach of the Analytic School from the conventional approach to Jewish law. With the exception of the use of the *haqira* and certain linguistic peculiarities, none of these features of the school is unique to it. The conjunction of all or most of the features is, however, rarely if ever found elsewhere, and each individual feature is more common in this school than elsewhere:

1. The use of the *haqira*.
2. *Harifut* ("sharpness," "penetrating thought"). This term covers the ideas of "on-the-spot" approach, analysis, conceptualism.
3. Definition and classification assume special importance.
4. Terminology. A number of characteristic technical terms are used, and there is a marked tendency towards reification of legal concepts. Some analysts use philosophical terminology, some do not.
5. There is a sense among the Analysts that they are interpreters of the Rishonim, not innovators, or creators of law. This leads to subservience to the earliest Talmudic commentators, a somewhat dismissive attitude to later authorities,[15] and hesitancy to reach practical decisions.
6. Rationalization—the relationship between law and reason, between Halakhah and logic, arises in speculations as to what is the "cause of obligation" or "cause of exemption" in a particular situation.

*Haqira* **contrasted with casuistry (pilpul):** The Analysts are often accused by those superficially acquainted with their work of being "pilpulistic," that is, of focusing upon the resolution of minute inconsistencies between Talmudic passages. But they themselves, following in the tradition of the Vilna Gaon, decried pilpul and claimed merely to be uncovering the plain meaning of the text. Indeed, an analysis of their procedure will make clear how it contrasts with traditional casuistry.[16] For illustration, we consider an extract from the work of Naftali Trop, a disciple of Shkop and J.L. Bloch, and head of the Hafetz Hayyim's yeshiva at Radin.

In the first section of his notes on Tractate Bava Qama,[17] Trop discusses two apparently contradictory rulings of Maimonides. The first ruling concerns an ox whose owner has been cautioned by the court to keep it under control. If such an ox—referred to as *muad*—gores and kills a man, not only must the ox be killed, but its owner must pay *kofer* (ransom) for the life of the victim. But how can such a case arise? Since an ox has to be killed even on the first occasion it kills a man, how can it ever become a known killer—and so called *muad*—in respect of men? Maimonides indicates several possibilities, one of which is that the ox takes on this status if it has killed three other animals, even if it has never killed a man; in this circumstance, the owner is liable to pay *kofer* if, on the next occasion, the victim is human (Mishneh Torah, *Nizqe Mamon* 10:3).

The second ruling is: "If an ox is *muad* for its species, it is not [thereby] *muad* for other species; if it is *muad* for man, it is not *muad* for animals." Several commentators highlight an apparent discrepancy, since this second ruling states that in no case is an ox that is *muad* for victims of class *x* necessarily *muad* for victims of class *y*, while the first states that there is a category of being *muad* such that if an ox is *muad* for victims of class *x* it is *muad* for victims of class *y*.

How is such a flagrant contradiction handled by conventional casuistry? Karo[18] states that the second ruling of Maimonides applies only to cases of injury, not killing. Karo has thus weakened the original universal proposition of Maimonides ("there is *no* type . . ."). He has in effect reduced Maimonides' general principles to *ad hoc* rules for what happens in particular instances.

Now let us examine what the Analyst does. Trop first proposes a *haqira* as to whether the responsibility for payment when one's property has caused damage arises (a) from negligence or (b) from the mere fact that one's property caused the damage, though if one had taken reasonable precautions one would be exempt from payment.[19] His decision is that the basis of responsibility in cases of loss

of life differs from the basis in cases of mere damage to property. The payment of *kofer* for loss of life of one's fellow human being arises from a breach in a duty of care the Torah imposes on us towards other people; this duty applies in respect of *persons*, not things or animals. Now, so long as an ox is *tam*—"innocent;" has no record of goring—in every respect, the general duty of care does not arise. One is not obliged constantly to supervise a normal ox to ensure that it does not attack anyone. However, as soon as the ox leaves its state of being *tam*, even though it is not yet positively *muad* with regard to people, the duty of care arises, and, from it, the liability to *kofer* should the ox gore a human being.

Trop actual posits two forms of being *muad*. The first covers strict liability in tort; the second the special duty of care towards humans. Each applies with perfect generality in its appropriate sphere, not as an *ad hoc* rule but as a statement of legal principle. They are, in addition, both amenable to a still higher level of generalization, which is apparently Trop's aim. He is telling us, first, that liability for damage to property is strict and, second, that liability for homicide is subject to breach of a duty of care. Like the scientist who rejects the *ad hoc* hypothesis but constructs a more general hypothesis to account for what previously appeared to be an anomaly, he has put forward a general theory of tortious liability that ought to accommodate without strain all the rules and instances with which he is concerned. Where Karo, the conventional casuist, *narrowed* the application of the rules, *increasing* their number, Trop *widened* the application, *decreasing* the number. Such an increase in the generality of statements of law is at the same time a demonstration of the rationality of the system as a whole, since it is seen to derive from a small number of general, equitable principles.

**Functional definition:** We see that a *haqira* in the Analytic fashion asks precisely what the concept under discussion is; that is, it seeks a *definition*. Definition—the answer to the question "what exactly *is* . . .?"—is therefore very important to the Analysts, who sometimes write as if there is an object in the front of them that they are attempting to describe, leading to the reification of Halakhah.

There are several types of definition. The analytic definition describes the essence of a thing, what distinguishes it from other, similar, things. For instance, the zoologist may describe a whale as "a mammal that spouts;" this says enough to distinguish the whale from all other animals. But there is a looser sort of definition that does not uniquely define the object under consideration but helps one recognize it by indicating what it does. "A whale is an animal that gets about by swimming" would be a functional definition of this type; it tells us something about how a whale functions but does not give enough information to distinguish a whale from, say, a dolphin or an otter. The germ of this type of definition appears in M. Mak. 1:4:

> Witnesses are not deemed *zommim* [refuted] until they themselves [and not merely their evidence] are refuted. How does this happen? They said: "We testify that so-and-so killed someone." [A subsequent pair of witnesses] said: "How can you give such evidence? The victim, or the murderer, was with us on that day in such-and-such a place!" [The first pair of witnesses] does not become *zommim* in this way. [If, however, the second pair of witnesses] said to them: "How can you testify! You were together with us on that day in such-and-such a place!"—they do become *zommim*.

Rather than analyzing what *hazama*—refutation—is, the passage tells us only how it functions.

A similar approach appears at B. Ned. 68a. In accordance with Num. 30, the vows of a minor girl may be annulled by her father; those of a married woman may be annulled by her husband; if a girl is betrothed when still a minor, her father and husband may jointly, but not separately, annul her vows. But what is "annulment" (*hafara*)? The Talmud discusses the effect of attempted annulment by the husband alone as follows:

> They asked: "Does the husband cut off [the vow] or does he [merely] weaken it?" Of what circumstances do we speak? If, for instance, she vowed [not to eat] two [particular] olive-sizes [of a certain foodstuff]— if we say he cuts off [the vow] she will be

liable to flagellation; if, however, we say he [merely] weakens it, it is only forbidden [for her to eat it, but she is not liable to flagellation].

This fails as an analytic definition of *hafara* because it is incomplete. It does not completely describe what *hafara* is but only how it functions. But the Amoraic passage marks a development from the Tannaitic example in two ways. First, it is of a more abstract nature. Second, the analysis seems to be sought for its own sake; apart from the unlikelihood of the practical illustration of the differences between the two theories, it is significant that the question first put is the theoretical and not the practical one.

**Functional definition in the Middle Ages:** Rabbinic law has several rules for the treatment of cases of doubt. Generally speaking, a doubtful case (*safeq*) in a matter having Pentateuchal authority is resolved *l'humra*— that is, the more stringent alternative must be followed. Where the doubt is compounded, so that two separate matters of doubt are involved (*s'feq s'feqa*), however, the more lenient view prevails.[20] Solomon ben Abraham Adret (Rashba, thirteenth century Spain), in a well-known responsum,[21] states that *s'feq s'feqa* functions as a majority view (*rov*). To put it simply, if one doubt reduces the possibility of, e.g., a prohibition to one in two, a further doubt concerning the same matter reduces it to one in four, yielding a statistical majority in favor of the more lenient view.

This is clearly a functional definition of *s'feq s'feqa*. It is not analytical, as it tells us nothing of the nature of *safeq* or *s'feq s'feqa* but only about how it operates. Even so, its conceptual nature is noteworthy—it contrasts strongly with other medieval discussions of *safeq* and *s'feq s'feqa*, which are generally limited to arguments concerning which rule to apply in a given circumstance, with little or no regard for the intrinsic nature of the concept.

**Functional definition in the Analytic School:** In few ways is it possible to appreciate the originality of the Analytic School more than by its use of functional definitions. Far from being a rare, exceptional phenomenon, this type of definition is of the very life

1404 TALMUD, NINETEENTH AND TWENTIETH CENTURY APPROACHES

stuff of the legal discussions of the school. For example, the Talmud rules that if two things are not permitted to follow each other, they also may not take place simultaneously (B. Ned. 69b). If, for instance, a man simultaneously performs an act of betrothal upon two sisters, neither is effectively betrothed, since, as long as the former is alive, the betrothal of one after the other is impermissible.

Soloveitchik[22] says that this principle may be understood in either of two ways. It may mean that two acts whose validity is mutually contradictory cannot be valid if performed simultaneously, or it might mean that if the validity of each act prevents the other's taking effect and they are both performed simultaneously, neither will be valid, since each invalidates the other. The difference between these two explanations is clear in a case in which only one of the acts impedes the other. According to the first explanation, if both are performed simultaneously, neither will take effect, since they cannot co-exist; but according to the second, the first act would still be effective, since, although it invalidates the second, the second does not invalidate the first. Such a situation occurs, claims Soloveitchik, in the simultaneous authorization and annulment of a vow. In Maimonides' view, he explains, the authorization of a vow legally precludes its annulment. The annulment, on the other hand, does not legally preclude authorization—it "removes" the vow so that nothing remains that could be the subject of subsequent authorization. Consequently, if a vow is simultaneously authorized and annulled, it is valid—the rule at hand merely ensures that annulment, which is legally precluded by the authorization, is not effective. The authorization, which is not legally precluded by the annulment—though if it preceded the annulment it would in fact preclude it—stands. Soloveitchik ingeniously explains that the two ways he suggests of understanding this rule are the basis of the dispute between Maimonides, who holds that a vow is valid under such conditions, presumably because he understands the principle in the second way; and Nissim of Gerona, who holds that the vow would not be valid, and presumably understands it in the first way.

Wasserman,[23] in another context, comes to a similar conclusion with regard to the principle that if two things are not permitted to follow each other, they also may not take place simultaneously. He says that the underlying idea is: "Which should be excluded and which included? Now this is only relevant where both are of equal status, for otherwise why should one take preference over the other?" Where there is some basic inequality, however, whichever is stronger should prevail. Soloveitchik's explanations are respectively the denial and affirmation of a particular instance of Wasserman's inequality concept.

Let us examine second example. The Talmud (see B. Git. 3b) discusses at some length the Tannaitic dispute between Meir and Eleazar on whether the witnesses who *sign* a bill of divorce are the decisive factor in effecting the divorce, or whether the witnesses of the *delivery* of the writ effect the divorce. Before the Analysts, no-one appears to have asked, "*How* do the signatories effect the divorce?" Trop, by contrast, gives a clear answer:

> It would appear that just as, according to Rabbi Meir, who holds that the witnesses who sign are the effective ones, if they do not sign the document it does not possess the legal status of a document at all; so, according to Rabbi Eleazar, who holds that it is the witnesses of transference who are effective, it is the witnesses of transference who give the document its legal status as a document, and if there are no witnesses of transference [the bill of divorce] does not have the status of a document at all.[24]

Trop assumes that according to Meir, who holds that the witnesses who sign are the effective ones, the document would not only be invalid if they failed to sign, it would *not be a document at all* in the eyes of the law. This is comparable to the Talmudic distinction between a bill of divorce that is invalid but possesses what the Talmud calls "the smell of a *get*"—a trace, or element, of validity—(B. Git. 86b), the recipient of which, like divorcees in general, is not subsequently permitted to marry a member of the priestly caste (Kohen), and a bill of divorce considered to have no effect at all, the recipient of which is permitted subsequently to marry a Kohen.

**Halakhah as a comprehensive logical system:** The Analysts' interest in building a comprehensive system of concepts varies. J.L. Bloch felt that such an attempt would distort the essence of Torah, as it would impose on it categories and criteria that are not intrinsic to the law. Soloveitchik and Leibowitz, similarly, believed that Torah should be expounded only in its own vocabulary, and therefore they would have opposed an attempt of this kind; Soloveitchik was rumored to have condemned Shkop's attempts in this direction, finding them contrived.

Only Shkop and Amiel made serious efforts at systematization. Shkop's *Sha'are Yosher* attempts systematically to clarify the basic concepts of doubt, majority, presumption, and evidence; it derives from Aryeh Löb Ha-Cohen's *Shev Shema'at'ta*, first published in 1804 at Lemberg. Amiel follows a highly original plan, especially in *Ha-Middot L'Heqer Ha-Halakha*. In his earlier work, *Darke Moshe*, he had attempted to formulate the basic concepts of the laws of sacrifices and of acquisition, but the preface to *Ha-Middot* shows that he felt that such an attempt presupposed a more basic analysis of the fundamental concepts governing the whole of the Rabbinic system of law, which he ambitiously attempts to provide. His work may owe something to Reines or Rozin, the latter of whom he cites several times.

**Dispute over the use of philosophical terminology in Halakhah:** Beyond personal idiosyncrasies, such as Soloveitchik's use of the term *shem* ("name," that is, the essence of a concept) and Shkop's use of *hithadshut* ("renewal," the way in which an aspect or quality persists), the Analysts are divided on the fundamental question of whether or not to use philosophical terms.

Ibn Tibbon's translation of Maimonides' logical work, under the title of *Millot ha-Higgayon*, defines the following terms utilized by some Analysts (not always in their original connations): *hiyyuv, shelila* (positive, negative); *peula, m'tziut* (act, existence); *siba, y'sod* (cause, foundation); *miqre, etzem*, *gader* (accident, essence, concept); *b'khoah, b'foal, he'eder* (potential, actual, absence).

The technical vocabulary used by some Analysts in interpreting Halakhic concepts includes the terms *gader, hagdara, he'eder, hiyyuvi, b'khoah, mahut, m'tziut, miqre, siba, etzem, b'foal* and *shelili*—remarkably close to the (incomplete) Tibbonide list. But apart from *mahut* and *etzem*, these words are almost completely absent from the writings of Soloveitchik, Leibowitz, J.I. Rabbinowitz, Trop, Epstein, and Meltzer, though Wasserman makes occasional use of *siba* and *b'foal*. Shkop, on the other hand, uses most of the terms, if in some cases infrequently. J.L. Bloch, A.I. Bloch, Hayyim Rabbinowitz, and Amiel use them frequently.

Clearly, then, Soloveitchik and five of the Analysts do not use what they perceived as "philosophical" terminology. The term *hallut*, which they commonly use, was in fact coined by the philosophers, but evidently Soloveitchik did not associate it with philosophy, but thought of it merely as an abstract noun derived from a verb common even in the Mishnah. The terms *hiyyuvi* and *shelili* ("positive;" "negative"), on the other hand, were not perceived to have a Halakhic basis but to belong to the realm of philosophy.

Most Analysts would have been familiar with such terms, whether directly from medieval philosophy, through the later Musar literature, or through contact with colleagues who used them; ignorance does not explain their non-use. Furthermore, one sometimes gets the impression that circumlocutions are used where matters might have been simplified by employment of the appropriate philosophical term; for instance, in Soloveitchik's *de facto/de jure haqira* and Trop's *essence/accident haqira*, we do not find the helpful word pairs *m'tziut/din* and *etzem/miqre*. Thus the avoidance of philosophical terminology apparently was deliberate, most probably a reaction to the association of philosophy with Haskala. Undoubtedly, it stands in the tradition of the Vilna Gaon, whose opposition to philosophy led him to state that it had misled Maimonides.

But how is it, then, that six Analysts nevertheless made at least some use of these terms, and who was responsible for their introduction into Halakhah? All six were connected with Telz; four as teachers, two as students. No Analyst who was at Telz—with the possible exception of Trop, who was there only for a few months as a young student and was apparently dissatisfied—completely rejects the philosophical vocabulary. On the other hand, none who was not at Telz uses it. Telz, evidently, is deeply implicated in the story.

For chronological reasons, only J.L. Bloch and Shkop come into question as the original advocates at Telz of the use of philosophical terms in Halakhic analysis. Of the two, Bloch is more likely to have been the prime mover. His three volumes of *Shiure Daat*[25] show his mastery of ethico-philosophical literature, and it is likely that this preoccupation with Musar made him receptive to the incorporation of some of its philosophical terminology into the realm of Halakhah.

Yet, as with so much in the story of the Analytic School, probing its origins leads us back to Reines and Rozin. Unfortunately, neither debt is acknowledged other than by Amiel, who received ordination from Rozin and does cite his written works.[26] The real story seems to be that philosophical terminology was associated with Analysis, in particular with the *haqira*, from its earliest development by Reines in the 1870s; it was rejected by Soloveitchik at Volozhin, whether for "purist" motives or as a reaction to Haskala; at Kelm and Telz, by contrast, the dominance of the Musar movement meant that philosophical classics such as Bahya's *Duties of the Heart* were read, philosophical terminology was not felt to be foreign to Torah, and its use was accepted even in the domain of Halakhah.

**Historical significance—A Counter-Enlightenment:** The genesis of the Analytic Movement was closely connected with Volozhin and can be dated within a few years of 1880. It took place in the context of the Orthodox reaction to Haskala, at that time and place perceived as the main threat to traditional Judaism. As with other movements of reaction, the attitude to the new movement was ambivalent. At the same time as it discredited the new ideas, the reactionaries were attracted by them; they adopted some of them, convincing themselves that these ideas

had not come from the "revolution" but belonged to the pristine tradition. Thus, the Analysts were attracted by the techniques and vocabulary of Haskala, such as the use of a high-sounding philosophical vocabulary or critical analysis, which they saw not as the adoption of Haskala methods but as a reversion to the "pure" tradition. The message is that Torah, and not Haskala, is the true path of wisdom.

There is an echo here of the Counter-Reformation. Just as Ignatius Loyola saw the salvation of the Roman Church in its propagation of educational institutions devoted to orthodox Christian thought, so the reactionary leaders of Jewry sought to rescue tradition by nurturing the yeshiva movement and by opening academies of higher learning (*Kolelim*), like those of Isaac Elhanan Spektor at Kovno and the Hafetz Hayyim at Radin, where outstanding young men might be trained as traditional spiritual leaders for the next generation. Just as the Index Expurgatorius banned the reading of literature that might weaken the faith of the true believer, so leading rabbis discouraged and even banned secular and heretical literature. The rigorous self-discipline and spiritual exercises of the Jesuit order, coupled with their practical mission to the world, are reflected in the Musar movement; the Council of Trent has its counterpart in the Rabbinical conferences of Kattowitz (1902), St. Petersburg (1911), and Frankfurt (1912).

The analogy must not be pushed too far; there was no perceived need, as at the Tridentine Councils, to take measures to raise the moral standards of the clergy, and the profligacy of some of the Hasidic houses in no way matched the excesses of the Renaissance Papacy. The value of conceiving the Analytic Movement as a facet of a general Counter-Enlightenment or Counter-Haskala, comparable to the Counter-Reformation, is that it enables us to perceive it as part of a widespread reaction to the secularist and assimilationist tendencies of nineteenth and early twentieth century European Jewry.

**The new concept of Torah:** We have seen that study of the legal sections of the Talmud underwent a radical transformation towards the end of the nineteenth century in the yeshivot of Lithuania and Belorus. This new method, with its emphasis on conceptual analysis, became, in the century since its origin, the dominant approach to advanced Talmudic study in the yeshiva world. But by no means did everyone accept the new approach. Even among the rabbis of non-Hasidic orientation, many found it contrived. Avraham Yeshayahu Karlitz (known as the Hazon Ish; 1878-1953), for instance, a leading legal decisor of modern Israel, rejected it in favor of the approach known as "developing the subject according to the Halakhah" (B. Yom. 26a), which he understood to refer to careful textual exposition, leading to correct Halakhic decisions, in the tradition of the Vilna Gaon and the Hafetz Hayyim.[27]

The main weakness of the conceptual approach, as perceived in the orthodox world, has been the difficulty of applying it in actual decision making. This is the consequence not so much of the personal preference of members of the Soloveitchik family not to act as decisors as of the inherent nature of the analytic process. If a *haqira* shows two contrary opinions to be equally reasonable, how do you choose between them? Because it undermines the decision-making process, the analytic approach has been far more successful in the Talmudic academy, where study it undertaken for its own sake, than in the Rabbinic court, where the law must be applied.

**The analytic paradigm—Rationality of Torah:** The analytic paradigm is distinguished from other Torah-law paradigms precisely in the manner in which it asserts the *rationality* of the Torah system. Its characteristic form of argument contrasts with the more traditional approach by providing solutions in terms of universal rather than particular propositions, as we saw through Trop's excursus on the goring ox. *Ratio decidendi*, or at least *ratio legis*, has become ingrained in the system; hence the frequent recourse to concepts such as "the *ground* of liability" or equivalent phrases among those who reject "philosophical" terminology.

Some Analysts bemoan the inadequacy of the human intellect to plumb the depths of Torah: "The Torah cannot be understood by the logic of human reason," avers Leibovitz,[28] "but by the ways and principles of the Torah; therefore one should adapt one's understanding to the Torah, not the Torah to one's understanding." But Leibovitz is not denying that there are discernible principles in Torah that enable us to perceive how the law operates. What he is denying—and this is an aspect of the reaction to Haskala—is the power of the human intellect to fathom the profound wisdom that, he insists, underlies the divine commandments. Moshe Mordecai Epstein, indeed, goes so far as to argue that purely rationalist ethics is inadequate for the comprehension even of those commandments, such as helping the needy, that have in the past been categorized as "rational"—for, as he asks, surely such a commandment is an invitation to interfere with God's will, for if God did not wish a particular person to be needy, does God not have an infinite number of ways to help him or her?[29] He is not so much rejecting rational ethics as declaring its inadequacy to tell the glory of God: "The world and intelligence were both created by the word of Torah; for the fact that men despise theft and murder and so on is because a portion of the Torah has been placed within them."[30] In the context of reaction to Haskala, the analytic approach has rendered Torah impervious to moral criticism; it is inherently rational but beyond our mere mortal ken.

**The Analytic paradigm—Immunity of Torah to history:** The main thrust of the Enlightenment's critique of traditional interpretation of Torah was that the Torah consists of documents that reflect changing social and economic conditions. It is "culture-bound;" its provisions relate to particular stages of the development of Israelite and Jewish society and so should be either abandoned or modified in the present world. The Analytic response to this is most clearly articulated by Joseph Dov (Baer) Soloveitchik (1913-93), the grandson of Hayyim, and it is articulated in philosophical terms. No one should be misled, however. Soloveitchik's account of the nature of Halakhah, though couched in philosophical terms, expresses the yeshiva milieu of his grandfather.

Though antipathetic towards the Enlighteners, many of the Analysts were fascinated by western culture.[31] In the 1920s, Weimar Berlin[32] hosted many aspiring young yeshiva trained Jews who were to become leaders of Orthodoxy, among them Soloveitchik, who wrote a thesis on Hermann Cohen. Cohen held that thought produced everything out of itself; sensation—such as what you feel when you place your feet on the ground—was merely an inconvenient problem posed to thought. Pure thought, rather than perception, imagination, or intuition, was the only legitimate source of knowledge; objects in the world were themselves constructs of thought, with no Kantian thing-in-itself behind them to generate sensation. Central to Cohen's logic was the comparison between logical thought and the mathematical sciences. Soloveitchik remained faithful, throughout his life, to the Cohenian enterprise of establishing the foundations of knowledge on a secure *a priori* basis. His extraordinary theory of Halakhah attempts to confer on the system of Halakhah precisely the invulnerability that appeared to characterize logic and the mathematical sciences.

No one before Soloveitchik had thought to defend tradition on the grounds that it comprised a set of *a priori* truths akin to geometry. Even Moses Mendelssohn, who presented the "Seven Laws of Noah" as a "religion of nature and reason" consisting of truths that should be recognized by any rational human being, neither suggested that such truths are logical certainties nor extended the concept to the system of Halakhah as a whole. To Mendelssohn, Halakhah was but one aspect of Torah, "revealed legislation," tailored to the specific needs and calling of the people of Israel; the laws were, in modern jargon, socially bound or situated and had no place within the universal "religion of nature and reason." But to Soloveitchik, *all* Torah is Halakhah. Torah narratives have as their purpose the determination of Halakhah;[33] even the creation story is not cosmogony or metaphysics but Halakhah—the Halakhah that we should engage in the creative activity of Torah.[34]

Halakhah is a distinct realm of truth, confronting the world independently of natural science or of "religion:"

> When Halakhic Man approaches the real world, he comes with his Torah, given to him on Sinai, in his hand. He connects himself to the world through fixed laws and through principles cast in a mold ... armed with his statutes, laws, principles and judgments in a priori fashion. ... What is this like? It is like a mathematician who forms an ideal world and utilizes it to determine a relationship between himself and the real world. ... The nature of halakha which he has received from the Holy One, blessed be He!, is the creation of an ideal world, and the recognition of the relationship which prevails between it and the real world. There is no phenomenon ... which a priori halakha does not approach with its ideal measuring rod ... When Halakhic Man stumbles upon a spring of water ... he has an a priori relationship with this phenomenon in the real world ... he aspires to harmonize the a priori concept with the a posteriori phenomenon.[35]

One may compare this with Max Scheler's attempt in his 1926 essay "Problems of a Sociology of Knowledge"[36] to set up an *a priori* sociology of knowledge, or perhaps with Hans Kelsen's "pure law" theory, first propounded in 1911.[37] According to Kelsen, law is free from ethical, political, sociological, historical, and other extraneous considerations. Law consists of a hierarchy of norms or legal propositions, the validity of each of which is determined deductively from higher order propositions, ultimately from an ultimate principle (Grundnorm) that does not depend on any rule of law; a typical Grundnorm would be the will of Parliament or the dictates of the Politburo. The analogy fails, though, when we consider the nature of the system as a whole. To Kelsen, the law as such is not *a priori*; given a different Grundnorm, there would be different laws, a situation impossible for Halakhah, according to Soloveitchik. Within the system, moreover, Soloveitchik would not consider that all cases can be solved deductively from one basic premise.

During his years in Berlin, if not before, Soloveitchik must have become acquainted with the problems posed to traditional belief by historical criticism of the Bible; Orthodox commentators, from Malbim to Hoffman and Breuer had consciously tried to rebut the "Higher Criticism;" Yehiel Yaakov Weinberg, a leading Orthodox rabbi among his contemporaries, studied under and worked closely with Paul Kahle.[38] Yet Soloveitchik simply brushes it aside. Once he had defined Torah as Halakhah, and characterized Halakhah as *a priori*, he had rendered Torah impervious to historical criticism.

This indeed is the logical outcome of the Analytic approach. The Vilna Gaon's insistence on careful textual study, though this was not his intention, left sacred texts open to historical criticism. The paradigm change effected by the Analysts evaded historical criticism by interpreting Torah texts as formulations of clear, unchallengeable, *a priori* legal concepts. In this way, the Analysts enabled the yeshiva world to retain its faith in the inherent, superhuman "rationality" of Torah and to achieve a sense of immunity to the moral and historical criticisms leveled at it by the Maskilim.

## Notes

[1] Norman Solomon, *The Analytic Movement: Hayyim Soloveitchik and His Circle* (Atlanta, 1993).

[2] I. Klausner, *Vilna bi-Tekufat ha-Ga'on* (1942) and *Ha-Gaon Rabbi Eliyahu mi-Vilna* (1969); I. Unna, *Rabbenu Eliyahu mi-Vilna u-Tekufato* (1946).

[3] Israel Klausner, *Historia shel ha-sifrut ha-'ivrit he-hadasha* vol. 3, 11.

[4] On the development of the Lithuanian yeshivot, especially those of Volozhin, Telz, and Sloboka, see Shaul Stampfer, *He-Yeshiva ha-Lita'it b'Hithavutah* (Jerusalem, 1995).

[5] I have no evidence for the pilpul Fried encouraged. The style of Fried's successor in the pilpul stakes, Joseph Baer Soloveitchik, cannot be reproached as artificial or arid; at the same time, Soloveitchik definitely did not foreshadow the Analytic movement, as we know both from his *Bet ha-Levi* and from his comments on what he regarded as his son's radical innovations.

[6] On this Soloveitchik, see Chaim Karlinsky, *Ha-Rishon l'shalshelet Brisk* (Jerusalem, 1984).

[7] A. Sorsky, *Marbitzei Torah uMusar*, vol. 1 (Israel, 1976), pp. 19 and 66-67, plays down the personal aspects of the controversy.

[8] See Stampfer, op. cit., and Hillel Goldberg, *Between Berlin and Slobodka: Jewish Transition Figures from Eastern Europe* (Hoboken, 1989).

[9] I at first believed Hayyim Soloveitchik originated the analytic technique associated with his name. But my attention was drawn to the works of Reines by the late Montagu Newman when he was working under my supervision on a doctoral thesis on Joseph Rozin.

[10] Joseph Rozin's notes on Maimonides, and also his volumes of responsa, share the title *Tzofnat Pa'aneah*, the Egyptian name conferred upon Joseph (Gen. 41:45), traditionally understood as "revealer of secrets." The best study is M.M. Kasher's *M'fa'aneah Tzefunot* (New York, 1958).

[11] Yosef Salmon, "The Yeshivah of Lida: A Unique Institution of Higher Learning," in *YIVO Annual* 15 (1974), pp. 106-125.

[12] Sorsky, op. cit., p. 152.

[13] A.J. Heschel, *God in Search of Man* (New York, 1955), p. 328.

[14] *Halakhic Man* was first published in Hebrew in 1944 in *Talpiyot*, vol. 4 (New York), pp. 651-735. Lawrence Kaplan translated it into English (Philadelphia, 1983).

[15] This attitude characterizes also the Vilna Gaon and Rozin.

[16] See Norman Solomon, "Anomaly and Theory in the Analytic School," in *The Jewish Law Annual* (VI) 1987, pp. 126-147, from which the example below is extracted.

[17] *Hiddushei HaGaRNaT Neziqin* (the volume carries no details of publication but is uniform with a volume on *Nashim* published in Jerusalem in 1945.

[18] *Kesef Mishneh* on Maimonides, ad loc.

[19] This parallels the debate in western jurisprudence on the nature of tortious liability. Trop's teacher, Shkop, was apparently aware of this, as he writes (*Hiddushe Rabbi Shimon Yehuda Ha-Cohen* to *Bava Qama*, New York, 1947, 1) of a "consensus between the laws of the Torah and the laws of the peoples that whoever brings something new into the world is its owner with regard to rights . . ." and develops this into something like a theory of strict liability.

[20] *Shulhan Arukh Yore De'ah* 110.

[21] Rashba *Responsa* 1:401.

[22] Soloveitchik, *Hiddushei Rabbenu Hayyim haLevi*, *Nedarim* 13:22.

[23] E.B. Wasserman, *Qovetz He'arot* (Pietrkow, 1932), #25.

[24] N. Trop, *Shi'ure haGaRNaT* on *Nashim*, *Gittin*, p. 70.

[25] J.L. Bloch, *Shi'ure Da'at*, 3 vols. (Tel Aviv, 1949).

[26] E.g., M.A. Amiel, *Ha-Middot l'Heqer ha-Halakha*, 3 vols. (Tel Aviv, 1939, 1942, 1945), vol. 1, p. 15 and vol. 3, p. 203.

[27] See Lawrence Kaplan, "The Hazon Ish: Haredi Critic of Modern Orthodoxy," in J. Wertheimer, ed., *The Uses of Tradition* (New York, 1992), pp. 145-173. Karlitz rejected newly discovered manuscripts on the grounds that, if they had disappeared, this was God's providence. See Moshe Bleich, "The Role of Manuscripts in Halakhic Decision-Making: Hazon Ish, His Precursors and Contemporaries," in *Tradition* 27 (Winter, 1993), pp. 37-115.

[28] The remark is reported by Reuben Gros-sovsky on page 6 of his biographical introduction to Baruch Dov Leibovitz' *Birkat Shmuel*, vol. 2 (New York, 1954).

[29] M.M. Epstein, Introduction to *Levush Mordecai* on *Bava Qama* (Jerusalem, 1929).

[30] Leibovitz, loc. cit.

[31] This is brought out strongly in Marc Shapiro's biography of Yehiel Yaakov Weinberg, shortly to be published in the Littman Library of Jewish Civilization.

[32] See Gershom Scholem, *From Berlin to Jerusalem* (New York, 1980); Gershom Scholem, *Walter Benjamin: The Story of a Friendship* (Philadelphia, 1981); Hillel Goldberg, *Between Berlin and Slobodka: Jewish Transition Figures from Eastern Europe* (Hoboken, 1989).

[33] *Ish ha-Halakha*, pp. 83f.

[34] *Ish ha-Halakha*, p. 84.

[35] *Ish ha-Halakha*, p. 28.

[36] Chapter 8 of *On Feeling, Knowing and Valuing: Selected Writings*, ed. H.J. Bershady (Chicago and London, 1992), pp. 166-200.

[37] Hans Kelsen, *Hauptprobleme der Staatsrechtslehre* (Tübingen, 1911). For a more mature version of the theory, see his *Pure Theory of Law* (Berkeley, 1967), which is an updated version of *Reine Rechtslehre*, first published in Leipzig in 1934.

[38] Shapiro, op. cit.

NORMAN SOLOMON

**THEODICY IN CLASSICAL JUDAISM:** The term theodicy refers to a justification of the ways of God, the proof that—despite what might appear to be the case—God's justice governs the world order. The need for such a proof comes about by reason of the character of monotheism. For, while a religion of numerous gods finds many solutions to one problem, a religion of only one God presents one to many. Life is seldom fair. Rules rarely work. To explain the reason why, polytheisms adduce multiple causes of chaos, a god per anomaly. Diverse gods do various things, so, it stands to reason, outcomes conflict. Monotheism, by contrast, explains many things in a single way. One God rules. Life is meant to be fair, and just rules are supposed to describe what is ordinary, all in the name of that one and only God. So in monotheism a simple logic limits ways of making sense of things. But that logic contains its own dialectics. If one true God does everything, then, since that God is all-powerful and omniscient, all things are credited to, and blamed on, him. In that case, God can be either good or bad, just or unjust—but not both.

Responding to the generative dialectics of monotheism, the Oral Torah systematically reveals the justice of the one and only God of all creation: God is not only God but also good. Appealing to the facts of Scripture, Rabbinic sages in the first six centuries C.E. constructed a coherent theology, a cogent structure and logical system, to expose the justice of God by arguing that the flaws in the perfectly created world are the result of human defiance of God, with the sin that results from their rebellion flawing creation and disrupting the world order. But people also have the power to initiate the process of reconciliation with God, so that, through repentance, an act of humility, they restore the perfection of the order that, through arrogance, they marred. God, in response, will renew the perfection that embodied the divine plan for creation. In this work of restoration, death that comes about by reason of sin will die, the dead will be raised and judged for their deeds in this life, and most of them, having been justified, will go on to eternal life in the world to come.

Within the framework of this story of God's justice, the theodicy of classical Judaism is worked out. But the claim that God orders the world through justice accessible to human reason confronts an everywhere acknowledged obstacle: justice seems to prevail only now and then. People's fate rarely accords with the fundamental principle of a just order but mostly discredits it. The problem is that, if the human condition embodied in Israelites' lives one by one defies the smooth explanations that intend to justify the condition of Israel in the abstract, then the entire logic of the Oral Torah fails.

How, then, to locate God's justice in the chaotic, scarcely-manageable detritus of private lives? This is accomplished through articulation of a doctrine of reward and punishment, the insistence on the justice of God in whatever happens. Within the logic at hand, reward and punishment not only precipitate, but define the teleology, of all thought. God is always God, but by no means good to all. This is stated in so many words, as is every critical proposition of the entire theological system animating the Oral Torah (Lam. Rabbah LXXXVII.i):

> 1.A. "The Lord is good to those who wait for him, to the soul that seeks him" (Lam. 3:25):
> B. Might one suppose that God is good to all?
> C. Scripture says, "to the soul that seeks him."

May we distinguish Israel from the gentiles? Not at all:

> 2.A. Along these same lines: "Surely God is good to Israel" (Ps. 73:1).
> B. Might one suppose that God is good to all?
> C. Scripture says, "Even to those who are pure in heart" (Ps. 73:1).
> D. That is, those whose heart is pure and in whose hand is no wickedness.

Then to whom is God good? To those who keep the Torah:

> 3.A. Along these same lines: "Happy is the one whose strength is in you" (Ps. 84:6).
> B. Might one suppose that God is good to all?
> C. Scripture says, "In whose heart are the highways" (Ps. 84:6)—those in whose heart the paths of the Torah are kept.

God is selective and elects those that ought to be selected, punishes and rewards those that deserve the one or the other. So God's justice is what is explained. God is good to those who deserve it and punishes those who deserve it.

Sages never for one minute doubted that the world order of justice encompassed private lives. This they stated in countless ways, the simplest being the representation of Hillel's statement encased in a fragmentary narrative (M. Ab. 2:6):

> [One day he was walking along the river and] he saw a skull floating on the water and said to it, "Because you drowned others, they drowned you, and in the end those who drowned you will be drowned."

Somewhere, somehow, the wicked get their comeuppance. The just God sees to it. But what about the righteous? Is their just reward equally certain? However dubious the former of the two propositions—the ultimate triumph of justice over the wicked when a crime or sin has been committed—that the righteous get their just reward certainly conflicted, then as now, with everyday experience. Indeed, the basic conviction of world order defined by justice violated every intuition, every perception, every reflection upon human fate, that private lives provoked. Then as now, people lived in a world of caprice and, right or wrong, discerned no justice at all.

Explaining how God's justice is worked out in private lives required a complex and diverse construction of thought. The thin, one-dimensional solution to the challenge to the theology of world order posed by gentile rule—the gentiles serve God's will in ruling Israel, thereby punishing Israel for its sin, but will themselves give way to Israel at the last—nicely served. But a much thicker explanation would be required to encompass the diverse cases all bundled together in the phrase "righteous in a bad way, wicked in a good way," or covered by the question, "why do the wicked prosper?" For when it comes to everyday life, the anomaly represented by a random, not a just, fate, encompassed many cases, each with its own special traits, none easily resolved by appeal to a single overriding principle of reward and punishment. And the cases pressed in, near at hand, in the next house, the next room. So the human condition presented its own anomalies to the rule of the just order. Suffering, illness, and death come to all, the wicked and the righteous alike. So, responding to that cliché of everyday life, Ecclesiastes among many sages surely forbade framing easy answers and making facile distinctions.

Everything begins with the insistence that people are responsible for what they do, therefore for what happens to them, as much as the people Israel dictates its destiny by its own deeds. Justice reigns, whatever happens. The reason that individuals (therefore, groups formed by individuals) are responsible for their own actions is that they enjoy free will. People are constantly subject to divine judgment; they have free choice, hence may sin; God judges the world in a generous way; but judgment does take place (M. Ab. 3:15):

A. R. Aqiba says, "Everything is foreseen, and free choice is given. In goodness the world is judged. And all is in accord with the abundance of deeds."

B. He would say, "All is handed over as a pledge, and a net is cast over all the living. The store is open, the storekeeper gives credit, the account book is open, and the hand is writing.

C. "Whoever wants to borrow may come and borrow. The charity collectors go around every day and collect from man whether he knows it or not. And they have grounds for what they do. And the judgment is a true judgment. And everything is ready for the meal."

God may foresee what is to happen, but people still exercise free will. The individual's attitude and intentionality make all the difference. Because people are not coerced to sin, nor can they be forced to love God or even obey the Torah, an element of uncertainty affects every life. That is the point at which human will competes with God's. It follows that, where humans give to God what God wants but cannot coerce, or what God wants but cannot command—love, generosity, for instance—there, the theology of the Oral Torah alleges, God responds with an act of uncoerced grace. But in all, one thing is reliable, and that is the working of just recompense for individual action. Expectations of a just reward or punishment, contrasting with actualities, therefore precipitate all thought on the rationality of private life: what happens is supposed to make sense within the governing theology of a just order.

People are responsible for their own actions. But who bears responsibility when an infant dies, or a woman in childbirth, or a man before his appointed time (prior to sixty in the Talmud's estimation)? And how do sages reasonably explain the anomalies round about, those manifested by Scripture and embodied in the here and now of everyday life? Several distinct explanations serve, depending on the circumstance. In one, the individual's fate is said to be bound up with that of the group, Israel, or of the particular generation; in a second type of explanation, a specific malady or affliction is associated with a particular sort of sin; and other approaches appear as well. Since, moreover, old age,

sickness, suffering, and death come to all, sages do not concede that these common mediators of fate are punishment for sin at all.

The doctrine of reward and punishment is spelled out in close detail. First let us take up the matter of punishment for specific sins or crimes. Here is a clear statement that individuals shape their own fate. The person afflicted with the ailment described at Lev. 13-14, here translated as "plagues" or "plague of leprosy," has brought the illness upon himself by gossiping, and Scripture contains ample proof of that fact (Sifra CLV:i.8):

A. "... saying" (Lev. 14:35)—

B. The priest will say to him words of reproach: "My son, plagues come only because of gossip, as it is said, 'Take heed of the plague of leprosy to keep very much and to do, remember what the Lord God did to Miriam' (Deut. 24:8).

C. "And what has one thing to do with the other?

D. "But this teaches that she was punished only because of gossip.

E. "And is it not an argument *a fortiori*?

F. "If Miriam, who did not speak before Moses' presence, suffered so, one who speaks ill of his fellow in his very presence, how much the more so?"

Not only gossip, but other sins bring on specific penalties, arrogance too:

G. R. Simeon b. Eleazar says, "Also because of arrogance do plagues come, for so do we find concerning Uzziah,

H. "as it is said, 'And he rebelled against the Lord his God and he came to the Temple of the Lord to offer on the altar incense and Azariah the priest came after him and with him priests of the Lord, eighty strong men, and they stood against Uzziah and said to him, It is not for you to do, Uzziah, to offer to the Lord, for only the priests the sons of Aaron who are sanctified do so. So forth from the sanctuary. And Uzziah was angry,' etc. (2 Chron. 26:16)."

A gossip is penalized by an attack of whatever disease, if any, is represented by the word "plagues" or by the skin-ailment under discussion here. God has spelled out in the Torah both sins and the penalty attaching to them. So what happens to the individual will naturally be explained as a consequence of what he has done.

Suffering forms an atonement for sin, which by definition is to be desired. First, suffering on its own constitutes a form of expiation and atonement, no less than an offering in the Temple in olden times. Second, suffering alerts people to their having sinned, telling them to find out what sin they committed and to repent for it. The prophets said the same thing as the sages. Such suffering represents an act of benevolence and is to be desired; it requires no justification beyond its own purpose. Sifre Deut. XXXII:V.5ff. states:

> 5.A. And, furthermore, a person should rejoice in suffering more than in good times. For if someone lives in good times his entire life, he will not be forgiven for such sin as may be in his hand.
> B. And how shall he attain forgiveness? Through suffering.

Suffering serves a just purpose and does not have to be explained further. Now a sequence of statements underscores the benevolence of God, expressed when he brings suffering to the sinner:

> 6.A. R. Eliezer b. Jacob says, "Lo, Scripture says, 'For whom the Lord loves he corrects, even as a father corrects the son in whom he delights' (Prov. 3:12).
> B. "What made the son be pleasing to the father? You must say it was suffering [on account of correction]."
> 7.A. R. Meir says, "Lo, Scripture says, 'And you shall consider in your heart, that as a man chasten his son, so the Lord your God chastens you' (Deut. 8:5).
> B. "'You know in your heart the deeds that you did, and also the suffering that I brought upon you, which was not in accord with the deeds that you did at all.'"

Suffering forms a mark of God's special engagement with the person:

> 8.A. R. Yose b. R. Judah says, "Beloved is suffering, for the name of the Omnipresent rests upon the one upon whom suffering comes,
> B. "as it is said, 'So the Lord your God chastens you' (Deut. 8:5)."

Suffering forms a covenant with God, no less than the covenant at Sinai or at circumcision:

> 9.A. R. Nathan b. R. Joseph says, "Just as a covenant is made through the Land, so a covenant is made through suffering, as it is said, 'The Lord, your God chastens you' (Deut. 8:5).
> B. "And it says, 'For the Lord your God brings you into a good land' (Deut. 8:7)."

That conception broadens the range of discourse. Now the entire repertoire of positive categories contributes, for suffering also serves as the prerequisite of certain gifts that Israel is given, the Torah, the land of Israel, and the world to come, the three most important components of Israel's public life then depending upon the condition of the Israelite:

> 10.A. R. Simeon bar Yohai says, "Suffering is precious. For through suffering three good gifts were given to Israel, which the nations of the world desire, and these are they: the Torah, the land of Israel, and the world to come.

Another approach to the same matter, also finding that suffering forms an act of divine grace, compares suffering to the offerings on the altar: with the Temple in ruins, suffering forms the counterpart to the sacrifices offered when the Temple stood. As the latter atoned for sin, so the former atones for sin. That turns suffering into a valued occasion, not to be rejected or explained away but appreciated. Suffering as punishment for sin is to be valued, because through suffering one atones. Hence a doctrine of suffering encompasses not only the cause—rebellion—but also what is achieved—humility, yielding repentance. Suffering as divine chastisement and instruction thus is to be received gratefully (no. 5, above). Not only does suffering yield atonement, it also appeases the way offerings do.

Suffering forms the equivalent to a sacrifice, a means of atonement for sin. Why should suffering be valued as a medium of atonement? For it provokes introspection and serves as a source of reflection on the sins one has committed, so providing the occasion for repentance, which yields atonement. Accordingly, the most important reason that suffering is precious is that it changes one's attitude. When suffering comes, it brings about submission to God, a point demonstrated here (Sifre Deut. 32):

A. Now when R. Eliezer was sick, four sages, R. Tarfon, R. Joshua, R. Eleazar b. Azariah, and R. Aqiba, came to visit him.

The first responses fail, because they merely commiserate and compliment the sufferer, which hardly addresses the issue of suffering at all:

B. Responded and said to him R. Tarfon, "My lord, you are more precious to Israel than the sun's orb. For the sun's orb gives light to this world, but you give light to us in this world and the world to come."
C. Responded and said to him R. Joshua, "My lord, you are more precious to Israel than the gift of rain, for rain gives life in this world, but you give life to us in this world and the world to come."
D. Responded and said to him R. Eleazar b. Azariah, "My lord, you are more precious to Israel than a father or a mother. For a father or mother bring one into this world, but you bring us into this world and the world to come."

The three miss the point. The fourth hits the bulls-eye:

E. Responded and said to him R. Aqiba, "My lord, suffering is precious."
F. R. Eliezer said to his disciples, "Lift me up."
G. R. Eliezer went into session, saying to him, "Speak, Aqiba."

The proof for the announced proposition derives from a specific case of Scripture:

H. He said to him, "Lo, Scripture says, 'Manasseh was twelve years old when he began to reign, and he reigned for fifty-five years in Jerusalem. And he did what was evil in the eyes of the Lord' (2 Chr. 33:1). And it further says, 'These are the proverbs of Solomon, which the men of Hezekiah, king of Judah, copied out' (Prov. 25:1).
I. "Now can anyone imagine that Hezekiah taught Torah to all Israel, while his son, Manasseh, he did not teach Torah?
J. "But one must conclude that, despite all of the learning that his father taught him, and all the work that he put into him, nothing worked for him except suffering.
K. "For it is said, 'And the Lord spoke to Manasseh and to his people, but they gave no heed. Therefore the Lord brought upon them the captains of the host of the king of Assyria, who took Manasseh with

hooks and bound him with fetters and carried him to Babylonia. And when he was in distress, he besought the Lord, his God, and humbled himself greatly before the God of his fathers and prayed to him, and he was entreated of him and heard his supplication and brought him back to Jerusalem into his kingdom' (2 Chr. 33:10-13).
L. "That proves that suffering is precious."

From such a perspective, suffering represents not an anomaly in, but a confirmation of, the theological logic that begins with the principle of God's justice and benevolence. Suffering helps individuals help themselves, returns them to God, precipitates their repentance. What more can one ask of a just God than the opportunity to shape one's own will?

No wonder, then, that the Oral Torah's framers, focused as they are on the patriarchs as paradigms for their children, Israel, and enduring sources for a heritage of virtue, go so far as to invoke the fathers as the founders of suffering. Here, the patriarchs themselves ask God to bestow old age, suffering, and sickness, because the world needs these things. These components of the human condition not only do not form challenges to the logic of God's just governance of the world but express that very benevolence that infuses justice (Gen. Rabbah LXV:IX.1):

A. "When Isaac was old, and his eyes were dim, so that he could not see, he called Esau his older son, and said to him, 'My son,' and he answered, 'Here I am'" (Gen. 27:1):
B. Said R. Judah bar Simon, "Abraham sought [the physical traits of] old age [so that, from his appearance, people would know that he was old]. He said before him, 'Lord of all ages, when a man and his son come in somewhere, no one knows whom to honor. If you crown a man with the traits of old age, people will know whom to honor.'
C. "Said to him the Holy One, blessed be he, 'By your life, this is a good thing that you have asked for, and it will begin with you.'
D. "From the beginning of the book of Genesis to this passage, there is no reference to old age. But when Abraham our father came along, the traits of old age were given to him, as it is said, 'And Abraham was old' (Gen. 24:1).

So much for old age, but what about what goes with it, the suffering of infirmities? Here Isaac makes his contribution, now being credited with that very conception that explains the justice of human suffering:

E. "Isaac asked God for suffering. He said before him, 'Lord of the age, if someone dies without suffering, the measure of strict justice is stretched out against him. But if you bring suffering on him, the measure of strict justice will not be stretched out against him. [Suffering will help counter the man's sins, and the measure of strict justice will be mitigated through suffering by the measure of mercy.]'

F. "Said to him the Holy One, blessed be he, 'By your life, this is a good thing that you have asked for, and it will begin with you.'

G. "From the beginning of the book of Genesis to this passage, there is no reference to suffering. But when Isaac came along, suffering was given to him: 'his eyes were dim' (Gen. 27:1).

Finally, what of sickness, the third in the components of human fate? That is Jacob's contribution, and the wisdom and good will of God come once more to full articulation in suffering:

H. "Jacob asked for sickness. He said before him, 'Lord of all ages, if a person dies without illness, he will not settle his affairs for his children. If he is sick for two or three days, he will settle his affairs with his children.'

I. "Said to him the Holy One, blessed be he, 'By your life, this is a good thing that you have asked for, and it will begin with you.'

J. "That is in line with this verse: 'And someone said to Joseph, "Behold, your father is sick"' (Gen. 48:1)."

K. Said R. Levi, "Abraham introduced the innovation of old age, Isaac introduced the innovation of suffering, Jacob introduced the innovation of sickness.

We proceed now to a further case of the same classification, now chronic illness and its origin in the wisdom of the saints, now Hezekiah:

L. "Hezekiah introduced the innovation of chronic illness. He said to him, 'You have kept a man in good condition until the day he dies. But if someone is sick and

gets better, is sick and gets better, he will carry out a complete and sincere act of repentance for his sins.'

M. "Said to him the Holy One, blessed be he, 'By your life, this is a good thing that you have asked for, and it will begin with you.'

N. "'The writing of Hezekiah, king of Judah, when he had been sick and recovered of his sickness' (Is. 38:9)."

O. Said R. Samuel b. Nahman, "On the basis of that verse we know that between one illness and another there was an illness more serious than either one."

Old age, suffering, and sickness do not represent flaws in creation but things to be desired. Each serves a good purpose. All form acts of divine mercy. The mode of explanation appeals to reason and practical considerations attached thereto.

Still, matters do not come out even; all die, but not everyone suffers premature death or sickness. Much more galling: sometimes wicked people live long, healthy, and prosperous lives, happily making everyone around them miserable, then die peacefully in their sleep at a ripe old age. And—then or now—one need not visit a cancer ward to find misery afflicting genuinely good and pious people. So while the doctrine of the benevolence expressed by sickness, suffering, and old age serves, it hardly constitutes a universal and sufficient justification. And, however reasonable suffering may be shown to be, in the end reason hardly suffices in the face of the raw agony of incurable illness. That is why, in sages' view, further responses to Job, Jeremiah, and Ecclesiastes are called for. One further effort to bring suffering within the framework of the rational, to show the justice of the matter, is called forth. Specifically, the same anomalies in the just order encompassing private life may come about for yet another reason, which is, God's own plan: when the righteous suffer, God is testing them (Gen. Rabbah LV:II.1f.):

1.A. "The Lord tries the righteous, but the wicked and him who loves violence his soul hates" (Ps. 11:5):

This is now embodied in metaphors drawn from the potter, the flax maker, and the farmer:

B. Said R. Jonathan, "A potter does not
test a weak utensil, for if he hits it
just once, he will break it. What
does the potter test? He tests the
strong ones, for even if he strikes
them repeatedly, they will not break.
So the Holy One, blessed be he,
does not try the wicked but the righteous: 'The Lord tries the righteous'
(Ps. 11:5)."

C. Said R. Yose bar Haninah, "When
a flax maker knows that the flax is
in good shape, then the more he
beats it, the more it will improve and
glisten. When it is not of good quality, if he beats it just once, he will
split it. So the Holy One, blessed be
he, does not try the wicked but the
righteous: 'The Lord tries the righteous' (Ps. 11:5)."

D. Said R. Eleazar, "The matter may be
compared to a farmer [lit.: house-
holder] who has two heifers, one
strong, one weak. On whom does he
place the yoke? On the one that is
strong. So the Holy One, blessed be
he, does not try the wicked but the
righteous: 'The Lord tries the righteous' (Ps. 11:5)."

We conclude the exercise with the juxtaposition of the base-verse, Gen. 22:1, and
the intersecting-verse, Ps. 11:5, at the meeting of which the point just now stated was
triggered:

III.1.A. Another interpretation: "The Lord
tries the righteous, but the wicked
and him who loves violence his soul
hates" (Ps. 11:5):

B. The cited verse speaks of Abraham:
"And it came to pass after these
things God tested Abraham" (Gen.
22:1).

The suffering of the righteous pays tribute to
their strength and is a mark of their virtue.
That is shown by appeal both to analogies
(potter, flax maker, householder) and Scripture. Suffering shows God's favor for the one
who suffers, indicating that such a one is worthy of God's attention and special interest.

That suffering is a valued gift explains the
critical importance of the theological principle that one should accept whatever God
metes out, even suffering. In a context defined by the conviction that suffering forms
a gift from a benevolent and just God, we

cannot find surprising that a person's loving
God should involve accepting punishment as
much as benefit. This is stated in so many
words (M. Ber. 9:4A-E):

A. One is obligated to bless over evil as
one blesses over the good, as it is said,
"And you shall love the Lord your God
with all your heart, with all your soul,
and with all your might" (Deut. 6:5).

B. "With all your heart"—with both of
your inclinations, with the good inclination and with the evil inclination.

C. "And with all your soul"—even if he
takes your soul.

D. "And with all your might"—with all of
your money.

Accordingly, the correct attitude toward suffering entails grateful acknowledgment that
what God metes out is just and merciful. The
same matter is amplified in the following exegesis of the same verses of Scripture (Sifre
Deut. XXXII:V.1-12):

1.A. R. Aqiba says, "Since it is said, 'with
all your soul,' it is an argument *a fortiori* that we should encompass, 'with
all your might.'

B. "Why then does Scripture say, 'with all
your might'?

C. "It is to encompass every single measure that God metes out to you, whether
the measure of good or the measure of
punishment."

People are expected to accept suffering as a
mark of divine favor and love, as an indication that God has special confidence in them,
or that God has a particular purpose in dealing with them as he does. If the patriarchs
asked for sickness, old age, and other forms
of suffering, all the more reason gratefully to
accept as a mark of divine justice the miser-
ies of the human condition.

So the sages mounted argument after argument. They framed and found scriptural
bases for doctrine after doctrine. All this was
to try to persuade themselves that somehow
the world conformed to rationality defined by
justice. True, the claim that anguish and illness, premature death and everyday suffering
fit under the rules of a reasonable world order,
the insistence that when the wicked prosper,
justice still may be done—these propositions,
necessary to the system, may well have tran-

scended the here and now and conformed to a higher reality. But still, when all is said and the day is done, the doctrine of suffering could not encompass all cases, let alone persuade everybody who raised the question, why me? why now? Nor did sages so frame matters as to suggest they found theology's panglossean solutions, if necessary, wholly sufficient let alone compelling. True, suffering is to be accepted as a mark of God's grace, a gift, an occasion, a mode of atonement and reconciliation with God. True, the patriarchs found much good in human fate and asked God to arrange matters as they are. And yet—and yet the fact remains that some suffer more than others, and, not uncommonly, the wicked prosper and the righteous do not.

So the doctrine of suffering on its own could not, and did not, complete the Oral Torah's account of the confrontation with the key-dilemma of sages' theology of world-order, the anomalies that manifestly flaw private lives, viewed in comparison and contrast with one another. Say what they would, sages in the end had to complete the circle: some do not get what they deserve, whether for good or for ill, and, if their time is replicated in our own, those some were very many. To that protean problem sages found in their larger theology a commensurate and predictable response.

Sages identified with adherence to Torah the promise of life eternal, with idolatry the extinction of being. This would come about at the last days, which will correspond with, and complete, the first days of creation. Justice will be done only when the world is perfected. With that conviction's forming the foundation of their very definition of world order, divided between those who will overcome the grave, Israel with the Torah, and those who will not, the gentiles with idolatry, sages found in hand a simple solution. The righteous suffer in this world and get their just reward in the world to come, but the wicked enjoy this world and suffer in the world to come. Since the theology of the Oral Torah to begin with distinguished the Torah and life from idolatry and death, what happens in this world and in this life does not tell the whole story. And when that entire

story is told, the received formulation of the problem of evil no longer pertains, and the final anomalies are smoothed out.

Since that theology contemplated a world beyond the grave—the world to come, in which individuals would resume the life they knew, but now for eternity—that conviction provided a solution to the problem of the prosperity of the wicked and the misery of the righteous. By insisting that this world does not tell the whole story of a private life, sages could promise beyond the grave what the here and now denied. The simplest statement of that position is at B. Hor. 3:3 I./11a:

6.A. Expounded R. Nahman bar Hisda, "What is the meaning of the verse of Scripture, 'There is a vanity that occurs on the earth, for there are the righteous who receive what is appropriate to the deeds of the wicked, and there are the wicked who receive what is appropriate to the deeds of the righteous' (Eccl. 8:14).

B. "Happy are the righteous, for in this world they undergo what in the world to come is assigned as recompense for the deeds of the wicked, and woe is the wicked, for in this world they enjoy the fruits of what is assigned in the world to come to the deeds of the righteous."

The righteous will enjoy the world to come all the more, and the wicked will suffer in the world to come all the more; the one has saved up a reward for eternity, the others have in this transient world already spent such reward as they may ever get. But that still begs the question:

C. Said Raba, "So if the righteous enjoy both worlds, would that be so bad for them?"

Raba acts in the model of Abraham facing God before Sodom! But he has a better solution, making still more radical claim:

D. Rather, said Raba, "Happy are the righteous, for in this world they get what is set aside for the [meritorious] deeds of the wicked in this world, and woe to the wicked, for in this world they get what is assigned for the deeds of the righteous in this world."

Raba's solution takes account of the theory of atonement through suffering. The righteous atone in the here and now; that is why they suffer. Then the world to come is all the more joyful. Now follows a story that shows how disciples of sages enjoy in this world such benefit as the wicked ought to have had in the world to come, and the rest follows.

> E. R. Pappa and R. Huna b. R. Joshua came before Raba. He said to them, "Have you mastered such and such tractate [of Torah] and such and such tractate?"
> F. They said to him, "Yes."
> G. "Have you gotten a bit richer?"
> H. They said to him, "Yes, because we bought a little piece of land."
> I. He recited in their regard, "Happy are the righteous, for in this world they undergo what in the world to come is assigned as recompense for the deeds of the wicked."

To grasp how, in massive detail, ultimate justice pervades the here and now, the premise of this passage should not be missed. It is that of a steady-state moral economy: a finite store of rewards and punishments awaits the righteous and the wicked alike, so what comes to the one is denied the other. World order defined by reasoned justice serves to justify— show God's justice in—even humble, everyday experience. It follows that the rules that govern and account for everyday experience are supposed to make sense of the nonsense of the present age.

But sages were no fools, and hope for the at-present-intangible future did not dim their dark vision of the ordinary experience of life, its nonsense, its anomalies. While pursuing philosophical modes of thought, in the end sages valued sagacity beyond reason, however compelling. For all their insistence upon the rule of God through a just order, sages accepted that beyond the known and reasonable lay the unknowable, the realm of God beyond the part set forth in the revealed Torah. They affirmed, in the end, their own failure, which makes them plausible and human in their claims to account for much, if not all, of the anguish of which private lives even of the most holy of men are comprised. In the end we all die, and who knows how long the interval until the resurrection? So sages last word on the reasonable rule of the just order consists of a single imperative: humility, the gift of wisdom, not of wit. Here is a

passage that generations of Talmud-students have found sublime, the statement of all things, all in all (B. Men. 3:7 II.5/29b):

> 5.A. Said R. Judah said Rab, "At the time that Moses went up on high, he found the Holy One in session, affixing crowns to the letters [of the words of the Torah]. He said to him, 'Lord of the universe, who is stopping you [from regarding the document as perfect without these additional crowns on the letters]?'
> B. "He said to him, 'There is a man who is going to arrive at the end of many generations, and Aqiba b. Joseph is his name, who is going to interpret on the basis of each point of the crowns heaps and heaps of laws.'
> C. "He said to him, 'Lord of the Universe, show him to me.'
> D. "He said to him, 'Turn around.'
> E. "He went and took a seat at the end of eight rows, but he could not grasp what the people were saying. He felt faint. But when the discourse reached a certain matter, and the disciples said, 'My lord, how do you know this?' and he answered, 'It is a law given to Moses from Sinai,' he regained his composure.
> F. "He went and came before the Holy One. He said before him, 'Lord of the Universe, How come you have someone like that and yet you give the Torah through me?'
> G. "He said to him, 'Silence! That is how the thought came to me.'
> H. "He said to him, 'Lord of the Universe, you have shown me his Torah, now show me his reward.'
> I. "He said to him, 'Turn around.'
> J. "He turned around and saw his flesh being weighed out at the butcher-stalls in the market.
> K. "He said to him, 'Lord of the Universe, 'Such is Torah, such is the reward?'
> L. "He said to him, 'Silence! That is how the thought came to me.'"

God rules, and people, in the end, cannot explain, account for the rationality of, everything God decrees. Sages offer more than reasonable explanations for the perceived violation of justice. They offer also the gift of humility in the form of is silence. That forms the barrier before the ultimate terror—not understanding, not making sense of things.

Accordingly, sages placed humility before God above even the entire theological enterprise with its promise of explanation, understanding, and justification. But the last word must register: that God's decrees, however inexplicable those decrees to the human mind, bear the comforting message that God cares. And since the premise of the mystery of suffering is formed by the conviction of God's justice, that God cares also means God loves. And it is a love for humankind, taken care of one by one, a love so deep as not to leave anybody ever unattended—even Aqiba in his martyrdom, but especially ordinary folk, when they suffer, when they bleed, when they die, as all do.

### Bibliography
Jacob Neusner, *The Theology of the Oral Torah* (Kingston and Montreal, 1998).

JACOB NEUSNER

**THEOLOGICAL ANTHROPOLOGY OF JUDAISM:** Humanity not only complements God, but also corresponds to, is like, God. When sages read in the Torah that humankind is created in God's image, they understood that to mean, God and humans correspond, bearing comparable traits. The theological anthropology of the Oral Torah defined correspondence between God and humans in three ways: [1] intellectually, sharing a common rationality; [2] emotionally, sharing common sentiments and attitudes, and [3] physcally, sharing common features. That is why, to begin with, God and Israel relate. They think alike. They feel the same sentiments. And they look alike. Like God, humans are in command of, and responsible for, their own will and intentionality and consequent conduct. The very fact that God reveals himself through the Torah, which humans are able to understand, there to be portrayed in terms and categories that people grasp, shows how the characteristics of God and humankind prove comparable. The difference between humans and God is that God is God.

We begin with that theological anthropology that sees humankind in God's image in a concrete way. Correspondence encompasses not only intangible, but material qualities. How do God and humans compare in physical presence? Because theology in its philosophical mode has long insisted on the incorporeality of God, let us begin with the Oral Torah's explicit claim that God and humans look exactly alike, being distinguished only by actions performed by the one but not the other (Gen. Rabbah VIII:X.1):

A. Said R. Hoshayya, "When the Holy One, blessed be he, came to create the first man, the ministering angels mistook him [for God, since man was in God's image,] and wanted to say before him, 'Holy, [holy, holy is the Lord of hosts].'

B. "To what may the matter be compared? To the case of a king and a governor who were set in a chariot, and the provincials wanted to greet the king, "Sovereign!' But they did not know which one of them was which. What did the king do? He turned the governor out and put him away from the chariot, so that people would know who was king.

C. "So too when the Holy One, blessed be he, created the first man, the angels mistook him [for God]. What did the Holy One, blessed be he, do? He put him to sleep, so everyone knew that he was a mere man.

D. "That is in line with the following verse of Scripture: 'Cease you from man, in whose nostrils is a breath, for how little is he to be accounted' (Is. 2:22)."

Man—Adam—is in God's image, interpreted in a physical way, so the angels did not know man from God. Only that humans sleeps distinguishes them from God. The theme derives from the verse that states, ". . . in our image, after our likeness" (Gen. 1:26), cited previously in Genesis Rabbah. Accordingly, "In our image" yields two views, first, that the complete image of humankind is attained in a divine union between humanity—man and woman—and, further, that what makes humans different from God is that people sleep, and God does not sleep.

But was the "face" that people and God have in common understood in a physical way, and are other human, physical characteristics ascribed to God? An affirmative answer emerges entirely clearly in the following (B. Ber. 7A, LVI):

A. "And he said, 'You cannot see my face'" (Exod. 33:20).

B. It was taught on Tannaite authority in the name of R. Joshua b. Qorha, "This is

what the Holy One, blessed be he, said
to Moses:

C. "'When I wanted [you to see my face],
you did not want to, now that you want
to see my face, I do not want you to.'"

D. This differs from what R. Samuel bar
Nahmani said R. Jonathan said.

E. For R. Samuel bar Nahmani said R. Jonathan said, "As a reward for three things
[Moses] received the merit of three things.

F. "As a reward for: 'And Moses hid his
face' (Exod. 3:6), he had the merit of
having a glistening face.

G. "As a reward for: 'Because he was afraid
to' (Exod. 3:6), he had the merit that
'They were afraid to come near him'
(Exod. 34:30).

H. "As a reward for: 'To look upon God'
(Exod. 3:6), he had the merit: 'The simili-
tude of the Lord does he behold' (Num.
12:8)."

I. "And I shall remove my hand and you
shall see my back" (Exod. 33:23).

J. Said R. Hana bar Bizna said R. Simeon
the Pious, "This teaches that the Holy
One, blessed be he, showed Moses [how
to tie] the knot of the phylacteries."

That God is able to tie the knot indicates that
(in the present context at least) God has fingers and other physical gifts. God furthermore is portrayed as wearing phylacteries as
well. It follows that God has an arm and a
forehead. There is no element of a figurative
reading of the indicated traits, no defense or
apology for invoking a mere metaphor. Quite
the opposite, in passage after passage, without the slightest trace of embarrassment or
reservation, the correspondence of God and
humanity yields a variety of physical traits.
Indeed, the entirety of the Song of Songs is
read as an account of God's love for Israel,
and Israel's for God, and for the sages the
most suitable way of expressing that account
required the physicalization of God and of
Israel alike.

Second, God and humans intellectually
correspond in the common logic and reason
that they share. That is in two aspects. First,
like Abraham at Sodom, sages simply took
for granted that the same rationality governs.
God is compelled by arguments people find
persuasive, appeals to which humans respond: "Will not the judge of all the
world. . . ." Second, meeting God through the
study of the record of God's self-revelation,

the Torah, sages worked out their conviction
that the human mind corresponded to God's,
which is why humankind can receive the
Torah to begin with. That people can study
the Torah proves they have the capacity to
know God intellectually.

Through their critical, analytical inquiry,
sages thought to gain access to the modes of
thought that guided the formation of the Torah and its law. This involved, for instance,
dialectical argument concerning comparison
and contrast in this way, not in that, identification of categories in one manner, not in
another. Those were the modes of thought
that, in sages' conception, dictated the structure of intellect upon which the Torah rested.
Sages thus could meet God in the Torah:
in their analysis of the deepest structures
of intellect of the Torah, they supposed to
enter into the mind of God, showing how
God's mind worked when God formed the
Torah. And so, in the intellect of God, humans gained access to God. In discerning
how God's mind worked, sages claimed for
themselves a place in that very process of
thought that had given birth to the Torah.

God not only follows and joins in the argument of the laws of the Torah conducted
by sages. God is party to the argument and
subjects himself to the ruling formed by the
consensus of sages—and says so. God not
only participates in the debate but takes pride
when his children win the argument over
him. The miracles of nature convey his vote.
He is outweighed by reason, which people exercise and which takes priority in the reading
of the Torah's laws even over God's judgment! In the following story, we find an explicit affirmation of the priority of reasoned
argument over all other forms of discovery
of truth (B. B.M. 59A-B):

A. There we have learned: If one cut [a
clay oven] into parts [so denying it its
normal form as an oven] but put sand
between the parts [so permitting it to
function as an oven]:

B. Eliezer declares the oven [broken-down
and therefore] insusceptible to uncleanness. [A broken utensil is deemed null,
and so it cannot receive the uncleanness that pertains only to whole and useful objects.]

C. And sages declare it susceptible [because while it is formally broken, it is functionally useful and therefore retains the status of an ordinary utensil].

D. And this is what is meant by the oven of Akhenai [M. Kel. 5:10].

E. Why [is it called] the oven of Akhenai?

F. Said R. Judah said Samuel, "It is because they surrounded it with argument as with a snake and proved it was insusceptible to uncleanness."

G. It has been taught on Tannaite authority:

H. On that day R. Eliezer produced all of the arguments in the world, but they did not accept them from him. So he said to them, "If the law accords with my position, this carob tree will prove it."

I. The carob was uprooted from its place by a hundred cubits—and some say, four hundred cubits.

J. They said to him, "There is no proof from a carob tree."

K. So he went and said to them, "If the law accords with my position, let the stream of water prove it."

L. The stream of water reversed flow.

M. They said to him, "There is no proof from a stream of water."

N. So he went and said to them, "If the law accords with my position, let the walls of the school house prove it."

O. The walls of the school house tilted toward falling.

P. Joshua rebuked them, saying to them, "If disciples of sages are contending with one another in matters of law, what business do you have?"

Q. They did not fall on account of the honor owing to R. Joshua, but they also did not straighten up on account of the honor owing to R. Eliezer, and to this day they are still tilted.

R. So he went and said to them, "If the law accords with my position, let the heaven prove it!"

S. An echo came forth, saying, "What business have you with R. Eliezer, for the law accords with his position under all circumstances!"

T. Joshua stood up on his feet and said, "'It is not in heaven' (Deut. 30:12)."

U. What is the sense of, "It is not in heaven" (Deut. 30:12)?

V. Said R. Jeremiah, "[The sense of Joshua's statement is this:] For the Torah has already been given from Mt. Sinai, so we do not pay attention to echoes, since you have already written in the Torah at Mt. Sinai, 'After the majority you are to incline' (Exod. 23:2)."

W. Nathan came upon Elijah and said to him, "What did the Holy One, blessed be he, do at that moment?"

X. He said to him, "He laughed and said, 'My children have overcome me, my children have overcome me!'"

Here the human is not only like God but, in context, equal to God, who is subject to the same logic. God is bound by the same rules of logical argument, of relevant evidence, of principled exchange, as the sages. So humans can argue with the mere declaration of fact or opinion—even God's claims must be measured against God's own reason, set forth, we see, within the written part of the Torah. That is why the (mere) declaration of matters by heaven is dismissed. Why? Because God is bound by the rules of rationality that govern in human discourse, and because humanity in the person of the sage thinks like God, as God does; so right is right, and nature has no call to intervene, nor even God to reverse the course of rational argument.

Next comes the matter of how God and humans are alike in their attitudes and emotions. What moves God, and moves God to action, are emotions that people too feel, attitudes that guide their actions as much as God's. Uncoerced love matched by an act of grace—that transaction above all tells us what really matters, and it is precisely there that the correspondence of humankind and God extends to emotional or attitudinal traits. God emerges in the Oral Torah as a fully-exposed personality. The common character of divinity and humanity, therefore, encompassed God's virtue, the specific traits of character and personality that God exhibited above and here below. Above all, humility, the virtue sages most often asked of themselves, characterized the divinity. God wanted people to be humble, and God therefore showed humility, as B. Shab. 89a suggests:

A. Said R. Joshua b. Levi, "When Moses came down from before the Holy One, blessed be he, Satan came and asked [God], 'Lord of the world, where is the Torah?'"

B. "He said to him, 'I have given it to the earth . . .' [Satan ultimately was told by God to look for the Torah by finding Moses.]

C. "He went to Moses and asked him,

'Where is the Torah that the Holy One, blessed be he, gave you?'

D. "He said to him, 'Who am I that the Holy One, blessed be he, should give me the Torah?'

E. "Said the Holy One, blessed be he, to Moses, 'Moses, you are a liar!'

F. "He said to him, 'Lord of the world, you have a treasure in store that you have enjoyed every day. Shall I keep it to myself?'

G. "He said to him, 'Moses, since you have acted with humility, it will bear your name: "Remember the Torah of Moses, my servant" (Mal. 3:22).'"

God here is represented as favoring humility and rewarding the humble with honor. God does not here cite Scripture or merely paraphrase it; the conversation is an exchange between two lifelike personalities. True enough, Moses, not God, is the hero. But the personality of God emerges in a vivid way, with arrogance, the denial of God, taking a critical role. This is because sin forms the action of which arrogance is the attitude, and catastrophe for humanity, on the one side, and for Israel, on the other, is the result. So what provokes the calamitous transaction that is the story of humankind to begin with originates in the attitude of arrogance. This, quite naturally, is linked to idolatry, the supreme act of arrogance, the quintessential sin (B. Sot. 5b, XVI):

P. And R. Yohanan said in the name of R. Simeon b. Yohai, "Whoever is arrogant is as if he worships idolatry.

Q. "Here it is written, 'Everyone who is arrogant in heart is an abomination to the Lord' (Prov. 16:5), and elsewhere it is written, 'You will not bring an abomination into your house' (Deut. 7:26)."

R. And R. Yohanan on his own account said, "He is as if he denied the very principle [of the world],

S. "as it is said, 'Your heart will be lifted up and you will forget the Lord your God' (Deut. 8:14)."

T. R. Hama bar Hanina said, "He is as if he had sexual relations with all of those women forbidden to him on the laws of incest.

U. "Here it is written, 'Everyone who is arrogant in heart is an abomination to the Lord' (Prov. 16:5), and elsewhere it is written, 'For all these abominations . . .' (Lev. 18:27)."

V. Ulla said, "It is as if he built a high place,

W. "as it is said, 'Cease you from man, whose breath is in his nostrils, for wherein is he to be accounted of' (Is. 2:22).

X. "Do not read, 'wherein,' but rather, 'high place.'"

God hates idolatry as an act of arrogance and rebellion against him, so God is capable of hatred. So too, God is made angry by idolatry, proving God possesses the quality of anger. These and other traits of emotion in God then find their correspondence in humans, who are to learn from God's emotions and attitudes and imitate them.

God enters into transactions with human beings and accords with the rules that govern those relationships. So God exhibits precisely the social attributes that human beings do. A number of stories, rather protracted and detailed, tell the story of God as a social being, living among and doing business with mortals. These stories provide extended portraits of God's relationships, in particular arguments, with important figures, such as angelic figures, as well as Moses, David, and Hosea. Like people, God negotiates, persuades, teaches, argues, exchanges reasons. God engages in arguments with humans and angels, and so enters into the existence of ordinary people. These disputes, negotiations, transactions yield a portrait of God who is reasonable and capable of give and take, as in the following (B. Ar. 15A-B):

F. Rabbah bar Mari said, "What is the meaning of this verse: 'But they were rebellious at the sea, even at the Red Sea; nonetheless he saved them for his name's sake' (Ps. 106:7)?

G. "This teaches that the Israelites were rebellious at that time, saying, 'Just as we will go up on this side, so the Egyptians will go up on the other side.' Said the Holy One, blessed be he, to the angelic prince who reigns over the sea, 'Cast them [the Israelites] out on dry land.'

H. "He said before him, 'Lord of the world, is there any case of a slave [namely, myself] to whom his master [you] gives a gift [the Israelites], and then the master goes and takes [the gift] away again? [You gave me the Israelites, now you want to take them away and place them on dry land.]'

I. "He said to him, 'I'll give you one and a half times their number.'

J. "He said before him, 'Lord of the world, is there a possibility that a slave can claim anything against his master? [How do I know that you will really do it?]'

K. "He said to him, 'The Kishon brook will be my pledge [that I shall carry out my word. Nine hundred chariots at the brook were sunk (Judg. 3:23) while Pharaoh at the sea had only six hundred, thus a pledge one and a half times greater than the sum at issue.]'

L. "Forthwith [the angelic prince of the sea] spit them out onto dry land, for it is written, 'And the Israelites saw the Egyptians dead on the sea shore' (Exod. 14:30)."

Willing to give a pledge to guarantee his word, God sees the right claim of the counterpart actor in the story. Hence we see how God obeys precisely the same social laws of exchange and reason that govern other incarnate beings.

Still more interesting is the picture of God's argument with Abraham. God is represented as accepting accountability, by the standards of humanity, for what he does (B. Men. 53b):

A. Said R. Isaac, "When the Temple was destroyed, the Holy One, blessed be he, found Abraham standing in the Temple. He said to him, 'What is my beloved doing in my house?'

B. "He said to him, 'I have come because of what is going on with my children.'

C. "He said to him, 'Your children sinned and have been sent into exile.'

D. "He said to him, 'But wasn't it by mistake that they sinned?'

E. "He said to him, 'She has wrought lewdness' (Jer. 11:15).

F. "He said to him, 'But wasn't it just a minority of them that did it?'

G. "He said to him, 'It was a majority' (Jer. 11:15).

H. "He said to him, 'You should at least have taken account of the covenant of circumcision [which should have secured forgiveness despite their sin]!'

I. "He said to him, 'The holy flesh is passed from you' (Jer. 11:15).

J. "And if you had waited for them, they might have repented!'

K. "He said to him, 'When you do evil, then you are happy' (Jer. 11:15).

L. "He said to him, 'He put his hands on his head, crying out and weeping, saying to them, 'God forbid! Perhaps they have no remedy at all!'

M. "A heavenly voice came forth and said, 'The Lord called you "a leafy olive tree, fair with excellent fruit"' (Jer. 11:16).

N. "'Just as in the case of an olive tree, its future comes only at the end [that is, it is only after a long while that it attains its best fruit], so in the case of Israel, their future comes at the end of their time.'"

God relates to Abraham as to an equal. That is shown by God's implicit agreement that he is answerable to Abraham for what has taken place with the destruction of the Temple. God does not impose on Abraham silence, saying the decree is not to be contested but only accepted. God as a social being accepts that he must provide sound reasons for his actions, as must any other reasonable person in a world governed by rules applicable to everyone. Abraham is a fine choice for the protagonist, since he engaged in the argument concerning Sodom. His complaint is expressed at B: God is now called to explain himself. At each point then Abraham offers arguments in behalf of sinning Israel, and God responds, item by item. The climax of course has God promising Israel a future worth having. God emerges as both just and merciful, reasonable but sympathetic. The transaction attests to God's conformity to rules of reasoned transactions in a coherent society.

Among the available models for the comparing humankind to God—warrior, teacher, young man—the one that predominated entailed representation of God as sage. That is because the sage in the Oral Torah embodied the teachings of the Oral Torah, did the deeds that the Torah required, such as Torah-study, and so conformed to God's image of man as set forth in the Torah. We already realize that that representation of the correspondence of God and the sage takes a subordinate position behind the representation of the correspondence of God's emotions and humankind's to the opportunity of grace. But an important chapter in any picture of correspondences encompasses the one between God and the sage. In this connection, God is represented as a school master (B. A.Z. 3b): "He sits and teaches school children, as it is said, 'Whom shall one teach knowledge, and whom shall one make to understand the message? Those who are weaned from milk' (Is. 28:9)." But this is not the same thing as God as a master-sage teaching mature disciples, that is, God as rabbi and sage.

God's personality merged throughout with the personality of the ideal master or sage. That representation proves detailed and specific. A sage's life—Torah first learned through discipleship in the chain extending backward to Sinai, then taught, through discipleship—encompassed both the correct modes of discourse and ritual argument, on the one side, and the recasting of all relationships in accord with received conventions of courtesy and subservience. God is represented in both dimensions, as a master requiring correct conduct of his disciples and as a teacher able to hold his own in arguments conducted in accord with the prevailing ritual. For one example, a master had the right to demand an appropriate greeting, and God, not receiving that greeting, asked why (B. Shab. 89a states):

A. Said R. Joshua b. Levi, "When Moses came up on high, he found the Holy One, blessed be he, tying crowns onto the letters of the Torah. He said to him, 'Moses, don't people say hello in your town?'
B. "He said to him, 'Does a servant greet his master [first]?'
C. "He said to him, 'You should have helped me [at least by greeting me and wishing me success].'
D. "He said to him, "'Now I pray you let the power of the Lord be great, just as you have said' (Num. 14:17).'"

Moses here plays the role of disciple to God the teacher, a persistent pattern throughout. Not having offered the appropriate greeting, the hapless disciple is instructed on the matter. Part of the ritual of "being a sage" thus comes to expression.

The Oral Torah deems humanity to be divided into two parts, Israel with the Torah, the nations with idolatry. We may hardly find surprising that, while God corresponds to humankind in general, the relationship of correspondence, shading over into intimacy and union, takes place with Israel in particular. Where there is love, there is true identification. But for the most part, in the Oral

Torah's representation of matters, God's person forms the counterpart to Israel's person, and the two are complementary but not one. The two, when equally hypostatized, are deemed counterparts, forming a relationship of deep love for one another. God indeed attains person-hood in relationship to Israel, God's twin (Pesiqta deRab Kahana V:VI.2):

A. Said R. Hiyya bar Abba, "How do we know that the Holy One is called 'the heart of Israel'?
B. "On the basis of this verse: Rock of my heart and my portion is God forever (Ps. 73:26)."

The amplification of the foregoing yields the picture of God as Israel's kin and lover, so both parties—the abstraction, "Israel," along with the abstraction, divinity—take on the traits of personhood, personality in particular (Pesiqta deRab Kahana V:VI.3):

A. ". . . My beloved is knocking" (Song 5:2) refers to Moses: "And Moses said, Thus said the Lord, At about midnight I shall go out in the midst of Egypt" (Exod. 11:4).
B. "Open to me:" said R. Yose, "Said the Holy One, blessed be he, 'Open to me [a hole] as small as the eye of a needle, and I shall open to you a gate so large that troops and siege-engines can go through it.'"
C. ". . . my sister:" [God speaks:] "My sister—in Egypt, for they became my kin through two religious duties, the blood of the Passover-offering and the blood of circumcision."
D. ". . . my dearest"—at the sea, for they showed their love for me at the sea, "And they said, the Lord will reign forever and ever" (Exod. 15:19).
E. ". . . my dove"—my dove at Marah, where through receiving commandments they became distinguished for me like a dove.
F. ". . . my perfect one"—My perfect one at Sinai, for they became pure at Sinai: "And they said, all that the Lord has spoken we shall do and we shall hear" (Exod. 24:7)."
G. R. Yannai said, "My twin, for I am not greater than they, nor they than I."
H. R. Joshua of Sikhnin said in the name of R. Levi, "Just as in the case of twins, if one of them gets a headache, the other one feels it, so said the Holy One, blessed be he, 'I am with him in trouble' (Ps. 91:15)."

I. "... for my head is drenched with dew." "The heavens dropped dew" (Judg. 5:4).

J. "... my locks with the moisture of the night:" "Yes, the clouds dropped water" (Judg. 5:4).

K. When is this the case? In this month: "This month is for you the first of the months" (Exod. 12:2).

The notion of God and Israel as twins, the one formed as the counterpart of the other, involves the hypostatization of both parties to the transaction.

Accordingly, the final focus of correspondence between God and humanity concerns Israel, unique among nations and holy to God. How do God and, within humanity, Israel correspond? It is, first, that Israel forms on earth a society that corresponds to the retinue and court of God in heaven. No surprise, then, that, just as Israel glorifies God, so God responds and celebrates Israel. Here correspondence of people and God, now Israel and God, in physical, emotional, and social traits, comes to expression. God wears phylacteries, as does Israel, but while Israel's phylacteries contain verses of Scripture in praise of God, God's choice of Scripture praises Israel. God further forms the correct attitude toward Israel, which is one of love, an indication of an attitude on the part of divinity corresponding to right attitudes on the part of human beings. Finally, to close the circle, just as there is a "you" to whom humanity prays, so God too says prayers—to himself, to God, and the point of these prayers is that God should elicit from himself forgiveness for Israel. If there is sublimity in the Oral Torah, this is where it is (B. Ber. 6a-b, XXXIX):

A. Said R. Nahman bar Isaac to R. Hiyya bar Abin, "As to the phylacteries of the Lord of the world, what is written in them?"

B. He said to him, "'And who is like your people Israel, a singular nation on earth' (1 Chr. 17:21)."

C. "And does the Holy One, blessed be he, sing praises for Israel?"

D. "Yes, for it is written, 'You have avouched the Lord this day ... and the Lord has avouched you this day' (Deut. 26:17, 18).

E. "Said the Holy One, blessed be he, to Israel, 'You have made me a singular entity in the world, and I shall make you a singular entity in the world.

F. "'You have made me a singular entity in the world,' as it is said, 'Hear O Israel, the Lord, our God, the Lord is one' (Deut. 6:4).

G. "'And I shall make you a singular entity in the world,' as it is said, 'And who is like your people, Israel, a singular nation in the earth' (1 Chr. 17:21)."

H. Said R. Aha, son of Raba to R. Ashi, "That takes care of one of the four subdivisions of the phylactery. What is written in the others?"

I. He said to him, "'For what great nation is there. ... And what great nation is there . . .' (Deut. 4:7, 8); 'Happy are you, O Israel . . .' (Deut. 33:29); 'Or has God tried . . .,' (Deut. 4:34). And 'To make you high above all nations' (Deut. 26:19)."

J. "If so, there are too many boxes!

K. "But the verses, 'For what great nation is there' and 'And what great nation is there,' which are equivalent, are in one box, and 'Happy are you, O Israel' and 'Who is like your people Israel' are in one box, and 'Or has God tried . . .,' in one box, and 'To make you high' in one box.

L. "And all of them are written in the phylactery that is on the arm."

We proceed to God's saying prayers, as do people, and the contents of those prayers (B. Ber. 7A, XLIX):

A. Said R. Yohanan in the name of R. Yose, "How do we know that the Holy One, blessed be he, says prayers?

B. "Since it is said, 'Even them will I bring to my holy mountain and make them joyful in my house of prayer' (Is. 56:7).

C. "'Their house of prayer' is not stated, but, rather, 'my house of prayer.'

D. "On the basis of that usage we see that the Holy One, blessed be he, says prayers."

E. What prayers does he say?

F. Said R. Zutra bar Tobiah said Rab, "'May it be my will that my mercy overcome my anger, and that my mercy prevail over my attributes, so that I may treat my children in accord with the trait of mercy and in their regard go beyond the strict measure of the law.'"

God seeks the blessing of the sage as well (B. Ber. 7a, L):

A. It has been taught on Tannaite authority:

B. Said R. Ishmael b. Elisha, "One time I

went in to offer up incense on the inner-most altar, and I saw the crown of the Lord, enthroned on the highest throne, and he said to me, 'Ishmael, my son, bless me.'

C. "I said to him, 'May it be your will that your mercy overcome your anger, and that your mercy prevail over your attributes, so that you treat your children in accord with the trait of mercy and in their regard go beyond the strict measure of the law.'

D. "And he nodded his head to me."

E. And from that story we learn that the blessing of a common person should not be negligible in your view.

God's wearing phylacteries treats him as physically comparable to man; but the consubstantial traits of attitude and feeling—just as humanity feels joy, so does God, just as humanity celebrates God, so does God celebrate Israel—are the more urgent. Just as Israel declares God to be unique, so God declares Israel to be unique. And just as Israel prays to God, so God says prayers. What God asks of himself is that he transcend himself—which is what, in prayer, humanity asks for as well. It would be difficult to find more ample evidence of a theological system that deems God and humanity to share a great many traits.

Among these traits, however, in the Written Torah, the point of greatest correspondence concerns attitudes, feelings, and emotions. Tractate Abot presents the single most comprehensive account of religious affections. These turn out to pertain to God's as much as to humankind's feelings. The reason is that, in that document above all, how we feel defines a critical aspect of virtue. A simple catalogue of permissible feelings comprises humility, generosity, self-abnegation, love, a spirit of conciliation of the other, and eagerness to please. A list of impermissible emotions is made up of envy, ambition, jealousy, arrogance, sticking to one's opinion, self-centeredness, a grudging spirit, vengefulness, and the like. People should aim at eliciting from others acceptance and good will and should avoid confrontation, rejection, and humiliation of the other. This they do through conciliation and giving up their own claims and rights. So both catalogues

form a harmonious and uniform whole, aiming at the cultivation of the humble and malleable person, one who accepts everything and resents nothing. And, time and again, the compilation underscores, one who conciliates others is favored by God, who respects and honors those who give up what no one can demand (M. Ab. 2:4):

A. [Rabban Gamaliel, son of R. Judah the Patriarch] would say, "Make his wishes into your own wishes, so that he will make your wishes into his wishes.

B. "Put aside your wishes on account of his wishes, so that he will put aside the wishes of other people in favor of your wishes."

God protects from the ill-will of others those who do that which God wishes. God further favors those who seek to please others (M. Ab. 3:10):

A. [Haninah b. Dosa] would say, "Anyone from whom people take pleasure—the Omnipresent takes pleasure.

B. "And anyone from whom people do not take pleasure, the Omnipresent does not take pleasure."

Aqiba at T. Ber. 3:3 goes over the same ground: "One in whom mankind delights, God delights. One in whom mankind does not delight, God does not delight. One who is content with his own portion, it is a good sign for him. One who is not content with his own portion, it is a bad sign for him."

A sequence of paradoxes—strength is marked by weakness, wisdom by the capacity to learn, wealth by making do, honor by the power to honor others—yields the picture of traits that humans should cultivate, to which God will respond (M. Ab. 4:17-19):

A. Ben Zoma says, "Who is a sage? He who learns from everybody,

B. "as it is said, 'From all my teachers I have gotten understanding' (Ps. 119:99).

C. "Who is strong? He who overcomes his desire,

D. "as it is said, 'He who is slow to anger is better than the mighty, and he who rules his spirit than he who takes a city' (Prov. 16:32).

E. "Who is rich? He who is happy in what he has,

F. "as it is said, 'When you eat the labor of your hands, happy will you be, and it will go well with you' (Ps. 128:2).

G. ("Happy will you be in this world, and it will go well with you in the world to come.")

H. "Who is honored? He who honors everybody,

I. "as it is said, 'For those who honor me I shall honor, and they who despise me will be treated as of no account' (I Sam. 2:30)."

A. R. Simeon b. Eleazar says, "Do not try to make amends with your fellow when he is angry,

B. "or comfort him when the corpse of his beloved is lying before him,

C. "or seek to find absolution for him at the moment at which he takes a vow,

D. "or attempt to see him when he is humiliated."

A. Samuel the Small says, "Rejoice not when your enemy falls, and let not your heart be glad when he is overthrown, lest the Lord see it and it displease him, and he turn away his wrath from him (Prov. 24:17)."

These virtues derive from knowledge of what really counts, which is what God wants. God favors those who—like God—aspire to please others. The point of correspondence then is clear: virtues appreciated by human beings prove identical to the ones to which God responds as well. And what single virtue of the heart encompasses the rest? Restraint, the source of self-abnegation, humility, serves as the antidote for ambition, vengefulness, and, above all, for arrogance. It is restraint of our own interest that enables us to deal generously with others, humility about ourselves that generates a liberal spirit towards others.

So the emotions prescribed in Abot turn out to provide variations of a single feeling, which is the sentiment of the disciplined heart, whatever affective form it may take. And where does the heart learn its lessons, if not in relationship to God? So, as we saw, "Make his wishes yours, so that he will make your wishes his" (M. Ab. 2:4). Applied to the relationships between human beings, this inner discipline of the emotional life will yield exactly those virtues that the framers of Abot spell out in one example after another. Imputing to heaven exactly those responses felt on earth—"Anyone from whom people take pleasure, God takes pleasure"

(M. Ab. 3:10)—makes the point at the most general level.

Do sages really mean that people and God correspond, or do we deal with some sort of figurative or poetic metaphor representing relationships of a less tangible character? I should claim that the entire system of theology, with its account of world order based on God's pervasive justice and rationality, means to portray exactly how things actually are—or can be made to be, with humankind's correct engagement. For sages deal with the true reality that this world's corruption obscures. We see an application of a large-scale, encompassing exercise in analogical thinking—something is like something else, stands for, evokes, or symbolizes that which is quite outside itself. It may be the opposite of something else, in which case it conforms to the exact opposite of the rules that govern that something else. The reasoning is analogical or it is contrastive, and the fundamental logic is taxonomic. The taxonomy rests on those comparisons and contrasts we should call parabolic. In that case what lies on the surface misleads, just as we saw how sages deem superficial the challenges to God's justice that private lives set forth. Conceding the depth of human suffering, sages also pointed out that sometimes, suffering conveys its own blessing. And so throughout, what lies beneath or beyond the surface—there is the true reality. People who see things this way constitute the opposite of ones who call a thing as it is. Self-evidently, they have become accustomed to perceiving more—or less—than is at hand.

God and humankind corresponded in the call to each for forbearance, patience, humiliation, self-abnegation. God, disappointed with creation, challenged by the gentiles with their idolatry, corresponded with Israel, defeated and subjugated, challenged by the worldly dominance of those who rejected the Torah. Both, sages maintained, dealt with failure, and both had to survive the condition of defeat. To turn survival into endurance, pariah-status, for Israel, into an exercise in Godly living, the glory lavished on idols into an occasion for forbearance and restraint on God's part, the sages' affective program served full well. Israel would see power in submission, wealth in the gift to be grateful, wisdom in the confession of ignorance. For God as for Israel, ultimate degradation was made to stand for ultimate power. Israel in exile served God through suffering.

True, the condition of Israel then would represent a scandal to the nations and foolishness too. That is why people and God corresponded at just that present failure that, for the here and now so concretely understood by sages, both parties to the cosmos shared. That is why from both God and Israel was demanded humility as a mark of strength, feelings of conciliation, restraint, and conformity as a mark of ultimate dignity. God and the Israelite person corresponded at heart. The heart would serve as the best defense, inner affections as the police who are always there when needed, the tamed attitude as the ultimate arbiter of what would come about in the future.

JACOB NEUSNER

**THEOLOGY OF JUDAISM—HALAKHAH AND AGGADAH:** The normative law, or *Halakhah*, of the Oral Torah defines the principal medium by which the Rabbinic sages of antiquity founded set forth their message. Norms of conduct, more than norms of conviction, served to convey the sages' statement. But the exposition of matters of religious belief, or Aggadah, undertakes a critical task as well, so that the Halakhah and the Aggadah together set forth the whole theology of Judaism. One without the other leaves the work incomplete.

The theology of the Written and Oral Torah—that is, Judaism—conveys the picture of world order based on God's justice and equity. The categorical structure of the Oral Torah encompasses the components, in sequential order: God and humanity; the Torah; Israel and the nations. The working-system of the Oral Torah's Aggadah finds its dynamic in the struggle between God's plan for creation—to create a perfect world of justice—and humanity's will. That dialectics embodies in a single paradigm the events contained in the sequences: rebellion, sin, punishment, repentance, and atonement;

exile and return; or the disruption of world order and the restoration of world order. The Halakhah manifestly means to form Israel in particular into the embodiment of God's plan for a perfect world of justice and so corresponds in its principal divisions to the three categories of the Aggadic theology.

**The Aggadah's Theology:** Now, as a matter of fact, none of these categories and propositions God, Torah, Israel, a struggle between God's word and human will, Israel and the Torah and the gentiles and their idolatry, for instance, is new. Anyone familiar with the principal components of the faith and piety of Judaism, the Written Torah, the Oral Torah, and the liturgy of home and synagogue, will find them paramount. In this context theology concerns not only proposition but principle, its task takes up not identifying normative beliefs alone but forming them into a logos—a sustained, rigorous, coherent theory, embodied in actualities (facts of Scripture, just as natural history appeals to facts of nature) joined to a compelling argument that can be set forth in narrative-sequential form.

Four principles of the theology of the Oral Torah emerge in the documents of mainly Aggadic character. These principles are not only necessary but sufficient to encompass the entirety of the theology set forth in the Aggadic writings, overspreading some of the Halakhic ones, and, not only so, but, the order in which they are given is absolutely required; any other order would violate the simplest rules of logic and yield complete chaos, which is to say, polytheism, not monotheism:

[1] God formed creation in accord with a plan, which the Torah reveals. World order can be shown by the facts of nature and society set forth in that plan to conform to a pattern of reason based upon justice. Those who possess the Torah—Israel—know God and those who do not—the gentiles—reject him in favor of idols. What happens to each of the two sectors of humanity, respectively, responds to their relationship with God. Israel in the present age is subordinate to the nations, because God has designated the gentiles as the medium for penalizing Israel's rebellion, meaning through Israel's subordi-

nation and exile to provoke Israel to repent. Private life as much as the public order conforms to the principle that God rules justly in a creation of perfection and stasis.

[2] The perfection of creation, realized in the rule of exact justice, is signified by the timelessness of the world of human affairs, their conformity to a few enduring paradigms that transcend change (theology of history). No present, past, or future marks time, but only the recapitulation of those patterns. Perfection is further embodied in the unchanging relationships of the social commonwealth (theology of political economy), which assure that scarce resources, once allocated, remain in stasis. A further indication of perfection lies in the complementarity of the components of creation, on the one side, and, finally, the correspondence between God and humanity, in God's image (theological anthropology), on the other.

[3] Israel's condition, public and personal, marks flaws in creation. What disrupts perfection is the sole power capable of standing on its own against God's power, and that is human will. What humans control and God cannot coerce is the human capacity to form intention and therefore choose either arrogantly to defy, or humbly to love, God. Because humans defy God, the sin that results from this rebellion flaws creation and disrupts world order (theological theodicy). The paradigm of the rebellion of Adam in Eden governs, the act of arrogant rebellion leading to exile from Eden thus accounting for the condition of humanity. But, as in the original transaction of alienation and consequent exile, God retains the power to encourage repentance through punishing human arrogance. In mercy, moreover, God exercises the power to respond to repentance with forgiveness, that is, a change of attitude evoking a counterpart change. Since, commanding their own will, humans also have the power to initiate the process of reconciliation with God, through repentance, an act of humility, they may restore the perfection of that order that through arrogance they have marred.

[4] God ultimately will restore that perfection that embodied his plan for creation. In the work of restoration death that comes about by reason of sin will die, the dead will be raised and judged for their deeds in this life, and most of them, having been justified, will go on to eternal life in the world to come. In the paradigm of humankind restored to Eden is realized in Israel's return to the land of Israel. In that world or age to come, however, that sector of humanity that through the Torah knows God will encompass all of humanity. Idolaters will perish, and humanity that comprises Israel at the end will know the one, true God and spend eternity in his light.

Now, recorded in this way, the story told by the Oral Torah proves remarkably familiar, with its stress on God's justice (to which his mercy is integral), humanity's correspondence with God in its possession of the power of will, human's sin of rebellion against God and God's response. If we translate into the narrative of Israel, from the beginning to the calamity of the destruction of the (first) Temple, the picture of matters that is set forth in both abstract and concrete ways in the Oral Torah, we turn out to state the human condition in terms of Israel. Then we find a reprise of the Authorized History laid out in Genesis through Kings and amplified by the principal prophets. Humanity set its will against God's word, sinned, and was exiled from Eden. The human's counterpart, Israel formed by the Torah, entered the Land, sinned, and was exiled from the Land.

Not only is the story familiar—Eden, fall, restoration, first Adam, then Israel, working through the same pattern—but the category-formation, creation, revelation, and redemption, imparting the dynamic ("the system") through which the story unfolds, is equally familiar. That is because the liturgy of synagogue and home recapitulates characteristic modes of thought of the Oral Torah and reworks its distinctive constructions of exemplary figures, events, and conceptions. The governing liturgical-creedal category-formation, creation, revelation, redemption, set forth in the proclamation of the Shema and its accompanying blessings, fore and aft, matches in structure and in system. That is how sages defined the Torah, which we call "Judaism," when they maintained from the very beginning that they possessed the

Torah revealed by God to Moses at Mt. Sinai ("Moses received Torah at Sinai and handed it on to Joshua, Joshua to elders, and elders to prophets, and prophets handed it on to the men of the great assembly"). So, in contemporary language, the theology of the Oral Torah recapitulates the theology of Scripture, when Scripture is read forward toward the Oral Torah, and adumbrates the theology of the liturgy, thus Judaism pure and simple.

So here, beginning with the integrating basics, encompassing the entire expanse of creation and humanity, from first to last things, are the ideas that impart structure and order to, and sustain, the whole. Starting with the doctrine of world order that is just and concluding with eternal life, here is the simple logic that animates all the parts and makes them cohere. The generative categories defined just now prove not only imperative and irreducible but, in the context of the narrative, also logically sequential. Each of the four parts of the theology of the Oral Torah—[1] the perfectly just character of world order, [2] indications of its perfection, [3] sources of its imperfection, [4] means for the restoration of world order and the result of the restoration—belongs in its place and set in any other sequence the four units become incomprehensible. Not only so but each component of the whole in order, drawing upon its predecessor, pointing toward its successor, forms part of an unfolding story that can be told in only one direction and in the dictated order and in no other way. Shift the position of a generative component and place it before or after some other, and the entire flow of thought is disrupted. That is the mark of a well-crafted theology, a coherent structure, a compelling system.

So much for the religious system, culminating in a systematic theology, that is set forth by a thorough reading of the mainly-Aggadic documents and the Aggadic passages of the Halakhic documents that all together comprise the entire corpus of the Oral Torah of the formative age. Sages themselves declare that truly to know the One-Who-by-Speaking-Brought-the-World-into-Being, we should turn to the Aggadah. But with prophets and Psalmists the sages also insisted that we see God's face in justice, and justice concerns not only abstractions concerning creation and world order but equity in everyday transactions. So we turn to the distinct, and complementary, perspectives of the Aggadah and the Halakhah as these focus upon the condition of holy Israel in relationship to God, community, and self.

**The Theology of the Halakhah:** The Aggadic statement addresses exteriorities, the Halakhic one, interiorities, of Israel's life with God. When we consider the program of the Halakhah, the topics that define its native categories, we find a quite distinct and autonomous construction, one that hardly intersects, *categorically*, with the Aggadah. How so? If the native categories of the Aggadah find definition in the story of mankind, derive their dynamism and energy in the conflict of God's word and human will, compose their system in the working of repentance and (ultimate) restoration of humanity to Eden, none of these categories is matched by a counterpart in the Halakhah's category-formation—not repentance, not redemption, not Eden and the fall and the restoration. If the Aggadah organizes large components of its entire system within such categories as Eden/land of Israel or Adam/Israel or fall/exile, the Halakhah responds with large categories that deal with Kilayim, mixed seeds, Shebiit, the Sabbatical year, and Orlah, produce of a tree in the first three years after its planting. What can one thing have to do with the other? Indeed only a few principal native-categories in the Aggadic theology intersect with principal native-categories of the Halakhah. Since the native- or organizing categories of the Halakhah are defined by the Mishnah and confirmed by the consequent exegetical documents, the Tosefta, the Yerushalmi, and the Bavli, we turn out to deal with two quite separate constructions.

The Aggadah's structure and system and those of the Halakhah address a single topic, but from different angles of vision of Israel's existence, one, outward-looking and the other, inner-facing, both engaged by relationships, the one transitive and the other intransitive. It is the Aggadah, fully set forth, that affords perspective on the Halakhah—and vice versa. The Halakhah in its way makes exactly the same statement about the same matters that the Aggadah does in its categories and terms. But the Aggadah speaks in large and general terms to the world at large, while the Halakhah uses small and particular rules to speak to the everyday concerns of ordinary Israelites. The Aggadah addresses exteriorities, the Halakhah, interiorities, of Israel in relationship with God.

Look again at the focus of the Aggadic theology summarized just now in the four principal units spelled out above. Categorically, the Aggadah faces outward, toward humanity in general and correlates, shows the relationship of, humanity in general and Israel in particular. The theological system of a just world order answerable to one God that animates the Aggadah, specifically, sets forth the parallel stories of humanity and Israel, each beginning with Eden (Israel: the land of Israel), marked by sin and punishment (Adam's, Israel's respective acts of rebellion against God, the one through disobedience, the other through violating the Torah), and exile for the purpose of bringing about repentance and atonement (Adam from Eden, Israel from the Land). The system therefore takes as its critical problem the comparison of Israel with the Torah and the nations with idolatry.

It comes to a climax in showing how the comparable stories intersect and diverge at the grave. For from there Israel is destined to the resurrection, judgment, and eternity (the world to come), the nations (that is, the idolaters to the end) to death. When we examine the category-formation of the Halakhah, by contrast, what we see is an account of Israel not in its external relationship to the nations but viewed wholly on its own. The lines of structure impart order from within. The Halakhah portrays intransitive Israel, focusing upon its inner life. That fact further explains why the category-formation of the Aggadah does not correspond with that of the Halakhah. Each formation is responds to the rules of construction of the same social order—God's justice—but the Aggadic one concerns Israel's social order in the context of God's transaction with humanity, the other, Israel's social order articulated within its own interior architectonics, thus, the one, transitive, the other, intransitive.

**Halakhic interiority and Aggadic exteriority:** The theology of the Oral Torah that the Aggadic documents and Aggadic segments of Halakhic ones portray focuses our attention upon one perspective and neglects the other. The outward-facing theology that coheres in the Aggadic documents investigates the logic of creation, the fall, the regeneration made possible by the Torah, the separation of Israel and the Torah from the nations and idolatry, the one for life through repentance and resurrection, the other for death, and the ultimate restoration of creation's perfection attempted with Adam at Eden, but now through Israel in the Land of Israel. Encompassing the whole of humanity that knows God in the Torah and rejects idolatry, Israel encompasses nearly the whole of mankind, along with nearly the whole of the Israel of the epoch of the Torah and of the Messiah that has preceded.

The Aggadah tells about Israel in the context of humanity, and hence speaks of exteriorities. Its perspectives are taken up at the border between outside and inside, the position of standing at the border inside and looking outward—hence [1] God and the world, [2] the Torah, and [3] Israel and the nations. That other perspective, the one gained by standing at the border, inside and turning, looking still deeper within, responds to the same logic, seeking the coherence and rationality of all things. That perspective focuses upon relationships too. But now they are not those between God and humankind or Israel and the nations, but the ones involving [1] God and Israel, [2] Israel in its own terms, and [3] the Israelite in his own situation, that is, within the household in particular—terms to be amply defined in the Halakhic context.

Israel relates to God in the encounter of enlandisement, where Israel takes its place in the land of Israel and confronts its relationship with God in the very terms of the creation, when Adam take his place in Eden, with catastrophic results. But now, Israel, entering the Land, shows how, regenerate, the

Israelite realizes repentance, confronting the occasion of the original sin but responding in obedience, rather than rebellion as at the outset. Israel in the Land moreover reconstructs Eden by recapitulating creation and its requirements. All of this takes on detail and forms a cogent, and compelling, statement through the Halakhah.

Thus the Aggadah describes exteriority, the Halakhah, interiority. The Aggadah answers the questions posed to justice by Israel's relationships with the world beyond. To complete the theological account, Aggadah having accomplished its task, the logic of a coherent whole requires that the Halakhah describe interior Israel. That logic must answer the questions posed to justice by Israel's relationships within itself. Specifically, the Halakhah must respond to issues posed by the monotheism of justice to

> [1] Israel's relationships with God when these relationships do not take place in the intersection of God, Israel, and the nations, but within Israel's own frame of reference; and
> [2] to Israelites' relationships with one another; and
> [3] to the interior life of the individual Israelite household on its own, with God.

Neither the Aggadah nor the Halakhah makes articulate categorical provision for the radically isolated individual, that is, the Israelite not within the household or not as part of "all Israel." That accounts for the reference to "the Israelite household," where the Hebrew counterpart would prefer to speak of "*ben adam le'asmo*," that is, "between a man and himself," or relationships within the heart and conscious of the individual. One cannot identify a tractate of the Mishnah that could yield a theory of the life of the private person, in abstraction from the household, hence the resort to "household" rather than "individual Israelite."

When the Aggadah's account of the exteriority of matters and the Halakhah's of the interiority ultimately join, then we may indeed see the coherence of that one whole Torah of Moses, our rabbi, oral and written, Aggadic and Halakhic, the unity of which defines as unique the hermeneutics of the sages.

So this account of the theology that imposes upon monotheism the logical requirements of justice in the formation of world order by nature deals with the public issues: God and humanity, the Torah to remedy the flaw of creation in humanity, Israel and the nations.

But what about Israel within? The Halakhah embodies the extension of God's design for world order into the inner-facing relationships of [1] God and Israel, [2] Israel's inner order in its own terms, and [3] the Israelite's household viewed on its own in time and space and social circumstance. If we wish to explore the interiority of Israel in relationship with God, as a shared order, and of Israel's autonomous building block, the household, we are required to take up the norms of everyday conduct that define Israel and signify its sanctification. One can discern in the theoretical structure of the Halakhah no smaller unit of social construction than the household. Households relate to comprise, all together, the house of Israel; Israel relates to God. Through the house of Israel, households interact with one another—that is the relationship that imposes obligations and restraints, for example. Through God, Israel relates to the gentiles-idolaters (apart from some marginal exceptions and figures, there is no other category in the Halakhah for the outsider than the idolater, though the Aggadah differentiates among gentiles, identifying the ones that matter to Israel: Babylonia, Media, Greece, Rome, in particular).

**Where does the Halakhah take up issues of the interior life of Israel?** If the Aggadah takes up exteriorities, then what are the counterparts within the interior structure constructed by the Halakhah? A consideration of the divisions and most, though not all, tractates thereof shows the simple correlation.

[1] BETWEEN GOD AND ISRAEL: the interior dimensions of Israel's relationships with God—the division of Agriculture, the division of Holy Things. The division of Agriculture defines what Israel in the land of Israel owes as God's share of the produce of the Holy Land, encompassing also Israel's conformity to God's regulation on how that produce is to be garnered; the anomalous tractate, Berakhot, concerns exactly the same set of

relationships. The division of Holy Things corresponds by specifying the way in which the gifts of the Land—meat, grain, oil, wine—are to be offered to Heaven, inclusive of the priesthood, as well as the manner in which the Temple and its staff are supported and the offerings paid for. Two tractates, moreover, describe the Temple and its rite, and one of them sets forth special problems in connection with the same. The sole anomalous tractate, Hullin, which takes up the correct slaughter of animals for secular purposes, belongs, because its rules pertain, also, to the conduct of the cult.

[2] WITHIN ISRAEL'S SOCIAL ORDER: the social order that is realized by Israelites' relationships with one another—the division of Damages: That division spells out the civil law that maintains justice and equity in the social order, the institutions of government and the sanctions they legitimately impose.

[3] INSIDE THE ISRAELITE HOUSEHOLD: INTERIOR TIME AND SPACE AND CIRCUMSTANCE; SUSTAINING LIFE: The inner life of the household, encompassing the individual Israelite, with God—the division of Women, the division of Appointed Times, and the division of Purities, as well as some singleton-tractates such as Hullin. The division of Women deals with the way in which relationships of man and woman are governed by the rules of sanctification enforced by Heaven, which takes an interest in how family relationships are formed, maintained, and dissolved, and the affects, upon the family, of invoking Heaven's name in vows. The division of Appointed Times addresses the affect upon the conduct of ordinary life of the advent of holy time, with special reference to the Sabbath and the pilgrim festivals (Passover, Tabernacles), the pilgrimage, and the intermediate days of festivals, the New Year and Day of Atonement, Fast Days, and Purim. While parts of some of these tractates, and nearly the whole of a few of them, concern conduct in the Temple, the main point of the tractates is to explore the impact upon the household and village of the Appointed times. The same interstitial position—between household and village, on the one side, and Temple and cult, on the other—serves

the division of Purity. The laws of the tractates concern mainly the household, since the cleanness-rules spelled out in those tractates concern purity at home. But, it goes without saying, the same uncleanness that prevents eating at home food that is to be preserved in conditions of cultic cleanness also prevents the Israelite from entering the restricted space of the Temple. But in the balance, the division concerns cleanness in that private domain that is occupied by the Israelite household.

The native-categories of the Halakhah as spelled out by the Mishnah and affirmed in the Tosefta, beginning to end, in the Yerushalmi, and in the Bavli (for those tractates of the Mishnah treated in the two Talmuds, respectively), on the whole fall quite naturally within the category-formation that is yielded by the Halakhah viewed in the context of the Aggadah. The Aggadah took shape within a tripartite category-formation involving [1] God and the world, [2] the Torah, and [3] Israel and the nations. Here we see the contrast between exteriorities and interiorities. Among the native categories of the Halakhah. One cannot point to a single systematic exposition of relationships between God *and the world*, though we find ample exposition, within the proposed category-formation, of relationships between God *and Israel*, specifically, what Israel owes God. Nor do we find any sustained halakhic exposition that is pertinent to the Torah, the turning point in God's relationship with man. Part of one tractate alone concerns itself with Israel's relationships with the gentiles, and that is the opening unit of tractate Abodah Zarah.

While an account of the theology of the Oral Torah formed within the logical category-formation of the Aggadah appeals to Halakhic passages and even to entire tractates, the fact is that the Halakhah takes shape around another set of perspectives than the ones that guide the Aggadah's category-formation. And the governing categories—God and Israel, Israel on its own, the Israelite household seen from within—naturally and with little strain accommodate the native-categories of the Halakhah.

[1] BETWEEN ISRAEL AND GOD: Israel engages with God in the possession of the land of Israel in particular. That is where God's presence locates itself, in the Temple. It is the gift of the Land to holy Israel that sets the conditions of Israel's relationship with God. Israel in the Land is a sharecropper, for example. In connection with tractate Maaserot and the general rules of tithing, for one example, we shall want to know how God and the Israelite farmer relate, when they intersect and what precipitates their encounter in partnership—the general theory embodied by the details of the law. Israel returns to God, through the altar, the principal gifts in which the Land glories, wine, oil, grain, meat. The principal tractates of the two divisions that work out the details of how Israel relates to God, the First, on Agriculture, and the Fifth, on Holy Things, embody in the details of the law a variety of religious principles. Here we learn about how God and man correspond, just as much as, within the theological anthropology set forth by the Aggadah, dimensions of that correspondence are set forth.

[2] WITHIN ISRAEL'S SOCIAL ORDER: In connection with the Babas (Baba Qamma, Baba Mesia, Baba Batra), which deal with the regulation of the social order, we shall want to identify those governing principles of equity that dictate the character of the details, both laws that deal with the imperfections of the social order, conflict for instance, and the ones that regulate the social order in all its balance and perfection, properly-conducted transactions, for example.

[3] INSIDE THE ISRAELITE HOUSEHOLD: And when we examine tractates Shabbat and Erubin, out of the specific rules we shall ask for a general theory of the interplay of space and time in the grid defined by the advent of sanctified time with the coming of the Sabbath for example: where am I now, where am I then, and what dictates my condition? How, in holy time, do I continue the life-sustaining activities of nourishment? The sources of the rules at hand, not in a literary but in a metaphysical sense, will have to be located, the modes of thought that govern to be identified. Such a theory will form a component of an account of the situation, in world order, of the Israelite household, a focus of holiness comparable in its way to the locus of sanctification in the Temple.

In more general terms, Rabbinic Judaism in the formative age through the Halakhah offered a restorationist program, not a messianic one. The Halakhah as set forth in its formative age aims to describe how in concrete terms holy Israel is to construct a social order in the land of Israel to realize that just and perfect world order that God had in mind in creating the world. The Halakhah is so framed, its category-formation so constituted, as to yield an account of how man in paradise, Adam in Eden, ought to have lived. Speaking in monumental dimensions, the Halakhah makes a teleological, but not a messianic, statement. And the promise of the Halakhah speaks to not Israel's messianic so much as to its restorationist aspiration: to form Eden not in time past nor in time future but in the here and now of everyday Israel, but this time we shall do it right. And here is how—in concrete detail.

**The messiah, the halakhah, and the Aggadah:** In this context we take up the allegation that Judaism is a messianic religion. In fact, the Messiah-theme to begin with plays itself out in the Aggadah, not in the Halakhah. But Israel's salvation depends upon Israel's sanctification, in concrete terms, the coming of the messiah is contingent on Israel's keeping the law of the Torah (e.g., the messiah will come when all Israel keeps a single Sabbath). In the generative writing of the Halakhah, the messiah-theme plays no formidable role. When constructing a systematic account of Judaism—that is, the world-view and way of life for Israel presented in the Halakhah—the philosophers of the Halakhah did not make use of the messiah-myth in the construction of the teleology for their system. Themes and doctrines, myths and rites, important in the continuator-documents of Mishnah- and Scripture-exegesis that reached closure from 400 onward do not register. The Mishnah's framers, for example, found it possible to present a statement of goals for their "Israel of hierarchical classification, from the many to the one, from the one to the many," that was entirely separate from appeals to history and eschatology. Time and change took a subordinated role to enduring paradigms, built upon the sanctification of Israel.

The Halakhah presented a system in which history did not define the main framework by which the issue of teleology took a form other than the familiar eschatological one, and in which historical events were absorbed, through their trivialization in taxonomic structures, into an ahistorical system. In the Halakhah, messiahs played a part. But these "anointed men" had no historical role. They undertook a task quite different from that assigned to Jesus by the framers of the Gospels. They were merely a species of priest, falling into one classification rather than another. The Halakhic documents, beginning with the Mishnah, find little of consequence to say about *the* messiah as savior of Israel, one particular person at onetime. On the contrary the Halakhah manages to set forth its system's teleology without appeal to eschatology in any form. For the Halakhah, "messiah" stands for a category of priest or general. The messiah-theme proved marginal to the Halakhic program.

Answering questions of purpose and history out of the resources of the Halakhah is not possible. The Halakhah presents no large view of history. It contains no abstract reflection whatever on the nature and meaning of the destruction of the Temple in 70 C.E., an event that surfaces only in connection with some changes in the law explained as resulting from the end of the cult. The Halakhah pays no attention to the matter of the end time. The word "salvation" is rare, "sanctification" commonplace. More strikingly, the framers of the Halakhah are virtually silent on the teleology of the system; they never tell us why we should do what the Halakhah tells us, let alone explain what will happen if we do. Incidents in the Halakhah are preserved either as narrative settings for the statement of the law, or, occasionally, as precedents. Historical events are classified and turned into entries on lists. But incidents in any case come few and far between. True, events do make an impact. But it always is for the

Halakhah's own purpose and within its own taxonomic system and rule-seeking mode of thought. To be sure, the framers of the Halakhah may also have had a theory of the messiah and of the meaning of Israel's history and destiny. But they kept it hidden, and their document manages to provide an immense account of Israel's life without explicitly telling us about such matters. All of these issues are addressed by the Aggadah, particularly the compositions and documents of an Aggadic character set forth in documents from the fifth century C.E. and later.

The messiah in the Halakhah does not stand at the forefront of the framers' consciousness. The issues encapsulated in the myth and person of the messiah are scarcely addressed. The framers of the Halakhah do not resort to speculation about the messiah as a historical-supernatural figure. So far as that kind of speculation provides the vehicle for reflection on salvific issues, or in mythic terms, narratives on the meaning of history and the destiny of Israel, we cannot say that the Halakhah's philosophers take up those encompassing categories of being: Where are we heading? What can we do about it? That does not mean questions found urgent in the aftermath of the destruction of the Temple and the disaster of Bar Kokhba failed to attract the attention of the Halakhah's sages. But they treated history in a different way, offering their own answers to its questions. To these we now turn.

When it comes to history and the end of time, the Halakhah absorbs into its encompassing system all events, small and large. With them the sages accomplish what they accomplish in everything else: a vast labor of taxonomy, an immense construction of the order and rules governing the classification of everything on earth and in heaven. The disruptive character of history—onetime events of ineluctable significance—scarcely impresses the philosophers. They find no difficulty in showing that what appears unique and beyond classification has in fact happened before and so falls within the range of trustworthy rules and known procedures. Once history's components, onetime events, lose their distinctiveness, then history as a didactic intellectual construct, as a source of lessons and rules, also loses all pertinence.

So lessons and rules come from sorting things out and classifying them from the procedures and modes of thought of the philosopher seeking regularity. To this labor of taxonomy, the historian's way of selecting data and arranging them into patterns of meaning to teach lessons proves inconsequential. Onetime events are not important. The world is composed of nature and supernature. The laws that count are those to be discovered in heaven and, in heaven's creation and counterpart, on earth. Keep those laws and things will work out. Break them, and the result is predictable: calamity of whatever sort will supervene in accordance with the rules. But just because it is predictable, a catastrophic happening testifies to what has always been and must always be, in accordance with reliable rules and within categories already discovered and well explained. That is why the lawyer-philosophers of the mid-second century produced the Halakhah—to explain how things are. Within the framework of well-classified rules, there could be messiahs, but no single messiah.

JACOB NEUSNER

**THEOLOGY, BIBLICAL—THE RELIGIOUS SYSTEM OF THE ANCIENT ISRAELITE SCRIPTURES:** The word "theology," consisting of the Greek roots *theós*, "God," and *lógos*, "word," "knowledge," or "doctrine," means "knowledge of God." Since the Hebrew Scriptures repeatedly speak about *daat elohim*—"knowledge of God" (Hos. 4:1; 6:6; cf., Num. 24:16; Is. 53:11; Jer. 22:16), God's will, and God's ways—there can be no question that Scripture presents theological statements. The issue, rather, is whether Scripture can be said actually to formulate this "knowledge" in the manner of theological doctrines, allowing us rightly to speak of "biblical theology." Many Biblical scholars answer this question negatively, pointing out that, while Scripture consists of a rich variety of literary forms—stories, legal statutes, prophetic oracles, poetry, proverbs— one looks in vain for theological doctrines about God and God's activity similar to those

of medieval theologians such as Maimonides and Aquinas.

And yet, even if there is not in the Hebrew Scriptures a complete system of theological doctrines, clearly there are elements that can be described as *theological notions*—ideas and themes that later on were developed into full-fledged doctrines. Thus, under the rubric of biblical theology, we profitably can explore the ideas and themes that became building blocks of Jewish, and Christian, theology. We do this by bringing together in larger complexes elements referred to briefly in a variety of biblical contexts. The biblical ideology of "the Land of Israel," for instance, emerges from many components: sayings about God's promise to give the land to the people, about God's threats to exile the people should they not keep the covenant, and concerning God's promise to bring them back to the land once they repent. We must be careful, at the same time, not to harmonize and homogenize distinctive theological statements found in different layers of the biblical text. The notion of "God," for instance, must be considered in its varying, distinct contexts. For the Bible contains no separate book or even chapter that focuses solely on God. Rather, the notion of God has different aspects depending on particular authors' frames of thought and experience.

Although they are not combined into the kinds of systems and structures found in later Jewish and Christian teachings, the various theological ideas in the Hebrew Scriptures already form certain patterns of thought. For instance, even the composition of the Hebrew Scriptures into the Torah, the Prophets, and the Writings reveals a theological understanding that goes beyond the mere repetition of history: first we have the creation, then God's prehistory with man, then God's history with Israel, starting with the Exodus, and so on. The Torah is presented first because it gives the *foundations*. Then the books of the prophets, because of their critical roles in trying to warn the king and the people of the consequences if Israel does not keep the Torah.

True to the perspective presented by Scripture itself, the following roughly follows the Bible's own order. Even so, this is a *theolog-*

*ical*, not *historical*, presentation. Our primary concern is how Scripture's themes and notions relate to each other theologically, not what is primary or secondary from a historical point of view. Similarly, because we are interested in the religious system of the Hebrew Scriptures, we do not generally refer to parallel material from the ancient Near East. But, obviously, historical remarks and comparisons cannot entirely be left out, since the ancient Near East is Scripture's historical setting and cultural and religious context.

**God, creation, and humanity:** Rather than with God's names or attributes, which appear later, the Torah begins by describing the deity's primeval acts: the creation of the world, and, as its climax, the creation of humankind. Two versions of the creation story stand side by side (Gen. 1:1-2:3 and Gen. 2:4-25), differing in many details, but both stressing God's special concern for humanity. Neither of the versions gives many details about how it all came about, though a characteristic of the first version is that God creates through his word, and, of the second, that God makes the cosmos out of chaos. Both stories place humans at the center: God provides for people's nutrition and gives them a suitable place to live.

In the first and younger creation story, the Hebrew word for "create" (*br'*) is used only with God as subject and without any mention of the material out of which anything was created. This does not, however, dictate *creatio ex nihilo*, "creation out of nothing," as a biblical theme. Only in the apocryphal books of Wisdom (11:17) and 2 Maccabees (7:28) does this theme come to the surface. In contrast to the common verb for "make" (*'sh*), which is also used for God's creating, the verb *br'* is a specific theological term that distinguishes God's creating from what usually happens when something is made or formed out of a certain material. Reference to God's role as creator of the world is very common in the Hebrew Scriptures.[1]

The first creation story underlines the fact that God created humankind (*adam*) as a pair, man and woman, and "in the image" of God. The expression "in our image, to our likeness" (Gen. 1:26-27) seems not so much a statement about the nature of humans as about God's making people the deity's *partner* in the creation project. Accordingly, human beings enjoy a high status within creation, as God's foremost counterpart, to whom God entrusts the earth, to "master" and "rule" (Gen. 1:28).

Although humans enjoy a significant place within creation, they cannot really be called the "crown of creation," for this role is allotted to the Sabbath (Gen. 2:1-3).[2] In the same vein, according to the second creation story, the human being is formed "from the dust of the earth" (Gen. 2:7) to which he is to return when he dies (Gen. 3:19). This seems to imply that humans, from the very outset, are weak and transient creatures, contrasted to God, who is eternal. Humans receive life or breath (*nishmat hayyim*)[3] as a gift from God, on whom they are totally dependent (Gen. 2:7). This dependence accounts for people's obligation to obey God's will.

The creation narratives are followed by stories of why humans could not remain in their original home, the Garden of Eden. Their departure is a consequence of Adam and Eve's disobeying the restrictions God placed on them (Gen. 3). After their initial rebellion against God, it does not take more than a generation before one of their sons kills his brother (Gen. 4). The general attitude of humankind thus seems to entail disobedience of God's will (Gen. 6:5; 8:22), with Enoch (Gen. 5:22) and Noah (Gen. 6:9) the only exceptions mentioned. In the end, God harshly punishes humanity's accumulated transgressions and crimes. Noah and his family are made the instrument of God in saving small remnants of humankind and animals from the planned destruction (Gen. 6:13-8:22).

From this point on, the biblical narrative presents God's dealings with humankind in a new framework. It introduces the category of "covenant," the first of which is established between God and all living creatures, with humankind represented by Noah and his sons (Gen. 9:1-17). A number of commandments are listed. Only now are people explicitly allowed to eat meat, though a prohibition against eating blood remains (Gen.

9:4). And a very strong prohibition is stated against shedding the blood of another human being (Gen. 9:6). God adds a personal promise, never again to send a deluge to destroy all life on earth. This does not, however, prevent humans from rebelling against God, as the story of the tower of Babel (Gen. 11) shows. As a result of people's persistent inclination to rebellion against God and the divine will, the relationship between God and humans did not turn out to be harmonious. Although, through Noah, God made a covenant with humankind, the relationship it intended to create seems to fail again. If this relationship is not to come to a dead end, a new initiative has to be taken by God.

**Election and Exodus:** The election of one man, Abram, who is asked to leave his country—Mesopotamia—for another—Canaan—constitutes a new creative act of God. In Canaan Abram will at first live as a stranger, but there he also will enter into a new relationship with God, conceived as a covenant (Gen. 15 and 17). Abraham[4] will become the ancestor of a numerous people, with Canaan as his possession. But this is not to happen immediately, only after a four hundred year sojourn of his descendants as slaves in Egypt. Then the "God of the fathers"—also called the "God of Abraham, Isaac and Jacob"—will be revealed as God of a whole people. While in Egypt, Abraham's descendants, also called Hebrews, are given a leader in Moses. Through his leadership and the Exodus from Egypt, they are united as a people, enter into a covenant with God at Sinai, and receive the Torah. It appears that, in Egypt, the Hebrews had no living contact with the God of the patriarchs. Moses needs to remind them of their long forgotten religious heritage and of the promises God made to their forefathers.

Confronted by the burning bush (Exod. 3), Moses is the first to ask God's name, to be used as a credential in front of the Israelites in Egypt. Moses receives the enigmatic answer "*Ehye asher ehye*," which has been interpreted variously, including as "I am that I am" or "I am the one who is." The root *hyh* seems to indicate that the name's bearer "is" or better "is active." This may be a clue to God's identity: this is a living and active

God. But an explication follows of the name: "The Lord (*YHWH*), the God of your fathers, the God of Abraham, the God of Isaac, and the God of Jacob, has sent me to you. This shall be my name forever, this my appellation for all eternity" (Exod. 3:13-15). Thus this is the same God known to and worshipped by the forefathers. A later, priestly source makes a similar point, that people did not previously use the name YHWH, but instead *El Shaddai* (Exod. 6:3). The main point in the revelation of the name thus appears to be not so much to indicate something about God but that this is the *same* God as previously worshipped, the God of the fathers, who promised to be with the Israelites and to protect them as God protected their ancestors.

The Hebrew verb for "choose" or "elect" expresses a central theme, that the initiative in creating the special relationship between God and Israel is God's alone.[5] God's reason for choosing Israel is explicit: "It is not because you are the most numerous of peoples that the Lord set his heart on you and chose you; indeed, you are the smallest of peoples; but it was because the Lord loved you and kept the oath he made to your fathers that the Lord freed you . . ." (Deut. 7:7-8). In the same way, the reason for giving the land of Canaan to Israel was not that Israel had been especially righteous, even though the other peoples are said to have been driven out because of their wickedness. The only reason mentioned is that God wanted to keep the promises made to Abraham, Isaac, and Jacob (Deut. 9:4-6).

Similarly, no explicit *reason* appears for God's choice of Abraham and his family; indeed the text does not even state that he was "chosen." But there is an explicit *purpose* in God's "calling" him out from Mesopotamia, namely, that he shall be "a blessing to all families on earth" (Gen. 12:3). Perhaps this is the model for the similar task thought to have been assigned to Israel. This seems to be the essence of what Is. 42:1 and 6 say about "the servant," understood as Israel: that he shall "teach righteousness to the nations" and be "a covenant-people, a light of nations." The most important choice, the choosing of the people of Israel, can even be compared to God's act of creation (Is. 43:19-25; 44:2). In fact, the unknown prophet referred to as Second Isaiah (ch. 40-55) repeats the pattern of Genesis: the creation leads to the call of Abraham as the witness of God in the world. The only difference is that in Second Isaiah, Israel has the role of Abraham.

The Exodus from Egypt is seen simultaneously as an *historical event* and a *saving act* of God (Exod. 12-15). The God of the fathers is experienced as a God who in the moment of truth chooses a capable leader for the people and, when the escape seems to fail, brings disaster upon the enemies' army. This saving act is the first to apply to the whole people; it is in fact the act that creates the people as a people. It does not remain unique but, rather, becomes a model, referred to as the "Exodus pattern." Theologically the shift "from slavery to freedom" interprets or anticipates similar acts of God that occur later, when the Judeans are exiled to Babylonia. Thus the Exodus theme becomes important again, especially in Second Isaiah (Is. 40:3-5; 41:17-20; 43:16-21, etc.). Similarly, the experience of slavery in Egypt becomes a model and is also to be remembered, in this case, to teach the people to treat their own slaves humanely (Deut. 15:15). Alongside its theological importance, the Exodus thus is invested with a strong socio-ethical motif.

**Covenant and Torah:** God's election of a certain family that was to become the people of Israel led eventually in the covenants at Sinai, described as a *treaty*, but not quite in the manner of a treaty between equals. A closer model is in Hittite and Assyrian treaties between the great king and his vassals. The king, the stronger party, offers to protect the vassals, who commit themselves to be loyal to the king. If either party fails to fulfill the terms of the commitment, the other is also freed from the obligation.

The character of the Sinai covenant as a treaty is made clear at Deut. 26:17-18: "You have affirmed this day that the Lord is your God, that you will walk in his ways, that you will observe his laws, commandments and norms, and that you will obey him. And the Lord has affirmed this day that you are, as he promised you, his treasured people which shall observe all his commandments." The purpose and meaning of the covenant is also expressed in the formula "I shall be your God and you shall be my people" (Exod. 6:7; Jer. 24:7; 30:22). The reciprocity of the covenant is clear: both parties are committed to each other. The Sinai covenant is different from the usual ancient Near Eastern examples only in that it is *permanent*. If Israel fails to fulfill its obligations, God will certainly punish the people; but God will remember the covenant and not revoke it (Lev. 26:44-45).

The founding document of the covenant is the *Torah*, given to Moses and accepted by Israel (Exod. 24:1-8). The word "Torah" means "instruction" or "law" and is derived from the root *yrh*, "aim," "direct," or "point out." Historically, several collections of laws were formulated at different stages, such as the Decalogue (Exod. 20:1-17; Deut. 5:6-21), the Book of Covenant (Exod. 20:22-23:19), the Law of Holiness (Lev. 17-26), and Deuteronomy, an independent statement. While Torah originally stood for a specific decision, e.g., of priestly law, in Deuteronomy Torah often has the meaning "law-book," distinguished from specific rulings and injunctions. Thus Deut. 4:44-45 states: "This is the *torah* which Moses set before the children of Israel; these are the testimonies, statutes, and the ordinances, which Moses spoke to the Israelites when they came out of Egypt. . . ."

The Torah as a whole is a binding document directed to all Israel, governing Israel's relationship to God within the covenant. For the individual Israelite, the Torah is a consequence of belonging to the chosen people of God, which obligates one to know the Torah, to understand it correctly, and to be reminded of it regularly. The well-being of the whole people depends on the sincerity and willingness of the individual Israelite to follow the Torah.[6]

Unlike the word Torah, the meaning of the name "Israel" is not clear, for we are not certain which verb stem the word combines with the element *el*, referring to God. According to the Biblical etymology at Gen. 32:9

(cf., Hos. 12:4), the verb intended is *srh*, and the word's meaning thus is "God fights." This name was probably initially applied to a group of tribes (Josh. 10:14, 42; Judg. 5) and then to the entire people prior to the rise of the monarchy. After that it designated the kingdom of Saul, David, and Solomon, and, after this kingdom's division, the northern kingdom alone. The name later was transferred, perhaps by Isaiah, to the southern kingdom, Judah, probably in connection with the northern kingdom's fall. The name "Israel" also is used in the Deuteronomist's (Jos. through 2 Kgs.) and Chronicler's (Ezra through 2 Chr.) accounts of the people in exile, now representing "all Israel" (Deut. 1:1; 11:6; Josh. 23:2; 1 Sam. 12:1; 1 Chr. 9:1; 2 Chr. 18:16). After the return from the exile, "Israel" becomes a spiritual appellation of the people (Is. 43:1, 15; 44:1, 5, 23; Mal. 1:1, 5; Ezra 2:70; 6:17; 1 Chr. 28:8).

In all these settings, "Israel" never was purely an ethnic name but always had theological connotations. Thus the Lord is said to be "the God of Israel," never "The God of Judah," and reference to "Israel" as "The people (*am*) of the Lord" usually indicates the nation of the Israelites. But sometimes the term *am* also refers to a "flock" to be "herded" (e.g. 2 Sam. 5:2; 7:7) or a religious congregation (Num. 11:29; Judg. 20:2). Additionally, *am* and *goy*, both meaning "people," sometimes are equivalent to terms such as *qahal* and *edah*, both meaning "congregation."

Israel, especially in Deuteronomy, is called "a holy people" or "a treasured people." Israel is "holy" because the Lord chose and rescued it from Egypt, and it therefore belongs to God (Exod. 19:6; Deut. 7:6; 14:2, 21; 26:19; 28:9). Israel is expected to behave according to its holy status, which requires imitating God: "you shall be to me a kingdom of priests and a holy nation" (Exod. 19:6; see too Lev. 11:44f.; 18:3; 19:36; 20:24-26). This probably means that Israel, like the priests, has immediate access to God and possibly also serves the role of a mediator between God and humankind. Sometimes the word "property" is used in the sense that Israel belongs to God, who has a claim on

the people (Deut. 4:20; 9:26, 29; 1 Kgs. 8:51).

The Sinai covenant includes some new statements on the nature of Israel's God. The passage beginning at Deut. 6:4, first, states that the Lord is *ehad*, meaning the *only* God of Israel, who is to be worshipped *alone*, not in a pantheon together with other deities. It was also important to understand that Israel's God is the same to all Israel, that is, God is to be worshipped in the same way by everyone and only at the Jerusalem Temple, not at local shrines. It is also forbidden to make "graven image" of God (Exod. 20:4). According to new research, this aniconism is not the result of theological reflection. It should rather be seen as an inherited convention of religious behavior that only later formed the basis for theological reflection. It is not peculiar to ancient Israel, either, but here it developed to its very extreme.[7]

Scholars have debated whether the worship of foreign gods was condemned from the beginning or whether it was the result of a so called "the Lord alone" movement. The rich variety of theophoric names that include the elements *-yah* or *-yahû* suggests that Yahweh was worshipped widely already in the time before king David. On the other hand, in these earlier times there was no exclusive worship of Yahweh, nor was the cult concentrated to one place (Jerusalem). This concentration was the result of a long development, starting with the Deuteronomistic movement and completed during postexilic times. We encounter the final breakthrough to a "theoretical" or "principal" monotheism only in Second Isaiah and in certain Deuteronomistic texts (Is. 40:18, 25, 44:6-8, 45:14, 18, 21ff., 46:9; Deut. 4:1-40; cf. 2 Sam. 7:22).

Certain prophetic texts present the view that Israel failed to live up to the requirements of the covenant, which it broke through social oppression and apostasy. Hos. 1:3 compares this apostasy with the unfaithfulness of a wife. Is. 5:1ff. relates Israel to a vineyard, which the owner (God) had planted and tended but which did not produce good fruit in due time. He also uses the image of a father and his children (1:2): "I reared children and brought them up, and they rebelled against me!" Jeremiah, again, uses the image of a bride forsaking the love of her youth (2:2ff.). As punishment for this, Israel must go into exile. But this was not to be the end: in the future God will again "remember" the covenant with Israel, gathering the exiles and bringing them back to the land God once gave them. The covenant will be renewed or reestablished as "a new covenant," through which the people will enjoy an immediate knowledge of and intimacy with their God (Jer. 31:31-34). This new covenant is thought even to surpass the Sinai covenant, guaranteeing the continuity of the people of Israel as the people of Yahweh (31:35-37).

**The land of Israel, exile, and return:** The covenant at Sinai includes God's promise to give the people of Israel the land of Canaan as an inheritance. This reflects the original promise to the patriarchs, and it finds its simplest expression in Gen. 12:7: "I will give this land to your offspring." In references to this promise, Exod. 6:8 says that God "swore to give it to Abraham, Isaac, and Jacob," and "I will give it to you for a possession." Many other biblical texts also refer to the promises to the fathers. But when the Sinai covenant is cited, this promise is usually connected with the condition that Israel keep the Torah (Deut. 6:10-19). There seems to be a difference between the promises made to Abraham and King David (see below), on the one hand, and those made to the Israelites, on the other hand. Only the former are often unconditional. One can perhaps say that the first mentioned are referred to in critical situations (the exile), whereas the others pertain to times when the people are established in the land.

Beginning with the Exodus from Egypt, Israel sets out for the "Promised Land." Remarkably, such a key event as the covenant at Sinai takes place *en route* to the land. The fulfillment of the promise of the land is told in great detail (Num. 32; 34; Josh.). The land is Yahweh's gift to his covenant people and the goal of its wanderings. It is beautiful and abundant; its fertility is God's special gift. No less than 21 times, starting with Exod.

3:8, it is characterized as "a land flowing with milk and honey." This is, however, not a description of a paradise but of a cultivated land in contrast to the desert.[8] It nevertheless makes good sense for the Israelites to rejoice and thankfully bring the first fruits of the land before God in the Temple (Deut. 26:1-11). The land is in this text understood and expressed in its twofold meaning, as "territory" (*'eres*) and "soil" (*adamah*).

The land belongs to God, and it remains God's (Lev. 25:23). Therefore the Israelites are not free to do with it as they wish. Only gardens and vineyards seem to have been regarded as private property, whereas fields belonged to the community. The giving of the first fruits to God is a symbolic expression of God's possession of the land. Also, the institution of the sabbatical year (Lev. 25:1-7), during which the land is left fallow, acknowledges God's ownership. The same seems to be the case with the jubilee, every fiftieth year, when acquired land returns to its former owners. These laws seem to have been practiced seldom, if ever. They nonetheless express a strong notion of God's ownership of the land.

The people of Israel are mythically and historically bound to the land. They did not belong to it from the beginning; instead they entered it at a certain point in history, when other peoples already inhabited it. This corresponds to the Israelites' consciousness of not being God's chosen people since times immemorial, but having become God's people at a certain stage in history. Israel thus has God alone to thank for the opportunity to conquer and settle the land (Gen. 12:6, 15:19-21, etc.). It can, therefore, be more easily understood that the covenant between God and Israel also makes their remaining in the land conditional to their keeping the Torah of God.

When the Israelites failed to keep the covenant, the prophets threatened—and then the people actually experienced—exile. There now naturally arose a need for the people to understand the nature of the covenant that had allowed exile to occur. In explaining this, the prophets again refer to God's promise to the patriarchs (Ezek. 33:23-24; Is. 41:8; 51:2;

63:16). Second Isaiah describes the promise as unconditional. Thus a return to the promised land is vouchsafed. But Ezekiel explains the people's exile by underscoring that, should they break the covenant, the promise to Abraham does not guarantee their remaining in the land. Still, the promise to Abraham provided hope of a renewed covenant with God under which the people once again could enter the land.[9] In the meantime, the specific locals Zion or Jerusalem took the place of the land in general.[10] On the whole, however, the land retained its status as the promised, beautiful, and abundant home for the people of Israel.

**The monarchy:** Unlike other nations, the Israelites did not think that their monarchy came from heaven, and Scripture accordingly reveals a somewhat ambivalent attitude toward it. The monarchy was not created "in the beginning" but appeared at a critical moment in the history of the people,[11] introduced in order to help Israel fight its enemies, especially the Philistines (Judg. 17:6; 18:1; 19:1; 21:25). Economical and social changes also contributed to its introduction. Monarchy thus seems to have been at the same time necessary and problematic. On the one hand, its introduction is described in a very hesitant and even critical way (1 Sam. 8-12; especially, 1 Sam. 12:15, 25). Indeed, Israel is warned against introducing kingship (1 Sam. 8:11-18), for God is the only real king of Israel (Judg. 8:23). Still, the first two kings, Saul (1 Sam. 10:24) and David (1 Sam. 16:8-13; 2 Sam. 6:21), are said to have been "chosen" by God.

Despite this ambivalence, the Israelite monarchy, and above all David and his dynasty, played a decisive role in their own time and in promises and expectations for the future (2 Sam. 7:18-29). The dynasty of David enjoys a special covenant with God (1 Kgs. 11:32; 2 Kgs. 19:34), and it stands for all that is good about the monarchy. Thus, the Davidic king is called the "son of God" (Ps. 2:7) and a priest of a unique order (Ps. 110:4). The king's obedience towards God could be a source of life, salvation, and blessing (1 Sam. 12:13-14; Ps. 72; 132:12). The king has free access to God in prayer, he is

"the anointed one of the Lord," the "servant," "the lamp," and "the redeemer" of the people. God is the "Father," the "stronghold," the "shield" of the king.

A constant tension exists between what the ideal king was expected to be and do and how the kings of Israel and Judah actually behaved. The Deuteronomistic writers evaluated them one by one according to their conduct, the criteria being whether or not they kept the covenant with the God of Israel. Some kings are severely criticized (1 Kgs. 11:7-13; 12:26-33), especially by the prophets Hosea (13:4-11) and Jeremiah (22-23). However, the Davidic kingship is never rejected, even by the prophets.

The main attitude towards the monarchy remained positive, for God had once and for all entrusted the governance of Israel into the hands of David and his descendants. This act by God could not easily be frustrated by the shortcomings of individual kings. When the prophets threatened the people with coming disaster, the Deuteronomistic writers could hope for a delay in the divine punishment, counting on the merits of David and Solomon. They even said that, because of his servant David, God did not destroy Judah (2 Kgs. 8:19; cf. 1 Kgs. 11:36; 15:4). Also individuals like Hezekiah and Josiah were regarded as ideal kings (2 Kgs. 18-20; 22-23). In Chronicles, the Davidic kings were regarded more or less as viceroys for God (1 Chr. 17:14; 28:5; 29:23; 2 Chr. 6:40-42; 9:8; 13:8).

With the fall of Jerusalem and the first Temple in 587/586 B.C.E., the royal family was exiled, punished by the Babylonians, and kept in custody. Nevertheless, the hope for restoration of the Davidic dynasty was not forgotten, and it was revived already when king Jehoiachin was released from prison (2 Kgs. 25:27) and strengthened when some exiles returned to their country and started to rebuild Jerusalem and its Temple (Jer. 33:14-26; Ezek. 37:24-25). As restoration of full independence became an increasingly distant goal, the people's hopes continued to be tied to the restoration of the dynasty of David. The ideal king more and more became a figure projected into the future, imagined as a final and transcendent descendant of David. Thus the idea of the Davidic king remained symbolic of Israel's continuing election.[12]

**Jerusalem and the Temple:** The city of Jerusalem became a visible sign of Israel's elected status (Is. 62:11-12; Jer 3:17). God chose Zion—originally a name for the Ophel hill, but then used for the city of Jerusalem—in the same way God chose Israel and the dynasty of David (Ps. 68:16-17; 74:2; 84:5-7; 87:1-3; 132:13-14). In the theological framework of the Deuteronomist, the idea that God chose this special place to "set his name there" is often repeated (Deut. 12:5, etc.). The place received its sacred status by king David's installation there of the Ark of the Covenant (2 Sam. 6:1-15; 1 Kgs. 6:19), and this location was made more permanent by Solomon's building there of the Temple (1 Kgs. 6:1-38; 7:15-51). The Temple mount is called God's "inheritance" (Exod. 15:17). From this nucleus of holiness, the belief in the holiness of the entire city of Jerusalem seems to have developed.

Ps. 125:1-2 expresses the close relationship between God and Zion as follows: "Those who trust in the Lord are like Mount Zion, and cannot be moved, enduring forever. Jerusalem, hills enfold it, and the Lord enfolds his People, now and forever." Zion is the foremost stronghold of the Israelites against their enemies. They are exhorted to trust in it (Ps. 46; 48; 76; Ezek. 38-39; cf. Joel 2; Zech. 8:22; 12; 14.). Part of the so-called "theology of Zion" is constituted by the contention that God protects the city of Jerusalem and from there will judge the enemies. Prophets, such as Micah and Jeremiah, criticized this theology but at the same time themselves witnessed its impact.[13] Jerusalem's destruction was deeply lamented and considered God's punishment (Lam. 1-5; Ps. 74; 79). However, God would "again" choose Jerusalem, and the rebuilt Temple would once more be the focus of promises of future salvation (Is. 14:1; Zech. 1:17; 2:16; 3:2). Jerusalem and its Temple were eventually to become places of pilgrimage, not only for Israelites but for people of many nations.[14]

The Temple cult was especially regarded as a sign of the chosenness of the holy city, with the Temple considered the place where the divine "glory" dwelled (Is. 6, cf. Ps. 24:29; 102:17) and where God's presence on earth was effected. This awareness encouraged the view that Jerusalem itself was a source of life and prosperity for God's people (Ps. 92:12-15; Ezek. 47:1-12). From Zion justice was distributed also to the nations (Is. 2:3-4). The well-being of Israel would eventually spread to all humankind (Zech. 14:16-21).

There seems to have existed a tension between the notion that God actually dwells in the Temple and that God simply appears or is somehow represented there. Originally, the idea was perhaps simply that the worshipper was expected to meet God in the Temple, because God was present there (1 Kgs. 6:11-13; Is. 8:18; Ps. 43:3; 74:2; 76:3; Joel 4:21). This is corrected, however, in Solomon's speech at 1 Kgs. 8:27-30:

> "But will God indeed dwell on the earth? Behold, heaven and the highest heaven cannot contain thee; how much less this house which I have built! Yet have regard to the prayer of thy servant and to his supplication, O Lord my God . . .; that thy eyes may be open night and day toward this house, the place of which thou hast said, 'My name shall be there'. . . . And hearken thou to the supplication of thy servant and of thy people Israel, when they pray toward this place; yea, hear thou in heaven thy dwelling place; and when thou hearest, forgive."

Here we meet an early reflection upon God's relation to the Temple. A kind of "Name theology" was developed that did not directly deny the presence of God in the Temple but indicated that God was, so to speak, represented there only by his name, the deity in actuality being transcendent.

There thus was a remarkable difference between ancient Near Eastern temples with statues of gods and the Jerusalem Temple without any image of God. The Holy of Holies in the Temple of Jerusalem was dark, containing only the throne of God, represented by the Ark and the Cherubim (1 Kgs. 6:23). God himself was, of course, not represented by any visible image, although the Psalmist could sing about going to the

Temple "to see his face" (Ps. 11:7; 17:15) or to "appear before his face" (Ps. 42:3). Such expressions became a technical terms for visiting the Temple.

**Cult and priest:** In the Temple cult, Israel relives its history, its chosenness, and above all the divine presence there. Accordingly, much of Scripture's theological vocabulary is originally cultic. Such pairs as "holiness/profanity," "acceptable gift/abomination," "cleanness/uncleanness" all originally belonged to the cult and were not intelligible outside the sanctuaries. Over time, these terms acquired a broader range of metaphoric meanings and so eventually took on an ethical and theological significance.[15] The cult thus was the cradle of theology: the sacrificial acts came first, and theology, a reflection on what one was doing and why, came later. This does not mean, of course, that the cultic praxis always set the standard for beliefs about God. Rather, religious ceremony and theology seem to have stimulated each other. The cult was interpreted differently as times changed, so that old practices and concepts took on new meanings in an ongoing interaction between cult and thought. Later in the development of biblical religion, the process of theologizing cultic concepts went even further.

Worship within the framework of the Temple cult enjoys such a central place in Scripture because the presence and help of God are all important. God was present in the Temple, and the Israelite visited there to "see God's face." To worship thus is to stand directly in God's presence. This does not imply that God appeared in a regular theophany at the Temple. Rather, contact with God primarily was achieved through the offering of sacrifices (Exod. 23:15, 19) accompanied by the prayers and songs of the devotee. Over time, there seems to have been a gradual shift from a concern with physical action towards a concern with spiritual intention. In line with this, the verbal elements in the cult, such as prayer and song, grew in significance.

The patriarchs, according to Scripture, performed sacrifices themselves (Gen. 12:7f.; 13:4, 18; 15:9f., etc.). An altar was built and sacrifice performed in a place in which God had appeared to a patriarch, judge, or king (2 Sam. 24:16ff.). God personally determined where the divine name was to be recalled (Exod. 20:24), and the cult therefore can be said to have been initiated directly by God. This is shown in detail by the stipulations concerning the "Tent of Meeting" and the sacrificial laws (Exod. 25, Num. 10). This also means that God was regarded as the one who gives the cult its meaning. The ceremonies of worship are never thought to function automatically. Cultic and ethical commandments are equally binding and they are related to each other.

A teacher of Torah, the priest declares the will of God (Deut. 31:9, 26; 33:10; Jer. 18:18; Ezek. 7:26, 44:23; Hos. 4:6; Mic. 3:11; Mal. 2:7). He is the expert on how properly to carry out the sacrificial cult (Lev. 4:1-35), and decisions about what is "holy" and "profane," "clean" and "unclean," belong to him (Lev. 10:10; 11-15). His decisions appear in declaratory formulas stating whether a certain cultic act is legitimate or whether something is clean or unclean, holy or profane. But the priests also used ethical criteria, e.g., to decide whether pilgrims were to be allowed to enter the Temple area (Pss. 15 and 24). Also the giving of oracles was included in the instruction administered by the priests (Exod. 28:30; Lev. 8:8; Num. 27:21; Deut. 33:8; 1 Sam. 23:9; Ezra 2:63). Overall, the importance of the priesthood derives from the significance of the cult together with the conviction that ritual cleanness is essential for the proper way of approaching God. The priest ensures that the conduct of the worshipper before God in the holy Temple is appropriate. As the guarantor of the right order, it is no coincidence that, according to Scripture, the priesthood was entrusted to certain families chosen by God (Exod. 28f.; 39f.; Lev. 8; Num. 3; 8).

Several kings initiated cultic reforms, but only those of Hezekiah and Josiah are described in some detail by the Deuteronomistic and Chronistic historians.[16] The reforms aimed to remove the syncretistic cults and to centralize Israelite worship around the cult of Yahweh in Jerusalem. This program was interrupted by the destruction of Jerusalem and its Temple in 587/586 B.C.E. However, when the Temple was rebuilt by the returning exiles, the cult became as central as ever before. Now, during postexilic times, the cultic laws and the festival calendars received their definitive forms.

The Sabbath developed into a holy day even more important than the pilgrimage festivals. During the Sabbath people rest in the same way that God rested after completing the work of creation. Thus, humans imitate God and, so to speak, activate the image of God within themselves. Through the Sabbath rest, everything created reaches its goal. Thus the Sabbath is an anticipation of messianic time.

**Prophets and prophecy:** The prophets have a double role within ancient Israelite society. They represent, on the one hand, the critical voice—Israel took for granted the covenant with God and ignored the commitments connected to election—and they speak about the coming judgment of God. On the other, they utter promises of future salvation and remind the people of God's will and continuing covenant mercy. Usually one of these functions is dominant, and this, naturally, has to do with the historical situation in which each prophet appears. These situations often are times of crisis, when Israel and Judah are threatened by enemy armies. To count on God's protection, Israel needed to review its fulfillment of its obligations towards God. Of course, the prophets often declared the people to be wanting, for which reason they could no longer take for granted that God would help them. God had, perhaps, even chosen Israel's enemies to carry out punishments against the people.

The prophets saw themselves as chosen and authorized to confront the people (Amos 7:10ff.; Is. 6; Jer. 1; Ezek. 1-3). Indeed, the Hebrew word for "prophet" means "called as a speaker" or "one who calls," implying that the prophets speak or interpret God's word and activity. Thus, they can be said to "see words" (Amos 1:1; Is. 2:1), and some prophets were called "seers." This may imply that they "see through" rather than "foresee." One way or the other, because they see the real condition of their people, they can also fore-

see what is going to happen if the people do not repent and turn back to God.

Broadly speaking, speech about judgment and punishment dominates the early prophets, while a message of salvation is central among the exilic and postexilic ones. Judgment, according to the early prophets, was the inevitable consequence of the social, religious, and political evils prevailing among the people, on the one hand, and of God's unmet demands for holiness, on the other. Their notion that judgment was inevitable is not to be understood in the sense that the people's turning back was not deemed possible. Even Amos was not quite categorical,[17] although he surely saw his people as approaching their end (8:2). But punishment was not understood as a goal in itself. It is not about annihilation but purification (Is. 1:24-26). Therefore, punishment and salvation are not contradictory. When punishment has been meted out, salvation arrives, showing God's true intention. There will be a new Exodus, a new Jerusalem, a new descendant of David, a new covenant. The exiles will be brought back to their land, they will be renewed, idolatry and war will disappear, God will again reign from Zion.[18]

Thus, one can say that, although the prophets differed from each other in many respects, they had in common their shared life situation. They lived in the midst of their people and interpreted the word of God as they understood it. The fact that the pupils and heirs of the prophets in their religious traditions preserved the prophets' most dire threats, shows that they, as well as the following generations, considered the prophets to be right, to be the true servants of the people and God alike. The Deuteronomistic theologians saw the prophets as successors of Moses himself, as true interpreters of the Torah (Deut. 18:15, 18).

In the context of prophecy a few words should be said about apocalypticism. Whereas prophecy is concerned with the past, present, and future, apocalypticism is mainly concerned with the future.[19] Whereas prophecy remains within history, apocalypticism envisages the end of history or, rather, a radical new beginning. In Scripture, apocalypticism tried to bridge the gap between the beginning, when God was dealing with all humankind (Gen. 1-11), and the end, when God would again appear as the Lord of world history (Dan. 4-5). God shall overcome all enemies in a final battle (Joel 3; Zech. 12; 14; Ezek. 38-39), and, in this drama, the final judgment will take place. To those who are saved, God will be all merciful, whereas God's enemies will meet only with destruction. To Israel, or its saved remnant, there will be salvation and restoration as the people of God. In contrast to the prophetic visions in Isaiah and Ezekiel, the apocalyptic visions do not connect God's restoration of Israel to people's conversion and God's forgiveness. Thus apocalypticism, while stemming from the same sources as prophecy, represents in several respects a clear departure from prophecy.

**Ethics and wisdom:** "Everything that the Lord has said we shall do and we shall hear," the Israelites declare when accepting the Torah at Sinai (Exod. 24:7). Remarkably, as reflected in his statement, Israel is told in so many ways how to act, but hardly ever is instructed concerning how or what to believe[20] (unless, of course, we are to take everything Israel does as an expression of beliefs). Still, since Israel is not only a people, but a religious community, its ethics has a religious foundation, deriving from the will of God.

Individual's ethical conduct has an effect upon the whole people, and it therefore is not possible to distinguish private from communal ethics. The people of Israel were in fact expected to be egalitarian,[21] all members of the people could be called "brothers." All are obliged to take care of the weak members in society, such as orphans, widows, strangers, and Levites. God too is the guardian of the weak (Ps. 68:6). In a society living in accordance with God's will, justice and peace were to be maintained. The prophets sharply criticized unsocial behavior.

There is, however, another ethical tradition in Scripture, the so-called *wisdom literature*, including Proverbs, Ecclesiastes, Job, and some Psalms. This literature does not obtain its themes directly from the Torah or from the covenant between God and Israel but is part of the larger body of Near Eastern wisdom literature, derived from the circles of the royal court. This means that "wisdom" is not common knowledge but the privilege of a special group of higher officials. Still, its ethics is largely based upon personal experience of, and reflection on, life, and its content does not differ very much from that of Torah instruction, even though the wisdom literature is more concerned with practical aspects of everyday life not requiring legal formulation.

Proverbs discusses how to behave wisely, how to be modest, and so on. It seldom refers to God directly, but since God has created the order of the world, knowledge about this order is also knowledge about God and God's will. There is a conviction that "fear of God" and right ethical behavior are rewarded through a blessed life (11:31). "No evil shall happen to the just; but the wicked are filled with mischief" (12:21). This is the voice of the older wisdom. But this opinion did not become a dogma, even in Proverbs, which sometimes admits that you really cannot see any connection between how you lead your life and what happens to you (Prov. 16:1, 9, 33, 20:24, 21:1f., 25:2).

Thus the wisdom tradition contains a radical critique of the optimistic view of "the good life," with Ecclesiastes declaring that the richness of "the good life" is not really what it is thought to be.[22] The idea that no correspondence exists between ethical behavior and a blessed life lies at the foundation of Job. Still, there, as in Prov. 1-9, we meet a late, theologized wisdom that combines sapiential cultivation and personal piety. This special form of wisdom comes to its fullest expression in the speeches of Job's friends. Humanity is not allowed to question God's justice, no matter how much injustice is suffered. God will reward the truly pious person, who will not suffer. But the Job of the prologue (Job 1-2) is such a pious sufferer, and the dialogues of the book show that this traditional teaching does not suffice to explain why people suffer injustice and sickness. And Job's encounter with God shows no easy answers to be available: God is God, and people are people. Humans cannot totally comprehend God and so cannot expect to understand God's choices regarding their fate on earth.

**Conclusion:** In Scripture we do not find theological doctrines, only short formulations expressing thoughts about God, the election of Israel, and the giving of the Torah, all of which provide a foundation for later theological reflection. Still, such reflections in the Hebrew Scriptures can be understood as theology, as what Scripture itself calls *daat elohim*, "knowledge of God." For through them, Scripture depicts how and why God created the world and explains what God expects of human beings in their life in that world. As has emerged clearly in this thematic account, the themes of the Exodus and covenant are central: through the Exodus from Egypt God makes a people out of the Hebrew slaves; and through the covenant at Sinai, God enters into an eternal relationship with them. The rest can be regarded either as preludes to or consequences of these focal points.

### Bibliography

Brueggemann, W., *Theology of the Old Testament. Testimony, Dispute, Advocacy* (Minneapolis, 1997).

Clements, R.E., *Old Testament Theology. A Fresh Approach* (London, 1978).

Weinfeld, Moshe, *Deuteronomy and the Deuteronomic School* (Oxford, 1972).

### Notes

[1] The verb *br'* occurs 48 times in Scripture. Other verbs used for creation are *'sh, ysr, kun, ysd.*

[2] See H.D. Preuss, *Theologie des Alten Testaments* (Stuttgart, Berlin, Köln, 1991-1992), vol. 1, p. 267.

[3] The more usual expression for "breath" is *ruah*; this term is also used for "wind" and "spirit."

[4] The original name "Abram" probably means "the father is exalted," but this name is in Gen. 17:5 changed into "Abraham," understood as "father of a multitude."

[5] Preuss, op. cit., vol. 1, pp. 31-35.

[6] R.E. Clements, *Old Testament Theology. A Fresh Approach* (London, 1978), pp. 106-110.

[7] T.N.D. Mettinger, *No Graven Image? Israelite Aniconism in Its Near Eastern Context* (Stockholm, 1995), pp. 195-196.

[8] Preuss, op. cit., vol. 1, pp. 135-136.

[9] Is. 11:10-16; 14:1-2; 60:21; 65:9; Jer. 12:15; Ezek. 47:13-23; Mic. 2:12-13; Obad. 19-21.

[10] See, e.g., Is. 40:9-11-17, 19ff., 51:3-11; 52:1-10, 54:1-3; Zech. 14:6-11; Ps. 69:36-37.

[11] Clements, op. cit., pp. 89-91; Preuss, op. cit., vol. 2, pp. 19-40.

[12] Clements, ibid., p. 90.

[13] See Is. 1:4-9, 3:16-26, 8:5-15, 10:27b-32, 29:1-4; Jer. 26:1-6.

[14] See Is. 2:2-4; Mic. 4:1-2; Is. 60; cf., Hag. 2:6-9; Ps. 68:29f.; 72:10f.; Jer. 3:17; Zech. 14:16-19.

[15] Clements, op. cit., p. 42.

[16] On Hezekiah's reform, see 2 Kgs. 18:3f.; 2 Chr. 29-31; on Josiah's reform, 2 Kgs. 22:3-23:25.

[17] Note the word "perhaps" at Amos 5:15, Zeph. 2:3, and Joel 2:14.

[18] See Is. 9:4; Mic. 2:1213, 4:6-8; Hos. 11:11; Jer. 31:31-34; Ezek. 36:26-30, 37:23, 43:7-9; Zech. 9:10, 13:2, etc.

[19] Apocalyptic texts in Scripture are at Is. 24-27, 66, Zech. 1-8, 12-14, certain texts in Ezek. 38-39, Joel 2-4, and the Book of Daniel.

[20] Preuss, op. cit., vol. 2, p. 201.

[21] See Exod. 21:4-11,16,18-32; 22:20-26; 23:1-9; Lev. 19:15; Deut 10:18; 13:18; 16:19; 27:19.

[22] E.g., Eccl. 1:16-18, 2:4-11, 2:24, 3:12f., 5:17f., 8:15, 9:7f., 11:9f.

KARL-JOHAN ILLMAN

**TORAH IN JUDAISM, THE CLASSICAL STATEMENT:** Torah means "teaching," and in Scripture refers to the teaching that God revealed to Moses at Mount Sinai. The most familiar meaning of the word is the five books of Moses or Pentateuch (Genesis, Exodus, Leviticus, Numbers, Deuteronomy). "The Torah" may also refer to the entirety of the Hebrew Scriptures (called by Christianity, "the Old Testament"). Since at Sinai, Judaism maintains, God revealed the Torah to Moses in two media, written and oral, with the written part corresponding to the Pentateuch, a further, oral part of the Torah is included in the meanings Jews assign to the word. This oral part is held to encompass the teachings ultimately written down by the sages of the Torah in ancient times and is contained, in part, in the Mishnah, Talmud, and Midrash-compilations.

But in Judaism, the term Torah—encompassing both Scripture, the written Torah, and the Rabbinic writings of ancient times called the oral Torah—has come to stand for what in secular language is called "Judaism." That is to say, what the world calls "Judaism" the faithful know as "the Torah," in the usage, "the Torah teaches." But that to which "Torah" makes reference proves far more encompassing than Scripture and even transcends the limits of the whole Torah, written and oral, extending as it does to the teachings of the authoritative sages, that is, "our sages of blessed memory."

Rabbinic or Classical Judaism as we know it at the end of late antiquity reached its now familiar definition when "*the* Torah"—meaning, a particular book or compilation of books—lost its capital letter and definite article and ultimately became "torah." What for nearly a millennium had been a particular scroll or book thus came to serve as a symbol of an entire system. Thus Rabbinic Judaism became and remained the religion of the Torah. As the system reached maturity, when a rabbi spoke of torah, he no longer meant only a particular object, a scroll and its contents. Now he used the word to encompass a distinctive and well-defined worldview and way of life. Torah had come to stand for something one does. Knowledge of the Torah promised not merely information about what people were supposed to do, but ultimate redemption or salvation.

Every detail of Judaism at hand exhibits essentially the same point of insistence, captured in the simple notion of the Torah as the generative symbol, the total, exhaustive expression of the system as a whole. That is why the definitive ritual of Rabbinic Judaism consisted in studying the Torah, and that is why the definitive myth explained that one who studied Torah would become holy, like Moses "our rabbi," and like God, in whose image humanity was made and whose Torah provided the plan and the model for what God wanted of a humanity created in his image.

**Seven meanings of the word Torah:** Here are the meanings assigned to the word Torah in the classical writings:

[1] When the Torah refers to a particular thing, it is to a scroll containing divinely revealed words.

[2] The Torah may further refer to revelation, not as an object but as a corpus of doctrine.

[3] When one "does Torah" the disciple "studies" or "learns," and the master "teaches," Torah. Hence while the word Torah never appears as a verb, it does refer to an act.

[4] The word also bears a quite separate sense, torah as category or classification or corpus of rules, e.g., "the torah of

driving a car" is a usage entirely acceptable to some documents.

[5] The word Torah very commonly refers to a status, distinct from and above another status, as "teachings of Torah" as against "teachings of scribes." For the two Talmuds that distinction is absolutely critical to the entire hermeneutic enterprise. But it is important even in the Mishnah.

[6] Obviously, no account of the meaning of the word Torah can ignore the distinction between the two Torahs, written and oral. It is important only in the secondary stages of the formation of the literature.

[7] Finally, the word Torah refers to a source of salvation, often fully worked out in stories about how the individual and the nation will be saved through Torah. In general, the sense of the word "salvation" is not complicated. It is simply salvation in the way in which Deuteronomy and the Deuteronomic historians understand it: kings who do what God wants win battles, those who do not, lose. So too here, people who study and do Torah are saved from sickness and death, and the way Israel can save itself from its condition of degradation also is through Torah.

Let us trace the documentary history of this symbol, Torah, from its beginnings in the Mishnah to its fulfillment in the Bavli.

**The Mishnah and the Torah:** Since the first document of Rabbinic Judaism, beyond Scripture, is the Mishnah, we should not find surprising the fact that the advent of the Mishnah precipitated deep thought about the definition of the Torah. That is because the Mishnah itself proved remarkably silent about the status of its own teachings. Upon its closure, the Mishnah gained an exalted political status as the constitution of the Jewish government of the Land of Israel. Accordingly, the clerks who knew and applied its law had to explain the standing of that law, meaning its relationship to the law of the Torah. But the Mishnah provided no account of itself. Unlike biblical law codes, the Mishnah begins with no myth of its own origin, like the one contained in the repeated phrase of the Pentateuch, "The Lord spoke to Moses saying, speak to the children of Israel and say to them. . . ." The Mishnah thus lays no claim to the power of prophecy in behalf of its authorities. It also fails to situate itself in any other way. It ends with no doxology. Discourse commences in the middle of things and ends abruptly. What follows from such laconic mumbling is that the exact status of the document required definition entirely outside the framework of the document itself. The framers of the Mishnah gave no hint of the nature of their book, so the Mishnah reached the political world of Israel without a trace of self-conscious explanation or any theory of validation.

The one thing that is clear is negative. The framers of the Mishnah nowhere claimed, implicitly or explicitly, that what they had written forms part of the Torah, enjoys the status of God's revelation to Moses at Sinai, or even systematically carries forward secondary exposition and application of what Moses wrote down in the wilderness. Later on, two hundred years beyond the closure of the Mishnah, the need to explain the standing and origin of the Mishnah led some to posit two things. First, God's revelation of the Torah at Sinai encompassed the Mishnah as much as Scripture. Second, the Mishnah was handed on through oral formulation and oral transmission from Sinai to the framers of the document as we have it. These two convictions, fully exposed in the ninth-century letter of Sherira, in fact emerge from the references of both Talmuds to the dual Torah. One part is in writing. The other was oral and now is in the Mishnah.

As for the Mishnah itself, however, it contains not a hint that anyone has heard any such tale. The earliest apologists for the Mishnah, represented in Abot and the Tosefta alike, know nothing of the fully realized myth of the dual Torah of Sinai. It may be that the authors of those documents stood too close to the Mishnah to see the Mishnah's standing as a problem or to recognize the task of accounting for its origins. Certainly they never refer to the Mishnah as something out there, or speak of the document as autonomous and complete. Only the two Talmuds reveal that conception—alongside their mythic explanation of where the document came from and why it should be obeyed. So the Yerushalmi marks the change. In any

event, the absence of explicit expression of such a claim in behalf of the Mishnah requires little specification. It is just not there.

But the absence of an implicit claim demands explanation. When ancient Jews wanted to gain for their writings the status of revelation, of torah, or at least to link what they thought to what the Torah had said, they could do one of four things. They could sign the name of a holy man of old, for instance, Adam, Enoch, Ezra. They could imitate the Hebrew style of Scripture. They could claim that God had spoken to them. They could, at the very least, cite a verse of Scripture and impute to the cited passage their own opinion. These four methods—pseudepigraphy, stylistic imitation (hence, forgery), claim of direct revelation from God, and eisegesis— found no favor with the Mishnah's framers. On the contrary, they signed no name to their book. Their Hebrew was new in its syntax and morphology, completely unlike that of the Mosaic writings of the Pentateuch. They never claimed that God had anything to do with their opinions. They rarely cited a verse of Scripture as authority. It follows that, whatever the authors of the Mishnah said about their document, the implicit character of the book tells us that they did not claim God had dictated or even approved what they had to say. Why not? The framers simply ignored all the validating conventions of the world in which they lived. And they failed to make explicit use of any others.

It follows that we do not know whether the Mishnah was supposed to be part of the Torah or to enjoy a clearly defined relationship to the existing Torah. We also do not know what else, if not the Torah, was meant to endow the Mishnah's laws with heavenly sanction. To state matters simply, we do not know what the framers of the Mishnah said they had made, nor do we know what the people who received and were supposed to obey the Mishnah thought they possessed.

A survey of the uses of the word Torah in the Mishnah, to be sure, provides us with an account of what the framers of the Mishnah, founders of what would emerge as Rabbinic Judaism, understood by that term. But it will not tell us how they related their own ideas to the Torah, nor shall we find a trace of evidence of that fully articulated way of life—the use of the word Torah to categorize and classify persons, places, things, relationships, all manner of abstractions—that we find fully exposed in some later writings.

True, the Mishnah places a high value upon studying the Torah and upon the status of the sage, as M. Hor. 3:8 illustrates.

> A. A priest takes precedence over a Levite, a Levite over an Israelite, an Israelite over a *mamzer* [one whose parents cannot legally marry by reason of consanguinity], a *mamzer* over a *Netin* [descendant of a Temple slave], a *Netin* over a proselyte, a proselyte over a freed slave.
> B. Under what circumstances?
> C. When all of them are equivalent.
> D. But if the *mamzer* was a disciple of a sage and a high priest was an *am haares* [that is, unlearned], the *mamzer* who is a disciple of a sage takes precedence over a high priest who is an *am haares*.

But that judgment, at M. Hor. 3:8D, distinctive though it is, cannot settle the question. All it shows is that the Mishnah pays due honor to the sage. But if the Mishnah does not claim to constitute part of the Torah, then what makes a sage a sage is not mastery of the Mishnah in particular. What we have in hand merely continues the established and familiar position of the wisdom writers of old. Wisdom is important. Knowledge of the Torah is definitive. But to maintain that position, one need hardly profess the fully articulated Torah-myth of Rabbinic Judaism. Proof of that fact, after all, is the character of the entire wisdom literature prior to the Mishnah itself.

So the issue is clearly drawn. It is not whether we find in the Mishnah exaggerated claims about the priority of the disciple of a sage. We do find such claims. The issue is whether we find in the Mishnah the assertion that whatever the sage has on the authority of his master goes back to Sinai. We seek a definitive view that what the sage says falls into the classification of Torah, just as what Scripture says constitutes Torah from God to Moses. That is what distinguishes wisdom from the Torah as it emerges in the context of Rabbinic Judaism. To state the outcome

in advance: we do not find the Torah in the Mishnah, and the Mishnah is not part of the Torah.

When the authors of the Mishnah surveyed the landscape of Israelite writings down to their own time, they saw only Sinai, that is, what we now know as Scripture. Based on the documents they cite or mention, we can say with certainty that they knew the Pentateuchal law. We may take for granted that they accepted as divine revelation also the Prophets and the Writings, to which they occasionally make reference. That they regarded as a single composition, that is, as revelation, the Torah, Prophets, and Writings appears from their references to the Torah, as a specific "book", and to a Torah-scroll. Accordingly, one important meaning associated with the word Torah, was concrete in the extreme. The Torah was a particular book or sets of books, regarded as holy, revealed to Moses at Sinai. That fact presents no surprise, since the Torah-scroll(s) had existed, it is generally assumed, for many centuries before the closure of the Mishnah in 200.

What is surprising is that everything from the formation of the canon of the Torah to their own day seems to have proved null in their eyes. Between the Mishnah and Mount Sinai lay a vast, empty plain. From the perspective of the Torah-myth as they must have known it, from Moses and the prophets, to before Judah the Patriarch, lay a great wasteland. So the concrete and physical meaning attaching to the word Torah, that is, the Torah revealed by God to Moses at Mount Sinai (including the books of the Prophets and the Writings), bore a contrary implication. Beyond The Torah there was no torah. Besides the Pentateuch, Prophets, and Writings, not only did no physical scroll deserve veneration, but no corpus of writings demanded obedience. So the very limited sense in which the words "the Torah" were used passed a stern judgment upon everything else, all the other writings that we know circulated widely, in which other Jews alleged that God had spoken and said "these things."

The range of the excluded possibilities that other Jews explored includes not only the Gospels (by 200 C.E. long since deemed to belong in the hands of outsiders), but secret books, history books, psalms, wisdom writings, rejected works of prophecy—everything excluded from any biblical canon by whoever determined there should be a canon. If the library of the Essenes at Qumran tells us what might have been, then we must regard as remarkably impoverished the (imaginary) library that would have served the authors of the Mishnah: The Book of Books, but nothing else. We seldom see so stern, so austere a vision of what commands the status of holy revelation among Judaisms over time. The tastes of the Mishnah's authors express a kind of literary iconoclasm, but with a difference. The literary icons did survive in the churches of Christendom. But in their own society and sacred setting, the judgment of Mishnah's authors would prevail from its time to ours. Nothing in the Judaisms of the heritage from the Hebrew Scripture's time to the Mishnah's day would survive the implacable rejection of the framers of the Mishnah, unless under Christian auspices or buried in caves. So when we take up that first and simplest meaning associated with the word Torah, "The Torah," we confront a stunning judgment: this and nothing else, this alone, this thing alone of its kind and no other thing of similar kind.

We confront more than a closing off of old possibilities, ancient claims to the status of revelation. For, at the other end, out of the Torah as a particular thing, a collection of books, would emerge a new and remarkably varied set of meanings. Possibilities first generated by the fundamental meaning imputed to the word Torah would demand realization. How so? Once the choice for the denotative meaning of the Torah became canonical in the narrowest possible sense, the ranges of connotative meaning imputed to the Torah stretched forth to an endless horizon. So the one concrete meaning made possible many abstract ones, all related to that single starting point. Only at the end shall we clearly grasp, in a single tableau, the entire vista of possibilities. But to begin with, it suffices to note that the Mishnah's theory of the Torah not only closed, but also opened, many paths.

**Torah in Tractate Abot:** Abot draws into the orbit of Torah-talk the names of authorities of the Mishnah. But even having taken that critical step, tractate Abot does not claim that the Mishnah forms part of the Torah. Nor, obviously, does the tractate know the doctrine of the two Torahs. Only in the Talmuds do we begin to find clear and ample evidence of that doctrine. Abot, moreover, does not understand by the word Torah much more than the framers of the Mishnah do. Not only does the established classification scheme remain intact, but the sense essentially replicates already familiar usages, producing no innovation. On the contrary, we see a diminution in the range of meanings.

Yet Abot in the aggregate does differ from the Mishnah. The difference has to do with the topic at hand. The other sixty-two tractates of the Mishnah contain Torah-sayings here and there. But they do not fall within the framework of Torah-discourse. They speak about other matters entirely. The consideration of the status of Torah rarely pertains to that speech. Abot, by contrast, says a great deal about Torah-study. The claim that Torah-study produces direct encounter with God forms part of Abot's thesis about the Torah. That claim, by itself, will hardly have surprised Israelite writers of wisdom books over a span of many centuries, whether those assembled in the Essene commune at Qumran, on the one side, or those represented in the pages of Proverbs and in many of the Psalms, or even the Deuteronomistic circle, on the other.

A second glance at tractate Abot, however, produces a surprising fact. In Abot, Torah is instrumental. The figure of the sage, his ideals and conduct, by contrast, forms the goal, focus, and center. To state matters simply: Abot regards study of Torah as what a sage does. The substance of Torah is what a sage says. That is so whether or not the saying relates to scriptural revelation. The content of the sayings attributed to sages endows those sayings with self-validating status. The sages usually do not quote verses of Scripture and explain them, nor do they speak in God's name. Yet, it is clear, sages talk Torah. What follows is that if a sage says something, what he says is Torah. More accurately, what he says falls into the classification of Torah. Accordingly, Abot treats Torah-learning as symptomatic, an indicator of the status of the sage, hence, as merely instrumental.

The simplest proof of that proposition lies in the recurrent formal structure of the document, the one thing the framers of the document never omit and always emphasize: (1) the name of the authority behind a saying, from Simeon the Righteous on downward, and (2) the connective-attributive "says." So what is important to the redactors is what they never have to tell us. Because a recognized sage makes a statement, what he says constitutes, in and of itself, a statement in the status of Torah. Let me set forth the opening statements of tractate Abot, so we shall see what "receiving" and "handing on" Torah consists of—that is to say, the contents of "Torah."

1:1 Moses received Torah at Sinai and handed it on to Joshua, Joshua to elders, and elders to prophets.
And prophets handed it on to the men of the great assembly.
They said three things:
"Be prudent in judgment.
"Raise up many disciples.
"Make a fence for the Torah."

1:2 Simeon the Righteous was one of the last survivors of the great assembly.
He would say:
"On three things does the world stand:
"On the Torah,
"and on the Temple service,
"and on deeds of loving-kindness."

1:3 Antigonos of Sokho received [the Torah] from Simeon the Righteous.
He would say,
"Do not be like servants who serve the master on condition of receiving a reward,
"but [be] like servants who serve the master not on condition of receiving a reward.
"And let the fear of Heaven be upon you."

1:4 Yose b. Yoezer of Seredah and Yosé b. Yohanan of Jerusalem received [it] from them.
Yose b. Yoezer says,
"Let your house be a gathering place for sages.
"And wallow in the dust of their feet.

"And drink in their words with gusto."

1:5 Yose b. Yohanan of Jerusalem says,
"Let your house be wide open.
"And seat the poor at your table ["make them members of your household"].
"And don't talk too much with women."
(He spoke of a man's wife, all the more so is the rule to be applied to the wife of one's fellow. In this regard did sages say, "So long as a man talks too much with a woman, he brings trouble on himself, wastes time better spent on studying Torah, and ends up an heir of Gehenna.")

1:6 Joshua b. Perahiah and Nittai the Arbelite received [it] from them.
Joshua b. Perahiah says,
"Set up a master for yourself.
"And get yourself a fellow disciple.
And give everybody the benefit of the doubt."

1:7 Nittai the Arbelite says,
"Keep away from a bad neighbor.
"And don't get involved with a wicked man.
And don't give up hope of retribution."

1:8 Judah b. Tabbai and Simeon b. Shatah received [it] from them.
Judah b. Tabbai says,
"Don't make yourself like one of those who make advocacy before judges [while you yourself are judging a case].
"And when the litigants stand before you, regard them as guilty.
"And when they leave you, regard them as acquitted (when they have accepted your judgment)."

1:9 Simeon b. Shatah says,
"Examine the witnesses with great care.
"And watch what you say,
"lest they learn from what you say how to lie."

To spell out what this means, let us look at the opening sentences. "Moses received Torah," and it reached "the Men of the Great Assembly." "The three things" those men said bear no resemblance to anything we find in written Scripture. They focus upon the life of sagacity—prudence, discipleship, a fence around the Torah. And, as we proceed, we find time and again that, while the word Torah stands for two things, divine revelation and the act of study of divine revelation, it produces a single effect, the transformation of unformed man into sage. One climax comes in Yohanan ben Zakkai's assertion that the purpose for which a man (an Israelite) was created was to study Torah, followed by his disciples' specifications of the most important things to be learned in the Torah. All of these pertain to the conduct of the wise man, the sage:

2:8   Rabban Yohanan b. Zakkai received [it] from Hillel and Shammai.

He would say,

"If you have learned much Torah, do not puff yourself up on that account, for it was for that purpose that you were created."

He had five disciples, and these are they: R. Eliezer b. Hyrcanus, R. Joshua b. Hananiah, R. Yosé the priest, R. Simeon b. Netanel, and R. Eleazar b. Arakh.

He would list their good qualities:

R. Eliezer b. Hyrcanus: A plastered well, which does not lose a drop of water.

R. Joshua: Happy is the one who gave birth to him,

R. Yosé: A pious man.

R. Simeon b. Netanel: A man who fears sin.

And R. Eleazar b. Arakh: A surging spring.

He would say, "If all the sages of Israel were on one side of the scale, and R. Eliezer b. Hyrcanus were on the other, he would outweigh all of them."

Abba Saul says in his name, "If all of the sages of Israel were on one side of the scale, and R. Eliezer b. Hyrcanus was also with them, and R. Eleazar [b. Arakh] were on the other side, he would outweigh all of them."

2:9   He said to them, "Go and see what is the straight path to which someone should stick."

R. Eliezer says, "A generous spirit."

R. Joshua says, "A good friend."

R. Yosé says, "A good neighbor."

R. Simeon says, "Foresight."

R. Eleazar says, "Good will."

He said to them, "I prefer the opinion of R. Eleazar b. Arakh, because in what he says is included everything you say."

He said to them, "Go out and see what is the bad road, which someone should avoid."

R. Eliezer says, "Envy."

R. Joshua says, "A bad friend."

R. Yosé says, "A bad neighbor."

R. Simeon says, "Defaulting on a loan."

(All the same is a loan owed to a human being and a loan owed to the Omnipresent, blessed be he, as it is said, The wicked borrows and does not pay back, but the righteous person deals graciously and hands over [what he owes] (Ps. 37:21].)

R. Eleazar says, "Bad will."

He said to them, "I prefer the opinion of R. Eleazar b. Arakh, because in what he says is included everything you say."

We have to locate the document's focus not on Torah but on the life of sagacity (including, to be sure, Torah-study). But what defines and delimits Torah? It is the sage himself. So we may simply state the tractate's definition of Torah: Torah is what a sage learns. Accordingly, the Mishnah contains Torah. It may well be thought to fall into the classification of Torah. But the reason, we recognize, is that authorities whose sayings are found in the Mishnah possess Torah from Sinai. What they say, we cannot overemphasize, is Torah. How do we know it? It is a fact validated by the association of what they way with their own names.

So we miss the real issue when we ask Abot to explain for us the status of the Mishnah or to provide a theory of a dual Torah. The principal point of insistence—the generative question—before the framers of Abot does not address the status of the Mishnah. And the instrumental status of the Torah, as well as of the Mishnah, lies in the net effect of their composition: the claim that through study of the Torah sages enter God's presence. So study of Torah serves a further goal, that of forming sages. The theory of Abot pertains to the religious standing and consequence of the learning of the sages. To be sure, a secondary effect of that theory endows with the status of revealed truth things sages say. But then it is because they say them, not because they have heard them in an endless chain back to Sinai. The fundament of truth is passed on through sagacity, not through already formulated and carefully memorized truths. That is why the single most important word in Abot also is the most common, the word "says."

At issue in Abot is not the Torah, but the authority of the sage. It is that standing that transforms a saying into a Torah-saying, or to state matters more appropriately, that places a saying into the classification of the Torah. Abot then stands as the first document of the doctrine that the sage embodies the Torah and is a holy man, like Moses "our rabbi," in the likeness and image of God. The beginning is to claim that a saying falls into the category of Torah if a sage says it as Torah. The end will be to view the sage himself as Torah incarnate.

**The Oral Torah, the Dual Torah:** The Mishnah is held in the Talmud of the Land of Israel to be equivalent to Scripture (Y. Hor. 3:5). But the Mishnah is not called Torah. Still, once the Mishnah entered the status of Scripture, it would take but a short step to a theory of the Mishnah as part of the revelation at Sinai—hence, oral Torah. In the first Talmud we find glimmerings of an effort to theorize in general, not merely in detail, about how specific teachings of the Mishnah relate to specific teachings of Scripture. The citing of scriptural proof-texts for the Mishnah's propositions, after all, would not have caused much surprise to the framers of the Mishnah; they themselves included such passages, though not often. But what conception of the Torah underlies such initiatives, and how do the Yerushalmi's sages propose to explain the phenomenon of the Mishnah as a whole? The answer is, these sages drew the outlines of the final solution to the problem of defining the Torah, distinguishing between the Torah in writing and the Torah in the medium of memory, further bearing the implication that the Mishnah formed part of that other Torah, the oral one.

The following passage of Y. Hag. 1:7 gives us one statement. It refers to the assertion at M. Hag. 1:8D that the laws on cultic cleanness presented in the Mishnah rest on deep and solid foundations in the Scripture.

A. [The laws of the Sabbath: R. Jonah said R. Hama bar Uqba raised the question in reference to M. Hag. 1:8D's view that there are many verses of Scripture on cleanness], "And lo, it is written only, 'Nevertheless a spring or a cistern holding water shall be clean; but whatever touches their carcass shall be unclean (Lev. 11:36). And from this verse you derive many laws. [So how can the Mishnah-passage say what it does about many verses for laws of cultic cleanness?]"

B. R. Zeira in the name of R. Yohanan: "If a law comes to hand and you do not know its nature, do not discard it for another one, for lo, many laws were stated to Moses at Sinai, and all of them have been embedded in the Mishnah."

The truly striking assertion appears when the Mishnah now is claimed to contain statements made by God to Moses. Just how these statements found their way into the Mishnah, and which passages of the Mishnah contain them, we do not know. That is hardly important, given the fundamental assertion at hand. The passage proceeds to a further, and far more consequential, proposition. It asserts that part of the Torah was written down, and part was preserved in memory and transmitted orally. In context, moreover, that distinction must encompass the Mishnah, thus explaining its origin as part of the Torah. Here is a clear and unmistakable expression of the distinction between two forms in which a single Torah was revealed and handed on at Mount Sinai, part in writing, part orally.

The Yerushalmi is the first document in the canon of the Judaism of the dual Torah to represent the Mishnah as equivalent to Scripture. And once the Mishnah entered the status of Scripture, it would take but a short step to a theory of the Mishnah as part of the revelation at Sinai—hence, oral Torah. Short of explicit allusion to Torah-in-writing and Torah-by-memory, which we find mainly in the Talmud of Babylonia, the ultimate theory of Torah of formative Judaism is at hand in what follows, Y. Hag. 1:7.V:

D. R. Zeirah in the name of R. Eleazar: "'Were I to write for him my laws by ten thousands, they would be regarded as a strange thing' (Hos. 8:12). Now is the greater part of the Torah written down? [Surely not. The oral part is much greater.] But more abundant are the matters that are derived by exegesis from the written [Torah] than those derived by exegesis from the oral [Torah]."

E. And is that so?

F. But more cherished are those matters that rest upon the written [Torah] than those that rest upon the oral [Torah]. . . .

J. R. Haggai in the name of R. Samuel bar Nahman, "Some teachings were handed on orally, and some things were handed on in writing, and we do not know which of them is the more precious. But on the basis of that which is written, "And the Lord said to Moses, Write these words; in accordance with these words I have made a covenant with you and with Israel' (Ex. 34:27), [we conclude] that the ones that are handed on orally are the more precious."

K. R. Yohanan and R. Yudan b. R. Simeon—

L. One [of the named authorities] said, "If you have kept what is preserved orally and also kept what is in writing, I shall make a covenant with you, and if not, I shall not make a covenant with you."

M. The other said, "If you have kept what is preserved orally and you have kept what is preserved in writing, you shall receive a reward, and if not, you shall not receive a reward."

N. [With reference to Deut. 9:10: "And on them was written according to all the words that the Lord spoke with you in the mount,"] said R. Joshua b. Levi, "He could have written, 'On them,' but wrote, 'And on them.' He could have written, 'All,' but wrote, 'According to all.' He could have written, 'Words,' but wrote 'The words.' [These then serve as three encompassing clauses, serving to include] Scripture, Mishnah, Talmud, laws, and lore. Even what an experienced student in the future is going to teach before his master already has been stated to Moses at Sinai."

O. What is the Scriptural basis for this view?

P. "There is no remembrance of former things, nor will there be any remembrance of later things yet to happen among those who come after" (Ec. 1:11).

Q. If someone says, "See, this is a new thing," his fellow will answer him, saying to him, "This has been around before us for a long time."

Here we have absolutely explicit evidence that people believed part of the Torah had been preserved not in writing but orally. Linking that part to the Mishnah remains a matter of implication. But it surely comes fairly close to the surface, when we are told that the Mishnah contains Torah-traditions revealed at Sinai. From that view it requires only a small step to the allegation that the Mishnah is part of the Torah, the oral part.

In the canonical documents up to the Yerushalmi, we look in vain for sayings or stories that fall into such a category. True, we may take for granted that everyone always believed that, in general, Israel would be saved by obedience to the Torah. That claim would not have surprised any Israelite writers from the first prophets down through the final redactors of the Pentateuch in the time of Ezra and onward through the next seven hundred years. But, in the rabbinical corpus from the Mishnah forward, the specific and concrete assertion that by taking up the scroll of the Torah and standing on the roof of one's house, confronting God in heaven, a sage in particular could take action against an invasion, protecting a city by his prayers—that kind of claim is not located in any composition surveyed so far.

What is critical here is the concrete assertion—the speciation of the genus—that in the hands of the sage and under conditions specified, the Torah may be utilized in pressing circumstances as his disciple, and the disciple of his disciple, used it. That is what is new.

**The sage as the Torah incarnate:** This stunningly new usage of Torah found in the Talmud of the Land of Israel emerges from a group of stories that treat the word Torah (whether scroll, contents, or act of study) as source and guarantor of salvation. Accordingly, evoking the word Torah forms the centerpiece of a theory of Israel's history, on the one side, and an account of the teleology of the Yerushalmi's entire system, on the other. Torah indeed has ceased to constitute a specific thing or even a category or classification when stories about studying the Torah yield not a judgment as to status (i.e., praise for the learned man) but promise for supernatural blessing now and salvation in time to come.

To the rabbis the principal salvific deed was to "study Torah," by which they meant memorizing Torah-sayings by constant repetition, mastering their meaning through discipleship to an established sage, and, as the Talmud itself amply testifies (for some sages) profound analytic inquiry into the meaning of those sayings. The innovation now is that this act of "study of Torah" imparts supernatural power of a material character. For example, by repeating words of Torah, the sage could ward off the angel of death and accomplish other kinds of miracles as well. So Torah-formulas served as incantations. Mastery of Torah transformed the man engaged in Torah-learning into a supernatural figure, who could do things ordinary folk could not do. The category of "Torah" had already vastly expanded so that through transformation of the Torah from a concrete thing to a symbol, a Torah-scroll could be compared to a man of Torah, namely, a rabbi. Now, once the principle had been established, that salvation would come from keeping God's will in general, as Israelite holy men had insisted for so many centuries, it was a small step for rabbis to identify their particular corpus of learning, namely, the Mishnah and associated sayings, with God's will expressed in Scripture, the universally acknowledged medium of revelation.

The key to the first Talmud's theory of the Torah lies in its conception of the sage, to which that theory is subordinate. Once the sage reaches his full apotheosis as Torah incarnate, then, but only then, the Torah becomes (also) a source of salvation in the present concrete formulation of the matter. That is why we traced the doctrine of the Torah in the salvific process by elaborate citation of stories about sages, living Torahs, exercising the supernatural power of the Torah, and serving, like the Torah itself, to reveal God's will. Since the sage embodied the Torah and gave the Torah, the Torah naturally came to stand for the principal source of Israel's salvation, not merely a scroll, on the one side, or a source of revelation, on the other. And that fact underlines two still more weighty ones. First, the Messiah, as we shall see, will be a sage. But, second, the systemic fulfillment comes with the attainment not of Torah but of merit—zekhut—which (among other things) the study of Torah secures for the learned man, as much as, but no more than, the wisdom of the chaste wife secures zekhut for such a woman.

**The formative history of the Torah in Rabbinic Judaism:** The history of the symbolization of the Torah, therefore, proceeds from its removal from the framework of material objects, even from the limitations of its own contents, to its transformation into something quite different and abstract, quite distinct from the document and its teachings. The Torah stands for this something more, specifically, when it comes to be identified with a living person, the sage, and endowed with those particular traits that the sage claimed for himself. While we cannot say that the process of symbolization leading to the pure abstraction at hand moved in easy stages, we may still point to the stations that had to be passed in sequence. The word Torah reached the apologists for the Mishnah in its long-established meanings: Torah-scroll, contents of the Torah-scroll.

But even in the Mishnah itself, these meanings provoked a secondary development, status of Torah as distinct from other (lower) status, hence, Torah-teaching in contra-distinction to scribal-teaching. With that small and simple step, the Torah ceased to denote only a concrete and material thing— a scroll and its contents. It now connoted an abstract matter of status. And once made abstract, the symbol entered a secondary history beyond all limits imposed by the concrete object, including its specific teachings, the Torah-scroll.

Abot stands at the beginning of this process. In the history of the word Torah as abstract symbol, a metaphor serving to sort out one abstract status from another regained concrete and material reality of a new order entirely. For the message of Abot, as we saw, was that the Torah served the sage. How so? The Torah indicated who was a sage and who was not. Accordingly, the apology of Abot for the Mishnah was that the Mishnah contained things sages had said. What sages said formed a chain of tradition extending back to Sinai. Hence it was equivalent to the Torah. The upshot is that words of sages enjoyed the status of the Torah. The small step beyond was to claim that what sages said was Torah, as much as what Scripture said was Torah.

A further small step (and the steps need not have been taken separately or in the order here suggested) moved matters to the position that there were two forms in which the Torah reached Israel: one [Torah] in writing, the other [Torah] handed on orally, that is, in memory. The final step, fully revealed in the Talmud at hand, brought the conception of Torah to its logical conclusion: what the sage said was in the status of the Torah, was Torah, because the sage was Torah incarnate. So the abstract symbol now became concrete and material once more. We recognize the many, diverse ways in which the Talmud stated that conviction. Every passage in which knowledge of the Torah yields power over this world and the next, capacity to coerce to the sage's will the natural and supernatural worlds alike, rests upon the same viewpoint.

The first Talmud's theory of the Torah carries us through several stages in the processes of the symbolization of the word Torah. First transformed from something material and concrete into something abstract and beyond all metaphor, the word Torah finally emerged once more in a concrete aspect, now as the encompassing and universal mode of stating the whole doctrine, all at once, of Judaism in its formative age. While both the national and the individual dimensions of salvation mark the measure of the word Torah in the Babylonian Talmud, the national proves the more interesting. For the notion of private salvation through "Torah" study and practice, of which we hear much, presents no surprise. When, by contrast, we find God himself saying, "If a man occupies himself with the study of Torah works of charity, and prays with the community, I account it to him as if he had redeemed me and my children from among the nations of the world" (B. Ber. 8A), we confront a concept beyond the imagination of the framers of Abot and the other compositions of that circle. That forms the final step in the historical evolution of the Torah into a powerful instrument of theological regeneration. It was at this point that the doctrine of the dual Torah reached its definitive statement, expressed in the passage at B. Shab. 31A (= The Fathers According to Rabbi Nathan XV:V.1):

11.A. *Our rabbis have taught on Tannaite authority:*

B. There was the incident of a certain gentile who came before Shammai. He said to him, "'How many Torahs do you have?"

C. He said to him, "Two, one in writing, one memorized."

D. He said to him, "As to the one in writing, I believe you. As to the memorized one, I do not believe you. Convert me on condition that you will teach me only the Torah that is in writing."

E. He rebuked him and threw him out.

F. He came before Hillel. He said to him, *"Convert me."* [ARN: My lord, how many Torahs were given?" He said to him, "Two, one in writing, one memorized." He said to him, "As to the one in writing, I believe you. As to the memorized one, I do not believe you."]

G. *On the first day he said to him, "Alef, bet, gimel, dalet." The next day he reversed the order on him.*

H. He said to him, "Well, yesterday, didn't you say it differently?"

 I. He said to him, "Didn't you depend on me then? Then depend on me when it comes to the fact of the memorized Torah too." [ARN: He said to him, "My son, sit." He wrote for him, *Alef, bet.* He said to him, "What is this?" He said to him, "An *alef.*" He said to him, "This is not an *alef* but a *bet.*" He said to him, "What is this?" He said to him, *"Bet."* He said to him, "This is not a *bet* but a *gimel.*" He said to him, "'How do you know that this is an *alef* and this a *bet* and this a *gimel*? But that is what our ancestors have handed over to us—the tradition that this is an *alef,* this a *bet,* this a *gimel.* Just as you have accepted this teaching in good faith, so accept the other in good faith."]

That is the point at which the Mishnah was fully absorbed into the Torah as a whole and given its rightful place even in the prophetic heritage, as its laws were correlated with the virtues of the moral life, as B. Shab. 31a states:

14.A. *Said R. Simeon b. Laqish, "What is the meaning of the verse of Scripture, 'And there shall be faith in your times, strength, salvation, wisdom, and knowledge' (Is. 33:6)?*

B. "'faith:' this refers to the Mishnah-division of Seeds.

C. "'in your times:' this refers to the Mishnah-division of Holy Seasons.
D. "'strength:' this refers to the Mishnah-division of Women.
E. "salvation:' this refers to the Mishnah-division of Damages.
F. "wisdom:' this refers to the Mishnah-division of Holy Things.
G. "'and knowledge:' this refers to the Mishnah-division of Purities.
H. "Nonetheless: 'the fear of the Lord is his treasure' (Is. 33:6)."

Now the message of Isaiah provides a categorical structure to encompass the laws of Judah the Patriarch, and the Torah is made whole. No wonder that the sage, in his person, could stand for the unity of what to begin with was eternally one and the same.

JACOB NEUSNER

**TRADITION IN JUDAISM:** The term tradition generally signifies the theological and ritual content of a religion, its beliefs, doctrines, cultural values, moral standards, and especially the particular behaviors through which individuals and communities express their participation in the religion. Tradition thus may refer to everything from modes of dress and choices of cuisine to language and approaches to rearing children. Insofar as these elements of communal life are transmitted from generation to generation, the term tradition signifies not only the content of the religious culture but also the process through which that culture is passed on from generation to generation. The designation of religious beliefs and practices as tradition implies that religious culture preserves a past way of life, continuously transmitted to contemporary times.[1]

In accordance with this definition, Judaism associates the term tradition with its concept of Torah, that is, the code of law and practice understood to have been revealed by God to Moses at Sinai and subsequently transmitted—whether in writing or by word of mouth or by example—from generation to generation. Especially insofar as the Hebrew Bible, the written component of that revelation, does not fully detail how the content of the covenant with God is to be enacted in the everyday life of the Jew, in conceiving of tradition, Judaism always refers to the in-

terpretation of that written law, embodied in what it refers to as Oral Torah. Like the Written Torah, this oral law is understood to derive from God's revelation to Moses at Sinai. It therefore is viewed as equal in authority and holiness to the Written Torah, represented by the Pentateuch as well as the other writings of the Hebrew Scriptures.

The Oral Torah appropriately is referred to as "tradition" in both of the two senses already described. First, it defines in exacting detail the practices, attitudes, theologies, and life styles that define Judaism, detailing, that is, the "tradition" by which Jews are to lead their lives. Second, the Oral Law is understood to have been originally transmitted orally and, even once committed to writing, it has been the subject of a continual process of analysis and interpretation through which it is handed down from age to age. Oral Torah therefore embodies the concept of tradition as a process of transmission, through which new generations receive and accept the ways of life of prior ages but also reevaluate, add to, and revise those same practices, as appropriate to and necessary within their particular situation in each age and context.

**The concept of oral tradition:** As just explained, Judaism maintains that God's revelation to Moses at Sinai, described in the Book of Exodus, contained two distinct parts. One component was the written law, embodied in the text of the Pentateuch. This component was transmitted in writing and made accessible to all of the people of Israel. The other part was the Oral Law, which was formulated for memorization and transmitted orally by successive generations of sages. Judaism holds that God taught the oral tradition to Moses, who repeated it to Joshua. After Joshua, the chain of tradition lists "elders" and the Biblical prophets and states that ultimately the oral materials were passed into the hands of Rabbinic authorities (M. Ab. 1:1). To assure that this tradition of revelation would not be lost as a result of war, national strife, or other physical or intellectual calamity, beginning in the second century C.E. the rabbis codified the oral materials and preserved them in written form.

The first and principal document of the

Oral Torah, the Mishnah, is a Hebrew-language law code, edited in the land of Israel ca. 200 C.E., but containing statements attributed to rabbis who flourished over the preceding two hundred years. Other Rabbinic texts, including the Tosefta, Midrashic documents, and the Talmuds of the land of Israel and of Babylonia are deemed also to embody the originally oral revelation.[2] The Rabbinic theory of Oral Torah thus holds that statements and principles expressed by sages who lived over a period of close to six hundred years preserve teachings that derive from God's original revelation to Moses at Sinai.

In this theory, the Written and Oral Torahs are part of a single, uniform revelation and are, accordingly, of equal authority and importance. When a second century rabbi in the Mishnah or a fifth century sage in the Midrash or Talmud responds to a discussion or question from his own day, his judgment does not comprise his own thinking and analysis. Rather, it is part and parcel of the divine revelation of Torah at Sinai. Even though the sage's comment is expressed in his own words and responds to a question or issue raised in his own day, it is understood to derive, in detail, from what God told Moses at the time of the original revelation. The statement in every respect has the authority of divine revelation.

The notion of the closed transmission of an esoteric tradition functions polemically within Rabbinic Judaism. The rabbis' claim to possess an otherwise unknown component of God's revelation legitimates Rabbinic authority and promotes the Israelite people's acceptance of Rabbinic leadership. The Rabbinic concept of an oral tradition claims that Rabbinic leaders are direct successors to Moses, whom Rabbinic authorities call "our rabbi," thus designating him the first Rabbinic sage. According to this notion of oral tradition, furthermore, only under Rabbinic guidance can the Israelite people correctly observe God's will. The Written Torah, available to all of Israel, contains only half of God's revelation. Access to the written Scriptures alone does not provide the people with all of the information needed properly to observe the law. Correct observance is pos-

sible only under the guidance of Rabbinic authorities, who, in the Oral Torah, have the revealed key to understanding the written Scripture. So from the earliest period in the emergence of Rabbinic Judaism, the concept of an oral tradition is essential to the rabbis' program for the people of Israel.

In comprehending the emergence of this concept of tradition in Judaism, we should be clear that the idea of oral tradition described here is uniquely Rabbinic. Other post-biblical Jewish writings know nothing comparable. This is evident, for instance, in Josephus' descriptions of the Pharisees, whom the later rabbis understand to be the direct recipients and transmitters of the oral tradition. In his first book, *The Jewish War*, Josephus says nothing about the Pharisees' knowledge of inherited traditions. He states only that, of the several Jewish philosophical schools, the Pharisees are "considered the more accurate interpreters of the laws" (1:97).[3] Josephus' later work, *Antiquities*, reworks his earlier descriptions, apparently to encourage the Roman government to support the Pharisees as leaders of the Jewish people.[4] To substantiate his case that the Pharisees are the nation's legitimate rulers, Josephus observes that they preserve and follow certain traditions developed in accordance with their distinctive philosophical doctrine (13:171):

> They follow the guidance of that which their doctrine has selected and transmitted as good, attaching the chief importance to the observance of those commandments which it has seen fit to dictate to them.[5]

Elsewhere, Josephus is explicit that, in that they accept teachings that are not explicitly stated in Scripture, the Pharisees are different from the Sadducees (*Antiquities* 13:297):

> For the present I wish merely to explain that the Pharisees had passed on to the people certain regulations handed down by former generations and not recorded in the Laws of Moses, for which reason they are rejected by the Sadducaean group, who hold that only those regulations should be considered valid which were written down (in Scripture), and that those which had been handed down by former generations need not be observed.[6]

The perspective attributed to the Pharisees, that the Jews should preserve and follow certain commandments or practices received from past generations, is in line with the general function of tradition within religious cultures. The same general idea is found in Philo, who reflects upon the Jews' adherence to laws and traditions handed down from Moses, their law-giver. But these ideas are quite different from the notion of tradition as it emerges in Rabbinic Judaism, which claims that *all* of the legal and exegetical dicta of a particular group have been passed down by tradition and derive, ultimately, from divine revelation. Outside of the Rabbinic writings, such a notion is absent from early Jewish discussions of tradition, which, as in the case of Josephus, are quite clear that what makes "tradition" unique is that it transmits rules and practices that derive from the people and not directly from revelation.

The Rabbinic theory of oral tradition thus legitimates all Rabbinic statements about the meaning of Scripture and the content of revelation. Under this theory, Rabbinic interpretations have the authority of the word of God.[7] At the same time, the Rabbinic concept of Oral Torah de-legitimizes interpretations that derive from outside of Rabbinic circles. These are viewed as (simply) the work of fallible human intellect and are distinguished from the interpretations of the rabbis, the product of whose intellect is held to comprise the word of God as revealed at Sinai. By establishing the rabbis as the only authoritative source for correct practice and understanding of the divine word, the Rabbinic theory of oral tradition promotes and justifies the rabbis' spiritual and political leadership over the Israelite people. As a result, within Judaism, all rules of law and practice are determined by Rabbinic study of the received tradition, not by independent examination and analysis of the written Torah, performed, for instance, by lay people, or carried out without reference to the existing body of rabbinical teachings.

**The character and antiquity of the oral tradition:** If we are to comprehend the actual processes through which tradition emerges in Judaism, on the one hand, and is comprehended by Jews, on the other, then we must consider the historicity of the rabbis'

claims regarding Oral Torah. For as we shall see, the nature and content of the documents of Rabbinic Judaism lead to conclusions quite different from those suggested by the Rabbinic ideology that their teachings actually originate in hoary antiquity. What the rabbis conceive of as an oral tradition originating at Sinai in fact takes the form of arguments and discussions among Rabbinic sages of the first centuries, just as later amplifications of this Rabbinic tradition continue to take place in every age and place in which Jewish communities exist. The earliest Rabbinic discussions, found in the Mishnah, took place for the most part in the aftermath of the destruction of the Jerusalem-Temple in 70 C.E. and the failed Bar Kokhba revolt of 133-135 C.E. During this decisive period in Jewish history, Rabbinic sages studied and interpreted Scripture, working out a program of ritual and legal practice that eventually would shape Judaism according to the rabbis' own ideals and aspirations. By the end of the Mishnaic period, the rabbis came to consider the results of their deliberations to be part of a divinely revealed oral tradition. But from the principles, rules, and issues actually at play in the Rabbinic documents, it is apparent that this Oral Torah is the product of the rabbis' own day and of their own distinctive attitudes and philosophies.[8] To illustrate this point, let us examine M. Ber. 1:1:

A. From what time may they recite the Shema-prayer in the evening?

B. From the hour that the priests enter [their homes] to eat their heave offering,

C. "until the end of the first watch"—the words of Rabbi Eliezer.

D. But sages say, "Until midnight."

E. Rabban Gamaliel says, "Until the rise of dawn."

F. There was an incident: His [that is, Gamaliel's] sons returned from a banquet hall [after midnight].

G. They said to him, "We did not [yet] recite the Shema."

H. He said to them, "If the dawn has not yet risen, you are obligated to recite [the Shema].

I. "And [this applies] not only [in] this [case]. Rather, [as regards] all [commandments] which sages said [may be performed] 'Until midnight,' the obligation [to perform them persists] until the rise of dawn."

J. [For example] the offering of the fats and entrails—their obligation [persists] until the rise of dawn [see Lev. 1:9, 3:3-5].

K. And all [sacrifices] which must be eaten within one day, the obligation [to eat them persists] until the rise of dawn.

L. If so why did sages [D] say [that these actions may be performed only] until midnight?

M. In order to protect man from sin.

Rabbinic sages discuss the time frame within which the Shema, an obligatory prayer, must be recited. As presented here, this issue clearly was live in the period of the discussion's named authorities, the early second century C.E. Since the matter is still under dispute, it appears hardly to represent the end product of a tradition of revealed law, intended by God to define exactly how the rules of the Written Torah are to be carried out. The Shema-prayer—although derived from passages of Scripture—is known as a liturgical formulation only from the Rabbinic literature itself. Accordingly, there is no reason to posit a long history of legislation concerning its recitation. And if there were an existing "tradition" that informed people in general of what they should do, that tradition appears to be ignored here.

While Eliezer, B-C, suggests Temple-practice as the guide to answering A's question, neither he nor the other cited authorities argue or imply that these positions represent the way things always—or even recently—had been done. Quite to the contrary, L-M explains that the opinion of sages (that is, anonymous Rabbinic authorities), D, is not meant to represent the true law at all. These unnamed authorities give an early time—midnight—for completion of the requirement, in order to prevent people from becoming lax and failing to fulfill their obligation. So here matters are explicit: the sages do not simply repeat what they know to be a revealed law, passed on through tradition. Rather, they intentionally refrain from indicating the correct parameters for proper practice, preferring, instead, to give their own reasoned opinion as to what the people should be taught.

What this means is that, in the hands of the rabbis, traditions of practice are not only transmitted but also created. In the case at hand, the notion that the Shema-prayer should be recited well before the point by which it in fact *must* be said becomes an authoritative statement of how Jews centuries later will actually do things. So we see the formation of tradition in Judaism as a live process of interpretation of existing texts.

The point of this observation must be clearly stated. It is not that traditions regarding ritual practice and the meaning of Scripture did not exist in late antiquity. Certainly the communal and religious life of the Jews depended upon traditions of how specific biblical precepts would be followed. Observance of the nation's religion required determinations of how ritual and social activities never discussed in Scripture at all were to be done. So the point is not that Jews did not pass on "traditions" from age to age. It is, rather, that, so far as the literary evidence indicates, in creating what turned out to be the foundation of all later forms of Judaism, the rabbis did not simply take up and preserve all of these traditions, making them significant components of their own legislation. Rather than a compendium of prior oral traditions, the Mishnah and all later Rabbinic writings, as they have come down to us, are the independent intellectual and literary creations of Rabbinic circles.

In sum, the documents of Rabbinic Judaism do not simply preserve an ancient tradition of law. Rather, they develop themes and ideas suggested by Scripture and worked out by the rabbis themselves. In this way, Jewish practice, while anchored in antecedent texts and inherited modes of behavior, also comprises a live and evolving tradition. As a result of the intellectual activities of rabbis and the fluid attitudes of Jews, Jewish beliefs and practices in each age were shaped by the changing needs of the Jews themselves. This was the case even as the evolving tradition always was authenticated by the understanding that each of its practices and beliefs was part and parcel of the original revelation at Sinai.

**The concept of tradition in the evolution of Rabbinic Judaism:** Within Rabbinic Judaism as it developed in Talmudic and post-Talmudic times, the concept of tradition took on an added significance, reflected in the general term *masoret*, a word based on the biblical Hebrew root 'SR, meaning to bind or imprison. This root yields the biblical Hebrew term *masoret*, found at Ezek. 20:37, which refers to the "bond of the covenant"[9] into which God promises to return the rebellious people of Israel. This sense of the term tradition, as a bond or fetter that assures correct practice of the law, appears as well in Rabbinic sources. Aqiba in particular, calls tradition a "fence around the Torah" (M. Ab. 3:13), reflecting the frequent implementation of restrictive measures that assure compliance with the actual word of the Torah (as we saw already at M. Ber. 1:1, above). Tradition, in this interpretation, protects people from violating the Torah.

But in post-biblical Hebrew, a secondary root—*MSR*[10]—emerged from 'SR, a term that expresses specifically the sense of "transmission" or "handing on." This root appears in its verbal form in references to the chain of tradition through which a statement of Torah is passed from age to age. As a noun, the Talmudic literature employs this term to refer to the variety of practices, rituals, and laws described in this transmitted knowledge. "Tradition" thus comes to encompass both that which is understood to derive directly from the written or oral Torah and also to embrace customs, folkways, and other practices or understandings that, while not explicitly derived from Torah, are comprehended as true or obligatory by virtue of their acceptance by the people.

B. Sot. 10b presents an example of an interpretation of Scripture accepted as authoritative because it derives from past generations. This is the case even though, apparently, it had not been verified through Scriptural exegesis: "R. Levi said, 'It is a tradition in our possession from our ancestors that Amoz [Isaiah's father] and Amaziah [a king of Judah] were brothers.'" Similarly, B. R.H. 31a distinguishes that which is known through the exegesis of Scripture from that

which has another source, which is called "tradition:"

> A. Said Rab Judah bar Idi said R. Yohanan, "The divine presence [Shechina] made ten journeys [in leaving Israel prior to the destruction of the first Temple].
> B. "[This we know from] Scripture.
> C. "And corresponding to these [stages], the Sanhedrin was exiled [successively to ten places of banishment].
> D. "[This we know from] tradition."

The point of these passages is that authoritative knowledge can emerge from the intellectual activities of the people, separate from revelation or even from the direct exegesis of Scripture or other historical records. Similarly, the Talmud understands it to be possible for that which begins simply as popular behaviors eventually to take on the status of law. This is exemplified at B. Hul. 63b, which reports on a dietary practice that is not prescribed by Torah but that has, by virtue of the practice of the people, taken on the standing of law. The issue of the passage emerges from the fact that Scripture lists the birds that are considered unclean and therefore forbidden for consumption but does not specifically enumerate which birds are clean and may be eaten. How therefore do we know what sorts of fowl may be consumed?

> A. Said R. Isaac, "Birds [are deemed] clean [so as to be permitted] for consumption on the basis of tradition.
> B. "A hunter is believed when he says, 'My master transmitted to me that this bird is clean.'"
> C. Said R. Yohanan, "[This is the case] provided that he was familiar with them [that is, birds] and their nomenclature."
> D. R. Zera asked, "[At B does] 'his master' [refer to] a sage or a hunter?"
> E. Come and learn, for said R. Yohanan, "This [B] applies provided he was familiar with them [that is, birds] and their nomenclature."
> F. Now if you say, granted, "his master" refers to a hunter, this makes sense, [since a hunter would in fact be familiar both with birds and their nomenclature].
> G. But if you say "his master" refers to a sage, granted, he would have learned their nomenclature, but would he actually know [that is, recognize] them [when he saw one in the wild]?
> H. No!

I. Therefore you must learn from this: "his master" refers to a hunter!

J. So you must learn from this.

The passage makes two important points concerning the emergence of cultural practices, in this case, the determination of what foods are permitted or forbidden. The first point is the Talmud's recognition that not all practices derive directly from Scripture or even can be validated through reference to the Bible. The question of what sorts of birds are permitted for consumption, rather, is determined by the tradition of practice within the community, a tradition validated by consistency over time rather than direct support in the biblical text. Associated with this is the point made here at D-J. The legitimate source of knowledge of the correct tradition here is not the Rabbinic sage, the master of Torah learning, at all. It is rather the common person, here the hunter who knows which birds people in fact have deemed over time to be clean. The determination of the hunter is legitimated not by reference to holy books or rabbinical courts but by the fact that his knowledge derives from past generations of hunters. It represents a tradition of community practice and so is both legitimate and incumbent upon all members of the community.

The Talmudic literature additionally recognizes the existence of practices, initiated to meet some particular need, that, as a result of their acceptance by successive generations of Jews, have become authoritative and immutable. Even when the original impetus for their practice no longer exists, these practices remain binding. This is the case, for instance, with the diaspora custom of observing two days of festivals, a custom that originally was necessitated by the determination of the calendar through observation of the new moon in the land of Israel. Since fixing the beginning of the month depended upon a witness's actual observation of the new moon, far-flung diaspora communities could not be informed of the correct date in time to assure that they could celebrate the festival on the correct day. Two-day observances accordingly were instituted, allowing the celebration to span the actual day and one adjacent day, although the community involved would not know which was which. At issue is the status of such two day observances after the calendar was fixed, such that observation of the moon was no longer necessary. If the diaspora communities knew well in advance the correct day on which to observe the festival, did they still need to observe two days? B. Bes. 4b holds that, because of the power of tradition, they do:

A. And now that we are knowledgeable in the fixing of [the date of] the new moon, what is the reason that we [continue to] observe two [festival] days?

B. It is because they sent word from there [in the land of Israel, stating], "Be careful [to follow] the customs of your ancestors [that have come down] into your hands.

C. "At time [the government] might enforce [a period of] religious persecution [preventing study of the texts needed to calculate the calendar] and, [should you not maintain the tradition of two festival days], this will cause confusion."

The passage argues in favor of continued acceptance of a seemingly outdated practice. This practice, a custom that has come down through the generations, has taken on an importance and immutability that overshadows the original reasons for its institution. While the original reason for this practice no longer applies, it is now in the status of a tradition, and therefore can no longer can be annulled. C offers an excuse for this power of tradition: things *might* go back to the way they once were, so that the traditional practice might again become necessary. But even in proposing this reasoning, the Talmud makes clear its authorities' own understanding that the practice in fact currently is unnecessary and has no special spiritual or religious significance. Its validity derives first and foremost from the fact that it is what Jews for generations have done, secondarily that it might be needed again. If the latter reason were decisive, by contrast, it could be argued that the practice should in fact currently be dropped, to be taken up again only if it actually is again needed.

In the thinking of Talmudic Judaism, people's behaviors over time thus define the folkways according to which they and subsequent generations must lead their lives. Once created, traditions of practice and behavior take on a permanence and immutability that defines them as part of the essence of Judaism, the tradition by which all Jews are to lead their lives. The Talmud accordingly is explicit that, to know the law, one should examine what the people actually do (B. Ber. 45a, top) and that, when a custom conflicts with an established legal practice, the custom frequently takes precedence (Soferim 14:18). Thus God is understood to have buried Moses in accord not with the law but with accepted practice (B. San. 46a), and even the messengers from God who visited Abraham partook of the meal he prepared (Gen. 18) only so as to follow the particular custom of Abraham's locale (B. B.M. 86b). Divine messengers, of course, do not really need to eat at all.

**The function of tradition in medieval Jewish society:** We see in the Talmudic literature the extent to which, in determining proper ritual practices, the Jewish community increasingly resorted to tradition, that is, lent authority to practices that emerged in the day-to-day life of the Jewish people but that could not be directly derived from the authoritative codes of law, whether Scripture or the Rabbinic literature. These community customs were granted an authority of almost equal weight to rules derived directly from the Written Law (see Shulhan Aruch, Yoreh Deah, 376, 4, Isserles' gloss). Thus Prov. 22:28's directive, "Remove not the ancient landmark which your fathers have set" was understood to refer to the inherited customs of the Jewish people, which were to be accepted and followed like all other dictates of the Torah.

This aspect of the development of Jewish communal practice was particularly important in medieval Jewish society, where problems in Jewish communal self-rule added an additional dimension to the problem of determining proper practice. The existing law neither covered all areas of communal life nor always provided appropriate precedents for deriving new laws. Accordingly, emerging community practice often was accepted as legitimate on the basis of its constituting an accepted custom—*minhag*—of the community. Such practices were not and could not be justified through reference to the explicit law of Torah. Their authority, rather, derived from their coming to be accepted by the community itself as appropriate and fair responses to specific problems.

Jacob Katz explains how this process of the adaptation of new modes of practice worked for the particular example of the allocation of the burden of a poll tax among different groups in the Jewish community in the late middle ages:[11]

> Legal precedents and principles were unable to provide for an equitable distribution of the tax burden among different groups and classes without disputes and clashes. The *kehilla* executive body had to combat the pressure exerted by various interested parties by use of concepts of the general and local tradition. The experts in religious law represented the principles of tradition, and they sometimes issued decisions on specific points of dispute. But, in general, these were matters in which they had difficulty in basing their decisions on Jewish law. Instead of issuing binding judgments, they would propose a compromise or explicitly refer a decision to the *kehilla* leaders. The decision was reached as a result of the operation of pressure groups, and it was executed through the coercive powers vested in the communal leaders.

The problem for the community was equitably to resolve current problems that had not been faced in the inherited legal and exegetical literature. In these cases, reason and, ultimately, the coercive powers of community leaders, rather than inherited practices, defined the approach the community would take. Accepted and promoted by religious leaders, this approach in turn ultimately would be vested with the authority of tradition.

At the same time that this approach resolved many problems in communal self-governance and other areas of religious and social practice, it led in the post-Talmudic period to significant problems. For as the centers of Jewish life spread throughout medieval Europe, local customs became more and more divergent. While the Jewish communal leaders of the seventh through eleventh centuries, the Geonim, generally advocated the retention of communal custom, the proliferation of such practices soon created problems:[12]

> In the course of time the customs increased in number; and the differences between them became very marked and portended danger of schism. Superstitions prevalent among the people of the dark ages frequently crept in among Jewish usages; and the Rabbis then became alarmed, and began to raise their voices against the multiplicity of customs. Maimonides vigorously decried this "minhag sickness," as Güdemann calls it, and Rabbenu Jacob Tam (1100-1171) said, in his epigrammatic style, that "minhag," when inverted, spells "gehinnam"; and that if fools are accustomed to do certain things, it does not follow that the wise should do likewise. During the thirteenth and fourteenth centuries many scholars endeavored to trace the origin of and the reason for the different customs; and a critical spirit prevailed even in the response of that period. This effort, the personal example of famous Rabbis, and the synods that assembled at different places during that period, greatly helped toward introducing some uniformity in Jewish customs. The most important figure in this age is MhRIL, or Rabbi Jacob Levi Molin, who was born in the middle of the fourteenth century in Mayence and died in Worms in 1427. His book on minhagim, which was published after his death, became the standard for many generations for synagogal and communal customs.

The result of these medieval developments was the codification of what had emerged initially as the customary practices of common people. While hardly completely eradicating the differences between local customs of nearby communities, this codification established a method of evaluating the legitimacy of specific practices so as to determine what was and was not an accepted and appropriate aspect of Jewish life.[13] Thus, while allowing regional differences to remain, developments within medieval and post-medieval Jewish law also have assured that Jewish law, and with it, Jewish custom, can be understood to represent what the Rabbinic tradition had always stood for, a single truth and mode of communal and personal living that reflect God's way as revealed in Torah.

## Notes

[1] On the preceding, see Leon Yagod, "Tradition," in *EJ*, vol. 15, col. 1308.

[2] For detailed descriptions of these literatures see RABBINIC JUDAISM. FORMATIVE CANON OF.

[3] H. Thackeray, translator, *The Jewish War* (Cambridge, 1956), p. 385.

[4] Morton Smith, "Palestinian Judaism in the First Centuries," in Moshe Davis, ed., *Israel: Its Role in Civilization* (New York, 1956), p. 81.

[5] Translation: R. Marcus, *Antiquities*. (Cambridge, 1957), vol. VII, p. 311.

[6] Pp. 377. See similarly Mark 7:8, where Jesus states that the Pharisees "leave the commandment of God, and hold fast the tradition of men." The later rabbis, by contrast, hold that this "tradition" has the same ultimate source, and hence the same validity, as the written law.

[7] That Rabbinic teaching is part and parcel of God's revelation to Moses at Sinai is explicitly asserted in the chain of tradition at M. Ab. 1:1ff. For a full discussion of this passage, see TORAH IN JUDAISM, THE CLASSICAL STATEMENT.

[8] For a complete and detailed account of this topic, see TORAH IN JUDAISM, THE CLASSICAL STATEMENT.

[9] The Septuagint for this verse reads, "I will let you go in by number." RSV here translates the Greek rather than the Hebrew. On this term, see Francis Brown, et al., *A Hebrew and English Lexicon of the Old Testament* (Oxford, reprint, 1974), p. 64, s.v., *msrt*.

[10] In its few biblical Hebrew appearances, this root means "to deliver up" or to "offer," especially in the sense of "to offer (commit) a transgression against" (Num. 31:16). See Brown, ibid., p. 588, s.v., *msr*.

[11] Jacob Katz, *Tradition and Crisis: Jewish Society at the End of the Middle Ages* (New York, 1958), pp. 93-94.

[12] Julius H. Greenstone, "Custom," in *Jewish Encyclopedia* (New York, reprint, n.d.), vol. IV, p. 397.

[13] Indeed, despite this codification of customary practices, a basic and consequential division remains between Jews who adhere to Spanish and Portuguese ritual (Sephardim) and those who follow the German and Polish practices (Ashkenazim). On the history and practices of these forms of Judaism see JUDAISM, HISTORY OF. PT. V.B. JUDAISM IN MODERN TIMES IN THE MUSLIM WORLD and EASTERN EUROPE, PRACTICE OF JUDAISM IN.

ALAN J. AVERY-PECK

# V

**VIRTUE IN FORMATIVE JUDAISM:** For Judaism, the account of virtue begins in the Torah's picture of world order based on God's virtue, not the virtue of humanity. God's traits of justice and equity, love and compassion, form the model for those of God's creatures. Moreover, the Torah knows humanity as the children of Adam via Noah to Abraham. Accordingly, Judaism in its classical statement treats virtue as a component of a much larger doctrine that concerns the meaning of the life of humanity. The Torah tells the story of humanity's life from creation through Sinai to redemption at the end of time, and from birth to the grave and ultimate resurrection. Within that doctrine, what Judaism identifies as virtue in men and women finds its context.

Who "we"—humanity—really are is simply said: we are "children of Adam and Eve, descendants of Noah," and, for the supernatural social entity Scripture knows as "Israel," children of Abraham and Sarah as well." Using the language, "children of . . .," conveys the meaning, "modeled after." As soon as we introduce the name of Adam and Eve—created by God "in our image-after our likeness" (Gen. 1:26), the matter of virtue finds its context in Adam's and Eve's relationship with God. That relationship was disrupted by Adam's and Eve's disobedience to God's commandment. So who are we really? On the one side, like Adam and Eve, we too are in God's image, after God's likeness. In their model, we by our nature both enjoy free will and disobey God's commandments.

Consequently, virtue stands for those traits that bring about reconciliation between Adam and Eve and God, and vice for those that disrupt the relationship. So the working-system of the Torah finds its dynamic in the struggle between God's plan for creation—to create a perfect world of justice—and the free will of humanity. All virtuous traits then find their place within that encompassing vision that explains who we are by telling the story of creation culminating in Adam, Eve, and Eden.

That is to say, in Judaism "we" are Adam and Eve, fallen from Eden, and, when possessed of the Torah, able to regain Eden. All virtue is defined in that context, and the story that Scripture tells sets forth that context.

When sages wish to investigate a question, they turn to Scripture, their principal source of facts concerning the record of humanity. There they meet God and in Scripture they amass those established data that supply the answer to any important question. In the Torah they find out that arrogance is a vice and causes sin, while humility is a virtue, and there they learn the reason why: virtue begins in our relationship to God, commencing with that of Adam and Eve: humility and obedience or arrogance and rebellion. Here is how the sages discover the governing principles of virtuous living, a full picture of the matter (B. Sot. 1:1-2 V.13ff./5A):

> 13.A. Whence [in Scripture] do we derive an admonition against the arrogant?
>
> B. Said Raba said Zeiri, "'Listen and give ear, do not be proud' (Jer. 13:15)."
>
> C. R. Nahman bar Isaac said, "From the following: 'Your heart will be lifted up, and you will forget the Lord your God' (Deut. 8:14).
>
> D. "And it is written, 'Beware, lest you forget the Lord your God' (Deut. 8:11)."
>
> 15.A. "With him also who is of a contrite and humble spirit" (Is. 57:15).
>
> B. R. Huna and R. Hisda:
>
> C. One said, "I [God] am with the contrite."
>
> D. The other said, "I [God] am the contrite."
>
> E. Logic favors the view of him who has said, "I [God] am with the contrite," for, lo, the Holy One, blessed be he, neglected all mountains and heights and brought his Presence to rest on Mount Sinai,
>
> F. and he did not raise Mount Sinai upward [to himself].
>
> G. R. Joseph said, "A person should always learn from the attitude of his Creator, for, lo, the Holy One, blessed be he, neglected all mountains and heights and brought his Presence to rest on Mount Sinai,

H. "and he neglected all valuable trees and brought his Presence to rest in the bush."

17.A. And R. Eleazar said, "Whoever is arrogant—his dust will not be stirred up [in the resurrection of the dead]. [Such a person will be judged for eternal death, when the dead are resurrected.]

B. "For it is said, 'Awake and sing, you that dwell in the dust' (Is. 26:19).

C. "It is stated not 'you who lie in the dust' but 'you who dwell in the dust,' meaning, one who has become a neighbor to the dust [by constant humility] even in his lifetime."

D. And R. Eleazar said, "For whoever is arrogant the Presence of God laments,

E. "as it is said, 'But the haughty he knows from afar' (Ps. 138:6)."

18.A. R. Avira expounded, and some say it was R. Eleazar, "Come and take note of the fact that not like the trait of the Holy One, blessed be he, is the trait of flesh and blood.

B. "The trait of flesh and blood is that those who are high take note of those who are high, but the one who is high does not take note of the one who is low.

C. "But the trait of the Holy One, blessed be he, is not that way. He is high, but he takes note of the low,

D. "as it is said, 'For though the Lord is high, yet he takes note of the low' (Ps. 138:6)."

24.A. Said R. Ashi, "Whoever is arrogant in the end will be diminished,

B. "as it is said, 'For a rising and for a scab' (Lev. 14:56), and rising refers only to elevation, as it is said, 'Upon all the high mountains and upon all the hills that are lifted up' (Is. 2:14).

C. "Scab means only 'attachment,' as it is said, 'Attach me, I ask you, to one of the priests' offices, so that I may eat a piece of bread' (1 Sam. 2:36)."

25.A. Said R. Joshua b. Levi, "Come and take note of how great are the humble in the sight of the Holy One, blessed be he.

B. "For when the sanctuary stood, a person would bring a burnt-offering, gaining thereby the reward for bringing a burnt-offering, or a meal-offering, and gaining the reward for a meal offering.

C. "But a person who is genuinely humble does Scripture treat as if he had made offerings of all the sacrifices,

D. "as it is said, 'The sacrifices [plural] of God are a broken spirit' (Ps. 51:19).

E. "And not only so, but his prayer is not rejected, as it is said, 'A broken and contrite heart, O God, you will not despise' (Ps. 51:19)."

F. And R. Joshua b. Levi said, "Whoever properly sets his ways in this world will have the merit of witnessing the salvation of the Holy One, blessed be he,

G. "as it is said, 'To him who orders his way I will show the salvation of God' (Ps. 50:23).

H. "Do not read 'orders' but 'properly sets' [his] way."

Arrogance embodies the bad attitude, and reason leads to the expectation that the arrogant will be cut down to size. If the arrogant person repents, however, then he abandons the bad attitude and adopts the good one, of humility, which is the condition of repentance. God is the model of humility, so too Moses. The resurrection of the dead involves the exaltation of the humble—dust itself. Scripture and parable serve to convey these points, but the system at its core insists upon them.

Three important doctrines define the setting of arrogance within the theological framework of the Torah:

[1] God formed creation in accord with a plan, which the Torah reveals. World order can be shown by the facts of nature and society set forth in the Torah's plan to conform to a pattern of reason based upon justice. Those who possess the Torah—Israel, defined as the people to whom God is made manifest through the Torah—know God. Those who do not—the gentiles, defined as idolaters—reject God in favor of idols. What happens to each of the two sectors of humanity, respectively, responds to their relationship with God. Israel in the present age is subordinate to the nations, because God has designated the gentiles as the medium for penalizing Israel's rebellion, intending through Israel's subordination and exile to provoke Israel to repent. Private life as much as the public order conforms to the principle that God rules justly in a creation of perfection and stasis.

[2] What disrupts the perfection of creation is the sole power capable of standing on its own against God's power, and that is

humanity's will. What humanity controls and God cannot coerce is humanity's capacity to form intention and therefore choose either arrogantly to defy, or humbly to love, God. This is where Judaism's definition of virtues makes its appearance. In the context established by the pattern of human creation and conduct, the principal virtue is humility, not arrogance. Because humanity defies God, the sin that results from human rebellion flaws creation and disrupts world order. The paradigm of the rebellion of Adam in Eden governs, the act of arrogant rebellion leading to exile from Eden thus accounting for the condition of humanity.

[3] But, as in the original transaction of alienation and consequent exile, God retains the power to encourage repentance by punishing arrogance. In mercy, moreover, God exercises the power to respond to repentance with forgiveness, that is, a change of attitude evoking a counterpart change. Since, commanding its own will, humanity also has the power to initiate the process of reconciliation with God, through repentance, an act of humility, humanity may restore the perfection of that order that through arrogance it has marred. Here we meet a divine virtue that humanity can replicate: mercy, forgiveness, reconciliation. And yet a third class of virtues, those involved in repentance and atonement, the confession of sin and the determination to do good, will surely follow. But everything begins in the virtue of humility.

But let us not neglect the end of the story. God ultimately will restore that perfection that embodied his plan for creation. In the work of restoration, death that comes about by reason of sin will die, the dead will be raised and judged for their deeds in this life, and most of them, having been justified, will go on to eternal life in the world to come. The paradigm of humanity restored to Eden is realized in Israel's return to the land of Israel. That is the view of the Oral Torah. In that world or age to come, however, that sector of humanity that through the Torah knows God will encompass all of humanity. Idolaters will perish, and humanity that comprises Israel at the end will know the one, true God and spend eternity in his light. The dead will rise out of their graves, and the age to come will see humanity restored to Eden.

Now, recorded in this way, the story told by the Torah proves remarkably familiar, with its stress on God's justice (to which his mercy is integral), humanity's correspondence with God in his possession of the power of will, humanity's sin and God's response. It follows that Judaism forms its conception of who we are to begin with out of the story of the creation of man and woman in Eden, and it answers the question, who are we really, by reflecting on the story of humanity's beginning, middle, and ending. All of us, Judaism maintains, are formed in the model of Adam and Eve.

If humble obedience to God's will defines virtue, and arrogant rebellion vice, then the question arises, on what account does humanity act with so much pride? For it is not as though humanity had much in which to take pride or foundation for its arrogant attitude. On the contrary, Aqabiah b. Mehalalel says, if we reflect on whence we come and whither we go, we shall attain humility (M. Abot 3:1):

> Aqabiah b. Mehalalel says, "Contemplate three things, and you will not come to commit a transgression. Know whence you have come, from a fetid drop; and where you are going, to worms and corruption; and before whom you are going to have to give a full accounting of yourself, before the King of kings of kings, the Holy One, blessed be he."

An amplification of Aqabiah's saying by a later authority links the definition of humanity to the story of creation, birth, and death. Conscience—not sinning—comes about through consciousness of who we really are.

But the sages set forth a doctrine that compares in its grand vision to the one that finds humanity in God's image and likeness. They further maintain that the human being is formed in the model of nature, created as the counterpart to the natural world, so that whatever characterizes the creation of nature also marks the creation of humans. The sage then treats the human being as a microcosm of nature, as much as in God's image, after God's likeness. It would be difficult to state a more elevated conception of who we really are than this invocation of nature and God as embodied in humanity. Here is how, in concrete language, the sage makes the statement that humanity forms the counterpart to the natural world (Abot d'Rabbi Nathan XXXI:III.1):

> R. Yose the Galilean says, "Whatever the Holy One, blessed be he, created on earth, he created also in man. To what may the matter be compared? To someone who took a piece of wood and wanted to make many forms on it but had no room to make them, so he was distressed. But someone who draws forms on the earth can go on drawing and can spread them out as far as he likes. But the Holy One, blessed be he, may his great name be blessed for ever and ever, in his wisdom and understanding created the whole of the world, created the heaven and the earth, above and below, and created in man whatever he created in his world.
>
> "In the world he created forests, and in man he created forests: the hairs on his head. In the world he created wild beasts and in man he created wild beasts: lice. In the world he created channels and in man he created channels: his ears. In the world he created wind and in man he created wind: his breath. In the world he created the sun and in man he created the sun: his forehead. Stagnant waters in the world, stagnant waters in man: his nose [namely, rheum]. Salt water in the world, salt water in man: his urine. Streams in the world, streams in man: man's tears. Walls in the world, walls in man: his lips. Doors in the world, doors in man, his teeth. Firmaments in the world, firmaments in man, his tongue. Fresh water in the world, fresh water in man: his spit. Stars in the world, stars in the man: his cheeks. Towers in the world, towers in man: his neck. masts in the world, masts in man: his arms. Pins in the world, pins in man: his fingers. A King in the world, a king in man: his heart. Grape clusters in the world, grape clusters in man: his breasts. Counselors in the world, counselors in man: his kidneys. Millstones in the world, millstones in man: his intestines [which grind up food]. Mashing mills in the world, and mashing mills in man: the spleen. Pits in the world, a pit in man: the belly button. Flowing streams in the world and a flowing stream in man: his blood. Trees in the world and trees in man: his bones. Hills in the world and hills in man: his buttocks. Pestle and mortar in the world and pestle and mortar in man: the joints. Horses in the world and horses in man: the legs. The angel of death in the world and the angel of death in

man: his heels. Mountains and valleys in the world and mountains and valleys in man: when he is standing, he is like a mountain, when he is lying down, he is like a valley.

> "Thus you have learned that whatever the Holy One, blessed be he, created on earth, he created also in man."

Here is a vision of humanity that recalls the Psalmist's cry, "What is man that you are mindful of him, and the son of man that you pay attention to him? Yet you have crowned him with glory and honor." So much for humanity in God's image, formed in the model of nature and its glories, a remarkable vision.

**What are the social virtues?** The social virtues begin with righteousness, which bears the meaning in Hebrew of charity. To be righteous is to love God. That love is best expressed through acts of charity (philanthropy), which define righteousness better than any other. The mark of righteousness is to desire God, and the righteous always direct their hearts to God (Lev. Rabbah XLI:I.1):

> "But the Lord afflicted Pharaoh and his house with great plagues because of Sarai, Abram's wife" (Gen. 12:17):
>
> "The righteous shall flourish like the palm-tree, he shall grow like a cedar in Lebanon" (Ps. 92:13).
>
> Just as a palm tree and a cedar produce neither crooked curves nor growths, so the righteous do not produce either crooked curves or growths. Just as the shade of the palm tree and cedar is distant from the base of the tree, so the giving of the reward that is coming to the righteous seems distant. Just as, in the case of the palm tree and the cedar, the very core of the tree points upward, so in the case of the righteous, their heart is pointed toward the Holy One, blessed be he.
>
> That is in line with the following verse of Scripture: "My eyes are ever toward the Lord, for he will bring forth my feet out of the net" (Ps. 25:15). Just as the palm tree and cedar are subject to desire, so the righteous are subject to desire. And what might it be? What they desire is the Holy One, blessed be he.

Charity and righteousness are called by one and the same word, *sedaqah*, because the act of philanthropy represents righteousness above all else. Charity and righteous deeds outweigh all other commandments in the

Torah (T. Pe. 4:19). Acts of charity are to be conducted with dignity and respect for the poor. Any one who gives a penny to the poor is blessed with six blessings, and anyone who speaks to him in a comforting manner is blessed with eleven (B. B.B. 1:5 IV.28-29/9b). God responds to acts of charity, so that, in the verse, "Thus says the Lord, do not enter into the house of mourning, nor go to lament, nor bemoan them, for I have taken away my peace from this people . . . even loving kindness and tender mercies" (Jer. 16:4), "loving kindness" is said to refer to acts of mercy, and "tender mercies" to charity (B. B.B. 1:5 IV.37-38/10a).

But what God really admires is acts of selflessness, and the highest virtue of all, so far as the Torah is concerned, is the act that God cannot coerce but very much yearns for, that act of love that transcends the self.[1] Virtue begins in obedience to the Torah, but reaches its pinnacle through deeds beyond the strict requirements of the Torah, and even the limits of the law altogether, that transform the hero into a holy man, whose holiness served just like that of a sage marked as such by knowledge of the Torah To understand how sages make their statement, we have to keep in mind two facts. First, they believed that God hears and answers prayer and that if God answers prayer, it is a mark of heaven's favorable recognition of the one who says it. Therefore, if someone has the reputation of saying prayers that are answered, sages want to know why. Second, sages believed that Torah-study defined the highest ideal a man could attain, and they maintained that God wanted them to live a life of Torah-study. But they discover people who could pray with effect in ways that they, the sages themselves, could not. And they further discovered that some people won heaven's favor not by a lifelong devotion to divine service but by doing a single remarkable action. So the sages themselves are going to tell us stories about how one enormous deed outweighed a life of Torah-study. The word *zekhut* stands for "the merit, source of divine favor." An act that generates *zekhut* for the individual is the counterpart and opposite: what one does by one's own volition

that also is beyond all requirements of the law. The ultimate act of virtue turns out to be an act of pure grace, to which God responds with pure grace.

We turn to the opposite of restraint and self-abnegation, which is arrogance. If acts of humility, embodied in prayer, charity, and repentance, right the relationship with God, acts of arrogance upset it. The sages identify as an act of supreme arrogance losing one's temper. God's presence is offended by displays of temper, and temper is a mark of arrogance, a source of sin (M. Ned. 4:4 I.16-18/22b.

Sages admire restraint and temperance, marks of humility, so it stands to reason that loss of restraint and intemperance will signify arrogance. Sages do not treat respectfully people who take vows, for they yield to the undisciplined will, to emotion unguided by rational considerations. But intentionality must (ideally) take form out of both emotion and reflection. Vows explode, the fuel of emotion ignited by the heat of the occasion. "Qonam be any benefit I get from you" hardly forms a rational judgment of a stable relationship; it bespeaks a loss of temper, a response to provocation with provocation. Right at the outset, the halakhah gives a powerful signal of its opinion of the whole: suitable folk to begin with do not take vows, only wicked people do. That explains in so many words why, if one says, something is subject to "the vows of suitable folk," he has said nothing. Suitable people—*kesheyrim*—make no vows at all, ever.

A distaste for vowing and disdain for people who make vows then characterize the law. People who take vows are deemed irresponsible, adults who have classified themselves as children. They possess the power of intentionality but not the responsibility for its wise use. That is why they are given openings toward the unbinding of their vows; they are forced at the same time to take seriously what they have said. Vows are treated as a testing of heaven, a trial of heavenly patience and grace. Sanctification can affect a person or a mess of porridge, and there is a difference. Expletives make that difference; these are not admired. To sages, language is holy, how God forms a relationship with humanity, the medium of divine communication. Vows constitute a disreputable use of the powerful and the holy. And language is holy because language gives form and effect to intentionality. That is why we do admit intentionality—not foresight but intentionality as to honor—into the repertoire of reasons for nullifying vows, as we note in the law of vows (M. Ned. 9:9):

A. They unloose a vow for a man by reference to his own honor and by reference to the honor of his children.
B. They say to him, "Had you known that the next day they would say about you, 'That's the way of So-and-so, going around divorcing his wives,'
C. "and that about your daughters they'd be saying, 'They're daughters of a divorcée! What did their mother do to get herself divorced' [would you have taken a vow]?"
D. And [if] he then said, "Had I known that things would be that way, I should never have taken such a vow,"
E. lo, this [vow] is not binding.

The normative law rejects unforeseen events as a routine excuse for nullifying a vow; foresight on its own ("had you known . . . would you have vowed?") plays a dubious role. But when it comes to the intentionality involving honor of parents or children, that forms a consideration of such overriding power as to nullify the vow.

Our final encounter with the social virtues carries us to the notion that the higher virtue is the one that encompasses lesser ones. And the highest virtue is good will, which encompasses every other social virtue of generosity, foresight, neighborliness, and the rest. The worst vice is not envy, bad neighborliness, defaulting on a loan, but ill-will (M. Abot 2:8-9):

A. [Rabban Yohanan ben Zakkai] said to [his disciples], "Go and see what is the straight path to which someone should stick."
B. R. Eliezer says, "A generous spirit."
C. R. Joshua says, "A good friend."
D. R. Yose says, "A good neighbor."
E. R. Simeon says, "Foresight."
F. R. Eleazar says, "Good will."
G. He said to them, "I prefer the opinion of

R. Eleazar b. Arakh, because in what he says is included everything you say."
H. He said to them, "Go out and see what is the bad road, which someone should avoid."
I. R. Eliezer says, "Envy."
J. R. Joshua says, "A bad friend."
K. R. Yose says, "A bad neighbor."
L. R. Simeon says, "Defaulting on a loan."
M. (All the same is a loan owed to a human being and a loan owed to the Omnipresent, blessed be he, as it is said, "The wicked borrows and does not pay back, but the righteous person deals graciously and hands over [what he owes]" [Ps. 37:21].)
N. R. Eleazar says, "Bad will."
O. He said to them, "I prefer the opinion of R. Eleazar b. Arakh, because in what he says is included everything you say."

The reason behind the position is explicit: the comprehensive definition is preferred over the episodic one. Yohanan finds in the attitude of good will the source of all specific virtues, because in his view attitude and intention in the end define the human being: we are what we want to be, the world is what we want to make of it. The entire message of the Torah for the virtuous man and woman is summed up in that conviction, which, furthermore, is embodied in the law of Judaism governing the social order.

**What is personal virtue?** The system of Judaism set forth by the sages forms a tight fabric, so that what sages say in a theological setting comes to expression also in the norms of behavior, guided by law not only by will, that they set forth. We see that fact when we take up the matter of hope. That defines one of the highest personal virtues—not to despair—and one of the personal virtues that Israel, a defeated and broken-hearted people, most required for itself. To make that statement, sages resorted to a legal point. The message is, When hope is abandoned, then, but only then, all is lost. This point is made in connection with the law of ownership of property. Ownership of property depends upon one's attitude toward the property. This comes to expression in several ways. If one consecrates the property, God through the Temple becomes the owner. An act of will alienates the rights of ownership. If squatters have taken one's field or house, when does the original owner lose title? One relinquishes ownership by reason of despairing of recovering possession of the property. So one may give up property either as a gift to heaven or as a surrender to bad fortune. Ownership by itself therefore makes little difference; one's attitude toward one's property, on the one side, and one's disposition of possessions, on the other, govern. One does well, therefore, to hold with open arms; one does better to give up ownership of property to heaven as an act of donation than relinquish ownership to violence as an act of despair.

In addition to hope, sages identified personal virtues as cleanliness, cultic cleanness, leading to spiritual achievements, holiness, humility, fear of sin, true piety, and onward. These are set forth in a hierarchy, leading from one upward to the next, finally to the day of judgment and eternal life. They did not differentiate the carnal from the spiritual but saw all personal virtue as forming a single coherent whole, from the humble quality of promptness onward up to the resurrection of the dead (Song Rabbah I:V.3):

A. In this connection R. Phineas b. Yair would say, "Promptness leads to [hygienic] cleanliness, cleanliness to [cultic] cleanness, [cultic] cleanness to holiness, holiness to humility, humility to fear of sin, fear of sin to true piety, true piety to the Holy Spirit, the Holy Spirit to the resurrection of the dead, the resurrection of the dead to Elijah the prophet [bringing the day of judgment]" [M. Sot. 9:15].

B. "Promptness leads to [hygienic] cleanliness:" "And when he made an end of atoning for the holy place" (Lev. 16:20).

C. ". . . cleanliness to [cultic] cleanness:" "And the priest shall make atonement for her, and she shall be clean" (Lev. 12:8).

D. ". . . cleanness to holiness:" "And he shall purify it and make it holy" (Lev. 16:9).

E. ". . . holiness to humility:" "For thus says the High and Lofty One, who inhabits eternity, whose name is holy, 'I dwell in the high and holy place, with the one who is of a contrite and humble spirit'" (Is. 57:15).

F. ". . . humility to fear of sin:" "The reward of humility is the fear of the Lord" (Prov. 22:4).

G. ". . . fear of sin to true piety:" "Then you spoke in a vision to your saints" (Ps. 89:20).

H. ". . . true piety to the Holy Spirit:" "Then you spoke in a vision to your saints" (Ps. 89:20).

I. ". . . the Holy Spirit to the resurrection of the dead:" "And I will put my spirit in you and you shall live" (Ezek. 37:14).

J. ". . . the resurrection of the dead to Elijah the prophet of blessed memory:" "Behold I will send you Elijah the prophet" (Mal. 3:23).

What we see once more is how the system supplies context to all the details. The virtue of personal cleanliness so far as Judaism teaches it finds its meaning in the ladder that leads to holiness, encounter with the Holy Spirit, and ultimately the resurrection of the dead.

But, as we saw earlier, the right attitude, the appropriate intention—these matter most of all. How does individual virtue encompass matters of attitude and emotion? The Written Torah answers the question decisively. Certainly the right attitude that the individual should cultivate begins in the commandment, "You will love your neighbor as yourself," (Lev. 19:18). Here is how sages amplify that matter (Sifra CC:III):

I.A. "You shall not hate your brother in your heart, [but reasoning, you shall reason with your neighbor, lest you bear sin because of him. You shall not take vengeance or bear any grudge against the sons of your own people, but you shall love your neighbor as yourself: I am the Lord]" (Lev. 19:17-18).

B. Might one suppose that one should not curse him, set him straight, or contradict him?

C. Scripture says, "in your heart."

D. I spoke only concerning hatred that is in the heart.

Sages' first point is to define loving one's neighbor as oneself as loving the neighbor in the heart, not harboring a secret enmity, but expressing openly and honestly one's own grievance. So we bear responsibility for those actions that shape our intentionality and attitude; there are things we can do to improve our attitude toward the other and so to foster a proper intentionality toward him or her, and not bearing a grudge is critical. But that involves expressing what troubles us, not holding things in and secretly conspiring, in our own heart, to get even. So we are required to speak forthrightly to the person against whom we have a grievance (Sifra CC:III):

2.A. And how do we know that if one has rebuked him four or five times, he should still go and rebuke him again?

B. Scripture says, "reasoning, you shall reason with your neighbor."

C. Might one suppose that that is the case even if one rebukes him and his countenance blanches?

D. Scripture says, "lest you bear sin."

That means not taking vengeance or bearing a grudge. As is their way, sages translate their teachings into narratives, which exemplify the point in a clear way:

4.A. "You shall not take vengeance [or bear any grudge]:"

B. To what extent is the force of vengeance?

C. If one says to him, "Lend me your sickle," and the other did not do so.

D. On the next day, the other says to him, "Lend me your spade."

E. The one then replies, "I am not going to lend it to, because you didn't lend me your sickle."

F. In that context, it is said, "You shall not take vengeance."

5.A. ". . . or bear any grudge":

B. To what extent is the force of a grudge?

C. If one says to him, "Lend me your spade," but he did not do so.

D. The next day the other one says to him, "Lend me your sickle,"

E. and the other replies, "I am not like you, for you didn't lend me your spade [but here, take the sickle]!"

F. In that context, it is said, "or bear any grudge."

6.A. "You shall not take vengeance or bear any grudge against the sons of your own people:"

B. "You may take vengeance and bear a grudge against others."

7.A. ". . . but you shall love your neighbor as yourself: [I am the Lord]:"

B. R. Aqiba says, "This is the encompassing principle of the Torah."

C. Ben Azzai says, "'This is the book of the generations of Adam' (Gen. 5:1) is a still more encompassing principle."

And we note, at the end, that the first century authority, Aqiba, deems love of neighbor to form the most important principle of the entire Torah.

In addition to love of neighbor, one other personal virtue takes priority, and that is love of God. But sages also value fear of God, that is to say, reverence. Then they ask, which is the better motive for serving God, fear or love? The one coerces, like it or not; the other appeals to our own will, making God's will into our will, rather than our will into God's will. So sages admire those who serve God out of love, but they identify with those who serve God out of reverence. Here is how they state the matter (M. Sot. 5:5):

A. On that day did R. Joshua b. Hurqanos expound as follows: "Job served the Holy One, blessed be he, only out of love,

B. "since it is said, 'Though he slay me, yet will I wait for him' (Job 13:15).

C. "But still the matter is in doubt [as to whether it means], 'I will wait for him,' or, 'I will not wait for him.'

D. "Scripture states, 'Until I die I will not put away mine integrity from me' (Job 27:5).

E. "This teaches that he did what he did out of love."

F. Said R. Joshua, "Who will remove the dirt from your eyes, Rabban Yohanan b. Zakkai. For you used to expound for your entire life that Job served the omnipresent only out of awe,

G. "since it is said, 'The man was perfect and upright and one who feared God and avoided evil' (Job 1:8).

H. "And now has not Joshua, the disciple of your disciple, taught that he did what he did out of love."

Joshua b. Hurqanos holds that Job served God out of love, and Joshua does not share that view, valuing service out of reverence more. He refers to his master, Yohanan b. Zakkai, now deceased, who has not lived to hear the exegesis of which he would have disapproved. Fear or reverence is the greater personal virtue because the one who fears will not rebel, that is, such a one is not going to be arrogant. If we serve God out of love, then our own feelings enter into the transaction; we can deny love. But if we serve God out of fear, then obligation takes over, and humility sets in.

**How does formative Judaism define character, good and bad?** Good character is defined in various ways, all of them deriving from the Torah. The basic question of good character is answered by appeal to the commandments that, if one does them, mark a person as Godly. But the Torah contains many commandments. Here is how sages define the truly good character. They affirm that all of the commandments serve to form good character, and disobedience to any of them marks bad character. But they recognize a hierarchy of character-forming obligations, a hierarchy that they find in the Written Torah (B. Mak. 23b-24a).

> B. R. Simelai expounded, "Six hundred and thirteen commandments were given to Moses, three hundred and sixty-five negative ones, corresponding to the number of the days of the solar year, and two hundred forty-eight positive commandments, corresponding to the parts of man's body.
>
> D. "David came and reduced them to eleven: 'A Psalm of David: Lord, who shall sojourn in thy tabernacle, and who shall dwell in thy holy mountain? (i) He who walks uprightly and (ii) works righteousness and (iii) speaks truth in his heart and (iv) has no slander on his tongue and (v) does no evil to his fellow and (vi) does not take up a reproach against his neighbor, (vii) in whose eyes a vile person is despised but (viii) honors those who fear the Lord. (ix) He swears to his own hurt and changes not. (x) He does not lend on interest. (xi) He does not take a bribe against the innocent' (Ps. 15).
>
> V. "Isaiah came and reduced them to six: '(i) He who walks righteously and (ii) speaks uprightly, (iii) he who despises the gain of oppressions, (iv) shakes his hand from holding bribes, (v) stops his ear from hearing of blood (vi) and shuts his eyes from looking upon evil, he shall dwell on high' (Is. 33:25-26).
>
> FF. "Micah came and reduced them to three: 'It has been told you, man, what is good, and what the Lord demands from you, (i) only to do justly and (ii) to love mercy, and (iii) to walk humbly before God' (Mic. 6:8).
>
> KK. "Isaiah again came and reduced them to two: 'Thus says the Lord, (i) Keep justice and (ii) do righteousness' (Is. 56:1).
>
> LL. "Amos came and reduced them to a single one, as it is said, 'For thus says the Lord to the house of Israel. Seek Me and live' (Amos 5:4).

> NN. "Habakkuk further came and based them on one, as it is said, 'But the righteous shall live by his faith' (Hab. 2:4)."

Living by one's faith should not be misunderstood. Simelai does not mean by "faith" one's personal opinions or beliefs, and he is not commending the individual who stands against the world by reason of personal conviction. By "faith," Simelai understands Habakkuk to mean, "faithfulness," that is, trust in God, and "the righteous shall live by his faith" means, "by confidence in God's providence." That accords with Amos's "Seek Me and live," and Micah's recommendation to walk humbly with God. Naturally, faithfulness to God yields, also, adherence to justice and mercy, as we have seen earlier, and the actions of those recommended as embodiments of self-abnegation—the ones whose prayers are answered—fit well into the picture before us.

What defines bad character? Once more, we are used to sages' preference for definition through deed. But, all together, sages find bad character to embody traits of selfishness and pride and arrogance. These are the attitudes that yield idolatry, fornication, love for gossip, and other forms of self-aggrandizement. Above all else, idolatry, fornication, and murder represent the cardinal sins— the actions by which one manipulates the world round about, trying to govern God, exploit and even eliminate the other (Gen. Rabbah XXXI:VI.1):

> A. Another matter: "For the earth is filled with violence" (Gen. 6:13):
> B. Said R. Levi, "The word for violence refers to idolatry, fornication, and murder.
> C. "Idolatry: 'For the earth is filled with violence' (Gen. 6:13).
> D. "Fornication: 'The violence done to me and to my flesh be upon Babylonia' (Jer. 51:35). [And the word for 'flesh' refers to incest, as at Lev. 18:6].
> E. "Murder: 'For the violence against the children of Judah, because they have shed innocent blood' (Joel 4:19).
> F. "Further, the word for 'violence' stands for its ordinary meaning as well."

And yet, there is a social vice that matters even more, being commonplace and easy to carry out. When it comes to assessing a person's character, gossip outweighs even idolatry, fornication, and murder (T. Pe. 1:2):

A. These are four things for the performance of which one is punished in this world, while the principal [i.e., eternal punishment] remains for the world to come, and these are they:

B. 1) idolatrous worship, 2) sexual misbehavior, 3) murder, and 4) gossip, which is worse than all of them [together].

The three cardinal sins nonetheless are forgivable, but rejection of the Torah is not (Y. Hag. 1:7/I:3):

A. R. Huna, R. Jeremiah in the name of R. Samuel bar R. Isaac: "We find that the Holy One, blessed be he, forgave Israel for idolatry, fornication, and murder. [But] for their rejection of the Torah he never forgave them."

B. What is the scriptural basis for that view?

C. It is not written, "Because they practiced idolatry, fornication, and murder," but, rather, "And the Lord said, 'Because they have forsaken my Torah.'"

D. Said R. Hiyya bar Ba, "'If they were to forsake me, I should forgive them, for they may yet keep my Torah. For if they should forsake me but keep my Torah, the leaven that is in [the Torah] will bring them closer to me.'"

E. R. Huna said, "Study Torah [even if it is] not for its own sake, for, out of [doing so] not for its own sake, you will come [to study it] for its own sake."

Why is rejection of the Torah not forgivable? Because the Torah affords knowledge of God and God's will, and rejecting the Torah then brings about all other vices and sins, constituting the ultimate act of arrogance.

Why, then, do people sin, and what is the key to bad character? Sages see two conflicting impulses in the human being, the impulse to do good and the impulse to do evil. That impulse is identified in many passages of the Oral Torah with sexual sins (not sexuality per se). Sages identify the mark of bad character as the dominant trait not only of the gossip but also of the fornicator (Song Rabbah XCVI:i.1):

B. R. Hunia in the name of R. Dosa b. R. Tebet: "Two impulses to do evil did the Holy One, blessed be he, create in his

world, the impulse to worship idols, and the impulse to fornicate. The impulse to worship idols has already been eliminated, but the impulse to fornicate still endures.

C. "Said the Holy One, blessed be he, 'Whoever can withstand the impulse to fornicate do I credit as though he had withstood them both.'"

D. Said R. Judah, "The matter may be compared to the case of a snake-charmer who had [two] snakes. He charmed the larger and left the smaller, saying, 'Whoever can withstand this one is certainly credited as though he had withstood them both.'

E. "So the Holy One, blessed be he, eliminated the impulse to worship idols but left the impulse to fornicate. He said, 'Whoever can withstand the impulse to fornicate do I credit as though he had withstood them both.'"

The impulse to do evil also bears a good side, as explained at Gen. R. IX:VII.1:

A. Nahman in the name of R. Samuel: "'Behold, it was very good' refers to the impulse to do good.

B. "'And behold, it was very good' encompasses also the impulse to do evil.

C. "And is the impulse to do evil 'very good'? Indeed so, for if it were not for the impulse to do evil, a man would not build a house, marry a wife, and produce children.

D. "So does Solomon say, 'Again I considered all labor and all excelling in work, that is rivalry with his neighbor' (Ec. 4:4)."

The person of poor character pays a heavy price: that person will never see God. Who are such types? They are scoffers, flatterers, liars, and slanderers (B. San. 11:2 X.4/103a). What these have in common is the use of the power of language for wicked purposes. These are not people who murder, fornicate, or worship idols. These persons will not see God because of things that they say, not do. Once more, we return the basic conviction that attitude and intentionality, reaching expression in language as much as in deed, make all the difference. What is the antidote? It is the shaping of one's attitude and intentionality in the proper way. And how is this done? Through close study of the Torah, both the written and the oral parts thereof.

Everything is captured in a single statement, "God wants the heart," which is amplified by another, "The commandments were given only to purify the heart of humanity." Then who is the person who ought to embody and represent that pure heart that the Torah so highly appreciates? It must be the master of Torah, the sage.

**Beyond the normal virtues: who is the extraordinary person?** The type of person who transcends the normal virtues and serves as the model for the rest of humanity is the sage. He[2] is valued in heaven by reason of his learning on earth. Sages on earth may not occupy positions of power and influence, but in heaven they do. The arrogant on earth are humbled in heaven, the humble on earth are exalted in heaven (B. Pes. 50A 3:7-8 II:4):

> A. Joseph b. R. Joshua fell sick and went into a coma. Afterward his father said to him, "So what did you see?"
> B. "I saw an upside down world, what is [exalted] on high is down [humble] below, and what is [humble] below is [exalted] on high."
> C. He said to him, "You saw a world of clarity."
> D. "And as to us, how are we perceived?"
> E. He said to him, "As we are valued here, so we are valued there. I heard them saying, 'Happy is he who comes here with his learning fully in hand.' And I heard them saying, 'As to those put to death [as martyrs] by the government, no creature can stand within their precincts.'"

The sage enjoyed heaven's high esteem because he spent his life trying to know God through mastery of God's self-manifestation in the Torah. He was sanctified through study of the Torah in discipleship, a link in the chain of Oral Torah from Sinai. Because they embody the law of the Torah, the actions of the sage define norms and supply exemplary models; the sage then constitutes a native category, holding together a vast corpus of exemplary statements, e.g., of what this or that named master did or refrained from doing.

Because of his mastery of the Torah, a disciple of a sage is equivalent to an actual Torah-scroll, the physical object, and is treated with the same respect that is paid to the Torah. He who sees a disciple of a sage who has died is as if he sees a scroll of the Torah that has been burned (T. Ta. 3:7 I.10). With special reference to the death of a sage, we additionally have the following (B. Ket. 23:1-2 I.19/17a):

> R. Sheshet, and some say, R. Yohanan, said, "Removing the Torah contained in the sage must be like the giving of the Torah: just as the giving of the Torah involved six hundred thousand, so taking away the Torah involves six hundred thousand. But this is with regard to one who has recited Scripture and repeated Mishnah traditions. But in the case of one who repeated Tannaite statements to others, there is no upper limit at all."

Why should the sage make such a difference? Because through what he masters in Torah, he meets God; he brings God's presence to rest upon Israel. This is expressed at Lev. Rabbah XI:VII.3:

> A. "And it came to pass in the days of Ahaz" (Is. 7:1).
> B. What was the misfortune that took place at that time?
> C. "The Syrians on the east and the Philistines on the west [devour Israel with open mouth]" (Is. 9:12).
> D. The matter [that is, the position of Israel] may be compared to a king who handed over his son to a tutor, who hated [the son]. The tutor thought, "If I kill him now, I shall turn out to be liable to the death penalty before the king. So what I'll do is take away his wet nurse, and he will die on his own."
> E. So thought Ahaz, "If there are no kids, there will be no he-goats. If there are no he-goats, there will be no flock. If there is no flock, there will be no shepherd. If there is no shepherd, there will be no world.
> F. So did Ahaz plan, "If there are no children, there will be no disciples; if there are no disciples, there will be no sages; if there are no sages, there will be no Torah; if there is no Torah, there will be no synagogues and schools; if there are no synagogues and schools, then the Holy One, blessed be he, will not allow his presence to come to rest in the world."
> G. What did he do? He went and locked the synagogues and schools.

Through the Torah, God comes into the world, and the sages, who master the Torah and teach it, therefore bring God into the world. That is why to deny the teachings of the sages is to deny God.

Why such heavy emphasis on the sainthood of the sage and on his Torah? The reason is that, through study, the sage entered into the mind of God, learning how God's mind worked in forming the written and oral Torah, which (in the explicit view of Gen. Rabbah 1:1) God consulted in creating the world. And there in the intellect of God, in sages judgment, humanity gained access to the only means of uniting intellect with humanity's existential condition as to salvation. The Mishnah had set forth the rules that governed the natural world in relationship to heaven. But knowledge of the Torah now joined the one world, known through nature, with the other world, the world of supernature, where, in the end, intellect merely served in the quest for salvation. Through Torah-study, sages claimed for themselves a place in that very process of thought that had given birth to nature; but it was a supernatural process, and knowledge of that process on its own terms would transform and, in the nature of things, save. That explains the integrative power of imputing supernatural power to learning.

One becomes a disciple of a sage by hearing and repeating and memorizing the words of the sage set forth as Torah. Reciting words of Torah is obligatory for the disciple, and doing so in constant interchange with colleagues is the sole valid way. Thus, "If two disciples of sages go along without words of Torah between them, they are worthy of being burned in fire, as it is said, 'And it came to pass, as they still went on, that, behold, a chariot of fire' (2 Kgs. 2:11). The reason that the chariot of fire appeared is that they were talking. Lo, if there had not been talk of Torah, they would have been worthy of being burned" (B. Sot. 9:12 V.3). What is the mark of a sage? A sage exhibits traits of intelligence and civility (M Ab. 5:7):

A. There are seven traits to an unformed clod, and seven to a sage.
B. (1) A sage does not speak before someone greater than he in wisdom.
C. (2) And he does not interrupt his fellow.
D. (3) And he is not at a loss for an answer.

E. (4) He asks a relevant question and answers properly.
F. (5) And he addresses each matter in its proper sequence, first, then second.
G. (6) And concerning something he has not heard, he says, "I have not heard the answer."
H. (7) And he concedes the truth when the other party demonstrates it. And the opposite of these traits apply to a clod.

So much for the sage, whose intellectual capacities—ability to learn what the Torah says and to reason in a rational way about it—are supposed to—and in some cases do—impart those qualities of character and conscience that realize what it means to be "in our image, after our likeness." But sages themselves paint yet another, and conflicting, picture of the extraordinarily virtuous person. They have the notion that the most ignorant of ignorant persons, who devote their lives to sin, can through a single action accomplish what a life devoted to Torah-study cannot achieve. And that brings us back to our starting point, the merit of the act of selfless love, the act God cannot compel or coerce but craves of humanity. The commandment to love God—"you shall love the Lord your God with all your heart, your soul, and your might" (Deut. 4:9)—and to love the other—"you shall love your neighbor as yourself" (Lev. 19:18)—meet and form a single statement. It is that to which God aspires for us, but which God cannot impose upon us. God can command love, but not coerce it, favor but not force it. But then God responds to the act of selfless generosity with an act of grace—precisely that act that humanity for its part cannot compel or coerce out of God, cannot cajole from God, but can only beseech.

And no wonder, in sages' account of matters, such a remarkable action done once not only makes up for a dissolute life but in that single moment wins heaven's perpetual favor. This is the center of the virtue attained through an action that yields *zekhut*, of sufficient importance to bear repetition, the same story occurring in the entry under ZEKHUT (Y. Ta. 1:4.I):

Q. In a dream of R. Abbahu, Mr. Pentakaka ["Five sins"] appeared, who prayed that rain would come, and it rained. R. Abbahu sent and summoned him. He said to him, "What is your trade?"

R. He said to him, "Five sins does that man [I] do every day, [for I am a pimp]: [1] hiring whores, [2] cleaning up the theater, [3] bringing home their garments for washing, [4] dancing, and [4] 'performing' before them."

S. He said to him, "And what sort of decent thing have you ever done?"

T. He said to him, "One day that man [I] was cleaning the theater, and a woman came and stood behind a pillar and cried. I said to her, 'What's with you?' And she said to me, 'That woman's [my] husband is in prison, and I wanted to see what I can do to free him,' so I sold my bed and cover, and I gave the proceeds to her. I said to her, 'Here is your money, free your husband, but do not sin.'"

U. He said to him, "You are worthy of praying and having your prayers answered."

Mr. Five-Sins has done everything sinful that (within sages' imagination) one can do, and, more to the point, he does it every day. What he should do is carry out the commandments, and he should study the Torah every day. So what he has done is what he should not have done, and what he has not done is what he should have done—every day. And yet in a single action, in a moment, everything changes. So the singularity of the act of *zekhut*, which suffices if done only one time, encompasses its power to outweigh a life of sin—again, an act of *zekhut* as the mirror-image and opposite of sin. Here again, the single act of saving a woman from a "fate worse than death" has sufficed. Mr. Five-Sins has carried out an act of grace, to which heaven, uncoerced and uncompelled, responds with that love in which God so richly abounds for humanity. The extraordinary person is the one who sacrifices for the other in an act of selfless love—and that can be anybody, at any time, anywhere.

### Notes

[1] See ZEKHUT.

[2] In the formative age of which we speak, the first seven centuries C.E., sages were men; the modes of acquiring knowledge of the Torah, involving study in a relationship of discipleship to a master, were not open to women. Hence here we speak of "him," not "him or her." In our own times the doors of the schools where the Torah is taught have opened to women as well. Women become rabbis in Reform, Reconstructionist, Conservative, and other Judaisms, and most of the various Orthodox Judaisms makes provision for women to study Torah as well.

JACOB NEUSNER

**WOMEN AND JUDAISM:** Feminist study of Jewish women is based on the premise that women's lives and experiences have often differed from the lives and experiences of men. Since the history of Judaism has most frequently been written from the point of view of the male Jew, documenting his religious obligations and spiritual strivings, most scholars have assumed that female religious experience was either subsumed in the experiences of men or have ignored it entirely. Yet as Susan Starr Sered has demonstrated in her anthropological study of elderly illiterate Middle Eastern Jewish women in Jerusalem, Jewish women have often constructed their own female-oriented traditions, developing ways to sacralize and enrich their lives religiously despite their historic exclusion from the communal spheres of synagogue ritual and Jewish learning. As opposed to the "great" tradition of normative, male-centered Judaism, Sered calls this "women's" Judaism the "little" tradition, noting that it incorporates piety based on philanthropy, domestic rituals, and nurturing of family members as well as individual worship.[1]

Because few Jewish women before modern times possessed the skills or authority to preserve their own voices for posterity, our access to information about the "little traditions" of the past is frequently limited. Hence we must utilize a wide range of primary sources and scholarship not only to describe changing attitudes towards women in "official" Judaism but also to delineate what can be known about Jewish women's spirituality, piety, and religious practice in many different eras and locations. Additionally, underlying this discussion of women in Judaism and women's Judaisms is a recognition of the perpetual tension between Judaism, a constantly evolving religious system, and the demands of everyday life, which often led to divergences from prescribed practice. Thus we shall see that Jews have negotiated ongoing and varying accommodations between attitudes and ordinances directed towards women in Jewish tradition and the customs and mores of the different cultures in which they have lived.

**Women in the Hebrew Bible:** The Hebrew Bible is a composite document containing a variety of types of literature, reflecting the attitudes and concerns of numerous authors writing in very different times and places. An example of such significant diversity as it applies to women is evident in the two creation stories placed at the beginning of Genesis. While the first account of the origin of human beings (Gen. 1:1-2:3) recounts that both male and female were created simultaneously, in the divine image, and equally charged to multiply and to dominate the earth and their fellow creatures, the second narrative (Gen. 2:4ff.) preserves a tradition of male priority. Here, woman is a subsequent and secondary creation, formed from man's body to fulfill male needs for companionship and progeny. Such divergent understandings of female status and capacities, and the contradictions they engender, appear throughout the biblical literature.

Recent scholars have utilized a number of strategies to contextualize the diverse portrayals of women in biblical texts. Studying women's status in biblical law, Tikva Frymer-Kensky writes that biblical legislation, like ancient Near Eastern social policy in general, assumes a woman's subordination to the dominant male in her life, whether father or husband.[2] This man controls her sexuality, including the right to challenge with impunity both her virginity and her marital faithfulness (Deut. 11:28-29; Num. 5:11-31). Indeed, legislative concerns about women's sexual activity primarily have to do with relations between men. A man is executed for having intercourse with another's wife (Lev. 20:10), because he has committed a crime of theft against a man; but a man who seduces or rapes a virgin pays a bride-price to her father and marries her (Deut. 22:28). This is not a crime in the same sense at all, not because of a dissimilarity in what the man did but because of the difference in who "owned" the right to the women's sexuality.

Not surprisingly, in a patriarchal culture in which women function primarily as daughters, wives, and mothers of particular men, women have virtually no property rights. Unmarried women inherit from their fathers only if they have no brothers; and, in such cases, they must subsequently marry within their father's clan to prevent the dispersal of tribal property among outsiders (Num. 36:2-12). Widows do not inherit from their husbands at all, but are dependent on their sons or the generosity of other heirs. According to the practice of levirate marriage, childless widows are the legal responsibility of their husband's oldest brother (Deut. 25:5-10).

Susan Niditch notes that the most noticeable laws of fencing off and boundary making vis-à-vis women are the priestly laws pertaining to purity.[3] According to these regulations menstruating and postpartum women are unclean and sexually unavailable to their husbands for prescribed periods of times (Lev. 12, 15), during which they also have the potential to render ritually impure people and objects around them. A woman is also unclean for a period of seven days after giving birth to a male child and fourteen after a girl. For thirty-three additional days after a boy and sixty-six after a girl, she is forbidden to enter the Temple or to touch hallowed things (Lev. 12:1-8). Although such priestly ordinances reflect a cultic stance in which all discharges—those of men as well as of women—are regarded as rendering unclean, these regulations apply particularly to women, who are regularly subject to the biological consequences of fertility, pregnancy, and childbirth. Biblical texts provide little information as to when, how, and whether such prohibitions were actually observed.

Carol Meyers has applied insights gleaned from sociology, anthropology, and archaeology to reconstruct models of Israelite social life and the ordinary women's place within it in various periods of biblical history. She argues that when agricultural work and childbearing, two spheres in which women played an active role, were central to biblical society, social and religious life in ancient Israel was relatively egalitarian. When the political state and the monarchy emerged, and religious life was institutionalized in the Temple cult and priestly bureaucracy (beginning in the tenth century B.C.E.), however, women were increasingly excluded from the public arena and lost access to communal authority. The negative images of wealthy and leisured urban women in Proverbs and some of the prophetic books may reflect this new reality, in which women's traditional roles have been transformed and devalued.[4]

Indeed, biblical writers have little to say about women's participation in organized cultic worship. We have references to women's participation in communal festivals, to women bringing sacrifices, and to women serving various functions in the ritual surrounding the Tabernacle cult in the premonarchic period, when it was common for women to sing and dance at festivals and as part of victory celebrations (Exod. 15; Judg. 5:1-31; Judg. 21:19-23; 1 Sam. 18:6-7).[5] Hannah, who becomes the mother of Samuel, Israel's last judge, is depicting as praying alone at the Tabernacle at Shiloh (1 Sam. 1:19). Her prayer (1 Sam. 2:1-10) becomes the model for supplicative prayer in Rabbinic tradition (B. Ber. 31a).

But there is far less information on women's participation in Temple rituals during the monarchical period. Although it seems likely that women tended to gather with other women, no mention is made of enforced segregation of the sexes either at Shiloh or in the First Temple. During the Herodian period (first century B.C.E.-first century C.E.), the Women's Court, to the east of the Second Temple's inner Court, provided a large gathering space for both men and women. Rabbinic sources indicate that during the Water-Drawing festival held on the second night of the autumn pilgrimage festival, Tabernacles, women were confined to the balconies in the Women's Court, apparently to prevent licentious behavior (T. Suk. 4:1; B. Suk. 51b-52a; Y. Suk. 55b). Although post-biblical sources indicate that women brought sacrifices and other offerings to the Second Temple, they appear to have been excluded from the Temple's central areas of sanctity, which were, by contrast, accessible to ordinary Israelite males.

References to girls' puberty rites (Judg. 11:39-40), harvest dances (Judg. 21:20-21), and childbirth rituals (Lev. 12:6-8) give fleeting illumination to exclusively female ceremonies that were not of interest to male biblical writers and editors.[6] A number of scholars additionally have discussed the persistence of goddess worship in ancient Israel and the particular place of the Near Eastern fertility goddess, Asherah. While Frymer-Kensky argues that biblical monotheism was generally successful in absorbing the central ideas of polytheism and the functions and roles of goddesses, she agrees that remnants of goddess worship remained. Jeremiah's condemnations of worship practices involving "the Queen of Heaven" (Jer. 7:17-18, 44:15-25) and frequent archaeological discoveries of ancient Israelite female clay figurines, particularly prominent in the period of the monarchies, indicate that aspects of such worship may have lingered, if only as unconscious affirmations of the power of fertility that was seen as the reward of devotion to the "invisible, transcendent God."[7]

Niditch suggests that the female personification of Wisdom in Proverbs also preserves residual elements of female divinity. Although she serves as a divine emissary (Prov. 1:29) and not a fully independent deity, Wisdom, God's confidante and delight (Prov. 8:30), is portrayed as having been created before the world and its inhabitants (Prov. 8:22ff.) and functions as an essential intermediary to divine favor (Prov. 8:35-37). As Niditch has written,[8] "This goddess-like figure in Proverbs directs her attention to male adherents, but also offers a source of identification and empowerment for women by suggesting that the female . . . can be a source of wisdom and life."

Although divine manifestations of female and male sexuality were major components of many ancient Near Eastern religious systems, the Bible treats sexuality essentially as a question of social control: "who with whom and in what circumstances." While a number of biblical narratives demonstrate the strength of sexual attraction and its potentially destructive consequences, only the Song of Songs preserves an idyllic vision of human sexuality beyond normal societal constraints and offers an established vocabulary of female-male erotic love. More typically, Proverbs warns young men to shun the snares of enticing and seductive women (Prov. 5; 7; 31:2-3). While acknowledging that sexual attraction and love underlie the powerful biblical metaphor of God and Israel as husband and wife, Frymer-Kensky notes the absence in the Hebrew Bible of a considered discourse on the dynamics and implications of human sexuality. She suggests that this vacuum was ultimately filled in Hellenistic/ Rabbinic times by the Greek-derived "anti-woman, anticarnal ideas that had such a large impact on the development of Western religion and civilization."[9]

**Women in the system of Rabbinic Judaism:** Rabbinic Judaism, which recorded its legal and literary traditions in the first six centuries C.E., is the basis of all contemporary forms of Jewish religious practice. The literary documents of this Judaism— Mishnah, Talmud, Midrash—are multistranded texts that interweave traditions, motifs, and influences from a variety of sources, time periods, and diverse geographic and cultural environments, reflecting the extended duration of their composition and redaction. It is difficult to extract from this complex and highly edited literary corpus precise historical information about how people actually lived at any given point or at any given location. As Jacob Neusner has demonstrated, even Rabbinic attributions of traditions and anecdotes to specific individuals, linked to express times and places, must be regarded as unreliable.[10]

Rabbinic discourse is far from monolithic in the views and attitudes expressed within its canon, preserving a variety of competing interpretations and opinions. While majority views are generally privileged, minority opinions are perpetuated as well. Given this multivocal literary structure, it is not surprising that Rabbinic literature expresses diverse attitudes towards women and their activities. What unites these views, however, is the conviction that women are essentially different from men both in innate capacities and in legal, social, and spiritual status. Since the interpreters and expositors of Rabbinic literature were men and the ideal human society they imagined was decidedly oriented towards the centrality of their own sex, this is not particularly surprising. Indeed, Rabbinic tradition believes that male Judaism *is* Judaism. Women did not play an active part in its development, nor were they granted a significant role in any aspect of Rabbinic Judaism's communal life of judicial leadership, study, and worship. Women's understandings of their own lives, experiences, and spirituality are not retrievable in any significant way from Rabbinic Judaism's androcentric writings.

Rabbinic legislation is in many ways extra-historical, depicting an ideal vision of how people should live rather than reflecting any contemporary reality. It is not possible to know which of the numerous laws and ordinances were actually in effect at the time they were recorded. The discernible anxiety in the Rabbinic literature regarding control of women's activities thus may reflect dissonance between what many women actually did and what the sages believed that they should do. Be this as it may, we should be clear that, in the course of the Middle Ages, the mandates of the Babylonian Talmud became normative for virtually all Jewish communities. Thus the ideal models of the relation between male and female, as between the divine and the human, that were imagined but not necessarily lived in every detail at the start of the Rabbinic period ultimately became the guidebook and practical pattern of life for ensuing forms of Jewish culture.

B. Shab. 62a expresses the basic Rabbinic conviction that "women are a separate people." Despite the egalitarian vision of human creation found in the first chapter of Genesis, in which both male and female appear to share equally in the divine image, Rabbinic tradition is far more comfortable with the view of Gen. 2:4ff., that women are a secondary conception, unalterably other from men and at a further remove from the divine. This certainty of woman's ancillary place in the scheme of things permeates Rabbinic thinking, and the male sages who produced Rabbinic literature accordingly apportioned separate spheres and separate responsibilities to women and men, making every effort to confine women and their activities to the private realms of the family and its particular concerns.[11]

These obligations included economic activities that would benefit the household, so that undertaking business transactions with other private individuals was an expected part of a woman's domestic role. Women also participated in the economic life of the marketplace, worked in a number of productive enterprises, trades, and crafts,[12] brought claims to the courtroom, met in gatherings with other women, and attended social events. But whatever women did in public, they did as private individuals. Not only by custom but as a result of detailed legislation, women were excluded from significant participation in most of Rabbinic society's communal and power-conferring public activities. Since these endeavors had mostly to do with participation in religious service, communal study of religious texts, and the execution of judgments under Jewish law, women were simultaneously isolated from access to public authority and power and from the communal spiritual and intellectual sustenance available to men.

The male formulators of Rabbinic Judaism primarily considered woman in her relationship to man, as she fell under his control and could contribute to his comfort, the sustenance of his household, and to the bearing and nurturing of his children. As Jacob Neusner has pointed out, Rabbinic legislation concerning women is particularly devoted to those liminal moments at which a woman's status changes due to betrothal, marriage, or the dissolution of a marriage due to death or divorce, with the property settlements such changes of state entail. Women are anomalous in a world-view in which men constitute normality, and they are most anomalous and threatening when they move from one setting and status to another. Writing of the Mishnaic Division of Women, he notes that, "the regulation of the transfer of women is Mishnah's way of effecting the sanctification of what, for the moment, disturbs and disorders the orderly world."[13]

As long as women satisfied male expectations in their assigned roles, they were revered and honored for enhancing the lives of their families and particularly for enabling their male relatives to fulfill their religious obligations. As B. Ber. 17a relates, women earn merit "by sending their children to learn in the synagogue, and their husbands to study in the schools of the rabbis, and by waiting for their husbands until they return from the schools of the rabbis." This remains the case even as Rabbinic jurisprudence goes beyond biblical precedents in its efforts to ameliorate some of the disadvantages and hardships women faced as a consequence of biblical legislation, devoting particular attention to extending special new protections to women in such areas as the formulation of marriage contracts that provided financial support in the event of divorce or widowhood and, in specific circumstances, in allowing a woman to petition a Rabbinic tribunal to compel her husband to divorce her.[14]

Generally, however, women are disadvantaged in the area of personal status, subject to the legal requirement of levirate marriage in the case of a childless widow, unable to divorce a husband or to contest a husband's wish to divorce, and in the case of the *agunah*, a woman whose husband has disappeared but cannot be proven dead, forbidden to remarry. Rabbinic society tolerated polygyny, although it is difficult to know its frequency, and both unmarried and married men were permitted significant sexual freedom, as long as their liaisons were with unmarried women. Thus a married man's relations with an unmarried woman were not considered illicit, nor were the children of such a union considered illegitimate. Adultery applied only when a man had relations with a woman married to someone else; children of such a union, including the children of an *agunah*, are *mamzerim* (often, though incorrectly, translated "bastards") and suffer significant legal disabilities.

Woman's otherness and less desirable status are assumed throughout the Rabbinic literature. While women are credited with more compassion and concern for the unfortunate than men, perhaps as a result of their nurturing roles, they also are linked with witchcraft (M. Ab. 2:7; Y. Qid. 4, 66b), foolishness (B. Shab. 33b), dishonesty (Gen. Rab. 18:2), and licentiousness (M. Sot. 3:4, and B. Ket. 65a), among a number of other inherent negative qualities (Gen. Rab. 45:5). Sometimes the secondary and inferior creation of women is cited as explaining their disagreeable traits (Gen. Rab. 18:2); elsewhere Eve's culpability in introducing death into the world accounts for women's disabilities in comparison to male advantages (Gen. Rab. 17:8). Aggadic exegeses of independent biblical women tend to criticize their pride and presumption. Thus, the biblical judge Deborah is likened to a wasp, and the prophetess Huldah to a weasel (B. Meg. 14b); other biblical heroines are similarly disparaged, and women who display unusual sagacity often meet early deaths (B. Ket. 23a). Women do utter words of wisdom in Rabbinic stories, but generally such stories either confirm a Rabbinic belief about women's character, such as women's higher degree of compassion for others (B. A.Z. 18a; B. Ket. 104a), or deliver a rebuke to a man in need of chastisement (B. Erub. 53b; B. San. 39a).

Both qualities are present in traditions about Beruriah, the wife of the second century C.E. rabbi, Meir, known for her unusual learning and quick wit (B. Pes. 62b; B. Erub. 53b-54a). Yet Beruriah's scholarship was a problem for Rabbinic culture, and in later Rabbinic tradition she is shown to reap the tragic consequences of the "lightmindedness" inherent in woman's makeup: in his commentary on B. A.Z. 18b, Rashi (eleventh century) relates that Beruriah was seduced by one of her husband's students and subsequently committed suicide. Contemporary scholars have shown that the scholarly Beruriah is a literary construct with little historical reality,[15] yet they agree that the traditions about her articulate profound disquiet about the role of women in the Rabbinic enterprise. Rachel Adler suggests that Beruriah's story expresses Rabbinic ambivalence about the possible place of a woman in their wholly male scholarly world, in which her sexuality was bound to be a source of havoc.[16] Daniel Boyarin writes that for the Amoraic sages of the Babylonian Talmud, Beruriah serves as proof of "R. Eliezer's statement that 'anyone who teaches his daughter Torah, teaches her lasciviousness' (M. Sot. 3:4);" in Rabbinic culture, he writes, "The Torah and the wife are structural allomorphs and separated realms . . . both normatively to be highly valued but also to be kept separate."[17]

This is not to say that women were granted no spiritual status. Women, like men, were not only responsible for obeying all of Judaism's negative commandments but also for observing the Sabbath and all of the festivals and holidays of the Jewish calendar—although male and female obligations on these days often differed. According to B. Ber. 20a-20b, women are exempt from participation in communal prayers that must be said at a fixed time. But they were not free from the obligation incumbent on each individual to pray (B. Ber. 20b). Later Jewish tradition understood that women were to make a personal address to God as they started their day and that the content of women's prayers might be spontaneous and could be voiced in a vernacular language rather than according to an established liturgy.[18] We do not find extant versions of specific formulations of prayers for women, however, until the end of the medieval period.

Judith Hauptman has suggested that woman's exemption from performing ritual acts at specific times is emblematic not only of her household duties but of her subordinate social position. Her being obligated to these acts "would lessen her husband's dominance over her because she would have to cease temporarily from serving him and instead serve God."[19] The gender asymmetry inherent within Rabbinic social policy thus demands that women's roles be subsidiary to those of men, with female religious observance taking second place to family responsibility. Some contemporary scholars have argued that not all Rabbinic authorities were agreed on this isolation of women from learning and communal prayer; minority strands more supportive of women's intellectual and spiritual abilities and needs also weave through the tradition, particularly from sources in the land of Israel.[20] Still, it is obvious that attitudes directed towards limiting women's activities in the communal sphere, including worship and serious study, represent the preponderance of Rabbinic thinking on this matter.

Women participated in their own religious observances, including abstention from work on *Rosh Hodesh*, the New Moon (Y. Ta. 1:6, 64c); the details of such rituals particular to women, which would have taken place in the private domain, are now mostly lost to us. Women also observed a number of ritual regulations within the domestic sphere, especially preparation and serving of food according to Rabbinic dietary laws (*kashrut*) and the observance of the limitations on marital contact during the menstrual period (*niddah*). Similarly, women were expected to set aside and burn a piece of the dough used in making bread (*hallah*), a reminder of the system of priestly tithes, and to kindle Sabbath lights (*hadlaqah*). Doubtless, for many women these rituals provided satisfying spiritual avenues for sanctification of aspects of daily life. Yet at least some strands of Rabbinic tradition do not regard women's performance of these ordinances as *mitzvot* at all. In these sources they are not divine commandments the observance of which enhances the religious life of the observer and assures divine favor, but, rather, eternal punishments brought upon woman to remind her of Eve's responsibility in the death of Adam and therefore in all human mortality (Gen. Rab. 17:8).

Female physical and biological differences from men are fundamental to the exclusion of women from Rabbinic Judaism's central spiritual endeavors. Anthropologists such as Michelle Rosaldo have pointed out that cultural notions of the female often center around natural or biological characteristics such as fertility, maternity, sexuality, and menstrual blood; women, therefore, may "be seen as anomalous and defined as dangerous, dirty, polluting, as something to be set apart."[21] Certainly, significant voices within Rabbinic Judaism are anxious to circumscribe, defuse, and control the biological/sexual attributes of the female as both polluter and temptress. Rabbinic Judaism saw ritual purity as a religious ideal, while ritual uncleanness necessitated a separation from the divine. The biblical strictures (particularly Lev. 12, 15, and 18) that limit contact with a menstruating or post-partum woman are fundamental to the Rabbinic separation of women from male religious activities.

While men are also subject to discharges and to states of ritual impurity, physical ailments and events imparting male impurity are unusual and sporadic. But for women, such discharges are characteristic; they are normal and expected rather than an accident that may temporarily affect a man. That women regularly menstruate constitutes an indispensable component of the Rabbinic construction of the female. Shaye Cohen has pointed out that such attitudes, expressive of folk piety as much as legal formulation, confirm "the marginality of all women, menstruating or not, in the organized, public expressions of Jewish piety."[22]

Women constitute an additional source of danger in Rabbinic thinking, because their sexual appeal to men can lead to social disruption. A significant argument for excluding women from synagogue participation rests on the Talmudic statement, "The voice of a woman is indecent" (B. Ber. 24a). This idea emerges from a ruling that a man may not recite the *Shema* while he hears a woman singing, since her voice might divert his concentration from the prayer. Extrapolating from hearing to seeing, Rabbinic prohibitions on male/female contact in worship eventually led to a physical barrier (*mehitzah*) between men and women in the synagogue, to preserve men from sexual distraction during prayer. Indeed, viewing women always as a sexual temptation, Rabbinic Judaism overall advises extremely limited contact between men and women who are not married to each other. This is to prevent inappropriate sexual contact, whether adulterous, incestuous, or simply outside of a married relationship.

In her detailed study of the legal status of women in the Mishnah, Judith Wegner points out the role of women's sexuality. She demonstrates that in all matters that affect a man's ownership of her sexuality—whether as minor daughter, wife, or levirate widow—a woman is presented as belonging to a man. In nonsexual contexts, by contrast, the wife is endowed with a high degree of personhood. Her legal rights as a property holder are protected, and she is assigned rights and privileges that are denied even to non-Israelite males.[23]

Notably, Mishnaic legislation always treats as an independent "person" a woman on whose sexuality no man has a legal claim. Such an autonomous woman—who might be an emancipated daughter of full age, a divorcée, or a widow—may arrange her own marriage, is legally liable for any vows she may make, and may litigate in court. Free from male authority, she has control over her personal life and is treated as an independent agent. Wegner emphasizes, however, that while the autonomous woman has some latitude in the private domain of relationships between individuals, Mishnaic rules governing women's relationship to the public domain tell quite a different story. Here, all women are systematically excluded from the religiously prestigious male domains of communal leadership, collaborative study, and public prayer.

**Women in non-Rabbinic Jewish communities in late antiquity:** From the third century B.C.E. on, large numbers of Jews lived in the Greek-speaking diaspora of the Hellenistic and Roman worlds. Evidence suggests that a number of aspects of Jewish life in these communities, including possibilities available for women, diverged significantly from the norms and prescriptions found in Rabbinic Judaism. While it seems

likely that most Jewish women of these milieus lived their lives in the relative seclusion of the domestic realm, Ross S. Kraemer's examination of funerary and other inscriptions demonstrates that some of them acted independently in social, economic, and religious spheres.[24] Kraemer and others have also found evidence for wide ranging female activities in the prominent and diverse roles played by female characters in the Hellenistic Jewish literature of late antiquity, such as Judith, Tobit, Asenath ("Joseph and Asenath"), and in the story of the mother of seven sons (2 and 4 Maccabees).[25]

In a number of Greek and Latin inscriptions dating from the first century B.C.E. to the sixth century C.E., and ranging from Italy to Asia Minor, Egypt, and Phoenicia, women bear such titles as "head of the synagogue," "leader," "elder," "mother of the synagogue," and "priestess." On this basis, Bernadette Brooten has suggested that contrary to the previous scholarly consensus informed by Rabbinic texts, Jewish women assumed positions of leadership in the very public sphere of the ancient synagogue.[26] Although it is not clear if these synagogue titles were simply honorific, in recognition of significant philanthropy, or whether they imply that women had meaningful leadership and/or ritual obligations, Kraemer suggests that Jewish communities in the Greco-Roman diaspora may have been particularly accepting of women's leadership in areas of public affairs, where "civic responsibility and religion intersected," as in synagogue activities. She also notes the possibility "that women's leadership was particularly likely in Jewish synagogues with relatively high numbers of proselytes (both male and female), for whom the participation of women in public life, including religious *collegia*, was familiar and acceptable."[27] Similarly, Brooten's analysis of archaeological, literary, and epigraphical evidence relating to women and the synagogue reveals no evidence from antiquity that women were routinely separated from men in Jewish worship, nor that women sat in upstairs galleries or adjacent rooms.

A few Jewish women of this milieu may also have possessed significant Jewish learning. The first century C.E. writer Philo of Alexandria relates that a small number of upper-class, well-educated Jewish women joined the contemplative monastic Therapeutic community that was located outside of Alexandria, Egypt. Apparently, most of those women were older virgins, who, like their male counterparts, spent their days reading Jewish scriptures and allegorical commentaries and living a life of rigorous asceticism, interrupted only by Sabbath and festival observances. When men and women prayed together on the Sabbath, they were separated by a partial wall that prevented visual contact but allowed the women to participate equally with the men in prayer and song.[28]

**The Middle Ages:** The main expectations for a Jewish woman of the Middle Ages were domestic: "May she sew, spin, weave, and be brought up to a life of good deeds" is the prayer with which one set of parents in medieval Northern Europe recorded their daughter's birth. With the additional desire, expressed in this same period but in Muslim Egypt, that a newborn daughter "might come into a blessed and auspicious home," that is, marry well, the essential hopes for medieval Jewish women have been expressed.[29] Yet the evidence shows, particularly in Christian Europe, that women were also active in economic endeavors, sometimes supporting their husbands and families, and that some fulfilled religious leadership roles such as teaching other women and leading them in prayer. Despite Jewish women's essential contributions as individuals to their families and communities, however, negative attitudes towards women in general are prevalent in medieval Jewish secular, religious, and mystical writings.

In medieval times most Jews lived outside the land of Israel, with significant populations in the Muslim worlds of North Africa, the Middle East, Western Asia, and Spain (Sepharad); smaller numbers of Jews lived in Christian Europe (Ashkenaz). Jewish communities were governed by the Babylonian Talmud, its laws developed by rabbis' answers to legal questions (responsa literature), by legal codes, and through biblical and Talmudic commentaries. These sources continued the Rabbinic pattern of ordaining separate gender roles and religious obligations for men and women and relegating females to secondary, enabling positions. However, norms and customs of local environments were also factors in how Jewish social life developed. Jews assumed the language, dress, and many of the mores of their gentile neighbors, including cultural attitudes towards appropriate female behavior. Still, recovering Jewish women's personal or spiritual aspirations or their feelings about the expectations imposed upon them is all but impossible, since beyond some examples of personal correspondence, virtually no documents written by medieval Jewish women survive.

Jewish social life in the Muslim realm was strongly influenced by Islamic customs, and polygyny was not uncommon. While Jewish women of prosperous families were not literally isolated in women's quarters, community norms dictated that women remain out of the public eye. The observation of the preeminent sage of medieval Judaism, Moses Maimonides (1135-1204), who lived much of his life in Cairo, that, "There is nothing more beautiful for a wife than sitting in the corner of her house," reflects the high degree of Jewish acculturation to Islamic custom. While Maimonides held that a woman is not a prisoner to be prevented from going and coming, he suggested that visits to family and friends should not exceed one or two a month.

Still, as accounts of marital disputes found in the Cairo genizah make clear, Jewish women had significant freedom of movement for visits to the synagogue, bathhouse, social and condolence calls, and business activities, such as the buying and selling of flax.[30] Married quite young and frequently to considerably older men, women were often protected by social safeguards written into the marriage contract (*ketubah*). These altered Jewish laws and practices unfavorable to women, particularly as protection against desertion and divorce, ordinarily a solely male prerogative. Such additions to the standard contract also attempted to provide security against many of the known pitfalls of married life and included guarantees that, in case of separation, a divorce document (*get*) freeing the wife would be produced by her husband without delay, that the husband would not marry another wife, that he would not beat his wife, separate her against her will from her parents, or travel anywhere without her consent. Quite frequently, the contract also stipulated that the husband would write a conditional bill of divorce before setting out on a journey, so that his wife would be free to remarry should he fail to return after a specified length of time. He might also be required to deposit the delayed installment of her marriage gift as well as the sums needed for her maintenance during his absence.

The *ketubah* obligated the husband to provide his wife with food and clothing and to maintain her in general. Following biblical custom, Jewish grooms in the Muslim milieu also contributed a marriage gift (*mohar*), part of which was payable to the bride's father at the time of the wedding, with a portion reserved for the bride in the event of a divorce or her husband's death. Similarly the bride brought property into the marriage in the form of her dowry and trousseau. This dowry, which was also to be returned to the wife in case of divorce or her husband's death, was generally far more valuable than the husband's marriage gift and gave the bride's family "significant leverage in finding her a suitable match and insuring her proper treatment during marriage."[31] In addition to the normative unilateral marriage contract issued in the husband's name alone, the Cairo genizah preserves some contracts from the land of Israel that define marriage as a partnership based on mutual consent, which even permit wives to initiate divorce proceedings.

Although boys were usually educated in both religious and secular subjects, Jewish women were rarely literate. There is no evidence in the Muslim milieu either of the development of liturgical language or a spiritual literature for Jewish women or of women prayer leaders, as in medieval Ashkenazic communities. Genizah documents report that women, who had no obligation to worship communally, were pious in observing home-based laws incumbent upon them. Women who chose to attend the synagogue prayed in a gallery separated from male worshippers.

Prosperous women often donated Torah scrolls or left legacies for the upkeep of the synagogue. Such donations to the synagogue may be understood as both expressions of piety and as reflecting women's strategies for asserting themselves in a realm of communal activity from which they were otherwise excluded. Generally, however, it was as a mother of sons learned in Jewish law that the Jewish woman in the Islamic world earned her spiritual reward in the eyes of her family and her society.[32]

The small Jewish communities of medieval Christian Europe lived in an atmosphere of religious suspicion and legal disability. Following the Crusades, Jews were barred from virtually any source of livelihood but money lending and were often compelled to wear distinctive clothing and badges. By the end of the Middle Ages, Jews were expelled from areas in which they had long lived (including England in 1290 and Spain in 1492), or were forced to live in crowded ghettoes. Despite their political insecurity, Jews enjoyed a high standard of living and were significantly acculturated. Jewish women participated in the family economy, sometimes as independent financiers, and their status was higher than that of Jewish women in the Muslim milieu, as indicated by larger dowries, significant freedom of movement, and the eleventh century ruling of Gershom ben Judah of Mainz forbidding polygyny for Jews in Christian countries. Gershom also ruled that no woman could be divorced against her will. In fact, divorce appears to have been less common among Jews in medieval Christian Europe than in the Muslim milieu, perhaps because it was not sanctioned within Christian society. Here too husbands who set out on a journey customarily left their wives with a conditional divorce document, so that the wives would be free to remarry should they fail to return after a specified length of time.

Jews in Christian Spain retained significant aspects of Muslim culture, including the attitude that women should remain at home, a feature of Sephardic Jewish life well into the early modern period, even after the expulsion from Spain (1492), when Jews lived in very different locations. The Muslim practice of polygyny also had a significant impact on Spanish Jewry, who never wholly accepted Gershom's ban on the practice. Even under Christian rulers, Spanish Jews who wished to take second wives, usually as a result of fertility problems or unhappy relationships with their first spouse, could obtain special royal permission by paying a fee. While second marriages were more frequent among the wealthy, who could most easily afford the expenses of an expanded household, their prevalence indicates the lower status of the Sephardic woman as compared to Jewish women in the rest of Europe.[33]

But this was not always the case. Under Jewish law, widows do not inherit their husband's property but instead either receive back their dowry or are supported by their husband's estate. Widows who chose to remarry generally had to give up custody of their minor children to their late husband's family. During the late medieval period it was not uncommon for Jewish men in Spain to file Latin wills with Christian courts to ensure that their wives could inherit their property and maintain custody of children. This is an example of Jewish willingness to circumvent the disadvantages for women inherent in the *halakhah* when it conflicted with personal circumstances and the norms of the majority culture. Especially those widows who benefited from their husbands' recourse to the generous inheritance laws of Christian Spain often controlled significant resources. Some powerful Sephardic widows, such as Benvenida Abarvanel and Dona Gracia Nasi, both of the sixteenth century, successfully continued their deceased husbands' businesses, intervened with rulers on behalf of threatened Jewish communities, and were renowned for their philanthropy and support of Jewish culture and learning.[34]

Positive Jewish attitudes towards marriage and sexuality expressed in medieval Jewish literature were at odds with medieval Christian teachings, which enjoined celibacy on the representatives of the Church and taught that the only purpose of marital sexuality should be procreation; it is not surprising that Christian writers criticized Jewish sexual behavior, real and imagined.[35] Influence from the Christian environment may account for the ambivalence towards sexuality characteristic of the German-Jewish pietists of the twelfth and thirteenth centuries. The writings of the *Hasidei Ashkenaz*, such as *Sefer Hasidim* ("Book of the Pious"), express not only an obsessive concern with the ubiquity of extramarital sexual temptations but also a profound ambivalence about the joys of licensed sexual activities. Although a happy marital relationship lessened the likelihood of illicit sexual activity and was, therefore, a good thing, they were concerned that it might also distract a man from God, who should be the focus of one's greatest and most intense devotion.

Religious education for girls usually centered on domestic knowledge essential for running a Jewish household, including not only the rudiments of cooking, needlework, and household management, but also the Rabbinic rules applicable to home and marriage. Basic religious training was considered essential so that a woman would know how to observe dietary laws, domestic regulations pertaining to the Sabbath and festivals, and the other commandments relevant to her intimate life with her husband. The New Moon continued to be a holiday from household responsibilities for women, but one more given to leisure and games of chance than spiritual activities. Although women's involvement in business required literacy in the vernacular language and bookkeeping skills, training in Hebrew and the study of Jewish texts was rare for girls and was limited to a few women from Rabbinic families. Learned women, such as the twelfth century Dolce (wife of the medieval Rabbinic leader and mystic, Eleazar of Worms), Richenza of Nuremberg, and the thirteenth century Urania, a cantor's daughter, also of Worms, often taught and led prayers for women in their communities, sometimes in a separate room in the synagogue. From the male point of view, however, such women were irrelevant to scholarship or communal life. Women's testimony on legal or religious matters was considered only if they were regarded as reliable witnesses to the practices of distinguished fathers or husbands.[36]

Figure 169. Alder wood charity box made by Lourie and Company for the Beth Jacob schools, Vienna, Austria. Founded in 1917, Beth Jacob schools were the first to provide an Orthodox education for girls.

Figure 170. Teachers and students at a Hebrew Gymnasium, Kaunas, Lithuania, c. 1939-1940.

Figure 171. Seamstresses in Kosino, Czechoslovakia, are (left to right) Magda Espan, Ilon Grosz, Jolan Braun, Margit Braun, Eszti Einczig, and a child, Aliz Braun, April 14, 1935.

Figure 172. Women's prayer group, New York City, undated. Photograph by Barbara Pfeffer.

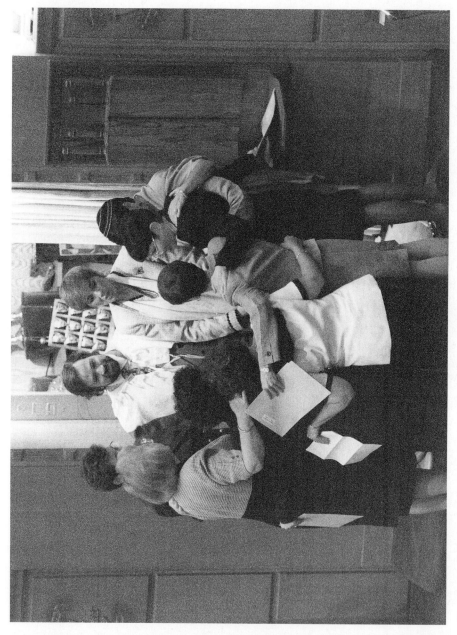

Figure 173. Women who did not have an opportunity to mark their coming of age at thirteen celebrate their bat mitzvah as adults at Stephen Wise Free Synagogue, New York City, June 7, 1996. Photograph by Peter Goldberg.

Figure 174. Tambourine made for feminist Passover seders. United States, 1999. The illustration by Betsy Platkin-Teutsch shows the prophetess Miriam dancing with a tambourine in the midst of other dancing women of all ages.

Figure 175. Cotton and wool needlepoint skullcap (kippah) made by Amy Levin, a rabbinical student at the Jewish Theological Seminary of America. New York City, 1990-1991. Increasingly, women have adopted ritual objects and clothing once worn only by men.

Figure 176. Lecture notice by the Student Zionist Organization on the theme, "Are the tactics of Brith-Shalom justified in today's times?" The lecture took place at the Hall of the Jewish Students Union, Vilna, Poland, February 15, 1930.

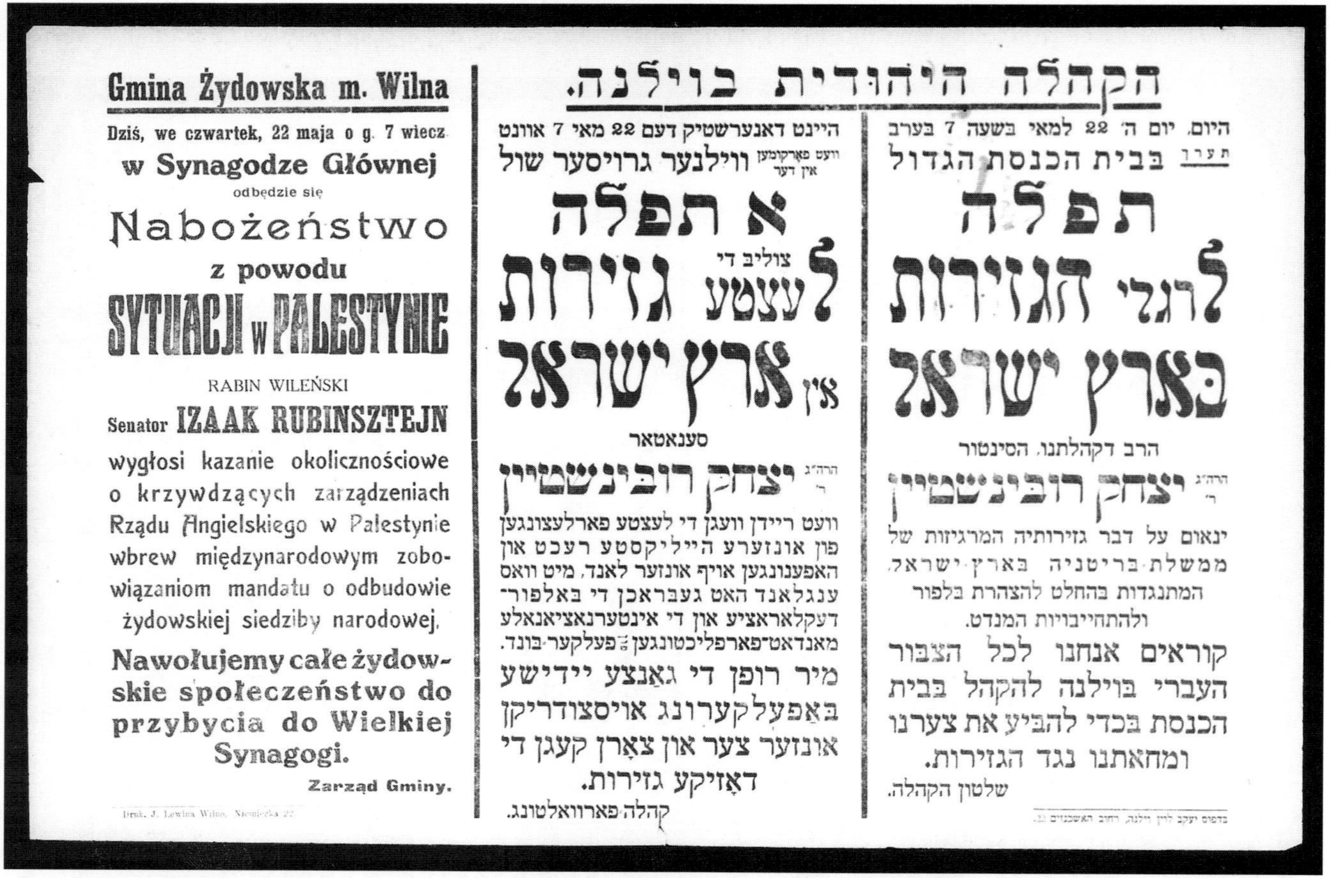

Gmina Żydowska m. Wilna

Dziś, we czwartek, 22 maja o g. 7 wiecz.

w Synagodze Głównej

odbędzie się

Nabożeństwo

z powodu

SYTUACJI w PALESTYNIE

RABIN WILEŃSKI

Senator IZAAK RUBINSZTEJN

wygłosi kazanie okolicznościowe o krzywdzących zarządzeniach Rządu Angielskiego w Palestynie wbrew międzynarodowym zobowiązaniom mandatu o odbudowie żydowskiej siedziby narodowej.

Nawołujemy całe żydowskie społeczeństwo do przybycia do Wielkiej Synagogi.

Zarząd Gminy.

Druk. J. Lewina Wilno, Niemiecka 22

הקהלה היהודית בווילנה.

היינט דאנערשטיק דעם 22 מאי 7 אוונט ווערט פארקומען אין דער ווילנער גרויסער שול

א תפלה

צוליב די לעצטע גזירות אין ארץ ישראל

סענאטאר הרה״ג ר׳ יצחק רובינשטיין

וועט ריידן וועגן די לעצטע פארלעצונגען פון אונזערע הייליקסטע רעכט און האפענונגען אויף אונזער לאנד, מיט וואס ענגלאנד האט געבראכן די באלפור־דעקלאראציע און די אינטערנאציאנאלע מאנדאט־פארפליכטונגען צו פעלקער־בונד.

מיר רופן די גאנצע יידישע באפעלקערונג אויסצודריקן אונזער צער און צארן קעגן די דאזיקע גזירות.

קהלה־פארוואלטונג.

היום, יום ה׳ 22 למאי בשעה 7 בערב תער״ג בבית הכנסת הגדול

תפלה

לרגלי הגזירות בארץ ישראל

הרב דקהלתנו, הסינטור הרה״ג ר׳ יצחק רובינשטיין

ינאום על דבר גזירותיה המרגיזות של ממשלת בריטניה בארץ ישראל, המתנגדות בהחלט להצהרת בלפור ולהתחייבויות המנדט.

קוראים אנחנו לכל הצבור העברי בוילנה להקהל בבית הכנסת בכדי להביע את צערנו ומחאתנו נגד הגזירות.

שלטון הקהלה.

בדפוס יעקב לוין ווילנא, רחוב האשכנזים 22.

Figure 177. Notice of prayer meeting and discussion in the Big Vilna synagogue in response to the British anti-Zionist policy in Palestine; Vilna, Poland, May 22, 1930.

Figure 178. Soccer poster announcing the opening of the Maccabi sports club soccer season, Grodno, Poland, April 25, 1931. Many Zionist groups emphasized sports and physical skills in their effort to prepare Jews for building new lives in a renewed homeland in Palestine.

Figure 179. Members of the Bardejov, Czechoslovakia, branch of Ha-shomer ha-Za'ir, a Socialist-Zionist youth organization, posing in front of their tent on a camping trip, undated.

Figure 180. First Zionist Congress held after World War II, London, 1945. Chaim Weitzman is at the microphone; David Ben Gurion and Rabbi Leo Baeck are seated at right.

While celibacy and monastic living allowed a significant number of Christian women and, to a certain extent, some Muslim women to cross gender boundaries and secure a place alongside men as scholars, saints, and mystics, Rabbinic insistence on universal marriage denied Jewish women any access to such alternatives. Formal Judaism offered no adult avenues through which Jewish women could express their spiritual aspirations beyond marital devotion, maternal solicitude, observance of domestic Jewish rituals, and acts of charity to others. As Ada Rapoport-Albert has observed, despite Jewish ambivalence towards asceticism in general, Jewish mystical circles sanctioned ritualistic practices for men, which could include prolonged periods of sexual abstinence. For women, on the other hand, such conduct was considered "inherently false, hypocritical or self-deluding."[37] Jewish religious leaders criticized women who adopted such ascetic practices as fasting, prayer, and acts of personal deprivation. These signs of single-minded devotion to God were seen as a dereliction of a woman's primary duties to her husband and family and were suspect, as well, even in the unmarried girl and the widow (cf. B. Sot. 22a).

Given these prohibitions, it is not surprising that medieval Jewish mysticism was an essentially male endeavor. As Gershom Scholem has written, "There have been no women Kabbalists; Rabia of early Islamic mysticism, Mechtild of Magdeburg, Juliana of Norwich, Theresa de Jesus, and the many other feminine representatives of Christian mysticism have no counterparts in the history of Kabbalism."[38] Moreover, in the gender imagery that pervades medieval Jewish mystical writings, the male, created in the divine image, is construed as the dominant, primary sex, while females are deemed passive and secondary. In sexual union female distinctiveness, and by analogy the feminine aspect of the divine, the *Shekhinah*, is effaced and absorbed by the preeminent male entity, the *Ayn Sof*, or infinite aspect of God, from which she was originally derived. While the *Shekhinah* as bride is a positive symbol, pointing to divine unity, the *Shekhinah* alone, sometimes represented as a menstruant (*niddah*), is dangerous, since the unconstrained female and her menstrual blood are linked to the demonic forces responsible for evil in the world.[39]

Religious and secular medieval Jewish literatures often represent women as untrustworthy, sources of sexual temptation, and demonic; negative attitudes already present in Talmudic tradition are often intensified.[40] Jewish customary law concerning the menstruating woman becomes more exclusionary in the Middle Ages, particularly in the Christian sphere. According to the sixth or seventh century *Baraita de Niddah*, the menstruant was forbidden to enter a synagogue, to come into contact with sacred books, to pray, or to recite God's name. These customs were followed in many locales during the medieval period, although they have no *halakhic* basis, and were endorsed by Rabbinic authorities who praised compliant women for their piety. Even where menstruating women did attend and enter fully into synagogue services, it is reported that, "They take care only not to look at the Torah scroll when the sexton displays it to the congregation."[41] As Cohen notes, the exclusion of menstruants confirmed that the sacred space of the synagogue was male space and that women "because they are women, are not its natural occupants."

Similarly, traditions about the demon Lilith are synthesized in the eleventh century *Alphabet of Ben Sira*. Here Rabbinic speculation about the "first Eve," who refused to submit to Adam's mastery and established herself as an independent sexual entity, merges with legends about demons who kill infants and endanger women in childbirth. This defines Lilith in later Jewish folklore and mysticism as the exemplar of rebellious wives and the fiendish enemy of properly submissive women and their children.[42] Similarly, *Sefer Hasidim* associates women with sorcery and witchcraft and assumes that even the most pious have the potential, however unwitting, to tempt a man to sin or sinful thoughts.

**Jewish women's spiritual literature in the early modern period:** The invention of printing in the fifteenth century, which made the dissemination of popular literature practicable and inexpensive, played an important role in expanding Jewish women's religious lives in Central and Eastern Europe. Rabbinic injunctions against women's learning applied to Talmud study but not to the Bible or legal rulings necessary for women's everyday activities. While Jewish women were generally ignorant of Hebrew, most were literate in the Jewish vernacular (Judaeo-German in Central Europe, Yiddish in Eastern Europe, written in Hebrew characters), which was essential to women's economic activities.

Translations of the Hebrew Bible, the first books to be printed in the Jewish vernacular, gave women access to Judaism's holy texts. Particularly popular were the *Taytsh-khumesh*, first published by Sheftl Hurwitz in Prague in 1608 or 1610, and the *Tsene-rene*, by Yankev ben Itzkhok Ashkenazy (c.1590-1618), both of which included homilies on the weekly biblical readings from the Torah and Prophets, as well as stories, legends, and parables drawn from Rabbinic literature, the Zohar and other mystical texts, and histories and travel accounts. *Musar* books, ethical treatises that discussed proper conduct, woman's religious obligations, and her relations with her husband, such as the *Brantshpigl* ("Burning Mirror") by Moses ben Henoch Altschuler (1596), and the *Meneket Rivkah* of Rebecca bas Meir Tiktiner of Prague (d. 1550; posthumously published in the early seventeenth century), were also available to female readers. These vernacular books intended for women were also read by Jewish men, many of whom were not possessed of significant Jewish scholarship; they were printed in a special typeface, *vayber taytsh* ("women's vernacular"), based on the cursive Hebrew hand women were taught for business contracts, marriage agreements, and correspondence.[43]

Although all the Hebrew and Aramaic prayers of the standard liturgy were translated into Judaeo-German/Yiddish, they were never as central to women as *tkhines*, supplicatory prayers intended for female use in Jewish rituals and in worship, both in the synagogue and at home. Collections of such prayers began to appear in the sixteenth century. While much of this literature was written by men for women and represents men's conceptions of women's religious lives, *tkhines* do demonstrate what women prayed about and offer insight into how they understood the meanings of their religious acts. A similar phenomenon was also present in Italy, where Deborah Ascarelli translated Hebrew liturgical poetry into rhymed Italian, presumably for use by female worshippers. Her *Abitacolo degli oranti*, completed in 1537 and published in 1601, may be the earliest published work in Jewish literature written by a woman.[44]

Some of the *tkhines* were written for use in the synagogue and follow the regular liturgy of daily and Sabbath prayers. Liturgical *tkhines* also exist for the penitential season (from the beginning of the month of Elul, one month before the New Year, through the Day of Atonement), confessions of sins, fast days, and the festivals, indicating that women were in regular attendance at the synagogue year round.[45] It was customary for a learned woman, known as the *firzogerin* or *zogerke*, often a rabbi's wife or daughter, to lead the women's section of the synagogue in reciting prayers that would include vernacular *tkhines* as well as the Hebrew liturgy.

Non-liturgical *tkhines*, written to hallow women's domestic activities, often address the special "women's commandments," the three religious duties especially incumbent on women: *hallah* (separating out a small portion of dough in memory of the priestly tithes), *hadlaqah* (lighting candles on the eve of Sabbaths and festivals); and *niddah* (marital separation during menstruation and ritual immersion afterwards). The *tkhines* for pregnancy and childbirth are similar in addressing central events in women's lives. Petitioning the dead, overwhelmingly associated with women, was also an important topic for *tkhines*. Most *tkhines* were intended to be recited individually, at home, or in other private settings, such as the ritual bath or the cemetery, an indication that women's religious lives were less public and communal than men's.[46]

Although some attributions of *tkhines* to

female authors or editors seem doubtful, women like Rebecca Tiktiner did write and publish *tkhines* collections.[47] Weissler has written that Eastern European *tkhines* that are generally accepted as having been written by women sometimes articulate both the sanctification of women's traditional roles and a critique of them. Sarah Rebecca Rachel Leah Horowitz (c. 1720-c. 1800), the highly educated author of the *Tkhine Imohes* ("Tkhine of the Matriarchs"), emphasizes the power and importance of women's prayer. Influenced by mystical teachings, she believed that through their devoted and tearful synagogue prayers, women could help end the exile of the *Shekhinah* and reunite her with her divine consort in the era of messianic redemption. Sarah bas Tovim (probably eighteenth century) made use of Rabbinic and mystical texts in Yiddish to construct a new vision of women's religious lives, in which women's prayer was as significant as men's. In the *Shloyse She'orim* ("Three Gates") she invokes the authority of meritorious women of the past in a complex description of a multi-chambered women's paradise; in each chamber an outstanding female biblical figure presides over thousands of joyous women studying the divine word.[48]

Collections of prayers and religious texts in Yiddish and in European vernacular languages, intended for female use, were produced into the twentieth century. *Stunden der Andacht* ("Hours of Devotion"), a German prayer book for women written by Fanny Neuda (d. 1894) went through twenty-eight editions by the 1920s and was also translated into English. These prayers for women reflect a personal rather than a communal understanding of Judaism, one in which women often called upon the biblical matriarchs to intercede with God on behalf of the worshipper and her family. Inasmuch as some of these prayers were written by women, they also represent some of the earliest extant expressions of female spirituality in Jewish tradition.[49]

Another early modern woman who wrote in her own voice is Glikl bas Judah Leib of Hameln (1646-1724), whose autobiography, written to drive away the melancholy that followed her husband's death and to let her children know their ancestry, is an engrossing document that interweaves and juxtaposes pious tales and moralizing with Glikl's accounts of events in her own life and those of her loved ones. Born into the prosperous Court Jew milieu of Central Europe, Glikl was extremely well read in Yiddish literature and had some knowledge of Hebrew and German as well; her memorial notice characterizes her as "a learned woman" (*melumedet*), unusual praise in her time and place.[50] Betrothed at twelve, married at fourteen, the mother of fourteen children, Glikl was active in business and pious in religious observance, including regular synagogue attendance. At the threshold of modernity, both as a woman and as a Jew, Glikl's business activities reflect the growing economic participation of Jews in the non-Jewish world, while her religious and secular education speaks to the broader horizons and new educational opportunities available to some seventeenth century Jews—including women.

**Hasidism:** The development of the pietistic/mystical movement of Hasidism in eighteenth century Poland had a profound and lasting impact on Eastern European Jewry. Hasidism brought no improvements for women's status, however, and in some ways intensified negative views of women already present in Jewish mysticism and traditional Rabbinic Judaism. Although Hasidic tradition preserves descriptions of daughters, mothers, and sisters of Rabbinic leaders who are said to have themselves led Hasidic communities and to have adopted rigorous standards of personal piety, Ada Rapoport-Albert has pointed out that there is little written documentation about them. She does not doubt that some of these prominent women existed, but suggests that their authority was based on their connection to revered male leaders. Thus "Hasidism did not evolve an ideology of female leadership, any more than it improved the position of women within the family or set out to educate them in Yiddish."[51]

The one apparent example of a woman who crossed gender boundaries to achieve religious leadership in a Hasidic sect on her own is, in fact, a story of female failure. The well-educated, pious, and wealthy Hannah Rachel Verbermacher (b. 1815), known as "the Holy Maid of Ludmir," acquired a reputation for saintliness and miracle-working, attracting both men and women to her "court," where she would lecture from behind a closed door. Reaction from the male Hasidic leaders of her region was uniformly negative, and pressure was successfully applied on Hannah to resume her rightful female role in marriage. Although her marriages were unsuccessful, they had the intended result of ending her career as a religious leader, and Hannah ended her life in obscurity.

In its emphasis on mystical transcendence and on male attendance on the Rabbinic leader, the *zaddik* or *rebbe*, to the exclusion of the family unit, Hasidism contributed significantly to the breakdown of the Jewish social life in nineteenth century Eastern Europe. Similar tensions between family responsibility and devotion to Torah were also present among the non-Hasidic learned elite of this milieu, where wives tended to assume the responsibility for supporting their families while husbands were studying away from home.[52] David Biale has noted that the sexual asceticism of the homosocial Hasidic courts and Rabbinic yeshivot of the eighteenth and nineteenth centuries offered young men a welcome withdrawal from family tensions and the threats of modernity. He writes that the negative attitudes toward human sexuality they found in these environments were often openly misogynistic, incorporating many demonic images of women from Rabbinic, Kabbalistic, and Jewish folklore traditions.[53]

**Enlightenment and bourgeois Jewish culture:** *Haskalah*, the Jewish Enlightenment movement that began in late eighteenth century Germany, brought enormous changes to Jewish religious, political, and social life in Western and Central Europe. Open to modernity and European culture, *Haskalah* insisted that Jewish acculturation to the mainstream mores and customs of the public sphere was not incompatible with adherence to Jewish tradition and rituals in the private domain of home and synagogue. While the goals of

Jewish political emancipation and achievement of full civil rights, with their accompanying economic benefits, were central to this movement, some of its supporters also championed religious change within the Jewish community. Most modern forms of Jewish religious practice, Reform Judaism, Conservative Judaism, and Modern Orthodoxy, were shaped in this milieu. Moses Mendelssohn, the founder of *Haskalah* in Central Europe, and others of his circle also advocated social change in gender relations, opposing arranged marriages and advocating love matches.[54]

Adoption of the language and values of the non-Jewish world tended to occur first among the wealthiest Jews, who had frequent financial dealings with non-Jews. Deborah Hertz has chronicled the lives of a number of women from Berlin's wealthy Jewish elite in the last decades of the eighteenth century. In a Jewish society in which girls received only minimal religious training, exposure to a new world of secular novels, poetry, and plays, together with instruction in music and modern languages, distanced young women from brothers and husbands whose lives were restricted narrowly to commerce and finance. Not surprisingly, many of these wealthy and accomplished women found success in a salon society in which gentiles and Jews mixed socially, and divorces from Jewish husbands were followed by conversions to Christianity and marriage to gentile suitors, often from the nobility. The number of women who followed this course was small and their motives extremely complex, but as Hertz has written, for these Jewish salon women, abandoning Judaism meant integration into the dominant upper-class culture and society. In making their choices these women experienced at an early date and in a gender-specific way the basic conflict between group loyalty and individual emancipation that would torment so many European Jews in the two centuries to follow.[55]

The experience of the salon Jewesses was not typical for most Western and Central European Jewish women. Rather, the processes of acculturation and assimilation, followed in some cases by dissolution of minority ties through conversion and/or intermarriage, were generally quite different for women and men. Gender tended to limit the assimilation of Jewish women, rendering their progress to integration halting and incomplete in comparison to that of Jewish men. Confined to the domestic scene, restricted in their educational opportunities, and prevented from participating in the public realms of economic and civic life, Jewish women had far fewer contacts with the non-Jewish world. Rather, women were encouraged to cultivate a home-based Judaism in which spirituality was expressed in domestic activities.

As Marion Kaplan demonstrates through memoirs, diaries, personal correspondence, and cookbooks, at a time at which male synagogue attendance and ritual performance was declining, women in Germany most often transmitted Jewish values to their families through a form of domestic religion that united traditional Jewish cooking and some form of home observance of the Sabbath and other holidays. Perhaps because they had been excluded from so many public rituals to begin with, women's Judaism was essentially domestic, and in secularized homes they were the last to preserve elements of Jewish tradition. Sigmund Freud, for example, persuaded his wife to drop all religious practices, but throughout their marriage Martha Freud and her husband argued over her wish to light candles on the Sabbath.[56]

Ellen Umansky and Michael Galchinsky have documented the somewhat different situation in England, where a significant number of Jewish women did work in the public domain to hasten Jewish enlightenment and emancipation and to further religious reform. These include active advocates of liberal Judaism like Lily Montagu and writers of both fiction and non-fiction with Jewish themes directed to Jewish and gentile audiences, such as Grace Aguilar (d. 1847) and Marion and Celia Moss (1840s).[57] In her extremely popular book, *The Women of Israel*, Aguilar defended the exalted position of women in Judaism, highlighting what she described as women's traditional role in hastening redemption as "teachers of chil-

dren" and through other domestic activities.[58] Yet, despite their uplifting messages, Jewish women's success in the world of literature was profoundly upsetting to the men of their milieu; while the Jewish reformers were compelled to support at least a degree of female emancipation in principle, they were determined to limit, trivialize, and undermine women's writing and influence in the public sphere.[59]

Hyman points out that nineteenth century domestic Judaism not only reflected traditional Judaism's preferred positioning of women in the private realm of husband and family but was also a form of Jewish conformity to the Christian bourgeois model of female domesticity that put religion in the female sphere. Jewish literature and the Jewish press of the late nineteenth century, both in Europe and the United States, where the Jewish community prior to 1881 was overwhelmingly of Central European origin, described the Jewish woman as the "guardian angel of the house," "mother in Israel," and "priestess of the Jewish ideal," and assigned her primary responsibility for the Jewish identity and education of her children. This was a significant indication of acculturation in an ethnic group in which men had historically fulfilled most religious obligations, including the Jewish education of their sons. Moreover, this shifting of responsibility for inculcating Jewish identity and practices to women led rapidly from praise to denigration, as commentators began to blame mothers for their children's assimilation. Such criticisms not only allowed men to ignore the implications of their own assimilationist behavior but also revealed central tensions in the project of acculturation itself, including a communal inability to prevent individual defections into the larger society.[60]

Reform Judaism offered nineteenth century Western and Central European Jews a modernized form of Jewish belief and practice emphasizing personal faith and ethical behavior rather than ritual observance. It proclaimed that women were entitled to the same religious rights and subject to the same religious duties as men in both home and synagogue. Emphasis on religious education for girls and boys, including the introduction of a confirmation ceremony for young people of both sexes and an accessible worship service in the vernacular, also made the new movement attractive to many women. Pressure from young women may have prompted the Reform rabbinate to adopt the innovation of double ring wedding ceremonies, in which not only men but also women made a statement of marital commitment. In fact, however, European Reform Judaism made few substantive changes in women's actual synagogue status, offering no extension to women of ritual participation in worship and maintaining separate synagogue seating for men and women well into the twentieth century.[61] This was not so much the case in the United States, where mixed seating was the norm and where, as the nineteenth century progressed, women were afforded increasing opportunities to assume some synagogue leadership roles. However, the Reform movement was only prepared to go so far. While a few young woman undertook and even completed Rabbinic training during the first half of the twentieth century, American Reform Judaism did not ordain its first female rabbi, Sally Priesand, until 1972.

Emulation of Christian models of female philanthropy and religious activism played a significant role in middle-class Jewish women's establishment of service and social welfare organizations in the nineteenth and early twentieth century centuries in Germany, England, and North America. Such organizations as the Jüdischer Frauenbund in Germany (founded in 1904 by Bertha Pappenheim), the Union of Jewish Women in Great Britain (founded in 1902), and the National Council of Jewish Women in the United States (founded in 1893) cooperated in the international campaign against coercion of poor women into prostitution and argued for greater recognition of women within their respective Jewish communities as "sustainers of Jewish communal life and guardians against defection from Judaism." In the process, their members blurred the boundaries between traditional male and female spheres as women acquired administrative expertise and assumed authoritative and

responsible public roles.[62] In her study of Jewish feminist movements and their leaders in England and the United States between 1881 and 1933, Linda Gordon Kuzmack has shown how women's activism directly affected the Jewish community in such areas as social welfare services, feminist trade unionism, support for women's suffrage, and agitation for religious change.[63]

In the United States the proliferation of Jewish women's organizations also included synagogue sisterhoods, which devoted themselves to the "domestic management" of the synagogue, decorating the sanctuary for festivals, catering synagogue events, and performing many other housekeeping functions. National organizations of sisterhoods, separated by denomination, encouraged local groups in their activities and provided a forum for public female leadership. While the Reform movement's National Federation of Temple Sisterhoods provided a platform for women to demand greater synagogue participation, including the ordination of women rabbis, the Conservative movement's Women's League emphasized the role of women in enhancing the Jewishness of their homes. Sisterhoods of all denominations, however, recognized that females must be Jewishly educated in order to strengthen Jewish observance at home and instill Jewish values in their children, and they encouraged expanded educational opportunities for women of all ages. Similarly, as they had throughout American Jewish history, Jewish women played a central role in establishing, supervising, and teaching in Jewish religious schools.[64] Through these activities, as well as through involvement with other Jewish women's groups, such as the Zionist organization Hadassah (founded by Henrietta Szold in 1912), middle-class American Jewish women found opportunities to articulate their Jewish identity and values through service and philanthropy.

**Eastern European Jewish women in the modern period:** The Jewish Enlightenment movement in Eastern Europe, which began in the last few decades of the nineteenth century, was very different from *Haskalah* in the West. It lacked both the emphasis on

Jewish achievement of political rights and civic equality and the impetus for religious reform, for neither were likely to be achieved in the conservative Eastern European environment. Nor was the impoverished and predominantly rural Jewish population an appropriate constituency for the middle-class norms and values of the West. Rather, *Haskalah* in Eastern Europe was a secularizing process that led to a discontinuation of religious observance while fostering a Jewish national/ethnic identity, often linked to socialist political goals. Eastern European women were frequently in the forefront of this movement of cultural transformation. This was partly a result of education: the customary exclusion of girls from substantive Jewish educations often led prosperous parents to provide secular instruction for their daughters. The Orthodox community did not begin to provide vehicles for female religious education until after the First World War (figs. 169-170). Moreover, girls and women in Eastern European Jewish society, where the strong capable woman's shrewd interaction with the outside world was the dominant cultural ideal, were also secularized by their active participation in public economic life (fig. 171). In many ways, late nineteenth century Eastern European women were far more involved in the process of Jewish assimilation than women in Western Europe or the United States. This is evident in the large numbers of Eastern European Jewish women who sought higher education in Western Europe, a significantly higher percentage of female conversions to Christianity, and particularly in female involvement in a wide range of political movements, including Zionism and the socialist Bund, which offered women opportunities for activism and leadership unavailable in traditional Jewish society.[65]

Similarly, as Jewish women at the end of the nineteenth and in the early decades of the twentieth century began to explore the greatly enlarged opportunities for self-expression offered by modern secular culture, many began to write poetry and prose, in Hebrew, Yiddish, English, and many other languages, from the raw material of their own experiences and feelings. But with the opportunity for self-realization came estrangement from traditional Jewish culture: to become a Jewish woman writer was to become a cultural anomaly; often the price of such an achievement was equivocal exile from a male culture profoundly uncomfortable with female intellectual assertiveness.[66]

**East European Jewish women in North America:** Of the almost two million Eastern European Jewish immigrants to arrive in the United States between 1880 and 1914, 43% were women, a far higher proportion than among other immigrant groups. The values these immigrants brought with them, even as they were gradually transformed by America, permitted women to play a complex role in helping their families adjust to their new environment. Most women contributed to the family income in one way or another. A significant number sought the benefits of higher education; others took advantage of a variety of public secular activities. Among the agents of change were earlier arrived Jews of Western and Central European origin, who sought to socialize the immigrants in their own image. As Hyman has written, "Americanization of young immigrant women, as Jewish reformers understood it, entailed adoption of American middle-class gendered norms and values." The Educational Alliance, accordingly, ran separate programs for boys and girls, teaching athletics to the former and domestic science to the latter.[67] Also facilitating acculturation was the ubiquity of advertising in the Yiddish press for consumer goods; women were responsible for most of the purchases that provided their families with the trappings of American identity. Hyman believes, however, that young Jewish immigrant women were most influenced by the world of work, where they were exposed to union issues and socialist ideas, and where many were ardent participants and leaders in labor activism. After their marriages Jewish women continued their public roles, through rent strikes, the 1902 kosher meat boycott, agitation for the availability of birth control information, and support for women's suffrage. Hyman notes that "This communal acceptance of women as active subjects, rather than passive objects, of history recognized, and promoted, the status of women as partners in negotiating the public role of Jews in American society."[68]

As Eastern European Jewish immigrants and their children became increasingly successful economically and began to enter the middle class, particularly in the period after World War II, they tended to follow the educational, occupational, residential, and religious patterns of previous waves of Jewish settlers in North America. This often included affiliation with Conservative and Reform synagogues and a preference that women should not work outside the home. Many of these women, who now had leisure for volunteer activities, became members of the earlier founded national Jewish women's organizations or became involved in synagogue sisterhood activities.

**Jewish women in pre-State and post-1948 Israel:** Inequality in the treatment of the sexes has been a reality in the modern Jewish settlement of the land of Israel since the first pioneers, inspired by the fervor of Labor Zionism, began arriving from Eastern Europe at the end of the nineteenth century. Many of these idealistic young people had learned farming in Zionist training schools in Russia that stressed the equality of women and men. Even so, young single women found their options limited and their choices narrowed. Betrayed by their male comrades who did not support their struggle, and limited by male perceptions of their biological inequality, unmarried women found themselves virtually unemployable as agricultural workers and were forced to survive by providing the men with kitchen and laundry services. Denied membership as single women in most collective settlements and refused employment as agricultural workers, a few founded successful female agricultural and urban collectives and women's training farms. Most, however, were compelled to accept their secondary roles and take whatever employment they could find, often in urban settings. They thus sacrificed their egalitarian ideals and fervent Labor Zionism for what they saw as the more pressing task of the building up the state.[69] As Deborah Bernstein has written of pre-State Israel, women's un-

equal and marginal position in the labor market and their sole responsibility for family care created a distinctly different life pattern for women from that of men. Women's secondary and intermittent visibility in the all important public sphere, and the invisibility of the private sphere where women were central, reinforced female exclusion from power and influence.[70]

Modern Israel continues to be far from progressive where the status of women is concerned. Despite popular mythology to the contrary, on women's issues it is, at the end of the twentieth century, more conservative than most other western democracies. The secondary status of Israeli women is a result of generations of past discrimination in Jewish tradition as well as of contemporary disadvantages for women in the workplace, mandated by paternalistic legislation and the expectation that women will also assume most household responsibilities. Israeli women continue to fulfill the traditional Jewish role of enablers, supporting their husbands and sons, who hold the primary power and powerful jobs and whose lives are at risk in defending the State. Only a small number of Israeli women reject women's subsidiary roles, but they recognize that women will not achieve equality as long as war and conflict are a dominant reality in Israeli society.[71]

Jewish women in Israel are also significantly disadvantaged in matters of personal status. When the State was established in May, 1948, the Declaration of Independence stated that "The State of Israel will maintain equal social and political rights for all citizens, irrespective of religion, race, or sex." This sentiment was reiterated in 1949 in the basic guidelines of the first government of Israel. Yet 1953 legislation awarded the Orthodox religious establishment monopolistic control over marriage and divorce for all Jewish citizens, thus legalizing women's substantial legal disadvantages in the *halakhah*, particularly in areas of family law.[72] There is no civil marriage or divorce in Israel, nor do Reform or Conservative Judaism, with their more egalitarian approaches, have any official standing. The issue of the over ten thousand *agunot*—women who cannot get a divorce because their husbands cannot be located or refuse to grant one—is the best known instance of the inability of the Orthodox rabbinate to deal with real social problems that cause immense pain and suffering to women and their families. Only recently have women begun to fight back, forming an International Coalition for *Agunah* Rights, reflecting an intensive effort to reform what are perceived as unjust and discriminatory divorce proceedings in rabbinical courts worldwide. Israel's nascent feminist movement has also brought cases to Israel's Supreme Court on issues as diverse as access to abortion, women's right to be elected to and hold seats on municipal religious councils, and the ability of women's prayer groups to hold services at the Western Wall.[73] This increased feminist activity, influenced by the women's movement throughout the Western world, and the hostility it has generated are indicative of the gender and religious tensions that characterize Israeli society at the end of the twentieth century.

**The Holocaust:** Scholarly explorations of the particularities of women's experiences during the Holocaust are still at an early stage. Until recently, as Joan Ringelheim has written, "The similarity among Jewish victims of the Nazi policy of destruction has been considered more important than any differentiation, including (or especially) that of gender."[74] Yet as Sara Horowitz has noted, the testimonies of female survivors reveal experiences and concerns absent in male narratives, including accounts of menstruation and pregnancy in the concentration camps, sexual victimization, women's strategies of survival, and the effects of their ordeals on women's postwar family, friendship, and communal relationships.[75] Ongoing research based on survivors' testimonies and a variety of historical and literary sources is beginning to provide a denser and far more nuanced picture of the ways in which gender played one part among many in the fates of female victims of Nazi brutality.

**North American Judaism in the last quarter of the twentieth century:** The resurgent feminist movement of the early 1970s brought both religious renewal and bitter controversy to contemporary western Judaism, especially in North America. Significant numbers of Jewish women, linking feminism's mandate for female equality in all areas of human endeavor with an explicit commitment to Jewish identification and the Jewish community, have begun to seek full participation in and access to a tradition that has rarely considered women central figures in its history, thought, religious practice, or communal life (figs. 172-175). This movement for change comes at a time when American Jewish women are facing previously unimagined challenges in the areas of family formation, unprecedented higher education and career path opportunities, increased communal acceptance of homosexuality and other alternative lifestyles, and a wide range of options in religious and spiritual expression and political and civic activism. Significant transformations in all of these spheres result from revolutionary changes in technology, social attitudes, and economic expectations over the half century since World War II.

The Jewish feminist movement has had a significant impact on Jewish religious practice. Egalitarian worship is the norm in Reform and Reconstructionist Judaisms, and it is almost universal now in Conservative practice as well. One of the most visible changes for women in the past two decades is the opportunity now offered them in the Reform, Reconstructionist, and Conservative movements to undertake Rabbinic and cantorial studies and to receive Rabbinic ordination. A long battle took place for female ordination both in Germany and the United States, and strong resistance came from within the Jewish community.[76] It seems clear that only major shifts in public attitudes and female possibilities brought about by the American feminist movement of the 1960s prompted the leadership of the Reform movement to sanction the ordination of Sally Priesand in 1972. Twenty-five years later, several hundred women have been ordained as rabbis, and as many as half of Rabbinic students in Reform, Conservative, and Reconstructionist seminaries are now female. Their paths, however, have not been free of obstacles. Fishman has discussed the challenges that women rabbis encounter in their professional and personal lives, noting that thus far female clergy have mostly held subordinate positions, a reflection not only of persistent cultural and prestige-oriented prejudices but also of many women's choices of options that allow them time for home and family.[77] On the other hand, as increasing numbers of women become rabbis, some observers have expressed fears that an imminent "feminization of the rabbinate" will diminish the respect in which the rabbi and the rabbi's functions are held, and that "men will relegate religious life to women and cease being active in the synagogue."[78]

Another example of the significant impact of feminism on Jewish religious life in North America is alterations in liturgical language. The traditional *siddur*, the Jewish prayer book, portrays worship as a prerogative for men and filters female needs and activities through a male perspective. Translations into English have until recently been couched in solely masculine terms, while women have tended to be portrayed as objects of prayer rather than as participating in prayer themselves.[79] The 1972 Reform movement Task Force on Equality recommended the elimination of unnecessary and inaccurate masculine references in prayer, whether referring to humanity in general or to God, suggesting that such language misleads worshippers about the nature of both human beings and the divine. Thus, "Sovereign" or "Ruler" might replace "Lord" or "King," while "God of our Fathers" could give way either to "God of our Fathers and Mothers," "God of our ancestors," or "God of Israel." Changes in both the Hebrew and English liturgies reflecting some of these guidelines have appeared in a number of new liturgical works, including the Reform movement's 1975 *Gates of Prayer* series; similar English formulations characterize the Conservative movement's 1985 *Sim Shalom* prayerbook, in which Hebrew prayers are unchanged.[80] Ongoing revisions continue in both movements.

Feminist advocates of liturgical changes have developed imagery that conceives God in female as well as male terms—for example, as a nurturing mother—in addition to

creating new prayers and blessings that delineate women's experiences and describe their search for spirituality. Some liturgical writers have experimented with references to God as "*Shekhinah*" and have alternated between using masculine and feminine forms in divine address. Others suggest that gender issues can by obviated by addressing God in the second person as "You." Among contemporary liturgists, Marcia Falk's many new blessings in Hebrew and English have enhanced and revitalized the spiritual lives of women and men across a wide spectrum of the Jewish community.[81]

Alongside changes in liturgical language has been the recovery of the traditional observance of *Rosh Hodesh*, the New Moon, now observed as a day on which groups of Jewish women meet for study and prayer.[82] Similar is the development of new rituals in connection with milestone events in women's biological and personal lives, including the establishment of rituals for women that parallel those long established for men.[83] The *Bat Mitzvah*, first introduced by Mordechai Kaplan, the founder of Reconstructionist Judaism, in 1922, to celebrate his daughter Judith's religious coming of age, became widespread in the decades following World War II (fig. 117). In Reconstructionist and Reform congregations, it is now fully equivalent to the boy's *Bar Mitzvah* ceremony, and it is also the norm in Conservative synagogues, although the details of what girls may and may not do ritually vary somewhat. Some Orthodox congregations are also beginning to offer girls an opportunity to publicly affirm their Jewish knowledge and commitment, although not in a format parallel to male *Bar Mitzvah*.[84] Ceremonies welcoming baby girls into the covenant of Israel (*Simhat Bat*) are also becoming increasingly common throughout the Jewish community.

A second category of ritual change is altering or supplementing traditional rituals related to life cycle events in ways that include women as equals. Such changes include alternative marriage contracts that emphasize mutuality and supplemental divorce rituals that allow a woman a role in acknowledging the final dissolution of her marriage.

Inclusion of women as recognized mourners whose obligations are the same as those of men also falls into this category. A third type of liturgical innovation recognizes the sacred nature of events of a woman's biological cycle and ritualizes such milestone events as menarche, menses, childbirth, miscarriage, and menopause. And finally, rituals have been developed to sacralize passages not previously considered in Jewish tradition, including ceremonies celebrating elder wisdom or healing from sexual abuse.[85] Which of these rituals, and in what forms, will ultimately become part of normative Jewish practice remains unknowable at this time, but their wide variety is testimony to the creative impact of feminist spirituality on contemporary Judaism.

Jewish feminism at century's end also has its theoretical aspect that looks beyond issues of ritual innovation and egalitarian practice. Judith Plaskow, a central figure in the development of Jewish feminist theology believes that ordination of women as rabbis and cantors is not a sufficient response to normative Judaism's inherent androcentrism. She urges feminists to move beyond their study of women's status in Jewish law and their demands for legal and institutional equality in Judaism as presently constituted, insisting that the origins of women's oppression in the core of Judaism itself must be exposed. For Plaskow, the future of Judaism demands transformations of the basic Jewish theological concepts—God, divine revelation, and the believing community—in directions that recognize the full and equal humanity of all Jews, that reflect and voice the female experience, and that reintegrate the female aspects of the divine into Jewish conceptions of the Godhead.[86]

Feminist efforts at expanding women's roles in traditional Judaism have prompted hostile reactions in many sectors of the Orthodox community, where they are perceived as contrary to centuries of Jewish tradition and as undermining women's customary roles. Yet there can be no doubt of feminism's profound impact even on contemporary Orthodoxy. As the dissonance between possibilities for women in the secular and tra-

ditional worlds has become more obvious, quality Jewish education for girls has become a central priority in a number of traditional Jewish communities; some Orthodox leaders are working with women, through *halakhah*, to increase their participation in such areas as Torah study and female prayer groups.[87] Still, Orthodox feminists often feel psychologically split as they simultaneously champion and attempt to reconcile the spiritual equality of women with the fundamentally androcentric Jewish tradition.[88]

Debra Kaufman has studied contemporary Jewish women who have chosen to become Orthodox Jews (*baalot teshuvah*). The "return" of most of her college educated subjects represented a conscious rejection of a secular culture devoid of the coherent and timeless moral values they believe they have found in Orthodoxy. These women, who are convinced that in Orthodoxy "the female and the feminine are central" also bring secular skills and concerns to their new communities, including the belief that girls should receive educations commensurate with boys, that daughters should be able to pursue advanced studies, and the hope expressed by some that eventually there will be changes in the structure of gender-related roles connected with communal prayer.[89]

Kaufman's findings are reinforced by Tamar Frankiel, herself a *baalat teshuvah*, in her elucidation of the spiritual benefits she finds in woman's distinctive role in traditional Judaism. She writes that through the bearing and nurturing of children, the preparation and serving of food, the creation and preservation of *shalom bayit* (household harmony), and the woman's special affinity to the Sabbath, New Moons, and other Jewish festivals, women participate in a cycle of Jewish life "richly interwoven with feminine themes."[90] Frankiel speaks in exalted terms of the special benefits of family purity rituals, finding in monthly immersion an experience of renewal, and in enforced marital separation a safeguard for the spirituality of sexual expression. Yet she also looks toward a future when women's Jewish educations will be of the same quality as men's and when women's spiritual impact on Jewish law, rituals, and custom will be recognized and appreciated.

Feminism altered all sectors of Jewish communal life as many women have given up the hours they once devoted to volunteer activities for full-time employment. Moreover, many women who continue to volunteer prefer to divert their energies to causes beyond the Jewish community, particularly those that support and further gender equality. The significant decline in female volunteers in Jewish women's organizations and synagogue sisterhoods at century's end has grave consequences for the future of these enterprises and those they serve.[91]

Although an increasing number of qualified women professionals are employed in Jewish communal agencies, several observers have noted that the Jewish communal sphere has proved particularly reluctant to recognize and encourage female leadership potential. According to Hyman, this resistance to women in positions of authority is indicative of the sexual politics of contemporary Jewish identity in general.[92] While some men will continue to resist what they perceive as female encroachment on male hegemony in the public domain, others may simply abandon Jewish communal institutions and Judaism to women altogether. As Fishman cautions,[93] the stakes for American Jews are significant, since "The American Jewish community not only shares in all the human consequences of feminism but also carries with it the additional responsibility of preserving three thousand years of Jewish history and culture and confronting the problems of a numerically challenged population as well." However, if the past is any indication, forces from outside the Jewish community will be as influential as any from within in determining the roles of women in American Judaism and American Jewish life in the twenty-first century.

### Bibliography

Baskin, Judith R., ed., *Jewish Women in Historical Perspective* (Detroit, 1998).

Baskin, Judith R., ed., *Women of the Word: Jewish Women and Jewish Writing* (Detroit, 1994).

Fishman, Sylvia Barack, *A Breath of Life: Feminism in the American Jewish Community* (New York, 1993).

Grossman, Susan, and Rivka Haut, eds., *Daughters of the King: Women and the Synagogue* (Philadelphia, 1992).

Hyman, Paula, *Gender and Assimilation in Modern Jewish History: The Roles and Representation of Women* (Seattle, 1995).

Swirski, B., and M. Safir, eds., *Calling the Equality Bluff: Women in Israel* (New York, 1991).

### Notes

[1] Susan Starr Sered, *Women as Ritual Experts: The Religious Lives of Elderly Jewish Women in Jerusalem* (New York, 1992).

[2] Tikva Frymer-Kensky, *In the Wake of the Goddesses: Women, Culture and the Biblical Transformation of Pagan Myth* (New York, 1992), p. 121.

[3] Susan Niditch, "Portrayals of Women in the Hebrew Bible," in Judith Baskin, ed., *Jewish Women in Historical Perspective* (Detroit, 1998) [hereafter: *JWHP*], p. 30.

[4] Carol Meyers, *Discovering Eve: Ancient Israelite Women in Context* (New York, 1988), pp. 189-191.

[5] Susan Grossman, "Women and the Jerusalem Temple," in Susan Grossman and Rivka Haut, eds., *Daughters of the King: Women and the Synagogue* (Philadelphia, 1992) [hereafter, *DK*], pp. 17-20. On the following paragraph, see pp. 20-29.

[6] Meyers, op. cit., p. 161.

[7] See Frymer-Kensky, op. cit., pp. 158-161; cf., Niditch, op. cit., p. 38; and Meyers, op. cit., pp. 162-163.

[8] Op. cit., pp. 37-38.

[9] Op. cit., pp. 197-198.

[10] Jacob Neusner, *In Search of Talmudic Biography: The Problem of the Attributed Saying* (Chico, 1984). Other scholars have argued that some historical information about women in Roman Palestine can be recovered from Rabbinic texts and utilized in conjunction with other literary evidence and archaeological data. See Tal Ilan, *Jewish Women in Greco-Roman Palestine* (Peabody, 1995), and Miriam Peskowitz, *Stories about Spinners and Weavers: Gendering the Everyday in Roman-period Judaism* (Berkeley, 1997).

[11] See Judith R. Baskin, "Woman as Other in Rabbinic Literature," in Jacob Neusner and Alan J. Avery-Peck, eds., *Where We Stand: Issues and Debates in the Study of Ancient Judaism* Vol. 2 (Leiden, 1999), pp. 177-196.

[12] See Peskowitz, op. cit.

[13] Jacob Neusner, *Method and Meaning in Ancient Judaism* (Missoula, 1979), p. 97.

[14] See Judith Hauptman, *Rereading the Rabbis: A Woman's Voice* (Boulder, 1998) and Jacob Neusner, *How the Rabbis Liberated Women* (Atlanta, 1998); cf., Rachel Biale, *Women and Jewish Law: An Exploration of Women's Issues in Halakhic Sources* (New York, 1984).

[15] David Goodblatt, "The Beruriah Traditions," in *JJS* 26 (1975), pp. 68-85.

[16] Rachel Adler, "The Virgin in the Brothel and

Other Anomalies: Character and Context in the Legend of Beruriah," in *Tikkun* 3/6 (1988), p. 32.

[17] Daniel Boyarin, *Carnal Israel: Reading Sex in Talmudic Culture* (Berkeley, 1993), pp. 188-189, 196.

[18] Biale, op. cit., p. 20.

[19] Judith Hauptman, "Women and the Conservative Synagogue," in *DK*, p. 169.

[20] Hauptman, *Rereading the Rabbis*; Boyarin, op. cit., p. 169.

[21] Michelle Zimbalist Rosaldo, "Woman, Culture, and Society: A Theoretical Overview," in M.Z. Rosaldo and Louise Lamphere, eds., *Women, Culture and Society* (Stanford, 1974), pp. 31-32.

[22] Shaye J.D. Cohen, "Purity and Piety: The Separation of Menstruants from the Sancta," in *DK*, pp. 103-116, p. 113.

[23] Judith Romney Wegner, *Chattel or Person? The Status of Women in the Mishnah* (Oxford, 1992), pp. 38, 87-91. On the following paragraph, see pp. 143-45.

[24] Ross S. Kraemer, *Her Share of the Blessings: Women's Religions Among Pagans, Jews, and Christians in the Greco-Roman World* (New York, 1992).

[25] See Amy-Jill Levine, ed., *"Women Like This:" New Perspectives on Jewish Women in the Greco-Roman World* (Atlanta, 1991).

[26] Bernadette Brooten, *Women Leaders in the Ancient Synagogue* (Chico, 1982).

[27] Kraemer, op. cit., p. 123. On the following, see Brooten, op. cit., pp. 103-38.

[28] Philo, *On the Contemplative Life* 27-29, 30, 34-39; Kraemer, op. cit., pp. 113-115.

[29] Judith R. Baskin, "Jewish Women in the Middle Ages," in *JWHP*, p. 101.

[30] S.D. Goitein, *A Mediterranean Society, Vol. 3, The Family* (Berkeley, 1978), pp. 153-155; Mordechai A. Friedman, "Marriage as an Institution: Jewry Under Islam," in David Kraemer, ed., *The Jewish Family: Metaphor and Memory* (New York, 1989) [hereafter: *JewFam*], p. 34. On the following, see pp. 105-106.

[31] Friedman, op. cit., p. 33. On the following, see pp. 34-35.

[32] Baskin, op. cit., p. 108; Goitein, op. cit., p. 358.

[33] Renée Levine Melammed, "Sephardi Women in the Medieval and Early Modern Periods," in *JWHP*, p. 131.

[34] On the preceding, see Robert I. Burns, *Jews in the Notarial Culture: Latinate Wills in Mediterranean Spain 1250-1350* (Berkeley, 1996), p. 31; Cheryl Tallan, "Medieval Jewish Widows: Their Control of Resources," in *Jewish History* 5 (1991), p. 116; and Melammed, op. cit., pp. 135-136.

[35] Kenneth R. Stow, *Alienated Minority: The Jews of Medieval Latin Europe* (Cambridge, 1992), pp. 207-209.

[36] On the preceding, see Baskin, op. cit., pp. 116-118; Emily Taitz, "Women's Voices, Women's Prayers: The European Synagogues of the Middle Ages," in *DK*, p. 64; and Judith R. Baskin, "Some Parallels in the Education of Me-

dieval Jewish and Christian Women," in *Jewish History* 5 (1991), pp. 45-46.

[37] Ada Rapoport-Albert, "On Women in Hasidism: S.A. Horodecky and the Maid of Ludmir Tradition," in A. Rapoport-Albert and S.J. Zipperstein, eds., *Jewish History. Essays in Honour of Chimen Abramsky* (London, 1988), p. 507. On the following, see Howard Adelman, "Finding Women's Voices in Italian Jewish Literature," in Judith R. Baskin, ed., *Women of the Word: Jewish Women and Jewish Writing* (Detroit, 1994) [hereafter: *WomWord*], p. 54.

[38] Gershom Scholem, *Major Trends in Jewish Mysticism* (New York, 1941), p. 37.

[39] Sharon Koren, "A Mystical Rationale for the Laws of Niddah," in R. Wasserfall, ed., *Women and Water: Menstruation in Jewish Life and Law* (Hanover, 1999).

[40] Judith Dishon, "Images of Women in Medieval Hebrew Literature," in *WomWord*, pp. 35-49.

[41] Cohen, "Purity and Piety," p. 111. The following quote is from p. 113.

[42] Aviva Cantor, "The Lilith Question," in Susannah Heschel, ed., *On Being a Jewish Feminist: A Reader* (New York, 1983) [hereafter: *BJF*], pp. 41-43.

[43] On the preceding, see Shmuel Niger, "Yiddish Literature and the Female Writer," in *WomWord*, pp. 76-77; Taitz, op. cit., pp. 66-67; Natalie Zemon Davis, *Women on the Margins: Three Seventeenth-Century Lives* (Cambridge, 1995), p. 24.

[44] On the preceding, see Chava Weissler, "Prayers in Yiddish and the Religious World of Ashkenazic Women," in *JWHP*, p. 172; Howard Adelman, "Italian Jewish Women," in *JWHP*, p. 154; and Taitz, op. cit., p. 66.

[45] Weissler, op. cit., p. 173.

[46] Ibid., pp. 173-174.

[47] Niger, op. cit., p. 90; Taitz, op. cit., p. 67.

[48] Weissler, op. cit., pp. 179-186.

[49] Paula E. Hyman, *Gender and Assimilation in Modern Jewish History: The Roles and Representation of Women* (Seattle, 1995), p. 34; Ellen Umansky, "Piety, Persuasion and Friendship: A History of Jewish Women's Spirituality," in Ellen M. Umansky and Dianne Ashton, eds., *Four Centuries of Jewish Women's Spirituality: A Sourcebook* (Boston, 1992) [hereafter: *FCJW*], p. 5.

[50] Davis, op. cit., pp. 24-26.

[51] Rapoport-Albert, op. cit., pp. 501-502. On the following, see pp. 502-506

[52] Jacob Katz, *Tradition and Crisis: Jewish Society at the End of the Middle Ages* (New York, 1971), p. 243; Immanuel Etkes, "Marriage and Torah Study among the *Lomdim* in Lithuania in the Nineteenth Century," in *JewFam*.

[53] David Biale, *Eros and the Jews: From Biblical Israel to Contemporary America* (New York, 1992), p. 136.

[54] Ibid., pp. 153-158.

[55] Deborah Hertz, "Emancipation through Intermarriage in Old Berlin," in *JWHP*, p. 204.

[56] Marion A. Kaplan, *The Making of the Jewish*

*Middle Class: Women, Family, and Identity, in Imperial Germany* (New York, 1991), pp. 69-84.

[57] Ellen Umansky, *Lily H. Montagu and the Advancement of Liberal Judaism: From Vision to Vocation* (Lewiston, 1983); Michael Galchinsky, *The Origin of the Modern Jewish Woman Writer: Romance and Reform in Victorian England* (Detroit, 1996).

[58] Hyman, op. cit., pp. 35-36; cf., Dianne Ashton, "Grace Aguilar and the Matriarchal Theme in Jewish Women's Spirituality," in Maurie Sacks, ed., *Active Voices: Women in Jewish Culture* (Urbana, 1995), pp. 79-93.

[59] Galchinsky, op. cit., p. 83.

[60] Hyman, op. cit., pp. 46-49.

[61] Kaplan, op. cit., pp. 67-68; Riv-Ellen Prell, "The Vision of Women in Classical Reform Judaism," *JAAR* 50:4 (Dec., 1982). On the following, see Ellen Umansky, "Piety, Persuasion and Friendship: A History of Jewish Women's Spirituality," in *FCJW*, p. 9.

[62] Kaplan, op. cit., pp. 211-219; Hyman, op. cit., pp. 40-41; Umansky, *FCJW*, pp. 17-18.

[63] Linda Gordon Kuzmack, *Women's Cause: The Jewish Woman's Movement in England and the United States, 1881-1933* (Columbus, 1990).

[64] On this, see Hyman, op. cit., pp. 42-44; Umansky, op. cit., pp. 15-17; and Umansky, "Spiritual Expressions: Jewish Women's Religious Lives in the Twentieth-Century United States," in *JWHP*, pp. 343-345.

[65] Hyman, op. cit., pp. 71-81.

[66] Baskin, *WomWord*, pp. 17-19; cf., Naomi Sokoloff, Anne Lapidus Lerner, and Anita Norich, eds., *Gender and Text in Modern Hebrew and Yiddish Literature* (New York, 1992).

[67] Hyman, op. cit., p. 109.

[68] Op. cit., p. 114, and see Andrew Heinze, *Adapting to Abundance: Jewish Immigrants, Mass Consumption, and the Search for American Identity* (New York, 1990).

[69] Leslie Hazleton, "Israeli Women: Three Myths," in *BJF*, pp. 65-69.

[70] Deborah S. Bernstein, ed., *Pioneers and Homemakers: Jewish Women in Pre-State Israel* (Albany, 1992), pp. 17-18.

[71] Hazleton, ibid., pp. 77-78; cf., B. Swirski and M. Safir, eds., *Calling the Equality Bluff: Women in Israel* (New York, 1991).

[72] Hazelton, ibid., pp. 71-72.

[73] Rivka Haut, "Women's Prayer Groups and the Orthodox Synagogue," in *DK*, pp. 159-82.

[74] Joan Ringelheim, "Women and the Holocaust: A Reconsideration of Research," in *Signs: Journal of Women in Culture and Society* 10:4 (1985), p. 741; cf., Dalia Ofer and Lenore J. Weitzman, eds., *Women and the Holocaust* (New Haven, 1988).

[75] Sara Horowitz, "Memory and Testimony of Women Survivors of Nazi Genocide," in *WomWord*, p. 264.

[76] Pamela S. Nadell, *Women Who Would Be Rabbis: A History of Women's Ordination, 1889-1985* (Boston, 1998).

[77] Sylvia Barack Fishman, *A Breath of Life: Feminism in the American Jewish Community* (New York, 1993), pp. 216-218.

[78] Laura Geller, "Reactions to a Woman Rabbi," in *BJF*, pp. 210-11.

[79] Rela Geffen Monson, "The Impact of the Jewish Women's Movement on the American Synagogue: 1972-1985," in *DK*, p. 229.

[80] Annette Daum, "Language and Liturgy," in *DK*, pp. 188-89. On the following, see p. 201.

[81] Marcia Falk, *The Book of Blessings: New Jewish Prayers for Daily Life, the Sabbath, and the New Moon Festival* (San Francisco, 1996).

[82] Cf., Penina V. Adelman, *Miriam's Well: Rituals for Jewish Women Around the Year* (New York, 1990).

[83] Debra Ornstein, ed., *Lifecycles: Jewish Women on Life Passages and Personal Milestones* (Woodstock, 1994), p. xviii.

[84] Ellen M. Umansky, "Piety, Persuasion and Friendship: A History of Jewish Women's Spirituality," in *FCJW*, p. 22.

[85] Ornstein, ibid., p. xviii.

[86] Judith Plaskow, *Standing Again at Sinai: Judaism from a Feminist Perspective* (San Francisco, 1990); cf., Rachel Adler, *Engendering Judaism: An Inclusive Theology and Ethics* (Philadelphia, 1998).

[87] Avraham Weiss, *Women at Prayer: A Halakhic Analysis of Women's Prayer Groups* (Hoboken, 1990); Rivka Haut, "Women's Prayer Groups and the Orthodox Synagogue," in *DK*, pp. 159-82.

[88] Fishman, ibid., pp. 158-159.

[89] Debra Renee Kaufman, *Rachel's Daughters: Newly Orthodox Jewish Women* (New Brunswick, 1991), p. 58; cf., Lynn Davidman, *Tradition in a Rootless World: Women Turn to Orthodox Judaism* (Berkeley, 1991).

[90] Tamar Frankiel, *The Voice of Sarah: Feminine Spirituality and Traditional Judaism* (San Francisco, 1990), p. 58.

[91] Fishman, ibid., pp. 72-78, 222-24. On the following, see p. 229.

[92] Paula E. Hyman, *Gender and Assimilation in Modern Jewish History: The Roles and Representation of Women* (Seattle, 1995), pp. 168-69.

[93] Op. cit., p. 247.

JUDITH R. BASKIN

**WORK IN FORMATIVE JUDAISM:** The sages see Israel as a sacred society, "a kingdom of priests and a holy people," and, within that context, quite logically, they view work not as a mere secular necessity but as a sacred activity. Thus they situate their definition of work within their larger statement of what it means to form holy Israel, God's first love on earth. Work is not merely something we are supposed to do in the interests of the community, so that the tasks of the world will be carried out and each of us will earn a living. Of greatest importance is that the Hebrew word for "work" is *abodah*, the same word used for "divine service," "liturgy," or the labor of the priests in the Temple in making offerings to God. In a moment, we shall understand why *abodah* can be a component of the life of the holy people, what work has to do with God.

But, first, we must face a striking fact, the Torah's answer to the question, why must we work? We must work, so far as Judaism is concerned, not merely so that we do not fall as a burden onto the backs of others. Rather, work is natural to the human condition, what we are created to do, and everyone, by definition, has useful work to carry out, if not in a secular then in a sacred framework. "Unemployment" meaning, having absolutely nothing of worth to do, no assigned task that possesses any value whatsoever, is a concept that the sages do not imagine (for a reason I shall give in a moment). Incumbent upon every human being are tasks of intrinsic merit, and no one can ever *be* unemployed in the sense of having no socially useful tasks to perform. Everyone from the smallest child to the oldest widow can and does contribute to sustaining the life of the community. But the scarce resource that must be rationally disposed of, so far as the Torah is concerned, has nothing to do with gold or silver; the scarce resource is piety, and that is to be "produced" and valued. Everyone is capable of acts of piety, for example, prayer or study of Torah, constituting *abodah* in the deepest sense: work in God's service. Thus unemployment in the contemporary sense is incomprehensible. That fixed idea comes to expression in a curious passage about the definition of a large town as against a village (M. Meg. 1:3):

A. What is a large town?
B. Any in which there are ten men available at all times [to form a prayer quorum].
C. [If there are] fewer than this number, lo, this is a village.

What is the point? If you are a person of leisure, with resources to permit your being available at all times, it means you have no job; in a secular world you are "unem-

ployed." But the idle rich, no less than the idle poor, have valued tasks to carry out. The Hebrew that I translate as "men available at all times" is *batlanim*, a word that in living Hebrew today means unemployed people, or, in a broader sense, time-wasters, worthless louts. But in the Mishnah, men with no fixed obligations, people with no jobs to go to, form a public asset. That is because, without fixed schedules, they are always available to form a quorum for public prayer. Their presence defines a large town; a village cannot afford such a luxury as a permanent quorum for prayer; a town, with its amenities, can. What these people do, then, is say prayers and make it possible for others to do so in a quorum (there being certain prayers that can only be said in community, among ten Israelites). By the definition of work of value that lies before us, every one of the faithful has valuable work to do, whether or not that work is conventional and whether or not it is compensated in an everyday way.

This brings us back to the connection between "work" and the life of holiness that the Torah demands of holy Israel. In the Torah, to be "holy" is to be like God, as at Lev. 19:1: "You shall be holy, for I the Lord your God am holy," and to be Israel means to aspire to imitate God. To understand the connection between work and sanctification, therefore, we have to realize how sages frame the issue. Rather than explaining why we must work, sages ask, is work natural to the human condition? They find the answer in the Torah's account of creation.

In the model of creation of the world in six days, with repose on the Sabbath, the whole sanctified at the very instant of perfection, sunset on the sixth day, work finds its context in the rhythm of the week. Six days are devoted to labor and one day to rest. That is how God made the world, and it is how we are to live our lives, six days of creation, a day of repose, called by the untranslatable Hebrew word, *Shabbat* (English: Sabbath). Just as it is a religious duty to rest on the Sabbath, so it is a religious duty to work during the week. That is how we imitate God in everyday life. The Ten Commandments include that admonition: "Six days shall you labor and do all your work" (Exod. 20:9). When people work for the six days of creation, they act like God, and when they rest on the seventh day, they imitate God as well. But there is work, and then there is real labor. The Torah recognizes the difference and accounts for it. In Judaism, we must work so that there can be the Sabbath. When you fully explore the depths of that proposition, you can understand any other statement that Judaism makes on any other critical subject: you enter the heart and soul of the Torah's system.

But, it goes without saying, the theology is one thing, the concrete activity, something else again. Most people do not feel that they are imitating God when they go to their jobs in the morning or in the middle of the night for that matter. But when the Sabbath defines the context of work, and creation the framework, the issue is not fatigue but something more (Mekhilta deR. Ishmael LIII:II.17):

A. "and rested on the seventh day:"
B. And does fatigue affect God? Is it not said, "The creator of the ends of the earth does not faint and is not weary" (Is. 40:28); "He gives power to the faint" (Is. 40:29); "By the word of the Lord the heavens were made" (Ps. 33:6)?
C. How then can Scripture say, "and rested on the seventh day"?
D. It is as if [God] had it written concerning himself that he created the world in six days and rested on the seventh.
E. Now you may reason *a fortiori*:
F. Now if the one who is not affected by fatigue had it written concerning himself that he created the world in six days and rested on the seventh, how much the more so should a human being, concerning whom it is written, "but man is born to trouble" (Job 5:7) [also rest on the Sabbath]?

So work and repose form the framework within which life is lived, like God.

Women who manage the household and raise children are understood to work, and no one imagines that they are unemployed or denigrates what they do as less essential than work conventionally defined. Their work in the home carries out their obligation to their husband, which they undertook in agreeing to the marriage. Work is deemed a natu-

ral right that a woman has and that cannot be denied her. For one principal reason we must work is that idleness corrupts. Even a wealthy woman, who does not have to work, and for whom, in the imagination of the sages of the Torah, a career outside of the home is unimaginable, has the right to work, not only the obligation. A husband who tries to keep his wife at leisure must divorce her and give her the opportunity to find a more humane world, in which she too may do things of value (M. Ket. 5:5):

A. These are the kinds of labor which a woman performs for her husband:
B. she (1) grinds flour, (2) bakes bread, (3) does laundry, (4) prepares meals, (5) gives suck to her child, (6) makes the bed, (7) works in wool.
C. [If] she brought with her a single slave girl, she does not (1) grind, (2) bake bread, or (3) do laundry.
D. [If she brought] two, she does not (4) prepare meals and does not (5) feed her child.
E. [If she brought] three, she does not (6) make the bed for him and does not (7) work in wool.
F. If she brought four, she sits on a throne.
G. R. Eliezer says, "Even if she brought him a hundred slave girls, he forces her to work in wool,
H. "for idleness leads to unchastity."
I. Rabban Simeon b. Gamaliel says, "Also: He who prohibits his wife by a vow from performing any labor puts her away and pays off her marriage contract. For idleness leads to boredom."

We see that the law assigns a fixed obligation of work to the wife; the burden may be diminished but not removed, for the reason Eliezer states. But Simeon b. Gamaliel gives a still more compelling explanation: idleness leads to boredom.

So much for why we must work. But, in all candor, the real question is not why we must work but why we must work at jobs we do not necessarily like. Why is work a burden and not a joy? The answer to these cutting questions derives not from everyday experience but from the theology that animates Judaism in its classical statement. Specifically, the Torah answers all questions by appeal to its own picture of the human condition, beginning with creation in Eden and the fall of humanity from grace by reason of sin. The classical statement of Judaism, in that reading of Scripture contained within the documents of the Oral Torah, points to the tragedy of Eden in explaining why we have to work. There the Judaic sages find that servile labor defines the human condition because of man's and woman's rebellion against God: "In the sweat of your face you shall eat bread until you return to the ground, for out of it you were taken; you are dust and to dust you shall return" (Gen. 3:19). The natural world ought to sustain man without his having to work. That is shown by the fact that nature sustains itself without menial labor. But with sin man has found it necessary to work, nature having lost its abundance (T. Qid. 5:16):

E. R. Simeon b. Eleazar says, "In your whole life, did you ever see a lion working as a porter, a deer working as a fruit-picker, a fox working as a storekeeper, a wolf selling pots, a domestic beast or a wild beast or a bird who had a trade?

F. "Now these are created only to work for me, and I was made only to work for my master.

G. "Now is there not an argument *a fortiori*: Now if these, who were created only to work for me, lo, they make a living without anguish, I who have been created to work for my master, is it not reasonable that I too should make a living without anguish!

H. "But my deeds have ruined things, and I have spoiled my living."

The natural order has each species doing what it is created to do. Humans are created to live without much trouble, but because of sin (Adam in Eden), they are condemned to hard labor.

Now if we examine work in the required context, namely, the work-week's ending with the Sabbath of rest and repose, matters take on a different appearance. When we work, it is with the knowledge that we are destined to the Sabbath rest, so, while we must work, we are not imprisoned by that obligation (Mekhilta deR. Ishmael LIII:II.9-10):

A. "Six days you shall labor and do all your work:"

B. But can a mortal carry out all of one's work in only six days?

C. But the nature of Sabbath rest is such that it should be as though all of your labor has been carried out.

A. Another teaching [as to "Six days you shall labor and do all your work:"]

B. "Take a Sabbath rest from the very thought of work."

C. And so Scripture says, "If you turn away your foot because of the Sabbath" (Is. 58:13), and, then, "Then you shall delight yourself in the Lord" (Is. 58:14).

Man and woman have left Eden and entered the world of work. But the Sabbath restores them for the moment to that world of Eden that they have lost. It gives them a foretaste of the age to come, when, the dead having been raised and life eternal having come, humanity will recover Eden.

But how to do so? Adam's sin finds its antidote in the Torah, which, sages maintain, is given to purify the heart of humanity. By keeping the Torah, humanity learns to accept God's will, so to overcome the natural propensity to rebel. When humanity, in full freedom of will, accepts God's commandments, beginning with "You will love the Lord your God with all your heart, with all your soul, and with all your might" (Deut. 6:5), then humanity regains Eden. The one thing God craves but cannot coerce is our love, freely given. That is what the Torah means to bring about. What appears to digress explains the very center of Judaism's doctrine of work: the most important work a person can do is study the Torah. For that is where God and humanity are to be reconciled: where humanity meets God in God's own self-revelation. In the Torah, God sets forth what he wants us to know about himself, and it is in the labor of learning that we meet him, where he talks with us.

That fundamental conviction explains why, from sages' perspective, the kind of work that Israelites were made to carry out is labor in Torah-study. That position is expressed in so many words by a principal figure in the formation of the oral part of the Torah, Yohanan ben Zakkai, who flourished in the first century, at about the time of the destruction of the Jerusalem Temple in 70 C.E. (M. Ab. 2:8):

A. Rabban Yohanan b. Zakkai received [the tradition of the Oral Torah] from Hillel and Shammai.
B. He would say, "If you have learned much Torah, do not puff yourself up on that account, for it was for that purpose that you were created."

Now the picture is complete, or so it would seem. We must work for three reasons, each quite distinct from the others. First, we must work to be like God, who created the world in six days of labor and rested on the seventh. Second, we must do servile labor because we are party to the human condition, cast from Eden by reason of our rebellion against God. Third, we ought to conduct the labor of divine service, particularly Torah-study, because that is how we may regain Eden. So work finds its place within a restorationist-theology that aims at bringing Adam and Eve back to Eden.

**How ought we work?—Kinds of work to be preferred or avoided:** The kind of work to be preferred unambiguously defines itself: Torah-study. Then the urgent question is, if we spend our time making a living, how are we to find the time to study the Torah? And that question brings us to one of the great, and on-going, debates in classical Judaism, which concerns what sort of work we must do. May we divide our time between Torah-study and gainful labor, or must we devote our time only or mainly to Torah-study and let the world bring what it may? What about knowledge of Torah as a way of making one's living? The answers to these questions lead us into the Torah's theory of the kind of work to be preferred and avoided. The first position is the most practical (M. Qid. 4:14):

E. R. Meir says, "A man should always teach his son a clean and easy trade. And let him pray to him to whom belong riches and possessions.
G. "For there is no trade that does not involve poverty or wealth.
H. "For poverty does not come from one's trade, nor does wealth come from one's trade.
I. "But all is in accord with a man's merit."

Meir would hold that so far as one can provide for an easy living for one's children, one

should do so, but, in the end, everything is in God's hands, and God decides matters by reference to a person's merit. So the "clean and easy trade," such as tailoring, is to be preferred, but not for religious reasons, only for the simple, secular fact that it does not involve any heavy lifting.

J. R. Simeon b. Eleazar says, "Have you ever seen a wild beast or a bird who has a trade? Yet they get along without difficulty. And were they not created only to serve me? And I was created to serve my Master. So is it not logical that I should get along without difficulty? But I have done evil and ruined my living."

Here, in a passage parallel to one we examined above, is the direct reference to the fall of Adam from Eden. How in practical, everyday terms that makes a difference is explicit. One's merit makes the difference between poverty and wealth. A more practical position follows in the continuation of the passage:

K. Abba Gurion of Sidon says in the name of Abba Gurya, "A man should not teach his son to be an ass-driver, camel-driver, barber, sailor, herdsman, or shopkeeper. For their trade is the trade of thieves."
L. R. Judah says in his name, "Most ass-drivers are evil, most camel-drivers are decent, most sailors are saintly, the best among physicians is going to Gehenna, and the best of butchers is a partner of Amalek."

Now comes the centerpiece, the view that "Torah"—meaning, perpetual study of the Torah—suffices as a means for making a living:

M. R. Nehorai says, "I should lay aside every trade in the world and teach my son only Torah.
N. "For a man eats its fruits in this world, and the principal remains for the world to come.
O. "But other trades are not that way.
P. "When a man gets sick or old or has pains and cannot do his job, lo, he dies of starvation.
Q. "But with Torah it is not that way.
R. "But it keeps him from all evil when he is young, and it gives him a future and a hope when he is old.
S. "Concerning his youth, what does it say? 'They who wait upon the Lord shall

renew their strength' (Is. 40:31). And concerning his old age what does it say? 'They shall still bring forth fruit in old age" (Ps. 92:14).

T. "And so it says with regard to the patriarch Abraham, may he rest in peace, 'And Abraham was old and well along in years, and the Lord blessed Abraham in all things' (Gen. 24:1).

U. "We find that the patriarch Abraham kept the entire Torah even before it was revealed, since it says, 'Since Abraham obeyed my voice and kept my charge, my commandments, my statutes, and my laws' (Gen. 26:5)."

Why Torah works as it does is made explicit at R: "It keeps him from evil when he is young." That is to say, the position of Meir and Simeon is repeated, only in a fresh way. If I know the Torah, I will not sin. The conception that, if I study Torah, I automatically get the food I need to eat and the roof I need for shelter is not at issue here, where our concern is with being kept from evil in youth and enjoying God's blessing in old age on account of keeping the Torah—a very different thing. But that position will emerge, as the successive documents record opinion unfolding over time.

Should one abandon all worldly occupations and only study the Torah? That is the position of hundreds of thousands of contemporary Orthodox Jews, men who spend all their time in yeshiva-learning, wives and children who live on whatever the yeshiva can give to support the men in their study. Within the society of Judaism are many, therefore, living out their lives in sacred service. But the view that Torah-study suffices as the work one should do took shape only over time. Indeed, the first apologia for the Mishnah, tractate Abot, ca. 250 C.E., holds that one should *not* make one's living this way. That is explicit in sayings that reject the use of Torah-study to avoid one's obligation to earn a living, holding instead that Torah-study along with labor at a craft is the ideal way of life (M. Ab. 2:2, 3:17):

A. Rabban Gamaliel, a son of Rabbi Judah the Patriarch, says: "Fitting is learning in the Torah along with a craft, for the labor put into the two of them makes one forget sin. And all learning of the Torah which is not joined with labor is destined to be null and causes sin."

A. R. Eleazar b. Azariah says, ". . . If there is no sustenance [lit.: flour], there is no Torah-learning. If there is no Torah-learning, there is no sustenance."

The way of virtue lies rather in economic activity in the conventional sense, joined to intellectual or philosophical activity in sages' sense. The labor in Torah is not an economic activity and produces no solutions to this-worldly problems of getting food, shelter, clothing. To the contrary, labor in Torah defines the purpose of human life, but it is not the medium for maintaining life and avoiding starvation or exposure to the elements.

That the context of Torah-study is religious and not economic in any sense is shown by Hananiah's saying, which is explicit: if people talk about the Torah, the presence of God joins them (M. Ab. 3:2):

B. R. Hananiah b. Teradion says, "[If] two sit together and between them do not pass teachings of the Torah, lo, this is a seat of the scornful, as it is said, 'Nor sits in the seat of the scornful' (Ps. 1:1). But two who are sitting, and words of the Torah do pass between them—the presence is with them, as it is said, 'Then they that feared the Lord spoke with one another, and the Lord hearkened and heard, and a book of remembrance was written before him, for them that feared the Lord and gave thought to his name' (Mal. 3:16). I know this applies to two. How do I know that even if a single person sits and works on the Torah, the Holy One, blessed be he, sets aside a reward for him? As it is said, 'Let him sit alone and keep silent, because he has laid it upon him' (Lam. 3:28)."

Do worldly benefits accrue to those who study the Torah? The rabbi cited in the following statement maintains that it is entirely inappropriate to utilize Torah-learning to gain either social standing or economic gain (M. Ab. 4:5):

C. R. Sadoq says, "Do not make [Torah-teachings] a crown in which to glorify yourself or a spade with which to dig."

D. So did Hillel say, "He who uses the crown perishes.

E. "Thus have you learned: Whoever derives worldly benefit from teachings of the Torah takes his life out of this world."

The bulk of opinion in the Mishnah and in M. Abot identifies Torah-learning with status within a system of hierarchical classification, not with a medium for earning a living. Admittedly that is not the only position that is represented. The following contrasts "working for a living" with "studying Torah" and maintains that the latter will provide a living, without recourse to hard labor (M. Ab. 3:15):

> A. R. Nehunia b. Haqqaneh says, "From whomever accepts upon himself the yoke of the Torah do they remove the yoke of the state and the yoke of hard labor. And upon whomever removes from himself the yoke of the Torah do they lay the yoke of the state and the yoke of hard labor."

But the prevailing view, represented by the bulk of sayings, treats Torah-study as an activity that competes with economic venture and insists that Torah-study take precedence, even though it is not of economic value in any commonplace sense of the words. That is explicitly imputed to Meir in the following (M. Ab. 4:10):

> A. R. Meir says, "Keep your business to a minimum and make your business the Torah. And be humble before everybody. And if you treat the Torah as nothing, you will have many treating you as nothing. And if you have labored in the Torah, [the Torah] has a great reward to give you."

Torah-study competes with, rather than replaces, economic activity. That is the simple position of Abot, extending the conception of matters explicit in the Mishnah. If I had to make a simple statement of the situation prevailing at ca. 250, sages contrast their wealth, which is spiritual and intellectual, with material wealth; they do not deem the one to form the counterpart of the other, but only the opposite. But matters shift in the later documents of the Oral Torah in the formative age, for there are passages that are quite explicit that Torah-study is tantamount to wealth.

A profound shift is represented by a story about first-century authorities that appears in the fifth century compilation, Leviticus Rabbah. To understand the passage, we must recall that in antiquity, "wealth" meant land, and people who had surplus to invest ordinarily bought land. Here, by contrast, we find a fundamental debate on the very definition of "wealth," or, in secular language, "scarce resources." It is a debate without precedent in any prior compilation, only adumbrated, as we saw, by minority opinion in tractate Abot. In this debate, the lesser figure, Tarfon, thought wealth took the form of land, while the greater figure, Aqiba, explained to him that wealth takes the form of Torah-learning. That the sense is material and concrete is explicit: land for Torah, Torah for land (Lev. Rabbah XXXIV:XVI):

> B. R. Tarfon gave to R. Aqiba six silver centenarii, saying to him, "Go, buy us a piece of land, so we can get a living from it and labor in the study of Torah together."
> C. He took the money and handed it over to scribes, Mishnah-teachers, and those who study Torah.
> D. After some time R. Tarfon met him and said to him, "Did you buy the land I mentioned to you?"
> E. He said to him, "Yes."
> F. He said to him, "Is it any good?"
> G. He said to him, "Yes."
> H. He said to him, "And do you not want to show it to me?"
> I. He took him and showed him the scribes, Mishnah teachers, and people who were studying Torah, and the Torah that they had acquired.
> J. He said to him, "Is there anyone who works for nothing? Where is the deed covering the field?"
> K. He said to him, "It is with King David, concerning whom it is written, 'He has scattered, he has given to the poor, his righteousness endures forever' (Ps. 112:9)."

When "Torah" substitutes for real estate, what, exactly, do sages know as scarce resources, and how is the counterpart-category constructed? We should err if we supposed that sages spoke in figurative or metaphorical language. When they identified "wealth" with "Torah-learning," they took a very concrete view. Just as "wealth" in real estate supports those who have it, so "wealth" in Torah-learning sustains those who have it. The spiritualization of the matter that we noted earlier—the Torah keeps us from sin—now moves to its logical next step, with the claim that, if we study the Torah, we gain that scarce resource that matters (Lev. Rabbah XXX:I.4-5):

> 4.A. R. Yohanan was going up from Tiberias to Sepphoris. R. Hiyya bar Abba was supporting him. They came to a field. He said, "This field once belonged to me, but I sold it in order to acquire merit in the Torah."
>
> B. They came to a vineyard, and he said, "This vineyard once belonged to me, but I sold it in order to acquire merit in the Torah."
>
> C. They came to an olive grove, and he said, "This olive grove once belonged to me, but I sold it in order to acquire merit in the Torah."
>
> D. R. Hiyya began to cry.
>
> E. Said R. Yohanan, "Why are you crying?"
>
> F. He said to him, "It is because you left nothing over to support you in your old age."
>
> G. He said to him, "Hiyya, my disciple, is what I did such a light thing in your view? I sold something which was given in a spell of six days [of creation] and in exchange I acquired something which was given in a spell of forty days [of revelation].
>
> H. "The entire world and everything in it was created in only six days, as it is written, 'For in six days the Lord made heaven and earth' [Exod. 20:11].
>
> I. "But the Torah was given over a period of forty days, as it was said, 'And he was there with the Lord for forty days and forty nights' [Exod. 34:28].
>
> J. "And it is written, 'And I remained on the mountain for forty days and forty nights'" (Deut. 9:9).

Land is the counterpart—and clearly the opposite—of the Torah.

One can sell a field and acquire "Torah," meaning in the context established by the exchange between Tarfon and Aqiba, the opportunity to gain leisure to (acquire the merit gained by) the study of the Torah. That the sage has left himself nothing for his support in old age makes explicit the material meaning of the statement, and the comparison of the value of land, created in six days, and the Torah, created in forty days, is equally explicit. The comparison of knowl-

edge of Torah to the merchandise of the merchant simply repeats the same point, but in a lower register. So too does the this-worldly power of study of the Torah make explicit in another framework the conviction that study of the Torah yields material and concrete benefit, not just spiritual renewal. Thus R. Huna states, "All of the exiles will be gathered together only on account of the study of Mishnah-teachings" (Pesiqta deRab Kahana VI:III.3.B). The point should not be missed: the in-gathering of the exiles marks the return of humanity to Eden, embodied in the return of holy Israel to the Land of Israel at the end of time. So Huna's statement fits into the larger system. It is defined by sages' contrast of Torah-study with land-ownership, intellectual prowess with physical power, the superiority of the one over the other. No wonder sages would in time claim that their power protected cities, which then needed neither police nor walls. These were concrete claims, affecting the rational utilization of scarce resources as much as the use and distribution of land constituted an expression of a rationality concerning scarce resources, their preservation and increase.

This brings us back to the matter of teaching one's son a trade. The contrast between the received position and that before us is found in the Talmud of the Land of Israel, which came to closure ca. 400 C.E., in the same period as the passages of Leviticus Rabbah we have examined (Y. Pe. 1:1.VII):

> D. It is forbidden to a person to teach his son a trade, in as much as it is written, "And you shall meditate therein day and night" (Josh. 1:8).
>
> E. But has not R. Ishmael taught, "'You shall choose life" (Deut. 30:19)—this refers to learning [Torah] and practicing a trade as well?

There is no harmonizing the two views. In fact, study of the Torah substituted for practicing a craft, and it was meant to do so. In all, therefore, the case is firmly established in favor of the proposition that Torah is a material good. Torah has now been transformed into the ultimate scarce resource, explicitly substituting for real estate, even in the Land of Israel.

No wonder then that it can be claimed that sages are the guardians of cities, a notion that later on yields the further allegation that sages do not have to pay taxes to build walls around cities, since their Torah-study itself offers protection (Pesiqta deRab Kahana XV:V.1):

A. R. Abba bar Kahana commenced discourse by citing the following verse: "'Who is the man so wise that he may understand this? To whom has the mouth of the Lord spoken, that he may declare it? Why is the land ruined and laid waste like a wilderness, [so that no one passes through? The Lord said, It is because they forsook my Torah which I set before them; they neither obeyed me nor conformed to it. They followed the promptings of their own stubborn hearts, they followed the Baalim as their forefathers had taught them. Therefore these are the words of the Lord of hosts the God of Israel: I will feed this people with wormwood and give them bitter poison to drink. I will scatter them among nations whom neither they nor their forefathers have known; I will harry them with the sword until I have made an end of them]' (Jer. 9:16)."

B. It was taught in the name of R. Simeon b. Yohai, "If you see towns uprooted from their place in the land of Israel, know that [it is because] the people did not pay the salaries of teachers of children and Mishnah-instructors.

C. "What is the verse of Scripture that indicates it? 'Why is the land ruined and laid waste like a wilderness, [so that no one passes through?]' What is written just following? 'It is because they forsook my Torah [which I set before them; they neither obeyed me nor conformed to it.]'"

2.A. Rabbi sent R. Yose and R. Ammi to go and survey the towns of the land of Israel. They would go into a town and say to the people, "Bring me the guardians of the town."

B. The people would bring out the head of the police and the local guard.

C. [The sages] would say, "These are not the guardians of the town; they are those who destroy the town. Who are the guardians of the town? They are the teachers of children and Mishnah-teachers, who keep watch by day and by night, in line with the verse, 'And you shall meditate in it day and night' (Josh. 1:8)."

D. "And so Scripture says, 'If the Lord does not build the house, in vain the builders labor' (Ps. 127:1)."

7.A. Said R. Abba bar Kahana, "No philosophers in the world ever arose of the quality of Balaam ben Beor and Abdymos of Gadara. The nations of the world came to Abnymos of Gadara. They said to him, 'Do you maintain that we can make war against this nation?'

B. "He said to them, 'Go and make the rounds of their synagogues and their study houses. So long as there are there children chirping out loud in their voices [and studying the Torah], then you cannot overcome them. If not, then you can conquer them, for so did their father promise them: 'The voice is Jacob's voice' (Gen. 27:22), meaning that when Jacob's voice chirps in synagogues and study houses, the hands are not the hands of Esau [so Esau has no power].

C. "'So long as there are no children chirping out loud in their voices [and studying the Torah] in synagogues and study houses, The hands are the hands of Esau [so Esau has power].'"

To understand the message, we have to know that, when sages in the documents that reached closure in the fifth and later centuries referred to "Esau," they meant Rome. This was Christian Rome, Rome guided by the same Scriptures of ancient Israel that sages valued as "the Written Torah." So now Israel (Jacob) competed with Esau, as contemporary Israel of the fifth century competed with Rome. They were brothers and enemies. Then Rome was Christian, which accounts for the conviction that Rome was the brother, hence Esau, competing with Jacob, who is Israel, for the inheritance, the birthright of the Torah. The reference to Esau, that is, Rome thus links the whole to the contemporary context and alleges that if the Israelites will support those who study the Torah and teach it, then their cities will be safe, and, still more, the rule of Esau/Rome will come to an end; then the messiah will come, so the stakes are not trivial.

So much for the work that really matters, the work that people should aspire to do. Sages also recognize that there are categories of work people should avoid, as we already have noticed. But what is the principle that explains which kind of work is to be avoided? It is work that demeans, and that means work that makes one dependent or work that brings one into disrepute. A man should not depend on his wife's earnings (B. Pes. 4:1-2 I.6-10/50B):

I.6A. Our rabbis have taught on Tannaite authority:
B. He who depends on the earnings of his wife or of a mill will never see a sign of blessing.
C. The earnings of his wife: this refers to her selling wool by weight.
D. A mill: this refers to renting it out.
E. But if she makes woolen things and sells them, Scripture certainly praises her: "She makes linen garments and sells them" (Prov. 31:24).

Another kind of living that sages, for obvious reasons, condemn, brings the worker into disrepute. It is not necessarily illegal, but it is certainly destructive of the common interest. That may be because they trade in what is free for the taking, which is the produce of the seventh year of the seven-year-cycle of agriculture, when the Holy Land is deemed ownerless, its produce available at no cost to everyone. Or it may be because they make a living by destroying the environment; sages condemn raising small cattle, particularly goats, which denude the land of trees and other sustaining growth, and cutting down trees. Or it may be, people who want to rise beyond their assigned station and lot in life, as the continuation of the preceding passage states:

I.8A. Our rabbis have taught on Tannaite authority:
B. Those who trade in produce of the Seventh Year, breed small cattle, cut down beautiful trees, or look for something better than their portion will never see a sign of blessing.
C. How come?
D. People are scandalized by them.

The striking point is the inclusion of people who try to better themselves. Sages valued private property, regarding the right of ownership as a given. But they did not think that people should aspire to enrich themselves; they did not see as a worthy goal the increase

of wealth defined as either gold or real estate. That is because, as we have seen, they defined wealth in other terms altogether. So they saw no point in trying to get more of what is worth less than something else, gold than Torah. Some money brings its own curse, as sages explain, and if people who work in the sacred professions, such as scribes, do the work just to make a living, they are profiting from God's interest. Here is how sages identify disreputable professions (B. Pes. 4:1-2 I.6-10/50B):

I.9A. Our rabbis have taught on Tannaite authority:
B. Four pennies will never carry a sign of blessing.
C. The fee for a clerk, the fee for an interpreter, the fee paid by orphans to those who trade in their capital, and money that comes from overseas.
D. Now there is no problem understanding why that is the case for the fee for interpreters [who announce in a loud voice the teachings of the master], since it appears to be a fee paid for work on the Sabbath; there is no problem understanding the case of orphans' money, since they cannot renounce ownership [and the minor cannot renounce an excessive fee]; and there is no problem understanding the case of money from overseas, since miracles don't happen every day. [Overseas trading is so perilous that to make money in it requires a miracle from God, on which people should not depend.] But what's the problem with the fee for a clerk?
E. Said R. Joshua b. Levi, "Twenty-four fasts did the men of the great assembly conduct on account of those who write out scrolls, phylacteries, and doorpost Scriptures, so that they should never get rich, for if they get rich, they'll never write the necessary religious articles again."
I.10A. Our rabbis have taught on Tannaite authority:
B. Those who write out scrolls, phylacteries, and doorpost Scriptures, they, those who trade in what they make, and those who trade in what those who trade in what they make, and all who trade in the work of Heaven—including those who sell blue wool—will never see a sign of blessing. But if they do it for its own sake, they do.

So much for work that the Torah does not advise or value; the reasons derive from the coherent system that identifies one kind of work as meritorious, another as neutral, and a third as disreputable. What sages condemn out of hand, for reasons that theology supplies, is sloth, and a simple statement of the matter, at Abot DeRabbi Natan XXI, suffices to show what is at stake:

I.1.A. R. Dosa b. Harkinas says, "Sleeping late in the morning, drinking wine at noon, chatting with children, and attending the synagogues of the ignorant drive a man out of the world."
   B. Sleeping late in the morning: how so?
   C. This teaches that a person should not intend to sleep until the time of reciting the *Shema* has passed.
   D. For when someone sleeps until the time for reciting the Shema has passed, he turns out to waste time that should be spent studying the Torah.
   E. As it is said, "The lazy one says, There is a lion in the way, yes, a lion is in the streets. The door is turning on its hinges and the lazy man is still in bed" (Prov. 26:13-14).
IV.1.A. And attending the synagogues of the ignorant drive a man out of the world: how so?
   B. This teaches that a person should not plan to join with the idle in the corners of the market place.
   C. For if someone sits around with the idle in the corners of the market place, he turns out to waste time that he should spend in studying the Torah.
   D. For so it is said, "Happy is the one who has not walked in the counsel of the wicked, stood in the way of the sinners, or sat in the seat of the scornful. . . . But his delight is in the Torah of the Lord" (Ps. 1:1-2).
V.1.A. There was the case of R. Aqiba who was in session and repeating teachings for his disciples. He remembered something that he had done in his youth.
   B. He said, "I give thanks for you, O Lord my God, that you have placed my portion among those who sit in the house of study and have not placed my portion with those who sit idly in the market place."

It would be difficult to state the matter more clearly than Aqiba does: work to be desired is Torah-study, work to be avoided demeans.

**Why must we help others? Private gain and public benefit:** The Torah contemplates Israel within the land of Israel, the Promised Land, and the Torah further regards God as the owner of the land: "The earth is the Lord's, and the fullness thereof" (Ps. 24:1). Hence when we help others, it is because we are using what God owns and has given to us in such a way as to carry out the will of the one who owns it all. Viewing holy Israel as a society made up of households engaged in farming, the Torah therefore provides for sharing crops with the needy as well as those engaged in public service. Scripture forms the basis for that provision, with its program of offerings and tithes to support the poor, the priesthood, and pilgrimage to Jerusalem on the festivals. Farmers are to leave the corner of the field, not taking every last bit of grain; the poor then are free to glean the remnant of the crops. Within this system, why must we help others? It is because what we have belongs to God. God has designated his share for those who need his help, especially the poor. So the poor have a special claim on society, but it is not because they are unemployed. It is because they are poor.

How does the Torah situate charity in the hierarchy of virtues and meritorious deeds? As in Islam, charity (called by the same Hebrew word used for "righteousness," *sedaqah*) forms a principal religious obligation. But when it comes to hierarchizing the virtues of charity, loving kindness, and justice, when they are to be compared with one another, they are shown in the end to be equivalent in God's eyes:

J. Said R. Eleazar, "Greater is the one who carries out an act of charity than one who offers all the sacrifices.
K. "For it is said, 'To do charity and justice is more desired by the Lord than sacrifice' (Prov. 21:3)."

So far we have set the world on its head, by declaring charity for the poor a greater act of service to God than the offering of sacrifices to God in heaven. But an act of loving kindness takes priority over an act of charity:

L. And R. Eleazar said, "An act of loving kindness is greater than an act of charity.

M. "For it is said, 'Sow to yourselves according to your charity, but reap according to your loving kindness' (Hos. 10:12).

N. "If a man sows seed, it is a matter of doubt whether he will eat a crop or not. But if a man harvests the crop, he most certainly will eat it."

O. And R. Eleazar said, "An act of charity is rewarded only in accord with the loving kindness that is connected with it.

P. "For it is said, 'Sow to yourselves according to your charity, but reap according to your loving kindness' (Hos. 10:12)."

The point is, if an act of charity is done out of a sense of obligation and devotion to the other, then it has value, but if it is done in a spirit of arrogance and condescension, it does not. Not only so, but an act of personal service takes priority over an act of charity in the form of mere money:

9.A. Our rabbis have taught on Tannaite authority:

B. In three aspects are acts of loving kindness greater than an act of charity.

C. An act of charity is done only with money, but an act of loving kindness someone carries out either with his own person or with his money.

D. An act of charity is done only for the poor, while an act of loving kindness may be done either for the poor or for the rich.

E. An act of charity is done only for the living. An act of loving kindness may be done either for the living or for the dead.

Charity and justice are the same thing. We give to the poor because it is an act of righteousness; it is owing from us, not a matter of volition but of obligation. The hierarchizing of loving kindness and charity produces the result that the former takes priority, for specified reasons, deriving from Scripture.

**Unemployment, exploitation, and alternatives to proper work:** Even as the situation of unemployment simply lies beyond the imagination of the sages of the Torah, they fully appreciated the mutual obligations of worker and employer. Employers exploit

workers when they pay them less than the going wage. Workers swindle workers when they do not show up for work they have contracted to do. How then to sort out the conflicting claims? In some cases the deceived party may complain but not gain reparations (M. B.M. 6:1):

A. He who hires craftsmen,

B. and one party deceived the other—

C. one has no claim on the other party except a complaint [which is not subject to legal recourse].

But what if one can demonstrate that the worker has caused the employer a genuine loss? Then the employer has recourse even to deception:

D. [If] one hired an ass driver or wagon driver to bring porters and pipes for a bride or a corpse,

E. or workers to take his flax out of the steep,

F. or anything which goes to waste [if there is a delay],

G. and [the workers] went back on their word—

H. in a situation in which there is no one else [available for hire],

I. he hires others at their expense,

J. or he deceives them [by promising to pay more and then not paying more than the originally stipulated commitment].

This principle of equity governs not only workers but also craftsmen. At the same time, these individuals are protected by the rule that if the employer changes the terms of the original agreement, he must pay up (M. B.M. 6:2):

A. He who hires craftsmen and they retracted—

B. their hand is on the bottom.

C. If the householder retracts,

D. his hand is on the bottom.

E. Whoever changes [the original terms of the agreement]—

F. his hand is on the bottom.

G. And whoever retracts—

H. his hand is on the bottom.

The extent to which workers bear responsibility for deceit is spelled out in the Tosefta. We see that the Mishnah's treatment of the basic transaction—one party deceives another, neither then has much of a concrete claim—applies only if the workers did not show up. But if these day-workers did show up, then they have lost a day of work, and, living from pay check to pay check and day to day, they cannot afford to lose the salary. The householder must pay it (T. B.M. 7:1):

B. He who hires workers and they deceived the householder, or the householder deceived them, they have no claim on one another except a complaint. Under what circumstances? When the workers did not show up.

C. But if ass-drivers came but did not find grain, workers but found the field too wet to work and not suitable for plowing, he pays them their wages in full.

D. But one who actually travels with a load is not the same as one who travels empty-handed, and one who does the work is not treated as equivalent to one who comes and sits and does nothing.

What happens if the work has gotten under way? Then we proportion the settlement, paying for the work actually done. But if time is of the essence, then the generous provision of the Mishnah's law pertains (T. B.M. 7:1):

I. Under what circumstances? If it is a case of something that does not go to waste. But in the case of something that goes to waste if there is a delay, he hires others at their expense or deceives them by promising to pay more and then not paying more than his originally stated commitment.

J. How so? He says to the worker, "I agreed to pay you a *sela*. Lo, I'm going to give you two." He then goes and hires workers from another location and comes and takes the money from this party and hands it over to that party. To what extent? Even up to forty or fifty *zuz*.

K. Under what circumstances? In a situation in which he comes to an agreement with him while he cannot find others to hire. But if he saw ass-drivers coming along, the worker may say to him, 'Go and hire one of these for your needs," and the employer has no claim on him except a complaint.

In this way we see how the law provides fair arrangements for both parties to the transaction of work, the employer and the employee. And we note, further, that the law limits the workers' liability: if other workers are at hand, those that have chosen not to work cannot be penalized.

Exploitation involves not only the employer's deceiving the workers, it also covers the employer's adhering to the accepted practices of the locale. The employer may not impose upon the workers regulations that are not generally required (M. B.M. 7:1):

A. He who hires day workers and told them to start work early or to stay late—in a place in which they are accustomed not to start work early or not to stay late, he has no right to force them to do so. In a place in which they are accustomed to provide a meal, he must provide a meal. In a place in which they are accustomed to make do with a sweet, he provides it.

The Torah provides that one may not muzzle an ox when it is plowing (Deut. 25:4). The ox has the right to nibble on the crop that it is helping to produce. The same rule applies to workers. If they are working in vineyards, they have the right to nibble on the grapes while they work; that is not deemed thievery (M. B.M. 7:2).

A. And these have the right to eat the produce on which they work by right accorded to them in the Torah: he who works on what is as yet unplucked may eat from the produce at the end of the time of processing; and he who works on plucked produce may eat from the produce before processing is done; in both instances solely in regard to what grows from the ground.

B. But these do not have the right to eat the produce on which they labor by right accorded to them in the Torah: he who works on what is as yet unplucked, before the end of the time of processing; and he who works on plucked produce after the processing is done, in both instances solely in regard to what does not grow from the ground.

But here too, the employer has rights; the workers may not gorge themselves or take advantage, and they also may eat only the crop on which they are working. Workers may not exploit their rights, and the employers may not limit those same rights. A further form of exploitation of workers involves not paying them promptly. Scripture forbids such a practice, "In his day you shall give him his fee" (Deut. 24:15), so too, "The wages of a hired worker will not abide with you at night until the morning" (Lev. 19:13). Rabbinic law interprets this to mean, one who has worked all day must be paid by night fall, and one who has worked all night must be paid by dawn (M. B.M. 9:11):

> B. (1) A day worker collects his wage any time of the night. (2) And a night worker collects his wage any time of the day. (3) A worker by the hour collects his wage any time of the night or day.
> C. A worker hired by the week, a worker hired by the month, a worker hired by the year, a worker hired by the septennate—if he completed his period of labor by day, collects any time that day. If he completed his period of labor by night, he collects his wage any time during the rest of that night and the following day.

Not paying promptly is deemed oppression of the workers (T. B.M. 10:3A-C):

> A. He who holds back the wages of a hired hand transgresses on account of five negative commandments, because of not oppressing (Lev. 19:13),
> B. because of not stealing (Lev. 19:13),
> C. because of the verse that says, "The wages of a hired worker will not abide with you all night until morning" (Lev. 19:13);
> D. "you shall give him hire on the day he earns it before the sun goes down, because he is poor" (Deut. 24:15)

But that is the case only if the worker lays claim for his wages. If he does not do so, the employer does not violate the law of paying promptly. The worker's responsibility to take care of himself triggers the working of the law.

The Torah takes account of all manner of exploitation of workers in its quest for justice for poor and rich alike. But, as we have seen, the sages find little to say about matters that fall outside of their categorical structure. Just as unemployment lies beyond their imagination, so they would find it difficult to differentiate "proper" from "improper" work. True, the Torah as sages interpret it values some kinds of work over others. It further recognizes the difference between hard physical labor and the less physically-enervating demands of certain crafts. But, in the end, work is work, and the system treats workers with dignity and respect, without regard to the kind of work that they do.

**Unconventional work—Working for God:** Who in formative Judaism are the people who work for God? The priests and Levites of the Temple would certainly present themselves as candidates. Their work is hard, involving much heavy lifting. To do the work properly, they must be punctilious, for example avoiding those sources of cultic contamination or uncleanness that Scripture specifies at Leviticus Chapters Eleven through Fifteen. And the children of Aaron, the priests, bring peace to the community and work for peace between Israel and their father in heaven (M. Ab. 1:12):

> Hillel says, "Be disciples of Aaron, loving peace and pursuing peace, loving people and drawing them near to the Torah."

The leaders of the community, judges and administrators, would offer themselves as a choice. They provide for the general welfare; they hold things together; they make provision for the needs of the community. They work not only for themselves but for everyone, realizing Hillel's famous saying (M. Ab. 1:14):

> Hillel would say, "If I am not for myself, who is for me? And when I am for myself, what am I? And if not now, when?"

The householders, responsible for the working of the social order, organizing and maintaining the natural processes that feed the community and sustain the entire life of Israel—they too would say they do God's work. And all would present a strong case for themselves, one that no one would reject.

The Torah identifies as those who work for God, above all, the disciples of the sages, who provide the model of true piety, studying the Torah in poverty and among nonbelievers. To make that point, the fourth century sage Raba refers to Song of Songs 7:12, "Come . . . let us go forth into the fields." Since all of Judaism knows that the Song of Solomon speaks of the intense, passionate love of God for Israel and Israel for God, the meaning of the verse will prove self-evident. Here Israel speaks to God and asks God to join Israel in the fields, not in the cities but in the villages—where the disciples of the Torah, in penury, labor at study of the Torah (B. Erub. 2:1-2 V.16/21B-22A):

A. Expounded Raba, "What is the meaning of the verse of Scripture, 'Come my beloved, let us go forth into the field, let us lodge in the villages, let us get up early to the vineyards, let us see whether the vine has budded, whether the vine blossom be opened, and the pomegranates be in flower; there will I give you my love' (Song 7:12)?

B. "'Come my beloved, let us go forth into the field:' Said the congregation of Israel before the Holy One, blessed be He, 'Lord of the world, don't judge me like those who live in the cities, who are full of thievery and fornication and vain oaths and false swearing.'

C. "'Let us go forth into the field:' 'Come and I shall show you disciples of sages, who are engaged in the Torah in the midst of want.'

D. "'Let us lodge in the villages:' Read the letters for villages as though they bore vowels to yield, 'among the infidels,' 'come and I shall show you those upon whom you have bestowed much good, and who have denied you.'

E. "'Let us get up early to the vineyards:' This refers to the synagogues and study houses.

F. "'Let us see whether the vine has budded:' This refers to masters of Scripture.

G. "'Whether the vine blossom be opened:' This refers to masters of the Mishnah.

H. "'And the pomegranates be in flower:' This refers to the masters of analysis.

I. "'There will I give you my love:' 'I shall show you my glory, my greatness, the praise of my sons and my daughters.'"

So the Oral Torah is explicit in the matter: those who do God's work are those who spend their lives at Torah-study.

When, at the outset, we placed the matter of work—what we owe the community—into the larger context of the theology of the Torah, we turned out to predetermine our results at every point. We cannot explain why we must work, what kinds of work are to be preferred or avoided, why we must help others through our work, what constitutes exploitation of workers, or what it means to work for God—we cannot explain anything to do with Israel in community without invoking the governing principle throughout. It is that Israel through the Torah will make of itself that community faithful to God such that God will respond with the work of restoration: Adam and Eve lost Eden, as Israel has lost the land (so matters appeared to the sages after 70 C.E., when the Temple was destroyed, and in the centuries thereafter). Through the regeneration brought about by the Torah, Israel will so purify its heart as to accept God's will over its own will—and the restoration of holy Israel to the land, signifying the return of Adam and Eve to Eden, is sure to follow. To the drama of humanity's restoration to grace, work forms a worthy overture.

JACOB NEUSNER

# Z

**ZEKHUT:** In classical Judaism *zekhut*—"the heritage of supererogatory virtue and its consequent entitlements"—stands for the empowerment, of a supernatural character, that derives from the virtue of one's ancestry or from one's own virtuous deeds, specifically, those not commanded but impelled by utter generosity of the heart, done without hope let alone prospect of recompense and without pressure of any kind. No single word in English bears the same meaning, nor is there a synonym for *zekhut* in the canonical writings, only the antonym, which is sin. Sin represents an act of rebellion, *zekhut*, an act of humble and willing, gratuitous submission; so the two represent binary opposites.

The meaning of *zekhut* is conveyed not in such familiar Rabbinic media as systematic exegetical or propositional expositions but in simple stories. Here the language of *zekhut* figures and the meaning of that language is conveyed in context. In the opening text, when the beggar asks for money, he says, literally, "acquire *zekhut* through me," referring in context to the action he solicits. But the same word, as noun or verb, in other contexts takes on other meanings, always with the same deeper significance for the relationship of grace, for the unearned, uncoerced love, that is besought. The difficulty of translating a word of systemic consequence with a single word in some other language (or in the language of the system's documents themselves) tells us we deal with what is unique (Y. Ta. 1:4.I):

> F. A certain man came before one of the relatives of R. Yannai. He said to him, "Rabbi, attain *zekhut* through me [by giving me charity]."
>
> G. He said to him, "And didn't your father leave you money?"
>
> H. He said to him, "No."
>
> I. He said to him, "Go and collect what your father left in deposit with others."
>
> J. He said to him, "I have heard concerning property my father deposited with others that it was gained by violence [so I don't want it]."
>
> K. He said to him, "You are worthy of praying and having your prayers answered."

The point of K, of course, is self-evidently a reference to the possession of entitlement to supernatural favor, and it is gained through deeds that the law of the Torah cannot require but does favor: what one does on one's own volition, beyond the measure of the law. Here I see the opposite of sin, the refusal to take what was gained through violence. A sin is what one has done by one's own volition beyond all limits of the law. So an act that generates *zekhut* for the individual is the counterpart and opposite: what one does by one's own volition that also is beyond all requirements of the law.

> L. A certain ass driver appeared before the rabbis [the context requires: in a dream] and prayed, and rain came. The rabbis sent and brought him and said to him, "What is your trade?"
>
> M. He said to them, "I am an ass driver."
>
> N. They said to him, "And how do you conduct your business?"
>
> O. He said to them, "One time I rented my ass to a certain woman, and she was weeping on the way, and I said to her, 'What's with you?,' and she said to me,

'The husband of that woman [me] is in prison [for debt], and I wanted to see what I can do to free him.' So I sold my ass, and I gave her the proceeds, and I said to her, 'Here is your money, free your husband, but do not sin [by becoming a prostitute to raise the necessary funds].'"

> P. They said to him, "You are worthy of praying and having your prayers answered."

The ass-driver clearly has a powerful lien on heaven, so that his prayers are answered, even while those of others are not. What he did to get that entitlement? He did what no law could demand: impoverished himself to save the woman from a "fate worse than death."

> Q. In a dream of R. Abbahu, Mr. Pentakaka ["Five sins"] appeared, who prayed that rain would come, and it rained. R. Abbahu sent and summoned him. He said to him, "What is your trade?"
>
> R. He said to him, "Five sins does that man [I] do every day, [for I am a pimp:] hiring whores, cleaning up the theater, bringing home their garments for washing, dancing, and performing before them."
>
> S. He said to him, "And what sort of decent thing have you ever done?"
>
> T. He said to him, "One day that man [I] was cleaning the theater, and a woman came and stood behind a pillar and cried. I said to her, 'What's with you?' And she said to me, 'That woman's [my] husband is in prison, and I wanted to see what I can do to free him.' So I sold my bed and cover, and I gave the proceeds to her. I said to her, 'Here is your money, free your husband, but do not sin.'"
>
> U. He said to him, "You are worthy of praying and having your prayers answered."

Q moves us still further, since the named man has done everything sinful that one can do, and, more to the point, he does it every day. So the singularity of the act of *zekhut*, which suffices if done only one time, encompasses its power to outweigh a life of sin—again, an act of *zekhut* as the mirror-image and opposite of sin. Here again, the single act of saving a woman from a "fate worse than death" has sufficed.

> V. A pious man from Kefar Imi appeared [in a dream] to the rabbis. He prayed for

rain and it rained. The rabbis went up to him. His householders told them that he was sitting on a hill. They went out to him, saying to him, "Greetings," but he did not answer them.

W. He was sitting and eating, and he did not say to them, "You break bread too."

X. When he went back home, he made a bundle of faggots and put his cloak on top of the bundle [instead of on his shoulder].

Y. When he came home, he said to his household [wife], "These rabbis are here [because] they want me to pray for rain. If I pray and it rains, it is a disgrace for them, and if not, it is a profanation of the name of heaven. But come, you and I will go up [to the roof] and pray. If it rains, we shall tell them, 'We are not worthy to pray and have our prayers answered.'"

Z. They went up and prayed, and it rained.

AA. They came down to them [and asked], "Why have the rabbis troubled themselves to come here today?"

BB. They said to him, "We wanted you to pray so that it would rain."

CC. He said to them, "Now do you really need my prayers? Heaven already has done its miracle."

DD. They said to him, "Why, when you were on the hill, did we say hello to you, and you did not reply?"

EE. He said to them, "I was then doing my job. Should I then interrupt my concentration [on my work]?"

FF. They said to him, "And why, when you sat down to eat, did you not say to us, 'You break bread too'?"

GG. He said to them, "Because I had only my small ration of bread. Why would I have invited you to eat by way of mere flattery [when I knew I could not give you anything at all]?"

HH. They said to him, "And why when you came to go down, did you put your cloak on top of the bundle?"

II. He said to them, "Because the cloak was not mine. It was borrowed for use at prayer. I did not want to tear it."

JJ. They said to him, "And why, when you were on the hill, did your wife wear dirty clothes, but when you came down from the mountain, did she put on clean clothes?"

KK. He said to them, "When I was on the hill, she put on dirty clothes, so that no one would gaze at her. But when I came home from the hill, she put on clean clothes, so that I would not gaze on any other woman."

LL. They said to him, "It is well that you pray and have your prayers answered."

The pious man of V, finally, enjoys the recognition of the sages by reason of his lien upon heaven, able as he is to pray and bring rain. What has so endowed him with *zekhut*? Acts of punctiliousness of a moral order: concentrating on his work, avoiding an act of dissimulation, integrity in the disposition of a borrowed object, his wife's concern not to attract other men and her equal concern to make herself attractive to her husband. None of these stories refers explicitly to *zekhut*, but all of them tell us about what it means to enjoy not an entitlement by inheritance but a lien accomplished by one's own supererogatory acts of restraint.

The critical importance of the heritage of virtue together with its supernatural entitlements emerges in a striking claim. Even though a man was degraded, a single remarkable deed, exemplary for its deep humanity, sufficed to win for an ordinary person the *zekhut* that elicits supernatural favor enjoyed by some rabbis on account of their Torah-study. *Zekhut* represents a power that only God can ultimately grasp: the power of weakness. It is what the weak and excluded and despised can do that outweighs what the great masters of the Torah—impressed with the power of the ass-driver to pray and get his prayers answered—have accomplished. *Zekhut* also forms the inheritance of the disinherited: what you receive as a heritage when you have nothing in the present and have gotten nothing in the past, that scarce resource that is free and unearned but much valued.

Thus far we have treated the relationship of complementarity—a transaction of reciprocal grace—between humans and God. But the theology of the Oral Torah differentiates humanity into Israel[ites] and gentiles, those who know God and those who worship idols. Therefore, it follows, the relationship of complementarity through acts of uncoerced generosity and love has likewise to be defined in the particular context of holy Israel. That takes place with the addition, to the word *zekhut*, of the Hebrew word for patriarchs, *abot*, thus *zekhut abot*. The phrase refers to the relationship of complementarity as worked out between God and Israel in particular. That relationship works itself out within the principle that God not only responds freely to what we do as an act of grace, but remembers in our favor what our progenitors, the patriarchs, did to express selfless love and loyalty to God. The patriarchs form an abiding presence within Israel, so at stake is not an inheritance by reason of genealogy but a heritage by reason of shared virtue.

The conception of a heritage of grace to which Israel has access is entirely familiar. Scripture for example knows that God loves Israel because he loved the patriarchs (Deut. 4:37); the memory or deeds of the righteous patriarchs and matriarchs appear in a broad range of contexts, e.g., "Remember your servants, Abraham, Isaac, and Jacob" (Exod. 32:13), for Moses, and "Remember the good deeds of David, your servant" (2 Chr. 6:42), for Solomon. But more specific usages of the concept in the context of a heritage of unearned grace derive only from the documents of the Oral Torah. Here there is clear indication of the presence of a conception of an entitlement deriving from some source other than one's own deed of the moment (M. Sot. 3:4-5):

> 3:4E. There is the possibility that *zekhut* suspends the curse for one year, and there is the possibility that *zekhut* suspends the curse for two years, and there is the possibility that *zekhut* suspends the curse for three years.
>
> F. On this basis Ben Azzai says, "A man is required to teach Torah to his daughter.
>
> G. "For if she should drink the water [that reveals whether she has committed adultery, Num. 5:12-22], she should know that [if nothing happens to her], *zekhut* is what suspends [the curse from taking effect]."
>
> 3:5A. R. Simeon says, "*Zekhut* does not suspend the effects of the bitter water.
>
> B. "And if you say, '*Zekhut* does suspend the effects of the bitter water,' you will weaken the effect of the water for all the women who have to drink it.
>
> C. "And you give a bad name to all the women who drink it who turned out to be pure.

> D. "For people will say, 'They are unclean, but *zekhut* suspended the effects of the water for them.'"
>
> E. Rabbi says, "*Zekhut* does suspend the effects of the bitter water. But she will not bear children or continue to be pretty. And she will waste away, and in the end she will have the same [unpleasant] death."

Now if we replace the term *zekhut* at each point with the phrase "the heritage of virtue and its consequent entitlements," we have good sense. That is to say, the woman may not suffer the penalty to which she is presumably condemnable not because her act or condition (e.g., her innocence) has secured her acquittal or nullified the effects of the ordeal but because she enjoys some advantage extrinsic to her own act or condition. She may be guilty, but she may also possess a benefice deriving by inheritance, hence, heritage of virtue, and so be entitled to a protection not because of her own but because of someone else's action or condition.

Now, as noted above, we find one antonym for *zekhut*, which is sin. A person by his or her action brings about *zekhut* for the community or may, similarly, cause the community to sin (M. Ab. 5:18):

> A. He who causes *zekhut* to the community never causes sin.
>
> B. And he who causes the community to sin—they never give him a sufficient chance to attain penitence.

Here the contrast is between causing *zekhut* and causing sin, so *zekhut* is the opposite of sin. The continuation is equally clear that a person attained *zekhut* and endowed the community with *zekhut*,—or sinned and made community sin:

> C. Moses attained *zekhut* and bestowed *zekhut* on the community.
>
> D. So the *zekhut* of the community is assigned to his [credit],
>
> E. as it is said, "He executed the justice of the Lord and his judgments with Israel" (Deut. 33:21).
>
> F. Jeroboam sinned and caused the community to sin.
>
> G. So the sin of the community is assigned to his [debit],
>
> H. as it is said, "For the sins of Jeroboam which he committed and wherewith he made Israel to sin" (1 Kgs. 15:30).

The sense is simple. Moses, through actions of his own (of an unspecified sort), acquired *zekhut*, which is the credit for such actions that accrued to him and bestowed upon him certain supernatural entitlements; and he, for his part, passed on as an inheritance that credit, a lien on heaven for the performance of these same supernatural entitlements. The upshot is to present *zekhut* as [1] an action, as distinct from a (mere) attitude, that [2] is precisely the opposite of a sinful one; it is, moreover, an action that [3] may be done by an individual or by the community at large, and one that [4] a leader may provoke the community to do (or not do).

What is it that Israelites as a nation do to gain a lien upon heaven for themselves or entitlements of supernatural favor for their descendants? Here is one representative answer to that question (Gen. Rabbah LXXIV:XII.1):

> A. "If the God of my father, the God of Abraham and the Fear of Isaac, had not been on my side, surely now you would have sent me away empty-handed. God saw my affliction and the labor of my hand and rebuked you last night" (Gen. 31:41-42):
> B. Zebedee b. Levi and R. Joshua b. Levi:
> C. Zebedee said, "Every passage in which reference is made to 'if' tells of an appeal to the *zekhut* accrued by the patriarchs."
> D. Said to him R. Joshua, "But it is written, 'Except we had lingered' (Gen. 43:10) [a passage not related to the *zekhut* of the patriarchs]."
> E. He said to him, "They themselves would not have come up except for the *zekhut* of the patriarchs, for if it were not for the *zekhut* of the patriarchs, they never would have been able to go up from there in peace."
> F. Said R. Tanhuma, "There are those who produce the matter in a different version," [as follows]:
> G. R. Joshua and Zebedee b. Levi:
> H. R. Joshua said, "Every passage in which reference is made to 'if' tells of an appeal to the *zekhut* accrued by the patriarchs except for the present case."
> I. He said to him, "This case too falls under the category of an appeal to the *zekhut* of the patriarchs."

So much for *zekhut* that is inherited from the patriarchs, a now familiar notion. But what about the deeds of Israel in the here and now?

> J. R. Yohanan said, "It was on account of the *zekhut* achieved through sanctification of the divine name."
> K. R. Levi said, "It was on account of the *zekhut* achieved through faith and the *zekhut* achieved through Torah.

Faith despite the here and now, study of the Torah—these are what Israel does now with the result that the people gains an entitlement for themselves or their heirs.

> L. "The *zekhut* achieved through faith: 'If I had not believed . . .' (Ps. 27:13).
> M. "The *zekhut* achieved through Torah: 'Unless your Torah had been my delight' (Ps. 119:92)."
> 2.A. "God saw my affliction and the labor of my hand and rebuked you last night" (Gen. 31:41-42):
> B. Said R. Jeremiah b. Eleazar, "More beloved is hard labor than the *zekhut* achieved by the patriarchs, for the *zekhut* achieved by the patriarchs served to afford protection for property only, while the *zekhut* achieved by hard labor served to afford protection for lives.
> C. "The *zekhut* achieved by the patriarchs served to afford protection for property only: 'If the God of my father, the God of Abraham and the Fear of Isaac, had not been on my side, surely now you would have sent me away empty-handed.'
> D. "The *zekhut* achieved by hard labor served to afford protection for lives: 'God saw my affliction and the labor of my hand and rebuked you last night.'"

Here is as good an account as any of the theology that finds a probative, exemplary detail in the category, *zekhut*. The issue of the *zekhut* of the patriarchs comes up in the reference to the God of the fathers. The conception of the *zekhut* of the patriarchs is explicit, not general. It specifies what later benefit to the heir, Israel the family, derived from which particular action of a patriarch or matriarch. But acts of faith and Torah-study form only one medium; hard labor, that is, devotion to one's calling, defines that source of *zekhut* that is going to be accessible to those many Israelites unlikely to distinguish themselves either by Torah-study and acts of faith, encompassing the sanctification of God's name, or by acts of amazing gentility and restraint.

Genesis Rabbah, where sages set forth their doctrine of origins, creation, and Israel in particular, provides the best systematic account of the doctrine of *zekhut*. Here *zekhut abot* draws in its wake the notion of the inheritance of an on-going (historical) family, that of Abraham and Sarah, and *zekhut* worked itself out in the moments of crisis of that family in its larger affairs. So the Israelites later on enjoy enormous *zekhut* through the deeds of the patriarchs and matriarchs. That conception comes to expression in what follows (Gen. Rabbah LXXVI:V):

> 2.A. ". . . for with only my staff I crossed this Jordan, and now I have become two companies" (Gen. 32:10):
> B. R. Judah bar Simon in the name of R. Yohanan: "In the Torah, in the Prophets, and in the Writings, we find proof that the Israelites were able to cross the Jordan only on account of the *zekhut* achieved by Jacob:
> C. "In the Torah: '. . . for with only my staff I crossed this Jordan, and now I have become two companies.'
> D. "In the prophets: 'Then you shall let your children know, saying, "Israel came over this Jordan on dry land"' (Josh. 4:22), meaning our father, Israel [that is, Jacob].
> E. "In the Writings: 'What ails you, O you sea, that you flee? You Jordan, that you turn backward? At the presence of the God of Jacob' (Ps. 114:5ff.)."

Here is a perfect illustration of *zekhut* as an entitlement one enjoys by reason of what someone else—an ancestor—has done; and that entitlement involves supernatural power. Jacob did not only leave *zekhut* as an estate to his heirs. The process is reciprocal and on-going. *Zekhut* deriving from the ancestors had helped Jacob himself (Gen. Rabbah LXXVII:III.3):

> A. "When the man saw that he did not prevail against Jacob, [he touched the hollow of his thigh, and Jacob's thigh was put out of joint as he wrestled with him]" (Gen. 32:25):
> B. Said R. Hinena bar Isaac, "[God said to the angel,] 'He is coming against you with five "amulets" hung on his neck, that

is, his own *zekhut*, the *zekhut* of his father and of his mother and of his grandfather and of his grandmother.

> C. "'Check yourself out; can you stand up against even his own *zekhut* [let alone the *zekhut* of his parents and grandparents]?'
> D. "The matter may be compared to a king who had a savage dog and a tame lion. The king would take his son and sic him against the lion, and if the dog came to have a fight with the son, he would say to the dog, 'The lion cannot have a fight with him, are you going to make out in a fight with him?'
> E. "So if the nations come to have a fight with Israel, the Holy One, blessed be he, says to them, 'Your angelic prince could not stand up to Israel, and as to you, how much the more so!'"

The collectivity of *zekhut*, not only its transferability, is illustrated here as well: what an individual does confers *zekhut* on the social entity. It is, moreover, a matter of the legitimate exercise of supernatural power. And the reciprocity of the process extended in all directions. Accordingly, what we have in hand is first and foremost a matter of the exercise of legitimate violence, hence a political power.

*Zekhut* might project not only backward, deriving from an ancestor and serving a descendant, but forward as well. Thus Joseph accrued so much *zekhut* that the generations that came before him were credited with his *zekhut*: (Gen. Rabbah LXXXIV:V.2):

> A. "These are the generations of the family of Jacob. Joseph [being seventeen years old, was shepherding the flock with his brothers]" (Gen. 37:2):
> B. These generations came along only on account of the *zekhut* of Joseph.
> C. Did Jacob go to Laban for any reason other than for Rachel?
> D. These generations thus waited until Joseph was born, in line with this verse: "And when Rachel had borne Joseph, Jacob said to Laban, 'Send me away'" (Gen. 30:215).
> E. Who brought them down to Egypt? It was Joseph.
> F. Who supported them in Egypt? It was Joseph.
> G. The sea split open only on account of the *zekhut* of Joseph: "The waters saw you, O God" (Ps. 77:17). "You have with your arm redeemed your people, the sons of Jacob and Joseph" (Ps. 77:16).

> H. R. Yudan said, "Also the Jordan was divided only on account of the *zekhut* of Joseph."

The passage asks why only Joseph is mentioned as the family of Jacob. The inner polemic is that the *zekhut* of Jacob and Joseph would more than suffice to overcome Esau. Not only so, but Joseph survived because of the *zekhut* of his ancestors (Gen. Rabbah LXXXVII:VIII.1):

> A. "She caught him by his garment. . . but he left his garment in her hand and fled and got out of the house. [And when she saw that he had left his garment in her hand and had fled out of the house, she called to the men of her household and said to them, 'See he has brought among us a Hebrew to insult us; he came in to me to lie with me, and I cried out with a loud voice, and when he heard that I lifted up my voice and cried, he left his garment with me and fled and got out of the house']" (Gen. 39:13-15):
> B. He escaped through the *zekhut* of the fathers, in line with this verse: "And he brought him forth outside" (Gen. 15:5).
> C. Simeon of Qitron said, "It was on account of bringing up the bones of Joseph that the sea was split: 'The sea saw it and fled' (Ps. 114:3), on the *zekhut* of this: '. . . and fled and got out.'"

*Zekhut*, we see, is both personal and collective, involving the Israelite and Israel as a whole. B refers to Joseph's enjoying the *zekhut* he had inherited, C to Israel's enjoying the *zekhut* that they gained through their supererogatory loyalty to that same *zekhut*-rich personality. The issue of the *zekhut* of the patriarchs comes up in the reference to the God of the fathers. The conception specifies what later benefit to the heir, Israel the family, derived from which particular action of a patriarch (rarely: matriarch) (Gen. Rabbah XLIII:VIII.2):

> A. "And Abram gave him a tenth of everything" (Gen. 14:20):
> B. R. Judah in the name of R. Nehorai: "On the strength of that blessing the three great pegs on which the world depends, Abraham, Isaac, and Jacob, derived sustenance.
> C. "Abraham: 'And the Lord blessed Abraham in *all* things' (Gen. 24:1)—on account of the *zekhut* that 'he gave him a tenth of *all* things' (Gen. 14:20).

> D. "Isaac: 'And I have eaten of *all*' (Gen. 27:33)—on account of the *zekhut* that 'he gave him a tenth of *all* things' (Gen. 14:20).
> E. "Jacob: 'Because God has dealt graciously with me and because I have all' (Gen. 33:11)—on account of the *zekhut* that 'he gave him a tenth of *all* things' (Gen. 14:20)."

Now we account for the *zekhut* that brings to Israel the grace involving in the priestly blessing, an example of how the sages of the Oral Torah try to identify, in Scripture, the links between *zekhut* and the virtuous actions of the ancestors (Gen. Rabbah XLIII:VIII.3):

> A. Whence did Israel gain the *zekhut* of receiving the blessing of the priests?
> B. R. Judah said, "It was from Abraham: '*So* shall your seed be' (Gen. 15:5), while it is written in connection with the priestly blessing: '*So* shall you bless the children of Israel' (Num. 6:23)."
> C. R. Nehemiah said, "It was from Isaac: 'And I and the lad will go *so* far' (Gen. 22:5), therefore said the Holy One, blessed be he, '*So* shall you bless the children of Israel' (Num. 6:23)."
> D. And rabbis say, "It was from Jacob: '*So* shall you say to the house of Jacob' (Exod. 19:3) (in line with the statement, '*So* shall you bless the children of Israel' (Num. 6:23)."

This links the priestly blessing with the history of Israel, and the picture is clear. "Israel" constitutes a family as a genealogical and juridical fact. It inherits the estate of the ancestors. It hands on that estate. It lives by the example of the patriarchs, and its history exemplifies events in their lives. *Zekhut* forms that entitlement that one generation may transmit to the next, in a way in which the heritage of sin is not to be transmitted except by reason of the deeds of the successor-generation. The good that one does lives onward, the evil is interred with the bones.

This statement appeals to the binding of Isaac as the source of the *zekhut*, deriving from the patriarchs and matriarchs, that will in the end lead to the salvation of Israel. What is important here is that the inherited *zekhut* joins together with the *zekhut* of one's own deeds; one inherits the *zekhut* of the past, and, moreover, if one does what the progenitors did, one not only receives an entitlement out of the past, one secures an entitlement on one's own account. So the categorical difference between *zekhut* and sin lies in the sole issue of transmissibility (Gen. Rabbah LVI:II.5):

A. Said R. Isaac, "And all was on account of the *zekhut* attained by the act of prostration.
B. "Abraham returned in peace from Mount Moriah only on account of the *zekhut* owing to the act of prostration: '. . . and we will worship [through an act of prostration] and come [on that account] again to you' (Gen. 22:5).
C. "The Israelites were redeemed only on account of the *zekhut* owing to the act of prostration: And the people believed . . . then they bowed their heads and prostrated themselves' (Exod. 4:31).
D. "The Torah was given only on account of the *zekhut* owing to the act of prostration: 'And worship [prostrate themselves] you afar off' (Exod. 24:1).
E. "Hannah was remembered only on account of the *zekhut* owing to the act of prostration: 'And they worshipped before the Lord' (1 Sam. 1:19).
F. "The exiles will be brought back only on account of the *zekhut* owing to the act of prostration: 'And it shall come to pass in that day that a great horn shall be blown and they shall come that were lost . . . and that were dispersed . . . and they shall worship the Lord in the holy mountain at Jerusalem' (Is. 27:13).
G. "The Temple was built only on account of the *zekhut* owing to the act of prostration: 'Exalt you the Lord our God and worship at his holy hill' (Ps. 99:9).
H. "The dead will live only on account of the *zekhut* owing to the act of prostration: 'Come let us worship and bend the knee, let us kneel before the Lord our maker' (Ps. 95:6)."

The entire history of Israel flows from its acts of worship ("prostration") beginning with that performed by Abraham at the binding of Isaac. Every sort of advantage Israel has ever gained came about through that act of worship done by Abraham and imitated thereafter. Israel constitutes a family and inherits the *zekhut* laid up as a treasure for the descendants by the ancestors. It draws upon that *zekhut* but, by doing the deeds they did, it also enhances its heritage of *zekhut* and leaves to the descendants greater entitlement

than they would enjoy by reason of their own actions.

But one's own deeds can generate *zekhut* for oneself, with the simple result that *zekhut* is as much personal as it is collective. Specifically, Jacob reflects on the power that Esau's own *zekhut* had gained for Esau. He had gained that *zekhut* by living in the land of Israel and also by paying honor and respect to Isaac. Jacob then feared that, because of the *zekhut* gained by Esau, he, Jacob, would not be able to overcome him. So *zekhut* worked on its own; it was a credit gained by proper action, which went to the credit of the person who had done that action. What made the action worthy of evoking heaven's response with an act of supernatural favor is that it was an action not to be required but if done to be rewarded, an act of will that cannot be coerced but must be honored. In Esau's case, it was the simple fact that he had remained in the holy land (Gen. Rabbah LXXVI:II):

A. "Then Jacob was greatly afraid and distressed" (Gen. 32:7): [This is Jacob's soliloquy:] "Because of all those years that Esau was living in the land of Israel, perhaps he may come against me with the power of the *zekhut* he has now attained by dwelling in the land of Israel.
B. "Because of all those years of paying honor to his father, perhaps he may come against me with the power of the *zekhut* he attained by honoring his father.
C. "So he said: 'Let the days of mourning for my father be at hand, then I will slay my brother Jacob' (Gen. 27:41).
D. "Now the old man is dead."

The important point, then, is that *zekhut* is not only inherited as part of a collective estate left by the patriarchs. It is also accomplished by an individual in his or her own behalf. The sages thus open a place for recognition of the individual, both man and woman as a matter of fact, within the system of *zekhut*. As we shall now see, what a man or a woman does may win for that person an entitlement upon heaven for supernatural favor of some sort. So there is space, in the system, for a private person, and the individual is linked to the social order through the shared possibilities of generating or inheriting an entitlement upon heaven.

Torah-study is one—but only one—means for an individual to gain access to that heritage, to get *zekhut*. There are other equally suitable means, and, not only so, but the merit gained by Torah-study is no different from the merit gained by acts of a supererogatory character. If one gets *zekhut* for studying the Torah, then there is no holy deed that does not generate its share of *zekhut*. But when it comes to specifying the things one does to get *zekhut*, the documents before us speak of what the Torah does not require but does recommend: not what people are commanded to do in detail, but what the right attitude, formed within the Torah, leads them to do on their own volition (Y. Ta. 3:11.IV):

C. There was a house that was about to collapse over there [in Babylonia], and Rab set one of his disciples in the house, until they had cleared out everything from the house. When the disciple left the house, the house collapsed.

D. And there are those who say that it was R. Adda bar Ahwah.

E. Sages sent and said to him, "What sort of good deeds are to your credit [that you have that much merit]?"

F. He said to them, "In my whole life no man ever got to the synagogue in the morning before I did. I never left anybody there when I went out. I never walked four cubits without speaking words of Torah. Nor did I ever mention teachings of Torah in an inappropriate setting. I never laid out a bed and slept for a regular period of time. I never took great strides among the associates. I never called my fellow by a nickname. I never rejoiced in the embarrassment of my fellow. I never cursed my fellow when I was lying by myself in bed. In the marketplace I never walked over to someone who owed me money.

G. "In my entire life I never lost my temper in my household."

H. This was meant to carry out that which is stated as follows: "I will give heed to the way that is blameless. Oh when wilt thou come to me? I will walk with integrity of heart within my house" (Ps. 101:2).

Striking in this story is that mastery of the Torah is only one means of attaining the merit that enabled the sage to keep the house from collapsing. For what the sage did to gain such remarkable merit is not to master such-and-so many tractates of the Mishnah. Nor does the story-teller refer to carrying out specific commandments of the Torah. It was rather acts of that expressed courtesy, consideration, restraint. These acts, which no specification can encompass in detail, produced the right attitude, one of gentility, that led merit. Acts rewarded with an entitlement to supernatural power are those of self-abnegation or the avoidance of power over others—not taking great strides among the associates, not using a nickname, not rejoicing in the embarrassment of one's fellow—and the submission to the will and the requirement of self-esteem of others.

The systemic statement made by the usages of *zekhut* speaks of relationship, of function, the interplay of humanity and God. One's store of *zekhut* derives from a relationship, that is, from one's forebears. That is one dimension of the relationships in which one stands. *Zekhut* also forms a measure of one's own relationship with heaven, as the power of one person, but not another, to pray and so bring rain attests. What sort of relationship does *zekhut*, as the opposite of sin, then posit? It is one of autonomous grace, for heaven cannot force us to do those types of deeds that yield *zekhut*, and that, story after story suggests, is the definition of a deed that generates *zekhut*: doing what we ought to do but do not have to do. But then, we cannot coerce heaven to do what we want done either, for example, by carrying out the commandments. These are obligatory, but do not obligate heaven.

Whence then the lien on heaven? It is through deeds of a supererogatory character—to which heaven responds by deeds of a supererogatory character. Self-abnegation or restraint shown by man precipitates a counterpart attitude in heaven, hence generating *zekhut*. The relationship measured by *zekhut*—heaven's response by an act of uncoerced favor to a person's uncoerced gift—contains an element of unpredictability for which appeal to the *zekhut* inherited from ancestors accounts. So while one cannot coerce heaven, one can through *zekhut* gain acts of favor from heaven, and that is by doing what heaven cannot require but only desire. Heaven then responds to people's attitude in carrying out what transcends their duties. The simple fact that rabbis cannot pray and bring rain, but a simple ass-driver can, tells the whole story. That act of pure disinterest—giving the woman means of livelihood—is the one that gains heaven's deepest interest. And, we must not miss the starting point of the transaction, the woman's act of utter and tangible self-sacrifice in behalf of her husband, which wins the ass-driver's empathy and provokes the action to which heaven responds.

"Make his wishes yours, so that he will make your wishes his . . . Anyone from whom people take pleasure, God takes pleasure" (M. Ab. 2:4). These two statements hold together the two principal elements of the conception of the relationship to God that the single word *zekhut* conveys. Give up, please others, do not impose your will but give way to the will of the other, and heaven will respond by giving a lien that is not coerced but evoked. By the rationality of discipline within, humans have the power to form rational relationships beyond ourselves, with heaven; and that is how the system expands the boundaries of the social order to encompass not only the natural but also the supernatural world. The conviction that, by dint of special effort, one may so conduct oneself as to acquire an entitlement of supernatural power turns one's commonplace circumstance into an arena encompassing heaven and earth. God responds to holy Israel's virtue, filling the gap that people leave when they forebears, withdraw, and give up: their space, their self-hood. Then God responds; people's sacrifice evokes memories of Abraham's readiness to sacrifice Isaac.

World order is ultimately attained by transcending the very rules of order. In order to establish the moral order of justice, therefore, God breaks the rules, accords an entitlement to this one, who has done some one remarkable deed, but not to that one, who has done nothing wrong and everything right. So a life in accord with the rules—even a life spent in the study of the Torah—in heaven's view is outweighed by a single moment, a gesture that violates the norm, extending the outer limits of the rule, for instance, of virtue. Humanity on earth incarnates God on high, the Israelite family in particular, and, in consequence, earth and heaven join—within.

**Bibliography**
Neusner, Jacob, *The Transformation of Judaism. From Philosophy to Religion* (Champaign, 1992).

JACOB NEUSNER

**ZIONISM AND ORTHODOX JUDAISM:** The Zionist national revolution confronted traditional Jewry with a unique, unforeseen historical situation: Jewish political sovereignty in the heart of the Holy Land prior to messianic times, under the leadership of non-practicing, rebellious Jews. Moreover, while Zionism began the process of returning the dispersed exiles, this was within a context far removed from the traditional theological concepts of exile and messiah, covenant and promise, reward and punishment, sin and atonement. It is no surprise, then, that these transformations were not received by traditionalist Jews with equanimity. Rather, they catalyzed an intense ideological ferment, leading to the creation of a series of new interpretations of classical Jewish sources and ultimately refocusing divisive issues and refashioning conflicting camps of thought.

**Sacred and profane:** Zionism incorporated many of the attributes of a revolutionary movement, while also containing many features typical of a renaissance. Interestingly, in both of these regards, the revolutionary and the restorational, it displayed radical tendencies. On the one hand, Zionism set out to affect a sweeping reform, more far reaching and comprehensive than those attempted by other modern revolutions. Compare, for example, the French or even the Bolshevik revolution. In those cases, the insurrectionists appealed to members of existing nations, who spoke established languages and lived within defined territorial and cultural boundaries. They aimed to transform certain aspects of the social reality, such as the political or economic system; on occasion, these changes were even depicted as leading to salvation. But whatever the program, it was contained within an existing territorial and historical framework: it did not extend to every imaginable sphere of existence.

The Zionist movement, by contrast, needed to generate a far-reaching, almost total revolution. The sons and daughters of the Jewish people needed to be taken from their countries of residence, learn a revived Hebrew language for everyday discourse, adopt new modes of life, and assume new professions. Zionism thus had to wage its battle on all fronts, social, cultural, political, legal, and economic, and to do so without an existing structure that could serve as the foundation for the new order. In the political arena, for example, not only did the Zionists, like other revolutionaries, have to reform a political system and turn out a foreign power, but they had to create a entirely new political entity after a 1900-year absence of Jewish sovereignty (figs. 176-179).

At the very same time, however, Zionism was a renaissance movement aspiring to restore a bygone reality. Whereas other modern revolutions forged a future-oriented mythos and a forward-looking ethos with symbols suggestive of a better tomorrow, Zionism drew its symbols primarily from the past. While not entirely free of utopian visions, the main building blocks of Zionism's radical myths and ethos were the stuff of the historical and collective memory: ancient landscapes, old proverbs, kings, heroes, and prophets. Like a boomerang, the movement burst forth in quest of a radical revolution while turning its face towards ancient memories and images.

Admittedly, Zionism was not very different in this respect from other nationalist movements that followed a similar trajectory, utilizing historical memory and traditional symbols to build national awareness and collective consciousness. Even the use of religious symbols is not unique to Zionism; these can be found in the Polish, Irish, and Czech national movements or, for that matter, in most related movements in Europe. Nevertheless, as the revolutionary elements of the Zionist movement extended further than those of other revolutions, its retrospective gaze penetrated deeper and was more demanding. But this was to be expected, since, unlike other national renaissance movements, Zionism is the product of a nation whose ethnic and religious identities were for countless generations fused into a single whole. The Jewish religion is particular to one nation, and in the present era (as opposed to the messianic one) the religion does not pursue a universal constituency but focuses its messages and meanings on this specific nation, the "Chosen People."

Similarly, throughout its history, the Jewish people has seldom operated in anything other than a religious context: its memories have, for the most part, been filtered through the prism constructed by classical Jewish texts. Its collective national identity and its religious identity thus have always been essentially interchangeable, as Ruth 1:16 ("Your people are my people, your God is my God") and Jonah 1:9 ("I am a Hebrew, and I revere God, the Lord of Heaven") intimate. The Jews' laws, culture, language, politics, and social norms were rooted in a joint religious and ethnic heritage. Any attempt to resurrect symbols from the nation's past thus perforce unearthed certain religious claims, as it is the nature of the religious consciousness to see the past not only as the source of history and existence but as the source of obligation. From this spring follow not only memories but beliefs and commandments as well.

Consider the dualistic nature of the land of Israel as a national homeland and as a holy land. Birthplace and home bring to mind a sense of intimacy, of comfort and of naturalness, of protection and shelter; the holy conjures up feelings of reverence and transcendence, awe and fear. The first is a distinctly national category; the second, a distinctly religious one: birth is an existential term, while holiness is metaphysical and laden with demand. But despite there distinct resonances, throughout Jewish history, the two ideas have always gone hand-in-hand, with all the internal tension inherent in the coupling. Accordingly, when Zionism reawakened the desire for a concrete homeland, it concomitantly aroused from its slumber the yearning for the Holy Land. And the latter is now risen and staking its claim.

The dualistic intertwining of nationhood and religion expresses itself in a number of ways, in the relationship between modern Hebrew and the holy tongue, between Herzl's "State of the Jews" and the classic visions of redemption, more recently in the contrast between the modern, secular Tel-Aviv and its life and Jerusalem and its symbols. Moreover, the dualistic tension in question here is not merely the result of conflict between sacred and profane or between the religious and national spheres. It is woven into the very fabric of modern Zionism and built into the national revolution itself. A central themes of Zionist rhetoric was the "normalization" of the Jewish people, the creation of a people that would reside in its own land, speak its own language, control its own destiny, be free of political subservience, and establish a healthy social order, the kind of people that all the nationalist movements worked to create. But what process did the Jewish people in particular have to undergo to attain such normality? A singular and "abnormal" process, apparently without precedent in world history.

A short example illustrates this point. In 1911, the great linguist Theodor Noeldeke published in the *Encyclopaedia Brittanica* a survey of ancient Semitic languages. The article included sections on Accadian, Canaanite, Phoenician, and the like, and, next to them, an examination of Hebrew language and its history from biblical times on. As the modern Zionist movement was just then emerging, the author saw fit to comment on the call of contemporary Zionists to revive the Hebrew language as the everyday spoken tongue of the Jewish people. "The dream," wrote Noeldeke, "of some Zionists that Hebrew—a would-be Hebrew, that is to say—will again become a living, popular language in Palestine, has still less prospect of realization than their vision of a restored Jewish empire in the Holy Land." An objective scholar without any particular biases, Noeldeke deemed the attempt to revive Hebrew and to establish a political entity in Palestine as far-fetched, even fantastic. The historical record has, of course, shown his assessment to be mistaken. Yet Noeldeke could find no precedent for the rebirth of a sacred tongue as an everyday spoken language, nor for the mass migration of a people to an ancient homeland after an absence of many centuries. What alternative did he have but to pronounce it unlikely?

Since Noeldeke, many rich studies of the revival of spoken Hebrew have been conducted. Yet, to date, no real analogy has been found. Take modern Greek, for example. While it boasts many similarities to its ancestor, a speaker of the contemporary language will struggle to read texts written in ancient Greek, whereas the modern Hebrew speaker progresses through the Bible without any particular difficulty. Similarly, recent attempts to revive the use of Gaelic in Ireland have enjoyed only modest success, and the language is used today mostly in poetry.

To repeat, the return to the homeland and the rebirth of the Hebrew language were described by Zionists as steps in the direction of normality, which was accorded a certain moral stature (that is, normality was conceived as a norm!). To achieve normality, however, it was necessary to undergo a completely unprecedented historical process, unique in human history. What was considered routine, proper, and normal to other nations—a national territory and spoken language—for the Jews demanded the expenditure of incredible energy and the playing out of a singular historical drama. Normality, as it were, was inextricably bound with anomaly.

To be sure, throughout the century, centrifugal social forces have sought to resolve the dichotomies inherent in the Zionist enterprise: old or new, sacred or profane, particular or universal, "in favor of normalcy" or "in favor of singularity." While Zionism succeeded in reshaping the Jewish public domain, movements and individuals have always sought to mold this domain in different and conflicting ways. Thus, in particular, the conflict between Orthodox and secular Jews in the modern state of Israel.

**Zionism and messianism:** Alongside all the other tensions, the greatest question has concerned the relationship between the Zionist idea and the classical Jewish messianic vision. In 1770, a non-Jew, "a man of rank," wrote to the Jewish philosopher Moses Mendelssohn proposing the establishment of a Jewish state in Palestine. Mendelssohn, in a polite reply, expressed his esteem for this "great idea," lauding the courage of this individual, "who speaks of the realization of such a bold project." Not surprisingly, however, he rejected the idea, noting certain external, practical elements that would hinder the plan' implementation. But the decisive obstacle was the mental makeup of the Jews themselves, the passivity and spirituality that, over the course of generations, had so stamped itself on the Jewish people that it had become virtually a second nature. As a result, the Jewish people would *ipso facto* be incapable of executing a historical breakthrough or of undertaking a political initiative on a national scale. In the words of this Jewish philosopher:

> The greatest obstacle in the way of this proposal is the character of my people. It is not ready to attempt anything so great. The pressure under which we have lived for centuries has removed all vigor from our spirit . . . the natural impulse for freedom has ceased its activity within us. It has been changed into a monkish piety, manifested in prayer and suffering, not in activity.

Mendelssohn thus ascribed the Jews' submissiveness and political impotence to their difficult straits and the travails of exile.

Interestingly, on a different occasion, when Mendelssohn wished to reassure gentiles of the Jews' absolute civic loyalty, he offered a very different explanation for their a-political behavior. The traditional Jewish passivity, he observed, was grounded in the binding provisions and stipulations of the Jewish religion—*ab initio* not *ex post facto*—reflecting the common sense of the ancients, who deferred collective, national activity until the advent of the messiah, thereby enabling the Jews to adjust to a life of dispersion and exile. "The hoped-for return to Palestine," argued Mendelssohn, is reserved only "for synagogue and prayer," for the Jews' inner religious feeling alone, but "it has no influence on our conduct as citizens." Thus he states:

> The Talmud forbids us to even think of a return to Palestine by force [to hasten the End by human effort]! Without the miracles and signs mentioned in the Scripture, we must not take the smallest step in the direction of forcing a return and a restoration of our nation. The Song of Songs expresses this prohibition in a somewhat mystical, yet captivating way, in the verse (Cant. 2:7): "I adjure you, O daughters of Jerusalem, by the gazelles and by the hinds of the field, that ye awaken not, nor excite my love, till it please [to come of itself]."

In brief, whether we speak of an acquired Jewish trait—the suppression of the "natural impulse toward freedom," engendered by hardship and oppression, about which Mendelssohn complained—or of an inherent Jewish viewpoint—the Talmudic injunction against "forcing the End," a viewpoint praised by Mendelssohn—the traditional political passivity of the Jews is perceived by this thinker as a basic characteristic of the Jewish people in exile.

Actually, a full century before Mendelssohn, Benedict Spinoza bemoaned the same mental trait, which denied the Jews the ability to engage in political initiative (and in military activity). He, too, held that this trait was the barrier to the renewal of the Jews' kingdom. Spinoza, however, did not consider this Jewish attribute to be the result either of hardship and distress or of any particular religious interdiction. He ascribed it to the overall nature of the Jewish religion—a religion that renders its adherents obeisant and servile: "If the foundations of their religion have not emasculated their minds, [the Jews] may even, if occasion offers—so changeable are human affairs—raise up their empire afresh, and God may a second time elect them." (This last phrase is, of course, intended metaphorically, as a way of saying that the Jews will ultimately achieve a normal political existence). Spinoza's criteria for examining Jewish history are historical and sociological categories, not theological or metaphysical ones. Scholars have noted that the conclusion to be inferred is that the Jews must make a fateful choice between two alternative paths. They may continue to follow their religion, with all its inherent traits, thereby forfeiting any prospect of a national-political revival. Or they may abandon their ancient faith and customs, thus reacquiring the greatness of spirit that is a *sine qua non* for their future national rebirth. In any event, according to Spinoza, the hypothetical rebuilding of the Jewish commonwealth is incontrovertibly dependent upon the prior secularization of the Jewish people.

The remarks of these philosophers, Spinoza and Mendelssohn, adumbrate and incarnate an array of questions that, in time, would be at the center of the religious controversy concerning Zionism and messianism: What is the nature of the prohibited "forcing of the End"? How is one to interpret a non-messianic Jewish national renewal that occurred at a historically propitious moment ("if occasion offers") and not "at the End of Days"? Is a naturalistic return to Zion possible—"without miracles and great wonders"—that does not inherently defy Jewish uniqueness and abjure the metaphysical dimension of Jewish history? Furthermore, does the traditional Jewish passivity reflect an historical "accident" and decline, which then evolved under the hardships of the exile? Or should it be seen as the result of the judicious practical guidance of the sages of Israel? Alternatively, is that passivity rooted in a substantive religious principle and a binding imperative? Finally, what is the true aim of Zionism? Do the Zionists rebel only against the Jewish fate and Jewish passivity, or does their revolt entail the eradication of Judaism itself—that is, the uprooting of the entire religious tradition, which (like Spinoza before them) they blamed for the national disposition to political submission and historical inaction?

In light of these many problems, the majority of Orthodox leaders condemned Zionism from its very outset, their criticism leveled first and foremost at the secularity of the national idea and the Zionist leaders' and settlers' repudiation of religious practice. While some prominent rabbis also opposed the Zionist initiative for pragmatic reasons, depicting it as hopelessly deluded and unrealistic, it was on theological grounds that some of the most important critics took the new movement to task, striking it at its root from the standpoint of traditional messianic faith. At base, even when they did not say so explicitly, the Orthodox opponents of Zionism saw it as a direct threat to traditional ways of thought, a danger, that is, not only to traditional practices but to nothing less than the entire theological interpretation of Jewish history. No wonder, then, that the issue of the relationship between Zionism and messianism soon became a central question: no longer confined to the realm of intuitive aversion and protest, it now became a subject for direct debate and eloquent ideological formulation.

**Zionism as an anti-messianic undertaking:** To illustrate the ways in which Orthodox Jews have responded to Zionism, we turn directly to positions that have been fully shaped and articulated in the last generation. We begin with the religious philosophies espoused by those at the two poles of the Jewish religious ideological axis, radical anti-Zionism, on the one hand, and messianic religious Zionism, on the other.

The anti-Zionist world-view of the ultraorthodox groups Neturei Karta and Satmar Hasidism perceives Zionism and the establishment of the state of Israel as an anti-messianic act, conceived and born from sin. These groups vigorously deny the very legitimacy of the collective political return to the Holy Land and to Jewish sovereignty. For this is the handiwork of humans, violating the Jewish people's oath of political quietism. In the words of the Midrash (as expounded by Rashi), the people were adjured not to return collectively to the land of Israel by the exertion of physical force, nor to "rebel against the nations of the world," nor to "hasten the End." In short, they were required to wait for the heavenly, complete, miraculous, supernatural, and meta-historical redemption that is totally distinct from the realm of human endeavor. This waiting over two millennia manifests the very essence and singularity of the Jewish people, expressing their faith in divine providence, in the assurances of the prophets, and in messianic destiny.

In this understanding, the Jewish people have been removed from the causal laws that govern nature and history and are exclusively bound by another set of religio-ethical laws within a causal process of reward and punishment, exile and redemption: "Unless the Lord build the house, its builders labor in vain; unless the Lord watches over the city, the watchman keeps vigil in vain" (Ps. 127:1). Accordingly, any Jewish political revival that is not messianic intrinsically represents a denial of divine providence and of the hope of redemption; it is a betrayal of the destiny and uniqueness of Israel. The attempt to hasten the End, to return by physical power to the sphere of political—and certainly military—history is a collective revolt against the kingdom of heaven, an aggressive aspiration to overstep human bound-aries into the realm reserved for God—just like the deeds of the generation of the Tower of Babel (Gen. 11:1-9). This is an act of the devil, a demonic outburst of unclean forces that may not be corrected. It is ultimately doomed to failure, regardless of human deeds: "The Lord shall rebuke you—the Satan who has chosen Jerusalem" (paraphrasing Zech. 3:2).

In other words, these groups' fierce opposition to the state of Israel is not directed against its secular nature or its laws and mores but, rather, against its very existence, regardless of its nature. In the words of the late Satmar rebbe, Yoel Teitelbaum, "even if the members of the Knesset were righteous and holy, it is a terrible and awful criminal iniquity to seize redemption and rule before the time has come." According to this logic, the concepts "Torah state" or "Halakhic state" are oxymorons; any Jewish state prior to the messianic age—by the very nature of its human, natural, mundane provenance—undermines and denies the Torah and takes a stand against the Halakhah. The faithful, therefore, are not enjoined to struggle for the refashioning of the Jewish character of the society and the state but are required to unqualifiedly isolate themselves, to separate themselves socially from the majority of the people of Israel and politically from the state of Israel. Consequently, any use of Zionist budgets and institutions is utterly forbidden, the members of these circles doing their utmost to deny themselves any benefit from them.

In this orthodox anti-Zionist view, then, the only hope for the Jewish state is its total destruction: "But [we] need mercy that this kingdom will be destroyed only by a force from above, by the Lord, may He be blessed, not by the [non-Jewish] nations; for if, God forbid, this is to be done by the nations, it will, of course, constitute a great danger for [the people of] Israel." The Zionist endeavor is destined to make way for the true, complete, miraculous salvation, for the redemption that will rise on its ruins as its total negation.

Numerically speaking, this ideology is marginal. All told, the extremists number today twenty thousand in Israel and several tens of thousands in the United States and in Europe. But their indirect influence, the challenge posed by their radical views, is widely felt in ultra-Orthodoxy. They project an image of consistency and unwavering faith, of a kind of avant-garde whose demands disturb the bourgeois complacency of others.

**Zionism as a messianic enterprise:** At the other end of the ideological continuum, we find an opposing image of historical realty that, paradoxically, shares an identical theological premise with the former school of thought. The redemptionist Zionism of the school of Merkaz Harav Yeshivah and Gush Emunin settlers in the West Bank (that is, Judea and Samaria) perceives the Zionist enterprise and the establishment of the State as a messianic step, conceived and born in sanctity. At bottom, these groups, like the anti-Zionist ones, deny the legitimacy of any Jewish revival or return to Zion that is not within the category of the decisive, ultimate redemption; they do not, however, admit to any dichotomy between the current and the messianic return. In the words of Rabbi Zvi Yehudah Hakohen Kook, the late head of the Merkaz Harav Yeshivah, "Our reality is a messianic reality," and "The true redemption is revealed in the settlement of the Land and the rebirth of Israel in it." Accordingly, we are called on to discern in the as-yet-incomplete processes of the present far more than meets the eye. The return to Zion and Jewish political independence are intrinsically sanctified, for they embody a human response to a divine call. Zionism thus is not insolence toward heaven or "hastening the End;" on the contrary, the Jewish state is built by force of the redeeming divine providence, which leads by "historical necessity" and by "cosmological decisiveness" towards perfect fulfillment in all spheres, both material and spiritual.

This philosophy accords inherent religious content to the fact of Jewish political sovereignty, a normative meaning that is not conditioned on specific laws and mores of the state or on the choices and decisions of its members. According to the logic of the Neturei Karta, the original sin is rooted in the very existence of the state and cannot be corrected or purified. By contrast, in the logic of the messianic approach, the inherent, positive essence of the state cannot be destroyed or damaged, no matter what politicians or citizens do. The Zionist enterprise, rather, inevitably will lead to repentance and redemption. The times thus bespeak the ultimate realization of history, the revealed End from which there is no turning back; the beginning guarantees the end. True, we are empowered to accelerate the process or delay it, to remove obstacles or to erect them. But nothing can alter the preordained direction or inevitable destination. A favorite metaphor used to explain this idea depicts a person traveling by train who can assist or hold back the engine's progress but is powerless to change the course of the tracks or the final destination of the journey. These have been laid in advance, by the Cause of all Causes, leading towards repentance and redemption.

The common denominator of the two contrary conceptions we have reviewed is that, *a priori*, they impart theological significance to the very existence of the state of Israel; both react to historical events through the messianic perspective and the hope of redemption, and both reject any return to Zion and Jewish revival that is not complete and ultimate. Each adopts an out-and-out deterministic approach to the historical process: the future is fixed and clearly revealed in accordance with ultimate destiny; the fate of the Zionist enterprise is predestined and predictable, either as curse or blessing, according to its inherent religious essence.

In the words of Rabbi Zvi Yehudah Kook (1891-1981), mentor of the "redemptionist" religious-Zionist camp during the decades following the establishment of the State:

> How is it that the movement for concrete redemption in our time, including the settlement and conquest of the Land and the abandonment and abolition of exilic existence did not originate with the religious? How is it that some religious spokesmen even withheld their support for Zionism and the movement for redemption?. . . . They failed to recognize that it was not that we mortals were forcing the End, but rather that the Master of the House, the Lord of the Universe, was forcing our hand; that it was not human voices that broke down the wall separating us from our land, but the voice of the living God calling upon us to "Go up!"

This declaration sums up concisely and eloquently the way this camp reacted to ultra-Orthodox theological criticism of Zionism. The Zionist undertaking did not stem from a merely human initiative or breakthrough, from nationalistic arrogance or self-assertion. Rather, it sprang from a divine thrust towards redemption, a compelling higher call to which the people of Israel responded with historic fidelity. Zionism, "the movement for concrete redemption in our time," is thus part of a new phase of Jewish history in which the people are released from their age-old, enforced decree of passivity. Zionism actively assaults "the wall separating us from our land" and goes on to build on the strength of a new religious imperative not heard in previous generations. "No, it is not we who are forcing the End," Kook would say to his disciples, "but the End that is forcing us!"

It is true, the rabbi and his followers would say, that many God-fearing Jews have not heard the voice charging them with "the divine historic imperative of ending the exile." They have not discerned the signs of the new era with its urgent messianic tidings. It is also true that many Zionists, including some of the most devoted pioneers, have not seen fit to acknowledge the divine origin of the call. They are not aware of the religious meaning of their undertaking and at times even deny it vehemently. Yet, on a deeper level, both groups, religious and secular alike, are moving in unison towards the fulfillment of a single, well-laid-out messianic purpose. In their subjectively different ways, they all fit into one objective plan. Whether they are aware of it or not, it is divine providence that grips them, guiding them inexorably toward the final redemption of Israel.

The nationalist ideology of Rabbi Kook and his followers views the history of Zionism as an inevitable and decidedly messianic process, "the state of Israel as the fulfillment of the biblical vision of redemption." Messianism, in this approach, is no longer to be seen as the antithesis of concrete reality. It is no longer merely a critique of what is, nor is it only addressed to the future. Rather, messianic redemption springs from present events, is embodied and realized in them. "Our reality is one of *teshuvah* [return to God; repentance], and it is a messianic one," writes Kook. In other words, the traditional religious categories of holiness, redemption, and repentance have assumed concrete form in the Zionist endeavor itself. They are given living, dynamic expression as part of the process of the return to Zion and the Jewish national revival.

To be sure, this is "messianism" without a messiah, a redemptive process that takes place in the absence of a living human redeemer, for, in these circles, immediate religious expectation does not center on a personal messiah. Without abandoning traditional beliefs, attention is focused in a new way on the realm of collective history. One seeks the signs of divine providence amid contemporary events in the life of the nation.

**Exile in the Holy Land:** The two opposing views discussed above attributed a distinctive, inherent religious significance to the Zionist movement and the state of Israel, for good or for evil. Both views also professed to foresee—each from its own point of view—the destiny of Zionism and the future of Israeli society. However, the majority of ultra-Orthodox Jews referred to as Haredim utterly reject both of these ideological stances and dismiss their judgments regarding these questions. From their point of view, the state of Israel is religiously neu-

tral, part of the secular realm still belonging to the age of exile. The state's conception and birth were neither holy nor profane, neither a messianic awakening nor an anti-messianic eruption. Rather, the State should be judged like any other historical phenomenon: according to its actual relationship to the Torah and the attitude of its leaders and adherents to the precepts of the Halakhah.

"There is no independent absolute value in the Torah except for the Holy One, blessed be he, and his service," the Haredi perspective holds. "Even the Holy Land, with all its importance and virtues, is not an independent value like a 'homeland' among the nations. The value of the Yishuv framework and its institutions is measured only by the degree to which they bring the people of the Lord closer to the Torah, the commandments, and the faith," explains Rabbi Shlomo Volpe. Accordingly, the future of the Jewish state is not preordained or predetermined by God. The people is invited to choose its own path and, accordingly, its destiny. God's judgment remains suspended and conditional. According to this conception, even life in the Jewish state in the land of Israel should be viewed and experienced as exile, the exile of Israel in the Holy Land.

Those who share this perception, in all its various shadings, deny the possibility of an interim historical situation that is neither exile nor redemption. They unequivocally reject the validity of such a hybrid and recognize no Halakhic or theoretical model appropriate to it. Any reality that is not totally messianic is, by definition, totally exilic. For exile is not a geographical condition that can be overcome by Aliyah and settlement alone. Neither is exile a political condition that can be corrected by the attainment of national sovereignty and independence. It is, rather, a theological and metaphysical concept, the exile of the Shekhinah—the divine presence—that will expire only when humanity and the world finally are set right. The responsibility imposed by exile on the Jewish people thus focuses exclusively on religious-spiritual activity, not on mundane political activity. The concept "exile" represents, first and foremost, a reality that has not yet been redeemed from sin, as the liturgy puts it: "Because of our sins we were exiled from our land;" and "Israel will only be redeemed by repentance."

This perception of the present historical reality as exile is not limited solely to a theological awareness. It is also reflected in a psychological and existential stance towards the secular environment, represented in a sense of personal and communal alienation. "Exile" does not merely denote the opposite of the destined messianic redemption; it also denotes the lack of a home, the home of one's parents and grandparents, as well as a sense of estrangement from the external society, its lifestyles and culture, and from the secular government and its institutions. These are depicted in many instances as having completely lost all Jewish characteristics, with nothing to distinguish them from the gentile environment in any country—in other words, exile.

The currently prevalent position among most Haredi circles in the state of Israel (in a variety of versions) thus recognizes the secular Jewish state *de facto* but does not grant it *de jure* recognition. Haredi representatives cooperate in a circumscribed and conditional manner with the institutions that are the outcome of the Zionist idea and movement but deny the validity of the Zionist doctrine *per se*; that is, they reject the founding ideology of the national enterprise. The state of Israel as a political entity and act of political organization by Jews is deemed devoid of religious significance, whether positive or negative; it is in itself a neutral phenomenon, existing within the secular realm; it is neither within the sphere of transgression nor that of obligation, but rather within a neutral, voluntary sphere. In this regard, the position of the outstanding scholar and leader of the previous generation, Rabbi Avraham Yeshayahu Karelitz (known as the Hazon Ish), was recently summed up: "The Hazon Ish did not view the state as the height of the darkness of exile, and certainly not as redemption, but rather as something merely technical and administrative; it therefore has no significance in principle, neither as a success nor as a disaster, and it

has no connection with the redemption."

The distinction drawn between the idea of an Israeli state and the actual political institution, between values and "technical and administrative" tools and instruments, intends to avoid the need to take any *a priori*—and certainly theological—position vis-a-vis the Jewish state in pre-messianic times. The distinction permits a clearly pragmatic approach to the State and its enterprises as well as to life within the State and cooperation with its institutions, openly based on accommodation, that is, on *post factum* acceptance of the given political reality. This life is supposed to be free of ideological commitment or identification, innocent of any normative decision and *a priori* recognition:

> We stand before the fact that they established a state on a part of our Holy Land, and hence we do not have here a Halakhic question of permitted or prohibited, for this question has already been resolved by those who do not ask [religious] questions. All that remains is for us to clarify our position and our attitude towards the reality with which we have been presented. . . . And we have not found, either in the Torah or the Talmud or in the later Halakhic authorities, any concepts or laws indicating when to recognize or not to recognize a state. This is nothing but a custom employed by gentiles for propaganda purposes.

Thus explains Rabbi Avraham Weinfeld, one of the distinguished ethical preachers within the world of the Lithuanian style Talmudic academies.

Accordingly, every assessment regarding the state and its actions (like any other mundane phenomenon) must be made *ad hoc* according to the merits of the case: based on its link with, and assistance to, the Torah and its students, and according to the attitude of the state's leaders to the demands of the Halakhah. If the state, its institutions, and it budgets support Torah students and bring into the fold those distant from the tradition, they are judged favorably. If they deny Torah-true Jews their due and cause those close to the tradition to abandon it, they are judged unfavorably. When the state rescues Jews and helps protect their lives and wellbeing, wherever they are, the evaluation is positive, since the saving of life is a religious value. But when it endangers the safety of Jews, whatever the reason, the evaluation will be negative. This criterion is used to evaluate every collective Jewish enterprise in the lands of their dispersion and remains valid for Jewish activity in the exile of Israel in the Holy Land. It follows that when Haredi circles make their support of one government or another conditional on increased financial allocations to yeshivot and Torah institutions, for example, they are merely being faithful to their philosophy. Of what use is a Jewish state, of what use are public institutions and parliamentary committees, if not for the purpose of promoting Torah study in the Holy Land?

**Moderate religious Zionism:** None of the religious outlooks discussed acknowledge an intermediate historical model—a concrete mode of Jewish being that is neither exile nor redemption. Rather, all maintain a dichotimistic approach—exile or redemption—thereby entirely rejecting the more complex option of a partial Jewish revival within history that continuously hovers between the two extremes. By contrast, a number of moderate alternative approaches seek religious significance specifically within the realm of historical, pre-messianic realization, doing so precisely because of what such a realization opens up and invites, demands and promises. This approach is manifested primarily within some ideological groups within religious Zionism as well as in certain Rabbinic circles among Oriental Jewry. The advocates of this viewpoint see the present return to Zion as taking place at an "opportune moment," as a Halakhic challenge based precisely on this maverick condition—that is, no longer "exile" but not yet "redemption." Hence, these groups' model for the modern return to Israel—of the present "Third Commonwealth" (in Hebrew, *bayit*; "home" or "house")—is that of the First Commonwealth and, even more so, the Second Commonwealth, rather than an absolute messianic one. These historical commonwealths were always portrayed by the collective Jewish memory as legitimate and desirable, even if not whole and total.

In other words, in this, as opposed to the ultra-Orthodox paradigm, the new national awakening has cured the psychological, existential element of exile by building a Jewish homeland. By the same token, however, unlike the Zionist-messianic outlook, Zionism has not yet cured the metaphysical, theological element of exile. It has brought about a national revival, but not religious redemption. On the contrary, the supporters of this stance would claim Jews have always distinguished themselves from Christians precisely in that they taught their children to find positive religious meaning even in a pre-messianic world, to search it out even in a historical reality that has not yet been saved. Of course, they will say, the partial achievement can eventually lead to the perfect one, step by step. But this does not detract from the innate value of the part in itself. Historical time is not to be judged only from the perspective of eschatological time.

Second, this moderate stance places the concept of covenant in the focus of its religious awareness. How so? The biblical covenant between the God of Israel and the people of Israel is, by its very nature, conditional, based upon a "two-sided" obligation of mutual responsibility and commitment. The very idea of the covenant thus negates religious determinism; it is inconsistent with the concept of a predestined fate or a predetermined future. The covenant contains neither an unlimited guarantee to the people nor an evil, unconditional decree. Therefore, as opposed to the radical outlooks that foresee an inevitable destiny for Zionism and the state of Israel—whether for good or for ill—the present outlooks emphasize the uncertainty of the future and the human freedom to influence and alter events. It is true, its advocates would say, that the prophetic promise for redemption is absolute. But its definite realization in a specific society or a given generation is conditional and contingent.

Furthermore, as opposed to the prevalent ultra-Orthodox approach, the covenant was not made between God and righteous individuals or God and pious communities alone, but, rather, between God and the entire people of Israel—"from your hewers of wood to your water drawers" (Deut. 31:10). More-over, the covenant covers the entire spectrum of the Jewish community, in its real exist-ence, from the saints to the ignorant. There-fore, according to this alternative stance, the present revival of the Jewish people enables the re-establishment of the covenant commu-nity. It is indeed intended for its perfection, even though it is not a guarantee thereof, until the End of Days.

**Social charter:** We have thus far dealt with different religious conceptions of Zion-ism and the state of Israel. Of course, in real life, the boundaries among purely ideologi-cal positions are sometimes obscured, espe-cially considering that members of all of these streams live within a Jewish state with a non-Orthodox majority. How is this shared life to be conducted?

Just after the establishment of the State, the secular and religious communities engi-neered a kind of compromise, which has been termed the "status quo." More than just a political agreement, it was an unwritten so-cial charter, designed to enable the two sides to live together despite their theological and ideological disagreements. And despite, or perhaps because of, its internal ambiguities and inconsistencies, the arrangement worked well for a long time. For example, Israel's Declaration of Independence concludes: "Out of trust in the Rock of Israel, we sign our names. . . ." Who or what is the "Rock of Is-rael"? Is it the God of Israel, or is it perhaps the genius of the Jewish people? The disputes concerning the phrasing of the Declaration drove its authors to settle for this intention-ally ambiguous term, which each individual camp was free to interpret as it saw fit. At the time, one of Israel's leading thinkers derided this ambiguity and deemed it hypoc-risy. That very ambiguity, however, is what gives the document its advantage, providing a point of identification for people of differ-ent factions and denominations. Similarly, what is the "trust" described in the Declara-tion? In the religious tradition, it connotes a belief in God and suggests a passive nod towards the redeemer of Israel. In modern Hebrew, however, "trust" (*bitahon*) refers principally to physical and military power

and security. Again, the double meaning was most fruitful and has enabled different people to identify themselves with the text.

A concrete aspect of the "status quo" was the determination that public buses would not run on the Sabbath (following Orthodox religious prohibitions), even as travel was permitted in private cars and taxis. While difficult to justify either on Halakhic grounds or according to secular liberal doctrine, each side could claim in this arrangement a par-tial victory; no one came away from the table feeling alienated and defeated. If anything, the partial disappointment and partial satis-faction that resulted from the deal guaranteed its (at least partial) success.

An extremely important development in recent years is the politicization of the "reli-gious" and "secular" divide, expressed in the evolution of the "religious right" and "secu-lar left." In this, we see a deepening and coalescence of the two principal rifts that di-vide contemporary Israeli society: the ques-tion of peace (and territorial compromise) and issues of religion and state.

Moreover, the original political and social agreement in fact was grounded on a mistake common to both sides. The secular, religious, and ultra-Orthodox camps all assumed that their rivals represented a fleeting historical phenomenon, that the "others" were fated to diminish in strength and numbers and even-tually to disappear. Prime Minister David Ben-Gurion and his secular disciples, ultra-Orthodox rabbis and their followers, Rabbi Kook and his Zionist students all harbored essentially the same conviction (fig. 180). And while they may not have believed that their forecasts would be realized in the short-term, all were quite assured in their expecta-tions that any agreement they reached was temporary, a tactical compromise rather than a fundamental reconciliation.

Secularist leaders could not conceive that the future held any promise for what they considered the antiquated world of Ortho-doxy. They believed that the traditional-ist world—observant Jews, yeshivah boys, Hasidim or Mitnaggedim—was fated to be overwhelmed by the normalization process already transforming the nation. In the diaspora, such people served as cultural guardians; but no longer. Their children and grandchildren would conform to the profile of the new Jew being molded in the national homeland. Until that time, why not compromise with these representatives of a fading epoch? Why not even show them a degree of nostalgic empathy?

At the same time, the Orthodox, far from perceiving themselves on the brink of extinction, believed that secular Jews were doomed to disappear. Indeed, to various ultra-Orthodox groups, the very term "secular Jew" was an oxymoron. Some of these people would assimilate entirely, and some would return to God and the true faith. But the opposition between the concepts "Jew" and "secular" meant that they could not sustain themselves as a definable group.

The religious Zionists, finally, in their own way, subscribed to a similar assumption. True, they said, secular Zionists avow that they are staging a revolt against their parents and grandparents and are abandoning the messianic faith. But what, in fact, are they doing? They return from exile to the Holy Land, adopt the holy tongue in preference to foreign languages, and abandon the option of assimilation into the nations in favor of strengthening the congregation of Israel. The expectation, therefore, was that once the secularists accomplished their political and secular goals, they would quest for an even deeper, spiritual and religious return. No one could withhold affection and good-will from these potentially observant Jews, who were already playing an active role in the process that would ultimately lead to the redemption of Israel.

But such "optimistic" expectations of all the groups have not been realized. The supposedly "fleeting phenomena" have refused to disappear or to redefine their religious or secular identities. The "others," rather, now insist increasingly on asserting themselves as enduring and vital realities that will continue to reproduce and flourish; no longer, therefore, is it possible to imagine a future free of them. This realization, naturally, has led to an escalation of tensions. If it once was easy to display tolerance towards those who

would soon be trading in their colors for yours, it is not so simple, today, to negotiate with individuals and groups determined to have power and likely to preserve their own identities. This demands a kind of acknowledgment and acceptance much different from what was formerly required.

Jews of the diaspora are largely exempt from these demands. An ultra-Orthodox Jew living in Williamsburg for the most part does not encounter a Reform Jew from Manhattan, not in a synagogue or temple, not in a community center, and certainly not in the attempt jointly to govern a shared Jewish country or even simply to shape a single social space. And if one runs into the other on the street or in the subway, it is a chance meeting between two Americans and not between two Jews. Zionist nationalism, by contrast, assembled all of these Jews within, sometimes literally, a stone's throw of each other. While this created a forum, a common public space, so long as each expected the other to disappear, true face-to-face confrontation did not occur. Today, for the reasons given, that meeting is finally taking place— in rancor and anger, perhaps—but it is taking place.

**The contested arena:** The reevaluation to which the social agreement between religious and secular Israelis has been subjected in recent years is related to an additional change that has taken place in the Israeli reality and consciousness. Previously marginal social groups (Sephardic Jews, the religious, Revisionists), as well as certain streams of thought (ultra-Orthodoxy and Reform) that were once opposed to political Zionism have been brought into the mainstream of the Zionist enterprise. More and more, the Jewish state has become an arena in which the contemporary debate about Jewish identity is played out. Less and less does the State reflect the outlook and principles of a single victorious group.

In the Israel of 1948, it was possible to identify a single prototype of the "authentic" Israeli. It was easy to define what it meant to participate in the collective Israeli experience and what it meant to deviate from it, to declare who stood at its center and who on its margins. Thus, the nexus meant to bind all Israelis together was forged according to the mold of one elite Israeli group, while others—Sephardim, the religious, Revisionists—were judged according to their compatibility with this model. Only later did these groups gravitate towards center stage, first by challenging the dominant ethos and its monolithic ideal and later by penetrating the centers of national culture and government.

We have already noticed that this inclusionary process has not bypassed religious streams of Judaism that were initially inimical to the Zionist movement, but that have, over time, been integrated into its historic undertaking. Even those factions that formerly opted to stand to the side or even outside the national enterprise have joined the project (at least *de facto*). This point is made concrete when we call to mind the debate over "Who is a Jew?, spawned by the Law of Return, which grants to any Jew who requests it immediate citizenship in the state of Israel. The principal combatants in this fierce debate, which has already brought down more than one Israeli government, are, on the one side, ultra-Orthodox leaders and, on the other, leaders of the reform movements. This, of course, is no wonder, since the argument, after all, concerns how one becomes a member of the Jewish people, that is, who possesses the authority to convert non-Jews to Judaism. (Thus, more accurately put, the debate actually concerns, Who is a rabbi?) This issue inflames first and foremost the leaders of the competing Jewish streams in North America, all of whom attach inordinate importance to the question of who the state of Israel, its citizens, institutions, and laws, recognizes as a religious authority.

But remember that, at the beginning, the fiercest religious opponents of Zionism were none other than thes leaders of ultra-Orthodoxy and Reform Judaism. The latter greeted the movement with fury, viewing it as a backward nationalistic reaction that denied the universal mission of the Jewish people. And the ultra-Orthodoxy, for their part, angrily defined Zionism as a rebellious secularist movement with anti-messianic intentions. Thus, at the turn-of-the-century, Rabbi Sha-

lom Dov Baer Schneersohn of Lubavitch was an implacable foe of Zionism. He could not have imagined that one day the monumental struggle between the two opposed branches of Judaism would spread to the very core of a Jewish state. But indeed, these two movements, which once fought against the formation of a Jewish state, today bitterly debate the character of that state and argue how it should decide questions of Jewish identity and religious authority.

Does this mark the failure or the success of Zionism? Israel's founders were indeed disposed to see their creation as a manifestation of the triumph of one Jewish outlook (their own), as if a decisive verdict had been rendered in the debate concerning the future of the Jewish people. Yet the Israel of today has become an arena for the continuation of that very struggle. The state has increasingly come to include the various opinions and factions, who now argue their positions within the walls of the national home. There is no denying that this inclusivity exacts a toll. And the price may, in fact, be deemed too steep by those who expect Zionism to revive Jewish nationalism and normalize the Israelis. The price, however, is not too steep to those who see the movement as a means of reviving the Jewish people in its entirety.

As it turns out, most of the internal tensions that have been stirring within Judaism throughout history have been carried over to the state of Israel and are reflected in the community that is coming together there. Zionism did not create the fragmentation. On the contrary, from a historiosophical, dialectical point of view, it is possible to depict Zionism as a logical outcome of this division. The Jewish nation was able, until relatively recently, to exist as a nation without territorial concentration and in the absence of a solid political base. The Shulhan Arukh, the most widely accepted code of Jewish law, and the prayer book were sufficient to bind the people together. In recent generations, however, Halakhic principles and religious faith have become a source of contention. In this sense, one may see the Zionist act as a heroic gesture, an almost desperate measure, to reestablish a common denominator in a

non-virtual context, as a political and historical entity, to establish once again a national
and existential center, despite theological rifts
and ideological divides. If we adopt this point
of view, it emerges that the attempt of the
founders to shape the culture and identity of
a new society using as their mode a single,
victorious image was itself contradictory. It
was destined to alienate various segments of
the community. In fact, it was precisely those
political and social compromises, the gray
areas, as it were, designed to foster mutuality that most suited the internal logic of the
Zionist entity and the complexities of the
contemporary Jewish experience.

With the reconstitution of a public forum
for the Jewish people in the land of Israel,
an arena for contests and judgments was also
created. Outside of Israel, there are almost
limitless opportunities for individualistic and
pluralistic Judaism. Every family and community can pitch its own tent. As it is possible to avoid contact, so is it mostly possible
to avoid collision. There is no need of public showdowns or legal or political verdicts.
Not so in Israel, where such decisions are
demanded daily. And as it is impossible to
avoid confrontation, it is necessary to agree
on rules for dialogue and decision-making,
although not necessarily on belief and lifestyle. We must nurture one language, but not
necessarily a single vocabulary. It is enough
to encourage empathy and solidarity on an
existential level ("a covenant of fate") and
not necessarily on an ideological and theological one ("a covenant of faith").

### Bibliography

Luz, Ehud, *Parallels Meet: Religion and Nation-
    alism in the Early Zionist Movement* (New
    York, 1988).
Ravitzky, Aviezer, *Messianism, Zionism, and
    Jewish Religious Radicalism* (Chicago, 1996).
Friedman Menachem, "Israel as a Theological
    Dilemma," in Baruch Kimmerling, ed., *The
    Israeli State and Society* (New York, 1988).

AVIEZER RAVITZKY

# EPILOGUE

## A LIVING RELIGION LOVINGLY PRESERVED

### CHAIM BERMANT

Judaism is a celebration, a living religion lovingly preserved. Given the melancholy nature of Jewish history and the onerous demands of Jewish observance, this may seem a strange claim to make. But the very fact of survival in the face of adversity suggests a unique destiny and induces a sense of thanksgiving, even exultation.

> O come let us sing before the Lord; let us shout for joy to the rock of our salvation. Let us come before him with thanksgiving, let us shout for joy and raise our voices in song.

The life of the Jew is governed by the thought, "Know before whom thou art standing!," so that the day begins and ends with prayer, and there are prayers to cover almost every action and every contingency, prayers for joy and prayers for sorrow, prayers for dangers faced and dangers averted, prayers before meals and after meals, prayers even for the discharge of bodily functions. And they are more than a mark of appreciation for things one usually takes for granted. They are a reminder that one should take nothing for granted, and that life itself is a privilege.

> O my God, the soul which you gave me is pure. You created it, you shaped it, you breathed it into me, and you are preserving it within me, and you will take it from me, and return it to me in the hereafter. But while the soul is within me, I will give thanks unto you. . . .

The Ten Commandments are but the chapter headings of Jewish observance, and there are ordinances to cover feast days and fast days, the Jew's working life and private life, what Jews eat, what they drink, what they wear, what they must do and what they must shun, duties to God, to people, to beasts. Yet among true believers, what the rabbis call "the yoke of the Torah" feels more like a privilege.

The Jewish creed is summed up in a line from Deuteronomy, "Hear O Israel, the Lord our God, the Lord is one," which is repeated in the morning and evening services and which may be found even on the door-posts of Jewish homes that have discarded every other relic of Judaism. It has become almost a talisman and suggests that even Jews who do not believe in God like to think that God believes in them.

The idea of monotheism is possibly Judaism's greatest contribution to the well-being of humankind. It offers a solitary focus for devotion, an ultimate address, a final arbiter, though, if Scripture is to be our guide, it derived not from abstract speculation but from divine revelation and felt experience. God is not a remote deity but is involved in the life of humanity on a daily and intimate basis.

Yet it is in a sense a qualified monotheism, for it is accompanied by the belief that an omniscient and omnipotent God alighted on the Jews to make his will manifest on earth, as if God could not have managed without them. It almost suggests a partnership, with the Jews acting as a visible proof of an invisible presence. *The Jews are, therefore God is.*

The claim to be chosen by God invites human opprobrium, and though rabbis have argued that it implies obligations rather than privilege, obligations, as we have suggested, can also be a privilege, and if the believing Jew is always aware of God, it implies that God is always aware of the Jew, believing or otherwise.

Not all Jews who take pride in their Jewishness believe in God, and not all who believe in God believe in the God of Israel, or in the mission of Israel. But many do and most did, and where sufficient people believe with sufficient fervor for a sufficient period of time, the actual facts of the case, in so far as they can be established, are almost irrelevant. If there is no God in heaven then the Jews have virtually put him there by the very force of their convictions.

Central to this conviction is a belief that God is good or, in the words of one of the most familiar verses in Jewish liturgy, "The Lord, the Lord is a merciful and gracious God, slow to anger and abounding in lovingkindness and truth; keeping lovingkindness for thousands, forgiving iniquity and transgression and sin." All of which may suggest that Jewish belief transcends Jewish experience. Though again, if God is good—and he wouldn't be much of a God if he weren't—then everything he does must be for the good. There are sages—like the Lubavitcher Rebbe, for example—who have applied this belief even to the Holocaust.

There are various Yiddish expressions to deal with this problem, the most familiar of which is: *Freg nit by Got kashes*—don't ask God questions. There is also a more cynical saying: *Man tracht und Got lacht*—which may be roughly translated as man thinks and God winks.

The fear of God necessarily implies a belief in divine punishment, and a convincing example of such punishment came some ten generations after creation, when "God saw that the wickedness of man was great. . . . And the Lord said, I will destroy man whom I have created from the face of the earth."

And destroy them, God did.

God was disposed to do the same with the Israelites after the incident with the Golden Calf:

> And the Lord said to Moses, I have seen this people and behold it is a stiff-necked people. Now therefore, let me alone that my wrath may wax hot against them, that I may consume them. . . .

And he might have done just that, but for the intervention of Moses.

If this was the first time the Israelites incurred the wrath of Heaven it was not the last, even though they had been sufficiently warned:

> If ye walk in my statutes and keep my commandments and do them, then I will give you rain in due season, and the land shall yield her increase, and the trees of the field shall yield the fruit. . . . And I shall give peace in the land, and ye shall lie down and none shall make ye afraid. . . .

But if you don't:

> I will even appoint over you terror, consumption and the burning ague that shall consume the eyes, and cause sorrow to the heart; and ye shall sow your seeds in vain for your enemies will have eaten it. . . . And I will make your heaven as iron and your earth as brass. . . .

> And I will bring a sword among you that shall avenge the quarrel of my covenant; and when ye are gathered together in the cities I will send the pestilence among you. . . . And ye shall eat the flesh of your sons, and the flesh of your daughters shall ye eat. And I will destroy your high places, and cut down your images, and cast your carcasses upon the carcasses of your idols. . . . And I will scatter you among the heathen, and will draw out a sword after you: and your land shall be desolate and your cities laid waste. . . .

But it was of little avail, for if there is one recurring theme in Scripture, it is "that the people did evil in the sight of God," and what had occurred in the days of Moses recurred in the days of Joshua and Ehud, and Deborah and Gideon, and Samuel and Saul and David, and right down through the centuries to the destruction of the first Temple by the Babylonians and the second Temple by the Romans.

Nor, in general terms, did later Jewish history follow a significantly different pattern. "Because of our sins," go the words of a familiar prayer, "we were expelled from our homeland." But expulsion, apparently, did not make the Jews more pious; it merely made them more vulnerable. Jewish misfortune, explained the rabbis, as they explain it still, was the measure of Jewish iniquity.

Yet if a people sins and is punished and sins again and is punished again, and the process continues for four thousand years without either an improvement in their ways or an end to their misfortunes, then it might be reasonable to infer that the deterrent does not deter and that there was perhaps some imperfection in the divine plan—or possibly even that there was no divine plan at all.

It certainly confirms the reputation of Jews as a stiff-necked people, though the most remarkable fact of all is their continued affirmation of faith in spite of every misfortune. They may be troubled by the ways of God, but they forgive him for they know not what he is doing. They only hope that God does.

And thus where one might have expected the Holocaust to lead to a decline in Jewish belief, or even the collapse of Judaism as an organized religion, it has actually led to—or has at least witnessed—a religious revival.

It is almost as if Jews have accepted this latest and greatest example of divine wrath as the ultimate proof of divine selection.

There is no external evidence to confirm the formative events of early Jewish history, the covenant between God and Abraham—or even the existence of Abraham—the Exodus from Egypt, the revelation at Sinai, the wanderings in the wilderness, and, as we have suggested, little in Jewish experience to support the claim that God was "merciful and gracious, slow to anger and abounding in lovingkindness." But if there were, faith would hardly have entered into the equation, and Judaism would have been merely a quid pro quo, a *Te Deum* for benefits received and in anticipation of benefits to come. Or to put it more crudely, it would suggest that in alighting on God, the Jews had picked a winner and were merely celebrating their good fortune.

Devout Jews, however, need no external evidence and believe they have all the evidence they need in the Torah. But the evidence of the Torah suggests that the founding fathers of the faith had it easy. Abraham may have been ready to sacrifice his son, but then he had personal experience of divine intervention. Moses martyred himself for the sake of the Israelites, but he had met God face to face. The Israelites in the wilderness suffered endless travails, but they had witnessed and benefited from countless miracles.

The same was to an extent true of the Judges and Prophets, all of whom had received direct evidence of a divine presence. God made many demands but also bestowed many blessings. God had, so to speak, discharged his part of the contract and could reasonably expect the people to discharge theirs. So it could be argued that Jews only became true *believers* once the age of miracles was over, and more specifically after the fall of the Temple and the end of the sacrificial cult.

Maimonides argued that the cult, which went back to the earliest years of Jewish history, was designed to wean the Israelites from idol worship. If so the process was an exceedingly slow one, for the cult continued to thrive more than a thousand years after Sinai. It sustained folk memories of the wandering in the wilderness and of the Tabernacle, and when in later years the cult came to be centered on Jerusalem and the Temple itself, with all its glories, pageantry, and ceremonies, it came to be seen as a palpable emanation of the divine presence, a reassurance that Gold dwelled in the midst of God's people.

The fall of the Temple thus represented the first real test of faith, for not only was the glory gone out of Zion, but the Jewish people were removed from the setting of their faith and taken into captivity. The sense of continuity that had kept folk memories of divine beneficence alive was disrupted, and they were left only with the immediate experience of divine fury.

And yet Judaism persisted. If anything it was reinvigorated, for, as the Prophets complained, the sacrificial cult had become mechanical. The whole point of the commandments had been forgotten, rituals had replaced righteousness.

"Will the Lord be pleased with thousands of rams, or with ten thousands of rivers of oil?," asked Micah. "Shall I give my first born for my transgressions, the fruit of my body for the sins of my soul? He hath shown thee, O man, what is good; and what doth the Lord require of thee, but to do justly, and to love mercy, and to walk humbly with thy God?"

With the fall of the Temple, study and prayer became the principal outlets for devotion, while study in particular came to be regarded as the greatest good: *V'Talmud Torah keneged kulam*, the study of Torah is of equal weight to the practice of all the other commandments combined. Judaism as we know it thus dates not from Jewish statehood but Jewish exile.

In this context it may be useful to recall that exile was not entirely the result of expulsion or persecution. The Holy Land could not, as it cannot, contain the teeming energies and restless ambitions of the entire Jewish people, and in most cases exile was voluntarily assumed—as it still is.

Jewish communities in different parts of the world acquired different characteristics, but the one thing they had in common was a devotion to learning. As a result literacy among Jews was almost universal centuries before it spread in the societies around them, and during their two thousand years of dispersion the Torah became not only their common bond and their common guide but their portable homeland.

Which did not mean that the actual homeland faded from their collective memory. For together with the Temple and the sacrifices it was evoked in both study and prayer, and most Jewish feasts and fasts, and a great many Jewish ceremonies, are associated in one way or another with the Holy Land. Pesach, Shavuot, and Succot, for example, are still called the "three pilgrimage festivals," because in ancient times they were celebrated by pilgrims converging on the Temple Mount in Jerusalem. They only became family occasions after the fall of the Temple.

The word Torah as used among Jews refers not only to Scripture but to the Talmud and all the glosses, commentaries, annotations, and interpretations this literature has inspired, spoken of collectively as the Oral Law.

A belief in *Torah min Hashamayim*—Torah from heaven—implies faith in both the written and oral law, standard for the believing Jew. Maimonides additionally prescribed Thirteen Principles of the Jewish faith, which, among other things, demand a belief in the coming of the messiah and the resurrection of the dead. Yet dogmas are alien to Judaism, and, other than the belief in the one God, no profession of faith has ever been required of the believing Jew. Instead, certain usages have evolved that distinguish orthodox Jews from their coreligionists: Sabbath observance, kashrut (the dietary laws), and *Taharat Hamishpacha* (the laws of family purity).

Of the three only the first is listed in the Ten Commandments.

Judaism abhors excess, even excess of toil, but its stress on the day of rest, "Remember the Sabbath day to keep it holy," is a celebration of creation, for on the seventh day, "God rested from all his labors. And he blessed the seventh day and sanctified it," set it apart, as God set apart the people of Israel, so that the two—the Sabbath and the people—became interdependent, with the survival of the one resting upon the survival of the other.

The days of creation began not with the morning, but the evening, and it is the same with the Sabbath.

The hours that precede it, in observant households, are hours of frantic preparation, with floors to be scrubbed, food to be cooked, clothes to be ironed, tables to be laid, and no matter how early one starts, there is always a last minute rush to finish. But then as the sun begins to set, all work gradually ceases, and, as the sun sets and the Sabbath candles are lit, one can almost hear the divine presence descending.

In eastern Europe, where the dominant characteristic of Jewish life was abject poverty, families half starved during the week to make a show of plenty on the Sabbath, when they brought out their best table-linen, put out their best crockery, and put on their best clothes.

It was a day out of time, an occasion to withdraw from the cares and stresses of workaday life, and, where persecution was rife, an opportunity to draw assurance from divine protection, no matter how erratic its nature. On the Sabbath the husband was king for a day, his wife queen, their children princes. The sense of sanctity at such times became an almost palpable experience. In a way it was a form of escapism, but a benign one.

On the other hand if it was an escape from hardship and stress, it was also a cause of stress and hardship, because until the five day week became universal, many observant Jews were almost unemployable, and even where they owned their enterprises or were self-employed they couldn't always compete on equal terms. This hardly mattered in eastern Europe, where the outside world was largely closed to them. But it did matter once they moved to the west, and while many Jews adhered to the traditional Sabbath whatever the price, others modified it to cope with prevailing circumstances or abandoned it altogether. Rabbis warned that those who sought a new life in the new world did so at the peril of their mortal souls, and their warnings were often confirmed by events.

The commandment to observe the Sabbath is immediately followed by "Honor thy father and thy mother," and the two obligations are obviously connected. The Sabbath presumes a family, and a stable family presumes parental authority, though the fact that it was spelled out in the Decalogue almost suggests that parental authority is modeled on divine authority. But there is this difference: while divine authority stemmed from the fact of divinity, parental authority had to be earned; the father not only had to be the bread-winner, he had to be the exemplar. God is not answerable for his own actions; a father is.

The Jewish family is a walled garden within which the young flourish and the old decline. Judaism is almost an emanation of family life, and family life an expression of Judaism. No faith is so sustained by the family, and none so sustains it, and if traditional Judaism is particularly harsh to the adulterer and the homosexual it is partly because it regards both as a threat to family life.

The Jewish home, as conceived by the rabbis, is a temple, and so simple an occasion as a meal can assume the nature of a holy communion, which may, in part, explain the importance attached to the dietary laws.

To the forbidden foods listed in Scripture has been added the practice of ritual slaughter, so that even permitted meat and poultry may only be bought from kosher butchers. Additionally the strict interpretations given by the rabbis to the verse "thou shalt not seethe a kid in its mother's milk" has meant two sets of crockery and cutlery, two sets of pots and pans, two sets of table linen and, in modern times, two sinks and two dish-washers. Some have even carried the matter to the point of having two kitchens. It is no longer hard to be a Jew, but it is expensive, and while Jews have always had middle-class aspirations even where they had working-class incomes, any Jew on a working class income, or a less than substantial professional income, would today find it difficult to conform at this level to Jewish usage.

Which does not mean that the utterly poor have been priced out of Judaism. Jews are required by the very nature of their faith to be mindful of the needy, and where a one is a self-confessed pauper, all basic needs, and even a few luxuries, will be provided. Accommodation, food, and clothing will be found. When daughters marry they will be found a dowry, and when the indigent dies he or she will receive a full kosher burial in a separate grave, with a separate tomb-stone. The hardships only arise when one is solvent, but not affluent.

"Family purity," the third pillar of Jewish observance, is based on the fact that Judaism insists not only on sexual abstinence outside marriage but on continence within it, which in turn is based on a verse in Leviticus:

And if a woman have an issue, and the issue in her flesh be blood, she shall be in her impurity seven days.

The sanctions against any breach of this ruling were extremely grave:

> And if a man shall lie with a woman knowing her sickness, and he shall uncover her naked-
> ness . . . both of them shall be cut off from among their people.

The rabbis therefore surrounded the scriptural enactment with a whole complex of *taqqanot*, by-laws. The seven days of impurity were extended to twelve, and even then a couple
may not resume sexual relations until the wife has immersed herself in a miqvah, a ritual
bath. The strongest epithet known to the Hebrew—or Yiddish—language is to call someone
a *mamzer ben niddah*, the bastard child of a menstrual woman.

It is claimed that the miqvah is both a means of curbing animal passions and of refreshing
marital relationships. It is also claimed that women who use the miqvah are less prone to
cervical cancer. None of the claims is unfounded, and the observant certainly enjoy more
stable and more wholesome family lives.

Similar claims can be made, and have been made, for the dietary laws, but like all Jewish
laws they have to be observed not because of any benefits they might offer but because the
Torah demands them—"You shall be holy because I the Lord thy God am holy." Yet underlying them all is the tacit belief that the Torah would not demand them if they were not
beneficial and that any immediate burdens they may entail are but a small price to pay for
the many blessings they will bring.

Jewish observance is to a greater or lesser extent preserved by a tacit system of mutual
policing, which can hardly apply to something so intimate as family purity. So one cannot
say how many couples abstained from sexual intercourse during the necessary twelve days
of separation, but it can be said that in modernity the miqvah all but vanished as an institution from most Jewish communities. In recent years it has been making a comeback.

Maimonides was inclined to group the dietary laws with the sexual laws as a necessary
restraint on bodily lust:

> It is well-known that it is intemperance in eating, drinking, and sexual intercourse that people
> mostly crave and indulge in; and these things counteract the ulterior perfection of man, impede at
> the same time the development of his first perfection, and generally disturb the social order of the
> country and the economy of the family.

Judaism is unquestionably puritanical. But it is not ascetic, and it frowns upon people—
Nazarites, for example—who deny themselves permitted pleasures. It may warn against excess
but does not call for abstemiousness. Thus there are three statutory meals to the Sabbath,
Jewish ceremonies call for a considerable intake of food and drink, and almost every festival has its culinary associations. Judaism not only impacts on the soul but can be tasted on
the tongue.

Though again the consumption of food for mere pleasure, even if it is kosher, is condemned: "Where three men have eaten at one table without uttering a word of Torah, it is as
if they have consumed the sacrifices to dead idols . . . their tables are full of vomit and filth."
The Jewish table must also serve as an altar.

The same is true of the Jewish bed. "Be fruitful and multiply," even if not contained in
the Decalogue, is the first of all commandments, and Judaism regards sexual intercourse
between husband and wife as an act of holy communion.

Sex is thus not only permitted but is mandatory, and the husband is required to satisfy his
wife at regular intervals, varying with the nature of his occupation. Healthy, prosperous men,
living at home should, according to the Talmud "perform, their duties nightly;" laborers,
twice a week; commercial travelers at least once a month, "while the time appointed for
scholars is Friday eve to Friday eve." Friday eve, indeed, is a time when the wife has special
claims on the attention of her husband, and to this end he was required to eat garlic for,
according to the Talmud, "garlic promotes love and satisfies desire."

The rabbis aver that at Sinai the people of Israel were as "one man with one heart," but they were rarely, if ever, of one mind, and today the Jewish world can be divided into four main streams and any number of minor ones.

The first, and perhaps the largest, is composed of Jews who in an earlier century might have been nominal Christians but who no longer feel any compulsion to belong to any denomination at all. They are Jewish in the sense that they are of Jewish descent but are so removed from Jewish life, or, indeed any religious life, as to avoid the benefit of clergy even at their funerals.

There was a time when the ultimate act of dissociation was to marry out of the faith. Today it is to be buried out of it, though given the popularity of cremations, many are merely scattered to the winds.

The unaffiliated include half Jews and quarter Jews, the sort of people who are regarded as Jews only by gentiles (unless, of course, they should win the Nobel Prize, in which case they are claimed as coreligionists even by Jews). But they remain sensitive to attacks on Jews or the Jewish state, and if Jews may appear to have an influence out of all proportion to their number, it is partly because it is impossible to say what their number actually is. It depends on who is counting.

Next in number are what might loosely be called the liberals, which, in the American context, would include the Reform movement, the Conservative, and the Reconstructionists. They are not, of course, all of a piece. There is, for example, little to distinguish some Orthodox rabbis from some Conservative ones, or some Conservative rabbis from Reform ones, and, for that matter, there is little to distinguish some Reform rabbis from some Unitarian ministers. They all, however, look vaguely the same to the Orthodox, who regard them all as non-kosher.

In Israel, liberal Jews are accepted as Jews under the Law of Return, which grants all Jews the right of citizenship, but they are not regarded as a Jewish denomination by the Israeli rabbinate or as a religious denomination by the state, and if the political pressure to define a Jew in traditional legal terms should succeed, many of them would not be regarded as Jews at all.

The liberals, who have their origins in nineteenth century Germany, have sizable outcrops in England and others parts of the English-speaking world and minor ones elsewhere, but they are now largely an American phenomenon and constitute about 80% of the American Jewish community.

A great many of the Jews who crossed the Atlantic in the last years of the nineteenth century were not only fleeing from poverty and persecution but from the rule of orthodoxy. They may have created landsmanschafts for mutual support and to preserve some of the ways and institutions of the old country, but few of them were anxious to perpetuate the old time religion with all its restrictions. They were in a new world and were impatient to make use of the opportunities around them. In many instances they only retained their links with Judaism because to be non-religious was to be un-American.

In Europe even reformers felt bound to cling to the past out of fear of being swallowed up by the Christian society around them. In America, where Jews were newcomers among newcomers and where there was a division between church and state, the danger of Christianization was remote, so that they could be more adventurous. Of late they have possibly become a little too adventurous, and their rabbis, instead of defending old boundaries, have been mapping out new ones.

In the past while liberals reserved the right to reinterpret, and even ignore, the rulings of the Rabbinic tradition, they claimed to venerate Scripture. But that is no longer the case, and many rabbis, for example, now are prepared to officiate at mixed marriages and seem to operate on the principle that where one cannot check a trend one should sanctify it. Thus while orthodoxy seems to have lost all capacity for movement, liberals appear to be moving too far and too fast in too many directions.

On the other hand they are prepared to reverse direction if need be. Hebrew has thus been given a larger place in their liturgy, the sense of Jewish nationhood has been revived, and where liberals were non-Zionist or even anti-Zionist, they have for the past fifty years put all their weight and authority behind the Jewish state.

They stress prophetic teaching rather than rabbinical enactments, ethics rather than ritual, the universal aspects of Judaism rather than the particular ones, and while mindful of their loyalty to the Jewish people, they regard themselves—and are generally regarded—as fully integrated members of the society around them. Where the orthodox fight assimilation, they welcome it; the former assert their distinctiveness, the latter glory in their sameness. The orthodox are Jews who happen to be Americans, the liberals are Americans who happen to be Jews. And finally while most orthodox Jews stay in the fold through their remembrance of Sinai, not a few liberal ones are drawn to it through their remembrance of Auschwitz, so that Holocaust memorials have a larger place in these Jews' loyalties than synagogues.

There is a widespread belief, certainly among the orthodox, that liberal Judaism is a station on the road to Jewish oblivion. But it has been in existence now for nearly five generations and is continuing to grow. This is not only a matter of numbers. Their seminaries are among the foremost seats of learning in America, and they have enriched the cultural life not only of the Jewish community but of the world around them.

Liberal Judaism has barely made any headway among Sephardic Jews, but then Sephardic Judaism has never been subject to the obscurantism and rigors of the East European ghettoes. They lived in more tolerant lands and acquired more tolerant attitudes, and their rabbis were less harsh and oppressive. As a result there was less to rebel against.

There are Sephardim who feel that their brand of Judaism is not rigorous enough, and many of these have been drawn to Hassidic Yeshivot in Israel and elsewhere and have become Ashkenazic-style Haredim—the ultra-orthodox who reject even the legitimacy of the Jewish State, seen as solely the creation of human, not divine, hands. In the main, however, Sephardic Jews belong to our next group, which is variously referred to as centrist, modern, or moderate orthodoxy, to distinguish it from the immoderate, black-clad orthodoxy represented by the Haredim.

Both the centrists and Haredim claim to be governed by *Torah min Hashamayim*, and while both avoid definitive statements on the matter, to the former the concept conveys vague suggestions of divine revelation, while, to the latter, it designates the words of the rabbis. This does not mean that centrist rabbis are powerless. But they do have the measure of their flock and avoid pronouncements that they suspect may be ignored, or worse, treated with derision.

While all centrist rabbis are orthodox and some are Haredi, the same cannot be said of their congregants. There are Jews who eat kosher at home but non-kosher out, who attend synagogue on a Shabbat morning but drive to a sports event in the afternoon, and are totally oblivious to the laws of family purity. And there are not a few who limit their observances to attending synagogue on Yom Kippur, celebrating the Seder, and saying Kaddish for their parents. In other words, they are not orthodox at all, but even if they take their religion in small doses, they like those doses to have a familiar flavor, to taste of the real thing. They prefer to be sinners among saints than to pass for saints among sinners, possibly in the hope that something of the sanctity of their neighbors may rub off on to them.

Yom Kippur has come to feature in the Jewish imagination not only as the Day of Atonement but as a roll-call of the Jewish people. To be in synagogue at all is an expression of solidarity and a way of hedging bets, and to fast for a day, a small price for avoiding damnation—even if one doesn't believe in it.

Moreover, the solemnity of the day, the white-clad officiants, the ancient rituals, the beautiful, if somber, liturgy, the familiar melodies, the reading from the Book of Jonah, the surrounding mellowness of early autumn, the very size of the throng, can, and often does, impose a passing sense of awe. There is more to a large congregation than the sum total of its congregants, and even those with a limited capacity for prayer can be affected by the fervor of their neighbors.

Pesach has retained its hold on Jewish loyalties not only because it commemorates the Exodus from Egypt and the beginnings of Jewish nationhood but because it is the family occasion *par excellence* and as such functions almost as the Sabbath of Sabbaths.

It also commemorates childhood, for children are at the center of the celebrations. It evokes distant echoes of huge assemblies festively attired, of uncles and aunts now gone, of cousins now scattered, of the four questions asked under the glowing eyes of grandparents, of the four cups of wine and the first taste of intoxication, of tales retold and songs resung, of faded pictures in wine-stained Haggadot, and, of course, of food and plenty of it, lovingly prepared, lavishly displayed, and hungrily consumed.

It is a festival—*the* festival—of gladness and togetherness, recalling past humiliations—"We were slaves unto Pharaoh in Egypt"—and present joys, so that even many families who do not normally keep a kosher home go to the far greater trouble, and infinitely greater expense, of making it kosher for Pesach.

Kaddish, the memorial prayer for the dead, has always been treated religiously even by the fairly irreligious. It is concerned less with belief than filial loyalty and guilt, and a father anxious to keep his son at least nominally Jewish need only drop dead to have his way.

Until a generation or two ago the level of orthodoxy of a synagogue was determined not so much by the outlook of the congregation as the outlook of the rabbi who, in many instances was, so to speak, expected to be orthodox on behalf of his congregants. There was little to distinguish many centrist Jews from their liberal brethren, except that while the former may have been prone to passing pangs of conscience for their lack of observance, the latter didn't even know they had gone wrong. In recent years, however, Jewish life has undergone a transformation.

A decline in faith is always taken to be natural so that a revival calls for some explanation. We have suggested the Holocaust as one reason. Another, possibly, was the emergence of the State of Israel. The repercussions took a long time to sink in, because the Jews who had lived through the thirties and forties had been numbed by the sheer succession of traumas and dramas, and it was only when things had calmed down a little and a new generation had grown to maturity that they had the necessary peace of mind to absorb what had happened. And just then came the triumphs of the Six Day war, which seemed so swift, complete, and miraculous as to confirm God's promise to Abraham:

> And I will make thee a great nation, and I will bless thee, and make thy name great; and thou shalt be a blessing. And I will bless them that bless thee, and curse them that curse thee, and in thee shall all the families of the earth be blessed . . . and unto thy seed will I give this land. . . .

At the same time there has been a growing disenchantment with western culture, no longer confident of itself as the supreme expression of human progress. Where it had represented Plato and Aristotle, Goethe and Schiller, Bach and Beethoven, it also came to represent Auschwitz, and while it offered every imaginable material benefit, and not a few unimaginable ones, there was something hollow at its heart. The very idea of progress came into question as polities that claimed to strive for more just and more equitable order and that had attracted some of the best minds in the Jewish world were shown to be hideous tyrannies shored up by oppression and lies. And even in free societies many young people recoiled from the excesses, absurdities, obscenities, and depravities of the pagan world around them.

The rejection of the new led to a reappraisal of the old, and many Jews have found their way back to Judaism, if only through a process of elimination. One can almost hear the cry: "Come back God, all is forgiven!"

Old customs have been revived and old usages resuscitated and institutions that were regarded as moldering relics of a discarded past have acquired new life. Yeshivot are flourishing everywhere, and a larger proportion of young people are engaged in Jewish study than at any time in Jewish history. Where Judaism and Jewishness were regarded as obstacles to advancement, they now are cherished as ends in themselves. Orthodoxy, once the province of the old, the alien, the backward, and the poor is no longer incompatible with success, and centrist orthodoxy has to a large extent become truly orthodox.

Which does not mean that centrist Jews are wholly immune to the attractions of western culture, but they now can see it in fuller perspective and view it more critically.

Centrists still strive to enter the best universities, but where in the past Jewish students were usually lost to Judaism and Jewish life, they now often leave the universities with their faith enhanced. There is a Hebrew saying, *negad shemo, avad shemo*, a name made great is a name lost. This is no longer true, and many Jews have been able to rise in *this* world without forsaking their interest in the next.

But as centrists like to think they are rational, and often are, they are open to pressures from which the other brands of Judaism are free. They accept that Jewish laws are "immutable," but they are also aware that in some circumstances they can be, and have been, changed, or at least reinterpreted. Thus they are finding it particularly difficult to be silent in the face of the claims of Jewish women to a larger role in Jewish life.

Judaism has always been a man's religion, as men readily acclaim in their morning prayers: "Blessed art thou O Lord Our God, King of the Universe, who has not made me a woman."

Rabbis explain that the prayer acknowledges the greater scope offered to men in the performance of mitzvot, but as traditional Jewish life revolves round the mitzvot and their performance, women are obviously denied a privilege.

Dr. Johnson, though not writing specifically about Jewish women, argued that the law gave women too few privileges because nature gave her too many. Certainly Jewish women have always assumed a dominant role in Jewish life, even if tradition insisted that they be seen and not heard, and preferably not seen either.

It has also been argued that women are inherently spiritual and therefore have less need for external aids to devotion. Where men might stray without the yoke of the Torah, women are restrained by their own natural instincts. Be this as it may, no reasonable man would deny that tradition accords an inferior status to women, and many women—though otherwise loyal to tradition—are no longer prepared to accept this status. They demand a larger say in the running of their synagogues, a more equal role in Jewish rituals, and, most seriously of all, an end to the iniquities inherent in Jewish divorce law, where the man, and only the man, can initiate a divorce.

Orthodox rabbis are not entirely unsympathetic to these demands, but they are nervous of them, not only because they are nervous of change but because they are nervous of feminism as a threat to the continuity and character of Jewish family life.

There is also a tradition that rabbis cannot be seen to be bending to pressure, and thus where there is no demand for change they see no need to act, and where there is, they feel they cannot act and in the main they don't. As a result women are gradually taking the law into their own hands. They are forming their own prayer groups, where possible with the blessing of their rabbis, and where necessary without. And as they are more knowledgeable than they have ever been before, it cannot be long before they demand the right to be rabbis. In fact the first orthodox woman rabbi has already been ordained in Jerusalem, and it will not be all that long before we have orthodox women religious judges—*dayanim* (though of course Jews have already had a female judge in the person of Deborah).

Liberals are not troubled by feminism's claims because they have never denied them, while Haredi women accept—or have hitherto accepted—their traditional role with quiet resignation.

Which brings us finally to the Haredim (the name means tremblers, which is to say, they claim to tremble with the fear of God).

They may seem all of a piece because they are all bearded and all in black and their wives are all bewigged. They were, however, composed of two opposing streams, the Hassidim and the Mitnagdim, who were at war for the better part of a century until they made common cause in the face of Jewish emancipation and enlightenment in the course of the nineteenth century.

All orthodox Jews venerate their rabbis to a lesser or greater extent, but the Hassidim approached theirs with an adoration that the Mitnagdim once denounced as idol worship. But today such adoration is commonplace even among them. Similarly, in the past the Mitnagdim laid greater stress on learning than the Hasidim. But that is no longer the case, so that there is now little to distinguish the one from the other.

Haredim are Jews' Jews. If Jews in general tend to keep themselves apart, Haredim keep themselves apart from other Jews. They live among themselves, study among themselves, marry among themselves, and only make hurried forays into the outside world for business reasons. Yet in spite of their exclusiveness and the rigorous nature of their observances, they have grown faster than any of the other brands of Judaism we have examined.

They have always regarded contraception as a grievous sin and many children as the greatest blessing, so that families of eight or even ten children are not uncommon among them.

Alongside their high birth rate, they suffer few defections. Their sons, as we have noted, marry young (their daughters even younger), spend many years in Yeshiva, and by the time they are in their mid-twenties and have to look around for a living, they may have four or five children but no trade. Thus many of them would be lost without the system of mutual support that is one of the most attractive features of their society.

But they have also gained new adherents, often from the outer fringes of Jewish life and sometimes beyond, for they represent old tyme religion and what is generally thought of as "authentic Judaism," and the very demands they make on adherents are one of their attractions.

Their Judaism is authentic in so far as it reflects a way of life lived in the ghettoes of Eastern Europe in the eighteenth and nineteenth centuries, but it is inauthentic in that it represents a uniquely narrow and inward looking brand of Judaism insulated from any contact with external ideas. What do they know of Judaism who only Judaism know?

It is the world of *Fiddler on the Roof*, but with full freezers, central-heating, air-conditioning, Oldsmobiles, and no pogroms. It also offers certainties and a sense of community not claimed by any other brand of Judaism, and it has been doubling in size every fifteen years.

But the system of mutual support that keeps them together and intact depends in the last resort on those of their numbers who are in touch with the outer world, and the Haredi way of life is only viable because most Jews are outside it and are content to admire it—where they do admire it—from a distance.

Study, as we have noted, is central to their existence, but they confine themselves to the sacred texts—and mainly the Talmud—to the exclusion of everything else, and there are youngsters who can recite by heart whole tracts of the Mishnah but are unable to give the date of the French Revolution or even the creation of the State of Israel. Never in Jewish history has so much learning been combined with so much ignorance. And the ignorance derives not from a lack of intelligence, but, as we have suggested, an inculcated aversion to external ideas and an indifference to external events.

Even in Mishnaic times, two thousand years ago, Jews were wary of what was known as *chochmat yavan* (Greek wisdom), but the Talmud itself offers abundant evidence of external influence, and the very richness of Jewish culture suggests a readiness to learn from everyone. So this narrow, inward-looking self centeredness is a comparatively recent phenomenon.

It is a phenomenon evident, interestingly, in the ArtScroll series of Jewish publications, a large American undertaking designed to make sacred texts more accessible to the general reader, though it is aimed at centrists and the non-committed rather than Haredim.

In appearance Art Scroll books are of a quality hitherto unknown to Jewish learning. The typography is excellent and the bindings are handsome. But the volumes add absolutely nothing to the body of Jewish knowledge. Indeed they all carry a *hechsher*—a certificate of permissibility—from leading rabbis to reassure readers that they are free of any taint of originality. The style owes everything to the new world, the thinking is hemmed in by the old.

Their use of political power too suggests an odd mixture of the new and the old. The Haredim are non-Zionist or even anti-Zionist, while the Centrists have come to represent Zionism at its most militant. But in Israel, almost since the very inception of statehood, they have formed a tacit united front.

The vagaries of Israel's electoral system always gave the religious elements in the country an influence out of all proportion to their numbers. But they now also have numbers, comprising nearly a quarter of the electorate, and they have used their power to preserve and enhance the Jewish character of the state. At the same time they seem to have distanced themselves from the sort of Judaism enshrined in prophetic teaching. They have shown little or no concern for equality, ethics, or social justice in the wider community and have clung on to the idea of a Greater Israel without giving much thought to how it would affect the two million Palestinians in the occupied territories or the democratic character of the Jewish state.

The matter was highlighted during the invasion of Lebanon in 1982, which was largely opposed by secular Israel but was overwhelmingly supported by the orthodox, who have consistently backed the most aggressive policies of the government. And when 200,000 demonstrators compelled Mr. Begin to hold a public inquiry into the Sabra and Chatilla massacres, orthodox rabbis protested that no such inquiry was necessary because it was not a Jewish concern.

It might almost seem as if one has to forego one's duties to God before one becomes alive to one's duties to humankind. There is a German saying that culture is what's left after everything one has learned has been forgotten. It might equally be argued that Judaism is what is left after all the usages it inculcated for ages have been abandoned. But, to the contrary, the secular, or the *hilonim* as they are referred to in Hebrew, are not all Jews without faith. They are, for the most part, merely Jews with doubts or reservations, who, while part of the fold, are not prepared to take the word of the rabbis as the word of God or the ways of the Haredim as the ultimate expression of Judaism.

All of which might suggest that Judaism, instead of representing a clearly defined set of ideals, assumes different forms among different groups, and far from being a source of unity is a source of conflict, and that the Jewish world is fractious, troubled, and divided. Yet its divisions and conflicts arise out of the very fact that it is a living faith, or, as the Talmud puts it, "both this and that are the word of the living God."

Judaism as spelled out in detail may not always seem to make sense, even to its own adherents, and, as we have suggested, the ways of God trouble and confound as much as they reassure.

Not all Jews understand the import of their prayers or can explain the reasons for their loyalties. Not all who claim to believe in *Torah min Hashamayim* know exactly what they mean by it, and not everyone lives up to his or her beliefs. And some people speak of belief when they only mean veneration for the old, the familiar, and the tried. But in general terms Judaism works, and, even if it has its defects, it is possibly less deficient and more benign than any obvious alternative.

It may demand the impossible but does not expect it and looks for effort rather than attainment, or as Rabbi Tarfon put it, "It is not thy duty to complete the task, but neither art thou free to desist from it." The task is to emulate the good and to become thereby a source of emulation, to be blessed and a source of blessing.

Which leaves the final question: Even if we agree—as I think we can—that Judaism has deserved to survive, will it continue to do so? Can it survive in freedom as it survived in adversity?

The very question suggests that Jewish continuity depends less on inner cohesion than outer hostility, which is manifestly untrue.

Jewish history was not one long night of suffering, though it sometimes reads as if it were, for when a people that likes to keep itself to itself is scattered among the nations, it only impinges upon history when things go seriously wrong. When things go right, it prefers, wherever possible, to enjoy its good fortune in silence.

Jews have never enjoyed freedom in the sense that they enjoy it now, but then nobody has, and they lived comparatively untrammeled lives for long periods under Greek and Roman rule in North Africa, under Parthian rule in Babylonia, and under Moslem rule in North Africa and Spain. And American Jewry, though replenished by successive waves of newcomers, has now been around for nearly six generations.

The unique challenge to Jewish life in our time lies not in the absence of hostility or oppression but in the openness of external society and its rampant paganism. In earlier centuries one could only cease to be Jewish through a definite act of renunciation. In our time, one can lose one's Jewishness almost unconsciously through casual drift, unless one makes a positive effort to stay Jewish, and not everyone is prepared to make that effort.

But, as we have seen, a great many people are, some out of belief in the God of Israel, some who are prepared to give God the benefit of their doubts, some out of attachment to the heritage of Israel, some out of family loyalty, some out of habit, some because of the sheer hell of it.

The evidence of erosion may be undeniable, but prevailing trends do not always proceed to their logical conclusion and are sometimes reversed, and in so far as anything in life is beyond conjecture, we may be fairly certain that Jews and Judaism are here to stay.

# ABBREVIATIONS

| | | | |
|---|---|---|---|
| A.Z. | Abodah Zarah | Me. | Meilah |
| Ah. | Ahilot | Meg. | Megillah |
| Ar. | Arakhin | Men. | Menahot |
| B. | Bavli, Babylonian Talmud | Mic. | Micah |
| B.B. | Baba Batra | Mid. | Middot |
| B.M. | Baba Mesia | Miq. | Miqvaot |
| B.Q. | Baba Qamma | MS. | Manuscript (pl. MSS.) |
| Bek. | Bekhorot | Naz. | Nazir |
| Ber. | Berakhot | Ned. | Nedarim |
| Bes. | Besah | Neg. | Negaim |
| Bik. | Bikkurim | Neh. | Nehemiah |
| Chr. | Chronicles | Nid. | Niddah |
| Col. | Column | Num. | Numbers |
| Cor. | Corinthians | Obad. | Obadiah |
| Dan. | Daniel | Oh. | Ohalot |
| Dem. | Demai | Or. | Orlah |
| Deut. | Deuteronomy | Par. | Parah |
| Eccl. | Ecclesiastes | Pes. | Pesahim |
| Ed. | Eduyyot | Prov. | Proverbs |
| Erub. | Erubin | Ps. | Psalm (pl.: Pss.) |
| Esdr. | Esdras | Qid. | Qiddushin |
| Esth. | Esther | Qin. | Qinnim |
| Exod. | Exodus | R.H. | Rosh Hashanah |
| Ezek. | Ezekiel | Rab. | Rabbah |
| Gal. | Galatians | Rev. | Revelations |
| Gen. | Genesis | Rom. | Romans |
| Git. | Gittin | Sam. | Samuel |
| Hab. | Habakkuk | Shab. | Shabbat |
| Hag. | Hagigah | Shav. | Shavuot |
| Hal. | Hallah | Sheb. | Shebiit |
| Heb. | Hebrew | Sheq. | Sheqalim |
| Hor. | Horayot | Sir. | Sirach |
| Hos. | Hosea | Sot. | Sotah |
| Hul. | Hullin | Suk. | Sukkah |
| Is. | Isaiah | T. | Tosefta |
| Jer. | Jeremiah | T.Y. | Tebul Yom |
| Jdt. | Judith | Ta. | Taanit |
| Jer. | Jeremiah | Tam. | Tamid |
| Josh. | Joshua | Tan. | Tanhuma |
| Judg. | Judges | Tem. | Temurah |
| Kel. | Kelim | Ter. | Terumot |
| Ker. | Keritot | Thess. | Thessalonians |
| Ket. | Ketuvot | Tim. | Timothy |
| Kgs. | Kings | Toh. | Toharot |
| Kil. | Kilaim | Uqs. | Uqsin |
| Lam. | Lamentations | Vol. | Volume |
| Lev. | Leviticus | Y. | Yerushalmi, Palestinian Talmud |
| M. | Mishnah | Y.T. | Yom Tob |
| M.Q. | Moed Qatan | Yad. | Yadaim |
| M.S. | Maaser Sheni | Yeb. | Yebamot |
| Ma. | Maaserot | Yom. | Yoma |
| Macc. | Maccabees | Zab. | Zabbim |
| Mak. | Makkot | Zeb. | Zebahim |
| Makh. | Makhshirin | Zech. | Zechariah |
| Mal. | Malachi | Zeph. | Zephaniah |
| Mat. | Matthew | | |

# GENERAL INDEX

# INDEX OF TEXTUAL REFERENCES

## 1. *Jewish Bible*

*5. Ancient Writings (a. Jewish, b. Christian, c. non-Jewish, non-Christian)*

## 6. *Rabbinic Literature*

g. Medieval & Renaissance
Rabbinic literature